E6-9 1. Credit add'l. paid-in capital, $72,000
E6-10 1. $45,000; 2. c.
E6-11 $1,700,000
E6-12 d. $127,000
E6-13 $21,200,000
E6-14 c.
P6-1 3. Consolidated retained earnings, $60,000
P6-2 3. Consolidated retained earnings, $59,000
P6-3 1. Carrying value of investment at date of pooling, $128,000
P6-4 3. Consolidated net income, $1,620,000; Consolidated retained earnings, $2,130,000
P6-5 3. Consolidated net income, $1,600,000; Consolidated retained earnings, $2,079,000
P6-6 5. Consolidated net income, $102,000; Consolidated retained earnings, $156,000
P6-7 5. Consolidated net income, $105,000; Consolidated retained earnings, $168,000
P6-8 1. $730,000; 2. $646,500
P6-9 1. Combined assets, $37,700,000; Combined net income, $7,800,000; Retained earnings at Dec. 31, 19X3, $14,700,000
2. Combined assets, $42,270,000; Combined net income, $6,050,000; Retained earnings at Dec. 31, 19X3, $9,270,000

E7-1 Adjusted balances, $34,000
E7-5 2. Defer $9,000
E7-13 1a. $24,000; 1b. $22,000
E7-14 1. Defer $20,000
2. Reduce equity in net income by $14,000
P7-1 2. Consolidated net income, $57,000; Consolidated retained earnings, $236,000
P7-2 (Same check figures as for P7-1)
P7-3 3. Consolidated net income, $53,000; Consolidated assets, $694,000
P7-4 (Same check figures as for P7-3)
P7-5 2. Consolidated net income, $39,000; Consolidated assets, $145,000
P7-6 3. (Same check figures as for P7-5)
P7-7 3. Consolidated net income, $85,000; Consolidated assets, $977,000
P7-8 3. (Same check figures as for P7-7)
P7-9 3. Consolidated retained earnings, $4,317,000; Consolidated assets, $15,129,000
P7-10 3. (Same check figures as for P7-9)
P7-11 2. Adjusted balances, $118,000
6. Consolidated net income, $227,000; Consolidated assets, $6,572,000
P7-12 2. & 6. (Same check figures as for P7-11)

E8-5 1. Net book value, $500,000
2. Net book value, $525,000
P8-1 2. Consolidated net income, $45,000; Consolidated assets, $307,000
P8-2 3. (Same check figures as for P8-1)
P8-3 3. Consolidated net income, $168,000; Consolidated assets, $860,000
P8-4 3. (Same check figures as for P8-3)
P8-5 3. Consolidated net income, $257,800; Consolidated assets, $534,000
P8-6 3. (Sam
P8-7 3. Conso
Conso
P8-8 3. (Same check figures as for P8-7)

E9-1 1. Loss of $14,000
E9-2 1. Loss of $14,000
E9-3 1. Gain of $19,000
E9-4 1. Gain of $19,000
E9-5 1. Gain of $44,000
E9-6 1. Gain of $44,000
E9-7 1. Loss of $29,500
E9-8 1. Loss of $29,500
E9-9 1. Gain of $10,000
E9-10 1. Gain of $10,000
P9-1 1. Parent's net income, $1,899,000; Subsidiary's net income, $319,000
P9-2 1. Parent's net income, $1,850,000; Subsidiary's net income, $305,000
P9-3 1. Loss of $96,000
P9-4 1. Loss of $96,000
P9-5 1. Loss of $120,000
P9-6 1. Loss of $120,000
P9-7 1. Gain of $3,500
4. Consolidated net income, $170,500; Consolidated assets, $1,134,500
P9-8 (Same check figures as for P9-7)
P9-9 1. Loss of $20,000
4. Consolidated net income, $207,100; Consolidated assets, $1,146,000
P9-10 (Same check figures as for P9-9)
P9-11 1. Gain of $21,000
3. Dec. 31, 19X3 investment balance, $353,000
4. Consolidated net income, $213,000; Consolidated assets, $1,948,500
P9-12 1. Gain of $21,000
3. Dec. 31, 19X3 investment balance, $361,000
4. Consolidated net income, $213,000; Consolidated assets, $1,948,000

E10-1 Goodwill, $35,500
E10-2 Parent's equity interest decrease, $52,941; Minority interest equity decrease, $7,059
E10-4 Retained earnings, decrease of $160,000
E10-5 No changes.
E10-6 Goodwill, $78,000; Minority interest, $8,000
E10-7 Goodwill, $46,800; Minority interest, $116,800
E10-8 Goodwill, $285,000; Minority interest, $35,000
E10-9 Goodwill, $228,000; Minority interest, $308,000
P10-1 Carrying value of investment, $1,430,000
P10-2 1. Decrease in parent's equity interest, $360,000
2. Goodwill element at Jan. 1, 19X6, $165,000
P10-3 1. Goodwill element at Jan. 1, 19X6, $190,000
(continued on last page of book)
P10-4 1. Carrying value of investment at Dec. 31, 19X4, $1,411,500; Gain on sale of shares, $32,000

(continued on p. 1210)

ADVANCED ACCOUNTING
Concepts and Practice

THIRD EDITION

ADVANCED ACCOUNTING

Concepts and Practice

THIRD EDITION

Arnold J. Pahler

San Jose State University

Joseph E. Mori

San Jose State University

HBJ

HARCOURT BRACE JOVANOVICH, PUBLISHERS

San Diego New York Chicago Austin Washington, D.C.

London Sydney Tokyo Toronto

To my children, Laura and Brett

Arnold J. Pahler

To my family, Carol Ann, David, and Julie

Joseph E. Mori

ISBN: 0-15-501827-2

Library of Congress Catalog Card Number: 87-81162

Printed in the United States of America

PREFACE

The Third Edition of *Advanced Accounting: Concepts and Practice* is noticeably different from the Second Edition in many respects. We have updated the book for new technical pronouncements throughout, changed the emphasis on particular topics to suit current pedagogical and professional needs, and altered the chapter order for better comprehension.

Additionally, we have made the book more accessible and have added features designed to attract students' interest in contemporary trends in business and accounting theory and practice.

Among the general changes are the following:

- Twelve articles from *The Wall Street Journal*, *Forbes*, and *Business Week* have been added so that students can better relate the material to current events.
- All consolidation elimination entries are shown with a shaded background, to avoid possible confusion with general ledger entries.
- More of the problems are of intermediate difficulty (the easy ones slightly harder, the really hard ones slightly less difficult). In addition, numerous comprehensive consolidation problems have been added.
- Selected references to recent articles in accounting journals have been included at the end of many chapters.
- Because students are more motivated to work additional exercises and problems if check figures are provided, check figures for exercises have been included in addition to those for problems. (The Checklist of Key Figures appears on the endpapers and on page 1210.)
- A simplified format has been adopted for the income statement section of the consolidating statement worksheet in Chapters 1–12. The results are that (1) several needless subtotals are no longer used, (2) intercompany accounts are conveniently placed in one section, and (3) the format is consistent with the plus-and-minus scheme used in the LOTUS 1-2-3 spreadsheet software and on the Electronic Spreadsheet Templates diskette available for use with this edition. (See Illustration 7-1, page 306, for an example of this new format.)

Changes in Parts I and II on Consolidations (Chapters 1–13)

Adoption of the Three-tier Statement Format. The analysis of retained earnings in the consolidating statement worksheet is now shown between the income statement and the balance sheet, rather than directly in the balance sheet. (See page 149, for example.)

Isolation of Income Taxes (Chapter 12). To simplify the preparation of consolidation worksheets, all income tax aspects previously dealt with in Chapters 3–11 have been moved to Chapter 12. Two advantages result: (1) the additional complexity of accounting for taxes is delayed until students are well grounded in the basics of consolidation, and (2) instructors have greater flexibility in the selection of topics they choose to cover.

Primary Emphasis on the Complete Equity Method (Chapters 7–9). In the chapters dealing with intercompany inventory, fixed asset, and bond transactions, the complete equity method is now given primary emphasis over the partial equity method, which is presented in appendixes to these chapters. This change was made because it is easier for students to learn the complete equity method first. Additionally, students often find the "two different income statements" result of the partial equity method somewhat confusing when they are exposed to only this method.

This material is presented so that instructors have the option of covering only the complete equity method (the conceptually superior method), only the partial equity method (widely used in practice), or both methods (when time permits). The related exercises and problems are identified and grouped accordingly.

Containment of Branch Accounting (Chapter 1). Chapter 3 has been revised so that no references to branch accounting are needed or made. Accordingly, Chapter 1 may be conveniently bypassed if time does not permit its inclusion.

Interview with T. Boone Pickens (Chapter 2). In this chapter, "Introduction to Business Combinations," we have included an interview with T. Boone Pickens, general partner of Mesa Limited Partnership, who discusses several timely business combination issues.

Equal Emphasis on Push-down Accounting (Chapter 3). This topic is now discussed prominently in the chapter (it was formerly covered in the chapter's appendix), in light of the SEC's strong and unwavering position in enforcing the use of push-down accounting for publicly owned companies. (In class-testing this change, we noted that it had the added benefit of strongly reinforcing the students' understanding of the "change in basis of accounting" concept that is the focal point of the purchase method of accounting.)

Coverage of the FASB's Proposed Amendments to *ARB No. 51 and APB Opinion No. 18* (Chapter 3). The discussion of consolidated financial statements includes the FASB's December 16, 1986, proposed amendments to these pronouncements.

Capsule History of Accounting for Goodwill (Chapter 3). To provide students with a historical perspective and heighten their interest, Chapter 3 includes a capsule history of accounting for goodwill.

Addition of Financial and Managerial Analysis Problems (Chapters 1, 3, and 4). A financial or managerial analysis has been added to the Problems section of each of these chapters. Each problem lends itself to requiring a three- to four-page written assignment, the purpose of which is to enable students to sharpen their analytical and writing skills.

Expansion of Conceptual Analysis to Allow Keeping Track of the Minority Interest (Chapter 5). Thus the minority interest is easily established as a single amount in the balance sheet section of the worksheet (rather than being a residual amount). This change avoids the use of a separate entry to establish the minority interest. Furthermore, several conceptual benefits accrue to the students in understanding the minority interest. (For example, see page 189.)

Revaluation under the Entity Theory Moved to the Chapter's Appendix A (Chapter 5). Thus students must deal only with the parent company approach to revaluation in the main discussion. The only aspect of the entity theory that remains in the chapter is that of how to classify the minority interest in the financial statements.

Consolidated Statement of Cash Flows (Chapter 5). In light of the FASB's recent pronouncements in this area, the Third Edition uses a consolidated statement of cash flows rather than a consolidated statement of changes in financial position.

Fuller Discussion of the Pooling of Interests Concept (Chapter 6). A much more in-depth discussion of the pooling of interests concept has been added (pages 240–53).

Addition of Capsule History of Pooling of Interests Accounting (Chapter 6). To provide a historical perspective and heighten students' interest, a capsule history of this controversial subject has been included for the Third Edition.

Income Tax Coverage Based on the FASB's Proposed Changes to *APB Opinion No. 11* and *APB Opinion No. 18* (Chapter 12). The income tax discussion in this chapter is based on FASB's latest proposed changes to existing pronouncements, which are expected to be issued in final form by the time this book is published.

Dealing with tax differences at the date of combination is covered in this chapter. We have also added a comprehensive example of how to calculate income taxes on a consolidated basis.

Segment Reporting (Chapter 13) Moved. This chapter (formerly Chapter 15) is now placed at the end of the consolidations chapters, inasmuch as segment reporting deals with disaggregating the consolidated financial statements and determining unrealized intrasegment and intersegment profit (the latter being a further refinement of the unrealized intercompany profit topic discussed in Chapter 7).

Changes in Part III, "Omnibus Area" (Chapters 14–19)

Splitting Translation of Foreign Currency Financial Statements into Two Chapters (Chapters 14 and 15). For the Third Edition, the conceptual issues associated with the translation of foreign currency financial statements are now dealt with in Chapter 14, and the specific requirements of *FASB Statement No. 52* are now covered in Chapter 15. The change is intended to make this complex subject more digestible to students, as well as to provide greater flexibility to instructors who may wish to give additional or lesser emphasis to either the conceptual issues or the requirements of *FASB Statement No. 52*.

Comprehensive Translation and Consolidation Problem (Chapter 16). This chapter contains a new comprehensive problem involving foreign currency transactions, translation of foreign currency financial statements, intercompany inventory transfers, and the preparation of consolidated financial statements.

Better Coverage of SEC Reporting (Chapter 18). The discussion of the SEC's enforcement powers has been expanded, and many recent examples having been added. Also, the role of the SEC in the FASB's Emerging Issues Task Force (EITF) is discussed.

Changes in Part IV, "Governmental and Nonprofit Organizations" (Chapters 20–22)

More Relevant Placement. In light of the heavier emphasis on this material in the CPA examination, these chapters now precede, rather than follow, partnership chapters.

Citation of the 1987 Codification of Governmental GAAP. The AICPA's revised *Governmental Audit Guide* for 1986 cites the GASB and GFOA Codification of Governmental Accounting and Financial Reporting Standards (rather than the various NCGA statements and interpretations and the GASB's statements in force at the time of the codification). Therefore we cite the codification in the same manner.

Coverage of GASB *Statement No. 6*, "Special Assessments" (Chapter 21). The discussion of special assessments is now based on the GASB's 1987 *Statement No. 6*, which abolished the use of Special Assessment Funds.

Resequencing of Topics in Special Purpose Funds and Account Groups Chapter (Chapter 21). Several logical changes were made in the order of discussing the topics in this chapter. The most notable changes were moving the discussion of the General Fixed Asset Account Group to follow immediately the Capital Projects Funds topic, and moving the discussion of the General Long-Term Debt Account Group to follow immediately the Debt Service Funds topic.

Chapter on Nonprofit Organizations Extensively Revised (Chapter 22). The material in this chapter has been substantially restructured to place much greater emphasis on comparative financial statements and much less emphasis on detailed journal entries, which have been relegated to the chapter's appendixes).

Changes in Part V, "Partnerships" (Chapters 23–25)

Expanded Coverage of Limited Partnerships. The discussion of limited partnerships (in Appendix A to Chapter 23) has been expanded, and the master limited partnership (MLP) form of organization, to which many corporations are switching as a result of the Tax Reform Act of 1986, is introduced.

The Professional Corporation (Chapter 23). This material has been substantially revised.

Improved Major Consolidations Feature

In preparing consolidated financial statements, we have retained the use of **analyzing the investment account by its individual components, updating the analysis using the equity method of accounting, and then preparing the basic consolidation elimination entry from this updated analysis**. This approach, which was received favorably by adopters of the earlier editions, eliminates most of the time that otherwise would be spent developing elimination entry amounts.

Furthermore, the **conceptual analysis has been expanded to accommodate minority interest situations**, resulting in a much simpler approach to dealing with minority interests.

New Appendix: "Student Manual for Using Electronic Spreadsheet Software"

For the Third Edition, the revised and enhanced student manual for the Electronic Spreadsheet Templates becomes the Appendix to this book. The master templates diskette is available free to adopting instructors. It runs on the IBM PC (or IBM AT or IBM XT) computer using the LOTUS 1-2-3 electronic spreadsheet software.

The templates diskette contains eleven class-tested models individually tailored and customized for the following text chapters:

Chapter 1	Model 1
Chapter 3	Model 3
Chapter 4	Model 4
Chapter 5	Model 5
Chapter 6	Model 6
Chapter 7-10	Model 7
Chapter 15	Model 15T (translation)
Chapter 15	Model 15R (remeasurement)
Chapter 19	Model 19
Chapter 23	Model 23
Chapter 25	Model 25

Eight of the models have problem data from the text stored in the lower section of the model. At the touch of a key, this data can be loaded into the worksheet section of the model using a macro command (a preprogrammed stored instruction). Models 3, 4, 5, 6, and 7 also contain a conceptual analysis of the investment account, from which the primary elimination entry for consolidation can be readily prepared and then, using a macro command, posted to the worksheet.

The templates have been designed so that students must perform a limited amount of spreadsheet programming. **No prior computer experience is required,** however. Furthermore, using the manual in the Appendix, students can work problems on their own, **without instructor involvement.**

A student with no prior computer experience should be able to complete the first problem using the templates diskette and the step-by-step instructions in the Appendix, in about two hours. Later problems require from fifteen to thirty minutes of computer time, depending on complexity.

Student-oriented Features

In addition to the useful new Appendix, the improved Electronic Spreadsheets Templates themselves, and the expanded Checklist of Key Figures mentioned earlier, the Third Edition contains the following features designed to make the text easier for students to use:

- An **outline of topics** preceding each chapter
- An **overview and summary** in each chapter
- A **glossary of new terms** in most chapters
- Descriptive **overviews of discussion cases, exercises, and problems**
- Clearly marked **illustrations of key points** in the text
- Handy **vertical format** for consolidating statement worksheets

Time-saving **working papers** for selected problems in Chapters 1, 3–10, 15, 16, and 23

Ancillaries

For this edition, the ancillaries have been thoroughly revised in content and usefulness.

Transparencies. For all problems involving consolidation or translation worksheets, a transparency is available of that worksheet and, if applicable, of the related conceptual analysis of the parent's investment account (Chapters 1, 3–11, 15, and 16). In addition, selected solutions are provided for most of the other chapters.

Solutions Manual. To assist instructors in evaluating and selecting problem materials, the Solutions Manual contains a description of each discussion case, exercise, and problem. The **relative difficulty** and **estimated time** for completion of problem materials are also included. (The manual is perforated to facilitate the preparation of additional transparencies.)

Instructor's Resource Manual and Test Book. For this edition the manual is divided into four parts. Part I consists of outlines for a one-term and a two-term course. Part II contains teaching suggestions and additional items of current interest to students. Part III is an instructor's introduction to the enhanced Electronic Spreadsheet Templates diskette and student manual Appendix to this book. Part IV is a substantially upgraded test bank for each chapter of the text. The test bank contains approximately 330 true-or-false statements, 200 multiple-choice questions, 240 completion statements (fill-ins), and 140 short problems. Because CPA examinations consistently contain excellent questions pertaining to theory, we have obtained or adapted many of the multiple-choice questions from recent examinations.

Working Papers. Working Papers are provided, where appropriate, for problems in Chapters 1, 3–10, 15, 16, and 23. The time saved using the Working Papers in these chapters can be considerable.

Acknowledgments

We are indebted to the following instructors who thoroughly and conscientiously reviewed materials for the Third Edition before publication:

Ted D. Skekel	University of Texas at San Antonio
Jane F. Mutchler	Ohio State University

James P. Trebby	Marquette University
Lane A. Daley	University of Minnesota

We also thank these users of the Second Edition who passed along much-appreciated and valuable suggestions for the Third Edition:

William P. Stevens	DePaul University
Stewart Berkshire, Jr.	California State University, Long Beach
G. Lee Willinger	University of Oklahoma
Abraham J. Simon	Queens College, City University of New York
Stanley C. Martens	DePaul University
Evelyn M. Duesberry	University of Wisconsin, Platteville

We also thank the following users of the Second Edition who responded to a questionnaire relating to that edition: Dan Acton, Marist College; Mary Beth Armstrong, California Polytechnic State University; Virginia Bakay, University of Nevada, Las Vegas; Jan Bell, California State University at Northridge; John Biglin, Muhlenberg College; Calvin Cooke, Howard University; Wagih Dafashy, College of William and Mary; Michael Davis, Lehigh University; James Dear, University of Southern Mississippi; David Durkee, Central State University; Orapin Duangploy, Pittsburg State University; Mary Fleming, California State University at Fullerton; John Gehman, Moravian College; Richard Heffelfinger, Otterbein College; Jerry Langham, California State University, San Bernardino; Randall E. LaSalle, Salisbury State College; Fraser MacHaffie, Marietta College; Norbert Maler, California State University at Fullerton; Charles Mandeville, Carroll College; Joseph Marcheggiani, Butler University; Ula Motekat, Old Dominion University; John Otto, Grove City College; William Paxton, Case Western Reserve University;' Sharyll Plato, Central State University; Galen Rupp, Pittsburg State University; Clayton Sager, University of Wisconsin, Whitewater; Gene Shea, Olivet Nazarene College; Barbara Shiarappa, Trenton State College; David Sidaway, Oakland University; Frederic Stiner, Jr., University of Delaware; Charles Tritschler, Purdue University; Neal Ushman, University of Santa Clara; Charles Wagner, Mankato State University; Richard Wallace, University of Arkansas, Monticello; Reginald Washington, Morgan State University; Dwight Zulauf, Humboldt State University.

We thank Arthur Andersen & Co. for allowing us to use its professional libraries and materials. We express with appreciation our thanks to the American Institute of Certified Public Accountants, the Financial Accounting Standards Board, and the Government Finance Officers Association for their permission to quote material from their respective pronouncements and various other publications. We also thank the American Institute of Certified Public Accountants for their permission to use and adapt material from the CPA examinations.

Finally, we express our appreciation to Ken Rethmeier, our editor at Harcourt Brace Jovanovich, whose innovative approach to the review process yielded exceedingly valuable feedback; Craig Avery, manuscript editor; Jon Preimesberger, production editor; Jane Carey, designer; and Sharon Weldy, production manager. Their diligence was greatly appreciated.

We welcome all comments from users of the Third Edition.

Arnold J. Pahler

Joseph E. Mori

CONTENTS

I

Consolidated Financial Statements: Fundamentals

1
Branch Accounting

AN OVERVIEW OF BRANCH ACCOUNTING

A substantial portion of the subject matter of advanced accounting concerns businesses that increase the number of their outlying manufacturing, retailing, or service locations to increase sales and profits. A business may establish additional outlying locations in one of the following two ways: internal expansion and external expansion. **Internal expansion** means that a business constructs or leases additional outlying facilities. In most instances, the additional facilities increase the company's manufacturing, retailing, or service capacities in the same line of business in which it currently operates. Much of the growth of International Business Machines Corporation, Sears, Roebuck and Company, and Bank of America occurred through such internal expansion. **External expansion** takes place when two existing businesses combine into a unified larger business. Although many business combinations enable companies to increase their operations in the same line of business, an increasing proportion of business combinations occur among companies in unrelated fields. Such combinations enable companies to diversify their product lines. Much of the growth of International Telephone and Telegraph, Gulf and Western Industries, and Litton Industries came about through external expansion.

This chapter deals exclusively with the internal expansion of businesses. Subsequent chapters deal with external expansion. By discussing internal expansion first, we establish some fundamental principles of accounting for multilocation operations that will benefit us in later chapters. Accounting for outlying locations established in foreign countries through internal expansion involves special considerations; accordingly, we discuss these situations in Chapters 14 to 16, which deal with foreign operations and transactions.

Terminology

A business's outlying location established through internal expansion is not a separate legal entity but merely an extension of a legal entity. Accordingly, it cannot be referred to as a company, because it is only part of a company. Because the professional accounting pronouncements do not specify how outlying locations should be referred to, many terms have evolved over the years. Banks commonly refer to their outlying locations as *branches;* insurance companies commonly refer to them as *sales offices;* and manufacturing companies use the terms *division* and *plant.* Some companies, however, use division to refer to geographical area—for example, all outlying manufacturing plants in a designated eastern location might be called the East Coast Division. Some companies use *division* to refer to a particular product line. General Motors Corporation, for example, has five automobile divisions, and each division has several manufacturing plants. An outlying location of a retail establishment is a *store.* Companies in the computer-manufacturing industry often establish outlying locations to service computers; these locations may be referred to as *field engineering offices.* In some companies, the outlying locations carry only demonstration units and sales brochures—any sales that they generate are approved and filled by the home office; such outlying locations are called *sales offices* or *agencies.* In all these instances, the headquarters location of the legal entity that established the outlying location is referred to as the **home office.**

Delegation of Decision-making Authority

When an outlying location is established, the home office must decide the extent to which it will grant decision-making authority to management at the outlying location. Although companywide policies are established by the home office, many day-to-day operating decisions can be delegated to the outlying management. The extent of delegation is part of the broad topic of centralized versus decentralized management decision making. For example, varying degrees of delegation are found in the retail industry. At one extreme are some home offices that decide all the merchandise to be carried by each outlying retail outlet, and each retail outlet must purchase all such merchandise from the home office. At the other extreme are home offices that grant managements at the outlying retail outlets complete discretion over the merchandise they may carry and from where they may buy it. Between these extremes are situations in which outlying retail outlets must carry certain merchandise specified by the home office (which often must be purchased from the home office), but local managers have complete discretion over other merchandise and where they buy it. In the banking industry, branches usually are assigned dollar limits on the amount of money they may loan to a given customer; any loan requests above the designated limits must be approved by a higher regional office or the home office. Some home offices handle national and regional advertising, allowing outlying locations to do only limited local advertising. Other home offices make each outlying location responsible for its own local advertising.

Accounting Systems

The home office must decide how to account for the activities and transactions of the outlying location. This decision is based on what is most practical and economical in a given situation. Accounting systems can be categorized as either centralized or decentralized.

Centralized Accounting. Under a **centralized accounting** system, an outlying location does not maintain a separate general ledger in which to record its transactions. Instead, it sends source documents on sales, purchases, and payroll to the home office. Outlying locations usually deposit cash receipts in local bank accounts, which only the home office can draw upon. When the home office receives source documents, it reconciles sales information with bank deposits, reviews and processes invoices for payment, and prepares payroll checks and related payroll records. Inventory and fixed assets at each outlying location also are recorded in the home office general ledger, appropriately coded to signify the location to which they belong. Journal entries pertaining to each outlying location's transactions are then prepared and posted to the home office general ledger. These entries are usually coded so that accountants at the home office can readily prepare operating statements for each outlying location. Centralized accounting systems commonly use computers at the home office to minimize the clerical aspects of keeping records and preparing financial statements. The home office reviews operating statements for each outlying location and provides copies to outlying management. Centralized accounting systems are usually practical when the operations of the outlying location do not involve complex manufacturing operations or extensive retailing or service activities. Grocery, drug, and shoe store chains usually use centralized accounting systems. Because centralized accounting systems present no unusual accounting issues, they are not discussed any further.

Decentralized Accounting. Under a **decentralized accounting** system, an outlying location maintains a separate general ledger in which to record its transactions. Thus, the outlying location is a separate **accounting entity,** even though it is not a separate legal entity. It prepares its own journal entries and financial statements, submitting the latter to the home office, usually on a monthly basis. Decentralized accounting systems are common for outlying locations that have complex manufacturing operations or extensive retailing operations involving significant credit sales. In a decentralized accounting system, the following accounting issues must be resolved:

1. The manner in which transactions between the home office and the outlying locations are recorded.
2. The procedures by which the revenues, costs, and expenses of the outlying locations are reported for financial and income tax reporting purposes.

The remainder of this chapter deals with these two issues. As mentioned previously, many industries create outlying locations through internal expansion. We use the retail industry to illustrate the fundamental accounting principles for multilocation operations using a decentralized accounting system because retailing activities allow a complete discussion of the issues. In discussing and illustrating such issues, the outlying locations are referred to hereafter as **branches.**

BRANCH GENERAL LEDGER ACCOUNTS

Intracompany Accounts

A branch is established when a home office transfers cash, inventory, or other assets to an outlying location. Because the home office views the assets transferred to the branch as an investment, it makes the following entry:

Investment in Branch	xxx	
Asset(s)		xxx

This Investment in Branch account (sometimes called *Branch Current*) is used to keep track of and maintain control over (1) the assets transferred to the branch and (2) the increase or decrease in the branch's net assets as a result of the branch's operations.

On receipt of the assets from the home office, the branch makes the following entry:

Asset(s)	xxx	
Home Office Equity		xxx

The Home Office Equity account represents the equity interest of the home office in the branch. The use of such an account allows double-entry bookkeeping procedures to be used at the branch level. (Remember that branches are not separate legal entities and do not have Common Stock, Additional Paid-in Capital, and Retained Earnings accounts.)

The balance in the Investment in Branch account on the books of the home office always equals the balance in the Home Office Equity account on the books of the branch. In practice, these accounts are referred to as the **intracompany** or **reciprocal accounts.** At the end of each accounting period, the branch closes its income or loss to its Home Office Equity account. Upon receipt of the branch's financial statements, the home office adjusts its Investment in Branch account to reflect the branch's income or loss and makes the offsetting credit or debit to an income statement account called **Branch Income** or **Branch Loss.** As a result of this entry and upon closing the Branch Income or Branch Loss account to retained earnings, the branch's income or loss is included in the home office's Retained Earnings account.

Branches are usually financed entirely by the home office and typically do not establish relations with local banks. Thus, they do not incur interest expense. If a branch has cash in excess of its immediate needs, it usually transfers it to the home office, which is responsible for investing excess cash on a companywide basis. Thus, branches do not have interest income from investments.

Income Tax Accounts and Reporting

Because branches are not separate legal entities, they do not file their own income tax returns. The home office must include the income or loss from its branches along with its own income or loss from operations for federal income tax reporting purposes. If the home office has operations in states that impose income taxes, the home office must file branch income tax returns in those states. Federal and state income taxes are almost always computed at the home office and recorded exclusively in the home office general ledger. Few companies attempt to allocate or transfer income tax expense from the home office general ledger to branch general ledgers. This not only simplifies the tax recording procedures but also eliminates the need to make arbitrary allocation assumptions. Furthermore, the potential benefits, if any, from allocating income tax expense to the branches would be minimal in most instances.

Because branches do not have interest income, interest expense, or income tax expense, the income or loss from their operations is an **operating income** or **loss,** not a net income or loss. Hereafter, all references to a branch's income or loss are in this context.

Home Office Allocations

The home office usually arranges and pays for certain expenses that benefit the branches. The most common example is insurance. In theory, some portion of the insurance expense should be allocated to the various branches, so that the home office may determine the true operating income or loss of each branch. In practice, however, allocations of home office expenses vary widely. Some home offices allocate only those expenses that relate directly to the branch operations, such as insurance and national advertising costs. Some home offices without any revenue-producing operations of their own allocate all of their expenses (including salaries of home office executives, facilities costs, legal fees, audit fees, and interest expense) to the branches. Branch managers are therefore continually aware that branch operations must cover these costs. Some home offices do not allocate any home office expenses to the branches on the theory that because the branches have no control over them, arbitrary allocations serve no useful purpose. The home office records allocations by debiting the Investment in Branch account and crediting the applicable expense accounts. The branch debits the applicable expense accounts and credits its Home Office account. The end result is the same as though the home office had transferred cash to the branch and the branch had arranged for and incurred the expenses.

Inventory Transfer Accounts

When inventory is transferred from the home office to a branch, all that has really happened is that the inventory has physically moved from one location in the company to another. A sale has not occurred, because sales take place only between the company and outside customers. To measure the profitability of a branch, however, an **intracompany billing** must be prepared. The purpose of the intracompany billing is to transfer purchases from the books of the home office to the books of the branch. The branch uses a special purchases account called Shipments from Home Office to record these inventory transfers and makes the following entry:

Shipments from Home Office	XXX	
Home Office Equity		XXX

The home office uses a special contrapurchases account called Shipments to Branch to record inventory transfers. If the inventory is transferred and billed at the home office's cost, the home office makes the following entry:

Investment in Branch	XXX	
Shipments to Branch..		XXX

The branch's ending inventory, cost of goods sold, gross margin, and operating profit or loss depend on the amounts of these intracompany billings. If the intracompany billing is made at the home office's cost, then these special accounts should always agree. By using these special accounts, the home office can strengthen control over branch operations. If these special accounts do not agree, then at least one of the accounting entities has made an error or a shipment is in transit. Before the month-end closing can be properly completed, an adjusting entry must be made to bring the two special accounts into agreement. Using the home office's cost in pricing intracompany inventory transfers is quite common, primarily because it does not require any special considerations in the preparation of month-end combined financial statements for the home office and its branches.

Although the use of the Shipments to Branch and Shipments from Home Office accounts strengthen control over branch operations, the period-end closing procedures and the preparation of combined financial statements are more understandable and simpler if these accounts are closed to respective Cost of Goods Sold accounts at month-end. (The inventory accounts are also adjusted in this closing entry to arrive at Cost of Goods Sold.) These closing entries and the preparation of combined financial statements are discussed and illustrated later in the chapter, as are situations in which inventory transfers are made at above the home office's cost.

Fixed Asset Accounts

Some home offices require their branches' fixed assets to be recorded on the books of the home office instead of on the books of the branches. Such a procedure automatically ensures that uniform depreciation methods and asset lives are used for all branches. The home office usually charges the branch for the depreciation expense of its fixed assets. It does this by crediting Accumulated Depreciation and debiting the Investment in Branch account instead of debiting Depreciation Expense. The branch debits Depreciation Expense and credits the Home Office Equity account instead of crediting Accumulated Depreciation. When fixed assets are recorded on the home office's books, the fixed assets pertaining to the branch must be added to the Investment in Branch account to evaluate the profitability of branch operations in relation to the net assets invested in the branch.

Other General Ledger Accounts

The branch maintains the balance sheet and income statement accounts necessary to record transactions that take place between (1) the home office and the branch, and (2) the branch and its customers, creditors, and employees. The extent of the accounts required depends on the scope of the branch's operations.

Illustrative Entries

TYPICAL TRANSACTIONS FOR A BRANCH

Assume that Searbuck Company, which prepares financial reports at the end of the calendar year, established a branch on July 1, 19X1. The following transactions occurred during the formation of the branch and its first six months of operations, ending December 31, 19X1.

1. The home office sent $25,000 cash to the branch to begin operations.
2. The home office shipped inventory to the branch. Intracompany billings totaled $60,000, which was the home office's cost. (Both the home office and the branch use a periodic inventory system.)
3. The branch acquired merchandise display equipment costing $12,000 on July 1, 19X1. (Assume that branch fixed assets are not carried on the home office books.)
4. The branch purchased inventory costing $40,000 from outside vendors on account.
5. The branch had credit sales of $85,000 and cash sales of $35,000.
6. The branch collected $66,000 on accounts receivable.
7. The branch paid outside vendors $25,000.
8. The branch incurred selling expenses of $15,000 and general and administrative expenses of $12,000. These expenses were paid in cash when they were incurred and include the expense of leasing the branch's facilities.
9. The home office charged the branch $2,000 for its share of insurance.

10. Depreciation expense on the merchandise display equipment acquired by the branch is $1,000 for the six-month period. (Depreciation expense is classified as a selling expense.)
11. The branch remitted $45,000 cash to the home office.
12. The branch's physical inventory on December 31, 19X1, is $30,000 (there was no beginning inventory). The home office's physical inventory on December 31, 19X1, is $150,000 (the beginning inventory was $135,000). (Home office purchases were $285,000.) Cost of goods sold is determined and recorded in a separate account for each accounting entity. (Note that the year-end inventory accounts are adjusted in this entry to the year-end physical inventory balances.)
13. The branch closes its income statement accounts.
14. The home office prepares its adjusting entry to reflect the increase in the branch's net assets resulting from the branch's operations.

The journal entries for these transactions as they would be recorded by the home office and the branch are presented in Illustration 1-1.

COMBINED FINANCIAL STATEMENTS: INVENTORY TRANSFERS AT HOME OFFICE COST

Month-end Verification of Intracompany Account Balances

Before the branch prepares its closing entries and submits financial statements to the home office, it must verify that its Home Office Equity account and Shipments from Home Office account agree with the corresponding reciprocal accounts maintained by the home office. If the accounts do not agree, there are two possible explanations:

1. A transaction initiated by one of the accounting entities has been improperly recorded by the other accounting entity. The accounting entity that made the error must make the appropriate adjusting entry.
2. A transaction initiated by one of the accounting entities has been recorded by the initiating entity but not yet by the receiving entity—for example, cash transfers in transit, inventory shipments in transit, and intracompany charges. Normally, the receiving accounting entity prepares the adjusting entry as though it has completed the transaction before the end of the accounting period. (It would be more disruptive to have the initiating accounting entity reverse the transaction.)

These adjusting entries to bring the intracompany accounts into agreement are absolutely necessary for the proper preparation of combined financial statements. After making any necessary adjustments, the branch submits an income statement and a balance sheet to the home office.

The Primary Elimination Entry

After the home office general ledger is adjusted for the branch's income or loss, it reflects the overall net income earned by the home office and the

Illustration 1-1
Typical Transactions for a Branch

Home Office Books			Branch Books		
1. Investment in Branch	25,000		1. Cash	25,000	
Cash		25,000	Home Office Equity		25,000
2. Investment in Branch	60,000		2. Shipments from Home Office	60,000	
Shipments to Branch		60,000	Home Office Equity		60,000
			3. Equipment	12,000	
			Cash		12,000
			4. Purchases	40,000	
			Accounts Payable		40,000
			5. Cash	35,000	
			Accounts Receivable	85,000	
			Sales		120,000
			6. Cash	66,000	
			Accounts Receivable		66,000
			7. Accounts Payable	25,000	
			Cash		25,000
			8. Selling Expenses	15,000	
			Administrative Expenses	12,000	
			Cash		27,000
9. Investment in Branch	2,000		9. Administrative Expenses	2,000	
Administrative Expenses		2,000	Home Office Equity		2,000
			10. Selling Expenses	1,000	
			Accumulated Depreciation		1,000
11. Cash	45,000		11. Home Office Equity	45,000	
Investment in Branch		45,000	Cash		45,000
12. Inventory	15,000		12. Inventory	30,000	
Shipments to Branch	60,000		Cost of Goods Sold	70,000	
Cost of Goods Sold	210,000		Shipments from Home Office		60,000
Purchases		285,000	Purchases		40,000
			13. Sales	120,000	
			Cost of Goods Sold		70,000
			Selling Expenses		16,000
			Administrative Expenses		14,000
			Home Office Equity		20,000
14. Investment in Branch	20,000				
Branch Income		20,000			

branch. Generally accepted accounting principles require, however, that in reporting the results of operations to its shareholders, the home office combine the detail of the branch's income or loss with the detail of the accounts making up the net income or loss from the home office's own operations. In other words, the home office cannot report a one-line item amount called "branch income" or "loss for the branch's operations"; it must combine the sales, the cost of goods sold, and the operating expenses of both accounting entities and report the combined amounts. This is accomplished by substituting the branch's income statement for the Branch Income or Loss account in the home office general ledger. Likewise, generally accepted accounting principles require that in reporting the balance sheet amounts to its shareholders, the home office combine the individual assets and liabilities of both accounting entities and report the combined amounts. This is accomplished by substituting the individual assets and liabilities of the branch for the Investment in Branch account (which, by its nature, always equals the branch's net assets).

This substitution takes place on a worksheet used to eliminate the appropriate accounts so that the assets, liabilities, sales, cost of goods sold, and operating expenses of each accounting entity can be combined. Such a worksheet, called a **combining statement worksheet,** is shown in Illustration 1-2. A journal entry, which for instructional and ease of reference purposes we call the **primary elimination entry,** is posted to the worksheet to eliminate (1) the Investment in Branch account in the home office column, (2) the Branch Income account in the home office column, and (3) the preclosing balance of the Home Office Equity account in the branch column of the statement of retained earnings/analysis of home office equity section.

All worksheet entries in this book are shaded to differentiate them from general ledger entries. The worksheet entry is as follows:

Branch Income	**xxx**	
Home Office Equity (preclosing balance)	**xxx**	
Investment in Branch		**xxx**

The debit to Branch Income in the income statement section of the worksheet is totaled at the net income line and then carried forward to the net income line in the statement of Retained Earnings/Analysis of Home Office Equity section of the worksheet. Each account on the worksheet is then cross-totaled to arrive at the combined amounts. The amounts in the combined column are used to prepare the financial statements that are distributed to the company's stockholders.

Illustration

A COMBINING STATEMENT WORKSHEET

The worksheet in Illustration 1-2 combines the financial statements of a home office with those of its branch. The financial statement amounts for

Illustration 1-2
Inventory Transferred at Cost

SEARBUCK COMPANY
Combining Statement Worksheet
For the Year Ended December 31, 19X1

	Home Office	Branch[a]	Eliminations Dr.	Eliminations Cr.	Combined
Income Statement:					
Sales	380,000	120,000			500,000
Cost of goods sold	(210,000)	(70,000)			(280,000)
Selling expenses	(52,000)	(16,000)			(68,000)
Administrative expenses	(59,000)	(14,000)			(73,000)
Interest expense	(19,000)				(19,000)
Branch income	20,000		20,000(1)		–0–
Income before Income Taxes	60,000	20,000	20,000		60,000
Income tax expense @ 40%	(24,000)				(24,000)
Net Income	36,000	20,000	20,000		36,000
Statement of Retained Earnings/ Analysis of Home Office Equity:					
Retained earnings—January 1, 19X1	82,000				82,000
Home office equity (preclosing)		42,000	42,000(1)		–0–
+ Net income	36,000	20,000	20,000		36,000
− Dividends declared	(10,000)				(10,000)
Balances, December 31, 19X1	108,000	62,000	62,000		108,000
Balance Sheet:					
Cash	30,000	17,000			47,000
Accounts receivable, net	80,000	19,000			99,000
Inventory:[b]					
Acquired from vendors	150,000	6,000			156,000
Acquired from home office		24,000			24,000
Land	22,000				22,000
Buildings and equipment, net	124,000	11,000			135,000
Investment in branch	62,000			62,000(1)	–0–
Total Assets	468,000	77,000		62,000	483,000
Accounts payable and accruals	60,000	15,000			75,000
Long-term debt	200,000				200,000
Common stock	100,000				100,000
Retained earnings	108,000				108,000
Home Office Equity		62,000	62,000		–0–
Total Liabilities and Equity	468,000	77,000	62,000		483,000
Proof of debit and credit postings			62,000	62,000	

[a]The amounts in this column reflect the activity shown in Illustration 1-1.
[b]The separation of the inventory into these two categories is not necessary if transfers are made at cost. It is shown here only for later comparison with Illustration 1-4, where transfers are made above cost.

Explanation of entry:
(1) The primary elimination entry.

the branch reflect the transactions shown in Illustration 1-1. The primary elimination entry is:

Branch Income	20,000	
Home Office Equity	42,000	
Investment in Branch		62,000

The following points are important for understanding Illustration 1-2:

1. The combining worksheet is started *after* the home office has made its adjusting entry concerning the branch's income and after it has provided for income taxes on the branch's income.
2. The balance in the Retained Earnings account in the home office column includes the branch's income net of applicable income taxes. This retained earnings amount is the combined retained earnings.
3. The debit balance in the eliminations column of the worksheet at the net income line of the income statement is carried forward to the net income line in the statement of retained earnings/analysis of home office equity section.
4. The net income in the home office column is the same as the net income in the combined column.
5. The combining worksheet is not distributed to the home office's stockholders; only the financial statements, which can be readily prepared from the combined column of the worksheet, are distributed to them. (The formal balance sheet and income statement are not shown.)
6. The primary elimination entry is posted only to the worksheet, not to the general ledger.
7. The primary elimination entry is the same each time the combination is performed; only the amounts differ.

COMBINED FINANCIAL STATEMENTS: INVENTORY TRANSFERS ABOVE HOME OFFICE COST

Some home offices transfer inventory to their branches at costs above their own cost. In some instances, the mark-up is designed to absorb the costs of central purchasing, warehousing, and handling, or to have those operations show a profit. In other instances, the transfer costs reflect prices that the branches would pay if they acquired the merchandise directly from the manufacturers and distributors. In theory, large volume discounts generated by the central purchasing department of the home office should not be reflected in the branch income statements. In other instances, the mark-up is designed to achieve greater companywide profits because branch personnel base the mark-up to their customers on the inflated billing prices from the home office. (Often branch personnel are not informed of the extent of the home office's mark-up.)

In situations involving inventory transfers at above cost, it is necessary to distinguish carefully between a mark-up expressed in relation to cost and one expressed in relation to the transfer price. For example, inventory costing $1,000 and transferred at $1,250 has a 25% mark-up based on cost ($250 ÷ $1,000) but a 20% mark-up based on the transfer price ($250 ÷ $1,250).

Procedures for Transferring Inventory above Home Office Cost

Any time transfers are made at above cost, the home office must defer recognition of the mark-up until the branch sells the inventory to its customers. To do otherwise would result in the recognition of profit merely from transferring inventory from one location to another within the company. When inventory is transferred to the branch, the home office (1) credits the Shipments to Branch account at the home office's cost, (2) credits an account called Deferred Profit for the amount of the mark-up, and (3) debits the Investment in Branch account for the total intracompany billing amount. The proper journal entry is as follows:

Investment in Branch	xxx	
Shipments to Branch		xxx
Deferred Profit		xxx

The branch makes the same entry as it does when inventory transfers are made at the home office's cost. Thus, the branch debits the Shipments from Home Office account for the total intracompany billing amount and credits the Home Office Equity account. Journal entry 2 in Illustration 1-3 records an inventory transfer above cost.

When the branch submits its month-end financial statements to the home office, it must show separately that portion of its ending inventory that was acquired from the home office. The home office can then (1) determine the amount of mark-up in the ending branch inventory, (2) adjust the Deferred Profit account to this amount, and (3) credit the Branch Income account for the recognizable mark-up. This procedure still keeps the Investment in Branch account on the home office books and the Home Office Equity account on the branch books in agreement. However, the Shipments to Branch account on the books of the home office is always less than the Shipments from Home Office account on the books of the branch by the amount of the mark-up. As a result of the mark-up, the branch's cost of goods sold is greater and the branch reports a lower operating profit than if the transfer had been billed at the home office's cost. The lower profit reported by the branch is offset by the recognition of the deferred profit by the home office. This procedure results in the same net income being reported on companywide basis, just as though the inventory had been transferred at cost.

Illustrative Entries

INVENTORY TRANSFERS ABOVE COST

Assume that the inventory transferred to the branch from the home office in Illustration 1-1 was marked up 20% over the home office's cost of $60,000. In Illustration 1-2, we assumed that the branch had a $30,000 ending inventory, of which $6,000 represented purchases from outside vendors and $24,000 represented inventory obtained from the home office. In this case, the branch's ending inventory acquired from the home office is $28,800 ($24,000 + $4,800 mark-up). Thus, the branch's total ending inventory is $34,800 ($28,800 + $6,000 acquired from outside vendors). Illustration 1-3 shows the journal entries for the transfer of this inventory above cost, along with the appropriate year-end closing and adjusting entries. The journal entries are numbered to correspond to Illustration 1-1, which shows inventory transfers made at the home office's cost.

Illustration 1-3
Inventory Transfers above Cost

Home Office Books			Branch Books		
2. Investment in Branch	72,000		2. Shipments from Home Office...........	72,000	
Shipments to Branch...........		60,000	Home Office Equity.............		72,000
Deferred Profit....		12,000			
12. Inventory.................	15,000[a]		12. Inventory Acquired from Vendors.........	6,000[b]	
Shipments to Branch	60,000		Inventory Acquired from Home Office.....	28,800[c]	
Cost of Goods Sold....	210,000		Cost of Goods Sold.....	77,200	
Purchases..........		285,000	Shipments from Home Office......		72,000
			Purchases		40,000
			13. Sales........................	120,000	
			Cost of Goods Sold		77,200
			Selling Expenses..		16,000
			Administrative Expenses.........		14,000
			Home Office Equity		12,800
14. Investment in Branch	12,800				
Branch Income ...		12,800			
Deferred Profit.........	7,200[d]				
Branch Income ...		7,200			

[a]This is the increase in the inventory ($150,000 − $135,000).
[b]This is the increase in the inventory acquired from vendors ($6,000 − $–0–). (There was no beginning inventory.)
[c]This is the increase in the inventory acquired from the home office ($28,800 − $–0–). (There was no beginning inventory.)
[d]Adjusts the Deferred Profit account to the $4,800 mark-up in the ending inventory (total mark-up of $12,000 − $4,800 = $7,200).

In practice, the mark-up must be calculated from the amount of home office–acquired inventory reported by the branch at month-end. (The branch keeps track of and accounts for its inventory based on the transfer price—not the home office's cost.) Using the same facts as in the preceding paragraph, the branch would report home office–acquired inventory of $28,800. (This could be determined from perpetual inventory records or from a physical count.) Knowing that the mark-up is 20% of the home office's cost, the home office would calculate the mark-up in the branch's ending inventory as follows:

$$\frac{\$28{,}800}{1.20} = \$24{,}000 \text{ (the home office's cost)}$$

$$\$28{,}800 - \$24{,}000 = \$4{,}800 \text{ (the mark-up)}$$

The Secondary Elimination Entry

When inventory transfers are made above the home office's cost, an additional elimination entry must be used to prepare combined financial statements. For instructional and ease of reference purposes we call this the **secondary elimination entry.** Its purpose is to adjust the branch's cost of goods sold downward to the amount that it would be if the inventory were transferred from the home office at cost. The overstatement of the branch's cost of goods sold equals the amount of the deferred profit that was earned during the year and recognized by the home office. Accordingly, that portion of the credit balance in the Branch Income account pertaining to the recognition of profit from the Deferred Profit account must be reclassified to the Cost of Goods Sold account in the income statement. Because this entry takes place entirely within the income statement section of the worksheet, it is merely a reclassification entry.

Illustration

COMBINING STATEMENT WORKSHEET: INVENTORY TRANSFERRED ABOVE COST

Illustration 1-4 shows a worksheet that combines the financial statements of a home office with those of a branch when inventory transfers were made above cost. The financial statements of the home office and the branch are taken from Illustration 1-2, adjusted to reflect inventory transfers at 20% above cost, as in Illustration 1-3.

The following elimination entries are made:

1. The primary elimination entry:

Branch Income	**12,800**	
Home Office Equity (Preclosing Balance)	**54,000**	
Investment in Branch		**66,800**

Illustration 1-4
Inventory Transferred above Cost

SEARBUCK COMPANY
Combining Statement Worksheet
For the Year Ended December 31, 19X1

	Home Office	Branch	Eliminations Dr.	Eliminations Cr.	Combined
Income Statement:					
Sales	380,000	120,000			500,000
Cost of goods sold	(210,000)	(77,200)		7,200(2)	(280,000)
Selling expenses	(52,000)	(16,000)			(68,000)
Administrative expenses	(59,000)	(14,000)			(73,000)
Interest expense	(19,000)				(19,000)
Branch income	20,000		12,800(1) 7,200(2)		-0-
Income before Income Taxes	60,000	12,800	20,000	7,200	60,000
Income tax expense @ 40%	(24,000)				(24,000)
Net Income	36,000	12,800	20,000	7,200	36,000
Statement of Retained Earnings/ Analysis of Home Office Equity:					
Retained earnings—January 1, 19X1	82,000				82,000
Home office equity (preclosing)		54,000	54,000(1)		-0-
+ Net income	36,000	12,800	20,000	7,200	36,000
− Dividends declared	(10,000)				(10,000)
Balances, December 31, 19X1	108,000	66,800	74,000	7,200	108,000
Balance Sheet:					
Cash	30,000	17,000			47,000
Accounts receivable, net	80,000	19,000			99,000
Inventory:					
Acquired from vendors	150,000	6,000			156,000
Acquired from home office		28,800		4,800(3)	24,000
Deferred profit	(4,800)		4,800(3)		-0-
Land	22,000				22,000
Buildings and equipment, net	124,000	11,000			135,000
Investment in branch	66,800			66,800(1)	-0-
Total Assets	468,000	81,800	4,800	71,600	483,000
Accounts payable and accruals	60,000	15,000			75,000
Long-term debt	200,000				200,000
Common stock	100,000				100,000
Retained earnings	108,000				108,000
Home Office Equity		66,800	74,000	7,200	-0-
Total Liabilities and Equity	468,000	81,800	74,000	7,200	483,000
Proof of debit and credit postings			78,800	78,800	

Explanation of entries:
(1) The primary elimination entry.
(2) The secondary elimination entry.
(3) The deferred profit elimination entry.

2. The secondary elimination entry:

Branch Income	7,200	
Cost of Goods Sold		7,200

3. The deferred profit elimination entry:

Deferred Profit	4,800	
Inventory		4,800

The following analysis proves that the branch's cost of goods sold is $7,200 more than if the transfers had been made at the home office's cost:

	Transfers above Cost	Transfers at Cost	Mark-up
Shipments from home office	$ 72,000	$ 60,000	$12,000
Purchases (from vendors)	40,000	40,000	
Total inventory available for sale	$112,000	$100,000	$12,000
Less—Ending inventory	34,800	30,000	4,800
Cost of goods sold	$ 77,200	$ 70,000	$ 7,200

The following points are important for understanding Illustration 1-4:

1. The only change from Illustration 1-2 is that the merchandise shipments from the home office were billed at $72,000 instead of $60,000, with the $12,000 mark-up initially credited to the Deferred Profit account.
2. The combined balances are the same in Illustrations 1-2 and 1-4.
3. Regardless of the transfer price for intracompany billing, the combined financial statements are the same for financial reporting purposes.
4. In whichever subsequent accounting period the branch sells the remaining portion of the inventory acquired from the home office, a reclassification entry is required within the income statement section of the combining worksheet:

Branch Income	4,800	
Cost of Goods Sold		4,800

This entry reduces the branch's reported cost of goods sold to agree with the home office's cost.

OTHER MISCELLANEOUS AREAS

Perpetual Inventory Systems

When the home office and the branch both use perpetual inventory systems, the respective general ledger Inventory accounts are used instead of the Shipments to Branch and Shipments from Home Office accounts, as shown below:

	Transfers at Cost		Transfers above Cost	
Home office books:				
Investment in Branch	60,000		72,000	
Inventory		60,000		60,000
Deferred Profit				12,000
Branch books:				
Inventory	60,000		72,000	
Home Office Equity		60,000		72,000

As sales occur, each entity relieves inventory directly to its Cost of Goods Sold account. The primary and secondary elimination entries are the same as those shown previously.

Interbranch Transactions

Branches often transfer inventory to one another. Each branch records the transfer using an Interbranch Receivable or Payable account and a Shipments to or from Branch account. For example, assume Branch A transfers inventory costing $5,000 to Branch B. The entry to Branch A's books would be:

Interbranch Receivable	5,000	
Shipments to Branch B		5,000

Correspondingly, the entry to Branch B's books would be:

Shipments from Branch A	5,000	
Interbranch Payable		5,000

The Shipments to Branch B account offsets the Shipments from Branch A account when combined financial statements are prepared. Any unpaid interbranch receivables and payables at month-end also offset each other when combined financial statements are prepared. Some home offices do not require branches to make cash payments to one another for interbranch transfers, because this is not sound cash management on a companywide basis. Instead, company policy may require each branch to close its Interbranch Receivable or Payable accounts to its respective Home Office Equity accounts at month-end. Assuming no other transactions occurred between branches A and B for the month, the entries to close these accounts would be as follows, for Branch A:

Home Office Equity	5,000	
Interbranch Receivable		5,000

for Branch B:

Interbranch Payable	5,000	
Home Office Equity		5,000

The branch must inform the home office of the amounts that have been charged or credited to the Home Office Equity accounts. The home office would then make the following entry:

Investment in Branch B	5,000	
Investment in Branch A		5,000

Freight

Freight charges incurred in acquiring inventory from the home office or from outside sources are inventoriable. When a branch acquires inventory from another branch rather than from the normal source of supply, sound accounting theory dictates that any freight charges in excess of normal should be expensed currently. If the home office is responsible for a branch having to use another branch as a supply source, then such incremental freight charges should be borne by the home office, regardless of which accounting entity makes the cash payment for the freight charges.

Start-up Costs

Expenses incurred by a branch *before* it formally opens for business are start-up costs. An operating loss incurred for a period of time after the formal opening is not considered a start-up cost.

Start-up costs may be expensed as incurred, or they may be capitalized for subsequent amortization over a reasonably short period of time (usually no more than a 3- to 5-year amortization period). Most companies expense start-up costs as incurred.

Agencies

Some companies open outlying sales offices that carry only product samples, demonstration units, and brochures, all of which are used in obtaining sales orders. These offices are commonly referred to as *agencies*. Sales orders are forwarded to the home office for approval and filling.

Agency personnel are almost always paid from the home office. The home office may establish a nominal imprest cash fund for each of these outlying locations. The imprest funds, which may be in the form of petty cash or a local bank account, are used to pay for miscellaneous expenses incurred. As imprest funds are depleted, the outlying location sends invoices and receipts to the home office, which reviews them and sends a check to replenish the fund. The home office records these expenses in its general ledger, usually in accounts specially coded to signify the outlying location to which they pertain. This manner of accounting for sales offices is a predominantly centralized system.

SUMMARY

When a company establishes operations in outlying locations through internal expansion, the outlying locations can be accounted for using a centralized or a decentralized accounting system. Under a centralized accounting system, the assets, liabilities, revenues, and expenses of the outlying locations are recorded on the books of the home office. Under a decentralized accounting system, each outlying location uses its own general ledger to reflect its assets, liabilities, revenues, costs, and expenses. A decentralized accounting system requires the home office to use accounting procedures that effectively treat the outlying locations as investments to maintain control over their net assets and operations.

Management must evaluate the profitability of branch operations carefully when inventory is acquired from the home office, because intracompany billing prices established by the home office directly affect the profitability of the branches. Furthermore, the treatment of home office expenses—none, some, or all of which may be allocated to the branches—complicates the process of evaluating the profitability of branch operations.

In preparing financial statements for stockholders, the company must combine the financial statements of the home office and the outlying locations. Combined financial statements are prepared so that intracompany transactions are eliminated and the combined financial statements reflect only those transactions that occur between the company and outside parties.

Glossary of New Terms

Agency An outlying location that carries product samples, demonstration units, and brochures for the purpose of obtaining sales orders, which are approved and filled by the home office.

Branch An outlying manufacturing, service, or retailing location of a legal business entity.

Centralized Accounting A system whereby the accounting for outlying locations is performed at the home office; the outlying locations do not maintain general ledgers.

Decentralized Accounting A system whereby outlying locations maintain their own general ledgers and submit financial reports periodically to the home office.

External Expansion The expansion of a business by combining two existing businesses into a unified larger business.

Home Office The headquarters location of a legal business entity that establishes a branch.

Internal Expansion The expansion of a business through the construction or leasing of additional facilities at an existing or outlying location.

Primary Elimination Entry A worksheet entry that enables the separate financial statements of a home office and its branch to be combined by eliminating the reciprocal accounts (Investment in Branch and Home Office Equity) and the Branch Income recorded on the home office's books.

Secondary Elimination Entry A worksheet entry that reclassifies the realized intracompany profit in the Branch Income account to the Cost of Goods Sold account.

Review Questions

1. What is the difference between a centralized accounting system and a decentralized accounting system?
2. Why is the branch's operating income or loss not a net income or loss?
3. What is the function of the Shipments to Branch and Shipments from Home Office accounts?
4. If the intracompany accounts do not agree, what are some possible explanations? Which accounting entity must make the adjustments?
5. Why are the elimination entries not posted to any general ledger?
6. What does the primary elimination entry accomplish? The secondary elimination entry?
7. When is the secondary elimination entry necessary?
8. Why is the shipment of inventory to a branch not considered a reportable sale for combined financial reporting purposes?
9. Why does the intracompany inventory transfer price have no effect on the combined amounts for financial reporting purposes?
10. Define start-up costs.

Discussion Cases

DC 1-1

Mark-up of Intracompany Inventory Transfers

You are the controller of a company that is establishing its first branch, which will use a decentralized accounting system. A substantial portion of the branch's inventory will be purchased from the home office to take advantage of the additional volume discounts that the home office can obtain. You must advise top management on the billing prices of intracompany inventory shipments to the branch. This decision is important, because the billing prices selected will directly affect the branch's operating income or loss. The branch manager has told you that all of the company's additional savings on volume discounts resulting from the formation of the branch should be passed on to the branch, since without the branch, they would not have been realized.

Required:
What considerations should be taken into account in determining the intracompany transfer pricing policy?

DC 1-2

Determination and Treatment of Start-up Costs

Lemcoe Company has numerous branch outlets, which operate from leased facilities. A new branch outlet historically has taken approximately two months from inception of its facility lease until it starts to generate sales, and another four months before its monthly operations start showing a profit. The typical new branch incurs a loss of $80,000 during this six-month period. Near the beginning of the current year, Lemcoe established the Jadeville and Rubysville branches:

	Jadeville Branch	Rubysville Branch
Number of months from lease inception until operations showed a profit	5	11
Excess of costs and expenses over revenues until monthly operations showed a profit	$(65,000)	$(130,000)

Management intends to treat as a deferred charge $160,000 of the combined $195,000 excess of costs and expenses over revenues for the two new branches. Any amount in excess of $80,000 is considered an unfavorable start-up variance, which should be expensed as a period cost.

Required:
Evaluate the treatment proposed by the company.

Exercises

E 1-1

Journal Entry Preparation: Periodic Inventory System—Inventory Transfers at Cost

The following transactions pertain to a branch's first month's operations:

1. The home office sent $9,000 cash to the branch.
2. The home office shipped inventory costing $40,000 to the branch; the intracompany billing is at cost.
3. The branch purchased inventory from outside vendors for $30,000.
4. The branch had sales of $80,000 on account.
5. The home office allocated $2,000 in advertising expenses to the branch.
6. The branch collected $45,000 on accounts receivable.

7. The branch incurred operating expenses of $14,000, none of which were paid at month-end.
8. The branch remitted $17,000 to the home office.
9. The branch's ending inventory is $28,000.

Required:

1. Prepare the home office and branch journal entries for these transactions, assuming a periodic inventory system is used.
2. Prepare the month-end closing entries for the branch.
3. Prepare the month-end adjusting entry for the home office relating to the branch's operations for the month.

E 1-2

Journal Entry Preparation: Periodic Inventory System—Inventory Transfers above Cost

The following transactions pertain to a branch's first month's operations:

1. The home office sent $9,000 cash to the branch.
2. The home office shipped inventory costing $40,000 to the branch; the intracompany billing was for $50,000.
3. Branch inventory purchases from outside vendors totaled $30,000.
4. Branch sales on account were $80,000.
5. The home office allocated $2,000 in advertising expenses to the branch.
6. Branch collections on accounts receivable were $45,000.
7. Branch operating expenses of $14,000 were incurred, none of which were paid at month-end.
8. The branch remitted $17,000 to the home office.
9. The branch's ending inventory (as reported in its balance sheet) is composed of:

Acquired from outside vendors	**$12,000**
Acquired from home office (at billing price)	**20,000**
Total	**$32,000**

Required:

1. Prepare the home office and branch journal entries for these transactions, assuming a periodic inventory system is used.
2. Prepare the month-end closing entries for the branch.
3. Prepare the month-end adjusting entries for the home office relating to the branch's operations for the month.

E 1-3

Reconciliation of Intracompany Accounts

On December 31, 19X1, the Home Office Equity account on the branch's books has a balance of $44,000 and the Investment in Branch account on the home office's books has a balance of $85,000. In analyzing the activity in each of these accounts for December, you find the following differences:

1. A $10,000 branch remittance to the home office initiated on December 27, 19X1, was recorded on the home office books on January 3, 19X2.
2. A home office inventory shipment to the branch on December 28, 19X1, was recorded by the branch on January 4, 19X2; the billing of $20,000 was at cost.
3. The home office allocated $5,000 of expenses to the branch on December 15, 19X1. The branch has not recorded this transaction.
4. A branch customer erroneously remitted $3,000 to the home office. The home office recorded this cash collection on December 23, 19X1. Meanwhile, back at the branch, no entry has been made yet.
5. Inventory costing $43,000 was sent to the branch by the home office on December 10, 19X1. The billing was at cost, but the branch recorded the transaction at $34,000.

Required:
Prepare the entries to bring the intracompany accounts into balance as of December 31, 19X1. Assume that a periodic inventory system is in use.

E 1-4

Reconciliation of Intracompany Accounts

The following entries are reflected in the intracompany accounts of Clayton Company and its lone branch in Mooreville for June 19X2:

Home Office Equity

			6/1	Balance	50,000
6/2	Remittance	10,000	6/8	Inventory shipment	30,000
6/24	Purchase of equipment (carried on home office books)	7,000	6/10	Collection of home office receivable	2,000
6/29	Remittance	15,000	6/16	Inventory shipment	12,000
6/30	Inventory returned to home office	1,000	6/24	Inventory shipment	17,000
6/30	Depreciation allocation	2,000	6/28	Advertising allocation	400
			6/30	Balance	76,400

Investment in Mooreville Branch

6/1	Balance	50,000			
6/5	Inventory shipment	30,000	6/2	Remittance	10,000
6/12	Inventory shipment	12,000	6/8	Collection of branch receivable	1,000
6/20	Inventory shipment	17,000	6/27	Equipment purchase by branch	7,000
6/25	Advertising allocation to branch (50% of $8,000 incurred)	4,000			
6/28	Inventory shipment	14,000			
6/30	Depreciation allocation	2,000			
6/30	Balance	111,000			

Required:

1. Prepare a schedule to reconcile the intracompany accounts. Assume that inventory shipments to the branch are billed at 25% above the home office's cost.
2. Prepare the adjusting journal entries to bring the intracompany accounts into balance.

E 1-5

Analysis of Branch Inventory and Deferred Profit

A home office shipped inventory to its branch during the year. The following information has been obtained from the financial statements of the home office and the branch at the end of the current year:

	Total	Resold	On Hand
Shipments from home office	$90,000		$21,000
Shipments to branch	75,000		
Mark-up	$15,000		

Required:

1. Complete the analysis.
2. Prepare the branch's entry to record cost of goods sold, assuming the branch purchases all of its inventory from the home office and reported a beginning inventory of $12,000. (Assume the same mark-up percentage for last year as for this year.)
3. Prepare an analysis of the Deferred Profit account for the year.

E 1-6

Adjusting the Deferred Profit Account

Toddlin Company ships inventory to its State Street branch at 125% of cost. The Deferred Profit account balance at the beginning of the year was $4,000. During the year, the branch was billed $70,000 for inventory transfers from the home office. At year-end, the branch's balance sheet shows $16,000 of inventory on hand that was acquired from the home office.

Required:

1. Determine the amount of the branch's beginning inventory (as shown in its prior year-end financial statements).
2. Prepare the branch's entry to record cost of goods sold.
3. Calculate the year-end adjustment to the Deferred Profit account and show the adjusting journal entry.

E 1-7

Journal Entry Preparation: Periodic Inventory System—Inventory Transfers above Cost

The following transactions pertain to branch operations:

1. The branch purchased and paid for equipment costing $3,000. All fixed assets are recorded on the home office books.

2. The branch received and deposited a $1,000 remittance from a customer of a nearby branch.
3. The home office paid the monthly lease expense of $4,000 on the branch's facilities. Company policy is to allocate such expenses to the branch.
4. A branch customer made a payment of $2,000 directly to the home office. The home office notified the branch, which then made the appropriate entry.
5. The branch remitted $15,000 to the home office.
6. The home office computed the monthly depreciation expense pertaining to the branch's fixed assets, which are recorded on the home office books. The depreciation expense of $4,500 was charged to the branch.
7. The home office allocated overhead expenses of $8,000 to the branch.
8. The home office shipped inventory to the branch. The home office's cost was $55,000, and it billed the branch $66,000.
9. With respect to the inventory purchased from the home office in transaction 8, assume the branch had $3,600 of this inventory on hand at month-end, as reflected in its financial statements submitted to the home office. Assume the branch reported a beginning inventory of items purchased from the home office of $6,000, all of which was sold during the current year.
10. The home office received the branch's monthly financial statements, which showed the branch had operating income of $25,000.

Required:
Prepare the home office and branch journal entries for these transactions, assuming a periodic inventory system is used. For transaction 9, prepare the branch's entry to record cost of goods sold.

E 1-8

Calculating Beginning Inventory from Selected Data

The Casco Company transfers inventory to its Roseville branch at a 20% mark-up. During the current year, inventory costing the home office $80,000 was transferred to the branch. At year-end, the home office adjusted its Deferred Profit account downward by $18,200. The branch's year-end balance sheet shows $4,800 of inventory acquired from the home office.

Required:
Calculate the home office's cost of the branch's beginning inventory.

Problems

P 1-1*

Preparing a Combining Statement Worksheet: Periodic Inventory System—Inventory Transfers at Cost; Initial Year of Branch Operations

The December 31, 19X1, financial statements of Friscoe Company and its Grant Avenue branch (which was established in 19X1) are given below.

	Home Office	Branch
Income Statement:		
Sales	$ 700,000	$200,000
Cost of goods sold	(380,000)	(135,000)
Selling expenses	(42,000)	(11,000)
Administrative expenses	(28,000)	(4,000)
Interest expense	(50,000)	
Branch income	50,000	
Income before Income Taxes	$ 250,000	$ 50,000
Income tax expense @ 40%	(100,000)	
Net Income	$ 150,000	$ 50,000
Balance Sheet:		
Cash	$ 90,000	$ 10,000
Accounts receivable, net	80,000	20,000
Inventory		
Acquired from vendors	180,000	10,000
Acquired from home office		30,000
Fixed assets, net	770,000	140,000
Investment in branch	170,000	
Total Assets	$1,290,000	$210,000
Accounts payable and accruals	$ 200,000	$ 40,000
Long-term debt	350,000	
Common stock	500,000	
Retained earnings	240,000	
Home Office Equity		170,000
Total Liabilities and Equity	$1,290,000	$210,000
Dividends declared during 19X1	$ 110,000	

Required:
Prepare a combining statement worksheet as of December 31, 19X1, assuming inventory transfers to the branch from the home office are at cost.

P 1-2* Preparing a Combining Statement Worksheet: Periodic Inventory System—Inventory Transfers above Cost; Initial Year of Branch Operations

The December 31, 19X1, financial statements of Miracle-Mart and its 34th Street branch (which was established in 19X1) are as follows:

*The financial statement information presented for problems accompanied by asterisks is also provided on Model 1 (filename: Model 1) of the software file disk that is available for use with the text, enabling the problem to be worked on the computer.

	Home Office	Branch
Income Statement:		
Sales	$ 700,000	$200,000
Cost of goods sold	(380,000)	(149,000)
Selling expenses	(42,000)	(11,000)
Administrative expenses	(28,000)	(4,000)
Interest expense	(50,000)	
Branch income	50,000	
Income before Income Taxes	$ 250,000	$ 36,000
Income tax expense @ 40%	(100,000)	
Net Income	$ 150,000	$ 36,000
Balance Sheet:		
Cash	$ 90,000	$ 10,000
Accounts receivable, net	80,000	20,000
Inventory:		
Acquired from vendors	180,000	10,000
Acquired from home office		36,000
Deferred profit	(6,000)	
Fixed assets, net	770,000	140,000
Investment in branch	176,000	
Total Assets	$1,290,000	$216,000
Accounts payable and accruals	$ 200,000	$ 40,000
Long-term debt	350,000	
Common stock	500,000	
Retained earnings	240,000	
Home Office Equity		176,000
Total Liabilities and Equity	$1,290,000	$216,000
Dividends declared during 19X1	$ 110,000	

Required:

1. Prepare a combining statement worksheet as of December 31, 19X1.
2. Complete the following analysis of the branch's inventory:

	Transfers above Cost	Transfers at Cost	Mark-up
Shipments from home office	$	$	$
Purchases (from vendors)	75,000	75,000	–0–
Total inventory available for sale			
Less—Ending inventory			
Cost of goods sold	$	$	$

3. Prepare the entry the branch made to record the cost of goods sold.
4. Calculate the mark-up as a percentage of the home office's cost.

P 1-3*

COMPREHENSIVE Year-end Adjusting and Closing Entries and Preparing Combining Statement Worksheet: Periodic Inventory System—Inventory Transfers above Cost

The trial balances of Beverly Company and its Rodeo Drive branch for the year ended December 31, 19X3, prior to adjusting and closing entries are as follows:

	Home Office		Branch	
Accounts	Dr.	Cr.	Dr.	Cr.
Cash	$ 35,000		$ 10,000	
Accounts receivable, net	80,000		50,000	
Inventory, January 1, 19X3:				
Acquired from vendors	230,000		50,000	
Acquired from home office			20,000	
Deferred profit		$ 25,000		
Fixed assets, net	870,000		90,000	
Investment in branch	155,000			
Accounts payable and accruals		221,000		$ 45,000
Long-term debt		400,000		
Common stock		300,000		
Retained earnings, January 1, 19X3		350,000		
Home office equity				115,000
Sales		960,000		320,000
Purchases	800,000		120,000	
Shipments from home office			90,000	
Shipments to branch		84,000		
Selling expenses	81,000		34,000	
Administrative expenses	54,000		16,000	
Interest expense	35,000			
	$2,340,000	$2,340,000	$480,000	$480,000
Inventory per physical count on December 31, 19X3				
Acquired from vendors	$ 180,000		$ 20,000	
Acquired from home office			$ 30,000	

Additional Information:

1. Inventory transferred to the branch from the home office is billed at 125% of cost.
2. The home office billed the branch $15,000 for inventory it shipped to the branch on December 28, 19X3; the branch received and recorded this shipment on January 2, 19X4.
3. The branch remitted $25,000 cash to the home office on December 31, 19X3; the home office received and recorded this remittance on January 4, 19X4.
4. The Deferred Profit account is normally adjusted at the end of the year.
5. Income taxes are to be recorded at 40%.
6. No dividends were declared during the year.

Required:

1. Prepare the year-end adjusting entries to:
   a. Bring the intracompany accounts into agreement.
   b. Adjust the inventory accounts and record cost of goods sold.
   c. Record the Branch's income on the home office's books.
   d. Adjust the Deferred Profit account to the proper balance.
   e. Provide for income taxes.
2. Prepare the year-end closing entries for the home office and the branch.
3. Prepare a combining statement worksheet as of December 31, 19X3 after completing requirements 1 and 2.

P 1-4*

COMPREHENSIVE Year-end Adjusting and Closing Entries and Preparing Combining Statement Worksheet: Periodic Inventory System—Inventory Transfers above Cost

The preclosing trial balances at December 31, 19X5, for the Dessin Company and its Fifth Avenue branch office are as follows:

DESSIN COMPANY
Trial Balances
For the Year Ended December 31, 19X5

Accounts	Home Office Dr.	Home Office Cr.	Branch Dr.	Branch Cr.
Cash	$ 36,000		$ 8,000	
Accounts receivable, net	35,000		12,000	
Inventory, January 1, 19X5	70,000		15,000	
Inventory, deferred profit		$ 10,500		
Fixed assets, net	90,000			
Investment in branch	20,000			
Accounts payable		36,000		$ 13,500
Accrued expenses		14,000		2,500
Common stock		50,000		
Retained earnings, January 1, 19X5		53,500		
Dividends declared	12,000			
Home office equity				9,000
Sales		392,000		95,000
Purchases	290,000		24,000	
Shipments to branch		40,000		
Shipments from home office			45,000	
Expenses	43,000		16,000	
	$596,000	$596,000	$120,000	$120,000

Additional Information:

1. On December 23, the branch manager purchased $4,000 of furniture and fixtures but failed to notify the home office. The bookkeeper, knowing that all

fixed assets are carried on the home office books, recorded the proper entry on the branch records. It is the company's policy not to take any depreciation on assets acquired in the last half of the year.

2. On December 27, a branch customer erroneously paid his $2,000 account to the home office. The bookkeeper made the correct entry on the home office books but did not notify the branch.
3. On December 30, the branch remitted $5,000 cash, which the home office received in January 19X6.
4. On December 31, the branch erroneously recorded the December allocated expenses from the home office as $500 instead of $1,500.
5. On December 31, the home office shipped merchandise billed at $3,000 to the branch. The branch received this shipment in January 19X6.
6. The entire beginning inventory of the branch was purchased from the home office. The physical inventories on December 31, 19X5, excluding the shipment in transit, are:

Home office	**$55,000**
Branch (composed of $18,000 from home office and $2,000 from outside vendors)	**20,000**

7. The home office consistently bills shipments to the branch at 20% above cost.
8. The Deferred Profit account is adjusted at year-end.

Required:

1. Prepare December 31, 19X5 adjusting entries to:
   a. Bring the intracompany accounts into agreement.
   b. Adjust the inventory accounts and record cost of goods sold.
   c. Record the branch income on the home office books.
   d. Adjust the Deferred Profit account to the proper balance.
   e. Provide income tax expense at 40%.
2. Prepare the year-end closing entries for the home office and the branch.
3. Prepare a combining statement worksheet as of December 31, 19X5 after completing requirements 1 and 2.

(AICPA adapted)

Problem Involving Financial Analysis

P 1-5

Calculating Return on Investment on a Newly Formed Branch

Data for the J. C. Nickels Company for the year ended December 31, 19X1, follow:

Operating income	**$ 200,000**
Interest expense	**(50,000)**
Income before Income Taxes	**150,000**
Income tax expense @ 40%	**(60,000)**
Net Income	**$ 90,000**

Long-term debt, 10% (average balance)	$ 500,000
Stockholders' equity (average balance)	$ 500,000
Total assets (average balance)	$1,200,000

During the fourth quarter of 19X1, steps were taken for the opening of a branch in Dimesville. This branch opened for business on January 1, 19X2. Data for the Dimesville branch for the quarter ended March 31, 19X2, follow:

Income for the quarter, as reported to the home office	$ 60,000
Average balance in the Home Office Equity account	$1,000,000

Additional Information:

1. Because of its good location, the branch's sales for the first quarter of 19X2 were excellent; they were very close to those of the home office for the first quarter of 19X1 on the basis of sales per square foot of retail space.
2. All inventory shipments to the branch were billed at the home office's cost.
3. The Branch's operating expenses as a percentage of sales were comparable to those of the home office for 19X1.
4. To finance the new branch, on January 1, 19X2, the home office (a) issued 10,000 shares of its common stock, which raised $400,000; and (b) borrowed $600,000 at 10% interest, due in five years. (This debt is recorded on the home office books.)
5. The only expenses allocated to the branch were for insurance and advertising.

Required:

1. Calculate the return on investment for 19X1.
2. Calculate the home office's return on its investment in the branch for the first quarter of 19X2.
3. Compare the returns on investment in requirements 1 and 2 above and evaluate whether investing in the branch was worthwhile. Can you think of other items that should be considered in this evaluation?

2

Introduction to Business Combinations

AN OVERVIEW OF EXTERNAL BUSINESS EXPANSION

Stockholders expect management to increase a company's sales and profitability each year. Consequently, sales and profit growth is one of the major objectives of corporate management. As discussed in Chapter 1, many companies can attain this growth either by expanding their existing line of business or by entering into a new line of business through internal expansion. Internal expansion can be a lengthy and involved process, considering the problems of choosing a site location, designing facilities, preparing environmental impact reports, obtaining governmental permits, dealing with architects and contractors, hiring qualified employees, developing new channels of distribution and markets, and the likely prospect of incurring operating losses for some time before revenues reach expected levels. Furthermore, entering into a new line of business through internal expansion generally is considered much riskier than expanding in the same line of business. This is simply because, initially at least, management's degree of expertise in the new line of business is less than that of existing competitors. Also, becoming an additional competitor in the field is bound to be risky.

The alternative to internal expansion is **external expansion,** whereby all or a segment of an existing business combines with the business seeking growth. Bringing together two separate businesses under common ownership is known as a **business combination.** Most of the problems of internal expansion are not encountered in external expansion; only the assessment of the prospects of an existing business is involved. If the assessment is favorable, then efforts can be made to combine the businesses. Most business combinations are completed in far less time than it would take to develop a new product, build manufacturing facilities to produce it, and then successfully market it. Often the newly acquired business produces a profit from the start. The management of the newly acquired business may be retained, and no new competitor is introduced into the field.

Terminology

In the business community, business combinations are referred to as mergers and acquisitions. The company whose business is being sought is often called the **target company.** The company attempting to acquire the target company's business is referred to as the **acquiring company.** The legal agreement that specifies the terms and provisions of the business combination is known as the *acquisition, purchase,* or *merger agreement.* For simplicity, we refer to this legal agreement as the **acquisition agreement.** The process of trying to acquire a target company's business is often called a **takeover attempt.** Business combinations can be categorized as vertical, horizontal, or conglomerate. **Vertical combinations** take place between companies involved in the same industry but at different levels—for example, a tire manufacturer and a tire distributor. **Horizontal combinations** take place between companies that are competitors at the same level in a given industry—two tire manufacturers, for example. **Conglomerate combinations** involve companies in totally unrelated industries—such as a tire manufacturer and an insurance company. In recent years, conglomerate combinations have become much more prevalent as businesses seek to diversify their product lines and minimize the effects of cyclical sales and earnings patterns in their businesses. These categories of business combination have no bearing on how the combination is recorded for financial reporting purposes.

Legal Restrictions on Business Combinations

Before discussing business combinations any further, we should note that certain combinations are prohibited. Section 7 of the Clayton Act (1914) prohibits any business combination in which "the effect of such acquisition may be substantially to lessen competition or tend to create a monopoly." The Justice Department and the Federal Trade Commission, the two federal agencies with antitrust jurisdiction, enforce this law. In 1978, these agencies issued certain precombination notification regulations: A company with assets or sales of at least $10 million that plans to acquire a manufacturing company with assets or sales of at least $10 million must file a detailed 21-page form 30 days before the planned date of consummation. (If the target company is not a manufacturing company, notification is required only if one company has at least $100 million in sales or assets and the other company has sales or assets of at least $10 million.) Such regulations enable the regulatory agencies to review proposed business combinations before they occur and, if necessary, to obtain preliminary court injunctions to block proposed combinations. For example, in 1986 the Federal Trade Commission sought a preliminary court injunction against the proposed sale by Philip Morris Co. of Seven-Up Co., its subsidiary, to PepsiCo Inc., and against the proposed purchase of Dr. Pepper Co. by Coca-Cola Co., because the transactions would give Coke and Pepsi nearly 80% of the soft drink market in the United States. Shortly thereafter, Philip Morris announced it would seek another buyer.[1]

Even when a proposed business combination is not challenged by the government before it is consummated, the government can later issue a *divestiture order* requiring the acquiring company to dispose of its acquired business. If the acquiring company appeals the order, the courts may or may not uphold it.

Although the Clayton Act apparently applies only to horizontal and vertical combinations, the regulatory agencies have challenged certain con-

[1] "Philip Morris Ends Plan to Sell Seven-Up to Pepsi, but Coke Still Seeks Dr. Pepper," *The Wall Street Journal*, June 25, 1986, p. 3.

glomerate combinations too. For the most part, these challenges have not been successful, and companies expanding externally into unrelated fields generally have no problem complying with the Clayton Act. Many companies obtain a legal opinion on the application of this law to each contemplated business combination before taking steps that lead to consummation.

Are Large Mergers Bad by Definition? Many observers feel that certain mergers should be prohibited simply because of their size, even though the merger would not have the effect of reducing competition or creating a monopoly. Their concern is that huge combinations concentrate economic power in fewer hands, which is deemed undesirable. However, the courts and the governmental agencies have taken the position in recent years that mergers are not bad merely because they are large.[2]

Which Party Is in Power? The zeal with which antitrust laws are interpreted and enforced by the governmental agencies is greatly influenced by which political party is in the White House. In the 1980s, for example, with Republican Ronald Reagan as president, governmental agencies generally restricted their challenges to proposed mergers between competing companies. Even in these cases, however, the agencies have increasingly taken into consideration foreign (rather than simply domestic) competition in assessing market concentration. The result has been that fewer combinations between competing companies are challenged.

The Prevalence of Business Combinations

External expansion is a major vehicle of corporate growth. The number of business expansions occurring in a given year is largely a function of the state of the economy: Merger activity is usually low during recessionary periods and high during boom periods, when companies tend to accumulate healthy amounts of cash. Excess cash not used for dividends must be invested. Stock market prices tend to rise after a boom, which enables an acquiring company, using stock as consideration instead of cash, to issue fewer shares of its stock to acquire another company. The greatest number of business combinations to date for a given year was in 1969, when the Federal Trade Commission reported 4,542 mergers and acquisitions. In recent years, approximately 2,500 to 3,500 business combinations have occurred each year.[3] In most cases a large company combines with a significantly smaller company. Often such combinations enable a small company to expand more rapidly than would be possible with existing resources. Recently, however, an increasing number of business combinations have involved large companies combining with other large companies, in which the consideration given to effect the combination is in the

[2]"Hey, Mister, Need a Lawyer?" *Forbes*, April 23, 1986, p. 74.
[3]W. T. Grimm & Co., Corporate Acquisition, Mergers, and Divestitures Consultants, Chicago.

billions of dollars. Some recent large takeover attempts that became titanic struggles between the acquiring company and the target company are discussed later in the chapter in connection with fighting a takeover attempt.

The "Greener Pastures" Syndrome. Much of the impetus for business combinations comes from the belief that high asset returns and growth rates exist in other businesses. As a result, capital is redeployed; the less desirable companies are sold and the presumed emerging "stars" are bought. In fact, some companies have made hundreds of acquistions and divestitures—with the result that they are no longer in their original businesses or their main lines of business turn over (or *churn*) every 10 to 15 years. Unfortunately, managements often find they cannot manage a new business that they know nothing about any better than the businesses with which they are familiar.

When Combinations Become Unworkable

Bringing together two companies through a business combination is not without risks. As high as 40% of all acquired businesses do not achieve their projected sales and profit growth, and in such circumstances the acquiring companies find that they have grossly overpaid for these poorly performing firms. In numerous other cases, unanticipated problems and changing market conditions have proved disastrous to the combined companies.

The New Bureaucracy. Often the target company's top management and key employees become both frustrated at having to deal with the acquiring company's newly imposed rigid operating procedures and resentful of the unwanted involvement in daily operations. Many of them simply leave the firm rather than continue under the new management—draining the company of leadership and talent needed to remain competitive. Often major operating losses result. (This is most notable in the electronics industry, in which over 500 companies have been acquired since 1980.) A stunning example of such an ill-fated combination was Schlumberger Ltd.'s acquisition of Fairchild Camera & Instrument Corp. for $425 million, which has turned out to be a classic case of how not to manage an acquired company. In early 1986, Schlumberger reported a one-time charge to income of $486 million pertaining to its Fairchild operation, most of which resulted from reducing the carrying value of assets ("goodwill" of $250 million was written off).[4]

Attempts at Diversification—and Retrenchment. When the U.S.'s major oil companies became flush with cash in the 1970s as a result of rising oil prices, many of them became fearful of the day when the world's oil reserves

[4] "Schlumberger Reports a Loss for 4th Quarter," *The Wall Street Journal*, February 11, 1986, p. 12.

would run out and began diversifying into other industries. For example, Mobil Corp. purchased retailer Montgomery Ward, Exxon Corp. acquired a premier electric motor manufacturer for $1.2 billion in cash, and Atlantic Richfield Co. and Standard Oil Co. acquired mining companies. By 1987 most of the diversified operations had been written down in value, shut down, sold, or placed on the selling block.

Because their vast operations simply became unmanageable, conglomerates that were created in the 1960s and 1970s have now disposed of great numbers of the companies they so eagerly acquired. One example of this is General Electric Co., which disposed of 190 subsidiaries from 1981 to 1986.[5] (We discuss how to account for disposals of businesses in Chapter 13.)

Ill Will Spurs the Largest Corporate Blowup. One of the largest buyouts in corporate history is an example of the problems newly combined firms face in adjusting to one another. In 1984, General Motors Corp. (GM) acquired Electronic Data Systems (EDS) by issuing a new class of common stock, class E, valued at $2.5 billion to EDS's stockholders. Dividends on this class of stock are based on the earnings of EDS, which is to retain "substantial independence." Texas billionaire H. Ross Perot, EDS's founder, chairman of the board, and chief executive officer, became GM's largest stockholder and one of its directors. Disputes arose in 1986 over the "excessive prices" EDS was charging GM for its services (GM was EDS's largest customer), over conflicting interpretations of "substantial independence," and over whether Perot (who retained his chairmanship of EDS) should report to GM's board or GM's president. Perot publicly criticized GM, comparing it to a "lumbering elephant," and stated that GM's management is overpaid. Shortly thereafter, and apparently to silence Perot, GM paid $700 million to acquire Perot's Class E common stock and that of three other top EDS officers. In turn, Perot resigned his directorship of GM and his positions at EDS.[6] After this buyout was announced, disgruntled shareholders of GM filed lawsuits against GM alleging mismanagement, breach of fiduciary duty, and waste of corporate assets.

The Ultimate Merger Fiasco. Probably the most dramatic ill-fated business combination of all was LTV Corp.'s $714 million acquisition of Republic Steel Corp. in 1984. At the time, LTV was the third largest steelmaker in the country; the merger made LTV the second largest, and it predicted that the merger would become "a landmark in the annals of America's basic industries." Anticipating a highly efficient and economical operation

[5] "Can Jack Welch Reinvent GE?" *Business Week*, June 30, 1986, pp. 62–64.

[6] "EDS Was Too Independent, GM Officials Say," *San Jose Mercury News*, December 7, 1986, p. 1C; "Perot Quits GM for $700 Million," *San Jose Mercury News*, December 2, 1986, p. 1F; "The Biggest Bumblers, Blowups, and Blunders of '86," *San Jose Mercury News*, December 14, 1986, p. 4C; "Greenmail Blues," *The Wall Street Journal*, December 12, 1986, p. 26.

with its new division, LTV inadvertently ended up with tremendous overcapacity and encountered substantial unanticipated problems at Republic in attempting to integrate the separate operations. In 1986 LTV Corp., failing under the burden of Republic Steel, filed for Chapter 11 bankruptcy reorganization.[7] Shortly after the bankruptcy filing, LTV reported a $2 billion quarterly loss, one of the largest quarterly losses ever reported by a corporation.

Taking Defensive Steps to Prevent a Takeover Attempt

Because business combinations are so prevalent, managements in fear of a potential takeover have in the last few years taken steps (colloquially known as "shark repellant") to make it more difficult for an acquiring company to effect a takeover. Some of the more routine steps involve requesting stockholders to approve such articles of incorporation, charter, and bylaw provisions as the following:

1. **Elimination of cumulative voting.** Under cumulative voting, each stockholder has as many votes as the number of shares owned multiplied by the number of directors up for election. Thus, a potential acquiring company with a relatively small holding of common stock could get representation on the board of directors. Many companies have reincorporated in Delaware, which does not require cumulative voting.
2. **Use of staggered terms for directors.** If directors have staggered terms, changes in the composition of the board of directors occur more slowly, making it impossible for a successful suitor to gain control of the board on consummation of the business combination.
3. **Adoption of supermajority provisions.** For votes on statutory mergers and acquisitions of assets (specific types of business combinations that are discussed in detail later in the chapter), imposing a stipulated percentage in excess of a simple majority (80% is commonly used) makes it more difficult to be taken over by either of these types of business combinations.
4. **Authorization of blank check preferred stock.** Such authorization enables management to place the preferred stock privately in friendly hands. Typically, the owners of the preferred stock have either (1) the right to approve any proposed merger or sale of assets, or (2) multiple voting rights (such as three votes for each vote of common stock).

Such actions by management that tend to insulate a company from acquisition have not gone unnoticed by the Securities and Exchange Commission (SEC). In recognition of the possibility that the interests of management to stay in power may conflict with the interests of stockholders (who might be receptive to an acquisition), the staff of the SEC has indicated that it intends to review proxy materials in detail to ensure that management has made adequate disclosure to shareholders regarding its

[7]"LTV, Dragged Down by Steel Subsidiary, Struggles to Survive," *The Wall Street Journal*, January 6, 1986, p. 1.

proposals. Specifically, the staff has indicated that appropriate disclosures in proxy materials regarding such proposals should include the following:

1. The reason(s) for the proposal and the bases of such reason(s).
2. Whether the corporation's charter or bylaws presently contain other provisions having an anti-takeover effect, whether the . . . proposal is part of a plan by management to adopt a series of such amendments, and whether management presently intends to propose other anti-takeover measures in future proxy solicitations.
3. The overall effects of the proposal, if adopted.
4. The advantages and disadvantages of the proposal . . . both to incumbent management and to shareholders generally.
5. Disclosure of how the proposal will operate.[8]

A Continuous State of Readiness. In recent years, scores of companies that considered themselves potential takeover candidates started operating in a state of continuous readiness to fend off takeover attempts. Such steps include the following:

1. Arranging in advance for investment bankers and lawyers who specialize in takeover attempts to assist them in the event of a "hostile" offer.
2. Lining up extensive credit resources in case funds are needed.
3. Contracting with "stock watch" companies that closely monitor purchases of its stock to see if a "raider" is accumulating its stock.
4. Entering into management contracts known as "golden parachutes," whereby top executives are to receive substantial cash and other benefits (millions of dollars, in many instances) in the event of an unfriendly takeover or their dismissal after a takeover. These companies justify such contracts on the grounds that an executive with a secure financial future can more objectively evaluate a takeover offer without regard to the impact on his or her job. Others contend that it assures management stability in a troubled time and prevents a drain of talent during an attempted takeover. Critics charge that these contracts merely allow executives to walk away rich and also make the acquisition more expensive for the acquiring company, which effectively must pay for these costs if the takeover is successful.

Steps Leading to a Business Combination

Few business activities match the excitement that can be generated by an attempt to acquire a target company's business. Often an acquiring company must operate in strict secrecy until the last possible moment, in order to avoid attracting the attention of other companies that might be interested in acquiring the business. Such secrecy minimizes the possibility of a bidding war. (Some companies, as a matter of policy, immediately cease their takeover efforts if a bidding war starts; the presumption here is

[8]Release No. 34-15230, Disclosure in Proxy and Information Statements, "Anti-takeover or Similar Proposals" (Washington, D.C.: Securities and Exchange Commission, October 13, 1978), pp. 7–10.

that the successful bidder would probably wind up paying too much.) The acquiring company may start purchasing the common stock of the target company slowly, over a period of time, until it owns just under 5% of the target company's common stock (5% ownership requires public disclosure). Such secrecy also affects the target company: If it is opposed to the takeover, its management has less time in which to take defensive actions.

The Friendly Approach. In theory, a business combination should involve only the acquiring company and the stockholders of the target company. In its simplest terms, the stockholders of the target company must decide whether or not to accept the acquiring company's offer. In evaluating the offer, the stockholders consider the recommendation of their directors and management. Because of this, most acquiring companies attempt to obtain a favorable recommendation from the directors and management of the target company before they present the offer to the target company's stockholders. The usual procedure for this involves negotiating an acquisition agreement with the target company's management. If successful, and the agreement is also approved by the target company's directors, the offer is then submitted to the target company's stockholders for their approval or rejection. This sequence of events is characterized as a "friendly" takeover attempt.

The Refusal to Be Friendly. Less friendly situations occur when (1) the approval of the target company's directors and management is not sought; (2) the target company's directors and management refuse to negotiate an acquisition agreement; and (3) negotiations do not result in an offer that the target company's directors and management feel is in the best interests of the target company's stockholders. The acquiring company must then present its offer directly to the stockholders of the target company without the approval of its directors and management. These cases are characterized as "unfriendly" takeover attempts. Some companies have a policy of pursuing a target company only if it can be done on a friendly basis.

Resorting to the Tender Offer. An offer made by an acquiring company directly to the target company's stockholders is known as a **tender offer.** Under a tender offer, the stockholders of the target company are requested to give up their shares in exchange for cash or securities offered by the acquiring company. The usual features of a tender offer are the following:

1. The offer is made in newspapers.
2. The offering price substantially exceeds the current market price of the target company's common stock.
3. The offer must be accepted by a certain specified date, usually in the near future (such as 30 days).

4. The acquiring company reserves the right to withdraw the offer if a specified number of shares are not tendered. (If more than the specified number of shares are tendered, the acquiring company reserves the right to reject such excess shares.)

Because the stockholders send their shares to a financial institution, which holds the shares in a fiduciary capacity until the expiration date of the offer, the shares are said to have been *tendered* —not sold. At the expiration date, and provided the minimum number of shares have been tendered, the acquiring company then pays for the tendered shares.

Statutes Governing Tender Offers (Takeover Bids)

In 1968, Congress passed the Williams Act, which provides for federal regulation of tender offers, which are commonly called takeover bids. The purpose of the law, which is enforced by the SEC, is to protect the target company's shareholders by requiring the bidder to furnish detailed disclosures to the target company and its stockholders, including the following:

1. The number of shares being sought.
2. Background information about the bidder.
3. The source and amount of funds or other consideration for the acquisition of the securities for which the tender is made.
4. The purpose of the tender offer and any plans for the target company.
5. Recent financial statements.

Since 1968, 37 states have passed legislation ostensibly to provide further protection to stockholders of the target company. For the most part, these statutes require more detailed disclosures than the federal statutes. Furthermore, most of them do not permit a tender offer to be made until 20 days after the initial public disclosure, whereas the federal requirement is only five days. A great controversy has developed over whether these state laws are really essential to protect the stockholders or whether they merely favor the in-state targets over out-of-state bidders, since the additional disclosures and waiting period give the target company extra time to thwart the takeover bid if it desires. The constitutionality of these laws may be questioned on the grounds that they interfere with interstate commerce and that federal statutes preempt state statutes. The courts have generally declined to enforce these laws for these reasons. As a result, bidding companies routinely file suits (at the public announcement of their takeover bids) seeking injunctions against the enforcement of these laws. Still, the states continually revise their laws hoping to exert regulation in this area. Occasionally such efforts are quite successful. For example, in 1986 the Ohio legislature passed an emergency measure giving companies in the state sweeping powers to prevent being taken over. This legislation, along with other steps taken by the management of Goodyear Tire & Rubber Co., resulted in a hostile bidder abandoning its $4.7 billion offer.[9]

[9]"Takeover Mania Prompts Calls for Tougher Rules," *The Washington Post*, November 23, 1986, p. K1.

Defensive Tactics during Takeover Attempts

The board of directors of a target company may authorize management to take aggressive action to try to prevent a takeover. A common defensive action is the filing of lawsuits against the acquiring company on various grounds relating to probable violation of antitrust laws, violation of state takeover laws, and violation of securities laws pertaining to public disclosures. Even if a lawsuit by itself is not successful, it entangles the acquiring company in legal proceedings and usually gives management more time to fight the takeover attempt.

Prior to the 1980s, these **legalistic defenses** were reasonably successful and were often referred to as "show-stoppers" (a defense that stops a bidder dead in its tracks). Beginning in the 1980s, however, legalistic defenses lost much of their effectiveness as courts began taking the position that the stockholders must decide on such attempts. As a result, other types of defensive tactics emerged, most of which are considered **financial defenses.** They include the following:

1. **Seeking a "white knight."** When the bidder is unlikely to need the management of the target company after the takeover, management may seek a bidder (the "white knight") that *will* need management. For example, after Mobil Corp. sought to acquire Marathon Oil Co. in 1984 for $5.1 billion, Marathon attracted U.S. Steel Corp., which won the bidding war with a $6.4 billion offer. This tactic is also used when the management of the bidder is not to the liking of the target company's management, even though management is likely to be retained.
2. **The "scorched earth" (or "selling the crown jewels") defense.** When a bidder's primary interest in a target company is one or more prized segments, management may sell those segments to make itself less attractive as a target. For example, after GAF Corp. sought to acquire Union Carbide Corp. in 1986 for $4.1 billion, Union Carbide sold its cherished consumer products lines (which included Eveready batteries and Glad plastic bags) to other companies, causing GAF to abandon its takeover efforts. A variation of this tactic is the **lock-up option,** whereby a friendly company is granted the option to acquire the prized segment in the event the takeover succeeds.
3. **Making a self-tender offer.** When the bidder's offer is deemed unfairly low, the target company may make a higher tender offer to a large percentage of its shareholders. This tactic is usually paired with the "selling the crown jewels" defense, which raises money from which to pay for the shares acquired in the self-tender offer.
4. **The Pac-Man defense.** When the target company is fairly large relative to the acquiring company, it may attempt to acquire the acquiring company. For example, when Bendix Corp. sought to acquire Martin-Marietta Corp. in 1982 for $1.5 billion, Martin-Marietta then sought to acquire Bendix. Considered the most bizarre and spectacular takeover attempt to date, the two companies exhausted their liquid assets trying to gain control of each other and be the first to oust the other's management and directors. As it became evident that the two companies would

end up owning each other and the result would be a unified but financially ailing enterprise, Bendix sought refuge by being acquired by Allied Chemical Corp. Martin-Marietta successfully resisted the takeover attempt.

5. **The mud-slinging defense.** When the acquiring company offers stock instead of cash, the target company's management may try to convince the stockholders that the stock would be a bad investment. In several recent takeover attempts, the fierce attacks on the integrity and ability of the acquiring company's management (in light of certain past transactions and recent performance) put the acquiring company on the defensive to such a degree that it abandoned its takeover attempts. In many cases, private investigators are hired to discover information that would be embarrassing and discrediting to the management of the hostile bidder.
6. **The defensive acquisition tactic.** When a major reason for an attempted takeover is the target company's favorable cash position, the target company may try to rid itself of this excess cash by attempting a takeover of its own. Such an action may also result in a combined business that the initial acquiring company is not interested in acquiring. For example, acquiring a competitor of the initial acquiring company creates anti-trust issues that would probably derail the takeover attempt with prospective litigation.
7. **The leveraged buyout defense.** When management desires to own the business, it may arrange to buy out the stockholders using the company's assets to finance the deal. (This increasingly common tactic is discussed in detail in Chapter 13, "Segment Reporting," as it is more commonly associated with disposals of subsidiaries.)
8. **Adopting a "poison pill" provision.** Although many variations exist, the common procedure is to grant the company's stockholders—excluding shares owned by the acquiring company—the right to purchase additional common shares of the company (or of an acquiring company) at bargain prices (typically at 50% of the market price of the stock). The rights usually become exercisable (or *triggered*) when an "unfriendly" acquiring company acquires 20% of the common stock or makes a bid to acquire 30% of the common stock. The purpose of the provision is to make the acquisition prohibitively expensive to the unfriendly company (or make it suffer unwanted dilution of its own shares if the rights pertain to its own common stock). The provision customarily enables the company to redeem the rights if it chooses to complete a friendly merger. A Delaware Supreme Court decision of 1985 upheld the right of managements to use the "poison pill" defenses without shareholder approval. Since then, this tactic has become so widely used (both during takeover attempts and to prevent future takeover attempts) that 1986 became known as "the year of the 'poison pill' defense."
9. **Paying "greenmail."** When a bidder acquires perhaps 10–20% of the target company's stock, the company may agree to purchase these stockholdings at a premium, allowing the bidder (most commonly called a **corporate raider**) to walk away with a hefty profit (on the condition that it not buy any stock in the future). For example, Walt Disney Productions paid a $60 million premium in 1984 to a bidder that had

acquired 11% of Disney's stock (a total buyback of $325 million). (Over 20 antigreenmail stockholder lawsuits have since been filed against Disney.)

Defensive Tactics: Whose Interest Is Served?

Sometimes turning down an offer or even refusing to negotiate results in the acquiring company's making a higher offer. This is clearly in the best interest of the target company's stockholders. In some cases, however, such actions by management are self-serving; managers oppose the takeover because they want to remain top executives of an independent company rather than become top executives of a small part of a much larger company—or they fear the loss of their jobs. In some instances, management's actions in defending against takeover attempts are irresponsible, especially when their stockholders are overwhelmingly tendering their shares and thereby accepting the offer.

As evident by preceding examples, more and more stockholders of target companies file lawsuits against their managers and directors alleging one of two things: (a) misuse of corporate resources in resisting takeover attempts (in a great number of instances, millions have been spent fighting the takeover attempt); or (b) violation of their fiduciary duty to stockholders by refusing to negotiate for the highest price possible. For the most part, the courts have been reluctant to find managements and directors guilty of these charges. Some companies attempt to protect their directors from such potential actions by dissatisfied stockholders by having the stockholders require the board of directors (through an amendment to the articles of incorporation) to consider factors other than the value and type of consideration offered when determining whether or not to accept an offer. Such factors might include the economic effects on employees and communities in which the target company has its operations.

The Debate over Takeovers Heats Up

The years 1984 through 1986 saw mergers and acquisitions, divestitures, buybacks, leveraged buyouts, and recapitalizations (collectively called *restructurings*) reach a record high in terms of the value of the transactions. The frenzied pace and sheer magnitude of these deals has focused attention on several issues:

1. Is all this restructuring good or bad for the long-term growth of the country? (Some observers contend it is revitalizing industry; others contend it is forcing companies to become overleveraged. Still others are concerned that it causes substantial disruption of the job market and has consequent adverse social impact on the communities affected.
2. Should some restrictions be imposed on the financing of hostile bids by investment bankers? Some observers contend that investment bankers, with their ability to raise billions of dollars through the use of high-

yield, low-rated "junk bonds," are as powerful as traditional economic forces, if not more so. Such power, they argue, requires controls.
3. Should Congress pass tougher rules to discourage corporate raiders?
4. Should certain defensive tactics—most notably "poison pill" provisions and "greenmail"—be allowed only if voted for by stockholders?

As this book goes to print, Congress (in light of a massive Wall Street insider-trading scandal that was exposed in late 1986 and early 1987) is drafting legislation to curb alleged takeover excesses. Below is an interview with T. Boone Pickens, formerly president and chairman of Mesa Petroleum and currently general partner of Mesa Limited Partnership. Pickens is commonly referred to as the "king of the corporate raiders." He discusses his view of management interest versus shareholder rights, touching on these issues from his unique perspective.

PERSPECTIVE

"Management Interest versus Shareholder Rights"

An Interview with T. Boone Pickens

Q: Do you consider any of the so-called "management entrenchment devices" to be good for the stockholders?

A: If the stockholders want management entrenchment devices, golden parachutes, or whatever, that is their right. But I believe these devices should be put to a vote each year. The composition of a company's stockholder group changes from year to year, and it is only democratic that the current owners decide what is in their best interest. If management is convinced that the devices are justified, then voting each year should not be a problem.

I might add that as the investing public better understands entrenchment devices, the effect will be reflected in the marketplace. The SEC is currently studying this subject.

As one of the major players in the corporate restructuring which some say is altering much of U.S. industry, how do you think history will treat you in this phenomenon?

I think there are two ways of answering that question. In a general sense, I believe I'll get favorable review in the history books as a person who was on the leading edge of a significant change in corporate America. What we are seeing is a new breed of manager replacing the "Good Old Boys Club" in this country. People who came out of our universities in the 1960s are moving into top positions at many corporations and they bring with them the frustrations of the 1960s, particularly their frustration with how the establishment is run and how they can alter it. The Good Old Boys are on the way out and a new management team will bring accountability back to corporate America.

Source: From "T. Boone Pickens, Jr.: Management vs. Shareholder Rights," in *American Thought Leader*, Winter 1985, pp. 1–6. Reprinted by permission of the publisher, BB&T Center for Leadership Development, East Carolina University, Greenville, N.C.

(continued)

On a more specific note, Mesa's role in the restructuring of the oil industry will also be seen favorably, I believe. Essentially what has happened is that the managers of the companies in which we have invested are making their companies' assets more productive than before. Again, accountability is being brought back to the system. What is interesting is that many of these managements didn't even know how productive or non-productive some of their assets were. Our economy can prosper from this, and I believe that is why the Dow Jones is trading at about 1400 currently. The market is reflecting what managements are going to have to do with the assets they are responsible for.

Recently a *Wall Street Journal* reporter noted that no corporate adventurer in modern time has so profoundly altered a single industry as T. Boone Pickens has in oil. Do you agree that you have been such a change agent in the oil industry? Have these been drastic changes and are they over?

I don't believe the changes are over. In fact, we've only seen the first steps being taken. For instance, Arco has undergone a significant restructuring, but it is only the first of several steps. The reason is that the management of the company has still not realized all of the value it can. Currently, the major oil companies sell at about 50% of appraised value. If you took the ten largest oil and gas companies and restructured them to raise their market value to 75% of appraised value, the 4 million stockholders of those companies would realize a $70 billion market value enhancement. That's a significant sum, and we're only talking about the ten largest companies.

The problem for these companies is that they have more cash flow than investment opportunity. They are not replacing their reserves and are, therefore, in a state of liquidation. When oil prices were rising in the mid-1970s, this problem could be hidden because revenues continually increased. Now that the price of oil is relatively steady, the problem becomes apparent. The investment community realizes this and, therefore, the stock trades at a low market to appraised value ratio.

As long as the value gap exists, there will be inherent pressure on managements to take action. That not only applies to the oil and gas industry, but all of corporate America. If we are to compete internationally, we must become more efficient. Protectionism will not alter the fundamentals. Only management has the power to make these companies more efficient and competitive.

I believe you have stated that the timing of your appearance on the corporate takeover scene was precipitated, at least to some degree, by the Cities Service attempt to take over Mesa. If Cities Service hadn't come after you and got your "back to the wall," how long would it have been before the acquisition strategies you envisioned earlier would have materialized?

When Mesa invested in Cities Service, we were trying to do the best we could with the capital available to us. At the time, we had decided that the future of exploration was poor; we couldn't justify the investment based on the returns that not only we, but the rest of the industry was experiencing. That fact was quantified last week in a speech given by Bernard Picchi of Salomon Brothers

"Management Interest versus Shareholder Rights" ***(continued)***

at the International Association of Drilling Contractors in Houston. Picchi cited a study that showed for every dollar invested by the domestic oil industry since 1980, only eighty cents of discounted present value was returned. That is a horrible record, and we realized it at the time.

So in 1981 we took a position in Cities Service, believing that we could do better for our stockholders by making such an investment. Cities was selling at about 35% of appraised value, and we were confident that we could upgrade the value significantly. As it turned out, Cities knew we were on their trail and they made a tender offer for Mesa first. We raised enough money to counter with a partial tender offer.

It was what I call a real plumber's job. We were groping in the dark trying to find our way. Fortunately, I had a group of smart people who catch on very quickly. We were a freshman basketball team, to be sure, but a freshman team with a lot of talent is going to do two things. They will have some heartbreaking losses and they will have some big victories. There is no doubt that they will make some mistakes, but they also mature very quickly. And that's what happened in the Cities deal. We took some green people in who were young, tough players. We found that they could play hard, understand things, learn quickly, were well-educated and were committed. Cities was a learning experience for them, and by the time we invested in Gulf, Phillips and Unocal, we had seasoned veterans to play. That's the way I mark it down in history: lots of mistakes in the Cities deal and very few afterwards.

Senator William Proxmire was quoted: "I believe the rising tide of takeovers threatens the very foundations of our American business system. They serve little purpose but to make millions for professional raiders and their lawyers and investment bankers." How do you react to his statement about the amount being paid to the investment bankers particularly?

I spent two hours with Senator Proxmire and the Senate Banking staff. One fellow on the staff was obviously out to expose Boone Pickens. He said that only raiders, investment bankers and lawyers make money from takeovers. That's not true. The 950,000 stockholders of the companies in which Mesa has invested made $15 billion in profits. Mesa's portion of that came to $750 million, hardly an overwhelming percentage of the profit, even though we were the largest stockholder in each case.

Many of the Senators and Congressmen keep searching for a loser in the deal. There aren't any. A few management egos may have been bruised, but I'm not really concerned about that. The assets of these companies were undervalued in the market and then upgraded through outside action. Stockholders made money, which they immediately channeled back into the economy. Everybody won.

The point is that these actions shake the foundation of America's corporations because they force management to go back to work. After World War II, stockholders became identified as investors, not owners, and their interests were separated from those of management, who quietly made off with the assets to do with as they pleased. I believe that if you were to polygraph a

(continued)

number of CEOs in corporate America today, asking them if they believed stockholders own the company, 90 out of 100 wouldn't pass the test. These managers believe they own the company, even when they aren't significant stockholders themselves.

Do you have any interest in acquisitions outside the oil and gas industry? Would you feel comfortable in a management/leadership role outside the oil industry?

I've always believed that if you can manage, there are a number of industries in which you can work. I'm a very well-organized person, although I won't say that I wouldn't have some doubts about changing industries. But that could very well happen to me. On December 4, Mesa shareholders will vote on whether to transform Mesa Petroleum into a Master Limited Partnership. I'll be the general partner of the MLP, but I'll also be allowed to go outside the MLP for other interests, as well.

Assume that you were asked to gauge the public's perception of takeover styles. Where do you feel the public would place you on a continuum which had "White Knight" on one pole and "Hostile Raider" on the opposite pole?

In the middle or better. I receive a tremendous amount of mail thanking me for working for stockholders. While I was in London and Zurich recently, I was told, "If you think it's bad for stockholders in the U.S. companies who live in the United States, you should try being a foreigner. The managements won't even communicate with us over here."

The attitude of managements is terrible. A very bright money manager in New York who handles $100 to $200 million of investment capital was approached by representatives of Unocal after he had voted against management in last spring's proxy contest. The representative's 20-minute pitch was that the money manager had made a mistake. He told them that he had made up his mind and would vote against management. They suggested that if he didn't like management's opinion, he should sell his Unocal stock. The money manager responded: "If I owned an estate and didn't like the way the gardener cut the lawn, I wouldn't sell the estate. I'd fire the gardener. Go back to your chairman and tell him he's analogous to the gardener."

You have had tremendous exposure in the financial press recently, having been both praised and criticized. What criticism has stung the most, and what praise has been the most welcomed and appreciated by you?

I would like to be identified as working for the stockholder. Our moves are never altruistic—we want to make money. But our record shows that all stockholders make money in our deals.

In one of the Senate hearings at which I testified, a Senator commented, "You know, Mr. Pickens, you make money so fast." I asked if it would make them happier if Mesa just broke even. Their reply: "Yes." Then I asked if our losing money would make them happy. They said, "No, we don't want you to lose anything."

"Management Interest versus Shareholder Rights" ***(continued)***

Probably more than anything, I would like to establish that I am an honest and sincere person. If the press would say, "This guy is honest, sincere, not arrogant, doesn't talk down to people, doesn't think he's smarter than other people, and wants to hear what others have to say," then I would be happy.

Then have you been satisfied with the way the media has portrayed your activity?

If I could have written it, I would have written it differently. But basically, yes.

In preparation for this interview, I asked a media executive whether I should request questions from a professional financial journalist. I was advised if I did get a good hard-hitting question, it would likely be one that Pickens would duck. What type of questions have you "ducked" in the past?

I never duck a question. In fact, that brings to mind a subject we haven't covered that I'd like to address. While I was in London a fellow said that one question had been avoided all evening and he thought I was skirting it. When I asked what it was, he said, "Junk bonds."

Only 15% of the corporations in America qualify for investment grade bonds, and in that group you're basically talking about the Fortune 500. Eighty-five percent have below investment grade bonds, also called high-yield or junk bonds. What is interesting is that when you look at where jobs are created among these corporations, it isn't among the investment grade companies. Since 1965, 35 million jobs were created in this country. The below investment grade companies—that 85% I mentioned—created 38 million jobs and the Fortune 500 lost 3 million. What that tells you is that the entrepreneurs are in the 85% group—the group whose paper could be termed junk bonds.

People are very confused about junk bonds. Many think that junk bonds are sold by grabbing some poor guy in a wheelchair on the corner and taking his last $1,000 on a junk bond deal. The people who invest in these securities are sophisticated investors because junk bonds are sold in $5 million or larger increments. And of all junk bonds sold, only 12% are used for acquisitions; 88% are corporate financing not used on acquisitions.

You were trained and educated as a geologist. What would you advise the young person who wants to go in business today to pursue in his or her college and university studies as the optimum preparation for a business career?

I used to advise young people to get a degree in engineering and then get an MBA. Today, I'm inclined to advise going to a business school. But let me add something to that. There are two things you must be able to do. One is this: you have to be able to get up on your feet and explain something briefly. You have to be accurate and to the point because you don't often have time to make a lengthy presentation.

Secondly, learn how to write. I'll guarantee you that there are not many people who can write. When we find them in our organization, they get noticed

(continued)

very quickly. Few executives will take the time to read a 40-page report, but a one or two-page well-written summary will get their attention.

What do you think is causing the enterpreneurial interest and enthusiasm currently being displayed on college campuses?

In the mid-1970s, I was broken-hearted with what I saw on college campuses. Many students said they wanted to get into the corporate bureaucracy and would be satisfied there, or thought they would. What I see now are young people wanting to start their own businesses, and I sense a feeling of entrepreneurism coming back. That's good news because that spirit will save this country. An entrepreneur, upon seeing an opening, will take advantage of it. When the economics are right, entrepreneurs will find the money to get the job done. I think we're entering a period that is going to be fantastic.

I am convinced that today's college students see themselves as well-educated, confident, committed and ready to get out and go to work and make money—nothing more than the American dream.

Assume that a group of graduating college students—not just business students, all scholars—were going to be meeting in a three-day forum to discuss the issues which were most important to contemporary society. In your opinion, what issues should they address—just enumerate two or three issues that really need to be dealt with because they are going to be important to society over the next decade.

The most significant issue is the national debt. I apologize to the young people because they are the ones who are stuck with the debt. It's going to be theirs to wrestle with. What can we devise to deal with it? A one-time tax? Maybe. Once and once only we say, "Here's the money. Pay off the debt and don't ever do it again." But if you go that way, make sure there are no trap doors because I guarantee that a politician with money is going to spend it, probably three or four times.

So, debt is the big issue?

That's right. People in this country are very interested in the business climate. Ten years ago, how many business television programs were there? None. Today, you can watch them from five in the morning until noon. Part of the increased interest stems from the larger stockholder pool we now have. There are 42 million stockholders in this country; that's one out of every six people. And we'll continue to see those numbers grow.

And if the entrepreneurial spirit is reviving, you'll also see more students in business schools and, ultimately, a change in corporate America. People will want to be educated about business because they'll be investing their money. A guy told me years ago, "Boone, be very serious now because we're getting ready to talk about something important—money. And it's really serious because it's my money."

That brings to mind another point, which has nothing to do with issues but is important for young people's futures. People experiences will be one of

"Management Interest versus Shareholder Rights" *(continued)*

your biggest problems in years to come. Watch anybody who is spending someone else's money, whether it's a corporate executive or a politician. When someone is spending another person's money—not money they've made personally or that they would suffer a loss from—be careful. Those people bear watching.

ACCOUNTING METHODS

The two basic methods of accounting for business combinations are the **pooling of interests method** and the **purchase method.** They are discussed in detail in *APB Opinion No. 16,* "Accounting for Business Combinations," which became effective in November 1970. When the value of the consideration given by the acquiring company is above or below the book value of the target company's net assets, these two methods produce dramatically different reporting of results of operations and financial position. Acquiring companies are fully aware of these consequences and often attempt to use the method that maximizes future earnings and earnings per share amounts. A major result of this pronouncement, however, was to eliminate the considerable latitude that previously existed in the use of either the purchase method or the pooling of interests method. If one of these methods is desired, then the terms and provisions of the acquisition agreement must be structured accordingly. This is a key point because **for a given set of terms and provisions only one accounting method will apply.** The methods used in a given set of circumstances are no longer elective.

In this respect, company accountants must be thoroughly familiar with *APB Opinion No. 16,* so they can properly advise top management during the negotiations. Many corporate controllers routinely obtain an opinion from their certified public accountants concerning whether or not a proposed set of terms and conditions will allow the use of the desired accounting method. This is practically essential, considering the complexity of the pronouncement. The objective of this practice is to prevent a situation in which a combination is completed under the assumption that it will be accounted for under a desired method only to have the certified public accountants later uncover something in the acquisition agreement that disallows the use of that method.

The Pooling of Interests Method

The theory underlying pooling of interests accounting is that **a sale and purchase of a business have not occurred.** Two companies have simply pooled their financial resources and managerial talents in such a manner that the owners of each of the separate businesses are now the owners of an enlarged business. This fusion of equity interests is the foundation of the pooling of interests concept. Continuity of interests exists only if the target company's shareholders receive common stock of the acquiring company as consideration for their business. This is the most important condition of the pooling of interests method. Specifically, twelve conditions must be met for pooling of interests accounting to be allowed. These conditions involve the attributes of the combining companies, the mechanics of the exchange, and transactions that are prohibited in periods subsequent to the exchange. If any one of these twelve rules is not met, then the pooling of interests method cannot be used. If all twelve rules are complied with, then the pooling of interests method *must* be used. These twelve rules are discussed in detail in Chapter 6, which discusses and illustrates the application of this method in detail.

When a combination qualifies for the pooling of interests treatment, the recorded assets and liabilities of the separate companies are carried forward to the combined corporation at their historically recorded amounts. Goodwill is never created, and future income statements of the combined, enlarged business never include goodwill amortization expense. Furthermore, in the event future income statements are presented for periods before the combination date, the separate income statements of each constituent company are combined, restated, and then reported as income of the combined corporation.

The Purchase Method

If the transaction does not qualify for pooling of interests treatment, then the purchase method must be used. The underlying concept of the purchase method is that **one company has acquired the business of another company and a sale has occurred.** Under this method, the acquiring company's cost (essentially the value of the consideration given for the acquired business) must be allocated to the individual assets acquired. In most situations, the acquired assets are valued at their current values. To the extent that the acquiring company's cost exceeds the current value of the identifiable assets, then goodwill arises, which must be amortized to income over a period not to exceed 40 years. In an economy that has experienced inflation, the acquiring company usually pays in excess of the book value of the net assets of the acquired company. If this excess relates to assets other than land (a nondepreciable asset), greater depreciation and amortization charges are reflected in future income statements than if the pooling of interests method had been used. Accordingly, future earnings are lower under the purchase method. This upward revaluation of the acquired business's assets and the possible creation of goodwill are the major disadvantages of the purchase method compared with the pooling of interests method from the viewpoint of future earnings and earnings per share.

Criticism of *APB Opinion No. 16*

APB Opinion No. 16 received barely the required two-thirds majority vote. Since its issuance, it has been widely criticized for not being a sound or logical solution to the issues associated with business combinations. The main criticism is that the results produced under the pooling of interests method often do not accurately portray the underlying economics of the business combination. For example, a company that has sales and assets of $100,000 could "pool" its resources and management with a company having sales and assets of $100,000,000. Many accountants feel that to treat such a combination as a pooling is just not sensible. In this situation, the substance of the combination is obviously the acquisition of the small business by the large business—a reality that is ignored under the pooling of interests method.

Most accountants agree with the fundamental concept of the purchase method, except for the treatment of goodwill. Many accountants and corporate executives think that goodwill should not be shown as an asset of the acquiring company but should be charged to the equity section of the acquiring company at the acquisition. Their reasoning is that the acquiring entity has, in substance, given up some of its equity with the hope of recouping it in subsequent years through the acquired company's superior earnings (which may or may not materialize). Also criticized are the arbitrary rules relating to the amortization of goodwill, as set forth in *APB Opinion No. 17,* "Intangible Assets." Goodwill created before November 1, 1970, does not have to be amortized at all, whereas goodwill created after October 31, 1970, must be amortized over a period no longer than 40 years.

About three years after these two controversial pronouncements were issued, the rule-making authority for the accounting profession was transferred to the Financial Accounting Standards Board (FASB), with the hope that a more independent organization (whose members are not tied to the public accounting profession that serves the public corporations) would be more effective in resolving current accounting issues.

Reevaluation of Issues by the FASB

In 1975, the FASB considered the possibility of completely reevaluating the pooling of interests criteria set forth in *APB Opinion No. 16.* The board later decided to reexamine the entire issue of business combinations, and in August 1976 it issued a discussion memorandum. In 1978 the FASB removed this project from its active agenda because of its low priority in relation to other projects. As this book goes to print, the project remains off the active agenda.

SPECIFIC TERMS AND PROVISIONS OF THE ACQUISITION AGREEMENT

Types of Consideration Given

The consideration given by the acquiring company can be the same as that used to pay for or finance internal expansions — namely, cash, other assets, or issuance of debt, preferred, or common stock. Under the purchase method, the consideration may consist of various combinations of cash, debt, and common stock. As stated earlier, the consideration given in a transaction that qualifies for pooling of interests treatment is the acquiring company's common stock.

Types of Assets Acquired

A business may be acquired in one of two ways, the acquisition of assets or the acquisition of common stock:

1. The **acquisition of assets.** The acquiring company acquires the target company's assets and simultaneously assumes responsibility for paying existing, specific liabilities of the target company. If the pooling of interests treatment is desired, 100% of the assets must be acquired; no such requirement exists for the purchase method.
2. The **acquisition of common stock.** The acquiring company must purchase more than 50% of the target company's outstanding common stock for a business combination to have occurred. With an ownership interest greater than 50%, the acquiring company can control the target company.

Many circumstances affect the determination of whether the acquiring company should acquire assets or common stock of the target company. Some of the more common considerations are the following:

1. Transferring stock certificates is easier than transferring assets. The transfer of assets may require the preparation of separate bills of sale for each asset or class of asset; also, state laws concerning bulk sales must be observed.
2. If the target company's contracts, leases, franchises, or operating rights cannot be transferred through the sale of assets, common stock must be acquired.
3. If the acquiring company does not wish to acquire all of the target company's assets, the acquisition of assets allows the acquiring company to obtain only those assets it desires. (To arrange for the acquisition of its common stock, the target company could dispose of the unwanted assets, but it may not always be feasible to do so in the time specified in the acquisition agreement.)
4. If the target company has significant contingent liabilities, the acquiring company can best insulate itself from responsibility for these

contingencies by acquiring assets. (If assets are acquired, the acquiring company usually clearly specifies in the acquisition agreement those liabilities for which it assumes responsibility.)

5. When the sale of the target company's business to the acquiring company is treated as a taxable event (taxable versus nontaxable treatment is discussed later in the chapter), there are several considerations from the seller's viewpoint. The most important consideration is when there is a taxable gain and the seller insists on structuring the transaction in such a manner that the gain is reportable on the installment basis for tax purposes. In this case the acquiring company must acquire common stock to accommodate the seller.
6. If the acquiring company offers cash as consideration and the target company has substantial cash and short-term investment assets, the acquisition of assets makes the target company's cash and short-term investment assets available to the acquiring company to either help replenish its cash or repay loans obtained to finance the acquisition. In effect, the acquisition can be partially paid for using the funds of the target company. If common stock were acquired, the target company's cash and short-term investment assets would not be available to the acquiring company, except to the extent that the target company (as a subsidiary and a separate legal entity) could pay dividends to the acquiring company (as the parent).

THE RESULTING ORGANIZATIONAL FORM OF THE ACQUIRED BUSINESS

Accounting for business combinations focuses on **how the acquiring company initially records the transaction that brings about the combination.** The detailed accounting entries for the acquiring company require substantial explanation under both the purchase method and the pooling of interests method; these are discussed and illustrated in detail in Chapters 3 and 6, respectively. The entries made by the target company, on the other hand, are quite simple. The following discussion is general in nature, so that an overall understanding can be grasped of the organizational effects of business combinations.

Acquisitions of Assets

Centralized Accounting. One manner of accounting for the operations of the acquired business is called **centralized accounting,** whereby the assets acquired and the liabilities assumed are recorded in the existing general ledger of the acquiring company. This is common, however, only when the acquiring company already has similar operations that are accounted for on a centralized basis. Thus, this method would most likely be found only in a horizontal combination. When centralized accounting is used, only two general ledgers are involved in the transaction—the acquiring company's and the target company's. (Assets and liabilities are simply transferred from the target company's general ledger to the acquiring company's general ledger.) For example, assume Punn Company acquired all of the assets and assumed all of the liabilities of Sunn Company by giving cash as the consideration. The following entries (in condensed format) would be made by each company:

Punn Company (the acquiring company)				Sunn Company (the target company)		
Assets	xxx[a]		←	Assets		xxx
Liabilities		xxx[a]	←	Liabilities	xxx	
Cash		xxx	→	Cash	xxx	
				Gain (if cash exceeds book value of net (assets)		xxx
				Loss (if cash is less than book value of net assets)	xxx	

[a]Because cash is the consideration given, the transaction must be accounted for as a purchase. Accordingly, the assets acquired and liabilities assumed are recorded at their current values based on the purchase price. (This is discussed further in Chapter 3.)

Decentralized Accounting. Another manner of accounting for the operations of the acquired business is called **decentralized accounting,** whereby the assets acquired and the liabilities assumed are recorded in a new general ledger maintained at the location of the newly acquired business. The newly acquired business is normally referred to as a **division** of the acquiring company. The difference between the assets acquired and the liabilities assumed are reflected in the division's Home Office account. The balance in this account always equals the balance in the Investment in Division account in the general ledger maintained at the acquiring company's headquarters. (At this point, the division refers to the acquiring company as the "home office.") Note that under this approach, three general ledgers are involved in the transaction—the two general ledgers of the acquiring company (one maintained at the home office and one maintained at the division) and the general ledger of the target company (which is still a separate legal entity). (Assets and liabilities merely are transferred from the target company's general ledger to the newly formed division's general ledger.)

Continuing with the preceding example, the following entries (in condensed format) would be made by the acquiring company, its newly established division, and the target company. For the home office's books:

Punn Company			Sunn Company		
Investment in Sunn Division	xxx				
Cash		xxx	Cash	xxx	
For Sunn Division's books:					
Assets	xxx		Assets		xxx
Liabilities		xxx	Liabilities	xxx	
Home Office Equity		xxx	Gain (if cash exceeds book value of net assets)		xxx
			Loss (if cash is less than book value of net assets)	xxx	

Forming a Wholly Owned Subsidiary to Acquire the Assets. In some cases, the acquiring company forms a wholly owned subsidiary to effect the acquisition of the target company's assets. This is done in situations in which it is not possible, practicable, or desirable to acquire the target company's common stock, but it is desirable to operate the acquired business as a separate legal entity insulated from the existing operations of the acquiring company.

Removal of Records. The target company must pack up its records (including its general ledger) and remove them from the location of the business that was sold.

Subsequent Courses of Action for the Target Company. If all its assets are disposed of and all its liabilities are assumed, the target company's remaining assets consist solely of the consideration received from the acquiring company. At this point, the target company (still a separate legal entity) is referred to as a **nonoperating company,** because it has no operating business—only passive assets. The following three courses of action are available:

1. Continue as a nonoperating company.
2. Use the assets to embark in a new line of business.
3. Distribute the assets to its shareholders. (This option is the most common one selected.)

If it chooses option 3, the target company becomes a **"shell" company** because it has no operating business and no assets. However, it still is a separate legal entity until steps are taken to have its charter withdrawn (which is usually done).

Tax Treatment on Any Gain by the Target Company. The target company is taxed on any gain resulting from the sale of its assets only if the transaction is a taxable combination. (Taxable versus nontaxable combinations are discussed later in the chapter.)

Acquisitions of Common Stock

A company owning more than 50% of the outstanding common stock of another company is referred to as the **parent** of that company. Conversely, a company whose outstanding common stock is more than 50% owned by another company is referred to as a **subsidiary** of that company. A subsidiary (as opposed to a division) is a separate legal entity that must maintain its own general ledger. Accordingly, the subsidiary's operations must be accounted for on a decentralized basis. The acquisition of the outstanding common stock of the acquired company is a personal transaction between the acquiring company and the acquired company's shareholders. For the target company, all that has happened is that the company's ownership is concentrated in the hands of significantly fewer stockholders, or even one stockholder if 100% of the outstanding common stock has been acquired. Consequently, only the acquiring company (the parent) must make an entry relating to the business combination.

Assuming that Punn Company acquired more than 50% of the outstanding common stock of Sunn Company, the relationship would be depicted as follows:

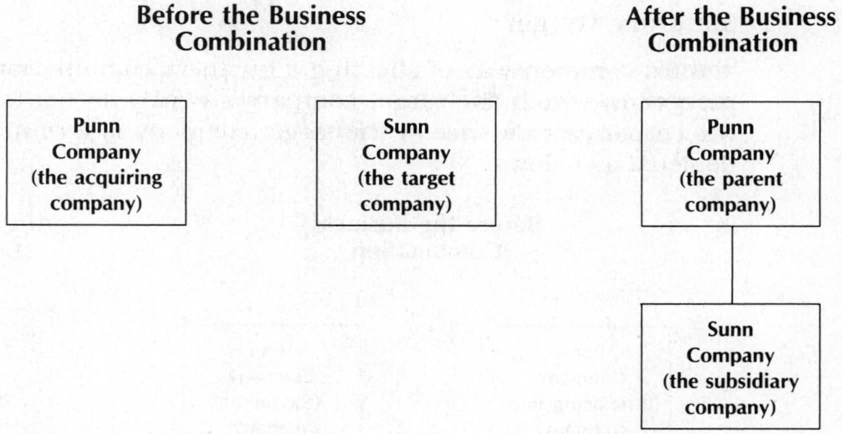

Cash for Stock Exchange. If the acquiring company gives cash as consideration for the target company's outstanding common stock (which would automatically disqualify the transaction for pooling of interests treatment), it makes the following entry:

Investment in Subsidiary	xxx	
Cash		xxx

Stock-for-Stock Exchange. If the acquiring company gives common stock as consideration (a necessary condition for pooling of interests treatment) for the target company's outstanding common stock, it is necessary to use what is known as the **exchange ratio** in accounting for the exchange. The number of common shares to be issued by the acquiring company for each common share of the target company determines the exchange ratio. This ratio is usually set forth in the acquisition agreement. An exchange ratio of 3 to 1, for example, means that the acquiring company issues three shares of its common stock for each share of the target company's common stock acquired. If the target company has 200,000 shares of common stock outstanding and all of the stockholders agree to exchange their shares for shares of the acquiring company's common stock, then the acquiring company would have to issue 600,000 shares of common stock to effect the business combination. The following entry would be made by the acquiring company:

Investment in Subsidiary	xxx	
Common Stock (600,000 × the par value)		xxx
Additional Paid-in Capital		xxx

This entry is slightly more involved if pooling of interests treatment applies (more about this in Chapter 6).

Statutory Merger

A third common way of effecting a business combination is the **statutory merger** in which the target company's equity securities are retired and the corporate existence of the target company is terminated. This can be depicted as follows:

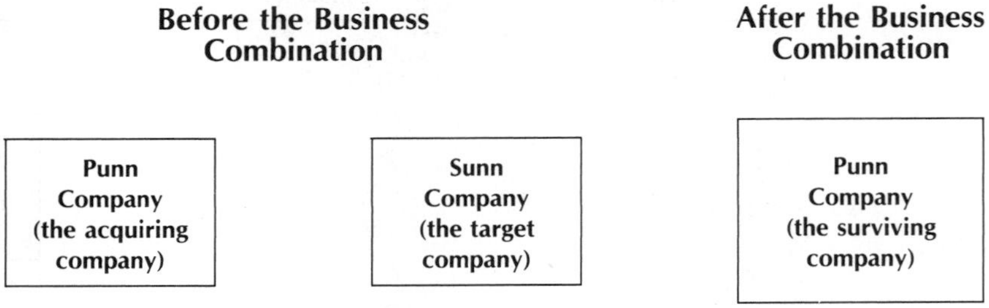

The assets and liabilities of the target company are transferred to the acquiring company. Because the acquiring company is the only surviving legal entity, the target company is said to have been "merged" into the acquiring company. Because these combinations take place pursuant to state laws, they are called statutory mergers. The primary requirements of the state statutory merger laws are as follows:

1. The board of directors of each company must approve the plan of proposed merger before the plan can be submitted to the shareholders of each company.
2. The required percentage (usually a simple majority to 80%) of the voting power of each company must approve the plan of proposed merger.

The end result of a statutory merger is the same as though the acquiring company had acquired directly the target company's assets and the target company had then ceased its legal existence. The reasons for using this roundabout manner of acquiring a target company's assets are explained in the following paragraphs.

Forcing out Dissenting Shareholders. In most cases in which the acquiring company acquires common stock, it desires 100% of the outstanding common stock of the target company. In some of these situations, this outcome may be unlikely because some shareholders of the target company object to the business combination and refuse to sell their shares. However, if the acquiring company acquires the required percentage of outstanding shares to approve a statutory merger, it can force out the dissenting shareholders by taking the necessary steps to liquidate the target company. (In some tender offers, the acquiring company clearly specifies that if all of the target company's shareholders do not accept the offer, the acquiring company intends to effect a statutory merger of the target company into the acquiring company, once the required ownership percentage is attained. This is a "tender your shares now or get forced out later" message.)

In these cases, the business combination technically occurs when the acquiring company acquires more than 50% of the target company's outstanding common stock, which creates a parent–subsidiary relationship. Thus, the statutory merger takes place after the business combination date, a process that normally can be completed within 30 to 60 days after approval of the plan of merger.

When the statutory merger subsequently becomes effective, entries are made to: (1) transfer the target company's assets and liabilities to the acquiring company, and (2) close out the equity accounts in the target company's general ledger. In addition, it is necessary to make a settlement with the dissenting shareholders of the target company (who did not tender their shares). State laws pertaining to statutory mergers generally provide that dissenting shareholders have the right to receive (in cash) the fair value of their shares as of the day before shareholder approval of the merger. Such value may have to be established through a judicial determination as provided under state law if the dissenting shareholders and the acquiring company cannot agree on the value of these shares.

Forcing out Shareholders Who Cannot Be Located. The company acquiring common stock toward a takeover cannot always locate all of the target company's shareholders; in most publicly-held companies, a small number of shareholders simply cannot be found. When the acquiring company desires 100% ownership notwithstanding, it may take the statutory merger route in order to liquidate these interests in the target company.

Acquiring Assets Indirectly. In unfriendly takeover atempts, the acquiring company is prevented from acquiring the assets directly from the target company, because the directors' refusal of the offer prevents the shareholders of the target company from voting on it. The acquiring company must then make a tender offer to the shareholders. If the acquiring company acquires the required percentage of outstanding shares through the tender offer and it does not wish to maintain a parent–subsidiary relationship, the acquiring company can then take the necessary steps to liquidate the target company via a statutory merger.

Formation of a Holding Company

Infrequently, two companies (generally of comparable size) combine in such a manner that a new corporate entity is established that controls the operations of both combining companies. This is done when the existing name of each corporation would not indicate the scope of operations of the combined business or it is desired to have the top-level corporation operate as a **holding company.** (A holding company has no revenue-producing operations of its own, only investments in subsidiaries.) To illustrate, assume Punn Company and Sunn Company wish to combine. They form Integrated Technology Company, which issues its stock for the stock of Punn Company and Sunn Company. Punn Company and Sunn Company are now subsidiaries of Integrated Technology Company. This would be depicted as follows:

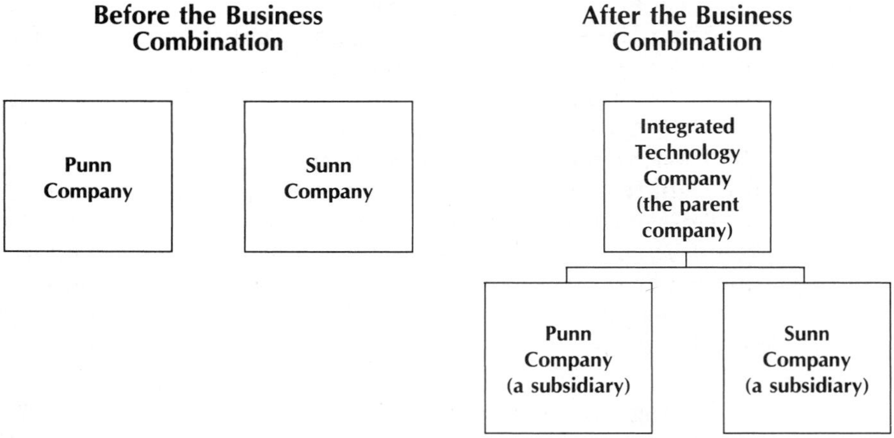

Statutory Consolidation

More infrequent than forming a holding company is statutory consolidation. A **statutory consolidation** results in a new legal entity that takes over the assets and assumes the liabilities of each of the combining companies. The combining companies simultaneously cease their separate corporate existences. Because the new legal entity is the only surviving legal entity, the combining companies are said to have been "consolidated" into the new corporation. Because these combinations take place pursuant to state laws, they are called statutory consolidations. The primary requirements of the state statutory consolidation laws are the same as for statutory mergers.

For example, assume Punn Company and Sunn Company agree to combine using a statutory consolidation. The surviving company is called Integrated Technology Company. This would be depicted as follows:

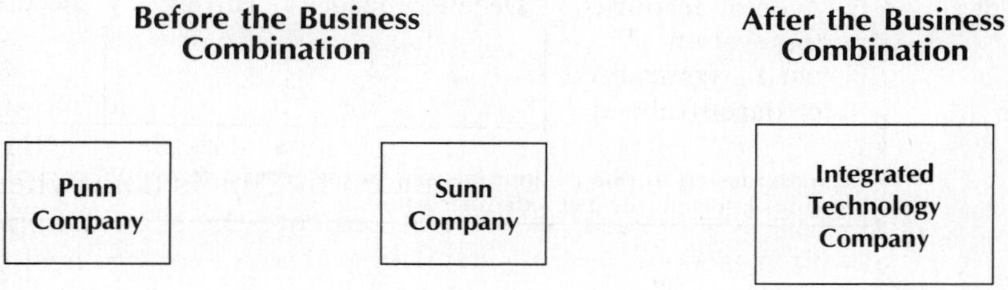

Illustration

SUMMARY OF BUSINESS COMBINATIONS

Illustration 2-1 presents the interrelationships of the various topics discussed up to this point.

TAX RAMIFICATIONS

The income tax rules for business combinations are quite complex and thus more properly the topic of an advanced income tax course. However, it is important at this point to understand the relationship and similarities between the accounting rules and the income tax rules—an understanding that does not always result when the tax rules are dealt with solely in an advanced tax course. Accordingly, the following discussion is limited, general in nature, and designed to accomplish this objective.

For financial reporting purposes, the terms and provisions in the acquisition agreement determine whether the purchase method or the pooling of interests method is used to record the combination. For income tax reporting purposes, the same terms and provisions in the acquisition

Illustration 2-1
Summary of Business Combinations

	Business Combinations			
1. Accounting methods	Purchase		Pooling of interests[a]	
2. Type of consideration given	Cash, other assets, debt, preferred stock, common stock—in any combination		Common stock	
3. Type of asset acquired	Common stock	Assets	Common stock	Assets
4. Resulting organizational form of the acquired business	Subsidiary	Division	Subsidiary	Division
5. Type of accounting system used—centralized or decentralized	Decentralized	Either	Decentralized	Either

[a]The discussion in this chapter focuses on the general concept of pooling of interests. Chapter 6 explores in detail this method's finer points.

agreement determine whether the combination is treated as a **taxable combination** or as a **tax-deferrable combination.** The latter is commonly referred to as a **tax-free combination.**

Taxable Combinations

The Underlying Concept: *A Sale Has Occurred.* The underlying concept of purchase accounting—that one company has acquired the business of another company—is essentially the same concept as that embodied in the Internal Revenue Code with respect to taxable combinations. For income tax reporting purposes, **a taxable combination is a completed and closed transaction in that a sale is deemed to have occurred.** Accordingly, the acquired business reports, or its shareholders report, a gain or loss in the year of the transaction. The fair value of the consideration received by the acquired business or its shareholders is compared with the tax basis of the assets sold to the acquiring business to compute the taxable gain or tax-deductible loss.

The Resulting Change in Basis. The acquiring company's tax basis for the acquired property (whether assets or common stock) is the purchase price paid. If assets are acquired for more than their carrying value as of the acquisition date, the acquired assets are stepped up in basis for tax depreciation and amortization purposes. If common stock is acquired, the assets of the acquired business can be stepped up in basis only if the acquiring company elects to treat the acquisition of the target company's common stock as an asset purchase. Accordingly, if it elects to do so, the basis of the common stock is effectively transferred to the assets of the acquired business. (A more detailed discussion of this election is contained in Chapter 12.) This allows the acquirer to be in the same position as it would be if assets had been acquired rather than common stock.

Accounting and Tax Rules Compared. Although the underlying concept of the purchase method for financial reporting purposes is the same as that embodied in the Internal Revenue Code for taxable combinations, it is important to recognize that the specific rules of *APB Opinion No. 16* regarding the purchase method are different from the specific rules of the Internal Revenue Code regarding taxable combinations. In other words, each set of rules is independent; the treatment for financial reporting purposes does not determine the treatment for tax reporting purposes and vice versa. Accordingly, some combinations that are accounted for under the purchase method for financial reporting purposes are treated as taxable combinations for income tax reporting purposes, whereas other combinations that are accounted for under the purchase method of accounting for financial reporting purposes are treated as tax-free combinations for income tax reporting purposes. Because of this similarity of the concepts but the difference in their specific rules, the only generalization that can be made is that **combinations accounted for under the purchase method for financial reporting purposes are more likely to be taxable combinations than tax-free combinations.**

Tax-free Combinations

The Underlying Concept: *No Sale Has Occurred*. The underlying concept of pooling of interests accounting—that the two equity interests of the combining companies pool together in such a manner that there is a continuity of interest in the new, enlarged business—is essentially the same concept as that embodied in the Internal Revenue Code with respect to tax-free combinations (referred to as *tax-free reorganizations* in the Internal Revenue Code). For income tax reporting purposes, **a tax-free reorganization is not a completed or closed transaction in that a sale is not deemed to have occurred.** Accordingly, the acquired business (or its shareholders) does not report a gain or loss in the year of the transaction. Only the form of the investment has changed; the investment in the business itself is maintained even though such business is now part of a larger business. At some later time, when the property that was received in the combination (typically the acquiring company's common stock) is disposed of in a completed taxable transaction, a gain or loss is reportable for income tax reporting purposes. Accordingly, in a tax-free reorganization income taxes are merely deferred or postponed until a later date.

No Resulting Change in Basis. With respect to the continuing enlarged business, the basis of the property acquired is not changed for income tax reporting purposes, regardless of whether assets or common stock is received in the exchange. The tax rules relating to tax-free reorganizations can accommodate acquisitions of assets and acquisitions of common stock. Section 368a of the Internal Revenue Code describes the various procedures by which tax-free combinations may be attained. Three specific procedures for accomplishing this are set forth in subsections a1A, a1B, and a1C. In practice, these are referred to as "A," "B," and "C" reorganizations. *Type A reorganizations* pertain to statutory mergers and statutory consolidations that take place under a specific state statute. *Type B reorganizations* pertain to stock for stock exchanges. *Type C reorganizations* pertain to an exchange of stock for assets. If the combining companies agree on tax-free reorganization, the terms and provisions of the acquisition agreement must be structured carefully around one of these three specific procedures. The requirements of the Internal Revenue Code must be fully complied with before tax-free treatment is allowed. The safest course of action is to secure a specific ruling in advance from the Internal Revenue Service. Because this is a highly specialized area of tax practice, competent tax advice should be obtained.

Accounting and Tax Rules Compared. The underlying concept of the pooling of interests method for financial reporting purposes is the same as that embodied in the Internal Revenue Code with respect to tax-free reorganizations. The same independent relationship exists between the pooling of interests method (for financial reporting purposes) and tax-free reorganizations (for income tax reporting purposes) as was explained for purchase accounting (for financial reporting purposes) in relation to taxable combinations (for income tax reporting purposes). The pooling of interests requirements, however, are much more stringent than the tax-free reorganization rules. The generalization can be made that **combinations accounted for under the pooling of interests method for financial reporting purposes almost always qualify for tax-free reorganization treatment.**

Conflicting Interests of Combining Businesses

Conflicting interests often exist between the acquiring company and the target company or its stockholders with respect to the desired accounting and tax treatments. The most common **accounting conflict** occurs when the acquiring company desires to use pooling of interests accounting (which requires that it issue common stock to the acquired business or to its shareholders), whereas the acquired business or its shareholders want to receive cash or other nonstock consideration.

The **tax conflicts** center around two issues: (1) whether the acquiring company desires to change the tax basis of the property received in the combination (assets or common stock) to its current value based on the consideration given by the acquiring company; and (2) whether the acquired company or its shareholders want a tax-free treatment. The ultimate resolution of these conflicting accounting interests and conflicting tax interests depends on the relative bargaining strengths and positions of each party.

The Value of Consideration Exceeds Tax Basis. The most common situation in an economy which has experienced inflation is that the acquiring company gives consideration that is greater in value than the tax basis of the property it is to receive. In such situations, the acquiring company would prefer a taxable treatment so that it can step up the basis of the property it is to receive. Thus, it will have greater depreciation and amortization deductions for income tax reporting purposes (or a higher basis in the acquired company's stock if a parent–subsidiary relationship is to be maintained). The acquired company or its shareholders, however, may prefer a tax-free treatment to defer or postpone the recognition of a gain for income tax reporting purposes.

The Value of Consideration Is below Tax Basis. The roles are usually reversed when the acquiring company gives consideration that is lower in value than the tax basis of the property it is to receive. In such a situation, the acquiring company would prefer a tax-free treatment, so that the higher basis of the property it is to receive will carry over. Thus, it would have greater depreciation and amortization deductions for income tax reporting purposes (or a higher basis in the acquired company's stock if a parent–subsidiary relationship is to be maintained). The acquired company or its shareholders, however, may prefer a taxable treatment to immediately recognize a loss for income tax reporting purposes.

The Impact of the Tax Reform Act of 1986. The Tax Reform Act of 1986 eliminated the long-standing doctrine that allowed a corporation selling its assets in a taxable transaction to not pay taxes at the corporate level. Previously, only the corporation's stockholders were taxed upon distribution to them of the proceeds of the sale. According to the 1986 act, taxes are now imposed at the corporate level (as well as at the stockholder level); therefore, structuring the transaction with a view to stepping up the basis of the assets for tax purposes becomes less desirable to the target company's stockholders. The tax-free (deferred) treatment now enables taxes at the corporate level (as well as taxes at the individual stockholder level) to be deferred.

SUMMARY

Business combinations are a major means of attaining corporate growth. The acquiring company may account for the acquired business using either the purchase method or the pooling of interests method. The purchase method treats the combination as a purchase of the acquired business, whereby the acquired assets of the target company are recorded at the acquiring company's cost, which is based essentially on the fair value of the consideration given. In contrast, the pooling of interests method treats the combination as a fusion of equity interests, whereby the acquired assets of the target company are recorded at the target company's historical book values as of the acquisition date. This fusion of equity interests is accomplished through the issuance of the acquiring company's common stock as consideration. Whether the acquiring company acquires the target company's assets or outstanding common stock has no bearing on the accounting treatment; only the resulting organizational form of the acquired business is different.

Business combinations are treated as either taxable or tax-free transactions. Under a taxable transaction, the acquiring company establishes a new basis for the acquired assets. Under a tax-free transaction, the basis to the acquired company carries over to the acquiring company. Tax considerations are often of primary consideration in negotiating the terms of the acquisition agreement, as is the desired accounting treatment from the acquiring company's point of view.

Glossary of New Terms

Acquiring Company A company attempting to acquire the business of another company.

Acquisition Agreement The legal agreement that specifies the terms and provisions of a business combination.

Conglomerate Combination A business combination that takes place between companies in unrelated industries.

Division In this chapter, a newly acquired business that does not maintain its separate legal existence.

Exchange Ratio The number of common shares issued by the acquiring company in exchange for each outstanding common share of the target company.

Horizontal Combination A business combination that takes place between companies involved as competitors at the same level in a given industry.

Parent A company that owns more than 50% of the outstanding common stock of another company.

Pooling of Interests Method A method of accounting for a business combination whereby the assets of the acquired business are carried forward to the combined corporation at their historically recorded amounts. A fusion of equity interests is deemed to have occurred as opposed to a sale.

Purchase Method A method of accounting for a business combination whereby the assets and liabilities of the acquired business are valued at their current values based on the consideration given by the acquiring company. A sale is deemed to have occurred.

Statutory Consolidation A legal term referring to a specific type of business combination in which a new corporation is formed to carry on the businesses of two predecessor corporations that are liquidated.

Statutory Merger A legal term referring to a specific type of business combination in which a newly acquired target company is liquidated into a division at the time of the business combination.

Subsidiary A company whose outstanding common stock is more than 50% owned by another company.

Takeover Attempt The process of trying to acquire the business of a target company.

Target Company The company whose business a company is seeking to acquire.

Tax-free Combination A specific type of business combination in which the acquired business or its shareholders do not report a gain or loss at the time of the business combination for income tax reporting purposes.

Tender Offer An offer made by an acquiring company directly to the stockholders of the target company, whereby the stockholders of the target company are requested to give up their common shares in exchange for the consideration offered by the acquiring company.

Vertical Combination A business combination that takes place between companies involved at different levels in a given industry.

Selected References

"The Accountant's Role in Acquisition Analysis," by Lisa M. Allison. *Management Accounting* (June 1984), 56–60.

"Acquisition Valuation: DCF Can Be Misleading," by James S. Ritchey. *Management Accounting* (January 1983), 24–28.

"Financial Implications of Offense and Defense in Corporate Takeovers," by Harry Friedman and J. Tomilson Hill. *Corporate Accounting* 3, no. 3 (Summer 1985), 54–59.

"How to Determine the Value of a Firm," by Dev Strischek. *Management Accounting* (January 1983), 32–37.

"Pre-Acquisition Audit: Verifying the Bottom Line," by John J. Welsh. *Management Accounting* (January 1983), 32–37.

"Taxes and Takeovers," by Robert Willens. *Journal of Accountancy* (July 1986), 86–95.

Review Questions

1. What is the difference between horizontal, vertical, and conglomerate combinations?
2. Contrast the purchase method with the pooling of interests method of accounting.
3. Why is the acquisition agreement so important in determining the ultimate accounting method used in recording a business combination?
4. On what grounds has *APB Opinion No. 16* been criticized?

5. What types of consideration can be given under purchase accounting and under pooling of interests accounting?
6. What types of assets can the acquiring company obtain in business combinations?
7. What various organizational forms can result from a business combination?
8. What is the difference between centralized and decentralized accounting systems?
9. How is the selling entity's gain or loss computed on the disposition of its assets?
10. Explain the relationship between *APB Opinion No. 16* and the income tax rules relating to business combinations.
11. What is meant by a tax-free combination?
12. Why does a conflict often exist between the acquiring company and the target company or its stockholders with respect to whether the combination should be treated in a taxable or nontaxable manner?
13. For the acquiring company, what is "the best of both worlds" from the standpoint of financial reporting and tax reporting?
14. Does a target company that sells its assets have to pay taxes if there is a gain?

Technical Research Question

15. Raider Company acquired 15% of the outstanding common stock of Fite-off Company. In a defensive move to prevent being taken over, Fite-off entered into an agreement with Raider to purchase the stock acquired by Raider at a 20% premium above market value. As part of this agreement, Raider agrees to not acquire any more common stock of Fite-off for the next ten years. How should the premium be accounted for and classified?

Discussion Cases

DC 2-1

Purchase versus Pooling of Interests

On July 1, 19X1, Pilex Company acquired all of the outstanding common stock of Stax Company by issuing 80,000 shares of common stock as consideration (valued at $4,000,000). Pilex's controller informed you of the business combination in August 19X1 and indicated that management has not yet decided whether to use the purchase method or the pooling of interests method to account for this business combination. The controller has asked you to assist him in evaluating the alternative accounting treatments between now and December 31, 19X1, the end of Pilex's reporting period.

Required:
How would you advise the controller?

DC 2-2

Accounting versus Tax Treatment

Dunno Company plans to embark on a business acquisition program to diversify its product lines. The controller has indicated to you that she is unclear on whether the tax treatment determines the accounting treatment or whether the accounting treatment determines the tax treatment.

Required:
How would you advise the controller?

DC 2-3

Limiting Legal Liability and Consistency

PT&T Company is having merger discussions with Swayco Company. All of PT&T's business acquisitions to date have been acquisitions of common stock resulting in parent–subsidiary relationships. PT&T prefers to legally insulate each of its acquired businesses from all other operations. Swayco has been and still is involved as a defendent in several lawsuits. As a result, PT&T plans to acquire Swayco's assets to insulate itself from any current or potential legal entanglements.

Furthermore, the controller indicates to you that if the merger is consummated in this manner, the company will not be accounting for its acquisitions consistently, which will violate a fundamental accounting principle. All businesses acquired to date have been consistently recorded as poolings of interests; the acquisition of Swayco will not qualify for pooling of interests treatment, which means an additional inconsistency will be created.

Required:

1. How could PT&T achieve the objective of insulating the business of Swayco?
2. Is the consistency principle being violated as a result of acquiring assets? Why or why not?
3. Is the consistency principle being violated as a result of the combination not qualifying for pooling of interests treatment? Why or why not?

Exercises

E 2-1

Terminology

Indicate the appropriate term or terms for each of the following:

1. The expansion of a business by constructing a manufacturing facility.
2. A business combination in which a company acquires one of its suppliers.
3. A business combination in which a company acquires one of its competitors.
4. A business combination in which a company acquires businesses to diversify its product lines.
5. The broad terms used to refer to business combinations.
6. A business combination in which the target company's corporate existence is terminated in conjunction with the transfer of its assets and liabilities to the acquiring company.

7. A business combination in which a new corporation is formed to acquire the businesses of two existing corporations.
8. The two methods of accounting for business combinations as set forth in *APB Opinion No. 16.*
9. The two types of assets that can be acquired in a business combination.
10. The expansion of a business by the acquisition of an existing business.
11. An acquired business that maintains its separate legal existence.
12. An acquiring business that acquires common stock of the acquired business, the latter maintaining its separate legal existence.
13. An acquired business that ceases to be a separate legal entity but continues to use a separate general ledger.
14. The primary type of consideration given in a business combination that is accounted for as a pooling of interests.
15. The allowable types of consideration that can be given in a business combination accounted for as a purchase.

E 2-2

Pooling of Interests Method: Acquisition of Assets

Pertex Company acquired all of the assets of Sassco Company in a business combination that qualified for pooling of interests treatment. The current value of the common stock issued by Pertex exceeded the book value of Sassco's net assets by $300,000.

Required:

Explain the general accounting procedures to be followed by Pertex in recording the acquisition of the assets.

E 2-3

Purchase Method: Acquisition of Assets

Plugg Company acquired all of the assets of Stopper Company in a business combination that did not qualify for pooling of interests treatment. Plugg paid $800,000 cash. The book value of Stopper's net assets is $600,000, and their current value is $750,000.

Required:

Explain the general accounting procedures to be followed by Plugg in recording the acquisition of the assets.

E 2-4

Divestiture Accounting: Sale of Common Stock

Pyroid Company acquired all of the outstanding common stock of Supperware Company from its shareholders by issuing common stock.

Required:

Explain in general how Supperware should account for this change in ownership of its outstanding common stock.

E 2-5

Divestiture Accounting: Sale of Assets

Poole Company acquired all of the assets of Swimco Company by issuing common stock (and assuming Swimco's liabilities).

Required:
Explain in general how Swimco Company should account for this transaction.

E 2-6

Statutory Merger and Statutory Consolidation

Plite Corporation is considering a merger or consolidation with Scooter Corporation. Both methods of acquisition are being considered under applicable corporate statutory law. Plite is the larger of the two corporations and is in reality acquiring Scooter Corporation.

Required:
Discuss the meaning of the terms *merger* and *consolidation* as used in corporate law with particular emphasis on the legal difference between the two.

(AICPA adapted)

Problems

P 2-1

COMPREHENSIVE Acquisition of Assets for Cash

Payola Company acquired all of the assets of SDS Company by assuming responsibility for all of its liabilities and paying $1,500,000 cash. Information with respect to SDS at the date of combination follows:

	Book Value	Current Value
Cash	$ 10,000	$ 10,000
Accounts receivable, net (including $30,000 due from Payola Company)	90,000	90,000
Inventory	200,000	200,000
Land	400,000	500,000
Building and equipment	2,500,000	1,600,000
Accumulated depreciation	(1,200,000)	
Total Assets	$2,000,000	$2,400,000
Accounts payable and accruals	$ 300,000	$ 300,000
Long-term debt	800,000	800,000
Total Liabilities	$1,100,000	$1,100,000
Common stock, $1 par value	$ 150,000	
Additional paid-in capital	450,000	
Retained earnings	300,000	
Total Stockholders' Equity	$ 900,000	$1,300,000
Total Liabilities and Equity	$2,000,000	$2,400,000

Required:

1. Does the acquisition appear to be a horizontal, vertical, or conglomerate type of combination?
2. Would the transaction be accounted for as a purchase or a pooling of interests?
3. Is Payola Company the parent company of SDS Company? Why or why not?
4. Is SDS a subsidiary? Why or why not?
5. Is SDS a separate legal entity after the transaction has been consummated?
6. Can the acquired business be accounted for on a centralized or a decentralized basis?
7. Prepare the journal entry that would be made by SDS on the date of the combination. Assume a 40% income tax rate.
8. Prepare a balance sheet for SDS after recording the entry in requirement 7.
9. What is SDS's book value before and after the combination?
10. What options are available to SDS after the business combination?
11. Prepare the entry—in condensed form—that Payola would make, assuming that centralized accounting is to be used.
12. Why did Payola pay $1,500,000 for a company whose net assets are worth only $1,300,000?
13. How could Payola have determined the current value of SDS's assets and liabilities?
14. Tax questions (optional):
    a. What is the treatment for income tax reporting purposes?
    b. From your answer in requirement 14a, what is Payola's tax basis of the land, buildings, and equipment it obtained?

P 2-2

COMPREHENSIVE Acquisition of Assets for Common Stock

Assume the same information as in Problem 2-1, except that Payola Company gave as consideration 30,000 shares of its $10 par value common stock (of which 970,000 shares are already outstanding) having a market value of $50 per share. Assume that all conditions for pooling of interests are met.

Required:

Respond to requirements 2 through 10 in Problem 2-1. Then continue with the following requirements:

11. At what amount would Payola record the assets acquired from SDS? (Do not prepare Payola's entry to record the combination; doing so requires an understanding of material in Chapter 6.)
12. Reevaluate your answer to requirement 7 in light of your answer to requirement 11. (Hint: Does Payola's accounting treatment affect SDS's accounting treatment—that is, is symmetry required?)
13. Tax questions (optional):
    a. What is the probable treatment for income tax reporting purposes?
    b. From your answer in requirement 13a, what is Payola's tax basis of the land, buildings, and equipment it obtained?
    c. What is SDS's tax basis in the Payola common stock it received?

P 2-3

COMPREHENSIVE Acquisition of Common Stock for Cash

Assume the same information as in Problem 2-1, except that Payola Company acquired all of the outstanding common stock of SDS Company rather than all of its assets.

Required:

Respond to requirements 2 through 10 in Problem 2-1. Then continue with the following requirements:

11. Prepare the entry that Payola would make to record the combination.
12. Where is the goodwill recorded that Payola paid for?
13. Tax questions (optional):
    a. What is the treatment for income tax reporting purposes?
    b. In what asset does Payola have a tax basis?
    c. How much is its tax basis in this asset?
    d. Does the tax basis of SDS's land, buildings, and equipment change?

P 2-4

COMPREHENSIVE Acquisition of Common Stock for Common Stock

Assume the same information as provided in Problem 2-1, except that Payola Company gave as consideration 30,000 shares of its $10 par value common stock (of which 970,000 shares are already outstanding) having a market value of $50 per share. Assume all conditions for pooling of interests are met.

Required:

Respond to requirements 2 through 10 in Problem 2-1. Then continue with the following requirements:

11. At what amount would Payola record the SDS common stock it obtained? (Do not prepare Payola's entry to record the combination; doing so requires an understanding of material in Chapter 6.)
12. What is the exchange ratio used in the transaction?
13. Tax questions (optional):
    a. What is the probable tax treatment?
    b. In what asset does Payola have a tax basis?
    c. How much is its tax basis in this asset?
    d. Nick Tymer acquired 3,000 shares of SDS's common stock for $24,000 (shortly before the announcement of the business combination). What is his tax basis of the Payola shares he received in the exchange?
    e. Did Tymer gain from his investment?

P 2-5

COMPREHENSIVE Acquisition of Common Stock for Common Stock

Assume the same information as provided in Problem 2-1, except that Payola Company gave as consideration 30,000 shares of its $10 par value common stock (of which 970,000 shares are already outstanding) having a market value of $50 per share. Also, one of the remaining eleven conditions for pooling of interests was *not* met.

Required:

Respond to requirements 2 through 11 in Problem 2-1. Then continue with the following requirements:

12. What is the exchange ratio used in the transaction?
13. Tax questions (optional):
    a. What is the probable treatment for income tax reporting purposes?
    b. In what asset does Payola Company have a tax basis?
    c. How much is its tax basis in this asset?
    d. Nick Tymer acquired 3,000 shares of SDS's common stock for $24,000 (shortly before the announcement of the business combination). What is his tax basis of the Payola shares he received in the exchange?
    e. Did Tymer gain from his investment?

3

The Purchase Method of Accounting: Date of Acquisition

Chapter 2 introduced the purchase method and the pooling of interests method of accounting for business combinations. Because these two methods are conceptual opposites, they are best discussed and illustrated separately. Consequently, this chapter and Chapters 4 and 5 cover the purchase method; Chapter 6 focuses on the pooling of interests method.

The purchase method, like the pooling of interests method, can be applied to either form of business combination, the acquisition of assets and the acquisition of common stock; with either, the results of reporting operations and the financial position of the enlarged business are the same. To prove this point, we discuss and illustrate each form of business combination. In the illustrations we must compare a situation in which all of the assets are acquired with one in which all of the common stock is acquired; otherwise, a comparison is not possible. Acquisition of less than 100% of the common stock requires some additional considerations that are not relevant in situations in which all of the common stock is acquired. Discussion of these more involved situations is delayed until Chapter 5.

THE ESSENCE OF THE PURCHASE METHOD

The underlying concept of the purchase method of accounting is that one entity has purchased the business of another entity—that is, a sale has been consummated. The acquiring company records at its cost the assets or the common stock acquired. The cost is based essentially on the value of the consideration given. If the cost is above the current value of the target company's net assets (determined by valuing its tangible assets, identifiable intangible assets, and liabilities at their current values, which may involve qualified appraisers), then goodwill exists, which must be amortized over a period not to exceed 40 years. Thus, **goodwill is determined in a residual manner.** In the far less frequent circumstances in which the acquiring company's cost is below the current value of the target company's net assets, a **bargain purchase element** exists, which must be allocated against the current value of certain noncurrent assets. If the bargain purchase element is so great that it reduces the applicable noncurrent assets to zero, the remaining amount is recorded as a **deferred credit** and amortized over a period not to exceed 40 years.

The purchase method parallels accounting for the acquisition of individual assets—that is, historical cost is used. Consequently, some assets and liabilities of the enlarged business are recorded at their historical cost (the assets and liabilities of the acquiring company), whereas some assets and liabilities of the enlarged business (the assets and liabilities of the acquired business) are reported at their current values as of the acquisition date. These current values become the acquiring company's historical cost. From the date of acquisition, the income of the acquired business is combined with the income of the acquiring company. The acquired business's preacquisition earnings are never combined with the preacquisition earnings of the acquiring company.

The purchase method can be neatly divided into two questions:

1. What is the total cost of the acquired business to the acquiring business?
2. What specifically is acquired for the total cost incurred?

The rest of this chapter discusses the procedures for answering these questions, in addition to the procedures for presenting the financial position of the enlarged business as of the acquisition date.

DETERMINING THE TOTAL COST OF THE ACQUIRED BUSINESS

The total cost of the acquired business equals the sum of the following:

1. The **fair value of the consideration given.**
2. The **direct costs** incurred in connection with the acquisition, excluding costs of registering with the Securities and Exchange Commission any securities given as consideration by the acquiring company.
3. The **fair value of any contingent consideration** that is given subsequent to the acquisition date.

Each of these areas is discussed below.

The Fair Value of the Consideration Given

The following three types of consideration may be given in any combination:

1. **Cash or other assets.** Cost is the amount of cash or the fair value of other assets given.
2. **Debt.** Cost is the present value of the debt issued, determined by applying the provisions of *APB Opinion No. 21*, "Interest on Receivables and Payables."
3. **Equity securities.** Cost is the fair value of the equity securities issued. However, if the fair value of the property acquired is more clearly evident than the fair value of the equity securities issued, then the fair value of the property acquired is used to determine cost.[1]

As a practical matter, when equity securities issued are identical with the acquiring company's outstanding publicly traded securities, the fair value of the equity securities given is readily determinable and is almost always used to determine cost. If the acquiring company's equity securities are not publicly traded or a new class of stock is issued, it is usually

[1]*Opinions of the Accounting Principles Board, No. 16*, "Accounting for Business Combinations" (New York: American Institute of Certified Public Accountants, 1970), par. 67.

necessary to obtain either (a) an appraisal of the fair value of the equity securities issued (usually obtainable from an investment banker) or (b) an appraisal of the property acquired, the latter alternative being preferable.

Direct Costs

Acquiring companies commonly use outside lawyers and accountants in various capacities throughout the course of events leading to a completed acquisition. Travel costs are common during acquisition negotiations, as are finders' fees. Such **costs and fees,** as well as any other direct costs, **that pertain to the acquisition** are added to the cost of the acquired business. In situations in which the consideration given is equity securities, **costs and fees that pertain to the issuance or registration of the equity securities** are not added to the cost of the acquired business. Instead, they are charged to additional paid-in capital.[2] (Recall from intermediate accounting that the costs incurred to issue and register equity securities in nonbusiness combinations are treated in this manner because they are considered a reduction of the fair value of the securities issued.) Indirect and general expenses, including salary and overhead costs of an internal acquisitions department, are not direct costs of an acquisition and are expensed as incurred.[3]

Contingent Consideration

Contingent consideration is often used as a compromise when the buyer and seller disagree on the purchase price or the form of consideration to be given, or both. Contingent consideration may be divided into two mutually exclusive categories: (1) contingencies whose outcomes are currently determinable, and (2) contingencies whose outcomes are not currently determinable.

Contingencies Whose Outcomes Are Currently Determinable. If it can be determined beyond a reasonable doubt at the acquisition date that the outcome of the contingency will be such that the contingent consideration will have to be paid, then the fair value of the additional consideration should be recorded at that time as part of the cost of the acquired business.[4] Relatively few contingencies fall into this category.

Contingencies Whose Outcomes Are Not Currently Determinable. If it cannot be determined beyond a reasonable doubt at the acquisition date that the contingent consideration will have to be paid, the contingent consideration should be disclosed but not recorded as a liability or shown as

[2] *APB Opinion No. 16*, par. 76.
[3] *APB Opinion No. 16*, par. 76, and Accounting Interpretation No. 33 to *APB Opinion No. 16*.
[4] *APB Opinion No. 16*, par. 78.

outstanding securities until it is determinable beyond a reasonable doubt.[5] An example of an appropriate disclosure is given later in the chapter in the section on disclosures. (This **"determinable beyond a reasonable doubt" criterion** of *APB Opinion No. 16* is more demanding than the "probable" criterion set forth in *FASB Statement No. 5*, "Accounting for Contingencies," which applies only to loss and gain contingencies.[6]) Contingencies that are not currently determinable can be divided into two categories:

a. **Contingencies based on other than security prices.** This type of contingency often is based on sales or earnings goals for the acquired business. It is commonly used when the target company or its shareholders want to protect themselves from selling out too cheaply in the event that the acquired business later realizes the potential they feel it possesses and the buyer wants to protect itself from paying too much in the event that the acquired business does not realize such potential. Contingent consideration is the compromise whereby an additional amount of consideration is given to the seller(s) at a later date if the acquired business achieves certain agreed-upon sales or earnings levels within a specified period of time. Later, when the contingency is resolved and any additional consideration is distributable, **the current value of the additional consideration is added to the acquiring company's cost of the acquired business.**[7] (Usually this increases the amount of goodwill.)

b. **Contingencies based on security prices.** This type of contingency is common when the target company or its shareholders receive as consideration the acquiring company's equity securities, which must be held for a certain period of time. In this situation, the target company or its shareholders want protection in the event the market price of the securities at the expiration of the holding period is below the market price of the securities at the acquisition date. The acquiring company must issue an additional number of securities if the market price at the end of the holding period is below the market price that existed on the acquisition date. The result is to bring the total value of the holdings of the target company or its shareholders at that time up to the total value existing on the acquisition date. If additional securities are later issued, the current value of the additional consideration is added to the acquiring company's cost of the acquired business. "However, the amount previously recorded for securities issued at the date of acquisition should simultaneously be reduced to the lower current value of those securities.[8] **The net effect of this procedure is not to increase the cost of the acquired business above what was recorded at the acquisition date.** The rationale is that the initial recorded cost represents the amount that would have been paid for the business in a straight cash transaction. Illustration 3-1 gives an example of the accounting entries for this type of contingency.

[5] *APB Opinion No. 16*, par. 78.
[6] *Statement of Financial Accounting Standards, No. 5*, "Accounting for Contingencies" (Stamford: Financial Accounting Standards Board, 1975).
[7] *APB Opinion No. 16*, par. 79.
[8] *APB Opinion No. 16*, par. 82.

Illustration 3-1
An Example of Contingent Consideration Based on Security Prices

Pine Company acquires the business of Spruce Company. (Whether assets or common stock is acquired is irrelevant.) The total consideration paid by Pine is $1,000,000 worth of its $5 par value common stock. The market price of Pine's common stock on the acquisition date is $50 per share; thus, 20,000 shares are issued at that time. A condition of the purchase is that the common stock issued be held by the seller for two years. If, at the end of two years, the market price of the common stock is below $50 per share, then an appropriate additional number of shares must be issued so that the total value of the issued shares equals $1,000,000. Two years later, the market price of Pine's common stock is $40 per share. Thus, $1,000,000 divided by $40 per share equals 25,000 shares. Because 20,000 shares have already been issued, an additional 5,000 shares are issued at that time.

Entry at the acquisition date:		
Cost of acquired business[a]	1,000,000	
Common stock		100,000
Additional paid-in capital		900,000
To record the issuance of 20,000 shares of $5 par value common stock.		
Entries required two years later:		
Cost of acquired business[a]	200,000	
Common stock		25,000
Additional paid-in capital		175,000
To record the issuance of 5,000 shares of $5 par value common stock as additional consideration.		
Additional paid-in capital	200,000	
Cost of acquired business[a]		200,000
To reflect the reduction in value of the previously issued shares from $50 per share to $40 per share.		

Note that the effect of the entries recorded two years after acquisition is to debit additional paid-in capital for $25,000 and credit common stock for $25,000. Thus, there is no effect on the cost of the acquired business, as initially recorded on the acquisition date.

[a]Later in the chapter, a more descriptive term is used, depending on whether assets or common stock is acquired.

TOTAL COST IN RELATION TO CURRENT VALUE AND BOOK VALUE OF ACQUIRED NET ASSETS

After determining the acquiring company's total cost of the acquired business, we must determine the current value of the acquired business's net assets. When the acquiring company's total cost is greater than the current value of the acquired business's net assets, such excess amount is considered **goodwill.** The current value of the acquired business's net assets and the residual amount determined as goodwill are reported in the financial statements of the enlarged, combined business. (A look at the use of goodwill in major firms appears on page 86. A capsule history of accounting for goodwill is on page 117.)

If the acquiring company's total cost is below the current value of the acquired business's net assets, then a **bargain purchase element** exists. This bargain purchase element is allocated as much as possible against the current values of certain noncurrent assets. If this allocation does not extinguish the bargain purchase element, then a deferred credit exists. The current value of the acquired business's net assets (adjusted for the bargain purchase element), along with any remaining deferred credit, is reported in the financial statements of the enlarged, combined business.

Illustration 3-2 summarizes all the possible situations with respect to the relationships among (1) the total cost of the investment, (2) the current value of the acquired business's net assets, and (3) the book value of the acquired business's net assets. The **book value** is the value recorded on the target company's books as of the acquisition date. These situations will be referred to continually throughout the chapter.

Illustration 3-2
Summary of Relationships among Total Cost, Current Value, and Book Value of Acquired Assets

		Net Assets of Acquired Business	
Category	Total Cost	Current Value	Book Value
1. **Neither goodwill nor a bargain purchase element exists (total cost equals current value)**			
A. Current value equals book value......	$60,000	$60,000	$60,000
B. Current value is above book value ...	$80,000	$80,000	$60,000
C. Current value is below book value ...	$50,000	$50,000	$60,000
2. **Goodwill exists (total cost is above current value)**			
D. Current value equals book value......	$70,000	$60,000	$60,000
E. Current value is above book value ...	$90,000	$80,000	$60,000
F. Current value is below book value ...	$55,000	$50,000	$60,000
3. **Bargain purchase element exists (total cost is below current value)**			
G. Current value equals book value......	$50,000	$60,000	$60,000
H. Current value is above book value ...	$75,000	$80,000	$60,000
I. Current value is below book value ...	$45,000	$50,000	$60,000

Note: The book-value column is relevant to the acquiring company only in situations in which common stock is acquired, as explained later in the chapter.

The rest of this chapter deals with recording business combinations and preparing combined and consolidated financial statements as of the date of the business combination. In an economy that has experienced inflation over many years, the net assets of an acquired business are usually undervalued. Thus, situations B, E, and H of Illustration 3-2 are most common. Not all of the situations in Illustration 3-2 are covered individually. Instead, one situation from each major category is discussed and illustrated—namely, situations A, E, and H—to develop the general procedures applicable to each major category. For situations A and E, acquisition of assets and acquisition of common stock are discussed and illustrated, so that these two methods of acquisition are compared. In addition, situation F is discussed for an acquisition of common stock, to explain the procedures for accounting for a situation in which the net assets are overvalued.

When assets are acquired, the procedures to record the business combination and to prepare financial statements reflecting the enlarged, combined operations are not complicated. This is because the assets acquired and liabilities assumed are recorded directly by the acquiring company in its own general ledger (or in the general ledger of a newly established division) at their current values.

When common stock is acquired, the procedures used to record the business combination are also relatively simple. However, the procedures to prepare financial statements reflecting the enlarged, combined operations *are* somewhat involved, because the acquired subsidiary continues to account for its assets and liabilities using its recorded book values. Stated differently, the parent does not directly record the assets and liabilities of the acquired business in its own general ledger. The only account in which the parent records the cost of the acquired business is called Investment in Subsidiary. As a result, the parent must deal with the book value of the subsidiary's net assets (recorded on the books of the subsidiary) in preparing financial statements that reflect the enlarged, combined operations.

PERSPECTIVE

What's Invisible and Worth $55 Billion?

When an overexcited management purchases a business at a silly price . . . the silliness ends up in the goodwill account. Considering the lack of managerial discipline that created the account, under the circumstances it might better be labeled no-will.

—Warren E. Buffett,
Chairman, Berkshire Hathaway Inc., in a recent message to shareholders

When Philip Morris Inc. completes its $5.8 billion acquisition of General Foods Corp., the tobacco giant will add about $2.8 billion worth of goodwill to its own balance sheet. Corporate silliness? Not this time, says Buffett, one of America's most intrepid stalkers of hidden assets. "We saw a lot of very enduring goodwill in the brands that General Foods had," he recalls, when his company bought 4 million shares of General Foods at 37 a few years back.

(continued)

Buffett has just made a $300 million profit by investing in a company whose principal asset—brand loyalty—escaped its balance sheet. By accounting convention, the value of General Foods' brand names didn't appear anywhere until Philip Morris paid a premium over tangible assets to acquire it. But after the takeover, those values will loom large on the Philip Morris balance sheet. Goodwill—that wispy, ethereal asset—will constitute nearly 80% of the cigarette maker's net worth. So far, investors don't see this as Jell-O: In the two days following the announcement, Philip Morris shares rose two points, to 78.

Until recently, investors ignored goodwill, calling it a phantom asset. But now companies are piling it up in unprecedented amounts. According to Standard & Poor's Compustat Services Inc., intangible assets on the books of 5,500 companies jumped 37% last year, to $55.3 billion. The culprit: takeover fever.

Where Goodwill Looms Large on the Balance Sheet

	1984 Goodwill	
Company	Millions of Dollars	Percent of Net Worth
Tiger International	$ 57	2,850%
Financial Corp. of America	1,106	570
Rapid-American	234	241
A. H. Belo	453	158
Beatrice	2,607	111
Philip Morris	3,200	78*
Gelco	163	78
Hasbro	178	61
Gannett	629	55
Allis-Chalmers	37	52
Texas Eastern	621	40
Avon	447	39
IC Industries	541	35
American Brands	598	28
Fluor	423	25
GM	5,939	24*
Allied	702	23
Warner-Lambert	282	20
Cooper Industries	232	19
United Technologies	523	13

*Including pending 1985 acquisition

Source: *Business Week*, October 14, 1985, p. 134. Used by permission.

Daunting Task

When one company buys another, it creates goodwill if it pays more than the appraised value of physical assets, such as inventory, equipment, and land. Goodwill is then written off, usually over 40 years, on the premise that a brand name or franchise will gradually lose its value.

What's Invisible and Worth $55 Billion? *(continued)*

There is no question that the intangibles that go into goodwill ordinarily have some value. "I don't think the market dismisses goodwill anymore," says Anton J. Brenner, an analyst at Cyrus J. Lawrence Inc. Diana K. Temple, an analyst at Salomon Bros., agrees. "If you had to go out and create a brand like Jell-O, it would cost you a lot more than what Philip Morris is paying for it," she says. "It is very expensive to establish brands today, and the casualty rate on new launches is very high."

The daunting task for investors is to distinguish the valuable goodwill from the silly—the kind that ends up on balance sheets as a result of bidding wars. "It has all the earmarks of the watered stock craze of the 1920s," when companies issued stock backed by phony assets, charges Abraham J. Briloff, an accounting professor at the City University of New York's Bernard Baruch College.

Briloff criticizes United Technologies Corp. for not immediately writing off $234 million in goodwill associated with its $345 million purchase of semiconductor maker Mostek Corp. in 1979. At the time, UTC thought Mostek would generate an ever-growing stream of earnings. Instead, Mostek has done poorly. Nevertheless, the goodwill remains on United Technologies' books as an asset. A UTC spokeswoman responds that Briloff's is a minority view. At this point, it is unlikely that the accounting treatment is artificially boosting UTC's stock, since Mostek's problems have been widely reported. And goodwill is a small component of UTC's net worth.

But what can investors make of General Motors Corp.'s $5 billion purchase of Hughes Aircraft Co.? Since Hughes's assets were appraised at $1 billion, that leaves $4 billion in goodwill. So far, investors have not penalized GM for paying the premium. One reason: The $100 million-a-year goodwill write-off, which is not tax-deductible, pales beside the automaker's 1984 profits of $4.5 billion. Indeed, GM stock has traded within a $5 range since the deal was announced.

Big Bath

However, Hughes owners, who will get GM's Class H stock in exchange, may suffer a very real loss. Class H dividends are to be distributed based on Hughes's profits, which totaled $266 million in 1984. But the Securities & Exchange Commission ruled last month that Hughes, which will continue to keep its own set of books, must also write off $100 million in goodwill every year. That's a 40% dent right off the top.

To GM's common shareholders, $100 million will only look like real money if Detroit has another downturn. But if Hughes is unable to continue at its past performance levels, GM investors will take a big bath. That's the kind of uncertainty facing all shareholders as goodwill looms larger and larger.

Source: Stuart Weiss, "What's Invisible and Worth $55 Billion?" Article and accompanying table reprinted from the October 14, 1985, issue of *Business Week*, pp. 132–34, by special permission.

THE ACQUISITION OF ASSETS

The acquisition of assets is merely the purchase of the target company's assets. Part of the purchase price takes the form of assuming responsibility for the target company's existing liabilities. Before the acquiring company can record the acquisition of assets, it must determine whether the operations of the acquired business will be accounted for on a centralized or a decentralized basis. This decision is based on what is most practical and economical. In most instances, decentralized accounting is most practical unless the acquisition is a horizontal combination and the acquiring company already has similar outlying operations accounted for on a centralized basis. Decentralized and centralized accounting systems are discussed in the following illustrations.

Illustration

ACQUISITION OF ASSETS WHERE:

- **Neither Goodwill nor a Bargain Purchase Element Exists (Total Cost Equals Current Value of Net Assets)**
- **Current Value Equals Book Value**

To illustrate the recording of the acquisition and the preparation of combined financial statements as of the acquisition date when cost equals current value of net assets, and current value equals book value (situation A of Illustration 3-2), we assume the following information:

1. P Company acquired all of S Company's assets on January 1, 19X1, by assuming responsibility for all of its liabilities and paying $60,000 cash.
2. Total cost $60,000
3. Current value of net assets $60,000
4. Book value of net assets $60,000
5. The balance sheets for each company as of January 1, 19X1—immediately prior to the business combination—are as follows:

	P Company	S Company
Assets:		
Cash	**$110,000**	**$ 20,000**
Accounts receivable, net	**70,000**	**23,000**
Inventory	**100,000**	**32,000**
Land	**200,000**	**30,000**
Buildings and equipment	**500,000**	**190,000**
Accumulated depreciation	**(280,000)**	**(45,000)**
	$700,000	**$250,000**

	P Company	S Company
Liabilities and stockholders' equity:		
Liabilities	$300,000	$190,000
Common stock	300,000	40,000
Retained earnings	100,000	20,000
	$700,000	$250,000

Decentralized Accounting. Under a decentralized accounting system, the individual assets acquired and liabilities assumed are recorded at their current values in a new general ledger maintained at the location of the acquired business. This location is usually referred to as a *division* of the acquiring company. The acquiring company, referred to as the *home office*, charges the cost of the acquired business to an account called Investment in Division.

This is the entry on the home office's books:

Investment in Division S	60,000	
Cash		60,000

This is the entry on Division S's books:

Cash	20,000	
Accounts Receivable	23,000	
Inventory	32,000	
Land	30,000	
Buildings and Equipment	145,000	
Liabilities		190,000
Home Office Equity		60,000

The following points are important for understanding these entries:

1. Each asset and liability is recorded at its current value, which in this illustration coincides with its book value.
2. The accumulated depreciation accounts relating to the fixed assets recorded on S Company's books do not carry over to the acquiring company. The current values of these assets are the new cost basis for P Company.
3. At no time did P Company make any entries on S Company's books.
4. After S Company records the receipt of the cash and the sale of its assets, its sole asset is $60,000 cash, which most likely will be distributed to its stockholders. S Company will then end its legal existence.
5. From the acquisition date on, division earnings are combined with the earnings of the home office. Any income statements presented by P Company for periods prior to the acquisition date will not include any preacquisition earnings of S Company.

Combined Financial Statements. For financial reporting purposes, the financial statements of the home office and the division must be combined. This is done outside the general ledger on a worksheet. An entry is made on the worksheet to eliminate the Investment in Division and Home Office Equity accounts (the two accounts that were created to enable decentralized accounting to be done on a double-entry bookkeeping basis). All worksheet entries are shown in shading, so as to differentiate them from general ledger entries. The elimination entry to combine the two balance sheets as of the acquisition date is as follows:

Home Office Equity	60,000	
Investment in Division S.........................		60,000

Illustration 3-3 shows a combining statement worksheet, which combines the balance sheets of the home office and the newly established division as of the acquisition date.

Illustration 3-3
The Acquisition of Assets in Situation A

P Company
Combining Statement Worksheet
As of January 1, 19X1

	Home Office	Division	Eliminations Dr.	Eliminations Cr.	Combined
Balance Sheet:					
Cash	50,000	20,000			70,000
Accounts receivable, net .	70,000	23,000			93,000
Inventory......................	100,000	32,000			132,000
Investment in Division S	60,000			60,000(1)	–0–
Land	200,000	30,000			230,000
Buildings and equipment	500,000	145,000			645,000
Accumulated depreciation	(280,000)	–0–			(280,000)
	700,000	250,000		60,000	890,000
Liabilities	300,000	190,000			490,000
Home office equity..........		60,000	60,000(1)		–0–
Common stock..............	300,000				300,000
Retained earnings	100,000				100,000
	700,000	250,000	60,000		890,000
Proof of debit and credit postings..........................			60,000	60,000	

Explanation of entry:
(1) The primary elimination entry.

Centralized Accounting. Under a centralized accounting system, the acquiring company does not establish a separate general ledger at the location of the acquired business. Instead, it records the assets acquired and liabilities assumed directly in the general ledger maintained at its headquarters offices. In such situations, the preparation of combined financial statements through the use of the combining statement worksheet does not apply.

Illustration

ACQUISITION OF ASSETS WHERE:

- **Goodwill Exists (Total Cost Is above Current Value of Net Assets)**
- **Current Value Is above Book Value**

To illustrate recording the acquisition and preparing combined financial statements as of the acquisition date when cost is above current value and current value is above book value (situation E of Illustration 3-2), we revise our assumptions of the previous illustration as follows:

1. Total cost $90,000
2. Current value of net assets $80,000
3. Book value of net assets $60,000
4. The current values of S Company's assets and liabilities are assumed to equal their book values, except for the following assets:

	Book Value	Current Value	Current Value over Book Value
Inventory	$ 32,000	$ 34,000	$ 2,000
Land	30,000	42,000	12,000
Buildings and Equipment.....	145,000	151,000	6,000[a]
			$20,000

[a]For simplicity, we have combined buildings and equipment in the balance sheet. (Also for simplicity, we will later assume that the entire $6,000 pertains to equipment.)

Accordingly, $20,000 of the cost in excess of the book value of the net assets is attributable to these assets. The remaining $10,000 of cost in excess of the book value of the net assets represents goodwill.

Because goodwill is not deductible for income tax reporting purposes, acquiring companies often try to include in the acquisition agreement a tax-deductible feature known as a **covenant not to compete.** Covenants not to compete are intangible assets similar to goodwill. Such a covenant prevents the target company from reentering the same line of business for a specified period of time.

Decentralized Accounting. Under a decentralized accounting system, the individual assets acquired and liabilities assumed are recorded in the new division's newly established general ledger at their current values.

The entry on the home office's books is:

Investment in Division S	90,000	
Cash		90,000

The entry on Division S's books is:

Cash	20,000	
Accounts Receivable	23,000	
Inventory	34,000	
Land	42,000	
Buildings and Equipment	151,000	
Goodwill	10,000	
Liabilities		190,000
Home Office Equity		90,000

Combined Financial Statements. A combined balance sheet as of the acquisition date is prepared using the following elimination entry:

Home Office Equity	90,000	
Investment in Division S		90,000

Illustration 3-4 shows a combining statement worksheet, which combines the balance sheets of the home office and the division as of the acquisition date. The following points are important for understanding Illustration 3-4:

1. As in Illustration 3-3, the assets acquired and the liabilities assumed are recorded at their current values.
2. No revaluation has been made of P Company's assets and liabilities that existed immediately before the acquisition date. They are stated at historical cost. Thus, the combined column includes some assets and liabilities recorded at historical cost and some at current values.

Centralized Accounting. Under a centralized accounting system, the acquiring company records the assets acquired and liabilities assumed at their current values directly in the general ledger maintained at its own headquarters offices.

Illustration

ACQUISITION OF ASSETS WHERE:

- **Bargain Purchase Element Exists (Total Cost Is below Current Value of Net Assets)**
- **Current Value Is above Book Value**

Illustration 3-4
The Acquisition of Assets in Situation E

P Company
Combining Statement Worksheet
As of January 1, 19X1

	Home Office	Division	Eliminations Dr.	Eliminations Cr.	Combined
Balance Sheet:					
Cash	20,000	20,000			40,000
Accounts receivable, net .	70,000	23,000			93,000
Inventory......................	100,000	34,000			134,000
Investment in Division S	90,000			90,000(1)	–0–
Land	200,000	42,000			242,000
Buildings and equipment	500,000	151,000			651,000
Accumulated depreciation	(280,000)				(280,000)
Goodwill		10,000			10,000
	700,000	280,000		90,000	890,000
Liabilities	300,000	190,000			490,000
Home office equity.........		90,000	90,000(1)		–0–
Common stock..............	300,000				300,000
Retained earnings	100,000				100,000
	700,000	280,000	90,000		890,000
Proof of debit and credit postings..........................			90,000	90,000	

Explanation of entry:
(1) The primary elimination entry.

To illustrate recording the acquisition and preparing combined financial statements as of the acquisition date when cost is below current value and current value is above book value (situation H of Illustration 3-2), we revise our assumptions of Illustration 3-4 as follows:

1. Total cost $75,000
2. Current value of net assets $80,000
3. Book value of net assets $60,000

The only change from the preceding situation is the lowering of the total cost from $90,000 to $75,000. Because the current value of the acquired business's assets is $80,000, a purchase price of $75,000 results in a bargain purchase element of $5,000.

Bargain purchase elements are treated arbitrarily under the provisions of *APB Opinion No. 16.* First, the bargain purchase element must be treated as a reduction of the current values assigned to any noncurrent assets acquired other than long-term investments in marketable securities. If the bargain purchase element is so large that the applicable noncurrent assets are reduced to zero (which rarely, if ever, happens), any remaining credit is recorded as a deferred credit and amortized to income over a period not more than 40 years. The rationale for attempting to eliminate the bargain purchase element is that the values assigned to the net assets as a whole should not exceed the purchase price paid. Under historical cost-based accounting, the purchase price constitutes cost. Were it not for this requirement, managements would have the opportunity to seek or use the highest possible appraisals for the assets to obtain the highest possible bargain purchase element. The high (artificial) bargain purchase element could then be amortized to income over a relatively short period of time in comparison with time periods assigned to the noncurrent assets. Thus, substantial opportunity for manipulating income would exist.

Because bargain purchase elements arise most frequently when the acquired business has recently experienced operating losses, this treatment results in a conservative valuation of the noncurrent assets other than long-term investments in marketable securities. This makes sense; such noncurrent assets acquired from a company experiencing operating losses are subject to greater realization risks than if the target company had not experienced operating losses.

In this situation, the $5,000 bargain purchase element is allocated to the land, building, and equipment, using their relative current values:

Appropriate Noncurrent Assets	Current Value[a]	Percentage to Total (Rounded)	Bargain Purchase Element	Percentage Times Bargain Purchase Element	Adjusted Current Value
Land............	$ 42,000	20%	$5,000	$1,000	$ 41,000
Buildings and Equipment.	151,000	80	5,000	4,000	147,000
	$193,000	100%		$5,000	$181,000

[a]As given in Illustration 3-4.

The entry to record the acquisition under a decentralized accounting system is as follows. Here is the entry on the home office's books:

Investment in Division S..............................	75,000	
Cash..		75,000

This is the entry on Division S's books:

Cash..	20,000	
Accounts Receivable......................................	23,000	
Inventory..	34,000	
Land..	41,000	
Buildings and Equipment...............................	147,000	
Liabilities..		190,000
Home Office Equity...................................		75,000

A combined balance sheet as of the acquisition date would be prepared in the same manner as shown in the preceding illustration; only the amounts would differ.

Some accountants incorrectly refer to an excess of current value over cost as *negative goodwill* rather than as a bargain purchase element. The use of this term is unfortunate and improper. Goodwill either does or does not exist; there is no such thing as a company having negative goodwill. We point this term out only because you may encounter it in practice.

THE ACQUISITION OF COMMON STOCK (WHOLLY OWNED SUBSIDIARY)

When common stock is acquired, the acquiring company charges its total cost to an account called Investment in Subsidiary. Assuming that the value of the consideration given by the acquiring company is $85,000 and direct costs incurred are $5,000 (that may be properly added to the cost of the acquisition), the entry to record the acquisition would be as follows. Assuming that $85,000 cash is the consideration given:

Investment in Subsidiary	90,000	
Cash		90,000

Assuming that 1,000 shares of $1 par value common stock (having a market value of $85,000) is the consideration given:

Investment in Subsidiary	90,000	
Common Stock		1,000
Additional Paid-in Capital		84,000
Cash		5,000

Note that if the common stock issued is registered with the Securities and Exchange Commission (SEC), the following additional entry would be made for the additional direct costs incurred to register the common stock:

Additional Paid-in Capital	XXX	
Cash		XXX

CONSOLIDATED FINANCIAL STATEMENTS

Consolidation is the process of combining the financial statements of the parent and the subsidiary. Combining the financial statements of a parent and a subsidiary is essentially the same as combining those of a home office and a division. However, because the subsidiary retains its status as a separate legal entity (thus retaining ownership of its assets and responsibilities for its liabilities), there are several conceptual issues for subsidiaries that do not exist for divisions:

1. **Appropriateness of consolidating.** Is it appropriate to present consolidated financial statements? (The alternative is to present the separate company financial statements of the parent and the subsidiary.)
2. **Minimum ownership level and conditions.** What level of ownership or other conditions must be met to permit consolidation?
3. **Limitations of consolidated financial statements.** Are there limitations of consolidated financial statements so that additional supplemental disclosures (such as industry segment information) are needed?
4. **Revaluation of assets and liabilities.** Should the subsidiary revalue its assets and liabilities to their current values (in its general ledger), or should the revaluation be made as part of the consolidation process (on the consolidating statement worksheet)?
5. **Manner of presenting subsidiary's separate financial statements.** If the subsidiary issues separate financial statements (perhaps because of a loan agreement requirement), on what basis should its assets and liabilities be reported—the subsidiary's historical cost or current values based on the parent's cost?

The rest of this chapter addresses these issues and discusses how to prepare consolidated financial statements.

The Purpose of Consolidated Statements

The purpose of consolidated financial statements is best expressed in *ARB No. 51:*

> The purpose of consolidated statements is to present, primarily for the benefit of the shareholders and creditors of the parent company, the results of operations and the financial position of a parent company and its subsidiaries essentially as if the group were a single company with one or more branches or divisions. There is a presumption that consolidated statements are more meaningful than separate statements and that they are usually necessary for a fair presentation when one of the companies in the group directly or indirectly has a controlling financial interest in the other companies.[9]

Thus, consolidation of subsidiaries is the general rule—not the exception.

The Conditions for Consolidation

The decision whether or not to consolidate a subsidiary is governed by the policy set forth in *ARB No. 51*, which is expected to be amended in 1987 as

[9]Accounting Research Bulletin No. 51, "Consolidated Financial Statements" (New York: American Institute of Certified Public Accountants, 1959), par. 1.

a result of the FASB's proposed statement, "Consolidation of All Majority-Owned Subsidiaries," which states:

> The usual condition for a controlling financial interest is ownership of a majority voting interest, and therefore, as a general rule ownership by one company directly or indirectly of over fifty percent of the outstanding voting shares of another company is a condition pointing toward consolidation. However, there are exceptions to this general rule. A majority-owned subsidiary shall not be consolidated if control is likely to be temporary or if it does not rest with the majority owners (as, for instance, if the subsidiary is in legal reorganization or in bankruptcy or operates under foreign exchange restrictions, controls, or other governmentally imposed uncertainties so severe that they cast significant doubt on the parent's ability to control the subsidiary).[10]

Until the proposed amendment becomes effective, an exception to consolidation is allowed for subsidiaries in different lines of business, such as an insurance or finance subsidiary of a parent that is a manufacturer. However, because of the diversity of practice and lack of comparability that have resulted under the increasingly criticized *ARB No. 51*, the Financial Accounting Standards Board took steps to eliminate this exception.

The accounting to be followed for unconsolidated subsidiaries is discussed in Chapter 4.

The Rules of the Securities and Exchange Commission. The consolidation rules of the Securities and Exchange Commission (SEC), which apply only to publicly owned companies, are slightly broader than the policy in the amended *ARB No. 51*. The reason for this is that in 1984 the SEC discovered the emerging practice of companies forming "nonsubsidiary subsidiaries." Such entities were formed to perform marketing or research and development. The entities were controlled not by majority voting interest, which would require consolidation, but through loan agreements and stock-option purchase agreements. The purpose was to exclude the operating expenses of these entities from the consolidated income statement of the parent. To end this emerging practice, the SEC broadened its consolidation rules in 1986 to require the following:

1. Ownership of a majority voting interest should not be the sole way of determining whether control of an entity exists.
2. Facts and circumstances of the realtionship between entities should be carefully analyzed when majority voting interest does not exist.
3. **Substance versus form** should be evaluated in deciding if consolidated financial statements are appropriate.[11]

[10]Proposed Statement of Financial Accounting Standards, "Consolidation of All Majority-owned Subsidiaries" (Stamford: Financial Accounting Standards Board, December 16, 1986), par. 16.
[11]Regulation S-X, Article 3A-02 (Washington, D.C.: Securities and Exchange Commission, 1986).

Therefore, a less-than-majority-owned entity may be deemed to be a subsidiary for which consolidation is appropriate.

A Subsidiary Having a Different Year-end. The subsidiary's fiscal year-end should be within three months of the parent's year-end. If not, the subsidiary (or possibly even the parent) must change its fiscal year-end.

Disclosure of Consolidation Policy. The parent must disclose its consolidation policy. A typical example of such disclosure in a note to the financial statements is as follows:

> The consolidated financial statements include the accounts of the company and its domestic and foreign subsidiaries. Significant intercompany accounts and transactions have been eliminated.

Foreign Subsidiaries. Foreign subsidiaries are exposed to several unique risks not faced by domestic subsidiaries. These additional circumstances are discussed in Chapter 15.

Limitations of Consolidated Financial Statements

Consolidated financial statements have limited usefulness in assessing the future prospects of companies with significant diversified operations in more than one industry or significant foreign operations. In recognition of this fact, *FASB Statement No. 14,* "Financial Reporting for Segments of a Business Enterprise," was issued in 1976. It requires specified information on industry segments and foreign operations to be presented as supplementary information to the consolidated financial statements. This pronouncement, which is discussed at length in Chapter 13, imposes extensive reporting requirements on companies with diversified or foreign operations.

The Consolidating Statement Worksheet

Unless the business combination occurs on the last day of the parent's reporting year (which rarely happens), there is no need to prepare consolidated financial statements as of the acquisition date. They are illustrated in the worksheets in this chapter for instructional purposes only.

The balance sheet is the only financial statement of the subsidiary that can be consolidated with the parent's financial statement as of the acquisition date. This is a fundamental concept of the purchase method—that is, the parent company can report to its stockholders only the operations of the subsidiary that occur subsequent to the acquisition date. (Combining the future income statements of a parent and a subsidiary is discussed in Chapter 4.)

The Primary Elimination Entry

The consolidation is prepared by posting an *elimination entry* to the consolidating statement worksheet. The entry eliminates the Investment in Subsidiary account and the subsidiary's capital accounts, substituting the asset and liability accounts of the subsidiary for the Investment in Subsidiary account. This substitution prevents the double counting of the subsidiary's net assets in arriving at the consolidated amounts. The entry is posted only to the worksheet, not to any general ledger accounts. (We call this entry the primary elimination entry for instructional and reference purposes only. In later chapters, other types of eliminations are encountered in preparing consolidated financial statements.)

THE PUSH-DOWN BASIS OF ACCOUNTING: THE PARENT REVALUES THE SUBSIDIARY'S ASSETS AND LIABILITIES TO THEIR CURRENT VALUES

Under the **push-down basis of accounting,** the subsidiary does the following as of the acquisition date:

1. Adjusts its assets and liabilities to their current values and records goodwill, if there is any. This makes the subsidiary's adjusted net assets equal the parent company's Investment in Subsidiary account.
2. Eliminates the balance(s) in its Accumulated Depreciation account(s). This recognizes that a new basis of accounting has been established for its fixed assets.
3. Closes its Retained Earnings account balance to Additional Paid-in Capital.
4. Uses this new basis of accounting in its separate financial statements. Retained earnings should be dated.

The Rationale for Using the Push-Down Basis of Accounting

The rationale for having the subsidiary adjust its assets and liabilities to their current values as of the acquisition date rests on an argument of substance over form. Advocates of push-down accounting contend that the relevant factor is the acquisition itself, not the form of consummating the acquisition. In their view, whether the parent company acquires assets or common stock is irrelevant. Recall that when assets are acquired, the individual assets and liabilities are revalued to their current values when they are recorded in the acquiring company's general ledger (or in the division's general ledger if decentralized accounting is used). As the acquisition itself is the relevant factor, a new basis of accounting has been established for the assets and liabilities. Merely because common stock is acquired instead of assets should not prevent this new basis of accounting from being reflected at the subsidiary level. Furthermore, in most cases **the parent controls the form of the ownership.** That is, it has the legal power to liquidate the subsidiary into a division. The fact that the parent chooses to maintain the acquired business as a separate legal entity should not have a bearing on whether a new cost basis should be established at the subsidiary level.

The SEC Leads the Way

Push-down accounting had not gained significant acceptance or use until 1983, when the Securities and Exchange Commission issued *Staff Accounting Bulletin No. 54.* This bulletin requires push-down accounting in the separate financial statements of a subsidiary acquired in a purchase transaction.

The SEC was convinced about the soundness of its position and concerned by the potentially misleading results from the many subsidiaries that had recently issued common stock based on historical cost-based financial statements using non-push-down accounting. The result of this practice was that these subsidiaries did not report their true cost of doing business and thus overstated their earnings. The SEC concluded that the time for substance over form had come.

General Motors Tests the Water. Perhaps to test the conviction of the SEC, General Motors Corp. argued before the commission that it should not have to apply push-down accounting to its $5 billion acquisition of all of Hughes Aircraft Co. in 1985 (in which there was $4 billion of cost in excess of book value). The SEC stood its ground.

Allowable Exceptions to Push-down Accounting. Despite its hard line in the matter, the SEC does not require the use of push-down accounting when the parent does not control the form of ownership in its subsidiary. When a significant minority interest, preferred stock, or outstanding public debt exists, the parent usually does not possess the legal power to liquidate the subsidiary into a division (and thus control the form of its ownership). (These exceptions are discussed in more detail in Chapter 5.)

Illustration

ACQUISITION OF COMMON STOCK UNDER THE PUSH-DOWN BASIS OF ACCOUNTING WHERE:

- **Goodwill Exists (Total Cost Is above Current Value of Net Assets)**
- **Current Value Is above Book Value**

Situation E of Illustration 3-2 is now used to illustrate the entries that would be made under the push-down basis of accounting and the elimination entry made in preparing consolidated financial statements as of the acquisition date. We assume that, rather than acquiring the target company's assets, common stock was acquired. Recall that in illustrating situation E for the acquisition of assets we used the following information:

1. Total cost $90,000
2. Current value of net assets $80,000
3. Book value of net assets $60,000
4. The current values of S Company's assets and liabilities are assumed to equal their book values, except for the following assets:

	Book Value	Current Value	Current Value over Book Value
Inventory	$ 32,000	$ 34,000	$ 2,000
Land	30,000	42,000	12,000
Buildings and Equipment	145,000[a]	151,000	6,000
			$20,000

[a]Net of $45,000 accumulated depreciation.

5. Goodwill of $10,000 ($90,000 − $80,000) exists.

The subsidiary would make the following entries as of the acquisition date.

1. To adjust assets to their current values and record goodwill:

Inventory	2,000	
Land	12,000	
Equipment	6,000	
Goodwill	10,000	
Additional Paid-in Capital		30,000

2. To eliminate the balance in the Accumulated Depreciation account:

Accumulated Depreciation	45,000	
Buildings and Equipment		45,000

3. To close out the balance in Retained Earnings:

Retained Earnings	20,000	
Additional Paid-in Capital		20,000

If consolidated financial statements were prepared as of the acquisition date, the following primary elimination entry would be made on the worksheet:

Common Stock	40,000	
Additional Paid-in Capital	50,000	
Investment in Subsidiary		90,000

Illustration 3-5 shows a consolidating statement worksheet, which consolidates the balance sheets of the parent company and the subsidiary as of the acquisition date (the subsidiary having already applied push-down accounting). Note that except for the equity accounts, the amounts in Illustration 3-5 are identical to the amounts in Illustration 3-4, when assets were acquired and recorded directly in the division's general ledger at their current values.

Illustration 3-5
The Acquisition of Common Stock (Push-down Accounting Applied by Subsidiary)

P COMPANY AND SUBSIDIARY (S COMPANY)
Consolidating Statement Worksheet
As of January 1, 19X1

	P Company	S Company	Eliminations Dr.	Eliminations Cr.	Consolidated
Balance Sheet:					
Cash	20,000	20,000			40,000
Accounts receivable, net	70,000	23,000			93,000
Inventory	100,000	34,000			134,000
Investment in S Company	90,000			90,000(1)	–0–
Land	200,000	42,000			242,000
Buildings and equipment,	500,000	151,000			651,000
Accumulated depreciation	(280,000)	–0–			(280,000)
Goodwill		10,000			10,000
	700,000	280,000		90,000	890,000
Liabilities	300,000	190,000			490,000
P Company:					
Common stock	300,000				300,000
Retained earnings	100,000				100,000
S Company:					
Common stock		40,000	40,000(1)		–0–
Additional paid-in capital		50,000	50,000(1)		–0–
Retained earnings		–0–			–0–
	700,000	280,000	90,000		890,000
Proof of debit and credit postings			90,000	90,000	

Explanation of entry:
(1) The primary elimination entry.

The consolidation process could not be any simpler than it is in Illustration 3-5. In the following sections, in which the subsidiary does *not* revalue its assets and liabilities, the consolidation process is more involved.

THE NON-PUSH-DOWN BASIS OF ACCOUNTING: THE SUBSIDIARY RETAINS THE HISTORICAL COST BASIS OF ITS ASSETS AND LIABILITIES

The non-push-down basis of accounting holds that the subsidiary cannot revalue its assets and liabilities to their current values merely because its outstanding common stock has changed hands and has become concentrated in the hands of significantly fewer or even a single stockholder.

The obvious question, then, is this: How are the subsidiary's assets and liabilities revalued to their current values as required under the purchase method of accounting? The answer requires an understanding of the major conceptual elements of the parent's total cost of the investment as reflected in its Investment in Subsidiary account.

The Major Conceptual Elements of Total Investment Cost

The total cost of the investment as recorded on the parent's books must be separated into its major conceptual elements. We do this by analyzing the relationship among the total cost, the current value of the subsidiary's net assets, and the book value of the subsidiary's net assets. Assume the following information (from situation E of Illustration 3-2):

1. P Company acquired all of S Company's outstanding common stock on January 1, 19X1.
2. Total cost $90,000
3. Current value of net assets $80,000
4. Book value of net assets $60,000
5. The current values of S Company's assets and liabilities are assumed to equal their book values, except for the following assets:

	Book Value	Current Value	Current Value over Book Value
Inventory	$ 32,000	$ 34,000	$ 2,000
Land	30,000	42,000	12,000
Buildings and equipment......	145,000[a]	151,000	6,000
			$20,000

[a]Net of $45,000 accumulated depreciation.

Accordingly, $20,000 of the cost in excess of the book value of the net assets is attributable to these assets. The remaining $10,000 of cost in excess of the book value represents goodwill.

Thus, the total cost of the investment may be considered to comprise three major elements:

1. **The book value element.** The parent's ownership interest in the subsidiary's recorded net assets at their book value (100% of $60,000)	$60,000
2. **The current value over book value element.** The parent's ownership interest in the subsidiary's excess of the current value of its net assets over their book value (100% of $20,000)	20,000
3. **The goodwill element.** The parent's total cost in excess of the current value of the subsidiary's net assets ($90,000 − $80,000)	10,000
Total cost of the investment	$90,000

The $20,000 difference between the current value of the subsidiary's net assets and their book value is included in the parent's investment account. When the subsidiary's financial statements are consolidated with its parent's financial statements, this $20,000 difference is reclassified from the investment account to the specific assets with which it has been identified. (In this situation, $2,000 is identified with undervalued inventories, $12,000 is identified with undervalued land, and $6,000 is identified with undervalued equipment.) The parent accounts for the individual items that make up this difference in the same manner that the subsidiary accounts for the specific assets that are undervalued.

This treatment contrasts with push-down accounting theory—in which the subsidiary's assets and liabilities are adjusted to their current values in the subsidiary's general ledger—in the following ways:

1. The subsidiary continues to depreciate its assets at their historical cost as though the business combination had never occurred.
2. The parent amortizes to its future income that portion of its cost in excess of book value that is attributable to depreciable or amortizable assets (in this example, $2,000 pertaining to the inventory and $6,000 pertaining to the equipment). The $2,000 amount relating to inventory is amortized to income as the subsidiary sells its inventory. The $6,000 amount relating to the equipment is amortized to income using the same remaining life that the subsidiary uses to depreciate its historical cost.
3. The parent also amortizes that portion of its investment account that represents goodwill ($10,000 in this example).

In other words, depreciation and amortization of the subsidiary's assets take place on two sets of books instead of just one set, as when assets are acquired. These amortization procedures on the books of the parent company are necessary to charge the combined operations with the current value of the assets acquired, because the assets were not revalued on the subsidiary's books. In substance, the net effect on the enlarged business as a whole is the same as though the subsidiary had revalued its assets to their current values (push-down accounting).

Illustration

SEPARATING THE TOTAL COST OF THE INVESTMENT INTO ITS MAJOR CONCEPTUAL ELEMENTS

Separating the total cost of the investment into its major conceptual elements is possible for all common stock investments, regardless of the price paid by the parent. Three situations were presented in the discussion of the acquisition of assets. Each had a different total cost and assumed current value for the net assets:

1. **Neither goodwill nor a bargain purchase element exists**—total cost equals current value of net assets (situation A of Illustration 3-2). The total cost of $60,000 was equal to the current value of the subsidiary's net assets of $60,000, and current value was equal to the book value of the subsidiary's net assets.
2. **Goodwill exists**—total cost is above current value of net assets (situation E of Illustration 3-2). The total cost of $90,000 was above the current value of the subsidiary's net assets of $80,000, with certain assets undervalued. Goodwill of $10,000 was present.
3. **Bargain purchase element exists**—total cost is below current value of net assets (situation H of Illustration 3-2). The total cost of $75,000 was below the current value of the subsidiary's net assets of $80,000, with certain assets undervalued. A bargain purchase element of $5,000 was present.

Using these three situations—but assuming that all of the common stock was acquired instead of all of the assets—we would separate the total cost of the investment on the parent company's books into its major conceptual elements, as shown in Illustration 3-6. In addition, situation F of Illustration 3-2, in which net assets are overvalued by $10,000, is shown. For simplicity, the entire overvaluation of net assets in situation F is assumed to apply to equipment. This situation does not involve any principles or procedures other than those discussed for situations in which the net assets are undervalued. It is shown only to demonstrate the conceptual view of overvalued assets.

The following points are important for understanding Illustration 3-6:

1. In situation A, only one major conceptual element exists because total cost equals current value and current value equals book value.
2. In situation E, all three major conceptual elements exist. If the total cost of the investment had been $10,000 less, no goodwill element and only two major conceptual elements would have existed.
3. In situation F, all three major conceptual elements exist, but the parent has a credit balance instead of a debit balance for its current value under

Illustration 3-6
The Major Conceptual Elements of the Total Cost of the Investment

Situation from Illustration 3-2	Net Assets of Subsidiary: Current Value (1) (Given)	Net Assets of Subsidiary: Book Value (2) (Given)	Current Value over (under) Book Value (3) (1) − (2)	Separation of Total Cost into Its Major Conceptual Elements: Total Cost (4) (Given)	=	Book Value Element (5) (2)	+	Current Value over (under) Book Value Element (6) (3)	+	Goodwill (Bargain Purchase) Element (7) (Residual)
1. **Neither Goodwill nor a Bargain Purchase Element Exists—Total cost equals current value:**										
A. Current value equals book value	$60,000	$60,000		$60,000	=	$60,000				
2. **Goodwill Exists—Total cost is above current value:**										
E. Current value is above book value	80,000	60,000	$20,000	90,000	=	60,000	+	$20,000	+	$10,000
F. Current value is below book value	50,000	60,000	(10,000)	55,000	=	60,000		(10,000)		5,000
3. **Bargain Purchase Element Exists—Total cost is below current value:**										
H. Current value is above book value	80,000	60,000	20,000	75,000	=	60,000	+	20,000	+	(5,000)[a]

[a]This bargain purchase element must be allocated to the extent possible to noncurrent assets other than long-term investments. If all of it is allocated thus, then the amounts in the column to the left decrease by $5,000 and no deferred credit remains. (See Illustration 3-7, in which all of it is allocated to the appropriate noncurrent assets.)

book value element. This credit balance is identified with depreciable assets and is amortized in future periods to the parent's income statement, as are the debit balances in situations E and H, which are identified with depreciable assets.

Displaying the Major Conceptual Elements by Their Components

The analysis of the parent's total cost by its major conceptual elements can be expanded so that the components of the book value element and those of the current value over book value element are displayed. This expanded analysis can be used as the source of an elimination entry that consolidates the financial statements of the parent with those of the subsidiary. The preparation of consolidated financial statements has always been an involved process. However, the use of an expanded analysis of the total cost of the investment, *which displays the components of the major conceptual elements*, substantially simplifies the consolidation procedures. The procedures for expanding the analysis are explained below using situation E of Illustration 3-6, in which total cost is above current value and current value is above book value.

Separating the Book Value Element. The book-value element is easily separated into its components by multiplying the parent's ownership interest by the balance in each of the subsidiary's individual capital accounts—Common Stock, Additional Paid-in Capital, and Retained Earnings—as of the acquisition date. The capital accounts of S Company as of the acquisition date are as follows:

Common stock	$40,000
Retained earnings	20,000
Total stockholders' equity	$60,000

Because we assume P Company acquires 100% of S Company's outstanding common stock, the $60,000 book-value element comprises these two components.

Separating the Current Value over (under) the Book Value Element. As stated previously, the parent accounts for the components of the current value over (under) book value element—not for the total difference as a lump sum. Thus, the current value over (under) book value element can be thought of as comprising the following three components:

Inventory	$ 2,000
Land	12,000
Equipment	6,000
Total current value over book value	$20,000

The Goodwill Element and the Bargain Purchase Element. No separation is needed for goodwill, which is a residual amount accounted for as a lump sum. When a bargain purchase element exists, the initial bargain purchase element credit must be allocated as much as possible to noncurrent assets other than long-term investments in marketable securities. Any remaining bargain purchase element is amortized to income in future periods.

Recapping the Conceptual Elements. The analysis of the total investment cost in situation E of Illustration 3-6 is shown below by the major conceptual elements and their components:

	Analysis of Total Investment Cost	
	By the Major Conceptual Elements	By the Components of the Major Conceptual Elements
Book value element:		
Common stock..........		$40,000
Retained earnings		20,000
Total....................	$60,000	$60,000
Current value over book value element:		
Inventory		$ 2,000
Land.........................		12,000
Equipment................		6,000
Total....................	20,000	$20,000
Goodwill element	10,000	$10,000
Total cost............	$90,000	$90,000

Illustration 3-7 displays the major conceptual elements for the situations in Illustration 3-6 by their components. The following points are important for understanding Illustration 3-7:

1. In situation A, in which only the book value element exists, the parent has completed accounting for its investment under the purchase method of accounting. No additional accounting procedures are necessary because no other major conceptual elements exist.
2. In situations E and H, in which the current value of the net assets exceeds their book value and the parent pays more than the book value of the net assets, the amount applicable to the equipment is amortized to the parent's future income over the remaining life of these assets, using the same remaining life that the subsidiary uses to depreciate these items. The amount determined for inventory is amortized in the following year, assuming the subsidiary sells its inventory. The amount determined for the land is not amortized because land is never depreciated. If the land is ever sold, the amount determined for land is charged to income at this time. In summary, the parent accounts for each individual component in a manner consistent with the way the subsidiary

Illustration 3-7
The Major Conceptual Elements and Their Components

			Book Value Element			+	Current Value over (under) Book Value Element						+	Goodwill (Bargain Purchase) Element
Situation from Illustration 3-2	Total Cost	=	Common Stock	+	Retained Earnings	+	Inventory	+	Land	+	Equipment		+	
1. **Neither Goodwill nor a Bargain Purchase Element Exists—Total cost equals current value:**														
A. Current value equals book value..	$60,000	=	$40,000	+	$20,000									
2. **Goodwill Exists—Total cost is above current value:**														
E. Current value is above book value	90,000	=	40,000	+	20,000	+	$2,000	+	$12,000	+	$ 6,000		+	$10,000
F. Current value is below book value	55,000	=	40,000	+	20,000					+	$(10,000)		+	5,000
3. **Bargain Purchase Element Exists—Total cost is below current value:**														
H. Current value is above book value	75,000	=	40,000	+	20,000	+	2,000	+	12,000	+	6,000		+	(5,000)
									(1,000)[a]		(4,000)[a]			5,000[a]
	$75,000		$40,000		$20,000		$2,000		$11,000		$ 2,000			$ –0–

[a]This allocation is the same as that illustrated on page 95, in which assets were acquired at below their current value.

accounts for its historical cost. Goodwill is amortized over its expected life, up to 40 years.

3. In situation F, in which the current value of the net assets is below their book value, the parent has a credit amount instead of debit amounts to amortize to its subsequent income statements. Otherwise, the procedures are the same as in point 2 above. The amortization partially offsets the depreciation expense recorded on the subsidiary's books from the viewpoint of combined operations.
4. The expanded analysis of the investment account is maintained in a supportng schedule to the Investment in Subsidiary general ledger account.

Illustration

ACQUISITION OF COMMON STOCK UNDER THE NON-PUSH-DOWN BASIS OF ACCOUNTING WHERE:

- **Goodwill Exists (Total Cost Is above Current Value of Net Assets)**
- **Current Value Is above Book Value**

Using the information from situation E in Illustration 3-7 (in which cost is in excess of the current value of the subsidiary's net assets), the following primary elimination entry as of the acquisition date is obtained directly from the expanded analysis of the total investment cost:

Common Stock	40,000	
Retained Earnings	20,000	
Inventory	2,000	
Land	12,000	
Equipment	6,000	
Goodwill	10,000	
Investment in Subsidiary		90,000

Illustration 3-8 shows the preparation of the consolidating statement worksheet as of the acquisition date using the above primary elimination entry. In addition, the following accumulated depreciation entry is needed to recognize that a new cost basis has been established for the subsidiary's fixed assets for consolidated reporting purposes:

Accumulated Depreciation	45,000	
Buildings and Equipment		45,000

The following points are important for understanding Illustration 3-8:

1. The parent's investment cost in excess of the book value of the subsidiary's net assets becomes clear in the consolidation process. The

Illustration 3-8
The Acquisition of Common Stock (Non-push-down Accounting Used by Subsidiary)

P COMPANY AND SUBSIDIARY (S COMPANY)
Consolidating Statement Worksheet
As of January 1, 19X1

	P Company	S Company	Eliminations Dr.	Eliminations Cr.	Consolidated
Balance Sheet:					
Cash	20,000	20,000			40,000
Accounts receivable, net	70,000	23,000			93,000
Inventory	100,000	32,000	2,000(1)		134,000
Investment in S Company	90,000			90,000(1)	–0–
Land	200,000	30,000	12,000(1)		242,000
Buildings and equipment,	500,000	190,000	6,000(1)	45,000(2)	651,000
Accumulated depreciation	(280,000)	(45,000)	45,000(2)		(280,000)
Goodwill			10,000(1)		10,000
	700,000	250,000	75,000	135,000	890,000
Liabilities	300,000	190,000			490,000
P Company:					
Common stock	300,000				300,000
Retained earnings	100,000				100,000
S Company:					
Common stock		40,000	40,000(1)		–0–
Retained earnings		20,000	20,000(1)		–0–
	700,000	250,000	60,000		890,000
Proof of debit and credit postings			135,000	135,000	

Explanation of entries:
(1) The primary elimination entry.
(2) The accumulated depreciation elimination entry.

excess is effectively reclassified to the balance sheet accounts with which it has been identified.

2. The amounts in the consolidated column are composed of (a) the parent's items based on book values, and (b) the subsidiary's items based on the current value of those items as of the acquisition date.
3. The amounts shown in the consolidated column are the same as those in the consolidated column of Illustration 3-5—in which the push-down basis of accounting was used.
4. The only difference between Illustrations 3-5 and 3-8 is that here we are doing on the worksheet what was done in the subsidiary's general ledger: revaluing assets to their current values and eliminating the accumulated depreciation as of the acquisition date.

Illustration

ACQUISITION OF COMMON STOCK UNDER THE NON-PUSH-DOWN BASIS OF ACCOUNTING WHERE:

- **Goodwill Exists (Total Cost Is above Current Value of Net Assets)**
- **Current Value Is below Book Value**

When the current value of the net assets is below their book value, the consolidation procedures are the same as those illustrated for the case in which the current value is above the book value of the net assets, except that a net credit balance exists in the current value under book value section of the expanded analysis, which displays the individual components of the major conceptual elements. The extent of the credit balances depends on the current value of each asset and liability compared with its book value.

From the information in situation F of Illustration 3-6 (in which the current value is below the book value of the net assets), the primary elimination entry at the acquisition date is as follows:

Common Stock	**40,000**	
Retained Earnings	**20,000**	
Goodwill	**5,000**	
Equipment		**10,000**
Investment in Subsidiary		**55,000**

The preparation of consolidated financial statements for this situation is not shown, because the procedures are the same as for situations in which the current value is above the book value of the net assets.

Dealing with Over- or Undervalued Liabilities

For simplicity, the previous discussions and illustrations dealt only with certain over- and undervalued assets. The current values of accounts payable and accrued liabilities (using present value procedures) are usually so close to their book values—because of the relatively short period until payment of the obligation—that the difference is often ignored in the interest of practicality. The current value of borrowings that have a floating interest rate always equals the book value. If the borrowings have a fixed interest rate that is different from the interest rate existing at the acquisition date, however, the present value of the debt does not equal its book value. Thus, the difference must be reflected as one of the components of the current value over (under) book value element in the conceptual analysis of the Investment in Subsidiary account. (For liabilities, however, the description "current value over (under) book value element" is changed so that the description becomes "current value under (over) book value element.") For example, assume that a subsidiary has 8% bonds payable outstanding at the acquisition date. If the current interest rate is 12%, the present value of the debt is below the book value. (The low fixed interest rate of 8% in relation to the current interest rate of 12% means that the debt appears larger than it really is.)

Reporting the Debt at Its Present Value. To illustrate, assume that on the acquisition date of January 1, 19X1, the subsidiary has 8% bonds outstanding having a face amount of $100,000 and a maturity date of December 31, 19X2 (two years from now). If the current interest rate is 12%, the present value of the bonds would be calculated as follows:

Present value of $100,000 principle payment due December 31, 19X2 ($100,000 × 0.79719)	$79,719
Present value of two $8,000 interest payments due at the end of 19X1 and 19X2 ($8,000 × 1.69005)	13,520
Total	$93,239

Accordingly, the $6,761 difference between the book value of the bonds ($100,000) and their present value ($93,239) would be reflected as an individual component of the current value under (over) book value element. If consolidated financial statements were prepared as of the acquisition date, the bonds would be reported in the consolidated column at their present value of $93,239 because the $6,761 amount would be debited to the Bonds Payable account in consolidation:

	P Company	S Company	Eliminations Dr.	Eliminations Cr.	Consolidated
Bonds payable		100,000	6,761		93,239

Subsequent Treatment of the Difference. The $6,761 amount is analogous to a discount and would be amortized to interest expense over the next two years using the interest method of amortization. Over the next two years, interest expense would be reported at 12% of the debt's carrying value (rather than at 8% of the book value of $100,000). For 19X1, interest expense of $11,190 would be reported (12% × $93,239), and the $3,190 difference between the $11,190 and the $8,000 cash payment would be amortized out of the Investment account. At December 31, 19X1, this component of the Investment account would have an unamortized balance of $3,571, which results in a $96,429 carrying value of the debt in consolidation at that date. For 19X2, interest expense of $11,571 would be reported (12% × $96,429), which is made up of the $8,000 cash payment and $3,571 amortized out of the Investment account. In the following chapter, we show in detail how to amortize amounts out of the Investment account.

CONCLUDING COMMENTS CONCERNING CONSOLIDATIONS

As this book goes to press, the FASB is reexamining all remaining conceptual issues associated with preparing consolidated financial statements. (This includes issues not addressed in its 1987 pronouncement about consolidating all majority-owned subsidiaries, as discussed on page 98). A discussion memorandum has not yet been issued.

REQUIRED DISCLOSURES

The acquiring company must make the following footnote disclosures for each period in which a business combination is accounted for under the purchase method:

1. The name and brief description of the acquired business.
2. A statement that the purchase method has been used to record the combination.
3. The period for which the results of operations of the acquired business are included in the acquiring company's income statement. (This period is from the acquisition date to the acquiring entity's reporting year-end, except for situations involving a subsidiary that has a reporting year-end different from that of the parent company.)
4. The cost of the acquired business, including information about the number of shares issued, issuable, and their assigned value.
5. The life and method of amortizing any goodwill.
6. Contingent consideration, if any, and the related proposed accounting treatment.[12]

Here is an example of this basic disclosure for an acquiring company having a calendar year-end:

> On July 1, 19X1, the Pana Company acquired all of the outstanding common stock of Sonic Corporation, a manufacturer of small computers. The acquisition has been accounted for as a purchase; therefore, the results of operations of the acquired business for the period from July 1, 19X1, through December 31, 19X1, are included in the consolidated income statement of the Pana Company. The recorded cost of the acquisition was $5,200,000 (50,000 common shares issued times their then fair market

[12]*APB Opinion No. 16*, par. 95.

> value of $100 per share, plus legal and finders' fees of $200,000). Goodwill of $1,000,000 is being amortized over 40 years using the straight-line method. Additional common shares are issuable (a maximum of 100,000 shares), depending on the cumulative sales level of the acquired business for the three years subsequent to the acquisition date. If and when any or all of these contingent shares are distributable (June 30, 19X4), the current value of the shares issuable will be recorded as an additional cost of the acquired business, which will increase goodwill. As of December 31, 19X1, no additional shares would be issuable based on the sales level of the acquired business for the six months then ended.

Supplemental Disclosures for Publicly Owned Companies

In addition to basic footnote disclosures, certain supplemental information related to income statements (including revenues, net income, and earnings per share, among other items) must be disclosed by publicly owned companies for the following periods:

1. Income statement–related information that would have resulted had the combination occurred at the beginning of the current reporting period.
2. Income statement–related information that would have resulted had the combination occurred at the beginning of the preceding reporting period.[13]

This supplemental disclosure notifies readers of the financial statements that some percentage of the change in revenues and net income is the result of external expansion, not just the result of internal expansion.

Here is an example of a supplemental disclosure that relates to the preceding basic disclosure:

> Results of operations of the Pana Company combined on a pro forma basis with the operating results of Sonic Corporation for the years ended December 31, 19X1, and 19X0, as if the companies had been combined at January 1, 19X0, are as follows:

	19X1	19X0
Revenues	$53,500,000	$26,750,000
Net income	2,400,000	1,400,000
Net income per common and common equivalent share	$2.47	$1.27

Acquisition Near Beginning of the Year. When an acquisition occurs near the beginning of the acquiring company's reporting year, it may

[13] *APB Opinion No. 16*, par. 96. (*FASB Statement No. 79*, "Elimination of Certain Disclosures for Business Combinations by Nonpublic Enterprises," amended *APB Opinion No. 16* in 1984 by exempting nonpublic enterprises from the disclosure requirements of par. 96 of *APB Opinion No. 16*.)

include the operations of the acquired business from the beginning of the current reporting year to the acquisition date, and also show as a deduction in the income statement an amount equal to the net income for these operations for this period. Assume the following information for a business acquired on March 1, 19X1 (two months after the beginning of the acquiring company's current reporting period):

	Jan. 1–Feb. 28, 19X1	Mar. 1–Dec. 31, 19X1
Revenues	$15,000	$110,000
Cost of goods sold	(9,000)	(66,000)
Expenses	(4,000)	(33,000)
Net Income	$ 2,000	$ 11,000

The acquiring company automatically includes the operations of the acquired business from March 1, 19X1, through December 31, 19X1, with its own operations—this is a fundamental concept of the purchase method of accounting. The acquiring company may disclose the operations of the acquired business for January 1, 19X1, through February 28, 19X1, as supplemental information (explained previously). Or, using the more practical approach, it may include the following accounts and amounts with its own operations for the entire year:

Revenues	$125,000
Cost of goods sold	(75,000)
Expenses	(37,000)
Subtotal	$ 13,000
Less—Preacquisition earnings	(2,000)
Net Income	$ 11,000

This approach allows the acquiring entity to bypass the supplemental disclosure requirement for the current reporting year, but it does not violate the basic principle of purchase accounting that **preacquisition earnings are not reportable as part of an acquiring company's operations.**

PERSPECTIVE

A Capsule History of Accounting for Goodwill

Accounting for goodwill has been studied and debated since about 1880. Through the years, it has evolved from a state of "anything goes" to the restrictive, arbitrary, and uniform accounting requirements of *APB Opinion Nos. 16* and *17*, issued in 1970. No accounting topic has inspired more diversely held views (and fiercely strong ones) than goodwill. Consequently, students must not simply memorize the rules of the current pronouncements; they must also understand how and why we have arrived at the present rules from what was

A Capsule History of Accounting for Goodwill *(continued)*

tried in the past and rejected. And as their predecessors have done, they must continually question the logic and practicality of these rules and their current application.

Prior to 1917	The entire cost of an acquisition in excess of book value is treated as goodwill. Accountants favor charging goodwill to stockholders' equity at the acquisition date. There is no support for charging goodwill to income, either through amortization or in a lump sum).
1917	The American Institute of Accountants, the predecessor to the AICPA, "recommends" that goodwill be shown as a reduction to stockholders' equity (if it is not already charged to capital).
1918–1929	Companies begin capitalizing internally generated goodwill. (Amounts range from advertising costs to arbitrary estimates of the value of the goodwill.) Many abuses result.
1930–1944	Recording as goodwill only purchased goodwill becomes the prevalent thinking. Permanent retention of goodwill as an asset and periodic amortization to income, retained earnings, or additional paid-in capital become acceptable practice (in addition to immediately charging these to capital). Accounting writers begin advocating the analysis of the cost in excess of book value.
1944	*Accounting Research Bulletin No. 24* is issued. It states that only historical cost should be used to value goodwill. Arbitrary write-ups and capitalization of start-up costs as goodwill is thus banned. The door is left open for companies to capitalize advertising costs as goodwill.
1945	The Securities and Exchange Commission (SEC) begins encouraging companies to amortize goodwill if they have been using the permanent retention treatment.
1953	*Accounting Research Bulletin No. 43* is issued. It prohibits charging goodwill to stockholders' equity immediately after acquisition. Discretionary write-downs of goodwill are banned—a loss of value must take place for a write-down or write-off.
1968	*Accounting Research Study No. 5, Accounting for Goodwill* (written by two senior partners of Arthur Andersen and Co.) is issued. The study concludes that goodwill is not an asset and should be charged to stockholders' equity at the time of the acquisition.
1968–1970	A fierce and heated debate takes place within the accounting profession concerning accounting for business combinations and the related issue of goodwill.
1970	*ABP Opinion Nos. 16* and *17* are issued, the first by a vote of 12 to 6 and the second by a vote of 13 to 5. As a result: (1)

(continued)

goodwill can arise only from a business combination; (2) the cost in excess of book value must be analyzed; (3) goodwill existing as of October 31, 1970, need not be amortized to income; (4) goodwill arising after that date must be amortized to income over no more than 40 years; and (5) if goodwill loses its value, it must be written off to income as an extraordinary charge. (The strong positions of the various opposing factions of the APB were such that many members could not talk to one another for three months after the voting (a two-thirds vote was required). One of the largest CPA firms seriously considers not supporting these pronouncements in its practice but decides to continue to work within the profession to bring about needed changes.)

1971 The handling of the business combinations and goodwill issues by the APB (in which strong positions were taken only to be withdrawn because of pressure from client companies) ultimately leads to the demise of the APB and the establishment of the FASB in 1973.

1971–1980 Goodwill becomes a dead issue.

1981 A crisis develops in the savings and loan industry because of high interest rates. Over a thousand savings and loan associations become financially distressed—many actually exhausting their net worths and thus facing bankruptcy—and are forced to merge with stronger savings and loans. Seeking ways to report higher earnings, the acquiring firms take advantage of a quirk in *APB Opinion No. 16* and account for these arranged, regulatory mergers as purchases (rather than as poolings of interests, the usual practice for such mergers). Consequently, billions of dollars of goodwill are reported as being amortized over 30 to 40 years. (The offsetting loan discount is credited to income over 10 to 12 years.)

Undaunted by the peculiarity (some would say absurdity) that companies facing bankruptcy could possibly possess goodwill, auditors of these acquiring companies allow this reporting of artificial income without exception. Form prevails over substance.

1983 In response to public criticism of the reporting of artificial income in the savings and loan industry, the FASB amends *APB Opinion No. 17* in *FASB Statement No. 72*, "Accounting for Certain Acquisitions of Banking or Thrift Institutions." It requires much shorter lives for goodwill (10 to 12 years). Some savings and loans rush through their mergers to beat the effective date of the pronouncement, which is retroactive only to September 30, 1982. The auditors of these firms give unqualified ("clean") opinions on the financial

A Capsule History of Accounting for Goodwill *(continued)*

	statements presented under the old rules as well as those presented under the new rules—deeming all the statements to "present fairly." Analyzing and understanding the financial statements of such savings and loans becomes quite difficult. (Perplexed investors ask their stockbrokers, "What are the "real" earnings?")
1983–1985	Scores of companies that went on acquisition binges in the 1970s begin disposing of hundreds of previously acquired companies due to their operating problems and unprofitability. Billions of dollars of unamortized goodwill (most companies were choosing a 40-year life) must be written off.
1985–1986	A congressional committee headed by Rep. John Dingell holds hearings on the conduct of the accounting profession because of the rising number of collapses, corporate failures and abuses, and alleged auditing failures among large financial institutions.
1986–1987	The accounting profession explores ways to enhance public confidence in the accounting profession.

Source: A major portion of the capsule history prior to 1970 is based on Research Monograph No. 80, *Goodwill in Accounting: A History of the Issues and Problems*, by Hugh P. Hughes (Atlanta: Georgia State University, 1982).

SUMMARY

Under the purchase method of accounting, the acquisition of either assets or common stock results in a revaluation of the assets and liabilities of the acquired business to their current values. When assets are acquired, the assets acquired and liabilities assumed are recorded at their current values directly in the books of the acquiring company. If decentralized accounting is used, they are recorded in the books of the newly established division. When common stock is acquired, the revaluation to current values is done by either having the subsidiary adjust its general ledger accounts (push-down accounting), or making the adjustments in the consolidation process (non-push-down accounting). The latter approach involves analyzing the total cost of the investment in the subsidiary to determine how much of the total cost relates to under- or overvaluation of the subsidiary's net assets.

Glossary of New Terms

Bargain Purchase Element The amount by which the total cost of the investment is below the current value of an acquired business's net assets.

Consolidation The process of combining the financial statements of a parent and one or more subsidiaries, so that results of operations and financial position are presented as though the separate companies were a single company with one or more divisions or branches.

Contingent Consideration Consideration that must be paid if certain future conditions are satisfied.

Controlling Interest In general, a controlling interest exists when one company owns, either directly or indirectly, more than 50% of the outstanding voting shares of another company. However, in some cases, control may exist even though a majority voting interest does not exist.

Non-push-down Basis of Accounting The subsidiary retains its historical cost basis in accounting for its assets and liabilities. (Adjustments to current values are made in the consolidation process.)

Push-down Basis of Accounting The subsidiary's assets and liabilities are adjusted to their current values in the general ledger based on the parent's cost.

Selected References

Accounting Principles Board Opinion No. 16. "Business Combinations." New York: American Institute of Certified Public Accountants, 1970.

Accounting Principles Board Opinion No. 17. "Intangible Assets." New York: American Institute of Certified Public Accountants, 1970.

Financial Report Survey 31. "Illustrations of Push Down Accounting," by Hortense Goodman and Leonard Lorensen. New York: American Institute of Certified Public Accountants, 1985.

Goodwill in Accounting: A History of the Issues Problems, by Hugh P. Hughes. Research Monograph No. 80. Atlanta: Business Publishing Division, College of Business Administration, Georgia State University, 1982.

"Push Down" Accounting. Issues Paper. Task Force on Consolidation Problems, Accounting Standards Division. New York: American Institute of Certified Public Accountants, 1979.

SEC Staff Accounting Bulletin No. 54. "Application of 'Push Down' Basis of Accounting in Financial Statements of Subsidiaries Acquired by Purchase." Washington, D.C.: Securities and Exchange Commission, 1983.

Review Questions

1. What is the essence of the purchase method of accounting?
2. What two basic questions must be answered with respect to the purchase method of accounting?
3. What types of consideration can the acquiring entity give in a business combination?
4. When is it preferable in recording a business combination to use the fair value of the equity securities issued instead of the current value of the net assets of the acquired business?
5. How should direct costs incurred in a business combination be treated?
6. What is contingent consideration and how should it be accounted for?

7. What are the three major conceptual elements into which the total cost of an investment could possibly be separated?
8. In which situations would only one major conceptual element exist? In which situation would only two major conceptual elements exist?
9. What is the purpose of separating the total cost of the investment into the individual components of the major conceptual elements?
10. Why is there no separate account for goodwill on the parent company's books (under non-push-down accounting)?
11. Why are consolidated financial statements necessary?
12. What is the usual condition for a controlling interest?
13. What is the distinction between the basic disclosures and the supplemental disclosures required for business combinations accounted for under the purchase method of accounting?
14. How are preacquisition earnings of an acquired business treated under the purchase method of accounting?

Technical Research Questions

Here and elsewhere in the book, answers to technical research questions may be found by consulting the pronouncements of the FASB, the APB, and the SEC.

15. Pert Products purchases Sprig & Sons and immediately incurs costs to close Sprig's duplicate facilities. Should those costs be added to the cost of the acquisition?
16. Should the costs Pert incurs in question 1 be added to the cost of the acquisition if it closes its own duplicate facilities instead?

Discussion Cases

DC 3-1

Determining Whether Consolidation Is Appropriate

Patentex Company and its head engineer, Dee Ziner, form Secretex Company, which will perform research and development. Secretex issues 5,000 shares of common stock to Ziner. Patentex lends $450,000 to Secretex for initial working capital in return for a note receivable that can be converted at will into 95,000 shares of Secretex common stock. Patentex also grants Secretex a line of credit of $2,500,000. If Ziner wants to sell the 5,000 shares, Patentex has the right of first refusal.

Required:
Determine if consolidation of Secretex's financial statements is appropriate.

DC 3-2

Evaluating the Push-down Basis of Accounting

Press Company acquired all of the outstanding common stock of Search Company by issuing a new class of common stock (Class B) valued at $700,000,000. The terms of the issuance call for dividends to be based on Search's audited net income using Search's historical cost basis. Search will remain a separate legal entity under the terms of the acquisition. Search will also continue to use its own auditors.

For the year following the acquisition, assume that Search expected to do the following:

1. It will have net income of $100,000,000.
2. It will pay cash dividends of $80,000,000 to the Class B stockholders.
3. It will have net income of only $60,000,000 if push-down accounting is used.

Required:

1. Evaluate whether the push-down basis of accounting makes sense in this situation.
2. If push-down accounting were used, could the dividends still be based on the earnings excluding the additional depreciation and amortization of $40,000,000 resulting from push-down accounting?

DC 3-3

Treatment of Cost in Excess of Book Value of Acquired Subsidiary's Net Assets

Pomglomerate Company, a highly diversified company, acquired all of the outstanding common stock of three companies during the current year. In each case, Pomglomerate's total cost was $500,000 in excess of book value of the net assets. The reason it paid more than the book value of the net assets of each company is stated below:

1. **Acquisition of Ironex Company.** Ironex mines iron ore from land it owns. Pomglomerate acquired Ironex to assure itself a continual supply of iron ore for its steel-making operation.
2. **Acquisition of Memco Company.** Memco manufactures high-quality memory chips for computers. Few companies can manufacture high-quality chips of this type. Pomglomerate acquired Memco to assure itself of a continual supply of high-quality memory chips for its computer manufacturing operation.
3. **Acquisition of Farmco Company.** Farmco manufactures farm machinery. Farmco earns a return on investment that is average for its industry. On this basis, Farmco was not worth acquiring. Pomglomerate, however, feels it can bring about substantial efficiencies by integrating Farmco's operations with those of another subsidiary, which manufactures farm machinery. The combined results are expected to increase substantially the overall return on investment of each previously separate operation.

Required:

For each of these acquisitions, determine how you would classify Pomglomerate's cost and how you would account for it in future-period consolidated financial statements.

DC 3-4

Treatment of Goodwill

You are the controller of a company that has recently acquired a business having substantial goodwill. While determining whether the treatment prescribed by *APB Opinion No. 17,* "Intangible Assets," presents your company's financial statements fairly, you discover that the APB considered the following alternatives before it issued *No. 17:*

1. Allow goodwill to be reported as a "permanent" asset, with no amortization required unless impairment occurred.
2. Require goodwill to be amortized.
3. Require goodwill to be charged to stockholders' equity of the acquiring company at the acquisition date.

Required:

1. Briefly evaluate the soundness of each of these alternatives.
2. For alternative 2, evaluate the soundness of allowing up to 40 years to amortize goodwill.

DC 3-5

Manner of Reporting "Cost in Excess of Net Assets"

The December 31, 19X1, consolidated balance sheet of Hyde Company has the following described asset:

Excess of cost over related net assets of businesses acquired....................	**$75,000,000**

The related footnote reads as follows:

> The excess of cost over related net assets applicable to businesses acquired prior to November 1, 1970, amounts to $11,000,000 and is not amortized, as it is believed to have continuing value; the balance applicable to businesses acquired after October 31, 1970, is being amortized on a straight-line basis over 40 years.

Required:

1. Is the title of the asset accurate?
2. Is the title of the asset informative?
3. What does the asset represent?
4. What is the theoretical justification for amortizing only part of this amount?

DC 3-6

Treatment of Bargain Purchase Element

You are the CPA for a company that has recently acquired all of the assets of another company at an amount below their current value. The controller has indicated to you that the bargain purchase element will be accounted for in one of the following ways:

1. Credit it to income in the year of the acquisition, possibly classified as an extraordinary item.
2. Amortize it to income over the two-year period needed to turn the acquired operation into a profit-making operation.
3. Allocate it to the acquired assets based on relative current values, thereby lowering the recorded values of these items.
4. Credit it to contributed capital.

Required:
How would you respond to these proposed treatments? Be sure to evaluate the theoretical soundness of each alternative regardless of the requirements of *APB Opinion No. 16*.

DC 3-7

Treatment of Understated Liabilities

Primex acquires all of the outstanding common stock of Sumex. Shortly after the combination is consummated, Primex discovers that Sumex's liabilities are understated by $25 million. Prior to this discovery, goodwill was calculated to be $30 million.

Required:
How should the $25 million be accounted for?

Exercises

E 3-1

Recording Acquisition of Assets for Cash

Pomeroy Company acquired all of the assets (except cash) and assumed all of the liabilities of Stiles Company for $1,100,000 cash. The acquired business is to be accounted for as a division with a decentralized accounting system. The assets and liabilities of Stiles Company as of the acquisition date are as follows:

	Book Value	Current Value
Cash	$ 30,000	$ 30,000
Accounts receivable, net	80,000	80,000
Inventory	90,000	80,000
Land	100,000	150,000
Buildings and equipment	1,200,000	870,000
Accumulated depreciation	(500,000)	
	$1,000,000	$1,210,000
Accounts payable and accruals	$ 100,000	$ 100,000
Long-term debt	200,000	200,000
	$ 300,000	$ 300,000
Net assets	$ 700,000	$ 910,000

Required:

1. Prepare the entry to record the acquisition on the books of the home office and on the books of the newly formed division.
2. How would the entries be different if the accounting for the acquired business were centralized?

E 3-2

Recording Acquisition of Assets for Stock

Assume the same information as in Exercise 3-1, except that Pomeroy Company issued 10,000 shares of its common stock ($5 par value), which was selling for $110 per share at the acquisition date, instead of giving cash to effect the business combination.

Required:

1. Prepare the entry to record the acquisition on the books of the home office and on the newly formed division.
2. How would the entries be different if the accounting for the acquired business were centralized?

E 3-3

Recording Acquisition of Common Stock for Cash and Stock

Party Time acquired 100% of the outstanding common stock of Streamers for $2,300,000 cash and 10,000 shares of its common stock ($2 par value), which was traded at $40 per share at the acquisition date.

Required:
Prepare the entry to record the business combination on Party Time's books.

E 3-4

Recording Direct Costs

Assume the same information provided in Exercise 3-3. In addition, assume that Party Time incurred the following direct costs:

Legal fees for preparing the acquisition agreement	$ 47,000
Accounting fees for the purchase investigation	17,000
Travel expenses for meetings held with management of Streamers	8,000
Legal fees for registering the common stock issued with the SEC	32,000
Accounting fees for the review of unaudited financial statements and other data included in the registration statement	16,000
SEC filing fees	4,000
	$124,000

As of the acquisition date, $103,000 has been paid and charged to a Deferred Charges account. The remaining $21,000 has not been paid or accrued.

Required:
Prepare the journal entry to record the business combination and the direct costs.

E 3-5

Contingent Consideration Based on Future Sales

Polychrome acquired all of the outstanding common stock of Spectrum Company for $1,000,000 cash. If the cumulative sales of Spectrum for the three years subsequent to the acquisition date exceed $10,000,000, then additional cash of $200,000 is to be paid to the former shareholders of Spectrum.

Required:
Prepare the entry to record the business combination. Explain the accounting treatment of the contingent consideration.

E 3-6

Contingent Consideration Based on Future Security Prices: Existing Security Price to Be Maintained

Pratt Company acquired all of the outstanding common stock of Switney Company by issuing 80,000 shares of its common stock ($10 par value), which had a market value of $40 per share at the acquisition date. If the market value of Pratt's common stock is below $40 per share two years after the acquisition date, then Pratt must issue additional shares at that time to Switney's former shareholders so that the total value of the shares issued equals $3,200,000.

Required:
Note: You may want to review paragraphs 81 and 82 of *APB Opinion No. 16* before solving.

1. Prepare the entry to record the business combination. Explain the accounting treatment of the contingent consideration.
2. Assume the market value of Pratt Company's common stock is $32 per share two years later. Prepare the entry to record the additional shares issued.

E 3-7

Contingent Consideration Based on Future Security Prices: Higher Security Price to be Attained

Photo Company acquired all of the outstanding common stock of Snapco Company by issuing 60,000 shares of its common stock ($5 par value), which had a market value of $50 per share as of the acquisition date. If the market value of Photo's common stock is not at least $70 per share two years after the acquisition date, then additional shares must be issued to Snapco's former shareholders so that the total value of the shares issued equals $4,200,000.

Required:
Note: You may want to review paragraphs 81 and 82 of *APB Opinion No. 16* before solving.

1. Prepare the entry to record the business combination. Explain the accounting treatment of the contingent consideration.

2. Assume the market value of Photo Company's common stock is $60 per share two years later. Prepare the entry to record the additional shares issued.

E 3-8

Acquisition of Common Stock: Separating Total Cost into Major Conceptual Elements—Cost Is above Current Value and Book Value of Net Assets

Potasha Company acquired all of the outstanding common stock of Sulpha Company at a total cost of $1,000,000. Sulpha Company's net assets have a book value of $600,000 and a current value of $880,000 as of the acquisition date.

Required:
Separate the total cost of the investment into its major conceptual elements as of the acquisition date.

E 3-9

Acquisition of Common Stock: Separating Total Cost into Major Conceptual Elements—Cost Is below Current Value but above Book Value of Net Assets

Pomona Company acquired 100% of the outstanding common stock of Sonora Company, a manufacturing company with extensive manufacturing facilities, at a total cost of $2,000,000. Sonora's net assets have a book value of $1,800,000 and a current value of $2,100,000 as of the acquisition date.

Required:
Separate the total cost of the investment into its major conceptual elements as of the acquisition date.

E 3-10

Acquisition of Common Stock: Separating Total Cost into Components of the Major Conceptual Elements—Cost Is above Current Value and Book Value of Net Assets

Pending Company acquired all of the outstanding common stock of Sheb Company for $800,000 cash. (Assume there were no direct costs or contingent consideration.) Information about Sheb Company as of the acquisition date is as follows:

	Book Value	Current Value
Cash	$ 50,000	$ 50,000
Accounts receivable, net	100,000	100,000
Inventory	200,000	210,000
Land	300,000	420,000
Building, net	400,000	480,000
Equipment, net	150,000	200,000
Total Assets	$1,200,000	$1,460,000

(continued)

	Book Value	Current Value
Accounts payable and accruals	$ 100,000	$ 100,000
Long-term debt	600,000	625,000
Total Liabilities	$ 700,000	$ 725,000
Common stock	$ 50,000	
Additional paid-in capital	300,000	
Retained earnings	150,000	
Total Stockholders' Equity	$ 500,000	735,000
Total Liabilities and Equity	$1,200,000	$1,460,000

Required:

1. Separate the total cost of the investment into the individual components of the major conceptual elements as of the acquisition date.
2. Explain why the current value of the long-term debt is greater than its book value.

E 3-11

Calculating Goodwill

On April 1, 19X6, Place Company paid $400,000 for all the issued and outstanding common stock of Show Corporation in a transaction properly accounted for as a purchase. Show's assets and liabilities on April 1, 19X6, are as follows:

Cash	$ 40,000
Inventory	120,000
Property and equipment (net of accumulated depreciation of $160,000)	240,000
Liabilities	(90,000)

On April 1, 19X6, the current value of Show's inventory was $95,000, and its property and equipment (net) had a current value of $280,000.

Required:
What amount should Place record as goodwill as a result of the business combination?

a. 0
b. $25,000
c. $75,000
d. $90,000

(AICPA adapted)

Problems

P 3-1 Acquisition of Common Stock: Separating Total Cost into Components of the Major Conceptual Elements—Cost Is above Current Value of Net Assets and Current Value Is above Book Value

Perusal Company acquired all of the outstanding stock of Scanner Company for $2,500,000 cash. Information with respect to Scanner Company as of the acquisition date is as follows:

	Book Value	Current Value
Cash	$ 55,000	$ 55,000
Accounts receivable, net	180,000	180,000
Notes receivable	100,000	60,000
Inventory	300,000	330,000
Land	500,000	600,000
Buildings and equipment	600,000[a]	750,000
Patent	45,000	105,000
Goodwill, net of amortization to date	120,000	See note.
Total Assets	$1,900,000	
Accounts payable and accruals	$ 300,000	$300,000
Long-term debt (10% bonds)	700,000	650,000
Total Liabilities	$1,000,000	
Common stock	$ 100,000	
Additional paid-in capital	500,000	
Retained earnings	300,000	
Total Stockholders' Equity	$ 900,000	
Total Liabilities and Equity	$1,900,000	

[a]Net of accumulated depreciation of $123,000.

Note:
The $120,000 of unamortized goodwill arose from Scanner's acquisition two years ago of the net assets of a local competitor. The goodwill is being amortized over 10 years. During the negotiations with Perusal Company, the management of Scanner Company indicated that these acquired operations have produced superior earnings since acquisition, which are expected to continue for at least another eight years. (Refer to paragraph 88 of *APB Opinion No. 16* for treatment.)

Required:

1. For other than existing goodwill, what procedures and guidelines are used to determine current values of assets acquired and liabilities assumed? (Refer to paragraphs 87 and 88 of *APB Opinion No. 16*.)
2. As to the 10% bonds payable, is the current rate of interest more or less than 10%? Will future interest expense be at a rate more or less than 10%?

Required under the Push-down Basis of Accounting:

3. Prepare the entries the subsidiary would make under the push-down basis of accounting.
4. Prepare the primary elimination entry as of the acquisition date.

Required under the Non-push-down Basis of Accounting:

5. Separate the total investment cost into the individual components of the major conceptual elements.
6. Prepare the elimination entries required in consolidation as of the acquisition date.

P 3-2 Acquisition of Common Stock: Separating Total Cost into Components of the Major Conceptual Elements—Cost Is below Current Value of Net Assets and Current Value Is above Book Value

Pladd Company acquired all of the outstanding common stock of Stripes Company for $310,000 cash. Information about Stripes as of the acquisition date is as follows:

	Book Value	Current Value
Cash	$ 20,000	$ 20,000
Accounts receivable, net	40,000	40,000
Inventory	200,000	140,000
Land	90,000	300,000
Buildings, net	130,000[a]	180,000
Equipment, net	100,000[b]	120,000
Total Assets	$580,000	$800,000
Accounts payable and accruals	$100,000	$100,000
Long-term debt	280,000	280,000
Total Liabilities	$380,000	$380,000
Common stock	$ 30,000	
Additional paid-in capital	270,000	
Accumulated deficit	(100,000)	
Total Stockholders' Equity	$200,000	420,000
Total Liabilities and Equity	$580,000	$800,000

[a]Net of accumulated depreciation of $55,000.
[b]Net of accumulated depreciation of $44,000.

Required under the Push-down Basis of Accounting:

1. Prepare the entries the subsidiary would make.
2. Prepare the primary elimination entry as of the acquisition date.

Required under the Non-push-down Basis of Accounting:

3. Separate the total investment cost into the components of the major conceptual elements.
4. Prepare the elimination entries required in consolidation as of the acquisition date.

P 3-3 Acquisition of Common Stock: Separating Total Cost into Components of the Major Conceptual Elements—Cost Is below Current Value of Net Assets and Current Value Is below Book Value

Plugg Company acquired all of the outstanding common stock of Sparks Company for $150,000 cash. Information about Sparks, which leases its manufacturing facilities and is in poor financial condition as of the acquisition date, is as follows:

	Book Value	Current Value
Cash	$ 20,000	$ 20,000
Accounts receivable, net	380,000	380,000
Inventory	300,000	270,000
Equipment, net	100,000[a]	60,000
Total Assets	$800,000	$730,000
Accounts payable and accruals	$450,000	$450,000
Long-term debt	50,000	50,000
Total Liabilities	$500,000	$500,000
Common stock	$210,000	
Additional paid-in capital	340,000	
Accumulated deficit	(250,000)	
Total Stockholders' Equity	$300,000	230,000
Total Liabilities and Equity	$800,000	$730,000

[a]Net of accumulated depreciation of $77,000.

Required under the Push-down Basis of Accounting:

1. Prepare the entries the subsidiary would make under the ~~non~~-push-down basis of accounting.
2. Prepare the primary elimination entry as of the acquisition date.

Required under the Non-push-down Basis of Accounting:

3. Separate the total investment cost into the components of the major conceptual elements.
4. Prepare the elimination entries required in consolidation as of the acquisition date.

P 3-4* Acquisition of Common Stock: Preparing Consolidated Financial Statements—Cost Equals Current Value of Net Assets and Current Value Equals Book Value

Payles Company, which is a calendar-year reporting company, acquired all of the outstanding common stock of Selmore Company at a total cost of $600,000 (an amount equal to the current value and book value of Selmore's net assets) on December 31, 19X1. The financial statements of each company for the year ended on that date immediately after the acquisition are as follows:

	Payles Company	Selmore Company
Income Statement (19X1):		
Sales	$ 8,000,000	$ 700,000
Cost of goods sold	(5,000,000)	(300,000)
Expenses	(2,100,000)	(280,000)
Net Income	$ 900,000	$ 120,000
Balance Sheet as of December 31, 19X1:		
Cash	$ 500,000	$ 100,000
Accounts receivable, net	900,000	400,000
Inventory	1,200,000	700,000
Investment in Selmore Company	600,000	
Land	800,000	300,000
Buildings and equipment	5,000,000	900,000
Accumulated depreciation	(1,000,000)	(200,000)
	$ 8,000,000	$2,200,000
Accounts payable and accruals	$ 1,000,000	$ 500,000
Long-term debt	2,000,000	1,100,000
Common Stock	1,000,000	100,000
Additional paid-in capital	2,000,000	200,000
Retained earnings	$ 2,000,000	$ 300,000
	$ 8,000,000	$2,200,000

Required under the Push-down Basis of Accounting:

1. Prepare the entries the subsidiary would make.
2. Prepare the primary elimination entry as of December 31, 19X1.

Required under the Non-push-down Basis of Accounting:

3. Prepare the elimination entries required in consolidation as of December 31, 19X1.
4. Prepare a consolidating statement worksheet as of December 31, 19X1.
5. What amount of income does the parent company report to its stockholders for 19X1?

*The financial statement information presented for problems accompanied by asterisks is also provided on Model 3 (filename: Model3) of the software file disk that is available for use with the text, enabling the problem to be worked on the computer.

P 3-5* Acquisition of Common Stock: Preparing Consolidated Financial Statements—Cost Is above Current Value of Net Assets and Current Value Is above Book Value

Price Company, which is a calendar-year reporting company, acquired all of the outstanding common stock of Selle Company at a total cost of $300,000 on December 31, 19X1. The analysis of the parent company's investment account by the individual components of the major conceptual elements as of the acquisition date is as follows:

Book value element:	
Common stock	$100,000
Retained earnings	90,000
Current value over (under) book value element:	
Inventory	5,000
Land	30,000
Equipment	50,000
Patent	(15,000)
Goodwill element	40,000
Total cost	$300,000

The financial statements of each company for the year ended December 31, 19X1, immediately after the acquisition are as follows:

	Price Company	Selle Company
Income Statement (19X1):		
Sales	$2,500,000	$500,000
Cost of goods sold	(1,400,000)	(250,000)
Expenses	(860,000)	(202,000)
Net Income	$ 240,000	$ 48,000
Balance Sheet (as of December 31, 19X1):		
Cash	$ 100,000	$ 20,000
Accounts receivable, net	200,000	55,000
Inventory	350,000	80,000
Investment in Selle Co.	300,000	
Land	400,000	70,000
Buildings and equipment	800,000	200,000
Accumulated depreciation	(150,000)	(40,000)
Patent		15,000
	$2,000,000	$400,000
Accounts payable and accruals	$ 250,000	$ 60,000
Long-term debt	1,000,000	150,000
Common stock	300,000	100,000
Retained earnings	450,000	90,000
	$2,000,000	$400,000

Required under the Push-down Basis of Accounting:

1. Prepare the entries the subsidiary would make.
2. Prepare the primary elimination entry as of December 31, 19X1.

Required under the Non-push-down Basis of Accounting:

3. Prepare the elimination entries required in consolidation as of December 31, 19X1.
4. Prepare a consolidating statement worksheet as of December 31, 19X1.

P 3-6*

Acquisition of Common Stock: Preparing Consolidated Financial Statements—Cost Is Equal to Current Value of Net Assets and Current Value Is below Book Value

Pepper Company, which is a calendar-year reporting company, acquired all of the outstanding common stock of Salt Company, at a total cost of $400,000 on December 31, 19X1. The analysis of the parent company's investment account by the individual components of the major conceptual elements as of the acquisition date is as follows:

Book value element:	
Common stock	$ 50,000
Additional paid-in capital	200,000
Retained earnings	250,000
Current value over (under) book value element:	
Inventory	(70,000)
Land	30,000
Building	(100,000)
Long-term debt	40,000
Total cost	$400,000

The financial statements of each company for the year ended December 31, 19X1, immediately after the acquisition are as follows:

	Pepper Company	Salt Company
Income Statement (19X1):		
Sales	$6,000,000	$800,000
Cost of goods sold	(3,300,000)	(600,000)
Expenses	(1,500,000)	(250,000)
Net Income	$1,200,000	$ (50,000)
Balance Sheet (as of December 31, 19X1):		
Cash	$ 240,000	$ 30,000
Accounts receivable, net	360,000	50,000
Inventory	800,000	220,000
Investment in Salt Company	400,000	
Land	500,000	100,000
Buildings and equipment	2,600,000	550,000
Accumulated depreciation	(400,000)	(50,000)
	$4,500,000	$900,000
Accounts payable and accruals	$ 800,000	$100,000
Long-term debt	2,100,000	300,000
Common stock	20,000	50,000
Additional paid-in capital	480,000	200,000
Retained earnings	1,100,000	250,000
	$4,500,000	$900,000

Required under the Push-down Basis of Accounting:

1. Prepare the entries the subsidiary would make.
2. Prepare the primary elimination entry as of December 31, 19X1.

Required under the Non-push-down Basis of Accounting:

3. Prepare the elimination entries required in consolidation as of December 31, 19X1.
4. Prepare a consolidating statement worksheet as of December 31, 19X1.

P 3-7*

COMPREHENSIVE Acquisition of Common Stock: Analyzing the Investment and Preparing Consolidated Financial Statements

Pinnacle acquired all of the outstanding common stock of Summit for $900,000 cash on January 1, 19X1. Pinnacle also incurred $55,000 of costs in connection with the acquisition. Of this amount, $15,000 was a finder's fee, $12,000 was an allocation of overhead from the mergers and acquisition department, and $8,000 was an allocated portion of the president's salary (the president had devoted approximately 20% of his time during 19X0 to the merger). The remaining $20,000 was for legal and accounting fees and travel costs.

Financial data for each company immediately **before** the acquisition are as follows:

	Pinnacle Company	Summit Company	
	Book Value	Book Value	Current Value
Cash	$1,345,000	$ 100,000	$ 100,000
Accounts receivable, net	900,000	140,000	140,000
Notes receivable		80,000	60,000
Inventory	1,100,000	310,000	330,000
Land	500,000	250,000	410,000
Buildings and equipment	4,500,000	800,000	620,000
Accumulated depreciation	(1,400,000)	(300,000)	
Patent, net	200,000	40,000	100,000
Goodwill, net of amortization		80,000	
Deferred acquisition costs	55,000		
	$7,200,000	$1,500,000	$1,760,000
Accounts payable and accrued liabilities	$1,800,000	$ 250,000	$ 250,000
Long-term debt	4,000,000	600,000	660,000
Common stock	600,000	150,000	
Retained earnings	800,000	500,000	
	$7,200,000	$1,500,000	

If Summit's sales for 19X2 exceed $850,000 in 19X2, then Pinnacle must pay an additional $60,000 cash to Summit's stockholders. Management feels optimistic that this sales level can be attained.

Required under the Push-down Basis of Accounting:

1. Prepare the entries the subsidiary would make.
2. Prepare the primary elimination entry to consolidate as of the acquisition date.
3. Prepare a consolidating statement worksheet as of the acquisition date.

Required under the Non-push Down Basis of Accounting:

4. Analyze the investment account by the components of the major conceptual elements as of the acquisition date.
5. Prepare the elimination entries required in consolidation as of the acquisition date.
6. Prepare a consolidating statement worksheet as of the acquisition date.

P 3-8

COMPREHENSIVE Acquisition of Assets: Recording the Acquisition and Preparing Combined Financial Statements

Use the same information provided in Problem 3-7, except that all of the assets were acquired instead of all of the common stock.

Required:

1. Prepare the entries made by Pinnacle to record the acquisition, assuming a decentralized accounting system is used.
2. Prepare the primary elimination entry as of the acquisition date.
3. Prepare a combining statement worksheet as of the acquisition date.

Problem Involving Financial Analysis

P 3-9

Analyzing Financial Statements

In an actual acquisition in late 1983, Financial Corporation of America (FCA) acquired all of American Savings and Loan. FCA paid cash of $290,000,000 and issued common and preferred stock valued at $625,000,000. At the acquisition date, American had a net worth at book value of $600,000,000. In valuing American's loans at their current values (using current interest rates, which were higher than contractual rates), the current value was found to be $793,000,000 lower than the book value.

The consolidated balance sheet and certain income statement data for the two years ended December 31, 1985 follow in condensed form:

	1985	1984
	(in millions)	
Assets:		
Cash and security investments	$ 8,968	$ 7,249
Loans receivable	14,974	18,020
Property acquired through foreclosure	931	733
Real estate investments	1,030	934
Intangible assets arising from acquisition	1,068	1,105
Premises and equipment, net	225	258
Deferred charges and other assets	179	219
Total Assets	$27,375	$28,518
Liabilities:		
Deposits	$17,405	$20,308
All other liabilities	9,740	8,017
Total Liabilities	27,145	28,325
Stockholders' Equity:		
Common stock and paid-in capital	634	634
Retained deficit	(404)	(441)
Total Stockholders' Equity	230	193
Total Liabilities and Equity	$27,375	$28,518
Income Statement Data:		
Net income (loss)	53	(590)
Amortization of intangibles	(55)	(55)

Required:

1. Calculate the goodwill paid for by FCA.
2. As a potential depositor of FCA, evaluate the financial soundness of FCA. (Ignore the fact of deposit insurance.)

4

The Purchase Method of Accounting: Subsequent to Date of Acquisition

AN OVERVIEW OF ACCOUNTING FOR INVESTMENTS IN SUBSEQUENT PERIODS

Chapter 3 explained recording initially, under the purchase method of accounting, an investment in an acquired business, and preparing consolidated financial statements as of the acquisition date. This chapter focuses on how to account for such investments for periods subsequent to the combination date, and how to prepare consolidated financial statements in such subsequent periods.

As in Chapter 3, we discuss topics in the following order:

1. The acquisition of assets (home office–division accounting).
2. The acquisition of common stock where the push-down basis of accounting was applied by the subsidiary.
3. The acquisition of common stock where the **non**-push-down basis of accounting is used by the subsidiary.

Two methods are available for valuing acquisitions of common stock—the equity method and the cost method. These methods are at the opposite ends of the conceptual spectrum. However, the reporting of financial position and results of operations on a consolidated basis for periods subsequent to the acquisition date are the same regardless of whether (a) the acquisition takes the form of assets or common stock, (b) the subsidiary's assets and liabilities are revalued to their current values (push-down accounting), and (c) the equity or the cost method is used in accounting for a common stock investment.

We emphasize the equity method when discussing investments in common stock, because it is the predominant method in use. Further, when push-down accounting is not used (SEC Staff Accounting Bulletin No. 54 applies only to publicly owned companies), the equity method allows the analysis of the investment account to be updated for all later activity by each component of the major conceptual elements in a manner that simplifies the preparation of consolidated financial statements.

INVESTMENTS IN ASSETS

Recall from Chapter 3 that in acquisitions of assets, (a) the division always records the assets acquired and liabilities assumed at their current values, and (b) the home office's Investment in Division account always equals the net assets of the division. To maintain this equality in subsequent periods, the home office must adjust its Investment in Division account for the income or loss of the division. For example, assume that the division reported $11,000 of income for the year following the acquisition. The home office's entry would be:

Investment in Division	11,000	
Division Income		11,000

The debit side of the entry maintains the Investment in Division account equal to the division's net assets. The credit side of the entry allows the division's income to be included in the home office's retained earnings account. (Recall from Chapter 3 that a division is not a separate legal entity and thus has no retained earnings account—only the lone equity account, Home Office Equity.)

Preparing Combined Financial Statements

The process of combining home office and division financial statements after the acquisition is the same as it is at the acquisition date, except that the home office's income statement must be combined with the division's income statement. A combined statement of retained earnings must also be prepared.

Combining the Income Statements. In combining the details of the two income statements, we must eliminate the Division Income or Loss account balance in the home office column of the worksheet. The effect of eliminating this account is to substitute for this account balance the revenue, cost, and expense accounts of the division.

The Combined Statement of Retained Earnings. The combining worksheets in this chapter incorporate analyses of the home office's Retained Earnings account and of the division's Home Office Equity account between the income statement and the balance sheet. Because the company must issue a combined statement of retained earnings, the analysis of the home office's retained earnings in the worksheet readily provides the amounts for this statement. Because the home office records the division's income or loss on its books, the home office's Retained Earnings account contains all the information necessary to prepare this statement.

Illustration

COMBINED FINANCIAL STATEMENTS FOR A HOME OFFICE AND DIVISION

To illustrate the preparation of combined financial statements, we can use the facts presented in Illustration 3-4 (the acquiring company paid

$90,000 cash for net assets having a book value of $60,000). For simplicity, we assume that the home office and its division had no intracompany transactions during the year following the acquisition, and that the division had $11,000 in income. The following worksheet elimination entry would be made:

Division Income	**11,000**	
Home Office Equity (preclosing balance)	**90,000**	
Investment in Division		**101,000**

Illustration 4-1 is a combining statement worksheet for this company at December 31, 19X1. The following points are important for understanding this illustration:

1. The elimination entry substitutes the division's individual income statement accounts for the Division Income account; this prevents double-counting the division's income in the combined column.
2. The debit balance in the eliminations column at the net income line (of the income statement) is carried forward to the net income line in the statement of retained earnings/analysis of home office equity section.

INVESTMENTS IN COMMON STOCK

Accounting for long-term investments, as covered in intermediate accounting texts, requires that investments in common stocks be accounted for as follows:

1. **Ownership interest is below 20%:** Apply the rule of lower of cost or market in accordance with the provisions of *FASB Statement No. 12*, "Accounting for Certain Marketable Securities."
2. **Ownership interest is at least 20% but not over 50%:** Apply the equity method of accounting in accordance with the provisions of *APB Opinion No. 18*, "The Equity Method of Accounting for Investments in Common Stock." (Note: The equity method applies here only if the investor's interest is in *voting stock.*)
3. **Ownership interest is above 50%:** Use either the equity method or the cost method, with the following limitation:

   Unconsolidated subsidiaries: Under the FASB's proposed amendments to *ARB No. 51* and *APB Opinion No. 18*, the equity method cannot be used for subsidiaries that are not consolidated when the parent company issues consolidated financial statements (of itself and of other consolidated subsidiaries). In other words, in such statements, the investment in the subsidiary must be accounted for under the cost method.[1]

[1]Proposed Statement of Financial Accounting Standards, "Consolidation of all Majority-owned Subsidiaries" (Stamford: Financial Accounting Standards Board, December 16, 1987), par. 16.

Illustration 4-1
Combining Statement Worksheet for a Home Office and Division

P COMPANY
Combining Statement Worksheet
For the Year Ended December 31, 19X1

	Home Office	Division	Eliminations Dr.	Eliminations Cr.	Combined
Income Statement:					
Sales	600,000	200,000			800,000
Cost of goods sold	(360,000)	(120,000)			(480,000)
Expenses	(204,000)	(69,000)			(273,000)
Division income	11,000		11,000(1)		–0–
Net Income	47,000	11,000	11,000		47,000
Statement of Retained Earnings/ Analysis of Home Office Equity:					
Retained earnings—Beg.	100,000				100,000
Home office equity (pre-closing)		90,000	90,000(1)		–0–
+ Net income	47,000	11,000	► 11,000		47,000
– Dividends declared	(31,000)				(31,000)
Balances, December 31, 19X1	116,000	101,000	101,000		116,000
Balance Sheet:					
Cash	40,000	30,000			70,000
Accounts receivable, net	75,000	43,000			118,000
Inventory	110,000	40,000			150,000
Investment in Division	101,000			101,000(1)	–0–
Land	200,000	42,000			242,000
Buildings and equipment	500,000	151,000			651,000
Accumulated depreciation	(320,000)	(14,000)			(334,000)
Goodwill		9,000			9,000
Total Assets	706,000	301,000		101,000	906,000
Liabilities	290,000	200,000			490,000
Common stock	300,000				300,000
Retained earnings	116,000				116,000
Home office equity		101,000	► 101,000		–0–
Total Liabilities and Equity	706,000	301,000	101,000		906,000
Proof of debit and credit postings			101,000	101,000	

The Equity Method

The equity method of valuing an investment in a subsidiary is similar to the accrual method of accounting in that it reflects the substance of the economic activity that has occurred. Under the equity method, the parent's interest in the subsidiary's earnings and losses is reflected as upward and downward adjustments, respectively, to the Investment in Subsidiary account. The offsetting credit or debit is recorded in the parent's income statement. Any dividends on common stock declared by the subsidiary are credited to the Investment in Subsidiary account at their declaration, and an offsetting debit is made to Dividends Receivable. Thus, **all dividends (except stock dividends) declared by the subsidiary are treated as a liquidation of the investment.**

The Cost Method

Under the cost method, dividends declared by the subsidiary are recorded as dividend income by the parent at their declaration, with the offsetting debit to Dividends Receivable. (When dividends subsequently declared by the subsidiary exceed **postacquisition earnings,** the parent treats such excess dividends as a **liquidating dividend** and, accordingly, credits the investment account instead of Dividend Income.) The parent's interest in the subsidiary's earnings and losses is completely ignored unless the magnitude of the subsidiary's losses is such that realization of the parent's cost is in serious doubt. In such instances, a write-down of the investment may be necessary. If such a write-down is made and, subsequently, the subsidiary's operations improve to such a degree that, in retrospect, the original write-down was not required, no adjustment is made to write up the investment to its original cost.

The cost method is conceptually unsound. When a subsidiary continues to have profitable operations, this method can result in an overly conservative valuation of the investment, unless the subsidiary declares dividends equal to earnings each year. Furthermore, the parent's dividend income can be easily manipulated, because the parent controls the subsidiary's dividend policy.

Illustration

THE EQUITY METHOD AND THE COST METHOD COMPARED (PUSH-DOWN BASIS OF ACCOUNTING ASSUMED)

In this section we compare the equity method and the cost method for a period of two years subsequent to the acquisition date. We assume that all of the common stock of a target company was acquired on January 1,

19X1, and that the earnings, losses, and dividends of the subsidiary for the following two years are as shown below:

	19X1	19X2
Net income	**$11,000**	**$19,000**
Dividends (Declared December 15, 19X1, and paid January 15, 19X2	**5,000**	**–0–**

We also assume that the subsidiary's assets and liabilities were revalued to their current values as required under the push-down basis of accounting. (Later in the chapter, we focus on non-push-down situations.) The entries that would be made under the equity method and the cost method are presented in Illustration 4-2.

The equity method is the predominant accounting method in use. The remainder of this chapter discusses the preparation of consolidated financial statements for periods subsequent to the acquisition date when the parent uses the equity method of accounting. Appendix A of this chapter focuses on the preparation of consolidated financial statements for periods subsequent to the acquisition date when the parent uses the cost method of accounting for its investment.

Illustration 4-2
The Equity Method and the Cost Method Compared (Push-down Basis of Accounting Assumed)

Equity Method			Cost Method		
Entries for 19X1:					
1. Subsidiary has $11,000 of earnings:					
Investment in Subsidiary	11,000		No entry.		
Equity in Net Income of Subsidiary		11,000			
2. Subsidiary declares $5,000 of dividends:					
Dividends Receivable	5,000		Dividends Receivable	5,000	
Investment in Subsidiary		5,000	Dividend Income		5,000
Entries for 19X2:					
1. Subsidiary pays dividend declared in 19X1:					
Cash	5,000		Cash	5,000	
Dividends Receivable		5,000	Dividends Receivable.		5,000
2. Subsidiary has $19,000 of earnings:					
Investment in Subsidiary	19,000		No entry.		
Equity in Net Income of Subsidiary		19,000			

Note: If the subsidiary had a net loss instead of a net income, the entry under the equity method would be:

Equity in Net Loss of Subsidiary	xxx	
Investment in Subsidiary		xxx

PREPARING CONSOLIDATED FINANCIAL STATEMENTS WHEN THE SUBSIDIARY HAS APPLIED THE PUSH-DOWN BASIS OF ACCOUNTING

Whether or not the subsidiary applied the push-down basis of accounting as of the acquisition date, the manner of determining the amounts for the primary elimination entry is the same. In this section, we discuss situations in which push-down accounting was applied by the subsidiary. However, if the subsidiary did not apply push-down accounting, as shown in the next section, an additional elimination entry is required.

Updating the Expanded Analysis of the Investment Account Using the Equity Method to Obtain the Source of the Primary Elimination Entry

To prepare consolidated financial statements for periods subsequent to the acquisition date, we must first update the analysis of the investment account by the components of the major conceptual elements for the entries recorded under the equity method. Certain changes in format and assumptions are made to make the preparation of the consolidated financial statements easier. Two additional retained earnings columns are used: one column to isolate the parent company's interest in the subsidiary's current earnings, and one column to isolate the parent company's share of dividends declared by the subsidiary during the current year.

Updating the analysis of the investment account in this manner allows the balances at a given date to be the source of the primary elimination entry that effects the consolidation. This technique greatly simplifies the preparation of the consolidated financial statements. After the statements are prepared, the balances in the two additional retained earnings columns are reclassified to the "Prior Years" retained earnings column to facilitate the preparation of the consolidated financial statements in the following year.

Illustration

UPDATING THE EXPANDED ANALYSIS OF THE INVESTMENT ACCOUNT USING THE EQUITY METHOD (PUSH-DOWN ACCOUNTING WAS APPLIED BY SUBSIDIARY)

To illustrate the updating of the expanded analysis of the investment account using the equity method, we use the facts from Illustration 3-5 (the acquiring company paid $90,000 cash for all of the common stock of S Company, which in turn had a book value of $60,000). Recall that the $30,000 cost in excess of book value was pushed down to the subsidiary. Illustration 4-2 showed the subsidiary's subsequent earnings and dividends. From this we update the expanded analysis of the investment account for the two years subsequent to acquisition, using the equity method of accounting:

				Book Value Element		
				Retained Earnings		
					Current Year	
	Total Cost	= Common Stock	+ Additional Paid-in Capital	+ Prior Years	+ Earnings	− Dividends
Balance, Jan. 1, 19X1 .	$ 90,000	$40,000	$50,000	$ -0-		
Equity in net income	11,000				$11,000	
Dividends..............	(5,000)					$(5,000)
Subtotal..................	$ 96,000	$40,000	$50,000	$ -0-	$11,000	$(5,000)
Reclassification.......				6,000	(11,000)	5,000
Balance, Dec. 31, 19X1	$ 96,000	$40,000	$50,000	$ 6,000	$ -0-	$ -0-
Equity in net income	19,000				19,000	
Subtotal..................	$115,000	$40,000	$50,000	$ 6,000	$19,000	$ -0-
Reclassification.......				19,000	(19,000)	
Balance, Dec. 31, 19X2	$115,000	$40,000	$50,000	$25,000	$ -0-	$ -0-

Preparing the Primary Elimination Entry from the Updated Analysis of the Investment Account

The primary elimination entries that would be obtained from the preceding analysis to prepare consolidated financial statements as of December 31, 19X1 (one year after the acquisition date), and December 31, 19X2 (two years after the acquisition date), are as follows:

	Consolidation Date			
	December 31, 19X1		December 31, 19X2	
Common Stock	40,000		40,000	
Additional Paid-in Capital......	50,000		50,000	
Retained Earnings (beginning of year)	-0-		6,000	
Equity in Net Income of Subsidiary........................	11,000		19,000	
Dividends Declared......		5,000		-0-
Investment in Subsidiary................		96,000		115,000

The following points are important for understanding this entry:

1. **The debit to retained earnings:** Because push-down accounting was used and because this is the first year subsequent to the acquisition date, the debit posting to Retained Earnings (for the beginning balance)

in this case is \$-0-. In the following year, the debit posting to Retained Earnings for the beginning balance is \$6,000 (19X1 net income of \$11,000 − \$5,000 of dividends declared in 19X1).

2. **The debit to equity in net income:** Isolating the subsidiary's current-year earnings or losses in a separate column enables us to eliminate the Equity in Net Income or Loss of Subsidiary account balance in the parent's column of the consolidating statement worksheet by posting the balance in the current-year column directly to this account on the worksheet. (The posting is then totaled at the net income line and carried forward to the net income line in the analysis of retained earnings section of the worksheet.)
3. **The credit to dividends declared:** The dividends declared by the subsidiary are posted directly to the dividends declared line in the analysis of retained earnings section of the worksheet. This prevents the subsidiary's dividends from being added to the parent's dividends in arriving at the dividends to be reported for consolidated purposes. Any dividends declared by the wholly owned subsidiary are intercompany transactions that cannot be considered dividends from the consolidated group to outsiders. The only dividends to outsiders are the dividends declared by the parent.
4. **The effect on the subsidiary's retained earnings:** The direct postings to the analysis of retained earnings (for the beginning balance and dividends declared), and the carryforward from the income statement to the net income line in the analysis of retained earnings, combine to eliminate the subsidiary's retained earnings in consolidation.

Illustration

CONSOLIDATING STATEMENT WORKSHEET (PUSH-DOWN ACCOUNTING WAS APPLIED BY SUBSIDIARY)

From the primary elimination entry at December 31, 19X1, in the preceding section, Illustration 4-3 shows a consolidating statement worksheet at that date. The following points are important for understanding Illustration 4-3:

1. P Company's net income is the same as the consolidated net income.
2. P Company's retained earnings is the same as the consolidated retained earnings.
3. All of the subsidiary's equity accounts have been eliminated.
4. The amounts in the consolidated column are the same as the amounts in the combined column of Illustration 4-1, where assets were purchased instead of common stock.

Illustration 4-3
Consolidating Statement Worksheet (Push-down Accounting Was Applied by Subsidiary)

P COMPANY AND SUBSIDIARY (S COMPANY)
Consolidating Statement Worksheet
For the Year Ended December 31, 19X1

	P Company	S Company	Eliminations Dr.	Eliminations Cr.	Consolidated
Income Statement:					
Sales	600,000	200,000			800,000
Cost of goods sold	(360,000)	(120,000)			(480,000)
Expenses	(204,000)	(69,000)			(273,000)
Intercompany Account:					
Equity in net income of S Company	11,000		11,000(1)		–0–
Net Income	47,000	11,000	11,000		47,000
Statement of Retained Earnings:					
Balances, January 1, 19X1	100,000[a]	–0–			100,000
+ Net income	47,000	11,000	11,000		47,000
− Dividends declared	(31,000)	(5,000)		5,000(1)	(31,000)
Balances, December 31, 19X1	116,000	6,000	11,000	5,000	116,000
Balance Sheet:					
Cash	45,000	25,000			70,000
Accounts receivable, net	75,000	43,000			118,000
Inventory	110,000	40,000			150,000
Investment in S Company	96,000			96,000(1)	–0–
Land	200,000	42,000			242,000
Buildings and equipment	500,000	151,000			651,000
Accumulated depreciation	(320,000)	(14,000)			(334,000)
Goodwill		9,000			9,000
Total Assets	706,000	296,000		96,000	906,000
Liabilities	290,000	200,000			490,000
P Company:					
Common stock	300,000				300,000
Retained earnings	116,000				116,000
S Company:					
Common stock		40,000	40,000(1)		–0–
Additional paid-in capital		50,000[b]	50,000(1)		–0–
Retained earnings		6,000	11,000	5,000	–0–
Total Liabilities and Equity	706,000	296,000	101,000	5,000	906,000
Proof of debit and credit postings			101,000	101,000	

[a]This amount is the parent's retained earnings as of the acquisition date as shown in Illustration 3-5.
[b]This amount resulted from the application of push-down accounting as shown in Illustration 3-5.

Explanation of entry:
(1) The primary elimination entry.

PREPARING CONSOLIDATED FINANCIAL STATEMENTS WHEN THE SUBSIDIARY USES THE NON-PUSH-DOWN BASIS OF ACCOUNTING

When the subsidiary does not use the push-down basis of accounting as of the acquisition date, the parent must account for its cost in excess of book value in a manner that produces the same result as though push-down accounting had been applied. That is, it must make amortization entries that otherwise would have been made by the subsidiary.

Accounting for Amortization of Cost in Excess of (under) Book Value

Based on situation E of Illustration 3-7 (the parent's total cost of $90,000 was $30,000 in excess of the $60,000 book value of the subsidiary's net assets), the amortization for the two years subsequent to January 1, 19X1, is calculated as follows:

	Current Value over Book Value Element				
	Inventory	Land	Equipment	Goodwill Element	Total
Remaining life:	(3 months)	(Indefinite)	(6 years)	(10 years)	
Balance, January 1, 19X1....	$2,000	$12,000	$6,000	$10,000	$30,000
Amortization—19X1	(2,000)		(1,000)	(1,000)	(4,000)
Balance, December 31, 19X1	$ -0-	$12,000	$5,000	$ 9,000	$26,000
Amortization—19X2			(1,000)	(1,000)	(2,000)
Balance, December 31, 19X2	$ -0-	$12,000	$4,000	$ 8,000	$24,000

Accordingly, the following entries are required:

	19X1		19X2	
Amortization of Cost in Excess of Book Value[a]	4,000		2,000	
Investment in Subisidary...		4,000		2,000

[a]An income statement account.

Illustration

UPDATING THE EXPANDED ANALYSIS OF THE INVESTMENT ACCOUNT USING THE EQUITY METHOD (NON-PUSH-DOWN ACCOUNTING USED BY SUBSIDIARY)

The balances in the investment account at January 1, 19X1, as shown in situation E in Illustration 3-7, are updated in Illustration 4-4 using the equity method of accounting for the parent's investment. We use the net

Illlustration 4-4

Updating the Expanded Analysis of the Investment Account Using the Equity Method (Wholly owned subsidiary—Total cost is above current value of subsidiary's net assets [Current value is above book value])

			Book Value Element				Current Value over Book Value Element				
				Retained Earnings					Equipment		
					Current Year						
	Total Cost	= Common Stock	+ Prior Years	+ Earnings	− Dividends	+ Inventory	+ Land	+ Cost	Accum. Depr.	+ Goodwill Element
Balance, Jan. 1, 19X1	$ 90,000	$40,000	$20,000			$2,000	$12,000	$6,000		$10,000
Equity in net income.............	15,000			$15,000						
Dividends............	(5,000)				$(5,000)					
Amortization	(4,000)					(2,000)			(1,000)	(1,000)
Subtotal.................	$ 96,000	$40,000	$20,000	$15,000	$(5,000)	$ –0–	$12,000	$6,000	(1,000)	$ 9,000
Reclassification[a]....			10,000	(15,000)	5,000					
Balance, Dec. 31, 19X1	$ 96,000	$40,000	$30,000	$ –0–	$ –0–	$ –0–	$12,000	$6,000	$(1,000)	$ 9,000
Equity in net income.............	21,000			21,000						
Amortization	(2,000)								(1,000)	(1,000)
Subtotal.................	115,000	$40,000	$30,000	$21,000	$ –0–	$ –0–	$12,000	$6,000	$(2,000)	$ 8,000
Reclassification[a]....			21,000	(21,000)						
Balance, Dec. 31, 19X2	$115,000	$40,000	$51,000	$ –0–	$ –0–	$ –0–	$12,000	$6,000	$(2,000)	$ 8,000

Note: The beginning balances are taken from situation E of Illustration 3-7. The amounts used to update the analysis are from Illustration 4-2, as adjusted to reflect the use of the **non**-push-down basis of accounting by the subsidiary.

[a]This reclassification is made after the primary elimination entry is prepared and is analogous to a closing entry. No formal journal entry is recorded because the analysis of the total cost of the investment is maintained in a schedule outside the general ledger.

income and dividend amounts from Illustration 4-2, except that the net income amounts are increased:

	19X1	19X2
Net income in Illustration 4-2 under push-down accounting	**$11,000**	**$19,000**
Incremental amortization and depreciation recorded by subsidiary under push-down accounting (see the table on page 150 for calculations)	**4,000**	**2,000**
Net income reported by subsidiary under non-push-down accounting	**$15,000**	**$21,000**

The following points are important for understanding Illustration 4-4:

1. The entries pertaining to the amortization of the current value over book value element actually expense a portion of the total cost of the investment on the parent company's books. These entries bring the investment's total carrying value closer to the book value of the subsidiary's net assets.
2. The inventory component of the current value over book value element was completely expensed in 19X1. Therefore, this component does not exist after 19X1.
3. The land component of the current value over book value element is part of that element until the land is disposed of, at which time it is charged to income.
4. The equipment component of the current value over book value element is amortized to expense over 20 years. At the end of 20 years, the amount in the accumulated depreciation column will equal the amount in the equipment cost column. Thereafter, these offsetting amounts are part of the current value over book value element until the asset is disposed of.
5. The goodwill element is amortized to expense over 10 years. At the end of 10 years, the goodwill element will no longer exist.
6. All of the amortization expense is charged to a separate account on the parent company's books called Amortization of Cost in Excess of Book Value. We explain later in the chapter why and how this expense amount is reclassified in consolidation to the appropriate, traditional income statement classifications—for example, cost of goods sold and administrative expenses.

Preparing the Primary Elimination Entry from the Updated Analysis of the Investment Account

From the information in Illustration 4-4, in which the parent's cost exceeds the current value of the subsidiary's net assets and net assets are undervalued, the primary elimination entries as of December 31, 19X1 (one year after the acquisition date), and December 31, 19X2 (two years after the acquisition date), are as follows:

	Consolidation Date			
	December 31, 19X1		December 31, 19X2	
Common Stock	40,000		40,000	
Retained Earnings (beginning of year)	20,000		30,000	
Equity in Net Income of Subsidiary	15,000		21,000	
Land	12,000		12,000	
Equipment	6,000		6,000	
Goodwill	9,000		8,000	
Dividends Declared		5,000		–0–
Accumulated Depreciation		1,000		2,000
Investment in Subsidiary		96,000		115,000

The Secondary Elimination Entry

When the parent has recorded amortization of cost in excess of (or below) the book value of the subsidiary's net assets, an additional elimination entry must be made to reclassify this amortization to the appropriate traditional cost and expense accounts. For example, that portion of the amortization relating to inventory should be shown as part of cost of goods sold. That portion of the amortization relating to the building should be allocated among all departments that use the building—such as manufacturing, marketing, and administration. This elimination entry could be avoided if the parent initially charged the appropriate traditional cost and expense accounts when it recorded the amortization. Doing so would not be proper, however, because the amortization account relates solely to the parent's investment in the subsidiary and not to any of its own separate operations. Accordingly, amortization is charged only to one account, which is considered a contra account to the Equity in Net Income of Subsidiary account. Combining these two accounts reveals the subsidiary's true earnings in relation to the parent's investment in the subsidiary.

This treatment presents a problem, however, when consolidated financial statements are prepared; the amortization must be shown among the traditional income cost and expense classifications to which it relates. Accordingly, an additional elimination entry is made to reclassify the balance in the Amortization of Cost in Excess of or under Book Value account to the appropriate traditional cost and expense accounts. The entry does not affect net income, because it takes place entirely within the income statement section of the worksheet. For instructional and ease of reference purposes, we find it convenient to label this entry; accordingly, we call it the secondary elimination entry.

From Illustration 4-4, the secondary elimination entries as of December 31, 19X1 (one year after the acquisition date), and December 31, 19X2 (two years after the acquisition date), are as follows:

	Consolidation Date			
	December 31, 19X1		December 31, 19X2	
Cost of Goods Sold..........	4,000		2,000	
Amortization of Cost in Excess of Book Value.		4,000		2,000

For simplicity, we arbitrarily assumed that all of the goodwill amortization and all of the amortization relating to the building should be classified as part of cost of goods sold. The amortization relating to the inventory belongs in cost of goods sold.

Illustration

CONSOLIDATING STATEMENT WORKSHEET (NON-PUSH-DOWN ACCOUNTING USED BY SUBSIDIARY)

Illustration 4-5 shows a consolidating statement worksheet as of December 31, 19X1 (one year after the acquisition date), using the primary and secondary elimination entries for that date in the previous section. An elimination entry is also needed for the subsidiary's accumulated depreciation balances as of the acquisition date. That entry is for the same amount as shown in Chapter 3, page 111:

Accumulated Depreciation..............................	45,000	
Buildings and Equipment.......................		45,000

The following points are important for understanding Illustration 4-5:

1. As was the case in Illustration 4-3, in which push-down accounting was applied, the net income and retained earnings amounts in the P Company column are the same as in the consolidated column. This equality always exists under the equity method of accounting.
2. The amounts in the consolidated column are identical to the amounts in Illustration 4-3. This demonstrates that whether or not push-down accounting was applied at the acquisition date, the consolidated amounts will always be the same.

Illustration 4-5
Consolidating Statement Worksheet for First Year Subsequent to Acquisition Date (Non-push-down Accounting Used by Subsidiary)

P COMPANY AND SUBSIDIARY (S COMPANY)
Consolidating Statement Worksheet
For the Year Ended December 31, 19X1

	P Company	S Company	Eliminations Dr.	Eliminations Cr.	Consolidated
Income Statement:					
Sales	600,000	200,000			800,000
Cost of goods sold	(360,000)	(116,000)	4,000(2)		(480,000)
Expenses	(204,000)	(69,000)			(273,000)
Intercompany Accounts:					
Equity in net income of S Company	15,000		15,000(1)		–0–
Amortization of cost in excess of book value	(4,000)			4,000(2)	–0–
Net Income	47,000	15,000	19,000	4,000	47,000
Statement of Retained Earnings:					
Balances, January 1, 19X1	100,000	20,000	20,000(1)		100,000
+ Net income	47,000	15,000	19,000	4,000	47,000
− Dividends declared	(31,000)	(5,000)		5,000(1)	(31,000)
Balances, December 31, 19X1	116,000	30,000	39,000	9,000	116,000
Balance Sheet:					
Cash	45,000	25,000			70,000
Accounts receivable, net	75,000	43,000			118,000
Inventory	110,000	40,000			150,000
Investment in S Company	96,000			96,000(1)	–0–
Land	200,000	30,000	12,000		242,000
Buildings and equipment	500,000	190,000	6,000(1)	45,000(3)	651,000
Accumulated depreciation	(320,000)	(58,000)	45,000(3)	1,000(1)	(334,000)
Goodwill			9,000(1)		9,000
Total Assets	706,000	270,000	72,000	142,000	906,000
Liabilities	290,000	200,000			490,000
P Company:					
Common stock	300,000				300,000
Retained earnings	116,000				116,000
S Company:					
Common stock		40,000	40,000(1)		–0–
Retained earnings		30,000	39,000	9,000	–0–
Total Liabilities and Equity	706,000	270,000	79,000	9,000	906,000
Proof of debit and credit postings			151,000	151,000	

Explanation of entries:
(1) The primary elimination entry.
(2) The secondary elimination entry.
(3) The accumulated depreciation elimination entry.

3. On full amortization of the excess relating to the equipment and the goodwill, the Investment in Subsidiary account balance will be $12,000 over the subsidiary's net assets at book value. This amount is based on the land component.
4. If the subsidiary's land is sold, this $12,000 would be amortized in full at that time, and the investment account balance would then equal the book value of the subsidiary's net assets.

Current Value Is below Book Value of Net Assets

When the current value of the subsidiary's net assets is below their book value, the net overvaluation produces a negative amount in the second major conceptual element—the current value over (or under) book value element. Separating this major conceptual element into its individual components may reveal that certain assets are overvalued and certain assets are undervalued. For those depreciable and amortizable assets that are overvalued, a credit balance is amortized instead of a debit balance. Therefore, the secondary elimination entry involves reclassifying the *credit* balance in the Amortization of Cost *Below* Book Value account to the appropriate traditional accounts.

The procedures for preparing consolidated financial statements for these situations are the same as when the current value of the subsidiary's net assets is above their book value.

SUMMARY

Under the purchase method of accounting, any portion of the acquiring company's cost that relates to the acquired business's depreciable or amortizable assets and goodwill must be charged against, or credited to, the combined future earnings of the two companies. For acquisitions of assets, this occurs automatically when the acquired assets and liabilities are recorded at their current values. For acquisitions of common stock, the use of push-down accounting also enables this to occur automatically. But when common stock is acquired and non-push-down accounting is used, the procedures depend on whether the parent uses the equity method or the cost method to account for its investment in the subsidiary. The equity method is conceptually superior to the cost method because it reflects the economic activity of the subsidiary. Under this method, amortization of cost in excess of (or below) book value is recorded in the parent's general ledger to accomplish the desired result. The cost method ignores the economic activity of the subsidiary in most instances. Under this method, the necessary amortization occurs in the consolidation process.

The key to straightforward preparation of consolidated financial statements is maintaining the analysis of the investment account by the components of the major conceptual elements in a format that facilitates the preparation of the primary elimination entry.

Glossary of New Terms

Cost Method A method of accounting for an investment in a subsidiary whereby the carrying value of the investment is never changed unless it is permanently impaired.

Equity Method (as applied to subsidiaries) A method of accounting for an investment in a subsidiary whereby the carrying value of the investment is (1) increased as a result of the subsidiary's earnings; (2) decreased as a result of the subsidiary's losses; (3) decreased as a result of the dividends declared on the subsidiary's common stock; and (4) adjusted for the amortization of cost over or under the book value of the subsidiary's net assets.

Selected References

"Accounting for Baseball," by George H. Sorter. *Journal of Accountancy* (June 1986), 126–133.

Accounting Principles Board Opinion No. 18. "The Equity Method of Accounting." New York: American Institute of Certified Public Accountants, 1970.

Accounting Research Bulletin No. 51. "Consolidated Financial Statements" by Committee on Accounting Procedure. New York: American Institute of Certified Public Accountants, 1959.

"Consolidating Financial Systems in a Diversified MNC," by Robert E. Breen. *Corporate Accounting* (Summer 1986), 25–29.

"Consolidation and the Equity Method—A Time for an Overhaul," by Benjamin S. Neuhausen. *Journal of Accountancy* (February 1982), 54–66.

"Deferred Taxes and Consolidations—A Case for Change," by Leon B. Hoshower and William L. Ferrara. *Management Accounting* (December 1985), 57–60.

Appendix A
PREPARATION OF CONSOLIDATED FINANCIAL STATEMENTS WHEN THE PARENT ACCOUNTS FOR ITS INVESTMENT UNDER THE COST METHOD

Under the cost method of accounting for an investment in a subsidiary, the parent never changes the original cost of the investment unless either a liquidating dividend or a permanent impairment of the investment's value exists. If the same consolidated amounts are to be obtained as when the equity method is used, the consolidation elimination entries must be different from those used when the equity method is used.

Whether the parent uses the equity method or the cost method, the consolidated amounts are identical—only the procedures of preparing the consolidating statement worksheet are different. The cost method has two main conceptual points:

1. To arrive at consolidated net income each year, the net income of the parent must be reduced for any dividend income of the subsidiary that is included. This adjusted net income is then added to the subsidiary's net income to arrive at consolidated net income.
2. To arrive at consolidated retained earnings, the parent's retained earnings (which includes only those earnings of the subsidiary that have been remitted to the parent in the form of dividends since the acquisition date) must be added to the postacquisition earnings of the subsidiary that have not been remitted to the parent.

The Primary Elimination Entry

The primary elimination entry is always exactly the same as the primary elimination entry made on the acquisition date. Using the assumptions of Illustration 4-5, in which the parent's cost of $90,000 exceeded both the current value ($80,000) and the book value ($60,000) of the subsidiary's net assets, we determine the primary elimination for all future consolidation dates as follows:

Common Stock	**40,000**	
Retained Earnings (beginning of year).............	**20,000**	
Inventory	**2,000**	
Land..	**12,000**	
Equipment..	**6,000**	
Goodwill	**10,000**	
Investment in Subsidiary........................		**90,000**

If this entry is used for all future consolidation dates, the secondary entry must be revised so that the consolidated financial statements reflect subsequent, appropriate amortization of cost over the book value of the net assets.

The Secondary Elimination Entry

The secondary elimination entry reflects the amortization of cost over the book value of the net assets directly in the appropriate, traditional cost and expense accounts. Under the cost method, therefore, the secondary elimination entry is an *adjusting* entry (rather than a reclassifying entry as under the equity method). This accomplishes on the consolidating statement worksheet what is otherwise done in the parent's general ledger under the equity method.

For all periods after the year following the aquisition date, the credits are made to the individual components on a cumulative basis. The beginning-of-period cumulative amortization is charged to retained earnings. For the two years subsequent to the acquistion date, the secondary elimination entries are as follows:

	Consolidation Date			
	December 31, 19X1		December 31, 19X2	
Cost of Goods Sold.......	4,000		2,000	
Inventory		2,000		2,000
Accumulated Depreciation		1,000		2,000
Goodwill		1,000		2,000
Retained Earnings........			4,000	

The Dividend Income Elimination Entry

A third elimination entry is necessary to eliminate any dividend income recorded on the parent's books that results from dividends received from the subsidiary. This entry is necessary only in years in which the subsidiary declares a dividend. The entry is as follows:

	Consolidation Date			
	December 31, 19X1		December 31, 19X2	
Dividend Income	5,000		No entry	
Dividends Declared		5,000		

This entry does not effect the balance sheet because the debit is carried forward from the income statement to the net income line in the analysis of retained earnings section of the worksheet. The sole purpose of the entry is to eliminate the dividend income from the parent's income statement.

Illustration

A CONSOLIDATING STATEMENT WORKSHEET WHEN PARENT COMPANY USES THE COST METHOD (NON-PUSH-DOWN ACCOUNTING USED BY SUBSIDIARY)

Illustration 4-6 shows the consolidating statement worksheet as of December 31, 19X1 (the year subsequent to acquisition) prepared using the cost method. (The consolidating worksheet is not shown as of the acquisition date because it is identical with the one in Illustration 3-8.)

The following points are important for understanding Illustration 4-6:

1. The amounts in the parent's column are different from the amounts in Illustration 4-5 (the comparable consolidating worksheet as of this date

Illustration 4-6
Cost Method Used by Parent Company (Non-push-down Accounting Used by Subsidiary)

P COMPANY AND SUBSIDIARY (S COMPANY)
Consolidating Statement Worksheet
For the Year Ended December 31, 19X1

	P Company	S Company	Eliminations Dr.	Eliminations Cr.	Consolidated
Income Statement:					
Sales	600,000	200,000			800,000
Cost of goods sold	(360,000)	(116,000)	4,000(2)		(480,000)
Expenses	(204,000)	(69,000)			(273,000)
Intercompany Account:					
Dividend income	5,000		5,000(3)		–0–
Net Income	41,000	15,000	9,000		47,000
Statement of Retained Earnings:					
Balances, January 1, 19X1	100,000	20,000	20,000(1)		100,000
+ Net income	41,000	15,000	→ 9,000		47,000
− Dividends declared	(31,000)	(5,000)		5,000(3)	(31,000)
Balances, December 31, 19X1	110,000	30,000	29,000	5,000	116,000
Balance Sheet:					
Cash	45,000	25,000			70,000
Accounts receivable, net	75,000	43,000			118,000
Inventory	110,000	40,000	2,000(1)	2,000(2)	150,000
Investment in S Company	90,000			90,000(1)	–0–
Land	200,000	30,000	12,000(1)		242,000
Buildings and equipment	500,000	190,000	6,000(1)	45,000(4)	651,000
Accumulated depreciation	(320,000)	(58,000)	45,000(4)	1,000(2)	(334,000)
Goodwill			10,000(1)	1,000(2)	9,000
Total Assets	700,000	270,000	75,000	139,000	906,000
Liabilities	290,000	200,000			490,000
P Company:					
Common stock	300,000				300,000
Retained earnings	110,000				110,000
S Company:					
Common stock		40,000	40,000(1)		–0–
Retained earnings		30,000	→ 29,000	→ 5,000	6,000
Total Liabilities and Equity	700,000	270,000	69,000	5,000	906,000
Proof of debit and credit postings			144,000	144,000	

Explanation of entries:
(1) The primary elimination entry.
(2) The secondary elimination entry.
(3) The dividend income elimination entry.
(4) The accumulated depreciation elimination entry.

Recap of Retained Earnings:

P Company	$110,000
S Company	6,000
Total	$116,000

when the equity method is used), whereas the amounts in the subsidiary's column and the consolidated column are the same.
2. The parent's Retained Earnings account under the cost method includes only those postacquisition earnings that have been remitted to the parent through dividends, whereas the parent's Retained Earnings account under the equity method includes all postacquisition earnings of the subsidiary.
3. As under the equity method, the eliminations and adjustments made to the income statement section of the worksheet are subtotaled at the net income line and carried forward to the net income line in the retained earnings section of the worksheet.
4. The retained earnings of the subsidiary that did not get eliminated are added to the parent's retained earnings to obtain consolidated retained earnings.

Appendix B
PREPARATION OF THE CONSOLIDATING STATEMENT WORKSHEET USING THE TRIAL BALANCE APPROACH

Some companies prepare their consolidating statement worksheets from trial balances rather than from financial statements. The same elimination entries are used as when the worksheets are prepared from financial statements. To demonstrate the preparation of the worksheet using the trial balance approach, we have reformatted the financial statements used in Illustration 4-5 into the trial balance approach shown in Illustration 4-7. The primary and secondary elimination entries from Illustration 4-5 are repeated below for convenience.

The primary elimination entry:

Common Stock	**40,000**	
Retained Earnings (beginning of year)	**20,000**	
Equity in Net Income of Subsidiary	**15,000**	
Land	**12,000**	
Equipment	**6,000**	
Goodwill	**9,000**	
Dividends Declared		**5,000**
Accumulated Depreciation		**1,000**
Investment in Subsidiary		**96,000**

The secondary elimination entry:

Cost of Goods Sold	**4,000**	
Amortization of Cost in Excess of Book Value		**4,000**

Illustration 4-7
Consolidating Statement Worksheet When Parent Uses the Trial Balance Approach (Non-push-down Accounting Used by Subsidiary)

P COMPANY AND SUBSIDIARY (S COMPANY)
Consolidating Statement Worksheet
For the Year Ended December 31, 19X1

	P Company		S Company	
	Dr.	Cr.	Dr.	Cr.
Cash	45,000		25,000	
Accounts receivable, net	75,000		43,000	
Inventory	110,000		40,000	
Investment in S Company	96,000			
Land	200,000		30,000	
Buildings and equipment	500,000		190,000	
Accumulated depreciation		320,000		58,000
Goodwill				
Liabilities		290,000		200,000
P Company:				
Common stock		300,000		
Retained earnings, January 1, 19X1		100,000		
Dividends declared	31,000			
S Company:				
Common stock				40,000
Retained earnings, January 1, 19X1				20,000
Dividends declared			5,000	
Sales		600,000		200,000
Cost of goods sold	360,000		116,000	
Expenses	204,000		69,000	
Intercompany accounts:				
Equity in net income of subsidiary		15,000		
Amortization of cost in excess of book value	4,000			
	1,625,000	1,625,000	518,000	518,000
Consolidated net income				
Consolidated retained earnings				

Explanation of entries.
(1) The primary elimination entry.
(2) The secondary elimination entry.
(3) The accumulated depreciation elimination entry.

	Eliminations Dr.	Eliminations Cr.	Income Statement Dr.	Income Statement Cr.	Consolidated Retained Earnings (Dr.) Cr.	Balance Sheet
						70,000
						118,000
						150,000
		96,000(1)				–0–
	12,000(1)					242,000
	6,000(1)	45,000(3)				651,000
	45,000(3)	1,000(1)				(334,000)
	9,000(1)					9,000
						906,000
						490,000
						300,000
					100,000	
					(31,000)	
	40,000(1)				–0–	
	20,000(1)				–0–	
		5,000(1)			–0–	
				800,000		
	4,000(2)		480,000			
			273,000			
	15,000(1)			–0–		
		4,000(2)	–0–			
	151,000	151,000				
				47,000 →	47,000	
					116,000 →	116,000
						906,000

Review Questions

1. Contrast the equity method of accounting with the cost method.
2. When it is inappropriate to consolidate a subsidiary's financial statements with those of its parent, how must the parent company account for its investment in the subsidiary?
3. What are liquidating dividends? How are they treated under the equity method? Under the cost method?
4. Why must the consolidated amounts be the same regardless of whether the parent company uses the equity method or the cost method to account for its investment in a subsidiary?
5. In the expanded analysis of the investment account, why is a separate column used for the parent company's share of the subsidiary's current-year net income or loss?
6. What is the source of the primary elimination entry when the parent uses the equity method?
7. What is the purpose of the secondary elimination entry?

Discussion Cases

DC 4-1

Selecting the Accounting Method for Measuring Return on Investment

Presto Company acquired all of the outstanding common stock of Speedley Company on January 1, 19X1, for $1,000,000 cash. Presto views the Speedley operation as an investment and wants to account for its investment in a manner that will enable it to evaluate readily the profitability of the investment each year, using a return-on-investment approach. Assume that Speedley expects net income of $200,000 for 19X1 and $300,000 for 19X2, and that no dividends will be paid to the parent company during these two years.

Required:

1. Calculate the expected return on investment for 19X1 and 19X2 assuming the parent company uses (a) the equity method and (b) the cost method.
2. Which method allows the correct return on investment to be calculated?

DC 4-2

Treatment of Amortization of Cost in Excess of Book Value in Calculating Return on Investment under the Equity Method

Pinnex Company acquired all of the outstanding common stock of Stickles Company on January 1, 19X1, for $1,000,000 cash. For 19X1, Stickles reported net income of $150,000. On December 31, 19X1, Stickles paid a $75,000 dividend to Pinnex. Pinnex amortized $30,000 of cost in excess of book value during 19X1, which it recorded under the equity method of accounting.

Required:

1. Calculate the parent company's 19X1 return on investment.
2. Calculate the parent company's 19X1 return on investment assuming that the dividend was paid on June 30, 19X1. For simplicity assume the declaration date of the dividend is the same as the payment date.

DC 4-3

Treatment of Subsidiary Dividends in Preparing the Consolidated Statement of Retained Earnings

The controller of Plumex Company is preparing the consolidated statement of retained earnings. Plumex declared dividends of $100,000 on its common stock during the year. Plumex's wholly owned subsidiary, which was acquired at the beginning of the year, declared dividends of $20,000 on its common stock during the year ($10,000 of which was declared on the last day of the year and has not been paid). The controller wants to know whether the consolidated statement of retained earnings for the year should reflect dividends of $100,000, $110,000, or $120,000.

Required:
How would you advise the controller?

DC 4-4

Subsequent Accounting for "Cost in Excess of Net Assets"

Payton Company acquired the business of Simpson Company on January 1, 19X1, at a cost of $800,000 in excess of the current value of Simpson's net assets. Simpson's operations had been unprofitable for the two years preceding the business combination and thus did not possess superior earning power. Payton paid the $800,000 so that it could readily establish itself in this high-risk industry. Payton expects Simpson's operations to report profits within three years. The cost in excess of current value is being amortized over 10 years.

Required:
Assume that at December 31, 19X4, Simpson's operations are still unprofitable. Management is uncertain whether Simpson's operations will ever be profitable. What are the implications of this situation?

Exercises

E 4-1

Preparation of Comparative Entries under the Equity Method and the Cost Method

Pidgeon Company acquired 100% of the outstanding common stock of Seagull Company at a total cost of $550,000 on January 1, 19X1. Assume the current value of Seagull's net assets equals their book value of $510,000. Also assume goodwill is assigned a 40-year life. The net income (loss) and dividends declared by Seagull for 19X1 and 19X2 are as follows:

	Net Income (Loss)	Dividends Declared (and Paid)
19X1	30,000	10,000
19X2	(12,000)	5,000

Required:
Prepare in comparative form the parent company's entries for 19X1 and 19X2 under the equity method and the cost method.

E 4-2

Applying the Equity Method and Preparing the Primary Elimination Entry

On January 1, 19X1, Planet Company acquired 100% of the outstanding common stock of Solar Company at a total cost of $750,000. The general ledger balances of Solar's capital accounts on the acquisition date were as follows:

Common stock	$100,000
Additional paid-in capital	400,000
Retained earnings	250,000
	$750,000

Assume the current value of Solar's net assets equals their book value. The net income (loss) and dividends declared by Solar for 19X1 and 19X2 are as follows:

	Net Income (Loss)	Dividends Declared (and Paid)
19X1	$80,000	$25,000
19X2	(40,000)	10,000

Required:

1. Assuming that the parent company uses the equity method of accounting, prepare the journal entries it would make for 19X1 and 19X2 for its investment in the subsidiary.
2. Prepare an expanded analysis of the investment account as of the acquisition date and update it for the entries developed in requirement 1. (Assume the non-push-down basis of accounting is used.)
3. Prepare the primary elimination entry as of December 31, 19X1, and December 31, 19X2.
4. Explain why there is no secondary elimination entry.
5. Prepare the primary elimination as of December 31, 19X1, and December 31, 19X2, assuming the push-down-basis of accounting was used.

E 4-3

Applying the Equity Method and Preparing the Primary and Secondary Elimination Entries

On January 1, 19X1, Pele Company acquired 100% of the outstanding common stock of Soccerex Company at a total of $400,000. The analysis of Pele's investment in Soccerex by the individual components of the major conceptual elements as of the acquisition date is as follows:

		Remaining Life
Book value element:		
Common stock	$100,000	
Retained earnings	60,000	
Current value over book value element:		
Inventory	5,000	3 months
Land	105,000	Indefinite
Building	90,000	15 years
Goodwill element	40,000	40 years
Total cost	$400,000	

The net income (loss) and dividends declared by Soccerex for 19X1 and 19X2 are as follows:

	Net Income (Loss)	Dividends Declared (and Paid)
19X1	$35,000	$5,000
19X2	(10,000)	5,000

Required:

1. Assuming that the parent company uses the equity method of accounting, prepare the journal entries it would make for 19X1 and 19X2 for its investment in the subsidiary.
2. Prepare an analysis of the investment account by the components of the major conceptual elements as of the acquisition date, and update it for the entries developed in requirement 1.
3. Prepare the primary and secondary elimination entries as of December 31, 19X1, and December 31, 19X2.

E 4-4

Applying the Equity Method and Preparing the Primary and Secondary Elimination Entries

Patter Company acquired 100% of the outstanding common stock of Sprinkles Company at a total cost of $310,000 on January 1, 19X1. The analysis of Patter's investment in Sprinkles by the components of the major conceptual elements as of the acquisition date (after appropriate allocation of the bargain purchase element) is as follows:

		Remaining Life
Book value element:		
Common stock	$250,000	
Retained earnings	100,000	
Current value over (under) book value element:		
Inventory	5,000	3 months
Land	30,000	Indefinite
Building	(75,000)	25 years
Total cost	$310,000	

The net income (loss) and dividends declared by Sprinkles for 19X1 and 19X2 are as follows:

	Net Income (Loss)	Dividends Declared (and Paid)
19X1	$(15,000)	$1,000
19X2	30,000	5,000

Required:

1. Assuming the parent company uses the equity method of accounting, prepare the journal entries it would make for 19X1 and 19X2 with respect to its investment in the subsidiary.
2. Prepare an analysis of the investment account by the individual components of the major conceptual elements as of the acquisition date and update it for the entries developed in situation 1.
3. Prepare the primary and secondary elimination entries as of December 31, 19X1, and December 31, 19X2.

E 4-5

Theory: Multiple-choice Questions

1. What would be the effect of the financial statements if an unconsolidated subsidiary is accounted for by the equity method but consolidated statements are prepared with other subsidiaries?
   a. All of the unconsolidated subsidiary's account are included individually in the consolidated statements.
   b. The consolidated retained earnings amount does not reflect the earnings of the unconsolidated subsidiary.
   c. The consolidated retained earnings amount is the same as it would be if the subsidiary had been included in the consolidation.
   d. Dividend revenue from the unconsolidated subsidiary is reflected in consolidated net income.
   e. None of the above.

2. At which amount should a parent company carry its unconsolidated domestic subsidiary on its separate financial statements in periods subsequent to acquisition?
   a. Original cost of the investment to the parent company.
   b. Original cost of the investment adjusted for the parent's share of the subsidiary's earnings, losses, dividends, and amortization of cost over or under the book value of the subsidiary's net assets.
   c. Current market value of the investment adjusted for dividends received.
   d. Current market value of the investment.
   e. None of the above.
3. In a parent's unconsolidated financial statements, which accounts, other than Cash, are affected when a subsidiary's earnings and dividends are recorded?
   a. Dividend Revenue, Equity in Earnings of Subsidiary, and Retained Earnings.
   b. Dividend Revenue and Retained Earnings.
   c. Investment in Subsidiary, Equity in Earnings of Subsidiary, Dividend Revenue, and Retained Earnings.
   d. Investment in Subsidiary, Equity in Earnings of Subsidiary, and Retained Earnings.
   e. None of the above.

(AICPA adapted)

Exercise for Appendix A

E 4-6A

Applying the Cost Method and Preparing the Primary, Secondary, and Dividend Income Elimination Entries

On January 1, 19X1, Psi Company acquired all of the outstanding common stock of Seta Company at a total cost of $200,000. The analysis of Psi's investment in Seta by the individual components of the major conceptual elements as of the acquisition date is as follows:

		Remaining Life
Book value element:		
Common stock	$ 50,000	
Retained earnings	25,000	
Current value over book value element:		
Inventory	5,000	1 month
Land	45,000	Indefinite
Building	25,000	25 years
Equipment	10,000	5 years
Goodwill element	40,000	10 years
Total cost	$200,000	

The net income (loss) and dividends declared by Seta for 19X1 and 19X2 are as follows:

	Net Income (Loss)	Dividends Declared (and Paid)
19X1	$10,000	$6,000
19X2	(2,000)	2,000

Required:

1. Assuming that the parent company uses the cost method of accounting for its investment in the subsidiary, prepare the entries it would make for 19X1 and 19X2.
2. Prepare the primary, secondary, and dividend income elimination entries, as appropriate, as of December 31, 19X1, and December 31, 19X2.
3. Explain how your answer would change for 19X2 if $5,000 of dividends were declared and paid instead of $2,000.

Problems

P 4-1*

Preparing Consolidated Financial Statements (Continuation of Problem 3-4)

On December 31, 19X1, Payles Company, a calendar-year reporting company, acquired all of the outstanding common stock of Selmore Company at a total cost of $600,000 (an amount equal to the current value and book value of Selmore's net assets). The analysis of the investment account as of the acquisition date is as follows:

Book value element:	
Common stock	$100,000
Additional paid-in capital	200,000
Retained earnings	300,000
Total cost	$600,000

The financial statements of each company for the year ended December 31, 19X2, are as follows:

	Payles Company	Selmore Company
Income Statement (19X2):		
Sales	$ 8,500,000	$ 900,000
Cost of goods sold	(5,500,000)	(400,000)
Expenses	(2,400,000)	(320,000)
Equity in net income of subsidiary	180,000	
Net Income	$ 780,000	$ 180,000

(continued)

*The financial statement information presented for problems accompanied by asterisks is also provided on Model 4 (filename: Model4) of the software file disk that is available for use with the text, enabling the problem to be worked on the computer.

	Payles Company	Selmore Company
Balance Sheet (December 31, 19X2):		
Cash	$ 220,000	$ 140,000
Accounts receivable, net	1,000,000	500,000
Inventory	1,500,000	800,000
Investment in Selmore Company	680,000	
Land	800,000	300,000
Buildings and equipment	5,200,000	900,000
Accumulated depreciation	(1,200,000)	(240,000)
	$ 8,200,000	$2,400,000
Accounts payable and accruals	$ 700,000	$ 620,000
Long-term debt	2,100,000	1,100,000
Common stock	1,000,000	100,000
Additional paid-in capital	2,000,000	200,000
Retained earnings	2,400,000	380,000
	$ 8,200,000	$2,400,000
Dividends declared during 19X2	$ 380,000	$ 100,000

Required:

1. Update the analysis of the investment account through December 31, 19X2.
2. Prepare the consolidation elimination entries as of December 31, 19X2.
3. Prepare a consolidating statement worksheet at December 31, 19X2. (The parent's retained earnings as of January 1, 19X2, was $2,000,000.)
4. Assuming the subsidiary had applied the push-down basis of accounting at the acquisition date, prepare the primary elimination entry as of December 31, 19X2.

P 4-2 Preparing Consolidated Financial Statements (Continuation of Problem 3-5)

Price Company, a calendar-year reporting company, acquired all of the outstanding common stock of Selle Company at a total cost of $300,000 on December 31, 19X1. The analysis of the parent company's investment account as of the acquisition date is as follows:

		Remaining Life
Book value element:		
Common stock	$100,000	
Retained earnings	90,000	
Current value over (under) book value element:		
Inventory	5,000	2 months
Land	30,000	Indefinite
Equipment	50,000	10 years
Patent	(15,000)	3 years
Goodwill element	40,000	4 years
Total cost	$300,000	

The financial statements of each company for the year ended December 31, 19X2, are as follows:

	Price Company	Selle Company
Income Statement (19X2):		
Sales	$2,800,000	$600,000
Cost of goods sold	(1,500,000)	(300,000)
Expenses	(1,000,000)	(240,000)
Equity in net income of subsidiary	60,000	
Amortization of cost in excess of book value	(15,000)	
Net Income	$ 345,000	$ 60,000
Balance Sheet (December 31, 19X2):		
Cash	$ 120,000	$ 25,000
Accounts receivable, net	300,000	50,000
Inventory	500,000	120,000
Investment in Selle Company	290,000	
Land	400,000	70,000
Buildings and equipment	1,100,000	220,000
Accumulated depreciation	(210,000)	(65,000)
Patent		10,000
	$2,500,000	$430,000
Accounts payable and accruals	$ 320,000	$ 85,000
Long-term debt	1,300,000	150,000
Common stock	300,000	100,000
Retained earnings	580,000	95,000
	$2,500,000	$430,000
Dividends declared during 19X2	$ 215,000	$ 55,000

Required:

1. Update the analysis of the investment account through December 31, 19X2.
2. Prepare the consolidation elimination entries as of December 31, 19X2.
3. Prepare a consolidating statement worksheet at December 31, 19X2. (The parent's retained earnings as of January 1, 19X2, was $450,000.)
4. Assuming that the subsidiary had applied the push-down basis of accounting at the acquisition date, prepare the primary elimination entry as of December 31, 19X2.

P 4-3

Preparing Consolidated Financial Statements (Continuation of Problem 3-6)

Pepper Company, a calendar-year reporting company, acquired all of the outstanding common stock of Salt Company at a total cost of $400,000 on December 31, 19X1. The analysis of Pepper's investment account as of the acquisition date is as follows:

		Remaining Life
Book value element:		
Common stock	$ 50,000	
Additional paid-in capital	200,000	
Retained earnings	250,000	
Current value over (under) book value element:		
Inventory	(70,000)	6 months
Land	30,000	Indefinite
Building	(100,000)	20 years
Long-term debt	40,000	4 years
Total cost	$400,000	

The financial statements of each company for the year ended December 31, 19X2, are as follows:

	Pepper Company	Salt Company
Income Statement (19X2):		
Sales	$7,000,000	$850,000
Cost of goods sold	(3,800,000)	(600,000)
Expenses	(1,700,000)	(310,000)
Equity in net loss of subsidiary	(60,000)	
Amortization of cost below book value	65,000	
Net Income (Loss)	$1,505,000	$ (60,000)
Balance Sheet (December 31, 19X2):		
Cash	$ 295,000	$ 20,000
Accounts receivable, net	400,000	80,000
Inventory	700,000	130,000
Investment in Salt Company	405,000	
Land	500,000	100,000
Buildings and equipment	3,100,000	550,000
Accumulated depreciation	(600,000)	(80,000)
	$4,800,000	$800,000
Accounts payable and accruals	$ 495,000	$ 60,000
Long-term debt	2,000,000	300,000
Common stock	20,000	50,000
Additional paid-in capital	480,000	200,000
Retained earnings	1,805,000	190,000
	$4,800,000	$800,000
Dividends declared during 19X2	$ 800,000	$ -0-

Required:

1. Update the analysis of the investment account through December 31, 19X2.
2. Prepare the consolidation elimination entries as of December 31, 19X2.
3. Prepare a consolidating statement worksheet at December 31, 19X2. (The parent's retained earnings as of January 1, 19X2, was $1,100,000.)

4. Assuming the subsidiary had applied the push-down basis of accounting at the acquisition date, prepare the primary elimination entry as of December 31, 19X2.

P 4-4 CHALLENGER Evaluating the Future Results under the Purchase Method in a Business Combination with a Troubled Savings and Loan

You are the auditor for Pyramid Savings and Loan Association, which recently acquired all of the assets of Sham Savings and Loan Association. The combination was structured so that the transaction did not qualify for pooling-of-interests treatment. Sham had incurred losses for approximately two years prior to the combination as a result of paying a higher interest rate to its depositors than it was earning on its loan portfolio. The combination was arranged by the Federal Savings and Loan Insurance Corporation to prevent Sham's liquidation, as Sham had exhausted its net worth. Selected data for Sham as of the combination date are as follows:

	Book Value	Current Value
Assets	$300,000,000	$260,000,000
Liabilities	300,000,000	300,000,000
Common stock	12,000,000	
Accumulated deficit	(12,000,000)	

The current value of the assets is lower than the book value because the current lending rate on home mortgages is 12%, whereas the yield on the loan portfolio (which has an average remaining life of 10 years) is only 10%. Pyramid S & L did not have to pay any consideration; it merely took title to the assets and assumed responsibility for the liabilities. Management intends to amortize goodwill over 40 years.

Required:

1. Prepare an analysis of the investment account at the acquisition date.
2. Prepare the primary elimination entry as of the acquisition date. (Assume non-push-down accounting was used.)
3. For years 1–10 (in total) and for years 11–40 (in total), determine the effect on income of amortizations made from the parent company's investment account.
4. Evaluate the soundness of the results that are reported under the purchase method at the acquisition date and for future periods.
5. What, if anything, should be done differently?

P 4-5 COMPREHENSIVE Recording the Acquisition, Analyzing the Investment Account, Applying the Equity Method, and Preparing Consolidated Financial Statements

On January 1, 19X1, Pinchnell Company acquired 100% of the outstanding common stock of Squeezers Company by issuing 7,000 shares of $10 par value common stock (which was trading at $60 per share on that date). In addition, Pinchnell incurred direct costs of $95,000 relating to the acquisition, $25,000 of which was for the registration of the shares issued with the Securities and Exchange Commission. (All these direct costs were charged to the investment account.) The balances in the capital accounts of the subsidiary as of the acquisition date are as follows:

Common stock	$100,000
Retained earnings	402,000
	$502,000

All the assets and liabilities of the subsidiary have a current value equal to their book value, except for the following:

	Book Value	Current Value	Remaining Life
Land held for development	$600,000	$710,000	Indefinite
Deferred charges	42,000	–0–	3 years
Long-term debt	200,000	230,000	6 years

Additional Information:

1. The subsidiary is a real estate development company, which owns several parcels of land. None of the land owned was developed during 19X1. However, one parcel acquired eight years ago was sold in its undeveloped stage. This was the only sale for 19X1.
2. The parent company is privately owned and chose to use non-push-down accounting.
3. The parent's accounting policy is to amortize goodwill over 10 years.
4. The only entry the parent made in its books relating to subsidiary was at the acquisition date.

The financial statements of each company for the year ended December 31, 19X1, are as follows:

	Pinchnell Company	Squeezers Company
Income Statement (19X1):		
Sales	$ 950,000	$ 330,000
Cost of goods sold	(520,000)	(200,000)
Expenses	(204,000)	(45,000)
Net Income	$ 226,000	$ 85,000

(continued)

	Pinchnell Company	Squeezers Company
Balance Sheet (December 31, 19X1):		
Cash	200,000	19,000
Accounts receivable, net	300,000	
Notes receivable		350,000
Inventory	600,000	
Investment in Squeezers Company	515,000	
Land	500,000	
Buildings and equipment	2,700,000	5,000
Accumulated depreciation	(600,000)	(2,000)
Land held for development		400,000
Deferred charges		28,000
	$4,215,000	$ 800,000
Accounts payable/accruals	160,000	13,000
Dividends payable		35,000
Long-term debt	1,600,000	200,000
Common stock	700,000	100,000
Additional paid-in capital	1,015,000	
Retained earnings	740,000	452,000
	$4,215,000	$ 800,000
Dividends declared during 19X1	$ 100,000	$ 35,000

Required:

1. Analyze the investment account by the components of the major conceptual elements as of the acquisition date. Make any appropriate adjusting entries.
2. Update the analysis of the investment account to reflect activity under the equity method through December 31, 19X1.
3. Prepare the consolidation elimination entries as of December 31, 19X1.
4. Adjust the parent company's financial statements as shown above to reflect the equity method, and then prepare a consolidating statement worksheet at December 31, 19X1.
5. Assuming that the subsidiary had applied push-down accounting at the acquisition date, prepare the primary elimination entry as of December 31, 19X1.

P 4-6*

COMPREHENSIVE CHALLENGER Converting to the Equity Method from the Cost Method Two Years after the Acquisition Date: Analyzing the Investment Account and Preparing Consolidated Financial Statements

Phonetics Company acquired all of the outstanding common stock of Sounder Company for $820,000 cash on January 1, 19X1. Phonetics also incurred $47,000 of direct costs in connection with the acquisition. Selected information on Sounder as of the acquisition date is as follows:

	Book Value	Current Value	Remaining Life
Inventory	$ 303,000	$ 310,000	4 months
Buildings and equipment	1,400,000[a]	1,490,000	15 years
Patent	20,000	60,000	5 years
Goodwill	60,000	–0–	6 years
10% bonds payable	1,200,000	1,000,000	10 years

[a]Net of $300,000 of accumulated depreciation.

Additional Information:

1. The parent company is privately owned and chose to use non-push-down accounting.
2. The parent company has used the cost method since the acquisition date and has decided to change to the equity method to account for its investment in the subsidiary.
3. Assume a 40-year life for any goodwill paid in the transaction.

The financial statements of each company for the year ended December 31, 19X2 (two years after the acquisition date), are as follows:

	Phonetics Company	Sounder Company
Income Statement (19X2):		
Sales	$8,500,000	$ 980,000
Cost of goods sold	(4,500,000)	(530,000)
Expenses	(3,640,000)	(310,000)
Dividend income	50,000	
Net Income	$ 410,000	$ 140,000
Balance Sheet (December 31, 19X2):		
Cash	$ 458,000	$ 118,000
Accounts receivable, net	750,000	190,000
Inventory	820,000	380,000
Investment in Sounder Company	867,000	
Land	760,000	240,000
Buildings and equipment	6,260,000	1,720,000
Accumulated depreciation	(2,465,000)	(480,000)
Patent	100,000	12,000
Goodwill		40,000
	$7,550,000	$2,220,000
Accounts payable and accruals	$1,600,000	$ 370,000
Long-term debt	3,000,000	1,200,000
Common stock	2,000,000	250,000
Retained earnings	950,000	400,000
	$7,550,000	$2,220,000
Dividends declared during 19X2	$ 100,000	$ 50,000
Dividends declared during 19X1	$ 80,000	$ 40,000
Reported net income for 19X1	$ 200,000	$ 90,000

Required:

1. Analyze the investment account by the components of the major conceptual elements as of the acquisition date.
2. Update the analysis of the investment account to reflect activity under the equity method of accounting through December 31, 19X2 (a two-year period).
3. Prepare the journal entry to convert to the equity method from the cost method.
4. Prepare the consolidation elimination entries as of December 31, 19X2.
5. Adjust the parent company's financial statements to reflect the equity method, and then prepare a consolidating statement worksheet at December 31, 19X2.

Problem Involving Managerial Analysis

P 4-7

Analyzing Financial Statements and Calculating Return on Investment

The Sunn City Sluggers is a Triple-A league baseball team that was formed eleven years ago. Operations quickly reached expected levels. For years 8, 9, and 10, the team reported net income of approximately $1,000,000 each year. (For simplicity, ignore income taxes.)

At the end of year 10, the team was sold to a partnership that was formed with capital of $5,001,000 and is managed by Homer Runn. The purchase price was $5,000,000. For simplicity, assume that: (1) the initial capital of the team, when formed, was $1; (2) all earnings for the ten years had been distributed to the owners by the end of the tenth year; (3) assets therefore equaled liabilities at the time of sale; and (4) none of the assets or liabilities are over- or undervalued.

As the partnership's accountant, you assigned the $5,000,000 to goodwill having a ten-year life. The income statement for year 11 follows:

Revenues	8,100,000
Expenses	(7,000,000)
Operating income	1,100,000
Goodwill amortization	(500,000)
Net Income	$ 600,000

The players' union and the general manager are currently negotiating a new contract for year 12. Runn contends that players' salaries cannot be increased because of a lackluster return on investment earned in year 11. The union argues that the goodwill amortization should be ignored, since the operating income increased by $100,000 from the prior year, which indicates that the value of the business has increased during the year—not decreased. (This is supported by the fact that a group of investors offered to buy the team near the end of year 12 for $6,000,000.)

Additional Assumptions:

1. Revenues and earnings are expected to remain constant through year 22.
2. Cash is to be distributed to partners at the end of each year equal to net income.
3. For years 11 to 20, an additional $500,000 cash is to be distributed to partners at the end of each year as a return of capital.
4. The partnership sells the team at the end of year 22 for $6,000,000.

Required:

1. Using the reported or assumed net income for years 11, 12, 20, 21, and 22, calculate the return on investment. (For simplicity, ignore the impact of each year's earnings in determining the capital balances to be used in the denominator. In other words, use the beginning capital balances for the denominator.)
2. Assess the validity of management's argument that player salaries cannot be increased unless there is an adequate return on investment to the partner-owners.
3. Assess the validity of the union's argument that the goodwill amortization should be ignored in calculating return on investment.
4. Given that none of the team's assets or liabilities were under or overvalued at the acquisition date, what else might the $5,000,000 (or some portion of it) be assigned to?
5. Assuming revenues and earnings occurred as expected through the end of year 22 when the team is sold for $6,000,000, how accurately did the return on investment calculations in requirement 1 portray the economics of what transpired?
6. What was the true return on investment from the time the team was bought by partnership until the partnership sold the team?

Problems for Appendix A

P 4-8A

Preparing Consolidated Financial Statements (Problem 4-1 Revised to Reflect the Cost Method)

On December 31, 19X1, Payles Company acquired all of the outstanding common stock of Selmore Company at a total cost of $600,000 (an amount equal to the book value of Selmore's net assets). The financial statements of each company for the year ended December 31, 19X2, are as follows:

	Payles Company	Selmore Company
Income Statement (19X2):		
Sales	$8,500,000	$ 900,000
Cost of goods sold	(5,500,000)	(400,000)
Expenses	(2,400,000)	(320,000)
Dividend income	100,000	
Net Income	$ 700,000	$ 180,000

(continued)

	Payles Company	Selmore Company
Balance Sheet (December 31, 19X2):		
Cash	$ 220,000	$ 140,000
Accounts receivable, net	1,000,000	500,000
Inventory	1,500,000	800,000
Investment in Selmore Company	600,000	
Land	800,000	300,000
Buildings and equipment	5,200,000	900,000
Accumulated depreciation	(1,200,000)	(240,000)
	$8,120,000	$2,400,000
Accounts payable and accruals	$ 700,000	$ 620,000
Long-term debt	2,100,000	1,100,000
Common stock	1,000,000	100,000
Additional paid-in capital	2,000,000	200,000
Retained earnings	2,320,000	380,000
	$8,120,000	$2,400,000
Dividends declared during 19X2	$ 380,000	$ 100,000

Required:

1. Prepare the consolidation elimination entries at December 31, 19X2.
2. Why is there no secondary elimination entry at December 31, 19X2?
3. Prepare a consolidating statement worksheet at December 31, 19X2. (The parent's retained earnings on January 1, 19X2, was $2,000,000.)

P 4-9A Preparing Consolidated Financial Statements (Problem 4-2 Revised to Reflect the Cost Method)

Price Company acquired all of the outstanding common stock of Selle Company at a total cost of $300,000 on December 31, 19X1. The analysis of the parent company's investment account as of the acquisition date is as follows:

		Remaining Life
Book value element:		
Common stock	$100,000	
Retained earnings	90,000	
Current value over book value element:		
Inventory	5,000	2 months
Land	30,000	Indefinite
Equipment	50,000	10 years
Patent	(15,000)	3 years
Goodwill element	40,000	4 years
Total cost	$300,000	

The financial statements of each company for the year ended December 31, 19X2, are as follows:

	Price Company	Selle Company
Income Statement (19X2):		
Sales	$2,800,000	$600,000
Cost of goods sold	(1,500,000)	(300,000)
Expenses	(1,000,000)	(240,000)
Dividend income	55,000	
Net Income	$ 355,000	$ 60,000
Balance Sheet (December 31, 19X2):		
Cash	$ 120,000	$ 25,000
Accounts receivable, net	300,000	50,000
Inventory	500,000	120,000
Investment in Selle Company	300,000	
Land	400,000	70,000
Buildings and equipment	1,100,000	220,000
Accumulated depreciation	(210,000)	(65,000)
Patent		10,000
	$2,510,000	$430,000
Accounts payable and accruals	$ 320,000	$ 85,000
Long-term debt	1,300,000	150,000
Common stock	300,000	100,000
Retained earnings	590,000	95,000
	$2,510,000	$430,000
Dividends declared during 19X2	$ 215,000	$ 55,000

Required:

1. Prepare the consolidation elimination entries at December 31, 19X2.
2. Prepare a consolidating statement worksheet at December 31, 19X2. (The parent's retained earnings on January 1, 19X2, was $450,000.)

P 4-10A

Preparing Consolidated Financial Statements (Problem 4-3 Revised to Reflect the Cost Method)

Pepper Company acquired all of the outstanding common stock of Salt Company at a total cost of $400,000 on December 31, 19X1. The analysis of the parent company's investment account as of the acquisition date is as follows:

		Remaining Life
Book value element:		
Common stock	$ 50,000	
Additional paid-in capital	200,000	
Retained earnings	250,000	
Current value over (under) book value element:		
Inventory	(70,000)	6 months
Land	30,000	Indefinite
Building	(100,000)	20 years
Long-term debt	40,000	4 years
Total cost	$400,000	

The financial statements of each company for the year ended December 31, 19X2, are as follows:

	Pepper Company	Salt Company
Income Statement (19X2):		
Sales	$7,000,000	$850,000
Cost of goods sold	(3,800,000)	(600,000)
Expenses	(1,700,000)	(310,000)
Net Income (Loss)	$1,500,000	$ (60,000)
Balance Sheet (December 31, 19X2):		
Cash	$ 295,000	$ 20,000
Accounts receivable, net	400,000	80,000
Inventory	700,000	130,000
Investment in Salt Company	400,000	
Land	500,000	100,000
Buildings and equipment	3,100,000	550,000
Accumulated depreciation	(600,000)	(80,000)
	$4,795,000	$800,000
Accounts payable and accruals	$ 495,000	$ 60,000
Long-term debt	2,000,000	300,000
Common stock	20,000	50,000
Additional paid-in capital	480,000	200,000
Retained earnings	1,800,000	190,000
	$4,795,000	$800,000
Dividends declared during 19X2	$ 800,000	

Required:

1. Prepare the consolidation elimination entries at December 31, 19X2.
2. Prepare a consolidating statement worksheet at December 31, 19X2. (The parent's retained earnings as of January 1, 19X2, was $1,100,000.)

5

The Purchase Method of Accounting: Partially Owned Subsidiaries and Block Acquisitions

AN OVERVIEW OF ACCOUNTING FOR MINORITY INTERESTS

Most subsidiaries are wholly owned. However, there are numerous partially owned subsidiaries, for the following reasons: (1) the parent has chosen not to purchase all of the outstanding common stock; (2) the parent is unable to locate a small number of stockholders; (3) some stockholders refuse to sell their shares to the parent company at its offering price; and (4) the parent sells a portion of its holdings in a wholly owned subsidiary to raise cash or merely to reduce its holdings (the accounting for this is discussed in Chapter 10).

When the parent owns less than 100% of the subsidiary's common stock, the consolidation process outlined in Chapter 4 becomes more complicated because special procedures are required to account for the interest of the subsidiary's other stockholders, hereafter called **minority interest.** This chapter uses examples from Chapters 3 and 4, adjusted to reflect only partial ownership, to illustrate accounting for partially owned subsidiaries.

CONCEPTUAL ISSUES

Two key conceptual issues arise when a subsidiary is less than 100% owned: (1) whether to use proportional or full consolidation in the consolidated financial statements, and (2) whether to treat the minority interest using the parent company theory or the entity theory.

Conceptual Issue 1: Proportional or Full Consolidation?

Proportional Consolidation. Under *proportional consolidation*, the parent consolidates only its ownership in each of the items in the subsidiary's financial statement. In other words, for an 80%-owned subsidiary we would multiply the subsidiary's cash, accounts receivable, sales, and so forth by 80% to arrive at the amounts to be included in the consolidation. Under this method, accounting for the minority interest in the consolidated financial statements is not necessary because it is not reported there. The rationale underlying proportional consolidation is as follows:

1. The consolidated financial statements should be merely an extension of the parent's financial statements.
2. In substance (although not as a legality), the parent has a percentage interest in each of the subsidiary's assets, liabilities, revenues, and expenses.
3. The consolidated financial statements should be the same whether the acquiring company purchases 80% of the assets or 80% of the common stock.

In recent years, proportional consolidation has become one of several methods of accounting for investments in real estate partnerships and construction joint ventures. Moreover, it has been advocated increasingly for consolidated financial statements. Currently however, the requirements of *ARB No. 51* (presently under reconsideration by the Financial Standards Accounting Board [FASB]) allow only full consolidation.

Full Consolidation. Under *full consolidation*, the parent consolidates the entire amount of each of the subsidiary's individual assets, liability, and income statement accounts with those of the parent company. Because the subsidiary is only partially owned, however, the additional amounts consolidated constitute the minority interest. Therefore, the minority interest in the subsidiary's net assets and net income are reported as separate items in the consolidated financial statements. The rationale underlying full consolidation is as follows:

1. The parent does not have a separable percentage interest in each individual asset, liability, and income statement account of the subsidiary. Its ownership interest is a percentage of the net assets and net income as a whole.
2. The parent controls all of the subsidiary even though its ownership is less than 100%.
3. The purpose of consolidated statements is to combine the operations of the parent and the subsidiary as though they were a single company.

Conceptual Issue 2: Classification of Minority Interest under Full Consolidation

Two theories have evolved concerning the treatment of the minority interest under full consolidation in consolidated financial statements:

1. The parent company only theory and
2. The entity theory. Both methods of treatment are discussed below.

The Parent Company Theory. The *parent company theory* assumes that the reporting entity does not change as a result of the consolidation process. Consolidated reporting merely represents a different manner of reporting the parent's financial position and the results of its operations. Thus, **the parent company is still considered the reporting entity.** As a result, (1) the interest of the minority shareholders is not considered an equity interest of the consolidated reporting entity, and (2) consolidated net income equals the parent's net income (which includes its share of the subsidiary's net income through application of the equity method of accounting). Therefore, the minority interest is presented in the consolidated financial statements as follows:

1. **In the consolidated balance sheet:** The minority interest in the subsidiary's net assets is treated as an outside interest and is shown

outside the stockholders' equity section in one of the following two ways:

a. **Between liabilities and stockholders' equity:** This presentation reflects the unique nature of the minority interest. It is an equity interest, but not of the parent company, which is the reporting entity.
b. **Among liabilities:** This presentation has little or no supporting theory. However, if the minority interest is insignificant and a separate classification is unwarranted, companies commonly classify it among liabilities.

2. **In the consolidated income statement:** The minority interest in the subsidiary's net income is shown as a deduction in the consolidated income statement in arriving at the consolidated net income. For example, assuming that an 80%-owned subsidiary had net income of $15,000 for the year, the minority interest deduction would be $3,000 (20% of $15,000) and would be presented as follows:

	Consolidated Income Statement
Revenues	$800,000
Cost of goods sold	(476,000)
Expenses	(273,000)
Minority interest in net income of subsidiary	(3,000)
Net Income	$ 48,000

The Entity Theory. The *entity theory* assumes that the reporting entity has changed as a result of the consolidation process. **A new reporting entity is deemed to exist.** This new reporting entity has two classes of equity interests—the controlling interest (the parent's shareholders) and the minority interest. Because the nature of these interests is the same, they must be treated the same way in consolidated financial statements. As a result, (1) the interest of the minority shareholders is treated as an equity interest of the consolidated reporting entity, and (2) consolidated net income equals the combined net incomes of both companies (without the application of the equity method of accounting). The minority interest is presented in the consolidated financial statements as follows:

1. **In the consolidated balance sheet,** the minority interest in the subsidiary's net assets is shown as a separate category within the stockholders' equity section.
2. **In the consolidated income statement,** the minority interest in the subsidiary's net income is shown as a portion of the total net income of the consolidated entity. Using the same amounts as in the above example, we can present the consolidated income statement as follows:

	Consolidated Income Statement
Revenues	$800,000
Cost of goods sold	(476,000)
Expenses	(273,000)
Net Income	$ 51,000
Division of net income:	
To controlling interest	$ 48,000
To minority interest	3,000
Total Net Income	$ 51,000

Whether the parent company theory or the entity theory is correct depends on whether the reporting entity is considered to have changed as a result of the consolidation process—a purely subjective evaluation. The minority shareholders do not influence the parent's operating policies. Thus, the consolidated financial statements are usually of no benefit whatsoever to the minority shareholders. This group is entitled only to the financial statements of the partially owned subsidiary. Minority shareholders who desire a set of the consolidated financial statements must make a formal request to the parent.

ARB No. 51 does not indicate how minority interest should be presented in consolidated financial statements. However, it does state that consolidated financial statements are prepared primarily for the benefit of the parent's shareholders and creditors.[1] This provision is consistent with the parent company theory but not with the entity theory. In practice, the minority interest is presented in consolidated financial statements almost exclusively in accordance with the parent company theory. For these reasons, the income statement sections of the consolidating statement worksheets presented later in this chapter are consistent with the parent company theory, under which the minority interest in the subsidiary's net income is shown as a deduction in arriving at the consolidated net income. (As this book goes to print, the FASB is addressing the minority interest presentation issue in its project on consolidations and the equity method of accounting.)

A later section focuses on how the conceptual analysis of the investment account can be slightly modified to present the minority interest in the consolidated financial statements.

Treatment of Dividends Paid to Minority Shareholders

Chapter 4 stated that dividend payments from a wholly owned subsidiary to the parent constitute intercompany transactions and are therefore not

[1] *Accounting Research Bulletin No. 51*, "Consolidated Financial Statements" (New York: American Institute of Certified Public Accountants, 1959), par. 1.

reported as dividends in the consolidated statement of retained earnings. Such transactions do not take place between the consolidated group and outsiders. This is not the case, however, with dividends paid to minority-interest shareholders in partially owned subsidiaries. Such dividends cannot be added to those declared by the parent in preparing the consolidated statement of retained earnings. The reason is obvious. The consolidated retained earnings include only the earnings of the subsidiary that accrue to the parent. Including dividends paid to minority shareholders with dividends paid to the parent's shareholders would be inconsistent. Instead, the subsidiary's dividends that accrue to the minority shareholders are treated as a reduction of the minority interest.

Including Minority Interest in the Conceptual Analysis of the Investment Account

When a minority interest exists, an extra column (called "minority interest") is added to the conceptual analysis of the investment account. The column is placed to the left of the total cost column. The initial amount appearing in this column is the minority interest in the subsidiary's net assets at their book value. All subsequent amounts appearing in the column to update the analysis are based on the changes in the subsidiary's book value. The following sections illustrate this.

NEITHER GOODWILL NOR A BARGAIN PURCHASE ELEMENT EXISTS AND NET ASSETS ARE NOT OVER- OR UNDERVALUED

When the parent's cost equals the parent's ownership interest in the current value of the subsidiary's net assets and the current value equals the book value, only the book value element exists. The following illustration shows how to deal with the book value element in the conceptual analysis of the investment account when the subsidiary is partially owned.

Illustration

PREPARING CONSOLIDATED FINANCIAL STATEMENTS AS OF THE ACQUISITION DATE

Assume the same information for P Company and S Company as provided in situation A of Illustration 3-6 (in which total cost was $60,000 and the book value and current value were also $60,000), except assume that P Company acquired only 80% of S Company's outstanding common stock at a cost of $48,000 (rather than 100% at a cost of $60,000). The expanded analysis of the investment account as of the acquisition date is as follows:

Date		Total Cost	=	Common Stock	+	Retained Earnings
				Book Value Element		
January 1, 19X1		$48,000		$32,000 (80% of $40,000)		$16,000 (80% of $20,000)
Format modification for minority interest:						
	Minority Interest (20% of $60,000)					
Add minority interest	$12,000			8,000 (20% of $40,000)		4,000 (20% of $20,000)
Modified balances:	$12,000 +	$48,000	=	$40,000	+	$20,000

From this analysis of the investment account, the primary elimination entry as of the acquisition date is as follows:

Common Stock	40,000	
Retained Earnings..	20,000	
Investment in Subsidiary..........................		48,000
Minority Interest in Net Assets of S Company..		12,000

Reformatting the conceptual analysis of the investment account as shown above allows the minority interest to be established as one amount. This amount is always equal to the minority interest ownership percentage times the book value of the subsidiary's net assets (20% of $60,000 in this example).

Illustration 5-1 shows a consolidating statement worksheet as of January 1, 19X1 (the acquisition date), using the above information.

In addition to making the primary elimination entry, it is necessary to eliminate the subsidiary's accumulated depreciation as of the acquisition date to reflect that a new basis of accounting has been established. Even though only 80% of the common stock was acquired, the elimination is made at 100% of the accumulated depreciation balance of $45,000.[2]

Accumulated Depreciation..............................	45,000	
Buildings and Equipment		45,000

[2]In July 1986, the authors discussed with the staff of the Securities and Exchange Commission whether all of the accumulated depreciation should be eliminated or only a portion based on the parent's ownership percentage. The staff's unofficial position was that it makes the most sense to eliminate 100% of the accumulated depreciation.

Illustration 5-1
Consolidating Statement Worksheet as of the Acquisition Date

P COMPANY AND SUBSIDIARY (S COMPANY)
Consolidating Statement Worksheet
As of January 1, 19X1

	P Company	S Company	Eliminations Dr.	Eliminations Cr.	Consolidated
Balance Sheet:					
Cash	62,000	20,000			82,000
Accounts receivable, net	70,000	23,000			93,000
Inventory	100,000	32,000			132,000
Investment in S Company	48,000			48,000(1)	–0–
Land	200,000	30,000			230,000
Buildings and equipment	500,000	190,000		45,000(2)	645,000
Accumulated depreciation	(280,000)	(45,000)	45,000(2)		(280,000)
Total Assets	700,000	250,000	45,000	93,000	902,000
Liabilities	300,000	190,000			490,000
Minority interest in net assets of S Company				12,000(1)	12,000
P Company:					
Common stock	300,000				300,000
Retained earnings	100,000				100,000
S Company:					
Common stock		40,000	40,000(1)		–0–
Retained earnings		20,000	20,000(1)		–0–
Total Liabilities and Equity	700,000	250,000	60,000	12,000	902,000
Proof of debit and credit postings			105,000	105,000	

Explanation of entries:
(1) The primary elimination entry.
(2) The accumulated depreciation elimination entry.

Illustration

PREPARING CONSOLIDATED FINANCIAL STATEMENTS FOR FIRST YEAR SUBSEQUENT TO THE ACQUISITION DATE

Assume the subsidiary in the preceding illustration had a net income of $15,000 in 19X1 and declared dividends of $5,000 in that year. Under the equity method of accounting, the parent would report its share of these amounts. The expanded analysis of the investment account would be updated as follows:

				Book Value Element		
				Retained Earnings		
					Current Year	
	Minority Interest (20%) +	Total Cost =	Common Stock +	Prior Years	+ Earnings	− Dividends
Balance, January 1, 19X1	$12,000	$48,000	$40,000	$20,000		
Equity in net income:						
To Parent		12,000			$12,000	
To Minority Interest	3,000				3,000	
Dividends declared:						
To Parent		(4,000)				$(4,000)
To Minority Interest	(1,000)					(1,000)
Subtotal	$14,000	$56,000	$40,000	$20,000	$15,000	$(5,000)
Reclassification				10,000	(15,000)	5,000
Balance, December 31, 19X1	$14,000	$56,000	$40,000	$30,000	$ -0-	$ -0-

Consolidated financial statements as of December 31, 19X1, would be prepared using the following primary elimination entry:

Common Stock	40,000	
Retained Earnings	20,000	
Equity in Net Income of Subsidiary	12,000	
Minority Interest in Net Income	3,000	
Dividends Declared		5,000
Investment in Subsidiary		56,000
Minority Interest in Net Assets of S Company		14,000

The above entry is posted to the consolidating statement worksheet as of December 31, 19X1, in Illustration 5-2. (Also posted is the accumulated depreciation elimination entry for $45,000.)

The following points are important for understanding this illustration:

1. The same equalities and control features that existed for wholly owned subsidiaries exist for partially owned subsidiaries. That is, the net income and retained earnings amounts in the P Company column are the same as the comparable items in the consolidated column.
2. The minority interest in the net assets of the subsidiary ($14,000) can be proved by multiplying the minority interest ownership percentage (20%) by the total stockholders' equity of the subsidiary ($70,000).

Illustration 5-2
Consolidating Statement Worksheet for First Year Subsequent to Acquisition Date

P COMPANY AND SUBSIDIARY (S COMPANY)
Consolidating Statement Worksheet
For the Year Ended December 31, 19X1

	P Company	S Company	Eliminations Dr.	Eliminations Cr.	Consolidated
Income Statement:					
Sales	600,000	200,000			800,000
Cost of goods sold	(360,000)	(116,000)			(476,000)
Expenses	(204,000)	(69,000)			(273,000)
Intercompany Account:					
Equity in net income of S Company	12,000		12,000(1)		–0–
Income before Minority Int.	48,000	15,000	12,000		51,000
Minority interest			3,000(1)		(3,000)
Net Income	48,000	15,000	15,000		48,000
Statement of Retained Earnings:					
Balances, January 1, 19X1	100,000	20,000	20,000(1)		100,000
+ Net income	48,000	15,000	15,000		48,000
− Dividends declared	(31,000)	(5,000)		5,000(1)	(31,000)
Balances, December 31, 19X1	117,000	30,000	35,000	5,000	117,000
Balance Sheet:					
Cash	86,000	25,000			111,000
Accounts receivable, net	75,000	43,000			118,000
Inventory	110,000	40,000			150,000
Investment in S Company	56,000			56,000(1)	–0–
Land	200,000	30,000			230,000
Buildings and equipment	500,000	190,000		45,000(2)	645,000
Accumulated depreciation	(320,000)	(58,000)	45,000(2)		(333,000)
Total Assets	707,000	270,000	45,000	101,000	921,000
Liabilities	290,000	200,000			490,000
Minority interest in net assets of S Company				14,000(1)	14,000
P Company:					
Common stock	300,000				300,000
Retained earnings	117,000				117,000
S Company:					
Common stock		40,000	40,000(1)		–0–
Retained earnings		30,000	35,000(1)	5,000	–0–
Total Liabilities and Equity	707,000	270,000	75,000	19,000	921,000
Proof of debit and credit postings			120,000	120,000	

Explanation of entries:
(1) The primary elimination entry.
(2) The accumulated depreciation elimination entry.

GOODWILL EXISTS AND NET ASSETS ARE UNDERVALUED

When the parent company's cost is more (or less) than its share of the book value of the subsidiary's net assets, the immediate question is this: "Does the push-down basis of accounting have to be used?" For partially owned subsidiaries, the Securities and Exchange Commission (SEC) requires push-down accounting only in certain circumstances. Accordingly, we first focus on non-push-down accounting. Later we discuss when push-down accounting is required and how to apply it.

The Parent Company Theory: The Non-push-down Basis of Accounting

In the preceding two illustrations, the subsidiary's net assets were not over- or undervalued and goodwill did not exist. The cost to the parent of acquiring 80% of the outstanding common stock was 80% of the book value of the subsidiary's net assets. When the subsidiary has undervalued assets or goodwill, or both, the parent's cost in excess of its ownership interest in the book value of the subsidiary's net assets logically depends on the parent's ownership interest. For example, assume that the subsidiary has undervalued assets worth $20,000. If the acquiring company is willing to pay $20,000 in excess of the book value of the net assets for all of the outstanding common stock, then for an 80% ownership interest the acquiring company should be willing to pay only $16,000 in excess of its ownership interest in the book value of the net assets. Similarly, if the acquiring company is willing to pay $10,000 for goodwill in acquiring all of the common stock, then it should be willing to pay only $8,000 for goodwill if it acquired only an 80% ownership interest.

Separating Total Cost into the Major Conceptual Elements. Knowing the factors that help determine total cost in partial ownership situations, we may separate the total cost into its major conceptual elements using the following procedures:

1. The minority interest ownership percentage is multiplied by the book value of the subsidiary's stockholders' equity to obtain the amount for the minority interest column.
2. The book value element is maintained at 100% of the book value of the subsidiary's stockholders' equity.
3. The parent's ownership percentage is multiplied by the undervaluation of the subsidiary's net assets to obtain the current value over book value element.
4. The goodwill element is determined by:
   a. Adding together the parent's cost and the minority interest in the subsidiary's stockholders' equity.
   b. Subtracting from the total in (a) the totals in the book value element and the current value over (under) the book value element.

Thus, the goodwill element is determined in a residual manner.

In situation E of Illustration 3-6, P Company acquired 100% of the outstanding common stock of S Company at a cost of $90,000, which was $30,000 in excess of the book value of the subsidiary's net assets. The $30,000 excess payment was identified as undervalued assets ($20,000) and goodwill ($10,000). Assume instead that P Company purchased only 80% of the outstanding common stock for $72,000 (80% of $90,000). The separation of the total cost into its major conceptual elements is as follows:

Minority Interest (20% of $60,000)	+	Total Cost	=	Book Value Element (100% of $60,000)	+	Current Value over Book Value Element (80% of $20,000)	+	Goodwill Element (Residual)
$12,000		$72,000		$60,000		$16,000		$8,000

Separating the Major Conceptual Elements into Their Components. We separate the current value over book value element into its components by multiplying the parent's ownership percentages by the amount that each asset is undervalued. In Illustration 3-7, the $20,000 undervaluation was attributed to Inventory, Land, and Equipment accounts. This $20,000 is separated into its components as follows:

Asset	Total Current Value over Book Value	Parent's Ownership Percentage	Parent's Interest in Current Value over Book Value
Inventory	$ 2,000	80%	$ 1,600
Land	12,000	80%	9,600
Equipment........	6,000	80%	4,800
	$20,000		$16,000

The expanded analysis of the investment account by the components of the major conceptual elements is as follows:

Book value element:		
Common stock..	$40,000	
Retained earnings	20,000	$60,000
Current value over book value element:		
Inventory	$ 1,600	
Land	9,600	
Equipment...	4,800	16,000
Goodwill element		8,000
Total of major elements.......................		$84,000
Total cost (the parent's cost)........................		$72,000
Minority interest		12,000
		$84,000

The primary elimination entry obtained with this procedure (which would be used only if non-push-down accounting were used) revalues the subsidiary's assets to their current values **only to the extent that such undervaluation is paid for by the parent company** ($16,000 in this example). Likewise, goodwill is reflected in the consolidated financial statements only to the extent that it is paid for by the parent company ($8,000 in this example). This approach results in **partial revaluation** of the subsidiary's assets, which is consistent with the parent company theory.

A different revaluation result occurs under the entity theory, which is discussed in Appendix A. We now illustrate the preparation of consolidated financial statements (as of the acquisition date and in years subsequent to the acquisition date) using the partial revaluation results that occur under the parent company theory.

Illustration

PREPARING CONSOLIDATED FINANCIAL STATEMENTS AS OF THE ACQUISITION DATE WHEN THE SUBSIDIARY USES NON-PUSH-DOWN ACCOUNTING

For this example, the primary elimination entry as of the acquisition date, taken from the expanded analysis of the investment account, is as follows:

Common Stock	40,000	
Retained Earnings	20,000	
Inventory	1,600	
Land	9,600	
Equipment	4,800	
Goodwill	8,000	
Investment in Subsidiary		72,000
Minority Interest in Net Assets of S Company		12,000

This primary elimination entry is used in Illustration 5-3 to prepare a consolidating statement worksheet as of January 1, 19X1 (the acquisition date), for P Company and S Company.

The amount reported in consolidation for each of the subsidiary's undervalued assets is the book value of the asset plus 80% of the undervaluation—not 80% of the current value. For example, note the following for land:

Current value	$42,000
Amount reported in consolidation (100% of book value of $30,000 plus 80% of the undervaluation of $12,000)	$39,600
Book value	$30,000

Illustration 5-3
Consolidating Statement Worksheet: Non-push-down Accounting Used by Subsidiary

P COMPANY AND SUBSIDIARY (S COMPANY)
Consolidating Statement Worksheet
As of January 1, 19X1

	P Company	S Company	Eliminations Dr.	Eliminations Cr.	Consolidated
Balance Sheet:					
Cash	38,000	20,000			58,000
Accounts receivable, net	70,000	23,000			93,000
Inventory	100,000	32,000	1,600(1)		133,600
Investment in S Company	72,000			72,000(1)	–0–
Land	200,000	30,000	9,600(1)		239,600
Buildings and equipment	500,000	190,000	4,800(1)	45,000(2)	649,800
Accumulated depreciation	(280,000)	(45,000)	45,000(2)		(280,000)
Goodwill			8,000(1)		8,000
Total Assets	700,000	250,000	69,000	117,000	902,000
Liabilities	300,000	190,000			490,000
Minority interest in net assets of S Company				12,000(1)	12,000
P Company:					
Common stock	300,000				300,000
Retained earnings	100,000				100,000
S Company:					
Common stock		40,000	40,000(1)		–0–
Retained earnings		20,000	20,000(1)		–0–
Total Liabilities and Equity	700,000	250,000	60,000	12,000	902,000
Proof of debit and credit postings			129,000	129,000	

Explanation of entries:
(1) The primary elimination entry.
(2) The accumulated depreciation elimination entry.

Land is not reported in consolidation at 80% of the current value of $42,000 (or $33,600).

Illustration

UPDATING THE EXPANDED ANALYSIS OF THE INVESTMENT ACCOUNT USING THE EQUITY METHOD

Assume that S Company had the following earnings, losses, dividends, and amortization of cost over book value for the two years subsequent to the acquisition date:

	19X1	19X2
Net income	$15,000	$21,000
Dividends	5,000	–0–
Amortization of cost in excess of book value	3,200	1,600

Illustration 5-4 shows an expanded analysis of the investment account for two years following the acquisition date, using the above information.

Illustration

PREPARING CONSOLIDATED FINANCIAL STATEMENTS FOR THE FIRST AND SECOND YEARS SUBSEQUENT TO THE ACQUISITION DATE WHEN THE SUBSIDIARY USES NON-PUSH-DOWN ACCOUNTING

The consolidated financial statements as of December 31, 19X1 (one year after the acquisition date), and December 31, 19X2 (two years after the acquisition date), are prepared using the following primary, secondary, and accumulated depreciation elimination entries.

1. The primary elimination entry:

	Consolidation Date			
	December 31, 19X1		December 31, 19X2	
Common Stock	40,000		40,000	
Retained Earnings (beginning-of-year balance)	20,000		30,000	
Equity in Net Income of Subsidiary	12,000		16,800	
Minority Interest in Net Income of S Company	3,000		4,200	
Land	9,600		9,600	
Equipment	4,800		4,800	
Goodwill	7,200		6,400	
Dividends Declared		5,000		–0–
Accumulated Depreciation		800		1,600
Investment in S Company		76,800		92,000
Minority Interest in Net Assets of S Company		14,000		18,200

2. The secondary elimination entry:

Cost of Goods Sold	3,200		1,600	
Amortization of Cost in Excess of Book Value		3,200		3,200

Illustration 5-4
Updating the Expanded Analysis of the Investment Account Using the Equity Method: 80%-owned Subsidiary

					Book Value Element			Current Value over Book Value Element				
					Retained Earnings					Equipment		
						Current Year						
Remaining life	Minority Interest (20%) +	Total Cost =	Common Stock +	Prior Years +	Earnings −	Dividends +	Inventory (3 Mo.) +	Land (Indefinite) +	Cost	Accum. Depr. (6 Yrs.) +	Goodwill Element (10 Yrs.)
Balance, Jan. 1, 19X1	$12,000[a]	$72,000	$40,000	$20,000			$1,600	$9,600	$4,800		$8,000
Equity in Net Income:											
To Parent		12,000			$12,000						
To Minority Interest	3,000[a]				3,000						
Dividends:											
To Parent		(4,000)				$(4,000)					
To Minority Interest	(1,000)[a]					(1,000)					
Amortization		(3,200)					(1,600)			(800)	(800)
Subtotal	$14,000	$76,800	$40,000	$20,000	$15,000	$(5,000)	$ –0–	$9,600	$4,800	$ (800)	$7,200
Reclassification				10,000	(15,000)	5,000					
Balance, Dec. 31, 19X1	$14,000	$76,800	$40,000	$30,000	$ –0–	$ –0–	$ –0–	$9,600	$4,800	$ (800)	$7,200
Equity in Net Income:											
To Parent		16,800			16,800						
To Minority Interest	4,200[a]				4,200						
Amortization		(1,600)								(800)	(800)
Subtotal	$18,200	$92,000	$40,000	$30,000	$21,000	$ –0–	$ –0–	$9,600	$4,800	$(1,600)	$6,400
Reclassification				21,000	(21,000)						
Balance, Dec. 31, 19X2	$18,200	$92,000	$40,000	$51,000	$ –0–	$ –0–	$ –0–	$9,600	$4,800	$(1,600)	$6,400

[a]No general ledger entry is necessary in the parent's books.

3. The accumulated depreciation elimination entry:

Accumulated Depreciation........	45,000		45,000	
Buildings and Equipment......		45,000		45,000

Illustration 5-5 shows the consolidating statement worksheet as of December 31, 19X1.

The Parent Company Theory: The Push-down Basis of Accounting

When to apply it. When a subsidiary has preferred stock outstanding, public debt outstanding, or a substantial minority interest, the parent is presumed to be unable to control the form of its ownership in the acquired business. In other words, it probably could not legally liquidate the subsidiary into a division if it desired. In such cases, *SEC Staff Accounting Bulletin No. 54* does not require the push-down basis of accounting to be used.

In the absence of preferred stock or public debt outstanding, the SEC staff uses the following guidelines for determining when a firm should use push-down accounting:

Parent's Ownership Percentage	Guidelines
90% or more	Substantially owned. Push-down accounting is required.
80–89%	Push-down accounting is encouraged but not required.
Below 80%	Push-down accounting may not be appropriate.

How to apply it. The position of the staff of the SEC on how to apply push-down accounting for partially owned subsidiaries is that revaluation of the subsidiary's assets should be made only to the extent of the parent's cost in excess of book value. No revaluation should be made to the minority interest—it is still to be based on the book value of the subsidiary's stockholders' equity (excluding the credit made to Additional Paid-in Capital in the revaluation process). Thus, push-down accounting is to be applied using the parent company theory. From the information in Illustration 5-4, the following entries would be made as of the acquisition date:

Illustration 5-5
Consolidating Statement Worksheet: Non-push-down Accounting Used by Subsidiary

P COMPANY AND SUBSIDIARY (S COMPANY)
Consolidating Statement Worksheet
For the Year Ended December 31, 19X1

	P Company	S Company	Eliminations Dr.	Eliminations Cr.	Consolidated
Income Statement:					
Sales	600,000	200,000			800,000
Cost of goods sold	(360,000)	(116,000)	3,200(2)		(479,200)
Expenses	(204,000)	(69,000)			(273,000)
Intercompany Accounts:					
Equity in net income of S Company	12,000		12,000(1)		–0–
Amortization of cost in excess of book value	(3,200)			3,200(2)	–0–
Income before Minority Int.	44,800	15,000	15,200	3,200	47,800
Minority interest			3,000(1)		(3,000)
Net Income	44,800	15,000	18,200	3,200	44,800
Statement of Retained Earnings:					
Balances, January 1, 19X1	100,000	20,000	20,000(1)		100,000
+ Net income	44,800	15,000	→ 18,200	→ 3,200	44,800
− Dividends declared	(31,000)	(5,000)		5,000(1)	(31,000)
Balances, December 31, 19X1	113,800	30,000	38,200	8,200	113,800
Balance Sheet:					
Cash	62,000	25,000			87,000
Accounts receivable, net	75,000	43,000			118,000
Inventory	110,000	40,000			150,000
Investment in S Company	76,800			76,800(1)	–0–
Land	200,000	30,000	9,600(1)		239,600
Buildings and equipment	500,000	190,000	4,800(1)	45,000(3)	649,800
Accumulated depreciation	(320,000)	(58,000)	45,000(3)	800(1)	(333,800)
Goodwill			7,200(1)		7,200
Total Assets	703,800	270,000	66,600	122,600	917,800
Liabilities	290,000	200,000			490,000
Minority interest in net assets of S Company				14,000(1)	14,000
P Company:					
Common stock	300,000				300,000
Retained earnings	113,800				113,800
S Company:					
Common stock		40,000	40,000(1)		–0–
Retained earnings		30,000	→ 38,200	→ 8,200	–0–
Total Liabilities and Equity	703,800	270,000	78,200	22,200	917,800
Proof of debit and credit postings			144,800	144,800	

Explanation of entries:
(1) The primary elimination entry.
(2) The secondary elimination entry.
(3) The accumulated depreciation elimination entry.

1. To revalue assets:

Inventory	**1,600**	
Land	**9,600**	
Equipment	**4,800**	
Goodwill	**8,000**	
Additional Paid-in Capital		**24,000**

2. To eliminate retained earnings:

Retained Earnings	**20,000**	
Additional Paid-in Capital		**20,000**
(100% of $20,000)		

3. To eliminate the accumulated depreciation account:[3]

Accumulated Depreciation	**45,000**	
Buildings and Equipment		**45,000**
(100% of $45,000)		

After applying push-down accounting, the parent's conceptual analysis of the investment account would be comprised of only the book value element, as shown below:

				Book Value Element		
Date	Minority Interest (20%)	+	Total Cost	= Common Stock	+ Add'l Paid-in Capital	+ Retained Earnings
January 1, 19X1	$12,000		$72,000	$40,000	$44,000	$ –0–

From this analysis, the following primary elimination entry would be made in preparing consolidated financial statements as of the acquisition date:

Common Stock	**40,000**	
Additional Paid-in Capital	**44,000**	
Investment in Subsidiary		**72,000**
Minority Interest in Net Assets of S Company		**12,000**

[3]As mentioned in footnote 2, the unofficial position of the staff of the SEC is that it makes the most sense to eliminate 100% of the accumulated depreciation.

Consolidating statement worksheet illustrations under push-down accounting are not shown, as their preparation is less involved than earlier illustrations under non-push-down accounting.

COST IS BELOW THE PARENT'S OWNERSHIP INTEREST IN THE BOOK VALUE OF THE SUBSIDIARY'S NET ASSETS

When the parent's cost is below its ownership interest in the book value of the subsidiary's net assets, the procedures for analyzing the investment account by the components of the major conceptual elements are identical with those previously illustrated. The only difference is that the second major conceptual element — the current value over (under) book value element — has a negative rather than a positive balance. We do not illustrate preparing consolidated financial statements for these situations, because the procedures are the same as those in which the current value of the subsidiary's net assets exceeds their book value.

BLOCK ACQUISITIONS

All the business combinations illustrated so far (in which a parent–subsidiary relationship was formed) were assumed to result from a single acquisition of the acquired company's outstanding common stock. But in many cases companies gain control over an entity by acquiring blocks of its common stock over a period of time. When the acquiring company attains more than 50% ownership, the acquired company becomes a subsidiary and consolidation procedures are appropriate. Until then, the investor must account for the investment as follows:

1. For **less than 20% ownership,** use the lower of cost or market, as prescribed by *FASB Statement No. 12,* "Accounting for Certain Marketable Securities."
2. For **20% through 50% ownership,** use the equity method of accounting, as prescribed by *APB Opinion No. 18,* "The Equity Method of Accounting for Investments in Common Stock."

When blocks of stock are acquired, *ARB No. 51* governs the determination of the individual components as of the control date so that consolidated financial statements can be prepared:

> When one company purchases two or more blocks of stock of another company at various dates and eventually obtains control of the other company, the date of acquisition (for the purpose of preparing consolidated statements) depends on the circumstances. If two or more purchases are made over a period of time, the earned surplus [current terminology is "retained

> earnings"] of the subsidiary at acquisition should generally be determined on a step-by-step basis; however, if small purchases are made over a period of time and then a purchase is made which results in control, the date of the latest purchase, as a matter of convenience, may be considered as the date of acquisition.[4]

In the **step-by-step method,** the cost of each block of stock acquired is separated into its components of the major conceptual elements using data that apply to the date the block was purchased. Cumulative amounts are then determined for each of the components as of the control date, using the analysis of each block's cost by component. The procedures for analyzing the cost of each block of stock in this way are identical with those discussed earlier in the chapter when the purchase of a single (although large) block of stock resulted in control.

In the **date of latest purchase method,** the total carrying value of the investment, as of the control date, is separated into the components of the major conceptual elements using data that apply only to the date control is obtained. This approach makes the practical (although artificial) assumption that all of the acquired shares were purchased on the date control was obtained. It is identical with the procedures discussed earlier in the chapter when control was achieved in a single purchase. Therefore, it is not illustrated in this section.

It is important to realize that *ARB No. 51* was issued before *APB Opinion No. 18* was issued. When 20–50% ownership levels exist, *APB Opinion No. 18* requires the investor to separate its cost into the components of the major conceptual elements using the step-by-step approach. When less than 20% ownership exists and an additional purchase results in at least 20% ownership, the investor must adjust the investment account "retroactively in a manner consistent with accounting for a step-by-step acquisition of a subsidiary."[5] As a result of *APB Opinion No. 18,* the percentage of those using the date of the latest purchase as the acquisition date has been significantly reduced. In many instances, with several small purchases over a period of time, the investor must use the equity method of accounting on reaching the 20% ownership level. Any blocks acquired beyond the 20% ownership level would be accounted for using the step-by-step method. For the date of latest purchase method to be used, the investor would have to make several small purchases that, cumulatively, do not exceed the 20% ownership level, and then make a large purchase that gives more than 50% ownership—for example, 5%, 5%, 5%, and 40%. In other words, the 20–50% ownership range would have to be bypassed.

[4]*ARB No. 51*, par. 10.

[5]*Opinions of the Accounting Principles Board, No. 18* "The Equity Method of Accounting for Investments in Common Stock" (New York: American Institute of Certified Public Accountants, 1971), par. 19m.

The Step-by-step Method

In the following illustration, an investment accounted for under the equity method is increased until control over the investee is eventually obtained. The step-by-step method is used.

Illustration

PREPARING THE EXPANDED ANALYSIS OF THE INVESTMENT ACCOUNT AS OF THE CONTROL DATE USING THE STEP-BY-STEP METHOD

Assume the following block acquisition information:

			Information Relating to Investee		
					Net Assets
Date of Block Acquisition	Ownership Percentage Acquired	Cost	Common Stock	Retained Earnings[a]	Current Value over Book Value[b]
January 1, 19X1	20	$15,000	$40,000	$ 5,000	$20,000
January 1, 19X2	25	21,750	40,000	15,000	20,000
July 1, 19X2	30[c]	33,500	40,000	35,000	20,000

[a]We assume the investee paid no dividends during the time the block acquisitions were made. Accordingly, the earnings for 19X1 and the first six months of 19X2 are $10,000 and $20,000, respectively.
[b]For simplicity, we assume that the entire undervaluation of net assets relates to a parcel of land held by the subsidiary.
[c]If any additional shares are acquired after July 1, 19X2, the date control is established, the transaction would be considered the acquisition of some or all of the minority interest. The accounting for this is discussed in Chapter 10.

Illustration 5-6 separates the cost of each block of stock into its components using the above information. The following points are important for understanding this illustration:

1. *APB Opinion No. 18* requires investors to amortize the excess of cost over book value to the extent such excess relates to depreciable or amortizable tangible and intangible assets.
2. The information given assumes that the investor can obtain information on the current value of the subsidiary's net assets as of each block acquisition date. Often this is not possible or practicable. In such situations, the entire excess of cost over the investor's interest in the investee's net assets at book value must be assigned to goodwill.[6]
3. The purpose of the schedule is to determine the cumulative amounts in each component of the major conceptual elements as of the control date (July 1, 19X2). This has been done on a step-by-step basis.
4. The July 1, 19X2, balances (after the acquisition of the last block) are the starting point for the procedures the parent must use to account for its investment in the subsidiary.

[6]*APB Opinion No. 18*, par. 19n.

Illustration 5-6

Preparing the Expanded Analysis of the Investment Account as of the Control Date Using the Step-by-step Method

Ownership Percentage Acquired	Date		Total Cost =	Book Value Element: Common Stock +	Book Value Element: Retained Earnings +	Current Value over Book Value Element: Land	+ Goodwill Element[d]
20	Block purchase, January 1, 19X1		$15,000	$ 8,000[a]	$ 1,000[b]	$ 4,000[c]	$2,000)
	Equity in 19X1 net income (20% × $10,000)		2,000		2,000		
	Amortize cost in excess of book value		(500)				(500)
20	Balance, December 31, 19X1		$16,500	$ 8,000	$ 3,000	$ 4,000	$1,500
+25	Block purchase, January 1, 19X2		21,750	10,000	3,750	5,000[e]	3,000
	Equity in net income (6 mo.) (45% × $20,000)		9,000		9,000		
	Amortize cost in excess of book value:						
	Block 1 ($2,000 × ¼ × ½ yr.)		(250)				(250)
	Block 2 ($3,000 × ⅓ × ½ yr.)		(500)				(500)
45	Balance, June 30, 19X2		$46,500	$18,000	$15,750	$ 9,000	$3,750
+30	Block purchase, July 1, 19X2		33,500	12,000	10,500	6,000[f]	5,000
75	Balance, July 1, 19X2		$80,000	$30,000	$26,250	$15,000	$8,750
	Format modification for minority interest:	Minority Interest (25%)					
		$18,750		10,000	8,750		
	Adjusted Balance, July 1, 19X2	$18,750	$80,000	$40,000	$35,000	$15,000	$8,750

[a]Calculated at 20% of $40,000. (Subsequent additions to this column are based on ownership percentages and book values.)
[b]Calculated at 20% of $5,000. (Subsequent additions to this column are based on ownership percentages and book values.)
[c]Calculated at 20% of $20,000.
[d]A remaining life of four years from the initial acquistion date is used to amortize goodwill. Thus, the $3,000 of goodwill from the second block purchase has a three-year life.
[e]Calculated at 25% of $20,000.
[f]Calculated at 30% of $20,000.

5. The primary elimination entry that would be used in preparing consolidated financial statements as of July 1, 19X2, is as follows:

Common Stock	40,000	
Retained Earnings	35,000	
Land	15,000	
Goodwill	8,750	
Investment in Subsidiary		80,000
Minority Interest in Net Assets		18,750

6. For all subsequent periods, the two additional separate retained earnings columns must be used in the analysis of the investment account to isolate the parent's share of the subsidiary's future earnings and dividends. These additional columns were not necessary in prior periods, because consolidated financial statements could not be prepared (the ownership was not more than 50%).

CONSOLIDATED STATEMENT OF CASH FLOWS

When a consolidated balance sheet and income statement are presented, a consolidated statement of cash flows is also necessary. A few additional areas require special consideration when the statement of cash flows is prepared on a consolidated basis rather than on a separate-company-only basis. These areas of special consideration are discussed later in this chapter.

The Two Approaches

Two approaches can be used to prepare the consolidated statement of cash flows: (1) combining the separate statements and (2) analyzing the changes in the consolidated balance sheets. Regardless of which approach is taken, a parent company usually requires each subsidiary to submit a statement of cash flows to facilitate its preparation of the consolidated statement. Thus, information is provided for each company within the consolidated group as to property additions, retirements, depreciation expense, borrowings, and repayments—items commonly set out separately in a statement of cash flows.

Combining the Separate Statements Approach. A multicolumn worksheet can be used to consolidate the separate company statements of cash flows. The columnar headings for the worksheet would be as follows:

P Company	S Company	Eliminations		Consolidated
		Dr.	Cr.	

This approach is practical when no intercompany inventory, fixed asset, or bond transactions have occurred. (These topics are covered in Chapters 7, 8, and 9.) Elimination entries are needed only to: (1) eliminate the parent's interest in the subsidiary's net income (to prevent double-counting); (2) eliminate intercompany dividends; and (3) eliminate the minority interest in the subsidiary's net income and reflect the minority interest deduction as a charge that did not require the use of funds. (We explain the last point more fully later.)

Analyzing the Changes in the Consolidated Balance Sheet Approach. A company can use its consolidated balance sheets for the beginning and end of a year to prepare a statement of cash flows. The change in each individual account balance for the year is analyzed in terms of sources and uses of cash. (This approach was covered in intermediate accounting.) When transactions for intercompany inventory fixed assets, or bonds have occurred, this method is much quicker because these intercompany transactions have been eliminated (as shown in later chapters) in preparing the consolidated balance sheet and income statement. Thus, these intercompany transactions are not dealt with again in preparing the consolidated statement of cash flows, as they must be under the combining the separate statements approach.

Areas Requiring Special Consideration

The following areas require special consideration in preparing the consolidated statement of cash flows:

1. Amortization of cost in excess of book value.
2. Minority interest.
3. Subsidiary with preferred stock.
4. Changes in the parent's ownership interest.

Because items 3 and 4 are covered in Chapters 9 and 10, we now discuss only items 1 and 2.

Amortization of Cost in Excess of Book Value. Recall that when the non-push-down basis of accounting is used in purchase accounting situations, the parent will have amortization of cost in excess of (or below) book value. This amortization is added back to consolidated net income (along with depreciation expense and any other charges that do not require the use of cash) to arrive at the amount of cash provided from operations. (Amortization of cost below book value would be shown as a reduction from consolidated net income because it is a credit that does not result in an inflow of cash.)

Minority Interest. Recall that the minority interest in a subsidiary's net income is shown in the consolidated income statement as a deduction in arriving at consolidated net income. This minority interest deduction, however, does not require the use of cash. Accordingly, it is added back to consolidated net income to arrive at cash provided from operations. Dividends paid to minority shareholders constitute a use of cash and are shown as such in the consolidated statement of cash flows, along with dividends paid to the parent's stockholders.

Illustration

CONSOLIDATING STATEMENT OF CASH FLOWS

Illustration 5-7 shows a consolidating statement of cash flows worksheet using the combining the separate statements approach.

SUMMARY

Under current accounting rules, partially owned subsidiaries must be fully consolidated—proportional consolidation is not allowed. The parent company theory is the predominant way to account for minority interests. First, amounts for minority interest reported in the consolidated financial statements are always based on amounts shown in the subsidiary's separate financial statements. Second, assets and liabilities are revalued to their current values in consolidation only to the extent that the undervaluation is bought and paid for by the parent company. Third, goodwill is reported only to the extent it is paid for. The push-down basis of accounting is required if the parent company has the power to liquidate the subsidiary and thus control the form of ownership. Regardless of which theory is used to account for minority interests, dividends accruing to minority shareholders are treated as a reduction of the minority interest and not as dividends of the consolidated group.

Glossary of New Terms

Block Acquisitions Acquisitions in which blocks of an investee company's outstanding common stock are acquired over time until the ownership level exceeds 50%.

Date of Latest Purchase Method When control over a company is achieved as a result of block acquisitions, the carrying value of the investment as of the control date is separated into the components of the major conceptual elements, using the current values of the subsidiary's assets and liabilities at the date control is obtained.

Entity Theory A theory pertaining to how the assets and liabilities of partially owned subsidiaries and the related minority shareholders' interests in the

Illustration 5-7
Consolidating Statement of Cash Flows

P COMPANY AND SUBSIDIARY (S COMPANY)
Consolidating Statement of Cash Flows For the Year Ended December 31, 19X1

	P Company	S Company	Eliminations Dr.	Eliminations Cr.	Consolidated
Cash flows from operating activities:					
Net income	44,800	15,000	12,000(1)		44,800
Charges (credits) not affecting cash			3,000(3)		
Depreciation expense	40,000	13,000			53,000
Amortization of cost in excess of book value	3,200				3,200
Equity in net income of subsidiary	12,000			12,000(1)	–0–
Net increase in receivables, inventory, and payables	(25,000)	(38,000)			(63,000)
Minority interest in net income of S Company				3,000(3)	3,000
Net cash flow from operating activities	51,000	(10,000)	15,000	15,000	41,000
Cash flows from investing activities:					
Acquisition of 80% of the common stock of S Company	(72,000)			72,000(4)	–0–
Elimination of Investment in S Company at acquisition date:					
Assets of S Company			274,000(4)		(274,000)
Liabilities of S Company				190,000(4)	190,000
Minority interest in S Company				12,000(4)	12,000
Cash of S Company at acquisition date				20,000(5)	20,000
Dividends received from S Company	4,000		4,000(2)		–0–
Net cash flow from investing activities	(68,000)		278,000	294,000	(52,000)
Cash flows from financing activities:					
Increase in long-term debt	–0–	20,000			20,000
Dividends paid	(31,000)	(5,000)		4,000(2)	(32,000)
Net cash flow from financing activities	(31,000)	15,000		4,000	(12,000)
Net Increase (Decrease) in cash	(48,000)	5,000	293,000	313,000	(23,000)

Note: The data used here was taken from Illustrations 5-4 and 5-5. Because liabilities were given in total in Illustration 5-5 (and at January 1, 19X1, in Chapter 3), we assumed that: (1) the parent had long-term debt of $200,000 at the beginning and end of the year; and (2) the subsidiary had $140,000 of long-term debt at the beginning of the year and $160,000 at the end of the year.

Explanation of entries:

(1) To eliminate parent's equity in net income.
(2) To eliminate intercompany dividends.
(3) To eliminate minority interest share of S Company's net income and show the minority interest deduction (that is present in the consolidated income statement) as a charge that did not require the use of cash.
(4) To eliminate the Investment in S Company and reflect the assets, liabilities, and minority interest at the acquisition date.
(5) To show the cash of S Company at the acquisition date.

subsidiary's earnings and net assets should be valued and presented in consolidated financial statements. The foundation of the theory is that a new reporting entity (other than the parent) is deemed to exist as a result of consolidation. Minority interest, therefore, is treated as an equity interest of the new consolidated reporting entity. Assets and liabilities of partially owned subsidiaries are revalued to their full current values as of the date of the business combination. Goodwill value is based on total goodwill implicit in the purchase price.

Minority Interest The interest of the shareholders of a partially owned subsidiary, other than the parent, in the subsidiary's earnings, losses, and net assets.

Parent Company Theory A theory pertaining to how the assets and liabilities of partially owned subsidiaries and the related minority shareholders' interests in the subsidiary's earnings and net assets should be valued and presented in consolidated financial statements. The foundation of the theory is that the parent company is the consolidated reporting entity. Minority interest, therefore, is not treated as an equity interest of the consolidated reporting entity. Assets and liabilities of partially owned subsidiaries are revalued to their current values as of the business combination date only to the extent of the parent's cost over or under its ownership interest in the book value of the subsidiaries' net assets. Goodwill is reported only to the extent that it is paid for by the parent.

Step-by-step Method When control over a company is achieved as a result of block acquisitions, the total carrying value of the investment as of the control date is separated into the individual components of the major conceptual elements by analyzing the cost of each separate block of stock.

Selected References

"Minority Interest: Opposing Views," by Paul Rosenfield and Steven Rubin. *Journal of Accountancy* (March 1986) 78–89.

As evident by the single article listed above, there are few recent attempts to deal with minority interest.

Appendix A
PREPARATION OF CONSOLIDATED FINANCIAL STATEMENTS USING THE COMBINATION ENTITY–PARENT COMPANY APPROACH AND THE ENTITY THEORY

The Entity Theory

In the example used earlier in the discussions of the parent company theory and the push-down basis of accounting, the subsidiary's net assets were undervalued by $20,000 at the acquisition date, and the undervalued assets were revalued upward by $16,000 (80% × $20,000) in consolidation. Some accountants believe that the **subsidiary's identifiable assets**

and liabilities should be fully revalued in consolidation to 100% of their current values, regardless of the parent's ownership interest. They would revalue the subsidiary's assets upward by $20,000 instead of $16,000. The additional $4,000 valuation would be reflected as an increase in the minority interest in the balance sheet. Such additional valuation results in additional amortization charges in future consolidated income statements. However, a corresponding reduction in the amount of consolidated net income is allocated to the minority shareholders. Thus, the amount of consolidated net income allocated to the controlling interests (the parent's shareholders) is not affected. This approach comes under the entity theory, which was discussed earlier in the chapter. Theoretically, the approach has merit in that a partial revaluation of the subsidiary's assets and liabilities results in a hybrid valuation of such items somewhere between their historical costs and their current values. The proponents of this theory feel that it makes more sense to revalue the assets and liabilities to their current values, as this would be more informative. However, because most business combinations involve large companies acquiring significantly smaller companies, the consolidated financial statements would not be that much more meaningful under the full revaluation approach.

Under the entity theory, the value of goodwill in consolidation is based on the amount of goodwill implicit in the transaction. For example, if the parent paid $8,000 for goodwill in acquiring an 80% ownership interest, then the goodwill implicit in the transaction would be $10,000 ($8,000 ÷ 80%). Thus, goodwill would be valued at $10,000 instead of $8,000, and the additional $2,000 valuation would be reflected as an increase to the minority interest in the balance sheet. As in the case of undervalued assets, this additional goodwill results in additional amortization expense in future consolidated income statements. However, a corresponding reduction in the amount of consolidated net income is allocated to the minority shareholders. Therefore, the amount of consolidated net income allocated to the controlling interests (the parent's shareholders) is not affected.

The Combination Entity–Parent Company Approach

A third alternative adopts certain features of both the parent company theory and the entity theory. We refer to this approach as the **combination entity–parent company approach.** Under this approach, the subsidiary's identifiable assets and liabilities are fully revalued in consolidation to 100% of their current values, as is done under the entity theory. However, goodwill is valued in consolidation only to the extent that it is paid for by the parent company, as is done under the parent company theory.

Whether the minority interest should be presented in the consolidated financial statements in accordance with the entity theory or the parent company theory is an arbitrary decision, because the approach is a combination of the two theories. The minority interest is rarely presented under the entity theory; apparently companies that use this combination approach present the minority interest in accordance with the parent company theory.

The Selection of a Valuation Method

The Requirements of the Official Pronouncements. Neither *ARB No. 51* nor *Accounting Principles Board Opinion No. 16* provides explicit guidance on which of the three valuation methods to use. As mentioned in the chapter, however, the staff of the SEC requires push-down accounting to be applied using only the parent company theory. A survey by the staff of the Financial Accounting Standards Board (FASB) in 1976 (seven years before the SEC's *Staff Accounting Bulletin No. 54*) found overwhelming use of the parent company theory and negligible use of the other two valuation theories.[7]

Regardless of the theoretical soundness of the entity theory, we believe that it produces results that are not consistent with the historical cost basis of accounting (which underlies the purchase method) because values are imputed above and beyond cost. The answers to the CPA examination problems from the American Institute for Certified Public Accountants in this area support this position; they show assets and liabilities revalued and goodwill valued only to the extent of the parent company's cost over its ownership interest in the book value of the subsidiary's net assets.

The entity theory and the combination entity–parent company approach make the preparation of consolidated financial statements somewhat more involved. When the parent's ownership interest is close to 100%, using the entity theory or the combination entity–parent company approach usually has no appreciable effect on the balance sheet. (In most business combinations in which common stock is acquired, the parent's ownership is more than 90%.)

For these reasons—as well as for the requirements of *SEC Staff Accounting Bulletin No. 54*—we used the parent company theory instead of the entity theory or the combination entity–parent company approach to illustrate the preparation of consolidated financial statements earlier in the chapter. Consequently, the minority interest presented in the consolidated balance sheet always equals the ownership percentage of the minority shareholders multiplied by the book value of the subsidiary's stockholders' equity. Likewise, the minority interest presented in the consolidated income statement (which is shown as a deduction in arriving at consolidated net income under the parent company theory) is always based on the subsidiary's net income as shown in its separate income statement.

The FASB Looks into the Issue. The FASB is addressing the valuation method issue for minority interest situations in its project on consolidations and the equity method of accounting. It may choose any one of the three valuation methods. Accordingly, in this appendix we focus on how to deal with the additional values reported in consolidation under the entity theory and the combination entity–parent company approach.

[7]The survey results may be found in a FASB discussion memorandum, "Accounting for Business Combinations and Purchased Intangibles," pp. 107, E-8, and E-17.

Illustration

THE COMBINATION ENTITY–PARENT COMPANY APPROACH

Recall that under the combination entity–parent company approach:

1. The subsidiary's net assets are revalued in consolidation to 100% of their current values as of the acquisition date.
2. Goodwill is reported in consolidation only to the extent that it is paid for by the parent company.

In the chapter example that examined the parent company theory, the subsidiary's net assets were undervalued by $20,000. In consolidation, these assets were revalued upward by $16,000 (80% of $20,000). Thus an additional $4,000 of undervaluation must be dealt with under the combination entity–parent company approach. This $4,000 is analyzed as follows:

Asset	Total Current Value over Book Value	Parent's Interest in Undervaluation (80%)	Minority Interest in Undervaluation (20%)
Inventory........	$ 2,000	$ 1,600	$ 400
Land	12,000	9,600	2,400
Building.........	6,000	4,800	1,200
	$20,000	$16,000	$4,000

One way to deal with the $4,000 in consolidation is to add these values into the conceptual analysis of the investment account. Illustration 5-8 shows how this is done. Because the entire additional valuation of $4,000 is added to the minority interest column, no entry is made in the parent company's general ledger.

Illustration

PREPARING CONSOLIDATED FINANCIAL STATEMENTS FOR THE FIRST AND SECOND YEAR SUBSEQUENT TO THE ACQUISITION DATE

For the two years following the acquisition date, the following entries would be made in consolidation:

The primary elimination entry:

Illustration 5-8
Additional Valuation under the Combination Entity–Parent Company Approach

				Book Value Element			Current Value over Book Value Element				
				Retained Earnings					Equipment		
					Current Year						
Remaining life	Minority Interest (20%) +	Total Cost =	Common Stock +	Prior Years +	Earnings −	Dividends +	Inventory (3 Mo.) +	Land (Indefinite) +	Cost (6 Yrs.)	Accum. Depr. (6 Yrs.) +	Goodwill Element (10 Yrs.)
Balances, Jan. 1, 19X1											
(per Illustration 5-4)	$12,000[a]	$72,000	$40,000	$20,000			$1,600	$ 9,600	$4,800		$8,000
Additional valuation	4,000[a]						400[a]	2,400[a]	1,200[a]		
Adjusted Balances, Jan. 1, 19X1	$16,000	$72,000	$40,000	$20,000			$2,000	$12,000	$6,000		$8,000
Equity in Net Income:											
To Parent		12,000			$12,000						
To Minority Interest	3,000[a]				3,000[a]						
Dividends:											
To Parent		(4,000)				$(4,000)					
To Minority Interest	(1,000)[a]					$(1,000)[a]					
Amortization:											
Parent's Share		(3,200)					(1,600)			(800)	(800)
Minority Int.'s Share	(600)[a]						(400)			(200)	
Subtotal	$17,400	$76,800	$40,000	$20,000	$15,000	$(5,000)	$ –0–	12,000	$6,000	$(1,000)	$7,200
Reclassification				10,000	(15,000)	5,000					
Balance, Dec. 31, 19X1	$17,400	$76,800	$40,000	$30,000	$ –0–	$ –0–	$ –0–	$12,000	$6,000	$(1,000)	$7,200
Equity in Net Income:											
To Parent		16,800			16,800						
To Minority Interest	4,200[a]				4,200[a]						
Amortization:											
Parent's Share		(1,600)								(800)	(800)
Minority Int.'s Share	(200)[a]									(200)[a]	
Subtotal	$21,400	$92,000	$40,000	$30,000	$21,000	$ –0–	$ –0–	$12,000	$6,000	$(2,000)	$6,400
Reclassification				21,000	(21,000)						
Balance, December 31, 19X2	$21,400	$92,000	$40,000	$51,000	$ –0–	$ –0–	$ –0–	$12,000	$6,000	$(2,000)	$6,400

[a]No general ledger entry is necessary in the parent's books in keeping track of the minority interest.

	Consolidation Date			
	December 31, 19X1		December 31, 19X2	
Common Stock	40,000		40,000	
Retained Earnings (beginning of year balance)	20,000		30,000	
Equity in Net Income of Subsidiary	12,000		16,800	
Minority Interest in Net Income of S Company	3,000		4,200	
Land	12,000		12,000	
Equipment	6,000		6,000	
Goodwill	7,200		6,400	
Dividends Declared		5,000		–0–
Accumulated Depreciation		1,000		2,000
Investment in Subsidiary		76,800		92,000
Minority Interest in Net Assets of S Company		17,400		21,400

The secondary elimination entry:

Cost of Goods Sold	3,200		1,600	
Amortization of Cost in Excess of Book Value		3,200		1,600

The minority interest additional amortization entry:

Cost of Goods Sold	600		200	
Minority Interest in Net Income of S Company		600		200

The accumulated depreciation elimination entry:

Accumulated Depreciation	45,000		45,000	
Buildings and Equipment		45,000		45,000

Illustration 5-9 shows a consolidating statement worksheet as of December 31, 19X1.

The following points are important for understanding the illustration:

1. The primary elimination entry was obtained from the conceptual analysis of the investment as usually done.
2. Entries 2 and 4 are exactly the same as those used in Illustration 5-5, which illustrated the parent company approach.

Illustration 5-9
Combination Entity–Parent Company Approach (Non-push-down Basis of Accounting Used by Subsidiary)

P COMPANY AND SUBSIDIARY (S COMPANY)
Consolidating Statement Worksheet For the Year Ended December 31, 19X1

	P Company	S Company	Eliminations Dr.	Eliminations Cr.	Consolidated
Income Statement:					
Sales	600,000	200,000			800,000
Cost of goods sold	(360,000)	(116,000)	3,200(2)		(479,800)
Expenses	(204,000)	(69,000)	600(3)		(273,000)
Intercompany Accounts:					
Equity in net income of S Company	12,000		12,000(1)		–0–
Amortization of cost in excess of book value	(3,200)			3,200(2)	–0–
Income before Minority Int.	44,800	15,000	15,800	3,200	47,200
Minority interest			3,000(1)	600(3)	(2,400)
Net Income	44,800	15,000	18,800	3,800	44,800
Statement of Retained Earnings:					
Balances, January 1, 19X1	100,000	20,000	20,000(1)		100,000
+ Net income	44,800	15,000	→ 18,800	→ 3,800	44,800
− Dividends declared	(31,000)	(5,000)		5,000(1)	(31,000)
Balances, December 31, 19X1	113,800	30,000	38,800	8,800	113,800
Balance Sheet:					
Cash	62,000	25,000			87,000
Accounts receivable, net	75,000	43,000			118,000
Inventory	110,000	40,000			150,000
Investment in S Company	76,800			76,800(1)	–0–
Land	200,000	30,000	12,000(1)		242,000
Buildings and equipment	500,000	190,000	6,000(1)	45,000(4)	651,000
Accumulated depreciation	(320,000)	(58,000)	45,000(4)	1,000(1)	(334,000)
Goodwill			7,200(1)		7,200
Total Assets	703,800	270,000	61,200	113,800	921,200
Liabilities	290,000	200,000			490,000
Minority interest in net assets of S Company				17,400(1)	17,400
P Company:					
Common stock	300,000				300,000
Retained earnings	113,800				113,800
S Company:					
Common stock		40,000	40,000(1)		–0–
Retained earnings		30,000	→ 38,800	→ 8,800	–0–
Total Liabilities and Equity	703,800	270,000	78,800	26,200	921,200
Proof of debit and credit postings			140,000	140,000	

Explanation of entries:

(1) The primary elimination entry.
(2) The secondary elimination entry.
(3) The minority interest additional amortization entry.
(4) The accumulated depreciation elimination entry.

3. Entry 3 is a new entry necessary because of the additional values reported under the combination entity–parent company approach. The entry has no effect on the parent's net income or the consolidated net income. An additional $600 is reported for cost of goods sold. However, exactly $600 less is reported for the minority interest deduction in the income statement.
4. The parent company's net income and the consolidated net income are the same as in Illustration 5-5.
5. Consolidated assets and the minority interest in the consolidated balance sheet are $3,400 greater than in Illustration 5-5. The difference relates entirely to the additional values being accounted for ($4,000), net of amortization to date of $600.
6. Illustration 5-9 shows that a minority interest deduction of $2,400 is reported in consolidation. The proof of this amount is shown in the following calculations:

Subsidiary's reported net income	**$15,000**
Minority ownership percentage	**20%**
Minority interest in book income	**$ 3,000**
Less: Additional amortization relating to minority interest in undervalued assets	**(600)**
Minority interest in net income	**$ 2,400**

Here is an alternate calculation:

Subsidiary's reported net income	**$15,000**
Less: Total amortization on undervalued assets:	
Parent company's portion	**(2,400)**
Minority interest portion	**(600)**
Subtotal	**$12,000**
Minority ownership percentage	**20%**
Minority interest in net income	**$ 2,400**

The Entity Theory

Recall that under the entity theory:

1. The subsidiary's net assets are revalued in consolidation to 100% of their current values as of the acquisition date.
2. Goodwill is reported in consolidation based on the amount of goodwill implicit in the transaction.

The only difference between the combination entity–parent company approach and the entity theory is that additional goodwill must be accounted for under the entity theory. In the chapter example of the parent company theory, goodwill of $8,000 was determined. We also demonstrated in the discussion of the entity theory, at the beginning of this appendix, that $10,000 is the total goodwill implicit in the transaction ($8,000 ÷ 80% ownership interest). Thus, an additional $2,000 of goodwill is reported under the entity theory. Accounting for this additional goodwill presents no difficulty. We would merely add the $2,000 to the conceptual analysis of the investment account in the same manner that the $4,000 of additional value was added for the undervalued assets. Consolidated financial statements would be prepared in the same manner as shown for the combination entity–parent company approach.

Appendix B
PREPARATION OF CONSOLIDATED FINANCIAL STATEMENTS USING THE TRIAL BALANCE APPROACH

To demonstrate the preparation of the worksheet using the trial balance approach when a subsidiary is partially owned, we have reformatted the financial statements used in Illustration 5-5 (page 200) into the trial balance approach shown in Illustration 5-10. The elimination entries used in Illustration 5-5 are repeated below for convenience.

The primary elimination entry:

Common Stock	40,000	
Retained Earnings (beginning of year)	20,000	
Equity in Net Income of Subsidiary	12,000	
Minority Interest in Net Income of S Company	3,000	
Land	9,600	
Equipment	4,800	
Goodwill	7,200	
Dividends Declared		5,000
Accumulated Depreciation (building)		800
Investment in Subsidiary		76,800
Minority Interest in Net Assets of S Company		14,000

The secondary elimination entry:

Cost of Goods Sold	3,200	
Amortization of Cost in Excess of Book Value		3,200

The accumulated depreciation elimination entry:

Accumulated Depreciation	45,000	
Buildings and Equipment		45,000

Review Questions

1. Explain what proportional consolidation means.
2. What are the arguments for full consolidation?
3. What are the three possible ways of classifying minority interest in the balance sheet? Which way is used most often?
4. How are dividends that are paid to minority shareholders treated for consolidated reporting purposes?
5. Explain the difference between the parent company theory and the entity theory.
6. In which circumstances would push-down accounting be required for partially owned subsidiaries?
7. Under which theory is the minority interest reported in the consolidated financial statements based on the subsidiary's book value of the net assets?
8. How does the step-by-step method work when control is achieved after several block purchases?
9. When control is achieved after several block acquisitions, in which situations is the date of latest purchase method appropriate?

Discussion Cases

DC 5-1

Classification of Minority Interest in the Consolidated Balance Sheet

Pegco Company's controller has requested your advice on how to classify the minority interest of the company's recently acquired partially owned subsidiary. The controller is concerned that the minority shareholders may object to (1) being classified as creditors if a liability classification is used, and (2) being classified as other than stockholders if a classification above the stockholders' equity section but below the liabilities section is used. The controller is also concerned that the parent's stockholders may object to classifying the minority interest as part of stockholders' equity.

Required:

1. Evaluate the rationale behind each method of presentation.
2. How would you advise the controller?

Exercises

E 5-1

Calculation of Consolidated Net Income

Pushco Company owns 75% of the outstanding common stock of Shovex Company. Each company's 19X1 net income from its own separate operations, exclusive of earnings and amortization recorded under the equity method, is as follows:

Pushco Company	$1,000,000
Shovex Company	200,000

Illustration 5-10
The Trial Balance Approach (Illustration 5-5 Reformatted)

P COMPANY AND SUBSIDIARY (S COMPANY)
Consolidating Statement Worksheet
For the Year Ended December 31, 19X1

	P Company		S Company	
	Dr.	Cr.	Dr.	Cr.
Cash	62,000		25,000	
Accounts receivable, net	75,000		43,000	
Inventory	110,000		40,000	
Investment in S Company	76,800			
Land	200,000		30,000	
Buildings and equipment	500,000		190,000	
Accumulated depreciation		320,000		58,000
Goodwill				
Liabilities		290,000		200,000
Minority interest in net assets of S Company				
P Company:				
Common stock		300,000		
Retained earnings, January 1, 19X1		100,000		
Dividends declared	31,000			
S Company:				
Common stock				40,000
Retained earnings, January 1, 19X1				20,000
Dividends declared			5,000	
Sales		600,000		200,000
Cost of goods sold	360,000		116,000	
Expenses	204,000		69,000	
Intercompany accounts:				
Equity in net income of S Company		12,000		
Amortization of cost in excess of book value	3,200			
Minority interest in net income of S Company				
	1,622,000	1,622,000	518,000	518,000

Consolidated Net Income ....

Consolidated Retained Earnings........

Explanation of entries:
(1) The primary elimination entry.
(2) The secondary elimination entry.
(3) The accumulated depreciation elimination entry.

		Consolidated			
Eliminations		Income Statement		Retained Earnings	Balance Sheet
Dr.	Cr.	Dr.	Cr.	(Dr.) Cr.	
					87,000
					118,000
					150,000
	76,800(1)				–0–
9,600(1)					239,600
4,800(1)	45,000(3)				649,800
45,000(3)	800(1)				(333,800)
7,200(1)					7,200
					917,800
					490,000
	14,000(1)				14,000
					300,000
				100,000	
				(31,000)	
40,000(1)					–0–
20,000(1)					–0–
	5,000(1)				–0–
			800,000		
3,200(2)		479,200			
		273,000			
12,000(1)			–0–		
	3,200(2)	–0–			
3,000(1)		3,000			
135,800	135,800	755,200	800,000		
		44,800 →		44,800	
		800,000	800,000	113,800 →	113,800
					917,800

During 19X1, Pushco had $20,000 of amortization of cost in excess of book value.

Required:

1. Determine the amount of consolidated net income.
2. Determine the amount of the minority interest in the subsidiary's net income.

E 5-2

Calculation of Consolidated Net Income

Potter Company owns 80% of the outstanding common stock of Stainless Company and 90% of the outstanding common stock of Steele Company. Each company's 19X1 net income from its own separate operations, exclusive of earnings recorded under the equity method and amortization of cost over book value of net assets, is as follows:

Potter Company	$1,000,000
Stainless Company	100,000
Steele Company	10,000

Amortization of cost over book value of net assets on a full-year basis is $4,000 and $2,000 for Stainless and Steele, respectively.

Required:

1. Calculate the minority interest in each subsidiary's net income and the consolidated net income for 19X1, assuming the subsidiaries were owned during the entire year.
2. Calculate the minority interest in each subsidiary's net income and the consolidated net income for 19X1, assuming Stainless was acquired on April 1, 19X1, and Steele was acquired on July 1, 19X1. (Assume earnings occurred evenly throughout the year.)

E 5-3

Determining Amounts for the Consolidated Income Statement without Using a Consolidating Statement Worksheet

On January 1, 19X1, Palmer Company acquired 75% of the outstanding common stock of Snead Company at an amount equal to 75% of Snead's net assets at carrying value. Each company's 19X1 income statement, exclusive of earnings recorded under the equity method, is as follows:

	Palmer Company	Snead Company
Sales	$800,000	$200,000
Cost of goods sold	(400,000)	(100,000)
Marketing expenses	(80,000)	(20,000)
Administrative expenses	(40,000)	(10,000)
Interest expense	(30,000)	(10,000)
Net Income	$250,000	$ 60,000

Balance sheet amounts for each company at December 31, 19X1, are purposely not furnished; therefore, a formal consolidating statement worksheet cannot be prepared. However, the consolidated amounts still can be determined if the main concept of the chapter is understood.

Required:

1. Determine the consolidated income statement amounts.
2. Determine the consolidated income statement amounts assuming Palmer amortized $2,000 of cost in excess of book value of net assets that pertains to goodwill.

E 5-4

Separating Total Cost into Individual Components of the Major Conceptual Elements

On January 1, 19X6, Prima Company acquired 70% of the outstanding common stock of Seconde Company at a total cost of $180,000. Seconde's capital account balances at December 31, 19X5, are as follows:

Common stock	$100,000
Additional paid-in capital	50,000
Retained earnings	60,000
	$210,000

Each of Seconde's assets and liabilities has a current value equal to its book value, except for the following items:

	Book Value	Current Value
Land	$170,000	$240,000
Goodwill	50,000	-0-
10% Bonds payable	160,000	140,000

Required:
Prepare an expanded analysis of the investment account as of the acquisition date.

E 5-5

Determining Subsidiary's Equity from Consolidated Data

Popp Company acquired 70% of the outstanding common stock of Soda Corporation. Popp's separate balance sheet immediately after the acquisition and the consolidated balance sheet are as follows:

	Popp Company	Consolidated
Current assets	$106,000	$148,000
Investment in Soda (cost)	100,000	—
Goodwill	—	8,100
Fixed assets (net)	270,000	370,000
	$476,000	$526,100

(continued)

	Popp Company	Consolidated
Current liabilities	$ 15,000	$ 30,000
Minority interest	—	35,100
Capital stock	350,000	350,000
Retained earnings	111,000	111,000
	$476,000	$526,100

Of the excess payment for the investment in Soda, $10,000 was attributed to undervaluation of its fixed assets; the balance was attributed to goodwill.

Required:

1. Calculate the total stockholders' equity of the subsidiary when it was acquired.
2. Prepare a conceptual analysis of the investment account at the acquisition date.

(AICPA adapted)

Exercises for Appendix A

E 5-6A

Comparison of the Parent Company Theory and the Entity Theory for Treatment of Tangible Assets

On January 1, 19X1, Placido Company acquired 60% of the outstanding common stock of Scotto Company for $2,400,000. All cost in excess of Placido's share of net assets at carrying value is entirely attributable to a parcel of land owned by Scotto. Scotto acquired this land many years ago for $50,000; its current value is $1,050,000. (The book value of Scotto's net assets is $3,000,000.)

Required:

1. Under the parent company theory, at what amount would the land be reported in the consolidated balance sheet?
2. Under the entity theory, at what amount would the land be reported in the consolidated balance sheet?
3. Compare the results in requirement 1 with those in requirement 2. What is the effect on the stockholders' equity section and the minority interest in the subsidiary's net assets as reported in the consolidated balance sheet?

E 5-7A

Comparison of the Parent Company Theory and the Entity Theory for Treatment of Goodwill

Poem Company acquired 70% of the outstanding common stock of Sonnet Company on January 1, 19X3, for $4,200,000. The cost in excess of its share of book value is entirely attributable to Sonnet's expected superior earnings ability. (The book value of Sonnet's net assets is $5,000,000.)

Required:

1. Under the parent company theory at what amount would goodwill be reported in the consolidated balance sheet?
2. Under the entity theory, at what amount would the goodwill be reported in the consolidated balance sheet?
3. Compare the results in requirement 1 with those in requirement 2. What is the effect on the stockholders' equity section and the minority interest in the net assets of the subsidiary as reported in the consolidated balance sheet?

E 5-8A

Comparison of the Parent Company Theory and the Entity Theory for Treatment of Tangible Assets and Goodwill

Pocahontas Company purchased 80% of the outstanding common stock of Smith Company for $6,400,000. All of Smith's assets and liabilities have book values equal to current values, except that land has a book value of $400,000 and a current value of $700,000. (The book value of Smith's net assets is $7,500,000.)

Required:

1. Under the parent company theory, at what amount would the land and goodwill be reported in the consolidated balance sheet?
2. Under the entity theory, at what amount would the land and goodwill be reported in the consolidated balance sheet?
3. Compare the results in requirement 1 with those in requirement 2. What is the effect on the stockholders' equity section and the minority interest in the net assets of the subsidiary as reported in the consolidated balance sheet?

Problems

P 5-1

Preparing Consolidated Financial Statements as of the Acquisition Date

On December 31, 19X1, Payles Company, a calendar-year reporting company, acquired 75% of the outstanding common stock of Selmore Company at a total cost of $450,000. Each of Selmore's assets and liabilities has a current value equal to its book value. Each company's financial statements for the year ended December 31, 19X1, immediately after the acquisition date, are as follows:

	Payles Company	Selmore Company
Income Statement (19X1):		
Sales	$8,000,000	$ 700,000
Cost of goods sold	(5,000,000)	(300,000)
Expenses	(2,100,000)	(280,000)
Net Income	$ 900,000	$ 120,000

(continued)

	Payles Company	Selmore Company
Balance Sheet (as of December 31, 19X1):		
Cash	$ 650,000	$ 100,000
Accounts receivable, net	900,000	400,000
Inventory	1,200,000	700,000
Investment in Selmore Company	450,000	
Land	800,000	300,000
Buildings and equipment	5,000,000	900,000
Accumulated depreciation	(1,000,000)	(200,000)
	$8,000,000	$2,200,000
Accounts payable and accruals	$1,000,000	$ 500,000
Long-term debt	2,000,000	1,100,000
Common stock	1,000,000	100,000
Additional paid-in capital	2,000,000	200,000
Retained earnings	2,000,000	300,000
	$8,000,000	$2,200,000

Required under Push-down Accounting:

1. Prepare the entries the subsidiary would make.
2. Prepare the primary elimination entry as of December 31, 19X1.

Required under Non-push-down Basis of Accounting:

3. Prepare the elimination entries required in consolidation as of December 31, 19X1.
4. Prepare a consolidating statement worksheet at December 31, 19X1.
5. What amount of income does the parent company report to its stockholders for 19X1?

P 5-2*

Preparing Consolidated Financial Statements Subsequent to the Acquisition Date (Continuation of Problem 5-1)

As described in Problem 5-1, Payles Company acquired 75% of Selmore Company for $450,000 on December 31, 19X1. Each company's financial statements as of December 31, 19X2 (one year after the acquisition date) are as follows:

	Payles Company	Selmore Company
Income Statement (19X2):		
Sales	$ 8,500,000	$ 900,000
Cost of goods sold	(5,500,000)	(400,000)
Expenses	(2,400,000)	(320,000)
Equity in net income of subsidiary	135,000	
Net Income	$ 735,000	$ 180,000

*The financial statement information presented for problems accompanied by asterisks is also provided on Model 5 (filename: Model5) of the software file disk that is available for use with the text, enabling the problem to be worked on the computer.

Balance Sheet (as of December 31, 19X2):

Cash	$ 345,000	$ 140,000
Accounts receivable, net	1,000,000	500,000
Inventory	1,500,000	800,000
Investment in Selmore Company	510,000	
Land	800,000	300,000
Buildings and equipment	5,200,000	900,000
Accumulated depreciation	(1,200,000)	(240,000)
	$ 8,155,000	$2,400,000
Accounts payable and accruals	$ 700,000	$ 620,000
Long-term debt	2,100,000	1,100,000
Common stock	1,000,000	100,000
Additional paid-in capital	2,000,000	200,000
Retained earnings	2,355,000	380,000
	$ 8,155,000	$2,400,000
Dividends declared during 19X2	$ 380,000	$ 100,000

Required:

1. Prepare and update the expanded analysis of the investment account through December 31, 19X2.
2. Prepare the consolidation elimination entries at December 31, 19X2.
3. Prepare a consolidating statement worksheet at December 31, 19X2. (The parent's retained earnings at December 31, 19X1, was $2,000,000.)
4. Prepare a formal consolidated balance sheet and income statement to be included in the annual report to the stockholders.
5. Assuming the subsidiary had applied push-down accounting at the acquisition date, prepare the primary elimination entry as of December 31, 19X2.

P 5-3 Preparing Consolidated Financial Statements as of the Acquisition Date

On December 31, 19X1, Price Company, a calendar-year reporting company, acquired 80% of the outstanding common stock of Selle Company at a total cost of $240,000. The analysis of the parent company's investment account as of the acquisition date is as follows:

		Remaining Life
Book value element (at 80%):		
Common stock	$ 80,000	
Retained earnings	72,000	
Current value over book value equipment:		
Inventory	4,000	2 months
Land	24,000	Indefinite
Equipment	40,000	10 years
Patent	(12,000)	3 years
Goodwill element	32,000	4 years
Total cost	$240,000	

Each company's financial statements for the year ended December 31, 19X1, immediately after the acquisition date, are as follows:

	Price Company	Selle Company
Income Statement (19X1):		
Sales	$2,500,000	$500,000
Cost of goods sold	(1,400,000)	(250,000)
Expenses	(860,000)	(202,000)
Net Income	$ 240,000	$ 48,000
Balance Sheet (as of December 31, 19X1):		
Cash	$ 160,000	$ 20,000
Accounts receivable, net	200,000	55,000
Inventory	350,000	80,000
Investment in Selle Company	240,000	
Land	400,000	70,000
Buildings and equipment	800,000	200,000
Accumulated depreciation	(150,000)	(40,000)
Patent		15,000
	$2,000,000	$400,000
Accounts payable and accruals	$ 250,000	$ 60,000
Long-term debt	1,000,000	150,000
Common stock	300,000	100,000
Retained earnings	450,000	90,000
	$2,000,000	$400,000

Required under Push-down Accounting:

1. Prepare the entries the subsidiary would make.
2. Prepare the primary elimination entry as of December 31, 19X1.

Required under Non-push-down Accounting:

3. Prepare the elimination entries required in consolidation as of December 31, 19X1.
4. Prepare a consolidating statement worksheet at December 31, 19X1.
5. What amount of income does the parent company report to its stockholders for 19X1?

P 5-4* Preparing Consolidated Financial Statements Subsequent to the Acquisition Date (Continuation of Problem 5-3)

As described in Problem 5-3, Price Company acquired 80% of Selle Company for $240,000 on December 31, 19X1. Each company's financial statements as of December 31, 19X2, one year after the acquisition date, are as follows:

	Price Company	Selle Company
Income Statement (19X2):		
Sales	$2,800,000	$600,000
Cost of goods sold	(1,500,000)	(300,000)
Expenses	(1,000,000)	(240,000)
Equity in net income of subsidiary	48,000	
Amortization of cost in excess of book value	(12,000)	
Net Income	$ 336,000	$ 60,000
Balance Sheet (as of December 31, 19X2):		
Cash	$ 169,000	$ 25,000
Accounts receivable, net	300,000	50,000
Inventory	500,000	120,000
Investment in Selle Company	232,000	
Land	400,000	70,000
Buildings and equipment	1,100,000	220,000
Accumulated depreciation	(210,000)	(65,000)
Patent		10,000
	$2,491,000	$430,000
Accounts payable and accruals	$ 320,000	$ 85,000
Long-term debt	1,300,000	150,000
Common stock	300,000	100,000
Retained earnings	571,000	95,000
	$2,491,000	$430,000
Dividends declared during 19X2	$ 215,000	$ 55,000

Required:

1. Prepare and update the expanded analysis of the investment account through December 31, 19X2.
2. Prepare the consolidation elimination entries at December 31, 19X2.
3. Prepare a consolidating statement worksheet at December 31, 19X2. (The parent's retained earnings at December 31, 19X1, was $450,000.)
4. Prepare a formal consolidated balance sheet and income statement to be included in the annual report to the stockholders.
5. Assuming the subsidiary had applied push-down accounting at the acquisition date, prepare the primary elimination entry as of December 31, 19X2.

P 5-5 Preparing Consolidated Financial Statements as of the Acquisition Date

Pepper Company, a calendar-year reporting company, acquired 80% of the outstanding common stock of Salt Company at a total cost of $320,000 on December 31, 19X1. The expanded analysis of the parent company's investment in account as of the acquisition date is as follows:

		Remaining Life
Book value element (at 80%):		
Common stock	$ 40,000	
Additional paid-in capital	160,000	
Retained earnings	200,000	
Current value over (under) book value element:		
Inventory	(56,000)	6 months
Land	24,000	Indefinite
Building	(80,000)	20 years
Long-term debt	32,000	4 years
Total cost	$320,000	

Each company's financial statements for the year ended December 31, 19X1, immediately after the acquisition date, are as follows:

	Pepper Company	Salt Company
Income Statement (19X1):		
Sales	$6,000,000	$800,000
Cost of goods sold	(3,300,000)	(600,000)
Expenses	(1,500,000)	(250,000)
Net Income (Loss)	$1,200,000	$ (50,000)
Balance Sheet (as of December 31, 19X1):		
Cash	$ 320,000	$ 30,000
Accounts receivable, net	360,000	50,000
Inventory	800,000	220,000
Investment in Salt Company	320,000	
Land	500,000	100,000
Buildings and equipment	2,600,000	550,000
Accumulated depreciation	(400,000)	(50,000)
	$4,500,000	$900,000
Accounts payable and accruals	$ 800,000	$100,000
Long-term debt	2,100,000	300,000
Common stock	20,000	50,000
Additional paid-in capital	480,000	200,000
Retained earnings	1,100,000	250,000
	$4,500,000	$900,000

Required under Push-down Accounting:

1. Prepare the entries the subsidiary would make.
2. Prepare the primary elimination entry as of December 31, 19X1.

Required under Non-push-down Accounting:

3. Prepare the elimination entries required in consolidation as of December 31, 19X1.

4. Prepare a consolidating statement worksheet at December 31, 19X1.
5. What amount of income does the parent company report to its stockholders for 19X1?

P 5-6*

Preparing Consolidated Financial Statements Subsequent to the Acquisition Date

As described in Problem 5-5, Pepper Company acquired 80% of Salt Company for $320,000 on December 31, 19X1. Each company's financial statements as of December 31, 19X2, one year after the acquisition date, are as follows:

	Pepper Company	Salt Company
Income Statement (19X2):		
Sales	$7,000,000	$850,000
Cost of goods sold	(3,800,000)	(600,000)
Expenses	(1,700,000)	(310,000)
Equity in net loss of subsidiary	(48,000)	
Amortization of cost below book value	52,000	
Net Income (Loss)	$1,504,000	$ (60,000)
Balance Sheet (as of December 31, 19X2):		
Cash	$ 375,000	$ 20,000
Accounts receivable, net	400,000	80,000
Inventory	700,000	130,000
Investment in Salt Company	324,000	
Land	500,000	100,000
Buildings and equipment	3,100,000	550,000
Accumulated depreciation	(600,000)	(80,000)
	$4,799,000	$800,000
Accounts payable and accruals	$ 495,000	$ 60,000
Long-term debt	2,000,000	300,000
Common stock	20,000	50,000
Additional paid-in capital	480,000	200,000
Retained earnings	1,804,000	190,000
	$4,799,000	$800,000
Dividends declared during 19X2	$ 800,000	

Required:

1. Prepare and update the expanded analysis of the investment account through December 31, 19X2.
2. Prepare the consolidation elimination entries at December 31, 19X2.
3. Prepare a consolidating statement worksheet at December 31, 19X2. (The parent's retained earnings at December 31, 19X1 was $1,100,000.)
4. Prepare a formal consolidated balance sheet and income statement to be included in the annual report to the stockholders.
5. Assuming the subsidiary had applied push-down accounting at the acquisition date, prepare the primary elimination entry as of December 31, 19X2.

P 5-7*

COMPREHENSIVE Analyzing the Investment; Applying the Equity Method; Preparing Consolidated Financial Statements Subsequent to the Acquisition Date

Poor Company acquired 60% of the outstanding common stock of Stands Company for cash of $503,000 on January 1, 19X1. Poor also incurred $37,000 of direct out-of-pocket costs in connection with the acquisition. Information with respect to Stands as of the acquisition date is as follows:

	Book Value	Current Value	Remaining Life
Cash	$ 74,000	$ 74,000	
Accounts receivable, net	266,000	266,000	
Inventory	280,000	260,000	6 months
Land	780,000	780,000	Indefinite
Buildings and equipment	900,000	675,000	15 years
Accumulated depreciation	(300,000)		
Patent	40,000	165,000	5 years
Goodwill	60,000		2 years
	$2,100,000	$2,220,000	
Accounts payable and accruals	$ 380,000	$ 380,000	
Long-term debt	1,200,000	1,040,000	4 years
Common stock	200,000	800,000	
Retained earnings	320,000		
	$2,100,000	$2,220,000	

The parent company intends to use the equity method to account for its investment. The only entry it has made to the investment account since the acquisition date, however, is to reflect the receipt of its share of $55,000 of dividends declared and paid during 19X1 by the subsidiary. The parent assigned a six-year life to goodwill that it paid for. Non-push-down accounting was chosen by the parent company.

The financial statements of each company for the year ending December 31, 19X1, one year after the acquisition date, are as follows:

	Poor Company	Stands Company
Income Statement (19X1):		
Sales	$9,000,000	$ 870,000
Cost of goods sold	(5,000,000)	(470,000)
Expenses	(2,800,000)	(190,000)
Net Income	$1,200,000	$ 210,000

(continued)

	Poor Company	Stands Company
Balance Sheet (as of December 31, 19X1):		
Cash	$ 653,000	$ 168,000
Accounts receivable, net	840,000	270,000
Inventory	1,200,000	560,000
Investment in Stands Company	507,000	
Land	1,000,000	780,000
Buildings and equipment	4,800,000	1,050,000
Accumulated depreciation	(1,700,000)	(390,000)
Patent	300,000	32,000
Goodwill		30,000
	$7,600,000	$2,500,000
Accounts payable and accruals	$1,100,000	$ 625,000
Long-term debt	2,600,000	1,200,000
Common stock	2,000,000	200,000
Retained earnings	1,900,000	475,000
	$7,600,000	$2,500,000
Dividends declared during 19X1	$ 900,000	$ 55,000

Required:

1. Prepare an expanded analysis of the investment account as of the acquisition date.
2. Update the expanded analysis of the investment account to reflect activity under the equity method of accounting for the investment through December 31, 19X1.
3. Adjust the parent company's financial statements as of December 31, 19X1, to reflect the equity method of accounting.
4. Prepare the consolidation elimination entries at December 31, 19X1.
5. Prepare a consolidating statement worksheet at December 31, 19X1.

P 5-8

REVIEW (Chapters 4 and 5) Analyzing the Investment; Applying the Equity Method; Computing Minority Interest and Consolidated Retained Earnings

On January 1, 19X6, Puttnam Corporation made the following investments:

1. It acquired 75% of the outstanding common stock of Shaft Corporation for $14 cash per share. The stockholders' equity of Shaft on January 1, 19X1, consisted of the following:

Common stock, $10 par value	$100,000
Retained earnings	20,000

2. It acquired 60% of the outstanding common stock of Tee Corporation for $40 cash per share. The stockholders' equity of Tee on January 1, 19X1, consisted of the following:

Common stock, $20 par value	$60,000
Paid-in capital in excess of par value	10,000
Retained earnings	50,000

The current values of each subsidiary's net assets equal their book values except for a parcel of land owned by Shaft that has a current value of $40,000 *less* than its book value. At the time of these acquisitions, Puttnam expected both companies to have superior earnings for the next 5 years. Puttnam has accounted for these investments using the cost method. An analysis of each company's retained earnings for 19X1 is as follows:

	Puttnam	Shaft	Tee
Balance, January 1, 19X1	$300,000	$20,000	$50,000
Net income (loss)	190,000	36,000	(15,000)
Cash dividends declared and paid	(110,000)	(24,000)	(10,000)
Balance, December 31, 19X1	$480,000	$32,000	$25,000

Required:

1. Under the equity method, what entries should have been made on the books of the parent during 19X1 to record the following:
   a. Investments in subsidiaries.
   b. Parent's share of subsidiary income or loss.
   c. Subsidiary dividends received.
   d. Amortization of cost in excess of (under) book value, if any.
2. Compute the amount of minority interest in each subsidiary's stockholders' equity at December 31, 19X1.
3. What were the parent's earnings from its own operations for 19X1, excluding accounts relating to its ownership in these subsidiaries?
4. What amount should be reported as consolidated retained earnings as of December 31, 19X1?

(AICPA adapted)

Problems: Block Acquisitions

P 5-9 Block Acquisitions: The Step-by-step Method

Pommel Company acquired blocks of stock of Sorse Company over a period of several years. Information regarding such purchases along with pertinent information relating to the investee as of each purchase date is as follows:

			Information on Investee		
					Net Assets
Date of Block Acquisition	Ownership Percentage Acquired	Cost	Common Stock	Retained Earnings[a]	Current Value over Book Value[b]
January 1, 19X1	20	$ 35,000	$100,000	$25,000	[c]
January 1, 19X2	20	56,000	100,000	55,000	[c]
December 31, 19X2	50	132,000	100,000	90,000	$40,000[d]

[a]Sorse Company declared cash dividends on common stock of $10,000 per year during 19X1 and 19X2.
[b]Assume Pommel Company uses a 10-year life for any goodwill acquired; also, assume that goodwill associated with each block acquisition has its own separate life.
[c]It was impractical to obtain specific information from the investee as to the current value of its individual assets and liabilities at the time of this block purchase.
[d]This amount is identified entirely with land.

Required:

1. Using the step-by-step approach, determine the balances that should exist in the investment account by the individual components of the major conceptual elements as of the control date (December 31, 19X2). *Hint:* Refer to paragraph 19n of *APB Opinion No. 18* for treatment of cost over investor's share of the investee's net assets at book value that cannot be identified with specific assets or liabilities.
2. Prepare the primary elimination entry at December 31, 19X2.

P 5-10

Block Acquisitions: The Step-by-step Method

On January 1, 19X8, Plaza Company acquired 30% of the outstanding common stock of Storelle Company at a total cost of $380,000. At that time, Storelle's capital accounts were as follows:

Common stock	$ 600,000
Retained earnings	400,000
	$1,000,000

On April 1, 19X8, Plaza acquired 40% of Storelle's outstanding common stock at a cost of $604,000. Earnings and dividend information for Storelle for 19X8 is as follows.

	First Quarter	Remainder of Year
Net income	$60,000	$200,000
Dividends declared	50,000	140,000

Assume that Plaza uses a 10-year life for goodwill associated with each block of stock. Assume also that none of Storelle's recorded assets or liabilities is over- or undervalued at either block acquisition date.

Required:

1. Using the step-by-step method, determine the balances that should exist in the investment account by the individual components of the major conceptual elements as of the control date (April 1, 19X8).
2. Update the analysis of the investment account through December 31, 19X8, assuming the parent intends to include only the revenue and expense items of the subsidiary for the period April 1, 19X8, to December 31, 19X8, in preparing the consolidated income statement for 19X8.
3. Prepare the primary elimination entry at April 1, 19X8.
4. Prepare all the elimination entries required at December 31, 19X8.
5. Explain the two methods available to the parent in reporting the subsidiary's earnings for 19X8. Specifically, explain how the earnings recorded under the equity method of accounting for the first quarter are presented.

P 5-11

Block Acquisitions: Comparison of the Date of Latest Purchase Method with the Step-by-step Method

Pestex Company acquired two blocks of stock of Sprayco Company. Information regarding each purchase along with pertinent information about the investee as of each purchase date is as follows:

			Information on Investee		
					Net Assets
Date of Block Acquisition	Ownership Percentage Acquired	Cost	Common Stock	Retained Earnings[a]	Current Value over Book Value[b]
January 1, 19X4	10	\$100,000[b]	\$400,000	\$300,000	\$50,000[c]
December 31, 19X6	60	800,000	400,000	640,000	70,000[c]

[a]Sprayco Company declared cash dividends on common stock of \$90,000 per year in 19X4, 19X5, and 19X6.
[b]The carrying value of this block on Pestex Company's books has never been below cost from the date it was acquired.
[c]This amount is identified entirely with land.

Required:

1. Using the date of latest purchase method, determine the balances that should exist in the investment account by the individual components of the major conceptual elements as of the control date (December 31, 19X6).
2. Using the step-by-step method, determine the balances that should exist in the investment account by the individual components of the major conceptual elements as of the control date (December 31, 19X6).

Problem Involving Consolidated Statement of Cash Flows

P 5-12

Consolidated Statement of Cash Flows:

The 19X1 separate-company statements of cash flows for Pacific Company and its 90%-owned subsidiary, South Company, follow:

	Pacific Company	South Company
Statement of Cash Flows (19X1):		
Cash flows from operating activities:		
Net income	$127,000	$ 30,000
Charges (credits) not affecting cash:		
Depreciation expense	14,000	6,000
Goodwill amortization	4,000	
Equity in net income of subsidiary	(27,000)	
Net increase in receivables, inventory, and payables	(11,000)	(5,000)
Net cash flow from operating activities	$107,000	$ 31,000
Cash flows from investing activities:		
Purchase of equipment	$ (71,000)	$(19,000)
Dividends received from South Company	9,000	
Net cash flow from investing activities	$ (62,000)	$(19,000)
Cash flows from financing activities:		
Sale of common stock	$ 50,000	
Sale of preferred stock	40,000	
Sale of bonds at par		$ 20,000
Retirement of debt	(30,000)	(15,000)
Dividends on common stock	(60,000)	(10,000)
Dividends on preferred stock	(2,000)	
Net cash flow from investing activities	$ (2,000)	$ (5,000)
Net Increase (Decrease) in Cash	$ 43,000	$ 7,000

Additional Information:

1. The only intercompany transaction during 19X1 was the payment of dividends to the parent.
2. The parent acquired the 90% interest in the subsidiary two years ago.

Required:

Prepare a consolidated statement of cash flows using the combining the separate statements approach.

6

The Pooling of Interests Method of Accounting

An Overview of the Pooling of Interests Method

The Growth of Pooling of Interests: From Concept to Common Practice

Conceptual Issues

Criteria for Pooling of Interests: A Brief Overview

Specific Conditions for Pooling of Interests

Recording a Pooling of Interests

Preparing Consolidated Financial Statements

Disclosures

PERSPECTIVE: A Capsule History of Pooling of Interests Accounting

Summary

AN OVERVIEW OF THE POOLING OF INTERESTS METHOD

In this chapter, the pooling of interests method of accounting for a business combination is discussed, illustrated, and contrasted with the purchase method. Recall from Chapter 2 that the terms and provisions of the acquisition agreement determine whether the purchase method or the pooling of interests method is used to record a business combination. The terms and provisions that qualify a business combination as a pooling of interests are reviewed in general and then in detail.

Paragraphs 27 to 65 of *APB Opinion No. 16* deal with the pooling of interests method. Throughout these paragraphs, the terms "acquiring company" and "acquired company" are purposely not used because the word "acquiring" describes the purchase method of accounting in paragraphs 66 to 96. Instead, the discussion uses the terms "combining company," "combined company," and "company issuing stock to effect the combination."[1] This language is consistent with the underlying concept of pooling of interests accounting, which is that a combining, or pooling, of the equity interests occurs rather than an acquisition. The latter term refers to a situation in which one company acquires the business of another company, for which purchase accounting is appropriate.

However, it is more convenient in most instances to refer to a company that issues common stock to effect a business combination as the acquiring company and a company that gives up its assets (or whose stockholders give up their common stock) as the target company or the acquired business.

The Essence of a Pooling of Interests

Under the **pooling of interests method,** each company's stockholders are presumed to have combined or fused their ownership interests in such a manner that each group becomes an owner of the combined, enlarged business. To accomplish this fusing of ownership interests, the acquiring company must issue common stock as consideration for the business that it acquires. Under this pooling of interests concept, the fair value of the consideration given and the current value of the acquired company's net assets are completely irrelevant. Instead, the book value of the acquired company's net assets is used as the basis for recording the "cost" of the investment to the acquiring company. This approach is completely the opposite of that under the purchase method. As a result, the assets and liabilities of the acquired business are reported at their historical costs in

[1]*Opinions of the Accounting Principles Board, No. 16*, "Accounting for Business Combinations" (New York: American Institute of Certified Public Accountants, 1970).

the consolidated financial statements. Furthermore, goodwill is never created. In an economy in which inflation has occurred over many years, the assets of companies are usually undervalued. Thus, the pooling of interests method is popular because the acquired company's assets do not have to be reflected at their current values, along with any goodwill, in the future financial statements. Future charges to income are thereby avoided. The disadvantage—an understatement of the consolidated stockholders' equity—is almost always of secondary importance compared with the advantages that result in the income statement.

Presenting Precombination Earnings and Dividends. When financial statements are presented for periods prior to the combination date, **the earnings of each company are combined as though the combination had occurred at the beginning of the earliest period presented.** In presenting dividend information for periods before the combination date, dividends of each company are combined to the extent of the ownership interest acquired. This is just the opposite of the purchase method, which disallows presenting the two companies' operations results and dividend information together for preacquisition periods.

THE GROWTH OF POOLING OF INTERESTS: FROM CONCEPT TO COMMON PRACTICE

When the pooling of interests concept emerged in the early 1940s, it implementation was limited to businesses of comparable size. Here are simple examples of such poolings, one for similarly sized professional businesses and one for equally matched corporations:

1. Two CPAs practice as sole proprietorships. One CPA specializes in taxes, the other in auditing. Each realizes that by joining together as a partnership they would both achieve certain advantages, among them (a) economies related to overhead, (b) better servicing of clients, and (c) greater attractiveness to prospective clients. Because each CPA continues as an owner in the partnership, it is obvious that no buy-out of the other has occurred. The combination is one of association—not acquisition.
2. Two companies of approximately the same size are in the same industry. One company has an excellent research and development department; the other company has excellent manufacturing and marketing organizations. The owners of each company realize that their firm, on its own, will have a difficult time becoming a major force in the industry. By combining the strengths of the two companies, however, the unified firm could have a better chance of success. Accordingly, one of the combining companies issues common stock to the stockholders of the other company. Each owner in the formerly separate businesses is now a fellow owner in the same company, sharing the risks and rewards

of common ownership with the others. None of the owners sells his or her stock as a result of the combination. Thus, neither group has bought out the other group.

Because of the favorable effects on the income statement that often result in a pooling of interests compared to a purchase transaction, companies have tried over the years to broaden (and thereby alter) the original concept of a pooling of interests so that many other types of business combinations can be classified as poolings of interests and thereby obtain the more desirable accounting treatment. (Examples would be industrial giants combining with start-up companies and companies combining from unrelated industries.) These efforts have been so successful that pooling of interests is no longer considered in the abstract by business people (and probably to most accountants as well) but instead is simply another useful accounting method.

In fact, because most business combinations that are accounted for under the pooling of interests method involve companies of disproportionate sizes, they are viewed by the parties involved as acquisitions — in the sense that one entity acquires the business of another entity, and the acquiring entity is completely dominant. In other words, the transaction is viewed as an acquisition (from other than an accounting viewpoint) that is merely recorded as a pooling of interests.

CONCEPTUAL ISSUES

Although accounting authorities agree that a pooling of interests cannot take place without the equity interests of the two companies joining together, they differ widely and strongly over the relevance of several other factors, among them (1) the relative size of the combining interests, (2) the ready negotiability of each interest's common stock, (3) the similarity or complementary nature of the two lines of business, (4) the subsequent disposal of stock, and (5) interests in one or the other company that dissent from the combination.

1. **Relative size:** *Should the equity interests be approximately the same size for a pooling of interests to take place?* For example, could an eight-partner partnership have a pooling of interests with one having two partners? What about forty-eight partners and two? Could a combination between IBM Corporation, which has revenues approaching $50 billion, and an electronics company having revenues of only $100 million — a 500 : 1 ratio — be considered a pooling of interests? Or should this be considered a buy-out? Should a line be drawn? If so, where?
2. **Ready negotiability of common stock:** Assume that each group of former owners now holds common stock that is negotiable and readily exchangeable into cash. Does this mean that there is no real sig-

nificance to the fact that common stock was given to one of the equity interests instead of cash? In other words, *does a true pooling of interests occur just because common stock is given*?

3. **Similar or complementary lines of business:** *Should there be a compelling economic relationship (similar or complementary lines of business) between the combining companies to have a pooling of interests*? For example, in 1986 Burroughs Corp., which had the third largest revenues in its industry, and Sperry Corporation, with the seventh largest revenues, combined to create Unisys Corp., the world's second largest computer company. The reason these firms gave for their combination was to be able to compete aggressively with IBM, the world's largest, in the $7 billion mainframe market. Could a business combination between Burroughs and Ford Motor Co., for example, be considered a pooling of interests?
4. **Subsequent disposal of stock:** Some or all of the owners of one of the former businesses sell their newly received common stock holdings shortly after the combination, effectively "cashing out" rather than continuing as owners in the combined business. *Does a disposal of stock mean that the combination was really a buy-out and not a pooling of interests*?
5. **Dissenting interests:** Some members of one of the equity interests choose not to be a party to the combination. For example, two partnerships of ten partners each contemplate combining, but two of the ten from one firm choose to withdraw their capital from the partnership and not be parties to the combination. *Should dissenting interests in one firm prevent the remaining partners from having a pooling of interests with the other partnership*?

Grounds for Difference

At one end of the spectrum are accountants who would disregard all five of these factors. For them, as long as a fusion of equity interests occurs (through the issuance of common stock by one of the combining companies in exchange for the assets or common stock of the other combining company), a pooling of interests occurs. In general, *APB Opinion No. 16* takes this approach.

Critics of *Opinion No. 16* contend that for most combinations treated as poolings of interests, the fusion of the equity interests is irrelevant. They maintain that what is relevant is whether or not one company has acquired or obtained *control* over the business of another company. If this control is the substance of the transaction, then purchase accounting is appropriate, regardless of the type of consideration given. This is the primary conclusion of *Accounting Research Study No. 5*, "A Critical Study of Accounting for Business Combinations," By Arthur R. Wyatt, which the American Institute of Certified Public Accountants published in 1963. (Research studies do not constitute the official position of the AICPA; they are for discussion purposes only.) This group would allow poolings of interests only when the companies involved are of comparable size and it is evident that a buy-out is not occurring. Because most transactions accounted for as poolings of interests involve companies of significantly disproportionate sizes, few business combinations would be treated as poolings of interests with this approach.

In summary, each group views the economic substance of a business combination involving the issuance of common stock differently. As mentioned in Chapter 2, *APB Opinion No. 16* is a controversial pronouncement that has received such substantial criticism since its issuance that the Financial Accounting Standards Board is expected to reexamine the accounting issues involved in business combinations in the future.

CRITERIA FOR POOLING OF INTERESTS: A BRIEF OVERVIEW

Before *APB Opinion No. 16* was issued, only general guidelines determined when a business combination should be treated as a pooling of interests. Because the guidelines could not be logically supported for the most part, in practice they were often ignored or broadly interpreted. The relative looseness of accounting principles in this area resulted in substantial criticism of the accounting profession, which led to the issuance of a pronouncement that contained specific pooling of interests criteria. In addition, *Opinion No. 16* substantially narrowed management's ability to choose between accounting alternatives for a given set of terms and conditions:

1. It specifically defines the criteria under which a business combination is treated as a pooling of interests.
2. It requires all business combinations meeting each of these specific criteria to be accounted for as a pooling of interests.
3. It requires all business combinations failing to meet any one of the specific criteria to be accounted for using purchase accounting.

APB Opinion No. 16 outlines twelve specific conditions that the combining firms must meet before pooling of interests accounting is permitted. In many respects, the conditions are arbitrary and not totally clear or comprehensive. As a result, the AICPA and the FASB have issued numerous interpretations. With the possible exception of accounting for leases, more interpretations have been issued for this pronouncement than for any other professional pronouncement. In practice, it has been one of the most difficult professional pronouncements with which to work. Many large public accounting firms have prepared lengthy booklets for internal use that explain how certain areas of the pronouncement are to be interpreted for uniform application within their firms.

The twelve conditions generally allow pooling of interests treatment only when a combination of independent equity interests occurs rather than a buy-out of one of the common shareholder equity interests. As a result, most of the emphasis is placed on the form and manner of accomplishing the combination so that the two stockholder groups "pool" their equity resources. Most of the conditions pertain to the manner of effecting the combination. The more salient points of the criteria are as follows:

1. Common stock must be the primary consideration given by the acquiring company.
   a. If assets are acquired, 100% of the assets must be acquired solely in exchange for the acquiring company's common stock.
   b. If common stock is acquired, at least 90% of the outstanding common shares must be acquired solely in exchange for the acquiring company's common stock. (Cash or other consideration may be given to dissenting stockholders of the target company so long as this group does not hold more than 10% of the target company's outstanding common stock.)
2. The common stock issued must have the same rights and privileges as the already issued and outstanding common stock of the acquiring company. In other words, the acquiring company's new stockholders must be full-fledged stockholders of the enlarged business.
3. There can be no arrangements to reacquire the common stock issued as consideration for the assets or common stock acquired.

Interestingly enough, the stockholders receiving common stock from the acquiring company can sell the stock immediately after the combination is consummated, if they do not want to continue as owners in the combined business. No "continuity of ownership interest" is required whereby the new stockholders must remain shareholders of the combined business for any specified period of time. Thus, the "fusion" of equity interests may take place for only an instant.

SPECIFIC CONDITIONS FOR POOLING OF INTERESTS

The twelve conditions for the pooling of interests method in *APB Opinion No. 16* fit into three broad categories:

1. The attributes of the combining companies.
2. The manner of combining equity interests.
3. The absence of planned transactions.

Each condition is quoted below under the appropriate category and discussed in detail. Because all the conditions are found in *Opinion No. 16*, only paragraph references to that pronouncement are given. Note that many of the conditions are designed to prevent companies from circumventing the basic concept of having to combine substantially all common shareholder equity interests.

Attributes of the Combining Companies

Two conditions pertain to the necessary attributes of the combining companies:

A. **"Each of the combining companies is autonomous and has not been a subsidiary or division of another corporation within two years before the plan of combination is initiated"** (Paragraph 46a).

This condition presumes that the pooling of interests concept applies only to independent companies. For the most part, this condition is sound; most divestitures of subsidiaries or divisions are intended disposals of interests as opposed to intended poolings of equity interests.

A subsidiary that is spun off pursuant to a governmental divestiture order or a new company that acquires assets it must dispose of is an arbitrary exception to this condition and is deemed an "autonomous company." This exception does not appear to be based on logic, and its inclusion is apparently an accommodation to the disposing company for purposes of facilitating the disposal.

When a portion of a business is spun off to certain stockholders in exchange for some or all of their stock, the stockholders of the newly established corporation may wish to combine their equity interests with another company in the true sense of the pooling of interests concept. Such a combining of equity interests could not be accounted for as a pooling of interests unless two years had elapsed from the spin-off date. Thus, a portion of a business cannot be spun off in this manner and then pooled with another company shortly thereafter. This is because the spinning off and subsequent combination are viewed as mere steps of a single transaction, the substance of which is a disposal of an interest.

B. **"Each of the combining companies is independent of the other combining companies"** (Paragraph 46b).

This condition means that at the initiation date and until the business combination is consummated, the combining companies cannot hold more than 10% of the outstanding voting common stock of any combining company. Voting common stock that is acquired during this time interval in exchange for voting common stock issued in connection with the terms of the business combination agreement is excluded in the percentage computation.

This condition is intended to prevent a combining company from altering the equity interests of the other combining company. (Paragraph 47c, which is discussed later in the chapter, prohibits each combining company from altering the equity interest of its own voting common stock in contemplation of a pooling.) If this condition were not imposed, a combining company could circumvent the intended purpose of paragraph 47c by buying out a large group of dissenting shareholders of the other combining company and then effecting a pooling of interests with its remaining shareholders.

Independence Based on Net Worth Invested. Usually, each combining company is independent of the other if neither company owns more than 10% of the outstanding voting common stock of the other. Occasionally, however, neither company owns more than 10% of the outstanding common stock of the other and independence still does not exist. This can occur when the smaller company has a significant investment—**in terms of its own net worth**—in the acquiring company. For example, assume that Mini-Computer Company (the target company) owns 6% of IBMM Company's outstanding common stock. If this investment constitutes more than 10% of Mini-Computer's net worth, then the companies are not independent. The calculation to determine if the 10% figure is exceeded uses the following facts:

1. IBMM has 400,000 common shares outstanding.
2. Mini-Computer has 100,000 common shares outstanding.
3. IBMM will issue two shares of its common stock for each share of Mini-Computer's outstanding common stock—in other words, a 2-for-1 exchange ratio.
4. Mini-Computer owns 24,000 IBMM common shares, which is 6% of IBMM's outstanding common shares.

Because Mini-Computer's shareholders will receive 200,000 shares of IBMM common stock, Mini-Computer's net worth can be considered the equivalent of 200,000 shares of IBMM common stock. The following calculation is then made:

$$\frac{\text{Shares of IBMM common stock held by Mini-Computer}}{\substack{\text{Shares of IBMM common stock to be issued} \\ \text{(100,00 shares of Mini-Computer} \times 2)}} = \frac{24{,}000}{200{,}000} = 12\%$$

In an alternate approach, the 24,000 shares of IBMM owned by Mini-Computer are considered the equivalent of 12,000 shares of Mini-Computer common stock. The following calculation is then made:

$$\frac{\substack{\text{Equivalent number of Mini-Computer's} \\ \text{shares invested in IBMM (24,000} \div \text{2)}}}{\text{Shares of Mini-Computer common stock outstanding}} = \frac{12{,}000}{100{,}000} = 12\%$$

In this example, the companies are not independent because the 10% level has been exceeded.

Independence is evaluated not only from the perspective of how much of the other combining company's outstanding common stock is owned but also from the perspective of how much of a company's own net worth is invested in the other combining company.

Smaller Company Issues the Common Stock. In the preceding situation, the larger of the two companies issued common stock to bring about the combination (the typical case). In a stock-for-stock exchange, the relative holdings of each group of stockholders can be the same regardless of which company issues the common stock to effect the pooling of interests.

Let us change the facts of the preceding situation to make Mini-Computer the issuing company. The same relative holdings of each group of stockholders is maintained if Mini-Computer issues one share for each two shares of IBMM outstanding common stock (a 1-for-2 exchange ratio). In this case, the issuing company has the intercorporate investment. However, the companies are still not independent, for the reasons discussed in the preceding paragraph. The smaller of the two companies issues the common stock (and thereby becomes the parent company) when it is more desirable to use the smaller company's name than the larger company's name. For example, the larger company may have an unfavorable public image, or the smaller company may have a wider investor following.

Dual Intercorporate Investments. The 10% independence test must be performed in a cumulative manner when each company has an investment in the other. To illustrate, assume the following facts:

1. IBMM Company has 400,000 common shares outstanding.
2. Mini-Computer Company has 100,000 common shares outstanding.
3. IBMM will issue two shares of its common stock for each share of Mini-Computer's outstanding common shares—a 2-for-1 exchange ratio.
4. Mini-Computer owns 16,000 IBMM outstanding common shares, which is 4% of IBMM's outstanding common shares.
5. IBMM owns 3,000 shares of Mini-Computer's outstanding common shares, which is 3% of Mini-Computer's outstanding common shares.

Although neither company owns more than 10% of the other company's outstanding common stock and neither company has more than 10% of its own net worth invested in the other company, the *combination* of intercorporate investments exceeds the 10% level, as shown by the following calculation:

Percent of Mini-Computer's common stock owned by IBMM	3%
Percent of Mini-Computer's net worth invested in IBMM [16,000 shares ÷ 200,000 common shares to be received in the exchange, or alternately, 8,000 shares (adjusted for the 2-for-1-exchange ratio) ÷ 100,000 outstanding shares]....	8%
	11%

The manner of dealing with an investment in the company issuing the common stock is explained in connection with paragraph 47b of *APB Opinion No. 16.* The approach treats shares owned in the issuing company (adjusted for the exchange ratio) as a reduction of the target company's outstanding shares to determine if 90% of the target company's outstanding common stock has been acquired in exchange for the issuing company's common stock:

Mini-Computer's outstanding common shares	100,000
Less: Shares owned by IBMM	(3,000)
Equivalent number of shares invested in IBMM by Mini-Computer (16,000 ÷ 2)	(8,000)
	89,000
Shares needed to reach the 90% level	90,000

Thus, the 90% level has not been reached. This analysis is difficult to understand. Because the issue is *independence*, we presented the discussion of dealing with investments in the issuing company from paragraph 46b rather than paragraph 47b.

Manner of Combining Equity Interests

Seven conditions pertain to the manner of effecting the combination, as follows:

> A. **"The combination is effected in a single transaction or is completed in accordance with a specific plan within the year after the plan is initiated" (Paragraph 47a).**

Evidently the APB felt that the transaction should be consummated within a reasonable period of time—one year.

> B. **"A corporation offers and issues only common stock with rights identical to those of its outstanding voting common stock in exchange for substantially all of the voting common stock interest of another company at the date the plan of combination is consummated" (Paragraph 47b).**

This condition is the fundamental requirement for effecting a pooling of interests. It means that the company issuing common stock must acquire at least 90% of the other combining company's outstanding common stock subsequent to the initiation date in exchange for its own common stock. Thus, shares acquired prior to the initiation date—no matter how acquired—cannot be used to determine if the 90% requirement has been met. To illustrate how the 90% rule is applied, assume the following facts:

1. P is the company issuing common stock.
2. S has 102,000 common shares issued, of which 2,000 shares are held in treasury. Thus, S has 100,000 common shares outstanding.
3. P acquires common shares of S as follows:

a. Prior to the initiation date	3,000
b. Between the initiation date and the consummation date:	
For cash	4,000
For its common stock pursuant to the terms of the combination agreement	5,000

c. At the consummation date by exchanging its own common stock pursuant to the terms of the combination agreement	84,000
Total shares owned	96,000

Although P Company owns more than 90% of S Company's outstanding common shares, it did not acquire at least 90,000 shares (90% of S's 100,000 outstanding shares) after the initiation date by exchanging common stock. Only 89,000 were obtained after the initiation date through an exchange of common stock (5,000 + 84,000). Therefore, the combination must be accounted for as a purchase instead of a pooling of interests.

The 90% rule does not allow the issuing company to give any cash to the 90% group of shareholders. (An exception pertains to cash given for fractional shares.) Dissenting shareholders, which as a group cannot hold more than 10% of the acquired company's outstanding common shares, may be given cash or other consideration in acquiring their shares.

This condition implies a stock-for-stock exchange. However, assets of a combining company can be exchanged, providing 100% of the assets are exchanged. In these situations, the acquired company can retain assets to settle liabilities, contingencies, or disputed items that are not assumed by the acquiring company, providing any assets remaining after settlement are transferred to the acquiring company.

C. "None of the combining companies changes the equity interest of the voting common stock in contemplation of effecting the combination either within two years before the plan of combination is initiated or between the dates the combination is initiated and consummated; changes in contemplation of effecting the combination may include distributions to stockholders and additional issuances, exchanges, and retirements of securities" (Paragraph 47c).

The concept of a pooling of interests does not allow a change in or alteration of the equity interests of the voting common stock of either combining company; only a fusing of the existing ownership interests occurs. Thus, this condition is necessary so that the fundamental concept is not violated. Above-normal dividend distributions to common shareholders would be considered a "change in the equity interest." The spin-off of a subsidiary or division to certain existing shareholders in exchange for some or all of their common stock (technically called a *split-off* for tax purposes) is an example of a distribution and retirement of outstanding securities. (This condition does not pertain to the disposal of a subsidiary or division by other means, such as an outright sale to an unrelated party.)

D. "Each of the combining companies reacquires shares of voting common stock only for purposes other than business combinations [to be accounted for as poolings of interests], and no company reacquires more than a normal number of shares between the dates the plan of combination is initiated and consummated" (Paragraph 47d).

This condition has a twofold purpose:

1. It prevents a target company from buying out a large group of its own dissenting shareholders (more than 10%) so that its remaining shareholders can effect a combination as a pooling of interests in the manner set forth in paragraph 47b.
2. Sometimes an acquiring company desires to effect a combination as a pooling of interests and yet does not want to increase the number of its outstanding common shares at all or beyond a certain number. This condition prevents the acquiring company from using cash or other assets or incurring liabilities to reacquire common shares, and then using such reacquired shares to effect a combination as a pooling of interests. This would clearly be an alteration of the equity interest, which is prohibited by paragraph 47c.

The phrase "for purposes other than business combinations" as used in paragraph 47d seems to allow substantial subjective interpretation of the company's purpose for acquiring shares. For example, an acquiring company could assert that it reacquired some of its shares because the company was overcapitalized or the price of its stock was at an attractive level. On the surface, such reacquisitions would not appear to be for purposes of business combinations. Thus, the intended purpose of the condition could be easily circumvented. As a result, the AICPA issued the following interpretation to this condition:

> In the absence of persuasive evidence to the contrary . . . it should be presumed that all acquisitions of treasury stock during the two years preceding the date a plan of combination is initiated . . . and between the initiation and consummation were made in contemplation of effecting business combinations to be accounted for as a pooling of interests. Thus, lacking such evidence, this combination would be accounted for by the purchase method regardless of whether treasury stock or unissued shares or both are issued in the combination.
>
> The specific purposes for which treasury shares may be reacquired prior to consummation of a "pooling" include shares granted under stock option or compensation plans, stock dividends declared (or to be declared as a recurring distribution), and recurring distributions as provided in paragraph 47d. Likewise, treasury shares reacquired for issuance in a specific "purchase" or to resolve an existing contingent share agreement from a prior business combination would not invalidate a concurrent "pooling." Treasury shares reacquired for these purposes should be either reissued prior to consummation or specifically reserved for these purposes existing at consummation.[2]

Assessing the purpose of the reacquisition of treasury shares by an acquiring company generally involves evaluating the subsequent distribution of

[2]*Accounting Interpretation No. 20 to APB Opinion No. 16*, "Accounting for Business Combinations" (New York: American Institute of Certified Public Accountants, 1971).

such shares. In most instances, a systematic pattern of reacquisitions for specified distribution purposes must be established at least two years before the combination plan is initiated to constitute "persuasive evidence to the contrary."

E. "The ratio of the interest of an individual common stockholder to those of other common stockholders in a combining company remains the same as a result of the exchange of stock to effect the combination" (Paragraph 47e).

Each shareholder of the target company who exchanges common stock for voting common stock of the acquiring company must receive that voting common stock in exact proportion to his or her relative common stock interest in the target company before the combination is effected. Thus, a shareholder who owns 20% of the target company's outstanding common stock must receive 20% of the voting common shares that the acquiring company issues to effect the combination.

If a shareholder owning 20% of the target company were to receive more or less than 20% of the common stock issued by the acquiring company, then a reshuffling of the target company's equity interests would result, which was deemed contrary to a pure combining of the equity interests.

F. "The voting rights to which the common stock ownership interests in the resulting combined corporation are entitled are exercisable by the stockholders; the stockholders are neither deprived of nor restricted in exercising those rights for a period" (Paragraph 47f).

Any limitations on voting rights would obviously be inconsistent with the pooling of interests concept.

G. "The combination is resolved at the date the plan is consummated and no provisions of the plan relating to the issue of securities or other considerations are pending" (Paragraph 47g).

This condition is intended primarily to prohibit poolings of interests when contingent consideration is issuable based on future sales, earnings, or market prices. Such contingencies are incompatible with the mutual sharing of risks and rewards, which underlies the pooling of interests concept. An interpretation says the following:

> The only contingent arrangement permitted under paragraph 47g is for settlement of a contingency pending at consummation, such as the later settlement of a lawsuit. A contingent arrangement would also be permitted for an additional income tax liability resulting from the examination of "open" income tax returns.[3]

[3]*Accounting Interpretation No. 14 to APB Opinion No. 16*, "Accounting for Business Combinations" (New York: American Institute for Certified Public Accountants, 1971).

Absence of Planned Transactions

Three conditions pertain to certain types of postcombination transactions that cannot be included either explicitly or implicitly in either the negotiations or the terms of the combination agreement. The conditions are as follows:

A. **"The combining corporation does not agree directly or indirectly to retire or reacquire all or part of the common stock issued to effect the combination" (Paragraph 48a).**

This condition prevents an acquiring company from circumventing the intended purpose of paragraph 47b. Obviously, issuing common shares to effect a combination and subsequently repurchasing the shares issued would not be, in substance, a combining of equity interests.

APB Opinion No. 16 does not prohibit an acquiring company from reacquiring shares issued in a pooling of interests (or an equivalent number of shares issued). It is prohibited only from making an agreement to repurchase the shares issued. In this area, the Securities and Exchange Commission has taken the following position:

> In specific fact situations, subsequent reacquisitions may be so closely related to the prior combination that they should be considered part of the combination plan. Thus, significant reacquisitions closely following a plan of combination which otherwise qualified as a pooling of interests may invalidate the applicability of that method. . . .[4]
>
> The Commission does not intend to establish an additional criterion for determining the accounting treatment of a business combination. Rather it intended simply to caution registrants and auditors that the substance of reacquisitions closely following consummation of a combination should not be ignored. . . .[5]

B. **"The combined corporation does not enter into other financial arrangements for the benefit of the former stockholders of a combining company, such as a guaranty of loans secured by stock issued in the combination, which in effect negates the exchange of securities" (Paragraph 48b).**

Arrangements of this nature are considered "bailouts" of former stockholders of the acquired company. Such provisions are inconsistent with the pooling of interests concept.

C. **"The combined corporation does not intend or plan to dispose of a significant part of the assets of the combining companies within two years after**

[4]*Accounting Series Release No. 146*, "Effect of Treasury Stock Transactions on Accounting for Business Combinations," par. 10 (Washington, D.C.: Securities and Exchange Commission, 1973). This release is now part of *Financial Reporting Release No. 1* (Section 201.02), which was issued in 1982 and is a codification of all accounting-related releases in effect at that time.

[5]*Accounting Series Release No. 146-A*, "Statement of Policy and Interpretations in Regard to *Accounting Series Release No. 146*, paragraph 3 (Washington, D.C.: Securities and Exchange Commission, 1974). (Section 201.02 of *Financial Reporting Release No. 1*.)

the combination other than disposals in the ordinary course of business of the formerly separate companies and to eliminate duplicate facilities or excess capacity" (Paragraph 48c).

The apparent purpose of this condition is to prohibit acquiring companies from effecting pooling of interests with companies having substantially undervalued assets, when the intent is to sell the undervalued assets shortly after consummation and thereby report immediate profits from the sale. (Such widely criticized practices existed before *APB Opinion No. 16* was issued.)

RECORDING A POOLING OF INTERESTS

Assume the following information:

1. P Company and S Company have agreed to combine under terms that provide for P Company to issue common stock (in exchange for either the assets or the outstanding common stock of S Company).
2. Information with respect to each company as of the combination date (January 1, 19X1) is as follows:

	P Company	S Company
Common stock, $10 par value (30,000 shares outstanding)	$300,000	
Common stock, $3 par value (5,000 shares outstanding)		$ 15,000
Additional paid-in capital	12,000	5,000
Retained earnings	100,000	40,000
Total Stockholders' Equity	$412,000	$ 60,000
Book value of assets	Irrelevant	$250,000
Book value of liabilities	Irrelevant	$190,000
Current value of net assets	Irrelevant	$ 80,000[a]
Market price of stock on combination date	$30[a]	Irrelevant

[a]This amount is relevant only under the purchase method.

3. All conditions for pooling of interests have been met.
4. P Company issues 1,000 shares of its common stock.

The next two sections show the entries to record the pooling of interests assuming, first, that the assets are acquired and, second, that the common stock is acquired. In showing the entry when common stock is acquired, we also present the entry under the purchase method to emphasize the conceptual difference between the two methods. (To make this comparison, we must assume that the combination does not qualify for pooling in one minor respect, but that the terms and conditions relating to the exchange of stock are the same.)

Acquisition of Assets

When assets are acquired, the acquiring company records these assets and the liabilities assumed at their book values as shown on the acquired business's books. As in purchase accounting, a centralized or a decentralized accounting system may be used subsequently to account for the acquired business. Assuming a centralized accounting system, the entry is as follows:

Assets (record at book value)	**250,000**	
Liabilities (record at book value)		**190,000**
Common Stock (1,000 shares issued × $10 par value)		**10,000**
Retained Earnings (100% of the target company's retained earnings)		**40,000**
Additional Paid-in Capital (residual amount to balance)		**10,000**

The preceding entry would also be made if the combination were made pursuant to a **statutory merger,** in which the target company's legal existence is terminated (discussed in Chapter 2).

Acquisition of Common Stock

The entry when common stock is acquired is nearly the same as when assets are acquired. The only difference is that rather than recording assets and liabilities at their book values, the Investment in Subsidiary account is debited an amount equal to the book value of the net assets ($60,000 in the preceding example).

The residual balancing amount in the preceding example, is a credit to Additional Paid-in Capital. This is not always the case. The following illustration shows, among other things, what to debit when a debit is needed to balance the entry.

Illustration

COMPARISON OF ENTRIES UNDER THE POOLING OF INTERESTS METHOD AND THE PURCHASE METHOD—100% OF OUTSTANDING COMMON STOCK ACQUIRED

Illustration 6-1 shows the entries when 1,000, 2,000, 3,000, and 4,000 shares of common stock are issued by P Company (the latter two situations resulting in debit entries to balance the entry). In addition, for comparison we present the entries that would be made under the purchase method.

Illustration 6-1
Comparison of the Pooling of Interests Method with the Purchase Method—100% of Common Stock Acquired

	Situation A 1,000 Shares		Situation B 2,000 Shares		Situation C 3,000 Shares		Situation D 4,000 Shares	
	Dr.	Cr.	Dr.	Cr.	Dr.	Cr.	Dr.	Cr.
Pooling of interests:								
(1) Investment in S Company..............	60,000		60,000		60,000		60,000	
(4) Additional paid-in capital.....................					10,000		12,000	
(2) Common stock		10,000		20,000		30,000		40,000
(4) Additional paid-in capital................		10,000						
(3) Retained earnings..		40,000		40,000		40,000		32,000[a]
Purchase method:								
(5) Investment in S Company..............	30,000		60,000		90,000		120,000	
(2) Common stock		10,000		20,000		30,000		40,000
(6) Additional paid-in capital................		20,000		40,000		60,000		80,000

Note: Shares are assumed to be issued.

[a] $40,000 − $8,000 that could not be charged to the parent's additional paid-in capital account.

Explanation of entries:
(1) This amount always equals the parent's ownership interest in the subsidiary's net assets at book value.
(2) This amount always equals the number of shares issued multiplied by the par value of the issuing company's common stock.
(3) This amount always equals (a) the parent's ownership interest in the subisidary's Retained Earnings account less (b) any amount that cannot be charged to the parent's Additional Paid-in Capital account, inasmuch as a debit balance would be created in Additional Paid-in Capital.
(4) This is a residual amount to balance the entry; a debit plug cannot be greater than the Additional Paid-in Capital account balance on the parent's books. (Any additional debit is charged to Retained Earnings.)
(5) This amount always equals the number of shares issued multiplied by the market price on the date of the combination.
(6) This amount is always the difference between the amounts determined in entries 5 and 2.

The following points are important for understanding Illustration 6-1:

1. The pooling of interests method ignores both the fair value of the consideration given and the current value of the subsidiary's net assets in determining the "cost" of the investment.
2. The purchase method uses the fair value of the consideration given—the number of shares issued multiplied by the market price on the date of the combination—to determine the cost of the investment.
3. Under the pooling of interests method, the investment account has only one major element—the book value element. Thus, there is no cost

above or below book value to amortize against the combined income of future periods.

4. Under the purchase method, the current value over or under the book value element exists in all four situations in Illustration 6-1, the goodwill element existing only in situations C and D and a bargain purchase element existing in situation A.
5. The given information purposely assigned a low amount to P Company's additional paid-in capital to show the extreme situation of reducing P Company's Additional Paid-in Capital account to zero. In practice, this would rarely occur because companies usually assign a very low par value to their common stock.

Illustration

COMPARISON OF ENTRIES UNDER THE POOLING OF INTERESTS METHOD AND THE PURCHASE METHOD—90% OF OUTSTANDING COMMON STOCK ACQUIRED

Illustration 6-2 compares the recording of a business combination under both methods using the information given above, but assuming only 90% of the outstanding common stock is acquired in exchange for 10% fewer shares issued by P Company. Note that the manner of determining the amounts recorded is the same as that used in Illustration 6-1, except 90% instead of 100% is used to determine the amount of the investment in S Company and the credit to retained earnings.

Purchase of Shares from Dissenting Shareholders

Occasionally, some shareholders of the target company refuse to take common stock of the acquiring company as consideration. These shareholders are known as **dissenting shareholders.** To acquire these shares, the acquiring company must usually offer other types of consideration—cash is the most common. So long as the dissenting shareholders do not hold more than 10% of the target company's outstanding shares, consideration other than the acquiring company's common stock may be given to dissenting shareholders, and pooling of interests treatment is allowed.

The purchase of these shares is similar to the purchase of a block of stock as discussed and illustrated in the preceding chapter. Accordingly, the manner of acquiring these shares seems to dictate that purchase accounting be used to account for their acquisition. However, *APB Opinion No. 16* provides that when shares are acquired from dissenting shareholders at the same time the business combination is consummated, "a single method should be applied to an entire combination."[6] Thus, the purchase method cannot be used to account for the cost of acquiring these shares from the dissenting shareholders; the pooling of interests method

[6] *APB Opinion No. 16*, par. 43.

Illustration 6-2
Comparison of the Pooling of Interests Method with the Purchase Method—90% of Common Stock Acquired

	Situation A 900 Shares		Situation B 1,800 Shares		Situation C 2,700 Shares		Situation D 3,600 Shares	
	Dr.	Cr.	Dr.	Cr.	Dr.	Cr.	Dr.	Cr.
Pooling of interests:								
(1) Investment in S Company..............	54,000		54,000		54,000		54,000	
(4) Additional paid-in capital....................					9,000		12,000	
(2) Common stock		9,000		18,000		27,000		36,000
(4) Additional paid-in capital...............		9,000						
(3) Retained earnings..		36,000		36,000		36,000		30,000[a]
Purchase method:								
(5) Investment in S Company..............	27,000		54,000		81,000		108,000	
(2) Common stock		9,000		18,000		27,000		36,000
(6) Additional paid-in capital...............		18,000		36,000		54,000		72,000

Note: Shares are assumed to be issued.

[a]$36,000 − $6,000 that could not be charged to the parent's additional paid-in capital account.

Explanation of entries:
(1) This amount always equals the parent's ownership interest in the subsidiary's net assets at book value.
(2) This amount always equals the number of shares issued multiplied by the par value of the issuing company's common stock.
(3) This amount always equals (a) the parent's ownership interest in the subsidiary's Retained Earnings account less (b) any amount that cannot be charged to the parent's Additional Paid-in Capital account, inasmuch as a debit balance would be created in Additional Paid-in Capital.
(4) This is a residual amount to balance the entry; a debit plug cannot be greater than the Additional Paid-in Capital account balance on the parent's books. (Any additional debit is charged to Retained Earnings.)
(5) This amount always equals the number of shares issued multiplied by the market price on the date of the combination.
(6) This amount is always the difference between the amounts determined in entries 5 and 2.

is used to account for all of the shares acquired. In other words, **the combination cannot be recorded as part pooling, part purchase.**

Illustration

DISSENTING SHAREHOLDERS BOUGHT OUT WITH CASH AT COMBINATION DATE

In situation B of Illustration 6-2, we assumed that P Company issued 1,800 shares of its common stock in exchange for 4,500 shares of S Company's outstanding common stock (90% of the outstanding shares). Let us assume that P Company acquired the remaining 500 shares from the dissenting shareholders at the combination date by paying $10,000 cash. The entry to record the entire transaction as a pooling of interests is as follows:

Investment in S Company (100% of $60,000)........	60,000	
Additional Paid-in Capital (residual amount)........	8,000	
Cash...		10,000
Common Stock (1,800 shares × $10)..........		18,000
Retained Earnings (100% of $40,000)..........		40,000

Treatment of Direct Costs and Registration Expenses

Accounting Treatment. Under the purchase method of accounting, direct costs relating to the acquisition of the common stock or the assets are included in the cost of the investment. In contrast, under the pooling of interests method, direct costs are charged to income in the period in which they are incurred. In addition, the costs of registering equity shares issued by the acquiring company are charged to income as incurred instead of being charged to additional paid-in capital as under the purchase method. The rationale is that no new capital is raised—only a "pooling" of the existing capital occurs.[7] In practice, these costs and expenses are customarily deferred until the combination is consummated, so that the costs and expenses are charged against the first period in which income from the newly combined business is included in net income.

Income Tax Treatment. Recall from Chapter 2 that a combination that qualifies for pooling of interests treatment for financial reporting purposes is almost always treated as a tax-free reorganization for income tax reporting purposes. In almost all instances, direct costs are not currently deductible for income tax reporting purposes. The acquisition of assets is treated as a capital expenditure that results in the creation of a capital asset with an indeterminable useful life. This asset remains intact until it is totally worthless or is disposed of, at which time a tax deduction may be obtained. When common stock is acquired, direct costs are treated as an upward adjustment to the basis of the common stock received by the acquiring company. If the subsidiary is ever sold, these costs are effectively deducted against the proceeds from the sale.

[7] *APB Opinion No. 16*, par. 58.

PREPARING CONSOLIDATED FINANCIAL STATEMENTS

Illustration

COMBINATION DATE AND FIRST YEAR SUBSEQUENT—WHOLLY OWNED SUBSIDIARY

Assume that for 19X1, S Company had net income of $15,000 and declared dividends of $5,000. Using the information given in Illustration 6-1, we analyze P Company's investment account by the individual components of the book value element as of the combination date (January 1, 19X1), and then update the analysis for the subsequent year's activity (under the equity method of accounting) as follows:

Analysis of Investment Account

					Retained Earnings		
						Current Year	
	Total Cost		Common Stock	Additional Paid-in Capital	Prior Years	Earnings	Dividends
Balance, Jan. 1, 19X1 ..	$60,000	=	$15,000 +	$5,000	+ $40,000		
Equity in net income	15,000					$15,000	
Dividends..............	(5,000)						$(5,000)
Subtotal....................	$70,000	=	$15,000 +	$5,000	+ $40,000 +	$15,000	$(5,000)
Reclassification.......					$10,000	(15,000)	5,000
Balance, Dec. 31, 19X1	$70,000	=	$15,000 +	$5,000	+ $50,000 +	$ –0–	$ –0–

Note that this analysis is the same regardless of the number of shares issued by P Company.

The primary elimination entries as of January 1, 19X1 (the combination date), and December 31, 19X1 (one year subsequent to the combination date), are as follows:

	Consolidation Date			
	January 1, 19X1		December 31, 19X1	
Common Stock	15,000		15,000	
Additional Paid-in Capital.........	5,000		5,000	
Retained Earnings (beginning of year)	40,000		40,000	
Equity in Net Income of Subsidiary...........................			15,000	
Dividends Declared.........				5,000
Investment in S Company		60,000		70,000

Because the book value element is the only major element under pooling of interests accounting, there is no cost over or under book value to amortize, and thus no secondary elimination entry is necessary.

Illustrations 6-3 and 6-4 show consolidating statement worksheets as of the above dates, assuming that 3,000 shares were issued (situation C in

Illustration 6-3
Date of Combination

P COMPANY AND SUBSIDIARY (S COMPANY)
Consolidating Statement Worksheet
As of January 1, 19X1

	P Company	S Company	Eliminations Dr.	Eliminations Cr.	Consolidated
Balance Sheet:					
Cash	110,000	20,000			130,000
Accounts receivable, net	70,000	23,000			93,000
Inventory	100,000	32,000			132,000
Investment in S Company	60,000			60,000(1)	–0–
Land	200,000	30,000			230,000
Buildings and equipment	500,000	190,000			690,000
Accumulated depreciation	(280,000)	(45,000)			(325,000)
Total Assets	760,000	250,000		60,000	950,000
Liabilities	288,000	190,000			478,000
P Company:					
Common stock	330,000				330,000
Additional paid-in capital	2,000				2,000
Retained earnings	140,000				140,000
S Company:					
Common stock		15,000	15,000(1)		–0–
Additional paid-in capital		5,000	5,000(1)		–0–
Retained earnings		40,000	40,000(1)		–0–
Total Liabilities and Equity	760,000	250,000	60,000		950,000
Proof of debit and credit postings			60,000	60,000	

Note: The journal entry recorded by the parent for the pooling (which effect is included in the P Company column) is:

Investment in S Company (100% of $60,000)	60,000	
Additional Paid-in Capital (residual amount)	10,000	
Common Stock (3,000 shares × $10)		30,000
Retained Earnings (100% of $40,000)		40,000

Prior to the combination, the parent's Additional Paid-in Capital account had a balance of $12,000.

Explanation of entry:

(1) The primary elimination entry.

Illustration 6-4
First Year Subsequent to Combination Date

P COMPANY AND SUBSIDIARY (S COMPANY)
Consolidating Statement Worksheet
For the Year Ended December 31, 19X1

	P Company	S Company	Eliminations Dr.	Eliminations Cr.	Consolidated
Income Statement:					
Sales	600,000	200,000			800,000
Cost of goods sold	(360,000)	(116,000)			(476,000)
Expenses	(204,000)	(69,000)			(273,000)
Intercompany Account:					
Equity in net income of S Company	15,000		15,000(1)		–0–
Net Income	51,000	15,000	15,000		51,000
Statement of Retained Earnings:					
Balances, January 1, 19X1	100,000	40,000	40,000(1)		100,000
+ Effect of pooling	40,000				40,000
+ Net income	51,000	15,000	15,000		51,000
− Dividends declared	(31,000)	(5,000)		5,000(1)	(31,000)
Balances, December 31, 19X1	160,000	50,000	55,000	5,000	160,000
Balance Sheet:					
Cash	135,000	25,000			160,000
Accounts receivable, net	75,000	43,000			118,000
Inventory	110,000	40,000			150,000
Investment in S Company	70,000			70,000(1)	–0–
Land	200,000	30,000			230,000
Buildings and equipment	500,000	190,000			690,000
Accumulated depreciation	(320,000)	(58,000)			(378,000)
Total Assets	770,000	270,000		70,000	970,000
Liabilities	278,000	200,000			478,000
P Company:					
Common stock	330,000				330,000
Additional paid-in capital	2,000				2,000
Retained earnings	160,000				160,000
S Company:					
Common stock		15,000	15,000(1)		–0–
Additional paid-in capital		5,000	5,000(1)		–0–
Retained earnings		50,000	55,000	5,000	–0–
Total Liabilities and Equity	770,000	270,000	75,000	5,000	970,000
Proof of debit and credit postings			75,000	75,000	

Explanation of entry:
(1) The primary elimination entry.

Illustration 6-1) to effect the combination. The following points are important for understanding both illustrations:

1. The primary elimination entry is developed in exactly the same way as in purchase accounting, except that the updating of the expanded analysis of the investment account is simpler because only the book value element is involved.
2. The amounts in the consolidated column are composed of (a) the parent's items based on book values and (b) the subsidiary's items based on book values. No revaluation to current values has been made.
3. A secondary elimination entry is not needed when pooling of interests accounting is used.
4. The use of the equity method to account subsequently for the parent's investment maintains the investment account balance equal to the subsidiary's net assets at book value, which simplifies the consolidation process.
5. When ownership of the subsidiary is less than 100% (it must be at least 90% to qualify for pooling of interests treatment), the necessary minority interest deduction is determined and derived in the same manner as shown in the preceding chapter for situations in which purchase accounting is used.
6. The formal consolidated statement of retained earnings would be presented as follows:

Balance, December 31, 19X0, as previously reported........	$100,000
Effect of pooling of interests with S Company..............	40,000
Balance, December 31, 19X0, as restated........................	$140,000
Net income for the year..	51,000
Subtotal...	$191,000
Dividends..	(31,000)
Balance, December 31, 19X1...	$160,000

KEY POINTS:

a. The amount shown for the effect of pooling of interests—($40,000 in this case)—always equals the parent's share of the subsidiary's retained earnings as of the beginning of the year, regardless of the actual business combination date. This is because **the subsidiary's earnings for the entire year are combined with those of the parent, no matter when during the year the combination occurs.**
b. Dividends declared by the subsidiary prior to the combination date—none in this case—that went to those stockholders who pooled (thus excluding dividends to minority shareholders) would be combined with the parent's dividends in this statement.

The preceding illustration assumed that the parent company used the equity method to account for its investment in the subsidiary. The parent may, however, account for its investment in the subsidiary using the cost method. The cost method is not illustrated, because the procedures are the same as those shown in Appendix A to Chapter 4.

Comparative Income Statements: Pooling of Interests Versus Purchase Accounting

We assumed in Illustration 6-4 that 3,000 shares of common stock were issued to effect the combination (situation C in Illustration 6-1). The fair value of the consideration given was $90,000. If the combination did not qualify for pooling of interests treatment, then under purchase accounting the $90,000 total cost would consist of the following major conceptual elements:

1. The book value element (100% of $60,000)	$60,000
2. The current value over book value element ($80,000 − $60,000)	20,000
3. The goodwill element ($90,000 − $80,000)	10,000
	$90,000

Assume that $4,000 of amortization of cost in excess of book value would be recorded in 19X1 under the purchase method. Income statements for 19X1 are shown under both methods for comparison:

	Pooling of Interests*	Purchase Method
Revenues	$800,000	$ 800,000
Cost of goods sold	(476,000)	$(480,000)
Expenses	(273,000)	(273,000)
Net Income	$ 51,000	$ 47,000

*From Illustration 6-4.

Conforming Accounting Methods

Under the purchase method of accounting, a new valuation basis is established for the assets and liabilities of the acquired business. In these situations, the acquiring company's accounting methods can be imposed on the acquired business at the consummation date to have uniform accounting methods on a combined or consolidated basis. However, uniform accounting methods are not required. Thus, a parent using straight-line depreciation that acquires a subsidiary using an accelerated depreciation method has the following options:

1. Allow the subsidiary to use accelerated depreciation.
2. Direct the subsidiary to use straight-line depreciation.

The second alternative is more desirable, because the consolidated financial statements are presented using uniform accounting methods.

Under the pooling of interests method of accounting, a new valuation basis is not established for the assets and liabilities of the acquired business. The AICPA, however, recognized the merits of presenting combined or consolidated financial statements that use uniform accounting methods. Accordingly, it included the following provision pertaining to conforming accounting methods for situations involving pooling of interests:

> The separate companies may have recorded assets and liabilities under differing methods of accounting and the amounts may be adjusted to the same basis of accounting if the change would otherwise have been appropriate for the separate company. A change in accounting method to conform the individual methods should be applied retroactively, and financial statements presented for prior periods should be restated.[8]

This statement does not make conformity of accounting methods mandatory. It states that the amounts "**may be adjusted** to the same basis of accounting." Conforming accounting methods is optional, as in purchase accounting.

DISCLOSURES

The acquiring entity must make the following disclosures for each period in which a business combination accounted for under the pooling of interests method occurs.

Disclosure in the Financial Statements

The financial statements must indicate that a business combination accounted for under the pooling of interests method has occurred. This indication may be either by captions or by references to notes to the financial statements.[9]

Disclosure in the Notes to the Financial Statements

The following footnote disclosures, among others, are required:

1. The name and description of the business combined.
2. The fact that the pooling of interests method is used to account for the combination.
3. The number of shares issued and a description thereof.
4. Income information (including revenues and net income) for preacquisition periods of the acquired business that are included in the current combined income statement.
5. Reconciliations of revenues and earnings to amounts previously reported by the acquiring entity.[10]

[8] *APB Opinion No. 16*, par. 52.
[9] *APB Opinion No. 16*, par. 63.
[10] *APB Opinion No. 16*, par. 64.

PERSPECTIVE

A Capsule History of Pooling of Interests Accounting

Early 1940s The term *pooling of interests* emerges. In rate-base cases brought before it involving business combinations, the Federal Power Commission (FPC) prohibits companies from revaluing their assets upward to their current values when the separate parties have merely pooled their interests. This policy is applied to both related parties and unrelated parties. For revaluation to be allowed, the FPC requires that a sale must occur—one party must dispose of an interest and the other party must acquire that interest.

1945 The Committee on Accounting Procedure of the American Institute for Certified Public Accountants (AICPA) begins to address poolings of interests. Internal memos show that only combinations of two or more interests of comparable size are considered poolings of interests.

1950 *ARB No. 40*, "Business Combinations," is issued. It lists four factors to be considered in determining whether the transaction is a purchase or pooling of interests: (1) The **continuity of the former ownership:** Eliminating one of the ownerships or altering the equity interests of either interest immediately before or after the combination indicates a purchase transaction. (2) **Relative size:** One party that is "quite minor" in size compared to the other suggests a purchase transaction. (3) **Continuity of management:** If the management of one of the interests is eliminated or has little influence after the combination, a purchase transaction is indicated. (4) **Similar or complementary lines of business:** If the businesses are in similar or complementary lines of business, a presumption of a pooling of interests is strengthened.

No single factor is the deciding one—the presence or absence of each of the factors is to be considered cumulatively.

OBSERVATION: After *ARB No. 40* was issued, it was possible in most cases to have the assets reported at the same values regardless of whether purchase accounting or pooling of interests accounting were used. This occurred because it was acceptable practice to immediately charge to retained earnings the cost in excess of book value that arose under the purchase method. As a result, there was no major controversy at this time.

1953 *ARB No. 43*, a restatement and revision of *ARB Nos. 1 to 42*, is issued. No substantive changes are made concerning business combinations. Of great importance, however, is the prohibition of immediately charging intangibles arising from acquisition to retained earnings (or to additional paid-in capital). Capitalization as an asset is required and amortization to income is encourage.

A Capsule History of Pooling of Interests Accounting *(continued)*

OBSERVATIONS: The effect of *ARB No. 43* was to make pooling of interests much more desirable because the cost in excess of book value can be eliminated from accountability only under pooling of interests. Thus the stage was set for the explosive shift to the pooling of interests method that would occur during the 1950s and 1960s.

At this time, the accounting profession did not have detailed rules concerning pooling of interests—only factors to be evaluated. The burden of determining whether or not pooling of interest should be applied was placed squarely on the auditors' judgment and integrity.

1950–1956 Because of the manner in which *ARB Nos. 40* and *43* are written—no single factor determines the need for pooling of interests—companies and their auditors interpret them loosely. The result in most cases is that companies have almost complete discretion to account for a combination as a purchase or as a pooling of interests.

1957 *ARB No. 48*, "Business Combinations," is issued, superseding the business combinations section of *ARB No. 43*. The "similar or complementary" lines of business factor is dropped. Concerning the relative size of the combining interests, the wording "quite minor" is replaced by a range of percentages: if one of the combining interests ends up with 90–95% of the stock, purchase accounting is indicated.

OBSERVATIONS: The fast-growing trend toward diversification most likely played a role in the deletion of the similar or complementary business factor. Thus, one of the major reasons why companies might want to pool their interests was deemed nonessential. It was now considered perfectly reasonable for a CPA and a dentist to pool their interests, as could the shareholders of a medical equipment manufacturer and a toy manufacturer.

The insertion of the 90–95% wording removed the intent of *ARB No. 40* that the combining companies be of comparable size. Now, companies of greatly disproportionate size could have a pooling of interests.

1958–1962 The relative-size factor having been already weakened, it becomes virtually ignored in practice. Companies begin to use preferred stock to maintain the "continuity of ownership." An abuse known as "retroactive poolings" becomes widespread and is severely criticized.[a]

1963 *Accounting Research Study No. 5*, "A Critical Study of Accounting for Business Combinations" by Arthur R. Wyatt and sponsored by the American Institute of Certified Public

[a]Retroactive poolings is a technique in which poolings of interests consummated after the year-end but before the issuance of the year-end annual report are given effect in the current year's financial statements rather than in the year of the combination.

(continued)

Accountants, is issued.[b] It recommends the following: (a) The pooling of interests accounting treatment should be abolished unless the parties are related. (b) When the parties are unrelated and approximately the same size, a fresh start (termed "fair value pooling of interests") should be made by revaluing the assets of both companies to their current values.

1965 The Accounting Principles Board issues *APB Opinion No. 6*, "Status of Accounting Research Bulletins." Commenting on *ARB No. 48*, it states that the factors set forth therein are guidelines rather than literal requirements.

1966–1968 New abuses crop up, such as the part-purchase, part-pooling method. Finding a company with undervalued assets, recording a combination with it as a pooling of interests, and then later selling off the undervalued assets to report phenomenal gains becomes a popular practice. Many companies call upon their auditors to teach them the intricacies of pooling of interests accounting.

The profession comes under mounting criticism for not having adequate standards by which to judge pooling of interests, especially in light of the largest wave of business combinations in history. One of the most scathing articles during this period is "Dirty Pooling" by Abraham J. Briloff of Baruch College.[c] Briloff subsequently becomes one of the leading critics of the accounting profession and is often referred to as its conscience.

February 1969 The chairman of the Securities and Exchange Commission, testifying before a congressional committee, states that unless the accounting profession takes prompt action to resolve the business combinations controversy, the SEC would establish rules in this area.

June 1969 The AICPA holds a symposium on accounting for business combinations.

September 1969 The AICPA's executive vice president, Leonard Savoie, states in an address that a forthcoming exposure draft will propose abolishing pooling of interests. He also states:

> Anything less than this solution will mean simply a "repositioning" of the abuses which have become so rampant in recent years.[d]

November 1969 The Accounting Principles Board tentatively decides to abolish pooling of interests accounting. A Federal Trade Com-

[b] Wyatt was then a professor of accountancy at the University of Illinois. A short time later, he became a senior partner in the home office of Arthur Andersen & Co. and subsequently becomes one of the most respected accountants in the profession. In 1985 he became a member of the Financial Accounting Standards Board.

[c] *The Accounting Review* (July 1967), 489.

[d] "The Accounting Profession at the Hump of the Decades." By Abraham J. Briloff, *Financial Analysts Journal* (May–June 1970), 61.

A Capsule History of Pooling of Interests Accounting *(continued)*

	mission study (authorized by a Senate antitrust committee) released about the same time recommends that the SEC eliminate pooling of interests accounting when stock is given as consideration.
December 1969	The APB reverses itself and tentatively decides pooling of interests accounting should be allowed but not as an alternative that can be freely chosen if desired. For a given set of circumstances and conditions, only one method will apply.
February 1970	The APB issues an exposure draft. The detailed conditions set forth to be met for a pooling of interests will severely limit its use. A three-to-one comparable-size test is included. Lawsuits are subsequently threatened over this condition.
June 1970	The APB reduces the size test to nine to one (about what it was under *ARB No. 48*).
August 1970	*APB Opinion No. 16* is issued; it barely passes on a 12-to-6 vote. The requirement that the combining companies effect a continuity of interests becomes the cornerstone for pooling of interests treatment; the size test is dropped entirely, and there are no requirements for continuity of management or simiiar or complementary lines of business. The combining interests must meet twelve detailed conditions in order to effect a pooling of interests. If they do not meet any one of the twelve conditions, they must use purchase accounting in their combination. OBSERVATION: The fact that the conditions for pooling of interests treatment are spelled out in such detail clearly shows that setting guidelines requiring the use of professional judgment and integrity does not work very well. This may be because the judgment of so many is either questionable or compromised as a result of concern over loss of clients to other CPAs who are more willing to liberally construe (some would say ignore) the guidelines.
1970–1973	*APB Opinion No. 16* proves to be difficult to apply. Because of its complexity and in order to close loopholes, the AICPA issues 30 interpretations and the SEC issues four Accounting Series Releases. (Later, from 1974 to 1987, the FASB will issue three interpretations and three technical bulletins.)
1973	The FASB replaces the APB and immediately requests views on previous APB pronouncements. The responses show that *APB Opinion Nos. 16* and *17* are of greatest concern.
1974	The FASB decides to reevaluate the twelve conditions for pooling of interests in *APB Opinion No. 16*.
1975	The FASB expands the scope of the project to encompass all issues associated with business combinations and goodwill.
1976	The FASB issues a discussion memorandum on "Accounting for Business Combinations and Purchased Intangibles."

(continued)

1981 The FASB removes the project from its active agenda because of its "low priority in relation to other existing and potential projects."

1987 Business combinations and purchased intangibles continue to be low in priority for the FASB, even though 14 years have passed since respondents indicated that they were most concerned with these issues.

Sources: A good portion of the history prior to 1971 was based on information contained in the following scholarly publications:

A Critical Study of Accounting for Business Combinations, by Arthur R. Wyatt. (American Institute of Certified Public Accountants, New York; 1963).

Goodwill in Accounting: A History of the Issues and Problems, by Hugh P. Hughes. Research Monograph No. 80. Atlanta: Georgia State University, 1982. Because of the close relationship of the goodwill issue with pooling of interests accounting, this publication devotes considerable attention to the pooling of interests issue.

SUMMARY

Under the pooling of interests method, a business combination is viewed as a combining of equity interests. This combining of interests is possible only in situations in which the acquiring company issues substantially all common stock as consideration for the acquired business. In addition, numerous secondary conditions must be met before the pooling of interests treatment may be used. If all the conditions are met, then pooling of interests accounting must be used. If any one condition is not met, then purchase accounting must be used.

A business combination that qualifies for the pooling of interests treatment is recorded based on the book value of the acquired company's net assets. The acquired company's assets and liabilities are reported at their historical amounts in the future financial statements of the combined businesses. Consequently, goodwill is never created. The pooling of interests method is conceptually opposed to the purchase method because it completely ignores the fair value of the consideration given and the current value of the acquired company's net assets. The pooling of interests method is popular primarily because it usually results in reporting greater earnings, and earnings per share, in future periods than would be reported under the purchase method.

Glossary of New Terms

Dissenting Shareholders Target company shareholders who refuse to exchange their common shares for only common stock of the acquiring company.

Spin-off A divestiture of a portion of a business whereby certain assets, liabilities, or common stock holdings of a subsidiary are given to certain shareholders of a company in exchange for some or all of their outstanding common stock holdings in the company.

Review Questions

1. Why is the term *acquired business* not used in the discussion of pooling of interests accounting in *APB Opinion No. 16*?
2. What is the essence of a pooling of interests?
3. What accounts for the popularity of the pooling of interests method?
4. How has the original concept of a pooling of interests changed over the years?
5. Distinguish between a joining together of the equity interests and a continuity of ownership of the separate equity interests.
6. What are the major conceptual issues pertaining to pooling of interests?
7. What criteria determine whether a business combination is treated as a pooling of interests?
8. What is the major criticism of the pooling of interests criteria in *APB Opinion No. 16*?
9. How is the value of the consideration given by the acquiring company accounted for in a business combination that qualifies as a pooling of interests?
10. What primary consideration is given in a business combination that qualifies as a pooling of interests?
11. How many major elements exist in the investment account for a business combination accounted for as a pooling of interests?
12. Can cash be given to the shareholders of the acquired company in a business combination that is accounted for as a pooling of interests?
13. When the acquisition of a subsidiary has been accounted for as a pooling of interests, is a secondary elimination entry required in preparing a consolidating statement worksheet? Why or why not?
14. To what extent are the subsidiary's net assets reflected at their current values in a business combination accounted for as a pooling of interests?
15. How are preacquisition earnings of the acquired business treated in income statements for periods before the acquisition date when the combination has been accounted for as a pooling of interests?
16. When assets have been acquired, may pooling of interests accounting be used?

Technical Research Questions

Here and elsewhere in the book answers to technical research questions may be found by consulting the pronouncements of the Financial Accounting Standards Board, the Accounting Principles Board, and the Securities and Exchange Commission.

17. Immediately after a business combination, a third party buys all or a portion of the common stock issued to effect the combination. Would such an arrangement disqualify the use of the pooling of interests method?
18. Assuming that the acquiring company acquires 90% of the outstanding common stock of the target company, may an individual common stockholder of the target company exchange some of his or her shares for shares of the acquiring company and either retain the balance of the shares or sell them to the acquiring company for cash?
19. Would the accounting for a business combination be affected if the consummation is contingent upon the purchase by a third party or parties of all or part of the common stock issued in the combination?
20. Could the common stock issued in a business combination to be accounted for as a pooling of interests be designated as a class of stock different from the majority class (for example, Class A if the majority class has no designation)?
21. An acquiring company issues some maximum number of shares to stockholders of the target company under an agreement that part of the shares are to be returned if future earnings are below a certain amount or the future market price of the stock is above a stipulated price. Would this invalidate pooling of interests treatment?
22. Would the granting of an employment contract or a deferred compensation plan by the combined enterprise to former stockholders of the combining company invalidate pooling of interests treatment?
23. Does the conversion of a mutual savings and loan association to a stock savings and loan association within two years before a plan of combination is initiated, or between the dates it is initiated and consummated, preclude pooling of interests accounting treatment?

Discussion Cases

DC 6-1

A Lawsuit Alleging Deception

In January 19X5, Planner Company entered into a business combination transaction with Supresso Company. Planner issued the common stock to effect the transaction. The twelve conditions for pooling of interests treatment were met, so the transaction was recorded as a pooling of interests. Supresso had a substantial amount of undervalued assets as of the combination date.

Through December 31, 19X7, Planner had reported six consecutive years of increased profits and had attracted a wide following on Wall Street. In 19X8, its earnings from operations were down slightly from 19X7. To show a continued trend of higher profits, management sold Supresso's undervalued assets throughout 19X8 at a substantial profit. In 19X9, earnings from operations were the same as in 19X8, but the company had no undervalued assets to sell. Accordingly, 19X9 earnings were substantially below those of 19X8 and 19X7.

As a result of reporting lower profits in 19X9, the price of the company's common stock dropped sharply, and many investors lost substantial amounts of money. A class-action lawsuit was filed against the company shortly after earnings were reported for 19X9, alleging that the company had conspired to issue false and misleading financial statements for 19X8. The focal point of the lawsuit was that the use of the pooling of interests method in 19X5 resulted in deceptive financial reporting in 19X8 and that the purchase method of accounting should have been used instead. (Only a nominal gain would have been reported on the sale of the assets in 19X8 if the purchase method had been used.)

The parties named in the lawsuit are Planner's top management, including the controller, and its certified public accountants.

Required:

1. Does the company have an adequate defense that it used generally accepted accounting principles?
2. To use the pooling of interests method, did Planner's controller have to believe personally that it results in a fair presentation?
3. How might the lawyer for the plaintiffs use *Accounting Research Study No. 5*? What impact might its use have on the jury?
4. In reading *APB Opinion No. 16*, the lawyer for the plaintiffs found that one of the dissenting members of the Accounting Principles Board was a partner in the CPA firm named in the lawsuit. Further research revealed that this CPA firm was vehemently against the pooling of interests concept prior to the issuance of *APB Opinion No. 16*. Of what use might this information be?

DC 6-2

Pooling of Interests Criteria: Substantial Undervaluation of Acquired Company's Net Assets and Nonoperating Status

Presto Company recently acquired all of the outstanding common stock of Sonesta Realty Company in a transaction structured to qualify for pooling of interests treatment. Sonesta has substantial land holdings that were acquired many years ago. The current value of these holdings is several million dollars in excess of book value. The fair value of the consideration given to Sonesta's shareholders equaled the current value of its net assets. Presto's controller has indicated to you, Presto's certified public accountant, that the transaction was structured as a pooling of interests to prevent the revaluation of these land holdings to their current values, as would be done under purchase accounting. In this way, Presto can start selling holdings after the combination date and report substantial profit at that time.

Required:

1. How do these comments affect your opinion on whether the pooling of interests accounting treatment is appropriate?
2. Assuming the twelve specific conditions for pooling of interests treatment are met, would the fact that Sonesta has been relatively inactive for the preceding few years—that is, it had no activities or operations other than these existing land investments—raise any other issues that would preclude pooling of interests treatment?

DC 6-3

Conditions for Pooling of Interests

Pinolta Company is negotiating a business combination with Shutterex. You, Pinolta's certified public accountant, learn the following from Pinolta's controller during a lunch meeting:

1. Pinolta will issue common stock to effect the combination. (The book value of Shutterex's net assets is 1% of the book value of Pinolta's net assets; the same relationship exists on a current value basis.) After the combination, Shutterex's former shareholders will hold approximately 4% of Pinolta's total outstanding common shares. As a result, these shareholders cannot significantly influence the operations of the combined companies.
2. There will be no specified holding period during which Shutterex's former shareholders must not sell the Pinolta shares they receive in the transaction.
3. Shutterex is an industry leader, has remarkably high profits, and has a price-to-earnings ratio of 60 to 1 (indicating that it has substantial goodwill).
4. Pinolta Company's management intends to acquire Shutterex's business at any cost, regardless of whether or not pooling of interests treatment can be used. In other words, the objective is to acquire the business; the form of consideration to be given is of secondary importance.
5. Immediately after the combination, approximately 20% of Shutterex's former stockholders plan to sell the Pinolta common stock they receive in the combination, because they need the cash.

Required:
How does this information affect your opinion on whether pooling of interests accounting treatment is appropriate?

DC 6-4

Conditions for Pooling of Interests

The boards of directors of Paterno Corporation, Sata Company, Seta Company and Sita Company are meeting jointly to discuss plans for a business combination. Each corporation has one class of common stock outstanding; Sata also has one class of preferred stock outstanding. Although terms have not been settled, Paterno will be the acquiring or issuing corporation.

Required:
For question 1, determine which position is correct. For the remaining questions, determine how these facts affect the accounting method to the used. (Consider each question independently of the others.)

1. Some of the directors believe that the terms of the combination should be settled immediately and that the method of accounting to be used (whether pooling of interests, purchase, or a mixture) may be chosen at some later date. Others believe that the terms of the combination and the accounting method are closely related.
2. Paterno and Sata are comparable in size; Seta and Sita are much smaller.
3. Seta was formerly a subsidiary of Spinner Corporation, which is not related to any of the four companies discussing combination. Eighteen months ago, Spinner voluntarily spun off Seta.
4. Mr. Don Dissento who holds 5% of Sita's common stock, will almost certainly object to the combination. Assume that Paterno can acquire only 95% (rather than 100%) of Sita's stock, issuing Paterno common stock in exchange. (If Paterno can acquire the remaining 5% at some future time—in five years, for instance—in exchange for its own common stock, which accounting method will be applicable to this second acquisition?)

5. Because the directors feel that one of Sita's major divisions will not be compatible with the combined company's operations, they expect to sell it as soon as possible after the combination is consummated. They expect to have no trouble finding a buyer.
6. Twenty months ago, Sata acquired 12% of its common stock because the price of the stock was attractively low. Fourteen months ago, Sata retired this treasury stock.
7. Sata is in the same industry as Paterno. Seta is in a complementary industry; and Sita is in a totally unrelated industry.

(AICPA adapted)

Exercises

E 6-1

Conditions for Pooling of Interests

Indicate whether each of the following conditions or terms negates pooling of interests accounting treatment:

1. Acquisition of 90% of the assets.
2. Acquisition of 85% of outstanding common stock.
3. Pro rata distribution of cash and common stock to acquired company's shareholders.
4. Additional common stock to be issued by the acquiring company if its common stock has a fair market value below $50 per share two years after the combination date.
5. The acquired subsidiary is to be liquidated into a division. (No sell-off of assets is involved.)
6. After acquisition of 100% of the division's assets, its accounting is to be centralized.
7. Acquisition of 90% of outstanding common stock.
8. The common stock issued to the acquired company's shareholders has certain voting restrictions.
9. Additional common shares are to be issued by the acquiring company, depending on the subsequent sales level of the acquired business for three years after the acquisition date.
10. The acquiring company agrees to purchase for cash less than 10% of the shares issued within three years of the acquisition date.

E 6-2

Testing for Independence

Paine Company and Swebber Company are contemplating a business combination structured to qualify as a pooling of interests. Common stock information is as follows:

	Paine Company	Swebber Company
Outstanding common shares	300,000	100,000
Paine Company common stock owned by Swebber Company		15,000
Market price of stock	$20	

Required:

1. Determine whether the companies are independent. Assume Paine will issue three shares for every one outstanding share of Swebber Company.
2. Determine whether the companies are independent, but assume that Paine will issue one share for every one outstanding share of Swebber Company.
3. Explain why the answers in requirements 1 and 2 are different.

E 6-3

Testing for Independence: Dual Intercorporate Investments

Pecos Company and Slimm Company are contemplating a business combination structured to qualify as a pooling of interests. Common stock information is as follows:

	Pecos Company	Slimm Company
Outstanding common shares..............	600,000	100,000
Slimm Company common stock owned by Pecos Company	5,000	
Pecos Company common stock owned by Slimm Company		4,000
Market price of stock	$25	

Pecos will issue one common share for each two outstanding common shares of Slimm.

Required:

1. Determine whether the companies are independent.
2. If Slimm were the company issuing the common stock, what exchange ratio would it use to maintain the relative holdings between the two stockholder groups?

E 6-4

CHALLENGER Testing for Independence: Dual Intercorporate Investments

Pigital Company and Sterry Company are contemplating a business combination structured to qualify as a pooling of interests. Common stock information is as follows:

	Pigital Company	Sterry Company
Outstanding common stock	900,000	200,000
Pigital Company common stock owned by Sterry Company...............		9,000
Sterry Company common stock owned by Pigital Company...............	18,000	
Market price of stock	$10	

Pigital will issue three common shares for every two common shares of Sterry.

Required:

1. Determine whether the companies are independent.
2. Determine whether the companies are independent, but assume that Sterry will be the issuing company and will issue 600,000 shares to Pigital's stockholders. (These shares maintain the same relationship as when Pigital was the issuing company.)
3. Explain why the answers in requirements 1 and 2 are different even though the relative holdings between the two stockholder groups was held constant. Which answer must be used to determine independence?

E 6-5

Recording a Pooling of Interests: 100% of Outstanding Common Stock Acquired

On January 1, 19X1, Panhandle Company acquired 100% of the outstanding common stock of Stover Company by issuing 20,000 shares of its $5 par value common stock. Selected information as of the acquisition date is as follows:

	Panhandle Company	Stover Company
Common stock, $5 par value	$1,000,000	
Common stock, $1 par value		$200,000
Additional paid-in capital	3,000,000	400,000
Retained earnings	2,000,000	250,000
	$6,000,000	$850,000
Fair market value per share	$50	$25
Net assets at current value	$7,000,000	$900,000

Assume the business combination qualifies for pooling of interests treatment.

Required:

1. Prepare the entry to record the business combination.
2. Prepare an expanded analysis of the investment account as of the acquisition date.
3. Prepare the primary elimination entry at January 1, 19X1.

E 6-6

Recording a Pooling of Interests: 100% of Outstanding Common Stock Acquired

On January 1, 19X1, Pinkert Company acquired 100% of the outstanding common stock of Security Company by issuing shares of its common stock. Each company's equity accounts as of the acquisition date are as follows:

	Pinkert Company	Security Company
Common stock, $10 par value	$1,000,000	
Common stock, $5 par value		$ 80,000
Additional paid-in capital	25,000	20,000
Retained earnings	200,000	50,000
	$1,225,000	$150,000

Assume the business combination qualifies for pooling of interest accounting.

Required:

1. Prepare the entry to record the business combination, assuming Pinkert issued:
   a. 8,000 shares.
   b. 10,000 shares.
   c. 12,000 shares.
   d. 14,000 shares.
2. Prepare the primary elimination entry as of the acquisition date for each situation in requirement 1.

E 6-7 Recording a Pooling of Interests: 90% of Outstanding Common Stock Acquired

Assume the information provided in Exercise 6-6, except that Pinkert Company acquired only 90% of the outstanding common stock of Security Company.

Required:

1. Prepare the entry to record the business combination, assuming Pinkert issued:
   a. 7,200 shares.
   b. 9,000 shares.
   c. 10,800 shares.
   d. 12,600 shares.
2. Prepare the primary elimination entry as of the acquisition date for each situation in requirement 1.

E 6-8 COMPREHENSIVE Recording a Pooling of Interests: Applying the Equity Method; Preparing Primary Elimination Entries; 100% of Outstanding Common Stock Acquired

On January 1, 19X1, Platter Company acquired 100% of the outstanding common stock of Singer Company by issuing 20,000 shares of its common stock. Each company's equity accounts as of the acquisition date are as follows:

	Platter Company	Singer Company
Common stock, $1 par value	$ 100,000	
Common stock, $5 par value		$ 5,000
Additional paid-in capital	900,000	95,000
Retained earnings	500,000	60,000
	$1,500,000	$160,000

For the year ended December 31, 19X1, Singer had net income of $40,000 and declared cash dividends of $10,000. Assume the business combination qualifies for pooling of interests accounting.

Required:

1. Prepare the entry to record the business combination.
2. Prepare the primary elimination entry as of the acquisition date.
3. Prepare the entries for 19X1 required under the equity method of accounting.
4. Update the analysis of the investment account for 19X1, and prepare the primary elimination entry as of December 31, 19X1.

E 6-9 COMPREHENSIVE Recording a Pooling of Interests: Applying the Equity Method; Preparing Primary Elimination Entries; 90% of Outstanding Common Stock Acquired

Assume the information provided in Exercise 6-8, except that Platter Company acquired only 90% of the outstanding common stock of Singer Company on January 1, 19X1, by issuing 18,000 shares of its common stock.

Required:
The requirements are the same as those in Exercise 6-8.

E 6-10 Determining Consolidated Retained Earnings and Consolidated Net Income in Acquisition Year

On June 30, 19X5, Prospero Company acquired Success, Inc., in a business combination properly accounted for as a pooling of interests. Prospero exchanged six of its shares of common stock for each share of Success's outstanding common stock. June 30 was the fiscal year-end for both companies. No intercompany transactions occurred during the year. The balance sheets immediately before the combination are as follows:

	Prospero Company	Success, Inc.	
	Book Value	Book Value	Fair Value
Current assets	$ 40,000	$ 30,000	$ 45,000
Equipment (net)	150,000	120,000	140,000
Land	30,000		
	$220,000	$150,000	$185,000
Current liabilities	$ 35,000	$ 15,000	$ 15,000
Notes payable	40,000		
Bonds payable		100,000	100,000
Common stock ($1 par value)	75,000		
Common stock ($5 par value)		50,000	
Retained earnings	70,000	(15,000)	
	$220,000	$150,000	

Required:

1. What was the Retained Earnings account balance on the combined balance sheet at June 30, 19X5?
   a. $45,000
   b. $55,000

c. $70,000
d. $80,000

2. How should the combined net income for the year be computed?
   a. Use only Prospero's income because the combination occurred on the last day of the fiscal year.
   b. Use only Success's income because the combination occurred on the last day of the fiscal year.
   c. Add together both companies' incomes even though the combination occurred on the last day of the fiscal year.
   d. Add together both companies' incomes and subtract the annual amortization of goodwill.

(AICPA adapted)

E 6-11

Determining Consolidated Net Income in Acquisition Year

On January 1, 19X7, Preserve, Inc., issued 100,000 additional shares of $10 par value voting common stock in exchange for all of Stuckers Company's voting common stock in a business combination appropriately accounted for as a pooling of interests. Net income for the year ended December 31, 19X7, was $400,000 for Stuckers and $1,300,000 for Preserve, exclusive of any consideration of Stuckers. During 19X7, Preserve paid $900,000 dividends to its stockholders, and Stuckers paid $250,000 dividends to Preserve.

Required:
Determine the consolidated net income for the year ended December 31, 19X7.

(AICPA adapted)

E 6-12

Determining the Effect of Pooling on Parent's Stockholders' Equity

Panda Corporation issued voting common stock with a $90,000 stated value in exchange for all of the outstanding common stock of Soo-Soo Company. The combination was properly accounted for as a pooling of interests.

The stockholders' equity section in Soo-Soo's balance sheet at the combination date was as follows.

Common stock	$ 70,000
Capital contributed in excess of stated value	7,000
Retained earnings	50,000
	$127,000

Required:
What should be the increase in Panda's stockholders' equity at the acquisition date as a result of this business combination?

a. $-0-
b. $37,000
c. $90,000
d. $127,000

(AICPA adapted)

E 6-13

Determining Consolidated Stockholders' Equity

On January 1, 19X1, Platt Company issued 200,000 shares of $5 par value common stock in exchange for all of Slatter Company's common stock in a business combination that qualified as a pooling of interests. Immediately before the business combination, Platt's total stockholders' equity was $16,000,000 and of Slatter was $4,000,000. Other data for 19X1 are as follows:

	Platt Company	Slatter Company
Net income (excluding income recorded under the equity method)	$1,500,000	$450,000
Dividends declared	$ 750,000	$200,000

Required:
What is the consolidated stockholders' equity at December 31, 19X1?

(AICPA adapted)

E 6-14

Determining the Effect of Pooling of Interest on Parent's Equity

In a business combination accounted for as a pooling of interests, the combined corporation's retained earnings usually equals the sum of the retained earnings of the individual combining corporations.

Required:
Assuming there is no contributed capital other than capital stock at par value on each company's books, which of the following describes a situation in which the combined retained earnings must be increased or decreased?

a. Increased if the par value dollar amount of the outstanding shares of the combined corporation exceeds the total capital stock of the separate combining companies.
b. Increased if the par value dollar amount of the outstanding shares of the combined corporation is less than the total capital stock of the separate combining companies.
c. Decreased if the par value dollar amount of the outstanding shares of the combined corporation exceeds the total capital stock of the separate combining companies.
d. Decreased if the par value dollar amount of the outstanding shares of the combined corporation is less than the total capital stock of the separate combining companies.

(AICPA adapted)

Problems

P 6-1*

Recording a Pooling of Interests; Preparing Consolidated Financial Statements as of Acquisition Date; 100% of Outstanding Common Stock Acquired

On December 31, 19X2, Postal Company acquired 100% of the outstanding common stock of Service Company by issuing 1,000 shares of its common stock. The financial statements of each company for the year ended December 31, 19X2, *before the business combination*, are as follows:

	Postal Company	Service Company
Income Statement (19X2):		
Sales	$400,000	$120,000
Cost of goods sold	(200,000)	(70,000)
Expenses	(191,000)	(47,000)
Net Income	$ 9,000	$ 3,000
Balance Sheet (as of December 31, 19X2):		
Cash	$ 50,000	$ 33,000
Accounts receivable, net	60,000	20,000
Inventory	80,000	27,000
Fixed assets, net	610,000	120,000
	$800,000	$200,000
Accounts payable and accruals	$ 90,000	$ 25,000
Long-term debt	360,000	65,000
Common stock, $10 par value	100,000	
Common stock, $2 par value		20,000
Additional paid-in capital	200,000	80,000
Retained earnings	50,000	10,000
	$800,000	$200,000
Dividends declared in 19X2	$ 5,000	$ 1,000

Assume that the business combination qualifies for pooling of interests treatment. (Note that the combination occurred at the end of the year, not at the begining of the year as illustrated in the text. Thus, the equity method is not applied during 19X2.)

Required:

1. Prepare the entry to record the business combination.
2. Prepare the primary elimination entry at December 31, 19X2.
3. Prepare a consolidating statement worksheet at December 31, 19X2.
4. Prepare a formal consolidated statement of retained earnings for 19X2.

*The financial statement information presented for problems accompanied by asterisks is also provided on Model 6 (filename: Model6) of the software file disk that is available for use with the text, enabling the problem to be worked on the computer.

P 6-2* Recording a Pooling of Interests; Preparing Consolidated Financial Statements as of Acquisition Date—90% of Outstanding Common Stock Acquired

Assume the information provided in Problem 6-1, except that Postal Company acquired 90% of the outstanding common stock of Service Company on December 31, 19X2, by issuing 900 shares of its common stock.

Required:
The requirements are the same as for Problem 6-1. In addition, an entry to reflect minority interest in the income statement and exclude dividends paid in 19X2 to the minority shareholders is necessary.

P 6-3* Determining the Entry Used to Record a Pooling of Interests; Updating Analysis of Investment Account for Year Subsequent to Combination; Preparing Consolidated Financial Statements Subsequent to Acquisition Date: 100% of Outstanding Common Stock Acquired

Puppet Company acquired 100% of the outstanding common stock of Sesame Company on January 1, 19X4, by issuing 4,000 shares of its common stock. The financial statements of each company for the year ended December 31, 19X4, are as follows:

	Puppet Company	Sesame Company
Income Statement (19X4):		
Sales	$ 800,000	$100,000
Cost of goods sold	(500,000)	(50,000)
Expenses	(270,000)	(44,000)
Equity in net income of subsidiary	6,000	
Net Income	$ 36,000	$ 6,000
Balance Sheet (as of December 31, 19X4):		
Cash	$ 60,000	$ 10,000
Accounts receivable, net	90,000	20,000
Inventory	150,000	60,000
Investment in subsidiary	133,000	
Fixed assets, net	567,000	110,000
	$1,000,000	$200,000
Accounts payable and accruals	$ 76,000	$ 17,000
Long-term debt	300,000	50,000
Common stock, $10 par value	100,000	
Common stock, $1 par value		20,000
Additional paid-in capital	400,000	80,000
Retained earnings	124,000	33,000
	$1,000,000	$200,000
Dividends declared in 19X4	$ 10,000	$ 1,000

Assume the business combination qualifies for pooling of interests accounting.

Required:

1. Prepare an expanded and updated analysis of the investment account for 19X4, using the equity method of accounting.
2. Determine the entry Puppet made on January 1, 19X4, to record the business combination.
3. Prepare the primary elimination entry at December 31, 19X4.
4. Prepare a consolidating statement worksheet at December 31, 19X4.
5. Prepare a formal consolidated statement of retained earnings for 19X4.

P 6-4*

COMPREHENSIVE Recording a Pooling of Interests: Dissenting Shareholders; Direct Costs; Updating Analysis of Investment Account; Preparing Consolidated Financial Statements Subsequent to Acquisition Date: 100% of Outstanding Common Stock Acquired

On September 30, 19X2, Park Company acquired all of the outstanding common stock of Script Company by issuing 270,000 shares of its common stock to holders of 18,000 shares of Script common stock, and by giving $140,000 cash to dissenting holders of 2,000 shares of Script common stock. Direct costs incurred in connection with the business combination were $20,000. An additional $60,000 cost was incurred in registering the common stock issued with the SEC. Each company's financial statements for the year ended December 31, 19X2, are as follows:

	Park Company	Script Company
Income Statement (19X2):		
Sales	$9,000,000	$ 900,000
Cost of goods sold	(5,000,000)	(400,000)
Marketing expenses	(2,500,000)	(300,000)
Net Income	$1,500,000	$ 200,000
Balance Sheet (as of December 31, 19X2):		
Cash	$ 410,000	$ 100,000
Accounts receivable, net	900,000	200,000
Inventory	2,000,000	300,000
Fixed assets, net	3,500,000	1,400,000
Deferred charges	80,000	
Investment in Script Company	110,000	
	$7,000,000	$2,000,000
Accounts payable and accruals	$1,800,000	$ 280,000
Long-term debt	2,000,000	800,000
Common stock, $2 par value	700,000	
Common stock, $5 par value		100,000
Additional paid-in capital	800,000	340,000
Retained earnings	1,700,000	480,000
	$7,000,000	$2,000,000
Dividends declared and paid in 19X2	$ 800,000	$ 120,000

Other Information:

1. Script's income was earned evenly throughout the year.
2. Script declared and paid dividends of $30,000 each quarter.

3. The $80,000 of out-of-pocket costs were paid and charged to a Deferred Charges account.
4. No entry has been made to record the combination (which qualifies as a pooling of interests) other than for the amount paid to the dissenting shareholders. (The parent desires to use the equity method.)

Required:

1. Prepare the entry to record the business combination and any necessary year-end adjusting entries.
2. Prepare the primary elimination entry at December 31, 19X2. (Hint: Prepare an updated conceptual analysis of the investment account.)
3. Prepare a consolidating statement worksheet at December 31, 19X2.
4. Prepare a formal consolidated statement of retained earnings for 19X2.

P 6-5* COMPREHENSIVE Recording a Pooling of Interests: Direct Costs; Updating the Analysis of the Investment Account; Preparing Consolidated Financial Statements Subsequent to Acquisition Date; 90% of Outstanding Common Stock Acquired

Assume the information provided in Problem 6-4, except that Park Company acquired 90% of the outstanding common stock of Script Company by issuing 270,000 shares of its common stock. Park did not acquire the shares of the dissenting shareholders. (Adjust the parent's financial statements for (a) the $140,000 that was not paid to the dissenting shareholders, and (b) the dividends from the subsidiary that instead would have been paid to the minority interests.)

Required:
The requirements are the same as those for Problem 6-4.

P 6-6* COMPREHENSIVE Recording a Pooling of Interests: Updating Analysis of Investment Account; Preparing Consolidated Financial Statements Subsequent to Acquisition Date—100% of Outstanding Common Stock Acquired

On September 30, 19X4, Pana Company obtained a 100% interest in Sonic Company through an exchange of its common stock for Sonic common stock on a 1-for-4 basis. Pana's common stock was selling on the market for $8 per share at the time, and the investment was recorded on this basis using the following journal entry:

Investment in Sonic	80,000	
Common stock		50,000
Additional paid-in capital		30,000

The transaction qualified for pooling of interests treatment.

No market price was available for Sonic's common stock when Pana acquired it. Its book value was $1.60 per share at the combination date. Pana's board of directors justified the premium paid for the Sonic stock on the grounds that the fixed assets and inventory were undervalued.

Each company's financial statements for the year ended December 31, 19X4, are as follows:

	Pana Company	Sonic Company
Income Statement (19X4):		
Sales	$450,000	$200,000
Cost of goods sold	(250,000)	(110,000)
Expenses	(130,000)	(58,000)
Net Income	$ 70,000	$ 32,000
Balance Sheet (as of December 31, 19X4):		
Cash	$ 50,000	$ 12,000
Accounts receivable, net	110,000	68,000
Inventory	177,000	22,000
Investment in Sonic Company	80,000	
Fixed assets, net	318,000	180,000
	$735,000	$282,000
Accounts payable and accruals	$117,000	$ 98,000
Long-term debt	140,000	106,000
Common stock, $5 par value	200,000	
Common stock, $1 par value		40,000
Additional paid-in capital	160,000	
Retained earnings	118,000	38,000
	$735,000	$282,000
Dividends declared in 19X4	$ 55,000	$ -0-

Required:

1. Prepare the adjusting entry to reflect the combination as a pooling of interests at September 30, 19X4.
2. Prepare the entry resulting from the application of the equity method of accounting from September 30, 19X4, through December 31, 19X4.
3. Prepare an expanded analysis of the investment account as of September 30, 19X4, and update it through December 31, 19X4.
4. Prepare the primary elimination entry at December 31, 19X4.
5. Prepare a consolidating statement worksheet for 19X4 (after adjusting the financial statements for entries in requirements 1, 2, and 3).
6. Prepare a formal consolidated statement of retained earnings for 19X4.

(AICPA adapted)

P 6-7

COMPREHENSIVE CHALLENGER Conforming Accounting Methods for Inventory Added to Problem 6-6

Assume the same information given in Problem 6-6, except that the financial statements reflect the FIFO method of valuing inventories for the parent company and the LIFO method for the subsidiary. The parent desires to conform the subsidiary's inventory method to its own as of the combination date. The subsidiary has developed the following information pertaining to its inventory:

Date	LIFO	FIFO
December 31, 19X3	$18,000	$27,000
September 30, 19X4	20,000	30,000[a]
December 31, 19X4	22,000	34,000

[a]Assume this amount is equal to current value on this date.

Required:

1. Prepare the subsidiary's December 31, 19X4, entry to conform its inventory accounting practice to the parent's. Ignore income tax considerations. (Hint: Refer to par. 27 of *APB Opinion No. 20,* "Accounting Changes," and par. 52 of *APB Opinion No. 16.*)
2. The remaining requirements are the same as requirements 1 to 6 for Problem 6-6.

Problems Comparing the Pooling of Interests Method with Purchase Method

P 6-8

Calculation of Consolidated Net Income: Pooling of Interests Method Versus Purchase Method

Pomglomerates Company acquired several businesses during 19X1. Information relating to each business is as follows:

Company	Date Acquired	Percentage Acquired	Net Income (Loss) for 19X1
Able Company	1/1/X1	100	$90,000
Baker Company	4/1/X1	90	80,000
Charley Company	7/1/X1	100	20,000
Delta Company	11/1/X1	95	60,000
Echo Company	12/31/X1	90	(10,000)

Assume all earnings and losses occurred evenly throughout the year. Assume Pomglomerates had net income of $500,000 from its own separate operations, exclusive of earnings or losses recorded under the equity method of accounting.

Required:

1. Determine the amount of consolidated net income for 19X1, assuming all business combinations qualified for pooling of interests accounting.
2. Determine the amount of consolidated net income for 19X1, assuming none of the business combinations qualified for pooling of interests accounting. Assume Pomglomerates amortized $17,000 cost in excess of book value, which is not reflected in the $500,000 amount given above.

P 6-9 COMPREHENSIVE (Chapters 3, 4, and 6) Comparing the Purchase Method with the Pooling of Interests Method: Preparing Consolidated Financial Statements

Sparrow Company merged into Plover Company on June 30, 19X3, and Sparrow ceased to exist. Both companies report on a calendar year-end basis.

Additional Information:
As of the date of the merger:

1. The fair value of each corporation's assets and liabilities on June 30, 19X3, was as follows:

	Plover Company	Sparrow Company
Current assets	$ 4,900,000	$ 3,400,000
Land	3,000,000	1,000,000
Buildings and equipment	19,000,000	13,000,000
Patents	700,000	400,000
Total Assets	$27,600,000	$17,800,000
Liabilities	(2,500,000)	(2,100,000)
Net Assets	$25,100,000	$15,700,000

2. Plover has charged $70,000 of direct out-of-pocket costs relating to the merger and $30,000 of internally generated general expenses of the acquisitions department to the Prepaid Expenses account (part of current assets) pending the recording of the combination.
3. Revaluing Plover's and Sparrow's assets to their current values results in additional amortization and depreciation of $240,000 and $80,000 for the six months ended December 31, 19X3.
4. Dividends declared and paid for 19X3 were:

	Plover Company	Sparrow Company
First six months	$800,000	$400,000
Last six months	900,000	

The balance sheets immediately before the merger date and net income data for all of 19X3 are as follows:

	Plover Company	Sparrow Company
Balance Sheet (as of June 30, 19X3):		
Current assets	$ 4,200,000	$ 3,000,000
Land	2,000,000	1,000,000
Building and equipment	20,500,000	12,300,000
Accumulated depreciation	(4,000,000)	(2,000,000)
Patents	600,000	200,000
	$23,300,000	$14,500,000

	Plover Company	Sparrow Company
Balance Sheet (as of June 30, 19X3):		
Liabilities	$ 2,500,000	$ 2,000,000
Common stock, $10 par value	12,000,000	—
Common stock, $5 par value	—	3,800,000
Paid-in capital in excess of par value	4,200,000	3,200,000
Retained earnings	6,000,000	5,500,000
	$24,700,000	$14,500,000
Less treasury stock, at cost 100,000 shares	(1,400,000)	—
	$23,300,000	$14,500,000
Net Income:		
January 1, 19X3 to June 30, 19X3	$ 2,200,000	$ 1,500,000
July 1, 19X3 to December 31, 19X3 (excluding amounts that would be recorded as a result of the merger)	2,400,000	1,800,000
	$ 4,600,000	$ 3,300,000

Required:
Do the following for each of the independent situations given below: (a) prepare a combined balance sheet as of June 30, 19X3; (b) determine the combined net income to be reported for 19X3 (12 months); and (c) prepare a formal combined statement of retained earnings for 19X3 (12 months).

1. Plover Company exchanged 400,000 shares of previously unissued common stock and 100,000 shares of treasury stock for all the assets and liabilities (which were assumed) of Sparrow Company. All the conditions for pooling of interests accounting were met.
2. Plover purchased the assets and assumed Sparrow's liabilities of Sparrow by paying $3,100,000 cash and issuing debentures of $16,900,000 at face value.

(AICPA adapted)

P 6-10 COMPREHENSIVE REVIEW The Pooling of Interests Method versus the Purchase Method

1. In a business combination, how should the acquired corporation's plant and equipment be reported under each of the following methods?

	Pooling of Interests	Purchase Method
a.	At current value	At recorded value
b.	At current value	At current value
c.	At recorded value	At recorded value
d.	At recorded value	At current value

2. Perkins Company incurred a $20,000 finder's and consultation fee and $7,000 of SEC registration costs in acquiring Sayco Company. Of these costs, how much should be reported in the income statement as business combi-

nation expenses in the year of the acquisition under each of the following methods?
a. Pooling of interests.
b. Purchase method.

3. Using the information in the preceding question, how much would be capitalized as part of the acquisition cost?
a. Under pooling of interests.
b. Under the purchase method.

4. How would the retained earnings of a subsidiary acquired in a business combination usually be treated in a consolidated balance sheet prepared immediately after the acquisition under each of the following methods?

	Pooling of Interests	**Purchase Method**
a.	Excluded	Excluded
b.	Excluded	Included
c.	Included	Included
d.	Included	Excluded

5. A subsidiary may be acquired by issuing common stock in a pooling of interests transaction or by paying cash in a purchase transaction. Which of the following items would be reported in the consolidated financial statements at the same amount regardless of the accounting method used?
a. Minority interest.
b. Goodwill.
c. Retained earnings.
d. Capital stock accounts.

6. Ownership of 51% of the outstanding voting stock of a company would usually result in:
a. the use of the cost method.
b. the use of the lower of cost or market method.
c. a pooling of interests.
d. a consolidation.

7. A supporting argument for the pooling of interests method of accounting for a business combination is that:
a. one company is clearly the dominant and continuing entity.
b. goodwill is generally a part of any acquisition.
c. it was developed within the boundaries of the historical cost system and is compatible with it.
d. a portion of the total cost is assigned to individual assets acquired on the basis of their current value.

8. What minimum amount of an investee's common stock must be exchanged during the combination period for the investor's common stock under the following methods?
a. Pooling of interests.
b. Purchase method.

9. If all other conditions for consolidation are met, how should subsidiaries acquired in a business combination be shown under each of the following methods?

	Pooling of Interests	**Purchase Method**
a.	Consolidated	Not consolidated
b.	Consolidated	Consolidated
c.	Not consolidated	Consolidated
d.	Not consolidated	Not consolidated

10. A business combination between Ponder Company and Suspire Company occurs September 30, 19X1. How would the income statement accounts of both companies appear in Ponder's consolidated financial statements for the year ended December 31, 19X1, under each of the following methods?
    a. Pooling of interests.
    b. Purchase.
11. A business combination between P Company and S Company occurs September 30, 19X1. During 19X1, P Company declares dividends of $25,000 each quarter, and S Company declares dividends of $10,000 each quarter. Assume that S Company is wholly owned because there are no dissenting shareholders. What amount would appear in the consolidated statement of retained earnings for the year ended December 31, 19X1, under each of the following methods?
    a. Pooling of interests.
    b. Purchase.
12. Using the information in question 11 but assuming that S Company is only 90% owned, answer the same question.
    a. Pooling of interests.
    b. Purchase.
13. What minimum amount of a target company's assets must be exchanged by the acquiring company under the following methods?
    a. Pooling of interests.
    b. Purchase.
14. What is the maximum amount of contingent consideration allowed under each of the following methods?
    a. Pooling of interests.
    b. Purchase.

(AICPA adapted)

II

Consolidated Financial Statements: Specialized Subjects

7

Intercompany Inventory Transfers

AN OVERVIEW OF INTERCOMPANY TRANSACTIONS

As stated in Chapter 3, consolidated financial statements present the financial position and results of operations of a parent and its subsidiaries as though the group were a single entity with one or more branches or divisions. Therefore, transactions among companies within the consolidated group should be eliminated during the process of consolidation. Such eliminations cause the consolidated financial statements to reflect only transactions between the consolidated group and outside parties. Unless intercompany transactions are eliminated, companies would report profits on "sales" to themselves.

This chapter discusses (1) the conceptual aspects of eliminating intercompany transactions, and (2) the manner of accomplishing the eliminations in the consolidating statement worksheets.

Format of the Consolidating Statement Worksheet

To focus attention on the elimination entries covered in this chapter and the following two chapters, we arrange the format of the consolidating statement worksheets as follows:

P Company	S Company	Nonintercompany Transaction Eliminations (Entries relating to Chapters 3–6)		Partially Consolidated	Intercompany Transaction Eliminations (Entries relating to Chapters 7–9)		Consolidated
		Dr.	Cr.		Dr.	Cr.	

This format highlights the impact of the entries that eliminate intercompany transactions. In practice, when numerous intercompany transactions exist, preparing the consolidating statement worksheet in this manner significantly reduces the possibility of errors.

The financial statements and elimination entries needed for "partial consolidation" were obtained, to the extent possible, from illustrations in previous chapters, appropriately modified to reflect intercompany transactions. In dealing with the intercompany transactions discussed in Chapters 7–9, it is important to understand that these transactions constitute separate transactions that have nothing to do with how the business combination was recorded. The entries in Chapters 7–9 are the same regardless of whether the combination was a purchase or a pooling of interests.

Types of Intercompany Transactions

Intercompany transactions among parent companies and subsidiaries consist of the following types:

1. **Sales of Inventory.** Sales of inventory are most common in vertically integrated operations in which a customer–supplier relationship exists. Because the selling and buying entities are legally separate, the transfer prices almost always approximate outside market prices. Consequently, the selling entity usually records a gross profit at the time of sale.

   Inventory sales from a parent to one of its subsidiaries are referred to as **downstream sales.** Inventory sales from a subsidiary to its parent are referred to as **upstream sales.** Inventory sales between subsidiaries of a common parent are referred to as **lateral sales.** Because lateral sales are less frequent than upstream or downstream sales, they are not illustrated. The principles and procedures of eliminating intercompany transactions in lateral sales, however, are the same as those in downstream and upstream sales, which are discussed and illustrated.
2. **Transfers of long-lived assets.** Far less common than inventory transfers are transfers of long-lived assets. This type of transaction most often occurs when one entity has surplus assets or when one entity manufactures assets usable by another. In the latter situation, the consolidated group has widely diverse operations. The procedures to account for intercompany fixed-asset transfers are discussed in Chapter 8.
3. **Leasing of long-lived assets. Sales-type leases** are dealt with using the principles and procedures discussed in Chapter 8. **Operating leases** merely require some offsetting in the income statement, as shown later in this chapter.
4. **Loans.** Subsidiaries often do not have local banking relationships, because treasury functions are usually centralized at the parent's headquarters. This allows the parent to monitor closely the cash positions of its subsidiaries, which obtain needed cash from the parent in the form of **loans.** Practice varies widely as to the charging of interest on loans to subsidiaries.
5. **Services.** A parent may charge its subsidiaries for top management services, including centralized research and development services, central computer services, and legal and advertising expenses.
6. **Dividends.** When a parent uses the equity method to account for its investment in a subsidiary, no elimination entry is necessary because the dividend reduces the investment account. However, when a parent uses the cost method, the dividend is recorded as dividend income, which must be eliminated in preparing consolidated financial statements, as shown in Appendix A to Chapter 4.
7. **Bond investments.** Infrequently, an entity within a consolidated group purchases bonds of another entity within the group. The procedures to account for these intercompany bond holdings in consolidation are discussed in Chapter 9.

With respect to all of these types of intercompany transactions, *Accounting Research Bulletin No. 51* states:

> In the preparation of consolidated statements, intercompany balances and transactions should be eliminated. This includes intercompany open account balances, security holdings, sales and purchases, interest, dividends, etc. As consolidated statements are based on the assumption that they represent the financial position and operating results of a single business enterprise, such statements should not include gain or loss on transactions among the companies in the group. Accordingly, any intercompany profit or loss on assets remaining with the group should be eliminated; the concept usually applied for this purpose is gross profit or loss.[1]

Using Separate Intercompany Accounts

Intercompany transactions are normally recorded in separate general ledger accounts to make the consolidation process easier. The income statement usually has several intercompany accounts, such as Intercompany Sales, Intercompany Cost of Goods Sold, Intercompany Interest Income, Intercompany Interest Expense, and Intercompany Gain on Long-lived Asset Transfer). For the balance sheet, however, most intercompany transactions can be dealt with using one account, Intercompany Receivable/Payable, the balance of which can be either a debit or a credit.

Before the consolidation process begins, all intercompany accounts that are to have reciprocal balances (both in the income statement and the balance sheet) must be reconciled and adjusted, if necessary, to bring them into agreement. Only by being in agreement will they completely eliminate each other in consolidation.

CONCEPTUAL ISSUES

Elimination of Gross Profit, Operating Profit, or Profit before Income Taxes

As indicated in the preceding section, when inventory and fixed assets are transferred from one company to another within a consolidated group, *ARB No. 51* designates the amount of profit to be eliminated in consolidation as the selling entity's **gross profit.** In selecting gross profit as the amount to be eliminated, other measures of profit—such as **operating profit** and **profit before income taxes**—were rejected to prevent the effect of capitalizing the selling entity's marketing, administrative, and borrowing expenses. Such expenses are period costs on a separate-company basis, and there is no justification for treating them otherwise on a consolidated basis. From a consolidated viewpoint, the sale of inventory or equipment among entities within a consolidated group is considered merely the physical movement of the items from one location to another,

[1] *Accounting Research Bulletin No. 51*, "Consolidated Financial Statements" (New York: American Institute of Certified Public Accountants, 1959), par. 6.

and a bona fide transaction does not occur. When the entire gross profit is eliminated, the cost basis of the selling entity is reported in consolidation.

Transportation Costs

ARB No. 51 does not specifically address the consolidation treatment of transportation costs incurred in transferring inventory among entities of a consolidated group. Because normal transportation costs are inventoriable costs, there is no sound reason to treat them otherwise in consolidated financial statements.

When the buying entity incurs the transportation costs and treats them as inventoriable costs, the elimination of all the selling entity's gross profit makes the transportation costs part of inventory cost on a consolidated basis. (Thus, no special procedures or elimination entries relating to transportation costs are needed in consolidation.) However, when the selling entity incurs the transportation costs—which it considers marketing costs—the elimination of its gross profit results in the expensing of the transportation costs on a consolidated basis. Accordingly, in consolidation an additional elimination entry must be made in these latter cases to (1) eliminate the transportation costs being reported as marketing expenses and (2) charge the transportation costs to inventory.

For the sake of simplicity, the illustrations pertaining to inventory transfers assume transportation costs are insignificant. Such costs are therefore treated as period costs on a separate company and on a consolidated basis.

Income Tax Considerations

ARB No. 51 requires elimination of any income taxes that have been provided on gross profit eliminated in consolidation.[2] For simplicity, however, we asume in our illustrations for Chapters 7–8 that this year-end elimination entry has already been recorded in the general ledger of the parent or the subsidiary. Thus, a separate entry dealing with the tax effects of gross profit deferred in consolidation is not required on the consolidating statement worksheet. Chapter 12 discusses income tax considerations for consolidated entities as a separate topic. That chapter discusses the manner of eliminating income taxes on intercompany transfers and shows how this is accomplished.

Minority Interest Considerations

When a subsidiary is partially owned, the parent may question whether to eliminate all of the gross profit or only that portion that accrues to the parent company. We address this issue later in the chapter when dealing with partially owned subsidiaries.

[2]*ARB No. 51*, par. 16.

INTERCOMPANY LOANS, MANAGEMENT FEES, AND OPERATING LEASES

Intercompany Loans

When interest is charged on intercompany loans, the interest income on the parent's books equals the interest expense on the subsidiary's books. The following elimination entry is made on the consolidating statement worksheet:

Intercompany Interest Income	xxx	
Intercompany Interest Expense........................		xxx

When a loan remains unpaid as of the consolidation date, the intercompany loan receivable on the parent's books equals the intercompany loan payable on the subsidiary's books. The following elimination entry is made on the consolidating statement worksheet:

Intercompany Loan Payable.....................................	xxx	
Intercompany Loan Receivable..........................		xxx

Intercompany Management Charges

When the parent has charged management fees to the subsidiary, the intercompany management fee income on the parent's books equals the intercompany management fee expense on the subsidiary's books. The following elimination entry is made on the consolidating statement worksheet:

Intercompany Management Fee Income......................	xxx	
Intercompany Management Fee Expense..........		xxx

Intercompany Operating Leases

When an operating lease exists between entities within the consolidated group, the Intercompany Lease Expense account on the lessee's books equals the Intercompany Lease Revenue account on the lessor's book. The following elimination entry is made on the consolidating statement worksheet:

Intercompany Lease Revenues..................................	xxx	
Intercompany Lease Expense...........................		xxx

Elimination by Rearrangement

Each of the above elimination entries takes place entirely within one of the financial statements. Most companies arrange the individual accounts on the consolidating statement worksheet so that these entries do not have to be made there. It is only necessary to show in parentheses the intercompany accounts of one of the entities in the corresponding section of the worksheet. For example, by putting the subsidiary's intercompany loan payable amount in parentheses on the same line as the parent's intercompany loan receivable in the asset section of the balance sheet, the balances add across to zero in the consolidated column. (The intercompany accounts should agree before the consolidation process.) Elimination by rearrangement reduces the number of required elimination entires. An example of this procedure follows:

	P Company	S Company	Eliminations Dr.	Eliminations Cr.	Consolidated
Intercompany interest income (expense)	1,000	(1,000)			–0–
Intercompany receivable (payable)	10,000	(10,000)			–0–

INVENTORY TRANSFERS AT COST

Intercompany inventory transfers are usually recorded at amounts approximating outside market prices; thus, the selling entity records a profit at the time of sale. This is usually necessary to aid management's review of the operating performance of the individual companies. To illustrate the first basic purpose of the elimination of intercompany inventory transactions, the first several examples are of transfers at cost.

Downstream Transfers at Cost

The illustrations in this section show how the double-counting of sales and cost of goods sold is prevented in arriving at consolidated amounts.

None Resold by Subsidiary. Assume that inventory costing $50,000 is sold to a subsidiary for $50,000 and that it has resold none of the inventory. Because these transactions did not generate sales to third parties, no sales or amounts for cost of goods sold should appear in the consolidated column of the consolidating statement worksheet. Accordingly, the following elimination entry is necessary:

Intercompany Sales	50,000	
Intercompany Cost of Goods Sold		50,000

After this entry is posted to the consolidating statement worksheet, the appropriate worksheet accounts would appear as follows:

	P Company	S Company	Intercompany Transaction Eliminations Dr.	Intercompany Transaction Eliminations Cr.	Consolidated
Income Statement:					
Sales					
Cost of Goods Sold					
Intercompany Accounts:					
Sales	50,000		50,000		–0–
Cost of Goods Sold	(50,000)			50,000	–0–
Net Income	–0–		50,000	50,000	–0–
Statement of Retained Earnings:					
Beginning of year					
+ Net income	–0–		50,000	50,000	–0–
Balance Sheet:					
Inventory		50,000			50,000

100% Resold by Subsidiary. Assume the facts in the preceding illustration, except that the subsidiary has resold all of the inventory for $90,000 in the same period in which it was acquired from the parent. If no elimination entry is made, both consolidated sales and consolidated cost of goods sold would be overstated by $50,000. Accordingly, the following elimination entry is necessary:

	Dr.	Cr.
Intercompany Sales	50,000	
Intercompany Cost of Goods Sold		50,000

The elimination entry prevents the double-counting of these accounts and allows the consolidated amounts to reflect only transactions with third parties. After this entry is posted, the appropriate worksheet accounts would appear as follows:

	P Company	S Company	Intercompany Transaction Eliminations Dr.	Intercompany Transaction Eliminations Cr.	Consolidated
Income Statement:					
Sales		90,000			90,000
Cost of Goods Sold		(50,000)			(50,000)
Intercompany Accounts:					
Equity in Net Income	40,000[a]				–0–
Sales	50,000		50,000		–0–
Cost of Goods Sold	(50,000)			50,000	–0–
Net Income	40,000	40,000[a]	50,000	50,000	40,000
Statement of Retained Earnings:					
Beginning of year					
+ Net income	40,000		50,000	50,000	40,000

[a]This amount would be eliminated in the first set of eliminations columns, which for simplicity is not shown here. (Also not shown are amounts for the subsidiary's retained earnings, as they would also be eliminated in the first set of eliminations columns.)

80% Resold by Subsidiary. Assume the facts in the preceding illustrations, except that the subsidiary has resold 80% of the inventory for $72,000. The only amounts that should appear in the consolidated column are the sales to third parties, the cost of those sales at the parent company's cost, and the remaining unsold inventory at the parent company's cost. Accordingly, the following elimination entry is necessary:

Intercompany Sales	50,000	
Intercompany Cost of Goods Sold		50,000

After this entry is posted, the appropriate worksheet accounts would appear as follows:

	P Company	S Company	Intercompany Transaction Eliminations Dr.	Intercompany Transaction Eliminations Cr.	Consolidated
Income Statement:					
Sales		72,000			72,000
Cost of goods sold		(40,000)			(40,000)
Intercompany Accounts:					
Equity in net income	32,000[a]				–0–
Sales	50,000		50,000		–0–
Cost of goods sold	(50,000)			50,000	–0–
Net Income	32,000	32,000[a]	50,000	50,000	32,000
Statement of Retained Earnings:					
Beginning of year					
+ Net income	32,000		50,000	50,000	32,000
Balance Sheet:					
Inventory (balance sheet)		10,000			10,000

[a]This amount would be eliminated in the first set of eliminations columns, which for simplicity is not shown.

Concluding Observations. Whenever inventory is transferred at cost, the elimination entry is the same regardless of the percentage of the inventory that has been resold by the subsidiary. In each of the three preceding illustrations, the debit in the income statement section of the consolidating statement worksheet equals the credit, and there is no net effect on the income statement (or on consolidated retained earnings).

AN OVERVIEW OF THE COMPLETE EQUITY METHOD AND THE PARTIAL EQUITY METHOD FOR INVENTORY TRANSFERS ABOVE COST

The remainder of the chapter focuses on the second basic purpose of the elimination of intercompany inventory transactions, which is that any intercompany profit on transfers that have not been resold by the acquiring entity is unrealized and must be deferred. There are two techniques for eliminating unrealized intercompany profit on inventory transfers: The complete equity method and the partial equity method. The following table summarizes the similarities and differences of both methods:

	Complete Equity Method	Partial Equity Method
Produces the proper consolidated amounts	Yes	Yes
Requires general ledger adjusting entries in addition to worksheet elimination entries	Yes	No
Has built-in checking feature (parent company's net income and retained earnings equals consolidated net income and consolidated retained earnings, respectively)	Yes	No

We discuss the complete equity method next and leave the partial equity method for Appendix A at the end of the chapter, for two reasons: (1) The complete equity method is conceptually superior to the partial equity method. (2) It is much easier to learn the complete equity method first and then the partial equity method than to do so in the reverse order.

INVENTORY TRANSFERS ABOVE COST: THE COMPLETE EQUITY METHOD

Under the complete equity method, the parent's net income and retained earnings are the same as consolidated net income and consolidated retained earnings, respectively. For this to occur, any unrealized intercompany profit must be deferred in the financial statements of the parent. The following sections illustrate the appropriate deferral entries.

Downstream Transfers above Cost

None Resold by Subsidiary. Assume that in 19X1 inventory costing $50,000 is sold to a subsidiary for $75,000 and that none of the inventory acquired from the parent has been resold by the subsidiary. The parent would make the following **general ledger entry** at December 31, 19X1:

Deferral of Gross Profit on Intercompany Sales (income statement)	25,000	
Deferred Gross Profit (balance sheet)		25,000
To defer the reporting of unrealized intercompany gross profit on inventory transfers.		

In consolidation, the following worksheet elimination entries (correspondingly numbered here and in the partial worksheet) would be made:

1. Deferred Gross Profit (balance sheet)..............	**25,000**	
Deferral of Gross Profit on Intercompany Sales (income statement)		**25,000**
To reverse in consolidation the year-end general ledger entry deferring unrealized intercompany gross profit.		
2. Intercompany Sales.......................................	**75,000**	
Intercompany Cost of Goods Sold............		**50,000**
Inventory		**25,000**
To eliminate the intercompany transaction.		

After these worksheet entries are posted, the appropriate worksheet accounts would appear as follows:

	P Company	S Company	Intercompany Transaction Eliminations Dr.	Intercompany Transaction Eliminations Cr.	Consolidated
Income Statement:					
Sales..					
Cost of goods sold...................					
Intercompany Accounts:					
Sales....................................	75,000		75,000(2)		–0–
Cost of goods sold................	(50,000)			50,000(2)	–0–
Deferral of gross profit	(25,000)			25,000(1)	–0–
Net Income..............................	–0–		75,000	75,000	–0–
Statement of Retained Earnings:					
Beginning of year					
+ Net income..........................	–0–		→ 75,000	→ 75,000	–0–
Balance Sheet:					
Inventory		75,000		25,000(2)	50,000
Deferred gross profit	(25,000)		25,000(1)		–0–

The following points are important for understanding the preceding partial worksheet:

1. The two worksheet entries post equal debits and credits to the income statement ($75,000). As a result, a zero net effect occurs in the income statement and in the parent's retained earnings.
2. The result in consolidation is as though the inventory had been transferred to the subsidiary at the parent's cost of $50,000.
3. The $25,000 of unrealized profit is not reportable until the subsidiary resells the inventory.

100% Resold by Subsidiary. Assume the same facts as in the preceding illustration, except that the subsidiary has resold all of this inventory for $90,000 in the same period in which it was acquired from the parent. Because no unrealized intercompany profit exists at year-end, the parent does not have to make a general ledger entry to defer unrealized intercompany profit. However, to eliminate the intercompany transaction and to report the subsidiary's cost of goods sold of $75,000 at the parent's cost of $50,000 in consolidation, the following elimination entry is necessary:

Intercompany Sales	75,000	
Intercompany Cost of Goods Sold		50,000
Cost of Goods Sold (to third parties)		25,000

After this elimination entry is posted, the appropriate worksheet accounts would appear as follows:

	P Company	S Company	Intercompany Transaction Eliminations Dr.	Intercompany Transaction Eliminations Cr.	Consolidated
Income Statement:					
Sales		90,000			90,000
Cost of goods sold		(75,000)		25,000	(50,000)
Intercompany Accounts:					
Equity in net income	15,000[a]				–0–
Sales	75,000		75,000		–0–
Cost of goods sold	(50,000)			50,000	–0–
Net Income	40,000	15,000[a]	75,000	75,000	40,000
Statement of Retained Earnings:					
Beginning of year					
+ Net income	40,000		75,000	75,000	40,000

[a]This amount would be eliminated in the nonintercompany eliminations columns, which for simplicity is not shown.

Note that because the entry takes place entirely within the income statement section of the worksheet, there is no net effect on the income statement. Thus, all of the intercompany profit of $25,000 is reported in consolidation (none of it had to be deferred). As in the preceding illustration, the amounts reported in consolidation are the same as though the inventory had been transferred to the subsidiary at the parent's cost.

80% Resold by Subsidiary. Assume the facts in the preceding illustrations, except that the subsidiary has resold 80% of the inventory for $72,000 in the same period in which it was acquired from the parent. Because 80% of the inventory has been resold, 80% of the $25,000 of intercompany gross profit, or $20,000, is included in the cost of goods sold to third parties. Likewise, because 20% of the inventory is still on hand, 20% of the intercompany gross profit of $25,000, or $5,000, is included in the subsidiary's inventory. Accordingly, the parent would make the following **general ledger entry** at December 31, 19X1:

Deferral of Gross Profit on Intercompany Sales (income statement)................................	5,000	
Deferred Gross Profit (balance sheet)........		5,000
To defer the reporting of unrealized intercompany gross profit on inventory transfers.		

In consolidation at December 31, 19X1, this entry would be reversed and the normal intercompany inventory transaction elimination entry would be made:

Deferred Gross Profit (balance sheet)..............	5,000	
Deferral of Gross Profit on Intercompany Sales (income statement)....................		5,000
To reverse in consolidation the year-end general ledger entry deferring intercompany gross profit.		
Intercompany Sales.......................................	75,000	
Intercompany Cost of Goods Sold...........		50,000
Cost of Goods Sold (to third parties).......		20,000
Inventory		5,000
To eliminate current-year intercompany transactions.		

In this illustration, 80% of the inventory was resold by the subsidiary, leaving 20% still on hand. In practice, the appropriate percentages can only be determined by ascertaining the actual amount of inventory still on hand, either by making a physical count or by referring to perpetual inventory records. Usually a formal analysis, such as the one below, is prepared to show how the intercompany gross profit is divided between cost of goods sold to third parties and inventory still on hand.

Analysis of Intercompany Sales

	Total (Given)	Resold	On Hand
Intercompany sales	$75,000	$60,000	$15,000
Intercompany cost of goods sold......	(50,000)	(40,000)	(10,000)
Gross profit...........................	$25,000	$20,000	$ 5,000

The first line of the analysis, Intercompany Sales, shows what portion of the year's total intercompany purchases have been charged to cost of goods sold by the subsidiary and what portion remains on hand at year-end. This separation is made by determining the amount of intercompany inventory purchases on hand at year-end ($15,000) and then subtracting this amount from the total intercompany sales for the year ($75,000) to arrive at the amount charged to cost of goods sold ($60,000).

The second line of the analysis, intercompany cost of goods sold, shows what amount would have been charged to cost of goods sold and at what amount the ending inventory would be stated had the intercompany transfer been at the selling entity's cost. The percentage of inventory resold and the percentage of inventory still on hand (determined using the amounts on the first line) are applied to the total intercompany cost of goods sold ($50,000) to determine the amounts in the resold and on hand columns.

The difference between the first and second lines, gross profit, is the amount by which cost of goods sold and ending inventory are overstated, as to the consolidated entity, because the inventory transfer was made above cost.

Illustration

PREPARING CONSOLIDATED FINANCIAL STATEMENTS USING THE COMPLETE EQUITY METHOD: DOWNSTREAM TRANSFERS ABOVE COST

The information in the preceding example is used in Illustration 7-1 to get from the partially consolidated column to the consolidated column of the worksheet. The P Company and S Company financial statements presented in Illustration 4-5, along with the primary and secondary elimination entries in that illustration, are used to obtain the partially consolidated amounts. The P Company and S Company columns were modified to reflect the intercompany inventory transactions shown in the preceding example. The elimination entries used in Illustration 7-1 are shown below for convenience:

1. The primary elimination entry:

Common Stock	40,000	
Retained Earnings (beginning of year)	20,000	
Equity in Net Income of Subsidiary	15,000	
Land	12,000	
Equipment	6,000	
Goodwill	9,000	
Dividends Declared		5,000
Accumulated Depreciation		1,000
Investment in Subsidiary		96,000

Illustration 7-1
The Complete Equity Method: Downstream Transfer above Cost

P COMPANY AND SUBSIDIARY (S COMPANY)
Consolidating Statement Worksheet
For the Year Ended December 31, 19X1

	P Company	S Company	Nonintercompany Transaction Eliminations Dr.	Nonintercompany Transaction Eliminations Cr.	Partially Consolidated	Intercompany Transaction Eliminations Dr.	Intercompany Transaction Eliminations Cr.	Consolidated
Income Statement:								
Sales	525,000	200,000			725,000			725,000
Cost of goods sold	(310,000)	(116,000)	4,000(2)		(430,000)		20,000(5)	(410,000)
Expenses	(204,000)	(69,000)			(273,000)			(273,000)
Intercompany Accounts:								
Equity in net income of S Company	15,000		15,000(1)		–0–			–0–
Amortization of cost in excess of book value	(4,000)			4,000(2)	–0–			–0–
Sales	75,000				75,000	75,000(5)		–0–
Cost of goods sold	(50,000)				(50,000)		50,000(5)	–0–
Deferral of gross profit	(5,000)				(5,000)		5,000(4)	–0–
Net Income	42,000	15,000	19,000	4,000	42,000	75,000	75,000	42,000
Statement of Retained Earnings:								
Balances, January 1, 19X1	100,000	20,000	20,000(1)		100,000			100,000
+ Net income	42,000	15,000	19,000	4,000	42,000	75,000	75,000	42,000
− Dividends declared	(31,000)	(5,000)		5,000(1)	(31,000)			(31,000)
Balances, December 31, 19X1	111,000	30,000	39,000	9,000	111,000	75,000	75,000	111,000
Balance Sheet:								
Cash	45,000	25,000			70,000			70,000
Accounts receivable	75,000	43,000			118,000			118,000
Inventory:								
From vendors	110,000	25,000			135,000			135,000
Intercompany		15,000			15,000		5,000(5)	10,000
Deferred profit	(5,000)				(5,000)	5,000(4)		–0–
Investment in S Company	96,000			96,000(1)	–0–			–0–
Land	200,000	30,000	12,000(1)		242,000			242,000
Buildings and equipment	500,000	190,000	6,000(1)	45,000(3)	651,000			651,000
Accumulated depreciation	(320,000)	(58,000)	45,000(3)	1,000(1)	(334,000)			(334,000)
Goodwill			9,000(1)		9,000			9,000
Total Assets	701,000	270,000	72,000	142,000	901,000	5,000	5,000	901,000
Liabilities	290,000	200,000			490,000			490,000
P Company:								
Common stock	300,000				300,000			300,000
Retained earnings	111,000				111,000	75,000	75,000	111,000
S Company:								
Common stock		40,000	40,000(1)		–0–			–0–
Retained earnings		30,000	39,000	9,000	–0–			–0–
Total Liabilities and Equity	701,000	270,000	79,000	9,000	901,000	75,000	75,000	901,000
Proof of debit and credit postings			151,000	151,000		80,000	80,000	

Explanation of entries:

(1) The primary elimination entry.
(2) The secondary elimination entry.
(3) The accumulated depreciation elimination entry.
(4) The reversal of the general ledger deferral entry.
(5) The current-year intercompany transactions elimination entry.

2. The secondary elimination entry:

Cost of Goods Sold (to third parties)................	4,000	
Amortization of Cost in Excess of Book Value..		4,000

3. The accumulated depreciation elimination entry:

Accumulated Depreciation.............................	45,000	
Buildings and Equipment		45,000

4. The reversal of the general ledger deferral entry:

Deferred Gross Profit (balance sheet)..............	5,000	
Deferral of Gross Profit on Intercompany Sales (income statement)....................		5,000

5. The current-year intercompany inventory transactions elimination entry:

Intercompany Sales..	75,000	
Intercompany Cost of Goods Sold..........		50,000
Cost of Goods Sold (to third parties).......		20,000
Inventory		5,000

Subsequent-Year Treatment of Unsold Inventory

Inventory Not Resold in 19X2. If the inventory is still on hand at the end of 19X2, no entries are needed in consolidation relating to the unrealized intercompany gross profit. The deferral is already reflected in the general ledger.

Inventory Resold in 19X2. If the inventory has been resold by the end of 19X2, the following entry would be made **in the parent's general ledger** at the time of the sale:

Deferred Gross Profit (balance sheet).....................	5,000	
Recognition of Gross Profit on Intercompany Inventory Sales (income statement)		5,000
To recognize the gross profit on prior year's intercompany sales deferred in the prior year.		

In consolidation at December 31, 19X2, the following elimination entry would be made on the worksheet:

Recognition of Gross Profit on Intercompany Inventory Sales (income statement)	**5,000**	
Cost of Goods Sold (to third parties).............		**5,000**
To reclassify the credit balance in the Recognition of Gross Profit account to Cost of Goods Sold (to third parties).		

Note that in consolidation this entry posts an equal debit and credit to the income statement ($5,000). As a result, a zero net effect is carried forward to retained earnings. The $5,000 of gross profit being reported has already been reflected in the general ledger Retained Earnings account.

Dealing with Beginning Inventory and Current-Year Transfers

In a normal consolidation involving intercompany inventory transactions, intercompany sales of inventory usually occur each year. Accordingly, entries are required both (1) to recognize the profit on the beginning intercompany inventory, and (2) to eliminate the current-year intercompany transactions. In this regard, it is simpler to separate these entries rather than to handle them as a single, combined elimination entry.

Some of the beginning inventory may be physically part of the ending inventory. However, the consolidation effort is simplified if it is assumed that the beginning inventory has been sold and that all of the ending inventory came from the current-year intercompany inventory transactions. So long as the gross profit rates are the same (or very close) year to year, the assumption is a safe one.

Minority Interest Considerations

Downstream Transfers. Accountants agree that for downstream transfers all of the gross profit on assets remaining within the group should be eliminated, regardless of the parent's ownership interest in the subsidiary. This is because all of the gross profit accrues to the parent.

Upstream Transfers. When inventory transfers are upstream from a wholly owned subsidiary, accountants agree that all of the gross profit on assets remaining within the group should be eliminated for the same reason. However, when the upstream inventory sales are from a partially owned subsidiary, two schools of thought differ on the amount of gross profit that should be eliminated. In discussing these two views we assume that the subsidiary is 80% owned and the parent company has on hand at year-end $15,000 of intercompany-acquired inventory, which cost the subsidiary $10,000. Thus, a total intercompany gross profit of $5,000 exists, of which $4,000 accrues to the parent company and $1,000 accrues to the minority interest. The two schools of thought are as follows:

1. Under the **complete elimination approach,** all of the gross profit is eliminated on the grounds that to do otherwise would be inconsistent with the underlying purpose of consolidated financial statements, which is to report activities as though a single entity existed. As a result, consolidated net income and consolidated retained earnings would be reduced $4,000, and the minority interest would be reduced $1,000.
2. Under the **partial elimination approach,** only the portion of the gross profit that accrues to the parent is eliminated. The portion of the profit that accrues to the minority interest is not eliminated on the grounds that it has been realized from the viewpoint of the minority interest shareholders. It is irrelevant to whom the subsidiary sells as far as the subsidiary's minority shareholders are concerned. As a result, consolidated net income and consolidated retained earnings would be reduced $4,000. The minority interest would not be reduced $1,000.

Requirements of Professional Pronouncements. In *Accounting Research Bulletin No. 51*, the American Institute of Certified Public Accountants chose the first alternative, whereby all of the gross profit is eliminated:

> The amount of intercompany profit or loss to be eliminated . . . is not affected by the existence of a minority interest. The complete elimination of the intercompany profit or loss is consistent with the underlying assumption that the consolidated statements represent the financial position and operating results of a single business enterprise. The elimination of the intercompany profit or loss may be allocated proportionately between the majority and minority interests.[3]

This position is reaffirmed in *Accounting Interpretation No. 1* to *APB Opinion No. 18:*

> When an investor controls an investee through majority voting interest and enters into a transaction with an investee which is not on an "arm's length" basis,[4] none of the intercompany profit or loss from the transaction should be recognized in income by the investor until it has been realized through transactions with third parties.[5]

The interpretation also states:

> In other cases, it would be appropriate for the investor to eliminate intercompany profit in relation to the investor's common stock interest in the investee.[6]

[3] *ARB No. 51*, par. 14.
[4] That is, a transaction between completely independent parties.
[5] *Accounting Interpretation No. 1* to *APB Opinion No. 18* (New York: American Institute of Certified Public Accountants, 1971), par. 4.
[6] *Accounting Interpretation No. 1* to *APB Opinion No. 18*, par. 5.

However, this statement is immediately followed by an example of a 30% investment in an investee. "In other cases" obviously refers to situations in which less than majority ownership exists. Accordingly, all of the profit recorded on intercompany transactions with subsidiaries must be deferred until it has been realized through transactions with third parties. (All transactions with controlled companies are considered to be on less than an "arm's length" basis.)

Deferring Profit on Upstream Transfers. A strict application of the equity method (as described in par. 6b of *APB Opinion No. 18*) calls for the investor to adjust the investee's reported net income to eliminate any unrealized intercompany gross profit before applying the equity method. This adjustment is made by requiring the subsidiary to adjust its general ledger as follows:

Deferral of Gross Profit on Intercompany Sales (income statement)....................................	**5,000**	
Deferred Gross Profit (balance sheet)............		**5,000**
To defer the reporting of unrealized intercompany gross profit on inventory transfers.		

(The parent booked the same entry in its general ledger when the intercompany transfer was downstream.) Thus, the subsidiary's net income and retained earnings would be $5,000 lower. Accordingly, the equity method of accounting would then be applied to the lower net income amount. In consolidation at year-end, this entry would be reversed and the normal intercompany inventory transaction elimination entry would be made. These entries are not shown here, as they are identical to the entries shown for a downstream inventory transfer.

In summary, the procedures for upstream transfers are identical to those for downstream transfers, except that the adjusting entry to defer the reporting of the unrealized intercompany gross profit at year-end is made to the subsidiary's general ledger instead of in the parent's general ledger.

Subsidiary's Reporting to Its Minority Shareholders. Under existing generally accepted accounting principles, the subsidiary need not defer any of its intercompany profit in reporting to its minority shareholders. Insofar as the minority shareholders are concerned, such intercompany profit has been realized. Accordingly, for reporting to the minority shareholders, the subsidiary would make a "financial statement adjusting entry" to reverse the intercompany profit deferral entry.

The consolidation effort is greatly simplified when the subsidiary is required to maintain its general ledger for reporting to the parent rather than to the minority shareholders. If the subsidiary's general ledger were kept the opposite way, the parent would have to make a financial statement adjusting entry to the subsidiary's financial statements prior to the start of the consolidation process. Some companies have hundreds of subsidiaries and large numbers of intercompany inventory transfers; making such an entry for each subsidiary would put a substantial burden on the parent's accounting department. It is best to have the subsidiaries maintain their general ledgers for reporting to the parent.

Illustration

PREPARING CONSOLIDATED FINANCIAL STATEMENTS USING THE COMPLETE EQUITY METHOD: UPSTREAM TRANSFERS ABOVE COST

Illustration 7-2 shows a consolidating statement worksheet involving upstream inventory sales. The worksheet adapts the P Company and S Company financial statements presented in Illustration 5-5 so that S Company has upstream sales and its financial statements have been adjusted for $5,000 of unrealized intercompany profit at year-end. The intercompany transaction elimination entries are the same as those used in Illustration 7-1.

The following points are important for understanding Illustration 7-2:

1. The parent's net income and retained earnings equals the consolidated net income and retained earnings at each stage of the consolidation process.
2. No additional adjustment is required to the minority interest in dealing with the intercompany transaction eliminations.

Subsequent-Year Treatment of Unsold Inventory

The accounting to be followed for subsequent years is the same as that shown earlier for downstream transfers (page 307). The only difference is that the subsidiary, not the parent, would make a general ledger entry to recognize the intercompany profit upon resale of the inventory.

Lower of Cost or Market Adjustments

Occasionally, the buying entity makes an adjustment for intercompany-acquired inventory in its general ledger that is based on its own cost or the market value, whichever is less. For purposes of consolidated reporting, the appropriate valuation of this adjustment is the lower of the *selling* entity's cost or the market value.

Illustration 7-2
The Complete Equity Method: Upstream Transfer above Cost

P COMPANY AND SUBSIDIARY (S COMPANY)
Consolidating Statement Worksheet
For the Year Ended December 31, 19X1

	P Company	S Company	Nonintercompany Transaction Eliminations		Partially Consoli-dated	Intercompany Transaction Eliminations		Consoli-dated
			Dr.	Cr.		Dr.	Cr.	
Income Statement:								
Sales	600,000	125,000			725,000			725,000
Cost of goods sold	(360,000)	(66,000)	3,200(2)		(429,200)		20,000(5)	(409,200)
Expenses	(204,000)	(69,000)			(273,000)			(273,000)
Intercompany Accounts:								
Equity in net income of subsidiary	8,000		8,000(1)		–0–			–0–
Amortization of cost in excess of book value	(3,200)			3,200(2)	–0–			–0–
Sales		75,000			75,000	75,000(5)		–0–
Cost of goods sold		(50,000)			(50,000)		50,000(5)	–0–
Deferral of gross profit		(5,000)			(5,000)		5,000(4)	–0–
Income before Minority Interest	40,800	10,000	11,200	3,200	42,800	75,000	75,000	42,800
Minority interest			2,000(1)		(2,000)			(2,000)
Net Income	40,800	10,000	13,200	3,200	40,800	75,000	75,000	40,800
Statement of Retained Earnings:								
Balances, January 1, 19X1	100,000	20,000	20,000(1)		100,000			100,000
+ Net income	40,800	10,000	13,200	3,200	40,800	75,000	75,000	40,800
− Dividends declared	(31,000)	(5,000)		5,000(1)	(31,000)			(31,000)
Balances, December 31, 19X1	109,800	25,000	33,200	8,200	109,800	75,000	75,000	109,800
Balance Sheet:								
Cash	62,000	25,000			87,000			87,000
Accounts receivable	75,000	43,000			118,000			118,000
Inventory:								
From vendors	95,000	40,000			135,000			135,000
Intercompany	15,000				15,000		5,000(5)	10,000
Deferred profit		(5,000)			(5,000)	5,000(4)		–0–
Investment in subsidiary	72,800			72,800(1)	–0–			–0–
Land	200,000	30,000	9,600(1)		239,600			239,600
Buildings and equipment	500,000	190,000	4,800(1)	45,000(3)	649,800			649,800
Accumulated depreciation	(320,000)	(58,000)	45,000(3)	800(1)	(333,800)			(333,800)
Goodwill			7,200(1)		7,200			7,200
Total Assets	699,800	265,000	66,600	118,600	912,800	5,000	5,000	912,800
Liabilities	290,000	200,000			490,000			490,000
Minority interest in net assets of subsidiary				13,000(1)	13,000			13,000
P Company:								
Common stock	300,000				300,000			300,000
Retained earnings	109,800				109,800	75,000	75,000	109,800
S Company:								
Common stock		40,000	40,000(1)		–0–			–0–
Retained earnings		25,000	33,200	8,200	–0–			–0–
Total Liabilities and Equity	699,800	265,000	73,200	21,200	912,800	75,000	75,000	912,800
Proof of debit and credit postings				139,800	139,800		80,000	80,000

Explanation of entries:

(1) The primary elimination entry.
(2) The secondary elimination entry.
(3) The accumulated depreciation elimination entry.
(4) The reversal of the general ledger deferral entry.
(5) The current-year intercompany transactions elimination entry.

SUMMARY

Consolidated financial statements present the financial position and the results of operations of all companies within the consolidated group as though a single entity exists. Consequently, the consolidated financial statements should reflect only transactions that take place between the consolidated group and outside parties. All open intercompany account balances and intercompany transactions that affect the income statement must be eliminated.

Transfers of inventory between companies within a consolidated group at amounts other than the transferring entity's cost require that the recorded intercompany profit or loss not be reported on a consolidated basis until the acquiring entity has disposed of the inventory. Under the complete equity method, the deferral of the profit is reflected in the financial statements of the transferring entity. Under the partial equity method, the deferral takes place on the consolidating statement worksheet.

Both techniques result in the same amounts in consolidation. The concept of profit or loss for these purposes is gross profit or loss. In deferring any gross profit or loss pertaining to unsold intercompany-acquired inventory as of a consolidation date, the appropriate income tax effect on the amount deferred must be shown.

Glossary of New Terms

Arm's Length Transaction Transactions that take place between completely independent parties.

Downstream Sale The sale of an asset from a parent to one of its subsidiaries.

Lateral Sale The sale of an asset between subsidiaries of a common parent.

Upstream Sale The sale of an asset from a subsidiary to its parent.

Selected References

Accounting Research Bulletin No. 51. "Consolidated Financial Statements." New York: American Institute of Certified Public Accountants, 1959.

"International Transfer Pricing," by Michael P. Casey. *Management Accounting* (October 1985), 31–35.

Appendix A
THE PARTIAL EQUITY METHOD

The complete equity method, discussed earlier, is ideally suited to situations in which "parent company" financial statements are issued in addition to consolidated financial statements. However, in the early 1980s the Securities and Exchange Commission (SEC) dropped its requirement for the inclusion of parent company financial statements in annual reports and registration statements filed with the SEC. (Parent company financial information must still be presented in certain cases; however, it is now usually presented in a condensed manner in a schedule.) Consequently, the partial equity method has become so widely used that it is now more prevalent than the complete equity method.

HOW IS THE PARTIAL EQUITY METHOD DIFFERENT?

Under the partial equity method, no entries are made to the parent's general ledger (for downstream transfers) or to the subsidiary's general ledger (for upstream transfers) for intercompany profit that is unrealized from a consolidated viewpoint. Thus, no entry for unrealized intercompany profit must be reversed in consolidation, as it must under the complete equity method. Thus, the partial equity method is considered a shortcut approach because these two additional entries are bypassed. (Of course, the same entry used in the complete equity method to eliminate the intercompany sale is made in the partial equity method.) Although this approach produces the same consolidated amounts as the complete equity method, there is no built-in checking feature from the partially consolidated column to the consolidated column.

Illustration

PREPARING CONSOLIDATED FINANCIAL STATEMENTS USING THE PARTIAL EQUITY METHOD: DOWNSTREAM TRANSFER ABOVE COST

Illustration 7-3 is a modification of Illustration 7-1 (the complete equity method) that reflects the use of the partial equity method.

The following points are important for understanding this illustration:

1. The amounts in the P Company column and the partially consolidated column for net income and ending retained earnings, are the same. Thus, the built-in self-checking feature of unrealized intercompany profit exists through the partially consolidated stage.
2. From the partially consolidated column to the consolidated column, however, no built-in self-checking feature exists. Consolidated net income and consolidated retained earnings are both $5,000 lower than

Illustration 7-3
The Partial Equity Method: Downstream Transfers above Cost

P COMPANY AND SUBSIDIARY (S COMPANY)
Consolidating Statement Worksheet
For the Year Ended December 31, 19X1

	P Company	S Company	Nonintercompany Transaction Eliminations Dr.	Nonintercompany Transaction Eliminations Cr.	Partially Consolidated	Intercompany Transaction Eliminations Dr.	Intercompany Transaction Eliminations Cr.	Consolidated
Income Statement:								
Sales	525,000	200,000			725,000			725,000
Cost of goods sold	(310,000)	(116,000)	4,000(2)		(430,000)		20,000(4)	(410,000)
Expenses	(204,000)	(69,000)			(273,000)			(273,000)
Intercompany Accounts:								
Equity in net income of S Company	15,000		15,000(1)		–0–			–0–
Amortization of cost in excess of book value	(4,000)			4,000(2)	–0–			–0–
Sales	75,000				75,000	75,000(4)		–0–
Cost of goods sold	(50,000)				(50,000)		50,000(4)	–0–
Net Income	47,000	15,000	19,000	4,000	47,000	75,000	70,000	42,000
Statement of Retained Earnings:								
Balances, January 1, 19X1	100,000	20,000	20,000(1)		100,000			100,000
+ Net income	47,000	15,000	19,000	4,000	47,000	75,000	70,000	42,000
− Dividends declared	(31,000)	(5,000)		5,000(1)	(31,000)			(31,000)
Balances, December 31, 19X1	116,000	30,000	39,000	9,000	116,000	75,000	70,000	111,000
Balance Sheet:								
Cash	45,000	25,000			70,000			70,000
Accounts receivable	75,000	43,000			118,000			118,000
Inventory:								
From vendors	110,000	25,000			135,000			135,000
Intercompany		15,000			15,000		5,000(4)	10,000
Investment in S Company	96,000			96,000(1)	–0–			–0–
Land	200,000	30,000	12,000(1)		242,000			242,000
Buildings and equipment	500,000	190,000	6,000(1)	45,000(3)	651,000			651,000
Accumulated depreciation	(320,000)	(58,000)	45,000(3)	1,000(1)	(334,000)			(334,000)
Goodwill			9,000(1)		9,000			9,000
Total Assets	706,000	270,000	72,000	142,000	906,000		5,000	901,000
Liabilities	290,000	200,000			490,000			490,000
P Company:								
Common stock	300,000				300,000			300,000
Retained earnings	116,000				116,000	75,000	70,000	111,000
S Company:								
Common stock		40,000	40,000(1)		–0–			–0–
Retained earnings		30,000	39,000	9,000	–0–			–0–
Total Liabilities and Equity	706,000	270,000	79,000	9,000	906,000	75,000	70,000	901,000
Proof of debit and credit postings			151,000	151,000		75,000	75,000	

Explanation of entries:
(1) The primary elimination entry.
(2) The secondary elimination entry.
(3) The accumulated depreciation elimination entry.
(4) The current-year intercompany transactions elimination entry.

the comparable amounts in the partially consolidated column. This is the principal disadvantage of the partial equity method.

3. If P Company were to issue "**parent company**" **financial statements** in addition to consolidated statements, the parent's net income of $47,000 first would have to be adjusted downward by $5,000. It would not make sense for a parent company that has intercompany transactions to report

a greater profit by not consolidating a subsidiary. Accordingly, the parent would make the following adjustment to its financial statements:

Deferral of Gross Profit on Intercompany Sales (income statement)	**5,000**	
Deferred Gross Profit (balance sheet)		**5,000**
To defer the recognition of unrealized gross profit on intercompany inventory sales.		

Subsequent-Year Treatment of Unsold Inventory

This section explains the accounting treatment in 19X2 of the 20% of the intercompany inventory transfer that was unsold at December 31, 19X1. Covered separately are the possibilities that the inventory is not resold by December 31, 19X2, or that it is resold.

Not Resold at the End of 19X2. If the inventory is still on hand at the end of 19X2, the following elimination entry is required in consolidation at December 31, 19X2:

Retained Earnings—P Company (beginning of year)	**5,000**	
Inventory		**5,000**

The credit brings S Company's $15,000 inventory down to $10,000 in consolidation, just as the $5,000 credit did in consolidation at December 31, 19X1 ($10,000 is the parent's cost). The $5,000 debit to retained earnings eliminates the gross profit recorded in the general ledger in 19X1 that is still not reportable from a consolidated viewpoint. (This entry is made at every consolidation date after December 31, 19X1, until the inventory is resold by the subsidiary.) Note that this entry does not involve the Intercompany Sales or Intercompany Cost of Goods Sold accounts. The intercompany sales relating to this inventory took place in 19X1, and those accounts were eliminated in consolidation in 19X1.

Resold by the End of 19X2. If the inventory has been resold by the end of 19X2, then the gross profit deferred at the end of 19X1 is now reportable. In consolidation at December 31, 19X2, the following entry would be made:

Retained Earnings—P Company (beginning of year)	**5,000**	
Cost of Goods Sold (to third parties)		**5,000**

After this elimination entry is posted, the appropriate worksheet accounts (assuming the inventory is resold for $18,000) would appear as follows:

	P Company	S Company	Intercompany Transaction Eliminations Dr.	Intercompany Transaction Eliminations Cr.	Consolidated
Income Statement:					
Sales		18,000			18,000
Cost of goods sold		(15,000)		5,000	(10,000)
Intercompany Accounts:					
Equity in net income	3,000[a]				–0–
Net Income	3,000	3,000[a]		5,000	8,000
Statement of Retained Earnings:					
Beginning of year	37,000		5,000		32,000
+ Net income	3,000			5,000	8,000
End of year	40,000		5,000	5,000	40,000

[a]This amount would be eliminated in the first set of elimination columns, which for simplicity is not shown.

Note that this elimination entry has a "wash" effect on Retained Earnings. This allows the $5,000 of gross profit recorded in the general ledger in 19X1 to flow across and be reported in the consolidated column.

Upstream Transfers above Cost (80%-Owned Subsidiary)

Because the elimination of all of the gross profit in consolidation is required regardless of whether or not a minority interest exists, the only difference between upstream and downstream inventory transfers is that an additional worksheet adjustment is made to the minority interest in an upstream transfer to allocate a portion of the deferred intercompany gross profit to the minority interest. Without this adjustment, the consolidated net income and consolidated retained earnings would be reduced by the total amount of the deferred intercompany gross profit (rather than just the portion that accrues to the parent company).

Based on the intercompany inventory transaction information given for Illustration 7-3, but assuming that the intercompany sales are upstream and the subsidiary is 80% owned, the appropriate elimination entries are as follows:

	Dr.	Cr.
Intercompany Sales	75,000	
Intercompany Cost of Goods Sold		50,000
Cost of Goods Sold (to third parties)		20,000
Inventory (balance sheet)		5,000
To eliminate the intercompany transactions and defer the recognition of $5,000 of intercompany gross profit.		
Minority Interest (balance sheet)	1,000	
Minority Interest (income statement)		1,000
To allocate to the minority interest $1,000 of the $5,000 deferred intercompany gross profit.		

In the latter entry, the credit to the minority interest deduction in the income statement reduces that deduction and thereby results in consolidated net income being reduced by $4,000 ($5,000 from the first entry less the $1,000 in the second entry) rather than by $5,000.

Illustration

PREPARING CONSOLIDATED FINANCIAL STATEMENTS USING THE PARTIAL EQUITY METHOD: UPSTREAM SALES ABOVE COST (80%-OWNED SUBSIDIARY)

Illustration 7-4 is a modification of Illustration 7-2 (the complete equity method) to reflect the use of the partial equity method. The preceding two elimination entries are used in Illustration 7-4 to get from the partially consolidated column of the worksheet to the consolidated column. The primary, secondary, and accumulated depreciation entries are shown below.

1. The primary elimination entry:

Common Stock	40,000	
Retained Earnings (beginning of year)	20,000	
Equity in Net Income of Subsidiary (80% of $15,000)	12,000	
Minority Interest in Net Income of S Company	3,000	
Land	9,600	
Equipment	4,800	
Goodwill	7,200	
Dividends Declared		5,000
Accumulated Depreciation		800
Investment in Subsidiary		76,800
Minority Interest in Net Assets of S Company		14,000

2. The secondary elimination entry:

Cost of Goods Sold (to third parties)	3,200	
Amortization of Cost in Excess of Book Value		3,200
(80% of the $4,000 used in Illustration 7-1)		

3. The accumulated depreciation entry:

Accumulated Depreciation	45,000	
Buildings and Equipment		45,000

Illustration 7-4
The Partial Equity Method: Upstream Transfer above Cost (80%-Owned Subsidiary)

P COMPANY AND SUBSIDIARY (S COMPANY)
Consolidating Statement Worksheet
For the Year Ended December 31, 19X1

	P Company	S Company	Nonintercompany Transaction Eliminations Dr.	Nonintercompany Transaction Eliminations Cr.	Partially Consoli-dated	Intercompany Transaction Eliminations Dr.	Intercompany Transaction Eliminations Cr.	Consoli-dated
Income Statement:								
Sales	600,000	125,000			725,000			725,000
Cost of goods sold	(360,000)	(66,000)	3,200(2)		(429,200)		20,000(4)	(409,200)
Expenses	(204,000)	(69,000)			(273,000)			(273,000)
Intercompany Accounts:								
Equity in net income of S Company	12,000		12,000(1)		-0-			-0-
Amortization of cost in excess of book value	(3,200)			3,200(2)	-0-			-0-
Sales		75,000			75,000	75,000(4)		-0-
Cost of goods sold		(50,000)			(50,000)		50,000(4)	-0-
Income before Minority Interest	44,800	15,000	15,200	3,200	47,800	75,000	70,000	42,800
Minority interest			3,000(1)		(3,000)		(1,000)(5)	(2,000)
Net Income	44,800	15,000	18,200	3,200	44,800	75,000	71,000	40,800
Statement of Retained Earnings:								
Balances, January 1, 19X1	100,000	20,000	20,000(1)		100,000			100,000
+ Net income	44,800	15,000	18,200	3,200	44,800	75,000	71,000	40,800
− Dividends declared	(31,000)	(5,000)		5,000(1)	(31,000)			(31,000)
Balances, December 31, 19X1	113,800	30,000	38,200	8,200	113,800	75,000	71,000	109,800
Balance Sheet:								
Cash	62,000	25,000			87,000			87,000
Accounts receivable	75,000	43,000			118,000			118,000
Inventory:								
From vendors	95,000	40,000			135,000			135,000
Intercompany	15,000				15,000		5,000(4)	10,000
Investment in S Company	76,800			76,800(1)	-0-			-0-
Land	200,000	30,000	9,600(1)		239,600			239,600
Buildings and equipment	500,000	190,000	4,800(1)	45,000(3)	649,800			649,800
Accumulated depreciation	(320,000)	(58,000)	45,000(3)	800(1)	(333,800)			(333,800)
Goodwill			7,200(1)		7,200			7,200
Total Assets	703,800	270,000	66,600	122,600	917,800		5,000	912,800
Liabilities	290,000	200,000			490,000			490,000
Minority interest in net assets of S Company				14,000(1)	14,000	(1,000)(5)		13,000
P Company:								
Common stock	300,000				300,000			300,000
Retained earnings	113,800				113,800	75,000	71,000	109,800
S Company:								
Common stock		40,000	40,000(1)		-0-			-0-
Retained earnings		30,000	38,200	8,200	-0-			-0-
Total Liabilities and Equity	703,800	270,000	78,200	22,200	917,800	76,000	71,000	912,800
Proof of debit and credit postings			144,800	144,800		76,000	76,000	

Explanation of entries:
(1) The primary elimination entry.
(2) The secondary elimination entry.
(3) The accumulated depreciation elimination entry.
(4) The current-year intercompany transactions elimination entry.
(5) The adjustment to the minority interest to share deferral of profit.

The following points are important for understanding Illustration 7-4:

1. From the partially consolidated column to the consolidated column, net income and retained earnings have been reduced by $4,000 (80% of $5,000).

2. Likewise, the minority interest deduction has been reduced by $1,000, as has the minority interest in the balance sheet (20% of $5,000).
3. The $2,000 minority interest deduction in the consolidated column is equal to 20% of $10,000, which is the subsidiary's recorded net income of $15,000 less the $5,000 intercompany gross profit deferred in consolidation.
4. If the parent were to issue **"parent company" financial statements,** in addition to consolidated financial statements (which rarely occurs), it first would have to make the following financial statement adjusting entry to reflect that the subsidiary's book net income includes unrealized intercompany profit:

Equity in Net Income of Subsidiary	4,000	
Investment in Subsidiary		4,000
(80% of $5,000)		

Subsequent-Year Treatment of Unsold Inventory

Not Resold at the End of 19X2. If the intercompany-acquired inventory is still on hand at the end of 19X2, the following elimination entry is required in consolidation at December 31, 19X2:

Retained Earnings—P Company (beginning of year)	4,000	
Minority Interest in Net Assets of S Company	1,000	
Inventory		5,000

This entry is made at every consolidation date after December 31, 19X1, until the inventory is resold by the parent.

Resold by the End of 19X2. If the intercompany-acquired inventory has been resold by the end of 19X2, then the gross profit deferred at the end of 19X1 is now reportable. In consolidation at December 31, 19X2, the following entry would be made:

Retained Earnings—P Company (beginning of year)	4,000	
Minority Interest (income statement)	1,000	
Cost of Goods Sold (to third parties)		5,000

This entry in the income statement effectively reports $4,000 more consolidated net income ($5,000 − $1,000). The $1,000 debit and the $5,000 credit are subtotaled at the net income line and carried forward to the net income line in the analysis of the parent's retained earnings in the balance sheet section of the worksheet. These carryforward amounts offset the $4,000 direct posting to the parent's Retained Earnings account, resulting in a wash effect. This allows the $4,000 in the parent's Retained Earnings account—in the general ledger—to flow across to the consolidated column and be reported for consolidated reporting purposes.

Appendix B
THE TRIAL BALANCE APPROACH

To demonstrate the trial balance approach to the preparation of the worksheet when intercompany inventory transfers exist, the financial statements used in Illustration 7-4 have been reformatted for the trial balance approach and are shown in Illustration 7-5. The elimination entries used in Illustration 7-5 are repeated below for convenience.

1. The primary elimination entry:

Common Stock	40,000	
Retained Earnings (beginning of year)	20,000	
Equity in Net Income of Subsidiary	12,000	
Minority Interest in Net Income of S Company	3,000	
Land	9,600	
Equipment	4,800	
Goodwill	7,200	
Dividends Declared		5,000
Accumulated Depreciation (building)		800
Investment in Subsidiary		76,800
Minority Interest in Net Assets of S Company		14,000

2. The secondary elimination entry:

Cost of Goods Sold	3,200	
Amortization of Cost in Excess of Book Value		3,200

3. The accumulated depreciation elimination entry:

Accumulated Depreciation	45,000	
Buildings and Equipment		45,000

4. The current-year intercompany inventory transaction elimination entry:

Intercompany Sales	75,000	
Intercompany Cost of Goods Sold		50,000
Cost of Goods Sold (to third parties)		20,000
Inventory		5,000

Illustration 7-5
The Trial Balance Approach (Illustration 7-4 reformatted)
The Partial Equity Method: Upstream Transfer above Cost (80%-Owned Subsidiary)

P COMPANY AND SUBSIDIARY (S COMPANY)
Consolidating Statement Worksheet
For the Year Ended December 31, 19X1

	P Company		S Company	
	Dr.	Cr.	Dr.	Cr.
Cash	62,000		25,000	
Accounts receivable, net	75,000		43,000	
Inventory—From vendors	95,000		40,000	
—Intercompany	15,000			
Investment in S Company	76,800			
Land	200,000		30,000	
Buildings and equipment	500,000		190,000	
Accumulated depreciation		320,000		58,000
Goodwill				
Liabilities		290,000		200,000
Minority interest in net assets of S Company				
P Company:				
Common stock		300,000		
Retained earnings—January 1, 19X1		100,000		
Dividends declared	31,000			
S Company:				
Common stock				40,000
Retained earnings—January 1, 19X1				20,000
Dividends declared			5,000	
Sales		600,000		125,000
Cost of goods sold	360,000		66,000	
Expenses	204,000		69,000	
Intercompany Accounts:				
Equity in net income of S Company		12,000		
Amortization of cost in excess of book value	3,200			
Sales				75,000
Cost of goods sold			50,000	
	1,622,000	1,622,000	518,000	518,000
Income before Minority Interest				
Minority interest (income statement)				
Consolidated Net Income				
Consolidated Retained Earnings				

Explanation of entries:

(1) The primary elimination entry.
(2) The secondary elimination entry.
(3) The accumulated depreciation elimination entry.
(4) The current-year intercompany inventory transactions elimination entry.
(5) The adjustment to the minority interest to share deferral-of-profit entry.

Eliminations		Consolidated			
		Income Statement		Retained Earnings	Balance Sheet
Dr.	Cr.	Dr.	Cr.	(Dr.) Cr.	
					87,000
					118,000
					135,000
	5,000(4)				10,000
	76,800(1)				–0–
9,600(1)					239,600
4,800(1)	45,000(3)				649,800
45,000(3)	800(1)				(333,800)
7,200(1)					7,200
					912,800
					490,000
1,000(5)	14,000(1)				13,000
					300,000
				100,000	
				(31,000)	
40,000(1)					–0–
20,000(1)					–0–
	5,000(1)				–0–
			725,000		
3,200(2)	20,000(4)	409,200			
		273,000			
12,000(1)			–0–		
	3,200(2)	–0–			
75,000(4)			–0–		
	50,000(4)	–0–			
217,800	219,800	682,200	725,000		
			42,800		
3,000(1)	1,000(5)	2,000			
220,800	220,800				
			40,800 →	40,800	
				109,800 →	109,800
					912,800

5. The adjustment to the minority interest to share deferral of profit entry:

Minority Interest in Net Assets of S Company	1,000	
Minority Interest in Net Income of S Company...		1,000

Review Questions

1. List five types of intercompany transactions.
2. Why are intercompany transactions usually recorded in separate general ledger accounts?
3. Why are intercompany sales not considered arm's length transactions?
4. Why must intercompany transactions be eliminated?
5. Which intercompany accounts can be eliminated by the rearrangement process?
6. How much profit on an intercompany sale of inventory must be eliminated in consolidation?
7. If intercompany profit is deferred in consolidation, must income taxes that have been provided on that profit be deferred also? Why or why not?
8. What is a downstream sale? an upstream sale?
9. Why are intercompany inventory transfers usually recorded at amounts in excess of cost?
10. When may the profit on an intercompany inventory sale be recognized for financial reporting purposes?
11. Are elimination entries relating to intercompany inventory transactions recorded in the general ledger?
12. If a parent company sells inventory to a subsidiary at prices equal to competitive market prices, has a bona fide sale occurred? Why or why not?
13. Explain the difference between the partial equity method and the complete equity method.
14. When the partial equity method is used and parent company financial statements are issued, what additional step is necessary?

Discussion Cases

DC 7-1 Evaluation of the Manner of Determining Intercompany Transfer Prices and Accounting Ramifications of Pricing Disparities

Porta Company manufactures a standard line of minicomputers. A substantial portion of the domestic manufacturing output is marketed in numerous foreign countries through wholly owned foreign subsidiaries. The subsidiaries purchase the minicomputers from the domestic parent, which has only a single subsidiary in any one foreign country. You have recently been assigned the task of preparing the monthly consolidating statement worksheet, and you notice that the parent's gross profit rates are quite high for intercompany sales to foreign subsidiaries with high income tax rates (higher than the U.S. income tax rate) and quite low to foreign subsidiaries with low income tax rates (lower than the U.S. income tax rate). Considering that the product is highly standardized, this seems unusual. You query the vice president of marketing, who informs you of the following facts:

1. The transfer prices are negotiated by the marketing personnel at the parent's location and the individual managements of the foreign subsidiaries.
2. The parent could impose transfer prices, but company policy is to negotiate transfer prices so that meaningful evaluations of each separate company can be made.

Required:

1. What other reason might account for this disparity?
2. What are the potential ramifications, if any, of this disparity?

DC 7-2

Treatment of Expenses Incurred by Parent on Behalf of Subsidiary

Sadler Company is a wholly owned subsidiary of Painter Company. Sadler files a registration statement with the SEC in connection with a proposed sale of bonds. In the past, certain expenses incurred by the parent on behalf of the subsidiary have not been charged to the subsidiary.

Required:

1. Should the subsidiary's historical income statements reflect all of the expenses that the parent incurred on behalf of the subsidiary?
2. If yes, how should the amount of expenses incurred on the subsidiary's behalf by the parent be determined?

Exercises

E 7-1

Reconciling Intercompany Accounts

During 19X1, Pontos Company and Santini Company (a wholly owned subsidiary) had the following intercompany transactions:

1. The parent advanced the subsidiary $50,000 on a noninterest-bearing basis.
2. The parent charged the subsidiary management fees of $36,000.
3. The subsidiary sold inventory costing $85,000 to the parent for $140,000.
4. The subsidiary declared dividends of $25,000.
5. The subsidiary paid dividends of $20,000. (The remaining $5,000 was paid on January 7, 19X2.)
6. The parent charged the subsidiary $15,000 for legal expenses incurred on behalf of the subsidiary.

Required:
Prepare T-account analyses of the intercompany receivable and payable accounts for 19X1.

E 7-2

Downstream Transfers at Cost

In 19X1, Passer Company sold inventory costing $40,000 to its wholly owned subsidiary, Selkirk Company for $40,000.

Required:
Prepare the elimination entry required in consolidation at the end of 19X1, 19X2, and 19X3 relating to this intercompany inventory transfer under each of the following assumptions:

a. All of the inventory was resold by the subsidiary in 19X3 for $60,000.
b. All of the inventory was resold by the subsidiary in 19X1 for $60,000.
c. In 19X1, 75% of the inventory was sold for $45,000, and the remaining 25% was sold in 19X3 for $15,000.

E 7-3

The Complete Equity Method: Downstream Transfers above Cost

In 19X1, Petro Company sold inventory costing $60,000 to its wholly owned subsidiary, Synfuel Company for $100,000. The complete equity method is used.

Required:

1. Prepare the general ledger entries required for each year under the complete equity method for each assumption in requirement 2.
2. Prepare the elimination entry or entries required in consolidation at the end of 19X1, 19X2, and 19X3 relating to this intercompany inventory transfer under each of the following assumptions:
   a. All of the inventory was sold by the subsidiary in 19X3 for $120,000.
   b. All of the inventory was sold by the subsidiary in 19X1 for $120,000.
   c. In 19X1, 75% of the inventory was sold for $90,000, and the remaining 25% was sold in 19X3 for $30,000.
3. For assumptions 2a and 2c, determine the amount at which the inventory is reported in consolidation at the end of 19X1 and 19X2.

E 7-4

Exercise 7-3 Changed to the Partial Equity Method

Assume the information provided in Exercise 7-3, except that the partial equity method is used.

Required:
Complete requirements 2 and 3 of Exercise 7-3. (Requirement 1 is not applicable.)

E 7-5

The Complete Equity Method: Downstream Transfers above Cost

A parent company and its subsidiary had intercompany inventory transactions in 19X1. The following information has been obtained from the individual financial statements of each company:

	Total	Resold	On Hand
Intercompany sales	$240,000		$36,000
Intercompany cost of goods sold	180,000		
Gross Profit	$ 60,000		

The complete equity method is used.

Required:

1. Complete the analysis.
2. Prepare the general ledger entry required at the end of 19X1.
3. Prepare the elimination entry or entries required in consolidation at the end of 19X1, assuming the transfers are downstream.

E 7-6

Exercise 7-5 Changed to the Partial Equity Method

Assume the information provided in Exercise 7-5, except that the partial equity method is used.

Required:
Complete requirements 1 and 3 of Exercise 7-5. (Requirement 2 is not applicable.)

E 7-7

The Complete Equity Method: Downstream Transfers above Cost

In 19X1, Probe Company sold inventory costing $50,000 to its wholly owned subsidiary, Search Company, for $70,000. (Search resold a portion of the inventory for $65,000 in 19X1.) As of December 31, 19X1, Search's balance sheet showed $21,000 of intercompany-acquired inventory. It resold this remaining inventory in 19X3 for $28,000. The complete equity method is used.

Required:

1. Prepare the general ledger entry required for 19X1, 19X2, and 19X3 under the complete equity method.
2. Prepare the elimination entry or entries required in consolidation at the end of 19X1, 19X2, and 19X3 relating to this intercompany inventory transfer.
3. Determine the amount at which the inventory is reported in consolidation at the end of 19X1 and 19X2.
4. How would your answers in requirements 2 and 3 be different if the subsidiary were 75% owned instead of wholly owned?

E 7-8

Exercise 7-7 Changed to the Partial Equity Method

Assume the information provided in Exercise 7-7, except that the partial equity method is used.

Required:
Complete requirements 2 to 4 of Exercise 7-7. (Requirement 1 is not applicable.)

E
7-9

The Complete Equity Method: Upstream Transfers above Cost

Presidio Company owns 80% of the outstanding common stock of Safety Company. During 19X1, Presidio acquired inventory from Safety for $160,000. Safety's cost was $100,000. The complete equity method is used.

Required:

1. Prepare the general ledger entry required for 19X1, 19X2, and 19X3 under the complete equity method for each assumption in requirement 2.
2. Prepare the elimination entries required in consolidation at the end of 19X1, 19X2, and 19X3 relating to this intercompany inventory transfer under each of the following assumptions:
   a. All of the inventory was sold by the parent in 19X3 for $200,000.
   b. All of the inventory was sold by the parent in 19X1 for $200,000.
   c. In 19X1, 75% of the inventory was sold for $150,000, and the remaining 25% was sold in 19X3 for $50,000.
3. For assumptions 2a and 2c, determine the amount at which the inventory is reported in consolidation at the end of 19X1 and 19X2.

E
7-10

Exercise 7-9 Changed to the Partial Equity Method

Assume the information provided in Exercise 7-9, except that the partial equity method is used.

Required:
Complete requirements 2 and 3 of Exercise 7-9. (Requirement 1 is not applicable.)

E
7-11

The Complete Equity Method: Upstream Transfers above Cost

In 19X1, Potash Company acquired inventory from Saline Company, its 75%-owned subsidiary, for $100,000. Saline's cost was $80,000. At December 31, 19X1, Potash's balance sheet showed $40,000 of intercompany-acquired inventory on hand. (A portion of the inventory was resold during 19X1 for $90,000.) The remaining inventory was resold in 19X3 for $52,000. The complete equity method is used.

Required:

1. Prepare the general ledger adjusting entry required for 19X1, 19X2, and 19X3 under the complete equity method.
2. Prepare the elimination entries required in consolidation at the end of 19X1, 19X2, and 19X3 relating to this intercompany inventory transfer.
3. Determine the amount at which the inventory is reported in consolidation at the end of 19X1 and 19X2.

E
7-12

Exercise 7-11 Changed to the Partial Equity Method

Assume the information provided in Exercise 7-11, except that the partial equity method is used.

Required:
Complete requirements 2 and 3 of Exercise 7-11. (Requirement 1 is not applicable.)

E 7-13

Lower of Cost or Market Adjustment

In 19X1, Ponderosa Company sold inventory costing $60,000 to its subsidiary Saguaro Company, for $70,000. At the end of 19X1, the subsidiary recorded a lower of cost or market adjustment relating to this inventory, 60% of which had been sold during 19X1.

Required:
Determine the amount at which the inventory should be reported in consolidation assuming the adjustment was:

a. $3,000.
b. $6,000.

E 7-14

Issuing "Parent Company" Financial Statements

Polymeric Company and Solarus Company, a 70%-owned subsidiary, had intercompany inventory transfers during 19X5. At the end of 19X5, $20,000 of unrealized intercompany profit was deferred in consolidation. (The partial equity method is used.) Pursuant to a loan agreement, the parent also issues "parent company" financial statements.

Required:

1. Prepare the financial statement entry the parent must make before issuing "parent company only" financial statements assuming the transfers are downstream.
2. Prepare the financial statement entry as in requirement 1, but assume that the transfers are upstream.

Problems

P 7-1*

The Complete Equity Method: Completing the Consolidating Statement Worksheet; Downstream Transfers above Cost to 100%-Owned Subsidiary—Profit in Beginning and Ending Inventory

The partially consolidated financial statements of Puffin Company and its wholly owned subsidiary, Skylark Company, for the year ended December 31, 19X2, are as follows:

*The financial statement information presented for problems accompanied by asterisks is also provided on Model 7 (filename: Model7) of the software file disk that is available for use with the text, enabling the problem to be worked on the computer.

	Partially Consolidated
Income Statement (19X2):	
Sales	$699,000
Cost of goods sold	(400,000)
Expenses	(284,000)
Intercompany accounts:	
Sales	100,000
Cost of goods sold	(60,000)
Deferral of gross profit	(4,000)
Recognition of gross profit	6,000
Net Income	$ 57,000
Statement of Retained Earnings:	
Beginning of year	$204,000
+ Net income	57,000
− Dividends declared	(25,000)
End of year	$236,000
Balance Sheet (December 31, 19X2):	
Cash	$120,000
Accounts receivable, net	180,000
Inventory:	
From vendors	190,000
Intercompany	10,000
Deferred profit	(4,000)
Fixed assets, net	440,000
Total Assets	$936,000
Liabilities	$400,000
Common stock—Puffin Company	$300,000
Retained earnings—Puffin Company	236,000
Total Liabilities and Equity	$936,000

Skylark's December 31, 19X1, inventory included inventory it had acquired from Puffin in 19X1 at a cost of $15,000; Puffin's cost was $9,000. (Assume that Skylark resold all of this inventory in 19X2.) The complete equity method is used.

Required:

1. Prepare all worksheet elimination entries needed to complete the consolidation.
2. Complete the consolidating statement worksheet at December 31, 19X2. (Assume that the business combination was a purchase.)
3. How would the elimination entries for requirement 1 be different if the business combination had qualified as a pooling of interests?

P 7-2*

Problem 7-1 Changed to the Partial Equity Method

Assume the information provided in Problem 7-2, except that the partial equity method is to be used.

Required:

1. Adjust the partially consolidated amounts to reflect the partial equity method.
2. Prepare all worksheet entries needed to complete the consolidation.
3. Complete the consolidating statement worksheet.

P 7-3*

The Complete Equity Method: Preparing the Consolidating Statement Worksheet; Downstream Transfers above Cost to 100%-Owned Subsidiary—Profit in Beginning and Ending Inventory

On January 1, 19X1, Pillow Company acquired all of the outstanding common stock of Sandman Company for $100,000 cash. The following information concerns the subsidiary at that date:

Common stock	$10,000
Retained earnings	80,000

The entire cost in excess of book value was assigned to goodwill, which was deemed to have a 10-year life. Financial statements for 19X2 and at December 31, 19X2, follow.

	Pillow Company	Sandman Company
Income Statement (19X2):		
Sales	$200,000	$147,000
Cost of goods sold	(110,000)	(82,000)
Expenses	(84,000)	(53,000)
Intercompany Accounts:		
Equity in net income	12,000	
Amortization of cost in excess of book value	(1,000)	
Sales	70,000	
Cost of goods sold	(40,000)	
Net Income	$ 47,000	$ 12,000
Balance Sheet (December 31, 19X2):		
Inventory:		
From vendors	$ 55,000	
Intercompany		$ 14,000
Investment in Sandman Company	108,000	
Other assets	337,000	286,000
Total Assets	$500,000	$300,000
Liabilities	$170,000	$200,000
Common stock	150,000	10,000
Retained earnings	180,000	90,000
Total Liabilities and Equity	$500,000	$300,000
Dividends declared—19X2	$ 23,000	$ 7,000
—19X1	17,000	4,000

During 19X1, the parent sold inventory costing $35,000 to the subsidiary for $65,000. At December 31, 19X1, the subsidiary's balance sheet showed $26,000 of this inventory still on hand. All of this inventory was resold in 19X2. The complete equity method is to be used.

Required:

1. Prepare the general ledger entries the parent would make to reflect the complete equity method. (Then adjust the financial statements accordingly.)
2. Prepare the worksheet elimination entries required in consolidation at December 31, 19X2.
3. Prepare a consolidating statement worksheet at December 31, 19X2.
4. How would the elimination entry or entries pertaining to the intercompany transfers be different if the acquisition of the subsidiary had qualified for pooling of interests treatment? It wouldn't

P 7-4*

Problem 7-3 Changed to the Partial Equity Method

Assume the information provided in Problem 7-3, except that the partial equity method is to be used.

Required:
Complete requirements 2 through 4 of Problem 7-3.

P 7-5*

The Complete Equity Method: Completing the Consolidating Statement Worksheet; Upstream Transfers above Cost from 80%-Owned Subsidiary—Profit in Beginning and Ending Inventory

The partially consolidated financial statements of Palm Company and its 80%-owned subsidiary, Snowberry Company, for the year ended December 31, 19X2, are as follows:

	Partially Consolidated
Income Statement (19X2):	
Sales	$157,000
Cost of goods sold	(73,000)
Expenses	(59,000)
Intercompany Accounts:	
Sales	48,000
Cost of goods sold	(32,000)
Deferral of gross profit	(5,000)
Recognition of gross profit	7,000
Income before Minority Interest	$ 43,000
Minority interest	(4,000)[a]
Net Income	$ 39,000
Statement of Retained Earnings:	
Beginning of year	$ 20,000
+ Net income	39,000
− Dividends declared	(10,000)
End of year	$ 49,000

Balance Sheet (December 31, 19X2):	
Cash	$ 5,000
Accounts receivable, net	10,000
Inventory:	
From vendors	25,000
Intercompany	15,000
Deferred profit	(5,000)
Fixed assets, net	95,000
Total Assets	$145,000
Liabilities	$ 40,000
Minority interest in net assets of subsidiary	6,000
Common stock (parent)	50,000
Retained earnings (parent)	49,000
Total Liabilities and Equity	$145,000

[a]Based on the subsidiary's adjusted book income of $20,000.

The parent's December 31, 19X1, inventory included inventory it had acquired from the subsidiary in 19X1 at a cost of $18,000. The subsidiary's cost was $11,000. (Assume that all of this inventory was resold by the parent in 19X2.) The complete equity method is used.

Required:

1. Prepare all worksheet elimination entries required to complete the consolidation.
2. Complete the consolidating statement worksheet at December 31, 19X2. (Assume that the combination qualified as a pooling of interests.)
3. How would the elimination entries for requirement 2 be different if purchase accounting had been used.

P 7-6* Problem 7-5 Changed to the Partial Equity Method

Assume the information provided in Problem 7-5, except that the partial equity method is to be used.

Required:

1. Adjust the partially consolidated amounts to reflect the partial equity method as follows:

Balance Sheet:		
Deferred Profit	5,000	
Minority Interest in Net Assets		1,000
Retained Earnings		4,000
Income Statement and Statement of Retained Earnings:		
Recognition of Gross Profit	7,000	
Deferral of Gross Profit		5,000
Minority Interest		400
Retained Earnings (beginning of year)		5,600
Retained Earnings (net income line)	1,600	
Retained Earnings (end of year)		4,000

2. Prepare all worksheet entries needed to complete the consolidation.
3. Complete the preparation of the consolidating statement worksheet at December 31, 19X2.

P 7-7*

The Complete Equity Method: Preparing the Consolidating Statement Worksheet; Upstream Transfers above Cost from 90%-Owned Subsidiary—Profit in Ending Inventory

On January 1, 19X1, Planeco Company acquired 90% of the outstanding common stock of Sanders Company for $310,000 cash. Information regarding Sanders on that date is:

Common stock	$120,000
Retained earnings	80,000
Land—Book value	85,000
—Current value	185,000

Goodwill was assigned a 20-year life. Separate company financial statements follow for 19X1 and at December 31, 19X1:

	Planeco Company	Sanders Company
Income Statement (19X1):		
Sales	$330,000	$ 70,000
Cost of goods sold	(175,000)	(30,000)
Expenses	(95,000)	(42,000)
Intercompany Accounts:		
Equity in net income	43,200	
Amortization of cost in excess of book value	(2,000)	
Sales		250,000
Cost of goods sold		(200,000)
Net Income	$101,200	$ 48,000
Balance Sheet (December 31, 19X1):		
Inventory:		
From vendors	$ 65,000	$ 40,000
Intercompany	90,000	
Land	200,000	85,000
Other assets	112,000	275,000
Investment in Sanders Company	333,200	
Total Assets	$800,200	$400,000
Liabilities	$168,000	$172,000
Common stock	400,000	120,000
Retained earnings	232,200	108,000
Total Liabilities and Equity	$800,200	$400,000
Dividends declared in 19X1	$ 66,000	$ 20,000

The complete equity method is to be used.

Required:

1. Prepare the general ledger adjusting entry required at the end of 19X2 under the complete equity method. (Then adjust the financial statements accordingly.)
2. Prepare the worksheet elimination entries required in consolidation at December 31, 19X1.
3. Prepare a consolidating statement worksheet at December 31, 19X1.
4. How would the elimination entry or entries pertaining to the intercompany inventory transfer be different if the acquisition of the subsidiary had qualified for pooling of interests treatment?

P 7-8*

Problem 7-7 Changed to the Partial Equity Method

Assume the information in Problem 7-7, except that the partial equity method is to be used.

Required:
Complete requirements 2 through 4 of Problem 7-7.

P 7-9*

COMPREHENSIVE (Chapters 3–7) The Complete Equity Method: Preparing Consolidated Statements; Downstream Transfers above Cost to Wholly Owned Subsidiary. Intercompany Loans; Mid-year Pooling of Interests

Pearl, Inc., acquired all of the outstanding $25 par common stock of Sapphire, Inc., on June 30, 19X4, in exchange for 40,000 shares of its $25 par common stock. The business combination meets all conditions for a pooling of interests. On June 30, 19X4, Pearl's common stock closed at $65 per share on a national stock exchange. Both corporations continued to operate as separate businesses maintaining separate accounting records with years ending December 31.

On December 31, 19X4, after year-end adjustments and closing nominal accounts, the companies had condensed balance sheet accounts as follows:

	Pearl, Inc.	Sapphire, Inc.
Assets:		
Cash	$ 825,000	$ 330,000
Accounts and other receivables	2,140,000	835,000
Inventories	2,310,000	1,045,000
Land	650,000	300,000
Buildings and Equipment	5,575,000	2,380,000
Accumulated depreciation	(1,000,000)	(400,000)
Investment in Sapphire, Inc.	2,430,000	—
Long-term investments and other assets	865,000	385,000
	$13,795,000	$4,875,000
Liabilities and Stockholders' Equity:		
Accounts payable and other current liabilities	$ 2,465,000	$1,145,000
Long-term debt	1,900,000	1,300,000
Common stock, $25 par value	3,200,000	1,000,000
Additional paid-in capital	1,850,000	190,000
Retained earnings	4,380,000	1,240,000
	$13,795,000	$4,875,000

Additional Information:

1. Pearl uses the equity method of accounting for its investment in Sapphire. The investment in Sapphire has not been adjusted for any intercompany transactions.
2. On June 30, 19X4, Sapphire's assets and liabilities had fair values equal to the book balances with the exception of Land, which had a fair value of $550,000.
3. On June 15, 19X4, Sapphire paid a cash dividend of $4 per share on its common stock.
4. On December 10, 19X4, Pearl paid a cash dividend totaling $256,000 on its common stock.
5. On June 30, 19X4, immediately before the combination, the stockholders' equities were:

	Pearl, Inc.	Sapphire, Inc.
Common stock	$2,200,000	$1,000,000
Additional paid-in capital	1,660,000	190,000
Retained earnings	3,036,000	980,000
	$6,896,000	$2,170,000

6. Sapphire's long-term debt consisted of 10% 10-year bonds issued at face value on March 31, 19X1. Interest is payable semiannually on March 31 and September 30. Pearl had purchased Sapphire's bonds at face value of $320,000 in 19X1, and there was no change in ownership through December 31, 19X4. Note: Even though intercompany bond holdings are not discussed until Chapter 9, the facts given are such that you need to know only that intercompany bond holdings are the equivalent of an intercompany loan.
7. During October 19X4, Pearl sold merchandise to Sapphire at an aggregate invoice price of $720,000, which included a profit of $180,000. At December 31, 19X4, $252,000 of the merchandise was reported in Sapphire's inventory, and Sapphire had not paid Pearl for the merchandise purchased.
8. The 19X4 net income amounts per the separate books of Pearl and Sapphire were $890,000 (exclusive of equity in Sapphire's earnings) and $580,000, respectively.
9. The balances in retained earnings at December 31, 19X3, were $2,506,000 and $820,000 for Pearl and Sapphire, respectively.

Required:

1. Prepare the general ledger entry the parent would make at the end of 19X4 under the complete equity method. (Then adjust the balance sheet accordingly.)
2. Prepare all elimination entries required to prepare a consolidated balance sheet. (Because a consolidated income statement is not called for, prepare the entries in a manner so that they will be posted only to the balance sheet.)
3. Prepare a consolidated balance sheet as of December 31, 19X4.
4. Prepare a formal consolidated statement of retained earnings for the year ended December 31, 19X4. (Determine the proper balances from the information given and your elimination entries, rather than from using a formal consolidating statement worksheet.)

(AICPA adapted)

P 7-10*

COMPREHENSIVE (Chapters 3–7) Problem 7-9 Changed to the Partial Equity Method

Assume the information provided in Problem 7-9, except that the partial equity method is to be used.

Required:
Complete requirements 2 through 4 of Problem 7-9.

P 7-11*

COMPREHENSIVE (Chapters 3–7) The Complete Equity Method: Preparing Consolidated Statements: Upstream Transfers above Cost from 75%-Owned Subsidiary—Profit in Ending Inventory; Intercompany Loans and Management Fees; Adjustment of Statements to the Equity Method at the End of the Acquisition Year

On June 30, 19X3, Puntt Company acquired 75% of the outstanding common stock of Shank Company for $533,000 cash. At the purchase date, each of Shank's recorded assets and liabilities had a current value equal to its book value, except for the following items:

	Book Value	Current Value
Inventory	$ 90,000	$ 70,000
Equipment—Cost	400,000	320,000
—Accumulated depreciation	(160,000)	

As of June 30, 19X3, Shank's equipment had an estimated remaining life of 5 years. (Shank uses straight-line depreciation.) Puntt's policy is to amortize intangibles over 10 years. By December 31, 19X3, Shank's inventory on hand at June 30, 19X3, had been charged to cost of goods sold.

No intercompany transactions had occurred between Puntt and Shank prior to the acquisition date. During the six months ended December 31, 19X3, the following intercompany transactions occurred:

1. Shank sold inventory to Puntt for $150,000, none of which has been paid for at December 31, 19X3.
2. On October 1, 19X3, Puntt loaned Shank $200,000 for internal expansion. The borrowing is in the form of a note bearing interest at 10%. (No interest or principal payments have been made to Puntt.)
3. Certain of Shank's management functions are now performed by Puntt. As a result, Puntt charges Shank a management fee of $4,000 per month. (All intercompany management fees have been paid.)
4. On December 28, 19X3, Shank declared a $36,000 dividend payable on January 15, 19X4. The only entry Puntt has made with respect to the dividend is to record the receipt of its share of the dividend on January 17, 19X4.

Puntt's financial statements for the year ended December 31, 19X3, and Shank's financial statements for the six months ended December 31, 19X3, are as follows:

	Puntt Company	Shank Company July 1, 19X3– Dec. 31, 19X3
Income Statement (19X3):		
Sales	$3,500,000	$ 730,000
Cost of goods sold	(2,100,000)	(450,000)
Expenses	(1,249,000)	(259,000)
Intercompany Accounts:		
Sales		150,000
Cost of goods sold		(90,000)
Management fees	24,000	
Interest income	5,000	
Interest expense		(5,000)
Net Income	$ 180,000	$ 76,000
Balance Sheet (December 31, 19X3):		
Cash	$ 365,000	$ 35,000
Accounts receivable, net	290,000	160,000
Intercompany receivables		118,000
Intercompany note receivable	200,000	
Inventory:		
From vendors	402,000	205,000
Intercompany	50,000	
Investment in Shank Company	533,000	
Land	900,000	125,000
Buildings and equipment	4,680,000	900,000
Accumulated depreciation	(1,270,000)	(380,000)
Total Assets	$6,150,000	$1,163,000
Accounts payable	$ 625,000	$ 370,000
Dividend payable		9,000
Intercompany payables	145,000	
Intercompany note payable		200,000
Long-term debt	2,500,000	
Common stock	2,000,000	400,000
Retained earnings	880,000	184,000
Total Liabilities and Equity	$6,150,000	$1,163,000
Dividends declared in 19X3	$ 110,000	$ 36,000

Other Information:

1. Shank's depreciation expense for the six months ended December 31, 19X3, was $40,000. There were no retirements.
2. The parent desires to account for its investment in the subsidiary using the equity method; however it has not made any entries to the investment account since the acquisition date.
3. The complete equity method is to be used.
4. Except for the intercompany loan, each company is to maintain one Intercompany Receivable/Payable account.

Required:

1. Prepare the general ledger adjusting entry (relating to the intercompany inventory sales) required at the end of 19X3 under the complete equity method. (Then adjust the financial statements accordingly.)
2. Prepare T-account analyses of the activity that should be recorded in the Intercompany Receivable/Payable accounts for the six months. Make sure the accounts have the correct balances before you prepare the consolidating statement worksheet. (Also, make sure all income statement intercompany reciprocal accounts agree.)
3. Prepare an expanded analysis of the investment account as of the acquisition date. Update it through December 31, 19X3, using the equity method. (Adjust the parent's financial statements accordingly.)
4. Prepare the primary, secondary, and accumulated depreciation elimination entries at December 31, 19X3.
5. Prepare the elimination entries relating to intercompany transactions.
6. Prepare a consolidating statement worksheet.

P 7-12*

COMPREHENSIVE (Chapters 3–7) Problem 7-11 Changed to the Partial Equity Method

Assume the information provided in Problem 7-11, except that the partial equity method is to be used.

Required:
Complete requirements 2 through 6 of Problem 7-11.

8

Intercompany Transfers of Fixed Assets

AN OVERVIEW OF INTERCOMPANY TRANSFERS OF FIXED ASSETS

Fixed assets are occasionally transferred among entities of a consolidated group. If the transfers are made at the carrying values of the assets, then no entries are necessary in consolidation because no intercompany profit or loss is recorded. If transfers are made above or below the carrying value, special procedures are required to defer recognition of the gain or loss. The reason for deferring the gain or loss is the same as in the case of inventory transfers—no gain or loss is reportable on intercompany transactions from a consolidated viewpoint.

Because intercompany gain or loss is deferred, fixed assets are reported at the cost to the selling entity. Likewise, depreciation (for depreciable assets) is reported in consolidation based on this cost to the selling entity. From a consolidated viewpoint, the reported amount for a fixed asset cannot change merely because the asset has been moved to a different location within the consolidated group or because legal ownership within that group has changed.

As was done in Chapter 7, the discussion of income taxes is delayed until Chapter 12. For current purposes, note that if an intercompany gain or loss is deferred, then the tax (or tax benefit) pertaining to the gain or loss must also be deferred.

The Basic Approach for Developing the Elimination Entries

The approach used in this chapter to develop the elimination entries required in consolidation parallels the approach used to make correcting entries. The classic approach to correcting entries is to (1) determine the entry that was made, (2) determine the entry that should have been made; and (3) compare the accounts and amounts in steps 1 and 2. Their differences constitute the correcting entry.

To develop elimination entries for transfers of assets:

1. Determine the actual general ledger account balances of the selling and acquiring entities as a result of the transfer.
2. Determine the balances that would exist (a pro forma determination) had the intercompany transfer taken place at no gain or loss.
3. Compare the accounts and amounts in steps 1 and 2 at each consolidation date. Their differences constitute the elimination entries.

TRANSFERS OF NONDEPRECIABLE ASSETS: THE COMPLETE EQUITY METHOD

Recall from Chapter 7 that under the complete equity method, the deferral of intercompany profit is accomplished in the general ledger of the parent for downstream transfers or in the general ledger of the subsidiary for upstream transfers. Unlike intercompany inventory transfers, which involve accounts for both intercompany sales and intercompany cost of goods sold, transfers of fixed assets use only one income statement account, called Intercompany Gain. Accordingly, it is not necessary to use a Deferral of Profit account (as in Chapter 7). The general ledger entry to defer the intercompany gain is made by directly debiting the Intercompany Gain account.

For the example that follows, assume that land costing $20,000 is sold by a parent to its subsidiary for $30,000 on January 1, 19X1.

Consolidation at January 1, 19X1. If a consolidation is done as of January 1, 19X1—the transfer date in our example—the parent would make the following **general ledger entry:**

Intercompany Gain (income statement)............	**10,000**	
Deferred Gain (balance sheet)..................		**10,000**
To defer the intercompany gain.		

In consolidation, the following entry would be made:

Deferred Gain (balance sheet)........................	**10,000**	
Land..		**10,000**
To lower the carrying value of the land.		

Land Not Resold at the End of 19X2. If the subsidiary still owns the land at the end of 19X2, the following entry would be made in consolidation:

Deferred Gain (balance sheet)........................	**10,000**	
Land..		**10,000**
To lower the reported carrying value of the land.		

Land Resold by the End of 19X3. If the subsidiary subsequently sells the land in 19X3 for $32,000, it would report a gain of $2,000 ($32,000 – $30,000). However, the reportable gain in consolidation is $12,000 ($32,000 – $20,000). Accordingly, the following general ledger entry would be made by the parent:

Deferred Gain (balance sheet)..........................	**10,000**	
Intercompany Gain (income statement).....		**10,000**
To recognize intercompany gain on the 19X1 land transfer.		

No elimination entry or entries are necessary in consolidation, as the two gain accounts would be lumped together so that a $12,000 gain is reported.

Upstream Transfers. When the transfer is upstream, the procedures are exactly the same as for a downstream transfer, except that the adjusting entry to defer the intercompany profit is made to the subsidiary's general ledger rather than to the parent's general ledger.

Transfers below Cost. When land is transferred below cost, the loss must be deferred. The principle is the same as that for a transfer above cost; only the debits and credits are reversed.

TRANSFERS OF DEPRECIABLE ASSETS: THE COMPLETE EQUITY METHOD

Downstream Transfers above Book Value

When a depreciable asset is transferred downstream at above its carrying value, the gain recorded by the parent must be deferred in the same manner that a gain on the transfer of a nondepreciable asset is deferred.

Because the subsidiary uses the transfer price as its cost, its depreciation expense in future periods is greater than it would have been had the parent transferred the asset at its carrying value. This additional depreciation expense in future periods must be eliminated, because from a consolidated viewpoint, depreciation expense must be based on the parent's carrying value at the transfer date. This additional depreciation expense on the subsidiary's books eventually offsets the initial gain recorded on the parent's books.

After the elimination entries, the parent's cost and accumulated depreciation (based on that cost) are reported in consolidation in the fixed assets section of the balance sheet.

Illustration

DOWNSTREAM TRANSFER ABOVE BOOK VALUE

Assume the following facts:

	P Company	S Company
Sales price of equipment sold to subsidiary on January 1, 19X1		**$18,000**

	P Company	S Company
Carrying value on parent's books:		
Cost	$50,000	
Accumulated depreciation	(35,000)	15,000
Gain recorded by parent		$ 3,000
Remaining life		3 years

Note: For simplicity, we assumed that the equipment is used by an administrative department of the subsidiary. Thus, the acquiring entity's depreciation expense on this equipment is included in its administrative expenses.

The subsidiary bases its periodic depreciation expense on the $18,000 transfer price. As a result, the subsidiary records $6,000 of depreciation expense per year over the next three years rather than $5,000 per year (which is based on the parent company's $15,000 carrying value).

Consolidation at January 1, 19X1. Immediately after the transfer, the appropriate accounts of the parent and the subsidiary would be as follows:

	P Company	S Company
Intercompany gain on sale of equipment	3,000	
Retained earnings—P Company (net income line)	3,000	
Equipment		18,000
Accumulated depreciation		–0–

Under the complete equity method, however, the $3,000 gain would be deferred in the parent's **general ledger** as follows:

Intercompany Gain on Sale of Equipment	3,000	
Deferred Gain (balance sheet)		3,000
To defer the intercompany gain.		

If a consolidating statement worksheet is prepared on January 1, 19X1 (the transfer date), the following worksheet elimination entry is made to report the equipment at the parent's cost, along with the related accumulated depreciation based on this cost:

Deferred Gain (balance sheet)	3,000	
Equipment ($50,000 – $18,000)	32,000	
Accumulated Depreciation		35,000

After this entry is posted, the appropriate worksheet accounts would appear as follows:

	P Company	S Company	Intercompany Transaction Eliminations Dr.	Intercompany Transaction Eliminations Cr.	Consolidated
Income Statement:					
Gain on sale of equipment......	–0–				–0–
Net income.........................	–0–				–0–
Statement of Retained Earnings:					
Beginning of year..................					
+ Net income........................	–0–				–0–
Balance Sheet:					
Equipment............................		18,000	32,000		50,000
Accumulated depreciation......		–0–		35,000	(35,000)
Deferred gain........................	3,000		3,000		–0–

Note that the equipment is reported in consolidation as though it had been transferred at the parent's $15,000 carrying value and the subsidiary had recorded $50,000 and $35,000 as its cost and accumulated depreciation, respectively, rather than $18,000 and $–0–.

Consolidation at December 31, 19X1. At the end of 19X1, the appropriate accounts of the parent and subsidiary would be as follows:

	P Company	S Company
Intercompany gain on sale of equipment..	–0–	
Depreciation expense...........................		6,000
Retained earnings—P Company (net income line)...............................	(1,000)[a]	
Equipment..		18,000
Accumulated depreciation.....................		(6,000)

[a]This amount is the $1,000 incremental depreciation expense as a result of applying the equity method.

However, because the subsidiary has recorded $1,000 of incremental depreciation expense as a result of the transfer price being $18,000 instead of the parent's cost of $15,000, only $2,000 of the intercompany gain need be deferred at December 31, 19X1. Accordingly, the parent would make the following **general ledger** adjusting entry:

Deferred Gain (balance sheet)	1,000	
Intercompany Gain (income statement).....		1,000
To reduce the deferred gain account to a $2,000 balance at December 31, 19X1 as a result of $1,000 of the intercompany gain having been realized.		

If a consolidating statement worksheet is prepared at December 31, 19X1, the following two elimination entries would be made:

Intercompany Gain (income statement)...........	1,000	
Depreciation Expense............................		1,000
To eliminate the intercompany gain and the incremental depreciation expense.		
Deferred Profit (balance sheet)........................	2,000	
Equipment ($50,000 – $18,000)......................	32,000	
Accumulated Depreciation ($35,000 + $5,000 = $40,000; $40,000 – $6,000 = $34,000)............................		34,000
To report the equipment at the parent's cost, along with the related accumulated depreciation based on this cost.		

On posting this entry, the appropriate worksheet accounts would appear as follows:

	P Company	S Company	Intercompany Transaction Eliminations Dr.	Intercompany Transaction Eliminations Cr.	Consolidated
Income Statement:					
Gain on sale of equipment......	1,000		1,000		–0–
Depreciation expense		(6,000)		1,000	(5,000)
Net income.........................	1,000	(6,000)	1,000	1,000	(5,000)
Statement of Retained Earnings:					
Beginning of year					
+ Net income........................	–0–[a]		1,000	1,000	–0–
Balance Sheet:					
Equipment..........................		18,000	32,000		50,000
Accumulated depreciation		(6,000)		34,000	(40,000)
Deferred profit......................	(2,000)		2,000		–0–

[a]This amount is zero because the $1,000 of intercompany gain reported by the parent in 19X1 is exactly offset by the $1,000 of incremental depreciation expense recorded by the subsidiary, which would be reflected in the parent's Retained Earnings account under the equity method of accounting.

Note that consolidated depreciation expense is $5,000, which is the $15,000 carrying value of the equipment at the transfer date divided by the three-year remaining life.

Master Analysis. For a depreciable asset sold to a subsidiary at above carrying value, a company often prepares an overall analysis that readily develops the elimination entries necessary over the asset's remaining life. Such an analysis is shown in Illustration 8-1.

Section 1 of the analysis (the pro forma part) shows the balances and activity that would have existed if the asset had been transferred at its $15,000 carrying value. In preparing this part of the analysis, companies assume that the subsidiary recorded the asset at the parent's cost ($50,000) less the related accumulated depreciation on the parent's books at the transfer date ($35,000).

Section 2 shows the balances and activity that will occur in the subsidiary's general ledger as a result of the transfer at $18,000. In preparing sections 1 and 2, companies must use the assets' **new remaining assigned life,** if different from the old remaining life. The old remaining life is no longer relevant.

Section 3 is merely the differences between the amounts in sections 1 and 2. The balances produced in this section are the amounts used in the elimination entries at each consolidation date. Section 4 shows these elimination entries for each consolidation date.

Effect on Parent's Retained Earnings at the End of 19X3. In reviewing Illustration 8-1, you should realize that at December 31, 19X3 (the date the equipment is fully depreciated by the subsidiary), there will be no net effect on the parent's general ledger Retained Earnings account as a result of the intercompany equipment transfer at above carrying value. The $3,000 gain recorded by the parent has been completely offset by the $3,000 incremental depreciation expense recorded on the subsidiary's books, which under the equity method of accounting the parent has recorded as a reduction to its retained earnings.

Concluding Comments. An illustration of the full consolidation process for financial statements (as in Chapter 7) is not presented for downstream equipment transfers. In the following section, which deals with an upstream transfer, the full consolidation process for financial statements is illustrated.

Upstream Transfers above Book Value

When depreciable assets are transferred from the subsidiary to the parent (upstream), the general ledger entries and consolidation entries shown earlier for downstream transfers are used except that the general ledger

Illustration 8-1
Analysis of Equipment Sold to Subsidiary at above Carrying Value

	Asset: Cost	Asset: Accum. Depr.	Annual Depreciation Expense	Gain to be Deferred
1. Balances that would have existed if transferred at carrying value:				
January 1, 19X1	$50,000	$35,000		
19X1		5,000	$5,000	
December 31, 19X1	$50,000	$40,000		
19X2		5,000	5,000	
December 31, 19X2	$50,000	$45,000		
19X3		5,000	5,000	
December 31, 19X3	$50,000	$50,000		
2. Balances that will exist since transferred at above carrying value:				
January 1, 19X1	$18,000			
19X1		$ 6,000	$6,000	
December 31, 19X1	$18,000	$ 6,000		
19X2		6,000	6,000	
December 31, 19X2	$18,000	$12,000		
19X3		6,000	6,000	
December 31, 19X3	$18,000	$18,000		
3. Differences between 1 and 2 (basis for intercompany elimination entries):				
January 1, 19X1	$32,000	$35,000		$3,000
19X1			$1,000	
December 31, 19X1	32,000	34,000		2,000
19X2			1,000	
December 31, 19X2	32,000	33,000		1,000
19X3			1,000	
December 31, 19X3	32,000	32,000		–0–

4. Entries required in consolidation:

	Consolidation Date: Jan. 1, 19X1 Dr.	Jan. 1, 19X1 Cr.	Dec. 31, 19X1 Dr.	Dec. 31, 19X1 Cr.	Dec. 31, 19X2 Dr.	Dec. 31, 19X2 Cr.	Dec. 31, 19X3 Dr.	Dec. 31, 19X3 Cr.
General Ledger Entries (transferring entity):								
Intercompany Gain (income statement)	3,000							
Deferred Gain (balance sheet)		3,000						
Deferred Gain (balance sheet)			1,000		1,000		1,000	
Intercompany Gain (income statement)				1,000		1,000		1,000
Consolidation Entries (per 3. above):								
Intercompany Gain (Income statement)			1,000		1,000		1,000	
Depreciation Expense				1,000		1,000		1,000
Deferred Gain (balance sheet)	3,000		2,000		1,000		–0–	
Equipment ($50,000 – $18,000)	32,000		32,000		32,000		32,000	
Accumulated Depreciation		35,000		34,000		33,000		32,000

Note: The entry after December 31, 19X3 (until the asset is sold or retired), is as follows:

	Dr.	Cr.
Equipment	32,000	
Accumulated Depreciation		32,000

deferral entries take place on the subsidiary's books rather than on the parent's books.

Illustration

PREPARING CONSOLIDATED FINANCIAL STATEMENTS: UPSTREAM TRANSFER ABOVE BOOK VALUE

The December 31, 19X1, elimination entries in Illustration 8-1 are used in Illustration 8-2 in going from the partially consolidated column to the consolidated column. The worksheet begins with the P Company and S Company financial statements presented in Illustration 5-5. These financial statements were modified as follows:

1. The subsidiary's financial statements reflect a $3,000 gain on the equipment transfer, $2,000 of which has been deferred in its general ledger.
2. The parent's financial statements reflect the $6,000 of additional depreciation expense ($1,000 of which is the incremental depreciation resulting from the subsidiary's $3,000 intercompany gain).
3. The parent's financial statements reflect an additional $800 (80% of $1,000 of realized gain) recorded under the equity method of accounting.

The primary elimination entry (modified for the upstream transfer) along with the other elimination entries follow.

1. The primary elimination entry:

Common Stock	40,000	
Retained Earnings (beginning of year)	20,000	
Equity in Net Income of Subsidiary (80% of $16,000)	12,800	
Minority Interest in Net Income of S Company (20% of $16,000)	3,200	
Land	9,600	
Equipment	4,800	
Goodwill	7,200	
Dividends Declared		5,000
Accumulated Depreciation		800
Investment in S Company		77,600
Minority Interest in Net Assets of S Company		14,200

2. The secondary elimination entry:

Cost of Goods Sold	3,200	
Amortization of Cost in Excess of Book Value		3,200

Illustration 8-2
The Complete Equity Method: Upstream Transfer above Book Value

P COMPANY AND SUBSIDIARY (S COMPANY)
Consolidating Statement Worksheet
For the Year Ended December 31, 19X1

	P Company	S Company	Nonintercompany Transaction Eliminations Dr.	Nonintercompany Transaction Eliminations Cr.	Partially Consolidated	Intercompany Transaction Eliminations Dr.	Intercompany Transaction Eliminations Cr.	Consolidated
Income Statement:								
Sales	600,000	200,000			800,000			800,000
Cost of goods sold	(360,000)	(116,000)	3,200(2)		(479,200)			(479,200)
Expenses	(210,000)	(69,000)			(279,000)		1,000(4)	(278,000)
Intercompany Accounts:								
Equity in net income of subsidiary	12,800		12,800(1)		–0–			–0–
Amortization of cost in excess of book value	(3,200)			3,200(2)	–0–			–0–
Gain on sale of equipment		1,000			1,000	1,000(4)		–0–
Income before Minority Interest	39,600	16,000	16,000	3,200	42,800	1,000	1,000	42,800
Minority interest			3,200(1)		(3,200)			(3,200)
Net Income	39,600	16,000	19,200	3,200	39,600	1,000	1,000	39,600
Statement of Retained Earnings:								
Balances, January 1, 19X1	100,000	20,000	20,000(1)		100,000			100,000
+ Net income	39,600	16,000	19,200	3,200	39,600	1,000	1,000	39,600
− Dividends declared	(31,000)	(5,000)		5,000(1)	(31,000)			(31,000)
Balances, December 31, 19X1	108,600	31,000	39,200	8,200	108,600	1,000	1,000	108,600
Balance Sheet:								
Cash	44,000	43,000			87,000			87,000
Accounts receivable	75,000	43,000			118,000			118,000
Inventory	110,000	40,000			150,000			150,000
Investment in subsidiary	77,600			77,600(1)	–0–			–0–
Land	200,000	30,000	9,600(1)		239,600			239,600
Buildings and equipment	518,000	140,000	4,800(1)	45,000(3)	617,800	32,000(5)		649,800
Accumulated depreciation	(326,000)	(23,000)	45,000(3)	800(1)	(304,800)		34,000(5)	(338,800)
Goodwill			7,200(1)		7,200			7,200
Total Assets	698,600	271,000	66,600	123,400	914,800	32,000	34,000	912,800
Liabilities	290,000	200,000			490,000			490,000
Deferred gain		2,000			2,000	2,000(5)		–0–
Minority interest in net assets of subsidiary				14,200(1)	14,200			14,200
P Company:								
Common stock	300,000				300,000			300,000
Retained earnings	108,600				108,600	1,000	1,000	108,600
S Company:								
Common stock		40,000	40,000(1)		–0–			–0–
Retained earnings		31,000	39,200	8,200	–0–			–0–
Total Liabilities and Equity	698,600	271,000	79,200	22,400	914,800	3,000	1,000	912,800
Proof of debit and credit postings			145,800	145,800		35,000	35,000	

Explanation of entries:

(1) The primary elimination entry.
(2) The secondary elimination entry.
(3) The accumulated depreciation elimination entry.
(4) The incremental depreciation expense elimination entry.
(5) The change in carrying value elimination entry.

3. The accumulated depreciation elimination entry:

Accumulated Depreciation	45,000	
Buildings and Equipment		45,000

4. The incremental depreciation expense elimination entry:

Intercompany Gain on Sale of Equipment	1,000	
Depreciation Expense		1,000

5. The change in carrying value elimination entry:

Deferred Gain (balance sheet)	2,000	
Buildings and Equipment	32,000	
Accumulated Depreciation		34,000

SUMMARY

Transfer of a fixed asset between companies within a consolidated group cannot result in a reportable gain or loss from a consolidated viewpoint. Under the complete equity method, any recorded gain or loss on the transfer is eliminated in the general ledger of the transferring entity. Where a depreciable asset is involved, the recorded depreciation expense must be adjusted in consolidation to obtain an amount based on the selling entity's carrying value at the transfer date. In the consolidated balance sheet, the transferred asset must be reported at the selling entity's cost, with accumulated depreciation, if appropriate, based on this cost.

Appendix A
TRANSFERS OF NONDEPRECIABLE ASSETS: THE PARTIAL EQUITY METHOD

Recall from Chapter 7 that under the partial equity method, the deferral of intercompany profit is accomplished entirely in the consolidation process (rather than in the general ledger(s) as under the complete equity method).

Downstream Transfers above Carrying Value

When land is transferred at above its carrying value, the selling entity records a gain. In preparing the consolidated financial statements, the gain is not reportable and must be deferred until the acquiring entity resells the land. For example, assume land costing $20,000 is sold in 19X1 to a subsidiary for $30,000.

Consolidation at January 1, 19X1. In consolidation, the entry necessary to eliminate the gain and reduce the land to the parent's carrying value at the transfer date is as follows:

Intercompany Gain on Sale of Land	10,000	
Land..		10,000

On posting this entry to the worksheet, the appropriate worksheet accounts would appear as follows:

	P Company	S Company	Intercompany Transaction Eliminations Dr.	Intercompany Transaction Eliminations Cr.	Consolidated
Income Statement:					
Intercompany gain on sale of land....................................	10,000		10,000		–0–
Net Income......................	10,000		10,000		
Statement of Retained Earnings:					
Beginning of year.....................					
+ Net income..........................	10,000		10,000		–0–
Balance Sheet:					
Land..		30,000		10,000	20,000

Note that if the parent were to issue **"parent company" financial statements,** it first would have to make the following financial statement adjusting entry:

Deferral of Gain (income statement)....................	10,000	
Deferred Gain (balance sheet)....................		10,000

Land Not Resold at the End of 19X2. If the subsidiary still owns the land at the end of 19X2, the following elimination entry would be necessary:

Retained Earnings—P Company (beginning of year)......................................	10,000	
Land..		10,000

On posting this entry, the appropriate worksheet accounts would appear as follows:

	P Company	S Company	Intercompany Transaction Eliminations Dr.	Cr.	Consolidated
Statement of Retained Earnings:					
Beginning of year	10,000		10,000		–0–
+ Net income					
Balance Sheet:					
Land		30,000		10,000	20,000

The entry does not involve the income statement accounts because the income statement activity occurred in 19X1. This entry would be made in all periods after 19X1 until the land is sold by the subsidiary.

Land Resold by the End of 19X3. If the subsidiary subsequently sells the land in 19X3 for $32,000, it would report a $2,000 gain ($32,000 – $30,000). However, the reportable gain in consolidation is $12,000 ($32,000 – $20,000). Accordingly, the entry required in consolidation to recognize the previously deferred gain of $10,000 is as follows:

Retained Earnings—P Company (beginning of year)	10,000	
Gain on Sale of Land		10,000

On posting this entry, the appropriate worksheet accounts would appear as follows:

	P Company	S Company	Intercompany Transaction Eliminations Dr.	Cr.	Consolidated
Income Statement:					
Intercompany Accounts:					
Equity in net income	2,000[a]				–0–
Gain on sale of land		2,000		10,000	12,000
Net Income	2,000	2,000[a]		10,000	12,000
Statement of Retained Earnings:					
Beginning of year	10,000		10,000		–0–
+ Net Income	2,000			→ 10,000	12,000
End of year	12,000		10,000	10,000	12,000

[a]This amount would be eliminated in the first set of eliminations columns, which for simplicity is not shown.

Transfers below Carrying Value and Upstream Transfers. When land is transferred at below its carrying value, the loss must be deferred. The principle is the same as that for a transfer above its carrying value; only the debits and credits are reversed.

When the transfer is upstream, the procedures are exactly the same as for a downstream sale only if the subsidiary is wholly owned. If the subsidiary is partially owned, then an additional adjustment is necessary for the minority interest. Upstream transfers are discussed and illustrated in the next section on transfers of depreciable assets.

Appendix B
TRANSFERS OF DEPRECIABLE ASSETS: THE PARTIAL EQUITY METHOD

Downstream Transfers above Carrying Value

Recall that under the partial equity method the intercompany gain deferral takes place in the consolidation process rather than in the transferring entity's general ledger. Continuing with the example used in Illustration 8-1, the consolidation elimination entries under the partial equity method are shown in Illustration 8-3.

Upstream Transfers above Carrying Value

When depreciable assets are transferred from the subsidiary to the parent (upstream), the entries required in consolidation are the same as those previously shown for a downstream transfer, but only if the subsidiary is wholly owned. When the subsidiary is partially owned, the entries are modified so that the deferral of the gain can be shared with the minority interests if the parent chooses. This requires either modifying the previ-

Illustration 8-3
Journal Entries for Downstream Transfer

	Jan. 1, 19X1		Dec. 31, 19X1		Dec. 31, 19X2		Dec. 31, 19X3	
	Dr.	Cr.	Dr.	Cr.	Dr.	Cr.	Dr.	Cr.
Intercompany Gain.....	3,000		3,000					
Equipment	32,000		32,000		32,000		32,000	
Accumulated Depreciation..		35,000		34,000		33,000		32,000
Depreciation Expense				1,000		1,000		1,000
Retained Earnings—P Company (beginning of year)..					2,000[a]		1,000[a]	

[a]The unreportable retained earnings at the beginning of the year.

ously shown entries or adding an additional entry. For instructional purposes, we have chosen to do the latter.

Using the facts in Illustration 8-1, except that the sale is upstream from an 80% owned subsidiary, we determine the minority interest in the subsidiary's gain as $600 (20% of $3,000). This amount is reportable as an increase to the minority interest, but not at the transfer date. Instead, it is reported over the period that the parent depreciates the equipment. The subsidiary's gain is realized in the same manner as far as the minority interest is concerned. (Note that the net effect of the upstream transfer on the parent's general ledger Retained Earnings account is a decrease of $600, which is the total incremental depreciation expense of $3,000 recorded by the parent less its $2,400 share of the subsidiary's reported gain of $3,000 [80% of $3,000] that the parent records under the equity method of accounting.)

Illustration 8-4 shows the entries presented in Illustration 8-3, plus the additional entries needed to share the deferral of the gain with the minority interest. The entries assume that the minority interest—based

Illustration 8-4
Consolidation Entries for Upstream Transfer

	Consolidation Date							
	Jan. 1, 19X1		Dec. 31, 19X1		Dec. 31, 19X2		Dec. 31, 19X3	
	Dr.	Cr.	Dr.	Cr.	Dr.	Cr.	Dr.	Cr.
To Negate Equipment Transfer:[a]								
Gain on Sale........................	3,000		3,000					
Equipment	32,000		32,000		32,000		32,000	
Accumulated Depreciation		35,000		34,000		33,000		32,000
Depreciation Expense.....				1,000		1,000		1,000
Retained Earnings—P Company (beginning of year).........					2,000		1,000	
To Share Deferral with the Minority Interest:								
Minority Interest in net assets	600[b]		400[b]		200[b]		-0-	
Minority Interest (income statement)......		600		400	200		200	
Retained Earnings—P Company (beginning of year)......						400[c]		200[c]

[a]The amounts in this entry at each consolidation date are the same as those in Illustration 8-3.
[b]The unreportable minority interest at this consolidation date.
[c]The unreportable minority interest at the beginning of the year. (Note that this credit posting partially offsets the debit posting to this account in the preceding entry; if the two entries were combined, a net debit posting would be made to P Company's Retained Earnings account.)

on the subsidiary's reported net income—has already been established at the partially consolidated column of the worksheet.

Illustration

PREPARING CONSOLIDATED FINANCIAL STATEMENTS: UPSTREAM TRANSFER ABOVE CARRYING VALUE

The elimination entries at December 31, 19X1, in Illustration 8-4 are used in preparing a consolidating statement worksheet at December 31, 19X1, shown in Illustration 8-5. The primary elimination entry used in Illustration 8-2 was modified for use in Illustration 8-5 as a result of the subsidiary's reporting the full $3,000 intercompany gain rather than only $1,000 (as reported under the complete equity method); thus, the subsidiary's net income is $2,000 higher.

The following points are important for understanding Illustration 8-5:

1. The $3,200 minority interest deduction in the consolidated column can be determined as follows:

Subsidiary's reported net income	**$18,000**
Less—Intercompany gain not deemed realized as far as the minority interest is concerned ($3,000 total gain − $1,000 deemed realized in 19X1)	**(2,000)**
	$16,000
Minority ownership percentage	**20%**
Reportable minority interest deduction	**$ 3,200**

2. The net effect at the net income line in the intercompany transaction eliminations column is $1,600 ($3,000 − $1,400). This amount (which is the net effect on the parent's retained earnings from the carryforward process) can be viewed as follows:

Total intercompany gain	**$3,000**
Less—Incremental depreciation recorded through December 31, 19X1	**(1,000)**
Unreportable gain at December 31, 19X1	**$2,000**
Less—Minority interest in unrealized gain (20% of $2,000)	**(400)**
Unreportable retained earnings at December 31, 19X1	**$1,600**

Review of Entries at December 31, 19X2. The entries in Illustration 8-4 for periods after the year of transfer are slightly harder to visualize and

Illustration 8-5
The Partial Equity Method: Upstream Transfers above Carrying Value

P COMPANY AND SUBSIDIARY (S COMPANY)
Consolidating Statement Worksheet
For the Year Ended December 31, 19X1

	P Company	S Company	Nonintercompany Transaction Eliminations Dr.	Nonintercompany Transaction Eliminations Cr.	Partially Consolidated	Intercompany Transaction Eliminations Dr.	Intercompany Transaction Eliminations Cr.	Consolidated
Income Statement:								
Sales	600,000	200,000			800,000			800,000
Cost of goods sold	(360,000)	(116,000)	3,200(2)		(479,200)			(479,200)
Expenses	(210,000)	(69,000)			(279,000)		1,000(4)	(278,000)
Intercompany Accounts:								
Equity in net income of subsidiary	14,400		14,400(1)		–0–			–0–
Amortization of cost in excess of book value	(3,200)			3,200(2)	–0–			–0–
Gain on sale of equipment		3,000			3,000	3,000(4)		–0–
Income before Minority Interest	41,200	18,000	17,600	3,200	44,800	3,000	1,000	42,800
Minority interest			3,600(1)		(3,600)		400(5)	(3,200)
Net Income	41,200	18,000	21,200	3,200	41,200	3,000	1,4000	39,600
Statement of Retained Earnings:								
Balances, January 1, 19X1	100,000	20,000	20,000(1)		100,000			100,000
+ Net income	41,200	18,000	21,200	3,200	41,200	3,000	1,400	39,600
− Dividends declared	(31,000)	(5,000)		5,000(1)	(31,000)			(31,000)
Balances, December 31, 19X1	110,200	33,000	41,200	8,200	110,200	3,000	1,400	108,600
Balance Sheet:								
Cash	44,000	43,000			87,000			87,000
Accounts receivable	75,000	43,000			118,000			118,000
Inventory	110,000	40,000			150,000			150,000
Investment in subsidiary	79,200			79,200(1)	–0–			–0–
Land	200,000	30,000	9,600(1)		239,600			239,600
Buildings and equipment	518,000	140,000	4,800(1)	45,000(3)	617,800	32,000(4)		649,800
Accumulated depreciation	(326,000)	(23,000)	45,000(3)	800(1)	(304,800)		34,000(4)	(338,800)
Goodwill			7,200(1)		7,200			7,200
Total Assets	700,200	273,000	66,600	125,000	914,800	32,000	34,000	912,800
Liabilities	290,000	200,000			490,000			490,000
Minority interest in net assets of subsidiary				14,600(1)	14,600	400(5)		14,200
P Company:								
Common stock	300,000				300,000			300,000
Retained earnings	110,200				110,200	3,000	1,4000	108,600
S Company:								
Common stock		40,000	40,000(1)		–0–			–0–
Retained earnings		33,000	41,200	8,200	–0–			–0–
Total Liabilities and Equity	700,200	273,000	81,200	22,800	914,800	3,400	1,400	912,800
Proof of debit and credit postings			147,800	147,800		35,400	35,400	

Explanation of entries:
(1) The primary elimination entry.
(2) The secondary elimination entry.
(3) The accumulated depreciation entry.
(4) The intercompany gain elimination entry.
(5) The adjustment to the minority interest to share deferral of gain entry.

understand. The following portrays how the appropriate accounts would be dealt with on the worksheet as of December 31, 19X2:

	P Company	S Company	Intercompany Transaction Eliminations Dr.	Intercompany Transaction Eliminations Cr.	Consolidated
Income Statement:					
Depreciation Expense.	(6,000)			1,000(1)	(5,000)
Income before Minority Interest..		–0–		1,000	
Minority Interest........			200(2)		(200)
Net Income.............		–0–[a]	200	1,000	
Statement of Retained Earnings:					
Beginning of year....	2,400[b]		2,000(1)	400(2)	800
+ Net income..........			200	1,000	800
End of year............	2,400		2,200	1,400	1,600
Balance Sheet:					
Equipment................	18,000		32,000(1)		50,000
Accumulated depreciation...........	(12,000)			33,000(1)	(45,000)
Minority Interest in Net Assets of S Company.............			200(2)		14,400[c]

[a]For simplicity, we assume the subsidiary broke even during 19X2 and paid no dividends either.
[b]This is the parent's 80% share of the $3,000 gain, which it recorded under the equity method of accounting in 19X1.
[c]At December 31, 19X1, the subsidiary had net assets of $73,000. The minority interest share was $14,600. Because we assume the subsidiary broke even in 19X2 and declared no dividends, the minority interest at the partially consolidated column would be $14,600 at December 31, 19X2, as well.

Explanation of entries:
(1) To negate the equipment transfer.
(2) To share deferral with the minority interest.

The following points are important for understanding this review:

1. The parent's $2,400 share of the $3,000 intercompany gain is being recognized in consolidation over three years. At the beginning of the year, $800 had been recognized. Another $800 is recognized during 19X2. At the end of 19X2, $800 of the $2,400 general ledger balance is being deferred in consolidation.
2. In the consolidation column, the $14,400 of minority interest in the net assets of S Company is $200 more than the balance of $14,200 at December 31, 19X1 in Illustration 8-5. Thus the minority interest $600 share of the $3,000 intercompany gain is being recognized in consolidation over three years ($200 per year).

Discussion Cases

DC 8-1

Review of Procedures for Consolidation: An Upstream Sale of Equipment

Shadd Company, a wholly owned subsidiary of Pike Company, manufactures and installs air conditioning systems. Shadd's sales are normally to outside parties, but during the current year Shadd sold Pike an air conditioning system for its new corporate headquarters. Shadd charged Pike $600,000 for the system and a fee of $90,000 for its installation. (Shadd's manufacturing cost was $400,000 and its installation costs were $65,000.)

Required:
Explain the procedures for preparing consolidated financial statements for the current year and in future years with respect to this transaction.

DC 8-2

Review of Procedures for Consolidation: Lateral Sales; Unconsolidated Subsidiary

Sugar Company is a wholly owned subsidiary of Plum Company, which is a conglomerate. Sugar manufactures office copiers, and all of its sales are normally to outside parties. At the beginning of the current year, a wholly owned insurance subsidiary of Plum acquired several office copiers from Sugar for its sales offices at a cost of $800,000. (Sugar's manufacturing cost was $500,000.) Only the insurance subsidiary is not consolidated with Plum. Companywide policy is to take a full year of depreciation in the year of acquisition.

Required:
Explain Plum's procedures in preparing its financial statements for its stockholders for the current year and future years with respect to this transaction.

Exercises

E 8-1

The Complete Equity Method: Downstream Land Transfer above Cost

On January 1, 19X1, Pastoral Company sold land costing $40,000 to its wholly owned subsidiary, Shepherd Company, for $100,000. The complete equity method is used.

Required:

1. Prepare the general ledger deferral entries and consolidation elimination entries as of January 1, 19X1, December 31, 19X1, and December 31, 19X2, under the complete equity method.

2. Prepare the necessary general ledger and consolidation entry or entries at December 31, 19X3, assuming that S Company subsequently sold the land for $120,000.

E 8-2

Exercise 8-1 Changed to the Partial Equity Method

Assume the same information provided in Exercise 8-1, except that the partial equity method is to be used.

Required:
The requirements are the same as those for Exercise 8-1.

E 8-3

The Complete Equity Method: Land Transfer above Cost—Upstream from 80%-Owned Subsidiary

On June 30, 19X1, Praline Company purchased land from Saints Company, its 80%-owned subsidiary, for $90,000. Saints' cost was $60,000. The complete equity method is used.

Required:

1. Prepare the general ledger deferral entries and the consolidation elimination entries as of June 30, 19X1, December 31, 19X1, and December 31, 19X2, under the complete equity method.
2. Prepare the necessary general ledger and consolidation entry or entries at December 31, 19X3, assuming that P Company subsequently sells the land for $85,000.

E 8-4

Exercise 8-3 Changed to the Partial Equity Method

Assume the same information provided in Exercise 8-3, except that the partial equity method is to be used.

Required:
The requirements are the same as those for Exercise 8-3.

E 8-5

Calculating Consolidated Amounts: Downstream Equipment Transfer above Carrying Value

On January 1, 19X1, Pacific Company sold equipment to its wholly owned subsidiary, Southern Company for $800,000. The equipment cost Pacific $1,000,000; accumulated depreciation at the time of the sale was $400,000. Pacific has depreciated the equipment over 10 years using the straight-line method and no salvage value.

Required:
Determine the amounts at which the cost and accumulated depreciation should be reported in the consolidated balance sheet at December 31, 19X1, under each of the following assumptions:

1. The subsidiary does not revise the estimated remaining life.
2. The subsidiary estimates the remaining life as eight years.

E 8-6

The Complete Equity Method: Downstream Equipment Transfer above Carrying Value

On January 1, 19X1, Placid Company sold machinery to its wholly owned subsidiary, Sereno Company. Information related to the sale is as follows:

Sales price		$16,000
Cost	$40,000	
Less—Accumulated depreciation	(30,000)	10,000
Gain		$ 6,000
Original life used by Placid Company		8 years
Remaining life assigned by Sereno Company		3 years

The complete equity method is used.

Required:
Prepare the general ledger deferral entries and consolidation elimination entries required as of January 1, 19X1, December 31, 19X1, December 31, 19X2, December 31, 19X3, and December 31, 19X4, under the complete equity method.

E 8-7

Exercise 8-6 Changed to the Partial Equity Method

Assume the same information provided in Exercise 8-6, except that the partial equity method is used.

Required:
The requirements are the same as those for Exercise 8-6.

E 8-8

The Complete Equity Method: Equipment Transfer above Carrying Value—Upstream from 90%-Owned Subsidiary

On January 1, 19X1, Prawn Company purchased equipment from its 90%-owned subsidiary Shrimp Company. Information related to the sale is as follows:

Sales price		$42,000
Cost	$75,000	
Less—Accumulated depreciation	(60,000)	15,000
Gain		$27,000
Original life used by subsidiary		5 years
Remaining life assigned by parent		3 years

The complete equity method is used.

Required:
Prepare the general ledger deferral entries and the consolidation elimination entries as of January 1, 19X1, December 31, 19X1, December 31, 19X2, December 31, 19X3, and December 31, 19X4.

E 8-9

Exercise 8-8 Changed to the Partial Equity Method

Assume the same information provided in Exercise 8-8, except that the partial equity method is to be used.

Required:
The requirements are the same as those for Exercise 8-8.

Problems

P 8-1*

The Complete Equity Method: Completing the Consolidating Statement Worksheet; Downstream Equipment Transfer above Carrying Value

The partially consolidated financial statements of Picasso Company and its 80%-owned subsidiary, Sarto Company, for the year ended December 31, 19X2, are as follows:

	Partially Consolidated
Income Statement (19X2):	
Sales	$282,000
Cost of goods sold	(140,000)
Expenses	(95,000)
Intercompany Accounts:	
Gain on sale of equipment	1,000
Income before Minority interest	48,000
Minority interest	(3,000)[a]
Net Income	$ 45,000
Statement of Retained Earnings:	
Beginning of year	$ 42,000
+ Net income	45,000
− Dividends declared	(15,000)
End of year	$ 72,000
Balance Sheet (December 31, 19X2):	
Buildings and equipment	$160,000
Accumulated depreciation	(40,000)
Other assets	190,000
Total Assets	$310,000

*The financial statement information presented for problems accompanied by asterisks is also provided on Model 7 (filename: Model7) of the software file disk that is available for use with the text, enabling the problem to be worked on the computer.

Liabilities	**$125,000**
Deferred gain	**3,000**
Minority interest in net assets of subsidiary	**10,000**
Common stock	**100,000**
Retained earnings	**72,000**
Total Liabilities and Equity	**$310,000**

[a]Based on the subsidiary's book income of $15,000.

On July 1, 19X2, Picasso sold a piece of office equipment to Sarto. Information pertaining to this transfer follows:

Sales price		**$12,000**
Carrying value:		
Cost	**$30,000**	
Accumulated depreciation through July 1, 19X2	**(22,000)**	**(8,000)**
Gain recorded by parent		**$ 4,000**
Remaining life		**2 years**

The complete equity method is used.

Required:

1. Prepare the required elimination entries at December 31, 19X2.
2. Complete the preparation of the consolidating statement worksheet at December 31, 19X2.

P 8-2*

Problem 8-1 Changed to the Partial Equity Method

Assume the information provided in Problem 8-1, except that the partial equity method is used.

Required:

1. Adjust the partially consolidated amounts to reflect the partial equity method.
2. Prepare the elimination entry or entries required in consolidation at December 31, 19X2.
3. Complete the consolidating statement worksheet.

P 8-3*

MINI-COMPREHENSIVE (Chapters 3, 4, and 8) The Complete Equity Method: Full Consolidation; Downstream Equipment Transfer above Carrying Value

On January 1, 19X1, Paton Company acquired all of the outstanding common stock of Seaver Company for $90,000 cash. Seaver's book value was $70,000 at that date ($45,000 common stock + $25,000 retained earnings). The entire cost in excess of book value was assigned to goodwill, which was deemed to have a four-year life. On January 2, 19X1, Paton sold equipment to Seaver. Information related to the sale is as follows:

Sales price		$35,000
Cost	$50,000	
Less—Accumulated depreciation	(30,000)	20,000
Gain		$15,000
Original life used by Paton Company		10 years
Remaining life assigned by Seaver Company		5 years

Condensed financial statement information for 19X1 and at December 31, 19X1, follows:

	Paton Company	Seaver Company
Income Statement (19X1):		
Sales	$440,000	$150,000
Cost of goods sold	(230,000)	(80,000)
Expenses	(70,000)	(40,000)
Intercompany Accounts:		
Equity in net income of subsidiary	30,000	
Amortization of cost in excess of book value	(5,000)	
Gain on sale of equipment	15,000	
Net Income	$180,000	$ 30,000
Balance Sheet (December 31, 19X1):		
Investment in Seaver Company	$103,000	
Buildings and equipment	250,000	$ 75,000
Accumulated depreciation	(100,000)	(24,000)*
Other assets	597,000	59,000
Total Assets	$850,000	$110,000
Liabilities	$110,000	$ 22,000
Common stock	300,000	45,000
Retained earnings	440,000	43,000
Total Liabilities and Equity	$850,000	$110,000
Dividends declared	$ 80,000	$ 12,000

*The balance was $10,000 at the acquisition date.

The complete equity method is to be used.

Required:

1. Prepare the general ledger deferral entry needed at December 31, 19X1, to reflect the complete equity method. (Then adjust the financial statements accordingly.)
2. Prepare the elimination entry or entries required in consolidation at December 31, 19X1.
3. Prepare a consolidating statement worksheet at December 31, 19X1.

P 8-4*

MINI-COMPREHENSIVE (Chapters 3, 4, and 8) Problem 8-3 Changed to the Partial Equity Method

Assume the information provided in Problem 8-3, except that the partial equity method is to be used.

Required:
Complete requirements 2 and 3 of Problem 8-3.

P 8-5*

MINI-COMPREHENSIVE (Chapters 3, 4, 5, and 8) The Complete Equity Method: Full Consolidation; Equipment Transfer above Carrying Value—Upstream from an 80%-Owned Subsidiary

On January 1, 19X1, Pak Company purchased 80% of the outstanding common stock of Shipp Company for $143,000 cash. At that date, Shipp Company had (1) a book value of $150,000 ($100,000 common stock + $50,000 retained earnings) and (2) land that was undervalued by $10,000. Goodwill in the transaction was assigned a five-year life. On January 3, 19X1, Shipp sold equipment to Pak. Information related to the sale is as follows:

Sales price		$22,000
Cost	$25,000	
Less—Accumulated depreciation	(15,000)	10,000
Gain		$12,000
Original life used by Shipp Company		5 years
Remaining life assigned by Pak Company		4 years

Condensed financial statements for the year ended December 31, 19X1, follow:

	Pak Company	Shipp Company
Income Statement (19X1):		
Sales	$520,000	$168,000
Cost of goods sold	(210,000)	(80,000)
Expenses	(90,000)	(40,000)
Intercompany Accounts:		
Equity in net income of subsidiary	48,000	
Amortization of cost in excess of book value	(3,000)	
Gain on sale of equipment		12,000
Net Income	$265,000	$ 60,000
Balance Sheet (December 31, 19X1):		
Investment in Shipp Company	$172,000	
Buildings and equipment	130,000	$ 44,000
Accumulated depreciation	(40,000)	(14,000)*
Other assets	238,000	165,000
Total Assets	$500,000	$195,000

(continued)

	Pak Company	Shipp Company
Liabilities	$ 75,000	$ 5,000
Common stock	200,000	100,000
Retained earnings	225,000	90,000
Total Liabilities and Equity	$500,000	$195,000
Dividends declared	$135,000	$ 20,000

*The balance was $10,000 at the acquisition date.

The complete equity method is to be used.

Required:

1. Prepare the general ledger deferral entry needed at December 31, 19X1, to reflect the complete equity method. (Then adjust the financial statements accordingly.)
2. Prepare the elimination entry or entries required in consolidation at December 31, 19X1.
3. Prepare a consolidating statement worksheet at December 31, 19X1.

P 8-6*

MINI-COMPREHENSIVE (Chapters 3, 4, 5, and 8) Problem 8-5 Changed to the Partial Equity Method

Assume the information provided in Problem 8-5, except that the partial equity method is to be used.

Required:
Complete requirements 2 and 3 of Problem 8-5.

P 8-7*

COMPREHENSIVE (Chapters 3–8) The Complete Equity Method: Preparing Consolidating Statement Worksheet: Downstream Inventory Transfers above Cost—Profit in Beginning and Ending Inventory; Upstream Equipment Transfer above Carrying Value from 60%-Owned Subsidiary

On January 1, 19X1, Park Company acquired 60% of the outstanding common stock of Stall Company for $160,000 cash. An additional $12,000 of direct costs were incurred. At the time, Stall's common stock had a book value of $36 per share. Also, Stall's land was undervalued by $50,000, and its 5% long-term debt (due December 31, 19X4) had a current value of $40,000 less than its book value. Park assigned a 10-year life to goodwill.

Many of the management functions of the two companies have been consolidated since the acquisition date. Park charges Stall a management fee of $1,000 per month.

On January 3, 19X2, Stall sold office equipment to Park. Information related to this transfer is as follows:

Sales price		$25,000
Cost	$45,000	
Accumulated depreciation	(30,000)	15,000
Gain		10,000
Original life used by Stall Company		9 years
Remaining life assigned by Park Company		5 years

The financial statements of each company for the year ended December 31, 19X2 (two years after the acquisition), are as follows:

	Park Company	Stall Company
Income Statement (19X2):		
Sales	$910,000	$400,000
Cost of goods sold	(570,000)	(200,000)
Expenses	(302,000)	(158,000)
Intercompany Accounts:		
Equity in net income of subsidiary	24,000	
Amortization of cost in excess of book value	(7,000)	
Sales	50,000	
Cost of goods sold	(30,000)	
Gain on equipment sale		10,000
Management fee income	12,000	
Management fee expense		(12,000)
Net Income	$ 87,000	$ 40,000
Balance Sheet (December 31, 19X2):		
Cash	$ 40,000	$ 20,000
Accounts receivable, net	112,000	60,000
Intercompany receivable	70,000	
Inventory:		
From vendors	247,000	90,000
Intercompany		10,000
Investment in Stall Company	173,000	
Land	123,000	95,000
Buildings and equipment	355,000	140,000
Accumulated depreciation	(150,000)	(55,000)[c]
Total Assets	$970,000	$360,000
Accounts payable and accruals	$130,000	$ 15,500
Intercompany payable		70,000
Long-term debt	200,000	90,000
Common stock, $10 par value	400,000	
Common stock, $20 par value		100,000
Retained earnings	240,000	105,000
Less—Treasury stock (at cost) (500 shares)		(20,500)[a]
Total Liabilities and Equity	$970,000	$360,000
Dividends declared:[b]		
19X1	$ 30,000	$ 5,000
19X2	41,000	25,000

[a]The treasury stock was purchased at a very favorable price on December 31, 19X2.
[b]Assume all dividends were declared on December 10 and paid ten days later.
[c]The balance was $40,000 at the acquisition date.

Stall's December 31, 19X1, inventory included inventory costing $15,000 that had been acquired from Park in 19X1. Park's cost was $10,000. Assume that all of this inventory was resold by the subsidiary in 19X2. The complete equity method is to be used.

Required:

1. Prepare the general ledger deferral ~~entry~~ or entries needed for 19X2, to reflect the complete equity method. (Then adjust the financial statements accordingly.)
2. Prepare the elimination entry or entries required in consolidation at December 31, 19X2. Prepare any supporting analyses or schedules as needed.
3. Prepare a consolidating statement worksheet as of December 31, 19X2.

P 8-8

COMPREHENSIVE (Chapters 3–8) Problem 8-7 Changed to the Partial Equity Method

Assume the information provided in Problem 8-7, except that the partial equity method is to be used.

Required:
Complete requirements 2 and 3 of Problem 8-7.

9

Intercompany Bond Holdings

AN OVERVIEW OF INTERCOMPANY BOND HOLDINGS

A parent or a subsidiary that has outstanding bonds may want to retire some or all of the bonds before their maturity dates. This is common when interest rates have declined significantly since the original issue date and new bonds can be issued at a lower interest rate, or when excess cash has accumulated beyond foreseeable needs. The entity that issues the bonds, (referred to as the **issuing entity**), may not have the cash available to retire the bonds, or it may be impractical to issue new bonds to retire the old ones. In these situations, another company within the consolidated group that has available cash or the ability to issue debt can purchase some or all of the outstanding bonds in the open market. Although it is not unusual for a parent to purchase a subsidiary's bonds, a subsidiary purchases a parent's bonds only if directed to do so by the parent.

When bonds are acquired within a consolidated group, no amounts are owed to any party outside the group. Therefore, the purchase by one entity within the group of any or all of the outstanding bonds of another entity represents a retirement of the bonds. Any imputed gain or loss on this deemed retirement must be reported in the consolidated income statement in the period of the purchase, as required by *APB Opinion No. 26*, "Early Extinguishment of Debt."[1] If the gain or loss is material, it must be reported as an extraordinary item, as required by *FASB Statement No. 4*, "Reporting Gains and Losses from Extinguishment of Debt."[2]

The accounting in consolidation is complicated by the fact that the issuing entity continues to account for the bonds as though they were outstanding, which they are from its viewpoint. The acquiring entity continues to account for the bonds as an investment until the issuing entity actually retires them. Accordingly, the objective of the consolidation procedures is to make the necessary adjustments on the consolidating statement worksheets to reflect, in the consolidated financial statements, amounts that would have existed if the issuing entity, rather than the acquiring entity, had acquired the bonds. These adjustments must be made from the acquisition date of the bonds to the date that they are actually retired.

Determination of Gain or Loss on the Extinguishment of Debt

The procedure for calculating the gain or loss on the extinguishment of debt is the same for both the complete equity method and the partial equity method.

[1] *Opinions of the Accounting Principles Board, No. 26*, "Early Extinguishment of Debt" (New York: American Institute of Certified Public Accountants, 1972), par. 20.

[2] *Statement of Financial Accounting Standards, No. 4*, "Reporting Gains and Losses from Early Extinguishment of Debt" (Stamford: Financial Accounting Standards Board, 1975), par. 8.

The amount of the *imputed* gain or loss on the extinguishment of debt that is reported in the period in which the affiliate's bonds are purchased is determined by comparing the acquisition cost to the applicable percentage of the carrying value of the bonds payable as of the bond purchase date. For example, assume that P Company acquired in the open market 40% of the outstanding 10% bonds of its wholly owned subsidiary, S Company, for $19,400 on January 1, 19X4. (The assumed maturity date of the bonds is December 31, 19X6, which is three years later.) Interest is payable on July 1 and January 1. Thus, none of the purchase cost relates to interest. The gain or loss is calculated at that date as follows:

Calculation of Gain or Loss on Extinguishment of Debt at January 1, 19X4

		Unamortized		
	Face Amount	Premium (S Co.)	Discount (P Co.)	Carrying Value
Bonds payable..................	$50,000	$3,750		$53,750
Percent acquired...........	40%	40%		40%
Amount deemed retired.....	$20,000	$1,500		$21,500
Investment in bonds.........	20,000		$600	19,400
Unrecorded gain on extinguishment of debt		$1,500	$600	$ 2,100

The gain is attributable to the applicable percentage (40%) of the unamortized premium on the subsidiary's books and all of the discount on the parent's books. At the bond purchase date, the subsidiary would make the following **general ledger entry** to reflect the fact that the parent company now holds a portion of the bonds:

Bonds Payable..	20,000	
Bond Premium..	1,500	
Intercompany Bonds Payable......................		20,000
Intercompany Bond Premium		1,500

The preceding example involved a premium on the issuing company's books and a discount on the acquiring company's books. This combination always results in a gain. If the issuing company has the discount and the acquiring company has the premium, a loss on early extinguishment of debt always results. When each company has a discount or each company has a premium, the net effect is a gain or a loss, depending on which company has the greater discount or premium. In all of these situations, the correct procedures for preparing consolidated financial statements can be determined through careful application of the principles discussed and illustrated in this chapter.

Purchase between Interest Payment Dates

In the preceding example, we assumed for simplicity that the bond purchase occurred on an interest payment date. When an affiliate's bonds are acquired between interest dates, the only other item to account for is the additional amount that would be paid by the acquiring entity for interest from the last interest payment date to the purchase date. This additional amount is charged to interest receivable at the purchase date. The procedures to determine and account for the gains and losses do not change.

THE COMPLETE EQUITY METHOD OF ACCOUNTING FOR INTERCOMPANY BOND TRANSACTIONS

As in Chapter 7, we discuss the complete equity method next and leave the partial equity method for the Appendix at the end of the chapter because the complete equity method is conceptually superior and it is easier to learn the two methods in this order.

Recall that under the complete equity method, the parent company's net income and retained earnings always equal the consolidated net income and consolidated retained earnings, respectively. For this to occur, the gain or loss on the deemed extinguishment of intercompany bonds must be reflected in the parent's income statement. Two approaches can be used to accomplish this result:

1. Adjusting the general ledgers.
2. Adjusting the income recorded under the equity method of accounting.

The first approach is simple and practical, and it minimizes the consolidation effort. The second approach is somewhat involved and makes the consolidation effort more difficult, although it is probably more theoretically correct.

Approach 1: Adjusting the General Ledgers

In the previous example, the parent had a discount of $600 and the subsidiary had an intercompany bond premium of $1,500. This would be accomplished with the following **general ledger entries** on the bond acquisition date:

	P Company		S Company	
Subsidiary's Entry:				
Intercompany Bond Premium ..			1,500	
Gain on Extinguishment of Debt..........................				1,500

	P Company	S Company
Parent's Entries:		
Investment in Bonds of S Company..........................	600	
Gain on Extinguishment of Subsidiary's Debt..........		600
Investment in Common Stock of S Company......................	1,500	
Equity in Net Income of S Company....................		1,500
To apply the equity method of accounting.		

Note that the parent's income statement now reports $2,100 of income, which is equal to the gain on the extinguishment of debt that would be reported in consolidation.

The Rationale for Making the General Ledger Entries. The rationale for eliminating the discount on the parent's books and the intercompany bond premium on the subsidiary's books is that the accounting treatment should be no different than if the parent had formally exchanged $20,000 checks with the subsidiary. That is, the parent advances $20,000 to the subsidiary with the stipulation that the subsidiary retire the $20,000 face value of bonds held by the parent. Using this procedure, the parent would record a $600 gain on the extinguishment of the debt and the subsidiary would record a $1,500 gain.

Entries Required in Consolidation. After the general ledger entries shown earlier have been recorded, the parent's Investment in Bonds of S Company account has a balance of $20,000. Likewise, the subsidiary's intercompany bond accounts show only the $20,000 balance in the Intercompany Bonds Payable account. As a result, no amortization is necessary by either company in their general ledgers in subsequent periods. At each future consolidation date (preceding the actual retirement of the bonds), the following two entries would be made in consolidation:

Intercompany Bonds Payable..............................	20,000	
Investment in Bonds of S Company............		20,000
Intercompany Interest Income	2,000	
Intercompany Interest Expense..................		2,000

Illustration

PREPARING CONSOLIDATED FINANCIAL STATEMENTS AT THE END OF THE BOND ACQUISITION YEAR FOR A WHOLLY OWNED SUBSIDIARY

Illustration 9-1 presents a consolidating statement worksheet as of December 31, 19X4.

Partially Owned Subsidiaries. Even when the subsidiary is partially owned, the procedures are the same as those for wholly owned subsidiaries. The parent would use its percentage of ownership (rather than 100%) when applying the equity method.

Approach 2: Adjusting the Income Recorded under the Equity Method of Accounting

Under this approach to having the parent's net income equal consolidated net income, the gain or loss on extinguishment of debt is recorded by the parent as an adjustment to the income it records under the equity method of accounting. In the earlier example, a $2,100 gain on extinguishment existed. Consequently, under this approach the parent would make the following entry at the bond acquisition date:

Investment in Common Stock of S Company..........	**2,100**	
Equity in Net Income of S Company..............		**2,100**

In succeeding periods, the intercompany bond premium and discount are amortized to income in the general ledgers. In applying the equity method of accounting, however, the parent uses the subsidiary's net income adjusted to exclude the amortizations of the intercompany bond premium and discount. In consolidation, the amortizations are eliminated from the income statement and reclassified as retained earnings.

Although these procedures produce the same reported results in consolidation as the previous approach does, the continual recording of the intercompany bond discount and premium amortizations, and the resultant continual adjustment of the subsidiary's net income in applying the

Illustration 9-1
Bond Acquisition for a Wholly Owned Subsidiary (The Complete Equity Method)

P COMPANY AND SUBSIDIARY (S COMPANY)
Consolidating Statement Worksheet
For the Year Ended December 31, 19X4

	P Company	S Company	Nonintercompany Transaction Eliminations Dr.	Nonintercompany Transaction Eliminations Cr.	Partially Consolidated	Intercompany Transaction Eliminations Dr.	Intercompany Transaction Eliminations Cr.	Consolidated
Income Statement:								
Sales	680,000	280,000			960,000			960,000
Cost of goods sold	(380,000)	(120,000)			(500,000)			(500,000)
Expenses	(242,200)	(128,500)			(370,700)			(370,700)
Intercompany Accounts:								
Equity in net income of subsidiary	31,000		31,000(1)		–0–			–0–
Interest expense		(2,000)			(2,000)		2,000(2)	–0–
Interest income	2,000				2,000	2,000(2)		–0–
Gain on extinguishment of debt	600	1,500			2,100			2,100
Net Income	91,400	31,000	31,000		91,400	2,000	2,000	91,400
Statement of Retained Earnings:								
Balances, January 1, 19X4	163,000	65,000	65,000(1)		163,000			163,000
+ Net income	91,400	31,000	31,000		91,400	2,000	2,000	91,400
− Dividends declared	(51,000)	(10,000)		10,000(1)	(51,000)			(51,000)
Balances, December 31, 19X4	203,400	86,000	96,000	10,000	203,400	2,000	2,000	203,400
Balance Sheet:								
Investment in S Company:								
Common stock	126,000			126,000(1)	–0–			–0–
Bonds	20,000				20,000		20,000(3)	–0–
Intercompany interest receivable (payable)	1,000	(1,000)			–0–			–0–
Other assets	600,400	311,000			911,400			911,400
Total Assets	747,400	310,000		126,000	931,400		20,000	911,400
Accounts payable and accruals	244,000	132,500			376,500			376,500
Bonds payable		30,000			30,000			30,000
Bond premium		1,500			1,500			1,500
Intercompany bonds payable		20,000			20,000	20,000(3)		–0–
P Company:								
Common stock	300,000				300,000			300,000
Retained earnings	203,400				203,400	2,000	2,000	203,400
S Company:								
Common stock		40,000	40,000(1)		–0–			–0–
Retained earnings		86,000	96,000	10,000	–0–			–0–
Total Liabilities and Equity	747,400	310,000	136,000	10,000	931,400	22,000	2,000	911,400
Proof of debit and credit postings			136,000	10,000		22,000	22,000	

Explanation of entries:
(1) The primary elimination entry.
(2) The elimination of intercompany interest income and intercompany interest expense.
(3) The elimination of the bond investment and related intercompany bond payable.

equity method, result in a substantial amount of busywork—a needless complication in the consolidation process.

We do not illustrate the preparation of consolidating statement worksheets under this approach because it is rarely encountered in practice. Controllers of parent companies are much more likely to select the practical and efficient approach of adjusting the general ledgers.

SUMMARY

The acquisition of an affiliated company's outstanding bonds is accounted for in consolidation as a retirement of those bonds, even though they are not actually retired. When the bonds are deemed retired, there is a gain or loss on early extinguishment of debt to the extent of the intercompany portion of the combined unamortized premium or discount at the bond acquisition date, as reflected on each company's books. Such gain or loss is reportable in the income statement in the period in which the bond acquisition occurs.

Under the complete equity method, any intercompany premium or discount is eliminated and recorded in the income statement. Subsequent amortization of the premium or discount existing at the bond acquisition date is unnecessary.

Appendix
THE PARTIAL EQUITY METHOD

Recall that under the partial equity method, the parent's net income and retained earnings do not equal consolidated net income and consolidated retained earnings, respectively. In dealing with intercompany bond holdings, this comes about because the gain or loss on extinguishment of debt is reported only in consolidation. The following discussion uses the example from the chapter for the complete equity method. If consolidated financial statements are prepared on January 1, 19X4 (the bond acquisition date), the following elimination entry is required in consolidation to (1) reflect this deemed retirement of the bonds and (2) report the gain on extinguishment:

Intercompany Bonds Payable	**20,000**	
Intercompany Bond Premium	**1,500**	
Investment in S Company Bonds		**19,400**
Gain on Extinguishment		**2,100**

This entry produces the same results as though the subsidiary had acquired and retired the bonds.

Dealing with Subsequent Amortization of Bond Premium and Discount

In the preceding example, the substance of the deemed bond retirement is to accelerate reporting the $1,500 intercompany bond premium and the $600 bond discount as income. In other words, instead of the $1,500 bond premium being reported as income over the remaining life of the bonds (as a reduction of interest expense through the amortization process), it is reported as income in consolidation at the bond acquisition date. Likewise, instead of the $600 bond discount being reported as income over the remaining life of the bonds (as additional interest income through the amortization process), it is reported as income in consolidation at the bond acquisition date.

Because the $1,500 intercompany bond premium and the $600 discount are reported as income in consolidation at the bond acquisition date, the parent's consolidated retained earnings balance is $2,100 greater than its general ledger Retained Earnings account balance. The parent's general ledger Retained Earnings account balance equals the consolidated retained earnings balance only through the complete amortization of the $1,500 bond premium and $600 discount that takes place in the general ledgers over the remaining life of the bonds. At December 31, 19X6 (the bond maturity date), the entire intercompany bond premium of $1,500 and the discount of $600 have been amortized in the general ledgers. As a result, the parent's general ledger Retained Earnings account balance is $2,100 greater than at January 1, 19X4 (the bond acquisition date).

If nothing is done in consolidation at the end of 19X4, 19X5, and 19X6 concerning this amortization, then the $2,100 has been reported as income twice:

1. First, as a $2,100 gain on extinguishment in 19X4 as a result of the elimination entry made in consolidation to eliminate the bond investment and the related intercompany bond payable and premium accounts.
2. Second, as additional interest income ($600) and lesser interest expense ($1,500) from January 1, 19X4, to December 31, 19X6, as a result of amortizing the $600 discount and the $1,500 intercompany bond premium to income in the general ledgers.

Obviously, the $2,100 can be reported as income only once. Thus, in periods subsequent to the bond acquisiton date, elimination entries are needed in consolidation to eliminate this income resulting from the amortization process. This, of course, is consistent with the consolidated viewpoint that the bonds are deemed to be retired at the bond acquisition date. Future-period consolidated income statements cannot report any interest income or expense with respect to these bonds.

Entries Recorded in Books Subsequent to Bond Acquisition Date

Assume that P Company and S Company use the straight-line method of amortizing bond premium and discount (the results from the straight-line method are not materially different from results under the interest method). The entries that would be recorded in **each company's general ledger** during 19X4, 19X5, and 19X6 relating to the bonds are as follows:

	P Company		S Company	
Intercompany Interest Expense..........			2,000	
Interest Expense			3,000	
Intercompany Interest Payable/ Cash				2,000
Interest Payable/Cash				3,000
To record interest expense (10% of $50,000, 40% of which is intercompany).				
Intercompany Interest Receivable/Cash	2,000			
Intercompany Interest Income ...		2,000		
To record interest income (10% of $20,000).				
Intercompany Bond Premium			500	
Bond Premium................................			750	
Intercompany Interest Expense..				500
Interest Expense				750
To amortize bond premium.				
Investment in S Company Bonds	200			
Intercompany Interest Income ...		200		
To amortize bond discount.				

At the end of each of these years, the balances in the Intercompany Interest Expense and Intercompany Interest Income accounts would be as follows:

P Company

Intercompany Interest Income	
	2,000
	200
	2,200

S Company

Intercompany Interest Expense	
2,000	
	500
1,500	

The difference between the two accounts is a net credit of $700, which is the result of the amortization of the intercompany bond premium of $500 and the bond discount of $200. Because three such years of amortization occur, the cumulative three-year difference is $2,100 (equal to the gain on extinguishment of debt reportable at January 1, 19X4). As explained in the preceding section, these account balances must be eliminated in consolidation at the end of 19X4, 19X5, and 19X6.

Illustration:

PREPARING CONSOLIDATED FINANCIAL STATEMENTS AT THE END OF THE BOND ACQUISITION YEAR FOR A WHOLLY OWNED SUBSIDIARY

Assuming P Company is a calendar year-end reporting company, the elimination entries that would be made in consolidation at December 31, 19X4 (one year after the bond acquisition date), are as follows:

1. The elimination of intercompany interest income and intercompany interest expense:

Intercompany Interest Income	2,200	
Intercompany Interest Expense............		1,500
Gain on Extinguishment of Debt..........		700

2. The elimination of the investment in the bonds and the related bond liability and premium accounts:

Intercompany Bonds Payable........................	20,000	
Intercompany Bond Premium ($1,500 − $500 19X1 amortization)..................................	1,000	
Investment in bonds ($19,400 + $200 19X1 amortization).........................		19,600
Gain on Extinguishment of Debt..........		1,400

The combination of the two entries results in a $2,100 credit to the Gain on Extinguishment of Debt account, which was the amount of gain determined on January 1, 19X1 (the date the bond investment was made). Because of the actual $700 amortization that was recorded in the general ledgers during 19X1, only $1,400 of premium and discount remain "locked into" the balance sheet at the end of 19X1.

The two preceding entries are posted to the December 31, 19X4, consolidating statement worksheet in Illustration 9-2. The following assumptions were made for simplicity:

1. P Company acquired all of the outstanding common stock of S Company on January 1, 19X1, at an amount equal to book value of S Company's net assets. Accordingly, no secondary elimination entry is made for cost over or under book value. In 19X4, S Company had net income of $30,000 and declared dividends of $10,000. The primary elimination entry (assuming that P Company uses the equity method of accounting) is as follows:

Illustration 9-2
Bond Acquisition for a Wholly Owned Subsidiary (the Partial Equity Method)

P COMPANY AND SUBSIDIARY (S COMPANY)
Consolidating Statement Worksheet
For the Year Ended December 31, 19X4

	P Company	S Company	Nonintercompany Transaction Eliminations		Partially Consolidated	Intercompany Transaction Eliminations		Consolidated
			Dr.	Cr.		Dr.	Cr.	
Income Statement:								
Sales	680,000	280,000			960,000			960,000
Cost of goods sold	(380,000)	(120,000)			(500,000)			(500,000)
Expenses	(242,200)	(128,500)			(370,700)			(370,700)
Intercompany Accounts:								
Equity in net income of subsidiary	30,000		30,000(1)		–0–			–0–
Interest expense		(1,500)			(1,500)		1,500(2)	–0–
Interest income	2,200				2,200	2,200(2)		–0–
Gain on extinquishment of debt							700(2) 1,400(3)	2,100
Net Income	90,000	30,000	30,000		90,000	2,200	3,600	91,400
Statement of Retained Earnings:								
Balances, January 1, 19X4	163,000	65,000	65,000(1)		163,000			163,000
+ Net income	90,000	30,000	30,000		90,000	2,200	3,600	91,400
− Dividends declared	(51,000)	(10,000)		10,000(1)	(51,000)			(51,000)
Balances, December 31, 19X4	202,000	85,000	95,000	10,000	202,000	2,200	3,600	203,400
Balance Sheet:								
Investment in S Company:								
Common stock	125,000			125,000(1)	–0–			–0–
Bonds	19,600				19,600		19,600(3)	–0–
Intercompany interest receivable (payable)	1,000	(1,000)		–0–				–0–
Other assets	600,400	311,000			911,400			911,400
Total Assets	746,000	310,000		125,000	931,000		19,600	911,400
Accounts payable and accruals	244,000	132,500			376,500			376,500
Bonds payable		30,000			30,000			30,000
Bond premium		1,500			1,500			1,500
Intercompany bonds payable		20,000			20,000	20,000(4)		–0–
Intercompany bond premium		1,000			1,000	1,000(4)		–0–
P Company:								
Common stock	300,000				300,000			300,000
Retained earnings	202,000				202,000	2,200	3,600	203,400
S Company:								
Common stock		40,000	40,000(1)		–0–			–0–
Retained earnings		85,000	95,000	10,000	–0–			–0–
Total Liabilities and Equity	746,000	310,000	135,000	10,000	931,000	23,200	3,600	911,400
Proof of debit and credit postings			135,000	135,000		23,200	23,200	

Explanation of entries:

(1) The primary elimination entry.

(2) The elimination of intercompany interest income and intercompany interest expense.

(3) The elimination of the bond investment and related intercompany bond liability and premium accounts.

Common Stock	40,000	
Retained Earnings (beginning of year)...........	65,000	
Equity in Net Income of Subsidiary...............	30,000	
Dividends Declared..............................		10,000
Investment in Subsidiary.....................		125,000

2. Intercompany interest payable of $1,000 at December 31, 19X4 ($2,500 × 40%), is eliminated against intercompany interest receivable of $1,000 using the rearrangement procedure discussed in Chapter 7. S Company's intercompany payable is shown among its assets in parentheses. Accordingly, no elimination entry is needed for these accounts.

The following points are important for understanding Illustration 9-2.

1. Both consolidated net income and consolidated retained earnings are $1,400 greater than the corresponding account balances in the partially consolidated column. The difference is attributable to P Company's unamortized discount of $400 at December 31, 19X4, and S Company's unamortized intercompany bond premium of $1,000 at December 31, 19X4. (Under the equity method of accounting, the subsidiary's unamortized intercompany bond premium of $1,000 that is recognized in consolidation in 19X4 accrues to the parent and is properly reportable as part of consolidated net income and consolidated retained earnings.)
2. The $2,100 gain on extinguishment in the consolidated column is less than 3% of net income. Accordingly, the gain is not reported as an extraordinary item because it is immaterial.

Bond Elimination Entries for Periods Subsequent to the Bond Acquisition Year

For periods subsequent to the bond acquisition year, the bond-related elimination entries required in consolidation are nearly identical to the two bond elimination entries shown for Illustration 9-2. The differences are as follows:

1. The elimination entry pertaining to the bond investment and related intercompany bond payable and premium accounts contains updated amounts because of the amortization that was recorded in the general ledgers during the year.
2. Retained Earnings—P Company (beginning of year) account is credited in each of these elimination entries rather than Gain on Extinguishment of Debt. The gain was reported in 19X4 as part of consolidated retained earnings at December 31, 19X4. Thus, the credits to Retained Earnings merely reestablish on the worksheet the portion of the gain on extinguishment that had not yet been recorded in the parent's Retained Earnings account (through the amortization process) at the beginning of the year.

The bond-related elimination entries that would be made in consolidation at December 31, 19X5, and December 31, 19X6, are as follows:

	December 31,			
	19X5		19X6	
Intercompany Interest Income	2,200		2,200	
Intercompany Interest Expense		1,500		1,500
Retained Earnings—P Company (beginning of year)		700		700
Intercompany Bonds Payable	20,000		20,000	
Intercompany Bond Premium	500			
Investment in Bonds		19,800		20,000
Retained Earnings—P Company (beginning of year)		700		

Minority Interest Considerations at Bond Acquisition Date

In the preceding discussion, we assumed that S Company was a wholly owned subsidiary. When the subsidiary is partially owned, the entries made in consolidation in connection with intercompany bond transactions require an adjustment to the minority interest if part of the gain or loss on early extinguishment of debt is attributable to the subsidiary's unamortized discount or premium. No adjustment is necessary if the subsidiary issued or acquired bonds at their face amount.

Let us change our example to reflect an 80% ownership in S Company. Of the $2,100 gain on extinguishment of debt, we know that $1,500 is a result of the premium on the subsidiary's books. Only 80%, or $1,200 of this $1,500 accrues to the parent company. The remaining $300 accrues to the minority-interest shareholders. In consolidation, this $300 is reflected as additional minority interest in the subsidiary's net income. Accordingly, if consolidated financial statements are prepared at January 1, 19X4, an additional entry is required to adjust the minority interest. This worksheet entry is as follows:

Minority Interest in Net Income	300	
Minority Interest in Net Assets		300

As a result of a 20% minority interest in the subsidiary, the consolidated net income is greater by $1,800 ($1,200 + $600 discount) rather than by $2,100.

Minority Interest Considerations at the End of the Bond Acquisition Year

The minority interest deduction that is derived from the primary elimination entry made at December 31, 19X4 (one year after the purchase of the bonds by the parent), is based on the subsidiary's $30,000 recorded net income for 19X4. This $30,000 includes one year's amortization of the bond premium of $500 (intercompany portion only). However, the amortization of the remaining premium of $1,000 (intercompany portion only) must be accelerated for consolidated reporting purposes. Of this amount, 20%, or $200, accrues to minority shareholders. Consequently, an additional $200 minority interest deduction must be made in consolidation at December 31, 19X4, as follows:

Minority Interest in Net Income	200	
Minority Interest in Net Assets		200

Illustration

PREPARING CONSOLIDATED FINANCIAL STATEMENTS AT THE END OF THE BOND ACQUISITION YEAR FOR A PARTIALLY OWNED SUBSIDIARY

Illustration 9-3 shows Illustration 9-2, revised to reflect 80% ownership of the subsidiary. The preceding minority interest entry is used in going from the partially consolidated column to the consolidated column of the worksheet. The following primary elimination entry on the worksheet would be made to go from the P Company and S Company columns to the partially consolidated column:

Common Stock	40,000	
Retained Earnings—S Company (beginning of year)	65,000	
Equity in Net Income of Subsidiary (80% of $30,000)...	24,000	
Minority Interest in Net Income of S Company (20% of $30,000)...	6,000	
Dividends Declared...............................		10,000
Investment in Subsidiary........................		100,000
Minority Interest in Net Assets of S Company (20% of $125,000)...............		25,000

The following point is important for understanding Illustration 9-3:

- The $6,200 minority interest deduction in the consolidated column is determined as follows:

Subsidiary's reported net income......................................	$30,000
Plus—Unamortized intercompany bond premium at December 31, 19X4 recognized in consolidation in 19X4.......................	1,000
	$31,000
Minority interest ownership percentage	20%
Reportable minority interest deduction............................	$ 6,200

Illustration 9-3
The End of the Bond Acquisition Year for a Partially Owned Subsidiary with the Partial Equity Method

P COMPANY AND SUBSIDIARY (S COMPANY)
Consolidating Statement Worksheet
For the Year Ended December 31, 19X4

	P Company	S Company	Nonintercompany Transaction Eliminations Dr.	Nonintercompany Transaction Eliminations Cr.	Partially Consolidated	Intercompany Transaction Eliminations Dr.	Intercompany Transaction Eliminations Cr.	Consolidated
Income Statement:								
Sales	680,000	280,000			960,000			960,000
Cost of goods sold	(380,000)	(120,000)			(500,000)			(500,000)
Expenses	(242,200)	(128,500)			(370,700)			(370,700)
Intercompany Accounts:								
Equity in net income of subsidiary	24,000		24,000(1)		-0-			-0-
Interest expense		(1,500)			(1,500)		1,500(2)	-0-
Interest income	2,200				2,200	2,200(2)		-0-
Gain on extinguishment of debt							700(2) 1,400(3)	2,100
Income before Minority Interest	84,000	30,000	24,000		90,000	2,200	3,600	91,400
Minority Interest			6,000		(6,000)	200(4)		(6,200)
Net Income	84,000	30,000	30,000		84,000	2,400	3,600	85,200
Statement of Retained Earnings:								
Balances, January 1, 19X4	154,000	65,000	65,000(1)		154,000			154,000
+ Net income	84,000	30,000	30,000		84,000	2,400	3,600	85,200
− Dividends declared	(51,000)	(10,000)		10,000(1)	(51,000)			(51,000)
Balances, December 31, 19X4	187,000	85,000	95,000	10,000	187,000	2,400	3,600	188,200
Balance Sheet:								
Investment in S Company:								
Common stock	100,000			100,000(1)	-0-			-0-
Bonds	19,600				19,600		19,600(3)	-0-
Intercompany interest receivable (payable)	1,000	(1,000)			-0-			-0-
Other assets	610,400	311,000			921,400			921,400
Total Assets	731,000	310,000		100,000	941,000		19,600	921,400
Accounts payable and accruals	244,000	132,500			376,500			376,500
Bonds payable		30,000			30,000			30,000
Bond premium		1,500			1,500			1,500
Intercompany bonds payable		20,000			20,000	20,000(3)		-0-
Intercompany bond premium		1,000			1,000	1,000(3)		-0-
Minority interest in net assets of subsidiary				25,000(1)	25,000		200(4)	25,200
P Company:								
Common stock	300,000				300,000			300,000
Retained earnings	187,000				187,000	2,400	3,600	188,200
S Company:								
Common stock		40,000	40,000(1)		-0-			-0-
Retained earnings		85,000	95,000	10,000	-0-			-0-
Total Liabilities and Equity	731,000	310,000	135,000	35,000	941,000	23,400	3,800	921,400
Proof of debit and credit postings			135,000	135,000		23,400	23,400	

Explanation of entries:
(1) The primary elimination entry.
(2) The elimination of intercompany interest income and intercompany interest expense (entry 2 in Illus. 9-1).
(3) The elimination of the bond investment and related intercompany bond liability and premium accounts (entry 3 in Illus. 9-1).
(4) The adjustment to the minority interest.

Bond Elimination Entries for Periods Subsequent to the Bond Acquisition Year for Minority Interest Situations

When a minority interest is involved, the following bond-related elimination entries are required in consolidation for periods subsequent to the bond acquisition year:

	December 31, 19X5		December 31, 19X6	
Intercompany Interest Income	2,200		2,200	
Intercompany Interest Expense		1,500		1,500
Minority Interest in Net Income (20% of the $500 intercompany bond premium amortized during the year)		100		100
Retained Earnings—P Company (beginning of year)		600		600
Intercompany Bonds Payable	20,000		20,000	
Intercompany Bond Premium	500			
Investment in Bonds		19,800		20,000
Minority Interest in Net Assets		100		
Retained Earnings—P Company (beginning of year)		600		

These entries assume that the minority interest deduction in the income statement—based on the subsidiary's reported net income—has already been established at the partially consolidated column of the worksheet.

The credits to the parent's Retained Earnings account merely reestablish on the worksheet the portion of the gain on extinguishment that had not yet been recorded in the parent's retained earnings (through the amortization process) at the beginning of the year. Likewise, the credit to the Minority Interest (balance sheet) account merely reestablishes on the worksheet the portion of the gain on extinguishment that accrues to the minority interest but that has not yet been recorded in the subsidiary's retained earnings (through the amortization process) at this consolidation date; the amount here is 20% of the $500 unamortized intercompany bond premium at December 31, 19X5.

Reissuance of Intercompany Bond Holdings

Infrequently, an acquiring entity sells some or all of the intercompany bonds to an outside party instead of holding them until their maturity date. In these cases, the bonds sold by the acquiring entity are considered to be reissued from a consolidated viewpoint. The consolidation procedures are modified as follows:

1. Any difference between the carrying value of the bonds sold at the time of sale and the face value is treated as previously reported in consolidation.
2. Any difference between the proceeds (other than amounts that relate to interest income) and the face value is treated as a premium or discount, as the case may be, and amortized to income over the remaining term of the bond.

These procedures produce the same results as though the issuing entity redeemed the bonds at their face value and then reissued them to an outside party.

Summary

With respect to the acquired bonds, the consolidation procedures report the appropriate unamortized bond premium or discount in the period in which the bonds are acquired. In subsequent periods, steps must be taken to prevent the reporting of bond premium and discount amortization that is actually recorded in subsequent separate company income statements. Thus, amounts that are reported as interest income or interest expense in later periods in each company's general ledger are reported as a gain or loss on early extinguishment of debt in the bond acquisition period. When a partially owned subsidiary has a premium or a discount, special adjustments are made to the minority interest.

Review Questions

1. From a consolidated viewpoint, what is the substance of an intercompany bond purchase?
2. How is the gain or loss on the extinguishment of debt determined?
3. Are gains and losses on extinguishment of debt extraordinary items?
4. Indicate whether a gain or loss results when: (a) each company has a premium; (b) each company has a discount; and (c) one company has a discount and the other a premium.
5. To which entity should the gain or loss on extinguishment of debt be assigned?
6. Under the complete equity method, what general ledger entry or entries are made at the bond acquisition date?
7. Under the partial equity method, why are entries in consolidation necessary in periods subsequent to an intercompany bond acquisition?
8. Which method requires an adjustment of the minority interest in consolidation when the subsidiary has a discount or premium?

Discussion Cases

DC 9-1

Decision Whether or Not to Use Excess Cash to Purchase a Subsidiary's Bonds

Prose Company owns all of the outstanding common stock of Seth Company. Seth has outstanding $500,000 of 25-year, 10% debenture bonds, which it issued five years ago at a discount of $50,000. Prose has excess cash and is considering purchasing these bonds, which are currently selling at their face value. Its controller has indicated to the treasurer that a loss will be reflected in consolidation when these bonds are purchased. The treasurer replied later that it might be best to avoid this loss by investing the excess cash elsewhere.

Required:
Evaluate the validity of these comments.

DC 9-2

Decision Whether or Not to Purchase a Subsidiary's Bonds to Report a Gain on Extinguishment of Debt

Petcon Company owns all of the outstanding common stock of Satrex Company. Satrex has outstanding $1,000,000 of 15-year, 10% debenture bonds, which it issued five years ago at a premium of $75,000. Petcon Company's management anticipates that consolidated earnings for this year will be lower than expected. Accordingly, it is evaluating ways to increase earnings for the remainder of this year. The controller has suggested that Petcon issue $1,000,000 of bonds and use the proceeds to acquire Satrex's outstanding bonds, which are currently selling at 90. Thus, a $150,000 gain can be generated and reported. Petcon's anticipated borrowing rate is approximately 14%.

Required:
Evaluate the validity and merits of the controller's idea.

DC 9-3

Reissuance of Intercompany Bond Holdings (When Using the Partial Equity Method)

In 19X1, Prolight Company acquired for $480,000 bonds of its wholly owned subsidiary, Sender Company. The acquired bonds were initially issued at their face value of $500,000. Prolight needed cash and sold all of the bonds for $505,000 in 19X4, when the carrying value of the bond investment was $483,000. (The above purchase price and proceeds exclude amounts pertaining to interest income.)

Required:
Using the amounts determinable from the above information, explain the procedures that should be used in consolidation in 19X4 and later years to account for the reissuance of these bonds. Indicate why the procedures you recommend are appropriate.

Exercises

E 9-1

The Complete Equity Method: Calculating Gain or Loss and Preparing the Elimination Entry at the Bond Acquisition Date with a Wholly Owned Subsidiary

Pell Company owns 100% of the outstanding common stock of Sull Company. On January 1, 19X2, Pell acquired in the open market 40% of Sull's outstanding 10% bonds at a cost of $430,000. On January 1, 19X2, the carrying value of all of the bonds ($1,000,000 face amount) was $1,040,000, and the maturity date is December 31, 19X5. Assume the complete equity method is to be used.

Required:

1. Determine the gain or loss from early extinguishment of debt reported in consolidation for 19X2.

2. Prepare the general ledger entry or entries required at the bond acquisition date under the complete equity method.
3. Determine the entry required in consolidation at January 1, 19X2.

E 9-2

Exercise 9-1 Changed to the Partial Equity Method

Assume the information provided in Exercise 9-1, except that the partial equity method is to be used.

Required:
Complete requirements 1 and 3 of Exercise 9-1.

E 9-3

The Complete Equity Method: Calculating Gain or Loss and Preparing the Elimination Entry at the Bond Acquisition Date with a Wholly Owned Subsidiary

Parr Company owns 100% of the outstanding common stock of Subb Company. On April 1, 19X4, Parr acquired in the open market 25% of Subb's outstanding 10%, 10-year debentures ($4,000,000 face amount) at a cost of $1,015,000. The bonds were issued at a premium of $320,000. They mature June 30, 19X8, and pay interest semiannually on June 30 and December 31. Assume that the straight-line method is used to amortize the premium and the complete equity method is to be used.

Required:

1. Determine the gain or loss from early extinguishment of debt reported in consolidation for 19X4.
2. Prepare the general ledger entry or entries required at the bond acquisition date.
3. Determine the entry required in consolidation at April 1, 19X4.

E 9-4

Exercise 9-3 Changed to the Partial Equity Method

Assume the information provided in Exercise 9-3, except that the partial equity method is to be used.

Required:
Complete requirements 1 and 3 of Exercise 9-3.

E 9-5

The Complete Equity Method: Calculating Gain or Loss and Preparing the Elimination Entry at the Bond Acquisition Date with a Partially Owned Subsidiary

Pelt Company owns 75% of the outstanding common stock of Sable Company. On January 1, 19X4, Pelt acquired in the open market 20% of Sable's outstanding 10% bonds at a cost of $160,000. On that date, the carrying value of all of the bonds ($1,000,000 face amount) was $1,020,000. Their maturity date is December 31, 19X7. (Assume that the complete equity method is to be used.)

Required:

1. Determine the gain or loss from early extinguishment of debt reported in consolidation for 19X4.
2. Prepare the general ledger entry or entries required at the bond acquisition date under the complete equity method.
3. Determine the entry required in consolidation at January 1, 19X4.

E 9-6

Exercise 9-5 Changed to the Partial Equity Method

Assume the information provided in Exercise 9-5, except that the partial equity method is to be used.

Required:
Complete requirements 1 and 3 of Exercise 9-5.

E 9-7

The Complete Equity Method: Determining Gain or Loss and Preparing the Elimination Entries in the Year of Bond Acquisition with a Wholly Owned Subsidiary

Paddle Company owns 100% of the outstanding common stock of Snare Company. On January 1, 19X5, Paddle acquired in the open market 30% of Snare's outstanding 10% bonds at a cost of $340,000. On January 1, 19X5, the carrying value of all of the bonds ($1,000,000 face amount) was $1,035,000, and their maturity date is December 31, 19X9. Assume that each company uses straight-line amortization for bond discount and that the complete equity method is to be used.

Required:

1. Determine the gain or loss from early extinguishment of debt reported in consolidation for 19X5.
2. Prepare the general ledger entry or entries required at the bond acquisition date under the complete equity method.
3. Determine the entry required in consolidation at January 1, 19X5.
4. Determine the entries required in consolidation at December 31, 19X5.

E 9-8

Exercise 9-7 Changed to the Partial Equity Method

Assume the information provided in Exercise 9-7, except that the partial equity method is to be used.

Required:
Complete requirements 1, 3, and 4 of Exercise 9-7.

E 9-9

The Complete Equity Method: Determining Gain or Loss and Preparing the Elimination Entries in the Year of Bond Acquisition with a Partially Owned Subsidiary

Pladd Company owns 80% of the outstanding common stock of Shane Company. On January 1, 19X3, Pladd acquired in the open market 60% of Shane's outstanding 10% bonds at a cost of $620,000. On January 1, 19X3, the carrying value of all of the bonds ($1,000,000 face amount) was $1,050,000, and their maturity date is December 31, 19X7. Assume that each company uses straight-line amortization for bond discount and the complete equity method is to be used.

Required:

1. Determine the gain or loss from early extinguishment of debt reported in consolidation for 19X3.
2. Prepare the general ledger entry or entries required at the bond acquisition date under the complete equity method.
3. Determine the entry required in consolidation at January 1, 19X3.
4. Determine the entries required in consolidation at December 31, 19X3.

E 9-10

Exercise 9-9 Changed to the Partial Equity Method

Assume the information provided in Exercise 9-9, except that the partial equity method is to be used.

Required:
Complete requirements 1, 3, and 4 of Exercise 9-9.

Problems

P 9-1

The Complete Equity Method: Completing Separate Company Income Statements in the Year of Bond Acquisition with a Wholly Owned Subsidiary

The partially completed income statements of Place Company and its wholly owned subsidiary Show Company, for the year ended December 31, 19X6, are as follows:

	Place Company	Show Company
Sales	$7,000,000	$3,000,000
Cost of goods sold	(4,000,000)	(1,600,000)
Expenses	(1,500,000)	(1,000,000)
Interest expense		
Intercompany Accounts:		
Equity in net income		
Interest income		
Interest expense		
Gain on extinguishment of debt		
Net Income	$	$

Additional Information:

1. Assume Place Company's cost for Show Company's common stock equals its share of Show's net assets at book value.

2. On January 1, 19X6, Place acquired 40% of Show's outstanding 10% bonds ($1,000,000 face amount) at 90. Show had initially issued these 10-year bonds on January 1, 19X4, at 105.
3. Assume that neither company had any other investments or indebtedness that would give rise to interest income or interest expense.
4. Assume that corporate policy requires bond premium or discount amortization (if appropriate) to be on the straight-line method.
5. The complete equity method is to be used.

Required:

1. Fill in the blanks in the above income statements.
2. Prepare the entries required in consolidation at December 31, 19X6, relating to the intercompany bond holding.

P 9-2

Problem 9-1 Changed to the Partial Equity Method

Assume the information provided in Problem 9-1, except that the partial equity method is to be used.

Required:
The requirements are the same as those for Problem 9-2.

P 9-3

The Complete Equity Method: Calculating Gain or Loss and Preparing the Elimination Entries in the Year of Bond Acquisition and Later Years with a Wholly Owned Subsidiary

Point Company owns 100% of the outstanding common stock of Stealth Company. On January 1, 19X3, Stealth issues $10,000,000 of five-year, 10% bonds at 98. On January 1, 19X5 (two years later), Point acquires in the open market 30% of these bonds at 102. (To comply with corporate policy, Stealth uses straight-line amortization for its bond discount.) The maturity date of the bonds is January 1, 19X8. Assume that the complete equity method is to be used.

Required:

1. Determine the gain or loss from early extinguishment of debt reported in consolidation for 19X5.
2. Prepare the general ledger entry or entries required at January 1, 19X5.
3. Prepare the entry or entries required in consolidation at January 1, 19X5.
4. Determine the entries required in consolidation at December 31, 19X5.
5. Determine the entries required in consolidation at December 31, 19X6.
6. Determine the entries required in consolidation at December 31, 19X7.

P 9-4

Problem 9-3 Changed to the Partial Equity Method

Assume the information provided in Problem 9-3, except that the partial equity method is to be used.

Required:
Complete requirements 1 and 3 through 6 of Problem 9-3.

P 9-5

The Complete Equity Method: Calculating Gain or Loss and Preparing the Elimination Entries in the Year of Bond Acquisition and Later Years with a Partially Owned Subsidiary

Panda Company owns 90% of the outstanding common stock of Salamander Company. On January 1, 19X1, Salamander issued $10,000,000 of five-year, 10% bonds at 95. On January 1, 19X3 (two years later), Panda acquired in the open market 30% of these bonds at 101. (To comply with corporate policy, Salamander uses straight-line amortization for its bond discount.) The maturity date of the bonds is January 1, 19X6. Assume the complete equity method is to be used.

Required:

1. Determine the gain or loss from early extinguishment of debt reported in consolidation for 19X3.
2. Prepare the general ledger entry or entries required at January 1, 19X3.
3. Determine the entry required in consolidation at January 1, 19X3.
4. Determine the entries required in consolidation at December 31, 19X3.
5. Determine the entries required in consolidation at December 31, 19X4.
6. Determine the entries required in consolidation at December 31, 19X5.

P 9-6

Problem 9-5 Changed to the Partial Equity Method

Assume the information provided in Problem 9-5, except that the partial equity method is to be used.

Required:
Complete requirements 1 and 3 through 6 of Problem 9-5.

P 9-7*

The Complete Equity Method: Preparing Consolidated Statements in the Year of Bond Acquisition with a Wholly Owned Subsidiary

Pitchco Company acquires 100% of the outstanding common stock of Striker Company on January 1, 19X1. The cost of the investment is $10,000 in excess of the $60,000 book value of the net assets. This excess was assigned to goodwill and is being amortized over 10 years. On March 31, 19X6, Pitchco Company acquires in the open market 25% of Striker Company's outstanding 12%, 10-year bonds for a total cash payment (including interest) of $106,500. Information regarding Striker's bonds as of the bond acquisition date is as follows:

Total face amount	$400,000
Unamortized bond premium	$28,000
Maturity date	December 31, 19X7
Interest payment dates	July 1 and January 1
Amortization method (to comply with corporate policy)	Straight-line

*The financial statement information presented for problems accompanied by asterisks is also provided on Model 7 (filename: Model7) of the software file disk that is available for use with the text, enabling the problem to be worked on the computer.

The financial statements of each company for the year ended December 31, 19X6, are as follows:

	Pitchco Company	Striker Company
Income Statement (19X6)		
Sales	$800,000	$410,000
Cost of goods sold	(430,000)	(210,000)
Expenses	(270,000)	(141,000)
Intercompany Accounts:		
Equity in net income of subsidiary	50,000	
Amortization of cost in excess of book value	(1,000)	
Interest income	9,000	
Interest expense		(9,000)
Net Income	$158,000	$ 50,000
Balance Sheet (December 31, 19X6):		
Investments in Striker Company:		
Common stock	$154,000	
Bonds	106,500	
Other assets	539,500	600,000
Total Assets	$800,000	$600,000
Accounts payable and accruals	$170,000	$ 22,000
Long-term debt (including premium)	200,000	428,000
Common stock	300,000	50,000
Retained earnings	130,000	100,000
Total Liabilities and Equity	$800,000	$600,000
Dividends declared and paid in 19X6	$ 51,000	$ 20,000

Other information:

1. Neither company has recorded any bond premium or discount amortization since March 31, 19X6.
2. Because of a cash shortage, Striker did not make any bond interest payments to Pitchco during 19X6.
3. The complete equity method is to be used.

Required:

1. Prepare an analysis of the appropriate accounts as of the bond acquisition date that shows how the gain or loss on extinguishment of debt is determined.
2. Prepare the general ledger entry or entries required at March 31, 19X6 and December 31, 19X6. Then adjust the financial statements accordingly.
3. Prepare the entries required in consolidation at December 31, 19X6.
4. Prepare a consolidating statement worksheet at December 31, 19X6.

P 9-8*

Problem 9-7 Changed to the Partial Equity Method

Assume the same information as provided in Problem 9-7, except that the partial equity method is to be used.

Required:

1. Prepare an analysis of the appropriate accounts as of the bond acquisition date that shows how the gain or loss on extinguishment of debt is determined.
2. Prepare the bond premium or discount amortization entries required from the bond acquisition date to year-end. Then adjust the financial statements accordingly.
3. Prepare the entries required in consolidation at December 31, 19X6.
4. Prepare a consolidating statement worksheet at December 31, 19X6.

P 9-9*

The Complete Equity Method: Preparing Consolidated Statements in the Year of Bond Acquisition with a Partially Owned Subsidiary

Penn Company acquired 75% of the outstanding common stock of Select Company on January 1, 19X2, for $75,000 cash. The cost of the investment was equal to Penn's share of the $100,000 book value of the net assets. However, Select's Land account was overvalued by $12,000. (This was the only asset or liability having a current value different from its book value.) Goodwill was assigned a 3-year life.

On September 1, 19X4, Penn acquired in the open market 40% of Select's outstanding 10%, 10-year bonds for a total cash payment of $134,000. Information regarding Select's bonds as of the bond acquisition date is as follows:

Total face amount	$300,000
Unamortized bond discount	$ 20,000
Maturity date	December 31, 19X7
Interest payment dates	July 1 and January 1
Amortization method (to comply with corporate policy)	Straight-line

The financial statements of each company for the year ended December 31, 19X4, are as follows:

	Penn Company	Select Company
Income Statement (19X4):		
Sales	$900,000	$600,000
Cost of goods sold	(500,000)	(350,000)
Expenses	(250,000)	(146,000)
Intercompany Accounts:		
Equity in net income of subsidiary	75,000	
Amortization of cost in excess of book value	(3,000)	
Interest income	4,000	
Interest expense		(4,000)
Net Income	$226,000	$100,000
Balance Sheet (December 31, 19X4):		
Investments in Select Company:		
Common stock	$117,000	
Bonds	134,000	
Other assets	649,000	$510,000
Total Assets	$900,000	$510,000

	Penn Company	Select Company
Accounts payable and accruals	$ 72,000	$ 62,000
Bonds payable (including discount)		280,000
Notes payable	300,000	
Common stock	200,000	60,000
Retained earnings	328,000	108,000
Total Liabilities and Equity	$900,000	$510,000
Dividends declared and paid in 19X4	$100,000	$ 80,000

Other Information:

1. Neither company has recorded any bond discount or premium amortization since the intercompany bond purchase.
2. The January 1, 19X5, bond interest payment was made on January 2, 19X5.
3. The complete equity method is to be used.

Required:

1. Prepare an analysis of the appropriate accounts as of the bond acquisition date that shows how the gain or loss on extinguishment of debt is determined.
2. Prepare the general ledger entry or entries required at September 1, 19X4 and December 31, 19X4. Then adjust the financial statements accordingly.
3. Prepare the entries required in consolidation at December 31, 19X4.
4. Prepare a consolidating statement worksheet at December 31, 19X4.

P 9-10*

Problem 9-9 Changed to the Partial Equity Method

Assume the information provided in Problem 9-9, except that the partial equity method is to be used.

Required:

1. Prepare an analysis of the appropriate accounts as of the bond acquisiton date that shows how the gain or loss on extinguishment of debt is determined.
2. Prepare the bond premium or discount amortization entries from the bond acquisition date to year-end. Then adjust the financial statements accordingly.
3. Prepare the entries required in consolidation at December 31, 19X4.
4. Prepare a consolidating statement worksheet at December 31, 19X4.

P 9-11*

COMPREHENSIVE (Chapters 3–5, 7, 9) The Complete Equity Method: Preparing Consolidated Statements in the Year of Bond Acquisition with a Partially Owned Subsidiary

Pye Company acquired 80% of the outstanding common stock of Slice Company on January 1, 19X1, for $230,000 cash. In addition $14,000 of direct costs were incurred. At the acquisition date, Slice's only assets and liabilities that had current values different from book values were as follows:

	Book Value	Current Value	Remaining Life
Patent	$ 70,000	$160,000	6 years
12% Bonds Payable (face value of $500,000)	532,000	492,000	8 years

The difference between the parent's cost and the current value of the net assets was properly allocated to Land inasmuch as the appraisal report indicated that this was the least firm of the appraisal amounts. On January 1, 19X3, Pye paid $50,000 cash to the former owners because Slice's earnings of $90,000 for the two years ended December 31, 19X2, exceeded $80,000. At that date, it was determined that the land was actually undervalued by $30,000. (In retrospect, the conservatism and caution of the appraiser was unjustified.)

On October 1, 19X3, Pye acquired in the open market 50% of Slice's outstanding 12% bonds for a total cash payment of $236,500.

Other information:

1. The subsidiary uses straight-line amortization for its bond premium (in accordance with corporate policy). Unlike the subsidiary, the parent has not recorded any amortization of its discount since October 1, 19X3.
2. Goodwill is assigned a 10-year life.
3. The interest payment dates for Slice's bonds are July 1 and January 1. (The January 1, 19X4, payment was made on January 2, 19X4.)
4. Slice did not declare or pay any dividends in 19X1 and 19X2.
5. At December 31, 19X2, Pye held inventory it had acquired from Slice in 19X2 at a cost of $19,000. (Slice's cost was $14,000.)
6. The complete equity method is to be used.

The financial statements of each company for the year ended December 31, 19X3, are as follows:

	Pye Company	Slice Company
Income Statement (19X3):		
Sales	$800,000	$500,000
Cost of goods sold	(400,000)	(250,000)
Expenses	(250,500)	(192,000)
Intercompany Accounts:		
Equity in net income	60,000	
Amortization of cost in excess of book value	(21,000)	
Sales		80,000
Cost of goods sold		(56,000)
Interest income	7,500[a]	
Interest expense		(7,000)
Net Income	$196,000	$ 75,000

	Pye Company	Slice Company
Balance Sheet (December 31, 19X3):		
Investment in Slice Company:		
Common stock	$ 361,000	
Bonds	236,500	
Inventory:		
From vendors	135,000	$ 80,000
Intercompany	25,000	
Other assets	842,500	820,000
Total Assets	$1,600,000	$900,000
Accounts payable and accruals	$ 150,000	$ 30,000
Bonds payable (including premium)	700,000	520,000
Common stock, $1 par value	400,000	120,000
Retained earnings	350,000	230,000
Total Liabilities and Equity	$1,600,000	$900,000
Dividends declared and paid in 19X3	61,000	15,000

[a]Excludes bond premium or discount amortization.

Required:

1. Prepare an analysis of the appropriate accounts as of the bond acquisition date that shows how the gain or loss on extinguishment of debt is determined.
2. Adjust the financial statements to reflect the use of the complete equity method.
3. Prepare the entries required in consolidation at December 31, 19X3. (Prepare supporting analyses or schedules as necessary.)
4. Prepare a consolidating statement worksheet.

P 9-12*

COMPREHENSIVE (Chapters 3–5, 7, 9) Problem 9-11 Changed to the Partial Equity Method

Assume the information provided in Problem 9-11, except that the partial equity method is to be used.

Required:

1. Prepare an analysis of the appropriate accounts as of the bond acquisition date that shows how the gain or loss on extinguishment of debt is determined.
2. Adjust the parent's financial statements for the bond investment amortization.
3. Prepare the entries required in consolidation at December 31, 19X3. (Prepare supporting analyses or schedules as necessary.)
4. Prepare a consolidating statement worksheet at December 31, 19X3.

10

Changes in Parent's Ownership Interest and Subsidiary with Preferred Stock

CHANGES IN PARENT'S OWNERSHIP INTEREST

Changes in a parent's ownership interest in a subsidiary occur infrequently with respect to each parent–subsidiary relationship. The procedures used to account for some of these changes are based on principles discussed in earlier chapters. Other changes involve such new issues as how to determine and account for the effect of a change in the ownership interest. Although variations of certain types of changes can occur, only the basic principle involved in each type is discussed and illustrated.

The Acquisition of Minority Interest

APB Opinion No. 16 allows only the use of the purchase method to account for the acquisition of minority interests. It states:

> The acquisition . . . of some or all of the stock held by minority stockholders of a subsidiary — whether acquired by the parent, the subsidiary itself, or another affiliate — should be accounted for by the purchase method rather than by the pooling of interests method.[1]

The Parent Acquires Minority Interest. The parent's acquisition of any or all of the minority interest is merely a block acquisition. The cost of the block of stock acquired must be separated into its components in the same manner that the initial investment cost of a partially owned subsidiary is separated into its components (illustrated in Chapter 5). Thus, the parent's acquisition of any or all of the minority interest presents no new accounting issues. The acquisition of any or all of the minority interest by the subsidiary is also a block acquisition from a consolidated viewpoint; the procedures for this treatment will be explained.

The Subsidiary Acquires Minority Interest. When the subsidiary acquires any or all of the minority interest and retires the acquired shares (which it does only if directed to do so by the parent), the accounting in consolidation must reflect the purchase method of accounting for the shares acquired. The subsidiary's entries are the same as those made by any corporation acquiring and retiring its outstanding shares — that is, debit the capital accounts and credit Cash (assuming cash is the consideration given). The parent does not adjust the total carrying value of its Investment in Subsidiary account regardless of the price paid by the subsidiary to acquire the minority interest. However, if the subsidiary pays more or less than book value per share, the parent's total dollar interest

[1] *Opinions of the Accounting Principles Board, No. 16*, "Accounting for Business Combinations" (New York: American Institute of Certified Public Accountants, 1970), par. 43.

in the subsidiary's net assets at their book value decreases or increases respectively. Accordingly, the expanded analysis of the investment account by components must be adjusted to reflect that the parent's interest in the subsidiary's net assets at book value has changed. To the extent that the parent's total dollar interest decreases (when the subsidiary pays more than book value), the book value element must be decreased and the current value over book value element and/or the goodwill element must be increased by an offsetting amount. The reverse occurs when the subsidiary pays less than book value. Because this adjustment within the expanded analysis does not change the total carrying value of the investment, it is essentially a *reclassification* of amounts from one component to another.

Illustration

THE SUBSIDIARY ACQUIRES THE ENTIRE MINORITY INTEREST AT ABOVE BOOK VALUE

Assume the following information:

	Percent	Shares
Parent's ownership in subsidiary:		
Before acquisition of minority interest by subsidiary	80	800
After acquisition of minority interest by subsidiary	100	800
Purchase price paid by subsidiary to acquire all 200 outstanding shares held by minority interest shareholders	$40,000	

This information is used in Illustration 10-1 to calculate the decrease in the parent's interest in the subsidiary's net assets. (The procedure is the same when the parent's equity in the subsidiary's net assets increases.)

The following points are important for understanding Illustration 10-1:

1. The minority shareholders received an additional $11,000 in excess of their ownership interest in the subsidiary's net assets at book value.
2. This excess payment to the minority shareholders dilutes the parent's interest in the subsidiary's net assets at book value by $11,000.
3. The $11,000 excess payment must be treated as cost in excess of book value by the parent. From a consolidated viewpoint, it is irrelevant that the subsidiary acquired the minority interest rather than the parent.

To reflect the $11,000 payment as cost in excess of book value, the parent adjusts its expanded analysis of the investment account by the components of the major conceptual elements. Assuming the parent had $50,000 of unamortized cost in excess of its share of the subsidiary's net assets

Illustration 10-1
Calculation of Decrease in Parent's Interest in Subsidiary's Net Assets as a Result of Subsidiary's Acquisition of Entire Minority Interest at Amount in Excess of Book Value

	Subsidiary's Equity Accounts	Book Value per Share	Parent's Interest Percent	Parent's Interest Amount	Minority Interest Percent	Minority Interest Amount
Before acquisition of minority interest:						
Common stock..........	$ 70,000		80	$ 56,000	20	$ 14,000
Retained earnings.....	75,000		80	$ 60,000	20	15,000
	$145,000	$145		$116,000		$ 29,000
After acquisition of minority interest:						
Common stock..........	$ 56,000[a]		100	$ 56,000		—
Retained earnings.....	49,000		100	49,000		—
	$105,000	$131.25		$105,000		—
Decrease in equity........	$ (40,000)			$ (11,000)		$(29,000)

Note: The parent's new ownership percentage is derived by dividing the shares owned by the parent (800 shares) by the outstanding shares of the subsidiary (800 shares). In other words, the parent's holdings remain constant—only the outstanding shares of the subsidiary (the denominator used in calculating the parent's ownership percentage) decrease.

[a]For simplicity, we assume that the $40,000 payment for the shares acquired and retired was properly charged to the subsidiary's capital accounts as follows:

Common stock (20% of $70,000)	$14,000
Retained earnings (residual)..........	26,000
	$40,000

at book value as of the minority interest acquisition date, the required adjustment is determined as follows:

	Book Value Element: Common Stock	Book Value Element: Retained Earnings	Cost in Excess of Book Value[a]
Balances immediately *before the acquisition* of the minority interest..........	**$70,000[b]**	**$75,000[b]**	**$50,000**
Purchase of minority interest.....	**(14,000)**	**(26,000)[c]**	**11,000[d]**
Balances immediately *after the acquisition* of the minority interest..........	**$56,000[b]**	**$49,000[b]**	**$61,000**

[a]The breakdown of this cost into its individual components is not shown, because it is not necessary with respect to the principle involved.
[b]This amount was obtained from the analysis in Illustration 10-1.
[c]This change of interest in this component element is determined by using the balances *before* and the balances *after* the acquisition of the minority interest.
[d]This is the $11,000 excess payment. It equals the total dilution of the parent's interest in the subsidiary's net assets at book value.

The required adjustment takes place entirely within the expanded analysis of the investment account by the components of the major conceptual elements. The total carrying value of the parent's investment account is unchanged. This adjustment prevents the parent from reporting a loss on the acquistion of the minority interest related to the dilution of the parent's interest in the subsidiary's net assets at book value. The $11,000 cost in excess of book value must be separated into its components in accordance with the purchase method of accounting. After the required adjustment is made within the expanded analysis of the investment account, the analysis is updated in the normal manner. The ending balances as of any future consolidation date are the sources for the primary elimination entry, as illustrated in Chapters 4 and 5.

The following is a "before and after" presentation of the applicable accounts on the consolidating statement worksheet:

Before the Acquisition of the Minority Interest (thousands of dollars)

	P Company	S Company	Eliminations Dr.	Eliminations Cr.	Consolidated
Cash		40			40
Investment in S Company	166			166	—
Cost in excess of book value			50		50
Minority interest in net assets of S Company				29	29
Common stock		70	70		—
Retained earnings		75	75		—

After the Acquisition of the Minority Interest (thousands of dollars)

	P Company	S Company	Eliminations Dr.	Eliminations Cr.	Consolidated
Cash		—			—
Investment in S Company	166			166	—
Cost in excess of book value			61		61
Common stock		56	56		—
Retained earnings		49	49		—

We can see from this presentation that the effect on the consolidated financial statements is as though the following entry had been made from a consolidated viewpoint:

Minority Interest	29,000	
Cost in Excess of Book Value	11,000	
Cash		40,000

The Subsidiary Acquires Part of the Minority Interest. In the preceding example, the subsidiary acquired all of the minority interest. When the subsidiary acquires only a portion of the minority interest at more or less than book value per share, both the parent's and the remaining minority shareholders' total dollar interests in the subsidiary's net assets at book value decrease or increase respectively. Only the parent's decrease or increase results in an increase or decrease, respectively, of the current value over book value element and/or the goodwill element.

The Disposal of Interest in a Subsidiary

A parent may dispose of a portion or all of its common stock investment in a subsidiary. The former often occurs when the parent wants to raise cash, whereas the latter usually occurs when the parent decides either to dispose of a line of business or to contract (or reduce) its operations.

100% Disposals. The complete disposal of the investment in a subsidiary's common stock fits into two categories:

1. **Disposals of a segment:** This category includes subsidiaries whose activities represent a separate major line of business or class of customer. Special reporting requirements pertaining to disposals of segments are set forth in paragraphs 13–18 of *APB Opinion No. 30,* "Reporting the Results of Operations." These requirements are discussed in Chapter 13, "Segment Reporting."
2. **All other disposals:** This category includes disposals that constitute a contraction of operations—that is, the consolidated group remains in the line of business in which the subsidiary is engaged but at a reduced manufacturing, retailing, or service capacity. Such disposals are not extraordinary events; although infrequent, business contractions are not unusual. The reporting for disposals in this category is governed by the provisions of paragraph 26 of *APB Opinion No. 30*:

> A material event or transaction that is unusual in nature or occurs infrequently but not both, and therefore does not meet both criteria for classification as an extraordinary item, should be reported as a separate component of income from continuing operations.[2]

Partial Disposals. When a parent sells a portion of its common stock holdings in a subsidiary, the accounting problem is that of determining the amount of the reduction to the investment account. This amount is compared with the proceeds from the sale to determine the reportable gain or loss. The two categories of partial disposal are as follows:

1. **Shares acquired in a single acquisition.** When all of the shares owned were acquired at one time, the investment account should be reduced using the average cost of all shares owned.

[2]*Opinions of the Accounting Principles Board, No. 30,* "Reporting the Results of Operations" (New York: American Institute of Certified Public Accountants, 1973), par. 26.

2. **Shares acquired in block acquisitions.** When the shares owned were acquired at more than one time (in block acquisitions or when the minority interest was subsequently acquired), three methods of reducing the investment account are available:
   a. The average cost method
   b. The specific identification method
   c. The first-in, first-out method

Our preference is the average cost method, because the other two methods introduce an artificial element. For example, the gain or loss reported under the specific identification method could be partially determined by the particular block of stock selected for sale; whereas under the first-in, first-out method, we use an assumed flow concept initially intended for inventory pricing. Furthermore, the manner of acquiring the shares is irrelevant to the accounting for the disposal of shares—the issue is the amount of the total ownership interest that is disposed of. This percentage answer should also apply to the carrying value of the cost of the investment. (Although only the specific identification and the first-in, first-out methods are allowed for federal income tax reporting purposes, this has no bearing on which method should be used for financial reporting purposes.)

Regardless of the method selected to reduce the investment account, it must be applied to each individual component in the expanded analysis of the investment account. Before the investment account is reduced, however, it must be adjusted in accordance with the equity method of accounting up to the date of sale.

Illustration

PARTIAL DISPOSAL USING THE AVERAGE COST METHOD

Assume the following information:

	Percent	Shares
Parent's ownership in subsidiary:		
Before partial disposal	80	800
After partial disposal	60	600
Shares sold		200
Subsidiary's net income:		
Jan. 1, 19X8–June 30, 19X8	$20,000	
July 1, 19X8–Dec. 31, 19X8	10,000	
Total	$30,000	
Disposal date	July 1, 19X8	
Proceeds from sale	$40,000	

Subsidiary's dividends:
On the last day of the first three quarters, dividends of $5,000 were declared; no dividends were declared in the fourth quarter of the year.

The expanded analysis of the investment account in Illustration 10-2 is updated for the year in which a disposal of a portion of shares held in a subsidiary takes place. The following points are important for understanding the illustration:

1. The reportable gain on the disposal of the shares sold is determined as follows:

Proceeds from sale	$40,000
Average cost of shares sold	(25,000)
Gain	$15,000

2. The following journal entry on the parent's books records this disposal:

Cash	40,000	
Investment in S Company		25,000
Gain on Sale of Subsidiary's Stock		15,000

3. The December 31, 19X8, balance in the Equity in Net Income of Subsidiary account in the parent's general ledger is as follows:

Equity in earnings January 1, 19X8–June 30, 19X8	$16,000
Equity in earnings July 1, 19X8–Dec. 31, 19X8	6,000
Total	$22,000

4. The minority interest deduction for the year is determined as follows:

	Jan. 1, 19X8– June 30, 19X8	July 1, 19X8– Dec. 31, 19X8	Total
Subsidiary's net income	$20,000	$10,000	$30,000
Minority interest ownership percentage	20%	40%	
Minority interest	$ 4,000	$ 4,000	$ 8,000

5. The primary elimination entry used to prepare the December 31, 19X8, consolidated financial statements is from the analysis of the

Illustration 10-2
Updating the Expanded Analysis of the Investment Account for a Partial Disposal Using the Average Cost Method

			Book Value Element				Current Value over Book Value Element	
				Retained Earnings				
					Current Year			
	Minority Interest +	Total Cost =	Common Stock +	Prior Year +	Earnings −	Dividends +	Land (Indef.) +	Goodwill Element (3 yr.)
Remaining life as of January 1, 19X8:								
Balance, January 1, 19X8	$20,100	$92,400	$40,000	$60,500			$9,600	$2,400
Equity in net income:								
To Parent (80%)		16,000			$16,000			
To Minority Interest (20%)	4,000				4,000			
Dividends—first and second quarters:								
To Parent (80%)		(8,000)				$(8,000)		
To Minority Interest (20%)	(2,000)					(2,000)		
Amortization of cost over book value		(400)						(400)
Balance, June 30, 19X8	$22,100	$100,000	$40,000	$60,500	$20,000	$(10,000)	$9,600	$2,000
Disposal, July 1, 19X8	22,100[a]	(25,000)[b]					(2,400)[b]	(500)[b]
Balance July 1, 19X8	$44,200	$75,000	$40,000	$60,500	$20,000	$(10,000)	$7,200	$1,500
Equity in net income:								
To Parent (60%)		6,000			6,000			
To Minority Interest (40%)	4,000				4,000			
Dividends—third quarter:								
To Parent (60%)		(3,000)				(3,000)		
To Minority Interest (40%)	(2,000)					(2,000)		
Amortization of cost over book value		(300)						(300)[c]
Balance, December 31, 19X8	$46,200	$77,700	$40,000	$60,500	$30,000	$(15,000)	$7,200	$1,200

[a]This amount is 20% of the book value element at June 30, 19X8 ($40,000 + $60,500 + $20,000 − $10,000) = $110,500; $110,500 × 20% = $22,100).
[b]The June 30, 19X8, balance is reduced by 25%, which is the ratio of the shares sold to total shares held (200 ÷ 800 = 25%).
[c]The $1,500 balance at June 30, 19X8, amortized over 2½ years is $300.

investment account as of December 31, 19X8 (in illustration 10-2). The entry is as follows:

Common Stock	**40,000**	
Retained Earnings (beginning of year)	**60,500**	
Equity in Earnings of Subsidiary	**22,000**	
Minority Interest in Net Income of Subsidiary	**8,000**	
Land	**7,200**	
Goodwill	**1,200**	
Dividends Declared		**15,000**
Investment in Subsidiary		**77,700**
Minority Interest in Net Assets of S Company		**46,200**

6. By updating the investment account analysis as illustrated, the disposal of a portion of the holdings in a subsidiary's common stock does not affect the basic procedures used to prepare consolidated financial statements.

Illustration 10-3 shows a consolidating statement worksheet for the year ended December 31, 19X8, prepared using the above primary elimination entry. The secondary elimination entry is as follows:

Cost of Goods Sold	700	
Amortization of Cost in Excess of Book Value		700

Some real-world examples of partial disposals (partial spinoffs) are discussed in the article on page 409.

Illustration 10-3
Partial Disposal of Investment in Subsidiary During the Year

P COMPANY AND SUBSIDIARY (S COMPANY)
Consolidating Statement Worksheet
For the Year Ended December 31, 19X8

	P Company	S Company	Nonintercompany Transaction Eliminations Dr.	Nonintercompany Transaction Eliminations Cr.	Consolidated
Income Statement:					
Sales	615,000	350,000			965,000
Cost of goods sold	(309,300)	(180,000)	700(2)		(490,000)
Expenses	(202,000)	(140,000)			(342,000)
Gain on sale of subsidiary's stock	15,000				15,000
Intercompany Accounts:					
Equity in net income of subsidiary	22,000		22,000(1)		–0–
Amortization of cost in excess of book value	(700)			700(2)	–0–
Income before Min. Int.	140,000	30,000	22,700	700	148,000
Minority interest			8,000(1)		(8,000)
Net Income	140,000	30,000	30,700	700	140,000
Statement of Retained Earnings:					
Balances, January 1, 19X8	210,000	60,500	60,500(1)		210,000
+ Net income	140,000	30,000	30,700	700	140,000
− Dividends declared	(60,000)	(15,000)		15,000(1)	(60,000)
Balances, December 31, 19X8	290,000	75,500	91,200	15,700	290,000
Balance Sheet:					
Investment in subsidiary	77,700			77,700(1)	–0–
Land	200,000	30,000	7,200(1)		237,200
Goodwill			1,200(1)		1,200
Other assets	522,300	280,000			802,300
Total Assets	800,000	310,000	8,400	77,700	1,040,700
Liabilities	210,000	194,500			404,500
Minority interest in net assets of subsidiary				46,200(1)	46,200
P Company:					
Common stock	300,000				300,000
Retained earnings	290,000				290,000
S Company:					
Common stock		40,000	40,000(1)		–0–
Retained earnings		75,500	91,200	15,700	–0–
Total Liabilities & Equity	800,000	310,000	131,200	61,900	1,040,700
Proof of debit and credit postings			139,600	139,600	

Explanation of entries:
(1) The primary elimination entry.
(2) The secondary elimination entry.

PERSPECTIVE

Partial Spinoffs Offer Investors a Chance to Get in on a Real Winner—or Real Flop

Coca-Cola Co. may sell a piece of its bottling business to the public. Time Inc. is offering shares in a cable television subsidiary. American Can Co. has already sold a 17% stake in its mutual fund business.

The partial spinoff is in vogue. Companies big and small are selling shares in subsidiaries while holding onto majority control. Some are simply raising money. Others are hoping to boost the price of the parent's stock by demonstrating the worth of the offspring.

For investors who buy the shares, the partial spinoff can be a spectacular winner, or an equally spectacular flop. While no method for picking stocks is sure-fire, market professionals say past spinoffs offer some clues.

Some of the best opportunities for investors have occurred when a company decided to cash in on a promising business that was buried in a slower-growing parent. In 1982, for instance, Collins Food International Inc. of Los Angeles sold the public a 28% interest in Sizzler Restaurants International Inc., a fast-growing restaurant chain. Sizzler's earnings per share have since risen at an annual rate of nearly 31%. An investor who put $1,000 into Sizzler's initial offering holds stock worth more than $4,450 today.

"Shareholder Constituency"

"One of the primary motivations for doing a spinoff is that you recognize that a business that you want to spin off has a different shareholder constituency than the parent company," says Dennis Bovin, a managing director of Salomon Brothers Inc., which has handled several spinoffs. A big, mature company may appeal to conservative investors, a smaller unit to those willing to take more risk.

A subsidiary that goes public because the parent no longer wants to be in a particular type of business can also be an attractive investment. But such an offering deserves an especially careful look.

Fed up with the volatility of the property-casualty insurance business, American Express Corp. sold a 53% stake in Fireman's Fund Corp. last October and subsequently reduced its holdings to 27%. Investors willing to take the risks of investing in the insurance industry have seen Fireman's Fund shares climb 36% since the initial offer, while American Express shares have risen 30%.

Sometimes, however, the parent company's shares have turned out to be a better bet than those of the subsidiary, particularly when the parent was shedding a unit that was less attractive than its core business. Two retailers, Dart Group Corp. and Thrifty Corp., sold the public a minority interest in a jointly owned bookstore chain three years ago. Since then, shares of Crown Books Corp. have fallen 35%, while Dart shares have risen 52% and shares of Thrifty, which is being acquired by Pacific Lighting Corp., have risen 108%.

Partial Spinoffs *(continued)*

Hard To Tell

The safest spinoffs are in industries Wall Street likes, such as specialty chemicals or broadcasting, says Carol Coles, president of Mitchell & Co., a Cambridge, Mass., consulting firm that has been tracking spinoffs since 1977. "But you're better off if it's not a new industry," she adds. In a new industry, even well-informed investors find it hard to tell which young company will prosper.

Biotechnology, for instance, is a promising industry. But those who bought shares in Damon Biotech Inc., a Needham, Mass., maker of monoclonal antibodies, are still waiting to realize the promise. Damon Corp. sold a 30% stake in the company three years ago at $17 a share. The stock is currently trading just above $7.

The market value of the shares being offered should exceed $60 million, Ms. Coles says. Anything less, and the fledgling company isn't likely to draw the attention of analysts or institutional investors.

Take Gerber Systems Technology Inc., a computer-graphics vendor in which Gerber Scientific Inc. sold a 20% interest in 1981. Five years later, a $1,000 investment is worth about $175. Among the problems, Ms. Coles suggests, is that the initial $7.6 million offering wasn't big enough to draw serious attention. (The South Windsor, Conn., company has had other problems, too: It turned a profit in only one of the past five years.)

Price-Earnings Ratios

The pricing of a spinoff, as with any new issue, is paramount. "The early partial spinoffs, six or seven years ago, were generally priced too low," Ms. Coles says. "Then Wall Street started to take these out at a very high price-earnings ratio and the price of spinoffs fell" after the initial offering. (The ratio of earnings-per-share to the market price of a stock is commonly used to determine how expensive a stock is.) A high price-earnings ratio is justified only if a company's growth prospects are better than those of its peers, says Ms. Coles.

Similar logic, of course, applies to a decision to buy any stock. In some respects, however, partial spinoffs are unusual. Believers say they offer managers incentives to perform that usually aren't available in a bigger company.

"They feel it's their company, but they also have a large company to provide advice and support," says John Hatsopolous, senior vice president of Thermo Electron Corp. in Waltham, Mass. In 1983, the company sold a 20% interest in Thermedics, a medical-products unit.

"We have a much easier time recruiting new people," says Mr. Hatsopolous, who doubles as a vice president of Thermedics. "They feel they become a large part of a small thing rather than being a small cog in a big machine." Happy with its first spinoff, Thermo Electron has since sold shares in a second unit and is taking two others public, as well.

On the other hand, investors in Thermedics or Sizzler forgo what has become one of the best ways to make money in the stock market, the unfriendly takeover. With 70% or 80% of the shares still held by its parent, the offspring is invulnerable.

(continued)

Indeed, a more likely prospect is a too-friendly takeover by the parent company at a price unattractive to minority shareholders. MGM/UA Entertainment Co. last year raised its offer to buy back a 15% stake in its Home Entertainment Group, which owns pay-television and home-video rights to the studio's film library, only after a wealthy Massachusetts investor sued. That's an expensive step most investors aren't willing to take.

Source: David Wessel, "Partial Spinoffs Offer Investors a Chance to Get in on a Real Winner—or Real Flop," *The Wall Street Journal*, July 17, 1986, p. 25.

The Subsidiary Issues Additional Common Stock

Rather than disposing of a portion of its stock holdings in a subsidiary to raise funds for the consolidated group, a parent may direct the subsidiary to issue additional common stock to the public.

If the shares issued to the public are sold below the current book value per share of the subsidiary's common stock as of the issuance date, the parent's total dollar interest in the subsidiary's net assets at book value is diluted and thus decreases. On the other hand, when the subsidiary issues shares above the existing book value of its common stock as of the issuance date, the parent's total dollar interest in the subsidiary's net assets at book value increases. (This may be understood best by realizing that if the subsidiary were liquidated at no gain or loss in the liquidation process, the parent would receive either more or less than it would have received if the subsidiary had not issued the additional shares.) The issue is how to account for an increase or a decrease in the parent's interest in the subsidiary's net assets at book value as a result of the issuance of the additional shares.

Accountants agree that an increase or a decrease in the parent's interest in the subsidiary's net assets at book value should result in an increase or decrease, respectively, to the carrying value of the investment. Accountants do not agree on the treatment of the offsetting credit or debit. The two alternative accounting treatments are as follows:

1. Record it as an adjustment to the parent's additional paid-in capital. (This treatment carries through to the consolidated balance sheet.)
2. Record it as a gain or loss in the parent's income statement. (The gain or loss **is not eliminated in consolidation.**)

Rationale for the Additional Paid-in Capital Treatment. Under the first alternative, the issuance of additional common stock by the subsidiary is a capital-raising transaction for the consolidated group. Because capital-raising transactions do not cause either a gain or a loss on a separate-company basis, they should not cause either a gain or a loss on a consolidated basis. (Recall from intermediate accounting that *APB Opinion No. 9*, "Reporting the Results of Operations" [paragraph 28], requires that gains or losses from transactions in a company's own stock are to be excluded from the income statement.) An increase in the parent's interest in the subsidiary's net assets at book value is deemed in consolidation to be a capital contribution from the minority shareholders to the parent. Similarly, a decrease in the parent's interest in the subsidiary's net assets at book value is treated in consolidation as a capital contribution from the parent to the minority shareholders. This approach fits under the entity theory (see Chapter 5), which maintains that a new reporting entity with two classes of common shareholders results from the consolidation process.

Rationale for the Income Statement Treatment. Under the second alternative above, the parent is viewed as either gaining or losing as a result of a subsidiary's issuing additional common stock above or below the book value of its exisiting outstanding common stock. Gains and losses are reported in the income statement. Accordingly, this type of gain or loss also should be reflected in the income statement. In regard to the requirements of *APB Opinion No. 9*, the argument can be made that this is not a transaction in one's own stock—it is a transaction involving the investment in the subsidiary's stock; thus *APB Opinion No. 9* is not applicable. The advocates of this approach also contend that substantively the sale of a subsidiary's shares by the parent (pursuant to a partial disposal)—whereby a gain or loss is recorded in the income statement—is no different from the issuance of additional common shares by a subsidiary. This approach fits under the parent company theory (see Chapter 5), which views the parent as the reporting entity in consolidation.

The Position of the AICPA. In 1980, the Accounting Standards Executive Committee of the American Institute for Certified Public Accountants (AICPA) prepared an issues paper, "Accounting in Consolidation for Issuances of a Subsidiary's Stock." This paper's advisory conclusions are that such gains or losses should be reflected in the consolidated income statement. The position taken here seems to be that such transactions are not "transactions in one's own stock." Thus, *APB Opinion No. 9* is not applicable.

The Position of the Securities and Exchange Commission. In 1983, the staff of the Securities and Exchange Commission (SEC) issued *Staff Accounting Bulletin No. 51*, which expresses its views concerning the subsidiary's issuance of additional common stock. According to the SEC staff, companies may recognize gains or losses resulting from these transactions when the subsidiary's sale of shares is not a part of a corporate reorganization contemplated or planned by the parent company. (The staff had previously required, without benefit of any ruling or publication, that these transactions be accounted for in consolidated financial statements as capital transactions.) This change in position resulted from the SEC's acceptance of the advisory conclusions in the AICPA's 1980 issues paper. The SEC staff considers this paper to be appropriate interim guidance in the matter until the Financial Accounting Standards Board (FASB) addresses this issue as a part of its project "Accounting for the Reporting Entity, including Consolidations, the Equity Method, and Related Matters." According to *SAB No. 51*, then, companies must show any such gain or loss as a separate item in the consolidated income statement regardless of size. Furthermore, the gain or loss must be clearly designated as nonoperating. Companies also should include an appropriate description of the transaction in the notes to the financial statements.[3]

Illustration

ISSUANCE OF ADDITIONAL SHARES AT BELOW BOOK VALUE

The journal entry in the following illustration reflects the accounting treatment for additional shares prescribed in the AICPA's 1980 issues paper. Assume the following information:

	Percent	Shares
Parent's ownership in subsidiary:		
Before subsidiary issues additional shares to the public	**80**	**800**
After subsidiary issues additional shares to the public	**$66\frac{2}{3}$**	**800**
Minority ownership in subsidiary:		
Before subsidiary issues additional shares to the public	**20**	**200**
After subsidiary issues additional shares to the public	**$33\frac{1}{3}$**	**400**
Proceeds from issuance of 200 additional shares of the subsidiary's no-par common stock at $100 per share	**$20,000**	

This information is used in Illustration 10-4 to calculate the loss to the parent. (The procedure is the same when there is a gain.) The following points are important for understanding the illustration:

1. The entry to record the loss on the parent's books is as follows:

[3] *Staff Accounting Bulletin No. 51*, "Accounting by the Parent in Consolidation for Sale of Stock by Subsidiary," (Washington, D.C.: Securities and Exchange Commission, 1983).

Illustration 10-4
Calculation of Parent's Dilution of Equity in Net Assets of Subsidiary: Subsidiary Sells Additional Common Stock at below Book Value

	Subsidiary's Equity Accounts	Book Value per Share	Parent's Interest Percent	Parent's Interest Amount	Minority Interest Percent	Minority Interest Amount
Before issuance of additional shares:						
Common stock..........	$ 70,000		80	$ 56,000	20	$14,000
Retained earnings......	75,000		80	$ 60,000	20	15,000
	$145,000	$145		$116,000		$29,000
After issuance of additional shares:						
Common stock..........	$ 90,000[a]		66⅔	$ 60,000	33⅓	$30,000
Retained earnings......	75,000		66⅔	50,000	33⅓	25,000
	$165,000	$137.50		$110,000		$55,000
Difference....................	$ 20,000			$ (6,000)		$26,000
Proceeds from issuance	(20,000)	$100				(20,000)
Parent's dilution/minority interest accretion[b]......	$ –0–			$ (6,000)		$ 6,000

[a]For simplicity, we assume that the subsidiary's common stock is no-par. Thus, the $20,000 proceeds have been credited to the Common Stock account.
[b]The dilution suffered by the parent is offset by the accretion to the minority interest.

Loss Resulting from Dilution of Interest in Subsidiary's Net Assets	6,000	
Investment in Subsidiary		6,000

This loss is not eliminated in consolidation.

2. The conceptual analysis of the investment account would be adjusted as follows (all amounts are based on Illustration 10-4):

	Minority Interest +	Total Cost[a] =	Book Value Element: Common Stock +	Book Value Element: Retained Earnings
Balances before issuance of additional shares....	**$29,000**	**$116,000**	**$70,000**	**$75,000**
Issuance of additional shares....................	**20,000**		**20,000**	
Subtotal.......................	**$49,000**	**$116,000**	**$90,000**	**$75,000**
Adjustment for parent's dilution/minority interest accretion....	**6,000**	**(6,000)**		
Balances after issuance of additional shares....	**$55,000**	**$110,000**	**$90,000**	**$75,000**

[a]For simplicity, we assume that there is no cost in excess of book value.

3. After the adjustment is made for the dilution of the parent's interest in the subsidiary's net assets, the analysis of the investment account is updated in the normal manner. The ending balances as of any future consolidation date are the sources of the primary elimination entry, as illustrated in earlier chapters.

OTHER CHANGES IN THE SUBSIDIARY'S CAPITAL ACCOUNTS

Stock Dividends

The treatment of stock dividends is set forth in *ARB No. 51* as follows:

> Occasionally, subsidiary companies capitalize earned surplus [retained earnings] arising since acquisition, by means of a stock dividend or otherwise. This does not require a transfer to capital surplus [additional paid-in capital] on consolidation, inasmuch as the retained earnings in the consolidated financial statements should reflect the accumulated earnings of the consolidated group not distributed to the shareholders of, or capitalized by, the parent company.[4]

In other words, a stock dividend by a subsidiary has no effect on the parent's books or in consolidation. The subsidiary has merely reshuffled amounts within its equity accounts by reducing Retained Earnings and increasing Common Stock and Additional Paid-in Capital in accordance with procedures discussed in intermediate accounting texts. Although no entry is required to adjust the carrying value of the Investment in Subsidiary account, the parent must adjust these accounts as they exist within the expanded analysis of their investment account by components. Assume the following information:

	Subsidiary's Books	
	Common Stock	Retained Earnings
Balances immediately *before* stock dividend	$70,000	$75,000
Capitalization of retained earnings as a result of stock dividend..	25,000	(25,000)
Balances immediately *after* stock dividend.........	$95,000	$50,000

The balances in the expanded analysis of the investment account by individual components would be adjusted accordingly.

The reclassification within the parent's expanded analysis of the investment account by components is necessary so that the posting of the

[4] *Accounting Research Bulletin No. 51*, "Consolidated Financial Statements" (New York: American Institute of Certified Public Accountants, 1959), par. 18.

primary elimination entry used to prepare consolidated financial statements properly eliminates the subsidiary's equity accounts.

If the capitalization of retained earnings exceeds the total retained earnings as of the acquisition date, an interesting problem results. Under the equity method of accounting, the parent has included amounts in its Retained Earnings account that it cannot obtain from the subsidiary as a result of the capitalization. If this restriction on dividend availability is material, it should be disclosed in the consolidated financial statements.

Stock Splits

As with stock dividends, when a stock split occurs, no entry is required on the parent's books to adjust the carrying value of its investment in the subsidiary. However, the parent does not make any reclassifications within the expanded analysis of the investment account by individual components, because no changes were made to the subsidiary's capital accounts at the time of the stock split. The parent company makes only a memorandum notation of the stock split.

Changes from Par Value to No-par and Vice Versa

When a subsidiary changes the par value of its common stock to no-par or vice versa, changes are made on its books in the Common Stock and Additional Paid-In Capital accounts. As a result, the parent makes an adjustment within the expanded analysis of the investment account. The carrying value of the investment itself does not change.

Appropriation of Retained Earnings

Inasmuch as the amount of the subsidiary's retained earnings existing as of the acquisition date is eliminated in consolidation, any appropriation of retained earnings by the subsidiary that does not exceed the total amount of retained earnings existing as of the acquisition date (including any amount that accrues to minority interests) has no effect on the parent's books or the consolidated financial statements. However, when appropriations of retained earnings exceed this amount, the restriction on dividend availability must be disclosed in the consolidated financial statements if it is material.

SUBSIDIARY WITH PREFERRED STOCK

In consolidated financial statements, a subsidiary's preferred stock not held by the parent company is treated as part of the minority interest. However, the amount recorded on the subsidiary's books relating to its preferred stock is not necessarily the amount that is added to the minority interest in consolidation. That amount depends on the *features* of the preferred stock—that is, whether it is cumulative or noncumulative, whether it is participating or nonparticipating, and whether it is callable at amounts other than its par value. Additional amounts above the recorded amount of the preferred stock that need to be added to the minority interest are taken from the subsidiary's recorded retained earnings. The parent must use an amount other than the subsidiary's recorded retained earnings to calculate the amount initially assigned to this individual component in its expanded analysis of the Investment in Subsidiary account.

Parent companies do not usually invest in the preferred stock of their subsidiaries. Accordingly, we discuss the subject in the following order:

1. Determination of minority interest **as of the acquisition date,** assuming the parent does not have or make an investment in the subsidiary's preferred stock.
2. Determination of minority interest **subsequent to the acquisition date,** assuming the **parent does not invest** in the subsidiary's preferred stock in such subsequent period.
3. Determination of minority interest **subsequent to the acquisition date,** assuming the **parent does invest** in the subsidiary's preferred stock subsequent to the acquisition date.

The Determination of Minority Interest as of the Acquisition Date

PARENT OWNS NONE OF SUBSIDIARY'S PREFERRED STOCK

The amount of preferred stock used to ascertain the minority interest as of the acquisition date is determined using the procedures for calculating the book value of preferred stock discussed in intermediate accounting texts. Briefly, the recorded amount is increased for preferred stock with any of the following features:

- **For cumulative preferred stock:** Add any dividends in arrears through the acquisition date.
- **For participating preferred stock:** Add any unpaid participation amounts through the acquisition date.
- **For callable preferred stock:** Add any premium relating to the call feature.

To the extent that any or all of these features apply, the subsidiary's retained earnings amount as of the acquisition date is reclassified and attributed to the preferred stock to calculate the parent's interest in the retained earnings applicable to common stock. (No entry is made on the subsidiary's books.)

For example, assume that $3,000 in dividends are in arrears on S Company's 6% **cumulative** preferred stock on January 1, 19X1, the date P Company acquired 80% of the outstanding common stock of S Company. The following calculation of the minority interest as of January 1, 19X1, assumes S Company's capital accounts on the acquisition date are as follows:

	Total	Parent's Interest	Minority Interest
6% Preferred stock, cumulative..........	$ 50,000		$50,000
Common stock..................................	40,000	$32,000	8,000
Retained earnings:			
Allocable to preferred stock............	3,000		3,000
Allocable to common stock	17,000	13,600	3,400
Total Stockholders' Equity	$110,000	$45,600	$64,400

Thus, the parent's interest in the subsidiary's Retained Earnings account is $13,600 (80% of $17,000)—not 80% of $20,000. These added features of the preferred stock effectively force the parent company to view the subsidiary's retained earnings as comprising two amounts—the portion that is allocable to the preferred stock and the residual, which is allocable to the common stock. Even if the allocation to the preferred stockholders results in a negative balance for the common stockholders, the retained earnings are still separated in this manner.

Determination of Minority Interest Subsequent to the Acquisition Date

PARENT OWNS NONE OF SUBSIDIARY'S PREFERRED STOCK

In periods subsequent to acquisition, the subsidiary's net income must be allocated between the preferred stockholders' and the common stockholders' interests. Assuming S Company had net income of $10,000 for 19X1 and paid no dividends on its preferred stock, the allocation of the net income for 19X1 is as follows:

Total net income	$10,000
Less—Preferred stock dividend requirement	(3,000)
Residual allocable to common stockholders.....................	$ 7,000

The parent company applies the equity method of accounting to the $7,000 and records $5,600 (80% of $7,000) of the subsidiary's earnings. This procedure is in accordance with *APB Opinion No. 18:*

> When an investee has outstanding cumulative preferred stock, an investor should compute its share of earnings (losses) after deducting the investee's preferred dividends, whether or not such dividends are declared.[5]

As of December 31, 19X1 (one year after the acquisition date), the minority interest would be calculated as follows:

[5]*Opinions of the Accounting Principles Board, No. 18*, "The Equity Method of Accounting for Investments in Common Stock" (New York: American Institute of Certified Public Accountants, 1971), par. 19k.

	Total	Parent's Interest	Minority Interest
6% preferred stock, cumulative...	$ 50,000		$50,000
Common stock..........................	40,000	$32,000	8,000
Retained earnings:			
Allocable to preferred stock.....	6,000[a]		6,000
Allocable to common stock	24,000	19,200	4,800
Total Stockholders' Equity ...	$120,000	$51,200	$68,800

[a]Two years of dividends are assumed to be in arrears.

The Determination of Minority Interest Subsequent to the Acquisition Date

PARENT SUBSEQUENTLY ACQUIRES SOME OF SUBSIDIARY'S PREFERRED STOCK

Using the data in the preceding example, assume that P Company acquired 40% of the subsidiary's outstanding preferred stock on January 1, 19X2, for $21,000. As with an intercompany bond purchase, for consolidated reporting purposes the preferred stock acquired is treated as retired. The total book value of the preferred stock on that date is $56,000 ($50,000 + $6,000 dividends in arrears); 40% of this total book value is $22,400. Thus, the parent's cost of the preferred stock is less than its share of book value by $1,400. The issue now raised is how the parent should account for its cost under book value when consolidated financial statements are prepared. Two apparent possibilities exist:

1. Treat the cost under book value the same as an acquisition of a common stock minority interest, applying the purchase method of accounting. Under this approach, the "preferred stock" label is ignored. The substance of the transaction is the acquisition of minority interest, the class of which is irrelevant. This approach is not sanctioned by any official pronouncement.
2. Treat the cost under book value as though the preferred stock were that of the parent company. In that case, any amount by which cost is below book value is credited to Additional Paid-in Capital. (If cost exceeds the applicable share of book value, such excess would be charged to Additional Paid-in Capital to the extent available, with any remaining difference charged to Retained Earnings.) The argument here is that although the preferred stock is classified as part of minority interest, it is distinctively different from the common stock minority interest. Any difference between cost and book value is unrelated either to the difference between asset values and book values or to expected superior earnings. This approach makes the most sense.

Under the second approach, P Company makes the following worksheet elimination entry in consolidation as long as the $6,000 of dividends in arrears as of the preferred stock acquisition date remains unpaid:

Preferred Stock (40% of $50,000).....................	20,000	
Retained Earnings—S Company (40% of $6,000)[a]	2,400	
Investment in S Company Preferred Stock		21,000
Additional Paid-in Capital......................		1,400

[a]On the acquisition date, $6,000 of preferred dividends are in arrears.

Later, in Illustration 10-5 (a conceptual analysis of the investment account), we show how to keep track of the parent's interest in the dividends in arrears (the $2,400). When kept track of in this manner, we debit Parent's Preferred Stock Interest in Retained Earnings, rather than debiting Retained Earnings of S Company.

Subsequent Payment of Dividends in Arrears. If the subsidiary subsequently pays the $6,000 of preferred stock dividends that are in arrears as of the acquisition date, the parent would receive $2,400 (40% of $6,000). Because these dividends pertain to earnings prior to the date when the parent acquired some of the subsidiary's preferred stock, they are "preacquisition earnings" as far as the preferred stock investment is concerned. Thus, the parent could not report the $2,400 as income from its preferred stock investment. Besides, the $2,400—then part of the subsidiary's Retained Earnings account—was used in determining the parent's cost under book value. To be consistent then, the parent would make the following **general ledger entry** upon receipt of the $2,400:

Cash..	2,400	
Investment in Preferred Stock of S Company...		1,000
Additional Paid-in Capital........................		1,400

Thus, $1,000 is considered a realization of its premium. (Recall that the parent paid $21,000 for preferred stock having a stated value of $20,000.) The credit to Additional Paid-in Capital merely records in the parent's general ledger what was reflected previously in consolidation. This makes sense because $2,400 in the subsidiary's Retained Earnings account has been merely transferred to the parent's Retained Earnings account. The following entry would be made on subsequent consolidation dates:

Preferred Stock (40% of $50,000).....................	20,000	
Investment in S Company's Preferred Stock...		20,000

Illustration

PREPARING CONSOLIDATED FINANCIAL STATEMENTS: PARENT HOLDS SUBSIDIARY'S PREFERRED STOCK

Assume the information in the preceding example concerning the parent company's acquisition of the subsidiary's preferred stock on January 1, 19X2, as well as the following additional information:

1. S Company had net income of $24,000 for 19X2. Because $3,000 of these earnings relate to the preferred stock dividend requirement, only $21,000 is available for common shareholders. Consequently, the parent's share of this $21,000 is $16,800 (80% of $21,000).
2. S Company paid preferred stock dividends of $6,000 in 19X2, which leaves one year of dividends in arrears as of December 31, 19X2. (No dividends have been paid on common stock since the parent acquired it.)
3. P Company acquired its 80% interest in S Company on January 1, 19X1, for $45,600 (an amount equal to its share of the book value of the net assets). Thus, no amortization entry appears on P Company's books nor is any secondary reclassification entry required in consolidation.

Illustration 10-5 is an analysis of the parent's investment account from January 1, 19X1, through December 31, 19X2. The following points are important for understanding the illustration:

1. In 19X2, the parent recorded under the equity method of accounting its $1,200 share of earnings that accrue to it as a result of its ownership of 40% of the subsidiary's preferred stock. (Even though *APB Opinion No. 18* applies only to investments in common stock, it would not be sensible to record under the equity method only some of the subsidiary's earnings that accrue to the parent and not record the remainder.)
2. Although this $1,200 technically accrues to the preferred stock holdings (rather than the common stock holdings), the consolidation procedures are simplified if it is accounted for in the conceptual analysis of the investment in common stock.

The primary elimination entry is readily determinable from Illustration 10-5; that entry as of December 31, 19X2, is as follows:

Common Stock	40,000	
Retained Earnings (beginning of year)	30,000	
Equity in Net Income of Subsidiary ($1,200 + $16,800)	18,000	
Minority Interest in Net Income of S Company ($1,800 + $4,200)	6,000	
Dividends Declared		6,000
Investment in Subsidiary		69,200
Minority Interest in Net Assets of S Company		18,800

Illustration 10-5
Updating the Expanded Analysis of the Investment in S Company's Common Stock from January 1, 19X1 through December 31, 19X2 Using the Equity Method

	Parent's Preferred Stock Interest in Retained Earnings[b]	+ Minority Interest	+ Total Cost	= Common Stock (Book Value Element)	+ Prior Years (Retained Earnings)	+ Current Year Earnings	− Current Year Dividends
Balance, Jan. 1, 19X1		$14,400[a]	$45,600	$40,000	$20,000		
Equity in 19X1 net income:							
To Preferred		$ 3,000				$ 3,000	
To Common—							
Parent (80% of $7,000)			$ 5,600			5,600	
Minority Interest (20% of $7,000)		1,400				1,400	
Subtotal		$18,800	$51,200	$40,000	$20,000	$10,000	
Reclassification					10,000	(10,000)	
Balance, Dec. 31, 19X1		$18,800	$51,200	$40,000	$30,000	$ –0–	
Forfeiture of equity in dividends in arrears upon parent's purchase of 40% of preferred stock (40% of $6,000)	$2,400[b]	(2,400)					
Equity in 19X2 net income:							
To Preferred—							
Minority Interest (60% of $3,000)		1,800				1,800	
Parent (40% of $3,000)			1,200			1,200	
To Common—							
Parent (80% of $21,000)			16,800			16,800	
Minority Interest (20% of $21,000)		4,200				4,200	
Dividends paid on preferred stock:							
To Parent (40% of $6,000)	(2,400)						(2,400)
To Minority Interest (60% of $6,000)		(3,600)					(3,600)
Subtotal	$ –0–	$18,800	$69,200	$40,000	$30,000	$24,000	$(6,000)
Reclassification					18,000	(24,000)	6,000
Balance, Dec. 31, 19X2	$ –0–	$18,800	$69,200	$40,000	$48,000	$ –0–	$ –0–

[a]This amount is comprised of:

a.	100% of dividends in arrears	$ 3,000
b.	20% interest in common stock (20% × $40,000)	8,000
c.	20% interest in retained earnings that accrue to common stockholders (20% × $17,000)	3,400
		$14,400

[b]This column is used to keep track of only those dividends in arrears at the date the parent acquired its 40% interest is the subsidiary's preferred stock.

This primary elimination entry, along with the preferred stock elimination entry shown previously, is used in Illustration 10-6 to prepare consolidated financial statements as of December 31, 19X2. (We assume that no other intercompany transactions require elimination.)

CONSOLIDATED STATEMENT OF CASH FLOWS: ADDITIONAL CONSIDERATIONS

In Chapter 5, we discussed the preparation of the consolidated statement of cash flows in terms of the types of transactions covered to that point. We now discuss the preparation of this statement in terms of the transactions discussed in Chapters 7 to 10.

Recall that when intercompany inventory transactions concerning inventory, fixed assets, or bond holdings occur, it is usually quicker and more practical to prepare this statement by analyzing the consolidated balance sheets rather than by trying to consolidate the separate company statements of cash flows. The former approach does not deal with these intercompany transactions a second time, but the latter approach does. Thus, when these types of transactions occur, no special problems exist in preparing this statement, as long as the former approach is used.

Subsidiary with Preferred Stock

When a subsidiary issues preferred stock, the proceeds are reported as a source of cash in the consolidated statement of cash flows. (We discussed earlier that such preferred stock is classified as part of the minority interest in the consolidated balance sheet.) The purchase of the preferred stock by the parent, or its retirement by the subsidiary, is treated as a use of cash. Any dividends paid on the preferred stock owned by outsiders are shown as a use of cash in the consolidated statement of cash flows.

Changes in Parent's Ownership Interest

Similarly, when the parent (or the subsidiary) acquires some or all of a minority interest, the amount paid is reported as a use of cash in the consolidated statement of cash flows.

When a subsidiary issues additional common stock, the proceeds are reported as a source of cash in the consolidated statement of cash flows.

SUMMARY

Accounting for Changes in Parent's Ownership

The acquisition of any or all of a subsidiary's minority interest is treated as an acquisition of a block of stock for which purchase accounting must be used. This holds true whether the parent or the subsidiary acquires the

Illustration 10-6
Parent Having Investment in Subsidiary's Preferred Stock

P COMPANY AND SUBSIDIARY (S COMPANY)
Consolidating Statement Worksheet
For the Year Ended December 31, 19X2

	P Company	S Company	Eliminations Dr.	Eliminations Cr.	Consolidated
Income Statement:					
Sales	650,000	230,000			880,000
Cost of goods sold	(390,000)	(130,000)			(520,000)
Expenses	(218,000)	(76,000)			(294,000)
Intercompany Accounts:					
Equity in net income of S Company	18,000		18,000(1)		–0–
Income before Min. Int.	60,000	24,000			66,000
Minority interest			6,000(1)		(6,000)
Net Income	60,000	24,000	24,000		60,000
Statement of Retained Earnings:					
Balances, January 1, 19X2	111,000	30,000	30,000(1)		111,000
+ Net income	60,000	24,000	24,000		60,000
− Dividends declared	(41,000)	(6,000)		6,000(1)	(41,000)
Balances, December 31, 19X2	130,000	48,000	54,000	6,000	130,000
Balance Sheet:					
Investment in S Company:					
Common stock	69,200			69,200(1)	–0–
Preferred stock	20,000			20,000(1)	–0–
Other assets	671,000	276,000			947,000
Total Assets	760,200	276,000		90,200	947,000
Liabilities	328,800	138,000			466,800
Minority interest in net assets of S Company				30,000(3) 18,800(1)	48,800
P Company:					
Common stock	300,000				300,000
Additional paid-in capital	1,400				1,400
Retained earnings	130,000				130,000
S Company:					
Preferred stock		50,000	30,000(3) 20,000(2)		–0–
Common stock		40,000	40,000(1)		–0–
Retained earnings		48,000	54,000	6,000	–0–
Total Liabilities and Equity	760,200	276,000	114,000	24,800	947,000
Proof of debit and credit postings			114,000	114,000	

Explanation of entries:
(1) The primary elimination entry.
(2) The preferred stock investment elimination entry.
(3) To reclassify the remainder of the preferred stock as minority interest.

minority interest shares. When the subsidiary acquires minority interest shares above or below book value, the decrease or increase in the parent's interest in the book value of the subsidiary's net assets must be determined. The total dollar dilution of the parent's interest is treated as cost in excess of book value and must be assigned to the appropriate components. Any increase in the parent's interest is treated as a reduction to any existing cost in excess of the book value element.

For the partial disposal of a parent's interest in a subsidiary, the parent must select a method of determining the cost to be removed from the Investment account. Conceptually, the average cost method is the soundest method. Each component of the Investment account should be appropriately relieved to avoid disrupting the normal procedures used to determine the primary elimination entry for future consolidation purposes. Any gain or loss on partial disposal is reported currently in the income statement.

The sale of additional common stock to the public by a subsidiary above or below book value results in either an increase or a decrease, respectively, in the parent's interest in the subsidiary's net assets at book value. Under the entity theory, the increase or decrease is a shift of equity interests between the controlling interests and the minority interests; accordingly no gain or loss is reported. Under the parent company theory, the parent has realized a gain or suffered a loss, which should be reported.

Accounting for Subsidiary's Preferred Stock

A subsidiary's preferred stock is treated as additional minority interest in the consolidated financial statements. The special features of this stock may require that a portion of the subsidiary's retained earnings be shown as part of the minority interest in the consolidated financial statements. When a parent acquires some or all of a subsidiary's outstanding preferred stock, the acquired stock is treated as retired for consolidated reporting purposes. A gain on retirement of preferred stock is credited to Additional Paid-in Capital; a loss is charged to Additional Paid-in Capital to the extent available, with any remaining loss charged to Retained Earnings. When a parent owns some or all of a subsidiary's outstanding preferred stock, it records earnings that accrue to these holdings under the equity method of accounting.

Selected References

"Accounting in Consolidation for Issuances of a Subsidiary's Stock," an issues paper prepared by the Accounting Standards Executive Committee. (New York: American Institute for Certified Public Accountants, June 3, 1980.)

"Carving Out Subsidiaries: Uncommon Financing and New Disclosure Requirements," by Jonathan B. Schiff. *Corporate Accounting* 4, no. 2, Spring 1986, 73–75.

"An Unusual Financing Source: Will It Spur New Disclosure Rules?" by Jonathan B. Schiff. *Management Accounting* (October 1986), 42–45.

Review Questions

1. When some or all of a minority interest is acquired, is the purchase method or the pooling of interests method of accounting used?
2. Does the accounting method used for the acquisition of some or all of a minority interest depend on whether the parent or the subsidiary acquires the minority interest?
3. When a subsidiary has acquired some or all of its outstanding minority interest at an amount in excess of book value, has the parent's interest in the subsidiary's net assets increased or decreased?
4. Is a parent's sale of all of its common stock holdings in a subsidiary a disposal of a segment?
5. When a parent's interest in a subsidiary was acquired in blocks, and a portion of such holdings is sold, what three methods may be used to reduce the investment account?
6. Which of the three methods in Question 5 are acceptable for federal income tax reporting purposes?
7. When a parent disposes of a portion of its common stock holdings in a subsidiary, why must the equity method of accounting be applied up to the date of sale?
8. In which situations does a parent "lose" when a subsidiary issues additional common shares to the public?
9. Does a parent make a general ledger entry when a subsidiary declares a stock dividend?
10. Does a parent make a general ledger entry when a subsidiary effects a stock split?
11. Is the book value of a company's common stock computed differently solely because it is a subsidiary?
12. What reasons might explain why a portion of a subsidiary's retained earnings is considered not allocable to common shareholders?
13. Under the equity method of accounting, are preferred stock dividends always deducted from net income?
14. How is the acquisition of an 80%-owned subsidiary's preferred stock similar to the acquisition of 10% of the subsidiary's common shares? How is it different?
15. How is the analysis of a parent company's investment account by the components of the major conceptual elements prepared differently as a result of an acquired subsidiary having preferred stock with dividends in arrears that is callable at above par value?
16. When a partially owned subsidiary has preferred stock that is shown as additional minority interest in the consolidated financial statements, should the acquisition of some or all of the preferred stock above book value be treated as cost in excess of book value in accordance with the purchase method of accounting?

Technical Research Question

Here and elsewhere in the book, answers to technical research questions may be found by consulting the pronouncements of the Financial Accounting Standards

Board, the Accounting Principles Board, and the Securities and Exchange Commission.

17. Certain expenses incurred by a parent on behalf of its subsidiary have not been charged to the subsidiary. The subsidiary files a registration statement with the SEC in connection with a public offering of additional shares.
    a. Should the subsidiary's historical financial statements reflect all of the expenses that the parent incurred on behalf of the subsidiary?
    b. How should the amount of expenses incurred on the subsidiary's behalf by its parent be determined, and what disclosure is required in the financial statements?

Discussion Cases

DC 10-1 Acquisition of Minority Interest by Parent: Pooling of Interests versus Purchase Method

The controller of Paddle Company indicates to you that the company plans to acquire the entire minority interest of its 92%-owned subsidiary, Steamer Company, by issuing common stock. The terms of the acquisition are identical to those that were used to obtain the 92% interest in Steamer two years ago. The business combination qualified for pooling of interests accounting treatment at that time. The controller asks your advice about how to account for this acquisition.

Required:
How would you advise the controller? State your reasons.

DC 10-2 Manner of Acquiring Minority Interest: By Parent or by Subsidiary?

Port Company owns 70% of the outstanding common stock of Star Company. Port desires to purchase half of the minority interest shares. The purchase price of the shares will be in excess of book value. Port can purchase the shares itself or direct the subsidiary to acquire the shares.

Required:
Which course of action, if either, is more beneficial to the parent company?

DC 10-3 Statutory Merger to Eliminate Minority Shareholders: Rights of Minority Shareholders

Several years ago, Paso Company acquired 80% of the outstanding common stock of Sol Company. Paso now decides to merge with Sol. Under state law, the merger requires approval of only two-thirds of Sol's shareholders. Paso votes its 80% of Sol's stock in favor of the merger, which provides that each of Sol's minority stockholders receive one share of Paso's stock in exchange for three shares of Sol's. Your examination of Paso's financial statements after the merger reveals that some of the minority stockholders voted against it. You are concerned that Paso properly disclose in its financial statements the liability, if any, to these stockholders.

Required:

1. What are the rights of Sol's stockholders who opposed the merger?

2. What steps must minority stockholders ordinarily take to protect their rights in these circumstances?

(AICPA adapted)

DC 10-4

Treatment of Gain on Partial Disposal of Interest in a Subsidiary

Phalanx Company sold a portion of its common stock holdings in one of its subsidiaries at a gain of $80,000. The controller is considering the following options:

1. Crediting this gain to the investment account to reduce the remaining $240,000 of unamortized goodwill.
2. Reporting the gain as an extraordinary item, because this is the first such disposal.
3. Reporting the gain as a partial disposal of a segment under the special reporting provisions of *APB Opinion No. 30* for disposals of segments, because neither the parent nor its other subsidiaries are in the same line of business.

Required:
Evaluate the theoretical merits of these three options.

DC 10-5

Treatment of Parent's Dilution after a Sale of Additional Common Stock to the Public by the Subsidiary

Saunders Company is a partially owned subsidiary of Promo Company. In 19X8, Saunders issued additional shares of its common stock to the public at an amount below book value.

Promo is considering the following options in consolidation:

1. Computing the minority interest of these new shareholders based on the amounts they paid for their interest plus their share of earnings minus their share of dividends since the date the additional shares were issued.
2. Computing total minority interest by multiplying the total minority interest ownership percentage by the subsidiary's net assets at book value.
3. Treating the dollar effect of the parent's decrease in interest in the subsidiary's net assets as additional cost in excess of book value.
4. Treating the dollar effect of the parent's decrease in interest in the subsidiary's net assets as a loss in the current period.

Required:
Evaluate the theoretical merits of each option.

Exercises

E 10-1

Acquisition of Minority Interest by the Parent

Prost Company owns 80% of the outstanding common stock of Skol Company. The expanded analysis of the parent's investment account by components of the major conceptual elements at January 1, 19X6, is as follows:

Book value element:	
Common stock	**$100,000**
Retained earnings	**90,000**
Current value over book value element:	
Land	**40,000**
Goodwill element	**28,000**
	$258,000

Total Cost	**$220,000**
Minority Interest	**38,000**
	$258,000

On January 2, 19X6, Prost acquires 15% of Skol's outstanding common stock from its minority shareholders for $45,000 cash. All of Skol's assets and liabilities have a current value equal to their book value at January 2, 19X6, except land, which is worth $60,000 in excess of its book value.

Required:
Update the expanded analysis of the parent's investment account to reflect this acquisition of a portion of the minority holdings.

E 10-2 Acquisition of Minority Interest by the Subsidiary—Determining Parent's Increase or Decrease in Net Assets

Penner Company owns 75% of the outstanding common stock of Selff Company. On January 1, 19X6, Selff acquired 15% of that stock from the minority shareholders for $300,000 cash. These shares were immediately retired (the Common Stock account was charged $15,000, the Additional Paid-in Capital account was charged $135,000, and the Retained Earnings account was charged $150,000). The subsidiary's capital accounts immediately before the acquisition are as follows:

Common Stock, $1 par value	**$ 100,000**
Additional Paid-in Capital	**900,000**
Retained Earnings	**600,000**
	$1,600,000

Required:

1. Calculate the total change in the equity in the subsidiary's net assets for the parent and the remaining minority interests as a result of the acquisition of a portion of the minority interest.
2. Determine the changes that must be reflected in the expanded analysis of the investment account.

E 10-3 The Manner of Reporting the Complete Disposal of Interest in Certain Subsidiaries

Pantrex Company is a holding company that has all of its investments in its subsidiaries. Each subsidiary operates in one of the following four major business segments: electronic products (television sets, radios, fire and smoke detectors, and burglar alarms); specialty metal products (high-speed and alloy steels, tungsten, and molybdenum); meatpacking (cattle, lamb, and hogs); and wood products (primarily plywood). In 19X6, Pantrex sold one of its three television manufacturing subsidiaries (to bring its capacity into line with current market demand) and all of its wood products subsidiaries.

Required:
How would these disposals be reported in the 19X6 financial statements?

E 10-4

The Effect on the Parent's Investment of a Stock Dividend by the Subsidiary

On April 1, 19X7, Pembroke Company, a 75%-owned subsidiary of Systems Company, declared a 10% common stock dividend on its 10,000 outstanding shares of $20 par value common stock. Pembroke recorded the following entry:

Retained Earnings	**160,000**	
Common Stock		**20,000**
Additional Paid-in Capital		**140,000**

Required:
Determine the appropriate changes that the parent company should make to its expanded analysis of the investment account by individual components as a result of the stock dividend.

E 10-5

The Effect on the Parent's Investment of a Stock Split by the Subsidiary

On January 1, 19X3, Schism Company, a 60%-owned subsidiary of Pergolon Company, split its $10 par value common stock 4 for 1. At the time of the stock split, Schism's capital accounts were as follows:

Common stock	**$ 100,000**
Additional paid-in capital	**900,000**
Retained earnings	**400,000**
	$1,400,000

Required:
Determine the appropriate changes that the parent company should make to its expanded analysis of the investment account by components as a result of the stock split.

E 10-6

Preferred Stock: Determining Parent's Share of Retained Earnings—Wholly Owned Subsidiary (Parent Owns None of Subsidiary's Preferred Stock)

On January 1, 19X1, Prater Company acquires 100% of the outstanding common stock of Sergio Company for $350,000 cash. Assume that the total current value of

Sergio's net assets equals the total book value. Sergio's equity structure of Prater Company as of January 1, 19X1 is as follows:

50% Preferred stock, cumulative, callable at 103 (dividends of $5,000 in arrears)	$100,000
Common stock	10,000
Additional paid-in capital	190,000
Retained earnings	80,000
	$380,000

Required:
Prepare an analysis of the investment account by the individual components of the major conceptual elements as of January 1, 19X1.

E 10-7 Preferred Stock: Determining Parent's Share of Retained Earnings—Partially Owned Subsidiary (Exercise 10-6 Revised to Reflect Partial Ownership)

Assume the information in Exercise 10-6, except that Prater Company acquires only 60% of the outstanding common stock of Sergio Company for $210,000.

Required:
The requirement is the same as for Exercise 10-6.

E 10-8 Preferred Stock: Determining Parent's Share of Retained Earnings—Wholly Owned Subsidiary (Parent Owns None of Subsidiary's Preferred Stock)

On January 1, 19X1, Peg-bit Company acquires 100% of the outstanding common stock of Snap-mate Company for $1,650,000 cash. Assume that the total current value of Snap-mate's net assets equals the total book value. Snap-mate's capital structure as of January 1, 19X1, is as follows:

5% Convertible bonds	$ 500,000
10% Convertible bonds	1,000,000
4% Convertible preferred stock, cumulative, callable at 103 (dividends of $12,000 in arrears)	100,000
8% Preferred stock, cumulative, callable at 102 (dividends of $16,000 in arrears)	200,000
Common stock, $1 par value	300,000
Additional paid-in capital	700,000
Retained earnings	400,000

Note: Assume that the 5% convertible bonds are common stock equivalents under *APB Opinion No. 15*, "Earnings Per Share."

Required:
Prepare an expanded analysis of the investment account as of January 1, 19X1.

E 10-9

Preferred Stock: Determining Parent's Share of Retained Earnings—Partially Owned Subsidiary (Exercise 10-8 Revised to Reflect Partial Ownership)

Assume the information in Exercise 10-8, except that Peg-bit Company acquired only 80% of Snap-mate's outstanding common stock for $1,320,000.

Required:
The requirement is the same as for Exercise 10-8.

Problems

P 10-1

Acquisition of Minority Interest by the Parent

On January 1, 19X3, Peplite Company acquired all of the minority interest shares of its 90%-owned subsidiary, Spree Company, by issuing 10,000 shares of its $5 par value common stock. Peplite's common stock had a fair market value of $17 per share on January 1, 19X3. The business combination with Spree was recorded as a pooling of interests at the time of the combination. Spree's capital accounts on December 31, 19X2, were as follows:

Common stock	$1,000,000
Retained earnings	400,000
	$1,400,000

All of Spree's assets and liabilities have a current value equal to their book value at January 1, 19X3, except for its building, which is worth $70,000 in excess of book value.

Required:
Prepare and update the expanded analysis of the parent's investment account to reflect the acquisition of the minority interest.

P 10-2

Acquisition of Minority Interest by the Subsidiary: Determination of Parent's Increase or Decrease in Net Assets

Pebit Company owns 60% of the outstanding common stock of Scredit Company. On January 1, 19X6, Scredit acquired 20% of its outstanding common stock from its minority interest shareholders for $360,000 cash. (These shares were immediately retired by debiting Common Stock for $20,000, Additional Paid-in Capital for $80,000, and Retained Earnings for $260,000.) The expanded analysis of Pebit's investment account by components at December 31, 19X5, is as follows:

Book value element:	
Common stock	$ 100,000
Additional paid-in capital	400,000
Retained earnings	700,000

Current value over book value element:	
Land	60,000
Goodwill element	90,000
	$1,350,000
Total Cost	$ 870,000
Minority Interest	480,000
	$1,350,000

All of Scredit's assets and liabilities have a current value equal to their book value on January 1, 19X6, except for land, which has a current value $100,000 over its book value.

Required:

1. Calculate the amount of the decrease in the parent's interest in the subsidiary's net assets.
2. Update the expanded analysis of the investment account by components to reflect this acquisition of a portion of the minority interest.

P 10-3 Acquisition of Minority Interest by the Parent (Problem 10-2 Revised)

Assume the information provided in Problem 10-2, except that the parent acquired 20% of the subsidiary's outstanding common stock from the minority interest shareholders for $360,000 cash.

Required:

1. Update the expanded analysis of the investment account by components to reflect this acquisition.
2. Explain why the parent suffered dilution in Problem 10-2 but not in this case.
3. Explain why the parent's cost in excess of book value increased by a greater amount in this case than in Problem 10-2.

P 10-4 Partial Disposal of the Investment in a Subsidiary: Updating the Analysis of the Investment Account and Preparing Year-end Elimination Entries

On October 1, 19X4, Pyramid Company (a calendar-year reporting company) sold 25% of its common stock holdings in its 80%-owned subsidiary, Schemex Company, for $500,000 cash. All of Schemex's shares were acquired on January 1, 19X1, in a business combination that was accounted for as a purchase. The expanded analysis of the investment account by components as of January 1, 19X4, is as follows:

		Remaining Life as of January 1, 19X4
Book value element:		
Common stock	$1,500,000	
Retained earnings	500,000	

Current value over book value element:		
Land	200,000	Indefinite
Patent	30,000	5 years
Goodwill element	24,000	12 years
	$2,254,000	
Total Cost	$1,854,000	
Minority Interest	400,000	
	$2,254,000	

During 19X4, Schemex had net income of $85,000, $25,000 of which was earned in the fourth quarter, and declared dividends of $10,000 at the end of each quarter.

Required:

1. Update the parent company's expanded analysis of the investment account through December 31, 19X4, assuming that Pyramid Company uses the equity method.
2. Prepare the primary elimination entry as of December 31, 19X4.
3. Prepare the entry to record the partial disposal by the parent.

P 10-5 Partial Disposal of the Investment in a Subsidiary: Updating the Analysis of the Investment Account and Preparing Year-end Elimination Entries

On July 1, 19X7, Pro Company (a calendar-year reporting company) sold 3,000 of the 9,000 Samateur Company common shares it held for $170,000 cash. The 9,000 common shares, a 90% interest, were acquired on January 1, 19X1 in a business combination that was accounted for as a purchase. The expanded analysis of the investment account by components as of January 1, 19X7, is as follows:

		Remaining Life as of January 1, 19X7
Book value element:		
Common stock	$100,000	
Retained earnings	150,000	
Current value over book value element:		
Land	75,000	Indefinite
Bonds Payable	54,000	6 years
Goodwill element	50,000	5 years
	$429,000	
Total Cost	$404,000	
Minority Interest	25,000	
	$429,000	

During 19X7, Samateur had the following:

	Net Income	Dividends Declared
Jan. 1, 19X7–June 30, 19X7	$50,000	$10,000
July 1, 19X7–Dec. 31, 19X7	30,000	10,000

Required:

1. Update the parent's expanded analysis of the investment account through December 31, 19X7, assuming that the parent uses the equity method.
2. Prepare the primary elimination entry as of December 31, 19X7.
3. Prepare the entry to record the sale of the 3,000 shares by the parent.

P 10-6

Issuance of Additional Common Shares by the Subsidiary

On July 1, 19X5, Streeter Company, a 90%-owned subsidiary of Paver Company, issued 20,000 shares of its $10 par value common stock to the public for $1,200,000. The balances in Streeter's equity accounts immediately prior to the issuance are as follows:

Common stock	$1,000,000
Additional paid-in capital	4,000,000
Retained earnings	2,500,000
	$7,500,000

Required:

1. Determine the "gain" or "loss" that the parent incurs as a result of the issuance.
2. How should the gain or loss be reported?

P 10-7

Issuance of Additional Common Shares by the Subsidiary

On April 1, 19X8, Sweepco Company, an 80%-owned subsidiary of Prush Company, issued 10,000 shares of its $1 par value common stock to the public for $360,000. The balances in Sweepco's equity accounts immediately prior to the issuance are as follows:

Common stock	$ 50,000
Additional paid-in capital	450,000
Retained earnings	1,000,000
	$1,500,000

Required:

1. Determine the "gain" or "loss" that the parent incurs as a result of the issuance.
2. How should the gain or loss be reported?

P 10-8*

COMPREHENSIVE (Chapters 3–5, 7, 9, and 10) The Partial Equity Method: Inventory Transfers, Bond Holdings, and Changes in Ownership; Preparing Consolidated Financial Statements

On January 3, 19X3, Potus Company acquired 80% of the outstanding common stock of Supercal Company by paying $400,000 cash to William Braun, the com-

*The financial statement information presented for problems accompanied by asterisks is also provided on Model 7 (filename: Model7) of the software file disk that is available for use with the text, enabling the problem to be worked on the computer.

pany's sole stockholder. In addition, Potus acquired a patent from Braun for $40,000 cash. Potus charged the entire $440,000 to the Investment in Supercal Company Common Stock account.

Additional Information:

1. The book value of Supercal's common stock on the acquisition date was $500,000. The book values of the individual assets and liabilities equaled their current values.
2. The patent had a remaining legal life of four years as of January 3, 19X3. No amortization has been recorded since the acquisition date.
3. During 19X4, Supercal sold merchandise to Potus for $130,000, which included a markup of 30% over Supercal's cost. At December 31, 19X4, $52,000 of this merchandise remained in Potus's inventory. In February 19X5, Potus sold this merchandise at an $8,000 profit.
4. On July 1, 19X5, Potus reduced its investment in Supercal to 75% of Supercal's outstanding common stock by selling shares to an unaffiliated company for $70,000 at a profit of $16,000. Potus recorded the proceeds as a credit to its investment account.
5. In November 19X5, Potus sold merchandise to Supercal for the first time. Potus's cost for this merchandise was $80,000, and it made the sale at 120% of its cost. Supercal's December 31, 19X5, inventory contained $24,000 of the merchandise that was purchased from Potus.
6. On December 31, 19X5, a $40,000 payment was in transit from Supercal to Potus. Accounts receivable and accounts payable include intercompany receivables and payables. (Supercal still owes Potus $12,000.)
7. In December 19X5, Supercal declared and paid cash dividends of $100,000 to its stockholders.
8. Supercal had $140,000 of net income for the six months ended June 30, 19X5, and $160,000 of net income for the six months ended December 31, 19X5.
9. On July 1, 19X5, Potus paid $56,000 for 50% of the outstanding bonds issued by Supercal. The bonds mature on June 30, 19X9, and were originally issued at a discount. At December 31, 19X5, the unamortized discount on Supercal's books is $2,800. (Interest at 10% is due on June 30 and December 31 of each year.) The December 31, 19X5, interest payment was made on time. (Both companies use the straight-line method of discount amortization.)
10. The financial statements of each company for the year ended December 31, 19X5, are as follows:
11. The partial equity method is used.

	Potus Company	Supercal Company
Income Statement (19X5):		
Sales	$4,000,000	$1,700,000
Cost of goods sold	(3,000,000)	(1,000,000)
Expenses	(385,500)	(400,000)
Intercompany Accounts:		
Equity in net income of subsidiary	232,000	
Dividend income	75,000	
Interest income	3,500	
Net Income	$ 925,000	$ 300,000

	Potus Company	Supercal Company
Balance Sheet:		
Cash	$ 487,500	$ 250,000
Accounts receivable, net	235,000	185,000
Inventory	475,000	355,000
Fixed assets, net	2,231,000	530,000
Investments in Supercal Company:		
Common stock	954,000	
Bonds	56,500	
Total Assets	$4,439,000	$1,320,000
Accounts payable	$ 384,000	$ 62,800
Bonds payable		120,000
Unamortized bond discount		(2,800)
Common stock	1,200,000	300,000
Retained earnings	2,855,000	840,000
Total Liabilities and Equity	$4,439,000	$1,320,000
Dividends declared	$ 170,000	$ 100,000

Required:

1. Prepare the appropriate adjusting entries required at December 31, 19X5.
2. Adjust the financial statements for the entries developed in requirement 1. Modify the financial statements to reflect the use of intercompany accounts.
3. Prepare the appropriate elimination entries in consolidation at December 31, 19X5.
4. Prepare a consolidating statement worksheet at December 31, 19X5, using the partially consolidated column format demonstrated in Chapters 7, 8, and 9. (Parent and subsidiary columns should reflect the adjustments made in requirement 2.)

(AICPA adapted)

P 10-9*

COMPREHENSIVE (Chapters 3–5, 7, 9, and 10) Problem 10-8 Changed to the Complete Equity Method

Assume the information provided in Problem 10-8, except that the complete equity method is to be used.

Required:

The requirements are the same as in Problem 10-8, except that in requirement 1 it is also necessary to prepare entries to convert the financial statements to the complete equity method.

Problems: Preferred Stock

P 10-10

Preferred Stock: Determining Parent's Share of Retained Earnings—Wholly Owned Subsidiary (Parent Owns None of Subsidiary's Preferred Stock)

On January 1, 19X1, Pelt Company acquired 100% of the outstanding common stock of Sable Company for $600,000 cash. All cost in excess of book value is allocable to goodwill, which has a 10-year life. Sable's capital structure as of January 1, 19X1, is as follows:

5% Convertible bonds	$1,000,000
6% Convertible preferred stock, callable at 105, cumulative (dividends of $18,000 in arrears)	100,000
Common stock, $10 par value	500,000
Retained earnings	30,000

Sable had net income of $26,000 during 19X1. It declared and paid cash dividends of $12,000 on its preferred stock.

Required:

1. Prepare an analysis of the investment account as of January 1, 19X1.
2. Update the analysis of the investment account for 19X1 activity under the equity method of accounting.

P 10-11 Preferred Stock: Determining Parent's Share of Retained Earnings—Partially Owned Subsidiary (Problem 10-10 Revised to Reflect Partial Ownership)

Assume the information in Problem 10-10, except that Pelt Company acquired only 60% of the outstanding common stock of Sable Company for $360,000 cash.

Required:
The requirements are the same as for Problem 10-10.

P 10-12 Preferred Stock: Determining Parent's Share of Retained Earnings and Preparing Preferred Stock Elimination Entry—Wholly Owned Subsidiary (Parent Acquires Some of Subsidiary's Preferred Stock Subsequent to Business Combination Date)

On January 1, 19X1, Prometheus Company acquired all of the outstanding common stock of Samson Company for $450,000 cash. All cost in excess of the book value of the net assets is allocable to land. Samson capital structure at January 1, 19X1, is as follows:

5% Preferred stock, cumulative, callable at 102 (dividends of $15,000 in arrears)	$100,000
Common stock, $10 par value	350,000
Retained earnings	50,000
	$500,000

On December 31, 19X1, Prometheus acquired 20% of Samson outstanding preferred stock for $17,000. During 19X1, Samson had net income of $30,000 and declared cash dividends of $5,000 on its preferred stock.

Required:

1. Prepare an analysis of the investment account at January 1, 19X1.
2. Update the analysis of the investment account through December 31, 19X1.
3. Determine the entry required in consolidation at December 31, 19X1, relating to the preferred stock.

P 10-13 Preferred Stock: Determining Parent's Share of Retained Earnings and Preparing Preferred Stock Elimination Entry—Partially Owned Subsidiary (Problem 10-12 Revised to Reflect Partial Ownership)

Assume the information in Problem 10-12, except that Prometheus Company acquired only 80% of the outstanding common stock of Samson Company for $360,000 cash.

Required:
The requirements are the same as for Problem 10-12.

P 10-14 Preferred Stock: Preparing Consolidated Financial Statements; Parent Acquires Some of Subsidiary's Preferred Stock Subsequent to Business Combination Date—Wholly Owned Subsidiary

On January 1, 19X1, Perceval Company acquired 100% of the outstanding common stock of Suffolk Company for $450,000 cash. All cost in excess of book value is allocable to land. Suffolk's capital structure on January 1, 19X1, is as follows:

5% Preferred stock, cumulative, callable at 104	
(dividends of $10,000 in arrears)	$100,000
Common stock, $100 par value	350,000
Retained earnings	50,000
	$500,000

Also on January 1, 19X1, Perceval acquired 60% of Suffolk's outstanding preferred stock for $65,000. During 19X1, Suffolk declared cash dividends of $10,000 on its preferred stock. The financial statements for each company for the year ended December 31, 19X1, are as follows:

	Perceval Company	Suffolk Company
Income Statement (19X1):		
Sales	$750,000	$350,000
Equity in net income of Suffolk Company	55,000	
Dividend income (on Suffolk Company preferred stock)	6,000	
Cost of goods sold	(480,000)	(240,000)
Marketing, administrative, and interest expenses	(150,000)	(50,000)
Net Income	$181,000	$ 60,000

	Perceval Company	Suffolk Company
Balance Sheet (December 31, 19X1):		
Investments in Suffolk Company:		
Common stock	$505,000	
Preferred stock	65,000	
Other assets	380,000	$585,000
Total Assets	$950,000	$585,000
Liabilities	$300,000	$ 35,000
Preferred stock		100,000
Common stock	400,000	350,000
Retained earnings	250,000	100,000
Total Liabilities and Equity	$950,000	$585,000
Dividends declared on common stock	$100,000	$ –0–

Required:

1. Prepare an analysis of the investment in common stock of the subsidiary as of January 1, 19X1.
2. Update the analysis of the investment in common stock of the subsidiary through December 31, 19X1, under the equity method of accounting.
3. Prepare the primary elimination entry at December 31, 19X1.
4. Prepare the elimination entry related to preferred stock at December 31, 19X1.
5. Prepare a consolidating statement worksheet for the year ended December 31, 19X1.

Problem: Consolidated Statement of Cash Flows

P 10-15

Consolidated Statement of Cash Flows

The following consolidated income statement and comparative balance sheets are for Pumper Company and its 80% owned subsidiary, Stress-lok Company:

Income Statement (19X1):	
Sales	$600,000
Cost of goods sold	(350,000)
Marketing and administrative expenses	(141,000)
Interest expense	(22,000)
Gain on sale of equipment	3,000
Minority interest	(6,000)
Net Income	$ 84,000

	December 31, 19X1	December 31, 19X0
Balance Sheets:		
Cash	$ 75,000	$ 60,000
Receivables, net	90,000	70,000
Inventory	200,000	170,000
Fixed assets—Cost	506,000	465,000
—Accum. depr.	(103,000)	(100,000)

Goodwill	32,000	35,000
Total Assets	$800,000	$700,000
Accounts payable	$180,000	$164,000
Bonds payable—Current	20,000	20,000
—Long-term	160,000	180,000
Minority interest	66,000	36,000
Common stock	250,000	200,000
Retained earnings	124,000	100,000
Total Liabilities and Equity	$800,000	$700,000

Additional Information:

1. On January 1, 19X1, Pumper increased its ownership in Stress-lok from 70% to 80% by paying $17,000 cash to certain minority shareholders. (The cost in excess of book value was designated as goodwill.)
2. On December 31, 19X1, Stress-lok issued preferred stock at par totaling $40,000 (shown as part of the minority interest in the December 31, 19X1, consolidated balance sheet). Stress-lok had no preferred stock outstanding prior to this issuance.
3. As of January 1, 19X1, goodwill has a five-year remaining life (including the goodwill paid for on January 1, 19X1).
4. On July 1, 19X1, Pumper issued 5,000 shares of common stock for $10 per share.
5. During 19X1, dividends on common stock were declared and paid as follows:

Pumper Company	$60,000
Stress-lok Company	20,000

6. On January 2, 19X1, Pumper sold equipment to Stress-lok for $21,000. The equipment had cost Pumper $30,000 and was 60% depreciated at the time of the intercompany transfer. Stress-lok assigned a three-year life to the equipment. In consolidation at December 31, 19X1, the following elimination entry was made as a result of this transfer:

Gain on Sale of Equipment	9,000	
Equipment	9,000	
Depreciation Expense		3,000
Accumulated Depreciation		15,000

7. The only fixed-asset retirement during 19X1 was a machine that had cost $33,000, had accumulated depreciation of $22,000, and was sold for $14,000.

Required:

Prepare a consolidated statement of changes in cash flow for 19X1.

11

Indirect and Reciprocal Holdings

AN OVERVIEW OF INTERCOMPANY RELATIONSHIPS

The most common intercompany relationship is the parent company's direct investment in a subsidiary's common stock. Other types of relationships are encountered less frequently; they can be categorized as follows:

1. Indirect vertical holdings.
2. Indirect horizontal holdings.
3. Reciprocal (mutual) holdings.

These various relationships are shown in Illustration 11-1. Although this chapter discusses each category independently of the others, the categories are not mutually exclusive; any combination of relationships may occur. Accounting for special corporate relationships involving combinations of indirect vertical holdings, indirect horizontal holdings, and reciprocal holdings can be developed from a careful application of the principles discussed in this chapter.

The accounting procedures for indirect vertical holdings and indirect horizontal holdings follow the principles discussed in earlier chapters with respect to accounting for the investment and preparing consolidated financial statements. In these relationships, the **sequence** of procedures in the consolidation process is of paramount importance.

Two methods have evolved for presenting the combined earnings in the consolidated income statement for reciprocal holdings involving a partially owned subsidiary. Each method is discussed and illustrated in detail. Selecting the method that **presents the most meaningful financial information** is important.

Discussion of the ramifications of unrealized intercompany profits on asset transfers is delayed until the end of the chapter.

INDIRECT VERTICAL HOLDINGS

An **indirect vertical holding** occurs when P Company, for example, owns more than 50% of S Company, and S Company owns more than 50% of T Company. In such relationships, commonly referred to as **chains,** S Company, although a subsidiary of P Company, is a parent with respect to T Company.

The procedures used to consolidate the financial statements of the three companies are as follows:

1. T Company is consolidated into S Company.
2. S Company, which is now consolidated with T Company, is consolidated into P Company.

Illustration 11-1
Affiliation Diagrams

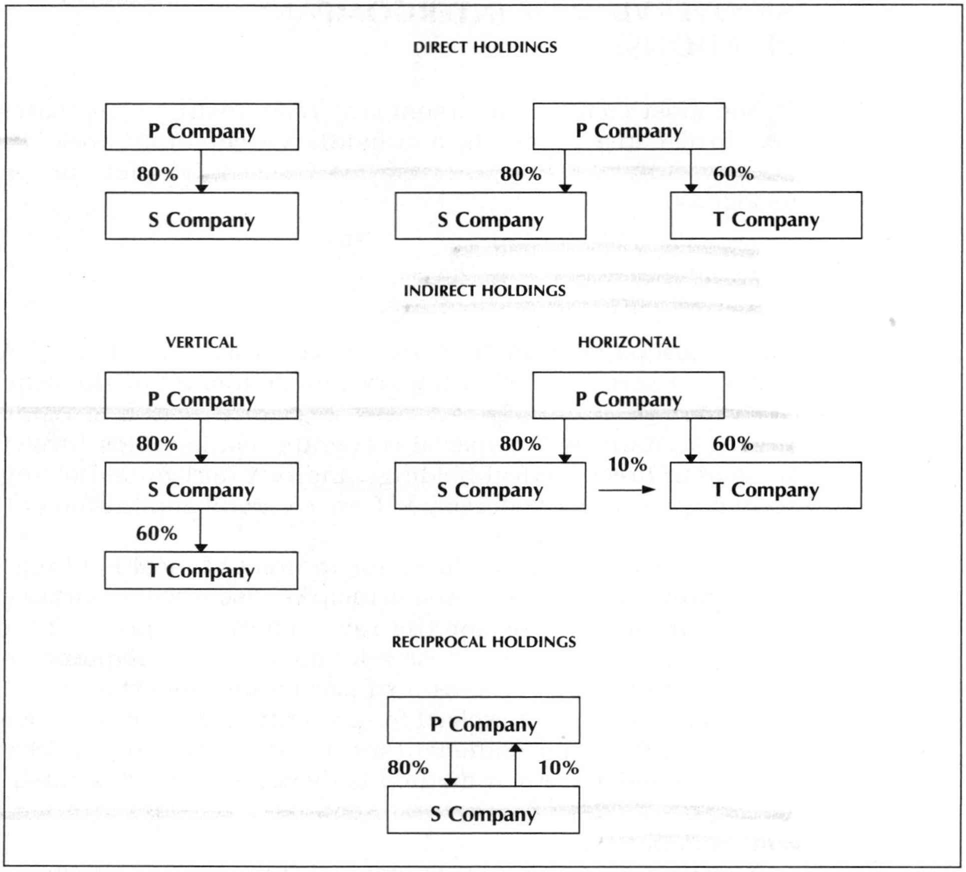

When minority interests exist at each level, the minority interest deduction in the income statement section and the minority interest in the balance sheet section of the consolidating statement worksheet increase at each higher level of consolidation.

Net income for P Company (the top-level parent) can be determined without consolidation by successive application of the equity method of accounting, starting with the lowest-level parent within the chain. For example, assume the following information for 19X1:

1. P Company owns 80% of S Company, and S Company owns 60% of T Company. The affiliation can be diagrammed as follows:

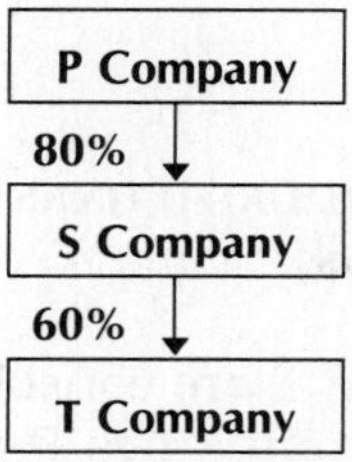

2. Net income from each company's operations, excluding equity in net income of subsidiary and amortization of cost in excess of book value, is as follows:

P Company	$1,000,000
S Company	100,000
T Company	10,000

3. All of P Company's $10,000 cost in excess of book value was allocable to land. All of S Company's $6,000 cost in excess of book value was allocable to goodwill—$1,000 was amortized during 19X1.

The successive application of the equity method of accounting is as follows:

S Company's income from its own operations	**$ 100,000**
S Company's equity in T Company's net income (60% of $10,000)	**6,000**
Less—Amortization of cost in excess of book value	**(1,000)**
Net Income of S Company	**$ 105,000**
P Company's income from its own operations	**$1,000,000**
P Company's equity in S Company's net income (80% of $105,000)	**84,000**
Net Income of P Company	**$1,084,000**

Note that only 48% of T Company's $10,000 net income is reflected in P Company's net income under the equity method of accounting [80% (60% × $10,000)]. Of the $1,000 amortization of cost in excess of book value expense recorded by S Company, 80%, or $800, accrues to P Company. Thus, the net amount that accrues to P Company is $4,000 ($4,800 − $800). Even though a majority of T Company's net income does not accrue to the consolidated group, successive consolidation is still appropriate, because T Company is controlled indirectly through S Company.

Illustrations

PREPARING CONSOLIDATED FINANCIAL STATEMENTS FOR INDIRECT VERTICAL HOLDINGS

Companies S and T are consolidated as of December 31, 19X1, in Illustration 11-2, and companies P and S are subsequently consolidated as of December 31, 19X1, in Illustration 11-3. The ownership and income information is from the preceding example. (We assume that no intercompany transactions requiring elimination occurred.) The primary and secondary elimination entries for these illustrations are as follows:

1. The primary elimination entry:

	Consolidation of			
	Companies S and T		Companies P and S	
Common Stock	40,000		300,000	
Retained Earnings (beginning of year)...........	20,000		100,000	
Equity in Net Income of Subsidiary......................	6,000		84,000	
Minority Interest in Net Income of S Company......	4,000		21,000	
Land..............................			40,000	
Goodwill	5,000			
Dividends Declared....		5,000		35,000
Investment in Subsidiary..............		44,000		416,000
Minority Interest in Net Assets of S Company		26,000		94,000

2. The secondary elimination entry:

Cost of Goods Sold.............	1,000	
Amortization of Cost in Excess of Book Value		1,000

The following points are important for understanding Illustrations 11-2 and 11-3:

1. At each higher level of consolidation, the minority interest deduction increases, as does the Minority Interest account in the balance sheet.
2. S Company treats the amortization of cost in excess of book value on its books as a normal expense, thereby reducing its net income, which in turn reduces the minority interest deduction when S Company is

Illustration 11-2
Indirect Vertical Holdings: Consolidation 1

S COMPANY AND SUBSIDIARY (T COMPANY)
Consolidating Statement Worksheet
For the Year Ended December 31, 19X1

	S Company	T Company	Eliminations Dr.	Eliminations Cr.	S and T Consolidated
Income Statement:					
Sales	790,000	200,000			990,000
Cost of goods sold	(360,000)	(120,000)	1,000(2)		(481,000)
Expenses	(330,000)	(30,000)			(360,000)
Intercompany Accounts:					
Equity in net income	6,000		6,000(1)		–0–
Amortization of cost in excess of book value	(1,000)			1,000(2)	–0–
Income before Min. Int.	105,000	10,000	7,000	1,000	109,000
Minority interest			4,000(1)		(4,000)
Net Income	105,000	10,000	11,000	1,000	105,000
Statement of Retained Earnings:					
Balances, January 1, 19X1	100,000	20,000	20,000(1)		100,000
+ Net income	105,000	10,000	11,000	1,000	105,000
− Dividends declared	(35,000)	(5,000)		5,000(1)	(35,000)
Balances, December 31, 19X1	170,000	25,000	31,000	6,000	170,000
Balance Sheet:					
Current assets	338,000	115,000			453,000
Investment in T Company	44,000			44,000(1)	–0–
Fixed assets, net	350,000	155,000			505,000
Goodwill			5,000(1)		5,000
Total Assets	732,000	270,000	5,000	44,000	963,000
Liabilities	262,000	205,000			467,000
Minority interest in net assets of subsidiary				26,000(1)	26,000
S Company:					
Common stock	300,000				300,000
Retained earnings	170,000				170,000
T Company:					
Common stock		40,000	40,000(1)		–0–
Retained earnings		25,000	31,000	6,000	–0–
Total Liabilities and Equity	732,000	270,000	71,000	32,000	963,000
Proof of debit and credit postings			76,000	76,000	

Explanation of entries:
(1) The primary elimination entry.
(2) The secondary elimination entry.

Illustration 11-3
Indirect Vertical Holdings: Consolidation 2

P COMPANY AND SUBSIDIARY (S COMPANY)
Consolidating Statement Worksheet
For the Year Ended December 31, 19X1

	P Company	S and T Consolidated[a]	Eliminations Dr.	Eliminations Cr.	P + S + T Consolidated
Income Statement:					
Sales	7,500,000	990,000			8,490,000
Cost of goods sold	(4,000,000)	(481,000)			(4,481,000)
Expenses	(2,500,000)	(360,000)			(2,860,000)
Intercompany Accounts:					
Equity in net income	84,000		84,000(1)		–0–
Income before Minority Interest	1,084,000	109,000	84,000		1,109,000
Minority interest		(4,000)	21,000(1)		(25,000)
Net Income	1,084,000	105,000	105,000		1,084,000
Statement of Retained Earnings:					
Balances, January 1, 19X1	1,700,000	100,000	100,000(1)		1,700,000
+ Net income	1,084,000	105,000	105,000		1,084,000
− Dividends declared	(700,000)	(35,000)		35,000(1)	(700,000)
Balances, December 31, 19X1	2,084,000	170,000	205,000	35,000	2,084,000
Balance Sheet:					
Current assets	2,068,000	453,000			2,521,000
Investment in S Company	416,000			416,000(1)	–0–
Fixed assets, net	2,600,000	505,000	40,000(1)		3,145,000
Goodwill		5,000			5,000
Total Assets	5,084,000	963,000	40,000	416,000	5,671,000
Liabilities	1,000,000	467,000			1,467,000
Minority interest in T Company and S Company		26,000		94,000(1)	120,000
P Company:					
Common stock	2,000,000				2,000,000
Retained earnings	2,084,000				2,084,000
S Company:					
Common stock		300,000	300,000(1)		–0–
Retained earnings		170,000	205,000	35,000	–0–
Total Liabilities and Equity	5,084,000	963,000	505,000	129,000	5,671,000
Proof of debit and credit postings			545,000	545,000	

[a]From Illustration 11-2.

Explanation of entry:
(1) The primary elimination entry.

consolidated with P Company. In other words, the amortization of cost in excess of book value by S Company is considered a bona fide expense in determining S Company's net income, and the minority interest deduction is based on this net income.

3. The consolidation process starts at the lowest parent–subsidiary level and then works upward.

INDIRECT HORIZONTAL HOLDINGS

Indirect horizontal holdings occur when one subsidiary holds an investment in another subsidiary of a common parent—for example, P Company owns more than 50% of companies S and T, and S Company has an investment in T Company, which obviously must be less than 50%.

Consolidating the financial statements of the three companies is accomplished as follows:

1. S Company (an investor) applies the equity method of accounting with respect to the earnings of T Company (an investee).
2. P Company applies the equity method of accounting to each of its subsidiaries and then consolidates S Company.
3. P Company then consolidates T Company.

When the three companies are consolidated in this sequence, the individual investments in T Company by companies P and S are added together when the latter are consolidated. This combined investment in T Company is then eliminated in a single step when T Company is consolidated with P Company, which is already consolidated with S Company. When eliminating the combined investment in T Company, the individual components of P Company's investment account must be combined with the individual components of S Company's investment account.

Regardless of one subsidiary's ownership percentage in another subsidiary, the equity method of accounting should be used by the investor subsidiary (even if the percentage is less than 20%), because the parent exercises significant influence over the investee subsidiary.

P Company's net income can be determined without consolidation by successive application of the equity method of accounting, starting with the lowest-level investor. Assume the following information for 19X1:

1. P Company owns 80% of S Company and 60% of T Company, and S Company owns 10% of T Company. The affiliations are diagrammed as follows:

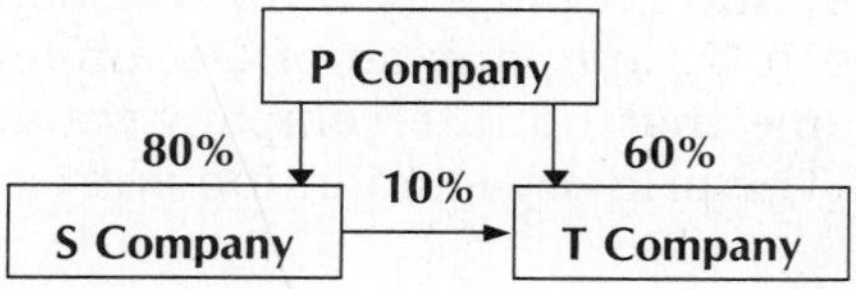

2. Income from each company's operations, excluding the equity in net income of any subsidiary or investee, is as follows:

P Company	$1,000,000
S Company	100,000
T Company	10,000

3. For simplicity, we assume that all cost in excess of book value was allocable to land. Thus, there is no amortization of cost in excess of book value.

The successive application of the equity method of accounting is as follows:

S Company's income from its own operations	$ 100,000
S Company's equity in T Company's net income (10% of $10,000)	1,000
Total Net Income of S Company	$ 101,000
P Company's income from its own operations	$1,000,000
P Company's equity in S Company's net income (80% of $101,000)	80,800
P Company's equity in T Company's net income (60% of $10,000)	6,000
Total Net Income of P Company	$1,086,800

Illustrations

PREPARING CONSOLIDATED FINANCIAL STATEMENTS FOR INDIRECT HORIZONTAL HOLDINGS

From the ownership and income information in the preceding example, companies P and S are consolidated as of December 31, 19X1, in Illustration 11-4, and P Company (now consolidated with S Company) is consolidated with T Company as of December 31, 19X1, in Illustration 11-5. (We assume that no intercompany transactions occurred requiring elimination.) The primary elimination entries are given as follows:

Illustration 11-4
Indirect Horizontal Holdings: Consolidation 1

P COMPANY AND SUBSIDIARY (S COMPANY)
Consolidating Statement Worksheet
For the Year Ended December 31, 19X1

	P Company	S Company	Eliminations Dr.	Eliminations Cr.	P + S Consolidated
Income Statement:					
Sales	7,500,000	790,000			8,290,000
Cost of goods sold	(4,000,000)	(360,000)			(4,360,000)
Expenses	(2,500,000)	(330,000)			(2,830,000)
Intercompany Accounts:					
Equity in net income—S	80,800		80,800(1)		–0–
Equity in net income—T	6,000	1,000			7,000
Income before Minority Interest	1,086,800	101,000	80,800		1,107,000
Minority interest			20,200(1)		(20,200)
Net Income	1,086,800	101,000	101,000		1,086,800
Statement of Retained Earnings:					
Balances, January 1, 19X1	1,700,000	100,000	100,000(1)		1,700,000
+ Net income	1,086,800	101,000	101,000		1,086,800
− Dividends declared	(700,000)	(35,000)		35,000(1)	(700,000)
Balances, December 31, 19X1	2,086,800	166,000	201,000	35,000	2,086,800
Balance Sheet:					
Current assets	2,029,000	368,000			2,397,000
Investment in Subsidiaries:					
S Company	412,800			412,800(1)	–0–
T Company	45,000	10,000			55,000
Fixed assets, net	2,600,000	350,000	40,000(1)		2,990,000
Total Assets	5,086,800	728,000	40,000	412,800	5,442,000
Liabilities	1,000,000	262,000			1,262,000
Minority interest in net assets of subsidiaries				93,200(1)	93,200
P Company:					
Common stock	2,000,000				2,000,000
Retained earnings	2,086,800				2,086,800
S Company:					
Common stock		300,000	300,000(1)		–0–
Retained earnings		166,000	201,000	35,000	–0–
Total Liabilities and Equity	5,086,800	728,000	501,000	128,200	5,442,000
Proof of debit and credit postings			541,000	541,000	

Explanation of entry:
(1) The primary elimination entry.

Illustration 11-5
Indirect Horizontal Holdings: Consolidation 2

P AND S COMPANIES (Consolidated)
AND SUBSIDIARY (T COMPANY)
Consolidating Statement Worksheet
For the Year Ended December 31, 19X1

	P and S Consolidated[a]	T Company	Eliminations Dr.	Eliminations Cr.	P + S + T Consolidated
Income Statement:					
Sales	8,290,000	200,000			8,490,000
Cost of goods sold	4,360,000)	(120,000)			(4,480,000)
Expenses	(2,830,000)	(70,000)			(2,900,000)
Intercompany Accounts:					
Equity in net income—T Company	7,000		7,000(1)		–0–
Income before Minority Interest	1,107,000	10,000	7,000		1,110,000
Minority interest	(20,200)		3,000(1)		(23,200)
Net Income	1,086,800	10,000	10,000		1,086,800
Statement of Retained Earnings:					
Balances, January 1, 19X1	1,700,000	20,000	20,000(1)		1,700,000
+ Net income	1,086,800	10,000	10,000		1,086,800
− Dividends declared	(700,000)	(5,000)		5,000(1)	(700,000)
Balances, December 31, 19X1	2,086,800	25,000	30,000	5,000	2,086,800
Balance Sheet:					
Current assets	2,397,000	115,000			2,512,000
Investment in T Company	55,000			55,000(1)	–0–
Fixed assets, net	2,990,000	155,000	9,500(1)		3,154,500
Total Assets	5,442,000	270,000	9,500	55,000	5,666,500
Liabilities	1,262,000	205,000			1,467,000
Minority interest in S Company	93,200			19,500(1)	112,700
P Company:					
Common stock	2,000,000				2,000,000
Retained earnings	2,086,800				2,086,800
T Company:					
Common stock		40,000	40,000(1)		–0–
Retained earnings		25,000	30,000	5,000	–0–
Total Liabilities and Equity	5,442,000	270,000	70,000	24,500	5,666,500
Proof of debit and credit postings			79,500	79,500	

[a]From Illustration 11-4.

Explanation of entry:
(1) The primary elimination entry.

	Consolidation of			
	Companies P and S		Companies P and T (See below for source of these amounts)	
Common Stock	300,000		40,000	
Retained Earnings (beginning of year)	100,000		20,000	
Equity in Net Income of Subsidiary	80,800		7,000	
Minority Interest in Net Income of Subsidiary	20,200		3,000	
Land	40,000		9,500	
Dividends Declared		35,000		5,000
Investment in Subsidiary		412,800		55,000
Minority Interest in Net Assets of Subsidiary		93,200		19,500

The primary elimination entry to consolidate companies P and T is obtained by combining the individual components of the major conceptual elements of P Company's investment in T Company and S Company's investment in T Company as shown below:

Analysis of the Investment Accounts by the Components of the Major Conceptual Elements

	P Company's Investment in T Company	S Company's Investment in T Company	Total
Common Stock	$36,000[a]	$ 4,000	$40,000
Retained Earnings (beginning of year)	18,000[a]	2,000	20,000
Equity in Net Income of T Company	6,000	1,000	7,000
Minority Interest in Net Income of T Company	3,000		3,000
Dividends	(4,500)	(500)	(5,000)
Land	6,000	3,500	9,500
	$64,500	$10,000	$74,500
Total Cost	$45,000	$10,000	$55,000
Minority Interest	19,500		19,500
	$64,500	$10,000	$74,500

[a]Because of the 10% horizontal investment, this amount is only 90% of the book value rather than 100%.

The following points are important for understanding Illustrations 11-4 and 11-5:

1. For the percentage investment held in T Company, S Company's cost in excess of book value was greater than that of P Company. We assumed that (1) S Company made its investment in T Company after P Company made its investment in T Company, and (2) the land appreciated in value during that interval.
2. The consolidation can also be performed using one consolidation worksheet in which companies S and T are simultaneously consolidated with P Company. This is the common procedure in practice; separate consolidations of each company are used here for instructional purposes.

RECIPROCAL HOLDINGS

Reciprocal holdings occur when a subsidiary invests in its parent company's common stock. Two accounting questions are raised by such holdings:

1. How should the subsidiary account for the investment in the parent company?
2. How should the investment in the parent company be accounted for in consolidation?

Accounting by the Subsidiary

An investment by a subsidiary in its parent's common stock must be considered a long-term investment. Because such investments rarely, if ever, reach the 20% level, ownership in the parent's common stock is usually less than 20%. In this situation, the subsidiary must account for the investment under the lower of cost or market method, as prescribed by *FASB Statement No. 12*, "Investments in Certain Marketable Securities."

Remember that a subsidiary, as a separate legal entity, must follow generally accepted accounting principles without regard to the fact that it is a subsidiary. Many subsidiaries must issue separate financial statements pursuant to loan indenture agreements. When contingent consideration based on the subsidiary's postcombination sales or earnings amounts is a provision of the business combination agreement, separate audited financial statements are often required.

Accounting in Consolidation

The subsidiary's method of accounting for its investment in the parent when preparing consolidated financial statements is prescribed by *ARB No. 51* as follows:

> Shares of the parent held by a subsidiary should not be treated as outstanding stock in the consolidated balance sheet.[1]

If the parent had acquired its own shares, then the cost would be treated as a cost of treasury shares. But the parent directed the subsidiary

[1]*Accounting Research Bulletin No. 51*, "Consolidated Financial Statements" (New York: American Institute for Certified Public Accountants, 1959), par. 13.

to acquire the shares, which is usually the way such investments are made. If the subsidiary is wholly owned, this treatment makes sense. However, if the subsidiary is partially owned, the requirement to treat all of the shares it owns as not outstanding ignores the reality that the subsidiary's minority shareholders are indirectly shareholders of the parent. This requirement can cause a misleading earnings-per-share amount to be reported, as demonstrated later in the chapter.

This requirement of *ARB No. 51*, therefore, means that in consolidation the cost of the investment in the parent's common stock is treated as a cost of treasury shares. Accordingly, a reclassification must be made in the balance sheet section of the consolidating statement worksheet as follows:

Cost of Treasury Stock	xxx	
Investment in Parent Company's Common Stock...		xxx

When a subsidiary has lowered the carrying value of its investment in its parent through a valuation allowance, the offsetting charge to its stockholders' equity section (required under *FASB Statement No. 12*) must be reclassified in consolidation as part of the total cost of the treasury shares. Until the subsidiary disposes of some or all of its investment in its parent, the balance of the cost of the treasury shares, as reported in the consolidated financial statements, remains unchanged.

When a subsidiary is wholly owned, consolidated net income is the sum of (1) the parent's earnings from its own operations, exclusive of earnings on its investment in the subsidiary and (2) the subsidiary's earnings from its own operations, exclusive of earnings on its investment in the parent. These situations present no accounting issues in preparing consolidated financial statements.

When a subsidiary is partially owned, the accounting issue is how to report the combined earnings for financial reporting purposes in view of the fact that the subsidiary's minority shareholders are indirectly shareholders of the parent. *ARB No. 51* does not specify the procedures for these situations. Two schools of thought explain how the combined earnings should be reported—one advocating the treasury stock method and the other advocating the traditional allocation method. Each of these methods is best discussed using an example. Assume the following information:

	P Company	S Company
Number of common shares outstanding...	100,000	20,000
Ownership interest in the other:		
Percentage..	70%	10%
Number of shares.................................	14,000	10,000
Net income for the year (from own separate operations, exclusive of earnings on investments in the other)...	$1,000,000	$500,000

The affiliation diagram is as follows:

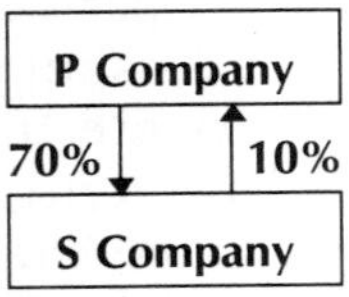

The Treasury Stock Method. The **treasury stock method** essentially comes under the parent-company theory, which is discussed in Chapter 5. Recall that under the parent company theory the parent is the reporting entity. The consolidation process is merely the substitution of the subsidiary's assets and liabilities for the parent's Investment in Subsidiary account. From this perspective, consolidated net income should be the sum of (1) the parent's earnings from its own separate operations, and (2) the parent's share of the subsidiary's earnings from its own separate operations.

From the above information, consolidated net income under this method is $1,350,000 [$1,000,000 + (70% × $500,000)]. Thus, the minority interest deduction is based solely on the percentage of minority interest ownership in the subsidiary's earnings from its own separate operations, exclusive of earnings on its investment in the parent. Thus, the minority interest deduction would be $150,000 (30% of $500,000).

The consolidated net income, therefore, is the amount by which the parent's retained earnings would increase if the subsidiary distributed as dividends all of its earnings from its own separate operations, exclusive of its earnings on its investment in the parent. Dividend distributions to the parent's stockholders are ignored in calculating the amount of this increase. Whether the parent uses the equity method or the cost method to account for its investment in the subsidiary is irrelevant.

When the parent accounts for its investment in the subsidiary under the equity method of accounting, it merely applies its ownership percentage in the subsidiary to the subsidiary's earnings from its own separate operations, not including the subsidiary's earnings on its investment in the parent. In the example, this would be $350,000 (70% of $500,000). As a result, the parent's $1,350,000 recorded net income equals the $1,350,000 consolidated net income.

The amount of earnings per share on a consolidated basis (assuming no other dilutive securities) is computed by dividing the consolidated net income of $1,350,000 by the 90,000 shares deemed outstanding (100,000 shares issued − 10,000 shares held by the subsidiary treated as not outstanding). This computation gives $15 per share. However, treating all 10,000 shares of the parent's stock held by the subsidiary as not outstanding results in a meaningless earnings-per-share amount. If the parent distributed as dividends all of its $1,350,000 consolidated net income, this amount would not be distributed solely to the holders of the

90,000 shares. Because 10,000 shares of the parent's stocks are held by the subsidiary and because the subsidiary is only 70% owned by the parent, the subsidiary's minority shareholders are effectively indirect shareholders of the parent to the extent of 3,000 shares (30% of 10,000). Assume that the subsidiary was liquidated immediately after it distributed as dividends its net income from its own separate operations. The 10,000 shares held as an investment in the parent would be distributed to the subsidiary's shareholders — 7,000 to the parent and 3,000 to the minority shareholders. Thus, the parent's consolidated net income of $1,350,000 would be distributed to holders of 93,000 shares, not 90,000 shares. Dividing $1,350,000 by 93,000 gives $14.52 per share. In terms of dollars, the holders of the 90,000 shares would receive $1,306,452 (90,000 ÷ 93,000) of the consolidated net income of $1,350,000. The minority interest shareholders would receive $43,548 (3,000 ÷ 93,000) of the $1,350,000 consolidated net income. The $14.52 earnings-per-share amount is therefore more meaningful.

The Traditional Allocation Method. The **traditional allocation method** essentially comes under the entity theory, which is discussed in Chapter 5. Recall that under the entity theory a "new reporting entity" is deemed to exist as a result of consolidation. This new reporting entity has two classes of shareholders:

1. The controlling interests (in the example, holders of 90,000 shares of the parent's outstanding common stock).
2. The subsidiary's minority shareholders (who indirectly own 3,000 shares of the parent's outstanding common stock in the example).

From this perspective, the combined earnings of the parent and the subsidiary should appear in the consolidated income statement so that the amount that accrues to each class of shareholders is shown. As demonstrated in the discussion of the treasury stock method, the holders of the 90,000 shares are entitled to $1,306,452 of the combined earnings of $1,500,000 ($1,000,000 + $500,000), and the minority shareholders are entitled to $193,548. The amount that accrues to the minority shareholders can be thought of as comprising two amounts, as follows:

1. The minority shareholders' interest in the subsidiary's earnings from its own separate operations, exclusive of earnings from its investment in the parent (30% of $500,000)		$150,000
2. The minority shareholders' interest in:		
a. The parent's earnings from its separate operations	$1,000,000	
b. The parent's share of the subsidiary's earnings of $500,000 from its own separate operations (70% of $500,000)	350,000	
	$1,350,000	

As shown in the discussion of the treasury stock method, the minority interest in these amounts is in the ratio of 3,000 shares to 93,000 shares (3,000 ÷ 93,000) × $1,350,000 =	43,548
Portion of combined earnings that accrues to the minority shareholders	$193,548

Recall from Chapter 5 that under the entity theory, the combined earnings of the parent and the subsidiary are presented in the consolidated income statement as follows:

Earnings accruing to controlling interests	**$1,306,452**
Earnings accruing to minority interests	**193,548**
Consolidated Net Income	**$1,500,000**

Some accountants advocate an alternative presentation that deducts the amount accruing to the minority interests from the combined earnings of $1,500,000 to arrive at a consolidated net income of $1,306,452. This presentation is inconsistent with the underlying premise of the traditional allocation method, in which the parent is not viewed as the reporting entity.

Reporting the combined earnings using either of these manners of presentation is obviously inconsistent with the equity method of accounting and the amount reported as consolidated net income. In a strict application of the equity method, the parent would record $350,000 as its share of the subsidiary's earnings (70% of $500,000). Thus, the parent's net income under the equity method would be $1,350,000, which is not reported using either of the above methods of presenting the combined earnings.

The amount of earnings per share on a consolidated basis (assuming no other dilutive securities) is computed by dividing the $1,306,452 earnings that accrue to the controlling interests by 90,000 shares deemed outstanding (100,000 shares issued − 10,000 shares held by the subsidiary treated as not outstanding). This computation gives $14.52 per share, which is a meaningful amount to the holders of the 90,000 shares. (The same earnings-per-share amount was calculated under the treasury stock approach using 93,000 as the denominator.)

Mathematically, the amount of the combined earnings that accrues to each class of shareholders is usually determined under this approach using simultaneous equations. In Illustration 11-6, the data from the example in this section are used with simultaneous equations to arrive at these amounts.

Whether to use the treasury stock method or the traditional allocation method depends on whether the parent company theory or the entity theory produces the more meaningful form of reported combined earnings. This purely subjective evaluation is based on whether or not the reporting entity is transformed into a new reporting entity by the consolidation pro-

Illustration 11-6
Application of Simultaneous Equations to Traditional Allocation Method

Let P equal P Company's net income from its own separate operations plus its share of S Company's net income that would accrue to it on S Company's liquidation. Let S equal S Company's net income from its own separate operations plus its share of P Company's net income that would accrue to it on P Company's liquidation. Thus:

$$P = \$1,000,000 + (.70 \times S)$$
$$S = \$500,000 + (.10 \times P)$$

Substituting for P:

$$S = \$500,000 + .10(\$1,000,000 + .70 \times S)$$
$$S = \$500,000 + \$100,000 + 0.07S$$
$$0.93S = \$600,000$$
$$S = \$645,161$$

S Company's minority shareholders would be entitled to \$193,548 (30% of \$645,161). Subtracting \$193,548 from the combined earnings of \$1,500,000 gives earnings of \$1,306,452, which accrue to the controlling interests.

Alternatively, the earnings that accrue to the controlling interests can be computed by solving the equation for P by substituting for S as follows:

$$P = \$1,000,000 + .70(\$500,000 + .10 \times P)$$
$$P = \$1,000,000 + \$350,000 + 0.07P$$
$$0.93P = \$1,350,000$$
$$P = \$1,451,613$$

Because P Company's existing shareholders (other than S Company) own 90% of its outstanding common stock, they would be entitled to \$1,306,452 (90% of \$1,451,613) in the event of a double liquidation.

cess. The treasury stock method is widely practiced, whereas the traditional allocation method is not, partly because of the simplicity of the treasury stock method and management's reluctance to treat part of the parent's earnings as accruing to the minority shareholders.

INTERCOMPANY PROFIT ON ASSET TRANSFERS

Regardless of the degree of complexity of the relationship among the entities within the consolidated group, any unrealized profit on intercompany asset transfers cannot be reported in the consolidated financial statements. When the complete equity method (explained in Chapters 7 and 8) is used, any unrealized intercompany profit is deferred in the general ledger or ledgers. Consequently, no special procedures are needed in consolidation merely because of the added complexity of the relationship among the entities within the consolidated group. However, when the partial equity method is used (it was explained in appendices to Chapters 7 and 8), a careful analysis must be made to determine how much of the total unrealized intercompany profit (being deferred *in the consolidation process*) is allocable to the minority interest.

SUMMARY

Indirect vertical holdings are chain holdings in which one company has more than 50% ownership interest in another company; the second company, in turn, has more than 50% ownership interest in a third company. In applying the equity method of accounting to these situations, the lowest-level parent must apply the equity method before it is applied at the next higher level in the chain.

In indirect horizontal holdings, a subsidiary has an ownership interest in another subsidiary of its parent. In applying the equity method of accounting to these situations, the investor-subsidiary must apply the equity method of accounting to its investee's earnings before the parent applies the equity method to the investor-subsidiary's earnings.

Reciprocal holdings are formed when a subsidiary invests in its parent company's common stock. When the subsidiary is partially owned, there are two theories concerning how the combined earnings of the parent and the subsidiary should be presented in the consolidated financial statements: the treasury stock method and the traditional allocation method. Under the treasury stock method, the minority interest deduction is based solely on the subsidiary's earnings from its own separate operations, excluding earnings on its investment in the parent. Under the traditional allocation method, the portion of the combined earnings that accrues to the minority shareholders includes a portion of the parent's earnings from its own separate operations.

Glossary of New Terms

Indirect Horizontal Holdings An intercorporate relationship in which a subsidiary has a common stock investment in another subsidiary of their common parent.

Indirect Vertical Holdings An intercorporate relationship in which a subsidiary has a controlling common stock interest in another company.

Reciprocal Holdings An intercorporate relationship in which two entities of an affiliated group of companies have common stock investments in each other.

Treasury Stock Method A procedure whereby the combined earnings of companies having reciprocal holdings (the controlled company being partially owned) are presented in a manner that portrays the parent as the reporting entity in consolidation. Under this method, the fact that the subsidiary's minority shareholders are indirectly shareholders of the parent is considered irrelevant.

Traditional Allocation Method A procedure whereby the combined earnings of companies having reciprocal holdings (the controlled company being partially owned) are presented in a manner that implies the existence of a new reporting entity from the consolidation process. Under this method, the combined earnings are divided between amounts that accrue to the controlling interests and amounts that accrue to the minority interests, based on their respective interests in the new reporting entity.

Review Questions

1. What is the difference between an indirect vertical holding and an indirect horizontal holding?
2. What are the two methods of accounting for reciprocal holdings?
3. Can a group of affiliated companies simultaneously have indirect vertical holdings, indirect horizontal holdings, and reciprocal holdings?
4. What is the sequence of the consolidation process when indirect vertical holdings exist?
5. What is the sequence of the consolidation process when indirect horizontal holdings exist?
6. How should a subsidiary account for an investment in its parent company?
7. From a consolidated viewpoint, are shares of a parent company that are held by a subsidiary considered issued stock or outstanding stock?
8. How is the cost of a subsidiary's investment in its parent's stock treated in consolidated financial statements?
9. Under the traditional allocation method, is the parent viewed as the reporting entity in consolidation? Why or why not?
10. Under the treasury stock method, why is it misleading to treat all of the parent's common shares held by a partially owned subsidiary as not outstanding when computing consolidated earnings per share?

Discussion Cases

DC 11-1

Reciprocal Holdings: Selection of Accounting Method

During 19X1, Piper Company acquired 80% of Sonoma Company's outstanding common stock, and Sonoma acquired 10% of Piper's outstanding common stock. Piper's top management has indicated to its controller that Sonoma's minority interest shareholders will probably not share in Piper's earnings for many years to come because Piper does not expect to pay any dividends on its common stock inasmuch as it intends to retain earnings for growth.

Required:
Decide whether to use the treasury stock method or the traditional allocation method. How does this dividend policy influence your decision?

DC 11-2

Reciprocal Holdings: Determining Dividends to Be Reported in the Consolidated Statement of Retained Earnings—Treasury Stock Method

Perk Company has an 80%-owned subsidiary that in turn owns 10% of the parent company's outstanding common stock. Perk uses the treasury stock method to determine consolidated net income. It declared and paid cash dividends of $100,000 on its outstanding common stock during 19X1, $10,000 of which went to its subsidiary. Perk's controller is uncertain whether the consolidated statement of retained earnings for 19X1 should show dividends declared of $100,000, $90,000, or $92,000.

Required:
How would you advise the controller?

DC 11-3

Reciprocal Holdings: Theory

Pey Company has a partially owned subsidiary that recently acquired some of Pey's outstanding common stock. You are the staff accountant in charge of preparing the consolidated financial statements for the first year after the reciprocal investment was established. Pey's controller has indicated that you should calculate the minority interest deduction by using the traditional allocation method.

Required:
How would you respond to this instruction?

DC 11-4

Reciprocal Holdings: Ramifications of Dual Intercorporate Control

Proofer Company owns 100% of Storm Company's outstanding common stock. Storm owns 100% of Proofer's outstanding common stock.

Required:
What are the ramifications of such intercorporate holdings?

Exercises

E 11-1

Indirect Vertical Holdings: Cost Equals Book Value of Net Assets

Pargo Company owns 90% of Solomon Company's outstanding common stock, and Solomon Company owns 80% of Tsar Company's outstanding common stock. Each company earned $100,000 during 19X1 from its own operations, exclusive of earnings on its investment in its subsidiary. (Assume there was no cost in excess of or below book value to amortize.)

Required:

1. Determine Pargo's consolidated net income for 19X1 through successive application of the equity method of accounting.
2. Determine the minority interest deduction in Pargo's consolidated income statement for 19X1.
3. Indicate the sequence of the consolidation process.

E 11-2

Indirect Vertical Holdings: Cost Equals Book Value of Net Assets

On January 1, 19X1, Delta Company acquired 80% of the outstanding common stock of Echo Company. On January 1, 19X2, Echo Company acquired 80% of the outstanding common stock of Fox Company. On January 1, 19X3, Pratt Company acquired 75% of the outstanding common stock of Delta Company. Each company's earnings for 19X3 (exclusive of earnings on investments in affiliates) are as follows:

Pratt Company	$400,000
Delta Company	300,000
Echo Company	200,000
Fox Company	100,000

Each company declared cash dividends on its common stock of $10,000 during 19X1, 19X2, and 19X3. (Assume there was no cost in excess of or below book value to amortize.)

Required:

1. Determine the net income of Pratt Company and its subsidiaries for 19X3 through successive application of the equity method of accounting.
2. Determine the total minority interest deduction shown in Pratt's consolidated income statement for 19X3.
3. Indicate the sequence of the consolidation process.

E 11-3

Indirect Horizontal Holdings: Cost Equals Book Value of Net Assets

On January 1, 19X1, Pulse Company acquired 80% of Sound Company's outstanding common stock and 70% of Tape Company's outstanding common stock. On July 1, 19X1, Sound acquired 10% of Tape's outstanding common stock. (Assume all investments were made at a cost equal to the applicable share of net assets at book value.) For 19X2, the following amounts were reported:

	Income from Own Operations (exclusive of earnings on investments in affiliates)	Dividends Declared
Pulse Company	$300,000	$50,000
Sound Company	100,000	20,000
Tape Company	50,000	10,000

Required:

1. Determine the consolidated net income of Pulse Company and its subsidiaries for 19X2 through successive application of the equity method of accounting.
2. Determine the total minority interest deduction shown in Pulse's consolidated income statement for 19X2.
3. Indicate the sequence of the consolidation process.

E 11-4 Several Indirect Horizontal Holdings: Cost Equals Book Value of Net Assets

Potter Company, a nonoperating holding company, is a parent of the following subsidiaries with the indicated ownership percentages:

Subsidiary Company	Ownership Percentage
B	90
C	80
D	70
E	60

In addition, B Company owns 10% of the outstanding common stock of C Company, D Company, and E Company; D Company owns 20% of the outstanding common stock of E Company. (Assume all investments were made at a cost equal to the applicable share of net assets at book value.)

Each company's net income from its own operations (exclusive of earnings on investments in affiliates) is as follows for 19X1:

Potter Company	$ –0–
B Company	10,000,000
C Company	1,000,000
D Company	100,000
E Company	10,000

Required:

1. Determine Potter Company's 19X1 net income through successive application of the equity method of accounting.
2. Determine the total minority interest deduction shown in Potter's consolidated income statement for 19X1.
3. Indicate the sequence of the consolidated process.

E 11-5 Reciprocal Holdings: Parent's Cost Equals Book Value of Net Assets

Premier Company owns 80% of the outstanding common stock of Smidgeon Company, which in turn owns 10% of the outstanding common of Premier. During 19X1, Premier earned $500,000 from its own operations, exclusive of earnings on its investment in Smidgeon. (Assume the cost of the parent company's investment equals its share of the net assets at book value). Smidgeon earned $100,000 from its own separate operations in 19X1. Neither company declared dividends during 19X1.

Required:

1. Compute the consolidated net income and the minority interest deduction for 19X1 under the treasury stock method.
2. Compute the amount of the combined earnings that accrues to the controlling interests and the minority interests for 19X1 under the traditional allocation method.

Problems

P 11-1

Indirect Vertical Holdings: Cost Exceeds Book Value of Net Assets

On January 1, 19X1, Posit Company acquired 80% of Syncron Company's outstanding common stock at a cost of $40,000 in excess of its share of net assets at book value. Assume that this excess is allocable to goodwill, which has a 10-year life.

On January 1, 19X2, Syncron Company acquired 60% of Techna Company's outstanding common stock at a cost of $20,000 in excess of its share of net assets at book value. Assume that this excess is allocable to goodwill, which has a 10-year life.

For 19X2, the companies reported the following:

	Income from Own Operations (exclusive of earnings and amortization on investments in affiliates)	Dividends Declared
Posit Company	$500,000	$100,000
Syncron Company	100,000	50,000
Techna Company	20,000	10,000

Required:

1. Determine the consolidated net income of Posit Company and its subsidiaries for 19X2 through successive application of the equity method of accounting.
2. Determine the total minority interest deduction shown in Posit's consolidated income statement for 19X2.
3. Indicate the sequence of the consolidation process.

P 11-2

Indirect Horizontal Holdings: Cost Exceeds Book Value of Net Assets

On January 1, 19X1, Packager Company acquired 80% of Shipper Company's outstanding common stock at a cost of $100,000 in excess of its share of net assets at book value. Assume that this excess is allocable to goodwill, which has an estimated 20-year life.

On January 1, 19X2, Packager acquired 65% of Tender Company's outstanding common stock at a cost of $20,000 in excess of its share of net assets at book value. Assume that this excess is allocable to goodwill, which has an estimated 10-year life.

On January 1, 19X3, Shipper acquired 20% of Tender's outstanding common stock at a cost of $5,000 in excess of its share of net assets at book value. Assume that this excess is allocable to goodwill, which has an estimated 10-year life.

Each company reported the following amounts during 19X3:

	Income from Own Operations (excluding income and amortization on investments in affiliates)	Dividends Declared
Packager Company	$1,000,000	$500,000
Shipper Company	100,000	50,000
Tender Company	10,000	5,000

Required:

1. Determine the amount of consolidated net income for Packager Company and its subsidiaries for 19X3 through successive application of the equity method of accounting.
2. Determine the total minority interest deduction shown in Packager's consolidated income statement for 19X3.
3. Indicate the sequence of the consolidation process.

P 11-3

Indirect Horizontal Holdings: Cost Exceeds Book Value of Net Assets

On January 1, 19X1, Polar Bank acquired 80% of the outstanding common stock of Solar Savings and 70% of the outstanding common stock of Tanner Trust. On January 2, 19X1, Solar acquired 20% of Tanner's outstanding common stock. The analysis of the investment accounts by the components of the major conceptual elements for each acquisition at the acquisition date is as follows:

	Polar's Investment		Solar's Investment
	Solar	Tanner	Tanner
Book value element:			
Common stock	$ 16,000	$ 7,000	$ 2,000
Additional paid-in capital	144,000	63,000	18,000
Retained earnings	40,000	21,000	6,000
Current value over book value element:			
Land	20,000	7,000	4,000
Goodwill element	40,000	10,000	5,000
Total Cost	$260,000	$108,000	$35,000

Assume goodwill has a five-year life from the purchase date. Data for 19X1 for each company are as follows:

	Income from Own Operations (exclusive of earnings and amortization on investments in affiliates)	Quarterly Dividends Declared
Polar	$600,000	$100,000
Solar	80,000	30,000
Tanner	40,000	10,000

Assume earnings for each company occurred evenly during the year.

Required:

1. Calculate the amount of Polar's consolidated net income for 19X1 through successive application of the equity method of accounting.
2. Determine the minority interest deduction shown in Polar's consolidated income statement for 19X1.
3. Indicate the sequence of the consolidation process.

P 11-4

Reciprocal Holdings: Parent's Cost Exceeds Book Value of Net Assets

Picolo Company owns 90% of Sayers Company's outstanding common stock. In turn, Sayers owns 10% of Picolo's outstanding common stock. Data for each company for 19X1 are as follows:

	Income from Own Operations (exclusive of earnings on investments in affiliates)	Dividends Declared
Picolo Company	$800,000	$200,000
Sayers Company	100,000	30,000

In addition, Picolo had $12,000 amortization of cost in excess of book value during 19X1, which is not reflected in its separate earnings of $800,000.

Required:

1. Calculate the consolidated net income and the minority interest deduction for 19X1 using the treasury stock method.
2. Calculate the amount of combined earnings that accrues to the controlling interests and the minority interests under the traditional allocation method.

P 11-5

CHALLENGER Reciprocal Holdings: Parent's Cost Exceeds Book Value; Preparing Consolidated Statement of Retained Earnings in Year Subsequent to Acquisition

Perigee Company acquired 60% of Syzygy Company's outstanding common stock on January 1, 19X1. On January 2, 19X1, Syzygy acquired 10% of Perigee's outstanding common stock. Data for each company for 19X1 are as follows:

	Perigee Company	Syzygy Company
Retained earnings, January 1, 19X1	$900,000	$300,000
Income from own operations for 19X1, exclusive of earnings on investments in affiliates and amortization of cost in excess of book value	400,000	100,000
Amortization of cost in excess of book value	10,000	
Dividends declared in 19X1	150,000	30,000
Common shares outstanding	100,000	20,000

Required:

1. Calculate the consolidated net income and the minority interest deduction for 19X1 under the treasury stock method.
2. Prepare a consolidated statement of retained earnings for 19X1 assuming that the parent uses the treasury stock method.
3. Calculate the amount of combined earnings that accrues to the controlling interests and the minority interests for 19X1 under the traditional allocation method.
4. Prepare a consolidated statement of retained earnings for 19X1 assuming the parent uses the traditional allocation method.

P 11-6

Indirect Vertical Holdings: Intercompany Inventory Profit in Ending Inventory from Upstream Sale

Peter Company acquired 75% of Steven Company's outstanding common stock on January 1, 19X1, and Steven acquired 80% of Theo Company's outstanding common stock on January 1, 19X2. The cost of these acquisitions was at the applicable percentage of net assets at book value.

During 19X2, each company reported $100,000 of income (after income taxes) from its own operations, exclusive of earnings on investments in affiliates. At December 31, 19X2, Steven's ending inventory included merchandise it had acquired from Theo at a cost of $50,000. Theo's cost was $30,000.

Required:

1. Determine the consolidated net income that Steven Company reports to its parent company for 19X2 through successive application of the equity method of accounting.
2. Determine the consolidated net income that Peter reports to its stockholders for 19X2 through successive application of the equity method of accounting.
3. Determine the total minority interest deduction for 19X2.

12

Income Taxes and Earnings per Share

Income Taxes

In the first section of this chapter we discuss accounting for income taxes for financial reporting purposes related to parent company investments in both domestic and foreign subsidiaries.

In late 1986, the Financial Accounting Standards Board issued a Proposed Statement of Financial Accounting Standards, "Accounting for Income Taxes" (dated September 2, 1986), which when finalized will supersede *APB Opinion No. 11*, "Accounting for Income Taxes," and *APB Opinion No. 23*, "Accounting for Income Taxes—Special Areas." In addition, several other pronouncements (including *APB Opinion No. 16*, "Business Combination") will be superseded or amended. As this book goes to print, the FASB has announced that it has tentatively reversed its position with respect to only one aspect of this proposed statement (which aspect we must deal with later in the chapter). The final statement is expected to be issued in late 1987. Accordingly, we have based our discussion of income taxes in this chapter on this proposed statement. Because passage of this proposed statement is a virtual certainty, we have chosen to refer to this proposed statement as *FASB Proposed Statement No. 00* (no number had been assigned at the time this chapter went to print). When the statement has passed, the word *proposed* should be deleted and a number substituted for the *00*.

AN OVERVIEW OF THE ISSUES AND GOVERNING PRONOUNCEMENTS

Purchase Business Combination

For purchase business combinations (as distinct from pooling of interests business combinations), the issue is whether or not deferred taxes should be recorded at the combination date for differences between the assigned values of assets and liabilities of the acquired business and the tax basis of those assets and liabilities. *FASB Proposed Statement No. 00* will amend paragraphs 87 to 89 of *Accounting Principles Board Opinion No. 16*, such that deferred income taxes must be recorded for these differences.

Earnings of Subsidiaries

For income tax reporting purposes, investor companies must pay income taxes on dividends *received* from investee companies. (Some exceptions to this requirement are discussed later in the chapter.) In this respect, the income tax rules are on the cash basis. The financial reporting issue is determining whether investor companies should record such income taxes in their books on the cash basis (consistent with income tax reporting) or on the accrual basis, whereby income taxes on an investor's share of an investee's net income are recorded in the year the investee reports its earnings. *FASB Proposed Statement No. 00* requires income taxes to be recorded on the accrual basis.

RECOGNIZING DEFERRED TAXES AT THE DATE OF THE BUSINESS COMBINATION

To properly account for income taxes on the accrual basis, *FASB Proposed Statement No. 00* takes the position that the tax consequences of an event must be recognized in the same period in which the event is recognized in the financial statements. For purchase business combinations, differences between the assigned values of assets and liabilities and the tax bases of those assets and liabilities will result in taxable or tax deductible amounts when the asset or liability in the financial statements is later recovered or settled at its reported amount. Under *FASB Proposed Statement No. 00*, a deferred tax liability or asset is to be recognized for such differences. (Goodwill and unextinguished bargain purchase elements are excluded from this requirement.)[1]

Taxable versus Nontaxable Purchase Business Combinations

Recall from Chapter 2 that most purchase business combinations are taxable combinations for tax reporting purposes; only a minor percentage are nontaxable (tax-deferred). Differences between the assigned values of assets and liabilities and the tax bases of those assets and liabilities nearly always exist in nontaxable purchase business combinations. For taxable purchase business combinations, however, such differences are the exception rather than the rule. This is because the acquiring entity assigns its purchase price to the assets and liabilities of the target company for both financial reporting and tax reporting purposes. (For this assignment to be done for tax purposes when common stock is acquired, the parent would have to make an election under Section 338 of the Internal Revenue Code, as explained on page 481, to step up the bases of the subsidiary's assets based on the purchase price.) The following section shows how deferred taxes are recognized in nontaxable purchase business combinations.

Nontaxable Purchase Business Combinations: The Acquired Business Has No Deferred Tax Accounts at the Combination Date

Assume that P Company and S Company's stockholders entered into a nontaxable purchase business combination on January 1, 19X1. Other assumptions follow:

[1]*Proposed Statement of Financial Accounting Standards [No. 00]*, "Accounting for Income Taxes" (Stamford: Financial Accounting Standards Board, September 2, 1986), par. 20.

1. P Company issued 1,000 shares of its $1 par value common stock, which has a market value of $90,000.
2. The book value of S Company's assets is $250,000, and the book value of its liabilities is $190,000. Thus the book value of the net assets is $60,000.
3. The book values of S Company's assets and liabilities are equal to their tax bases. Thus no deferred tax liability or asset accounts exist on S Company's books at the combination date.
4. S Company's assets have a current value of $20,000 in excess of their book values.
5. The enacted income tax rate for future years is 40%.

Because of the temporary difference of $20,000 between the assigned values of the assets and their tax bases, a deferred tax liability of $8,000 ($20,000 × 40%) must be recognized in recording the business combination. Illustration 12-1 presents the entries that would be made assuming that the assets are acquired (part 1) and the common stock is acquired (part 2). The analysis of the investment by its major conceptual elements is also shown for the latter situation.

Nontaxable Purchase Business Combinations: The Acquired Business Has a Deferred Tax Liability at the Combination Date

Based on the facts in the preceding illustration, let us assume that: (a) the acquired business has used accelerated depreciation for income tax report-

Illustration 12-1
Nontaxable Purchase Business Combination: The Acquired Business Has No Deferred Tax Accounts at the Combination Date

1. **Acquisition of Assets:**		
Assets ($250,000 + $20,000)	270,000	
Liabilities		190,000
Deferred Tax Liabilitity		8,000
Common Stock (1,000 shares × $1)		1,000
Additional Paid-in Capital		89,000
Goodwill (residual amount)	18,000	
2. **Acquisition of Common Stock:**		
Investment in Subsidiary	90,000	
Common Stock (1,000 shares × $1)		1,000
Additional Paid-in Capital		89,000

Conceptual Analysis of Investment Account by Major Conceptual Elements:

				Current Value over (under) Book Value Element				
Total Cost	=	Book Value Element	+	Various Assets	+	Deferred Tax Liability	+	Goodwill Element
$90,000		$60,000		$20,000		$(8,000)		$18,000

ing purposes; and (b) the acquired business has a $4,000 deferred tax liability on its books at the combination as a result of having deducted $10,000 more depreciation expense for tax purposes than for financial reporting purposes. Accordingly, there is a $30,000 difference between the assigned values and the tax bases of the assets. Thus a $12,000 deferred tax liability needs to be recognized at the combination date ($30,000 × 40%). However, because of the deferred tax situation, the target company would have $4,000 of additional assets in addition to the deferred tax liability of $4,000. In comparison to Illustration 12-1, in which the target company had no deferred tax liability, the only change would be in the acquisition of assets section. That is, the assets would be debited for an additional $4,000 ($274,000 instead of $270,000), and the Deferred Tax Liability account would be credited an additional $4,000 ($12,000 rather than $8,000).

RECORDING INCOME TAXES ON EARNINGS OF SUBSIDIARIES

Consolidated Income Tax Return Situations

A parent company and its **domestic** subsidiaries may file a consolidated federal income tax return if the parent owns directly or indirectly at least 80% of both the voting power of all classes of stock of each subsidiary and the value of all classes of stock of each subsidiary included in the consolidated return. (At least one subsidiary must be at least 80% directly owned by the parent.)[2] Filing a consolidated income tax return relieves each subsidiary of the responsibility of filing a separate federal income tax return.

Advantages of Consolidated Returns. Preparing a consolidated federal tax return is similar to preparing a consolidated income statement for financial reporting purposes. Often only an appropriate adjustment is needed to the consolidated income statement that was prepared for financial reporting purposes to arrive at consolidated taxable income. The two preparations are similar in other ways as well:

1. Losses of companies within the consolidated group that do not generate profits can offset the earnings of the other members of the consolidated group.
2. Intercompany profits and losses recorded on the sale of assets between entities are deferred until such assets are either sold (for inventory transfers) or depreciation occurs (for equipment transfers).
3. Intercompany dividends are **not taxable** to the parent at all. However, when a **domestic** subsidiary files a separate federal income tax return, dividends paid by a subsidiary to its parent **are taxable** to the parent. (However, an 80% "dividends received deduction" is allowed; thus, only 20% of the dividend is taxed.)

[2]The detailed requirements are set forth in the U.S. Internal Revenue Code of 1954, Sec. 1504(a).

Implications of Consolidated Tax Returns for Financial Reporting. The obvious implication for financial reporting purposes of a consolidated income tax return is that no income taxes need to be recorded by a parent with respect to the subsidiary's **net income.** This holds true whether or not the subsidiary actually makes dividend payments to the parent. Thus, from a consolidated viewpoint, these situations involve no accounting issues. From a separate-company viewpoint, the total consolidated income tax expense must be allocated among the companies included in the consolidated income tax return. For subsidiaries included in consolidated tax returns that issue separate financial statements, *FASB Proposed Statement No. 00* requires the following disclosures:

a. The amount of current and deferred tax expense for each income statement presented and the amount of any tax-related balances due to or from affiliates as of the date of each balance sheet presented.
b. The principal provisions of the method by which the consolidated amount of current and deferred tax expenses is allocated to members of the consolidated group and the nature and effect of any changes in that method (and in determining related balances to or from affiliates) during the years for which the disclosures in (a) above are presented.[3]

The following section focuses on situations in which subsidiaries file separate federal income tax returns. These situations involve accounting issues from a consolidated viewpoint.

Separate Income Tax Returns

The Accounting Issue. Subsidiaries that file separate federal income tax returns record the income taxes they will pay individually. Parent companies include in their tax return only **dividends received** from their subsidiaries, not their full share of subsidiary earnings. The accounting issue is determining if and when income taxes should be recorded by the parent on the subsidiary's **net income** for financial reporting purposes. There are two obvious possibilities:

1. Under the **cash basis,** income taxes are recorded in **the year in which the parent receives the dividends.** Thus, for a wholly owned domestic subsidiary with net income of $300,000 and paying dividends of $100,000 in a given year, the parent would record income taxes of $8,000, assuming a 40% income tax rate and the application of the 80% dividends received deduction [.40(1 − 0.80) × $100,000]. No income taxes would be recorded on the undistributed earnings of $200,000. (Of course, under the equity method of accounting, the parent would record $300,000 earnings.)

[3]*FASB Proposed Statement No. 00*, par. 26.

2. Under the **accrual basis,** income taxes are recorded in **the year in which the subsidiary reports income,** rather than the year in which it pays dividends. Timing differences result between financial reporting and tax reporting when current earnings are not distributed. Compared with the preceding example using the cash basis, the parent would record income taxes of $24,000 under the accrual approach [.40(1 − 0.80) × $300,000]. (Although the 80% dividends received deduction is an income tax provision applicable only to dividends actually received, we apply the concept to the full $300,000 of earnings in computing income tax expense for financial reporting purposes, not just to the $100,000 of dividends actually received. Hereafter, for financial reporting purposes, we refer to the 80% dividends received deduction as the 80% **dividend exclusion** to signify that the 80% is not applied solely to dividends received.)

To be consistent with the accrual basis of accounting, the apparent solution would have the parent record any required federal income taxes in the period in which the subsidiary reports the income. This is the approach adopted in *FASB Proposed Statement No. 00. FASB Proposed Statement No. 00,* as issued, would have eliminated a loophole available in *APB Opinion No. 23,* "Accounting for Income Taxes—Special Areas," whereby the parent does not have to provide income taxes on earnings of its subsidiaries when a certain condition is met. After a public hearing on the proposed statement was held in early 1987, the FASB decided to tentatively reverse its position in this respect. Because the final pronouncement will be modified in this respect, we must refer to *APB Opinion No. 23* in discussing this condition.

Tax-free Liquidations. U.S. federal income tax laws allow a subsidiary to remit its undistributed earnings to its parent in a tax-free liquidation, providing certain conditions are met. Under both *FASB Proposed Statement No. 00* (par. 46) and *APB Opinion No. 23,* a parent need not provide income taxes on such earnings if the earnings could be remitted tax-free.

Requirements of *APB Opinion No. 23.* Under *APB Opinion No. 23,* parent companies must provide income taxes on their share of their subsidiaries' net incomes unless evidence shows that **some** or **all** of the undistributed subsidiary earnings have been or will be invested indefinitely.[4] If this condition is satisfied, the parent records no income taxes on the applicable portion of the undistributed subsidiary earnings. Appropriate income taxes must always be recorded on subsidiary earnings that are distributed or are expected to be distributed. (Calculations are shown later in the chapter.) Note that *indefinitely* does not mean permanently. In other words, parent companies are not required to invest the undis-

[4]*Opinions of the Accounting Principles Board, No. 23,* "Accounting for Income Taxes—Special Areas" (New York: American Institute of Certified Public Accountants, 1972), par. 12.

tributed earnings of their subsidiaries forever—only for the forseeable future. Two examples of evidence required to satisfy this condition are **experience** and **future programs of operations.**[5]

In essence, the parent records income taxes only to the extent that their payment is reasonably expected. Thus, in addition to the extreme cases of either 100% reinvestment on an indefinite basis, or no intention to reinvest any earnings on an indefinite basis, possible hybrid situations exist in which a percentage of current earnings has been or is expected to be distributed as dividends and the remainder is reinvested indefinitely. With respect to changing circumstances, the pronouncement states:

> [1] If circumstances change and it becomes apparent that some or all of the undistributed earnings of a subsidiary will be remitted in the foreseeable future but income taxes have not been recognized by the parent company, it should accrue as an expense of the current-period income taxes attributable to that remittance; income tax expense for such remittance should not be accounted for as as an extraordinary item.
>
> [2] If it becomes apparent that some or all of the undistributed earnings of a subsidiary on which income taxes have been accrued will not be remitted in the foreseeable future, the parent company should adjust income tax expense of the current period; such adjustment of income tax expense should not be accounted for as an extraordinary item.[6]

Situation 1 typically occurs when a parent company anticipates either: (a) a significant decrease in the direct exchange rate of the currency of the country in which its subsidiary is located (whether from an expected weakening of the foreign currency or a strengthening of the dollar); or (b) the foreign government's imposition of currency transfer restrictions. Situation 2 typically occurs during a continuing increase in the direct exchange rate of the currency of the country in which the subsidiary is located or when the foreign government encourages the expansion of existing operations by granting inducements.

Rationale of *APB Opinion No. 23.* The rationale of *APB Opinion No. 23* is that a subsidiary may not distribute all of its earnings because funds are needed to finance internal growth. This situation is most common for newly established foreign subsidiaries, when parent companies desire to limit the amount of equity capital the subsidiary obtains directly from the parent. Thus, the parent views all or a large portion of the subsidiary's retained earnings as *permanent capital.* From this viewpoint, no U.S. income

[5] *APB Opinion No. 23*, par. 12.
[6] *APB Opinion No. 23*, par. 12.

taxes would ever be paid on the amount deemed permanent capital, because it would never be distributed as dividends. Consequently, the parent would not record any income taxes on that portion of a subsidiary's earnings that is invested in the subsidiary indefinitely.

Domestic versus Foreign Subsidiaries. When income taxes are to be recorded on earnings of subsidiaries, the calculation of income taxes is different for a domestic subsidiary than for a foreign subsidiary. The following sections illustrate these separate calculations.

Computing and Recording Income Taxes for Domestic Subsidiaries. Income taxes recorded on the parent's equity in a domestic subsidiary's net income are calculated using the 80% dividend exclusion. For a 90%-owned subsidiary with net income of $100,000, the calculation is as follows:

Net income of subsidiary	$100,000
Parent's ownership percentage	90%
Parent's equity in earnings of subsidiary	$ 90,000
Less—Dividend exclusion @ 80%	72,000
Net income subject to taxation	$ 18,000
Assumed income tax rate	40%
Income taxes	$ 7,200

To the extent that all of the current earnings are not distributed in the current year, timing differences result, and the Deferred Tax Liability account must be credited for the income taxes relating to the undistributed current earnings. Assuming the subsidiary paid total dividends of $25,000 (25% of its net income) during the year, the parent company's entries with respect to the subsidiary's operations for the year are as follows:

1. To record equity in earnings of subsidiary:

Investment in Subsidiary	90,000	
Equity in Net Income of Subsidiary		90,000
(90% of $100,000)		

2. To record dividend received from subsidiary:

Cash	22,500	
Investment in Subsidiary		22,500
(90% of $25,000)		

3. To record income tax expense on equity in earnings of subsidiary:

Income Tax Expense	7,200	
Income Taxes Currently Payable [($22,500 ÷ $90,000) × $7,200]		1,800
Deferred Tax Liability [($67,500 ÷ $90,000) × $7,200]		5,400

An Overview of Tax Rules for Foreign Subsidiaries. A foreign subsidiary files an income tax return in the country in which it is domiciled (that is, where incorporated). Dividends paid to a U.S. parent are not eligible for the 80% dividends received deduction. However, the parent pays U.S. federal income taxes on these dividends only if the subsidiary's foreign income tax credits cannot offset amounts otherwise payable to the U.S. government. For foreign subsidiaries, the income taxes recorded on the parent's equity in the subsidiary's net income are calculated as follows:

1. The subsidiary's net income is irrelevant; instead, the subsidiary's pretax income is treated as though it had been earned in the United States.
2. U.S. income taxes are calculated on this foreign pretax income using regular income tax rates.
3. Foreign tax credits are subtracted from the taxes calculated in step 2. If a positive balance exists, then that amount of U.S. income tax is payable. If a zero or negative balance exists, no U.S. income tax is payable. There are two kinds of foreign tax credits:
   a. Foreign income taxes.
   b. Dividend withholding taxes. These taxes are withheld by the foreign government when a dividend is remitted.

A table of statutory income tax rates for several countries appears in Illustration 12-2.

In addition to any U.S. income taxes, the parent must record on its books the dividend withholding tax payable. The dividend withholding tax is a tax to the recipient; accordingly, it is never recorded as an expense on the foreign subsidiary's books.

Computing and Recording Income Taxes for Foreign Subsidiaries. The following examples show how to calculate and record income taxes on earnings of foreign subsidiaries:

	Country A	Country B
Assumed foreign income tax rate	20%	50%
Assumed foreign dividend withholding rate	10%	15%
Foreign subsidiary's pretax income	$200,000	$200,000
Foreign income tax expense	(40,000)	(100,000)
Foreign subsidiary's net income	$160,000	$100,000

Illustration 12-2
Examples of Foreign Income Tax Rates

	Statutory Income Tax Rate[a] (percent)	Dividend Withholding Tax Rate[b] (percent)
Brazil	25–40	25
Canada		
Manufacturing	30	15
Other	36	15
France	50	5–15
Ireland (Republic of)		
Manufacturing	10	None
Other	50	None
Italy	36	5–30
Japan	46–56	10–15
Mexico	25–42	21
Switzerland	23–36	5–15
United Kingdom	40–52	None
United States	15–34	15–30
Venezuela	50	15
West Germany	36–56	15–25

Source: Latest available published statutory rates.

[a]For countries that have a range of income tax rates indicated, the exact rate is a function of one or more of the following factors: amount of income, amount of capitalization, whether earnings are distributed or retained, type of business, and whether the corporation is a resident or nonresident company.
[b]For foreign countries, the withholding tax rate indicated is that existing under tax treaties with the United States.

	Country A	Country B
U.S. income taxes at assumed rate of 34% on pretax income	**$ 68,000**	**$ 68,000**
Less foreign tax credits:		
Foreign income taxes (as above)	**(40,000)**	**(100,000)**
Dividend withholding taxes (10% and 15%, respectively, of subsidiary's net income)	**(16,000)**	**(15,000)**
U.S. income taxes recorded by the parent company	**$ 12,000**	**$ –0–**

Timing differences result when all current earnings are not distributed in the current year, and the Deferred Tax Liability account must be credited for taxes on the undistributed current earnings. Assuming each subsidiary paid $20,000 total dividends during the year (one-eighth and one-fifth of their respective net incomes), the parent's entries with respect to each subsidiary's operations for the year are as follows:

1. To record equity in earnings of subsidiary:

Investment in Subsidiary............	**160,000**		**100,000**	
Equity in Net Income of Subsidiary..................		**160,000**		**100,000**
(100% of $160,000 and $100,000, respectively.)				

2. To record the dividend withholding tax:

Income Tax Expense...................	**16,000**		**15,000**	
Income Taxes Payable—Foreign (1/8 and 1/5, respectively)...................		**2,000**		**3,000**
Deferred Tax Liability—Foreign (7/8 and 4/5, respectively)..................		**14,000**		**12,000**
(100% of $16,000 and $15,000, respectively.)				

3. To record dividend received from subsidiary:

Cash...	**18,000**		**17,000**	
Income Taxes Payable—Foreign..	**2,000**		**3,000**	
Investment in Subsidiary....		**20,000**		**20,000**

Note: Income taxes payable equal the taxes withheld at the time of remittance.

4. To record U.S. income taxes on equity in earnings of subsidiary:

Income Tax Expense...................	**12,000**	
Income Taxes Payable—U.S.		**1,500**
Deferred Tax Liability—U.S.		**10,500**
(1/8 and 7/8, respectively.)		

The greater the foreign income tax and dividend withholding tax rates, the greater are the credits against the U.S. income taxes otherwise payable. The preceding examples assume no limitations on the credit amount allowable against these taxes. However, on a per-country and an overall basis, the Internal Revenue Code does limit the credit amount allowable against U.S. income taxes otherwise payable. The specific limitations are beyond the scope of this text, but students should be aware that they exist.

TAX TREATMENT OF PARENT'S AMORTIZATION OF COST ABOVE OR BELOW ITS INTEREST IN SUBSIDIARY'S NET ASSETS AT BOOK VALUE

Chapters 4 and 5 illustrated the amortization procedures appropriate for that portion of a parent's cost that is in excess of or below its interest in the subsidiary's net assets at book value. (Recall that this occurs only under the non-push-down basis of accounting.) For income tax reporting purposes, the amortization of cost in excess of book value (which is recorded in the parent's general ledger) is not tax deductible. This holds true even though some amortization relates to depreciable, tangible assets. Likewise, when a parent's cost is below book value, the amortization (which is a credit to income in these situations) is not taxable.

However, under Section 338 of the Internal Revenue Code, an acquiring company in a taxable transaction may treat the acquisition of a target company's common stock as an asset purchase. If it does, the tax basis of the target company's assets is "stepped up" based on the purchase cost of the target company's common stock, just as though the assets had been acquired instead of common stock. (In substance, this is nothing more than applying push-down accounting for tax reporting purposes.) From a consolidated viewpoint, the end result is as though the parent's cost in excess of book value were tax deductible. (Note that it is the *subsidiary* that receives greater depreciation and amortization deductions—not the parent. The parent's cost of the investment in the subsidiary becomes the tax basis of its common stock investment in the subsidiary.)

Section 338 also includes the following requirements:

- The subsidiary must be 80% owned. (The 80% ownership level must have been obtained within a 12-month period.)
- The election must be made within 75 days after obtaining 80% ownership of the target company's common stock.
- Amounts assigned to goodwill are not tax deductible.

It would be simpler for the parent to acquire the assets rather than the common stock. Recall from Chapter 2, however, that there may be certain nontax reasons for not doing so.

CALCULATING CONSOLIDATED INCOME TAX EXPENSE

Income tax expense was not shown as a separate line item in the consolidating statement worksheet illustrations in Chapters 4 to 11. For the sake of simplicity, the tax expense was assumed to be included in the Expenses account in the worksheets. However, this is not the customary practice. Illustration 12-3 shows a consolidating statement worksheet with the income tax expense included as a separate line item. For simplicity, only one set of eliminations columns is shown. At year-end there is $40,000 of unrealized intercompany profit, which the parent has deferred in its general ledger under the complete equity method. Illustration 12-4 shows the calculation of the income tax expense amounts in Illustration 12-3 for the parent and the subsidiary, the total of which is consolidated income tax expense.

In reviewing Illustration 12-4, recall that the complete equity method was used by the parent. If the partial equity method had been used by the

Illustration 12-3
Consolidating Income Statement Showing Income Tax Expense (Wholly Owned Subsidiary)

P COMPANY AND SUBSIDIARY (S COMPANY)
Consolidating Income Statement
For the Year Ended December 31, 19X5

	P Company	S Company	Eliminations Dr.	Eliminations Cr.	Consolidated
Income Statement:					
Sales	900,000	600,000			1,500,000
Cost of goods sold	(500,000)	(300,000)	35,000(2)	60,000(4)	(775,000)
Expenses	(204,000)	(200,000)			(404,000)
Intercompany Accounts:					
Equity in net income of S Company	70,000		70,000(1)		–0–
Amortization of cost in excess of book value	(35,000)[a]			35,000(2)	–0–
Sales	200,000		200,000(4)		–0–
Cost of goods sold	(100,000)			100,000(4)	–0–
Deferral of profit	(40,000)			40,000(3)	–0–
Income before Taxes	291,000	100,000	305,000	235,000	321,000
Income tax expense	(104,000)[b]	(30,000)[b]			(134,000)
Net Income	187,000	70,000	305,000	235,000	187,000

[a] Illustration 12-4 assumes that $10,000 of this amount pertains to goodwill.
[b] See Illustration 12-4 for the calculation of this amount.

Explanation of entries:
(1) The primary elimination entry.
(2) The secondary elimination entry.
(3) The reversal of the parent's year-end general ledger unrealized intercompany profit entry (made under the complete equity method).
(4) The intercompany sales elimination entry.

Illustration 12-4
Calculation of Consolidated Income Taxes

Assumptions:

1. S Company is a wholly owned domestic subsidiary of P Company. (Thus the 80% dividend exclusion applies.)
2. Parent and subsidiary file separate income tax returns. (Thus unrealized intercompany profit at year-end must still be reported for tax reporting purposes—this will result in a deferred tax asset.)
3. The parent makes a Section 338 election under the Internal Revenue Code, whereby the subsidiary steps up the bases of its assets based on the parent's purchase price. (Thus the subsidiary has additional depreciation and amortization of $25,000; the other $10,000 of amortization of cost in excess of book value is goodwill, which is not deductible for tax reporting purposes resulting in a deferred tax asset.)
4. S Company declared no dividends during 19X5. However, the earnings are **not being reinvested indefinitely.** (Thus income taxes will be recorded by the parent on the earnings of the subsidiary; however, these taxes are not payable currently because no dividends were declared and paid—resulting in a deferred tax liability.)
5. The enacted income tax rate for the current and future years is 40%.

	P Company		S Company
	Tax Reporting	Financial Reporting	Tax and Financial Reporting
Income before income taxes (from Illustration 12-3)	$291,000	$291,000	$100,000
Dividend exclusion:			
($70,000 × 80%)		(56,000)	
($70,000 × 100%)	(70,000)		
Amortization of cost in excess of book value:			
Inventory and equipment.....	25,000	25,000	(25,000)
Goodwill	10,000		
Unrealized intercompany profit at year-end	40,000		
Taxable Income	$296,000	$260,000	$ 75,000
Income tax rate assumed	40%	40%	40%
Income Tax Expense	$118,400	$104,000	$ 30,000

General ledger entries to record income taxes:

	P Company		S Company	
Income Tax Expense	104,000		30,000	
Prepaid Income Taxes [40% of $50,000 ($10,000 and $40,000)]	20,000[a]			
Income Taxes Currently Payable		118,400		30,000
Deferred Tax Liability [40% of $14,000 ($70,000 − $56,000)] ...		5,600[a]		

[a]In the published balance sheet, the prepaid income taxes and the deferred tax liability would be netted and shown as one amount.

parent, its general ledger net income would have been $40,000 more. This would result in the following general ledger income tax entry:

Income Tax Expense....................................	120,000	
Prepaid Income Taxes ($10,000 × 40%)...........	4,000	
Income Taxes Currently Payable............		118,400
Deferred Tax Liability (40% of $14,000)...		5,600

In consolidation, the $40,000 of unrealized intercompany profit would be deferred. In addition, the related income tax effect of $16,000 (40% of $40,000) would also be deferred on the worksheet, as follows:

Prepaid Income Taxes....................................	16,000	
Income Tax Expense..............................		16,000

Earnings Per Share

Fundamentally, consolidated earnings per share is simply consolidated net income (income accruing to the benefit of the parent's shareholders) divided by the average number of the parent company's common shares outstanding (adjusted for the parent's common equivalent shares and its other potentially dilutive securities, if any).

Most subsidiaries are wholly owned and do not have outstanding any potentially dilutive securities such as stock options, warrants, convertible bonds, and convertible preferred stocks. The parent's calculation of earnings per share on a consolidated basis presents no special problems in these cases. To make the calculations, the parent company merely uses the income it has recorded under the equity method of accounting with respect to the subsidiary's earnings, along with the net income from its own operations.

When a subsidiary is partially owned and has no potentially dilutive securities outstanding, the procedures are identical to those in situations in which a subsidiary is wholly owned and has no potentially dilutive securities outstanding. The subsidiary's earnings that accrue to the minority shareholders and the minority interest shares outstanding are excluded in the calculation of consolidated earnings per share.

When a subsidiary has potentially dilutive securities outstanding (whether the subsidiary is wholly owned or partially owned), the above procedures are not proper. A parent company must follow different procedures to determine the amount of a subsidiary's earnings that may be included with a parent company's net income for purposes of computing earnings per share on a consolidated basis.

At this point, students should have a solid understanding of the procedures used to compute earnings per share as discussed in *APB Opinion*

No. 15, "Earnings per Share." This pronouncement is discussed in detail in intermediate accounting texts.

REQUIREMENTS OF *APB OPINION NO. 15*

APB Opinion No. 15 specifies the accounting procedures used to compute earnings per share on a consolidated basis:

> If a subsidiary has dilutive warrants or options outstanding or dilutive convertible securities which are common stock equivalents from the standpoint of the subsidiary, consolidated . . . primary earnings per share should include the portion of the subsidiary's income that would be applicable to the consolidated group based on its holdings and the subsidiary's primary earnings per share.
>
> If a subsidiary's convertible securities are not common stock equivalents from the standpoint of the subsidiary, only the portion of the subsidiary's income that would be applicable to the consolidated group based on its holdings and the fully diluted earnings per share of the subsidiary should be included in consolidated . . . fully diluted earnings per share.[7]

The procedures for determining "the portion of the subsidiary's income that would be applicable to the consolidated group based on its holdings" and the subsidiary's primary and fully diluted earnings per share are explained in the next section.

BASIC APPROACH

When a subsidiary has potentially dilutive securities outstanding, the effect of their potential dilution must be considered when computing earnings per share on a consolidated basis. This is done by substituting an earnings amount (the calculation of which is explained and illustrated later in this chapter) for the subsidiary's earnings that the parent has recorded under the equity method of accounting. The latter amount is usable for calculating consolidated earnings per share only when the subsidiary has no potentially dilutive securities outstanding.

This substitution effectively adjusts the numerator that the parent uses to calculate the primary and fully diluted earnings per share on a consolidated basis. Because this adjustment to the numerator is made only to compute earnings per share, it is accomplished on a worksheet outside the general ledger: the Equity in Earnings of Subsidiary account recorded on the parent company's books is not adjusted.

[7] *Opinions of the Accounting Principles Board, No. 15*, "Earnings per Share" (New York: American Institute of Certified Public Accountants, 1969), par. 66–67.

The denominator that the parent uses to calculate the primary and fully diluted earnings per share on a consolidated basis is determined using only the parent's outstanding common stock and potentially dilutive securities.

To determine how a subsidiary's potentially dilutive securities affect earnings per share on a consolidated basis, the subsidiary must make available to the parent (a) the numerator and denominator used in calculating its own primary earnings per share, and (b) the numerator and denominator used in calculating its fully diluted earnings per share. (The actual earnings per share amounts for the subsidiary are not used for our purposes—only the numerator and denominator used in each calculation are needed.) The numerator represents the earnings for purposes of earnings per share. The objective is to determine how much of this numerator accrues to the parent company so that earnings per share on a consolidated basis can be calculated.

This is done by developing a percentage from the denominator used to compute the subsidiary's earnings per share; this percentage is then applied to the numerator. The percentage is developed from the following ratio:

$$\frac{\text{Number of shares in denominator that are owned by or accrue to the parent}}{\text{Total number of shares in denominator}} = \text{Percentage}$$

This is the percentage of the numerator in the subsidiary's calculations of primary earnings per share and fully diluted earnings per share that accrues to the parent company.

This approach produces the same results as those illustrated in an unofficial accounting interpretation of *APB Opinion No. 15* issued by the American Institute of Certified Public Accountants.[8] However, the illustration in that interpretation uses a different and more involved mechanical procedure than the one illustrated here.

A COMPREHENSIVE ILLUSTRATION

Computing Earnings per Share on a Consolidated Basis when Subsidiary Has Potentially Dilutive Securities Outstanding

Assume the following information with respect to P Company and its 90%-owned subsidiary, S Company, for 19X1:

[8] *Unofficial Accounting Interpretations of APB Opinion No. 15*, "Computing Earnings per Share" (New York: American Institute of Certified Public Accountants AICPA, 1970), *Definitional Interpretation No. 93.*

1. For P Company:

Income data:	
Income from its own separate operations	$150,000
Equity in net income of subsidiary (90% of $80,000)	72,000
Amortization of cost in excess of book value	(12,000)
Consolidated net income	$210,000
Securities data:	
Average number of common stock shares outstanding during the year	250,000
Common equivalent shares deemed outstanding, net of shares assumed repurchased under the treasury stock method	50,000
Denominator for purposes of computing consolidated primary earnings per share	300,000
Other potentially dilutive securities	None
(On the basis of the structure of P Company's securities, fully diluted earnings per share on a consolidated basis is not necessary because P Company has no other potentially dilutive securities outstanding.)	

2. For S Company:

Income data:	
Net income	$100,000
Less—Preferred stock dividend requirement	(20,000)
Net income allocable to common stock	$ 80,000
Securities data:	
Average number of common stock shares outstanding during the year	60,000
Common equivalent shares deemed outstanding (stock options and warrants), net of shares assumed repurchased under the treasury stock method (P Company owns 40% of these outstanding securities)	20,000
Denominator for purposes of computing primary earnings per share	80,000
Other potentially dilutive securities:	
Preferred stock, convertible into 40,000 shares of common stock, annual cumulative dividend requirement is $20,000 (P Company owns none of these preferred shares)	40,000
Denominator for purposes of computing fully diluted earnings per share	120,000

S Company's primary and fully diluted earnings per share are calculated as follows:

Calculation of primary earnings per share—S Company:	
Net income	$100,000
Less—Preferred stock dividend requirements	(20,000)
Numerator	$ 80,000
Denominator	80,000 shares
Primary earnings per share	$1.00
Calculation of fully diluted earnings per share—S Company:	
Net income (numerator)	$100,000
Denominator	120,000 shares
Fully diluted earnings per share	$0.83

The calculation above of the amounts for earnings per share above is unnecessary. The numerator and denominator used in each calculation, however, are needed to determine the amount of the subsidiary's earnings that may be included with the parent's own separate earnings when computing consolidated earnings per share. This amount is calculated as follows:

	Shares Owned by or That Accrue to P Company	Total
Average number of common stock shares outstanding during the year	54,000	60,000
Common stock equivalents deemed outstanding, net of shares assumed repurchased under the treasury stock method	8,000 (40%)	20,000
	62,000	80,000

The ratio (62,000 ÷ 80,000) is equivalent to 77.5%, which is multiplied by the numerator used by S Company to compute its primary earnings per share as follows:

Numerator used by S Company to compute its primary earnings per share	$80,000
Percentage calculated above	77.5%
Amount of S Company earnings that P Company must use to compute consolidated primary earnings per share	$62,000

The consolidated primary earnings per share is calculated as follows:

Calculation of consolidated primary earnings per share:	
Amount of S Company's earnings that P Company can include in computing consolidated primary earnings per share (per preceding calculation)	$ 62,000
P Company's earnings from its own separate operations.	150,000
Less—Amortization of cost in excess of book value	(12,000)
Numerator for computing consolidated primary earnings per share	$200,000
Denominator	300,000 shares
Primary earnings per share (consolidated)	$0.67

The amount of the subsidiary's earnings that P Company can include in its numerator for purposes of computing consolidated fully diluted earnings per share is computed as follows:

	Shares Owned by or That Accrue to P Company	Total
Average number of common stock shares outstanding during the year	54,000	60,000
Common stock equivalents deemed outstanding, net of shares assumed repurchased under the treasury stock method	8,000 (40%)	20,000
Other potentially dilutive securities (preferred stock)		40,000
	62,000	120,000

The ratio (62,000 ÷ 120,000) is equivalent to 51.67%, which is multiplied by the numerator used by S Company to compute its fully diluted earnings per share as follows:

Numerator used by S Company to compute its fully diluted earnings per share	$100,000
Percentage calculated above	51.67%
Amount of S Company's earnings that P Company must use to compute consolidated fully diluted earnings per share	$ 51,667

The consolidated fully diluted earnings per share is calculated as follows:

Calculation of consolidated fully diluted earnings per share:	
Amount of S Company's earnings per share that the parent can include to compute consolidated fully diluted earnings per share (from preceding calculation)	$ 51,667
P Company's earnings from its own separate operations.	150,000
Less—Amortization of cost in excess of book value.......	(12,000)
Numerator for purposes of computing consolidated fully diluted earnings per share	$189,667
Denominator (same as in primary earnings per share because P Company has no other potentially dilutive securities outstanding)...	300,000 shares
Consolidated fully diluted earnings per share.................	$0.63

The following points are important for understanding the preceding illustration:

1. The equity in the subsidiary's earnings recorded by P Company was calculated after the preferred stock dividend requirement was subtracted from S Company's net income, as required by paragraph 19k of *APB Opinion No. 18*.
2. The $72,000 equity in the subsidiary's earnings, recorded by P Company under the equity method of accounting, was greater than both the $62,000 used to compute consolidated primary earnings per share and the $51,667 used to compute consolidated fully diluted earnings per share.
3. Initially, P Company did not have to calculate a fully diluted earnings per share amount, inasmuch as it does not have any "other potentially dilutive securities" outstanding. The subsidiary, however, does have such securities outstanding, which significantly reduce the parent's interest in the subsidiary's net income. Accordingly, a fully diluted earnings-per-share amount must be calculated on a consolidated basis.
4. We assumed that no unrealized profit existed pertaining to intercompany transactions that required eliminations in arriving at consolidated net income. Any unrealized profit deferred in consolidation would have to be subtracted from the numerators used above to compute consolidated primary and fully diluted earnings per share.

SUMMARY

Income Taxes

For purchase business combinations, a deferred tax liability or asset must be recognized at the combination date for differences between the assigned values of assets and liabilities and their tax bases. Consolidated tax returns have several advantages over separate-company tax returns, such as the ability to offset losses of one entity against the profits of another entity. Separate returns also require that the parent must record income taxes on the earnings of subsidiaries (although an 80% dividend exclusion is available for domestic subsidiaries and certain tax credits are available for foreign subsidiaries) under *FASB Proposed Statement No. 00* (unless certain conditions of tax-free liquidation or indefinite investment are met). Section 338 of the Internal Revenue Code allows an acquiring company (in a taxable business combination in which common stock is acquired) to step up the bases of the subsidiary's assets based on the parent's purchase price to obtain the same results as though the assets had been purchased.

Earnings per Share

When a subsidiary has common stock equivalents or other potentially dilutive securities, the parent company cannot use the earnings it has recorded in its general ledger under the equity method of accounting to compute consolidated primary and fully diluted earnings per share. Instead, another amount that reflects the parent's interest in the subsidiary's earnings must be used, assuming the subsidiary's common stock equivalents and other potentially dilutive securities had been exercised or converted into common stock. To determine this other amount involves analyzing the number of shares that the subsidiary uses as its denominators to compute the amounts for its individual primary and fully diluted earnings-per-share. This analysis produces a ratio, which when applied to the numerators used by the subsidiary to compute its individual primary and fully diluted earnings per share amounts, produces the proper amount the parent must use to compute consolidated primary and fully diluted earnings per share amounts.

Selected References

"Consolidated Returns and Affiliated Groups," by Robert Willens. *Journal of Accountancy* (February 1986), 60–69.

"Corporate Provisions of the TRA* of 1984," by Robert Willens. *Journal of Accountancy* (February 1985), 54–62. The subtopics covering Section 338 and consolidated returns are the relevant sections of this article.

"What to Do when Purchasing 80 Percent or More of Another Corporation's Stock," by Terence E. Kelly. *Corporate Accounting* 4, no. 3 (Summer 1986), 76–82.

*Tax Reform Act.

Review Questions

1. Under what conditions must a deferred tax liability or asset be recognized at the business combination date?
2. What bearing does the taxability or nontaxability of a combination have on recognizing a deferred tax liability or asset at the business conbination date?
3. What are the main advantages of a consolidated tax return?
4. What disclosures are required for a subsidiary that is included in a consolidated tax return and issues separate financial statements?
5. Explain how earnings of domestic subsidiaries are taxed at the parent company rate.
6. In general, how are the earnings of foreign subsidiaries taxed in the United States?
7. On whose books is the dividend withholding tax recorded? Why?
8. When a parent company's cost is in excess of its share of its subsidiary's net assets at book value, and such excess may be assigned to depreciable assets, is that excess deductible for income tax reporting purposes?
9. What steps are necessary to make cost in excess of book value deductible for income tax reporting purposes?
10. Summarize the basic approach to calculating consolidated earnings per share when a subsidiary has potentially dilutive securities outstanding.
11. When a subsidiary has potentially dilutive securities outstanding, is the denominator used by a parent company adjusted to compute consolidated earnings per share? Why or why not?

Discussion Cases

DC 12-1

Income Tax Planning

On January 1, 19X1, Paul Company acquired all of Saul Company's outstanding common stock in such a manner that the business combination did not qualify either as a pooling of interests for financial reporting purposes or as a tax-free reorganization for income tax reporting purposes. The value of the consideration given by Paul greatly exceeded the book value of Saul's net assets. The cost in excess of book value was assignable to land, depreciable fixed assets, and goodwill.

Required:
What important income tax consideration should be addressed?

DC 12-2

Determining If and When to Record Income Taxes

Expando Company is establishing a foreign subsidiary. The plans call for investing $500,000 to establish initial operations. The subsidiary will retain all earnings for the first five years to finance internal growth. At the end of the five-year period, future internal growth is expected to be more moderate, and all of the future earnings will not be needed to finance additional internal growth.

Required:
Evaluate if and when Expando Company should record income taxes on the foreign subsidiary's earnings, assuming foreign income tax credits will not offset income taxes that would otherwise be payable.

Exercises: Income Taxes

E 12-1

Recognizing Deferred Taxes at the Business Combination Date

Pirouette Company acquired the business of Swirl Company in a nontaxable purchase business combination on July 1, 19X5. Other information follows:

1. Pirouette issued 5,000 shares of its $1 par value common stock, which had a fair market value of $40 per share.
2. The book value of Swirl's net assets is $160,000.
3. The book value of Swirl's assets and liabilities equals their tax bases just prior to the combination.
4. Swirl's fixed assets have a current value of $330,000 and a book value of $355,000.
5. Swirl's liabilities of $500,000 equal their current value.
6. The enacted income tax rate for current and future years is 40%.

Required:

1. Prepare the entry made to record the acquisition assuming the assets are acquired.
2. Prepare the entry made to record the acquisition, assuming all the common stock is acquired. Also prepare a conceptual analysis of the investment account.

E 12-2

Recording Income Taxes on Earnings of a Subsidiary

Pann Company owns 100% of the outstanding common stock of Sluce Company a domestic company that had net income of $150,000 in 19X1. Sluce's earnings are not intended to be retained in the business indefinitely. In 19X1, Sluce paid cash dividends of $80,000 on its common stock. Assume a 40% income tax rate.

Required:
Prepare Pann Company's 19X1 entries with respect to its investment in Sluce Company.

E 12-3

Recording Income Taxes on Earnings of a Subsidiary

Assume the information in Exercise 12-2, except that all of Sluce Company's earnings are intended to be retained in the business for internal expansion and that Sluce has not paid any dividends on its common stock since its inception.

Required:
The requirement is the same as for Exercise 12-2.

E 12-4

Recording Income Taxes on Earnings of a Subsidiary

Pike Company owns 100% of the outstanding common stock of Shantal Company, a foreign subsidiary that had net income of $140,000 in 19X1. Shantal consistently declares no dividends on its common stock, because the earnings are used each year for internal expansion, which is expected to continue into the foreseeable future. Assume a 40% domestic income tax rate, a 30% foreign income tax rate, and a 10% withholding tax rate.

Required:
Prepare Pike Company's 19X1 entries with respect to its investment in Shantal Company.

E 12-5

Recording Income Taxes on Earnings of a Subsidiary

In 19X5, the Tosco Company formed a foreign subsidiary. Income before U.S. and foreign income taxes for this wholly owned subsidiary was $500,000 in 19X5. The income tax rate in the foreign subsidiary's country is 35%. None of the foreign subsidiary's earnings have been remitted to Tosco; however, nothing indicates that these earnings will not be remitted in the future.

The foreign country in which the subsidiary is located does not impose a tax on remittances to the United States. A tax credit is allowed in the U.S. for taxes payable in the foreign country.

Assuming the income tax rate in the U.S. is 40%, what total amount of income taxes related to the foreign subsidiary should be shown in Tosco's 19X5 income statement?

a. $0
b. $25,000
c. $175,000
d. $200,000

(AICPA adapted)

Exercises: Calculating Earnings per Share

E 12-6

Partially Owned Subsidiary with Warrants; Parent with Simple Capital Structure

Powell Company owns 75% of Somas Company's outstanding common stock. Income and securities data for each company for 19X1 are as follows:

	Powell Company	Somas Company
Income from own operations	$500,000	$100,000
Average number of common stock shares outstanding during 19X1	200,000	20,000
Common equivalent shares:		
Warrants—		
Average number of warrants outstanding during 19X1		15,000
Shares assumed repurchased under the treasury stock method		10,000

Required:

1. Calculate primary earnings per share on a consolidated basis assuming:
   a. The parent company owns none of the subsidiary's warrants.
   b. The parent company owns 20% of the subsidiary's warrants.
2. Determine consolidated net income.

E 12-7

Wholly Owned Subsidiary with Convertible Preferred Stock; Parent with Simple Capital Structure

Press Company owns 100% of Stamp Company's outstanding common stock. Income and securities data for each company for 19X1 are as follows:

	Press Company	Stamp Company
Income from own operations	$1,000,000	$500,000
Average number of common stock shares outstanding during 19X1	100,000	75,000
Common equivalent shares:		
Convertible preferred stock—		
Shares outstanding during 19X1		5,000
Dividends per share (cumulative)		$10
Number of common shares obtainable on conversion		25,000

Required:

1. Calculate primary earnings per share on a consolidated basis assuming:
   a. The parent company owns none of the subsidiary's convertible preferred stock.
   b. The parent company owns 40% of the subsidiary's convertible preferred stock.
2. Determine consolidated net income.

E 12-8

Wholly Owned Subsidiary with Convertible Bonds; Parent with Simple Capital Structure

Pandora Company owns all of Scylla Company's outstanding common stock. Income and securities data for each company for 19X1 are as follows:

	Pandora Company	Scylla Company
Income from own operations	$600,000	$ 200,000
Average number of common stock shares outstanding during 19X1	300,000	100,000
Preferred stock (nonconvertible)—		
Average number of shares outstanding during 19X1	25,000	
Dividends per share (cumulative)	$4	
Common equivalent shares:		
Convertible bonds—		
Face amount outstanding during 19X1		$1,000,000
Interest rate		10%
Assumed income tax rate		40%
Number of common shares obtainable on conversion		50,000

Required:

1. Calculate primary earnings per share on a consolidated basis assuming:
   a. The parent company owns none of the subsidiary's convertible bonds.
   b. The parent company owns 60% of the subsidiary's convertible bonds.
2. Determine consolidated net income and consolidated net income accruing to common stockholders.

Problems: Income Taxes

P 12-1

Recognizing Deferred Taxes at the Business Combination Date

Parrish Company entered into an agreement with the stockholders of Sermonetti Company providing for a nontaxable purchase business combination. Other information as of the combination date follows:

1. Parrish issued 10,000 shares of its $5 par value common stock, which had a fair market value of $70 per share on the combination date.
2. Sermonetti's net assets have a book value of $600,000.
3. Sermonetti has a deferred tax liability of $24,000 as a result of using accelerated depreciation for tax reporting purposes.
4. Sermonetti's fixed assets have a current value of $490,000 and a book value of $410,000.
5. Sermonetti's long-term debt has a current value of $500,000 and a book value of $450,000.
6. The enacted income tax rate for current and future years is 40%.

Required:

1. Prepare the entry made to record the acquisition assuming the assets are acquired.

2. Prepare the entry made to record the acquisition assuming all the common stock is acquired. Also prepare a conceptual analysis of the investment account.

P 12-2

Recording Income Taxes on Earnings of a Foreign Subsidiary

On January 1, 19X1, Problemex Company formed a wholly owned foreign subsidiary, Solvco. Solvco is domiciled in a foreign country that has a 27% corporate income tax rate and a 10% dividend withholding rate. Assume a 40% U.S. income tax rate. Problemex expects Solvco to be operational for five to ten years, after which its total accumulated earnings will be remitted to Problemex in a tax-free liquidation. The subsidiary had a net income of $200,000 in 19X1.

Required:
Prepare Problemex Company's 19X1 entries related to its investment in Solvco.

P 12-3

Recording Income Taxes on Earnings of a Foreign Subsidiary

Pavlov Company owns 100% of the outstanding common stock of Skinner Company, a foreign subsidiary domiciled in a foreign country that imposes a 20% corporate income tax and a 10% dividend withholding tax. Assume a 40% U.S. income tax rate. Skinner had net income of $200,000 in 19X1. Skinner's earnings are not being reinvested indefinitely; it declared and paid cash dividends of $120,000 on its common stock in 19X1.

Required:

1. Prepare Pavlov Company's 19X1 entries related to its investment in Skinner Company.
2. What amounts for the earnings of the subsidiary will be reported on the parent's U.S. Federal Form 1120 corporate income tax return for 19X1?

P 12-4

Recording Income Taxes on Earnings of a Foreign Subsidiary

Parias Company owns 100% of the outstanding common stock of Sonata Company, a foreign subsidiary that had net income of $600,000 in 19X1. The foreign country in which Sonata is domiciled has a 25% corporate income tax rate and a 15% dividend withholding tax. Assume a 40% U.S. income tax rate. Sonata consistently pays cash dividends on its common stock. Parias instructs this foreign subsidiary to remit dividends to the maximum extent possible, considering cash requirements for normal operations that are not expected to expand. In 19X1, it declared $500,000 of dividends but paid only $400,000.

Required:

1. Prepare Parias Company's 19X1 entries related to its investment in Sonata Company.
2. What amounts for the earnings of the subsidiary will appear on the parent's U.S. Federal Form 1120 corporate income tax return for 19X1?

P 12-5

Calculating Consolidated Income Taxes: Wholly Owned Domestic Subsidiary

The partially completed income statements of Plowe Company and Snowe Company (a wholly owned domestic subsidiary) for 19X7 follow:

	Plowe Company	Snowe Company
Income Statement:		
Sales	$2,000,000	$1,000,000
Cost of goods sold	(1,100,000)	(500,000)
Expenses	(400,000)	(310,000)
Intercompany Accounts:		
Equity in net income of S Company		
Amortization of cost in excess of book value	(50,000)	
Sales	400,000	
Cost of goods sold	(200,000)	
Deferral of profit	(80,000)	
Income before Taxes		190,000
Income tax expense		
Net Income		

Other Information:

1. Separate income tax returns are filed.
2. Snowe Company declared and paid dividends of $100,000 during 19X7. (The remainder of the net income will be remitted to the parent in 19X8.)
3. The acquisition of Snowe in 19X5 was a taxable combination. The parent made a Section 338 election under the Internal Revenue Code to step up the bases of the subsidiary's assets for tax reporting purposes. Of the $50,000 amortization of cost in excess of book value recorded by the parent, $40,000 pertains to depreciable assets, the remaining $10,000 is goodwill.
4. The enacted income tax rate for current and future years is 40%.

Required:

1. Calculate the income tax expense for each company for 19X7.
2. Prepare the general ledger entries to record income taxes.
3. Prepare a consolidating income statement. (Use only one set of eliminations column.)

P 12-6

Calculating Consolidated Income Taxes: Wholly Owned Foreign Subsidiary

The partially completed income statements of Powersburg Company and its wholly owned foreign subsidiary, Strongsville Company, for 19X8 follow:

	Powersburg Company	Strongsville Company
Income Statement:		
Sales	$4,000,000	$2,400,000
Cost of goods sold	(2,100,000)	(1,100,000)
Expenses	(900,000)	(800,000)
Intercompany Accounts:		
Equity in net income of subsidiary		
Amortization of cost in excess of book value	(100,000)	
Sales	600,000	
Cost of goods sold	(300,000)	
Deferral of profit		
Income before Taxes		
Income tax expense		
Net Income		

Other Information:

1. The subsidiary is located in a country that imposes a 20% income tax and a 10% dividend withholding tax.
2. Dividends of $300,000 were declared during 19X8, of which $240,000 was paid in 19X8. The remaining $50,000 was paid on January 10, 19X9. The remainder of the subsidiary's net income will be remitted to the parent in March 19X9.
3. Of the parent's 19X8 amortization of cost in excess of book value, $80,000 pertains to depreciable assets; the remaining $20,000 is goodwill.
4. At December 31, 19X8, the subsidiary reported $210,000 of intercompany acquired inventory in its balance sheet. (No unrealized intercompany profit existed at the beginning of the year.)
5. The acquisition of the subsidiary was a nontaxable transaction to the selling stockholders.
6. The enacted U.S. income tax rate for current and future years is 40%.

Required:

1. Calculate the income tax expense for each company for 19X8.
2. Prepare the general ledger entries to record income taxes.
3. Prepare a consolidating income statement. (Use only one set of eliminations column.)

Problems: Calculating Earnings per Share

P 12-7

Partially Owned Subsidiary with Warrants; Parent with Warrants

Powers Company owns 80% of Sanders Company's outstanding common stock. Income and securities data for each company for 19X1 are as follows:

	Powers Company	Sanders Company
Income from own operations	$2,000,000	$600,000
Average number of common stock shares outstanding during 19X1	1,450,000	200,000
Common equivalent shares:		
Warrants—		
Average number of warrants outstanding during 19X1	200,000	45,000
Shares assumed repurchased under the treasury stock method	150,000	25,000

Required:

1. Calculate primary earnings per share on a consolidated basis assuming:
   a. The parent company owns none of the subsidiary's warrants.
   b. The parent company owns 75% of the subsidiary's warrants.
2. Determine consolidated net income and consolidated net income accruing to common stockholders.

P 12-8

Partially Owned Subsidiary with Convertible Preferred Stock; Parent with Convertible Preferred Stock

Presco Company owns 60% of Slicex Company's outstanding common stock. Income and securities data for each company for 19X1 are as follows:

	Presco Company	Slicex Company
Income from own operations	$700,000	$250,000
Average number of common stock shares outstanding during 19X1	800,000	200,000
Common equivalent shares:		
Convertible preferred stock—		
Shares outstanding during 19X1	20,000	50,000
Dividends per share (cumulative)	$5	$1
Number of common shares obtainable on conversion	200,000	80,000

Required:

1. Calculate primary earnings per share on a consolidated basis assuming:
   a. The parent company owns none of the subsidiary's convertible preferred stock.
   b. The parent company owns 25% of the subsidiary's convertible preferred stock.
2. Determine consolidated net income and consolidated net income accruing to common stockholders.

P 12-9

Partially Owned Subsidiary with Warrants and Convertible Bonds; Parent with Warrants and Convertible Preferred Stock

Parker Company owns 80% of Sheldon Company's outstanding common stock. Income and securities data for each company for 19X1 are as follows:

	Parker Company	Sheldon Company
Income from own operations	$1,500,000	$470,000
Average number of common stock shares outstanding during 19X1	900,000	200,000
Common equivalent shares:		
Warrants—		
Average number of warrants outstanding during 19X1	250,000	80,000
Shares assumed repurchased under the treasury stock method	150,000	50,000
Convertible bonds—		
Face amount outstanding during 19X1		$500,000
Interest rate		10%
Assumed income tax rate		40%
Number of common shares obtainable on conversion		20,000
Other potentially dilutive securities:		
Convertible preferred stock—		
Shares outstanding during 19X1	80,000	
Dividends per share	$2.50	
Number of common shares obtainable on conversion	300,000	

Required:

1. Calculate primary and fully diluted earnings per share on a consolidated basis assuming:
   a. The parent company owns none of the subsidiary's warrants or convertible bonds.
   b. The parent company owns 75% of the subsidiary's warrants and none of the convertible bonds.
2. Determine consolidated net income and consolidated net income accruing to common stockholders.

13

Segment Reporting, Disposals of Segments, and Leveraged Buyouts

AN OVERVIEW OF SEGMENT REPORTING

The foregoing chapters focus on the preparation of combined and consolidated financial statements, which are important to investors and lenders in evaluating the overall performance and condition of an enterprise. Historically, financial statements have also been used by investors and lenders to prepare trends and ratios that are useful in assessing the future prospects of an enterprise. For companies that have expanded into different industries or geographic areas, this task is usually more complicated because of different opportunities for growth, degrees and types of risk, and return on investments among the various segments. As is discussed in Chapters 14 and 15, significant additional risks arise in conducting operations in foreign countries. Even when a company has only domestic operations, substantial differences in future prospects may exist among the industry segments.

Because of two major events, accountants feel that lenders and investors would be better served if combined or consolidated financial statements were supplemented with information concerning the industries and geographic areas in which an enterprise operates. The first event was the substantial foreign investment that occurred after World War II. The second event was the extensive diversification of products carried out by scores of companies beginning in the 1960s. In 1976, the Financial Accounting Standards Board (FASB) issued *Statement No. 14*, "Financial Reporting for Segments of a Business Enterprise," in response to these events. This pronouncement requires the disclosure of information in addition to the basic financial statements. This information fits into three broad categories:

1. Operations in different industries.
2. Foreign operations and export sales.
3. Major customers.[1]

If a complete set of the basic financial statements is presented for more than one year (for comparative purposes), then the information to be disclosed under *FASB Statement No. 14* must be presented for each such year.[2]

The reporting requirements of this pronouncement are substantial for companies obliged to comply (certain companies are exempted from this pronouncement's reporting requirements). Before *FASB Statement No. 14* was issued, the Securities and Exchange Commission (SEC) had imposed line of business reporting requirements on publicly owned companies. The current SEC reporting requirements in Regulation S-K, an integrated

[1]*Statement of Financial Accounting Standards, No. 14*, "Financial Reporting for Segments of a Business Enterprise" (Stamford: Financial Accounting Standards Board, 1976), par. 3.
[2]*FASB Statement No. 14*, par. 3.

disclosure regulation adopted in 1977, are closely patterned after *FASB Statement No. 14*. (Regulation S-K is discussed in detail in Chapter 18).

Applicability of *FASB Statement No. 14*

Public Enterprises Only. When it was issued, *FASB Statement No. 14* applied to all enterprises. Later, however, it was evident that (1) the reporting requirements of this pronouncement burdened small, closely held enterprises; and (2) its benefit to nonmanagement investors and creditors was too limited. Consequently, *FASB Statement No. 21*, "Suspension of the Reporting of Earnings per Share and Segment Information by Nonpublic Enterprises," was issued, suspending the requirements of *FASB Statement No. 14* for nonpublic enterprises. *FASB Statement No. 21* defines a nonpublic enterprise as follows:

> For purposes of this Statement, a nonpublic enterprise is an enterprise other than one (a) whose debt or equity securities trade in a public market on a foreign or domestic stock exchange or in the over-the-counter market (including securities quoted only locally or regionally) or (b) that is required to file financial statements with the Securities and Exchange Commission. An enterprise is no longer considered a nonpublic enterprise when its financial statements are issued in preparation for the sale of any class of securities in a public market.[3]

Interim Financial Statements. *FASB Statement No. 14* required that segment information be included in interim financial reports that constituted a complete set of financial statements—containing statements of financial position, results of operations, and changes in financial position in conformity with generally accepted accounting principles. However, *FASB Statement No. 18*, "Financial Reporting for Segments of a Business Enterprise—Interim Financial Statements," later rescinded this requirement.[4]

Financial Statements Presented in Another Enterprise's Financial Report. Many situations arise in which a complete set of an entity's financial statements is presented in another enterprise's financial report. The three most common such situations are the following:

1. "Parent company only" statements are presented in addition to the consolidated financial statements.

[3]*Statement of Financial Accounting Standards, No. 21*, "Suspension of the Reporting of Earnings per Share and Segment Information by Nonpublic Enterprises" (Stamford: Financial Accounting Standards Board, 1978) par. 13.

[4]*Statement of Financial Accounting Standards, No. 18*, "Financial Reporting for Segments of a Business Enterprise—Interim Financial Statements" (Stamford: Financial Accounting Standards Board, 1977), par. 7.

2. The financial statements of an unconsolidated subsidiary are presented in footnotes to the parent's financial statements (which may be consolidated with the financial statements of other subsidiaries).
3. The financial statements of a 50%-or-less-owned investee are presented in the footnotes to the investor's financial statements.

In a literal interpretation of paragraph 7 of *FASB Statement No. 14*, the separate "additional" set of financial statements described in the above three situations must include the information required by *FASB Statement No. 14*. *FASB Statement No. 24*, "Reporting Segment Information in Financial Statements That Are Presented in Another Enterprise's Financial Report," later amended this paragraph to delete this reporting requirement in certain situations. For the three situations listed above, the *FASB Statement No. 24* provisions are as follows:

1. The disclosure requirements of *FASB Statement No. 14* do not apply to "parent company" financial statements (because such statements are included in the consolidated statements).
2. The disclosure requirements of *FASB Statement No. 14* apply to the financial statements of unconsolidated subsidiaries "if that information is significant in relation to the financial statements of the primary reporting entity in that financial report.[5]
3. The disclosure requirements of *FASB Statement No. 14* in these situations depend on whether the 50%-or-less-owned investee is a domestic or foreign entity.
   a. **Domestic entity:** The requirements of *FASB Statement No. 14* apply to a domestic entity's financial statements "if that information is significant in relation to the financial statements of the primary reporting entity in that financial report.[6]
   b. **Foreign entity:** The requirements of *FASB Statement No. 14* do not apply to a foreign entity's financial statements "unless that foreign entity's *separately issued* financial statements disclose the information required by *FASB Statement No. 14*.[7]

In summary, the disclosure requirements of *FASB Statement No. 14* currently pertain to **annual** financial statements of **publicly held** companies. When the financial reports of these companies also include a complete set of financial statements of an unconsolidated subsidiary or a 50%-or-less-owned entity, then the requirements of *FASB Statement No. 14* may also apply to the investee's financial statements (as included in the financial report of the investor), depending on the individual circumstances.

[5]*Statement of Financial Accounting Standards, No. 24*, "Reporting Segment Information in Financial Statements That Are Presented in Another Enterprise's Financial Report" (Stamford: Financial Accounting Standards Board, 1978), par. 5.
[6]*FASB Statement No. 24*, par. 5.
[7]*FASB Statement No. 24*, par. 5.

The Principles Used to Present Segment Information

Recall that a basic principle in the preparation of consolidated financial statements is that all intercompany transactions (and intracompany transactions when divisions are used) are completely eliminated just as though the transactions had never occurred. This principle is also used in the preparation of segment information, with the modification that any **intersegment** sales should be separately **disclosed** but then also **eliminated** in reconciling to the consolidated revenues—and this disclosure and elimination must be shown together. Any **intrasegment** sales, (such as those within a vertically integrated operation), need not be disclosed.

With respect to reporting information by geographic areas, the modified basic principle requires separate disclosure of transfers between geographic areas with the elimination of these transfers in reconciling to consolidated revenues; this disclosure and elimination also are shown together. "Transfer" means shipments of inventory, whether or not accounted for as a sale by the shipping organization. (The statement ignores the organizational structure of companies—that is, whether divided into branches, divisions, or subsidiaries.)

The appendix to this chapter contains a comprehensive illustration of the type of disclosure required by *FASB Statement No. 14.* Before proceeding, lightly review this appendix to obtain a general understanding of the disclosure required under this pronouncement. Specific sections of the appendix are referred to later in the chapter as the material is discussed.

INFORMATION ABOUT DIFFERENT INDUSTRIES

FASB Statement No. 14 specifies detailed mathematical tests for determining the components of a business that must disclose certain information regarding their operations. Components that meet these tests are "reportable industry segments." Before discussing these mathematical tests, we present the information that must be disclosed for each reportable industry segment and the manner of reporting this information.

Information Presented for Reportable Industry Segments

The following information must be presented for each reportable industry segment and in total for all nonreportable industry segments:

1. *Revenue.* Sales to unaffiliated customers and sales or transfers to other industry segments....
2. *Profitability.* Operating profit or loss...[along with an explanation of] the nature and amount of any unusual or infrequently occurring items...that have been added or deducted in computing the operating profit or loss....

3. *Identifiable assets.* The aggregate carrying amount of identifiable assets. . . .
4. *Other related disclosures:*
   a. The aggregate amount of depreciation, depletion, and amortization expense. . . .
   b. The amount of . . . capital expenditures, i.e., additions to its property, plant, and equipment. . . .
   c. The . . . equity in the net income from and investment in the net assets of unconsolidated subsidiaries and other equity method investees whose operations are vertically integrated with the operations of that segment. . . .
   d. The effect . . . on the operating profit [of a change in accounting principle].[8]

The pronouncement defines items 1, 2, and 3 as follows:

> **Revenue.** The revenue of an industry segment includes revenue both from sales to unaffiliated customers (i.e., revenue from customers outside the enterprise as reported in the enterprise's income statement) and from intersegment sales or transfers, if any, of products and services similar to those sold to unaffiliated customers. . . .
>
> **Operating Profit or Loss.** The operating profit or loss of an industry segment is its revenue as defined . . . minus all operating expenses. As used herein, operating expenses include expenses that relate to both revenue from sales to unaffiliated customers and revenue from intersegment sales or transfers. . . .
>
> **Identifiable Assets.** The identifiable assets of an industry segment are those tangible and intangible enterprise assets that are used by the industry segment, including (1) assets that are used exclusively by that industry segment and (2) an allocated portion of assets used jointly by two or more industry segments. . . .[9]

The identifiable assets of segments that were acquired in a business combination accounted for as a purchase include the amount of the parent's cost of an investment in excess of its interest in a subsidiary's net assets. This is necessary so that the amount of a segment's identifiable net assets is the same whether assets or common stock was acquired.

Methods of Presenting Information on Reportable Segments

The required information pertaining to reportable segments must be included in the financial statements in one of the following ways:

1. Within the body of the financial statements, with appropriate explanatory disclosures in the footnotes to the financial statements.

[8] *FASB Statement No. 14*, pars. 22–27.
[9] *FASB Statement No. 14*, par. 10.

2. Entirely in the footnotes to the financial statements.
3. In a separate schedule that is included as an integral part of the financial statements.[10]

The information that must be presented for individual reportable industry segments and in the aggregate for industry segments not deemed reportable must be reconciled to the consolidated financial statements as follows:

1. Revenue shall be reconciled to revenue reported in the consolidated income statement. . . .
2. Operating profit or loss shall be reconciled to pretax income from continuing operations (before gain or loss on discontinued operations, extraordinary items, and cumulative effect of a change in accounting principle) in the consolidated income statement. . . .
3. Identifiable assets shall be reconciled to consolidated total assets, with assets maintained for general corporate purposes separately identified in the reconciliation.[11]

Reconciling items 2 and 3 to consolidated amounts requires the use of procedures discussed and illustrated in Chapters 7 and 8 for the recognition and deferral of gross profit or gain on intercompany asset transfers.

Transfer Pricing

The definition of revenue includes revenues from intersegment sales and transfers, if any, of products and services similar to those sold to unaffiliated customers. Accordingly, the reported profitability of each segment is directly affected by the sales or transfer prices used. Because such sales or transfers are not determined on an "arm's length" basis from a consolidated viewpoint, substantial latitude exists for top management to shift profits between the selling and buying segments.

It would be impractical for the FASB to try to establish a basis to set prices for sales or transfers between segments. Instead, the board requires companies to use the same transfer prices (for reporting purposes under the pronouncement) as those used internally to price the intersegment sales or transfers.[12] Because transfer pricing has been associated in the past with vertically integrated operations (which need not be disaggregated), the potential for shifting profits is of less apparent concern.

Furthermore, when sales or transfers take place between segments, most often the organizational structures of the segments are similar to profit centers. This organizational structure is a substantial motivating factor for each segment to sell or transfer at no more or no less than inde-

[10] *FASB Statement No. 14*, par. 28.
[11] *FASB Statement No. 14*, par. 30.
[12] *FASB Statement No. 14*, par. 10.

pendent market prices, as the case may be. The basis of accounting for sales or transfers between industry segments and between geographic areas must be disclosed. If the basis is changed, the nature and effect of the change must be disclosed in the period of change.[13]

Allocation of Common Costs

When determining an industry segment's operating profit or loss, the operating expenses subtracted from revenue (as defined in the pronouncement) include expenses related to both revenue from sales to unaffiliated customers and revenue from intersegment sales or transfers. Operating expenses not directly traceable to an industry segment are allocated on a reasonable basis among those industry segments for whose benefit the expenses were incurred.[14]

The methods used to allocate operating expenses among industry segments must be consistently applied from period to period. If the methods are changed, however, the nature of the change and the effect on the operating profit or loss of reportable segments must be disclosed in the period of change.[15]

Because many items would have to be allocated on an arbitrary basis, *FASB Statement No. 14* specifies that the following items are neither added nor deducted, as the case may be, in computing an industry segment's operating profit or loss:

1. Revenue earned at the corporate level and not derived from the operations of any industry segment.
2. General corporate expenses.
3. Interest expense.
4. Domestic and foreign income taxes.
5. Equity in income or loss from unconsolidated subsidiaries and other unconsolidated investees.
6. Gain or loss on discontinued operations.
7. Extraordinary items.
8. Minority interest.
9. The cumulative effect of a change in accounting principle.[16]

Note that items 3 to 9 appear below the operating income or loss line as that term is customarily used in income statements. Thus, the meaning of operating profit or loss for a segment is consistent with the customary definition of those terms.

In the appendix to this chapter, exhibits A and B and the note to exhibit B contain the industry segment information discussed to this point.

[13]*FASB Statement No. 14*, pars. 23 and 35.
[14]*FASB Statement No. 14*, par. 10.
[15]*FASB Statement No. 14*, par. 24.
[16]*FASB Statement No. 14*, par. 10.

Determination of Industry Segments

An industry segment is defined as follows:

> A component of an enterprise engaged in providing a product or service or a group of related products and services primarily to unaffiliated customers (i.e., customers outside the enterprise) for a profit. By defining an industry segment in terms of products and services that are sold primarily to unaffiliated customers, the Statement does not require the disaggregation of the vertically integrated operations of an enterprise.[17]

The products and services that are sold to outside customers must be grouped by industry lines to arrive at industry segments. Because the available classification systems are not entirely suitable, the grouping of products and services into appropriate industry segments is left to management's judgment,[18] with the following considerations:

1. The nature of the product.
2. The nature of the production process.
3. Markets and marketing methods.[19]

> Broad categories such as *manufacturing, wholesaling, retailing,* and *consumer products* are not per se indicative of the industries in which an enterprise operates, and those terms should not be used without identification of a product or service to describe an enterprise's industry segments.[20]

The underlying philosophy is to disaggregate the total business into segments with distinct markets and thus different profitability, growth potential, and/or risk patterns. The enterprise's internal data by organizational, divisional, or parent–subsidiary lines *may* be used, but only if consistent with this philosophy.

Determination of Reportable Industry Segments

A reportable industry segment is

> an industry segment (or, in certain cases, a group of two or more closely related industry segments . . .) for which information is required to be reported by this Statement.[21]

An industry segment is "reportable" simply if it is big enough. Any industry segment that satisfies **any one** of the following criteria is considered a reportable segment for which specific information should be disclosed:

[17] *FASB Statement No. 14*, par. 10.
[18] *FASB Statement No. 14*, par. 12.
[19] *FASB Statement No. 14*, par. 100.
[20] *FASB Statement No. 14*, par. 101.
[21] *FASB Statement No. 14*, par. 10.

1. Its revenue (including both sales to unaffiliated customers and intersegment sales or transfers) is 10% or more of the combined revenue (sales to unaffiliated customers and intersegment sales or transfers) of all of the enterprise's industry segments.
2. The absolute amount of its operating profit or operating loss is 10% or more of the greater, in absolute amount, of:
   a. The combined operating profit of all industry segments that did not incur an operating loss, or
   b. The combined operating loss of all industry segments that did incur an operating loss.
3. Its identifiable assets are 10% or more of the combined identifiable assets of all industry segments.[22]

To illustrate the application of the second test, assume that a company has eight industry segments, which are grouped as follows:

Industry Segment	Operating Profit	Operating Loss
A	$ 80,000	
B	300,000	
C	400,000	
D	220,000	
E	500,000	
F		$160,000
G		90,000
H		250,000
	$1,500,000	$500,000

The total of the operating profits is greater than the total of the operating losses. Applying the 10% test to the total of the operating profits gives $150,000. Any segment that has an operating profit or loss equal to or above $150,000 satisfies the test and is a reportable segment. In this situation, only segments A and G do not pass the test. Segments that do not satisfy the tests of a reportable segment are shown as a combined group of segments, appropriately described.

After applying the three 10% tests, an enterprise must exercise judgment in evaluating the results of the tests. In this respect, it may be appropriate to:

1. Exclude a segment that satisfies one of the tests if the result is a freak occurrence, such as an abnormally high revenue or operating profit or loss for the segment.
2. Include a segment that does not meet one of the tests if the result is a freak occurrence, such as an abnormally low revenue or operating profit or loss.

[22] *FASB Statement No. 14*, par. 15.

This latitude was granted so that interperiod comparability could be maintained. When a "reportable" segment is excluded or a "nonreportable" segment is included, appropriate disclosure of such circumstances is required.[23]

Enough individual segments must be shown so that at least 75% of the combined revenues (from sales to unaffiliated customers of all industry segments) is shown by reportable segments.[24] To illustrate how the 75% test is applied, assume a company with eight industry segments has the following revenues:

Industry Segment	Sales to Unaffiliated Customers	Intersegment Sales	Total
A	$ 100,000		$ 100,000
B	200,000		200,000
C	310,000	$ 40,000	350,000
D	340,000		340,000
E	550,000		550,000
F	600,000	60,000	660,000
G	700,000		700,000
H	800,000	300,000	1,100,000
	$3,600,000	$400,000	$4,000,000
	75%		
	$2,700,000		

Assume that the operating profit or loss test and the identifiable assets test do not result in any reportable segments other than those determined below in the 10% of total revenues test.

Industry Segment	Sales to Unaffiliated Customers
E	$ 550,000
F	600,000
G	700,000
H	800,000
	$2,650,000

An additional segment must be selected so that at least $2,700,000 of sales to unaffiliated customers is shown by individual segments. This 75% requirement is determined after the three tests pertaining to revenues, operating profit or loss, and identifiable assets have been performed.

[23]*FASB Statement No. 14*, par. 16.
[24]*FASB Statement No. 14*, par. 17.

There may be situations in which a substantial number of segments must be presented to comply with the 75% test. No specific limit is imposed on the number of segments for which information is reported. However, for practical reasons, the FASB has indicated that if more than ten industry segments are reportable segments, a company may combine "the most closely related industry segments into broader reportable segments."[25]

INFORMATION ABOUT FOREIGN OPERATIONS AND EXPORT SALES

Foreign Operations Defined

Foreign operations are revenue-producing operations (except for unconsolidated subsidiaries and other unconsolidated investees) that

> (a) are located outside of the enterprise's home country (the United States for U.S. enterprises) and (b) are generating revenue either from sales to unaffiliated customers or from intraenterprise sales or transfers between geographic areas.[26]

Determination of Reportable Foreign Operations

Information about foreign operations must be presented if either of the following criteria is met:

1. Revenue generated by the enterprise's foreign operations from sales to unaffiliated customers is 10% or more of consolidated revenue as reported in the enterprise's income statement.
2. Identifiable assets of the enterprise's foreign operations are 10% or more of consolidated total assets as reported in the enterprise's balance sheet.[27]

These two tests are based on the consolidated amounts, whereas the revenue and identifiable assets tests used to determine reportable industry segments are based on total industry segment amounts. Note that the 10% operating profit or loss test used for industry segments is not used for geographic segments. This test was apparently excluded because potential misinterpretations could occur as a result of significant differences in tax structures among geographic areas.

Determination of Geographic Areas

Disclosures required for foreign operations are presented in total or by geographic area. The grouping of foreign countries into geographic areas is

[25]*FASB Statement No. 14*, par. 19.
[26]*FASB Statement No. 14*, par. 31.
[27]*FASB Statement No. 14*, par. 32.

left to the judgment of management, which should consider the following factors: "proximity, economic affinity, similarities in business environment, and the nature, scale, and degree of interrelationship of the various countries."[28] These factors could create differing patterns of risk, profitability and growth.

Determination of Reportable Geographic Areas

When foreign operations are conducted in more than one geographic area, information must be presented for any geographic area meeting one of the following conditions:

1. Its revenues from sales to unaffiliated customers are 10% or more of consolidated revenues.
2. Its identifiable assets are 10% or more of consolidated total assets.[29]

Information Presented about Foreign Operations

The following information must be presented in total (when only one foreign geographic area exists) or for each reportable geographic area, and in the aggregate for all other foreign geographic areas that individually are not reportable as geographic areas:

> 1. Revenue . . . with sales to unaffiliated customers and sales or transfers between geographic areas shown separately. . . .
> 2. Operating profit or loss . . . or net income, or some other measure of profitability between operating profit or loss and net income. . . .
> 3. Identifiable assets. . . .[30]

With respect to item 2, a wide range of profitability can be used in lieu of operating profit and loss (as required for industry segment reporting). There are two apparent reasons for allowing this flexibility:

1. Companies already must disclose the incomes and losses of their foreign operations pursuant to the provisions of *ARB No. 43* (discussed in Chapter 15). Thus, the use of a net income or loss level would satisfy both reporting requirements.
2. When there are significant differences among the tax structures of foreign countries and the United States, misleading conclusions could result if the operating income or loss level alone were imposed.

A multinational company that has diversified operations may have to disclose both industry segment information *and* information about its foreign operations.

[28]*FASB Statement No. 14*, par. 34.
[29]*FASB Statement No. 14*, par. 33.
[30]*FASB Statement No. 14*, par. 35.

Information Presented about Export Sales

When sales to unaffiliated foreign customers by a domestic company (export sales) are 10% or more of total revenue from sales to unaffiliated customers as reported in the consolidated income statement, the total export sales must be separately reported, in total and by geographic area.[31]

Methods of Presenting Foreign Operations and Export Sales Information

Foreign operations and export sales information may be presented in any of the ways shown previously for presenting industry segment information. The information presented for foreign operations, however, must be presented with the same information for domestic operations. The information for domestic operations and for foreign operations must then be reconciled to the related amounts in the consolidated financial statements in a manner similar to that described for industry segment information.[32]

Information regarding export sales may have to be presented even though segment data need not be disclosed. In these cases, the information would normally be presented in a simple narrative footnote rather than as part of a more complex schedule dealing with segment data.

In the appendix to this chapter, exhibit C and the note to exhibit C illustrate the type of disclosure required with respect to foreign operations and export sales.

INFORMATION ABOUT MAJOR CUSTOMERS

Some enterprises rely heavily on major customers. *FASB Statement No. 14*, as amended by *FASB Statement No. 30*, "Disclosure of Information about Major Customers," requires enterprises having revenues from any single customer in excess of 10% of total revenues to disclose the following information:

1. The fact that the enterprise has revenues from one or more single customers in excess of 10% of total revenues.
2. The amount of revenues from each such customer but not the identity of each such customer.
3. The industry segment making the sales to each such customer.[33]

The federal government (including its agencies), a state government, a local government unit (such as a county or a municipality), a foreign government, and a group of entities under common control are each

[31]*FASB Statement No. 14*, par. 36.
[32]*FASB Statement No. 14*, par. 37–38.
[33]*Statement of Financial Accounting Standards, No. 30*, "Disclosure of Information about Major Customers" (Stamford: Financial Accounting Standards Board, 1979).

considered a single customer.[34] As in the case of export sales, information about major customers may have to be presented even though segment data need not be disclosed. A simple narrative footnote usually suffices in these cases.

REPORTING THE DISPOSAL OF A SEGMENT OF A BUSINESS

A Short History

The Professional Management Approach. In the 1960s and 1970s, a professional management approach became exceedingly popular. Under this approach, it was thought that acquired businesses could be managed by professional managers, whose skills could be applied successfully to almost any acquired business. Managing a diverse group of acquired businesses was likened to managing a portfolio of investments. This thinking contributed to the rapid rise in the number of conglomerates during this period (discussed in Chapter 2).

The Reversal of the Professional Management Approach and the Deconglomeration Trend. By the early 1980s, it was evident that this approach had not been that successful. After an acquisitions binge, many companies found that they had bitten off more than they could chew. Many companies had bought into the wrong industry, or they simply did not have the managerial talent to manage a diverse group of industries effectively. In fact, of the fourteen companies identified as having supremely excellent management by Peters and Waterman in their 1982 best-selling book *In Search of Excellence: Lessons from America's Best-Run Companies*, not one was a conglomerate.

In recent years, scores of top managements have undone much of the external expansion of their predecessors because the acquired businesses had lower than expected rates of return or continuous operating losses. Such undoings are referred to as "divestiture programs" rather than "selling your losers." In the 1980s, the number of disposals of unwanted businesses per year has increased dramatically (approaching a thousand for several of the recent years). Clearly, there is a trend away from "making deals" and toward operating businesses that managements know best. Recent notable divestiture programs include the following:

Income from continuing operations before income taxes	$xxxx	
Provision for income taxes	xxx	
Income from continuing operations		$xxxx

[34]*FASB Statement No. 30*, par. 6.

Discontinued operations (Note ____):		
Income (loss) from operations of discontinued Division X (less applicable income taxes of $ ____)	$xxxx	
Loss on disposal of Division X, including provision of $ ____ for operating losses during phase-out period (less applicable income taxes of $ ____).....	xxxx	xxxx
Net Income...		$xxxx

Amounts of income taxes applicable to the results of discontinued operations and the gain or loss from disposal of the segment should be disclosed on the face of the income statement or in related notes. Revenues applicable to the discontinued operations should be separately disclosed in the related notes.[35]

If prior-period income statements are presented for comparative purposes, such statements are **restated** to report the results of operations of the segment being disposed of as a separate component of income before extraordinary items, net of taxes.[36]

1. From 1979 until 1985, International Telephone and Telegraph (ITT), in a move to reverse an earnings decline in almost all of its lines of businesses, sold approximately 80 business units having estimated sales of $2 billion. (ITT has been called the "ultimate conglomerate"; from 1959 to 1977 it acquired approximately 350 businesses in nearly 20 countries; the products and services it made and offered included Hostess Twinkies, radar surveillance systems, and the Sheraton hotel chain.)
2. From 1983 to 1985, Gulf and Western Industries, Inc., a conglomerate, sold more than 60 of its business units to streamline and reshape the direction of the company.
3. From 1980 to 1985, General Electric Co. sold nearly 200 subsidiaries in a relentless divestiture of low-profit business units.

Results of Divestitures. Divesting companies are leaner and healthier after divesting unwanted units. New management may run the divested units more effectively. If existing management buys the business, it may be entrepreneurially oriented and able to make decisions faster than allowed in a major corporation's rigid and stifling reporting structure.

Manner of Divesting. Companies commonly employ investment advisers (at substantial fees) to assist them in their divestitures. Divestitures can take the following forms: (a) selling segments to other companies (a business combination for the acquiring company); (b) selling segments to managers, employees, or investors in a **leveraged buyout** (increasingly

[35] *Opinions of the Accounting Principles Board, No. 30,* "Reporting the Results of Operations" (New York: American Institute of Certified Public Accountants, 1973), par. 8. Copyright © 1973 by the American Institute of Certified Public Accountants, Inc.
[36] *APB Opinion No. 30,* par. 13.

common in recent years); (c) spinning off segments as separate companies (distributing the common stock of the subsidiary to the parent company's shareholders); and, when all else fails, (d) liquidating the business.

Accounting Issues

The following accounting issues are associated with the disposal of a segment of a business:

1. How should a gain or loss on the disposal of a segment be measured and classified in the income statement?
2. How should the results of operations of the discontinued operation be reported in the income statement?

The reporting and accounting for the disposal of a segment of a business are governed by *APB Opinion No. 30*, "Reporting the Results of Operations." This pronouncement introduced the idea that the results of operations of a discontinued segment and any gain or loss on the disposal should be reported separately from continuing operations. Before *APB Opinion No. 30* was issued, losses on the disposals of segments were commonly reported as extraordinary items, whereas gains were not commonly shown as extraordinary items; the results of operations of the discontinued segments were not separated from the continuing operations.

Manner of Reporting a Disposal of a Segment

Accounting Principles Board Opinion No. 30 specifies the manner of reporting the disposal of a segment as follows:

> For purposes of this Opinion, the term "discontinued operations" refers to the operations of a segment of a business . . . that has been sold, abandoned, spun off, or otherwise disposed of or, although still operating, is the subject of a formal plan for disposal. . . .
> The Board concludes that the results of continuing operations should be reported separately from discontinued operations and that any gain or loss from disposal of a segment of a business . . . should be reported in conjunction with the related results of discontinued operations and not as an extraordinary item. Accordingly, operations of a segment that has been or will be discontinued should be reported separately as a component of income before extraordinary items and the cumulative effect of accounting changes (if applicable) in the following manner:

Definition of a Segment of a Business

The precise definition of a segment of a business in *APB Opinion No. 30*, which is different from the definition in *FASB Statement No. 14*, is as follows:

> For purposes of this Opinion, the term "segment of a business" refers to a component of an entity whose activities represent a separate major line of

> business or class of customer. A segment may be in the form of a subsidiary, a division, or a department, and in some cases a joint venture or other nonsubsidiary investee, provided that its assets, results of operations, and activities can be clearly distinguished, physically and operationally and for financial reporting purposes, from the other assets, results of operations, and activities of the entity.... The fact that the results of operations of the segment being sold or abandoned cannot be separately identified strongly suggests that the transaction should not be classified as the disposal of a segment of the business. The disposal of a segment of a business should be distinguished from other disposals of assets incident to the evolution of the entity's business, such as the disposal of part of a line of business, the shifting of production or marketing activities for a particular line of business from one location to another, the phasing out of a product line or class of service, and other changes occasioned by technological improvements.[37]

This definition is apparently narrower than the definition used in *FASB Statement No. 14* in that the disposal of a discrete operation within a vertically integrated operation would be considered a disposal of a segment. (Actually, this would be a disposal of a portion of a segment as that term is used in *FASB Statement No. 14.*) This interpretation is consistent with the intent of *FASB Statement No. 14,* because an appendix to the statement illustrates the disposal of a portion of a segment (as that term is defined in *FASB Statement No. 14*), which is reported in accordance with the procedures set forth in *APB Opinion No. 30.*

Definition of Measurement and Disposal Dates

APB Opinion No. 30 distinguishes between the operations of a segment that occur before a decision to dispose of that segment and operations that occur after that time. The particular point in time, referred to as the **measurement date,** is defined as follows:

> The "measurement date" of a disposal is the date on which management, having authority to approve the action, commits itself to a formal plan to dispose of a segment of the business, whether by sale or abandonment. The disposal should include, as a minimum, identification of the major assets to be disposed of, the expected method of disposal, the period expected to be required for completion of the disposal, an active program to find a buyer if disposal is by sale, the estimated results of operations of the segment from the measurement date to the disposal date, and the estimated proceeds or salvage to be realized by disposal.[38]

The **disposal date** as used in the preceding definition is defined as follows:

[37] *APB Opinion No. 30,* par. 13.
[38] *APB Opinion No. 30,* par. 14.

> The "disposal date" is the date of closing the sale if the disposal is by sale or the date that operations cease if the disposal is by abandonment.[39]

The format for reporting the discontinued operations of a business includes two categories. The first category, the income or loss from operations of a discontinued segment of a business, includes all operations up to the measurement date. The second category, the gain or loss on disposal of a segment of a business, includes the following:

1. The income or loss from operations **during the phase-out period** (from the measurement date to the disposal date).
2. The gain or loss on the sale or abandonment of the segment.

The amount reported in the second category **as of the measurement date** depends on the relative amounts determined for items 1 and 2, above, and whether the amounts are positive or negative. The pronouncement requires companies to recognize losses currently and to recognize income and gains only when realized, but some offsetting is also required. Thus, an anticipated loss on the sale or abandonment of the segment is recognized as of the measurement date, whereas an anticipated gain is recognized when realized. However, estimated losses from operations during the phase-out period are included in this calculation. Estimated income from operations during the phase-out period is included only to the extent of the estimated loss on the sale or abandonment of the segment (with any remaining amount to be recognized when realized).[40]

To illustrate, assume that on October 1, 19X1, a company with a calendar year-end decides to dispose of a segment of its business. The expected sales date is March 31, 19X2. Illustration 13-1 shows the amounts reported for 19X1 and 19X2 under various assumptions.

Guidelines for Determining Gain or Loss on Disposal

APB Opinion No. 30 specifies the following guidelines to determine the amount of gain or loss on disposal:

> Estimated amounts of income or loss from operations of a segment between measurement date and disposal date included in the determination of loss on disposal should be limited to those amounts that can be projected with reasonable accuracy. In the usual circumstance, it would be expected that the plan of disposal would be carried out within a period of one year from the measurement date and that such projections of operating income or loss would not cover a period exceeding approximately one year.
>
> Gain or loss from the disposal of a segment of a business should not include adjustments, costs, and expenses associated with normal business activities that should have been recognized on a going-concern basis up to

[39] *APB Opinion No. 30*, par. 14.
[40] *APB Opinion No. 30*, par 15.

Illustration 15-1
Determining the Amount Reported for Category 2: Loss or Gain on Disposal (thousands of dollars)

	Estimated Income (Loss) from Operations during the Phase-out Period (October 1, 19X1 to March 31, 19X2)			Estimated Gain (Loss) on Sale of Segment	Category 2 Gain (Loss) to Be Reported	
	19X1	19X2	Total	March 31, 19X2	19X1	19X2
A.	$(30)	$(70)	$(100)	$(140)	$(240)[a]	
B.	(30)	(70)	(100)	80	(20)[a]	
C.	(30)	(70)	(100)	130		$ 30[b]
D.	30	70	100	(140)	(40)[a]	
E.	30	70	100	(90)		10[b]
F.	30	70	100	160	30[b]	230[b]

Note: For simplicity, income tax effects were not considered.

[a]Reported as of the measurement date (October 1, 19X1).
[b]Reported when realized.

the measurement date, such as adjustments of accruals on long-term contracts or write-down or write-off of receivables, inventories, property, plant, and equipment used in the business, equipment leased to others, . . . or other intangible assets. However, such adjustments, costs, and expenses which (a) are clearly a "direct" result of the decision to dispose of the segment and (b) are clearly not the adjustments of carrying amounts or costs, or expenses that should have been recognized on a going-concern basis prior to the measurement date should be included in determining the gain or loss on disposal. Results of operations before the measurement date should not be included in the gain or loss on disposal.

Costs and expenses "directly" associated with the decision to dispose include items such as severance pay, additional pension costs, employee relocation expenses, and future rentals on long-term leases to the extent they are not offset by sublease rentals.[41]

Disclosure

In addition to the manner of reporting in the income statement gains or losses on the disposal of a segment, the notes to the financial statements for the period encompassing the measurement date should disclose the following:

1. The identity of the segment of business that has or will be discontinued.

[41]*APB Opinion No. 30*, par. 15–17. Copyright © 1973 by the American Institute of Certified Public Accountants, Inc.

2. The expected disposal date, if known.
3. The expected manner of disposal.
4. A description of the remaining assets and liabilities of the segment at the balance sheet date, and
5. The income or loss from operations and any proceeds from disposal of the segment during the period from the measurement date to the date of the balance sheet.[42]

LEVERAGED BUYOUTS

A **leveraged buyout** (LBO) is a financing technique used in acquiring a business. Pioneered in the 1960s, it became immensely popular and widespread in the early 1980s when large conglomerates began their drive to divest marginal subsidiaries. Because of the recession and resultant depressed stock market from 1980 to 1982, numerous subsidiaries were purchased at bargain prices. As the technique grew in popularity it also began to be used widely to acquire privately and publicly owned companies.

"Management Buyouts." The buyers in an LBO usually retain the existing management. However, to make sure that management has sufficient commitment to the business, the buyers customarily require members of management to invest some of their own money and become part of the ownership. (If management is unwilling to do this, the business may not be worth acquiring.) In these situations, LBOs are often called "management buyouts." Allowing management to have a piece of the action and become entrepreneurs is usually essential in light of the buyers' not taking an active role in managing the business.

How They Work. The following steps are how a typical leveraged buyout is expected to work:

1. Investors, including management of the target company, put up a minimal amount of capital toward purchasing the target company.
2. To come up with the remainder of the purchase price, the investors borrow from a financial institution through the target company. (In some cases, the loans have been as high as for 99% of the purchase price.) The target company's assets are used as collateral to secure the loans. Thus the debt structure of the target company is refinanced simultaneously with the acquisition.
3. Banks are customary lending institutions. They earn loan fees and charge interest at one to two points above the prime rate. Insurance companies, pension plans, venture capitalists, and other investment companies may also participate in the financing package, usually on a subordinated basis with the option to convert such debt into common stock.

[42] *APB Opinion No. 30*, par. 18.

4. Because the purchase of the target company is a taxable transaction, the target company's assets are revalued to their current values (based on the purchase price). This allows greater depreciation charges for tax reporting purposes.
5. The combination of increased expenses for interest and depreciation often results in the target company not having to pay income taxes for several years.
6. With a rededicated management, the expectation is that the business's operations will improve and that the business (which may have been acquired at four to six times earnings) will be taken public at 20 to 30 times earnings or sold to another company.

A Spectacular Example. In 1981, two investors acquired Gibson Greetings Inc. (which was beginning to promote its Garfield the Cat cartoon character) from RCA for $80 million (at about five times earnings). The investors used $1 million of their own money and borrowed $79 million. Garfield became a sensation, and profits improved greatly. In the 1983 bull market, which was clamoring for new stock issues, the company was taken public at $27.50 per share, or 20 times earnings. The total sales price was $290 million—over four times the purchase price. Because of the leverage they used, the two investors made a phenomenal return on their $1 million investment.

Accounting Considerations. No special accounting rules are necessary for LBOs; purchase accounting as discussed in Chapter 3 is used. (We could have discussed LBOs in Chapter 3, but because they are most often associated with the disposal of subsidiaries, we chose to discuss them in this chapter.)

PERSPECTIVE

Leveraged Buyouts Aren't Just For Daredevils Anymore

Staid Wall Street Firms are Jumping In, Too

When it thinks it's on to a good thing, Wall Street really goes for broke. The latest example: the leverage buyout. It used to be faintly disreputable in some dealmaking circles; these days it's the game everybody wants to play. Investment banking firms are no longer content to locate promising LBO candidates for other investors—and watch them reap huge profits. So now they are emptying their own wallets to get a piece of the action. And insurance companies and pension funds, which don't want to be left on the sidelines, are committing cash to giant LBO funds. Complains Daniel J. Good, head of Shearson Lehman Brothers' LBO group: "There's more money available than deals."

LBOs can be mouth-watering money-makers. Returns on the equity portion of such deals have reached 50% or more annually. But that's just for starters. A firm participating in a "bust-up" LBO, in which the newly private company sells off pieces of itself, can collect a stream of fees from each spinoff. And when

Leveraged Buyouts Aren't Just For Daredevils Anymore *(continued)*

the LBO comes full cycle, usually after five or six years, the bankers happily underwrite its reentry as a public company or negotiate its sale to someone else.

Moreover the whiff of danger once associated with an LBO's mountainous debt burden has been blown away by the stunning success of such deals as Gibson Greetings Inc. and Simplicity Mfg. Inc., put together four or five years ago. "Once these companies go private and management has a meaningful stake, our record shows that they outperform their original forecast, even in recessionary periods," says Daniel O'Connell, co-head of First Boston Corp.'s LBO unit.

Lofty Offers

But the price investment bankers are paying for their enthusiasm is going up—literally. Just a few years ago, LBO prices were 9 to 10 times earnings. Growing competition has bid prices up to 14 times earnings or more, according to Martin Sikora, editor of *Mergers & Acquisitions*, a Philadelphia publication. The stock market's rise is responsible for some of the inflation, of course. So are lower interest rates, which enable LBO investors to afford richer prices. But the amount of money being thrown at deals, investment bankers concede, is driving prices even higher.

The buyouts of R. H. Macy & Co. and Safeway Stores Inc. are prime examples. At $68 per share, Macy's fetched 17 times earnings. Kohlberg Kravis Roberts & Co.'s $69 offer for Safeway is even loftier—20 times earnings. But higher prices aren't all bad. The flood of money seeking these deals has caused investors to boost the proportion of equity going into LBOs. That reduces the leverage and the risk, but also the expected returns.

Crowding in the market is changing dealmaking etiquette, too. While in the past deals were frequently negotiated privately, now "it's rare that an LBO player can purchase a company without any competition," says First Boston's O'Connell. Company directors, fearful of appearing unsophisticated or breaching their fiduciary duties, are fueling the auction process by marketing their company or its spinoffs to a large number of potential buyers.

The popularity of LBOs is also rewriting the rulebook. In the old days, the ideal LBO candidate was a mature, recession-resistant company with plenty of hard assets. Now most LBO investors are willing to base their decisions on cash flow and intangible assets. The unique franchise of a broadcast company, for example, should produce a relatively protected future cash flow to pay down debt. Similarly, Macy's and Safeway were valued, at least partly, on future developments. Both are expected to generate more cash after tax reform, and Macy's new owners plan to refinance the store's real estate at lower rates.

But in some cases, the criteria seem to be getting a little too relaxed. National Gypsum Co., for example, has been a classically cyclical company that prospers when homebuilding comes on strong. Nonetheless, Gypsum recently went private in a $1.6 billion LBO during what may turn out to have been the peak of the homebuilding cycle.

(continued)

More Transactions

Merrill Lynch, First Boston, Morgan Stanley, and Shearson are among the most aggressive of the firms that are acting as principal investors. To compete against KKR and Forstmann Little & Co., whose sheer size enables them to tackle a far broader array of transactions, Wall Street firms are pooling their money with cash from insurance companies and pension funds in "LBO funds." Explains Dan L. Hale, general manager of General Electric Credit Corp.'s corporate financial services division: "In this environment they have to have an ability to commit [cash] up front. Otherwise they don't get to see the transactions."

Because the appetites for deals are so ravenous, investment bankers are beginning to underwrite entire LBOs before knowing whether all the financing will be available. Over the past year, First Boston has closed more than $1 billion of LBOs in this way.

As the new LBO players muster more cash and cast their nets wider, it seems inevitable that they will drag up deals better left behind. Critics cite LBOs financed with deferred interest debt as evidence of deteriorating quality. In May, for example, Merrill Lynch, Pierce, Fenner & Smith Inc. took Jack Eckerd Corp., a specialty retailer, private for $1.4 billion.

Nearly $200 million was financed with discounted subordinated debentures that won't begin paying interest until 1991. Such interest deferrals "came about because the deals were basically unfinanceable with normal debt," claims one expert. "The company has to grow its way into making its first interest payments."

So far, maturing LBOs have been winners, proving the doomsayers wrong. But as the competition gets hotter and deals get pricier, the odds of LBOs collapsing will increase. Wall Street seems unconcerned now. But the Street has always found it hard to believe that there can be too much of a good thing.

Source: Ellyn E. Spragins, "Leveraged Buyouts Aren't Just for Daredevils Anymore." Reprinted from the August 11, 1986, issue of *Business Week*, p. 50, by special permission.

SUMMARY

Consolidated financial statements have limited usefulness in enabling investors and lenders to assess the future prospects of enterprises with diversified operations. Supplemental data on industry segments and foreign operations are considered necessary to assist users of financial statements to assess future prospects.

The process of supplying information by industry involves (1) identifying the various industry segments in which the enterprise operates; (2) applying three tests to each industry segment to determine if it is considered a reportable industry segment; and (3) presenting financial information for each reportable industry segment and all other industry segments combined in such a manner that the amounts shown tie into the consolidated financial statements. The basic criterion for determining whether a component of a business is an industry segment is whether or not that component sells products or provides services primarily to unaffiliated customers for a profit. The three major disclosures for a reportable industry segment pertain to revenues, operating profit or loss, and identifiable assets used by the segment. In addition, a fourth category of miscellaneous disclosures relates primarily to capital investments, depreciation, and effects of changes in accounting principles.

The process of disclosing information about foreign operations involves (1) grouping the various foreign countries in which the enterprise operates into meaningful, related geographic area; (2) applying two tests to each geographic area to determine if it is reportable; and (3) presenting financial information and data for each reportable geographic area and all other geographic areas combined in such a manner that the amounts shown tie into the consolidated financial statements. The three major disclosures for geographic areas pertain to revenues, operating profit or loss, and identifiable assets used by each segment.

Disposals of segments (or part of a segment) are reported in the income statement separately from all other operations, which are referred to as continuing operations.

Glossary of New Terms

Disposal Date "The disposal date is the date of closing the sale if the disposal is by sale or the date that operations cease if the disposal is by abandonment."*

Identifiable Assets "The identifiable assets of an industry segment are those tangible and intangible enterprise assets that are used by the industry segment, including (1) assets that are used exclusively by that industry segment and (2) an allocated portion of assets used jointly by two or more industry segments."†

Industry Segments "A component of an enterprise engaged in providing a product or service or a group of related products and services primarily to unaffiliated customers (i.e., customers outside the enterprise) for a profit. By defining an industry segment in terms of products and services that are sold primarily to unaffiliated customers, the Statement does not require the disaggregation of the vertically integrated operations of an enterprise."†

Leveraged Buyout Investors and management buy a controlling interest in a company, financing the purchase by borrowing from a financial institution and using the company's own assets as collateral.

*Definitions quoted from *APB Opinion No. 30*, par. 14.
†Definitions quoted from *FASB Statement No. 14*, par. 10.

Measurement Date "The measurement date of a disposal is the date on which management, having authority to approve the action, commits itself to a formal plan to dispose of a segment of the business, whether by sale or abandonment."*

Operating Profit or Loss "The operating profit or loss of an industry segment is its revenue as defined . . . minus all operating expenses. Operating expenses include expenses that related to both revenue from sale to unaffiliated customers and revenue from intersegment sales or transfers."†

Reportable Segments "An industry segment (or, in certain cases, a group of two or more closely related industry segments . . .) for which information is required to be reported by the Statement."†

Revenue "The revenue of an industry segment includes revenue both from sales to unaffiliated customers (i.e., revenue from customers outside the enterprise as reported in the enterprise's income statement) and from intersegment sales or transfers, if any, of products and services similar to those sold to unaffiliated customers."†

Suggested References

"Maximizing the Tax and Financial Benefits of Leveraged Buyouts," by Hugh J. Barry and Richard A. Stratton. *Corporate Accounting* 2, no. 1 (Winter 1984), 16–21.

"Why LBOs Are Popular," by Susan D. Harding, Leon Hanouille, Joseph C. Rue, and Ara G. Volkan. *Management Accounting* (December 1985), 51–56.

Appendix
COMPREHENSIVE ILLUSTRATION

This Appendix contains illustrations of the type of information required by *FASB Statement No. 14*, as follows:

- Exhibit A Consolidated income statement of a hypothetical company for the year ended December 31, 19X1.
- Exhibit B Information about operations in different industries and sales to major customers.
- Exhibit C Information about operations in different geographic areas and export sales.

The consolidated income statement in Exhibit A is not required pursuant to *FASB Statement No. 14;* it is included so that amounts in Exhibits B and C can be identified in the consolidated income statement.

Exhibits A, B, and C, and the notes to B and C in the text, were adapted from *FASB Statement No. 14*, "Financial Reporting for Segments of a Business Enterprise" (Stamford: Financial Accounting Standards Board, 1976), Appendix F. Amounts in the notes are in thousands.

Exhibit A

X Company
Consolidated Income Statement
For the Year Ended December 31, 19X1
(thousands of dollars)

Sales		$4,700
Cost of sales	$3,000	
Selling, general, and administrative expense	700	
Interest expense	200	(3,900)
		$ 800
Equity in net income of Z Company (25% owned)		100
Income from continuing operations before income taxes		$ 900
Income taxes		(400)
Income from continuing operations		$ 500
Discontinued operations:		
Loss from operations of discontinued farm machinery manufacturing business (net of $50 income tax effect)	$ 70	
Loss on disposal of farm machinery manufacturing business (net of $100 income tax effect)	130	(200)
Income before extraordinary gain and before cumulative effect of change in accounting principle		$ 300
Extraordinary gain (net of $80 income tax effect)		90
Cumulative effect on prior years of change from straight-line to accelerated depreciation (net of $60 income tax effect)		(60)
Net Income		$ 330

Note to Exhibit B

X Company operates principally in three industries—computers, food processing, and can manufacturing. Operations in the computer industry include the design, development, manufacture, and marketing of large computers. Operations in the food-processing industry include the cleaning, cooking, canning, and marketing of vegetables. Operations in the can-manufacturing industry include the production and sale of aluminum and steel cans for the canning industry. Total revenue by industry includes both sales to unaffiliated customers, as reported in the company's consolidated income statement, and intersegment sales, which are accounted for at negotiated prices between the segments. The company feels these negotiated prices approximate outside market prices.

Operating profit is total revenue less operating expenses. In computing operating profit, none of the following items has been added or deducted: general corporate expenses, interest expense, income taxes, equity in income from unconsolidated investee, loss from discontinued operations of the farm machinery manufacturing business (which was a separate industry), extraordinary gain (which relates to the company's operations in the computer industry, and the cumulative effect of the change from straight-

Exhibit B

X COMPANY
Information about the Company's Operations in Different Industries (thousands of dollars)

	Computers	Food Processing	Can Manufacturing	Other Industries	Adjustments and Eliminations	Consolidated
Sales to unaffiliated customers	$1,200	$2,000	$1,300	$ 200		$ 4,700
Intersegment sales			700		$(700)	
Total revenue	$1,200	$2,000	$2,000	$ 200	$(700)	$ 4,700
Operating profit	$ 200	$ 290	$ 600	$ 50	$ (40)[a]	$ 1,100
Equity in net income of Z Company						100
General corporate expenses						(100)
Interest expense						(200)
Income from continuing operations before income taxes						$ 900
Identifiable assets at December 31, 19X1	$2,000	$4,050	$6,000	$1,000	$ (50)[b]	$13,000
Investment in net assets of Z Company						400
Corporate assets						1,600
Total assets at December 31, 19X1						$15,000

See accompanying note in text.

[a]$10,000 of intersegment operating profit in beginning inventory, net of $50,000 of intersegment operating profit in ending inventory.
[b]$50,000 of intersegment operating profit in ending inventory.

line to accelerated depreciation, of which $30 relates to the company's operations in the computer industry, $10 to the food-processing industry, and $20 to the can-manufacturing industry). Depreciation for these three industries was $80, $100, and $150, respectively. Capital expenditures for the three industries were $100, $200, and $400, respectively.

Changing from straight-line to accelerated depreciation reduced the 19X1 operating profit of the computer industry, the food-processing industry, and the can-manufacturing industry by $40, $30, and $20, respectively.

Identifiable assets by industry are assets that are used in the company's operations in each industry. Corporate assets are principally cash and marketable securities.

The company has a 25% interest in Z Company whose operations are in the United States and are vertically integrated with the company's operations in the computer industry. The equity in Z Company's net income was $100; the investment in Z Company's net assets was $400.

To reconcile industry information with consolidated amounts, the following eliminations have been made: $700 of intersegment sales; $40 from the net change in intersegment operating profit in beginning and ending inventories; and $50 intersegment operating profit in inventory at December 31, 19X1.

Contracts with a U.S. government agency account for $1,000 of the sales to unaffiliated customers of the food-processing industry.

Note to Exhibit C

Transfers between geographic areas are accounted for at prices negotiated between the buying and selling units. The company feels such prices approximate outside market prices. Operating profit is total revenue less operating expenses. In computing operating profit, none of the following items has been added or deducted: general corporate expenses, interest expense, income taxes, equity in income from unconsolidated investee, loss from discontinued operations of the farm machinery manufacturing business (which was part of the company's domestic operations), extraordinary gain (which relates to the company's operations in Western Europe),

Exhibit C

X COMPANY
Information about the Company's Operations in Different Geographic Areas
For the Year Ended December 31, 19X1
(thousands of dollars)

	United States	Western Europe	South America	Adjustments and Eliminations	Consolidated
Sales to unaffiliated customers	$3,000	$1,000	$ 700		$ 4,700
Transfers between geographic areas	1,000			$(1,000)	
Total revenue	$4,000	$1,000	$ 700	$(1,000)	$ 4,700
Operating profit	$ 800	$ 400	$ 100	$ (200)	$ 1,100
Equity in net income of Z Company					100
General corporate expenses					(100)
Interest expense					(200)
Income from continuing operations before income taxes					$ 900
Identifiable assets at December 31, 19X1	$7,300	$3,400	$2,450	$ (150)	$13,000
Investment in net assets of Z Company					400
Corporate assets					1,600
Total assets at December 31, 19X1					$15,000

See accompanying note in text.

and the cumulative effect of the change from straight-line to accelerated depreciation (which relates entirely to the company's operations in the United States).

The company's identifiable assets are identified with the operations in each geographic area. Corporate assets are principally cash and marketable securities.

Of the $3,000 U.S. sales to unaffiliated customers, $1,200 were export sales, principally to South America.

Review Questions

1. Why are consolidated financial statements alone considered insufficient and inadequate financial reports?
2. What three basic disclosures relate to industry segment reporting?
3. Define *industry segment* according to *FASB Statement No. 14.*
4. Distinguish between an industry segment and a reportable segment.
5. What tests determine whether an industry segment is a reportable segment?
6. What amounts for industry segments must be reconciled to consolidated amounts?
7. Under *FASB Statement No. 14*, how should prices be determined for transfers between segments?
8. Name five items that cannot be allocated to industry segments in computing a segment's operating profit or loss.
9. What two tests determine whether foreign operations are reportable?
10. How are foreign countries grouped into geographic areas under *FASB Statement No. 14?*
11. What three types of information must be disclosed for a reportable geographic area?
12. Explain the difference between the definition of an industry segment under *FASB Statement No. 14* and the definition under *APB Opinion No. 30.*
13. Distinguish between the measurement date and the disposal date as those terms are used in *APB Opinion No. 30.*
14. How are revenues, cost of goods sold, and operating expenses from the beginning of the year to the measurement date reported for a segment being disposed of?

Discussion Cases

DC 13-1

Procedures Used to Determine Industry Segments

Knotter Company has the following operations: (1) planting and growing trees (2) harvesting trees (3) processing cut trees into building materials (lumber and plywood) (4) manufacturing paper and paper products, and (5) manufacturing container and packaging products.

The controller has asked your advice on determining industry segments.

Required:

1. How would you determine which operations constitute industry segments?
2. Make several possible assumptions as to the key determinant, and proceed accordingly.

DC 13-2

Treatment of Central Research and Development Costs

Foursome Company operates in four industries, each of which is conducted through subsidiaries. The operations of these subsidiaries are located some distance from the parent's headquarters location. Each subsidiary conducts research and development at its separate location. In addition, the parent maintains a central research department at its own headquarters location, which benefits all of the segments in the same manner that top management at the headquarters location benefits all segments.

Required:
Evaluate the treatment used to record the facilities and expenses of the central research department in preparing segment information disclosures.

DC 13-3

Manner of Reconciling Segment Information to Consolidated Amounts

Tres Company operates in three industry segments—A, B, and C. Industry segment A comprises three companies (X, Y, and Z), which constitute a vertically integrated operation. Company X sells solely to Company Y, which sells solely to Company Z, which sells solely to unaffiliated customers. In addition, Segment B sells about 10% of its production output to Segment C. Segments B and C are not vertically integrated operations. All of these intercompany sales are at prices approximating outside market prices. Assume Company Y, Company Z, and Segment C have intercompany inventory purchases on hand at the beginning and end of the current reporting year.

Required:
How are intercompany sales and intercompany profits on such intercompany inventory sales presented in disclosing industry segment information? Be specific as to the effect on presenting revenues, operating profit or loss, and identifiable assets.

Exercises

E 13-1

Segment Reporting: Multiple Choice

1. Select the items that are part of the additional information disclosure requirements of *FASB Statement No. 14.*
   a. Major customers
   b. Different industries
   c. Imports
   d. Major suppliers
   e. Export sales
   f. Foreign operations

2. Select the items that are used in one of the three 10% tests for determining reportable industry segments.
   a. Total revenues
   b. Operating profit or loss
   c. Segment net income
   d. Revenues to unaffiliated customers
   e. Identifiable assets
   f. Nonidentifiable assets
3. Select the items that are to be disclosed for reportable industry segments.
   a. Identifiable assets
   b. Capital expenditures
   c. Pretax accounting income
   d. Depreciation expense
   e. Operating profit or loss
   f. Total revenues
   g. Revenues from sales to unaffiliated customers and sales or transfers to other industry segments
4. Select the items reportable by industry segment that must be reconciled to consolidated amounts.
   a. Net income
   b. Identifiable assets
   c. Cost of goods sold
   d. Operating profit or loss
   e. Intersegment sales
   f. Revenues
5. Select the items that cannot be added or deducted, as the case may be, in computing the operating profit or loss of an industry segment.
   a. Income taxes
   b. General corporate expenses
   c. Interest expense
   d. Property taxes
   e. Research and development expenses
   f. Gain on early extinguishment of debt
   g. Extraordinary items

E 13-2

Segment Reporting: True or False

Indicate whether the following statements are true or false:

1. The definition of *revenue* under *FASB Statement No. 14* includes revenues from intersegment sales or transfers.
2. The FASB has established a basis that should be used to set prices for intersegment sales.
3. The FASB has allowed management to determine the procedures for allocating general corporate expenses to individual segments.
4. *FASB Statement No. 14* applies to companies having consolidated sales under $100,000,000.
5. The emphasis of *FASB Statement No. 14* is on organizational structure—that is, branches, divisions, and subsidiaries.
6. An industry segment is the component of a business that sells only to unaffiliated customers.
7. Revenue (as defined) minus all operating expenses equals the operating profit or loss of an industry segment.
8. The definition of operating expenses does not include expenses related to both revenues from sales to unaffiliated customers and revenues from intersegment sales or transfers.
9. Identifiable assets of an industry segment may include an allocated portion of assets used jointly by two or more segments.
10. Management determines the grouping of products and services into appropriate industry segments.

E 13-3

Segment Reporting: Fill-in

Fill in the blanks with the appropriate word or phrase.

1. If more than ________ reportable industry segments exist, a company may appropriately combine the most closely related segments into broader segments.
2. Enough individual segments must be presented so that at least ________% of the combined revenues (from sales to ________________ ________________ of all industry segments) is shown by reportable segments.
3. An industry segment is a component of an enterprise engaged in providing a ________________ or ________________ or a group of related ________________ and ________________ primarily to ________________ customers for a ________________.
4. Segment reporting is not required for ________________ companies.
5. The percentage used in the three tests for determining if an industry segment is reportable is ________________.
6. The revenues test used to determine if an industry segment is reportable is based on ________________ ________________, which includes sales to ________________ customers and ________________ sales.
7. The revenues test and the identifiable assets test used to determine if a geographic area is separately reportable are based on ________________ amounts.
8. The three basic types of information provided for a reportable geographic area are ________________, ________________, and ________________ ________________.

E 13-4

Segment Reporting: Treatment of Common Costs

Sulovsky Company operates in three different industries, each of which is appropriately regarded as a reportable segment. Segment 1 contributed 60% of Sulovsky's total sales. Sales for Segment 1 were $900,000 and traceable costs were $400,000. Total common costs for Sulovsky were $300,000. Sulovsky allocates common costs based on the ratio of a segment's sales to total sales, an appropriate method of allocation. Assume a 40% income tax rate.

Required:
Determine the operating profit presented for Segment 1.

(AICPA adapted)

E 13-5

Segment Reporting: Determining Reportable Segments—Revenues Test

Ming Company has the following revenues (stated in thousands of dollars) for its industry segments:

Segment	Sales to Unaffiliated Customers	Intersegment Sales	Total Sales
A	$ 170		$ 170
B	150		150
C	75		75
D	300	$125	425
E	80		80
F	125		125
G	200	175	375
	$1,100	$300	$1,400

Required:

1. Determine the reportable segments based on the revenues test.
2. Assuming the other two 10% tests based on operating profit or loss and identifiable assets do not result in any additional reportable segments, perform the 75% test.

E 13-6

Segment Reporting: Determining Reportable Geographic Areas—Revenues Test

Clover Company earns revenues (in thousands of dollars) in the following geographic areas:

Geographic Area	Sales to Unaffiliated Customers	Transfers between Geographic Areas	Total
Western Europe	$ 100	$100	$ 200
Africa	200	150	350
South America	300		300
Australia	400	100	500
Middle East	500		500
United States	1,000	150	1,150
	$2,500	$500	$3,000

Required:
Determine which foreign geographic areas are reportable areas based on the revenues test.

E 13-7

Disposal of a Segment: Determining Amounts to Be Reported

The following condensed income statement for Divesto Corporation, a diversified company, is presented for the two years ended December 31, 19X7 and 19X6:

	19X7	19X6
Net sales	$5,000,000	$4,800,000
Cost of goods sold	(3,100,000)	(3,000,000)
Gross profit	$1,900,000	$1,800,000
Operating expenses	(1,100,000)	(1,200,000)
Operating income	$ 800,000	$ 600,000
Gain on sale of division	450,000	
Income before Income Taxes	$1,250,000	$ 600,000
Provision for income taxes	(500,000)	(240,000)
Net Income	$ 750,000	$ 360,000

On January 1, 19X7, Divesto entered into an agreement to sell for $1,600,000 the assets and product line of its separate Data PC division. The sale was consummated on December 31, 19X7, and resulted in a pretax gain on disposition of $450,000. This division's contribution to Divesto's reported pretax operating income for each year was as follows: 19X6, $(250,000) loss; 19X7, $(300,000) loss. Assume an income tax rate of 40%.

Required:
Determine the following amounts that Divesto should report in its comparative income statement for 19X7 and 19X6:

a. Income from continuing operations (after income taxes).
b. Discontinued operations.
c. Net income.

(AICPA adapted)

E 13-8

Disposal of a Segment: Determination of Loss Related to Discontinued Operations

The Rodney Company is disposing of a segment of its business. With respect to this disposal, the following information is given:

Estimated operating loss from the measurement date to the end of the current year	$200,000
Severance pay	100,000
Relocation costs (for employees)	50,000
Actual operating loss from the beginning of the year to the measurement date	300,000
Estimated operating loss from the end of the current year to the estimated disposal date	400,000
Estimated loss on the sale of the segment's assets in the following year	500,000

The severance pay and the employee relocation costs are directly associated with the decision to dispose of this segment. Assume a 40% income tax rate.

Required:
Prepare the discontinued operations section of the income statement for the current year.

Problems

P 13-1

Segment Reporting: Determining Reportable Segments—Revenues Test, Operating Profit or Loss Test, and Identifiable Assets Test

Information (in thousands of dollars) with respect to Mogambu Company's industry segments for 19X1 follows:

Segment	Total Revenue	Operating Profit (Loss)	Identifiable Assets
A	$ 30	$ (10)	$ 75
B	210	100	400
C	80	(40)	125
D	190	20	100
E	170	(60)	250
F	70	10	100
G	250	110	450
	$1,000	$130	$1,500

The only intersegment revenues were $60,000 from segment E to segment D.

Required:

1. Determine which industry segments are reportable segments.
2. Perform the 75% test.

P 13-2

Segment Reporting: Presenting Industry Segment Information—Intersegment Inventory Sales (Intercompany Profit in Ending Inventory)

Kasagi Company operates in five major industry segments, all of which are reportable segments. Financial information for each segment for 19X8 follows:

	Segment				
	A	B	C	D	E
Total revenues	$70,000	$60,000	$50,000	$40,000	$30,000
Operating profit	30,000	25,000	20,000	15,000	10,000
Identifiable assets	40,000	35,000	30,000	25,000	20,000

Intersegment sales (included in the above total revenues) were as follows:

1. Segment C sold inventory costing $5,000 to segment D for $8,000. At December 31, 19X8, all of this inventory had been sold by segment D.
2. Segment A sold inventory costing $6,000 to segment B for $10,000. At December 31, 19X8, 20% of this inventory had not been sold by segment B.

Assume no intercompany inventory was on hand at December 31, 19X7, and assume a consolidated income tax return is filed. Data related to the corporate offices are as follows:

Corporate expenses	$12,000
Interest expense	18,000
Interest income	5,000
Corporate assets	15,000
Overall corporate income tax rate	40%

Required:

Prepare a report presenting industry segment information, reconciling, when required, to amounts that would appear in the consolidated financial statements. (Use the illustration in the appendix to this chapter as a guide.)

P 13-3

Segment Reporting: Presenting Industry Segment Information—Intrasegment and Intersegment Sales (Intracompany Profit in Beginning and Ending Inventories)

Dubbler Company operates in two industries, both of which qualify as reportable industry segments. Applicable data follow (amounts are in thousands):

	19X2
Segment A:	
Sales to unaffiliated customers	$500
*Inter*segment sales	400
*Intra*segment sales	200
Operating profit	300
*Inter*segment gross profit that could not be reported at the end of:	
19X2	60
19X1	20
*Intra*segment gross profit that could not be reported at the end of:	
19X2	10
19X1	–0–
Segment B:	
Sales to unaffiliated customers	800
Operating profit	100

Required:

Determine the proper amounts for revenues and operating profit to be presented in the industry segment information disclosure schedule for 19X2 shown below:

	Segment A	Segment B	Adjustments and Eliminations	Consolidated
Revenues				
Operating profit				

P 13-4 Segment Reporting: Presenting Industry Segment Information—Intrasegment and Intersegment Sales (Intercompany Profit in Beginning and Ending Inventories)

Maui Company has three industry segments—A, B, and C, each of which is a reportable industry segment. Data (in thousands of dollars) for these segments for 19X2 are as follows:

	Revenues			
	Intercompany	Unaffiliated Customers	Operating Profit	Identifiable Assets
Segment A:				
Company X	$100		$ 30	$240
Company Y		$700	170	660
Segment B:				
Company M		300	80	310
Company N	50	560	120	490
Segment C:				
Company T		300	50	200

Additional Information:

1. Segment A is a vertically integrated operation. Company X sells all of its output to Company Y.

2. Segments B and C are not vertically integrated operations. Company N's intercompany sales are to Company T.
3. All intercompany sales are at prices that approximate outside market prices. Assume a 40% gross profit margin on all intercompany sales.
4. At the end of the current reporting year, each company has 10% of its current-year intercompany inventory purchases on hand.
5. Data relating to the corporate offices are as follows:

Corporate expenses	$35,000
Interest expense	29,000
Corporate assets	40,000

6. Assume a consolidated federal income tax return is filed and a 40% income tax rate.

Required:

1. Present the above data in a schedule that satisfies the disclosure requirements of *FASB Statement No. 14*, assuming no intercompany inventory purchases were on hand at the beginning of the year. The following steps will help:
   a. Prepare the intercompany transaction elimination entry in consolidating Company X and Company Y.
   b. Post the entry in (a) to a mini-worksheet containing the sales and profit data provided in the problem.
2. Present the above data in a schedule that satisfies the disclosure requirements of *FASB Statement No. 14*, assuming that (a) Company Y had $25,000 of intercompany inventory on hand at the beginning of the year, and (b) Company T had $4,000 of intercompany inventory on hand at the beginning of the year. (Assume a 40% gross profit rate for the prior year.)
   a. Prepare the entries required in consolidation with respect to each company's beginning intercompany acquired inventory.

P 13-5 Segment Reporting: Presenting Geographic Area Information—Intrageographic and Intergeographic Transfers (Intercompany Profit in Ending Inventory)

Klaus Company has operations in the United States, Mexico, and England, each of which qualifies as a reportable geographic area. Data (in thousands of dollars) with respect to these areas for 19X3 are as follows:

	Revenues			
	Inter-company	Unaffiliated Customers	Operating Profit	Identifiable Assets
United States:				
Company A		$800	$200	$300
Company B	$150	450	150	200
Company C	60	600	240	350
Mexico:				
Company X	100		30	180
England:				
Company S		280	110	90

Additional Information:

1. Company X is part of a vertically integrated industry and sells all of its output to Company B.
2. Company B is part of a vertically integrated industry and sells part of its output to Company S.
3. Company C's intercompany sales are to Company A.
4. All intercompany sales are at prices that approximate outside market prices. Assume a 40% gross profit margin on all intercompany sales.
5. At the end of the current reporting year, each company has 10% of its current-year intercompany inventory purchases on hand.
6. Data as to the corporate offices are as follows:

General corporate expenses	$37,000
Interest expense	28,000
Corporate assets	65,000

7. Assume a 40% income tax rate.

Required:

Present the above data in a schedule that satisfies the disclosure requirements of *FASB Statement No. 14*, assuming no intercompany inventory purchases were on hand at the beginning of the year.

P 13-6

Disposal of a Segment: Determining Amounts to Report

On June 30, 19X1, Zapata Enterprises (a calendar year-end reporting company) announced plans to dispose of several of its segments. Data (in thousands of dollars) gathered at that time for these segments follow:

Segment	Year-to-Date Income (Loss) from Operations	Estimated Future Income (Loss) from Operations through the Disposal Date 19X1	Estimated Future Income (Loss) from Operations through the Disposal Date 19X2	Estimated Gain (Loss) on Disposal	Estimated Disposal Date
A	$(400)	$(300)	$(200)	$(100)	2/1/X2
B	(100)	(400)	(300)	800	2/1/X2
C	200	(500)	100	300	2/1/X2
D	(300)	(400)		200	10/1/X1
E	(300)	(200)		400	10/1/X1
F	300	200		(400)	10/1/X1
G	200	200	200	300	3/1/X2
H	200	400	200	(300)	3/1/X2
I	600	300	(100)	(300)	3/1/X2

These amounts do not reflect income taxes.

Required:
Determine the amounts to be reported in the two categories of the discontinued operations section of the income statement for each of the above segments. Use the following reporting periods:

First and Second Quarters — 19X1	Third and Fourth Quarters — 19X1	First Quarter — 19X2

For simplicity, assume future operations and sales of the segments proceed according to plan. Ignore income tax effects.

P 13-7 Disposal of a Segment: Preparing Income Statement and Statement of Retained Earnings — Variety of Events and Transactions

Variety Company had the following events and transactions in 19X5:

Sales	$10,000,000[a]
Cost of goods sold (corrected for inventory pricing error at December 31, 19X4)	5,700,000[a]
Understatement of December 31, 19X4 inventory (pricing error)	250,000
Marketing and administrative expenses	2,000,000[a]
Operating loss for 19X5 related to Gismo Division, $150,000 of which occurred after the decision to dispose of the division	500,000
Estimated 19X6 operating loss for Gismo Division	300,000
Estimated loss on sale of Gismo Division's net assets (a separate industry segment), disposal to be completed in 19X6	550,000
Gain on early extinguishment of debt	600,000
Flood loss, uninsured	700,000[b]
Settlement of lawsuit related to 19X3 activity (not accrued in prior years)	400,000[c]

[a]Excludes Gismo Division.
[b]The last major flood in the area was 60 years ago.
[c]From the time the lawsuit was filed in 19X3, legal counsel felt that the company would not win the lawsuit. Legal counsel could not estimate either the ultimate settlement amount or a likely range within which the settlement amount would fall. Future such lawsuits are possible.

Assume a combined federal and state income tax rate of 40%. Assume that no timing or permanent differences exist between pretax accounting income and taxable income. Retained earnings were $2,000,000 on January 1, 19X5, and cash dividends of $100,000 were declared during 19X5.

Required:
Prepare an income statement and a statement of retained earnings for 19X5.

III

Omnibus Area

14

Translation of Foreign Currency Financial Statements: Concepts

AN OVERVIEW OF FOREIGN OPERATIONS AND TRANSACTIONS

The expansion of international business in the last 40 years has been phenomenal. Total U.S. exports and imports are each approximately $300 billion. Investments overseas by U.S. companies total approximately $200 billion (up from approximately $12 billion in 1950), producing over $40 billion in earnings per year. As a result, export sales and foreign operations now constitute a significant part of the overall activities of a considerable number of domestic corporations. For many of these companies, foreign activities are limited to such operations as importing goods from unaffiliated foreign suppliers and exporting goods to unaffiliated foreign customers.

The Accounting Issues

Foreign Operations. Through internal or external expansion, some companies build or acquire overseas manufacturing or marketing organizations, which may conduct import or export activities with the domestic operation. Such foreign operations may be conducted through branches, divisions, or subsidiaries, but the most common form of organization is the subsidiary, because it best insulates legally the foreign operation from the domestic operation. There are three accounting issues for foreign operations of a domestic parent:

1. How should the earnings and losses of the foreign units be determined in U.S. dollars?
2. What additional risks must be considered in reporting earnings from foreign operations? Is consolidation appropriate?
3. Should supplemental information disclose the extent of a company's foreign operations?

Foreign-Currency Transactions. Importing and exporting situations that require settlement (payment) in a foreign currency raise the following accounting issues:

1. How should the transaction be recorded in U.S. dollars at the transaction date?
2. If credit terms are granted and used, how should the accounting consequences of the decision to grant or use credit be recorded?

This chapter lays the theoretical groundwork for dealing with currency exchange rates. Chapter 15 discusses and illustrates how to translate foreign-currency financial statements into U.S. dollars. Chapter 16 discusses how to translate foreign-currency transactions.

The Governing Pronouncements

Translation. The principles and procedures to be followed in accounting for the translation of foreign operations and transactions are set forth in *FASB Statement No. 52*, "Foreign Currency Translation." Issued in 1981 after three years of intensive research and extensive participation by professionals in industry, public accounting, higher education, and finance, *FASB Statement No. 52* addresses what is widely recognized as one of the most complex and controversial accounting issues. *FASB Statement No. 52* replaced *FASB Statement No. 8*, "Accounting for the Translation of Foreign Currency Transactions and Foreign Currency Financial Statements," which was issued in 1975. *FASB Statement No. 8* outlined uniform accounting procedures for an area previously characterized by numerous practices that often produced widely different results. However, the results under the uniform treatment prescribed by *FASB Statement No. 8* were widely criticized as not reflective of economic changes, and the business community's strong opposition to and continued criticism of the pronouncement resulted in FASB's decision in 1979 to reconsider the entire translation issue. Chapters 15 and 16 examine *FASB Statement No. 52* in detail.

Additional Risks and the Appropriateness of Consolidation. *Accounting Research Bulletin No. 43* addresses the additional risks associated with foreign operations and the appropriateness of consolidation. These aspects are discussed in Chapter 15.

Supplemental Disclosures. The issue of presenting in financial statements supplemental information pertaining to the extent of a company's foreign operations is addressed in *FASB Statement No. 14*, "Financial Reporting for Segments of a Business Enterprise." This pronouncement was discussed in detail in Chapter 13, which covers segment reporting.

CURRENCY EXCHANGE RATES

Conversion versus Translation

Actually changing one currency into another currency is called **conversion.** Foreign currencies are usually purchased through commercial banks. Likewise, when payment is received in a foreign currency, that currency may be converted into dollars at such institutions. Conversion must be differentiated from **translation,** which is the process of expressing amounts stated in one currency in terms of another currency by using the appropriate **currency exchange rates.**

Methods of Expressing Exchange Rates

The ratio of the number of units of one currency needed to acquire one unit of another currency constitutes the exchange rate between the two currencies. The exchange rate may be expressed in two ways, indirect quotation and direct quotation:

1. **Indirect quotation.** The number of units of the foreign currency needed to acquire one unit of the domestic currency is the **indirect** quotation of the exchange rate (for example, 1 dollar = 0.625 pounds). To determine the dollar equivalent of an amount stated in a foreign currency, the foreign currency is **divided** by the exchange rate. (Professional traders in foreign currencies use the indirect quotation rate.)
2. **Direct quotation.** The number of units of the domestic currency needed to acquire one unit of the foreign currency is a **direct** quotation of the exchange rate (for example, 1 pound = $1.60). To determine the dollar equivalent of an amount stated in a foreign currency, the foreign currency amount is **multiplied** by the exchange rate. (Travelers prefer the direct quotation rate.)

Banks and daily newspapers in the United States quote exchange rates both indirectly and directly. Translation of amounts stated in foreign currencies is usually performed using direct quotations. In all examples and illustrations in this chapter, we use the direct quotation of the exchange rate. Direct quotations of the exchange rates between the dollar and several major foreign currencies are as follows:

	Dollar Equivalent of One Unit of Foreign Currency			Percent Change	
Country (currency)	12/31/81	12/31/85	12/31/86	5 year	1 year
Brazil (cruzado)	$8.0100	$0.1005	$0.0685	−99	−32
Britain (pound)	1.9170	1.4452	1.4830	−23	+3
Canada (dollar)	0.8435	0.7153	0.7241	−14	−1
France (franc)	0.1757	0.1333	0.1551	−11	+16
Italy (lira)	0.0008	0.0006	0.0007	−12	+17
Japan (yen)	0.0045	0.0049	0.0063	+40	+28
Mexico (peso)	0.0381	0.0028	0.0011	−97	−61
Switzerland (franc)	0.5602	0.4859	0.6154	+11	+27
West Germany (mark)	0.4460	0.4090	0.5203	+17	+27

The Exchange Rate System: Floating versus Fixed Exchange Rates

Currency exchange rates are a function of market conditions, which in turn are a function of changing economic and political conditions such as the balance of payments surplus or deficit, the internal spending surplus or deficit, the internal inflation rate, and the imminence of various civil disorders. Exchange rates determined by market conditions are either **floating** or **free** rates.

Before 1974, the dollar was tied to gold, and most currencies were tied to the dollar. As a result, **fixed** or **official** exchange rates existed. When fixed rates no longer reflected economic conditions, governments were forced to devalue or revalue their currencies (as the U.S. government did in 1973 when it announced a 10% devaluation). Although devaluations of certain currencies were often expected, it was impossible to determine exactly when they would occur or the amount of the devaluation. This major drawback and the fact that the system could not deal with rapid inflation made the system unsustainable. In 1974, the dollar was taken off the gold standard (that is, the dollar was no longer backed by gold reserves), and most currencies that had not already been allowed to float were allowed to do so. As a result, changing international economic conditions are reflected in the currency exchange rates on a daily basis.

Even under the floating exchange rate system, governments may intervene in the exchange markets by buying and selling currencies (as the U.S. government did in the late 1970s to bolster the dollar). An extreme example of intervention is the Mexican peso. After nearly 25 years of stability, the Mexican government allowed the peso to float in 1976; it promptly declined 50% in value against the dollar. In theory, the peso became a floating currency in the international money markets at that time. However, by buying and selling dollars, the central bank of Mexico tried to control the value of the peso at a fairly fixed level against the dollar. In early 1982, the central bank's reserves of U.S dollars were nearly exhausted, and the government announced that it would withdraw temporarily from the foreign exchange markets. The peso promptly declined nearly 40% in value against the dollar. Two subsequent interventions and temporary withdrawals occurred in 1982; the peso declined approximately 85% in value against the dollar in 1982.

A change in a floating exchange rate is appropriately referred to as a **strengthening** or **weakening** of one currency in relation to another.

Strengthening Currencies. A foreign currency that is strengthening in value in relation to the dollar requires more dollars to obtain a unit of the foreign currency; accordingly, the direct exchange rate increases. A weakening of the dollar has the same effect on the direct exchange rate as does the strengthening of the foreign currency.

Weakening Currencies. A foreign currency that is weakening in value in relation to the dollar requires fewer dollars to obtain a unit of the foreign currency; accordingly, the direct exchange rate decreases. A strengthening of the dollar has the same effect on the direct exchange rate as does the weakening of the foreign currency.

Spot and Forward Exchange Rates. Exchange rates at which currencies could be converted immediately (for settlement in two days) are termed **spot rates.** Exchange rates also exist for transactions whereby conversion could be made at some stipulated date (normally up to 12 months) in the future. **Future,** or **forward, rates** are discussed in Chapter 16.

Exchange Rates Used in Translation

Before we discuss the specific issues and procedures for translating foreign currency transactions and foreign currency financial statements into dollars, we must define the currency exchange rates that are used in these translation processes.

Current Exchange Rate. For **transactions,** the current exchange rate is the rate at which one unit of currency can be exchanged for another currency. For **translation** of a foreign unit's financial statements into dollars, *FASB Statement No. 52* requires the use of a current exchange rate in most situations. Specifically, a company must use (a) the exchange rate existing at the balance sheet date for assets and liabilities and (b) the exchange rates in effect at the time of recognition of revenues, cost of goods sold, expenses, gains, and losses in the income statement.[1]

Average Exchange Rates. Because it is impractical to translate the various income statement items at the numerous exchange rates that could apply throughout a period, *FASB Statement No. 52* allows firms to use appropriately weighted average exchange rates for the period.

Historical Exchange Rate. *FASB Statement No. 52* requires the use of both the current exchange rate and the historical exchange rate (depending on the individual item) when the current rate method of translation is not appropriate. For example, the exchange rate in effect last year when a building was acquired (the current rate at that time) is now the historical exchange rate, which is used in translation rather than the current exchange rate existing at the balance sheet date. Likewise, the historical exchange rate would be used in translating depreciation expense related to the building rather than the rate in effect when the depreciation was recognized in the income statement.

Ignor

Multiple Exchange Rates. In addition to the floating rates, many countries declare one or more official rates for certain types of currency conversions. For example, to discourage the repatriation of dividends to a foreign

[1]*Statement of Financial Accounting Standards, No. 52,* "Foreign Currency Translation (Stamford: Financial Accounting Standards Board, 1981), par. 12.

parent company, a country would use a rate whereby the parent company would receive a lesser amount of its own currency than it otherwise would receive had the free rate been used. When such multiple rates exist, *FASB Statement No. 52* requires the following:

a. *Foreign Currency Transactions* — The applicable rate at which a particular transaction could be settled at the transaction date shall be used to translate and record the transaction. At a subsequent balance sheet date, the current rate is that rate at which the related receivable or payable could be settled at that date.[2]
b. *Foreign Currency Statements* — In the absence of unusual circumstances, the rate applicable to conversion of a currency for purposes of dividend remittances shall be used to translate foreign statements.[3]

GETTING IN STEP WITH U.S. GENERALLY ACCEPTED ACCOUNTING PRINCIPLES

Companies establish foreign operations with the expectation that these units will generate profits on the investments made. Domestic companies, therefore, want to isolate for analysis the profit or loss generated by their foreign units. Each foreign unit keeps its books and records in its own local currency. However, the profit or loss of a foreign unit as stated in the foreign currency is not meaningful to the domestic parent or home office; domestic companies must be able to determine the profit or loss of each of their foreign units in dollars. This is done by translating the foreign-currency financial statements into dollars, using appropriate currency exchange rates. However, translating profit or loss amounts of foreign units into dollars is complicated by the fact that foreign units use the accounting principles of the countries in which they are located — not U.S. generally accepted accounting principles.

The Diversity of Worldwide Accounting Principles

Accounting principles are not uniform worldwide. Different national laws, different tax laws, and varying degrees of formalization of accounting and reporting practices by standard-setting bodies in the private sector are the main reasons for these differences. The major differences involve the following four areas:

1. **LIFO inventory costing.** Although widely used in the United States, this method has virtually no acceptance in other countries.
2. **Interperiod income tax allocation.** Although mandatory in the United States, only a handful of other countries require it.

[2]Transactions are discussed in Chapter 16.
[3]*FASB Statement No. 52*, par. 27.

3. **Pooling of interests.** Although required in the United States when the specified criteria are met, it is allowed in only a few other countries and then only under rigid constraints. Pooling of interests is unheard of in many countries.
4. **Goodwill amortization.** Amortization is mandatory in the United States, but most foreign countries do not require it, allowing goodwill to appear on the balance sheet practically forever.

The following examples demonstrate the range and diversity of accounting practices in foreign countries.

Australia

- Land and buildings are reported at either cost or appraised values (or a mixture of both), less depreciation.
- Certain nonmanufacturing assets may not be depreciated.
- All cost in excess of an acquired business's net assets at book value is usually deemed to be goodwill. Goodwill may be shown as a deduction from capital or charged to capital.

Brazil

- All fixed assets are written up once a year, using indexes published by the federal government that are based on the percentage of inflation that occurred during the year. Depreciation for financial and tax reporting purposes is based on the revalued amounts.
- A provision for "maintenance of working capital" may be recorded to remove from profit the effect of inflation on current and long-term assets (excluding fixed assets) and liabilities. This provision is also deductible for tax-reporting purposes.

France

- Pension costs are provided only to the extent that such provisions are deductible for income tax purposes.

Italy

- The national legislative body periodically authorizes companies to revalue their fixed assets to reflect inflation.

Japan

- Goodwill may be expensed as incurred or amortized over no more than five years.
- Research and development costs may be deferred over a maximum of five years.
- Losses generally are not provided on obsolete or slow-moving inventory.

Mexico

- Most industrial and retail firms revalue their fixed assets annually to current appraised value.
- Some companies report income tax expense on the cash basis.
- All cost in excess of an acquired business's net assets at book value is deemed to be goodwill.

Switzerland

- The equity method is not used to account for long-term investments.
- Machinery and equipment may be expensed at the time of purchase.

United Kingdom

- Goodwill may be written off immediately to stockholders' equity or amortized to income. No maximum amortization period exists.

West Germany

- Intangible assets cannot be amortized over more than five years (compared to 40 years in the U.S.).
- Certain inventory valuation methods may result in a valuation lower than that produced by applying the lower of cost or market rule.

Just as it does not make sense to add together financial statement amounts in dollars and foreign currencies, it would not be meaningful financial reporting to report worldwide operations using one set of accounting principles for domestic operations and a variety of accounting principles for foreign operations. Accordingly, when foreign currency financial statements are prepared using accounting principles and practices that are materially different from U.S. generally accepted accounting principles, such statements must be **restated** to reflect U.S. generally accepted accounting principles **before they are translated into dollars.**

Obviously, the lack of worldwide uniform accounting principles and practices is unfortunate, as the article on page 553 reflects. Some international accounting organizations (most notably the International Accounting Standards Committee, which has issued nearly thirty international accounting standards) are seeking to promote worldwide uniform accounting principles and practices. The problem is not only one of reaching agreement on what the worldwide accounting principles should be but also of persuading countries to adopt uniform accounting principles. Both aspects of the problem are monumental, and efforts to date have produced only limited results. However, the increasing propensity of companies to try to raise captial in world markets (outside their home countries) is becoming a factor in internationalizing accounting principles.

PERSPECTIVE

Where Boards and Governments Have Failed, the Market Could Internationalize Accounting

A French manufacturing company listed recently on the Paris Bourse looks like a promising investment. Its financial statement shows booming international sales and a healthy profit. The company's earnings outshine the disappointing results of a comparable U.S. concern in the same business.

There's only one problem. The two companies used different foreign-currency translation methods during a year of wild exchange-rate fluctuations. Because the concerns took different paths to the bottom line, the figures there could differ by millions of dollars.

Accounting experts warn that this lack of uniformity in financial statements — the absence of a world-wide accounting language — threatens the growing internationalization of trade, investment and securities markets. If investors and managers of multinational enterprises can't get understandable financial information about foreign companies and subsidiaries, they are less likely to venture abroad.

Consequently, all kinds of international bodies are trying to harmonize accounting standards. But their success has been limited, and the real changes may come from the companies themselves. As more large European firms seek to raise funds on world markets, especially in the U.S., they have had to upgrade their accounting practices and, in many cases, adopt U.S. accounting standards to attract investors and meet government filing requirements.

Such de facto harmonization could force national governments and accounting bodies to harmonize their standards. "Economics may force something that has been lagging for the last 30 years," says Edmund Coulson, deputy chief accountant of the U.S. Securities and Exchange Commission.

Many groups are working on the problem. The Organization for Economic Cooperation and Development, which monitors developed economies, gathered international business and accounting leaders here recently to discuss the barriers to standardization. The International Accounting Standards Committee, representing accountants in 65 nations, has issued more than 20 nonbinding international accounting standards. The United Nations has a group working on the problem, and the European Common Market has issued several directives requiring European companies to standardize their financial statements.

But widely varying national laws, as well as national pride, still are roadblocks. "Given the complexity of the subject and the weight of the past, the goal of harmonization still seems to be a rather long way off," says Jean-Claude Paye, the OECD's secretary-general. Donald J. Kirk, chairman of the Financial Accounting Standards Board, the professional body that hammers out accounting standards for U.S. companies, says: "Harmonization even within the U.S. is difficult, so I have to be a pessimist about international prospects."

But the growing influence of standards issued by Mr. Kirk's group may spur that harmonization. U.S. accounting rules — the so-called generally accepted accounting principles — are observed in most audits by large U.S. accounting firms. In addition, the SEC requires all companies seeking a public

... The Market Could Internationalize Accounting ***(continued)***

listing in the U.S. to comply with these principles. Some European companies, anxious to tap the deep pool of funds available in U.S. markets, have adopted the guidelines.

The number of foreign companies seeking listings in the U.S. is growing rapidly. Transactions in the U.S. in stock of foreign companies rose from $2.03 billion in 1970 to nearly $30 billion in 1983. Eighteen companies located outside the U.S. and Canada raised about $1 billion in the U.S. in 1983.

Aside from capital, a U.S. listing "gives the impression that the company is on the move and a major player," says Alfredo Scotti, who helped direct Saipem S.p.A's adoption of U.S. accounting standards in anticipation of a New York Stock Exchange offering.

Mr. Scotti says Saipem, the engineering and oil services unit of Ente Nazionale Idrocarburi, Italy's state energy holding company, came out of the process a changed entity. For one thing, earnings increased because of different rules governing the depreciation of fixed assets. (Continental European accounting practices tend to minimize profits, with the aim of minimizing taxes, while U.S. practices tend to maximize profits, with the aim of impressing potential investors.)

Some of the differences in accounting practices have a national rationale that causes European accountants to resist the wholesale, "imperialistic" imposition of U.S. standards. While countries should seek to promote international harmonization of accounting standards, "each should be free to use the methods best suited to it and its traditions," says French Finance Minister Pierre Beregovoy.

"There's a danger in trying to apply in France standards hammered out for a different country—that is, America," says Bertrand d'Illiers, chief accountant at the Paris Bourse.

Even advocates of U.S. standards express concern that they may have become too detailed and rigid. The FASB, in its 12 years of existence, has issued 80 statements refining general accounting principles, a trend Mr. Kirk worries may lead to "standards overload."

In fact, the SEC has modified some of its requirements for offerings by foreign companies. For example, companies don't need to report the salaries of individual officers, but only aggregate executive compensation. And differences in national accounting practices are permitted if the required information is provided and a means exists to reconcile it with U.S. standards.

Source: Paul Hemp, "Where Boards and Governments Have Failed, the Market Could Internationalize Accounting," *The Wall Street Journal*, May 8, 1985, p. 38.

National preferences aside, adjusting a foreign subsidiary's financial statements to the U.S.'s generally accepted accounting principles is nothing more complicated than making correcting entries, a subject that is covered in intermediate accounting. However, the difficulty lies in the fact that there are usually many such restatement entries for each foreign subsidiary.

CONCEPTUAL ISSUES

The process of translating foreign currency financial statements into dollars is merely a mechanical process, once the exchange rate for each account has been determined. However, for many years a raging controversy has existed over the following two conceptual issues:

1. Which exchange rates should be used to translate the foreign currency financial statements into dollars?
2. How should the effect of a change in the exchange rate be reported?

In this section we devote considerable attention to the substance of this controversy and the solutions that have been tried and rejected. This background is a solid base for understanding the rationale for and the requirements of *FASB Statement No. 52*. More importantly, this section emphasizes thinking rather than memorization of detailed rules and requirements, thereby enabling you to better evaluate the requirements of *FASB Statement No. 52* independently.

CONCEPTUAL ISSUE 1: WHICH EXCHANGE RATES TO USE?

Criteria Used as a Frame of Reference

The first conceptual issue is determining the appropriate exchange rates for translating the individual assets and liabilities in the balance sheet. The translation of the stockholders' equity accounts is not part of the issue, because the total translated stockholders' equity is a forced residual amount that is the difference between the total translated assets and the total translated liabilities. Once the appropriate exchange rates have been determined for the assets and liabilities, consistency and logic dictate the appropriate exchange rates for translating the income statement accounts.

Balance sheet accounts may be conveniently grouped into **monetary** and **nonmonetary** classifications (the same classification scheme used in constant-dollar accounting). Monetary items include cash and accounts that are contractually obligated to be settled in cash—namely receivables and payables. All other accounts—Inventory, Fixed Assets, and the equity accounts, for example—are nonmonetary. This first conceptual issue is discussed shortly for each of these categories.

Accountants have used the following criteria as a frame of reference for determining the appropriate exchange rates:

1. Does the exchange rate selected for a specific account result in a meaningful dollar amount?

2. Does the exchange rate selected for a specific account change the basis of accounting in translation? (For example, is the historical cost basis for fixed assets in the foreign currency retained when translation is made into dollars?)
3. When a change has occurred in the exchange rate, do the translated results reflect the economic impact of the change?

The first two criteria require no explanation. For the last criterion, understand that when a U.S. company has invested money in a foreign country, an increase in the direct exchange rate is a favorable economic event that should result in a positive report. Likewise, a decrease in the direct exchange rate is an unfavorable economic event that should result in an adverse report. For example, assume someone invested $1,000 in a savings account in a Mexican bank when the direct exchange rate was $0.08 (as many U.S. citizens did in 1975–1976 because of the high interest rates). The bank would credit his account for 12,500 pesos ($1,000 ÷ $0.08). Assume that the direct exchange rate then dropped to $0.04 (as it did in 1976). If he then withdrew the 12,500 pesos and converted them into dollars, he would have only $500 (12,500 pesos × $0.04). This decrease in the direct exchange rate was indeed an adverse economic event that caused his net worth to decrease by $500.

In the discussion to follow of the first conceptual issue, we refer to the effect of a change in the exchange rate as a **translation adjustment.** How to report a change in the exchange rate is a controversial issue that we address in our discussion of the second conceptual issue.

Translating Monetary Accounts

Most accountants agree that the only sensible way to translate monetary items is to use the exchange rate in effect at the balance sheet date (a current exchange rate). This procedure effectively values these items on a current-value basis, which is considered the most timely reporting basis. For example, assume the following information:

1. A domestic company formed a West German subsidiary on December 1, 19X1.
2. The domestic company acquired the subsidiary's common stock for $450,000 on that date when the direct exchange rate was $0.45. (The subsidiary immediately converted the $450,000 into 1,000,000 marks.)
3. The subsidiary had no other transactions from its inception to December 31, 19X1 (the parent's and its year-end).
4. The direct exchange rate at December 31, 19X1, was $0.60. (Thus, either the mark strengthened or the dollar weakened during this period—from the companies' viewpoint it does not matter which occurred.)

What is the appropriate exchange rate to translate the 1,000,000 marks at December 31, 19X1, into dollars? The only meaningful dollar amount is the dollar equivalent of marks—that is, the number of dollars into which the 1,000,000 marks could be converted. Obviously, only the $0.60 direct exchange rate at December 31, 19X1, gives a meaningful answer ($600,000). Using the $0.45 exchange rate that existed at December 1, 19X1, would give $450,000, an amount that has absolutely no meaning or usefulness at this time. Accordingly, the translation process for the Cash and the Common Stock accounts as of December 1, 19X1, and December 31, 19X1, would be as follows:

	Amount (marks)	December 1, 19X1 Rate	December 1, 19X1 Amount	December 31, 19X1 Rate	December 31, 19X1 Amount
Cash	1,000,000	$0.45	$450,000	$0.60	$600,000
Common stock	1,000,000	0.45	450,000	0.45[a]	450,000
Translation adjustment (the effect of the change in the exchange rate).........					150,000

[a]The historical exchange rate of $0.45 must be used here to isolate the effect of the change in the exchange rate.

If the parent liquidated the foreign subsidiary on December 31, 19X1, it would receive $600,000, not the $450,000 it initially invested. The parent's investment actually increased in value during December 19X1 by $150,000. The use of the $0.60 exchange rate existing at the balance sheet date reflects the economics of what has transpired, and the increase in the direct exchange rate is a favorable economic event. In summary, all three criteria listed on pages 555–56 are satisfied.

Monetary Items Other Than Cash. To translate the remaining monetary items (receivables and payables), we use the logic that was applied to the Cash account. Because receivables are one step away from cash, the only meaningful dollar amount is the dollar equivalent of the receivables. Likewise, payables require the use of cash, so the only meaningful dollar amount is the dollar equivalent that would be needed to settle the payables. The direct exchange rate existing at the balance sheet date is the only exchange rate that produces meaningful dollar amounts. Furthermore, the use of the exchange rate existing at the balance sheet date does not change the valuation basis of these accounts in translation. (For example, the valuation basis of receivables in a foreign currency is *net realizable value,* and the use of the exchange rate existing at the balance sheet date produces the dollar equivalent of the net amount expected to be realized.) Finally, as with Cash, the use of the exchange rate existing at the balance sheet date reflects the economic impact of any change in the exchange rate. Thus, all three criteria listed on pages 555–56 are satisfied.

Translating Nonmonetary Accounts: An Introduction to the Controversy

Accountants do not agree on the appropriate exchange rates to translate nonmonetary accounts at the balance sheet date. Two schools of thought have evolved concerning the appropriate exchange rate to use at the balance sheet date to translate nonmonetary accounts into dollars: the **parent company perspective** and the **foreign perspective,** discussed shortly.

Is the Monetary–Nonmonetary Distinction Relevant? Under the parent company perspective, the distinction between monetary and nonmonetary items is crucial, and therefore the use of the exchange rate existing at the balance sheet date (a current exchange rate) is deemed inappropriate for nonmonetary accounts. Under the foreign perspective, the distinction between monetary and nonmonetary items is irrelevant, and the exchange rate existing at the balance sheet date may be used for nonmonetary accounts.

In deciding whether a distinction between monetary and nonmonetary is relevant, it is important to realize that a foreign unit's buildings and equipment, although classified as nonmonetary items, are actually transformed from nonmonetary into monetary assets. Nonmonetary assets generate a cash flow, part of which constitutes a recovery of the cost of these assets. Of course, the process takes as long as the depreciation lives selected, and the transformation is not as evident as when nonmonetary assets are sold (disposed of) outright for cash. Because of this transformation process, when the exchange rate changes, the cash flow generated by these nonmonetary assets is worth either a greater number of dollars (when the direct exchange rate increases) or a lesser number of dollars (when the direct exchange rate decreases). Thus, in determining the appropriate exchange rate to translate nonmonetary items into dollars, we may view nonmonetary assets as being on the way to becoming monetary assets.

The Parent Company (or U.S. Dollar) Perspective

To illustrate the parent company perspective, let us change slightly the facts from the example used in the discussion of monetary accounts by assuming the foreign subsidiary used the 1,000,000 marks from the issuance of the common stock to purchase a parcel of land on December 1, 19X1. Thus, at December 31, 19X1, it has Land reported at 1,000,000 marks in its balance sheet instead of Cash of 1,000,000 marks.

The Rationale. From the **parent company perspective,** foreign operations are viewed as extensions of the parent company. Therefore, **all transactions must be translated in a manner that produces the dollar equivalent of the transaction at the time the transaction occurred.** From this perspective, the historical cost of the land in dollars is the amount of dollars that were needed to acquire it on December 1, 19X1. Because we know this amount is $450,000, the only exchange rate that translates the 1,000,000 marks into this amount is the historical exchange rate of $0.45 (the rate in effect on December 1, 19X1). Using the historical exchange rate not only expresses the cost of the land in dollars, but it also **changes the unit of measure from the foreign currency to the dollar.** Thus, the cost of the land has been **"remeasured" and expressed in U.S. dollars.** (This concept is difficult to grasp now; at this point, you should understand it fully after you have studied the foreign perspective, discussed later, under which the foreign currency is retained as the unit of measure in the translation process.) The historical exchange rate retains or preserves the historical cost measurement basis in dollars. Fixed assets of the domestic parent and its foreign units are therefore reported in consolidation on the same historical cost basis in terms of the reporting currency (U.S. dollars). Proponents of this approach claim that the results are clearly meaningful dollar amounts.

Its Shortcoming. The shortcoming of the parent company perspective is that **it completely disregards how changes in the exchange rate affect the nonmonetary accounts.** Changes in the exchange rate are economic events that have considerable impact on the U.S. parent company, which has invested money in the foreign unit. This fact holds true regardless of whether the foreign unit holds all monetary assets, all nonmonetary assets, or any combination of the two. When the effects of a change in the exchange rate are not reflected in the reporting results, the parent is effectively pretending that the exchange rate did not change.

To illustrate this shortcoming, we first deal with a situation in which the exchange rate changes and nonmonetary assets are financed entirely by a capital (common stock) investment by the parent. In a second situation, the nonmonetary assets are financed entirely by a local loan in the foreign country, and the parent has a nil investment in the subsidiary.

Situation 1: Parent Company Financing of Nonmonetary Assets

Let us continue with the example in the preceding discussion to see how a favorable economic event (an increase in the direct exchange rate) is not reported because the historical exchange rate is used to translate the nonmonetary accounts into dollars. Using the information presented so far, we know the translation process for the Land and Common Stock accounts as of December 1, 19X1, and December 31, 19X1, would be as follows:

	Amount	December 1, 19X1		December 31, 19X1	
	(marks)	Rate	Amount	Rate	Amount
Land..............	1,000,000	$0.45	$450,000	$0.45	$450,000
Common stock	1,000,000	0.45	450,000	0.45	450,000

This presentation clearly shows that the economic impact of the change in the exchange rate is not reported under this approach. However, from an economic viewpoint, the parent's $450,000 initial investment has increased in value to $600,000, because the direct exchange rate has increased from $0.45 at December 1, 19X1, to $0.60 at December 31, 19X1. (The $150,000 increase would be considered an unrealized increase in value.)

This concept is more understandable if we assume that the land was sold on December 31, 19X1, for cash of 1,000,000 marks, its book value on that date. On the date of sale, cash of 1,000,000 marks would be translated at $0.60, resulting in $600,000. This translated amount is $150,000 more than the Land account would show if the land were still owned. (Note that we do not assume that the land has appreciated in value in marks—the value in marks holds constant at 1,000,000.) However, because historical exchange rates are used to translate nonmonetary accounts, this favorable economic event (the increase in the direct exchange rate) is never reported. What is equally misleading is that if the land is sold on January 1, 19X2 (instead of December 31, 19X1), for cash of 1,000,000 marks (its book value), a $150,000 favorable result would be reportable at that time (assuming the exchange rate did not change from December 31, 19X1), even though nothing happened economically on January 1, 19X2. (Likewise, a decrease in the exchange rate in December 19X1 from $0.45 to $0.30—an unfavorable economic event—would be ignored in the reporting process, even though from an economic veiwpoint the parent's $450,000 initial investment has decreased in value by $150,000 to $300,000.)

Situation 2: Foreign Financing of Nonmonetary Assets

To minimize the risk of investing in foreign companies (including the risk that the exchange rate could change adversely), U.S. companies commonly finance foreign operations through foreign borrowings to the extent possible, thereby keeping their investments in the foreign units as small as possible. To illustrate this situation, let us change the example in the preceding discussion as follows:

1. The foreign subsidiary was so thinly capitalized by the parent on December 1, 19X1, that we can ignore the translation of the Common Stock account.
2. The foreign subsidiary borrowed 1,000,000 marks from a local bank on December 1, 19X1, and used the proceeds to purchase the parcel of land. (The loan is payable in marks.)
3. For simplicity, interest expense on the loan is ignored.
4. No principal payments were made on the loan in December 19X1.

From this we determine the translation process for the Land and Notes Payable accounts (the loan is a monetary item) as of December 1, 19X1, and December 31, 19X1, as follows:

	Amount (marks)	December 1, 19X1 Rate	December 1, 19X1 Amount	December 31, 19X1 Rate	December 31, 19X1 Amount
Land	**1,000,000**	**$0.45**	**$450,000**	**$0.45**	**$450,000**
Notes payable	**1,000,000**	**0.45**	**450,000**	**0.60**	**600,000**
Translation adjustment (the effect of the change in the exchange rate)					**(150,000)**

An adverse result of $150,000 would be reported under this translation approach. We might conclude from this result that it would take $150,000 more to pay off the loan at December 31, 19X1, than were needed at December 1, 19X1. However, the adverse result exactly offsets the $150,000 increase in value of the land, which is completely ignored because of the use of the historical exchange rate of $0.45 for the land at December 31, 19X1.

We may more easily understand why nothing adverse has actually occurred from an economic viewpoint by assuming that the land was sold on December 31, 19X1, for cash of 1,000,000 marks, its book value on that date. On the date of sale, cash of 1,000,000 marks would be translated at $0.60 into $600,000 rather than at $0.45 into $450,000. The translated cash amount of $600,000 equals the translated note payable amount of $600,000, and no translation adjustment is needed. Interestingly, if the land is sold on January 1, 19X2 (rather than on December 31, 19X1), for cash of 1,000,000 marks (its book value), a favorable result of $150,000 would be reportable at that time (assuming the exchange rate does not change from December 31, 19X1), even though nothing happened economically on January 1, 19X2. Note also that this $150,000 favorable result for 19X2 completely offsets the $150,000 unfavorable result reportable for 19X1.

The most convincing proof that nothing adverse has happened during December 19X1, as far as the parent's investment in the subsidiary is concerned, is the fact that the parent's investment is negligible. It had nothing invested and therefore nothing at risk. To report a $150,000 adverse result for 19X1 under these conditions makes no sense. (The same logic would be applied if the exchange rate decreased during December from $0.45 to $0.30, but the reporting results would be reversed.) Accordingly, when the parent can finance the foreign unit's nonmonetary assets with foreign borrowings that are repayable in the foreign currency, a change in the exchange rate has no economic impact on the parent. In this situation, the reporting of favorable and unfavorable results is viewed as mere paper gains and losses that are reversed in later periods—in other words, timing differences. From this viewpoint, it is not sensible to report adverse results in one period that are offset by favorable results in later periods and vice versa.

The Two Translation Methods That Fit under the Parent Company Perspective. Two translation methods fit under the parent company perspective—the **temperal method** and the **monetary–nonmonetary** method. Under the **temporal method,** which can accomodate any measurement basis (historical cost, current replacement price, or current market price), a foreign currency measurement is changed into a dollar measurement without changing the measurement basis. Thus, **the accounting principles are not changed** (even though the unit of measure has been changed to the dollar). The measurement basis of an asset or liability determines the exchange rate used in translating that asset or liability. Accordingly, different exchange rates are used for different measurement bases (for example, historical exchange rates, for fixed assets and a current exchange rate for receivables). The **monetary–nonmonetary** method is merely a classification scheme whereby all monetary assets and liabilities are translated at the exchange rate existing at the balance sheet date, and all nonmonetary assets and liabilities are translated at historical exchange rates. Under current generally accepted accounting principles, the results of the temporal method coincide with those of the monetary–nonmonetary method. However, if accounting principles change so that nonmonetary assets (such as marketable equity securities) are measured at current prices instead of at historical prices or at the lower of cost or market, the results would be different. The temporal method could accommodate such accounting principles, whereas the monetary—nonmonetary method could not, because the measurement basis would not be maintained in the translation process.

The Focus for Both Methods: Net Monetary Position. Under both the temporal and the monetary–nonmonetary translation methods, the monetary or nonmonetary composition of the individual assets and liabilities is critical in determining whether a favorable or unfavorable result is reported as a consequence of a change in the exchange rate. In this respect, the focus is on the *net monetary position.* An excess of monetary assets over monetary liabilities is referred to as a **net monetary asset position;** an excess of monetary liabilities over monetary assets is referred to as a **net monetary liability position.** If the direct exchange rate has increased since the beginning of the period (a favorable economic event), a company in a net monetary asset position reports a favorable result; if it is in a net monetary liability position, the company reports an unfavorable result. On the other hand, if the direct exchange rate has decreased since the beginning of the period (an unfavorable economic event), a company in a net monetary asset position reports an unfavorable result, but if it is in a net monetary liability position, it reports a favorable result.

The FASB's First Attempt. In 1975, the Financial Accounting Standards Board (FASB) adopted the parent company perspective by requiring the temporal method of translation in all cases. The unusual results that occur under the parent company perspective led to a reconsideration of the entire translation issue in 1979. *FASB Statement No. 52* superseded *FASB*

Statement No. 8 in 1981, and the parent company perspective is now called for only in certain situations discussed in Chapter 15.

The Foreign (or Local) Perspective

The Rationale. From the foreign perspective, a foreign operation is a separate business unit whose only factual financial statements are those prepared in its foreign currency. From this premise, we reason that **the relationships of items must be maintained in the translation process.** The only way to maintain the relationships of items in translation is to use a single exchange rate for all assets and liabilities. The exchange rate existing at the balance sheet date (a current exchange rate) is presumably the single most meaningful exchange rate. For translation using a single exchange rate, **the foreign currency is the "unit of measure"** in the dollar financial statements. **Thus, the nonmonetary accounts are not translated to their dollar equivalent when the transactions were recorded.** Consequently, **the nonmonetary accounts are not remeasured in dollars—they are only expressed in dollars.** The use of the exchange rate existing at the balance sheet date clearly overcomes the objections raised for the parent company perspective—namely, that the economic impact of the change in the exchange rate is completely ignored in the translation of the nonmonetary accounts. As a result, the proponents of the foreign perspective assert that the translated amounts are obviously meaningful dollar amounts.

Is the Translated Amount Historical Cost? The most difficult result to understand under the foreign perspective is whether the amount expressed in dollars should be considered historical cost or some form of current value. Let us continue with the example of translating the value of land that we used in discussing the parent company perspective. Under the foreign approach, the foreign subsidiary's Land and Common Stock accounts would be translated into dollars at December 1, 19X1, and December 31, 19X1, as follows:

	Amount (marks)	December 1, 19X1 Rate	December 1, 19X1 Amount	December 31, 19X1 Rate	December 31, 19X1 Amount
Land	1,000,000	$0.45	$450,000	$0.60	$600,000
Common stock	1,000,000	0.45	450,000	0.45[a]	450,000
Translation adjustment (the effect of the change in the exchange rate)					150,000

[a]The historical exchange rate of $0.45 must be used here to isolate the effect of the change in the exchange rate.

Obviously, the $600,000 translated amount for the land at December 31, 19X1, is not historical cost in terms of the equivalent number of dollars that were needed to acquire the land on December 1, 19X1 (that is, $450,000). Advocates of the foreign perspective claim that **the $600,000 is the historical cost of the land using the foreign currency as the unit of measure rather than the dollar.** If the direct exchange rate were $0.70 at December 31, 19X2 (one year later), then the historical cost using the foreign currency as the unit of measure would be $700,000 (1,000,000 marks × $0.70). Thus, the land would be reported in the consolidated financial statements at a different amount every year as the exchange rate changed each year. Critics of the foreign perspective contend that, in substance, this is merely an abandonment of historical cost and a change to a form of current-value accounting.

Is the Translated Amount Current Value? Let us continue with the preceding example dealing with Land but assume that the land appreciated in value by 100,000 marks during December 19X1. Its current value in marks at December 31, 19X1, is 1,100,000 marks. To obtain the land's current value in dollars at that date, this amount would have to be multiplied by the $0.60 exchange rate existing at December 31, 19X1, which is $660,000. However, nonmonetary accounts are not adjusted for inflation prior to translation. Accordingly, the use of the exchange rate existing at the balance sheet date would result in current value only if the nonmonetary account were restated for the effects of inflation. Furthermore, when dealing with depreciable assets, the amounts expressed in dollars would approximate current value only if the depreciation lives and methods used gave results that closely corresponded to the decline in the assets' values.

The Disappearing Plant Problem. About fifteen countries (primarily in South America) currently have highly inflationary economies (approximately 100% or more over a three-year period). The use of the foreign perspective can result in meaningless figures in these situations. To illustrate, consider the following example of a manufacturing plant in Argentina that cost 10,000,000 australs when it was purchased on December 31, 1974:

	Amount (australs)	December 31, 1974		December 31, 1986	
		Rate	Amount	Rate	Amount
Plant......	10,000,000	$0.20	$2,000,000	$0.00000008	$0.80

Obviously, the application of the December 31, 1983, current exchange rate to the historical cost in australs produces an amount that bears no relationship to current value or a reasonable historical cost amount. The use of the current exchange rate would produce a meaningful amount only if it were applied to the inflation-adjusted historical cost in australs. However, this procedure would depart from historical cost in the foreign currency.

Accordingly, operations in highly inflationary economies require special consideration. Chapter 15 shows how *FASB Statement No. 52* deals with these situations.

The Current-rate Method of Translation. Only one translation method fits under the foreign perspective—the **current-rate method.** Under the current-rate method, an increase in the direct exchange rate results in a favorable translation adjustment, and a decrease in the direct exchange rate results in an unfavorable translation adjustment.

The Focus: The Net Investment. The current-rate method focuses on the parent's net investment (total assets − total liabilities), not on the composition of the individual assets and liabilities. In other words, the monetary or nonmonetary classification of the individual assets and liabilities is irrelevant. This approach emphasizes that the foreign operation's net assets are at risk (described as a **net investment** view as opposed to the individual asset and liability view under the temporal method).

Summary Illustration

THE EFFECT OF CHANGES IN THE EXCHANGE RATE

Illustration 14-1 summarizes the effect of exchange rate changes under both the parent company (U.S. dollar) perspective and the foreign (local) perspective.

Illustration 14-1
The Effect of Changes in the Exchange Rate

		Economic Result of Direct Rate	
Perspective	**Possible Financial Positions**	**Increase[a] (Foreign Currency Has Strengthened or Dollar Has Weakened)**	**Decrease[b] (Foreign Currency Has Weakened or Dollar Has Strengthened)**
Foreign (local)	Net asset	Favorable	Unfavorable
Foreign (local)	Net liability	Unfavorable	Favorable
Parent company (U.S. dollar)	Net monetary asset	Favorable	Unfavorable
Parent company (U.S. dollar)	Net monetary liability	Unfavorable	Favorable

[a]In all situations, the effect is favorable on the assets and unfavorable on the liabilities.
[b]In all situations, the effect is unfavorable on the assets and favorable on the liabilities.

The FASB's Second Attempt: The "Functional Currency" Concept. *FASB Statement No. 52* adopted the foreign perspective in addition to the parent company perspective. However, the foreign company perspective is dominant because its use is required far more often than the parent company perspective. *FASB Statement No. 52* introduced the "functional currency" concept as a basis for determining whether the foreign or the parent company perspective should be used for each foreign operation. In a nutshell, a foreign unit's functional currency is that currency in which it primarily conducts its operations. If a foreign unit's functional currency is its local currency, then the foreign perspective must be used. If a foreign unit's functional currency is the U.S. dollar, the parent company (or U.S. dollar) perspective must be used. Chapter 15 discusses the factors to consider in determining a foreign unit's functional currency.

CONCEPTUAL ISSUE 2: HOW TO REPORT THE EFFECT OF A CHANGE IN THE EXCHANGE RATE

The issue of how to report the effect of a change in the exchange rate centers on whether or not the translation adjustment should be reported in the income statement in the period in which the rate changes. There are arguments for both sides, and the FASB takes a dual approach to the issue in its *Statement No. 52.*

Arguments for Reporting It Immediately in the Income Statement

The following list contains the principal arguments for including the translation adjustment immediately in the income statement:

1. The possibility of changes in the exchange rate is a risk of investing in a foreign country. The effects of this possibility can be economically favorable or unfavorable. Favorable effects are gains; unfavorable effects are losses. Gains and losses should be recognized in the period in which they occur.
2. Recognizing in the income statement the effects of changes in the exchange rate is consistent with the all-inclusive income statement approach that has prevailed in accounting in recent years.
3. Past exchange rate changes are historical facts, and each accounting period should reflect the economic events that occurred during that time frame.
4. Exchange rates fluctuate. Not including the effects of such fluctuations in net income when they occur gives the impression that exchange rates are stable.

Arguments for Not Reporting It Immediately in the Income Statement

The following list contains the principal arguments for excluding the translation adjustment from the income statement:

1. If exchange rates are likely to reverse, the effect should be deferred. (This argument presumes that managements are reasonably adept at predicting future exchange rates; in reality, a high degree of uncertainty exists with future exchange rates.)
2. Exchange rate changes often reverse, causing unnecessary fluctuations in net income. (This argument implies that a function of accounting is to minimize the reporting of fluctuations.)
3. When the parent company perspective is used and when monetary liabilities exceed monetary assets (nonmonetary assets thus financed to some degree by borrowings), the translation adjustment should be deferred to offset (a) the unrecognized decrease in value on these assets (when the direct exchange rate decreases), and (b) the unrecognized increase in value of these assets (when the direct exchange rate increases). This approach would eliminate some of the unusual reporting results that occur under the parent company perspective; however, it is merely a disguised manner of revaluing the nonmonetary assets upward or downward. As a result, these items are translated at exchange rates that are between the historical exchange rate and the exchange rate existing at the balance sheet date, depending on the amount of borrowings to finance these nonmonetary assets.
4. For many foreign operations, translation adjustments do not affect the operations or cash flows of the foreign unit. They arise only in translation and thus do not affect directly the cash flows of the reporting currency (dollars). The effects of changes in the exchange rate are unrealized until the investment is disposed of or liquidated. Translation adjustments do not possess the characteristics of items normally included in determining net income.[4] (Comments in the following two paragraphs relate to this argument.)

The Dual Approach of *FASB Statement No. 52*. In *FASB Statement No. 52*, how to report the effect of a change in the exchange rate is a function of the perspective used for each foreign operation. When the foreign perspective is used (requiring the use of the current-rate method of translation), the effect of a change in the exchange rate is called a **translation adjustment** (in *FASB Statement No. 52*), and it is **reported as a separate component of stockholders' equity,** bypassing the income statement until disposal or liquidation of the investment. (Argument 4 above, which was first presented in *FASB Statement No. 52*, is the basis for this position.) When the parent company perspective is used (requiring the use of procedures that are nearly identical to the temporal method of translation), the effect of a change in the exchange rate is called a **foreign currency transaction gain or loss** (in *FASB Statement No. 52*), and it is **reported currently in the income statement.**

Why the Separate Component of Stockholders' Equity? Recall that the foreign perspective is now required more often than the parent company

[4]*FASB Statement No. 52*, par. 111 and 117.

perspective. Thus, one might think that the criticisms of *FASB Statement No. 8* (which required the parent company perspective in all cases) have been addressed. A major part of the business community's dissatisfaction with *FASB Statement No. 8* was not only the results produced under the parent company perspective but the requirement to report the effects of the change in the exchange rate currently in the income statement when subsequent reversals were expected (the paper gain and loss conclusion discussed earlier). Wild gyrations in adjustments often resulted on a quarter-to-quarter basis. Even under the foreign perspective (which requires the use of the current-rate method of translation), significant fluctuations in translation adjustments occur as long as exchange rates continue to change back and forth significantly; this is possible under the current floating exchange rate system. In fact, the fluctuations may be even greater under the foreign perspective—the only requirement is that a foreign operation's net asset position must be greater than its net monetary asset or liability position. Thus, although the business community has available a method that produces results that reflect the economics, it opposes reporting translation adjustments currently in the income statement because of the significant fluctuations. The FASB's decision to require companies to report translation adjustments resulting from the use of the current-rate method as a separate component of stockholders' equity may have been partly attributable to the practical aspects of the environment in which the FASB operates.

Glossary of New Terms

Conversion The exchange of one currency for another.

Foreign Operation "An operation (for example, subsidiary, division, branch, joint venture, and so on) whose financial statements (a) are prepared in a currency other than the reporting currency of the reporting enterprise and (b) are combined or consolidated with or accounted for on the equity basis in the financial statements of the reporting enterprise.*

Monetary Accounts Cash and receivables and payables to be settled in currency.

Net Asset Position Having assets in excess of liabilities.

Net Liability Position Having liabilities in excess of assets.

Net Monetary Asset Position Having monetary assets in excess of monetary liabilities.

Net Monetary Liability Position Having monetary liabilities in excess of monetary assets.

Nonmonetary Accounts All balance sheet accounts that are not monetary accounts.

**FASB Statement No. 52*, Appendix E, pp. 75–78.

Suggested References

"The Gaps in International GAAP," by John L. Kirkpatrick. *Corporate Accounting* 3, no. 4 (Fall 1985), 3–10.

"Competition Spurs Worldwide Harmonization," by Gary Meek. *Management Accounting* (August 1984), 47–49.

"IFAC's Traveling Salesmen," by Susan Jayson. *Management Accounting* (October 1986), 22–25.

"IASC Chairman Kirkpatrick on International Standards," by John N. Slipkowsky. *Management Accounting* (October 1986), 27–31.

"How U.S. and European Accounting Practices Differ," by Roger K. Doost and Karen M. Ligon. *Management Accounting* (October 1986) 38–41.

Review Questions

1. Differentiate between conversion and translation.
2. What is the direct quotation rate? the indirect quotation rate?
3. What is meant when a currency is said to be strengthening? weakening?
4. What is meant by the current exchange rate? historical exchange rate?
5. What is meant by the term *monetary accounts*?
6. Summarize the parent company (or U.S. dollar) perspective.
7. Summarize the foreign (or local) perspective.
8. What is meant by the term *functional currency*?

Discussion Cases

DC 14-1

Evaluation of the Impact of a Weakening Foreign Currency

Assume you are the controller of a domestic company that established operations in Mexico two years ago. These foreign operations are conducted through a Mexican subsidiary. The subsidiary has three operational manufacturing plants, all of which cost approximately the same amount and were financed as follows:

1. The first plant was financed entirely from a capital stock investment made by the parent in subsidiary.
2. The second plant was financed entirely from a long-term loan from a local Mexican bank, none of which has been repaid.
3. The third plant was financed entirely from an interest-bearing, long-term loan from the parent, none of which has been repaid. (The loan is payable in dollars.)

During the month preceding the annual shareholders' meeting, the Mexican peso declined approximately 30% in value. You are sure a question will arise at the shareholders' meeting concerning the financial consequences of this decline.

Required:

1. Without regard to whether the functional currency is the dollar or the peso, prepare a brief summary of the impact of the decline in the value of the peso on the company's foreign operations.
2. Indicate the effect of the change in the exchange rate that will be reported for the current year of each of the plants assuming that the functional currency is:
   a. the peso.
   b. the dollar.

DC 14-2

Evaluation of the Impact of a Weakening Dollar

Rosebud Corporation is a domestic company that established a manufacturing subsidiary in West Germany four years ago. In establishing this foreign operation, Rosebud minimized the number of dollars taken out of the United States by financing the subsidiary's manufacturing plant through a loan obtained from a West German financial institution. This loan is being repaid over 25 years. As a result, the subsidiary is thinly capitalized.

During the current year, the dollar weakened approximately 20% against the mark, as concerns arose over the sizable U.S. foreign trade deficit, the federal spending deficit, and the inability to control inflation. (The mark held steady against the other major currencies of the world.) In marks, the subsidiary had a profit for the current year comparable to the prior year. In dollars, the subsidiary had a loss for the current year, compared with a profit for the prior year.

Required:
Rosebud's president, Orson Wellsby, has asked you, the controller, to respond to the following questions:

1. How is it possible to report a loss on the foreign operation for the current year, considering the following:
   a. The parent minimized its dollars at risk by financing the foreign plant with local borrowings.
   b. The operation was run as efficiently this year as in the prior year.
2. Is this an economic loss or a paper loss? Explain your answer.
3. Is there any way the loss could have been avoided?

Exercises

E 14-1

Exchange Rates

On January 1, 19X1, 100,000 pesos could be converted into $400. On December 31, 19X1, 100,000 pesos could be converted into $500.

Required:

1. Express the relationship between the two currencies at each date directly and indirectly.

2. Did the peso strengthen or weaken during 19X1? Did the dollar strengthen or weaken during 19X1?

E 14-2 Getting in Step with U.S. Generally Accepted Accounting Practices

A foreign subsidiary must adjust its fixed assets annually for inflation. Amounts of these adjustments are maintained in separate general ledger accounts. The balances in these accounts at year-end are as follows:

	Debit	Credit
Land—revaluation	500,000	
Building—revaluation	800,000	
Accumulated depreciation—revaluation		200,000
Depreciation Expense—revaluation (19X1)	40,000	

The depreciation expense increment is deductible for foreign federal tax purposes. Assume the foreign tax rate is 40%.

Required:
Prepare the adjusting entry necessary to convert to U.S. generally accepted accounting principles at the end of 19X1.

E 14-3 Calculating the Effect of a Change in the Exchange Rate

The Berkshire Corporation has a foreign subsidiary in a country in which the direct exchange rate has decreased from $0.25 at January 1, 19X1, to $0.20 at December 31, 19X1. The average balances of the individual assets and liabilities during the year were as follows:

	Units of Foreign Currency
Cash	80,000
Accounts Receivable	220,000
Inventory	275,000
Fixed Assets, net	425,000
	1,000,000
Accounts Payable and Accruals	325,000
Current portion of Long-Term Debt	25,000
Intercompany Payable	100,000
Long-Term Debt	300,000
Deferred Income Taxes	50,000
	800,000

Required:
Determine the effect of the change in the exchange rate for 19X1 assuming the foreign operation's functional currency is:

a. the foreign currency.
b. the dollar.

E 14-4

Determining the Financial Position of Foreign Operations from Effect and Direction of Exchange Rate Changes

Information for Extent Corporation's overseas subsidiaries for 19X1 is presented below:

Country	Functional Currency	Direction of Direct Exchange Rate in 19X1	Effect of Change in Exchange Rate
Brazil	Dollar	Decreased	Favorable
Mexico	Dollar	Decreased	Unfavorable
Sweden	Krona	Increased	Favorable
Belgium	Franc	Increased	Unfavorable
Ireland	Punt	Decreased	Unfavorable
Spain	Peseta	Decreased	Favorable
Saudi Arabia	Dollar	Increased	Favorable
Japan	Dollar	Increased	Unfavorable

Required:

Determine the appropriate financial position that each of the above foreign operations was in during the year for the above listed effect to have resulted.

15

Translation of Foreign Currency Financial Statements: Practice

This chapter focuses on the requirements of *FASB Statement No. 52*, "Foreign Currency Translation."

THE FUNCTIONAL CURRENCY CONCEPT

The Objectives of Translation

FASB Statement No. 52 states the following objectives for translation of foreign currency financial statements:

a. Provide information that is generally compatible with the expected economic effects of a rate change on an enterprise's cash flows and equity.
b. Reflect in consolidated statements the financial results and relationships of the individual consolidated entities as measured in their *functional currencies* in conformity with U.S. generally accepted accounting principles.[1]

The first objective merely states that the selected exchange rate and the reporting of the effect of a change in the exchange rate should reflect the economics of what has transpired. The second objective allows for the use of both the parent company perspective (when the dollar is the foreign unit's functional currency) and the more prevalent foreign perspective (when the foreign currency is the foreign unit's functional currency). To achieve these two objectives, the **functional currency concept** was developed.

The Basis for the Functional Currency Concept

FASB Statement No. 52 presumes that an enterprise's foreign operations may be conducted in one or more economic and currency environments. The primary economic environment must be determined for each separate foreign operation. However, the pronouncement does not specifically define the economic environment concept. Each foreign country has its own economic environment composed of taxation policies, currency controls, government policies toward intervention in the international currency markets, economic instability, and inflation. The primary economic environment concept, however, pertains to the manner in which the foreign operation conducts its operations—the currency it primarily uses to generate and expend cash.[2] (This concept presumes that each foreign operation has a primary currency.)

[1]*Statement of Financial Accounting Standards, No. 52*, "Foreign Currency Translation" (Stamford: Financial Accounting Standards Board, 1981), par. 4.
[2]*FASB Statement No. 52*, par. 5 and 78.

The currency of the primary economic environment is then designated as that foreign operation's functional currency. The FASB has developed some economic factors that are to be considered individually and collectively in determining the functional currency for each foreign operation of an enterprise. (A list of these economic factors appears in Illustration 15-1.) The functional currency determined for each foreign operation is the basis for the method of translation into dollars. When the foreign currency is designated the functional currency (which occurs most of the time), the foreign perspective must be used; thus, the current-rate method is used to translate the foreign currency financial statements into dollars. When the dollar is designated the functional currency, the parent company perspective must be used; thus, translating foreign currency financial statements into dollars is accomplished using procedures that are nearly identical to the temporal method (which *FASB Statement No. 8* required for all situations).[3]

Two Categories of Foreign Operations. In reviewing Illustration 15-1, realize that most foreign operations conveniently fit into one of two categories. The **first category** includes **foreign operations that are relatively self-contained and independent of the parent's operations.** These operations primarily generate and expend the foreign currency of the country in which they are located. Earnings may be reinvested or distributed to the parent. In these cases, the foreign currency is obviously the functional currency. (An example would be a foreign subsidiary that manufactures automobiles for sale in the foreign country, purchasing no parts from the parent's operations.) The **second category** includes **foreign operations that are not relatively self-contained and independent of the parent's operations.** These operations may be viewed as direct extensions or integral components of the parent's operations. The day-to-day operations of these units directly affect the parent company's dollar cash flows. In these cases, the dollar is the functional currency. (An example would be a foreign subsidiary that manufactures automobile transmissions that are shipped to the parent for inclusion in cars produced domestically.)[4]

No Arbitrary Selection Allowed. The determination of the functional currency should be based on the economic facts—it cannot be an arbitrary selection. Because significant differences in reported net income can occur as a result of choosing the foreign currency or the dollar as the functional currency, managements must be prevented from arbitrarily choosing their accounting principles. When the economic factors listed in Illustration 15-1 do not clearly point to which functional currency a foreign operation should use, management can weigh the individual economic factors and use its judgment, considering the stated objectives of translation.[5]

[3]*FASB Statement No. 52*, par. 5, 10, 12, 47, and 48.
[4]*FASB Statement No. 52*, par. 79–81.
[5]*FASB Statement No. 52*, par. 8 and 82.

Illustration 15-1
Economic Factors to be Considered in Determining the Functional Currency

Type of Factor	Factors Pointing to a Foreign Functional Currency	Factors Pointing to a Dollar Functional Currency
Cash flows	Cash flows related to the foreign entity's individual assets and liabilities are primarily in the foreign currency and do not directly impact the parent company's cash flows.	Cash flows related to the foreign entity's individual assets and liabilities directly impact the parent's cash flows on a current basis and are readily available for remittance to the parent company.
Sales prices	Sales prices for the foreign entity's products are not primarily responsive on a short-term basis to changes in exchange rates but are determined more by local competition or local government regulation.	Sales prices for the foreign entity's products are primarily responsive on a short-term basis to changes in exchange rates; for example, sales prices are determined more by worldwide competition or by international prices.
Sales market	An active local sales market exists for the foreign entity's products, although significant amounts of exports might also be available.	The sales market is mostly in the parent's country, or sales contracts are denominated in the parent's currency.
Costs and expenses	Labor, materials, and other costs for the foreign entity's products or services are primarily local costs, even though imports from other countries might also be available.	Labor, materials, and other costs for the foreign entity's products or services, on a continuing basis, are primarily costs for components obtained from the country in which the parent company is located.
Financing	Financing is primarily denominated in foreign currency, and funds generated by the foreign entity's operations are sufficient to service existing and normally expected debt obligations.	Financing is primarily from the parent or other dollar-denominated obligations, or funds generated by the foreign entity's operations are not sufficient to service existing and normally expected debt obligations without the infusion of additional funds from the parent company. Infusion of additional funds from the parent company for expansion is not a factor, provided funds generated by the foreign entity's expanded operations are expected to be sufficient to service that additional financing.
Intercompany transactions and arrangements	There is a low volume of intercompany transactions, and an extensive interrelationship does not exist between the operations of the foreign entity and the parent company. However, the foreign entity's operations may rely on the parent's or affiliates' competitive advantages such as patents and trademarks.	There is a high volume of intercompany transactions, and an extensive interrelationship exists between the operations of the foreign entity and the parent company. Additionally, the parent's currency generally would be the functional currency if the foreign entity is a device or shell corporation for holding investments, obligations, intangible assets, and so on, that could readily be carried on the parent's or an affiliate's books.

Source: Adapted from *Statement of Financial Accounting Standards, No. 52*, "Foreign Currency Translation" (Stamford: Financial Accounting Standards Board, 1981), Appendix A. par. 42.

Highly Inflationary Economies. An exception to the approach of determining the functional currency from economic facts is made for operations in highly inflationary economies. *FASB Statement No. 52* defines an inflationary economy as "one that has cumulative inflation of approximately 100 percent or more over a 3-year period.[6] In these cases, the dollar is used as the functional currency. The purpose of the exception is to deal with the "disappearing plant" problem discussed in Chapter 14. Recall that applying the current exchange rate to historical cost amounts in foreign currency financial statements can produce meaningless dollar amounts for fixed assets in such economies. The problem is the foreign currency's lack of stability, which makes it completely unsuitable for use as a functional currency. In the exposure draft that preceded the issuance of *FASB Statement No. 52*, the FASB proposed restating the historical cost amounts for inflation prior to translation (and then allowing the use of the current-rate method). However, the proposal was dropped because of conceptual objections to mixing historical cost with inflation-adjusted amounts and the inadequacy of published indices for several countries. As a practical alternative, which is an acknowledged conceptual compromise, the FASB designated the dollar as the functional currency in highly inflationary economies (whereby the historical cost amounts are translated at historical exchange rates). The results are more reasonable dollar amounts for the fixed assets of these foreign operations.

Illustration 15-2 lists the countries whose cumulative inflation rates have recently exceeded 100% over three-year periods; countries approaching this 100% threshold are also listed. Although 100% may seem high, an annual inflation rate of only 26% results in 100% inflation cumulatively over a three-year period. The use of 100% is arbitrary, but the use of the modifier "approximately" in the pronouncement allows management some latitude in judgment. Thus, a cumulative inflation rate of 90%, for example, could be sufficient grounds for using the dollar as the functional currency, whereas a foreign unit operating with a cumulative inflation rate of

Illustration 15-2
Countries Having Highly Inflationary Economies

Recent Three-Year Inflation Rate Exceeds 100%		Recent Three-Year Inflation Rate Approaches 100%
Argentina	Mexico	Jamaica
Bolivia	Peru	Korea
Brazil	Somalia	Sudan
Chile	Turkey	Tanzania
Colombia	Uruguay	
Ghana	Yugoslavia	
Iceland	Zaire	

Source: *International Financial Statistics*, Bureau of Statistics, International Monetary Fund.

[6] *FASB Statement No. 52*, par. 11.

110% could still use the foreign currency as the functional currency. We must also consider management's latitude when the economic facts do not clearly indicate the functional currency. In such a case and when the cumulative inflation rate is high but below 100%, management may lean toward using the dollar as the functional currency.

Distinguishing "Translation" from "Remeasurement"

For simplicity, we have referred to the process of applying exchange rates to a foreign operation's financial statements to arrive at dollar amounts as *translation*. Historically, this has been the definition of the term. The use of the functional currency concept, however, has resulted in a narrower definition of this term in *FASB Statement No. 52*.

Translation (from the Functional Currency to the Reporting Currency). In *FASB Statement No. 52*, **translation** refers to the process of **expressing functional currency amounts in the reporting currency.** Accordingly, the term is restricted to situations in which the foreign currency is the functional currency. Recall that when the foreign currency is the functional currency, the current-rate method is required, and it merely *expresses* the foreign currency financial statements in dollars. (It does not "remeasure" the nonmonetary accounts to obtain their dollar equivalents at the time the transactions were recorded.) The effect of a change in the exchange rate in these "translation" situations is called a **translation adjustment.** Translation adjustments are reported separately in stockholders' equity (a less closely monitored section of the financial statements, unfortunately) pending sale or liquidation of the investment.[7]

Remeasurement (from a Nonfunctional Currency to the Functional Currency). In *FASB Statement No. 52*, **remeasurement** is the process of applying exchange rates to a foreign operation's financial statements when they are not stated in the functional currency. **Thus, amounts in a different currency are expressed in the functional currency.** The most common example occurs when the functional currency of the foreign operation is the dollar. Foreign operations normally maintain their books and prepare their financial statements in the currency of the country in which they are located, regardless of whether the dollar is their functional currency. Recall that when the dollar is the functional currency, a combination of current and historical exchange rates is used whereby the nonmonetary accounts are remeasured in dollars to obtain the dollar equivalent of the transactions at the time they were recorded. Thus, the remeasurement process in *FASB Statement No. 52* refers to the remeasuring in the functional currency. Note that when the dollar is the functional currency, translation (as narrowly defined in the preceding paragraph) is not neces-

[7]*FASB Statement No. 52*, par. 12–14.

sary because the functional currency is also the reporting currency. The effect of a change in the exchange rate from the remeasurement process is called a **foreign currency transaction gain or loss,** which must be reported currently in the income statement.[8]

Remeasurement and Translation Situations. Infrequently, a foreign operation's functional currency is a foreign currency that is different from the currency it uses to maintain its books and prepare its financial statements. An example would be a Swiss operation that keeps its books in Swiss francs (most likely because of tax laws) but uses the French franc as its functional currency. In such a case, the Swiss financial statements must be "remeasured" and expressed in French francs. Then, the French franc financial statements must be "translated" into dollars. Thus, a two-step process is required to obtain amounts in dollars. However, most foreign operations require only a one-step process—either the translation process or the remeasurement process.

Comparison Comment. The translation process is relatively simple because of the use of the current-rate method. In comparison, the remeasurement process is slightly more involved because of the use of current and historical exchange rates. When the remeasurement process is illustrated later in the chapter, we list the accounts to be remeasured using historical exchange rates. (For now, understand only that these are nonmonetary accounts and their amortizations.)

The following article reveals how *FASB Statement No. 52* is viewed by financial analysts.

PERSPECTIVE

Plenty of Opportunity to Fool Around

With the dollar off sharply against most major foreign currencies, investors in U.S. multinational corporations are already getting good news. Thanks to the falling dollar, IBM's year-end 1985 stockholders' equity account rose by $1.5 billion. Exxon's equity jumped $669 million, Ford Motor's $395 million. More such tidings will follow throughout the year, reflecting the dollar's drop since December.

These equity increases stem not so much from greater competitiveness overseas as from the accounting rules that tell companies how to translate foreign currencies into dollars. The rules are embodied in the Financial Accounting Standards Board's *Statement 52,* effective since 1983. *FASB 52,* you may recall, replaced the downright bizarre *FASB 8.* Still, *FASB 52* produces its own odd results.

Take those boosts to shareholder equity reported by IBM, Exxon and Ford, big multinationals all. But Texaco, Hewlett-Packard and Chrysler also run large

[8] *FASB Statement No. 52,* par. 15.

Plenty of Opportunity to Fool Around ***(continued)***

foreign operations. Yet none of these firms reported an equity increase from currency translation.

What gives?

Under *FASB 52*, managements have considerable leeway in choosing where to book currency translation gains and losses. *FASB 52* says management must designate for each of its foreign operations the "functional" currency in which that subsidiary does business. Several factors are considered. What currency are most of the sales and expenses in? Is management judged on foreign-currency sales or on performance translated back into dollars? How autonomous is the foreign sub? And so on. Note that management can specify the dollar as the functional currency.

"Within rather broad parameters," says Peat, Marwick, Mitchell partner James Weir, choosing the functional currency "is basically a management call." So much so, in fact, that Texaco, Occidental and Unocal settled on the dollar as the functional currency for most of their foreign operations, whereas competitors Exxon, Mobil and Amoco chose primarily the local currencies as the functional currencies for their foreign businesses.

Now for translating the financials.

Converting the income statement is straightforward enough. Say the West German subsidiary's 1984 revenue was DM 600 million and expenses were DM 420 million, and there were three marks to the dollar. Then sales would convert to $200 million, expenses to $140 million, income to $60 million.

But suppose in 1985 the dollar drops to a dollar-to-mark rate of 1:2. Then sales are $300 million, expenses $210 million, income $90 million—same mark sales and expenses, but $30 million more profit. Thus did IBM report an extra $140 million in earnings in this year's first quarter—23 cents a common share. That allowed IBM's earnings to increase 3%, rather than fall 11%, from a year earlier.

Translating the balance sheet gets a little hairier. Let's assume our German subsidiary has assets of DM 900 million and liabilities of DM 600 million. Equity: DM 300 million. With the dollar-to-mark at 1:3, that equity translates to $100 million. Fine. But now the dollar drops to $1:DM 2. Nothing has changed in Germany. But now the subsidiary's equity is $150 million.

Question: How to account for that extra $50 million in equity? (If you answer, "Look, the gain isn't real, so let's ignore it," your mind is not tidy enough to be an accountant's.)

This is where *FASB 52's* choice of functional currency comes in. If management chooses a local currency—marks, say—as its functional currency, gains and losses from translating foreign assets and liabilities go into a separate account in shareholders' equity. You don't get those crazy swings in net income you got from *FASB 8*.

Take Exxon, where most foreign operations are deemed to operate in the local currency. The falling dollar's effect on foreign asset and liability translations meant Exxon added $332 million to equity in the first quarter of this year. Had Exxon used the dollar as functional currency, *FASB 52* says it would have had to credit the $332 million balance sheet adjustment to earnings. Even

(continued)

after taxes and other adjustment, Exxon's first-quarter net would have jumped some 10%.

Confused? You aren't alone. "Suddenly people are going to be seeing book values going up, and nobody will be able to figure out why," says Oppenheimer & Co. analyst Norman Weinger "It didn't come through in earnings. It didn't come through in sales of stock. It came through in this idiot . . . uh . . . [he pauses] . . . in this bookkeeping entry.

What happens should the dollar rise? Then companies using local currencies for functional currency must make negative translation adjustments to equity. By the end of 1984, when the dollar was strong, Ford Motor's cumulative negative adjustment had reached $1.4 billion. (It has since come down to $970 million.) Note, however, that reducing Ford's equity artificially boosted Ford's return on equity from 25.9%, without the adjustment, to 29.5% for 1984. Mobil's cumulative negative adjustment of $2 billion gave it a 9.3% ROE in 1984, rather than 8.1% without the adjustment. Unrealistic? Of course. But tidy accounting is not always consistent with economic reality.

Should the dollar rise again, companies using the dollar as their functional currency may have to take big, if unreal, charges against earnings. But earnings can be hit even if the dollar falls, depending on a company's asset-liability mix. Consider Pan Am, which uses the dollar as functional currency. Pan Am has a large amount of yen-denominated debt but, after selling its Pacific operations to United, few offsetting yen assets. The dollar's fall against the yen increased the dollar value of the yen debt, forcing Pan Am to take a $17 million charge against first-quarter income.

But don't jump on the accountants. Whatever its weaknesses, *FASB 52* is a major improvement over *FASB 8*. Oppenheimer's Weinger puts it all in witty perspective when he says: "Nobody is happy with the current system, but as long as everybody is equally unhappy, it [*FASB 52*] is okay."

Source: John Heins, "Plenty of Opportunity to Fool Around," *Forbes*, June 2, 1986, pp. 139, 140.

THE TRANSLATION PROCESS

In this section, we deal with the actual translation of foreign currency financial statements into dollars. Recall that in the translation process the foreign currency is the functional currency.

Basic Procedures before Translation

Certain fundamental procedures must be performed before the financial statements of foreign subsidiaries or branches may be translated into dollars.

Adjustments to Conform to U.S. Generally Accepted Accounting Principles. Operations conducted in a foreign country must be accounted for using that country's accounting principles. When foreign currency financial statements use accounting principles that are different from U.S. generally accepted accounting principles, appropriate adjustments must be made to those statements before translation so that they conform to U.S. generally accepted accounting principles. These adjustments, which are **made on a worksheet,** are never posted to the general ledger of the foreign accounting entity. The adjustments are necessary regardless of (1) the organizational form through which foreign operations are conducted, and (2) whether or not the foreign operation's statements are consolidated (if a subsidiary) or combined (if a division or a branch) with the financial statements of the domestic accounting entity.

Similarly, when a domestic company has a 20% to 50% interest in a foreign operation, which must be accounted for under the equity method of accounting, the investee's foreign statements must be adjusted to conform to U.S. generally accepted accounting principles before translation into dollars. The equity method is then applied after the translation process in accordance with *FASB Statement No. 52.*

Adjustments to Receivables and Payables. A foreign operation's receivables or payables in other than its local currency must be adjusted to reflect the current rate between the local currency (of the foreign country) and the currency in which the receivable or payable is stated. (Chapter 16 covers how to make and account for such adjustments.) In the illustration of the translation process in this section, we assume that any such adjustments have already been made.)

Reconciliation of Inter- or Intracompany Receivable and Payable Accounts. Inventory and cash are commonly transferred between domestic and foreign operations. Such transactions (other than dividend remittances) are usually recorded in separate inter- or intracompany receivable and payable accounts by each accounting entity. Such accounts must be reconciled to each other before translation to ensure that no clerical errors or unrecorded in-transit items exist. Only by performing this reconciliation will these accounts completely offset each other after translation.

Furthermore, when the inter- or intracompany account is to be settled in dollars (rather than in the foreign unit's local currency), the foreign unit's accounts must be adjusted as described in the preceding section. If settlement is to be made in the foreign unit's local currency, the domestic operation must adjust its books. (Such adjustments are illustrated in Chapter 16, where the intricacies of intercompany transactions with foreign subsidiaries are discussed.)

Translating the Branch Home Office Account. Most foreign operations are conducted using subsidiaries. When branches are used instead, the

Home Office account on the books of the branch replaces the equity accounts otherwise used by a subsidiary. The simplest technique is to have the branch maintain its Home Office account and the home office maintain its Investment in Branch account in three categories. The first category is the amount of the preceding period's ending balances of all three categories. This amount is translated at the combined amount shown for the Home Office account in the translated financial statements of the preceding period. The second category reflects all current-year transactions with the home office and is, in substance, a combination Intracompany account (as discussed in the preceding two paragraphs) and quasi-Capital account. Although the activity in this category must be reconciled with that period's activity in the corresponding category of the home office's Investment in Branch account, no adjustments are made for changes in the exchange rate. If each accounting entity has recorded all current-period transactions properly, this category is readily translated into dollars using the amount in the corresponding category on the home office's books. The third category represents the branch's current-year income; the translated amount in dollars is obtained from the translation of the branch's income statement.

Specific Translation Procedures

In the translation process using the foreign perspective, current exchange rates are used.

Balance Sheet Accounts. The following procedures translate the individual balance sheet accounts:

1. All assets and liabilities are translated at the exchange rate existing at the balance sheet date.
2. Common stock and additional paid-in capital are translated at historical exchange rates (to isolate the effect of the change in the exchange rate for the current period).
3. Beginning retained earnings is the dollar balance in the Retained Earnings account at the end of the prior period. (Dividend payments, if any, reduce this balance using the exchange rate in effect at the time of the declaration.)

Revenue, Cost of Goods Sold, and Expense Accounts. All revenues, costs of sales, and expenses are translated using exchange rates that were in effect when these items were **recognized** in the income statement. Thus, exchange rates **in effect during the current period** are used. The following four paragraphs explain how this process can be simplified.

The Use of Average Exchange Rates. When translating income statement accounts, average exchange rates may be used, provided that approximately the same results can be obtained from translating each individual transaction into dollars using the exchange rate that was in effect when the transaction occurred. If the item being translated occurred evenly throughout the period (month, quarter, or year), a simple average is sufficient. Otherwise, a weighted average is necessary. (Most publicly owned companies achieve a weighted average result by multiplying each individual month's amount by each month's average exchange rate.) Average exchange rates must be calculated using the direct exchange rates that existed during the period; indirect exchange rates would not give the proper translated amounts.

The Substitution Technique. A simplifying technique commonly used to translate income statement accounts that arise from activity with the parent or home office is to **substitute the amount in the domestic company's account for the subsidiary's or branch's account.** For example, the Intercompany Interest Expense account on the foreign subsidiary's books would be translated at the amount recorded in the Intercompany Interest Income account on the parent company's books. Likewise, the Intercompany Sales account on the foreign subsidiary's books would be translated at the amount recorded in the Intercompany Purchases account on the parent's books. This procedure automatically translates these items at the rates in effect on each transaction date, thus negating the need to use average rates. (This technique cannot be used in the translation process for downstream sales because it would result in a cost of goods sold amount based on exchange prices in existence when the inventory was acquired by the foreign unit rather than when the foreign unit sold the inventory. The latter is required under the translation process.)

In most cases, inter- or intracompany revenue and expense accounts need not be reconciled before doing the substitution. By reconciling the inter- or intracompany receivable and payable accounts before this substitution is made (as discussed on page 582), any clerical errors or unrecorded in-transit items affecting these income statement accounts would have been detected.

"Forcing out" the Translation Adjustment. Recall that in the translation process, the effect of a change in the exchange rate is called a translation adjustment. It must be reported in a separate category of stockholders' equity. Under the fixed exchange rate system, translation adjustments could be calculated by multiplying the foreign operation's net asset position at the time of a devaluation or revaluation by the change in the exchange rate. Under the current floating exchange rate system, exchange rates change daily and no such calculation is possible. The only practical alternative is to "force out" the translation adjustment (the amounts used are from Illustration 15-3 on page 585 and discussed on pages 586–87):

1.	**Translated assets**	$300,000
2. Less	**Translated liabilities**	208,000

Illustration 15-3
Translation of Foreign Subsidiary's Financial Statements for the Year Ended December 31, 19X1

	Marks	Exchange Rates		Dollars
		Code	Rate	
Balance Sheet:				
Cash	50,000	C	$0.40	$ 20,000
Accounts receivable, net	150,000	C	0.40	60,000
Inventory	200,000	C	0.40	80,000
Fixed assets	400,000	C	0.40	160,000
Accumulated depreciation	(50,000)	C	0.40	(20,000)
Total Assets	750,000			$300,000
Accounts payable	230,000	C	0.40	$ 92,000
Income taxes payable	40,000	C	0.40	16,000
Long-term debt	250,000	C	0.40	100,000
Total Liabilities	520,000			$208,000
Common stock	100,000	H	0.50	$ 50,000
Retained earnings:				
Prior years	70,000		*	33,000
Current year	60,000	(Per net income below)		25,200
Cumulative translation adjustment, net:				
Prior years			*	(6,400)
Current year		(Forced amount)		(9,800)
Total Equity	230,000			$ 92,000
Total Liabilities and Equity	750,000	(Per above)		$300,000
Income Statement:				
Sales	800,000	A	0.42	$336,000
Cost of goods sold	(500,000)	A	0.42	(210,000)
Depreciation expense	(20,000)	A	0.42	(8,400)
Operating expenses	(180,000)	A	0.42	(75,600)
Income before Income Taxes	100,000			$ 42,000
Income tax expense @ 40%	(40,000)	A	0.42	(16,800)
Net Income	60,000			$ 25,200

Code:
C = Current rate existing at the balance sheet date.
A = Average rate, as given in the introduction to this illustration.
H = Historical rate.

*The amount in dollars is given in the introduction to this illustration.

3. Equals	**Total stockholders' equity**	**$ 92,000**
4. Less	**Translated common stock and additional paid-in capital accounts**	**50,000**
5. Equals	**Total retained earnings and the cumulative translation adjustment**	**$ 42,000**

6. Less	Beginning retained earnings in dollars as reported in the prior period's translated financial statements (reduced for any dividends declared)	33,000
7. Less	Translated net income (determined from translating the individual revenue and expense accounts)	25,200
8. Equals	The cumulative translation adjustment.........	$ (16,200)
9. Less	The cumulative translation adjustment as of the beginning of the period	(6,400)
10. Equals	The current-period translation adjustment ...	$ (9,800)

Illustration

TRANSLATION OF FOREIGN CURRENCY FINANCIAL STATEMENTS

Assume the following information for a wholly owned subsidiary located in West Germany.

1. **Conformity with U.S. generally accepted accounting principles:** The financial statements in marks have been adjusted to conform with U.S. generally accepted accounting principles. No adjustments are necessary on the worksheet before translation.
2. **Intercompany Receivable and Payable Accounts:** The parent company and the subsidiary have no intercompany transactions (other than dividends declared by the subsidiary). Accordingly, no intercompany receivable and payable accounts exist, and no adjustments must be made at the balance sheet date prior to the translation process relating to changes in the exchange rate.
3. **Exchange rates:** The direct exchange rate at the beginning of the year was $0.45. The mark weakened or the dollar strengthened during the year such that the direct exchange rate at year-end was $0.40. The average rate for the year was $0.42.
4. **Common stock:** The subsidiary was formed several years ago when the direct exchange rate was $0.50. No additional capital stock changes have occurred since then.
5. **Retained earnings—beginning of year:** No dividends were declared during 19X1. The translated amount of retained earnings at the end of the prior year was $33,000.
6. **Sales, costs, and expenses:** All sales, costs, and expenses occurred evenly throughout the year.
7. **Cumulative translation adjustment—beginning of year:** The amount of the cumulative translation adjustment at the end of the prior year was a debit balance of $6,400.

Illustration 15-3 uses the information above to translate the foreign subsidiary's financial statements into dollars. The following items are important for understanding how this is done:

1. The $300,000 translated amount for the assets was inserted at the Total Liabilities and Equity line (the first step in the "forcing" process).
2. The $25,200 translated net income amount was then inserted into the balance sheet to force out the current-period translation adjustment.
3. Because the exchange rate decreased from $0.45 at the beginning of the year to $0.40 at year-end—a decrease of $0.05—the subsidiary's average net asset position during the year was approximately 196,000 marks ($9,800 translation adjustment ÷ .05).
4. No amounts are shown for the income tax consequences relating to the translation adjustments. Such adjustments, if any, would be made to the dollar amounts on a worksheet prior to the consolidation process.
5. Under the equity method of accounting, the parent company would make the following entries:

Investment in Subsidiary....................................	25,200	
Equity in Net Income of Subsidiary............		25,200
To record equity in net income.		
Cumulative Translation Adjustment....................	9,800	
Investment in Subsidiary..........................		9,800
To record effect of change in exchange rate.		

Note: These entries always maintain the book value element of the investment account balance at the difference between the subsidiary's assets and liabilities.

6. The conceptual analysis of the parent's investment account would be updated in 19X1 as follows:

			Book Value Element		
			Retained Earnings		
	Total Cost	= Common Stock	+ Prior Years	+ Current Year Earnings	+ Cumulative Translation Adjustment
Balance, January 1, 19X1.....	$76,600[a]	$50,000	$33,000		$ (6,400)
Equity in net income........	25,200			$25,200	
Cumulative translation adjustment..................	(9,800)				(9,800)
Subtotal............................	$92,000	$50,000	$33,000	$25,200	$(16,200)
Reclassification...............			25,200	(25,200)	
Balance, December 31, 19X1	$92,000	$50,000	$58,200	$ –0–	$(16,200)

[a]For simplicity, we assumed that there was no cost in excess of book value.

7. The primary elimination entry to consolidate the subsidiary at December 31, 19X1, is developed from the preceding analysis and is as follows:

Common Stock	50,000	
Retained Earnings (beginning-of-year balance).....	33,000	
Equity in Net Income of Subsidiary.....................	25,200	
Cumulative Translation Adjustment...........		16,200
Investment in Subsidiary..........................		92,000

Disposition of Translation Adjustments

The translation adjustments reported as a separate component of stockholders' equity are removed from that component (along with any related income taxes) and reported in the income statement on (a) complete or substantially complete liquidation or (b) sale of the investment.[9] (*FASB Interpretation No. 37* requires such treatment on a pro rata basis when only part of the ownership in a foreign operation is sold.[10]) Further interpretations are needed in this area to address the following questions:

1. Does the conversion of all operating assets into cash constitute a liquidation?
2. Does the conversion of all operating assets into passive investments constitute a liquidation?
3. What percentage of the operating assets would have to be sold to constitute a substantially complete liquidation?

A company that has foreign operations in more than one foreign country must, of course, maintain the separate translation component of equity for each such foreign operation that has translation adjustments.

Income Tax Consequences of Rate Changes

Income taxes provided on translation adjustments are to be allocated to the separate component of stockholders' equity.[11]

THE REMEASUREMENT PROCESS

This section deals with the actual remeasurement of a foreign operation's financial statements into dollars, which in this case is the foreign unit's functional currency. The basic procedures required before translation that were discussed in the preceding section on the translation process also apply to the remeasurement process—that is, making adjustments to conform to U.S. generally accepted accounting procedures, adjusting foreign currency receivable and payable accounts, and reconciling inter- or intracompany accounts.

Specific Remeasurement Procedures

Recall that the intent of the remeasurement process is to produce the same results as though the foreign unit's transactions had been recorded in the

[9] *FASB Statement No. 52*, par. 14.
[10] *Financial Accounting Standards Board Interpretation No. 37*, "Accounting for Translation Adjustments upon Sale of Part of an Investment in a Foreign Entity" (Stamford: Financial Accounting Standards Board, 1983), par. 2.
[11] *Statement of Financial Accounting Standards, No. 52*, par. 23. (In the FASB Exposure Draft "Accounting for Income Taxes," dated September 2, 1986, which is scheduled for passage in late 1987, paragraph 23 is amended slightly, but the requirement remains the same.)

functional currency (dollars, in this case) using the exchange rates in effect when the transactions occurred. Thus a combination of current and historical exchange rates is used. To achieve this objective, the FASB specified which accounts are remeasured using historical exchange rates (the current rate is used for all other accounts). These accounts are listed in Illustration 15-4.

Forcing out the Foreign Currency Transaction Gain or Loss from Remeasurement. Recall that the effect of the change in the exchange rate under

Illustration 15-4
Accounts Remeasured Using Historical Exchange Rates

Assets:
- Marketable securities carried at cost:
  - Equity securities
  - Debt securities not intended to be held until maturity
- Inventories carried at cost
- Prepaid expenses, such as insurance, advertising, and rent
- Property, plant, and equipment
- Accumulated depreciation on property, plant, and equipment
- Patents, trademarks, licenses, and formulas
- Goodwill
- Other tangible assets

Liabilities:
- Deferred income

Equity:
- Common stock
- Preferred stock carried at issuance price

Revenues, costs, and expenses (examples of accounts related to nonmonetary items):
- Cost of goods sold
- Depreciation of property, plant, and equipment
- Amortization of intangible items, such as goodwill, patents, licenses, and so on
- Amortization of deferred charges or credits, except deferred income taxes and policy acquisition costs for life insurance companies

Source: Based on *FASB Statement No. 52*, par. 48.

Note: The above list excludes deferred income taxes; they would be remeasured using the current rate.

Comments:
1. **Additional Paid-in Capital:** Although not listed above, this account would be remeasured at historical exchange rates. (The Common Stock account listed was obviously intended to include this account.)
2. **Retained Earnings:** This account is not listed above, not because the current rate is used, but because it is a "forced out" amount.

the remeasurement process is reported in the income statement as a foreign currency transaction gain or loss. Because of the floating exchange rate system, this amount must be forced out in the income statement (the amounts used are from Illustration 15-5, discussed on page 592).

1.		Remeasured assets	$336,000
2.	Less	Remeasured liabilities	208,000
3.	Equals	Total stockholders' equity	$128,000
4.	Less	Remeasured common stock and additional paid-in capital	50,000
5.	Equals	Total retained earnings	$ 78,000
6.	Less	Beginning retained earnings in dollars as reported in the prior period's remeasured financial statements (reduced for any dividends declared)	46,400
7.	Equals	Current-period net income	$ 31,600
8.	Less	Remeasured revenues and expenses	16,600
9.	Equals	The current-period foreign currency transaction gain from remeasurement	$ 15,000

Illustration

REMEASUREMENT OF A FOREIGN OPERATION'S FINANCIAL STATEMENTS INTO DOLLARS

To compare the results of the remeasurement process with the results of the translation process illustrated in the previous section, we use the financial statements for the same West German foreign subsidiary in the following illustration. In addition, we reflect an Intercompany Payable account of 50,000 marks (long-term debt was reduced by 50,000 marks). The assumptions for this illustration, some of which are identical to those used in the translation process, are as follows:

1. **Conformity with U.S. generally accepted accounting principles:** The financial statements in marks have been adjusted to conform with U.S. generally accepted accounting principles. No adjustments are necessary on the worksheet before remeasurement.
2. **Intercompany Receivable and Payable accounts:** The parent company and the subsidiary have considerable intercompany transactions (involving mainly inventory transfers). The subsidiary's intercompany payable account is payable in marks. Accordingly, the parent company has a foreign currency transaction and is the entity that must adjust its intercompany receivable account at year-end to reflect the exchange rate existing at the balance sheet date. (Chapter 16 discusses how to make adjustments to intercompany payables and receivables.)

Illustration 15-5
Remeasurement of Foreign Subsidiary's Financial Statements into Dollars for the Year Ended December 31, 19X1

	Marks		Exchange Rates Code	Exchange Rates Rate	Dollars	
Balance Sheet:						
Cash		50,000	C	$0.40		$ 20,000
Accounts receivable, net		150,000	C	0.40		60,000
Inventory		200,000		*		81,000
Fixed assets		400,000	H	0.50		200,000
Accumulated depreciation		(50,000)	H	0.50		(25,000)
Total Assets		750,000				$336,000
Accounts payable		230,000	C	0.40		$ 92,000
Income taxes payable		40,000	C	0.40		16,000
Intercompany payable		50,000	C	0.40		20,000
Long-term debt		200,000	C	0.40		80,000
Total Liabilities		520,000				$208,000
Common stock		100,000	H	0.50		$ 50,000
Retained earnings:						
Prior years		70,000		*		46,400
Current year		60,000	(Forced amount)			31,600
Total Equity		230,000				$128,000
Total Liabilities and Equity		750,000	(Per above)			$336,000
Income Statement:						
Sales		800,000	A	0.42		$336,000
Cost of goods sold:						
Beginning inventory	100,000			*	$ 46,000	
Purchases	600,000		A	0.42	252,000	
Goods available for sale	700,000				$298,000	
Less: Ending inventory	(200,000)	(500,000)	(Per balance sheet)		(81,000)	(217,000)
Depreciation expense		(20,000)	H	0.50		(10,000)
Operating expenses		(180,000)	A	0.42		(75,600)
Income before Income Taxes		100,000				$ 33,400
Income tax expense @ 40%		(40,000)	A	0.42		(16,800)
Income before Transaction Gain from Remeasurement		60,000				$ 16,600
Transaction Gain from Remeasurement			(Forced amount)			15,000
Net Income		60,000	(Per balance sheet)			$ 31,600

Code:
C = Current rate existing at the balance sheet date.
H = Historical rate.
A = Average rate, as given in the introduction to this illustration.

*The amount in dollars is given in the introduction to this illustration.

3. **Exchange rates:** The direct exchange rate at the beginning of the year was $0.45. The mark weakened or the dollar strengthened during the year such that the direct exchange rate at year-end was $0.40. The average rate for the year was $0.42.
4. **Inventory:** The beginning inventory was remeasured at $46,000 in last year's financial statements. Ending inventory cost was below market in marks, resulting in no adjustment in marks for valuation purposes. The subsidiary determines that its ending inventory was acquired when the exchange rates were as follows:

Marks	Rate	Dollars
20,000	$0.42	$ 8,400
60,000	0.41	24,600
120,000	0.40	48,000
200,000		$81,000

5. **Fixed assets:** All fixed assets were acquired in prior years when the exchange rate was $0.50. No fixed assets were retired during the year.
6. **Common stock:** The subsidiary was formed several years ago when the exchange rate was $0.50. No additional capital stock changes have occurred since then.
7. **Retained earnings—Beginning of year:** No dividends were declared during 19X1. The translated retained earnings amount at the end of the prior year was $46,400.
8. **Sales, purchases, and expenses:** All sales, purchases, and expenses occurred evenly throughout the year.

Illustration 15-5 uses the above information to remeasure the foreign subsidiary's financial statements into dollars. The following items are important for understanding how this is done:

1. The $336,000 translated amount for the assets was inserted at the total liabilities and equity line (the first step in the "forcing" process). As a result, current-period net income can be forced out in the equity section.
2. The net income forced out in the equity section was then inserted at the bottom of the income statement (the second step in the forcing process). This allows the transaction gain from remeasurement to be forced out in the income statement.
3. The exchange rate decreased from $0.45 at the beginning of the year to $0.40 at year-end—a decrease of $0.05—and a $15,000 transaction gain from remeasurement was reported. Therefore, the foreign subsidiary was in an average net monetary liability position of 300,000 marks during the year ($15,000 ÷ $0.05). In other words, monetary liabilities exceeded monetary assets by 300,000 marks on the average during the year. (This average net monetary liability position approximates the December 31, 19X1 net monetary liability position, which is 320,000 marks [520,000 − 200,000].)
4. The decrease in the direct exchange rate was an adverse economic event; however, a $15,000 favorable result was reported for the effect of

the change in the exchange rate. (This unusual result situation was discussed in detail in the conceptual issues section of Chapter 14.)

5. The $15,000 transaction gain from remeasurement would not have resulted if the company had kept monetary assets and monetary liabilities at approximately the same level throughout the year. Doing this merely to minimize transaction gains and losses from remeasurement, however, counteracts the long-standing principle of minimizing the risks associated with foreign operations by financing them with foreign borrowings (payable in the foreign currency of the foreign operation) to the maximum extent possible. Obviously, companies must carefully weigh these conflicting objectives. (In Chapter 16, we discuss other means of minimizing gains and losses resulting from remeasurement.)
6. The equity method of accounting would be applied to the subsidiary's net income of $31,600 as follows:

Investment in Subsidiary	**31,600**	
Equity in Net Income of Subsidiary		**31,600**

Note: Recall that the $15,000 transaction gain from remeasurement is included in determining net income.

7. Total assets and total equity are both higher by $36,000 in Illustration 15-5 than in Ilustration 15-3, in which the translation process was shown. This difference is the result of using historical exchange rates in Illustration 15-5 for inventory (a $1,000 difference) and fixed assets (a $35,000 difference) rather than the rate existing at the balance sheet date (a current rate).

Income Tax Consequences of Rate Changes

Foreign currency transaction gains or losses from the remeasurement process that are not currently reported for tax purposes should be treated as **timing differences** for which interperiod tax allocation is necessary.[12]

Basic Procedures after Remeasurement

Because of the use of historical exchange rates for most nonmonetary assets, the results of the remeasurement process create a special problem that does not arise with the translation process. Nonmonetary assets remeasured at historical exchange rates are not necessarily realizable in dollars (even though no realizability problem exists in the foreign currency). Thus, the foreign operation's remeasured nonmonetary assets must be reviewed and evaluated for their realizability in dollars. Prior to consolidation, the dollar amounts of such assets on the worksheet must be adjusted to the extent that they are not realizable in dollars. *FASB Statement No. 52* discusses the realization of inventory in dollars in great detail;

[12]*FASB Statement No. 52*, par. 22.

however, it only briefly touches on the realization of fixed assets, which may be an even greater problem.

Inventory. The lower of cost or market test must also be performed in dollars, to ensure that the realizable value in dollars is not less than remeasured historical cost. Such situations usually arise when ending inventory is acquired before the direct exchange rate decreases significantly, and the inventory is thus priced at historical cost and remeasured at the historical rate. In applying the lower of cost or market test in dollars, we determine current replacement cost, net realizable value, and net realizable value reduced for a normal profit margin (a percentage concept) in the foreign currency and then express each one in dollars using the exchange rate existing at the balance sheet date. (These are current-value concepts; thus, the exchange rate existing at the balance sheet date is the only sensible rate.)

To illustrate this procedure, we must use a more drastic decrease in the exchange rate than the one assumed in Illustration 15-5. Let us use the 85% decline in the value of the Mexican peso that occurred in 1982. We assume that ending inventory was acquired for 1,000,000 pesos before the decrease in the direct exchange rate. The exchange rate before the decrease was $0.04, and the exchange rate after the decrease was $0.006. The lower of cost or market calculation in dollars is as follows:

	Pesos	Rate	Dollars
Historical cost	1,000,000	$0.04	$40,000
Replacement cost	1,000,000	0.006	6,000
Net realizable value	1,200,000	0.006	$ 7,200 (ceiling)
Net realizable value reduced for a normal profit margin	1,000,000	0.006	$ 6,000 (floor)

Accordingly, the inventory must be valued at $6,000, a write-down of $34,000. This write-down is made to the dollar column; it would never be posted to the peso general ledger. This process is necessary regardless of whether a write-down was needed in applying the lower of cost or market test in pesos. In an alternative view of the rationale for performing the lower of cost or market test in dollars, we assume that the inventory was sold on the last day of the year for 1,200,000 pesos. The 1,200,000 pesos (cash or receivables) would be remeasured to $7,200, which is below the remeasured historical cost of $40,000.

This example assumes that selling prices and purchase prices did not advance after the weakening of the peso. When selling prices neither advance nor decline, replacement cost always equals the floor. If selling prices had advanced in pesos after the weakening of the peso, the ceiling and floor would have been higher, thus necessitating a lower write-down.

(Inflation often increases after a sharp decline in the value of a foreign currency.) The process of performing a lower of cost or market test for inventory in dollars is discussed at length in paragraphs 49 to 53 of *FASB Statement No. 52*.

Assets Other than Inventory. Fixed assets may be realizable in the foreign currency, but the future cash flow that such assets generate (including that portion of the future cash flow that presumably represents a recovery of the investment in fixed assets) is worth significantly less (in dollars) as a result of a weakening of the foreign currency. Surprisingly, the use of historical rates in remeasuring assets other than inventory and the potential realization problems that may arise are given only footnote attention in *FASB Statement No. 52*. Footnote 5 to paragraph 49 states:

> An asset other than inventory may sometimes be written down from historical cost. Although that write-down is not under the rule of cost or market, whichever is lower, the approach described in this paragraph might be appropriate . . . .[13]

If a substantial decline in the direct exchange rate occurs (such as the 85% devaluation of the Mexican peso in 1982), the realization of fixed assets in dollars represents a major problem that could be a much greater one than the realization of inventory in dollars.

In practice, write-downs of fixed assets are rare. However, when an operation is losing money and the prospects of improving the situation are not good, such operations are often sold. If the operation is sold for less than book value, as could be expected, the loss in value of the fixed assets is reported as a loss on disposal of a segment (if a segment is being disposed of) or as a loss on disposal of fixed assets if the disposal does not qualify as a disposal of a segment. (Disposals of segments are discussed in Chapter 13.)

The direct exchange rate in Illustration 15-5 decreased during the year, and a $15,000 transaction gain resulted from the remeasurement process. Because of the decline in the exchange rate, the inventory and fixed assets must be reviewed for their realization in dollars. A write-down would offset (partially or fully) the transaction gain from remeasurement. Depending on the extent of the write-down, this procedure either minimizes or eliminates the reporting of a current-period transaction gain from remeasurement that will only be offset by the reporting of future-period transaction losses from remeasurement.

If the direct exchange rate had increased rather than decreased in Illustration 15-5, a transaction loss from remeasurement would have resulted; however, no provisions exist for revaluing inventory and fixed assets

[13]*FASB Statement No. 52*, par. 49, footnote 5.

upward to obtain the offsetting effect discussed in the preceding paragraph. Accordingly, the reporting of a current-period transaction loss from remeasurement is offset in later periods as the nonmonetary assets are realized (transformed into monetary assets).

THE MANNER OF REPORTING FOREIGN OPERATIONS

Disclosures Concerning Translation and Remeasurement

Translation. For the separate component of stockholders' equity containing the cumulative translation adjustments, the FASB requires an analysis of the following changes during the period:

a. Beginning and ending amount of cumulative translation adjustments.
b. The aggregate adjustment for the period resulting from translation adjustments and gains and losses from certain hedges and intercompany balances [the latter items are discussed in Chapter 16].
c. The amount of income taxes for the period allocated to translation adjustments.
d. The amounts transferred from cumulative translation adjustments [including all items above] and included in determining net income for the period as a result of the sale or complete or substantially complete liquidation of an investment in a foreign subsidiary.[14]

This analysis may be shown (1) in a separate financial statement, (2) in notes to the financial statements, or (3) as part of a statement of changes in stockholders' equity.

Remeasurement. The total of all transaction gains and losses from remeasurement (along with other foreign currency transaction gains and losses that are reported in the income statement—such as those resulting from importing and exporting transactions) is disclosed as a net amount either in the income statement or in notes to the financial statements.[15] Transaction gains and losses are not considered extraordinary items, no matter how material they might be.

Additional Risks in Reporting Earnings from Foreign Operations

An asset held in a foreign country is not the same as an asset held domestically. This is true for monetary assets (such as cash, receivables, or any other asset that will be settled by the payment of currency) and nonmen-

[14] *FASB Statement No. 52*, par. 31.
[15] *FASB Statement No. 52*, par. 15.

tary assets (such as land, buildings, equipment, and inventory). Assets held in foreign countries entail the following additional risks:

1. Expropriation, or the seizure of assets.
2. Devaluation, or the diminution of value of both monetary assets and the cash flows from future operations.
3. Currency transfer restrictions, or the limitation on repatriation of foreign profits and invested capital. The article below shows the lengths to which companies go in order to transfer their assets back to the United States.
4. Wars and civil disorders.

These risks must be considered in determining the earnings reported from foreign operations, regardless of the amounts determined under the procedures called for in *FASB Statement No. 52.* Of course, these factors also influence whether or not consolidation is appropriate. In practice, for example, a domestic company usually does not consolidate foreign operations located in a country that imposes currency exchange restrictions, because the assets are no longer under the domestic company's complete control.

PERSPECTIVE

Funds Blocked Abroad by Exchange Controls Plague Big Companies

In Western France, a Frenchman straps on a money belt loaded with French francs given to him by a multinational company operating in France. He hang glides over the Swiss border so he can get Swiss francs to deposit in a Swiss bank account.

In New Delhi, a major international airline gives a case of Scotch to a government official. The government thereupon permits the airline to convert $18 million worth of rupees into dollars to take to the airline's home country.

Corporations often must go to such lengths to get around foreign-exchange controls. It is one of the oldest games in international finance, and one of the riskiest. It also has become one of the most widely played.

Result of Debt Crisis

Countries have long limited the holding and purchase of foreign currency within their borders, often as a way to support the value of their own currencies. But since the global debt crisis came to a head two years ago, the controls have spread as developing countries have tried to allocate scarce dollars and other so-called hard currencies to specific imports or to pay interest on foreign debt.

The result is that multinational corporations often can't get their money out of the developing countries. These blocked funds represent everything from

Funds Blocked Abroad by Exchange Controls Plague Big Companies *(continued)*

uncollected bills and unpaid trade credits to royalties and dividends that companies want to convert to hard currency and ship home.

"Every multinational corporation is sitting on blocked funds somewhere, and every treasurer is ripping his hair out over some," says Philip S. Beckerman, a group vice president of MG Services Co., a New York trading company.

Nobody knows how much money is tied up in these blocked funds. Corporate treasurers estimate that the total exceeds $5 billion. If the definition includes the practical inability to liquidate any foreign assets and move the proceeds out of the country, the total could be in the hundreds of billions of dollars.

Breadth of Problem

Michael W. Liikala, special adviser to the undersecretary of commerce for international trade administration, says that when the Commerce Department surveyed Chicago-area companies about overdue receivables abroad, he received a "stack of papers the size of a phone book, one page a company."

The situation is causing some gigantic corporate headaches. "Blocked funds can be an insidious problem for multinationals around the world," says Jon W. Rotenstreich, the treasurer of International Business Machines Corp. in Armonk, N.Y. By preventing a company from deploying its capital where it can earn the highest return, exchange controls "downgrade the quality of a company's investment," he observes.

The problem also can put pressure on earnings, and it can force companies to make wrenching decisions: sell the blocked assets at a deep discount, wait out the crisis and possibly suffer even bigger losses, or close local operations altogether.

Airlines generally are the hardest hit because they are legally required to accept local currency payments for flights in or out of the country, when the flight is booked in that country. The International Air Transport Association estimates that at midyear its members had about $850 million blocked in various countries, up from $600 million in mid-1983.

Role of Central Banks

The initial tactic of a company with blocked assets is to argue its case at the country's central bank, which usually has responsibility for converting and releasing funds held in the country.

"Negotiate all the time, demonstrate your importance to the local economy, demonstrate your dependence on foreign sourcing if you're a manufacturing company," says Edward E. Matthews, executive vice president for finance at American International Group Inc., an insurance company based in New York. "The biggest thing you have to have is patience," Mr. Matthews says. He should know. AIG filed 15 times with Tanzania for $100,000 before getting paid.

(continued)

Peter L. Rapuzzi, a vice president of Chase Manhattan Bank, says, "To move a government it's best if you have some vital import to keep a factory running, to feed somebody, or a strategic interest."

Agricultural products and drugs usually lead the list, followed by imports for industries that either create a lot of employment or are economically strategic. Next come capital goods, followed by such things as trucks. Nonessential items such as liquor and expensive foods come last.

Some companies learn to play hardball. One U.S. electrical-products company bluntly threatened to close down a factory, throwing hundreds of Mexicans out of work, if government officials didn't allow it to exchange pesos for dollars. It got its greenbacks.

Pfizer Inc., a pharmaceutical company based in New York, says it argued with Brazilian officials last year that if they didn't release funds, Pfizer wouldn't be able to buy the imports necessary to protect Brazilian chickens from disease. A U.S. official recalls that Brazil "came back with double what Pfizer requested."

If these methods fail, J. Beresford Packham, the executive treasurer for United Brands, Co., a food-processing company based in New York, says a multinational's only options with blocked cash are to "spend it, lend it, try to transfer it, reinvest it, or give it away." And whatever the solution, he says, the cost is high.

Nearly all companies search for some other multinational concern that is willing to buy the blocked currency for dollars, even if at a discount. A pioneer, bankers say, was Walt Disney Productions, which arranged for U.S. companies investing in Japan after World War II to buy its blocked receivables amassed from showing Mickey Mouse and Donald Duck films. The money became known as Disney dollars.

Use of Middlemen

Today, banks, investment banks and private intermediaries such as the Robert Langworthy Group and Del Cristo & Co. earn fees by matching holders of blocked funds with companies and wealthy individuals that need the local currencies. Exeucutives from Pfizer, Exxon Corp., Du Pont Co. and Dow Chemical Co. set up an informal network in Coral Gables, Fla., to help each other out of blocked-money jams in Latin America.

In 1983, Helena Rubenstein Inc., burdened with the remains of a defunct subsidiary in Guatemala, sought to sell to Monsanto Co. $1.3 million in tax-loss carry-forwards and the rights that it had to remove $1.2 million from the country. Monsanto's local subsidiary was stuck with $800,000 to $1 million in blocked funds. But Monsanto wasn't interested in buying Rubenstein's subsidiary, which was the only way to obtain the tax credits.

Salomon Brothers Inc. structured the deal so that Monsanto would buy Rubenstein's removal rights at a discount, transfer receivables to Rubenstein's subsidiary and, finally, have Rubenstein repatriate the cash to the U.S.

Funds Blocked Abroad by Exchange Controls Plague Big Companies *(continued)*

Salomon intended to get Guatemalan government approval for the transaction, but the deal ultimately fell through. Bankers say that asset swaps similar to this go on all the time, however, often without the knowledge of local officials.

Variations on the currency-swap theme include so-called parallel loans. In the Third World, a cash-rich subsidiary of one multinational company lends local funds to the subsidiary of another, while the borrower's parent company simultaneously pays dollars to the lender's parent. That way, the lender unloads blocked funds quickly. At the same time, the borrower bypasses constraints of the local banking system, including borrowing limits and high interest rates.

Some companies, such as General Motors Corp., don't like swaps because the exchange rates are usually unattractive, and the arrangements can sometimes be a shade shy of the law. But companies sometimes are even prodded by local governments to evade the local laws.

More blatantly illegal tactics for evading exchange controls include invoicing games. A U.S. government official tells of how a German importer of Indian scrap metal was always offered two payment options: list price or a discount. If the German company chose the discount, it paid a false, very low bill and deposited additional funds in the Indian's Swiss bank account. Bankers say the practice is so common among Latin American exporters that they are known as the 15 percenters, because their trade partners routinely deposit 15% of an export's value in Miami Banks.

Many companies avoid such tactics. "In Spain and some other countries, you don't go to jail for tax evasion, but you can for currency violations," says Paul H. Boschma, international executive for Klynveld Main Goerdeler, a Dutch accounting firm.

Barter and Countertrade

Some multinational companies have turned to barter, or its more sophisticated version, countertrade. For instance, a developing country may permit a company to buy a local product with its blocked cash and sell the product abroad for dollars.

"But a country will only give you something it can't move," warns George S. Horton, a senior vice president at MG Services Co. The country usually won't permit barter with a product that can easily sell for hard currency, he explains.

Pierre Loze, now an international manager for Parfums Bourjois, a cosmetics firm in Paris, once had to accept Romanian trucks as payment for an oil sale to Morocco when he worked for a French chemical company. He couldn't sell the trucks. They were traded for oranges. He couldn't sell the oranges. "It was a business without end; we couldn't get any money," he says.

When multinational companies can't free their blocked funds or they believe the cost is too high, they hunker down and search for ways to protect their holdings from the Third World's dual devastations of devaluation and inflation. Some invest in local businesses that earn hard currency through exports; oth-

(continued)

ers, when permitted, buy gold. Pfizer held onto Buenos Aires real estate rather than sell it, figuring it may be the best hedge against rampant Argentine inflation. Argentina and Guatemala offer dollar-denominated bonds; Brazil offers inflation-adjusted bonds.

Using Funds on a Film

Columbia Pictures Industries Inc. early this year filmed "Sheena" in Kenya to use up blocked funds generated by its parent Coca-Cola Co.'s soft-drink operations. PepsiCo Inc. exports wine to the U.S. from Romania, Bulgaria and Hungary. It also sells Russian vodka.

Rather than try to repatriate $30 million to $40 million from liquidated Brazilian assets, Britain's Imperial Chemical Industries PLC in August reinvested the money in a polyester film factory. And in Argentina, the diversified chemical and pharmaceuticals company uses its pesos to rebuild inventories.

Companies can sometimes use blocked funds by holding sales conferences in the country, and to pay services rendered to the parent company, such as legal and accounting fees.

The head of international operations for a Dutch company says that when he travels to where his company has blocked cash, the local subsidiary always pays for his expenses, even if he's on vacation; he then reimburses the parent company in hard currency. Another executive says that for a while some companies were booking all of their airline tickets—wherever the destination or departure—out of Dar es Salaam, Tanzania, to spend currency blocked in that country.

GM Deal with Hertz

In the spring of 1983 General Motors helped Hertz Corp. protect about $6 million worth of blocked Mexican pesos from devaluation in a transaction that combined aspects of both a parallel loan and a counter-trade deal.

Here is how it worked: Hertz bought automobile engines from General Motors de Mexico with a dollar-denominated IOU that matured in 18 months. The engines were then placed in U.S.-made GM cars, which Hertz also purchased. At the same time that Hertz handed over its IOU (which, in effect, was a GM loan to Hertz), its Mexican affiliate lent GM de Mexico its blocked pesos. GM then sold the Hertz IOU at a discount and deposited the money with Mexico's central bank in a dollar-indexed account.

Although Hertz didn't actually get its blocked pesos out of Mexico, the deal effectively protected them from depreciation against the dollar. From GM's standpoint, the complicated transaction "increased the good will with one of our major customers at a time GM de Mexico was looking for volume," says Louis R. Hughes, assistant treasurer for GM.

Funds Blocked Abroad by Exchange Controls Plague Big Companies *(continued)*

Mr. Hughes concedes that it is sometimes difficult for multinational companies to decide whether to close shop or work out complicated transactions. "If you close up, the cost can be enormous—it can be in the hundreds of millions of dollars for a company GM's size—and you forgo a presence in that market for a long time." He adds: "It's crisis management."

Source: Michael R. Sesit, "Funds Blocked Abroad by Exchange Controls Plague Big Companies," *The Wall Street Journal*, December 3, 1984, p. 1.

Nonconsolidation of a Foreign Operation. If a foreign subsidiary is not consolidated, then the parent must evaluate whether or not it can realize its investment in the subsidiary. If a realization problem exists, the investment must be written down.

Disclosures Concerning Foreign Assets, Revenues, and Profitability. *FASB Statement No. 14*, "Financial Reporting for Segments of a Business Enterprise," requires disclosures of foreign assets, revenues, and profitability of consolidated foreign operations if specific tests are met. We discussed these tests and the disclosure requirements in Chapter 13, which deals with segment reporting.

CONCLUDING COMMENTS

Knowledgeable people, many with substantial experience in assessing and dealing with foreign operations, draw completely different conclusions concerning how to account for the effects of changes in the exchange rate in reporting foreign operations. For example, *FASB Statement No. 52* was passed by a mere 4 to 3 vote. We summarize the views of the dissenting members of the FASB below.

Views of the Dissenting FASB Members

The substantial objections and views of the three dissenting FASB members are presented in pages 15 to 23 of *FASB Statement No. 52.* They basically objected to allowing the use of a foreign currency as the unit of measure (when the dollar is not the functional currency). (This objection essentially rejects the functional-currency concept as a relevant factor in determining how foreign operations should be expressed in dollars.) In their view, the dollar should be used as the unit of measure in all cases. Furthermore, dissenting members felt that the translation adjustments should not be reported directly in stockholders' equity. In their view, translation adjustments are gains and losses from a dollar perspective that should be currently reported in the income statement. In summary, these members felt that *FASB Statement No. 8* was conceptually sound and that the temporal method of translation should be used in all cases. (They would have allowed a practical modification for inventory; locally acquired inventory could be translated at the current exchange rate.)

Has the Controversy Ended?

Whether *FASB Statement No. 52* is the last chapter concerning the foreign currency translation issue or merely the latest chapter remains to be seen. An adequate assessment of the reporting results from using the functional currency concept and not reporting translation adjustments currently in the income statement will probably require a fairly long period of time. Considering the extensive monumental effort that the FASB and its staff devoted to *FASB Statement No. 52*, it is likely that they will not want to readdress this issue for quite a while.

SUMMARY

The cornerstone of *FASB Statement No. 52* is the functional currency concept. The functional currency for each foreign operation must be determined. The currency in which the foreign operation primarily generates and expends cash is its functional currency, and this currency is not necessarily the one in which it maintains its books and prepares its financial statements. Illustration 15-6 contains a summary of accounting for the translation of foreign currency financial statements once the functional currency has been determined.

Glossary of New Terms

Current Exchange Rate "The current exchange rate is the rate at which one unit of a currency can be exchanged for (converted into) another currency. For purposes of translation . . . , the current exchange rate is the rate as of the end of the period covered by the financial statements or as of the dates of recognition in those statements in the case of revenues, expenses, gains, and losses."*

Foreign Currency Translation "The process of expressing in the reporting currency of the enterprise those amounts that are denominated or measured in a different currency.*

Remeasurement The process of measuring in the functional currency amounts denominated or stated in another currency.

Translation (distinguished from remeasurement) The process of expressing functional currency measurements in the reporting currency.

**FASB Statement No. 52*, Appendix E, pp. 75–78.

Illustration 15-6
Summary of Accounting for the Translation of Foreign Currency Financial Statements

	Functional Currency	
	Foreign Currency	**U.S. Dollar**
Perspective taken	Foreign	Parent Company
Name given to process	Translation	Remeasurement
Exchange rates to be used for:		
Assets and liabilities	Current rate[a]	Combination of current[a] and historical rates
Income statement accounts	Current rate[b]	Combination of current[b] and historical rates
Term used to describe the effect of a change in the exchange rate	Translation adjustment	Foreign currency transaction gain or loss
Treatment to be accorded the effect of a change in the exchange rate	Accumulate in separate component of stockholders' equity (pending liquidation or disposal of the investment)	Report currently in the income statement

Note: For operations located in countries that have highly inflationary economies, the dollar is deemed to be the functional currency.

[a]Current rate here means the exchange rate existing at the balance sheet date.
[b]Current rate here means the exchange rate existing when the items were recognized in the income statement.

Translation Adjustments Adjustments that result from the process of translating financial statements from the entity's functional currency into the reporting currency.

Unit of Measure The currency in which assets, liabilities, revenues, expenses, gains, and losses are measured.*

Review Questions

1. How does *FASB Statement No. 52* define a highly inflationary economy?
2. How are highly inflationary economies dealt with in *FASB Statement No. 52*?
3. Differentiate between translation and remeasurement.
4. How are the effects of changes in the exchange rate treated in translation situations? in remeasurement situations?
5. List the basic procedures required before the translation or remeasurement process begins.

6. Name six balance sheet accounts for which historical exchange rates are used in remeasurement.
7. What are some of the additional risks in reporting earnings from foreign operations?

Discussion Cases

DC 15-1

Determination of the Functional Currency

The Handy Company manufactures soap domestically and in a foreign country, which has low labor costs. The foreign operation (conducted through a wholly owned subsidiary) purchases all of its raw materials from the parent company, which can obtain volume discounts because of its size. (Were it not for the volume discount, the foreign subsidiary would purchase the raw materials directly from suppliers.) The foreign subsidiary's purchases from the parent company are denominated in dollars.

All of the subsidiary's sales are in its local currency, the mun, and all employees are paid in muns. The parent company has established that the subsidiary's dividend policy is to convert its available funds into dollars as quickly as possible each month for current or near-term distribution to the parent.

Required:
Determine whether the functional currency is the dollar or the mun.

DC 15-2

Criteria for Consolidation of Foreign Subsidiary

In 19X1, Poplar Company formed a subsidiary, Sycamore Company, in the emerging nation of Mulberria. Poplar owns 90% of Sycamore's outstanding common stock; the remaining 10% of Sycamore's outstanding common stock is held by Mulberria citizens, as required by Mulberria constitutional law. The investment in Sycamore, which Poplar accounts for using the equity method, represents about 17% of Poplar's total assets at December 31, 19X4, the close of the accounting period for both companies.

Required:
What criteria should Poplar Company use in determining whether to prepare consolidated financial statements? Explain.

(AICPA adapted)

Exercises

E 15-1

Selection of the Proper Exchange Rate: Balance Sheet Accounts

The following accounts exist in a foreign subsidiary's books:

1. Allowance for Doubtful Accounts
2. Inventory (carried at cost)
3. Inventory (carried at market, which is below cost)
4. Marketable Equity Securities (carried at cost)
5. Marketable Equity Securities (carried at market, which exceeds historical cost)
6. Patents
7. Equipment
8. Accumulated Depreciation
9. Intercompany Payable
10. Long-term Debt
11. Income Taxes Payable
12. Deferred Income Taxes
13. Common Stock
14. Additional Paid-in Capital
15. Retained Earnings

Required:

1. Assuming that the subsidiary's local currency is its functional currency, determine whether the historical exchange rate, the current exchange rate, an average exchange rate, or some other procedure should be used to translate the above accounts.
2. Assuming that the dollar is the subsidiary's functional currency, determine whether the historical exchange rate, the current exchange rate, an average exchange rate, or some other procedure should be used to remeasure the above accounts in dollars.

E 15-2

Selection of the Proper Exchange Rate: Income Statement Accounts

The following accounts exist in a foreign subsidiary's books:

1. Revenues
2. Intercompany Sales to Parent Company
3. Purchases
4. Intercompany Purchases from Parent Company
5. Cost of Goods Sold
6. Selling Expenses
7. Depreciation Expense
8. Income Tax Expense
9. Goodwill Amortization
10. Gain on Sale of Equipment
11. Intercompany Interest Expense
12. Depreciation Expenses (incremental amount resulting from adjusting assets for inflation)

Required:
The requirements are the same as those in Exercise 15-1.

E 15-3

Translation of Depreciation Expense

The Willinger Company owns a foreign subsidiary with 3,600,000 local currency units (LCU) of property, plant, and equipment before accumulated depreciation at December 31, 19X5. Of this amount, 2,400,000 LCU were acquired in 19X3 when the exchange rate was 5 LCU to $1; 1,200,000 LCU were acquired in 19X4 when the exchange rate was 8 LCU to $1.

The exchange rate in effect at December 31, 19X5, was 10 LCU to $1. The weighted average of exchange rates that were in effect during 19X5 was 12 LCU to $1. Assume that the property, plant, and equipment are depreciated using the straight-line method over a 10-year period with no salvage value.

Required:

1. Are the exchange rates given above the direct rates or the indirect rates?
2. Determine the dollar amount of depreciation expense for 19X5 assuming that the foreign operation's functional currency is
   a. the LCU.
   b. the dollar.

(AICPA adapted)

E 15-4

Translating/Remeasuring and Performing a Lower of Cost or Market Test in Dollars for Inventory

The following selected information is provided in connection with the translation of a Mexican subsidiary's December 31, 19X1, financial statements:
The December 31, 19X1, inventory was acquired when the following exchange rates existed:

Pesos	Direct Rate
1,000,000	$.009
3,000,000	.008
7,000,000	.007
10,000,000	.006
15,000,000	.005
36,000,000	

The replacement cost of the inventory is 38,000,000 pesos; the net realizable value is 60,000,000 pesos; and the net realizable value less a normal profit margin is 40,000,000 pesos.

The exchange rate at December 31, 19X1 is 200 pesos to $1; however, the average relationship for 19X1 was 150 pesos to $1.

Required:
Perform a lower of cost or market test in dollars assuming that:

a. the peso is the functional currency.
b. the dollar is the functional currency.

E 15-5

Translating/Remeasuring a Gain in Dollars for Fixed Assets

A Mexican subsidiary sold equipment acquired in prior years costing 4,000,000 pesos on April 1, 19X1, for 2,500,000 pesos when the exchange rate was $0.008. (The exchange rate existing when the equipment was purchased several years ago was $0.04.) A 1,000,000-peso gain relating to this disposal is recorded in the general ledger.

The exchange rate at December 31, 19X1, is 200 pesos to $1; however, the average relationship for 19X1 was 150 pesos to $1.

Required:
Determine the amount of the gain in dollars assuming that:

a. the peso is the functional currency.
b. the dollar is the functional currency.

Problems

P 15-1

MINI-COMPREHENSIVE Translation and Remeasurement

Following are certain items (accounts or account totals) that have been translated or remeasured into dollars at or for the year ended December 31, 19X2:

Total Assets	$200,000
Total Liabilities	110,000
Common Stock	20,000
Revenues	80,000
Expenses	50,000

	Functional Currency	
	Pound	Dollar
Amounts Reported at the End of the Prior Year (December 31, 19X1):		
Retained Earnings	$12,000	$30,000
Cumulative translation adjustment	$15,000	

Required:

1. Assuming that the pound is the functional currency, determine the following items:
   a. Ending balance for Retained Earnings at December 31, 19X2
   b. Current-period effect of the change in the exchange rate
2. Assuming that the dollar is the functional currency, determine the following items:
   a. Ending balance of Retained Earnings at December 31, 19X2
   b. Current-period effect of the change in the exchange rate

P 15-2*

Translation (Foreign Currency Is the Functional Currency)

The financial statements of the Maginot Company, a foreign subsidiary domiciled in France, for the year ended December 31, 19X2, are as follows:

		Francs	Exchange Rates	Dollars
Balance Sheet:				
Cash		200,000	.10	20,000
Accounts receivable, net		1,000,000	.10	100,000
Inventory		2,000,000	.10	200,000
Land		1,000,000	.10	100,000
Buildings and equipment		5,300,000	.10	530,000
Accumulated depreciation		(500,000)	.10	50,000
Total Assets		9,000,000	.10	900,000
Accounts payable		2,500,000	.10	250,000
Income taxes payable		200,000	.10	20,000
Long-term debt		2,800,000	.10	280,000
Total Liabilities		5,500,000		550,000
Common stock		1,500,000	.16	240,000
Retained earnings:				
Prior years		1,400,000		217,000
Current year		600,000	.10	72,000
Total Equity		3,500,000		
Total Liabilities and Equity		9,000,000		
Translation adjustment				(22,000) (137,000) 900,000
Income Statement:				
Sales		10,000,000	.12	1,200,000
Cost of goods sold:				
Beginning inventory	1,500,000			
Purchases	6,000,000			
	7,500,000			
Less—Ending inventory	(2,000,000)	(5,500,000)	.12	660,000
Depreciation expense (total)		(200,000)	.12	24,000
Operating expenses		(3,300,000)	.12	396,000
Income before Income Taxes		1,000,000		120,000
Income tax expense		(400,000)	.12	48,000
Net Income		600,000		72,000

Additional Information:

1. **Conformity with U.S. generally accepted accounting principles:** Assume the financial statements in francs have been adjusted to conform with U.S. generally accepted accounting principles.
2. **Exchange rates:**

	Direct Rate
Current rate at December 31, 19X1	$0.15
Average rate for 19X2	0.12
Current rate at December 31, 19X2	0.10

*The financial statement information presented for problems accompanied by asterisks is also provided on Model 15T (for translation problems) and Model 15R (for remeasurement problems) of the software file disk (filenames: Model15T and Model15R) that is available for use with the text, enabling the problem to be worked on the computer.

3. **Inventory:** The ending inventory is valued at the lower of cost or market in francs; however, no write-down to market was necessary on the subsidiary's books. Assume that the inventory at December 31, 19X2, was acquired when the exchange rate was $0.11. Inventory at December 31, 19X1, was acquired when the exchange rate was $0.16.
4. **Property, plant and equipment:** All were acquired in prior years when the exchange rate was $0.16, except equipment costing 300,000 francs, which was acquired in late December 19X2 when the exchange rate was $0.11. (No depreciation was recorded on this equipment for 19X2.)
5. **Sales, purchases, and operating expenses:** All occurred evenly throughout the year.
6. **Common stock:** The subsidiary was formed two years ago when the direct exchange rate was $0.16. No additional capital transactions have occurred since then.
7. **Retained earnings**—Beginning of year: The subsidiary did not declare any dividends during the year.

Required:

1. Translate the financial statements into dollars assuming that
   a. the franc is the functional currency.
   b. retained earnings at December 31, 19X1 (per the translated financial statements) was $217,000.
   c. the cumulative translation adjustment at December 31, 19X1 was $(22,000).
2. Calculate the average financial position that the subsidiary was in during the year to have the translation adjustment that resulted for 19X2.
3. Prepare the parent company's entry or entries at December 31, 19X2, relating to the equity method of accounting.

Remeasurement (Dollar Is the Functional Currency)

P 15-3*

Assume the information provided in Problem 15-2.

Required:

1. Remeasure the financial statements into dollars asuming that
   a. the dollar is the functional currency.
   b. from the dollar financial statements, retained earnings at December 31, 19X1, was $260,000.
2. Calculate the average financial position that the subsidiary was in during the year to have the transaction gain or loss from remeasurement that occurred for 19X2.
3. Prepare the parent company's entry or entries at December 31, 19X2, relating to the equity method of accounting.
4. After you have completed the remeasurement process, evaluate whether any other important areas should be addressed.

Translation (Foreign Currency is the Functional Currency)

P 15-4*

The financial statements of Tipperary Company, a foreign subsidiary domiciled in Ireland, for the year ended December 31, 19X4, are as follows:

		Punts
Balance Sheet (December 31, 19X4):		
Cash		200,000
Accounts receivable		600,000
Allowance for doubtful accounts		(50,000)
Inventory (Fifo)		900,000
Land		300,000
Buildings and equipment		1,000,000
Accumulated depreciation		(250,000)
Total Assets		2,700,000
Accounts payable and accrued liabilities		700,000
Accrued income taxes payable		100,000
Intercompany payable (to parent)		500,000
Long-term debt		600,000
Total Liabilities		1,900,000
Common stock		100,000
Retained earnings		700,000
Total Equity		800,000
Total Liabilities and Equity		2,700,000
Income Statement (19X4):		
Sales		4,000,000
Cost of goods sold:		
Beginning inventory	800,000	
Purchases	3,200,000	
	4,000,000	
Less—Ending inventory	(900,000)	(3,100,000)
Depreciation expense (in total)		(50,000)
Operating and interest expenses		(450,000)
Income before Income Taxes		400,000
Income tax expense @ 25%		(100,000)
Net Income		300,000

Additional Information:

1. **Conformity with U.S. generally accepted accounting principles:** Assume the financial statements in punts are in accordance with U.S. generally accepted accounting principles; thus no adjustments are required.
2. **Exchange rates:**

	Direct Rate
Current rate at December 31, 19X3	$1.25
Average rate for 19X4	1.40
Current rate at December 31, 19X4	1.50

3. **Inventory:** The ending inventory is valued at the lower of cost or market in punts; however, no write-down to market was necessary on the subsidiary's books. Assume that the inventory at December 31, 19X4, was acquired evenly during the last quarter of 19X4 (which had an average exchange rate of $1.45).

   The beginning inventory was all acquired when the exchange rate was $1.20, and no market adjustment in punts was necessary.

4. **Fixed assets:** The land, buildings, and equipment were acquired in 19X2 when the exchange rate was $1.60, except for some office equipment costing 50,000 punts that was acquired in late December 19X4 when the exchange rate was $1.48. (No depreciation was recorded on this equipment for 19X4.)
5. **Sales and operating expenses:** Assume sales and expenses occurred evenly throughout the year.
6. **Purchases:** Assume purchases occurred evenly throughout the year.
7. **Intercompany payable:** The intercompany payable is denominated in punts.
8. **Common stock:** The subsidiary was formed in 19X2, when the exchange rate was $1.60. No additional capital transactions have occurred since then.
9. **Dividends:** No dividends were declared during 19X4.

Required:

1. Translate the financial statements into dollars assuming the following:
   a. The punt is the functional currency.
   b. From the dollar financial statements, retained earnings at December 31, 19X3, were $560,000.
   c. The cumulative translation adjustment at December 31, 19X3, was $(95,000).
2. Calculate the subsidiary's average financial position during the year for it to have the translation adjustment that resulted for 19X4.
3. Prepare the parent company's entry or entries at December 31, 19X4, under the equity method of accounting.

P 15-5*

Remeasurement (Dollar is the Functional Currency)

Assume the information provided in Problem 15-4.

Required:

1. Remeasure the financial statements into dollars assuming the following:
   a. The dollar is the functional currency.
   b. From the dollar financial statements, retained earnings at December 31, 19X4, were $640,000.
2. Calculate the subsidiary's average financial position during the year for it to have the transaction gain or loss from remeasurement that resulted for 19X4.
3. Prepare the parent company's entry or entries at December 31, 19X4, under the equity method of accounting.

16

Translation of Foreign Currency Transactions

In this chapter we discuss accounting for (1) importing and exporting transactions that require settlement in a foreign currency; (2) transactions entered into to protect against adverse changes in exchange rates on those transactions; (3) transactions a domestic company may enter into to protect its investment in a foreign operation against adverse exchange-rate changes; and (4) transactions a domestic company may have with its foreign operation. The first two types of transactions above require an understanding only of pages 546–550 in Chapter 14; the second two types require a complete understanding of Chapters 14 and 15.

BASICS

Measured versus Denominated Transactions

The currency in which a transaction is to be settled must be stipulated. When the transaction is to be settled by the receipt or payment of a fixed amount of a specified currency, the receivable or payable, respectively, is said to be **denominated** in that currency. When the transaction is to be settled by the receipt or payment of a fixed amount of a currency other than the U.S. dollar, from the perspective of a U.S. reporting entity, the receivable or payable is denominated in a foreign currency. A party to a transaction **measures** and records the transaction in the currency of the country in which that party is located. A transaction may be measured and denominated in one currency, or it may be measured in one currency and denominated in another currency. The following examples illustrate this process:

1. A U.S. importer purchases goods on credit from a Swiss exporter, with payment to be made in a specified number of Swiss francs. The domestic importer measures and records the transaction in dollars, and the Swiss exporter measures and records the transaction in Swiss francs. The domestic importer's liability is denominated in a foreign currency, the Swiss franc. The Swiss exporter's receivable is denominated in Swiss francs. (If the terms of the transaction called for payment to be made in dollars, the transaction would be measured and denominated in dollars, from the perspective of the importer.)
2. A Swiss subsidiary of a U.S. company purchases goods on credit from another Swiss company, with payment to be made in a specified number of Swiss francs. The Swiss subsidiary measures the asset acquired and the liability incurred in Swiss francs. The Swiss subsidiary's liability is not denominated in a foreign currency, because the liability is denominated in Swiss francs. From the perspective of the U.S. parent, however, the Swiss subsidiary's liability is denominated in a foreign currency, because the liability is not payable in dollars.
3. A Swiss subsidiary of a U.S. company purchases goods on credit from an Italian company, with payment to be made in Italian lira. The Swiss

subsidiary measures the asset acquired and liability incurred in Swiss francs. The Swiss subsidiary's liability is denominated in a foreign currency. From the perspective of the U.S. parent, the Swiss subsidiary's liability is denominated in a foreign currency, because the liability is not payable in dollars.

Foreign Currency Transactions versus Foreign Transactions

For each foreign transaction, only one party has a foreign currency transaction, because payment is usually specified in only one currency. The party that must make or receive payment in other than its own local currency has the **foreign currency transaction.** For example, a domestic importer who pays for goods in the supplier's currency has a foreign currency transaction, whereas the supplier has only a **foreign transaction.** Likewise, a domestic exporter who receives payment in the customer's currency has a foreign currency transaction, whereas the customer has only a foreign transaction.

When the domestic company makes or receives payment in dollars, no special accounting procedures are necessary because no accounting issues exist. When the domestic company pays or receives in the foreign currency, however, several accounting issues arise. Before discussing these issues, we must define the following three dates that may be involved in a foreign currency transaction:

1. The **transaction date** is the date on which the transaction is initially recordable under generally accepted accounting principles.
2. **Intervening balance sheet dates** occur between the transaction date and the settlement date. A transaction recorded on August 20, 19X5, and settled on January 10, 19X6, would have five intervening balance sheet dates, assuming that monthly financial statements are prepared. Intervening balance sheet dates exist only for transactions in which credit terms are granted and used.
3. Payment is made on the **settlement date.** On this date, one currency is **converted** into the other currency. (When credit terms are not granted, the transaction date and the settlement date coincide.)

Conceptual Issues

In foreign currency transactions, the first accounting issue pertains to how the transaction should be recorded in dollars at the transaction date. Accountants generally agree that the transaction should be recorded at the transaction date using the exchange rate in effect at that date. For an import transaction, therefore, the acquired asset is initially recorded at the dollar amount needed to purchase the amount of foreign currency that would settle the transaction at the transaction date. For an export transaction, the export sale is recorded at the dollar amount that would be received from converting the foreign currency into dollars if full payment were made at the transaction date.

If credit terms are not granted, no other accounting issues exist. If credit terms are granted and used, the following additional accounting issues arise:

1. If the exchange rate used to record the transaction at the transaction date has changed between the transaction date and an intervening balance sheet date, should the receivable or payable pertaining to the unsettled portion of the transaction be adjusted to reflect the current rate at such intervening balance sheet date?
2. If the transaction is settled at an amount different from that at which it was initially recorded, how should the difference be recorded?

With respect to the first issue, most accountants agree that any unsettled portion of the transaction represented by a payable or receivable should be adjusted at intervening balance sheet dates to reflect the exchange rate in effect at those dates. It makes sense to carry the receivable or payable at the amount of dollars that would be received or paid, respectively, if the transaction were settled on that date. (This is essentially current-value accounting.) There are two viewpoints concerning the second issue:

1. Under the **one-transaction perspective,** all aspects of the transaction are viewed as part of a single transaction. A company's commitment to pay or receive foreign currency is considered a necessary and inseparable part of the transaction to purchase or sell goods, respectively. The amount initially recorded at the transaction date is considered an estimate until the final settlement. As a result, the initially recorded cost of goods acquired or revenue is subsequently adjusted for any difference between the amount recorded at the transaction date and the amount at which the transaction is ultimately settled.
2. Under the **two-transaction perspective,** the commitment to pay or receive foreign currency is considered a separate transaction from the purchase or sale of goods. The decision to grant or use credit is considered a separate decision from that of purchasing or selling goods. As a result, any difference between the amount initially recorded at the transaction date and the amount at which the transaction is ultimately settled is considered a foreign currency transaction gain or loss—no adjustment is made to the initially recorded cost of goods acquired or revenues recorded pertaining to goods sold, as the case may be.

From either perspective, the risk in a foreign currency transaction from potential adverse exchange rate changes can be eliminated by not granting or using credit or by using a *forward exchange contract* (discussed later in the chapter).

FASB Adopts the Two-Transaction Perspective. The Financial Accounting Standards Board rejected the one-transaction approach in *FASB Statement No. 52* (as it did in *FASB Statement No. 8*) on the grounds that the consequences of the risks associated with foreign currency transactions should be accounted for separately from the purchase or sale of goods. Thus, the requirements of *FASB Statement No. 52* reflect the two-transaction perspective, and a domestic importer or exporter would account for such transactions as follows:

1. At the **transaction date**, measure and record in dollars each asset, liability, expense, or gain arising from the transaction using the exchange rate in effect at that date.
2. At each **intervening balance sheet date,** adjust the recorded balances of any foreign currency receivable or payable to reflect the current exchange rate.
3. Report in the income statement a **foreign currency transaction gain or loss** resulting from (a) adjustments made at any intervening balance sheet dates, and (b) any adjustments from settling the transaction at an amount different from that recorded at the latest intervening balance sheet date (or the transaction date when there are no intervening balance sheet dates).[1]

In summary, the cost or the revenue arising from a transaction should be determined only once: when the transaction is initially recorded. The fact that credit terms are granted should not result in a later adjustment to the asset or service acquired, or to the revenue initially recorded, if the exchange rate changes between the transaction date and the settlement date. Any additional or lesser amount than that initially recorded represents a gain or loss that could have been avoided had the transaction been fully paid for when it occurred. Thus, any additional or lesser amount payable involves a decision to grant or exercise credit, which should be charged or credited to income in the period in which the exchange rate changes.

Illustration

IMPORT AND EXPORT TRANSACTIONS

Assume a domestic company has the following import and export transactions with suppliers and customers in Britain:

1. On December 11, 19X1, inventory is acquired from Vendor A for 100,000 pounds. Payment is due in pounds on January 10, 19X2.
2. Inventory is sold to Customer X for 200,000 pounds on December 21, 19X1. Payment is due in pounds on January 20, 19X2.

Illustration 16-1 shows these transactions as initially recorded and as adjusted at the intervening balance sheet date (December 31, 19X1).

[1] *Statement of Financial Accounting Standards, No. 52*, "Foreign Currency Translation" (Stamford: Financial Accounting Standards Board, 1981), pars. 15 and 16.

Illustration 16-1
Recording Foreign Currency Transactions

Entries Related to Vendor A

December 11, 19X1:

Inventory (or Purchases)	150,000	
Foreign Currency Payable		150,000
To record purchase of inventory. (100,000 pounds × \$1.50 = \$150,000)		

December 31, 19X1:

Foreign Currency Transaction Loss	5,000	
Foreign Currency Payable		5,000
To adjust foreign currency payable to the current spot rate. (\$1.55 − \$1.50 = \$0.05) (\$0.05 × 100,000 pounds = \$5,000)		

January 10, 19X2:

Foreign Currency Transaction Loss	2,000	
Foreign Currency Payable		2,000
To adjust foreign currency payable to the current spot rate. (\$1.57 − \$1.55 = \$0.02) (\$0.02 × 100,000 pounds = \$2,000)		
Foreign Currency	157,000	
Cash		157,000
To record purchase of foreign currency.		
Foreign Currency Payable	157,000	
Foreign Currency		157,000
To record payment to vendor.		

In an alternative (shortcut) approach at January 10, 19X2, Foreign Currency Payable is not adjusted, but the following entry is made (rather than the first and third entries shown above for January 10, 19X2):

Foreign Currency Payable	155,000	
Foreign Currency Transaction Loss	2,000	
Foreign Currency		157,000

Payments are made as required. The direct exchange rates (spot rates) for the applicable dates in December 19X1 and January 19X2 (when the pound was strengthening) are as follows:

December 11, 19X1	**\$1.50**
December 21, 19X1	**1.52**
December 31, 19X1	**1.55**
January 10, 19X2	**1.57**
January 20, 19X2	**1.60**

Illustration 16-1 (continued)

Entries Related to Customer X

December 21, 19X1:

Foreign Currency Receivable	304,000	
Sales		304,000
To record sale.		
(200,000 pounds × $1.52 = $304,000)		
December 31, 19X1:		
Foreign Currency Receivable	6,000	
Foreign Currency Transaction Gain		6,000
To adjust foreign currency receivable to the current spot rate.		
($1.55 − $1.52 = $0.03)		
($0.03 × 200,000 pounds = $6,000)		
January 20, 19X2:		
Foreign Currency Receivable	10,000	
Foreign Currency Transaction Gain		10,000
To adjust foreign currency receivable to the current spot rate.		
($1.60 − $1.55 = $0.05)		
($0.05 × 200,000 pounds = $10,000)		
Foreign Currency	320,000	
Foreign Currency Receivable		320,000
To record collection from customer.		
(200,000 pounds × $1.60 = $320,000)		
Cash	320,000	
Foreign Currency		320,000
To convert foreign currency into U.S. dollars.		

In the alternative (shortcut) approach at January 20, 19X2, Foreign Currency Receivable is not adjusted, but the following entry is made (rather than the first two entries shown above for January 20, 19X2):

Foreign Currency	320,000	
Foreign Currency Receivable		310,000
Foreign Currency Transaction Gain		10,000

The following points are important for understanding Illustration 16-1:

1. When its payments are due in pounds, the domestic company has a foreign currency transaction, not a foreign transaction.
2. Adjustments for the foreign currency transactions were necessary at December 31, 19X1, because the exchange rates had changed since the dates the transactions were initially recorded. Such adjustments would have been avoided if full payment had been made when the transactions were initially recorded.

3. The 19X1 net foreign currency transaction gain is $1,000 ($6,000 gain on receivable − $5,000 loss on payable). The net foreign currency transaction gain is credited to income in 19X1.
4. Foreign currency transaction gains are almost always taxable; thus, income taxes must be provided on the net foreign currency transaction gain. (Likewise, net foreign currency transaction losses are almost always tax deductible.)
5. When one of the parties to a foreign transaction incurs a foreign currency transaction gain or loss, the other party does not incur an opposite, offsetting foreign currency transaction gain or loss. Foreign currency transaction gains and losses, therefore, are one-sided.

SPECIAL AREAS

In addition to the basic importing and exporting transactions settled in a foreign currency, companies often enter into foreign currency transactions with dealers in foreign currency to hedge an existing foreign currency transaction (exposure), and to speculate. By *hedging*, a company can avoid a loss that may arise from an existing foreign currency transaction; the idea is to have a counterbalancing gain on the hedging transaction if a loss occurs on the existing foreign currency transaction. Three types of hedging transactions exist.

1. A hedge of a **recorded but unsettled** foreign currency transaction (such as from importing or exporting inventory).
2. A hedge of an **identifiable foreign currency commitment** (such as an order for inventory or equipment from a foreign company); in other words, a transaction that is **not yet recordable.**
3. A hedge of a **net investment** in a foreign operation or a hedge of a **net monetary position.**

The most common hedging or speculating transactions involve a forward exchange contract. (Other less frequently used methods are discussed next along with forward exchange contracts.)

Forward Exchange Contracts

A **forward exchange contract** is an agreement to buy or sell a foreign currency at a specified future date (usually within twelve months) at a specified exchange rate, commonly called the **forward rate.** Invariably, the forward rate is slightly above or slightly below the spot rate. The difference is primarily attributable to the difference in interest rates obtainable on the two currencies in the international money market for the duration of the contract.

When the interest rate obtainable on the dollar is higher than the interest rate obtainable on the foreign currency, the forward exchange rate is higher than the spot rate, and the foreign currency is said to be selling at a

premium on the forward market. On the other hand, when the interest rate obtainable on the dollar is lower than the interest rate obtainable on the foreign currency, the forward exchange rate is lower than the spot rate, and the foreign currency is said to be selling at a **discount** on the forward market. The premium or discount rate multiplied by the units of foreign currency to be received or delivered under the contract equals the total amount of premium or discount on the forward exchange contract. This interest parity system, in effect, prevents the transfer of money between international money markets merely to obtain a higher interest rate relatively risk-free through the use of a forward exchange contract.

The following table summarizes when premiums and discounts occur and whether a debit or credit balance for the premium or discount results in recording the forward exchange contract:

	Direct Rate		Result	
Buying or Selling Foreign Currency	Spot Rate	Forward Rate	Premium	Discount
Buying	$1.00	$1.01	x (Debit)	
Buying	$1.00	$ .99		x (Credit)
Selling	$1.00	$1.01	x (Credit)	
Selling	$1.00	$ .99		x (Debit)

When a currency is strengthening or weakening to a limited extent, the difference between the spot rate and the forward rate may also be attributable somewhat to expectations of what the spot rate will be at the specified future date. When a currency is strengthening or weakening to a greater extent and substantial economic or political uncertainties exist, the risks may be significant enough to cause the futures market to cease temporarily until stability is achieved.

Accounting for forward exchange contracts is different for the three types of hedging transactions and for speculative transactions. We discuss each of these areas separately.

Hedge of a Recorded but Unsettled Foreign Currency Transaction

A company that has a liability in a foreign currency is said to be in an **exposed liability position.** A company that has a receivable in a foreign currency is said to be in an **exposed asset position.** Because accounting for these situations is symmetrical, we illustrate only the first situation.

Exposed Liability Position. The domestic company in Illustration 16-1 agreed to pay Vendor A 100,000 pounds for inventory on January 10, 19X2; the domestic company is in an exposed liability position. To avoid the risk of an exchange rate increase during the period from the transaction date (December 11, 19X1) to the settlement date (January 10, 19X2), the domestic company could enter into a 30-day forward exchange contract on December 11, 19X1, whereby it agreed to purchase 100,000 pounds on January 10, 19X2, at the currently existing forward exchange rate. Thus, the domestic company can determine now, rather than on January 10, 19X2, how many dollars are needed to obtain 100,000 pounds.

Entering into a forward exchange contract is an immediately recordable transaction. The domestic company has (1) a fixed dollar liability to the foreign currency dealer that is determined by multiplying the forward rate by the number of units of foreign currency to be acquired; and (2) a foreign currency receivable that is initially valued at the spot rate multiplied by the number of units of foreign currency to be acquired. At subsequent balance sheet dates before the forward contract expiration date, the foreign currency receivable is adjusted to reflect **the spot rate on that date.**[2] The difference, if any, between the amounts initially recorded at 1 and 2 above represent either a premium or a discount that must be amortized over the life of the contract.[3]

At the end of the contract, the fixed liability to the foreign currency dealer is extinguished by the payment of cash (dollars) to the dealer, and the foreign currency receivable is extinguished by receipt of the foreign currency from the foreign currency dealer. The latter part of the exchange requires a debit to a Foreign Currency account. When the foreign currency is delivered to Vendor A, the Foreign Currency account is credited and the Foreign Currency Payable account is debited.

By valuing the foreign currency receivable at the current spot rate (both initially and subsequently), the foreign currency receivable always equals the amount payable to Vendor A, because that amount is always adjusted to the current spot rate, as shown in Illustration 16-1. Accordingly, any exchange loss on the payable to Vendor A exactly offsets an exchange gain on the foreign currency receivable—such is the purpose of the forward exchange contract. The shifting of risk to the foreign currency dealer also involves a commission charge that would be amortized over the life of the contract.

Illustration

HEDGE OF A RECORDED BUT UNSETTLED FOREIGN CURRENCY TRANSACTION

Illustration 16-2 shows the entries that would be made under a forward exchange contract entered into to protect the exposed liability position of the 100,000-pound purchase transaction with Vendor A. (For simplicity, we ignore commission charges.) The direct exchange rates for the applicable dates in December 19X1 and January 19X2 (when the pound was strengthening) were the following:

[2]*FASB Statement No. 52*, par. 18.
[3]*FASB Statement No. 52*, par. 18.

Illustration 16-2
Hedge of a Recorded but Unsettled Transaction

December 11, 19X1:		
Foreign Currency Receivable ($1.50 × 100,000 pounds)	150,000	
Deferred Premium on Forward Exchange Contract	4,000	
Liability to Foreign Currency Dealer ($1.54 × 100,000 pounds)		154,000
To record initially the forward exchange contract.		
December 31, 19X1:		
Foreign Currency Receivable	5,000	
Foreign Currency Transaction Gain		5,000[a]
To adjust the foreign currency receivable to the current spot rate. ($1.55 − $1.50 = $0.05) ($0.05 × 100,000 pounds = $5,000)		
Premium Amortization Expense	2,667	
Deferred Premium on Forward Exchange Contract		2,667
To amortize the premium on the contract. [(20 ÷ 30) × $4,000 = $2,667]		
January 10, 19X2:		
Foreign Currency Receivable	2,000	
Foreign Currency Transaction Gain		2,000[b]
To adjust the foreign currency receivable to the current spot rate. ($1.57 − $1.55 = $0.02) ($0.02 × 100,000 pounds = $2,000)		
Premium Amortization Expense	1,333	
Deferred Premium on Forward Exchange Contract		1,333
To amortize the premium on the contract. (10 ÷ 30 × $4,000 = $1,333)		
Liability to Foreign Currency Dealer	154,000	
Cash		154,000
Foreign Currency	157,000	
Foreign Currency Receivable		157,000
To pay the foreign currency dealer in exchange for the receipt of 100,000 pounds.		

Note: In addition to the preceding entries (which relate only to the forward exchange contract), the following entry is necessary to discharge the liability to Vendor A:

Foreign Currency Payable	157,000	
Foreign Currency		157,000

T-account Comparison: Note below how the receivable on the hedging contract is symmetrical to the payable on the inventory purchase transaction.

Hedging Contract — Foreign Currency Receivable

	Debit	Credit	
Dec. 11	150,000		
Dec. 31	5,000		
	155,000		
Jan. 10	2,000		
	157,000		
		157,000	Jan. 10
	–0–		

Inventory Purchase in Illustration 16-1 — Foreign Currency Payable

	Debit	Credit	
		150,000	Dec. 11
		5,000	Dec. 31
		155,000	
		2,000	Jan. 10
		157,000	
Jan. 10	157,000		
		–0–	

[a]This gain offsets the $5,000 foreign currency transaction loss on the importing transaction; see the journal entry on page 618.
[b]This gain offsets the $2,000 foreign currency transaction loss on the importing transaction; see the journal entry on page 618.

	Spot Rate	Forward Rate
December 11, 19X1 (the date the forward exchange contract was entered into)................	$1.50	$1.54
December 31, 19X1 (the intervening balance sheet date)..	1.55	n/a
January 10, 19X2 (the expiration date of the forward exchange contract)............................	1.57	n/a

The following points are important for understanding Illustration 16-2:

1. During the 30-day period of the forward exchange contract, the pound strengthened from $1.50 to $1.57. Without the forward exchange contract, the $7,000 additional amount payable to Vendor A would not have been offset by the $7,000 foreign currency transaction gain.
2. Inasmuch as the foreign currency transaction loss on the amount payable to Vendor A is offset by the foreign currency transaction gain on the forward exchange contract, the net cost of the forward exchange contract is the $4,000 premium.
3. The forward exchange contract is an independent transaction in relation to the transaction with Vendor A. Accounting for one is independent of accounting for the other.

Exposed Asset Position. An exposed asset position most often results from an exporting transaction in which payment is to be received in the foreign currency. In these situations, the domestic exporter agrees to **sell a specified number of foreign currency units at a specified future date.** Because the domestic company is selling foreign currency under the forward exchange contract, it has a fixed receivable amount from the foreign currency dealer and a foreign currency amount payable (which is valued at the spot rate) to the foreign currency dealer. Any premium or discount is amortized to income over the life of the contract, along with the commission.

Hedge of an Identifiable Foreign Currency Commitment

Commitment to Purchase. A domestic company often enters into an agreement with a foreign company whereby the domestic company purchases goods to be delivered and paid for in the future in the foreign currency. In such situations, the future transaction date may be known or reasonably determinable, but the exchange rate cannot be known. Accordingly, the domestic company may desire to protect itself from the risks of exchange-rate fluctuations by entering into a forward exchange contract under which the domestic importer agrees to **purchase a specified number of foreign currency units at a specified future date.** In these situations, any gain or loss that arises from the forward exchange contract must be deferred until the transaction is recorded. The gain or loss is then subtracted from or added to the cost of the goods acquired. In addition, the premium or discount on the forward exchange contract may be either amortized over the life of the contract (as is required in exposed asset or exposed liability situations) or treated the same as a gain or loss arising from the forward exchange contract—that is, it may be deferred and added to or subtracted from, respectively, the cost of the goods acquired.[4]

The rationale for deferring the foreign currency transaction gain or loss is that of the one-transaction perspective, introduced earlier. The one-transaction perspective makes sense in this situation because we are dealing with a commitment rather than a recorded purchase or sales transaction in which the cost or revenue has already been determined. This rationale also allows the premium or discount to be treated the same as a foreign currency transaction gain or loss. (Although *FASB Statement No. 52* does not specifically address them because of their immateriality, commission costs could also be treated in this manner under the one-transaction perspective.)

Illustration

HEDGE OF AN IDENTIFIABLE FOREIGN CURRENCY COMMITMENT (PURCHASE COMMITMENT)

Assume a domestic company with a calendar year-end entered into the following transactions on October 10, 19X1:

1. It ordered equipment built to its specifications from a French manufacturer. The purchase price is 1,000,000 francs. Delivery is to be in 90 days (January 8, 19X2), and the payment is due then.
2. It contracted with a foreign currency dealer to purchase 1,000,000 francs on January 8, 19X2, at the forward exchange rate of $0.098 plus a commission of $750.

Illustration 16-3 shows these transactions as initially recorded and as adjusted at the intervening balance sheet date (December 31, 19X1). Delivery and payments are made as required. The direct exchange rates for the applicable dates were the following:

	Exchange Rate	
	Spot	Forward
October 10, 19X1	$0.100	$0.098
December 31, 19X1	0.105	n/a
January 8, 19X2	0.104	n/a

The following points are important for understanding Illustration 16-3:

[4]*FASB Statement No. 52*, par. 21.

Illustration 16-3
Hedge of an Identifiable Foreign Currency Commitment

October 10, 19X1:

Foreign Currency Receivable (1,000,000 francs × $0.10)..	100,000	
Deferred Commission Costs	750	
Liability to Foreign Currency Dealer		
(1,000,000 francs × $0.098 + $750 commission)...		98,750
Deferred Discount on Forward Exchange Contract		
(1,000,000 francs × $0.002)................................		2,000
To record initially the forward exchange contract.		

December 31, 19X1:

Foreign Currency Receivable	5,000	
Deferred Foreign Currency Transaction Gain		5,000
To adjust the foreign currency receivable to the current spot rate.		
($0.105 − $0.100 = $0.005)		
($0.005 × 1,000,000 francs = $5,000)		

The deferred discount and deferred commission costs need not be amortized, as it is assumed that they will be treated as adjustments to the purchase price of the equipment at the time of delivery.

January 8, 19X2:

Deferred Foreign Currency Transaction Gain	1,000	
Foreign Currency Receivable		1,000
To adjust the foreign currency receivable to the current spot rate.		
($0.105 − $0.104 = $0.001)		
($0.001 × 1,000,000 francs = $1,000)		
Liability to Foreign Currency Dealer	98,750	
Cash		98,750
Foreign Currency	104,000	
Foreign Currency Receivable		104,000
To pay the foreign currency dealer in exchange for the receipt of 1,000,000 francs.		

Note: In addition to the preceding entries (which relate only to the forward exchange contract), the following entry would be made to record the purchase of the equipment on January 8, 19X2 (when delivery and payment were made):

Deferred Discount on Forward Exchange Contract	2,000	
Deferred Foreign Currency Transaction Gain..	4,000	
Equipment..	98,750	
Deferred Commission Costs		750
Foreign Currency..		104,000

1. The capitalized cost of the equipment ($98,750) is determined as follows:

Dollar equivalent of foreign currency paid to supplier (1,000,000 francs × $0.104)	**$104,000**
Less—Deferred transaction gain on forward exchange contract	**(4,000)**
Deferred discount on forward exchange contract	**(2,000)**
Plus—Deferred commission costs	**750**
	$ 98,750

2. If the forward exchange contract had not been entered into, the capitalized cost would have been $104,000.
3. The $4,000 foreign currency transaction gain can be treated as an adjustment to the $104,000 purchase price because the company's expected purchase price was $100,000 (based on the exchange rate existing when the equipment was ordered). The forward exchange contract merely locks in this price.
4. The discount and commission cost can be treated as adjustments to the locked-in purchase price of $100,000 because these items are necessary and incidental costs to protect or lock in the $100,000 purchase price.

Commitment to Sell. Parallel accounting procedures are used when (1) the domestic company has entered into an agreement to sell goods to a foreign company in the future, with payment to be received in the foreign currency, and (2) the domestic company wishes to protect itself from the risk of exchange rate fluctuations by entering into a forward exchange contract to **sell a specified number of foreign currency units at a specified future date.**

Qualifying Conditions. The following two conditions must be met for a forward exchange contract (or other foreign currency transaction) to qualify as a hedge of an identifiable foreign currency commitment:

a. The foreign currency transaction is designated as, and is effective as, a hedge of a foreign currency commitment.
b. The foreign currency commitment is firm.[5]

The "designation" part of the first condition merely means that **the company must identify the intent of the hedge with the foreign currency commitment.** Whether or not a hedge transaction is **effective** is an **after-the-fact determination.** Obviously, the hedge is effective if (1) the forward exchange contract is in the same currency as the transaction being hedged, and (2) the gain or loss on the hedging transaction is in the **opposite direction** to the loss or gain on the transaction being hedged.

[5]*FASB Statement No. 52*, par. 21.

The second condition is not defined in *FASB Statement No. 52.* However, it implies that the foreign currency commitment is either noncancelable or that the probability of cancellation is remote because of a severe monetary penalty.

Transactions Other Than Forward Exchange Contracts. The preceding two conditions are sufficiently broad that foreign currency transactions other than forward exchange contracts may qualify as hedges of foreign currency commitments. For example:

1. A U.S. company committed to constructing a building in France and receiving payment in francs could borrow francs to finance the construction and designate the borrowing as a hedge of the commitment.
2. A U.S. company committed to purchasing inventory or equipment from a Japanese company could convert dollars into yen, hold or invest the yen, and designate them as a hedge of the commitment.
3. A U.S. company, or its Spanish subsidiary, could designate a foreign currency receivable in Italian lira as a hedge against a foreign currency purchase commitment in Italian lira.

Other Technical Points. The hedging transaction need not be entered into at the same time as the foreign currency commitment; nor must it extend from the foreign currency commitment date to the anticipated transaction date. Other technical points include the following:

1. If the hedging transaction extends **beyond the foreign currency commitment transaction date,** any gain or loss on the hedging transaction that occurs after that date cannot be deferred; it must be reported in the income statement as it arises.
2. If the hedging is terminated **before the foreign currency transaction commitment date,** any deferred gain or loss on the hedging transaction up to that point is still deferred and treated as part of the cost of the asset acquired or as an adjustment to the sales price of the asset sold.
3. If the hedging transaction amount **exceeds the foreign currency transaction commitment amount,** only the gain or loss on the hedging transaction up to the foreign currency transaction commitment amount may be deferred and included as an adjustment to the cost of the asset acquired or as an adjustment to the sales price of the asset sold.
4. Losses on hedging transactions related to a foreign currency transaction commitment cannot be deferred (but must be reported currently in the income statement) if such deferral would lead to recognizing losses in a later period.[6]

Speculating in Foreign Currency

When a company enters into a forward exchange contract that does not relate to a foreign currency exposure, the forward exchange contract is

[6] *FASB Statement No. 52,* par. 21.

intended to produce an investment gain. Any gains or losses on such contracts are recognized currently in the income statement as they arise (no special deferral provisions exist for this type of hedging). In calculating gains and losses, the foreign currency receivable or payable must be **carried in the balance sheet at the current forward exchange rate for the remaining life of the forward exchange contract** (rather than at the current exchange rate existing at each intervening balance sheet date).[7] The current forward exchange rate is presumably a better indicator of the ultimate amount that will be received or paid when the contract expires. Because the foreign currency receivable or payable is initially recorded at the fixed liability to or receivable from the foreign currency dealer no accounting recognition is given to premiums and discounts.

Illustration

SPECULATING IN FOREIGN CURRENCY

Assume a domestic company with a calendar year-end concludes that the Swiss franc will strengthen within 90 days. Accordingly, it contracts with a foreign currency dealer on November 11, 19X1, to purchase 100,000 Swiss francs at the 90-day forward rate of $0.49. (For simplicity, we ignore the commission charge, which would be amortized over the life of the contract.) Illustration 16-4 shows the entries that would be made for this contract using the following assumed direct exchange rates:

	Spot Rate	Forward Rate for February 9, 19X2
November 11, 19X1 (the date the forward exchange contract was entered into)...	n/a	$0.49
December 31, 19X1 (the intervening balance sheet date)............................	n/a	0.52
February 9, 19X2 (the expiration date of the forward exchange contract)..........	$0.57	n/a

The following points are important for understanding Illustration 16-4:

1. The ultimate gain on the contract depends on the spot rate existing when the contract expires.
2. If the spot rate were used to value the foreign currency receivable at December 31, 19X1 rather than the forward rate available for February 9, 19X2) the $8,000 total gain would have been reported differently than as shown in the illustration.

[7]*FASB Statement No. 52*, par. 19.

Illustration 16-4
Speculating in Foreign Currency

November 11, 19X1:		
Foreign Currency Receivable	49,000	
Liability to Foreign Currency Dealer		49,000
To record initially the forward exchange contract. (100,000 francs × $0.49 = $49,000)		
December 31, 19X1:		
Foreign Currency Receivable	3,000	
Foreign Currency Transaction Gain		3,000
To adjust the foreign currency receivable to the forward rate available at the expiration of the contract. ($0.52 − $0.49 = $0.03) (100,000 francs × $0.03 = $3,000)		
February 9, 19X2:		
Foreign Currency Receivable	5,000	
Foreign Currency Transaction Gain		5,000
To adjust the foreign currency receivable to the spot rate at the expiration of the contract. ($0.57 − $0.52 = $0.05) (100,000 francs × $0.05 = $5,000)		
Liability to Foreign Currency Dealer	49,000	
Cash		49,000
Foreign Currency	57,000	
Foreign Currency Receivable		57,000
To pay the foreign currency dealer in exchange for the 100,000 francs.		

Note: At February 9, 19X2, the company could convert the foreign currency of 100,000 francs into $57,000.

Hedging a Net Investment

Companies with foreign operations normally have a person or department responsible for monitoring foreign currency changes and handling foreign currency operations. Because of the potentially substantial economic losses from adverse exchange-rate changes, the person in charge is often a vice-president.

Forward exchange contracts and other foreign transactions (such as borrowings in a foreign currency) are also commonly used to hedge a net investment in a foreign operation. For example, in 1982 before the Mexican peso declined sharply in value, some domestic companies with operations in Mexico correctly concluded that a decline was imminent. Accordingly, the parent company or the Mexican subsidiary borrowed pesos to hedge some or all of the company's net asset position. (The borrowings were immediately converted into dollars.) When the direct exchange rate then declined, the adverse effect on the net asset position was partially or fully offset by the fewer number of dollars required to buy pesos to repay the loan. Accounting for the gain or loss on such transactions depends on whether the foreign currency or the dollar is the foreign operation's functional currency

When the Foreign Currency is the Functional Currency. When the foreign currency is the functional currency, the gain or loss on the hedging transaction (net of the related tax effect) must be **accumulated in the separate component of equity.** This requirement allows a foreign currency translation adjustment to be offset partially or fully by the effect of a rate change on the hedging transaction. For the gain or loss to be deferred in this manner, however, **the transaction must be designated as a hedge of the net investment** and **it must be effective** (go in the opposite direction to the translation adjustment).[8]

Illustration

HEDGING A NET INVESTMENT POSITION: THE FOREIGN CURRENCY IS THE FUNCTIONAL CURRENCY

Assume a domestic company with a calendar year-end and a $500,000 investment in a wholly owned Japanese subsidiary expects the Japanese yen to weaken considerably within six months. Accordingly, it contracts with a foreign currency dealer on July 10, 19X1, to sell 100,000,000 yen in 180 days at the forward rate of $0.0049. Illustration 16-5 shows the accounting treatment for this contract. (For simplicity, we ignore commission costs and assume that the only intervening balance sheet date is December 31, 19X1.) The following direct exchange rates are assumed:

	Spot Rate	Forward Rate for January 6, 19X2
July 10, 19X1 (the date the forward exchange contract was entered into)	$0.0050	$0.0049
December 31, 19X1 (the intervening balance sheet date)..........................	0.0043	n/a
January 6, 19X2 (the expiration of the forward exchange contract).............	0.0042	n/a

The following points are important for understanding Illustration 16-5:

1. The following amount may be deferred and accumulated in the separate component of equity at December 31, 19X1:

[8] *FASB Statement No. 52*, par. 20.

Illustration 16-5
Hedging a Net Investment Position

July 10, 19X1:		
Receivable from Foreign Currency Dealer		
(100,000,000 yen × $0.0049)	490,000	
Deferred Discount on Forward Exchange Contract	10,000	
Foreign Currency Payable (100,000,000 yen × $0.005)		500,000
To record initially the forward exchange contract.		
December 31 19X1:		
Foreign Currency Payable	70,000	
Foreign Currency Transaction Gain		70,000
To adjust the foreign currency payable to the current spot rate.		
($0.0050 − $0.0043 = $0.0007)		
(100,000,000 yen × $0.0007 = $70,000)		
Discount Amortization Expense	9,667	
Deferred Discount on Forward Exchange Contract		9,667
To amortize the discount on the contract.		
(174 ÷ 180 × $10,000 = $9,667)		
January 6, 19X2:		
Foreign Currency Payable	10,000	
Foreign Currency Transaction Gain		10,000
To adjust the foreign currency payable to the current spot rate.		
($0.0043 − $0.0042 = $0.0001)		
(100,000,000 yen × $0.0001 = $10,000)		
Discount Amortization Expense	333	
Deferred Discount on Forward Exchange Contract		333
To amortize the discount on the contract.		
(6 ÷ 180 × $10,000 = $333)		
Foreign Currency	420,000	
Cash		420,000
To record purchase of 100,000,000 yen.		
(100,000,000 × $0.0042 = $420,000)		
Foreign Currency Payable	420,000	
Foreign Currency		420,000
Cash	490,000	
Receivable from Foreign Currency Dealer		490,000
To collect the amount due from the foreign currency dealer in exchange for the 100,000,000 yen.		

Foreign currency transaction gain	**$70,000**
Less—Discount amortization expense	**(9,667)**
Net deferrable amount	**$60,333**

2. Assuming a $68,000 unfavorable translation adjustment for 19X1 (determined by using the translation procedures discussed in Chapter 15), the net charge to the separate component of equity for 19X1 (ignoring income tax effects) would be $7,667 ($68,000 − $60,333). Obviously, the hedge was effective.

The Dollar is the Functional Currency. When the dollar is the functional currency, the gain or loss on the hedging transaction is **reported in the income statement.**[9] Recall that when the dollar is the functional currency the remeasurement process is required (instead of the "translation" process), and any gains or losses from remeasurement are reported currently in the income statement. Hedging a net asset position when the dollar is the functional currency may or may not cause an offsetting effect, which occurs when the foreign currency is the functional currency. The gain or loss resulting from the remeasurement process is **not based on the net asset position but on the net monetary position.** Being in a net monetary asset position causes an offsetting effect in the income statement. However, being in a net monetary liability position does not cause an offsetting effect in the income statement. Instead, two gains or two losses are reported—such as a gain on the hedging transaction and a gain resulting from the remeasurement process (or a loss on each). Some companies with foreign operations that use the dollar as the functional currency hedge the net asset position, wisely realizing that the gain or loss from remeasurement (in net monetary liability situations) is merely a paper gain or loss that will reverse itself in the future as the nonmonetary assets are financially transformed into monetary assets. (The amount of the gain or loss on the hedging transaction could be more, less, or equal to the gain or loss from remeasurement, depending on the amount of the net investment hedged and the amount of the net monetary position.)

Hedging a Net Monetary Position

When the dollar is the foreign unit's functional currency, a company may decide to hedge the net monetary position instead of the net asset position to ensure an offsetting effect in the income statement. An interesting dilemma occurs when the foreign operation is in a net monetary liability position and the foreign currency is expected to strengthen or the dollar is expected to weaken. To prevent the reporting of a transaction loss from remeasurement if the direct exchange rate increases, the company may decide to enter into a forward exchange contract (or other type of hedging transaction) to purchase foreign currency to the extent of the net monetary liability position. If the direct exchange rate increases as expected, the transaction loss from remeasurement offsets the gain on the forward exchange contract. However if the direct exchange rate decreases, a loss on

[9]*FASB Statement No. 52*, pars. 15 and 17.

the forward exchange contract and a transaction gain from the remeasurement process occur. As explained previously, the transaction gain from remeasurement (in net monetary liability position situations) may be viewed as a paper gain that will reverse itself in later periods. The loss on the forward exchange contract, however, is an actual loss that will not reverse in later periods.

One of the criticisms leveled at the temporal method of translation required under *FASB Statement No. 8* was that companies focused their attention on hedging net monetary positions to minimize the impact of currency exchange rate changes on consolidated income. (From an economic viewpoint, the net assets should be the focus of the hedging.) Because the remeasurement process procedures are nearly identical to the temporal method, this problem continues to exist when the dollar is the functional currency.

The following article reveals how Eastman Kodak Corp.'s foreign-exchange planning director manages foreign currency exposure.

PERSPECTIVE

By Trading Currencies, Kodak's Eric R. Nelson Saves the Firm Millions

ROCHESTER, N.Y.—On a recent cold morning in Honeoye Falls, N.Y., a hamlet 20 miles south of here, Eric R. Nelson crawled out of bed a few minutes before 5 A.M., fed two cats, put on an overcoat over his pajamas and went down to his unheated basement.

For 30 minutes, he read news reports from a rented newswire hooked into a video screen, while waiting for his routine 5:30 A.M. phone call from a London bank. When it came, Mr. Nelson bought $6.3 million in yen, $5.1 million in West German marks and $2.1 million in French francs. It was a normal morning for Mr. Nelson, who is neither an insomniac nor an eccentric millionaire. Over the course of a year, he manages $1.5 billion in foreign currencies for Eastman Kodak Co., based here.

As Kodak's foreign-exchange planning director, the 33-year-old Mr. Nelson is one of the people at the forefront of corporate America's struggle to stem the damage that volatile currency markets and a soaring dollar can inflict on company profits.

From the summer of 1976 to mid-1980, when the dollar was the leper of foreign-exchange markets, many U.S. exporters didn't give much thought to currency exposures—the net amount of overseas assets subject to changes in currency values. They just sat back and let their foreign receivables and dividends roll in. As the dollar fell, each mark, pound, or yen was worth that much more in the U.S.

But the dollar's surge against foreign currencies since July 1980 has sent exporters scrambling to find ways to neutralize its negative effects.

Kodak calculates that the strong dollar whacked $97.1 million, or 60 cents a share, off its 1984 net income of $923 million, or $5.71 a share. Over the past four years, such lost profits totaled $500 million, Kodak believes. Interna-

(continued)

tional Business Machines Corp. estimates that had the dollar stayed unchanged last year IBM earnings would have been increased by $278.1 million, or 45 cents a share; 1984 net was $10.77 a share.

Much Reticence

Many companies won't discuss how they deal in foreign exchange. Some fear that they might antagonize foreign governments. Others fear that shareholders might think that they are gambling rather than defending themselves against currency swings.

On Kodak's trading-room wall is a sign that reads: "Minimize your maximum regret." It's the maxim that drives Kodak's approach to currency markets.

"We are reacting to the market; we have no illusions as to our ability or desire to influence exchange rates," Mr. Nelson says, adding: "We create foreign-exchange positions because it makes business sense to market our product, not because we like to be long [own] the Spanish peseta."

Even so, Kodak is renowned among bankers and corporate money managers for attacking foreign-exchange markets the way the old Chicago Bears used to rush quarterbacks—aggressively. For good reason.

Heavy Exposure

Of Kodak's $10.6 billion in revenue last year, $3.71 billion, or 35%, came from sales outside the U.S., and about half of that came from products exported from the U.S. Because the photographic-products company bills its subsidiaries in their own currencies and sells its goods mostly in foreign currencies, Kodak has a "long" position in foreign currencies and a "short" one in dollars. In other words, it is owed more in nondollar currencies than it owes in them.

Thus, a rising dollar can produce losses, because Kodak's foreign receivables are worth less when converted to dollars. Conversely, a falling dollar makes the company's foreign sales more valuable in the U.S.

Mr. Nelson's team of seven people is responsible for protecting imports, receivables, royalties, dividends, service fees and processing costs in 16 currencies. It actively manages about $300 million at any one time.

The key to what Mr. Nelson calls Kodak's "market surveillance" is to monitor exchange rates hourly and "do what the market tells you to do; if the market tells you to sell British pounds, you sell pounds. If sterling continues to fall, you keep selling." But, when necessary, Kodak reverses course and gradually starts buying pounds.

In some ways, the procedure is the foreign-exchange market's version of three yards and a cloud of dust—dull but effective. Most of Kodak's currency trades are in the relatively small range of $3 million to $5 million. But it does a lot of them. "If we're in the market with a lot of transactions, we learn more

By Trading Currencies, Kodak's Eric R. Nelson Saves the Firm Millions *(continued)*

about the market; we can do better analysis on what's going on," Mr. Nelson explains. "We can avoid the maximum regret."

To constantly adjust to market volatility, Kodak buys and sells $10 billion to $12 billion a year to protect its $1.5 billion exposure.

Most big multinationals maintain "netting" operations, which allow them to balance exposures throughout the company. For example, one unit may have more British pounds than it needs, while another may have to pay a bill in sterling. By shifting funds internally, a company saves the costs of buying and selling currencies through a bank.

Companies also try to hedge against currency swings. The most common form of hedging involves the forward market, where currencies are bought and sold for preset prices for delivery at a future date. In nearly all major currencies, big international banks will quote a price, or exchange rate, for the dollar up to a year in the future, sometimes longer. It works like this:

Say a U.S. exporter expects to receive 50 million marks in two months from a German customer, but he is worried that the mark might weaken. So he arranges to sell 50 million marks two months from now to a bank at a set price. The price may be less than the current value of his marks but more than what he expects the marks to be worth in two months. In effect, the exporter nails down the number of dollars he gets for his marks, regardless of the exchange rate at the time.

Or the same exporter might take out an option to sell his marks at a set exchange rate for a period of time up to some future date. The advantage of the option is that if the mark rises, he doesn't have to exercise the option—as he does the forward contract—and can convert the marks, when he receives them, for more dollars. On the other hand, he has paid a premium, usually 1½% to 1¾% of the option's value, for a right that he hasn't exercised.

Because the dollar has increased in value for three years and because Kodak naturally holds large amounts of foreign currencies, hedging would have been profitable. Kodak declines to disclose its currency group's actual record, but Donald E. Snyder, Kodak's treasurer, says it has avoided more than $50 million in potential losses during the three years.

Relentless Job

Such success has its price. Decisions must be made at the moment, whether it be 3 A.M. because something is happening in Europe or 9 P.M. because the Tokyo market has taken a lurch. "My biggest problem," Mr. Nelson says, "is that it's a 24-hour market, unlike the stock market, which opens at 10 and closes at 4."

Mr. Nelson, a former Bankers Trust foreign-exchange trader who moved to Kodak in 1979, figures that he tracks 16 of those 24 hours daily, buying and selling currencies from home, if necessary. "It doesn't do me any good at all if it's the right position at 5 in the evening and the wrong one at 8 in the morning," he notes. Every night, he leaves instuctions with Tokyo and London

(continued)

banks to execute certain orders or call him at home if market conditions change.

"It's a schizophrenic job," Mr. Nelson concedes. On St. Valentine's night, he spent more time on the phone with Tokyo and London banks than he did with his wife. Catching a mere hour and a half of sleep, Mr. Nelson spent the night scrambling to undo hedges; the dollar, after setting record highs against a number of currencies for eight consecutive days, had plunged a relatively sharp 2% against the yen and also had dropped against European currencies.

Startled Audience

Another time, he was jammed into a small room at a local community center with about 20 other people challenging tax assessments on their houses. He called Tokyo from a pay phone on the wall. When the Japanese banker at the other end kept repeating that he couldn't hear, Mr. Nelson shouted: "Buy two billion (yen)." He says: "The whole room turned, looking at me with an expression of 'What's this guy doing here worrying about his assessments?' I wasn't about to get a lot of sympathy after that."

Theoretically, a company can manage its currency exposures in countless ways. It can, for instance, hedge 30%, 50%, 75% or all of its exposure, or not hedge at all. Hedging everything would avoid all currency risk except the cost of the hedging contracts. Hedging nothing would be a bet that the dollar will stay even or fall—saving the company the cost of hedging contracts and making a big profit if the dollar falls. But the company incurs a big loss if the dollar surges.

Kodak takes a more activist approach. It wants to hedge much of its exposure. But because it is in the market every day, it believes that it can spot opportunities to make a modest profit without much risk by leaving some of its exposure unhedged or, occasionally by overhedging. Profits made by anticipating correctly the direction that currencies will move offset the hedging costs. Thus, Kodak not only expects Mr. Nelson to protect against cash losses but also holds him responsible for missed opportunities. Mr. Nelson indicates that Kodak's aggressiveness is unusual among manufacturing companies.

A Cautious View

Some multinationals consider Kodak's trading style too aggressive. Says Richard Karl Goeltz, the treasurer of Seagram Co.: "One is as likely to gain as lose simply by waiting; I don't believe people can consistently outperform the market, looking at the short term." He adds that because some multinationals believe currency risks must be "eliminated at virtually any cost, exchange risks aren't subject to the same rigorous evaluation procedures" applied to other areas of their business.

By Trading Currencies, Kodak's Eric R. Nelson Saves the Firm Millions *(continued)*

Many companies, however, do long-term hedging. Advocates of that tactic term it an insurance policy that guarantees a known cash flow. It not only protects profits but also helps guide planning, pricing and budgeting decisions, the argument runs. And it shields a treasurer from surprises.

In fact, if a multinational had hedged its anticipated revenue on Jan. 3, 1984, and had stuck with the hedge all last year, it would have fared well. Say a U.S. exporter expected to receive 100 million marks around year-end. On Jan. 3, 1984, when trading began in Frankfurt, those marks were worth $36.4 million. If the exporter incorrectly expected the mark to strengthen against the dollar and didn't hedge, he would have received only $31.7 million on Dec. 31 because the mark had, in fact, weakened to 3.1570 to the dollar from 2.7458.

If, on the other hand, the U.S. exporter had hedged his receivables in the forward market on Jan. 3, he could have locked in an exchange rate of 2.6450 marks to the dollar at year-end. He thus would have made his marks worth $37.8 million, or $6.1 million more than in an unhedged transaction.

However, since nearly all forecasters predicted the dollar would fall in 1984, many companies didn't hedge their foreign income. They took a bath. Economists at one major U.S. multinational forecast that the dollar would be worth 2.45 marks by Dec. 31, 1984—22% below where it wound up the year.

The trouble with forecasts, Mr. Nelson contends, is that they can lull a company into staying with them too long. "You don't want to be making decisions at your threshold of pain," he notes. For example, just prior to the French franc's 8% devaluation in March 1983, the French central bank pushed the interest rate for certain short-term loans to a rate equivalent to 3,000% per year. For anyone holding or due to receive francs and wanting to hedge against the anticipated devaluation, it was too late. The interest rate on the franc had risen so high, compared with the yield on the dollar, that no one would be willing to buy dollars at the prevailing forward exchange rate.

Like other companies, Kodak has forecasts, and it analyzes economic and political news that can affect exchange rates. But Mr. Nelson's unit relies more on sophisticated technical analysis. An internally developed software package can chart, among other things, currency price and volatility correlations for the past 10 years.

Kodak's computers disgorge trend lines, moving averages and momentum measurements that show, for example, a currency's rate of change over time. Says Mr. Nelson: "These are simply clues, pieces of a puzzle we try to put together."

Source: Michael R. Sesit, "By Trading Currencies, Kodak's Eric R. Nelson Saves the Firm Millions," *The Wall Street Journal*, March 5, 1985, p. 1, 26.

Summary Illustration

Illustration 16-6 summarizes the accounting treatment of the special foreign currency transactions discussed so far.

Illustration 16-6
Summary of Accounting for Special Foreign Currency Transactions

	Accounting Treatment Accorded Gains and Losses	
Type of Transaction	**Recognize Currently in the Income Statement**	**Special Treatment**
A. Hedge of a recorded but unsettled foreign currency transaction	X	
B. Hedge of an identifiable foreign currency commitment		Defer and treat as an adjustment to cost of item acquired or sales price of item sold.
C. Speculation in foreign currency	X	
D. Hedge of a net investment:		
a. Foreign currency is functional currency		Accumulate in the special component of stockholders' equity.
b. Dollar is functional currency	X	
E. Hedge of a net monetary position (occurs when the dollar is the functional currency)	X	

Other considerations pertaining to foreign currency transactions involving forward exchange contracts include the following:

1. In determining the gain or loss on the contract, the foreign currency receivable or payable is carried at the current (spot) rate (except in speculation situations, for which the available forward rate is used).
2. Premiums and discounts on forward exchange contracts are recognized currently in the income statement if the gain or loss on the contract is treated in that manner. If the gain or loss is given special treatment (as shown above), the premium or discount *may be given the same special treatment* or be recognized currently in the income statement. (Premiums and discounts are not recognized in speculation situations.)

SUMMARY

A foreign currency transaction involves a commitment to receive or purchase foreign currency in settlement of the transaction. When the transaction involves credit, the party engaging in the foreign currency transaction assumes the risk that the currency exchange rate may change between the transaction date and the settlement date. The effect of exchange rate changes that occur between these two dates is called a foreign currency transaction gain or loss. Such gains or losses are accounted for separately from the purchase or sale of goods, as recorded on the transaction date. Transaction gains or losses are reported in the income statement in the period in which they occur.

A company usually enters into special foreign currency transactions to protect its exposure to exchange rate changes. (Illustration 16-6 summarizes how to account for gains and losses on such transactions.)

Glossary of New Terms

Discount or Premium on Forward Exchange Contract "The foreign currency amount of the contract multiplied by the difference between the contracted forward rate and the spot rate at the date of inception of the contract."*

Forward Exchange Contract "An agreement to exchange at a specified future date currencies of different countries at a specified rate (forward rate)."*

Forward Rate *See* Forward Exchange Contract.

Foreign Currency Transactions "Transactions whose terms are denominated in a currency other than the entity's functional currency."*

Settlement Date The date at which a receivable is collected or a payable is paid.

Spot Rate "The exchange rate for immediate delivery of currencies exchanged."*

Transaction Date "The date at which a transaction (for example, a sale or purchase of merchandise or services) is recorded in accounting records in conformity with generally accepted accounting principles."*

Transaction Gain or Loss "Transaction gains or losses result from a change in exchange rates between the functional currency and the currency in which a foreign currency transaction is denominated. They represent an increase or decrease in (a) the functional currency cash flows realized upon settlement of foreign currency transactions and (b) the expected functional currency cash flows on unsettled foreign currency transactions."*

Suggested References

"International Cash Management," by George M. Stetter. *Corporate Accounting* 3, no. 4 (Fall 1985), 11–17.

"Managing Multinational Exchange Risks," by James G. S. Yang. *Management Accounting* (February 1986), 45–52.

Appendix
INTERCOMPANY TRANSACTIONS WITH FOREIGN UNITS

This appendix discusses the specific reporting requirements pertaining to intercompany transactions between a parent company and a foreign subsidiary.

Adjusting Intercompany Receivables and Payables

When intercompany receivables and payables exist, the entity that makes or receives payment in the foreign currency (that is, in other than its own currency) must adjust its intercompany receivable or payable to reflect

**FASB Statement No. 52*, Appendix E. pp. 75–78.

the new exchange rate. In Illustration 15-5 (page 591), which dealt with the remeasurement process, the foreign subsidiary had an intercompany payable to the parent company. The payable was denominated in marks; thus, the parent company had the foreign currency transaction and was the entity that made the adjustment to reflect the current rate. Let us assume that the payable of 50,000 marks arose when the direct exchange rate was $0.45 (the parent's receivable was therefore $22,500). The direct exchange rate at December 31, 19X1, was $0.40, making the receivable worth only $20,000 (50,000 marks × $0.40). Accordingly, the parent would make the following adjustment:

Foreign Currency Transaction Loss	**2,500**	
Intercompany Receivable		**2,500**
To adjust intercompany receivable to reflect the new exchange rate of $0.40. ($22,500 − $20,000 = $2,500)		

If the intercompany payable had been repayable in dollars instead of marks, the foreign subsidiary would have made the adjustment at December 31, 19X1 ($22,500 ÷ $0.40 = 56,250 marks):

Foreign Currency Transaction Loss ...	**6,250 (marks)**	
Intercompany Payable		**6,250 (marks)**
To adjust the intercompany payable to reflect the new exchange rate of $0.40. (56,250 marks − 50,000 marks = 6,250 marks)		

When expressing the foreign subsidiary's financial statements in dollars, the parent company must use the direct exchange rate to which the intercompany payable was adjusted ($0.40) in dealing with the foreign currency transaction loss of 6,250 marks. This calculation gives $2,500 (6,250 marks × $0.40), which equals the amount of loss the parent company would have recorded if the payable had been repayable in marks instead of dollars. (Alternatively, we could obtain this answer by multiplying the 50,000 marks by the $0.05 change in the direct exchange rate.)

Of course, if the appropriate adjusting entries are not made at the balance sheet date, the intercompany receivable and payable accounts would not agree and would not eliminate in consolidation.

The Wash Effect. The preceding entries indicate that a $2,500 transaction loss would be reported as a result of adjustments to the intercompany receivable or payable accounts. **However, the parent company's equity is never affected by adjustments to the intercompany accounts.** This fact holds true whether the amounts are denominated in the dollar or in the foreign operation's local currency. The zero net answer results from the translation process or the remeasurement process, as the case may be.

When the dollar is the foreign operation's functional currency, a $2,500 transaction gain from remeasurement arises on the 50,000 mark intercompany payable (50,000 marks × $0.05 decrease in direct exchange rate). This amount offsets the $2,500 transaction loss in the income statement. When the foreign currency is the functional currency, a $2,500 translation adjustment arises on the 50,000 mark intercompany payable. This $2,500 translation adjustment, however, is reported in the translation adjustment component of stockholders' equity. Thus, the income statement contains no offsetting entry, but Stockholders' Equity does.

Long-term Intercompany Receivables and Payables. A long-term intercompany receivable on the parent company's books is, in substance, an addition to its investment. Likewise, a long-term intercompany payable on the parent company's books is, in substance, a reduction of its investment. When such receivables and payables exist **and settlement is not planned or anticipated in the foreseeable future,** *FASB Statement No. 52* requires that transaction gains and losses resulting from adjusting these accounts (as a result of exchange rate changes) should be treated as translation adjustments. They are **accumulated in the separate component of stockholders' equity** rather than reported currently in the income statement.[10] This provision ensures that the entire effect of a rate change on the true net investment in a foreign unit is shown as part of the separate component of stockholders' equity. This requirement applies **only when the "translation" process is involved, that is, when the foreign currency is the functional currency.**

Intercompany Profits

An intercompany profit from intercompany transactions must, of course, be eliminated. Under *FASB Statement No. 52,* no special problems are involved when the foreign unit has the dollar as its functional currency, because all foreign-unit account balances are remeasured into the equivalent dollar amounts. However, when the foreign unit has a foreign currency as its functional currency, the translated cost of any remaining intercompany-acquired inventory or fixed assets does not equal the parent's selling price if the exchange rate has changed since the transfer date. The difference between the translated cost at the transfer date and the translated cost at the balance sheet date is treated as part of the effect of the change in the exchange rate—that is, as part of the translation adjustment accumulated in the special component of stockholders' equity. *FASB Statement No. 52* requires that **any intercompany profit be eliminated using the exchange rate existing at the time of the transfer. The gross profit determined at the time of the transfer is used for subsequent eliminations, regardless of any subsequent exchange rate changes.**[11]

Intercompany Dividends

The parent company uses **the exchange rate existing when dividends are declared** to record a dividend receivable. Any changes in the exchange

[10] *FASB Statement No. 52,* par. 20.
[11] *FASB Statement No. 52,* par. 25.

rate between the declaration date and the remittance date result in a foreign currency transaction gain or loss recorded by one of the entities. Such gains and losses can be avoided if dividends are remitted at their declaration.

Summary

Gains or losses from adjusting intercompany receivable and payable balances for exchange rate changes are reported currently in the income statement unless (1) the adjustment pertains to long-term receivables and payables, and (2) the foreign unit's functional currency is *not* the dollar. When intercompany asset transfers occur, the gross profit eliminated is based on the gross profit determined at the time of the transfer. Subsequent changes in the exchange rate have no bearing in this respect.

Review Questions

1. What does *denominated* mean?
2. What is the difference between a foreign transaction and a foreign currency transaction?
3. Summarize the two-transaction perspective.
4. Summarize the one-transaction perspective.
5. Why would a company enter into a forward exchange contract?
6. How does a company treat gains and losses on forward exchange contracts related to hedges of identifiable foreign currency commitments?
7. What two conditions must be met to qualify a forward exchange contract as a hedge of an identifiable foreign currency commitment?
8. Distinguish between hedging a net investment and hedging a net monetary position.
9. How are gains and losses on hedging a net investment treated?

Exercises

E 16-1

Basic Understanding of Foreign Currency Exposure

The Docker Company has many importing and exporting transactions that require settlement in foreign currency (LCU). Credit terms are granted and used.

Required:

1. Docker should be concerned about whether the direct exchange rate:
   a. goes up.
   b. goes down.
2. Indicate in the following table what the foreign currency exposure concern should be:

Trans-action	Billing Currency	Whether the Dollar Will		Whether the LCU Will	
		Strengthen	Weaken	Strengthen	Weaken
Importing	Dollar	______	______	______	______
Importing	LCU	______	______	______	______
Exporting	Dollar	______	______	______	______
Exporting	LCU	______	______	______	______

E 16-2 Basic Understanding of Forward Exchange Contracts

The Hedgley Company has foreign operations and importing and exporting transactions that require settlement in a foreign currency. The company often enters into forward exchange contracts to hedge its foreign currency exposure and occasionally to speculate. Hedgley must determine whether it should contract to buy or sell a foreign currency in each of the following situations:

Area of Foreign Currency Exposure	Future Expectation		Buy	Sell
	Direct Rate or Currency	Direction		
1. Importing	Direct rate	Up	___	___
	Direct rate	Down	___	___
	U.S. dollar	Strengthen	___	___
	U.S. dollar	Weaken	___	___
	Foreign	Strengthen	___	___
	Foreign	Weaken	___	___
2. Exporting	Direct rate	Up	___	___
	Direct rate	Down	___	___
	U.S. dollar	Strengthen	___	___
	U.S. dollar	Weaken	___	___
	Foreign	Strengthen	___	___
	Foreign	Weaken	___	___
3. Net investment in a foreign subsidiary	U.S. dollar	Strengthen	___	___
	U.S. dollar	Weaken	___	___
	Foreign	Strengthen	___	___
	Foreign	Weaken	___	___
4. Net monetary asset position of a foreign subsidiary	U.S. dollar	Strengthen	___	___
	U.S. dollar	Weaken	___	___
	Foreign	Strengthen	___	___
	Foreign	Weaken	___	___
5. Net monetary liability position of a foreign subsidiary	U.S. dollar	Strengthen	___	___
	U.S. dollar	Weaken	___	___
	Foreign	Strengthen	___	___
	Foreign	Weaken	___	___
6. n/a—Speculation	Foreign	Strengthen	___	___
	Foreign	Weaken	___	___

Required:

Put and X in the appropriate buy or sell column in the table.

Exercises for Appendix

E 16-3

Adjusting Intercompany Accounts

The Sunset Company formed a foreign subsidiary on December 30, 19X1. The parent company lent the subsidiary $90,000 at that time when the direct exchange rate between the dollar and the widgetta (the foreign country's currency) was $0.10. The subsidiary immediately converted the $90,000 into widgettas and used the entire amount to purchase land on December 30, 19X1. At December 31, 19X1, the year-end of the parent company and the subsidiary, the direct exchange rate was $0.09.

Required:

1. Make the appropriate adjustments at December 31, 19X1, assuming the loan is denominated in widgettas.
2. Make the appropriate adjustments at December 31, 19X1, assuming the loan is denominated in dollars.
3. Express in dollars the effect of the adjustments made in requirement 2. (Show the calculations for the two ways of determining this amount.)

E 16-4

Accounting for a Dividend from the Foreign Subsidiary

For the year ended December 31, 19X5, Moonglow Corporation's foreign subsidiary had net income of 60,000,000 local currency units (LCU), which was appropriately translated into $2,900,000. On July 25, 19X5, when the exchange rate was 20 LCU to $1, the foreign subsidiary declared a dividend to Moonglow of 30,000,000 LCU. The dividend represented the foreign subsidiary's net income for the six months ended June 30, 19X5, during which time the weighted average of the exchange rate was 21 LCU to $1. The dividend was paid on August 3, 19X5, when the exchange rate was 19 LCU to $1. The exchange rate existing at December 31, 19X5, was 18.5 LCU to $1. Moonglow uses the equity method of accounting for the foreign subsidiary.

Required:

1. Prepare the parent company's entry to record the dividend receivable.
2. Prepare the entry related to the receipt of the dividend on August 3, 19X5.

Problems

P 16-1

Importing and Exporting Transactions: No Intervening Balance Sheet Date

During July 19X5, the Billings Company had the following transactions with foreign businesses:

Date	Nature of Transaction	Billing Currency	Exchange Rate (Direct)
Vendor A:			
July 1, 19X1	Imported merchandise costing 1,000,000 pesos from Mexico City wholesaler	Pesos	$0.0070
July 10, 19X1	Paid 50% of amount owed	Pesos	0.0071
July 31, 19X1	Paid remaining amount owed	Pesos	0.0066
Customer A:			
July 15, 19X1	Sold merchandise for 50,000 francs to French wholesaler	Francs	$0.130
July 20, 19X1	Received 50% payment	Francs	0.120
July 30, 19X1	Received entire payment	Francs	0.125

Required:
Prepare journal entries for the above transactions.

P 16-2 Importing and Exporting Transactions: Intervening Balance Sheet Date

During June and July of 19X1, the Quartex Company (which reports on a calendar year basis and issues quarterly financial statements) had the following transactions with foreign businesses:

Date	Nature of Transaction	Billing Currency	Exchange Rate (Direct)
Vendor A:			
June 15, 19X1	Imported merchandise costing 100,000 Canadian dollars from Canadian manufacturer	Canadian dollars	$0.80
July 15, 19X1	Paid entire amount owed	Dollars	0.77
Customer A:			
June 20, 19X1	Sold merchandise for 10,000 pounds to London retailer	Pounds	$1.55
June 30, 19X1	Received 50% payment	Pounds	1.52
July 10, 19X1	Received remaining amount owed.	Pounds	1.54

The exchange rate on June 30, 19X1, for Canadian dollars was $0.79.

Required:
Prepare journal entries for the above transactions. (Be sure to prepare journal entries at June 30, 19X1, when necessary.)

P 16-3 Hedge of an Exposed Liability Position: Intervening Balance Sheet Date

On October 17, 19X1, Bavaro Company purchased merchandise costing 40,000,000 lira from the Vinnie Company of Italy. The spot rate (direct) on that date was $0.00062. Payment is due in lira in 90 days.

Concurrently, Bavaro entered into a foreign exchange contract, whereby it agreed to purchase 40,000,000 lira for delivery in 90 days at $0.00065 (the forward rate). On December 31, 19X1, the spot rate was $0.00068, and on January 15, 19X2 (the date Vinnie was paid in full), the spot rate was $0.00066. Bavaro has a June 30 fiscal year-end and issues quarterly financial reports.

Required:
Prepare the journal entries to record the above transactions. (Be sure to prepare journal entries at December 31, 19X1, when necessary.)

P 16-4

Hedge of an Exposed Asset Position: Intervening Balance Sheet Date

On April 1, 19X3, Niagara Company, a calendar-year reporting company that issues quarterly financial reports, sold merchandise to a Canadian company for 100,000 Canadian dollars. The spot rate (direct) on April 1, 19X3, was $0.81. Payment is due in 120 days.

Concurrently, Niagara entered into a forward exchange contract to sell 100,000 Canadian dollars at $0.80 (the forward rate). The spot rate on July 30, 19X3, was $0.82. Assume that payment was made on July 30, 19X3. (The spot rate on June 30, 19X3, was $0.825.)

Required:
Prepare the entries related to the above transactions, including appropriate June 30, 19X3, adjustments.

P 16-5

Hedge of an Identifiable Foreign Currency Commitment: Intervening Balance Sheet Date

On October 1, 19X1, Vail Company, a calendar-year reporting company, entered into a noncancelable contract with a Swiss company, whereby the Swiss company would manufacture a custom-built aerial tram for 1,000,000 francs, with delivery to be in 180 days and payment to be in Swiss francs. On October 1, 19X1, the exchange rate (direct) was $0.47.

Concurrently, Vail entered into a forward exchange contract (at a commission cost of $1,000) to acquire 1,000,000 Swiss francs in 180 days at $0.48. At December 31, 19X1 (the only intervening balance sheet date for purposes of this problem), the current exchange rate was $0.463. Assume that delivery and payment were made in 180 days and that Vail desires to maximize earnings in 19X1. Assume that the spot rate on March 30, 19X2, was $0.45.

Required:
Prepare the entries related to the above transactions, including appropriate adjustments at the intervening month-end.

P 16-6

Hedging a Net Investment Position

The functional currency for Kimberly Company's foreign subsidiary is its local currency, the debita. For 19X1, the subsidiary's net income was 100,000 debitas, which translated into $35,000. (Earnings occurred evenly throughout the year and were remitted to the parent monthly.) An unfavorable translation adjustment of $75,000 resulted for 19X1.

On January 5, 19X1, in expectation that the debita would weaken throughout 19X1, management entered into a 360-day forward exchange contract with a foreign currency dealer to sell 600,000 debitas (which approximates its net investment in the subsidiary) on December 31, 19X1, at the forward rate of $0.41 plus a commission of $850. The following exchange rates are for 19X1:

	Exchange Rates	
	Spot	Forward (for 12/31/X1)
January 1, 19X1	$0.401	n/a
January 5, 19X1	0.400	$0.410
June 30, 19X1 (assumed to be the only intervening balance sheet date)	0.360	0.340
December 31, 19X1	0.300	n/a
Average rate for 19X1	0.350	n/a

Required:

1. Prepare the journal entries pertaining to the forward exchange contract.
2. Determine the amount to be charged or credited to the special component of stockholders' equity for 19X1.

P 16-7

Hedging Net Investments and Net Monetary Positions

McLaughlin Company's foreign subsidiary had the following average account balances for 19X1 (expressed in its local currency, the krebit):

Monetary Assets	400,000	Monetary Liabilities	300,000
Nonmonetary Assets	400,000	Stockholders' Equity	500,000

Net income for 19X1 was 100,000 krebits, earned evenly throughout the year and remitted to the parent monthly. During 19X1, the krebit weakened 25%, the direct (spot) rate going from $0.40 to $0.30. Various assumptions for different situations follow:

Situation	Functional Currency	Item Hedged
A	Krebit	Net investment
B	Krebit	Net monetary asset position
C	U.S. dollar	Net investment
D	U.S. dollar	Net monetary asset position
E	U.S. dollar	Net monetary liability position

(For situation E, assume average monetary liabilities were 500,000 krebits and average stockholders' equity was 300,000 krebits.

For situations A, B, C, and D, assume that management expected the krebit to weaken during 19X1 and it hedged the item indicated using forward exchange contracts entered into on January 1, 19X1, and terminated December 31, 19X1. For situation E, assume that management expected the krebit to strengthen during 19X1 and it hedged accordingly. (For simplicity, assume that the forward rate on January 1, 19X1, for a one-year forward exchange contract was $0.40.)

Required:
For each situation, determine the following and indicate how the amounts should be reported for 19X1:

1. The hedging gain or loss.
2. The translation adjustment or the gain or loss from the remeasurement process, as appropriate.

Problems for Appendix

P 16-8A

Determining the Net Effect of Adjustments to Intercompany Account

A domestic company formed a foreign subsidiary on December 1, 19X1. On that date, the parent company lent the foreign subsidiary $180,000; the subsidiary converted the $180,000 into laffers (its local currency) and used all of them to purchase land. The direct exchange rate was $0.40 at December 1, 19X1, and $0.45 at December 31, 19X1. For simplicity, assume that the subsidiary was so thinly capitalized that we can ignore the Common Stock account.

Required:

1. Make the appropriate December 31, 19X1, adjusting entry, assuming that the loan is denominated in dollars.
2. Translate the subsidiary's December 31, 19X1, financial statement into dollars, assuming that the laffer is the foreign subsidiary's functional currency.
3. Remeasure the subsidiary's December 31, 19X1, financial statements in dollars, assuming that the dollar is the foreign subsidiary's functional currency.
4. Considering the effect of the adjustment made for requirement 1, determine the net effect of the change in the exchange rate in the 19X1 consolidated statements assuming that:
   a. the laffer is the functional currency.
   b. the dollar is the functional currency.

P 16-9A

Determining the Net Effect of Adjustments to Intercompany Account

Assume the information in Problem 16-8, except that the subsidiary used the money from the loan to open a checking account rather than buying land.

Required:
The requirements are the same as in Problem 16-8.

Problem for Comprehensive Review

P 16-10*

COMPREHENSIVE (Chapters 4, 7, 14–16) Translation, Consolidation, and Intercompany Transactions (Foreign Currency Is Functional Currency)

The financial statements of Piper Company and its wholly owned subsidiary, Swan Company (located in Great Britain), for the year ended December 31, 19X5, are as follows:

	Piper Company (Dollars)	Swan Company (Pounds)
Balance Sheet (December 31, 19X5):		
Cash	$ 570,000	£ 50,000
Accounts receivable	800,000	300,000
Intercompany receivable	471,000	
Inventory:		
Vendor acquired	700,000	400,000
Intercompany acquired		100,000
Investment in Swan Company	359,000	
Land	200,000	150,000
Buildings and equipment	1,000,000	500,000
Accumulated depreciation	(300,000)	(100,000)
Total Assets	$3,800,000	1,400,000
Accounts payable	$ 700,000	160,000
Accrued liabilities	500,000	40,000
Intercompany payable		300,000
Long-term debt	1,500,000	500,000
Total Liabilities	$2,700,000	1,000,000
Common stock	500,000	100,000
Retained earnings	610,000	300,000
Cumulative translation adjustment	(10,000)	
Total Equity	$1,100,000	400,000
Total Liabilities and Equity	$3,800,000	1,400,000
Income Statement (19X5):		
Sales	$7,000,000	1,500,000
Cost of goods sold	(4,000,000)	(800,000)
Depreciation expense	(100,000)	(30,000)
Expenses	(1,900,000)	(470,000)
Intercompany Accounts:		
Sales	500,000	
Cost of goods sold	(300,000)	
Net Income	$1,200,000	200,000
Dividends declared	$ 900,000	100,000

*The financial statement information presented for this problem is also provided on Model 15T (filename: Model15T) of the software file disk that is available for use with the text, enabling the problem to be worked on the computer.

Additional Information:

1. **Conformity with U.S. generally accepted accounting principles:** Assume the financial statements of the subsidiary are in accordance with U.S. generally accepted accounting procedures.
2. **Exchange rates:**

	Direct Rate
Current rate at December 31, 19X4	$1.70
Average rate for 19X5	1.60
Current rate at December 31, 19X5	1.50

The pound is the functional.

3. **Inventory:** The ending inventory was acquired during the last quarter of 19X5 when the average exchange rate was $1.55. (No intercompany acquired inventory was on hand at the beginning of 19X5.)
4. **Fixed assets:** The fixed assets were acquired when the subsidiary was formed in 19X2, at which time the exchange rate was $1.75.
5. **Sales and operating expenses:** These occurred evenly throughout the year.
6. **Intercompany accounts:** All intercompany transactions are denominated in pounds. No adjustment has been made at year end because of changes in the exchange rate during the year.
7. **Common stock:** No common stock transactions have occurred since the formation of the subsidiary by the parent in 19X2.
8. **Retained earnings:** From the dollar financial statements the subsidiary's retained earnings account at December 31, 19X4, was $345,000.
9. **Cumulative translation adjustment:** The cumulative translation adjustment at December 31, 19X4 was $(10,000).
10. **Dividends:** The subsidiary declared its 19X5 dividends on December 20, 19X5 (when the exchange rate was $1.51), and paid the dividend on January 4, 19X6 (when the exchange rate was $1.48). (Intercompany dividends are recorded in the intercompany payable and intercompany receivable accounts and were properly recorded by both entities.)
11. **Income taxes:** For simplicity, ignore income tax considerations.
12. **Equity method of accounting:** The parent uses the complete equity method of accounting, but has yet to record the earnings of the subsidiary for 19X5 or reflect unrealized intercompany profit in its books.

Required:

1. Translate the subsidiary's financial statements into dollars.
2. Prepare the entries the parent would record under the equity method of accounting.
3. Prepare a conceptual analysis of the investment account as of December 31, 19X4, and update it through December 31, 19X5. (Hint: The components at December 31, 19X4, total $510,000.)
4. Prepare all entries needed at December 31, 19X5, in order to consolidate the subsidiary's financial statements properly.
5. Prepare a consolidating statement worksheet.

17

Interim Reporting

AN OVERVIEW OF INTERIM REPORTING

Applicability

Users of financial data need continuous, timely information about the performance of an enterprise to make investment or credit-related decisions. Although it has the benefit of an independent audit, an annual report is inadequate by itself in meeting these needs. Accordingly, the reporting of quarterly financial data has become a basic part of the corporate reporting process. Quarterly periods are sufficiently short to reveal business turning points, which may be obscured in annual reports. For companies that have significant seasonal variations in their operations, quarterly financial reports may give investors a better understanding of the nature of the business.

Quarterly financial reporting is not required by any official accounting pronouncement of the Financial Accounting Standards Board (FASB) or any of its predecessor organizations. However, the New York Stock Exchange and the American Stock Exchange require their listed companies to furnish interim quarterly operating results to their stockholders. Companies not subject to these stock exchange listing requirements usually furnish such reports voluntarily. In fact, many privately owned companies furnish financial information to their stockholders as often as monthly.

Requirements of the Securities and Exchange Commission. Publicly owned companies that are subject to the continuous reporting requirements of the Securities and Exchange Commission (SEC) must file interim financial statements with the SEC on Form 10-Q. This form must be filed for each of the first three quarters of each fiscal year within 45 days after the end of each such quarter.[1] Furthermore, the SEC requires specified quarterly financial data pertaining to operations for the latest two years to be presented in the annual report sent to stockholders and in the annual financial statements that must be filed with the SEC on Form 10-K.[2] (Forms 10-Q and 10-K are discussed in detail in Chapter 18.) Such disclosures inform investors of the pattern of corporate activities throughout the year.[3]

Official Accounting Pronouncements

The first and still current pronouncement specifically dealing with interim reports is *APB Opinion No. 28,* "Interim Financial Reporting," which was

[1]Companies whose securities are listed on a stock exchange and companies meeting certain size tests whose securities are traded in the over-the-counter market are subject to the continuous reporting requirements of the SEC.

[2]Proxy and Information Statement Rule 14a-3(b)(3); Form 10-K, Item 8; and Regulation S-K, Item 302 (a) (Washington, D.C.: Securities and Exchange Commission).

[3]*Accounting Series Release No. 177* (Washington, D.C.: Securities and Exchange Commission, 1975).

issued in 1973. This pronouncement has been amended by *FASB Statement No. 3*, "Reporting Accounting Changes in Interim Financial Statements," and interpreted by *FASB Interpretation No. 18*, "Accounting for Income Taxes in Interim Periods." Also, as this book goes to print, the FASB has an exposure draft outstanding ("Accounting for Income Taxes," dated September 2, 1986) that, if finalized, will slightly amend *APB Opinion No. 28*. *APB Opinion No. 28* is divided into the following two major parts:

1. Part I does not require interim financial reports to be issued but sets forth accounting standards to be used in preparing them.
2. Part II sets forth minimum disclosures to be included in interim financial reports issued by publicly owned companies.

Interim financial statements filed with the SEC on Form 10-Q must be prepared in accordance with the provisions of *APB Opinion No. 28* and any amendments. Before discussing the detailed requirements of this pronouncement and the related amendment and interpretation, we discuss the conceptual issues associated with interim reporting.

CONCEPTUAL ISSUES

The fundamental conceptual issue concerning interim financial statements (whether complete or condensed) is whether or not they should be prepared in accordance with the same accounting principles and practices used to prepare annual financial statements. This issue pertains almost solely to the recognition of costs and expenses, because accountants generally agree that for interim reporting purposes no sensible alternatives exist to the long-established practice of recognizing revenue when it is earned. The following examples of costs and expenses illustrate the problems associated with their treatment for interim reporting purposes:

1. **Major advertising expenditures.** Suppose that a major advertising compaign is launched early in the year. For interim reporting purposes, should the cost be deferred as an asset and amortized throughout the year, even though no portion of advertising costs can be deferred and reported as an asset at the end of the annual reporting period?
2. **Seasonal repairs.** Suppose a company historically makes major annual repairs late in the year. Accruing liabilities for future repair costs (other than warranty-related costs) is not proper at the end of an annual reporting period. Is it proper, therefore, to spread total estimated repairs throughout the year by accruing such costs in interim periods prior to their incurrence?
3. **Depreciation and rent.** In most cases, depreciation and rent expenses are computed for annual reporting purposes based on the passage of time. Should a year's depreciation and rent expense be assigned to interim periods for interim reporting purposes on this same basis, or should some other basis (such as sales) be used?

4. **Social Security taxes.** Social Security taxes are paid by the employer only during a portion of the year for employees who have incomes greater than the maximum amount on which employer Social Security taxes must be paid. Should the employer's Social Security taxes for these employees be charged to expense over the entire year, using deferrals?
5. **Year-end bonuses.** Should year-end bonuses be anticipated and accrued for interim reporting purposes?

There are three schools of thought concerning the approach used in interim reporting: the discrete view, the integral view, and the combination discrete–integral view.

The Discrete View

Under the **discrete view,** an interim period is a discrete, self-contained segment of history, just as an annual period is; therefore, an interim period must stand on its own. From this perspective, the results of operations for each interim period are determined using the same accounting principles and practices used to prepare annual reports. No special deferral or accrual practices are used for interim reporting purposes that cannot be used for annual reporting purposes. As a result, the components of Assets, Liabilities, Revenues, Expenses, and Earnings are defined for interim reporting purposes the same way as they are for annual reporting purposes. Under the discrete view, the function of accounting is to record transactions and events as they occur. Thus, the period of time for which results of operations are determined should not influence how such transactions and events are reported.

This approach is unacceptable to most accountants because it does not allow accruals, deferrals, and estimations at interim dates for annual items.

The Integral View

Under the **integral view,** an interim period is an integral part of an annual period. From this perspective, the expected relationship between revenues and expenses for the annual period should be reflected in the interim periods so that reasonably constant operating profit margins can be reported throughout the year. Under this "pure form" of the integral view, annual expenses are estimated and assigned to interim periods in proportion to revenues recognized. Special deferral and accrual practices are used for interim reporting purposes that may not be used for annual reporting purposes. As a result, the components of Assets, Liabilities, Revenues, Expenses, and Earnings are defined differently for interim reporting purposes than for annual reporting purposes. The costs of unforeseen events and certain other nonoperating items—such as settlement of litigation, discontinued operations, and asset disposals—are recorded in the interim period in which they occur.

This approach is also unacceptable to most accountants because of the artificial assumption that each dollar of revenue attracts the same rate of operating profit margin. Such an assumption is no more appropriate for periods within a year than it is over a company's entire life cycle.

The Combination Discrete–Integral View

Between the extremes of the discrete view and the pure form of the integral view are various combination **discrete–integral approaches.** Under these approaches, the integral view is used for some costs and the discrete view is used for the remaining costs. All methods of deciding which costs are treated with integral techniques and which are treated under the discrete view are arbitrary. The remainder of this chapter discusses *APB Opinion No. 28*, which prescribes a combination discrete–integral approach.

THE REQUIREMENTS OF *APB OPINION NO. 28*

Revenues

> Revenue from products sold or services rendered should be recognized as earned during an interim period on the same basis as followed for the full year.[4]

This provision, which requires that each interim period be viewed as an annual period, produces the following results:

1. Companies that have seasonal revenues must report such revenues in the interim period in which they are earned as opposed to allocating them over the full year.
2. When receipts at an interim date precede the earnings process, the revenues are deferred until the interim period in which the product is delivered or the service is rendered.
3. Companies using the percentage-of-completion method for long-term construction-type contracts must recognize revenues in interim periods using the same procedures that are used at the end of the annual period.

Costs Associated with Revenues (Product Costs)

> Those costs and expenses that are associated directly with or allocated to the products sold or to the services rendered for annual reporting purposes (including for example, material costs, wages and salaries and related fringe benefits, manufacturing overhead, and warranties) should be similarly treated for interim reporting purposes.... Companies should generally use the same inventory pricing methods and make provisions for

[4]*Opinions of the Accounting Principles Board, No. 28*, "Interim Financial Reporting" (New York: American Institute of Certified Public Accountants, 1973), par. 11.

write-downs to market at interim dates on the same basis as used at annual inventory dates....[5]

Although this provision appears to treat each interim period as though it were an annual period, the following four specified exceptions allow each interim period to be viewed as part of an annual period:

1. Estimated gross profit rates may be used to determine the cost of goods sold during interim periods. This procedure is merely a practical modification, as complete physical inventories are usually not taken at interim dates.
2. Liquidation at an interim date of LIFO base-period inventories that the company expects to replace by the end of the annual period does not affect interim results; that is, cost of goods sold for the interim reporting period should include the expected cost of replacing the liquidated LIFO base.
3. Declines in market price at interim dates that will probably be recovered by the end of the annual period (temporary declines) "need not" be recognized at the interim date. If inventory losses from market declines are recognized at an interim date, any subsequent recoveries should be recognized as gains in those periods, but only to the extent of previously recognized losses.
4. For companies using standard cost accounting systems, purchase price variances or volume or capacity variances of costs that are inventoriable "should ordinarily" be deferred at interim reporting dates, providing such variances are planned and expected to be absorbed by the end of the annual period.

With respect to exception 3 above, assume that a company has on hand at the beginning of the year 15,000 units of a particular inventory item, which are valued at their historical FIFO cost of $20 per unit. For simplicity, we assume that no additional purchases of this item are made during the year. Assumed sales for each quarter and replacement costs (assumed to be market) at the end of each quarter are as follows:

Quarter	Units Sold during Quarter	Replacement Cost at End of Quarter
1	1,000	$16 (Not considered a temporary decline)
2	2,000	14 (Considered a temporary decline)
3	3,000	17
4	4,000	21

Illustration 17-1 shows the adjustments that would be made to the Inventory account for this item during the year for market changes.

In reviewing Illustration 17-1, note that no market adjustment was made at the end of the second quarter. The market decline during that

[5] *APB Opinion No. 28*, pars. 13–14.

Illustration 17-1
Analysis of the Inventory Account for the Year

	Units			Amount
Balance, January 1	15,000	× $20		= $300,000
First quarter sales	(1,000)	× 20		= (20,000)
				$280,000
First-quarter market adjustment	14,000	× (4)	[$20 − $16] =	(56,000)
Balance, March 31	14,000	× 16		= $224,000
Second-quarter sales	(2,000)	× 16		= (32,000)
Balance, June 30	12,000	× 16		= $192,000
Third-quarter sales	(3,000)	× 16		= (48,000)
				$144,000
Third-quarter market adjustment	9,000	× 1	[$17 − $16] =	9,000
Balance, September 30	9,000	× 17		= $153,000
Fourth-quarter sales	(4,000)	× 17		= (68,000)
				$ 85,000
Fourth-quarter market adjustment	5,000	× 3	[$20 − $17] =	15,000
Balance, December 31	5,000	× 20		= $100,000

quarter was considered a temporary decline that was reasonably expected to disappear by the end of the annual period.

Note also that the use of the language "need not" in the pronouncement (rather than the mandatory term "should") permits companies to recognize temporary market declines in the interim period in which they occur if they choose to do so. Thus, alternative treatments for temporary market declines are sanctioned.

With respect to exception 4 that deals with companies using standard cost accounting systems, the use of the language "should ordinarily" in the pronouncement (rather than an unqualified "should") permits alternative treatments for purchase price and volume variances that are planned and expected to be absorbed by year-end. In summary, *APB Opinion No. 28* allows substantial leeway for dealing with certain aspects of inventory costing and manufacturing cost variances in interim reports.

All Other Costs and Expenses

The Accounting Principles Board (APB) developed the following standards for all costs and expenses other than product costs:

a. Costs and expenses other than product costs should be charged to interim periods as incurred, or be allocated among interim periods based on an estimate of time expired, benefit received or activity associated with the periods. Procedures adopted for assigning specific cost and expense items to an interim period should be consistent with the bases followed by the company in reporting results of operations at annual reporting dates. However when a specific cost or expense item charged to expense for annual reporting purposes benefits more than one interim period, the cost or expense item may be allocated to those interim periods.

b. Some costs and expenses incurred in an interim period, however, cannot be readily identified with the activities or benefits of other interim periods and should be charged to the interim period in which incurred. Disclosure should be made as to the nature and amount of such costs unless items of a comparable nature are included in both the current interim period and in the corresponding interim period of the preceding year.
c. Arbitrary assignment of the amount of such costs to an interim period should not be made.
d. Gains and losses that arise in any interim period similar to those that would not be deferred at year end should not be deferred to later interim periods within the same fiscal year.[6]

These standards do the following:

1. They prohibit the "normalizing" or "spreading" of expenditures over a fiscal year on a revenue basis as under a pure integral approach.
2. They require that most expenditures be treated as though each interim period were an annual reporting period.
3. They permit certain expenditures that clearly benefit more than one interim period to be allocated among the interim periods benefited. Note that this treatment is **permissive, not mandatory.** Some examples of expenditures that may qualify for allocation among interim periods are major annual repairs, costs of periodic advertising campaigns, Social Security taxes, and charitable contributions.

In addition to the preceding standards, the pronouncement requires that estimation procedures be used at interim dates for items that historically have resulted in year-end adjustments (usually charges to income) or that can be reasonably approximated at interim dates. Examples are allowances for uncollectible accounts, inventory shrinkage, quantity discounts, and accruals for discretionary year-end bonuses.[7] This requirement clearly attempts to prevent the reporting of material fourth-quarter adjustments that cast a shadow on the reliability of prior interim reports and undermine the integrity of the interim reporting process.

Seasonal Revenues, Costs, and Expenses

Many businesses—such as amusement parks, professional sports teams, farming corporations, department stores, and toy manufacturers—receive all or a major portion of their revenues in one or two interim periods. As a result, these companies report wide fluctuations in revenues and

[6] *APB Opinion No. 28*, par. 15.
[7] *APB Opinion No. 28*, par. 17.

profitability in their interim reports. Such companies must disclose the seasonal nature of their activities to avoid misleading inferences about revenues and profitability for the entire year. Furthermore, these companies should consider providing supplemental financial information for the 12-month periods ended at the interim date for the current and prior years.[8]

Income Tax Provisions

The basic provision for the computation of income taxes for interim periods is as follows:

> At the end of each interim period the company should make its best estimate of the effective tax rate expected to be applicable for the full fiscal year. The rate so determined should be used in providing for income taxes on a current year-to-date basis. The effective tax rate should reflect anticipated investment tax credits, foreign tax rates, percentage depletion, capital gains rates, and other available tax planning alternatives.[9]

The following points concerning this provision should be understood:

1. Each interim period is *not* a separate taxable period.
2. If the estimated tax rate for the year changes as the year proceeds, the effect of the change is included in the appropriate interim period as a change in estimate. No retroactive restatement of prior interim periods is made. The provision for income taxes for the third quarter of a company's fiscal year, for example, is the result of applying the expected tax rate to year-to-date earnings and subtracting the provisions reported for the first and second quarters.

The basic provision as stated above is supplemented for the tax effects of unusual or extraordinary items as follows:

> However, in arriving at this effective tax rate no effect should be included for the tax related to significant unusual or extraordinary items that will be separately reported or reported net of their related tax effect in reports for the interim period or for the fiscal year.[10]

Illustration 17-2 shows how to calculate the estimated effective annual income tax rate at interim periods and how to determine the income tax provision for the first interim quarter and subsequent interim quarters. For simplicity, the assumed facts do not involve any unusual or extraordinary items. Computing interim-period income taxes is more involved when one or more of the following items is present:

1. Unusual items reported separately.
2. Extraordinary items reported net of related tax effects.

[8] *APB Opinion No. 28*, par. 18.
[9] *APB Opinion No. 28*, par. 19.
[10] *APB Opinion No. 28*, par. 19.

Illustration 17-2
Calculation of Estimated Effective Annual Income Tax Rate and Interim Tax Provisions

1. Assumptions:

Income before income taxes for 19X1:	
First quarter (actual)	$100,000
Remainder of the year (estimated)	$500,000
Federal income tax rate	34%
State income tax rate	5%
Estimated federal research and development tax credits for 19X1	$ 11,500
Estimated officers' life insurance premiums not deductible for state or federal income tax	$ 10,000

2. Calculation of Estimated Effective Annual Income Tax Rate and First-quarter Income Tax Provision:

Calculation of estimated state income taxes for 19X1:	
Estimated annual income before income taxes ($100,000 + $500,000)	$600,000
Add—Officers' life insurance premiums	10,000
Estimated state taxable income for 19X1	$610,000
State income tax rate	5%
Estimated state income taxes for 19X1	$ 30,500
Calculation of estimated federal income taxes for 19X1:	
Estimated annual income before income taxes ($100,000 + $500,000)	$600,000
Add—Officers' life insurance premiums	10,000
Less—State income taxes	(30,500)
Estimated federal taxable income for 19X1	$579,500
Federal income tax rate	34%
	$197,030
Less—Research and development tax credits	(11,500)
Estimated federal income taxes for 19X1	$185,530
Calculation of estimated effective annual income tax rate for 19X1:	
Combined estimated federal and state income taxes for 19X1 ($185,530 + $30,500)	$216,030
Estimated income before income taxes for 19X1	$600,000
Estimated effective annual income tax rate ($216,030 ÷ $600,000)	36%
Calculation of income tax provision for the first quarter:	
Income before income taxes for first quarter	$100,000
Estimated effective annual income tax rate	36%
Income tax provision	$ 36,000

Illustration 17-2 (continued)

3. Calculation of Second-quarter Income Tax Provision:

At the end of the second quarter, another calculation would be made of the estimated effective annual income tax rate for 19X1 using the same procedures used at the end of the first quarter. Assume that the calculation at the end of the second quarter produces an estimated effective annual income tax rate of 35%. The calculation of the income tax provision to be reported for the second quarter, assuming second quarter income before income taxes of $180,000, is as follows:

Income before income taxes for the first six months ($100,000 + $180,000)	$280,000
Estimated effective annual income tax rate (calculated at the end of the second quarter)	35%
Cumulative income tax provision	$ 98,000
Less—Income tax provision reported for the first quarter	(36,000)
Income tax provision for second quarter	$ 62,000

Note that 35% of $180,000 is $63,000. The difference between this amount and the $62,000 amount calculated above is the 1% change in the estimated annual tax rate multiplied by the first quarter income before income taxes of $100,000.

3. Losses in one or more interim periods.
4. Prior year operating loss carryforwards available.
5. Discontinued operations.
6. Changes in accounting principles.
7. Effects of new tax legislation.

A discussion and illustration of each of these items is beyond the scope of this chapter. However, item 3 deserves some attention here as it relates to seasonal businesses that may have losses during early interim periods but that are expected to be profitable for the entire year. In these cases, the tax effects of losses arising in the early portion of a fiscal year are recognized only if (1) the carryback of such losses to prior years is possible, or (2) realization is assured beyond reasonable doubt as a result of profitable operations expected for the entire year. A historical pattern of losses in early interim periods that have been offset by profits in later interim periods normally constitutes sufficient evidence that realization is assured beyond a reasonable doubt, unless other facts indicate that the historical pattern will not repeat.[11]

Illustration 17-3 shows the income tax expense or benefit reported in each interim reporting period for an enterprise engaged in a seasonal business that shows a loss for the first interim reporting period. We assume that the enterprise anticipates being profitable for the entire year and that

[11] *APB Opinion No. 28*, par. 20.

Illustration 17-3
Income Tax Expense or Benefit to be Reported for a Seasonal Business (in thousands of dollars)

	Reporting Quarter				Fiscal
	1	2	3	4	Year
Income (loss) before income taxes.	$(200)	$100	$150	$950	$1,000
Income tax benefit (expense) @ 40%	80	(40)	(60)	(380)	(400)
Net income (loss)........................	$(120)	$ 60	$ 90	$570	$ 600

this expectation proves to be correct. Established seasonal patterns ensure realization of the tax benefit related to the loss in the first interim reporting period. For simplicity, we also assume that (1) the estimated annual effective tax rate is 40%, (2) this rate does not change during the year, and (3) no unusual or extraordinary items are present.

FASB Interpretation No. 18, "Accounting for Income Taxes in Interim Periods," clarifies the application of *APB Opinion No. 28* with respect to accounting for income taxes. This interpretation, containing more than 20 detailed examples spread over more than 40 pages, shows how to compute interim period income taxes involving the more complex areas listed on pages 660 and 662. Refer to that pronouncement for a complete discussion and related examples.

Disposal of a Segment of a Business and Extraordinary, Unusual, Infrequently Occurring, and Contingent Items

The effects of the disposal of a segment of a business and extraordinary, unusual, and infrequently occurring items are reported in the period in which they occur. If the effects are material in relation to the operating results of the interim period, they are reported separately.[12]

The basic thrust of *APB Opinion No. 28* concerning contingencies is a discrete approach; that is, disclosures are made in interim reports in the same manner as they are made in annual reports, except that the significance of a contingency should be judged in relation to annual financial statements.[13] *FASB Statement No. 5*, "Accounting for Contingencies," was issued after *APB Opinion No. 28*. The application of *FASB Statement No. 5* provisions to interim periods as though each interim period were an annual period is consistent with the basic thrust of *APB Opinion No. 28* in this area. Thus, the **probable** and **reasonably estimatable** criteria of *FASB Statement No. 5* would be used to determine in which interim period a loss contingency should be accrued.

[12] *APB Opinion No. 28*, par. 21.
[13] *APB Opinion No. 28*, par. 22.

Accounting Changes

Interim financial reports must disclose any changes in accounting principles or practices. The basic provisions of *APB Opinion No. 20*, "Accounting Changes," apply to interim reporting. Changes in accounting principles that require **retroactive restatement** of previously issued annual financial statements result in the similar restatement of previously issued interim financial statements when such accounting changes are made in other than the first interim reporting period.[14] (*APB Opinion No. 20* specifically sets forth the few changes that can be accorded retroactive restatement, such as a change in the method of accounting for long-term construction contracts.)

The **cumulative effect** of a change in accounting principles is reported as an adjustment in the current-year income statement as prescribed by *FASB Statement No. 3*, an amendment to *APB Opinion No. 28*. If such a change is made during the *first* interim reporting period, the cumulative effect as of the beginning of that year is included in the net income of that first interim reporting period. If such a change is made in *other than the first* interim reporting period, however, the prior interim reporting periods of the current year are restated by applying the new accounting principles, and the cumulative effect as of the beginning of that year is included in the restated net income of the first interim reporting period of the current year.[15] The end result, therefore, is as though all such changes had been made in the first interim reporting period.

Changes in accounting estimates must be accounted for in the interim period in which the change is made on a prospective basis, regardless of the interim period of the change. Thus, restatement of previously reported interim information is prohibited for such changes.[16]

Previously issued interim reports may be restated for corrections of an error just as previously issued annual financial statements may be restated for such items.[17]

Disclosures of Summarized Interim Financial Data by Publicly Owned Companies

The following minimum disclosures must be furnished to stockholders in interim reports (including fourth-quarter reports):

a. Sales or gross revenues, provision for income taxes, extraordinary terms (including related income tax effects), cumulative effect of a change in accounting principles or practices, and net income.

[14] *APB Opinion No. 28*, par. 25.
[15] *Statement of Financial Accounting Standards, No. 3*, "Reporting Accounting Changes in Interim Financial Statements" (Stamford: Financial Accounting Standards Board, 1974), par. 9–10.
[16] *APB Opinion No. 28*, par. 26.
[17] *APB Opinion No. 28*, par. 25.

b. Primary and fully diluted earnings per share data for each period presented . . .
c. Seasonal revenue, costs or expenses.
d. Significant changes in estimates or provisions for income taxes.
e. Disposal of a segment of a business and extraordinary unusual or infrequently occurring items.
f. Contingent items.
g. Changes in accounting principles or estimates.
h. Significant changes in financial position.[18]

Most publicly owned companies exceed these requirements by furnishing either a condensed or a complete income statement. These income statements (condensed or complete) are usually presented in comparative form. For reports other than the first quarter, quarterly data and **year-to-date** amounts are usually presented. Many companies also furnish complete or condensed balance sheets (usually in comparative form) in their interim reports. In addition to financial data, these interim reports usually contain a narrative discussion of interim period highlights.

Many publicly traded companies do not issue a separate report covering fourth-quarter interim results. Such companies often disclose fourth-quarter results (as outlined in paragraph 30 of *APB Opinion No. 28*) in the annual report. If the results of the fourth quarter are not furnished in a separate report or in the annual report, a company must disclose the following items recognized in the fourth quarter in a note to the annual financial statements:

1. Disposals of segments.
2. Extraordinary items.
3. Unusual or infrequently occurring items.
4. The aggregate effect of year-end adjustments that are material to the results of the fourth quarter.[19]

In addition, the effects of accounting changes made during the fourth quarter are disclosed in a note to the annual financial statements in the absence of a separate fourth-quarter report or disclosure in the annual report.[20]

The Requirements of *APB Opinion No. 28* and of SEC Form 10-Q Compared

The disclosure requirements of SEC Form 10-Q are more extensive than those of *APB Opinion No. 28.* Form 10-Q requires that the following condensed financial statements be included in interim reports filed with the SEC:

[18]*APB Opinion No. 28*, par. 30.
[19]*APB Opinion No. 28*, par. 31.
[20]*FASB Statement No. 3*, par. 14.

1. **Balance sheets.** Balance sheets are presented as of the end of the most recent fiscal quarter and for the end of the preceding fiscal year.
2. **Income statements.** Income statements are presented for the most recent fiscal quarter, for the period between the end of the last fiscal year and the end of the most recent fiscal quarter (year-to-date amounts in second- and third-quarter reports), and for corresponding periods of the preceding fiscal year.
3. **Statements of changes in financial position.** Statements of changes in financial position are presented for the period between the end of the last fiscal year and the end of the most recent fiscal quarter, and for the corresponding period of the preceding fiscal year. (In the near future, the SEC is expected to change this requirement to a statement of cash flows.)

As stated earlier, financial statements included in Form 10-Q reports are prepared in accordance with *APB Opinion No. 28* provisions and any amendments to the opinion that may be adopted by the FASB. Disclosures must be complete enough so that none of the information presented is misleading. Furthermore, management must provide an analysis of the quarterly results of operations. Information required in Form 10-Q may be omitted from that form if such information is contained in a quarterly report to the stockholders and a copy of that quarterly report is filed with Form 10-Q.

INVOLVEMENT OF CERTIFIED PUBLIC ACCOUNTANTS IN INTERIM REPORTING

Audited interim financial reports are virtually nonexistent. For many years prior to 1975, common deficiencies in unaudited reports included a preponderance of unusual charges and, less often, credits to income late in the year and corrections to previously issued interim financial data. In recognition of such significant, continuing deficiencies and abuses in the interim reporting process, the SEC took steps in 1975 to improve the quality of interim financial reports by effectively forcing the accounting profession to accept auditor involvement in the interim reporting process. At that time, most members of the profession did not want to be associated with interim financial reports on anything less than a complete audit basis, fearing potential lawsuits in the event interim financial report data proved to be false or misleading. The SEC obtained auditor involvement in quite an interesting way. First, it passed a rule requiring that quarterly financial data appear in a note to the annual financial statements included in the annual 10-K report filed with the SEC. This requirement caused auditors to be "associated" with these data by virtue of reporting on the financial statements in which the note was included. This occurred even though the SEC allowed the note to be labeled "unaudited" and the auditors had not audited the data in the note.

Second, the SEC passed a rule informing auditors that the SEC presumed that auditors applied "appropriate professional standards and procedures with respect to the data in the note." Thus, auditors had to perform some form of "review" of the data included in this note. Furthermore, the SEC indicated that unless the American Institute of Certified Public Accountants (AICPA) developed professional standards and procedures in connection with reviewing the data in this note, the SEC would do so. The AICPA chose to do so, and these standards and procedures are contained in *Statement on Auditing Standards No. 36*, "Review of Interim Financial Information."[21] Because this pronouncement is the subject of an auditing course, it is not discussed in detail here. Briefly, auditors must perform certain procedures that are **substantially less than an audit.**

Auditors are not specifically required as part of the interim reporting process to perform these review procedures during the year. Thus, the review can be made at year-end. The SEC took these steps, however, in the belief that companies would have the reviews made as part of the interim reporting process for the following reasons:

1. The likelihood of having to revise quarterly data when the annual statements are published should be less.
2. The likelihood of discovering needed adjustments on a timely basis should be greater, so that unusual charges and credits are less frequent in the last month of the year.
3. The added expertise of professional accountants increases the quality of the interim reporting process.[22]

To encourage auditors to be more involved in the interim reporting process, the SEC adopted a rule in 1979 that exempts interim financial reports from a federal securities law provision automatically making certified public accountants liable for a client's false and misleading financial statements unless such accountants can prove they were diligent. (Certified public accountants are not exempted, however, from the section of the federal securities law that deals with fraud.) Even before the adoption of this rule, the opposition of auditors to involvement in the interim reporting process had, for the most part, dissipated. Most auditors of publicly held companies now encourage their clients to have the review performed as part of the interim reporting process rather than at year-end.

In 1980, the SEC revised its reporting requirements, so that (a) quarterly financial data may be presented outside of the notes to the annual financial statements, and (b) auditors must follow the AICPA's review standards and procedures regardless of the placement of the quarterly financial data.[23]

[21] *Statement on Auditing Standards No. 36*, "Review of Interim Financial Information" (New York: American Institute of Certified Public Accountants, 1981). This pronouncement supersedes *Statement on Auditing Standards No. 24*, which was issued in 1979.
[22] *Accounting Series Release No. 177* (Washington, D.C.: Securities and Exchange Commission, 1975).
[23] Regulation S-K, Item 302(a)(1) and (4) (Washington, D.C.: Securities and Exchange Commission, 1980).

SUMMARY

Interim reporting raises the fundamental issue of whether or not interim financial statements should be prepared using the same accounting principles and practices used in preparing annual financial statements. Under the discrete view, each interim period must stand on its own without regard to the fact that it is part of an annual reporting period. Under the integral view, the fact that an interim period is part of an annual reporting period is a basis for assigning the total estimated annual costs and expenses to interim periods based on revenues to report reasonably constant operating margins. *APB Opinion No. 28* adopted a combination discrete–integral approach, whereby revenues, extraordinary items, gains or losses from the disposal of a segment, unusual items, and infrequently occurring items are treated under the discrete view. For costs associated with revenue (product costs), the discrete view is used. (Four specified exceptions to this rule produce integral results.) The discrete view must be used for all other costs and expenses, unless an item meets specified standards for integral treatment. If the standards are met, the company may use integral techniques. For income taxes, the integral view is prescribed.

Glossary of New Terms

Discrete View A manner of measuring interim period earnings by viewing each interim period as an independent period that must stand on its own.

Integral View A manner of measuring interim period earnings by viewing each interim period as an integral part of an annual reporting period. Under this view, each interim period should bear part of the annual expenses that are incurred in generating revenues for the entire year.

Combination Discrete–Integral View A manner of measuring interim period earnings by accepting the integral view for certain costs and expenses and using the discrete view for all other costs and expenses.

Review Questions

1. Do the principles and practices that apply to interim reporting apply only to publicly owned companies?
2. What is the fundamental issue pertaining to interim reporting?
3. Are the issues associated with interim reporting primarily related to revenues or to costs and expenses?
4. Name the three schools of thought that exist concerning the approach to interim reporting.

5. Under which approach must each interim period stand on its own?
6. Does *APB Opinion No. 28* impose integral techniques for costs and expenses not associated with revenue? Explain.
7. What factors could cause the estimated annual income tax rate to change from quarter to quarter?
8. If fourth-quarter results are not furnished in a separate report or in the annual report, which items recognized in the fourth quarter must be disclosed in a note to the annual financial statements?

Discussion Cases

DC 17-1

Treatment of Annual Furnace Relining Costs

Harth Company was formed in 19X1 to produce steel. Production commenced in October 19X2, and sales began in November 19X2. The company expects to close down its furnaces each September to reline them, which takes about a month. Members of the controller's staff disagree on how the costs of relining the furnaces should be reported. The following approaches are advocated:

1. Expense the costs in the period in which they are incurred.
2. Expense the costs over the company's calendar reporting year.
3. Expense the costs over a period from September to August of the following year.

Required:
Evaluate the theoretical soundness of these proposed treatments and comment on their conformity with the provisions of *APB Opinion No. 28.*

DC 17-2

Treatment of Accounting and Legal Fees Related to Reporting to Stockholders

Callex Company reports on a calendar year-end basis. The accounting firm that performs the annual year-end audit renders approximately one-third of its audit-related services in the fourth quarter of each calendar year and approximately two-thirds of its audit-related services in the first quarter of each calendar year. (The accounting firm renders an interim billing in the fourth quarter for services performed during that quarter.)

The legal firm that assists the company in preparing its annual 10-K report, which must be filed with the SEC within 90 days after year-end, renders all of its 10-K related services in the first calendar quarter of each year. (The legal firm renders its billing sometime in the second quarter.)

Required:
Determine how these accounting and legal fees should be reported in the quarterly financial statements.

DC 17-3

Material Year-end Physical Inventory Adjustment

Pilferex Company uses a periodic inventory system and takes an annual physical inventory at year-end. Historically, the company's adjustments from book value to physical inventory have been insignificant. Current-year sales and production increased substantially over the prior year, and a material book to physical inventory adjustment (a shortage) occurred. Management has not determined the cause of the physical inventory adjustment.

The market price of the company's common stock rose during the year due to the favorable sales and earnings pattern reported for the first three quarters. The market price declined sharply when the company announced that the annual earnings would be below estimated amounts as a result of the large physical inventory adjustment.

Required:

1. How should the physical inventory adjustment be reported?
2. What are the possible consequences of large fourth-quarter adjustments?

DC 17-4

Revising Previously Issued Quarterly Results

In November 1982, Tandem Computers, Inc., announced results for its fourth quarter (ended September 30, 1982) prior to the completion of its annual audit. (The company assumed that its outside auditors would not have any proposed adjustments.) In December 1982, after the auditors had completed their work, the company announced a restatement of third- and fourth-quarter results because (a) recorded sales included shipments that had occurred after the end of these quarters, and (b) previously recorded sales did not have sufficient documentation. Reported results (in millions of dollars) follow:

	Initially Reported	Restated	Decrease Amount	Decrease Percent
Sales	$336.9	$312.1	$(23.8)	(7)
Net income	37.3	29.9	(7.4)	(20)

After this announcement, the price of the company's common stock immediately fell 6 points, a 20% decline.[24]

Required:

1. What are the ramifications of restating results for these quarters?
2. If the auditors reviewed quarterly information at the end of each quarter, why did they not discover this problem at the end of the third quarter?

DC 17-5

Treatment of Unresolved Item

During its second quarter, Newby Company entered into a new type of transaction, which will result in the immediate reporting of substantial income. The company

[24] *The San Jose Mercury*, December 9, 1982, pp. 1F, 2F.

feels that its proposed accounting treatment is in accordance with generally accepted accounting principles. However, its outside auditors have been noncommittal as to whether the company's interpretation of the applicable FASB accounting standard is proper. At the end of the second quarter, the auditors indicate that they need more time to study the issue and do research. (Assume the auditors review quarterly results at year-end.)

Required:

1. Should the company record the transaction and report the income in the second quarter? State your reasons for your position.
2. What steps might the outside auditors take in doing research?
3. What other steps should the auditors consider?

Exercises

E 17-1

Inventory Loss from Market Decline

An inventory loss of $420,000 from market declines occurred in April 19X6. At that time, the market decline was not considered temporary. Of this loss, $100,000 was recovered in the fourth quarter ended December 31, 19X6.

Required:
How should this loss be reflected in the quarterly income statements for 19X6?

(AICPA adapted)

E 17-2

Annual Major Repairs and Property Taxes

On January 1, 19X6, Luca Company paid property taxes of $40,000 on its plant for calendar year 19X6. In March 19X6, Luca made its annual major repairs to its machinery amounting to $120,000. These repairs benefit the entire calendar year's operations.

Required:
How should these expenditures be reflected in the quarterly income statements for 19X6?

(AICPA adapted)

E 17-3

Year-end Bonuses

In January 19X7, Gelt Company estimated that its 19X7 year-end bonuses to executives would be $240,000. The actual amount paid for 19X6 year-end bonuses was $224,000. The 19X7 estimate is subject to year-end adjustment.

Required:
What amount, if any, of expense should be reflected in the quarterly income statement for the three months ended March 31, 19X7?

(AICPA adapted)

E 17-4

Percentage-of-completion Method on Long-Term Contracts

For annual reporting purposes, Candu Company appropriately accounts for revenues from long-term construction contracts under the percentage-of-completion method. In December 19X5, for budgeting purposes, Candu estimated that these revenues would be $1,600,000 for 19X6. As a result of favorable business conditions in October 19X6, Candu recognized revenues of $2,000,000 for the year ended December 31, 19X6. If the percentage-of-completion method had been used for the quarterly income statements on the same basis as followed for the year-end income statement, revenues would have been as follows:

Three months ended March 31, 19X6	$ 300,000
Three months ended June 30, 19X6	400,000
Three months ended September 30, 19X6	200,000
Three months ended December 31, 19X6	1,100,000
Total	$2,000,000

Required:
What amount of revenues from long-term construction contracts should be reflected in the quarterly income statement for the three months ended December 31, 19X6?
(AICPA adapted)

E 17-5

Severance Pay

During the second quarter of its current reporting year, Gilley Company announced that it would trim its work force by 7% as a result of below-normal demand for its products. Employees being laid-off are given 3 to 6 weeks severance pay, depending on their length of employment.

Required:
Assuming the severance pay was paid in the second quarter, how should it be accounted for in the quarterly reports for the current year?

Problems

P 17-1

Income Tax Provision: Change in Estimated Rate

Reviso Company had the following pretax income for the first two reporting quarters of 19X2:

First quarter	$500,000
Second quarter	700,000

Reviso's actual annual effective income tax rate for 19X1 was 40%. For budgeting purposes, Reviso estimated that the effective annual income tax rate for 19X2 would also be 40%. Near the end of the second quarter, Reviso changed its estimated effective annual income tax rate for 19X2 to 35%. Reviso issues its quarterly reports within 45 days of the end of the quarter.

Required:
Determine the amount of income tax expense reported for the first and second quarters of 19X2.

P 17-2 Incentive Compensation Plan for Sales Personnel

Pavlov Company uses an incentive system for its sales personnel whereby each salesperson receives:

1. A base salary of $1,000 per month.
2. A commission of 2% of the individual salesperson's sales.
3. A bonus of 10% on the individual salesperson's annual sales in excess of $1,200,000. (This bonus is paid in the first quarter of the year following the year on which the bonus is based.)

The company's sales do not occur in a seasonal pattern. Sales generated by certain sales personnel for the first and second quarters of 19X3 are as follows:

	First Quarter	Second Quarter	Cumulative
Buffet	$ 400,000	$ 350,000	$ 750,000
Cook	340,000	220,000	560,000
Dillon	260,000	380,000	640,000
Holly	280,000	290,000	570,000
Total	$1,280,000	$1,240,000	$2,520,000

Payments made during the first quarter of 19X3 for bonuses based on total 19X2 sales are as follows:

Buffet	$24,000
Holly	3,000

Required:
Determine the amount of compensation reported as expense for the first and second quarters of 19X3 using two different approaches for the bonuses.

P 17-3 Calculation of Estimated Effective Annual Income Tax Rate and Interim Tax Provisions

Domino Company has developed the following data for 19X2 at the end of its first reporting quarter:

Income before income taxes:	
First quarter (actual)	$200,000
Remainder of year (estimated)	$800,000
Federal income tax rate	40%
State income tax rate	10%
Estimated research and development tax credits	$ 44,600
Officers' life insurance premiums not deductible for state or federal purposes	$ 10,000
Excess of accelerated depreciation over straight-line depreciation for state and federal purposes	$ 50,000

Required:

1. Calculate the estimated effective annual income tax rate at the end of the first quarter.
2. Calculate the income tax provision for the first quarter.
3. Calculate the estimated effective annual income tax rate at the end of the second quarter assuming:
   a. Income before income taxes for the second quarter was $400,000.
   b. The estimated income before income taxes for the third and fourth quarters is $500,000 in total.
4. Calculate the income tax provision for the second quarter.

P 17-4 COMPREHENSIVE Identifying Weaknesses in an Interim Report and Evaluating Treatment of Selected Items

Budd Company, which is listed on the American Stock Exchange, budgeted activities for 19X5 as follows:

	Amount	Units
Net sales	$6,000,000	1,000,000
Cost of goods sold	(3,600,000)	1,000,000
Gross margin	$2,400,000	
Selling, general, and administrative expenses	(1,400,000)	
Operating income	$1,000,000	
Nonoperating revenue and expenses	-0-	
Income before Income Taxes	$1,000,000	
Estimated income taxes (current and deferred)	(400,000)	
Net Income	$ 600,000	
Earnings per share of common stock	$6.00	

The company has operated profitably for many years and has experienced a seasonal pattern of sales volume and production similar to the ones forecasted for 19X5. Sales volume is expected to follow a quarterly pattern of 10%, 20%, 35%, and 35%, respectively, because of the seasonality of the industry. Because of production and storage capacity limitations, production is expected to follow a pattern of 20%, 25%, 30%, and 25% per quarter, respectively.

At the conclusion of the first quarter of 19X5, the controller prepared and issued the following interim report for public release:

	Amount	Units
Net sales	$ 600,000	100,000
Cost of goods sold	(360,000)	100,000
Gross margin	$ 240,000	
Selling, general, and administrative expenses	(260,000)	
Operating loss	$ (20,000)	
Loss from warehouse fire	(140,000)	
Loss before Income Taxes	$(160,000)	
Estimated income taxes	–0–	
Net Loss	$(160,000)	
Loss per share of common stock	$(1.60)	

The following additional information is available for the first quarter just completed but was not included in the information released to the public:

a. The company uses a standard costing system, in which standards are set annually at currently attainable levels. At the end of the first quarter, an underapplied fixed factory overhead (volume variance) of $50,000 was treated as an asset at the end of the quarter. Production during the quarter was 200,000 units, of which 100,000 units were sold.
b. The selling, general, and administrative expenses were budgeted on a basis of $800,000 fixed expenses for the year plus $0.50 variable expenses per unit of sales. (An unfavorable variance of $10,000 was incurred in the first quarter.)
c. Assume that the warehouse fire loss met the conditions of an extraordinary loss. The warehouse had an undepreciated cost of $320,000; $180,000 was recovered from insurance on the warehouse. No other gains or losses are anticipated this year from similar events or transactions, nor has the company had any similar losses in preceding years; thus, the full loss is deductible as an ordinary loss for income tax purposes.
d. The effective income tax rate, for federal and state taxes combined, is expected to average 40% of earnings before income taxes during 19X5. No permanent differences exist between pretax accounting earnings and taxable income.
e. Earnings per share were computed on the basis of 100,000 shares of capital stock outstanding. Budd has only one class of stock issued, no long-term debt outstanding, and no stock option plan.

Required:

1. Without reference to the specific situation described above, what standards of disclosure exist for interim financial data (published interim financial reports) for publicly traded companies? Explain.
2. Identify the form and content weaknesses of the interim report without reference to the additional information.
3. Indicate for interim reporting purposes the preferable treatment for each of the five items of additional information and explain why that treatment is preferable.

(AICPA adapted)

18

Securities and Exchange Commission Reporting

AN OVERVIEW OF SEC REPORTING

Historical Background

The nature of securities is such that their purchase and sale can create substantial opportunities for misrepresentation, manipulation, and other fraudulent acts. In reaction to a rapidly increasing number of flagrant abuses in this area, all but one state enacted some form of legislation between 1911 and 1933 to regulate the purchase and sale of corporate securities. Commonly referred to as the **blue sky laws,** these laws vary widely among the states. In addition, because these laws apply only to intrastate transactions, from an overall standpoint in protecting the public, they have proved to be ineffective. The stock market crash of 1929, testimonial to the inadequacy of this type of regulation, was preceded by (1) the issuance of billions of dollars of securities during the preceding decade that proved to be worthless; (2) the excessive use of credit to purchase stocks on margin; (3) the extensive manipulation of stock prices by various means; (4) the extensive use of inside information by officers and directors for purposes of self-enrichment; and (5) lax standards governing the solicitation of votes from shareholders whereby managements were often able to perpetuate themselves in power. The magnitude of the inadequate financial reporting and questionable ethical standards that led to this financial collapse substantially undermined the integrity of the capital markets and thus raised serious questions concerning the survival of our system of free capital markets.

To restore investor confidence and reestablish integrity in the capital markets, Congress passed the Securities Act of 1933 ("the 1933 Act") and the Securities Exchange Act of 1934 ("the 1934 Act"). These two acts do not replace the intrastate regulation provided by the blue sky laws but merely supplement them. The 1933 Act applies to the initial distribution of securities to the public. The purpose of this act, as expressed in its preamble, is

> to provide full and fair disclosure of the character of securities sold in interstate and foreign commerce and through the mails, and to prevent frauds in the sale thereof...

This required disclosure is accomplished by "registering" securities with the Securities and Exchange Commission (SEC) before they may be offered to the public. The registration procedure involves filing specified financial and nonfinancial information with the SEC for examination.

The 1934 Act applies to the subsequent trading in outstanding securities that are listed on organized stock exchanges and in the over-the-counter markets. The purpose of this act, as expressed in its preamble, is

> to provide for the regulation of securities exchanges and of over-the-counter markets operating in interstate and foreign commerce and through the mails to prevent inequitable and unfair practices on such exchanges and markets...

Companies that come under the provisions of the 1934 Act must file periodic reports with the SEC of specified financial and nonfinancial information. In addition, certain practices are prohibited.

Because each act constitutes a major piece of legislation, we cannot discuss them in great detail in one chapter. Accordingly, this chapter provides a general familiarity with selected portions of each act and the means of complying with the financial reporting requirements established by the SEC.

The Functions of the SEC

Before discussing the two acts, we must examine the functions and organizational structure of the Securities and Exchange Commission. The SEC is a quasi-judicial agency of the U.S. government that was created in 1934 to administer the 1933 Act and the 1934 Act (the 1933 Act was administered for one year by the Federal Trade Commission). Since that time, the SEC's responsibilities have broadened so that it now administers and enforces the following additional acts:

1. **The Public Utility Holding Company Act of 1935** requires geographic integration of operations and simplification of unduly cumbersome and complex capital structures of public utility holding companies. Because these objectives were accomplished many years ago through the registration process, current efforts are directed toward maintaining the status quo.
2. **The Trust Indenture Act of 1939** requires the use of a trust indenture that meets certain requirements for debt securities offered to the public to protect the rights of investors in such securities. Although a separate act, it is substantively an amendment to the 1933 Act.
3. **The Investment Company Act of 1940** regulates investment companies, that is, companies engaged primarily in the business of investing, reinvesting, owning, holding, or trading in securities. Mutual funds are the most visible investment companies. Regulation is effected through the registration process.
4. **The Investment Advisers Act of 1940** regulates the conduct of investment advisers similarly to the manner in which the conduct of brokers and dealers is regulated under the 1934 Act. Regulation is effected through the registration process.

The Organizational Structure of the SEC

The Securities and Exchange Commission is composed of five members appointed by the president, with the advice and consent of the Senate, for a five-year term, with one term expiring each year. No more than three members may be of the same political party. An extensive professional staff—comprising primarily lawyers, accountants, and financial analysts—has been organized into the following separate offices and divisions:

Offices

Administrative Law Judges
Opinions and Review
Secretary
Chief Accountant
Chief Economic Adviser
General Counsel
Executive Director
The following additional offices report to the Executive Director:
- **Consumer Affairs**
- **Public Affairs**
- **Reports and Information Services**
- **Comptroller**
- **Data Processing**
- **Administrative Services**
- **Personnel**

Operating Divisions

Corporation Finance
Enforcement
Investment Management
Market Regulation
Corporate Regulation

These offices and divisions are responsible to the commission and carry out its orders and legal responsibilities. In addition to this bureaucracy located in Washington, D.C., nine regional offices and eight branch offices are located in major cities throughout the country. The roles of the office of the Chief Accountant and the division of Corporation Finance are pertinent to this chapter.

The Division of Corporation Finance. The division of Corporation Finance reviews the registration statements and reports that registrants file with the SEC. The review determines (1) that all required financial statements and supporting schedules have been included, and (2) that such financial statements apparently have been prepared in accordance with generally accepted accounting principles, as well as the rules, regulations, and policies issued by the SEC. Because the SEC does not perform audits of registrants' financial statements, it cannot absolutely determine whether they have been prepared in accordance with generally accepted accounting principles. For this it relies on the reports of registrants' outside certified public accountants (discussed later in the chapter).

The Chief Accountant. The Chief Accountant is the commission's chief accounting officer for all accounting and auditing matters in connection with the administration of the various acts. The Chief Accountant advises the commission of accounting problems and recommends courses of action. For example, in 1986 the Chief Accountant proposed that the full cost method used by oil and gas-producing companies be abolished. Following an outcry by two cabinet members and ten senators from oil- and gas-producing states, the SEC's commissioners voted to abandon the proposal. Accordingly, the power to establish accounting principles (discussed in detail in the following section) resides with the SEC's commissioners—not with the Chief Accountant. Administratively, the Chief Accountant drafts rules and regulations governing the form and content of the financial statements that must be filed with the commission under the various acts.

The following article discusses how the states are beginning to revise their "blue sky" laws to prevent securities fraud due to the perceived reduced role of the SEC.

PERSPECTIVE

Repainting Blue Skies

Florida's is only the latest in a series of public and private inquiries to find the SEC wanting when it comes to securities fraud enforcement. Florida's effort, chaired by the state's former governor, Reubin Askew, with former SEC Commissioner John Evans as vice chairman, may be among the more prestigious. Its conclusions, however, sound all too familiar. "The Securities & Exchange Commission is not doing the same job it used to do, and the states will have to step up their own enforcement," says Evans.

Florida, though long a happy hunting ground for investment con men, is not alone in questioning the quality of federal protection. Both New Jersey and Utah have recently installed stronger state securities statutes and beefed up enforcement. Every state has some form of so-called blue sky law named after one of the first, in Kansas in 1911, that was supposed to protect citizens against schemes having "no more basis than so many feet of blue sky."

But the new laws, like legislation proposed by the Florida task force, reflect a growing concern by the states and others that the SEC, because of budgetary constraints, staff cutbacks and a narrowing of the agency's role under SEC Chairman John Shad, does not do the job. This concern is only aggravated by booming stock markets, an explosion of new public securities offerings and the well-publicized flood of vastly more complicated securities products and markets.

Not surprisingly, Chairman Shad has publicly denied that the SEC's enforcement is lagging. But statistics from the agency illustrate its problems. Over the last ten years, while the SEC staff has declined slightly, the number of registered broker/dealers increased from 3,500 to 11,400, and the number of registered investment advisers went from 3,400 to 11,100. Moreover, last year the SEC received 31,200 complaints from the public, compared with 9,500 in 1975. Meanwhile, the commission in 1985 brought 265 cases, vs. 316 in 1975.

To be sure, many of the states themselves have been no great shakes in this area. Their regulatory agencies, when they exist at all, are frequently little more than skeletal shadows without meaningful budgets or staff. Chairman Shad recently told Congress that while the 50 states collected some $120 million in

(continued)

1985 through registration and other securities-related fees, they spent only $40 million on regulation (vs. an SEC budget of $106 million).

In New Jersey, as in other states, things may be changing. The legislature, prompted by a proliferation of boiler room scams, is increasing the staff of the state securities department from 11 to some 35 and the department's budget from under $300,000 to an expected $3 million this year. Most federally registered securities sold to New Jersey citizens now must be filed with the state bureau for review. The state also now requires full disclosure in new-offering papers of anyone associated with that offering who has ever had a record of securities fraud or other major violations of state or federal laws. By comparison, the SEC rules require such disclosure of violations only for the past five years.

Florida is hoping to go even further by setting up a so-called merit review of all federally registered securities that go public at $5 or less and are not traded in a national market system. Though 36 states now have them in one form or another, merit reviews are controversial because they usually contain some vague standards and allow state regulators, more or less subjectively, to judge whether a stock can be sold in their states.

The Securities Industry Association, Wall Street's industry group, and some members of the Florida Bar Association are expected to lobby against Florida's merit proposal and argue that federal disclosure laws provide investors with sufficient protection.

Despite the controversy, the fact that merit is even being considered is a clear indication of the new skepticism being directed at the SEC. "The pendulum definitely is swinging the other way," says former Massachusetts securities director Michael Unger. Indeed, in the past year attempts to restrict or overturn merit laws have been defeated in Texas and Washington State.

Whether the states really are up to the task of protecting their citizens from securities fraud remains to be seen. So many investment scams simply prey on the greed and stupidity of their victims, and it's fair to ask if any law can protect citizens from their own avarice and ignorance. At the same time, though, it is clear that many states are worried that budget restrictions at the SEC are leaving the public unnecessarily exposed. And in those states, taxpayers will foot the bill, one way or the other.

Source: Richard L. Stern, "Repainting Blue Skies," *Forbes*, May 5, 1986, p. 66.

THE ROLE OF THE SEC IN RELATION TO THE FASB

The Statutory Authority of the SEC

Under the 1933 Act and the 1934 Act, the SEC has the power to do the following:

1. Adopt, amend, and rescind rules and regulations as necessary to carry out the provisions of these Acts.

2. Prescribe the form or forms on which required information is filed with the SEC.
3. Prescribe the accounting methods to be followed in the financial statements filed with the SEC.
4. Prescribe the items or details to be shown in the financial statements filed with the SEC.

In item 3, the SEC has the statutory authority to prescribe accounting principles for companies falling under its jurisdiction. Recognizing the expertise and substantial resources of the public accounting profession, however, the SEC has usually looked to the accounting profession's standard-setting bodies to establish and improve accounting and reporting standards. When the Financial Accounting Standards Board (FASB) was established in 1973, for example, the SEC specifically announced that

> principles, standards and practices promulgated by the FASB in its Statements and Interpretations will be considered by the Commission as having substantial authoritative support and those contrary to such FASB promulgations will be considered to have no such support.[1]

This policy of looking to the private sector in establishing and improving standards is by no means an abdication of its responsibilities or authority. When the SEC has concluded that such bodies were moving too slowly or in the wrong direction, it has not hesitated to take one of the following courses of action:

1. Establish its own additional financial reporting requirements (calling for additional disclosures).
2. Impose a moratorium on accounting practices.
3. Overrule a pronouncement of the FASB.

Concerning items 1 and 2, in most instances the SEC has later rescinded its own action as a result of the passage of new or revised accounting principles or disclosure requirements by the profession's standard-setting bodies. The following two paragraphs contain examples of the most recent major actions of the SEC along these lines.

Examples of Additional Disclosures Required. The SEC imposed line-of-business disclosure requirements long before the 1976 issuance of *FASB Statement No. 14,* "Financial Reporting for Segments of a Business Enterprise." Shortly after this statement was issued, the SEC modified its previous line-of-business disclosure requirements to conform in most respects with the requirements of *FASB Statement No. 14.* In 1976, the SEC required certain large companies to disclose replacement cost data (*Account-*

[1] *Accounting Series Release No. 150,* "Statement of Policy on the Establishment and Improvement of Accounting Principles and Standards" (Washington, D.C.: Securities and Exchange Commission), 1973. In April 1982, *Accounting Series Release No. 150* was codified in *SEC Financial Reporting Release No. 1,* Section 101.

ing Series Release No. 190). After *FASB Statement No. 33*, "Financial Reporting and Changing Prices," was issued in 1979, the SEC rescinded its requirements in this area.

Examples of Prohibiting Accounting Practices. In 1974, the SEC imposed a moratorium on the capitalization of interest *(Accounting Series Release No. 163)*. It had noted with concern an increase in the number of companies changing their accounting methods to a policy of capitalizing interest cost. Because no authoritative statement on this subject existed at that time (except for two specific industries), this action stopped a developing trend until the FASB could deal with the issue. In 1979, after the FASB issued *FASB Statement No. 34*, "Capitalization of Interest Cost," the SEC rescinded its moratorium. In another action, in 1983 the SEC moved to halt the spread of a controversial accounting method that more than a dozen computer software companies were using to increase their earnings. The SEC had noticed a trend in the industry toward capitalization without adequate criteria—the accounting standards and related interpretation that existed then were somewhat fuzzy. Therefore, the SEC imposed a moratorium on the capitalization of software development costs for companies that had not publicly disclosed the practice of capitalizing those costs prior to April 14, 1983 (Financial Reporting Release No. 12). In 1985, after the FASB issued *FASB Statement No. 86*, "Accounting for the Costs of Computer Software to be Sold, Leased, or Otherwise Marketed," the SEC rescinded its moratorium.

Overruling the FASB. Only once has the SEC overruled a pronouncement of the FASB. This ruling occurred in 1978 when the SEC rejected the standards set forth in *FASB Statement No. 19*, "Financial Accounting and Reporting for Oil and Gas Producing Companies." The SEC favored developing a new system of "reserve recognition accounting" (RRA). The conflict between the requirements of *FASB Statement No. 19* and those of the SEC (as set forth in *Accounting Series Release No. 253*) resulted in an untenable situation. (Privately owned companies were subject to *FASB Statement No. 19* and publicly owned companies were subject to *ASR No. 253*. Lack of comparability resulted.) Accordingly, the FASB voluntarily (and to be practical) issued *FASB Statement No. 25*, which suspended the effective dates of most requirements in *FASB Statement No. 19*. In 1981, the SEC abandoned its effort to develop RRA and announced it would support FASB's efforts to develop disclosure requirements for oil and gas producers. In 1982, the FASB issued *FASB Statement No. 69*, "Disclosures about Oil and Gas Producing Activities," which amended *FASB Statements No. 19* and *No. 25*. Shortly thereafter, the SEC amended its disclosure requirements for oil and gas producers to require compliance with the provisions of *FASB Statement No. 69*.

Current Working Relationship. The Securities and Exchange Commission and the FASB now try to maintain a close working relationship to prevent any future conflicts. FASB members meet with the SEC's commissioners on a regular basis to exchange information on the status of projects and plans, and to discuss other matters of mutual interest. Members of the Chief Accountant's staff are responsible for keeping track of the development of specific FASB technical projects. SEC staff members participate in advisory task force meetings on those projects and frequently observe FASB meetings. When the SEC proposes changes to its rules and regulations, the FASB has occasionally expressed its views on such proposals. In summary, both organizations strive for a climate of mutual cooperation and no surprises.

SEC Involvement in the FASB's Emerging Issues Task Force. In 1984, the FASB responded to criticism that its lengthy due-process procedures were not dealing with emerging issues on a timely basis by forming the "emerging issues task force." The task force is comprised of representatives of eleven certified public accounting firms, (including senior technical partners from each of the eight largest accounting firms), four major companies, the Chief Accountant, and the FASB. The task force meets every six weeks in an open meeting. Since its inception it has debated more than 140 accounting issues. Designed to deal promptly with areas in which no standards exist, its consensus views have become generally accepted accounting principles for publicly owned companies even though the task force has no formal authority. This is primarily because the Chief Accountant has taken the position that the conclusions of the task force represent the best thinking on areas for which there are no specific standards. As a result, the SEC challenges any registrant's accounting practices that differ from the consensus views of the task force.

The Open Door Policy. The SEC encourages registrants to bring novel accounting treatments and new types of accounting transactions to its attention for immediate resolution before reporting the accounting effects to stockholders. Unfortunately, many registrants do not avail themselves of this opportunity (possibly fearing that the answer will be no). Instead, they try to slip liberal accounting practices and interpretations past the SEC—hoping that it will not notice these practices when making its reviews—and placing themselves in the position of having enforcement actions brought against them.

ENFORCEMENT ROLE

Actions against Registrants

The Securities and Exchange Commission does not hesitate to question the accounting and reporting practices of the financial statements filed with it, regardless of whether a registrant's outside auditors concur with the registrant's accounting treatment. Unlike the FASB, the SEC can order companies to revise their financial statements if it concludes that a particular accounting treatment is not proper. In this respect, the SEC pays great attention to assuring that substance prevails over form. Countless instances have occurred in which the SEC has cast aside a registrant's literal interpretation of generally accepted accounting principles that the SEC deemed superficial and unreflective of the economics. Some of the more notable and recent such actions are as follows:

1. Financial Corp. of America had to restate its net income for the first half of 1984 to a loss of $79.9 million from the previously reported profit of $73.3 million. The SEC required the company to change its method of accounting for its reverse repurchase agreement transactions.
2. BankAmerica Corp. had to reclassify as an extraordinary item a $30.8 million gain from a debt-equity exchange that it previously reported as part of operating income.
3. Aetna Life & Casualty Co. was prohibited from giving tax effects to items through the use of the operating loss carryforward provisions of *APB Opinion No. 11*.
4. Alexander and Alexander Services, Inc., had to report as an extraordinary loss an unanticipated $40 million it proposed to add to goodwill and amortize over 40 years. The registrant had purchased a target company and shortly after the consummation discovered that the acquired company's liabilities had been understated by $40 million.
5. Several financial institutions were ordered to reduce their goodwill amortization lives from 40 years to 25 years or less because of the SEC's perception that artificial income was being reported in the use of 40 years for goodwill and a much shorter life for loan discounts (the amortization of which increased income). (The FASB subsequently addressed the issue in *FASB Statement No. 72*, "Accounting for Certain Acquisitions of Banks or Thrift Institutions," with similar conclusions.)
6. Numerous companies having contractual arrangements with their research and development limited partnerships were required to recognize a liability for the eventual acquisition of the R&D product and charge a like amount to income as R&D expense. (The FASB later addressed the issue in *FASB Statement No. 68*, "Research and Development Arrangements" with similar conclusions concerning if and when a liability should be recognized.)
7. Several companies that formed "nonsubsidiary subsidiaries" (discussed in Chapter 3) to avoid recognition of expenses or losses in their statements during the early years of the affiliates' operations were ordered to consolidate such companies.

During economically troubled times, the SEC usually scrutinizes financial reports closely, because fraudulent and deceptive practices are much more likely when companies attempt to conceal their financial difficulties. Overall, the SEC is given high marks and has won the reputation as a tough police officer of corporate conduct.

Disciplinary Actions against Auditors

If the SEC finds that a registrant's certified public accountants are not qualified, lack integrity, have engaged in unethical or improper professional conduct, or have willfully violated or aided and abetted the violation of any provision of the federal securities laws or rules thereunder, the SEC is empowered to take the following steps:

1. Bar the auditor(s) from practicing before the SEC either permanently or for a specified period of time.
2. Bar the auditor(s) from accepting new publicly owned companies as clients for a stipulated period of time.
3. Censure the auditor(s).
4. Require the auditor(s) to submit to a peer review.
5. Recommend criminal proceedings against the auditor(s) (as the SEC did in the well-publicized Continental Vending case and the National Student Marketing case of the early 1970s in which partners of two large accounting firms were convicted and sent to prison).

SEC PROMULGATIONS

To carry out its responsibilities, the SEC issues various rules, regulations (a group of rules), releases, and staff accounting bulletins, and prescribes certain forms that companies must use in filing registration statements and reports. The 1933 Act and the 1934 Act have their own regulations, rules, releases, and forms. In addition, certain regulations and releases apply to both the 1933 Act and the 1934 Act. The Staff Accounting Bulletins also apply to both acts. An understanding of all of these items is essential to comply with the registration and reporting requirements of these acts.

The General Rules and Regulations, Forms, and Releases

General Rules and Regulations. The Securities Act of 1933 is divided into 26 sections, and the Securities Exchange Act of 1934 is divided into 35 sections. The SEC has adopted rules pertaining to the 1933 Act, which are assigned three-digit numbers starting with 100. The rules are grouped into various categories, most of which are designated *regulations.* For example, Rules 400–494 make up Regulation C, which deals with the mechanics of registering securities with the SEC.

Rules and regulations pertaining to the 1934 Act are assigned numbers that correspond to the section of the act to which they relate. The major sections are referred to as *regulations,* and the detailed rules within each regulation are *rules.* For example, Section 10(b) of the act is called Regulation 10B, and the individual rules within that section are referred to as Rule 10b-1 through Rule 10b-17.

Forms. The *forms* are enumerations of the form and content of the information included in registration statements and reports. (They are not blank forms to be filled out, as the term is used by the Internal Revenue Service and other taxing authorities.) Each act has its own forms.

Releases. *Releases* are announcements pertaining to the various rules, regulations, and forms. Releases are numbered sequentially as issued. To date, approximately 6,700 releases have been issued under the 1933 Act and approximately 24,000 under the 1934 Act. A release is formally designated as follows: Securities Act of 1933, Release No. 5307. A release is informally referred to simply as Release 33-5307, for example, under the 1933 Act, and Release 34-9310, for example, under the 1934 Act. Some SEC releases under the 1934 Act also apply under the 1933 Act. In these cases, a release is assigned a number under the 1933 Act and a different number under the 1934 Act. Except for Interpretative Releases, they are subject to the Administrative Procedures Act and must be exposed for public comment before becoming effective. The primary matters to which these releases pertain are as follows:

1. **Proposals to amend or adopt new rules and forms.** Changes are often necessary to keep up with the times. In some instances, better ways of disclosure are found. For example, to improve the readability of information provided to investors, the SEC issued Release 33-5164, which proposed certain amendments to Rules 425A and 426 of the Securities Act of 1933.

   Interested companies and certified public accountants usually make comments and suggestions to the SEC. The final adopted amendment or new rule or form probably reflects many of these comments and suggestions. Sometimes a proposed item is not adopted for various reasons.
2. **Adoption of amendments or new rules and forms.** To continue with the preceding example, the proposals contained in Release 33-5164 were revised to reflect the comments and suggestions that the SEC considered significant and were subsequently adopted in Release 33-5278.

Regulation S-K and Regulation S-X

All nonfinancial disclosure requirements are contained in Regulation S-K. All financial disclosure requirements are contained in Regulation S-X. Each form under the 1933 Act and the 1934 Act specifies the disclosures contained in Regulations S-K and S-X that are to be made for that form.

Regulation S-K (Nonfinancial Statement Disclosure Requirements). The major disclosure requirements contained in Regulation S-K deal with (1) a description of the company's business; (2) a description of the company's properties; (3) a description of the company's legal proceedings; (4) selected financial data for the last five years (including sales, income from continuing operations, cash dividends per common share, total assets, and long-term obligations); (5) supplementary financial information (quarterly financial data and information on the effects of changing prices); (6) information about the company's directors and management (including management remuneration); and (7) management's discussion and analysis (commonly referred to as the "MDA") of financial condition and results of operations.

Regulation S-X (Financial Statement Disclosure Requirements). Regulation S-X, which accountants deal with most often, not only lists the **specific financial statements** that must be filed under all Acts administered by the SEC but also details the **form and content of such financial statements.** The term **"financial statements"** as used in this regulation includes all notes to the financial statements and all related financial statement supporting schedules. The financial statements filed under Regulation S-X are (1) audited balance sheets as of the end of the two most recent fiscal years, and (2) audited statements of income and changes in financial position for the three fiscal years preceding the date of the most recent audited balance sheet being filed. (Variations from these requirements are permitted for certain specified filings.) In addition, the regulation contains requirements for filing interim financial statements. (Regulation S-X is discussed in more detail later in the chapter.)

Financial Reporting Releases

The Financial Reporting Releases (FRRs), numbered sequentially, pertain solely to accounting matters. Nearly 30 Financial Reporting Releases have been issued. Prior to 1982, such accounting matters (as well as enforcement matters) were dealt with in the now discontinued Accounting Series Releases (of which 307 had been issued). *Financial Reporting Release No. 1* is the codification of the earlier releases that had continuing relevance to financial reporting. This codification (with its topical index) makes thousands of pages of material available in a concise and much more accessible format. These releases pertain to the following major areas of accounting:

1. **Adoption of amendment or revision of Regulation S-X.** Many FRRs include financial reporting requirements that go beyond the pronouncements of the FASB and its predecessor organizations. In addition to setting forth an amendment or revision to Regulation S-X, such FRRs also discuss the purpose of the new reporting requirements and comments received in response to the SEC's proposed revisions to Regulation S-X (including the SEC's reaction to those comments). In some cases, an FRR contains exhibits and examples to assist companies in understanding and complying with the new reporting requirements of Regulation S-X.

   Many FRRs have been rescinded as a result of the issuance of subsequent accounting pronouncements. However, the SEC rescinds such requirements only when it concurs with an accounting pronouncement.

2. **Policy/interpretive statements regarding particular accounting areas.** *Accounting Series Release Nos. 130, 135, 146,* and *146A* (now part of *FRR No. 1*), for example, deal with how the SEC interprets certain provisions of *APB Opinion No. 16*, "Accounting for Business Combinations." Accountants must be familiar with such releases in addition to the provisions of the professional pronouncements. (Recall that *Accounting Series Release Nos. 146* and *146A* were discussed in Chapter 6 in connection with pooling of interests accounting.)

Accounting and Auditing Enforcement Releases

Accounting and Auditing Enforcement Releases (AAERs) announce accounting and auditing matters related to the SEC's enforcement activities. Because of their nature, AAERs are not codified.

Staff Accounting Bulletins

The Staff Accounting Bulletins (SABs) represent interpretations and practices followed by certain departments of the SEC that are responsible for reviewing the disclosure requirements of the federal securities laws. These bulletins do not constitute official rules or regulations, nor do they have the official approval of the SEC. The bulletins essentially accomplish on an informal basis what otherwise would be dealt with formally through releases. Much of the subject matter of the bulletins arises from specific questions raised by registrants. The dissemination of answers to these questions in this manner rather than solely to the company making an inquiry avoids needless repetition of inquiries pertaining to the same subject. Nearly 70 SABs have been issued to date. In 1981, the staff codified by topic all bulletins issued to date in *Staff Accounting Bulletin No. 40*, making the SABs substantially more easy to use. (Recall from Chapter 3 that push-down accounting was implemented as a result of the issuance of *Staff Accounting Bulletin No. 54.*)

THE SECURITIES ACT OF 1933

Registration

The Securities Act of 1933 prohibits sales of, or offers to sell, securities to the public (in interstate commerce or through the use of the mails) by an **issuer** or an underwriter unless the securities have been registered with the SEC. Certain exemptions to this prohibition are discussed later in the chapter. A **security** is defined broadly as:

> any note, stock, treasury stock, bond, debenture, evidence of indebtedness, certificate of interest or participation in any profit-sharing agreement, . . . transferable share, investment contract, voting trust certificate, . . . or in general any interest or instrument commonly known as a security . . . .

To avoid having a technical loophole in the law, the prohibition also applies to underwriters. An **underwriter** is defined as:

> any person who has purchased from an issuer with a view to, or offers or sells for an issuer in connection with, the distribution of any security, or participates [directly or indirectly]... in any such undertaking....

It is important at this point to understand that registration under the 1933 Act refers only to the **actual quantity of securities being registered** and not the registration of an **entire class of securities.** This is just the opposite of the 1934 Act, which is discussed in detail later in the chapter.

The Essence of Registration. **Registration** of a security offering under the 1933 Act begins with the filing of specified financial and nonfinancial information with the SEC using the appropriate form. The appropriate SEC form in a particular case is a legal determination. All specified financial and nonfinancial information submitted as set forth in the appropriate form is called a **registration statement.** The SEC examines the registration statement and almost always issues a **letter of comments** (commonly referred to as a **deficiency letter**). The registrant must respond to this letter of comments to the SEC's satisfaction before it may sell the securities to the public. Responding to a letter of comments usually involves a combination of direct written responses to the SEC in a letter, revision of certain information in the registration statement, and addition of information to the statement. The revised registration statement, called an **amended registration statement,** is filed with the SEC for reexamination. When the SEC is satisfied that the items in its letter of comments have been appropriately addressed, it permits the amended registration statement to become "effective," and the securities being offered are deemed registered under the 1933 Act and may be sold to the public.

Prospectuses. Prospective investors in a security being registered with the SEC under the 1933 Act must be furnished a **prospectus.** The registration statement is divided into two basic parts:

- Part I Information required to be included in the prospectus.
- Part II Information not required to be included in the prospectus.

Part I is the major part of the registration statement. It includes all required financial statements and related notes (according to the provisions of Regulation S-X), as well as reports by the registrant's auditors on financial statements that must have been audited. Part I also includes, among other things, such nonfinancial information as an extensive description of the registrant's business (including risk factors associated with the purchase of the securities offered) and properties, an explanation of how the proceeds are to be used, a description of any current legal proceedings, the names of the registrant's directors and officers (including their backgrounds), and the amount of their remuneration. The financial and nonfinancial disclosures included in the prospectus should provide potential investors with an adequate basis for deciding whether to invest in the securities offered. Preliminary prospectuses, which may be distributed to potential investors before the effective date, are commonly referred to as "red herrings" because certain information on the cover is printed in red ink.

Part II of the registration statement lists all exhibits filed with the registration statement and includes specified financial statement supporting schedules and other miscellaneous information not deemed necessary for distribution to potential investors.

Regulation C. Regulation C deals with the mechanics of registering securities under the 1933 Act. A company's legal counsel usually assumes responsibility for ensuring that the registration statement complies with Regulation C.

Unlawful Representations Relating to Registration Statements. The 1933 Act expressly states the responsibility of the SEC with respect to its examination of registration statements:

> Neither the fact that the registration statement for a security has been filed or is in effect . . . shall be deemed a finding by the Commission that the registration statement is true and accurate on its face or that it does not contain an untrue statement of fact or omit a material fact, or be held to mean that the Commission has in any way passed upon the merits of, or given approval to, such security. It shall be unlawful to make, or cause to be made, to any prospective purchaser any representation contrary to the foregoing provisions of this section [Section 23].

A statement to this effect must be made on the cover page of each prospectus. The SEC cannot evaluate the investment quality of the securities offered. This contrasts sharply with the blue sky laws of many states, which allow state regulatory commissions to prohibit the sale of securities considered potentially fraudulent, dangerously speculative, or lacking sufficient investment quality.

Exemptions from Registration

Certain types of securities and securities transactions, which have no practical need for registration or for which the benefits of registration are too remote, are exempt from the registration requirements. The major categories of exemptions are discussed below.

Regulation A Offerings. Regulation A (Rules 251–263 of the 1933 Act) pertains to offerings whose total amount, together with other exempt offerings within a one-year period, does not exceed $1,500,000. If the total offering price is more than $100,000, however, a Regulation A Offering Statement (containing specified financial and nonfinancial information) must be filed with a regional or branch office of the SEC for examination. Furthermore, an offering circular (Part II of the Offering Statement) must be furnished to prospective purchasers.

Regulation D Offerings. Regulation D (Rules 501–506 of the 1933 act) was adopted in 1982 to facilitate the capital-raising process for small companies. The amount of offerings exempted within a twelve-month period is $500,000 or $5,000,000, depending on the type of company and whether it is subject to the continuous reporting requirements of the SEC. Under Regulation D, only a notice of the sale must be filed with the SEC (on Form D).

Private Offerings. The 1933 Act exempts "transactions by an issuer not involving a public offering [Section 4(2)]." Such transactions are also commonly referred to as **private placements.** This exemption is available for offerings to persons (individuals, partnerships, and corporations) having access to substantially the same information concerning the issuer that registration would provide and who can fend for themselves.[2] The fundamental consideration in determining whether this exemption applies is the potential investor's level of sophistication and such investor's access to information about the issuer. Generally, sophisticated investors have either sufficient economic power or a family or employment relationship that enables them to obtain adequate information from the issuer for purposes of evaluating the merits and risks of the investment. Private offerings are commonly made to venture capital firms and insurance companies. Because the security is not sold through a public offering, it is referred to as a **restricted security.** The restrictions are discussed in the following exemption category.

Transactions by Individual Investors. The 1933 Act exempts "transactions by any person other than an issuer, underwriter or dealer [Section 4(1)]." This section was intended to exempt only transactions between individual investors with respect to securities already issued and not distributions by issuers or acts of other individuals who engage in steps necessary to such distributions.[3] Investors who acquire an issuer's securities by means that do not involve a public offering (such as a private offering) may resell the securities to the public other than through registration only if certain conditions are met. Otherwise, the sale is considered a distribution of securities to the public because the investor is acting as a conduit for sale to the public on behalf of the issuer—that is, as an underwriter. In

[2] *SEC* v. *Ralston Purina Co.*, 346 U.S. 119 (1953).
[3] *SEC* v. *Chinese Consol. Benev. Ass'n.*, 120 F. 2d 738 (2nd. Cir., 1941). *Certiorari* denied, 314 U.S. 618.

such cases, the resale of the security to the public must be registered. Rule 144 sets forth conditions that must be satisfied in order to resell restricted securities to the public other than through registration. This rule emphasizes that (1) the investor must have paid for and held the security for a reasonable period of time (a minimum of two to four years, depending on the category of the issuer), and (2) adequate current public information with respect to the issuer of the securities must be available.

Strictly Intrastate Issues. For intrastate issues, the security must be offered and sold only to the residents of the state in which the corporate issuer is incorporated and doing business [Section 3(11)].

Commercial Paper. This category, commercial paper, pertains to a borrowing "which arises out of a current transaction or the proceeds of which have been or are able to be used for current transactions, and which has a maturity at the time of issuance of not exceeding nine months... [Section 3(3)]." This category is a practical necessity; an example is a bank borrowing under a 90-day note.

Securities of Governments and Banks. According to Section 3(2), the governmental category of securities includes federal, state, and local governmental units (including municipalities) and agencies thereof.

Whether or not a security offering or transaction is exempt from registration under the 1933 Act is strictly a legal and factual determination and outside the expertise of accountants.

Forms Used in Registration

The Securities and Exchange Commission has devised numerous forms to deal with the diverse companies (and their maturity) seeking to offer securities to the public. Although the general contents of a registration statement have already been described, each form has its own detailed table of contents and related instructions. (Recall that the financial statement requirements for these forms are set forth in Regulation S-X.) Two categories of forms are used under the 1933 Act: general forms and special forms.

General Forms. The SEC has three **general forms:** S-1, S-2, and S-3. These three forms are set up on a tier system based on the issuer's following in the stock market. Although all three forms basically require the same information to be furnished to potential investors, the method of furnishing that information varies. Form S-1, the most widely used of the forms, is required when one of the special forms is not authorized or prescribed, or when a company eligible to use Form S-2 or S-3 chooses to use Form S-1 instead. Basically, Form S-1 is used by new registrants and by companies that are already registered under the 1934 Act but have been filing reports with the SEC for less than 36 months. All financial and nonfinancial disclosures must be included in the prospectus. (The detailed table of contents to Form S-1 appears in the appendix to this chapter.)

To be eligible to use Forms S-2 and S-3, a company must have been subject to the reporting requirements of the 1934 Act for at least 36 months and satisfy other conditions. Form S-3 is used by large companies having a wide following in the stock market; accordingly, such firms must meet an additional requirement based on annual trading volume and outstanding voting stock. The advantage to these forms is time and effort; that is, financial and nonfinancial information need not be included in the prospectus—it may simply be incorporated by reference to reports already filed with the SEC under the 1934 Act. Thus, these forms are effectively a simplified Form S-1.

Special Forms. The SEC has 12 **special forms,** five of which are commonly used:

1. **Form S-4,** for registration of securities issued in connection with most business combinations and reofferings. (Substantial information may be incorporated by reference.)
2. **Form S-8,** for securities offered to employees pursuant to employee benefit plans, such as stock option plans.
3. **Form S-11,** applicable to real estate investment trusts and real estate companies.
4. **Form S-15,** for securities issued in certain business combinations (involving a large company and a much smaller company). This streamlined form requires only an abbreviated prospectus.
5. **Form S-18,** for offerings up to $7.5 million. This form gives small initial registrants (including limited partnerships) a fast and simple method of raising capital in public markets because (1) the disclosure requirements are less extensive than in Form S-1, and (2) the filing may be made at an SEC regional office rather than in Washington, D.C.

Legal Liability for Filing a False Registration Statement

Section 6 of the Securities Act of 1933 requires that the registration statement be signed by the following persons:

1. The principal executive officer or officers.
2. The principal financial officer.
3. The controller or principal accounting officer.
4. The majority of the board of directors or persons performing similar functions.

The 1933 Act sets forth the following civil liabilities for a false registration:

> In case any part of the registration statement, when such part became effective, contained an untrue statement of a material fact or omitted to state a material fact required to be stated therein or necessary to make the statements therein not misleading, any person acquiring such security (unless it is proved that at the time of such acquisition he knew of such untruth or omission) may . . . sue [for recovery of losses suffered]—
>
> 1. every person who signed the registration statement;
> 2. every person who was a director of . . . the issuer . . . ;
> 3. every person who, with his consent, is named in the registration statement as being or about to become a director . . . ;
> 4. every accountant, engineer, appraiser, or any person whose profession gives authority to a statement made by him, who has with his consent been named as having prepared or certified any part of the registration statement, . . . with respect to the statement in such registration statement, report, or valuation, which purports to have been prepared or certified by him;
> 5. every underwriter with respect to such security [Section 11].

In addition to these civil proceedings whereby a purchaser may recover damages suffered, Section 24 of the 1933 Act provides for criminal penalties (monetary fines and imprisonment) if the untrue statement of a material fact or omission thereof was "willful."

Shareholders Often Sue if Stock Prices Fall. Countless instances have occurred in which stock prices have substantially declined from the offering price within six to twelve months of the offering. In such cases, it is common for disgruntled stockholders to file class-action lawsuits alleging that unfavorable information was purposely omitted from the prospectus. (Such information could include known problems in developing anticipated new products, or shipping and order delays.) In fact, many attorneys actively search out investors who have sustained losses on public offerings, hoping to represent them in such lawsuits, which have a high settlement potential.

Ramifications to Outside Auditors. This section of the 1933 Act has special significance to certified public accountants of companies registering securities. When securities are not registered, **gross negligence** must be proved for a company's certified public accountants to be held liable for civil damages. When a company registers securities under the 1933 Act, however, the focal point is not whether the outside auditors were grossly negligent in the performance of their duties. Instead, the issue is merely whether or not the financial statements and related notes in the registration statement **contained an untrue statement of a material fact or omitted a material fact.** Thus, the 1933 Act imposes an additional potential liability on the certified public accountants of companies registering securities. However, certain defenses are available to the outside auditors under Section 11 of the 1933 Act that relate to their having made a "reasonable investigation" and having "reasonable grounds for belief."

THE SECURITIES EXCHANGE ACT OF 1934

The Securities Exchange Act of 1934, which deals with the trading in (exchange of) securities, has two broad purposes:

1. To require publicly held companies to disclose on a continual basis current information to holders and prospective purchasers of their securities comparable to the information that must be disclosed in a registration statement under the 1933 Act. In this respect, the 1934 Act supplements the 1933 Act, which applies only to public offerings of securities and not to subsequent trading in such securities.
2. To regulate the public trading markets (organized exchanges and over-the-counter markets) and the broker-dealers who operate in such markets.

Major Provisions of the 1934 Act

Unlike the 1933 Act, which is a unified piece of legislation, the 1934 Act covers a wide range of areas. Its major provisions are discussed in the following paragraphs.

Registration of Securities Exchanges. Securities exchanges (such as the New York Stock Exchange) must be registered with the SEC, which has supervisory control over them.

Registration of Securities on Securities Exchanges. Securities exchanges cannot effect transactions in any security unless that security is registered on the exchange. The registration process involves filing a registration statement on Form 10 (or another appropriate form) with the securities exchange and with the SEC. Form 10 requires information comparable to that required in Form S-1 under the 1933 Act. A security that is traded on a securities exchange is referred to as a "listed" security. Companies having securities registered on a securities exchange are referred to as Section 12(b) companies.

Registration of Over-the-counter Securities. The *over-the-counter* market encompasses all securities transactions that do not take place on organized securities exchanges. The 1934 Act was amended in 1964 to require registration of securities traded in the over-the-counter market that meet certain size tests. Companies that have total assets exceeding $3 million *and* a class of equity security with 500 or more stockholders must register such security with the SEC by filing a registration statement (usually

Form 10). Securities traded in the over-the-counter market are referred to as "unlisted" securities. Companies meeting these tests are referred to as Section 12(g) companies. Once a company meets these size tests, it is subject to all the requirements of the 1934 Act that are imposed on listed companies.

A Section 12(g) company may deregister when it has (1) less than 500 shareholders for the class of equity security and total assets of less than $5 million at the end of each of its last three fiscal years; or (2) fewer than 300 shareholders.

Filing of Periodic and Other Reports. Issuers of securities that must be registered under the 1934 Act must file annual and quarterly reports with the SEC containing specified financial and nonfinancial information. In addition, reports describing specified important events must be filed promptly after they occur. These periodic reports are discussed in detail on pages 700–701.

Proxy Regulations. For companies subject to the registration requirements of the 1934 Act, the SEC is authorized to prescribe regulations and rules governing the solicitation of proxies by management from shareholders regarding matters to be voted on by shareholders. A **proxy** is merely a document empowering one person to vote for another. Because all shareholders do not normally attend annual or special shareholders' meetings, companies typically request each shareholder to sign a proxy empowering management to vote either as the shareholder indicates or in accordance with the recommendations of management. When soliciting proxies, a **proxy statement** containing information specified by the SEC must be furnished to the stockholders. Furthermore, preliminary proxy material must be filed with the SEC for review at least ten days before the proposed mailing date.

Antifraud and Insider Trading Provisions. Section 10 of the 1934 Act makes it unlawful for any person directly or indirectly to use deceptive or fraudulent practices or to misstate or omit any material fact in connection with the purchase or sale of a security. Criminal fines up to $100,000 can be imposed. Persons suffering losses as a result of fraud are entitled to sue for recovery of actual losses.

Corporate "insiders" are prohibited from trading in a corporation's securities using material information that has not been disseminated to the public. Inside traders can be forced to give up their profits and be fined up to three times their profits. Also, criminal fines of $100,000 can be imposed. An **insider** is any person who has material nonpublic information, including any officer or director or any person who obtains such information from others. In addition, under the "short-swing profit" rule in Section 16(b), any profit realized from any purchase and sale (or from any sale and purchase) of any such issuer's equity security within any period of less than six months by certain persons accrues to the issuer and is recoverable by the issuer, with certain exceptions. These certain persons are officers, directors, or any person who is the beneficial owner of more than 10% of any security that is registered under the 1934 Act. Under Section 16(a), officers, directors, and such 10% security holders must report to the SEC any changes in their beneficial ownership of registered securities.

The effect of fraud and insider trading on public confidence in the stock market is the subject of the following article.

PERSPECTIVE

Insider Trading: Backlash Is the Biggest Danger

The headline is the sort you might see blaring from the *National Enquirer* at supermarket checkout counters. In fact, it recently ran on the front page of *The New York Times*. It describes a 24-year-old man accused of putting rat poison in Contac capsules and buying options to sell the stock, hoping for a price decline.

The story broke not long after Dennis B. Levine, 33, a managing director at Drexel Burnham Lambert Inc., was accused of insider trading. A few weeks later, five other people, ages 23 to 27, were indicted for insider trading. One headline said: "Young, Eager and Indicted."

Although each case differs and each must be judged independently, the people involved are all relatively young—and most got on the fast track armed with MBA or law degrees from prestigious colleges. If the charges against them stand up in court, they share another characteristic: greed that blinded them to right and wrong.

To many, this cluster of criminal cases is simply additional evidence that the yuppie generation is callow, avaricious, materialistic, and amoral. The yuppie backlash has been under way for some time. But now the backlash threatens serious consequences.

The business schools that churn out tens of thousands of MBAs every year are beginning to worry about the ethical hollowness of many of their graduates. A yuppie backlash could easily translate into an MBA backlash. "We clearly can produce technical whiz kids. But are we doing enough to teach ethical values in the context of the business environment?" asks Kenneth E. Goodpaster who teaches "Ethical Aspects of Corporate Policy" at Harvard business school.

The most dangerous development, however, might be a public backlash against investment bankers and Wall Street itself. Anything that harms the distribution of capital in the economy is a matter of concern far beyond snide intergenerational sniping.

To judge by some public comments, many on Wall Street regard insider trading as nothing more serious than exceeding the 55-mph speed limit—a law that nobody really believes in or follows. There is even a modest body of legitimate academic opinion that supports the notion that, to make the markets

(continued)

more efficient, insider trading should be legal anyhow. The faster the information gets into the public domain, the argument goes, the smoother the market process.

Efficiency is certainly to be desired, but the myopia of many on Wall Street reeks of political naivete. Beyond the canyons of Wall Street, fairness is what people want from the stock market. As long as people believe they have an even shot at getting rich—as long as a level playing field exists—the public will put up with nearly anything, including ostentatious displays of wealth by Wall Street hotshots.

Insider trading challenges this sense of fairness. "There is a growing perception that in an increasingly unregulated marketplace, the little guy stands to lose," says Arthur Levitt Jr., chairman of the American Stock Exchange. "The notion that a small group of investors is taking advantage of its position of power is very dangerous."

Even before the insider trading cases, the little guy was beginning to chafe at the sight of Wall Street greenmailers squeezing a higher price for their stock from corporate managements than was available on the open market. Program trading has also made individual investors increasingly nervous. By trading stock-index futures and huge blocks of equities, large institutional investors can lock in guaranteed profits. But they also make the market extremely unpredictable for everyone else.

So far, public confidence in investment bankers and Wall Street in general remains positive. When the Dow Jones industrial average is flirting with 1900, almost every investor becomes richer and more forgiving. Congress, too, appears willing to give Wall Street the benefit of the doubt for now and is waiting for the SEC to send the bad guys to jail. The arbs and the merger-and-acquisition specialists have time to temper their hustling with a few quiet thoughts on ethics and justice, if not the law.

But unless Wall Street quickly cleans up its act, public confidence could easily turn against the investment bankers. This is especially true if the market drops, as it must eventually, and the little guys begin to feel victimized by powerful wheeler-dealers. Then there won't be much talk about the "efficiency" of the market. The freedom of the market itself will be in jeopardy.

Source: Bruce Nussbaum, "Insider Trading: Backlash Is the Biggest Danger." Reprinted from the June 16, 1986, issue of *Business Week*, p. 34, by special permission, © 1986 by McGraw-Hill, Inc.

Brokers and Dealers. The 1934 Act requires brokers and dealers to register with the SEC and to comply with regulations imposed on them. Certain trading practices are prohibited. Specific sections of the 1934 Act deal with unlawful representations, liability for misleading statements, and criminal penalties.

Forms Used in Reporting

The SEC has devised approximately 20 forms to be used by companies whose securities are registered under the 1934 Act. Because most of these forms are of a specialized nature, a complete list is not presented. By far the most commonly used forms are the following:

- Form 8-K, current reports
- Form 10-K, annual report
- Form 10-Q, quarterly report

Regulation 12B of the 1934 Act sets forth the mechanics of reporting in the same manner that Regulation C does under the 1933 Act.

Form 8-K, Current Reports

Form 8-K provides certain information to investors on a reasonably current basis. A report on this form must be filed when one of the following events occurs:

1. Changes in control of the registrant.
2. Significant acquisitions or dispositions of assets (including business combinations).
3. Bankruptcy or receivership.
4. Changes in the registrant's certifying accountant. (The disclosures here are designed to discourage "opinion shopping.")
5. Other events (that the registrant deems important to its security holders).
6. The resignation of a director.

Form 8-K reports must be filed within 15 days after the occurrence of the earliest event.

Form 10-K, Annual Report

Within 90 days after the end of the fiscal year, a company must file an annual report with the SEC, using Form 10-K if no other form is prescribed. Although it must be furnished to stockholders on request, this report is in addition to the company's annual report to its stockholders. Form 10-K must include substantially all nonfinancial statement disclosure requirements set forth in Regulation S-K (the major items were indicated on pages 687–88) and the financial statement information specified in Regulation S-X (described on page 688).

Form 10-K Compared with the Annual Report to Stockholders. As part of the SEC's three-year effort from 1980 to 1982 to streamline its reporting requirements, substantially all the information called for in the 10-K annual report also must be included in the annual report sent to the stockholders. Companies may omit information from the 10-K annual report if it is included in the annual report sent to the stockholders. A copy of the annual report sent to the stockholders must be filed with the 10-K annual report, and the 10-K annual report must indicate that the omitted information is included in the annual report sent to the stockholders. (This is known as **incorporation by reference.**)

Form 10-Q, Quarterly Report

Within 45 days of the end of each of the first three fiscal quarters of each fiscal year, a company must file a quarterly report with the SEC on Form 10-Q. No report is necessary for the fourth quarter. Form 10-Q calls for the interim financial statements specified in Regulation S-X. These financial statements, which may be condensed, are as follows:

1. An interim **balance sheet** as of the end of the most recent fiscal quarter, and a balance sheet at the end of the preceding fiscal year.
2. Interim **income statements** for the most recent fiscal quarter; for the period between the end of the last fiscal year and the end of the most recent fiscal quarter (year-to-date amounts in second- and third-quarter reports); and corresponding periods of the preceding fiscal year.
3. **Statements of changes in financial position** for the period between the end of the last fiscal year and the end of the most recent fiscal quarter and for the corresponding period of the preceding fiscal year.

Detailed footnotes are not required; however, disclosures must be complete enough so that the information presented is not misleading. In this respect, companies may presume that users of the interim financial information have read or have access to the audited financial statements for the preceding fiscal year. Thus, disclosures deal primarily with events after the end of the most recent fiscal year. The interim financial information need not be audited or reviewed by an independent public accountant.

Form 10-Q also calls for a *management discussion and analysis* (MDA) of the financial condition and results of operations pursuant to the nonfinancial statement disclosure requirements of Regulation S-K.

Form 10-Q Compared with the Quarterly Report to Stockholders. As with the rules concerning the 10-K annual report, information called for on Form 10-Q may be omitted if such information is contained in a quarterly report to the stockholders and a copy of that report is filed with Form 10-Q.

REGULATION S-X: A CLOSER LOOK

Recall from the introduction to Regulation S-X on page 688 that this regulation sets forth not only the financial statements filed with the SEC under the various acts but also the form and content of those financial statements. As a result of recent revisions to modernize Regulation S-X and integrate the various reporting requirements of companies, the regulation also applies to annual reports to stockholders. Accordingly, the financial statements included in Form 10-K annual report are now identical to the financial statements in annual reports to stockholders.

Because this regulation is approximately 100 pages long, a detailed discussion is beyond the scope of this book. The objective here is to provide a general familiarity with the contents of Regulation S-X.

Regulation S-X is composed of the following articles, each of which has its own rules:

Article	Description
1	Application of Regulation S-X
2	Qualifications and reports of accountants
3	General instructions for financial statements
3A	Consolidated and combined financial statements
4	Rules of general application
5	Commercial and industrial companies
5A	Companies in the development stage
6	Registered investment companies
6A	Employee stock purchase, savings, and similar plans
7	Insurance companies
9	Bank holding companies
10	Interim financial statements
11	Pro forma financial information
12	Form and content of schedules

Because Articles 5A, 6, 6A, 7, and 9 have at most only limited application to most companies, they are not discussed in this chapter. The remaining articles are discussed briefly.

Article 1: Application of Regulation S-X

Article 1 specifies the nature of Regulation S-X, states the Acts to which it applies, and defines the terms used in the regulation.

Article 2: Qualifications and Reports of Accountants

Article 2 discusses (1) the qualification of certified public accountants (primarily, conditions necessary for their independence), and (2) specific requirements concerning the content of a certified public accountant's report on audited financial statements included in one of the designated forms filed with the SEC.

Article 3: General Instructions for Financial Statements

Article 3 specifies the balance sheets, income statements, and statements of changes in financial position to be included in registration statements and reports filed with the SEC.

Article 3A: Consolidated and Combined Financial Statements

Article 3A deals with the presentation of consolidated and combined financial statements. It specifies which subsidiaries should not be consolidated and requires, in general, that all intercompany items and transactions be eliminated.

Article 4: Rules of General Application

Article 4, the rules of general application, pertains to a variety of items regarding form, classification, and the content of notes to the financial statements. Rule 4-08, "General Notes to Financial Statements," comprises most of this article. Rule 4-08 is an extensive rule specifying certain information to be set forth in notes to the financial statements. This rule is not a duplication of FASB disclosure requirements. Instead, the requirements pertain to items not specifically addressed in pronouncements of the FASB and its predecessor organizations. Generally, preparing the additional disclosures called for by this Article is not a major task.

Article 5: Commercial and Industrial Companies

Article 5 applies to all companies that are not required to follow Articles 5A, 6, 6A, 7, and 9. Rules 5-02 and 5-03 set forth the various line items and certain additional disclosures that should appear in the balance sheet, income statement, or related notes.

Rule 5-04 is a list and description of 13 financial statement supporting schedules (commonly referred to as **schedules**) that are filed in support of the basic financial statements. These schedules pertain to such things as analyses of property, plant, and equipment and analyses of valuation accounts for specified periods of time. In most cases, only four or five schedules apply. The exact form and content of the schedules are specified by Article 12.

Article 10: Interim Financial Statements

Article 10 deals with the form and content of presentation of interim financial statements (quarterly reports under the 1934 Act and interim financial statements in registration statements filed under the 1933 Act).

Article 11: Pro Forma Financial Information

Article 11 specifies when pro forma financial statements must be presented. Such financial statements are required when business combinations have occurred or are probable.

Article 12: Form and Content of Schedules

Article 12 prescribes the form and content of the financial statement supporting schedules required by Rule 5-04 under Article 5 and certain rules in other articles. The exact columnar headings used for each schedule are specified, along with detailed instructions on how to prepare each schedule.

SUMMARY

The Securities Act of 1933 and the Securities Exchange Act of 1934 protect investors from fraudulent actions and unethical practices by the promoters of securities and the managements of companies issuing securities. Companies subject to the registration and reporting requirements of these statutes must be familiar with a labyrinth of regulations, rules, releases, forms, and bulletins to comply with these statutes. For the disclosure of nonfinancial information, companies usually rely heavily on their legal counsel for assistance and guidance. For the disclosure of financial information, company accountants must be intimately familiar with the detailed requirements of Regulation S-X. In many respects, Regulation S-X imposes no additional reporting requirements beyond those required by generally accepted accounting principles as established in the private sector. In some areas, Regulation S-X imposes significant additional reporting requirements beyond those required under generally accepted accounting principles.

Glossary of New Terms

Blue Sky Laws State laws dealing with the purchase and sale of securities.

Exempt Offering An offering of securities that need not be registered with the SEC because of an available statutory exemption.

Forms Specific enumerations of the form and content of information included in registration statements and reports filed with the SEC.

Private Offering "Transactions by an issuer not involving a public offering."*

Prospectus The portion of a registration statement that must be furnished to prospective investors in connection with an offering of securities being registered with the SEC.

Proxy A document empowering a person to vote for another person.

Proxy Statement A statement containing specified information furnished to stockholders in connection with the solicitation of proxies for use at an annual meeting (or special meetings) of shareholders.

Registration Statement All of the specified financial and nonfinancial information filed with the SEC (set forth according to an appropriate form) for purposes of registering an offering of securities to the public.

Restricted Security Securities acquired by means that did not involve a public offering.

Security "Any note, stock, treasury stock, bond, debenture, evidence of indebtedness, certificate of interest or participation in any profit-sharing agreement, . . . transferable share, investment contract, voting trust certificate, . . . or in general any interest or instrument commonly known as a security . . ."*

Underwriter "Any person who has purchased from an issuer with a view to, or offers or sells for an issuer in connection with, the distribution of any security, or participates [directly or indirectly] . . . in any such undertaking . . ."*

*Securities Act of 1933.

Appendix
TABLE OF CONTENTS OF FORM S-1

The following is the table of contents from Form S-1, the most widely used of the SEC's forms. It is reprinted here in order to provide a more complete look at what is called for in a registration statement.

General Instructions

I. Eligibility requirements for use of Form S-1
II. Application of general rules and regulations
III. Exchange offers

Facing Sheet

I. Information Required in Prospectus

Item

1. Forepart of the registration statement and outside front cover page of prospectus
2. Inside front and outside back cover page of prospectus
3. Summary information, risk factors, and ratio of earnings to fixed charges
4. Use of proceeds
5. Determination of offering price
6. Dilution
7. Selling security holders
8. Plan of distribution
9. Description of securities being registered
10. Interest of named experts and counsel
11. Information with respect to the registrant[4]
12. Disclosure of commission position on indemnification for securities act liabilities

II. Information Not Required in Prospectus

13. Other expenses of issuance and distribution
14. Indemnification of directors and officers
15. Recent sales of unregistered securities
16. Exhibits and financial statement schedules
17. Undertakings

Signatures

Instructions as to Summary Prospectuses

[4]This item specifies (a) the nonfinancial disclosure requirements in Regulation S-K and (b) the financial statement requirements of Regulation S-X that are to be included.

Review Questions

1. How does the Securities Exchange Act of 1934 differ from the Securities Act of 1933?
2. What purpose is served by the SEC's Staff Accounting Bulletins?
3. What purpose do SEC releases serve?
4. Describe the SEC's role in the formation and improvement of generally accepted accounting principles.
5. Distinguish between a registration statement and a prospectus.
6. What is the distinction between Form S-1 and Form 10-K?
7. What do Regulations A and D have in common?
8. What do Forms 8-K, 10-K, and 10-Q have in common?
9. How is Regulation C under the 1933 Act similar to Regulation 12B under the 1934 Act?
10. What is the distinction between Regulation S-X and Regulation S-K?
11. Distinguish between a proxy and a proxy statement.
12. How are financial statements that are prepared in accordance with Regulation S-X requirements different from financial statements prepared in accordance with generally accepted accounting principles?

Exercises

E 18-1

SEC Promulgations

Complete the following statements:

1. The form and content of financial statements included with filings with the SEC are set forth in ________.
2. The pronouncements that announce the SEC's proposed revisions to its rules and regulations are called ________.
3. Nonfinancial statement disclosure requirements are set forth in ________.
4. An SEC regulation is merely a collection of ________.
5. The SEC rules and regulations that pertain to the various sections of the 1933 Act and the 1934 Act are referred to as the ________ rules and regulations.
6. The regulation that specifies the financial statements included in SEC filings is ________.
7. The interpretations and practices followed by certain departments of the SEC are called ________.
8. Accounting related releases used to be announced in ________, but now they are set forth in ________.
9. The promulgation of the SEC that accountants deal with more than any other is ________.
10. A list of instructions concerning what is included in a particular SEC filing is called a ________.

E 18-2

The 1933 and 1934 Acts: Terminology

Complete the following statements:

1. Under the 1933 Act, issuers of securities must furnish potential investors with a ______.
2. A registration statement is divided into the following two basic parts:
   a. Information ______.
   b. Information ______.
3. A "red herring" is a ______.
4. Stocks and bonds are ______.
5. A person who purchases an issuer's stock with a view to distributing that stock to the public is a(n) ______.
6. Security offerings that need not be registered with the SEC are considered ______ offerings.
7. All the information filed with the SEC using an appropriate form under the 1933 Act is called a ______.
8. The Securities Act of 1933 pertains to the ______ of securities.
9. The Securities Exchange Act of 1934 pertains to ______ of issued securities.
10. Securities acquired by means that did not involve a public offering are called ______.
11. A document authorizing one person to vote for another person is a ______.
12. A statement furnished to stockholders in connection with soliciting their votes is called a ______.

E 18-3

The 1933 and 1934 Acts: Forms Used in Registrations and Filings

Indicate the SEC form applicable to each of the following items:

1. The most commonly used annual reporting form under the 1934 Act.
2. The most commonly used registration form under the 1933 Act.
3. The quarterly reporting form under the 1934 Act.
4. The form used under the 1934 Act to report certain transactions or events that arise during the year.
5. The form that may be used to register stock option plans, providing certain other conditions are met.
6. The most commonly used registration form under the 1934 Act.
7. The three general forms used under the 1933 Act.
8. The item filed with the SEC when a Regulation A offering is involved.

E 18-4

Regulation S-X: True or False

Indicate whether the following statements are true or false.

1. Regulation S-X specifies the financial statements included in registration statements and reports filed with the SEC.
2. Some Financial Reporting Releases explain and illustrate certain rules in Regulation S-X.
3. Regulation S-X applies to the 1933 Act but not the 1934 Act.

4. Some Regulation S-X rules permit the deletion of certain notes to financial statements otherwise required by generally accepted accounting principles.
5. The form and content of financial statements included in registration statements and reports filed with the SEC are set forth in Regulation S-X.
6. The SEC automatically amends Regulation S-X to comply with any new FASB pronouncements.
7. Annual reports to shareholders need not present financial statements in compliance with Regulation S-X.
8. In general, it is a major task to convert financial statements and the related footnotes (prepared in accordance with generally accepted accounting principles) to meet the requirements of Regulation S-X.
9. Regulation S-X is a guide for preparing financial statements included in the registration statements and reports filed with the SEC—it need not be strictly followed.
10. Regulation S-X does not specify which SEC form is used in preparing reports filed under the 1934 Act.
11. Certain rules in Regulation S-X require additional financial disclosures above and beyond disclosures normally made pursuant to generally accepted accounting principles.
12. Changes in Regulation S-X can be announced through the issuance of a Financial Reporting Release.

Problems

P 18-1

The Role of the SEC in Relation to the FASB

Indicate whether the following statements are true or false. Discuss your reasons for your answers.

1. The pronouncements of the Financial Accounting Standards Board must be approved by the SEC before they can be issued.
2. The accounting related pronouncements of the SEC must be approved by the FASB before they are issued.
3. The SEC has given the FASB the statutory authority to prescribe accounting principles.
4. Publicly owned companies are subject to the financial reporting requirements of the SEC and FASB.
5. Privately owned companies are not subject to the financial reporting requirements of the SEC.
6. The SEC automatically rescinds a pronouncement when the FASB issues a Statement of Financial Accounting Standards involving a particular accounting issue.
7. When the SEC notices an emerging accounting practice that has not been addressed by the FASB, it most likely will establish accounting principles in that area until the FASB can address the issue.
8. Unlike the FASB, the SEC can order a company subject to its reporting requirements to alter its financial statements.

P 18-2

The Securities Act of 1933: The Role of the SEC and Responsibility of Outside Auditors

Select the best answer for each of the following items:

1. One of the SEC's functions is to
   a. judge the merits of the securities being offered to the public.
   b. ascertain the wisdom of investing in securities being offered to the public.
   c. warrant that registration statements contain all necessary financial and nonfinancial statement information required by the investing public to evaluate the merit of the securities being offered.
   d. warrant that the information contained in registration statements examined and approved by the SEC is true and accurate.
   e. none of the above
2. A company registers securities with the SEC under the 1933 Act. As this event concerns its outside auditors, which of the following is correct?
   a. The SEC will defend any action brought against certified public accountants who have reported on financial statements included in a registration statement examined and approved by the SEC.
   b. Any action brought against the auditors would have to be decided on the basis of ordinary negligence versus gross negligence.
   c. The auditors could be held liable in the event of ordinary negligence as well as gross negligence.
   d. The auditors could be held liable for misleading statements in the notes to the financial statements even if negligence is not involved.
   e. none of the above
3. One of the major purposes of the federal security statutes is to
   a. establish the qualifications for accountants who are members of the profession.
   b. eliminate incompetent attorneys and accountants who participate in the registration of securities offered to the public.
   c. provide a set of uniform standards and tests for accountants, attorneys, and others who practice before the Securities and Exchange Commission.
   d. provide sufficient information to the investing public who purchase securities in the marketplace.
   e. none of the above
4. Under the Securities Act of 1933, subject to some exceptions and limitations, it is unlawful to use the mails or instruments of interstate commerce to sell or offer to sell a security to the public unless
   a. a surety bond sufficient to cover potential liability to investors is obtained and filed with the SEC.
   b. the offer is made through underwriters qualified to offer the securities on a nationwide basis.
   c. a registration statement that has been properly filed with the SEC has been found to be acceptable and is in effect.
   d. the SEC approves of the financial merit of the offering.
   e. none of the above
5. A company registers securities with the SEC under the 1933 Act. As this event concerns its outside auditors, which of the following is correct?

a. The outside auditors may disclaim any liability under the federal securities acts by an unambiguous, boldfaced disclaimer of liability on its audit report.
b. The outside auditors must determine which SEC form the company should use in the filing.
c. As long as the outside auditors engage exclusively in intrastate business, the federal securities laws do not apply to them.
d. The outside auditors have primary responsibility for the nonfinancial statement portions of the registration statement as well as responsibility for the financial statement portions of the registration statement.
e. none of the above

P 18-3

The 1933 and 1934 Acts: Technical Understanding

Select the best answer for each of the following items:

1. Regulation A and Regulation D deal with
   a. the mechanics of registering securities under the 1933 Act.
   b. the responsibilities of outside auditors under the 1933 Act.
   c. the forms used under the 1933 Act.
   d. allowable exemptions from registration under the 1933 Act.
   e. none of the above
2. Concerning the relationship between the 1933 Act and the 1934 Act, which of the following is correct?
   a. Having once become subject to the reporting requirements of the 1934 Act, a company may offer securities to the public in the future without having to register such securities with the SEC under the 1933 Act.
   b. If a privately owned company having 200,000 common shares outstanding registers the sale of 50,000 new shares under the 1933 Act, then all 250,000 common shares are deemed to be registered under the 1933 Act.
   c. A company that registers securities under the 1933 Act becomes subject to the reporting requirements of the 1934 Act.
   d. If a privately owned company having 500,000 common shares outstanding registers the sale of 100,000 new shares under the 1933 Act, then only the 100,000 new shares may be registered under the 1934 Act.
   e. none of the above
3. Under the 1933 Act, which of the following is the most important criterion of whether a private placement to a limited number of persons or a public offering has been made?
   a. The size of the issuing corporation.
   b. The type of security offered.
   c. The prompt resale of the securities by the purchasers.
   d. Whether the company engages exclusively in intrastate business.
   e. none of the above
4. Which of the following is not exempt from registration under the 1933 Act?
   a. Securities offered through underwriters.
   b. Securities offered to a limited number of persons in a private placement.
   c. Securities offered only to residents of the state in which the company is located.

d. Securities offered by a governmental unit.
e. none of the above

5. Concerning the 1934 Act, which of the following is correct?
a. A company may be subject to the reporting requirements of the 1934 Act even though it never has registered securities under the 1933 Act.
b. A company that has been subject to the reporting requirements of the 1934 Act is always subject to such requirements unless the company becomes privately held again.
c. A company is no longer subject to the reporting requirements of the 1934 Act if its total assets are below $3 million at the end of its last three fiscal years.
d. A company that is no longer subject to the reporting requirements of the 1934 Act is also no longer subject to the requirements of the 1933 Act.
e. none of the above

P 18-4

The Securities Exchange Act of 1934: Stock Transactions by Employees

Discovery Corporation is a manufacturing company whose securities are registered on a national securities exchange. On February 6, 19X5, one of the company's engineers disclosed to management that he had discovered a new product that he believed would be quite profitable to the corporation. Messrs. Prescott and Trout, the corporation's president and treasurer and members of its board of directors, were quite impressed with the prospects of the new product's profitability.

Trout had such confidence in the corporation's prospects that on February 12, 19X5, he purchased on the open market 1,000 shares of the corporation's common stock at $10 per share. This purchase occurred before news of the new product reached the public in late February and caused a rise in the market price to $30 per share. Prescott did not purchase any shares in February because he had already purchased 600 shares of the corporation's common stock on January 15, 19X5, for $10 per share.

On April 16, 19X5, because of unexpected expenses arising from a fire in his home, Prescott sold on the open market the 600 shares of stock he purchased in January for $35 per share. Trout continues to hold his 1,000 shares.

Required:

1. What questions arising out of the federal securities laws are suggested by these facts? Discuss.
2. What would be a reasonable corporate policy designed to have employees buy and sell stock on the same basis as nonemployees?

P 18-5

The Securities Exchange Act of 1934: Public Disclosures

B&S Corporation's sole issue of stock is traded on a national exchange. In conducting the year-end examination of its financial statements, the auditor learned that B&S research department had perfected a manufacturing process that would have a positive material effect on future earnings. B&S did not announce the development.

When a rumor about the new process started in late January, B&S's president promptly telephoned financial papers in several states and announced that there was no substance to the rumor. A number of papers reported the president's denial of the rumor. Thereafter, B&S's stock traded in its normal narrow range. In February, relying on the information reported in the financial press, Sellinger (an outside shareholder) sold a large block of his B&S stock at the current market price.

B&S's president made a public announcement about the perfection of the new process the following June. The announcement precipitated a dramatic increase in both the price and volume of trading of B&S's stock. Neither B&S nor any person with knowledge of the process engaged in trading B&S's stock before the public announcement of the discovery.

Required:
What questions arising out of federal securities laws are suggested by these facts? Discuss.

(AICPA adapted)

19

Troubled Debt Restructurings, Bankruptcy Reorganizations, and Liquidations

An Overview

Bankruptcy Statutes

Troubled Debt Restructurings

Bankruptcy Reorganizations

PERSPECTIVE: "Chapter 11 Isn't So Chic Anymore"

Liquidations

Accounting by Trustees

Concluding Comments

Summary

AN OVERVIEW

Options for Financially Distressed Companies

Any type of economic entity (including corporations, partnerships, sole proprietorships, and municipalities) can encounter financial difficulties. Business entities in financial difficulty first usually retrench and undertake cost-cutting steps to conserve cash and reduce operating losses. Such steps may include revamping the organizational structure to eliminate or consolidate functions (often resulting in the termination of a substantial number of personnel, seeking wage and fringe-benefit concessions from employees, seeking relaxation of restrictive union work rules, and disposing of unprofitable segments. In addition, the entity may eventually need to (1) raise additional capital, (2) dispose of profitable segments, (3) combine with another business, (4) restructure its debt outside of the bankruptcy courts, (5) reorganize through the bankruptcy courts, or (6) liquidate.

This chapter deals with corporations that select the last three options. Option 4, restructuring debt outside of the bankruptcy courts, usually consists of extending due dates, forgiving some portion of debt, and reducing the interest rate on the debt. This option gives the business a reasonable chance to continue as a viable entity and recover from the financial difficulties, thereby avoiding liquidation, at least for the time being. Although option 5, reorganization through the bankruptcy courts, is identical in its objective to that of option 4, it is considered less desirable even though it usually results in a substantial forgiveness of debt. Option 6, liquidation, consists of converting all noncash assets into cash, paying creditors to the extent possible, and ending the legal existence of the corporation. In discussing the options of restructuring debt and reorganizing through the bankruptcy courts, we exclude railroads and municipalities because of their special nature. We also exclude these special entities from the discussion of liquidation, because public policy dictates that these entities not be liquidated.

BANKRUPTCY STATUTES

Their Purpose

Debt capital markets would be inhibited without some provisions for ensuring fair and equitable means of resolving rights and protecting public interests. This is the purpose of the bankruptcy laws. Distressed companies and their creditors must decide whether it is necessary to resort to the bankruptcy process. Accordingly, we now discuss the federal bankruptcy statutes.

Their Substance

Under the bankruptcy statutes, a company or an individual is placed under the protection of the court, whereby creditors (including creditors possessing security interests, unsecured creditors, tax collectors, and public utilities) are prevented from taking other legal action (such as foreclosing on loans, filing lawsuits, repossessing or seizing assets, and placing padlocks on the doors of the company's real property). When a company's rehabilitation and future viable operations are feasible, its debt is restructured under the supervision and control of the court in such a manner that the debtor may be legally freed from the payment of certain past debts. When rehabilitation and recovery are not feasible, an orderly liquidation takes place under the supervision and control of the bankruptcy court.

Federal Bankruptcy Statutes

Article I, Section 8 of the U.S. Constitution grants to the Congress the power to establish uniform laws throughout the United States pertaining to the subject of bankruptcies. Federal statutes pertaining to bankruptcy prevail over state laws that conflict with federal laws.

In 1978, the U.S. Congress rewrote the federal bankruptcy statutes under the Bankruptcy Reform Act of 1978. Taking effect on October 1, 1979, the new law replaced the National Bankruptcy Act of 1898. The new law established separate bankruptcy courts (adjuncts to the district courts) with special judges (commonly referred to as "bankruptcy judges") who supervise and review all bankruptcy petitions and proceedings. (If a case involves broad bankruptcy issues, however, such issues are to be decided by district judges, not the bankruptcy judges.)

The Bankruptcy Reform Act of 1978 (as amended in 1984) consists of the following eight chapters (even-numbered chapters do not exist):

Chapter 1	**General provisions**
Chapter 3	**Case administration**
Chapter 5	**Creditors, the debtor, and the estate**
Chapter 7	**Liquidation**
Chapter 9	**Adjustment of debts of a municipality**
Chapter 11	**Reorganization**
Chapter 13	**Adjustment of debts of an individual with regular income**
Chapter 15	**United States trustees**

The general provisions of Chapters 1, 3, and 5 pertain to Chapters 7, 9, 11, and 13, unless otherwise indicated. In this section, we discuss certain basic aspects of Chapters 1, 3, and 5. Chapters 9 and 13 do not pertain to corporations organized to make a profit; accordingly, they are not discussed in this chapter. (Chapter 9 applies only to municipalities that seek relief voluntarily—a municipality cannot be forced into bankruptcy proceedings against its will by its creditors.) Chapter 7 is discussed later in this chapter in the section dealing with liquidations. Chapter 11 is also discussed later in this chapter in the section dealing with bankruptcy reorganizations.

In the 1978 Act, the subject of the bankruptcy proceedings is referred to as a **debtor.** The commencement of a bankruptcy case creates an **estate.** The estate includes all of the debtor's property no matter where located (Section 541).[1]

Applicability of the Bankruptcy Statutes

The bankruptcy statutes apply to individuals, partnerships, corporations (all of which are collectively referred to as "persons"), and municipalities. Insurance companies and certain financial institutions (such as banks, savings and loan associations, building and loan associations, and credit unions) are excluded because they are subject to alternative regulations. Railroads may not use the liquidation provisions of Chapter 7, only the reorganization provisions of Chapter 11. Stockbrokers and commodity brokers are not eligible for the reorganization provisions of Chapter 11, only the liquidation provisions of Chapter 7 (Section 109[b]).

Voluntary Petitions

An eligible corporation (that is, a corporation other than an insurance company or certain financial institutions) may file a voluntary petition with the bankruptcy courts under Chapter 7 or 11 and thereby obtain the benefits available under the statutes (Section 109). Filing a voluntary petition constitutes an **order for relief,** which has the full force and effect as if the bankruptcy court had issued an order that the debtor be granted relief under the statutes (Section 301). However, the court can dismiss a voluntary filing if it is in the best interests of creditors (Section 707 and 1112[b]).

The petition initiates bankruptcy proceedings and is an official form that must be accompanied by a summary of the debtor's property (at market or current values) and debts, including supporting schedules, all on official forms. The supporting schedules for property consist of separate schedules for real property, personal property and property not otherwise scheduled. The supporting schedules for debts consist of separate schedules for *creditors with priority* (a special class of creditors explained later in the book), creditors holding security, and creditors having unsecured

[1]This reference is to the Bankruptcy Reform Act of 1978. Hereafter, only the section number of the act is provided.

claims without priority. Information also must include each creditor's address (if known), when the debt was incurred, and whether the debt is contingent, disputed, or subject to setoff. In addition, the petitioner must respond to a questionnaire regarding all aspects of its financial condition and operations. Although this questionnaire is called the *statement of affairs*, it should not be confused with the statement of affairs that accountants prepare regarding asset values and debts owed, which is explained later in the chapter.

Involuntary Petitions

Under Chapter 7 or 11, an eligible corporation may be forced into bankruptcy proceedings against its will by its creditors. One or more creditors may file an involuntary petition with the bankruptcy court. If a debtor has twelve or more creditors, at least three of them who have claims totaling a minimum of $5,000 more than the value of any lien on the property of the debtor securing such claims must sign the petition (Section 303[b][1]). If a company has fewer than twelve creditors, one or more creditors having such claims of at least $5,000 must sign the petition (Section 303[b][2]). These dollar amounts apply to both liquidation and reorganization cases.

For an involuntary petition filed under Chapter 7 or 11, the bankruptcy court enters an order for relief against the debtor only if either of the following conditions pertain:

1. The debtor is generally not paying its debts as they become due.
2. A custodian was appointed or took possession of the debtor's property within 120 days before the date of the filing of the petition. (This does not apply to a trustee, receiver, or agent appointed or authorized to take charge of less than the majority of the debtor's property for the purpose of enforcing a lien against such property.) (Section 303[h]).

The first test above is an equity insolvency test; that is, the debtor's assets equitably belong to the creditors to the extent of their claims. In the second test, the appointment of a custodian presumes that the debtor cannot pay its debts as they mature.

In practice, voluntary bankruptcies occur much more frequently than involuntary bankruptcies. Regardless of whether a company enters bankruptcy proceedings voluntarily or involuntarily, it should immediately obtain the assistance of an attorney who specializes in bankruptcy proceedings.

Creditors with Priority

A company entering bankruptcy proceedings can have two general classes of creditors—secured creditors and unsecured creditors. **Secured** creditors have been pledged certain of the company's assets as security on their claims. Creditors that have no right to any of the company's specific assets are **unsecured** creditors. In addition to these two general classes of creditors, the bankruptcy statutes create a special class of creditors termed **creditors with priority.** Debts with priority are listed in the order of their priority, as follows:

1. **Administrative expenses, fees, and charges assessed against the estate.** Administrative expenses are the actual and necessary costs and expenses of preserving the estate after the petition has been filed. This includes trustee's fees, legal, accounting, and appraisal fees incurred in connection with the bankruptcy proceedings, filing fees paid by creditors in an involuntary bankruptcy petition, and expenses incurred in recovering assets that were concealed or fraudulently transferred.
2. **Certain postfiling "gap" claims.** This category, which exists only for involuntary filings, includes unsecured claims arising in the ordinary course of the debtor's business after the involuntary filing but before the appointment of a trustee or an order of relief is entered, whichever occurs first.
3. **Wages, salaries, and commissions.** Wages, salaries, and commissions are limited to unsecured amounts earned by an individual within 90 days before the filing date or the date of the cessation of the debtor's business, whichever occurs first, but only up to $2,000 for each individual. This category includes vacation, severance, and sick leave pay.
4. **Employee benefit plans.** This category pertains to unsecured claims for contributions to employee benefit plans arising from services rendered by the employees within 180 days before the date of the filing of the petition or the date of the cessation of the debtor's business, whichever occurs first. The claims are limited to the number of employees covered by each such plan multiplied by $2,000, minus (a) the total amount paid to such employees as items in priority 3 above, and (b) the total amount paid by the estate on behalf of such employees to any other employee benefit plan.
5. **Deposits by individuals.** This category includes unsecured claims of up to $900 for each such individual, arising from the deposit of money before the commencement of the case in connection with the purchase, lease, or rental of property, or the purchase of services for the personal, family, or household use of such individuals, that were not delivered or provided.
6. **Taxes.** This category includes income taxes, property taxes, withholding taxes, employer payroll taxes, excise taxes, and customs duties. Most of these taxes are limited to amounts relating to a specified period of time preceding the date of the filing, usually one or three years, depending on the item.

Creditors with priority are given a statutory priority over the claims of other unsecured creditors with regard to payment. Later in the chapter, we illustrate this priority in a liquidation through the bankruptcy courts.

TROUBLED DEBT RESTRUCTURINGS

In troubled debt restructurings, steps are taken outside of the bankruptcy courts to give the distressed company a reasonable chance of surviving. This option is considered much more desirable than a Chapter 11 reorganization.

The Advantages of Restructuring versus Reorganizing

One advantage of restructuring outside of the bankruptcy courts is that the restructuring can be completed in far less time than a Chapter 11 reorganization, which takes a minimum of approximately 18 months. However, of greater importance is the desire to avoid the stigma associated with being or having been subject to bankruptcy proceedings. More uncertainty is associated with Chapter 11 reorganizations concerning the distressed company's chances of survival—many companies that file for Chapter 11 reorganizations are unable to work out a successful plan of reorganization and are liquidated instead. Thus, filing for reorganization under Chapter 11 is considered the last resort, short of liquidation.

Needless to say, filing for a Chapter 11 reorganization has far greater consequences to the distressed company in terms of its impact on suppliers, competitors, customers, and employees than does a restructuring outside of the bankruptcy courts. For example, a distressed company that is restructuring may be able to obtain some credit from suppliers; when a company reorganizes under Chapter 11, suppliers usually require payment on delivery. During restructuring, competitors tend to get sales leverage from a distressed company's problems; during a Chapter 11 reorganization, competitors have that much more ammunition. (Competitors often show customers press clippings of the distressed company's financial problems.)

When a company has filed for reorganization under Chapter 11, customers have that much less assurance of the company's survival—this can be critical for a distressed company that sells products requiring the company's continued existence for purposes of providing service and stocking spare parts. Employees are more likely to look for greener pastures once a company files for reorganization under Chapter 11 because of the uncertainty associated with bankruptcy proceedings. (Personnel placement firms tend to zero in on distressed companies to hire away their employees; their chances of success increase when a company files for a Chapter 11 reorganization.)

Working out a troubled debt restructuring agreement is usually a substantial and difficult undertaking, especially when major differences exist among various groups of creditors as to the sacrifices each is willing to make. A distressed company often resorts to a Chapter 11 reorganization when it is impossible to work out a troubled debt restructuring agreement with its creditors, when its lenders refuse to lend any more money, or when suppliers begin requiring payment on delivery. Although the advantages of restructuring debt outside of the bankruptcy courts are considerable, there are certain advantages in filing for reorganization under Chapter 11. These advantages are discussed later in the chapter when reorganization under Chapter 11 is discussed in detail.

The Nature of Troubled Debt Restructurings

The accounting procedures for most debt restructurings are prescribed by *FASB Statement No. 15,* "Accounting by Debtors and Creditors for Troubled Debt Restructurings." Before discussing the accounting issues and procedures in detail, we (1) define a troubled debt restructuring, (2) show transactions that may be considered troubled debt restructurings, and (3) show some ways in which a distressed company can restructure its debt.

Definition. *FASB Statement No. 15* defines a troubled debt restructuring as follows:

> A restructuring of a debt constitutes a **troubled debt restructuring** for purposes of this Statement if the creditor for economic or legal reasons related to the debtor's financial difficulties grants a concession to the debtor that it would not otherwise consider.[2]

The statement expounds on this definition as follows:

> Whatever the form of concession granted by the creditor to the debtor in a troubled debt restructuring, the creditor's objective is to make the best of a difficult situation. That is, the creditor expects to obtain more cash or other value from the debtor, or to increase the probability of receipt, by granting the concession than by not granting it.[3]

Categories of Transactions. The statement lists the following types of transactions that may constitute troubled debt restructurings:

a. Transfer from the debtor to the creditor of receivables from third parties, real estate, or other assets to satisfy fully or partially a debt (including a transfer resulting from foreclosure or repossession).
b. Issuance or other granting of an equity interest to the creditor by the debtor to satisfy fully or partially a debt unless the equity interest is granted pursuant to existing terms for converting the debt into an equity interest.

[2]*Statement of Financial Accounting Standards, No. 15,* "Accounting by Debtors and Creditors for Troubled Debt Restructurings" (Stamford: Financial Accounting Standards Board, 1977), par. 2.
[3]*FASB Statement No. 15,* par. 3.

c. Modification of terms of a debt, such as one or a combination of:
  1. Reduction (absolute or contingent) of the stated interest rate for the remaining original life of the debt.
  2. Extension of the maturity date or dates at a stated interest rate lower than the current market rate for a new debt with similar risk.
  3. Reduction (absolute or contingent) of the face amount or maturity amount of the debt as stated in the instrument or other agreement.
  4. Reduction (absolute or contingent) of accrued interest.[4]

Individual Creditor Agreements. The most frequently used manner of restructuring debt is the **individual creditor agreement** between a debtor and a creditor whereby the payment terms are restructured pursuant to negotiated terms. Within the last seven years, dozens of large companies have restructured their debt in this manner or have at least attempted to do so. Typically, the creditors involved are banks. The most major, widely publicized completed restructurings in the 1980s were those of Chrysler Corp., which owed $4.4 billion to more than 400 banks, and International Harvester Corp., which owed $3.4 billion to more than 200 banks.

Composition agreements. A **composition agreement** is a formal agreement between a debtor and its creditors (and among the creditors) whereby the creditors collectively agree to accept a percentage of their claims — such as 60 cents on the dollar — in full settlement of their claims. For example, a composition agreement may include only the debtor's major creditors, with all other creditors still entitled to full payment. The payment terms of the composition agreement may require immediate, partial, or full payment of the reduced amount. To the extent that payment of the reduced amount is deferred, a debtor may execute notes payable bearing interest on the deferred amount.

Composition agreements are usually negotiated when a company's filing for a Chapter 11 reorganization is imminent. As a result of the agreement, the company does not suffer the taint of having gone through a bankruptcy proceeding, a potentially lengthy and involved bankruptcy process is avoided, and the creditors expect to recover more than they would in a Chapter 11 reorganization.

Conceptual Issues

Troubled debt restructurings usually result in the creditors' substantial reduction of the debtor's financial obligations (required payments for principal and interest). This procedure requires a comparison of (a) the total amount owed (including unpaid interest) immediately before the restructuring, which is commonly referred to as the **carrying amount of the debt,** with (b) the **total future payments** (including amounts designated as

[4]*FASB Statement No. 15*, par. 5.

interest) to be made pursuant to the restructuring agreement. If the carrying amount of the debt exceeds the total future payments, the debtor's liabilities must be reduced. This reduction constitutes a **forgiveness of debt.** If the debtor's total future payments exceed the carrying amount of the debt, the excess is reported as interest expense in future periods. This situation presents no accounting issue. The accounting issues pertain solely to the forgiveness of debt and are as follows:

1. *How should any forgiveness of debt be measured?* The focus of this issue is primarily whether the new (post-restructuring) liability amount should be measured and reported as (a) the undiscounted total future payments to be made, or (b) the present value of total future payments. The difference between (a) or (b) and the carrying amount of the debt is the amount of the forgiveness. Obviously, the choice between (a) and (b) affects the amount of forgiveness.
2. *How should a forgiveness of debt be classified and reported?* This issue is concerned with whether a forgiveness of debt should be considered (a) a **gain** and, therefore, reported in the **income statement,** or (b) a **capital contribution** by the creditor or creditors and, therefore, credited directly to an **equity account.**

The resolution of these issues should be based on the **substance** of the restructuring, rather than its **form.** However, varying perceptions exist as to what constitutes the substance.

Conceptual Issue 1: Calculation of Forgiveness of Debt

In some situations, the calculation of forgiveness of debt is quite simple. For example, assume a creditor that is owed $100,000 agrees to cancel $40,000 of the debt in return for the immediate payment of the remaining $60,000. Obviously, the amount of debt forgiven is $40,000. Most situations, however, are more complex. For example, assume that (1) a creditor is owed $100,000 of principal related to a delinquent loan bearing interest at 10% (for simplicity, we assume no interest is owed); and (2) the creditor agrees to be paid in full in two years with no interest to be charged. Two approaches have been advocated for such situations—one that **imputes interest** and one that **does not impute interest.** When interest is not imputed, the calculation to determine any forgiveness of debt is as follows:

Carrying amount of debt	**$100,000**
Total future payments	**100,000**
Amount of forgiveness	**$ –0–**

Under this approach, the liability reported in the balance sheet immediately after the restructuring is $100,000, and it bears a zero interest rate. No interest expense would be reported in either year.

When interest is imputed (using present value techniques), the amount of forgiveness, if any, depends on the imputed interest rate used. Assuming that the 10% pre-restructuring interest rate is appropriate, the calculation to determine any forgiveness of debt is as follows:

Carrying amount of debt		**$100,000**
Total future payments	**$100,000**	
Present value factor (10%, 2 years)	**0.82645**	
Present value of total future payments		**82,645**
Amount of forgiveness		**$ 17,355**

Under this approach, the liability reported in the balance sheet immediately after the restructuring is $82,645, and it bears interest at 10%. Interest expense of $8,264 (10% of $82,645) would be reported in year one, and $9,091 [10% of ($82,645 + $8,264)] would be reported in year two.

Rationale for Not Imputing Interest. Arguments for not imputing interest are as follows:

1. Troubled debt restructurings *are not* "exchanges of debt" and, therefore, *do not* require the use of present value techniques as set forth in *APB Opinion No. 21*, "Interest on Receivables and Payables," which deals with "exchanges."
2. A creditor does not grant any forgiveness under the restructuring so long as the total future payments to be received equal or exceed the recorded investment in the receivable; that is, the **recoverability** of the recorded investment in the receivable is not affected.
3. A reduction of the debtor's financial obligations (before the restructuring) to the amount of the recorded investment in the receivable merely changes the creditor's **future profitability** on the loan. Thus, a creditor's effective interest rate after the restructuring could vary from the pre-restructuring interest rate of 10%, for example, down to zero.

Recall from the nonimputing example that no forgiveness of debt existed because the total future payments of $100,000 were not below the $100,000 carrying amount of the debt. Thus, from the creditor's perspective, the future profitability on the loan had been reduced to zero, but the recoverability of the recorded amount of the receivable had not been affected.

Rationale for Imputing Interest. Arguments for imputing interest are as follows:

1. The debtor's liability after restructuring ($82,645 in the imputing example) is reported on the same basis as the borrowings of all debtors—that is, the present value of the future cash outflows for principal and interest.

2. The debtor's future income statements will reflect a reasonable amount of interest expense, which should enhance comparability of those statements with the debtor's past income statements and with future income statements of other companies.

An implementation issue under this approach is whether the **pre-restructuring** interest rate or a current market interest rate should be used. Most accountants feel that the debtor's obligation after the restructuring results from a modification of an existing loan. Therefore, the pre-restructuring rate should be used. Other accountants who view the debtor's obligation after restructuring as arising from the execution of a new lending agreement conclude that a current market interest rate should be used. An advantage of the pre-restructuring approach is that the interest rate is known. However, the current market rate approach involves determining the interest rate at which a debtor in a precarious financial position might be able to borrow when, in fact, no lenders may be available.

Conceptual Issue 2: Reporting Forgiveness of Debt

A forgiveness of debt may be reported in the income statement. In this approach, a forgiveness of debt is a **gain on restructuring,** which is **similar to a gain on extinguishment of debt.** Under *APB Opinion No. 26,* "Early Extinguishment of Debt," gain on extinguishment of debt must be reported in the income statement. Most advocates of this position agree that such a gain should be reported as an extraordinary item because the criteria of unusual and infrequent would be met.

In a second alternative, a forgiveness of debt may be reported as a **direct addition to paid-in capital.** The arguments for this approach are as follows:

1. Because the transaction infuses capital to the debtor, in substance, the debtor has received a capital contribution from the creditor.
2. It should make no difference whether the additional capital needed to keep the debtor in business comes from stockholders or creditors.
3. A company in serious financial difficulty, which has probably reported substantial operating losses, should not report income on a transaction intended to assist it in eventually returning to profitable operations.

Requirements of *FASB Statement No. 15*

After considering the various viewpoints on imputing or not imputing interest, the Financial Accounting Standards Board (FASB) concluded that (1) **interest should not be imputed** in the calculation to determine if any forgiveness of debt exists; (2) the amount of debt forgiven should be reported as a **gain on restructuring**; and (3) such gain, if material, should be reported as an **extraordinary item,** net of its related income tax effect. Accordingly, in calculating the amount of debt forgiven, the carrying amount of the debt is compared with any one (or more) of the following that was included in the restructuring plan:

1. The total future cash payments specified in the new terms, **not discounted** back to their present value.
2. The fair value of the noncash assets transferred.
3. The fair value of the equity interest granted.

To the extent that the carrying amount of the debt exceeds the relevant factor or factors listed above, a gain on restructuring is reportable.

We now define in detail certain terms used in *FASB Statement No. 15.*

1. **The carrying amount of the debt** is the face, or principal, amount, plus any accrued interest payable, less any unamortized discount (or plus any premium), finance charges, or debt issuance costs.[5]
2. **Total future cash payments** include amounts that are designated principal and interest.[6] Thus, the labels traditionally assigned to amounts to be paid to creditors lose their significance for purposes of determining if a gain on restructuring of debt exists.
3. **Fair value** is defined as "the amount that the debtor could reasonably expect to receive . . . in a current sale between a willing buyer and a willing seller, that is, other than in a forced or liquidation sale."[7]

In most respects, this approach for calculating the amount of debt forgiven is relatively simple to apply. However, subsequent income statements reflect either no interest expense (when a forgiveness of debt is reportable) or unrealistically low interest expense (when no forgiveness of debt is reportable) until the maturity date of the restructured debt. Consequently, reported earnings are higher than the earnings reported if the company paid interest (or at least measured interest expense) at the current rate. Because of the potentially misleading inferences that can be made from subsequent income statements immediately after a complex restructuring, it is important to disclose in the notes to the financial statements of the appropriate subsequent periods the fact that reported interest expense is artificially low because the restructuring was accounted for in this manner.

Other Important Technical and Procedural Points. Other important technical and procedural points of *FASB Statement No. 15* are the following:

1. The *date of consummation* is the point in time at which the restructuring occurs.[8]
2. The restructuring of each payable is accounted for individually, even if the restructuring was negotiated and restructured jointly.[9]

[5]*FASB Statement No. 15*, par. 13.
[6]*FASB Statement No. 15*, par. 16, footnote 9.
[7]*FASB Statement No. 15*, par. 13.
[8]*FASB Statement No. 15*, par. 6.
[9]*FASB Statement No. 15*, par. 4.

3. When a noncash asset is transferred to a creditor in full settlement of a debt, the difference between the carrying amount of the noncash asset and its fair value is recognized as a gain or loss in the transfer of the asset. (Such gain or loss is reported in the income statement in the period of transfer as provided in *APB Opinion No. 30*, "Reporting the Results of Operations.")[10]
4. To the extent that the total future cash payments specified in the new terms exceed the carrying amount of the debt, the difference is reported as interest expense between the restructuring date and the maturity date.[11]
5. The "interest" method prescribed by *APB Opinion No. 21* is used to calculate the amount of the interest expense for each year between the restructuring date and the maturity date. This method causes a constant effective interest rate to be applied to the carrying amount of the debt at the beginning of each period between the restructuring date and the maturity date.[12]
6. When a gain on restructuring has been recognized, all future cash payments are charged to the carrying amount of the payable. In other words, if a gain on restructuring is reported, then there cannot be any future interest expense with respect to that debt.[13]
7. For determining if a gain on restructuring exists, the total future cash payments include amounts that may be contingently payable.[14]
8. When the debtor grants an equity interest to a creditor to settle fully a payable, the equity interest is recorded in the debtor's capital accounts at its fair value, and any remaining liability in excess of this fair value is recognized as a gain on restructuring of payables.[15]
9. When either noncash assets or an equity interest is given to a creditor in partial settlement of a payable and the payment terms of the remaining payable are modified, the fair value of the assets transferred or the equity interest granted is first subtracted from the carrying amount of the payable. The residual amount of the payable is then compared with the total future cash payments specified in the new terms to determine if a gain on restructuring exists.[16]

Illustration

APPLICATION OF *FASB STATEMENT NO. 15*

Assume that the financially distressed Never-Quit Company has consummated a troubled debt restructuring with substantially all of its unsecured creditors on August 31, 19X1. Never-Quit's August 31, 19X1, balance sheet before the restructuring is shown in Illustration 19-1. We assume that all

[10] *FASB Statement No. 15*, par. 14.
[11] *FASB Statement No. 15*, par. 16.
[12] *FASB Statement No. 15*, par. 16.
[13] *FASB Statement No. 15*, par. 17.
[14] *FASB Statement No. 15*, par. 18.
[15] *FASB Statement No. 15*, par. 15.
[16] *FASB Statement No. 15*, par. 19.

Illustration 19-1
Balance Sheet before Restructuring of Debt

NEVER-QUIT COMPANY
Balance Sheet
August 31, 19X1
(immediately before restructuring)

Assets		
Current Assets:		
Cash		$ 450,000
Accounts receivable	$ 650,000	
Less—Allowance for uncollectibles	(240,000)	410,000
Inventories		800,000
Total Current Assets		$ 1,660,000
Noncurrent Assets:		
Property, plant, and equipment	$2,700,000	
Less—Accumulated depreciation	(1,500,000)	1,200,000
Other assets		140,000
Total Assets		$ 3,000,000
Liabilities and Stockholders' Deficiency		
Current Liabilities:		
Note payable, secured by land and buildings		$ 1,000,000
Notes payable, unsecured		2,050,000
Accrued interest (all on unsecured notes)		540,000
Accounts payable		925,000
Other accrued liabilities		75,000
Total Liabilities		$ 4,590,000
Stockholders' Deficiency:		
Common stock, $1 par value, 200,000 shares issued and outstanding		$ 200,000
Additional paid-in capital		1,850,000
Accumulated deficit		(3,640,000)
Total Stockholders' Deficiency		$(1,590,000)
Total Liabilities in Excess of Stockholders' Deficiency		$ 3,000,000

notes payable (secured and unsecured) are currently due and payable as a result of defaults under related loan agreements.

The following items are part of the restructuring. For each of these items (except the last item), the application of *FASB Statement No. 15* is explained and the journal entry to reflect the restructuring is given. (All solutions ignore income tax effects.)

1. **Payment of cash in full settlement.** Never-Quit owes $600,000 to 80 vendors. These vendors have collectively agreed to settle their claims fully for 40 cents on the dollar. Payment of $240,000 was made on August 31, 19X1. Because the carrying amount of the $600,000 debt

exceeds the total future cash payments of $240,000, a $360,000 gain on restructuring of debt is reportable in the 19X1 income statement, recorded as follows:

Accounts Payable	600,000	
Cash		240,000
Gain on Restructuring of Debt		360,000
To record payment to vendors and gain on restructuring of debt.		

2. **Transfer of receivables in full settlement.** The company owes $325,000 to a vendor who has agreed to accept certain of the company's accounts receivable totaling $280,000. The company has an allowance of $100,000 recorded on the books against these receivables. The receivables were assigned to the creditor on August 31, 19X1. The company has not guaranteed the collectibility of these receivables.
   Because the $325,000 carrying amount of the debt exceeds the $180,000 fair value of the assets (the net amount expected to be collectible by the debtor), a gain on restructuring of $145,000 is reportable in the 19X1 income statement, recorded as follows:

Accounts Payable	325,000	
Allowance for Uncollectibles	100,000	
Accounts Receivable		280,000
Gain on Restructuring of Debt		145,000
To record transfer of assets to vendor and gain on restructuring of debt.		

3. **Grant of an equity interest in full settlement.** The company owes $500,000 ($430,000 principal and $70,000 interest) to a financial institution that has agreed to cancel the entire amount owed in exchange for 100,000 shares of the debtor's common stock. The market value of the common stock on August 31, 19X1, is $3.50 per share. The company issued the 100,000 shares to the creditor on this date.
   Because the $500,000 carrying amount of the debt exceeds the $350,000 fair value of the equity interest granted (100,000 shares × $3.50 per share), a gain on restructuring of debt of $150,000 is reportable in the 19X1 income statement, recorded as follows:

Notes Payable	430,000	
Accrued Interest Payable	70,000	
Common Stock		100,000
Additional Paid-in Capital		250,000
Gain on Restructuring of Debt		150,000
To record grant of equity interest and gain on restructuring of debt.		

4. **Modification of debt terms (no contingent interest).** The company owes $260,000 ($220,000 principal and $40,000 interest) to a financial institution that has agreed to cancel $20,000 of principal and the $40,000 of accrued interest and reduce the interest rate on the remaining principal to 5% for five years, at the end of which time the note is to be paid in full.

   Because the $260,000 carrying amount of the debt exceeds the $250,000 total future cash payments as specified in the terms of the agreement ($200,000 designated as a principal payment and $50,000 designated as interest payments), a gain on restructuring of debt of $10,000 is reportable in the 19X1 income statement, recorded as follows:

Notes Payable	**220,000**	
Accrued Interest Payable	**40,000**	
Restructured Debt		**250,000**
Gain on Restructuring of Debt		**10,000**
To record the restructuring of the debt and the resultant gain.		

   Because a gain on restructuring of debt exists, no interest expense is reported for the next five years on this debt.

5. **Modification of debt terms (contingent interest).** The company owes a total of $750,000 ($500,000 principal and $250,000 interest) to a financial institution that has agreed to the following:

   a. The $250,000 accrued interest is canceled.
   b. The due date of the $500,000 principal is extended six years from August 31, 19X1.
   c. The interest rate for the first three years is 5% (a reduction of 5% from the old rate).
   d. The interest rate for the following three years is 10%.
   e. If the debtor's cumulative earnings for the next six years exceed $1,000,000, then interest for the first three years must be paid at 10% rather than 5%. (The cumulative earnings will probably not exceed $1,000,000 for the next six years.)

   The total minimum and maximum future payments are determined as follows:

Principal	**$500,000**
Interest—years 1, 2, and 3 @ 5%	**75,000**
Interest—years 4, 5, and 6 @ 10%	**150,000**
Minimum Total Future Payments	**$725,000**
Contingent interest—years 1, 2, and 3	**75,000**
Maximum Total Future Payments	**$800,000**

The $750,000 carrying value of the debt does not exceed the $800,000 total maximum future payments that may be made under the new terms. Thus, no gain on restructuring of debt is reportable in 19X1:

Notes Payable	**500,000**	
Accrued Interest Payable	**250,000**	
Restructured Debt		**750,000**
To record the restructuring of the debt.		

If at the end of the sixth year the cumulative earnings have not exceeded $1,000,000, then a $25,000 gain on restructuring is reported at that time. If it becomes probable during the six years that the cumulative earnings will exceed $1,000,000, then additional interest expense of $50,000 ($800,000 − $750,000 carrying amount of the debt) must be provided over the remaining life of the loan.

6. **Combination grant of equity interest and modification of debt terms.** Never-Quit owes $1,080,000 ($900,000 principal and $180,000 interest) to some of its major stockholders, who have agreed to the following:

   a. Accrued interest of $80,000 is canceled.
   b. Principal of $400,000 is canceled in exchange for the issuance of 4,000 shares of 6%, $100 par value, convertible preferred stock with cumulative dividends. (We assume that the articles of incorporation were amended to approve the authorization for this new class of stock, which was issued on August 31, 19X1.)
   c. The remaining principal of $500,000 and the uncanceled interest of $100,000 bear interest at 5%, with $300,000 to be paid in six months and the remaining $300,000 to be paid in 18 months.

   Because no established market price is available for the preferred stock, we assume that the fair value of the preferred stock equals the $400,000 amount of the principal canceled. This assumed fair value of the preferred stock is subtracted from the $1,080,000 carrying value of the debt to arrive at an **adjusted carrying value** of $680,000. The adjusted carrying value of $680,000 is then compared with the total future payments to determine if a gain on restructuring exists. The total future payments are $630,000 ($600,000 designated as principal and $30,000 designated as interest). Accordingly, a gain on restructuring of debt of $50,000 ($680,000 − $630,000) is reportable in the 19X1 income statement, recorded as follows:

Notes Payable	**900,000**	
Accrued Interest Payable	**180,000**	
Preferred Stock		**400,000**
Restructured Debt		**630,000**
Gain on Restructuring of Debt		**50,000**
To record the restructuring of the debt.		

7. **Reclassification by secured creditor.** None of the preceding items pertains to the company's secured creditor (who is owed $1,000,000), because a secured creditor is under no economic compulsion to make concessions. Because of the preceding restructurings, however, this creditor agrees to allow Never-Quit to repay $960,000 of the $1,000,000 owed after August 31, 19X2, leaving only $40,000 as a current liability as of August 31, 19X1. (The interest rate was not changed.)

Never-Quit's August 31, 19X1, balance sheet, which reflects the financial terms of the restructurings, is shown in Illustration 19-2. In comparing Illustration 19-2 with Illustration 19-1, note that the stockholders' deficiency has been almost eliminated as a result of the restructuring. Although a substantial portion of the stockholders' deficiency is usually eliminated in a troubled debt restructuring, the entire deficiency need not be eliminated for the rehabilitation efforts to be successful.

Never-Quit's 19X1 income statement reflects the gain on restructuring as an extraordinary item, part of the period's income but separate from income (loss) from operations. The illustration has omitted tax effects, which we address in a later section.

Nonapplicability of *FASB Statement No. 15* to Quasi-Reorganizations

Although a debt restructuring may eliminate most or all of the stockholders' deficiency, some companies try to eliminate the accumulated deficit by using the "quasi-reorganization" procedures provided by many state laws.

Recall from intermediate accounting that adjustments made to restate (usually write down) assets in a quasi-reorganization are charged directly to equity.[17] Adjustments to restate (reduce) liabilities in a quasi-reorganization are similarly credited directly to equity. Treating such adjustments to assets and liabilities as capital transactions is desirable, because otherwise asset write-downs would be reported as capital transactions and liability reductions would be reported (per the general rule of *FASB Statement No. 15*) as noncapital (income statement) transactions.

FASB Statement No. 15 does not apply to a troubled debt restructuring that coincides with quasi-reorganization procedures if the debtor "restates its liabilities generally" in that quasi-reorganization.[18] The phrase **"restates its liabilities generally"** is a new term introduced into the accounting literature by *FASB Statement No. 15.* Although the pronouncement does not define the term, it means a restructuring that encompasses most of a company's liabilities, as would usually occur when restructuring is part of the quasi-reorganization plan. Although *FASB Statement No. 15*

[17]This procedure is required pursuant to the provision of *Accounting Research Bulletin No. 43*, Chapter 7, Section A, "Capital Accounts," par. 6. This position was reaffirmed in *Opinions of the Accounting Principles Board, No. 9*, "Reporting the Results of Operations," par. 28.
[18]*FASB Statement No. 15*, footnote 4.

Illustration 19-2
Balance Sheet after Restructuring of Debt

NEVER-QUIT COMPANY
Balance Sheet
August 31, 19X1
(after the restructuring)

Assets		
Current Assets:		
Cash		$ 210,000
Accounts receivable	$ 370,000	
Less—Allowance for uncollectibles	(140,000)	230,000
Inventories		800,000
Total Current Assets		$1,240,000
Noncurrent Assets:		
Property, plant, and equipment	$2,700,000	
Less—Accumulated depreciation	(1,500,000)	1,200,000
Other assets		140,000
Total Assets		$2,580,000
Liabilities and Stockholders' Deficiency		
Current Liabilities:		
Other accrued liabilities		$ 75,000
Current portion of secured note payable		40,000
Current portion of restructured debt, unsecured		300,000
Total Current Liabilities		$ 415,000
Long-Term Debt:		
Secured note payable		$ 960,000
Restructured debt, unsecured		1,330,000
Total Long-Term Debt		$2,290,000
Stockholders' Deficiency:		
Preferred stock, 6%, $100 par value, cumulative, 40,000 shares issued and outstanding		$ 400,000
Common stock, $1 par value, 300,000 shares issued and outstanding		300,000
Additional paid-in capital		2,100,000
Accumulated deficit		(2,925,000)
Total Stockholders' Deficiency		$ (125,000)
Total Liabilities in Excess of Stockholders' Deficiency		$2,580,000

does not explain why it does not apply to these situations, we may assume that the FASB wants to allow consistent treatment for both asset and liability adjustments in quasi-reorganizations.

This explanation does not help in the more common situation in which the stockholders' deficiency resulted from several years of large operating losses — that is, not from a restatement of the assets. Regardless of what caused the accumulated deficit (whether from restating assets or from operating losses), the following question is raised: Why should the (decision to eliminate the accumulated deficit using quasi-reorganization procedures (a mere formality under state law) change the perception of forgiveness of debt from an income statement gain (in *FASB Statement No. 15*) to a capital transaction? The answer evidently lies in the "fresh start" objective of a quasi-reorganization. A restructuring not involving a quasi-reorganization maintains the company's basic continuity. A quasi-reorganization results in the assumed death of the old company and the assumed creation of a new one. A "break" exists that usually destroys any pre- versus post-income statement comparability. Because of this fresh-start objective, treating the forgiveness as a capital transaction makes more sense.

Tax Consequences of Gains on Restructurings

The Internal Revenue Code treats gains on troubled debt restructurings as taxable only to the extent that such restructurings result in a positive balance in total stockholders' equity (not retained earnings). Any income taxes provided would be netted against the gain on the restructuring, because in financial reporting, the gain must be reported as an extraordinary item net of income tax effects.

Accounting by Creditors

Although this chapter is concerned with accounting by a debtor, *FASB Statement No. 15* applies to creditors as well. In most respects, accounting by a creditor is symmetrical to the accounting by a debtor. Thus, if the debtor reports a gain on restructuring, the creditor simultaneously reports an offsetting loss on restructuring of its receivables, except to the extent that such loss has already been provided for in allowances for uncollectibles or write-offs, or both.

Interestingly, the banking industry uniformly and vehemently opposed the imputed interest (discounted present value) approach of calculating the amount of debt forgiven as presented in the FASB discussion memorandum that preceded *FASB Statement No. 15.* This approach would have had creditors reporting much greater losses than under the "no-discount" alternative adopted by the FASB. How the banking industry's strong vocal position influenced the FASB in its deliberations is conjecture. It is interesting to note, however, that the FASB's first exposure draft on troubled debt restructurings (dated November 7, 1975, and encompassing only accounting by debtors) called for the imputed interest approach. Because of the obvious implications to creditors — that is, if a debtor reports a gain, the creditor should simultaneously report a loss — the project was expanded to include accounting by creditors as well.

Subsequent-Period Interest Expense in "No Reportable Gain" Restructurings

Procedural points 4 and 5 of *FASB Statement No. 15* (shown on page 726) indicate that when total future payments exceed the carrying amount of the debt, the excess is reported as interest expense between the restructuring date and the maturity date using the interest method prescribed by *APB Opinion No. 21*. In such cases, the effective interest rate must be calculated. Assume the following information:

1. Carrying amount of the debt at January 1, 19X1:	
Principal owed	$1,100,000
Interest owed	33,947
	$1,133,947
2. Cancellation of debt per restructuring agreement consummated January 1, 19X1:	
Principal	$ 100,000
Interest	33,947
	$ 133,947
3. Total future payments to be made:	
Amount designated as principal (due December 31, 19X2)	$1,000,000
Amounts designated as interest (10% of $1,000,000 payable annually at year-end for two years)	200,000
	$1,200,000

Because the $1,200,000 total future payments exceed the $1,133,947 carrying amount of the debt, $66,053 interest expense ($1,200,000 − $1,133,947) is reported in the income statements during the two years following the restructuring. What interest rate is needed for the total future payments of $1,200,000 to equal the present value of the carrying amount of the debt of $1,133,947? A trial-and-error approach to the present value tables reveals that the effective interest rate is 3%. The present value calculations are shown below:

Designation	Total Future Payments	Present Value Factor at 3%	Present Value
Principal	$1,000,000	0.94260	$ 942,600
Interest	200,000	1.91347[a]	191,347
	$1,200,000		$1,133,947

[a]Obtained from an annuity present value table (applied to the $100,000 annual amount).

This example was designed so that the effective interest rate would be an even number to avoid the additional complexity of interpolating. In practice, of course, interpolating is usually necessary.

The following entries would be made for the restructuring, the recording of interest using the effective interest rate, and the payments made under the restructuring agreement:

1. January 1, 19X1:		
Notes Payable	**1,100,000**	
Interest Payable	**33,947**	
Restructured Debt		**1,133,947**
To record the effect of the restructuring.		
2. December 31, 19X1:		
Interest Expense	**34,018**	
Restructured Debt	**65,982**	
Cash		**100,000**
To record interest expense at 3% of $1,133,947 and the first payment of $100,000.		
3. December 31, 19X2:		
Interest Expense	**32,035**	
Restructured Debt	**67,965**	
Cash		**100,000**
To record interest expense at 3% of $1,067,965 ($1,133,947 − $65,982) and the second payment of $100,000.		
Restructured Debt	**1,000,000**	
Cash		**1,000,000**
To record the $1,000,000 payment at its maturity date.		

The entries affecting the Restructured Debt account are recorded in the following T-account to illustrate how the use of the exact effective interest rate results in a zero balance after the last required payment.

Restructured Debt

		1,133,947	Jan. 1, 19X1
Dec. 31, 19X1	65,982		
		1,067,965	
Dec. 31, 19X2	67,965		
		1,000,000	
Dec. 31, 19X2	1,000,000		
		–0–	

BANKRUPTCY REORGANIZATIONS

Although Chapter 11 of the bankruptcy statutes is the reorganization chapter, the statutes do not define the term *reorganization*. However, we may assume from the Chapter 11 purpose and the procedures that the chapter allows that the term is intended to have a broad meaning. Basically, a **reorganization** encompasses the development of a plan—called a *plan of reorganization*—to alter the company's liability and/or equity structure so that the company has a reasonable chance of surviving bankruptcy proceedings and prospering on its own.

Most reorganization plans involve a negotiated settlement between the company and its unsecured creditors to repay debts, usually at so many cents on the dollar. Thus, the company is provided with a "fresh start" a unique opportunity in business. Approximately 10–20% of all business bankruptcy filings are Chapter 11 filings (the remainder being Chapter 7 filings).

Advantages and Disadvantages of Reorganizing under Chapter 11 versus Restructuring Outside of the Bankruptcy Courts

The primary advantage to a distressed company of a Chapter 11 reorganization is that it usually results in a massive reduction of the debtor's liabilities (forgiveness of debt) compared with the amount of debt forgiven in a restructuring outside of the bankruptcy courts. In addition, a considerable amount of cash is saved because interest on unsecured debt does not accrue during the period of the bankruptcy proceeding—the amount of unsecured creditors' claims is fixed at the bankruptcy filing. For example, Wickes Cos., a giant retailing conglomerate, saved more than $350 million of interest related to its unsecured debt during the 33 months that it was in Chapter 11 reorganization (concluded in 1985). Furthermore, filing for reorganization under Chapter 11 places a company in sanctuary from its creditors because they cannot sue for overdue payments. As a result, the distressed company has some "breathing room" to develop a plan of reorganization. When recessions and high interest rates occur, as they did in the early 1980s, increasing numbers of companies flee to the bankruptcy courts for protection from creditors and for the opportunity to salvage the potentially productive (profitable) portions of the existing organization. Also of major importance is that, with court approval, companies in Chapter 11 can make substantial wage reductions by rejecting or altering union contracts.

However, as the article on page 737 makes clear, increasingly the disadvantages of filing for Chapter 11 bankruptcy outweigh the advantages.

What Percentage Survive Chapter 11? To file for reorganization under Chapter 11 is to flirt with extinction. Of all Chapter 11 filings, about only 15% emerge as viable companies—and then usually with new top management; the remainder are transferred to Chapter 7 and liquidated.

PERSPECTIVE

Chapter 11 Isn't So Chic Anymore

Manville did it. Continental Airlines did it. Texaco threatened to do it. Each time an apparently viable company summoned the specter of Chapter 11, the strategy appeared to work. Suddenly, it seemed, bankruptcy had become just one more management tool.

But Chapter 11 is getting its bad name back. First, a landmark May 28 federal appeals court decision against Wheeling-Pittsburgh Steel Corp. will make it much more difficult for companies to use bankruptcy to cut wage costs. Second, Manville Corp.'s shareholders and some of its executives are now paying for their reorganization with huge dilution of their stock holdings and damage to their careers. And A. H. Robins Co.'s managers are fighting this month to keep control of their company, which went into Chapter 11 last summer. The cases, says New York bankruptcy specialist Richard Lieb, establish that "if you're in bankruptcy, you've got to pay for it. And sometimes it's a very big price."

Wrath and Praise

When Manville kicked off the brief era of bankruptcy chic with its unprecedented reorganization filing on Aug. 26, 1982, the dangers weren't so clear. No company as financially successful had ever filed under Chapter 11, and a federal bankruptcy law then only three years old encouraged reorganizations of large public companies by allowing managers to keep control in most circumstances. Manville's move drew wrath from some, but there were admirers in the business community who saw the reorganization as a creative response to the company's crushing asbestos liability.

A rash of imitators followed. In 1983 the managers of Oklahoma-based Wilson Foods Corp. filed under Chapter 11 and succeeded in slashing union wages. A few months later Continental Airlines Corp. Chairman Frank Lorenzo did the same thing and also succeeded. But other results are less clear. The Robins case was filed in 1985 in an effort to use Chapter 11 to handle thousands of claims that the Dalkon Shield intrauterine device caused injuries. It is still unresolved and threatens to backfire on Robins' management. And the Wheeling-Pitt decision is clearly a setback for efforts to get wage cuts through bankruptcy.

There has always been strong opposition to management–by–Chapter 11. On Capitol Hill, organized labor won a new law in 1984 that made a Continental-type wage cut possible in bankruptcy court only with the judge's prior approval. It wasn't clear until the new Wheeling-Pitt decision, however, that companies must also convince the court they would collapse without the proposed cuts. David M. Silberman, an AFL-CIO lawyer who worked on the case, says the ruling will "make companies who would use bankruptcy to avoid agreements think twice and three times. It will have impact across the board." Wheeling-Pitt hasn't yet decided whether to ask the Supreme Court to review the case.

Chapter 11 Isn't So Chic Anymore *(continued)*

The 1984 law says companies can get wage reductions in bankruptcy court only if they are "necessary." Many companies have argued that their financial condition didn't have to be life-or-death in order to win the relief they were seeking. The Wheeling-Pitt decision, the first appeals court decision interpreting the new law, rejects that argument. Federal appeals Judge Dolores K. Sloviter declared that "such an indulgent standard would inadequately differentiate between labor contracts, which Congress sought to protect, and other commercial contracts," which companies can discard in bankruptcy.

The Manville and Robins variations on creative bankruptcy didn't require an act of Congress to highlight the dangers of Chapter 11. Seven months after its filing, Robins enraged some of its creditors by paying creditors and several executives $6.8 million without first obtaining approval from the court. A U.S. attorney in Virginia is asking the judge hearing the case to appoint a trustee to take control from management because of what he charges are abuses.

Take No Prisoners

This spring Manville's executives were forced to negotiate their own futures with representatives of the asbestos claimants. The bitter negotiations ended with the resignation of Manville President Josh T. Hulce. Says Manville director Aaron A. Gold: "It was like executing captured soldiers. They weren't going to take any prisoners."

The Manville and Robins experiences point out dangers that managers overlooked as they experimented with Chapter 11, says Robert J. Rosenberg of Latham & Watkins, who represented the Manville asbestos victims until a few months ago. "In this wave of bankruptcy as a management technique, business people lost sight of what is wrong with Chapter 11, which is that you're not in there by yourself. You're in there with everyone, and they are given power to accomplish their own goals." That is not an oversight executives are likely to make as frequently from now on.

Source: William B. Glaberson, Matt Rothman, and Mark Ivey, "Chapter 11 Isn't So Chic Anymore." Reprinted from the June 16, 1986, issue of *Business Week* by special permission, © 1986 by McGraw-Hill, Inc.

The Sequence of Events in a Chapter 11 Filing

The typical sequence of events in a Chapter 11 filing is as follows:

1. **Filing the petition.** Either a voluntary or an involuntary petition can initiate bankruptcy proceedings. The company in question may prepare a statement showing asset values and amounts that would be paid to each class of creditor in the event of liquidation. As noted earlier, accountants call this a *statement of affairs.* We illustrate the preparation of this statement later in the chapter in connection with liquidations.

2. **Management of the company.** The debtor company's management usually continues to control and operate the debtor's day-to-day activities. Under certain conditions and for just cause (such as fraud, imcompetence, or gross mismanagement of the company), and if in the best interests of creditors, the court may appoint a trustee to manage the debtor's business (Section 1104[a]). **The appointment of a trustee in a Chapter 11 filing is infrequent.** We discuss the duties of trustees later in the chapter in connection with liquidations, for which trustees are always appointed.
3. **Creditors' and equity security holders' committees.** After an order for relief has been entered, the court appoints a committee of unsecured creditors. (The court may also appoint additional committees of creditors, or of equity security holders if necessary, to ensure adequate representation of these groups. Such a court-appointed committee may

   a. select and authorize [with the court's approval] the employment by such committee of one or more attorneys, accountants, or other agents, to represent or perform services for such committee [Section 1103(a)];
   b. consult with the trustee or debtor in possession concerning the administration of the case;
   c. investigate the acts, conduct, assets, liabilities and financial condition of the debtor, the operation of the debtor's business and the desirability of the continuance of such business, and any other matter relevant to the case or to the formulation of a plan;
   d. participate in the formulation of a plan [of reorganization], advise those represented by such committee of such committee's recommendations as to any plan formulated, and collect and file with the court acceptances of a plan;
   e. request the appointment of a trustee or examiner . . . if a trustee or examiner, as the case may be, has not previously been appointed . . . ; and
   f. perform such other services as are in the interest of those represented [Section 1103(c)].

4. **Plan of reorganization.** Under Chapter 11 of the 1978 act, a plan of reorganization may alter the legal, equitable, and contractual rights of any class of creditors' claims, secured or unsecured, or of equity interests. Such an alteration is known as **impairment** of a claim or an interest (Section 1124). In a common plan of reorganization, all unsecured creditors agree to accept payment at a percentage of their respective claims — for example, 25 cents on the dollar — with the remainder of the debt canceled.

The debtor has the exclusive right to propose a plan during the 120 days after the order for relief. At the end of this period, any party of interest — such as the trustee, committee, a creditor, or an equity security holder — may file a plan, provided certain conditions are met (Section 1121). The role of the Securities and Exchange Commission (SEC) is quite limited:

> The Securities and Exchange Commission may raise and may appear and be heard for any issue . . . but the SEC may not appeal from any judgment, order, or decree entered in the case [Section 1109].

5. **Disclosure statement.** Before acceptance of a plan of reorganization can be solicited, the debtor must furnish the plan or a summary of the plan to the various classes of creditors and equity interests, along with a written disclosure statement approved by the court as containing **adequate information** (Section 1125[b]). Adequate information is defined as "information of a kind, and in sufficient detail, as far as is reasonably practicable in light of the nature and history of the debtor and the condition of the debtor's books and records, that would enable a hypothetical reasonable investor . . . to make an informed judgment about the plan" (Section 1125[a][1]). This is obviously determined on a case-by-case basis.
6. **Acceptance of plan.** Each class of creditors and equity interests then votes to accept or reject the plan of reorganization. The requirements for approval are as follows:
   a. **Creditor's claims.** "A class of claims has accepted a plan if such plan has been accepted by creditors . . . that hold at least **two-thirds in amount and more than one-half in number** of the allowed claims of such class . . ." (Section 1126[c]).
   b. **Equity interests.** "A class of interests has accepted a plan if such plan has been accepted by holders of such interests . . . that hold at least **two-thirds in amount** of the allowed interests of such class . . ." (Section 1126[d]).
7. **Confirmation of the plan by the court.** After the plan of reorganization has been submitted to the court, a hearing is held. A plan must meet eleven specific requirements to be approved by the court. The overriding requirement is that the debtor must be unlikely to be liquidated or have need for further financial reorganization after the plan is confirmed. In other words, the plan of reorganization must be feasible. Another major requirement is that each class of claims or equity interests must have accepted the plan or must not be impaired under the plan. However, a provision in the law (referred to in House Committee Reports as "cram down"), allows the court to confirm the plan (if requested by the proponent of the plan) even if each class of claims or equity interests has not accepted it. For this to occur, the plan must not discriminate unfairly and must be fair and equitable with respect to each class of claims or equity interests that is impaired or has not accepted the plan (Section 1129).

   If the court does not confirm the plan of reorganization, it may, on request of a party of interest and after notice and a hearing, either dismiss the case or convert it to a Chapter 7 case (whereby the debtor is forced out of business through liquidation). Such action depends on which course is in the best interest of creditors and the estate (Section 1112).
8. **Discharge of indebtedness.** After the court confirms the plan of reorganization, the debtor is discharged of certain indebtedness as set forth in the plan. However, if the debtor has committed certain acts, then dis-

charge of indebtedness does not occur even though a plan has been confirmed (Section 1141[d]). In general, discharge of indebtedness is not granted if (a) the debtor has not fully cooperated with the court (for example, by not making all properties and records available to the court's representative, failing to explain losses satisfactorily, or refusing to obey court orders); and if (b) the debtor has performed certain specified acts involving the debtor's properties and records to hinder, delay, or defraud creditors (for example, concealing property, destroying records, failing to keep or preserve records, or obtaining money or property fraudulently) (Section 727[a]). A discharge is not granted if the debtor was granted a discharge in a case commenced within six years before the filing date of the petition (Section 727[a]).

9. **Exceptions to discharge of indebtedness.** Certain types of indebtedness cannot be discharged under the bankruptcy statutes. These debts, which eventually must be paid if the debtor survives Chapter 11 proceedings, are as follows:
   a. Taxes owed to the United States or any state, county, district, or municipality, and customs duties.
   b. Debts incurred in obtaining money, property, services, an extension renewal, or refinance of credit by either:
      (1) false pretenses, a false representation, or actual fraud, other than a statement concerning the debtor's financial condition.
      (2) use of a written statement that is materially false with respect to the debtor's financial condition on which the creditor reasonably relied and that the debtor made or published with intent to deceive.
   c. Debts that have not been duly scheduled in time for proof and allowance because a creditor had no notice or knowledge of bankruptcy proceedings.
   d. Debts for fraud or defalcation while acting in a fiduciary capacity, or larcency.
   e. Debts related to willful and malicious injury by the debtor to another entity or to the property of another entity.
   f. Fines, penalties, and forfeitures payable to and for the benefit of a governmental unit (Section 523).

Accounting Issues

The accounting issues in bankruptcy reorganizations are the same as those discussed earlier for troubled debt restructurings—that is, how to calculate and report the amount of debt forgiven. After some initial confusion about the application of *FASB Statement No. 15* to bankruptcy reorganizations, *FASB Technical Bulletin No. 81-6* was issued to clarify the matter. This bulletin states that *FASB Statement No. 15* does not apply to bankruptcy reorganizations that result in a "general restatement of the debtor's liabilities" (defined earlier as a restructuring of most of the amount of a company's liabilities).[19] Because this usually occurs in

[19] *FASB Technical Bulletin No. 81-6*, "Applicability of *Statement 15* to Debtors in Bankruptcy Situations" (Stamford: Financial Accounting Standards Board, 1981), par. 3.

bankruptcy reorganizations, *FASB Statement No. 15* will rarely apply. Consequently, the following questions must be addressed:

- What is meaningful accounting for a reorganized company?
- What, if any, guidance is contained in promulgated accounting standards?

We first address the calculation of the amount of debt forgiven and then the reporting of such forgiveness.

Calculation of Forgiveness of Debt. In reorganizations in which unsecured creditors are paid immediately at so many cents on the dollar, there is only one way to calculate the forgiveness. However, unsecured creditors may also be given cash and notes payable (and often equity securities as well). Traditionally, accountants have compared the amount owed with the fair value (discounted present value, in the case of debt) of the consideration given to determine the amount of debt forgiven. This method usually results in a much larger reported forgiveness ("gain") than would result under the *FASB Statement No. 15* approach of comparing the carrying amount of the debt (essentially the amount owed) with the undiscounted total future payments. To illustrate the dramatic difference that can occur, we assume that a company in bankruptcy reorganization proceedings proposes to settle with its unsecured creditors (who are owed $10,000,000) by paying $2,000,000 cash and giving $5,000,000 of 14% (assumed market rate) notes payable due in five years. The amount of debt forgiven under each approach is calculated as follows:

	Fair Value of Consideration Given Approach	Total Future Payments Approach of *FASB Statement No. 15*
Carrying amount of debt..........	$10,000,000	$10,000,000
Amounts to be compared with carrying amount of debt:	(fair value)	(total future payments)
Cash	$ 2,000,000	$ 2,000,000
Notes payable....................	5,000,000	5,000,000
Interest ($5,000,000 × 14% × 5 years)	n/a	3,500,000
	$ 7,000,000	$10,500,000
Post-reorganization carrying value of the debt	$ 7,000,000	$10,000,000
Amount of debt forgiven ("gain")	$ 3,000,000	None
Future interest expense...........	$700,000 per year for the next five years	$500,000 total over the next five years

Most reorganization plans attempt to structure a positive stockholders' equity (though not necessarily positive retained earnings) to place the company on firmer ground for emerging from bankruptcy proceedings. To measure and report this effect is exceedingly difficult under the approach of *FASB Statement No. 15*. The pronouncement itself, if applicable, might very well be counterproductive to obtaining an agreement with the unsecured creditors concerning necessary sacrifices. (If applicable, the pronouncement requires much greater sacrifices by creditors to achieve a positive net worth.) This possibility may have been part of the FASB's rationale for exempting bankruptcy reorganizations from *FASB Statement No. 15* guidance. Another possible reason for the exemption involves the "fresh start" purpose of reorganizations under Chapter 11. Future income statements should reflect a reasonable amount of interest expense on restructured debt. This occurs under the "fair value of consideration given" approach but rarely occurs under the *FASB Statement No. 15* approach.

Imputing of Interest. The imputing of interest issue, discussed earlier in connection with troubled debt restructurings, also pertains to bankruptcy reorganizations. Unfortunately, the current accounting literature gives no explicit guidance concerning whether or not to impute interest in bankruptcy reorganizations.[20] Our inquiries to practicing accountants who are involved in bankruptcy reorganizations reveal that some companies are imputing interest under the principles of *APB Opinion No. 21*, "Interest on Receivables and Payables," and others are not.

Reporting Forgiveness of Debt. Current accounting pronouncements also do not explicitly state how to report (classify) a forgiveness of debt in bankruptcy proceedings. Some practicing accountants perceive the forgiveness of debt as a "gain from extinguishment of debt" and report it as an extraordinary item, if material, pursuant to the requirements of *FASB Statement No. 4*, "Reporting Gains and Losses from Extinguishment of Debt," paragraph 8. Practicing accountants who perceive the forgiveness of debt as a capital contribution credit it directly to Paid-in Capital. The latter treatment is usually found when the common stockholder accounts are adjusted on reorganization to eliminate an accumulated deficit as in quasi-reorganization accounting.

The Role of Accountants in Bankruptcy Reorganizations

Certified public accountants are commonly employed in varying capacities in bankruptcy proceedings. Many accounting firms can generate substantial fees for their services in this area. (The new bankruptcy statutes eliminated the longstanding requirement that accountants set their fees in a

[20]This guidance was clear prior to the issuance of *FASB Statement No. 15*, because *FASB Interpretation No. 2*, "Imputing Interest on Debt Arrangements Made under the Federal Bankruptcy Act," extended the principles of *Opinions of the Accounting Principles Board, No. 21*, "Interest on Receivables and Payables," to bankruptcy reorganizations. Unfortunately, *FASB Interpretation No. 2* was expunged from the literature on the issuance of *FASB Statement No. 15* (supporting accountants who thought *FASB Statement No. 15* applied to bankruptcy reorganizations), and *FASB Technical Bulletin No. 81-6* did not reinstate it. It is not known whether this was an oversight or purposeful.

"spirit of economy"; bankruptcy assistance is no longer considered charity work.) The most common capacity for outside accountants is that of rendering advice and assistance on financial projections used in developing a plan of reorganization. Both the distressed company and its creditors' committee commonly hire their own outside accountants. Occasionally, outside accountants are responsible for determining the quality of the distressed company's accounts receivable. If management is suspected of improper actions, bankruptcy judges may need to appoint outside accountants to investigate such charges. The creditors' committee often hires outside accountants to determine the following:

1. Has the debtor made any transfers of assets that would constitute preferences to certain creditors?
2. Has management committed any acts that would constitute fraud, deception, or bad faith?
3. Has management committed any acts that would bar it from obtaining a discharge of certain indebtedness?
4. In what condition are the company's books and records?
5. What would be obtained in liquidation? Answering this question requires the preparation of a statement of affairs, which is discussed and illustrated later in the chapter.

The creditors' accountants need not perform an audit of the debtor's financial statements to be of assistance in these areas; a limited special purpose examination is usually sufficient. Obviously the scope of any such limited examination must be worked out with the creditors' committee.

LIQUIDATIONS

Large companies with common stock that is publicly traded on the New York Stock Exchange are seldom liquidated because they usually have adequate capital and managerial talent to deal with adverse developments. The growing trend toward diversification also works against liquidation. A large, diverse business is less apt to be affected overall by an adverse development resulting from poor management decisions in one of its industry segments. Furthermore, if management cannot deal effectively with such problems in one of its industry segments, that segment will most likely be disposed of through sale (or possibly abandonment), but the remainder of the business will continue. Consequently, liquidation is generally associated with small and moderately sized businesses. The smaller and more unseasoned a company is, the more likely it is to face liquidation.

Liquidation outside of the Bankruptcy Courts

In some instances, liquidation may take place outside of the bankruptcy courts. In these situations, a formal **general assignment for the benefit of**

creditors usually is executed, whereby the debtor's property is transferred to a designated assignee or assignees (who are often the debtor's creditors) for the purpose of converting the assets into cash and making appropriate distributions of cash to the creditors. Any assets that remain after creditors have been paid in full are returned to the debtor for ultimate distribution to its stockholders. However, if the proceeds from the conversion of assets into cash are insufficient to pay creditors in full, then the creditors have no other recourse and the stockholders receive nothing.

There are three possible advantages of liquidating outside of the bankruptcy court:

1. Legal fees are usually lower.
2. The debtor can designate the assignee or assignees.
3. There is greater flexibility in the conversion of assets into cash.

Under an *involuntary* proceeding, a general assignment for the benefit of creditors is considered grounds for the bankruptcy court to enter an order for relief. Accordingly, to avoid liquidation through the bankruptcy court, a general assignment must be agreed to by all of the creditors for all practical purposes. If a sufficient number of qualified creditors subsequently file an involuntary petition of bankruptcy, the general assignment for the benefit of creditors is null and void, and the bankruptcy court then supervises and controls the liquidation of the company.

Liquidation through Bankruptcy Court

After a company has filed for liquidation under Chapter 7, one of the court's first duties is to determine if the case should be dismissed. As we mentioned at the beginning of the chapter, the filing of a voluntary petition constitutes an order for relief. Dismissals of voluntary filings are infrequent. When the debtor does not dispute an involuntary petition, the court enters an order for relief against the debtor. Dismissals of uncontested involuntary filings are also infrequent. However, if the debtor disputes an involuntary petition, then a trial must be held to determine whether the case should be dismissed or an order for relief should be entered.

The Role of the Trustee. After an order for relief has been entered, the bankruptcy court must promptly appoint an interim trustee (Section 701[a]). In an involuntary filing, the debtor may continue to operate the business from the filing date until an order for relief is entered, just as though the petition had not been filed (Section 303[f]). However, the court may appoint an interim trustee during this period, if necessary, to preserve the property of the estate or to prevent loss to the estate, providing certain procedures are followed (Section 303[g]).

After an order for relief has been entered, the court must also call a meeting of the debtor's creditors (Section 341). In this meeting, the creditors first vote for a trustee and then select a creditor's committee that consults with the trustee in connection with the administration of the estate. If the creditors are unable to select a trustee, then the interim trustee becomes the trustee (Section 702[d]). Trustees are usually professionals, mostly practicing lawyers, who specialize in this type of work. The following duties of trustees are set forth under Section 704:

1. Collect and reduce to money the property of the estate for which such trustee serves, and close up such estate as expeditiously as is compatible with the best interests of parties of interest.
2. Be accountable for all property received.
3. Investigate the financial affairs of the debtor.
4. If a purpose would be served, examine proofs of claims and object to the allowance of any claim that is improper....
5. Unless the court orders otherwise, furnish such information concerning the estate and the estate's administration as is requested by a party of interest.
6. If the business of the debtor is authorized to be operated, file with the court and with any governmental unit charged with responsibility for collection or determination of any tax arising out of such operation, periodic reports and summaries of the operation of such business, including a statement of receipts and disbursements, and such other information as the court requires. (Under Section 721, "the court may authorize the trustee to operate the business of the debtor for a limited period, if such operation is in the best interest of the estate and consistent with the orderly liquidation of the estate.")
7. Make a final report and file a final account of the administration of the estate with the court.

Accounting by trustees is discussed in detail later in the chapter.

Technical Aspects of the Duties of Trustees. The following technical aspects of the duties of the trustee should be noted:

1. **Employment of professionals.** With the court's approval, the trustee may employ attorneys, accountants, appraisers, auctioneers, or other professional persons to represent or assist the trustee in carrying out his or her duties (Section 327).
2. **Avoidance powers.** A trustee is authorized to void both **fraudulent** and **preferential** transfers made by the debtor within certain specified periods preceding the filing date. (Such transfers include the giving of a security interest in a property.) Creditors, therefore, may be required to return monies and/or properties received or may lose their security interest, or both. The section of the act dealing with preferences is intended to prevent a debtor from giving certain creditors preferential treatment over other creditors. The 1978 act sets forth the conditions that must exist for a trustee to void a property transfer to a creditor. The act also sets forth certain transfers that a trustee cannot void.

3. **Setoffs.** With respect to mutual debts between the debtor and allowable claims of a creditor, the amount owed the debtor by the creditors is subtracted from or offset against the amount owed to the creditor (Section 553). (There are certain technical exceptions to this rule that we need not deal with now.)

Distribution of Cash to Creditors. The sequence of payments to creditors is as follows:

1. The proceeds from the sale of assets that have been pledged to secured creditors are applied to satisfy those claims. Note that the bankruptcy proceedings do not alter the rights of the secured creditors to the assets that have been pledged to them; these rights are only temporarily suspended.
2. If the proceeds exceed the secured creditors' claims, such excess is available for payment to creditors with priority and unsecured creditors.
3. If the proceeds are insufficient to satisfy the claims of the secured creditors, the secured creditors become unsecured creditors to the extent of the deficiency.
4. The proceeds from the sale of unpledged assets are used to pay creditors with priority.
5. After creditors with priority have been paid, payments are made to the unsecured creditors. Payments are always stated as a percentage of all allowed claims.
6. To the extent that any creditors are not paid in full, the deficiency represents a loss.

After the final payment has been made to the unsecured creditors, the corporation is a **shell** corporation without any assets or liabilities. In most instances, the corporation then ceases its legal existence. The bankruptcy court is not authorized to grant a formal discharge of indebtedness with respect to any unpaid claims when the debtor is other than an individual (Section 727[a][1]). According to House Bankruptcy committee reports, this change is intended to prevent trafficking in corporate shells and bankrupt partnerships.

The selling of assets and the payment of proceeds to the debtor's various creditors does not always conclude a liquidation. Trustees may file suit against former directors and officers, asking for monetary damages on the grounds of gross negligence in the management of certain aspects of the business. When a sudden collapse of a company occurs shortly after its outside auditors have issued an unqualified ("clean") audit report on the company's financial statements, serious questions may be raised concerning the performance of the audit. In such situations, the auditors may be sued for alleged breach of performance.

The Role of the Accountant in Liquidations. Bankruptcy trustees often employ certified public accountants to assist them in preserving the assets of the bankrupt's estate. The extent of the accountant's services usually depend on the complexity of the estate. If the debtor's in-house accountants have not resigned before the bankruptcy petition is filed, they generally leave shortly thereafter. A certified public accountant can provide the following types of services to the bankruptcy trustee:

1. Determining what accounting books and records exist at the debtor's offices.
2. Determining the condition of the accounting records, including the filing status of all tax reports.
3. Updating the debtor's accounting records as necessary.
4. Preparing current-year tax reports and informational forms.
5. Comparing creditors' claims (as filed with the court) with the debtor's books and records and with the schedule of liabilities filed with the court by the debtor.
6. In certain instances, if fraud is suspected or known, the accountant may examine certain of the debtor's books and records in detail and submit a formal report to the trustee.

This list is not exhaustive—the accountant may be called upon to perform any service within the realm of accounting expertise.

The Statement of Affairs

Regardless of whether liquidation takes place outside of or through bankruptcy court, a special **statement of affairs** is prepared showing the financial condition of the company. The statement of affairs is prepared on the basis that the company is going out of business. Because the company is not considered a going concern, the historical cost basis for carrying assets loses its significance, and the amount expected to be realized in liquidation is the relevant valuation basis.

The statement of affairs provides information concerning how much money each class of creditors can expect to receive on liquidation of the company, assuming assets are converted into cash at the estimated realizable values used in preparing the statements. Thus, conventional classifications such as current assets and current liabilities lose their significance. Instead, assets are classified as to whether they are pledged with creditors or not pledged with creditors; liabilities are classified by category of creditor—namely, creditors with priority, secured creditors, and unsecured creditors. Stockholders' equity also loses its significance because companies in the process of liquidation usually have a negative net worth. The specific categories of assets and liabilities in the statement of affairs are as follows:

Assets

1. **Assets pledged with fully secured creditors** are expected to realize an amount at least sufficient to satisfy the related debt.

2. **Assets pledged with partially secured creditors** are expected to realize an amount below the related debt.
3. **Free assets** are not pledged and are available to satisfy the claims of creditors with priority, partially secured creditors, and unsecured creditors.

Liabilities

1. **Liabilities with priority** have priority under the bankruptcy statutes (explained earlier in the chapter).
2. **Fully secured creditors** expect to be paid in full as a result of their having sufficient collateral (pledged assets) to satisfy the indebtedness.
3. **Partially secured creditors** have collateral (pledged assets), the proceeds of which are expected to be insufficient to satisfy the indebtedness.
4. **Unsecured creditors** have no collateral (pledged assets) relating to their indebtedness.

Contingent liabilities that are reasonably calculable and probable as to payment (the criteria under *FASB Statement No. 5,* "Accounting for Contingencies") are shown in the statement of affairs. Contingent liabilities that do not meet these criteria should be disclosed in a note to the statement of affairs.

Illustration

THE STATEMENT OF AFFAIRS

The balance sheet of Fold-up Company which filed a voluntary bankruptcy petition (for liquidation under Chapter 7) on September 23, 19X5, is shown in Illustration 19-3. Additional information regarding realization follows:

1. **Receivables.** The notes and accounts receivable are considered to have been adequately provided for in preparing the balance sheet; thus, the company expects to realize the amounts shown.
2. **Finished goods.** The finished goods can be sold for $47,000; however, the company expects to incur $4,000 of direct selling and shipping costs.
3. **Work in process.** The work in process can be completed if $3,000 of direct costs are incurred for labor. On completion, this inventory can be sold for $37,000; however, the company expects to incur $2,000 of direct selling and shipping costs.
4. **Raw materials.** The raw materials can be converted into finished goods if $7,000 of direct costs are incurred for labor. On completion, this inventory can be sold for $19,000; however, the company expects to incur $1,000 of direct selling and shipping costs.
5. **Supplies.** The supplies will be substantially consumed in the completion of the work in process and the conversion of raw materials into

Illustration 19-3
A Balance Sheet for a Company in Chapter 11 Bankruptcy Proceedings

FOLD-UP COMPANY Balance Sheet September 23, 19X5	
Assets	
Current Assets:	
Cash	$ 2,000
Notes receivable	5,000
Accounts receivable, net	25,000
Inventory:	
Finished goods	40,000
Work in process	30,000
Raw materials	20,000
Supplies	5,000
Prepayments	8,000
Total Current Assets	$135,000
Noncurrent Assets:	
Land	70,000
Building, net	110,000
Equipment, net	60,000
Deferred charges	15,000
Total Assets	$390,000
Liabilities and Stockholders' Deficiency	
Current Liabilities:	
10% Notes payable to bank, secured by accounts receivable	$ 35,000
Accounts payable	246,000
Accrued liabilities:	
Interest ($2,000 to bank, $6,000 to insurance company)	8,000
Salaries and wages	7,000
Payroll taxes	2,000
Total Current Liabilities	$298,000
Long-Term Debt:	
8% Notes payable to insurance company, secured by land and building	175,000
Total Liabilities	$473,000
Stockholders' Deficiency:	
Common stock, no par	$100,000
Accumulated deficit	(183,000)
Total Stockholders' Deficiency	$ (83,000)
Total Liabilities in Excess of Stockholders' Deficiency	$390,000

finished goods. The estimated realizable value of the remaining supplies after completion and conversion is $1,000.

6. **Prepayments.** The prepayments are expected to expire during the liquidation period.
7. **Land.** The land has a current market value of $90,000.

8. **Building.** The building has a current market value of $135,000.
9. **Equipment.** The equipment can be sold in auction for an estimated $35,000.
10. **Deferred charges.** Deferred charges include organization costs, issuance expenses relating to the notes payable to the insurance company, and plant rearrangement costs.
11. **Salaries and wages.** All salaries and wages were earned within the last 90 days, and no employee is owed more than $2,000.
12. **Liquidation expenses.** The company estimates that $15,000 in court and filing fees, appraisal fees, and legal and accounting fees will be incurred in connection with the liquidation. No amounts have been provided for these expenses at September 23, 19X5.
13. **Accounts payable.** Accounts payable include $6,000 to the company's attorneys for legal work incurred in connection with patent research and collection efforts on certain accounts receivable that have been written off. Accounts payable also include $5,000 owed to the company's certified public accountants in connection with the December 31, 19X4, audit of the company's financial statements.

A statement of affairs prepared using the above information is shown in Illustration 19-4. The following points are important for understanding Illustration 19-4.

1. The book value column is shown only for purposes of tying into the September 23, 19X5 balance sheet, which was prepared in the conventional manner.
2. Each asset and liability is assigned to its appropriate descriptive category. The categories themselves are the key to producing the desired information—that is, how much money can the unsecured creditors expect to receive in liquidation?
3. Accrued interest payable is classified with the debt to which it relates, because the pledged assets are security for both the principal and the interest.
4. Although the company has not recorded the $15,000 of estimated liquidation expenses in its general ledger at September 23, 19X5, the statement of affairs should reflect this estimate so that it is as useful as possible.
5. Legal and accounting fees incurred in connection with matters not related to the bankruptcy are not considered debts with priority under the bankruptcy statutes.
6. The bank is an unsecured creditor to the extent of $12,000, the amount by which the $25,000 collateral is insufficient to satisfy its $37,000 claim.
7. The unsecured creditors are estimated to receive $149,000 of the $258,000 owed them. This figure is often expressed in terms of recovery per dollar owed. In this situation, it would be 58 cents on the dollar ($149,000 ÷ $258,000).

Once a liquidation has occurred, no accounting issues exist for the former company. An accountant performing services for a trustee in liquidation, however, should have a basic familiarity with the liquidation process.

Illustration 19-4
A Statement of Affairs for a Company in Bankruptcy Proceedings

FOLD-UP COMPANY
Statement of Affairs
September 23, 19X5

Book Value	Assets	Estimated Current Value	Estimated Amount Available for Unsecured Creditors	Gain or Loss on Realization
	Assets pledged with fully secured creditors:			
$ 70,000	Land	$ 90,000		$ 20,000
110,000	Building	135,000		25,000
		$225,000		
	Less—Fully secured claims (from liability side)	(181,000)	$ 44,000	
	Assets pledged with partially secured creditors:			
25,000	Accounts receivable	$ 25,000		
	(Deducted on liability side)			
	Free assets:			
2,000	Cash	$ 2,000	2,000	
5,000	Notes receivable	5,000	5,000	
	Inventory:			
40,000	Finished goods	43,000[a]	43,000	3,000
30,000	Work in process	32,000[b]	32,000	2,000
20,000	Raw materials	11,000[c]	11,000	(9,000)
5,000	Supplies	1,000	1,000	(4,000)
8,000	Prepayments			(8,000)
60,000	Equipment	35,000	35,000	(25,000)
15,000	Deferred charges			(15,000)
	Estimated amount available for unsecured creditors, including creditors with priority		$173,000	
	Less—Liabilities with priority (from liability side)		(24,000)	
	Estimated amount available for unsecured creditors		$149,000	
	Estimated deficiency to unsecured creditors (plug)		109,000	
$390,000				$(11,000)
	Total Unsecured Debt		$258,000	

[a]Net of $4,000 of estimated disposal costs.
[b]Net of $3,000 of estimated labor to complete and $2,000 of disposal costs.
[c]Net of $7,000 of estimated labor to convert into finished goods and $1,000 of disposal costs.

Illustration 19-4 (continued)

FOLD-UP COMPANY
Statement of Affairs
September 23, 19X5

Book Value	Liabilities and Stockholders' Deficiency		Amount Unsecured
	Liabilities with priority:		
$ –0–	Estimated liquidation expenses	$ 15,000	
7,000	Salaries and wages	7,000	
2,000	Payroll taxes	2,000	
	(deducted from amount available for unsecured creditors on asset side)	$ 24,000	
	Fully secured creditors:		
175,000	Notes payable to insurance company	$175,000	
6,000	Accrued interest on notes	6,000	
	Total (deducted on asset side)	$181,000	
	Partially secured creditors:		
35,000	Note payable to bank	$ 35,000	
2,000	Accrued interest on note	2,000	
		$ 37,000	
	Less—Pledged accounts receivable (from asset side)	(25,000)	$ 12,000
	Unsecured creditors:		
246,000	Accounts payable and accruals		246,000
(83,000)	Stockholders' deficiency		
$390,000			
	Total Unsecured Debt		$258,000

ACCOUNTING BY TRUSTEES

The accountability of trustees to the bankruptcy court was set forth earlier in the discussion of liquidations under Chapter 7 of the Bankruptcy Reform Act of 1978. The same accountability exists in reorganizations under Chapter 11 of the 1978 act in which a trustee is appointed to operate the debtor's business. The act sets forth specific requirements concerning the type of report or reports rendered to the courts by trustees only when the debtor's business is operated by a trustee. In most liquidation cases, normal operations cease immediately. Accordingly, we discuss accounting by trustees in liquidations separately from reorganizations (when normal operations continue).

Accounting in Liquidation

When normal operations immediately cease, the preparation of an operating statement for the period covering the trustee's administration of the estate is inappropriate. This holds true even when a trustee, with the court's permission, continues the operations necessary to convert work in process (and possibly raw materials) into finished goods. Such activities by themselves do not constitute normal operations; accordingly, costs incurred in this regard are treated as bankruptcy administration costs. Because the 1978 act does not prescribe the type of report or reports rendered by trustees when normal operations are not conducted (as was the case under the old law), each bankruptcy court establishes its own requirements. Most bankruptcy courts simply require a written explanation as to the disposition of the various assets and a statement of cash receipts and disbursements. Such a statement typically shows the following: (1) cash balances of the debtor that were turned over to the trustee at the trustee's appointment; (2) the proceeds from the conversion of noncash assets into cash; (3) cash disbursements (which are usually limited to bankruptcy administration costs); (4) the remaining cash balance available for distribution to creditors; and (5) a summary of how the remaining cash balance should be distributed to the various classes of creditors (including creditors with priority). In most cases, only one report is rendered (called the *final report*). In some cases, cash is distributed to creditors on an interim basis, after an interim report proposing such a distribution is filed with and approved by the court. Some courts require the cash disbursements in summary form only; others require detail by check number, payee, and purpose of disbursement.

Most trustees find it expedient to (1) open a separate checking account for each estate they administer, and (2) use the related cash receipts and disbursements records to prepare the required statement of cash receipts and disbursements. Trustees usually do not use the debtor's general ledger or any of the debtor's journals to record transactions and events. If the court or creditors desire information that relates the trustee's activity with the book balances existing when the trustee was appointed, then a **statement of realization and liquidation** can be prepared. Such a statement for Fold-up Company is shown in Illustration 19-5. The beginning balances are taken from Illustration 19-3. The activity during the assumed period that the trustee administers the estate is consistent with the estimated amounts and information provided in the data used to prepare the statement of affairs in Illustration 19-4.

In some cases, a trustee may be authorized to operate the debtor's business. This is often done when a greater amount may be realized by selling the business in its entirety rather than in piecemeal, and when a greater amount may be realized by selling an active business rather than one that has been shut down. The accounting reports rendered during the time

Illustration 19-5
A Statement of Realization and Liquidation

FOLD-UP COMPANY
Statement of Realization and Liquidation
For the Period September 23, 19X5, to May 18, 19X6

	Assets		Liabilities				
	Cash	Noncash	With Priority	Fully Secured	Partially Secured	Unsecured	Stockholders' Deficiency
Book Balances, September 23, 19X5 (from Illustration 19-4)	$ 2,000	$388,000	$ 9,000	$181,000	$37,000	$246,000	$ (83,000)
Cash receipts:							
Collection of note receivable and related interest	5,200	(5,000)					200
Proceeds from sale of inventory, net of $16,700 "actual" direct costs	85,800[a]	(90,000)					(4,200)
Proceeds from sale of supplies	1,100[a]	(5,000)					(3,900)
Proceeds from sale of equipment	35,400[a]	(60,000)					(24,600)
Proceeds from sale of land and building, net of $181,000 withheld by title company to pay off fully secured creditor	45,500[a]	(180,000)		(181,000)			46,500
Cash disbursements:							
Payment of bankruptcy administration costs, net of $16,700 "actual" inventory conversion and selling costs shown above	(2,000)						(2,000)
Other:							
Amortization of prepaids		(8,000)					(8,000)
Write-off of deferred charges		(15,000)					(15,000)
Release of accounts receivable to partially secured creditor		(25,000)			(25,000)		
Reclassification of residual amount to unsecured status					(12,000)	12,000	
Accrual of bankruptcy administration costs			12,600				(12,600)
Book Balances, May 18, 19X6	$173,000	$ -0-	$21,600	$ -0-	$ -0-	$258,000	$(106,600)
Proposed distribution	$173,000		$21,600 (100%)			$151,400 (58.7%)	

[a]The actual proceeds here are purposely slightly different from the "estimated" current values shown in Illustration 19-4, inasmuch as it is highly unlikely that the actual proceeds would agree with the estimated proceeds in a real-world situation.

that a trustee operates the debtor's business are the same as those required in reorganizations, which are discussed in the following section.

Accounting in Reorganization

When a trustee is appointed in a Chapter 11 reorganization, the new law requires trustees to submit

> periodic reports and summaries of the operation of such business, including a statement of receipts and disbursements, and such other information as the court requires [Sections 704 and 1106].

In addition to these items, the courts usually require that a balance sheet be presented whenever operating statements or summaries are furnished. In most cases, trustees find it practical to use the debtor's books and records to record transactions and events. However, the date the trustee was appointed is usually recorded so that the activity during the trustee's administration can be reported separately. Also, a distinction is usually made between (1) assets on hand and liabilities owed at the trustee's appointment, and (2) assets acquired and liabilities incurred during the trustee's administration. This distinction is necessary because trustees are responsible for the acquisition and realization of new assets as opposed to only the realization of old assets, and for the incurrence and liquidation of new liabilities as opposed to only the liquidation of old liabilities.

The preparation of required reports and statements presents no unusual problems when the trustee uses the debtor's books and records. In some cases a trustee may account for some or all of the debtor's assets and operations in a new set of books. In this case, the transfer of assets to the new set of books and the accounting for subsequent operations parallels the accounting for a home office and a branch. Accordingly, the balances and activity on each set of books must be combined to the extent necessary in preparing financial reports. Traditionally, advanced accounting textbooks have included a discussion and illustration of a somewhat involved statement of realization and liquidation encompassing assets, liabilities, and operations. However, current practice favors the use of the separate conventional financial statements, and we do not present a discussion and illustration of this single comprehensive statement.

CONCLUDING COMMENTS

Most companies in serious financial difficulty never recover and must be liquidated. A company that can feasibly effect a successful recovery must show complete honesty and good faith with its creditors during this difficult period. Creditors should realize that often they can minimize their losses if a successful troubled debt restructuring can be achieved. The use of professionals in insolvency proceedings can minimize the procedural problems and help the company and its creditors to be realistic in arriving at an acceptable plan of recovery.

Not all proposed troubled debt restructurings succeed. Many are rejected as infeasible, with liquidation best serving the creditors' interests. Others are rejected as a result of evidence of management fraud, deception, or bad faith—again, liquidation best serves the creditors' interests. Consequently, an accountant furnishing assistance to a debtor or a creditors' committee must be skeptical, alert, and imaginative in carrying out this difficult assignment.

SUMMARY

The accounting issues involved with troubled debt restructurings include how to calculate whether any debt has been forgiven and how to report a forgiveness of debt. *FASB Statement No. 15* does not allow the imputing of interest in making this calculation. The total amount owed (the "carrying amount of the debt") is compared with the total amount to be paid back (the "total future payments"). If the total future payments exceed the carrying amount of the debt, the excess is reported as interest expense between the restructuring date and the maturity date. However, if the carrying amount of the debt exceeds the total future payments, a forgiveness of debt results. *FASB Statement No. 15* treats a forgiveness of debt as a gain reported as an extraordinary item, if material. As a result of these procedures, the debtor's future income statements reflect either no interest expense (when a forgiveness of debt results) or unrealistically low interest expense (when no forgiveness of debt results) until the maturity date of the debt.

In most instances, *FASB Statement No. 15* does not apply to either quasi-reorganizations or formal bankruptcy reorganizations under Chapter 11 of the bankruptcy statutes. In these situations, the amount owed is compared with the consideration given in settlement. Because the current accounting literature does not state specifically how to calculate and report a forgiveness of debt in formal reorganizations, some companies do not impute interest in making this calculation, whereas others do. Some companies treat the forgiveness of debt as a gain, whereas others treat it as a capital contribution.

Glossary of New Terms

Creditors with Priority A special class of creditors created by the bankruptcy statutes. These creditors are entitled to payment before a debtor's other unsecured creditors may be paid.

Debtor Under the bankruptcy statutes, a debtor is the party that is the subject of a bankruptcy proceeding.

Estate Under the bankruptcy statutes, all of a debtor's property.

Impairment The alteration of the rights of a creditor or equity holder in a bankruptcy reorganization case.

Involuntary Petition The filing of a petition by the creditors of a company in financial distress to have the distressed company liquidated or financially reorganized under the control and supervision of the bankruptcy court.

Liquidation The process of converting a company's assets into cash, paying off creditors to the extent possible, and ceasing operations.

Quasi-reorganization A process outside of bankruptcy court for eliminating a deficit balance in Retained Earnings (properly called an accumulated deficit) to give the entity a "fresh start."

Reorganization The altering of a distressed company's liability and/or equity structure under Chapter 11 of the bankruptcy statutes for purposes of financially rehabilitating the company to avoid liquidation.

Restatement of Liabilities Generally Restructurings or modifications of debt that encompass most of the debtor's liabilities coincidentally with either a reorganization under Chapter 11 of the bankruptcy statutes or a quasi-reorganization.

Setoffs In a bankruptcy proceeding, offsetting amounts owed to a debtor by a creditor against amounts owed to that creditor by the debtor.

Troubled Debt Restructuring The granting of a concession by a creditor because of a debtor's financial difficulties.

Voluntary Petition The filing of a petition with the bankruptcy court by a company in financial distress to have the company liquidated or financially reorganized under the control and supervision of the bankruptcy court.

Selected References

"A Different Approach to a Customer's Bankruptcy Reorganization," by Timothy Morris. *Corporate Accounting* 4, no. 2 (Spring 1986), 39–44.

"Financing in Chapter 11—Back from the Depths," by Gene P. Kaplan and Harvey C. Guberman. *Corporate Accounting* 4, no. 2 (Spring 1986), 26–37.

"Positioning for the Upturn after Surviving the Downturn," by Robert E. McCoy and Robert C. Robinson. *Management Accounting* (March 1984) 24–28.

Review Questions

1. Between what two broad categories are the bankruptcy statutes divided (as they pertain to business corporations)?
2. What fundamental objectives do the bankruptcy statutes accomplish?
3. Under what conditions may an involuntary petition be filed?
4. What is meant by the term *creditors with priority*?
5. List the order of priority of creditors with priority.

6. In an involuntary bankruptcy filing, do secured creditors lose their right to their security?
7. Why do companies try to restructure their debt outside of Chapter 11 of the bankruptcy statutes if at all possible?
8. What are the advantages of filing for reorganization under Chapter 11 of the bankruptcy statutes?
9. Summarize the general procedures for determining if a gain on the restructuring of debt exists as set forth in *FASB Statement No. 15*.
10. How are material gains on the restructuring of debt reported in the income statement?
11. To what extent are the present value procedures discussed in *APB Opinion No. 21* used in determining a gain on restructuring of debt under *FASB Statement No. 15*?
12. What is the essence of a composition agreement?
13. What is meant by a *discharge of indebtedness* in a bankruptcy reorganization?
14. Which debts cannot be discharged in a bankruptcy reorganization?
15. Is a discharge of indebtedness automatic in a liquidation proceeding? in a reorganization proceeding?
16. How is the statement of affairs different from the balance sheet?
17. State two purposes for which a statement of affairs may be used.
18. Contrast the statement of affairs with the balance sheet.
19. Give four classifications of liabilities that can appear in a statement of affairs.

Discussion Cases

DC 19-1

Troubled Debt Restructuring: Theory

Debtco Company has recently completed restructuring a substantial portion of its debt with one of its major lenders, which was owed $1,000,000 of principal and $100,000 of interest as of the date the restructuring was consummated. Under the terms of the restructured debt agreement, the accrued interest of $100,000 is forgiven and the principal of $1,000,000 is to be paid two years hence, with no interest to be paid for these two years.

Debtco Company's controller has indicated to you that the company intends to value the debt owed at $826,446, which is the present value of $1,000,000 using a discount rate of 10% (the interest rate before the restructuring). This valuation results in the reporting of (1) a gain on restructuring of debt of $273,554 in the current year, (2) interest expense of $82,645 in the first year following the restructuring, and (3) interest expense of $90,909 in the second year following the restructuring. The controller gives you the following reasons why this approach best reflects the economics of the restructuring:

1. The creditor's $1,000,000 note receivable is worth no more than what the note receivable can be sold for or discounted on a nonrecourse basis.
2. If the creditor sold the note receivable to a financial institution on a nonrecourse basis, it certainly could not sell it for more than its present value using an interest rate commensurate with the issuing company's risk.

3. Considering the poor financial condition of the company, a higher rate than 10% probably would be justified. However, the controller decided not to use a rate higher than 10% to be conservative in the computation of the gain on restructuring of the debt.
4. If the value of the note receivable on the creditor's books cannot be worth more than $826,446, the excess of the carrying amount of the note payable (including accrued interest) over this amount must represent the true value of the debt forgiveness.

Required:

1. Disregarding the requirements of *FASB Statement No. 15*, evaluate the soundness of the controller's approach.
2. Is the controller's approach conservative? What other reason might have prompted the controller to use a low interest rate?
3. What impact will this approach have on retained earnings at the end of the two years? What impact will the approach set forth in *FASB Statement No. 15* have on retained earnings?

DC 19-2

Troubled Debt Restructuring: Theory

Assume that *FASB Statement No. 15* required that income statements of periods subsequent to a troubled debt restructuring reflect interest expense related to restructured debt based on an interest rate commensurate with the risk associated with the restructured debt.

Required:
How would you determine an appropriate interest rate "commensurate with the risk"?

DC 19-3

Bankruptcy Reorganization: Theory

You are the controller of a company that has been attempting to work out a troubled debt restructuring at lengthy meetings with its major creditors. At the last meeting, the company's president told the creditors that if they did not agree to the restructuring plan proposed by the company, management would file for reorganization under Chapter 11 of the bankruptcy statutes.

Required:

1. How would the accounting change as a result of restructuring the debt through the bankruptcy courts versus outside of the bankruptcy courts?
2. What is the rationale for having different rules for the restructuring of debt in bankruptcy reorganizations?

DC 19-4

Bankruptcy Reorganization: Theory

Assume you are the controller for a company that, after several years of operating losses, filed for reorganization under Chapter 11 of the bankruptcy statutes. The company's plan of reorganization was confirmed 18 months after the filing, and unsecured creditors were paid 40 cents on the dollar ($30 million was owed to these creditors). You want to report the $18 million amount of debt canceled in the income statement.

Required:

1. Disregarding the accounting pronouncements, evaluate whether or not a company should report income from a bankruptcy reorganization. (Try to list arguments for and against this position.)
2. What other options does the company have?
3. Why might it not make much difference which way the company reports the $18 million canceled debt?

Exercises

E 19-1

Bankruptcy Law: Filing the Petition and Debts with Priority

1. Which of the entities listed below are entitled to file a voluntary bankruptcy petition under Chapter 7 or 11?
   a. A banking corporation.
   b. A partnership.
   c. A corporation that manufactures consumer goods.
   d. A corporation that provides personal services.
   e. A municipal corporation.
   f. A railroad.
   g. An insurance corporation.
2. Select the entities in question 1 that may have an involuntary bankruptcy petition filed against them.
3. In which of the following situations could an involuntary bankruptcy petition be filed?
   a. The debtor has debts of at least $5,000.
   b. The appropriate number of creditors required to sign the petition are owed at least $5,000.
   c. The debtor has committed a fraudulent act.
   d. The debtor has recently appointed a custodian.
   e. The debtor has made asset transfers that constitute a preference to one or more creditors.
   f. Wages are owed to employees for more than 90 days.
   g. The debtor is not paying its debts as they mature.
   h. The debtor has entered into discussions with its creditors to restructure its debt.
   i. The debtor's net worth is negative as a result of operating losses.
4. Which of the following debts have priority under the bankruptcy statutes?
   a. Amounts owed to secured creditors.

b. In an involuntary petition, amounts owed to the creditors who signed the petition.
c. Costs of administering the bankruptcy proceedings.
d. Debts incurred by issuing materially false statements as to financial condition.
e. All wages owed to employees that were earned within 90 days prior to filing the bankruptcy petition.
f. Wages of up to $2,000 per employee, no matter when earned.
g. Taxes owed to the United States or any state or subdivision thereof.

E 19-2

Bankruptcy Law: Reorganization under Chapter 11

Determine if the following statements are true or false. Explain why any false statements are false.

1. In a Chapter 11 reorganization, management usually continues to operate the business.
2. The legal and contractual rights of any class of creditors may be altered or impaired under a plan of reorganization.
3. A plan of reorganization must be approved by the Securities and Exchange Commission.
4. A simple majority of creditors in a class of claims is required to approve a plan of reorganization.
5. A simple majority in the amount of claims in a class of creditors is required to approve the dollar amount of claims in a plan of reorganization.
6. The bankruptcy court usually imposes a plan of reorganization on the creditors.
7. The rights of secured creditors are eliminated when a company files for reorganization under Chapter 11.
8. In a reorganization under Chapter 11, the discharge provisions have no meaningful application.

E 19-3

Bankruptcy Law: Liquidation under Chapter 7

Determine if the following statements are true or false. Explain why any false statements are false.

1. In involuntary filings under Chapter 7, the case is dismissed if the debtor contests the filing.
2. In a Chapter 7 filing, the bankruptcy court usually appoints a trustee.
3. In a Chapter 7 filing, management usually continues to operate the business until the liquidation is completed.
4. The primary function of a trustee in Chapter 7 filings is to settle disputes between the debtor and the debtor's creditors.
5. When a company is liquidated under Chapter 7, all unpaid debts (except those specified in the bankruptcy statutes) are discharged by the bankruptcy court.
6. In a Chapter 7 filing, trustees have the authority to dispose of the debtor's assets.
7. Trustees are authorized to void preferential transfers made to certain creditors.
8. The concept of creditors with priority does not apply to Chapter 7 filings.

E 19-4

Troubled Debt Restructuring: Modification of Terms

A company having serious financial difficulty executed an agreement with its bank whereby the currently due $500,000 note payable to the bank was extended for five years. The old interest rate of 10% was lowered to 4%. Interest is to be paid annually in arrears. Accrued interest of $20,000 as of the restructuring date was canceled.

Required:

1. Determine if a gain on restructuring of debt has resulted.
2. Prepare the journal entry related to the restructuring.

E 19-5

Troubled Debt Restructuring: Modification of Terms

A company having serious financial difficulty executed an agreement with one of its major vendors whereby the $800,000 account payable to the vendor was converted into a $600,000 note payable, all due and payable in two years. The interest rate on the note is 10%, with interest payable annually in arrears. The remaining $200,000 of the original note payable was canceled.

Required:

1. Determine if a gain on restructuring of debt has resulted.
2. Prepare the journal entry related to the restructuring.
3. How would your answer be different if the due date of the note payable were four years from the restructuring date?

E 19-6

Troubled Debt Restructuring: Modification of Terms—Use of Present Value Concepts

A company having serious financial difficulty has entered into a restructuring agreement with a creditor that is owed $1,000,000 of principal (now due and payable) and $28,000 of interest. In the restructuring agreement, the company agrees to pay the principal in three years, with interest paid annually in arrears at 4%. The accrued interest of $28,000 is canceled.

Required:

1. Determine if a gain on restructuring of debt has resulted.
2. Determine the total amount of interest expense reported over the next three years.
3. Using present value tables, calculate the approximate effective interest rate.
4. Prepare the journal entries made between the restructuring date and the maturity date, assuming all required payments are made on time.

E 19-7

Troubled Debt Restructuring: Equity Interest Granted

A company having serious financial difficulty executed an agreement with one of its note holders whereby a $100,000 note payable was converted into

30,000 shares of the company's $1 par value common stock. The common stock was traded at $2 per share on the date of the agreement.

Required:

1. Determine if a gain on restructuring of debt has resulted.
2. Prepare the journal entry related to the restructuring.

E 19-8

Troubled Debt Restructuring: Transfer of Noncash Assets

A company having serious financial difficulty executed an agreement with one of its creditors whereby a $200,000 note payable and the $25,000 related accrued interest was canceled in exchange for a parcel of land. The land had cost the company $100,000 and has a current appraised value of $150,000.

Required:

1. Determine the amount of "gain on restructuring" to be reported.
2. Prepare the required journal entry or entries.

E 19-9

Bankruptcy Reorganization: Settlement for Cash and Stock

New Life Company's plan of reorganization under Chapter 11 of the bankruptcy statutes calls for a cash payment of $4,000,000 and the issuance of 800,000 shares of its $1 par value common stock to its unsecured creditors on a pro rata basis. These unsecured creditors are composed of vendors (owed $8,000,000) and a bank (owed $3,500,000 principal and $500,000 interest). New Life's common stock is currently trading at $1.25 per share.

Required:
Prepare the journal entry related to this settlement.

E 19-10

Bankruptcy Reorganization: Settlement for Cash and Notes

Skiddex Company's plan of reorganization under Chapter 11 of the bankruptcy statutes calls for a cash payment of $1,500,000 and the issuance of $2,000,000 of 14% notes payable to its unsecured creditors on a pro rata basis. These unsecured creditors are composed of vendors (owed $2,300,000) and a bank (owed $3,300,000 principal and $400,000 interest). (The 14% interest rate on the notes is considered reasonable under the circumstances.) The notes are to be paid in full in three years.

Required:
Prepare the journal entry related to this settlement.

E 19-11

Statement of Affairs: Calculating Expected Settlement Amounts

The statement of affairs for Defuncto Company reflects the following amounts:

	Book Value	Estimated Current Value
Assets:		
Assets pledged with fully secured creditors	$150,000	$180,000
Assets pledged with partially secured creditors.....	80,000	60,000
Free assets	220,000	150,000
	$450,000	$390,000
Liabilities:		
Liabilities with priority..	$ 20,000	
Fully secured creditors	130,000	
Partially secured creditors	100,000	
Unsecured creditors..	260,000	
	$510,000	

Required:

Compute the amount that each class of creditors can expect to receive if assets are converted into cash at their estimated current values.

(AICPA adapted)

Problems

P 19-1 Troubled Debt Restructuring: Modification of Terms

Stallex Company, which is having serious financial difficulty, entered into an agreement with its major lender on December 31, 19X4. The amount owed to the lender was restructured as follows:

1. Of the $2,000,000 of principal owed to the lender (all of which was currently due), 10% was canceled.
2. Accrued interest of $300,000 was canceled.
3. The due date on the remaining principal amount was extended to December 31, 19X8.
4. The interest rate on the remaining principal amount was reduced from 12% to 3% for 19X5 and 19X6. For 19X7 and 19X8, the interest rate is 6%. All interest at these new rates is to be paid annually in arrears.

Required:

1. Determine if a gain on restructuring of debt has resulted.
2. Prepare the journal entry to record the restructuring.
3. Calculate the total amount of interest expense, if any, reported from the restructuring date to the maturity date.

P 19-2

Troubled Debt Restructuring: Combination of Equity Interest Granted and Modification of Terms

Ganes Company, which is having serious financial difficulty, entered into an agreement with holders of its notes payable on December 31, 19X5. The debt was restructured as follows:

1. Of the total $14,000,000 of notes payable (all of which was currently due), $7,000,000 of principal was canceled in exchange for 300,000 shares of the company's $1 par value common stock. (The common stock had a market value of $20 per share on December 31, 19X5.)
2. The remaining $7,000,000 of principal is to bear interest at 5%, payable annually in arrears. The maturity date of this $7,000,000 was extended to December 31, 19X8.
3. Accrued interest of $350,000 was canceled.

Required:

1. Determine if a gain on restructuring of debt has resulted.
2. Prepare the journal entry to record the restructuring.
3. Calculate the total amount of interest expense, if any, reported from the restructuring date to the maturity date.

P 19-3

Troubled Debt Restructuring: Combination of Equity Interest Granted and Modification of Terms

Lossco Company, which is having serious financial difficulty, entered into an agreement with its bondholders on December 31, 19X1. The debt was restructured as follows:

1. Of the total $25,000,000 in face value of bonds outstanding (which bear interest at 12%), $5,000,000 was canceled in exchange for 50,000 shares of a new class of preferred stock having a par value of $100.
2. The maturity date of the remaining $20,000,000 of bonds was extended to December 31, 19X3.
3. The interest rate on the $20,000,000 is 3% until maturity.
4. Of the $2,000,000 interest payable accrued at December 31, 19X1, $1,500,000 was canceled. The remaining $500,000 was paid when the restructuring agreement was signed (at the close of business on December 31, 19X1).

Other Information:

1. The bonds were issued at a $700,000 premium eight years ago. The straight-line method of amortization had been used.
2. The original life of the bonds was 10 years. The bonds were due in full during 19X1 as a result of a default in the interest payments.

Required:

1. Determine if a gain on restructuring of debt has resulted.
2. Prepare the journal entry to record the restructuring.
3. Calculate the total amount of interest expense, if any, reported from the restructuring date to the maturity date.

P 19-4 Troubled Debt Restructuring: Combination of Equity Interest Granted and Modification of Terms Involving Contingent Interest

Futura Company, which is having serious financial difficulty, entered into an agreement with its major lender on December 31, 19X3. The amount owed to the lender was restructured as follows:

1. Of the $100,000,000 of principal owed to the lender (all of which was currently due), $40,000,000 was canceled in exchange for 400,000 shares of a new class of preferred stock, having a par value of $100 per share.
2. The maturity date of the remaining $60,000,000 of principal was extended to December 31, 19X8.
3. The interest rate on the $60,000,000 of principal was reduced to 4% from 8%, with interest payable annually in arrears.
4. If the company's cumulative earnings before interest expense and income taxes from January 1, 19X4 through December 31, 19X8, exceed $25,000,000, then the interest rate reverts to 8% retroactive to January 1, 19X4. (As of December 31, 19X3, it is not probable that cumulative earnings during this period will exceed $25,000,000.)
5. Accrued interest payable of $15,000,000 as of December 31, 19X3, was forgiven.

Required:

1. Determine if a gain on restructuring of debt has resulted.
2. Prepare the journal entry to record the restructuring.
3. Determine the total amount of interest expense, if any, reported during the next five years, assuming that the company's cumulative earnings before interest expense and income tax expense during that period
   a. did not exceed $25,000,000.
   b. did exceed $25,000,000 as of September 30, 19X7.

P 19-5 Troubled Debt Restructuring: Modification of Terms—Use of Present Value Concepts

Defaulto Company, which is having serious financial difficulty, entered into a restructuring agreement with a creditor that is owed $3,000,000 of principal (now due and payable) and $427,000 of interest. The terms of the restructuring agreement (dated January 1, 19X1) call for:

1. Cancellation of $277,000 of accrued interest, with payment of the remaining $150,000 on signing the agreement. (This payment was indeed made at that time.)
2. Principal payments of $1,000,000 per year beginning January 1, 19X2 (one year from now), until the loan is paid in full on January 1, 19X4.
3. Interest to be paid annually in arrears, beginning January 1, 19X2, at 10% on the unpaid balance. (The interest rate prior to the restructuring was 14%.)

Required:

1. Determine if a gain on restructuring of debt has resulted.
2. Prepare the journal entry to record the restructuring.
3. Determine the total amount of interest expense reported over the next three years.
4. Using present value tables, calculate the approximate effective interest rate.
5. Prepare the journal entries made between the restructuring date and the maturity date, assuming all required payments are made on time.

P 19-6

COMPREHENSIVE Troubled Debt Restructuring

On July 1, 19X2, TDR Company entered into a troubled debt restructuring agreement with its creditors. Data pertaining to the various classes of creditors and equity interests prior to the restructuring are as follows:

Accounts payable, unsecured	$1,800,000
10% Note payable to bank, currently due and payable	3,000,000
Accrued interest on note payable	400,000
8% Debenture bonds (subordinated to bank loan)	2,000,000
Accrued interest on debenture bonds	100,000
6% Preferred stock, $100 par value, cumulative, dividends in arrears of $90,000; 5,000 shares outstanding	
Common stock, no-par value, 200,000 shares outstanding	

The terms of the restructuring are as follows:

1. Accounts payable of $400,000 are canceled outright. Accounts payable of $600,000 are canceled in exchange for 80,000 shares of common stock. Trading in the company's common stock was suspended on January 15, 19X2. Just before that time, the common stock was selling at $2 per share. Trading was resumed on July 2, 19X2, and the stock closed at 50 cents per share on that day. All remaining payables are to be paid within 180 days.
2. Principal of $500,000 on the bank note, along with all accrued interest, is canceled. The due date on the remaining principal is extended to July 1, 19X5. The interest rate is reduced to 5%. However, if TDR's cumulative earnings exceed $2,000,000 during the three years ended June 30, 19X5, then the interest rate reverts to 10% retroactively. (It appears unlikely that TDR's earnings will exceed $2,000,000 during this period.)
3. Principal of $1,000,000 on the debenture bonds is exchanged for a new class of 7% preferred stock. This new preferred stock, which is designated Series A, is

senior to the existing preferred stock with respect to dividends and distributions in the event of liquidation. The existing preferred stock (which was issued at par) is designated Series B. All accrued interest on the debentures is canceled. The June 30, 19X7, due date is unchanged. The interest rate on the remaining $1,000,000 of principal is reduced to 5% until maturity.

4. The dividends in arrears on the existing preferred stock is canceled, and the future dividend rate is reduced to 3% for a period of five years.

Required:

1. Prepare the accounting entries related to the above restructurings, assuming July 1, 19X2, is the consummation date.
2. What entry, if any, would be made on June 30, 19X5, if TDR's earnings do not exceed $2,000,000 from July 1, 19X2 to June 30, 19X5?
3. Calculate the total amount of interest expense reported in the income statement for the next five years with respect to the debenture bonds.

P 19-7

COMPREHENSIVE Bankruptcy Reorganization

Assume that the information in Problem 19-6 pertains to a Chapter 11 bankruptcy reorganization rather than a troubled debt restructuring outside of the bankruptcy courts.

Required:

1. Prepare the journal entries related to this plan of reorganization. Assume that it is *not* necessary to apply the provisions of *APB Opinion No. 21*.
2. With respect to the bank note, what entry, if any, would be made on June 30, 19X5 if TDR's earnings do not exceed $2,000,000 from July 1, 19X2 to June 30, 19X5?
3. Calculate the total amount of interest expense reported in the income statement for the next five years with respect to the debenture bonds.

P 19-8

Bankruptcy Reorganization: Settlement with Unsecured Creditors—Use of Present Value Concepts

Debtorex Corporation's plan of reorganization was confirmed by the bankruptcy court on June 30, 19X1. Under the plan, unsecured creditors (who are owed $850,000,000) are to receive the following:

Cash	**$300,000,000**
12% Unsecured notes	**$300,000,000**
Common stock, $1 par value	**10,000,000 shares**

The company's investment bankers have determined that the 12% unsecured notes will trade at a discount on issuance to yield a return of approximately 15%. These notes are to be paid off at $60,000,000 per year beginning June 30, 19X2, until their maturity five years from now. Interest is to be paid annually in arrears each June 30.

The company's common stock (2,000,000 shares now outstanding) traded at $1.50 per share when the company's plan of reorganization was confirmed.

Assume that *APB Opinion No. 21* applies to the 12% unsecured notes. Selected present value factors follow:

	Present Value Factors	
Periods	12%	15%
1	0.89286	0.86957
2	0.79719	0.75614
3	0.71178	0.65752
4	0.63552	0.57175
5	0.56743	0.49718
Five payments (annuity)	3.60478	3.35216

Required:

1. Prepare the journal entries related to the plan of reorganization.
2. Prepare the journal entries made for the first two years following confirmation of the plan, assuming all required payments are made on time. (Assume that the company has a June 30 fiscal year end.)

P 19-9*

Liquidation: Preparing a Statement of Affairs

As Die-hard Corporation's CPA, you are aware that it is facing bankruptcy proceedings. The company's balance sheet at June 30, 19X1, and supplementary data are presented below:

Assets	
Cash	$ 2,000
Accounts receivable, less allowance for uncollectibles	70,000
Inventory, raw materials	40,000
Inventory, finished goods	60,000
Marketable securities	20,000
Land	13,000
Buildings, net of accumulated depreciation	90,000
Machinery, net of accumulated depreciation	120,000
Goodwill	20,000
Prepaid expenses	5,000
Total Assets	$440,000
Liabilities and Equity	
Accounts payable	$ 80,000
Notes payable	135,000
Accrued wages	15,000
Mortgages payable	130,000
Common stock	100,000
Accumulated deficit	(20,000)
Total Liabilities and Equity	$440,000

*Problems accompanied by asterisks can be worked on the computer using Model 19 (filename: Model19) of the software file disk that is available for use with the text.

Additional Information:

1. Cash includes a $500 travel advance that has been expended.
2. Accounts receivable of $40,000 have been pledged to bank loans of $30,000. Credit balances of $5,000 are netted in the accounts receivable total.
3. Marketable securities consist of government bonds costing $10,000 and 500 shares of Bumm Company stock. The market value of the bonds is $10,000 and the stock is $18 per share. The bonds have accrued interest due of $200. The securities are collateral for a $20,000 bank loan.
4. Appraised value of raw materials is $30,000 and of finished goods is $50,000. For an additional cost of $10,000, the raw materials would realize $70,000 as finished goods.
5. The appraised value of fixed assets is land, $25,000; buildings, $110,000; and machinery, $75,000.
6. Prepaid expenses will be exhausted during the liquidation period.
7. Accounts payable include $15,000 of withheld payroll taxes and $6,000 owed to creditors who had been reassured by Die-Hard's president that they would be paid. Unrecorded employer's payroll taxes total $500.
8. Wages payable are not subject to any limits under bankruptcy laws.
9. Mortgages payable consist of $100,000 on land and buildings and $30,000 chattel mortgage on machinery. Total unrecorded accrued interest for these mortgages amounts to $2,400.
10. Estimated legal fees and expenses connected with the liquidation are $10,000.
11. Probable judgment on a pending damage suit is $50,000.
12. You have not rendered a $5,000 invoice for last year's audit, and you estimate a $1,000 fee for liquidation work.

Required:

1. Prepare a statement of affairs. (The book value column should reflect adjustments that properly should have been made at June 30, 19X1 in the normal course of business.)
2. Compute the estimated settlement per dollar of unsecured liabilities.

(AICPA adapted)

P 19-10*

Liquidation: Preparing a Statement of Affairs

Last-Legg Corporation is in financial difficulty because of low sales. Its stockholders and principal creditors want an estimate of the financial results of the liquidation of the assets and liabilities and the dissolution of the corporation.

LAST-LEGG CORPORATION
Postclosing Trial Balance
December 31, 19X3

	Debit	Credit
Cash	$ 5,000	
Accounts Receivable	82,000	
Allowance for Uncollectibles		$ 3,000
Inventories	160,000	
Supplies Inventory	12,000	

Investment in Hye-Flyer Company's 5% Bonds (at face value)	20,000	
Accrued Bond Interest Receivable	3,000	
Advertising	24,000	
Land	16,000	
Building	120,000	
Accumulated Depreciation—Building		20,000
Machinery and Equipment	184,000	
Accumulated Depreciation—Machinery and Equipment		32,000
Accounts Payable		104,000
Notes Payable—Bank		100,000
Notes Payable—Officers		80,000
Payroll Taxes Payable		3,000
Wages Payable		6,000
Mortgage Payable		168,000
Mortgage Interest Payable		2,000
Capital Stock		200,000
Accumulated Deficit	117,000	
Estimated Liability for Product Guarantees		25,000
	$743,000	$743,000

The following information has been collected for a meeting of the stockholders and principal creditors to be held on January 10, 19X4:

1. Cash includes a $2,000 protested check from a customer. The customer stated that funds to honor the check will be available in about two weeks.
2. Accounts receivable include accounts totaling $40,000 that are fully collectible and have been assigned to the bank in connection with the notes payable. Included in the unassigned receivables is an uncollectible account of $1,000. The Allowance for Uncollectibles account of $3,000 now on the books will adequately provide for other doubtful accounts.
3. Purchase orders totaling $36,000 are on hand for the corporation's products. Inventory with a book value of $24,000 can be processed at an additional cost of $2,000 to fill these orders. The balance of the inventory, which includes obsolete materials with a book value of $4,000, can be sold for $41,000.
4. In transit at December 31 but not recorded on the books is a shipment of defective merchandise being returned by a customer. The president of the corporation authorized the return and the refund of the $1,000 purchase price after the merchandise had been inspected. Other than this return, the president knows of no other defective merchandise that would affect the Estimated Liability for Product Guarantees account. The merchandise being returned has no salvage value.
5. The supplies inventory comprises advertising literature, brochures, and other sales aids, which could not be replaced for less than $14,000.
6. The investment in 10% bonds of Hye-Flyer Company is recorded at face value (two bonds each having a $10,000 face value). They were purchased in 19X1 for $8,500, and the adjustment to face value was credited to Retained Earnings. At December 31, 19X3, the bonds were quoted at 30.
7. The Advertising account represents the future benefits of a 19X3 advertising campaign. The account contains 10% of certain advertising expenditures.

The president stated that this figure was too conservative and that 20% would be a more realistic measure of the market that was created.

8. The land and building are in a downtown area. A firm offer of $200,000 has been received for the land, which would be used as a parking lot; the building would be razed at a cost of $48,000 to the buyer. Another offer of $160,000 was received for the real estate, which the bidder stated would be used for manufacturing that would probably employ some employees of Last-Legg.
9. The highest offer received from used machinery dealers was $72,000 for all of the machinery and equipment.
10. One creditor, whose account for $16,000 is included in the accounts payable, confirmed in writing that he would accept 75 cents on the dollar if the corporation paid him by January 10.
11. Wages payable are for amounts earned within the last 30 days.
12. The mortgage payable is secured by the land and building. The last two monthly principal payments of $800 each were not made.
13. Estimated liquidation expenses amount to $13,000.
14. For income tax purposes the corporation has the following net operating loss carryovers (the combined federal and state tax rate is 40%): 19X1, $40,000; 19X2, $48,000; and 19X3, $32,000.

Required:

1. Prepare a statement of affairs. (The book value column should reflect adjustments that should have been made at December 31, 19X3 in the normal course of business. Assume the company has a June 30 fiscal year-end.)
2. Prepare a schedule that computes the estimated settlement per dollar of unsecured liabilities.

(AICPA adapted)

IV

Government and Nonprofit Organizations

20

Governmental Accounting: Basic Principles and the General Fund

Accounting for state and local governmental units could be the subject of an entire textbook. A major portion of this chapter, therefore, is devoted to introductory material, to give you an overall understanding of (1) the historical development and current status of accounting principles applicable to governmental units; (2) the nature of governmental operations; and (3) the current shortcomings of governmental financial reporting.

ESTABLISHMENT OF ACCOUNTING PRINCIPLES

The GFOA, *GAAFR*, and NCGA

Before 1978, the Financial Accounting Standards Board (FASB) and its predecessor organizations restricted their efforts to the establishment of accounting principles for the private sector of the economy—that is, to enterprises engaged in a trade or business for a profit. To fill the void that existed with respect to the accounting principles and practices peculiar to governmental units, the National Committee on Municipal Accounting was established in 1934 through the efforts of the Government Finance Officers Association of the United States and Canada (GFOA).[1] The committee was not a permanent one, but was reestablished periodically as necessary to upgrade standards and address current problems. In 1949, the committee's name was changed to the National Committee on Governmental Accounting (NCGA) to signify the expansion of its activities to encompass all governmental units except the federal government and its agencies. Over the years, the committee issued numerous publications dealing with principles, practices, and procedures of accounting, budgeting, auditing, and financial reporting for state and local governmental units. In 1968, it combined most of its publications issued up to that time under a single title, *Governmental Accounting, Auditing and Financial Reporting* (referred to and cited as *GAAFR*).[2] In 1974, the American Institute of Certified Public Accountants (AICPA) issued an audit guide, *Audits of State and Local Governmental Units* (referred to as the AICPA governmental audit guide and cited *ASLGU*). This audit guide (which was revised in 1986) not only acknowledged GAAFR as "an authoritative publication in the area of accounting for governmental units," but also considered the principles set forth therein to "constitute generally accepted accounting principles [GAAP]," except as modified in the audit guide.[3]

[1]Prior to 1984, the GFOA was called the Municipal Finance Officers Association. In this chapter we use its new name.

[2]National Committee on Governmental Accounting, *Governmental Accounting, Auditing and Financial Reporting* (Chicago: Government Finance Officers Association of the United States and Canada, 1968).

[3]Committee on Governmental Accounting and Auditing, *Audits of State and Local Governmental Units* (New York: American Institute of Certified Public Accountants, 1974), pp. 8–9.

It was soon evident that major improvements in financial reporting were still needed. Accordingly, the National Council on Governmental Accounting was established in 1974 as the successor to the National Committee on Governmental Accounting. Certain structural changes were made and due-process procedures similar to those of the FASB were adopted.

Major Improvements Made. In 1979, the NCGA issued *NCGA Statement 1*, "Governmental Accounting and Financial Reporting Principles." This major pronouncement substantially upgraded the basic principles set forth in *GAAFR*. The most important revisions pertained to the manner of financial reporting. Narrative explanations and financial statements illustrate the application of the basic principles (which include the manner of financial reporting) and incorporate accounting provisions of *ASLGU*. We discuss these basic principles (grouped into seven broad categories) in detail later in the chapter. (In 1980, the AICPA issued *Statement of Position 80-2*, which amended *ASLGU* as a result of the issuance of *NCGA Statement 1*.)

***GAAFR* Reissued but Becomes a Guide.** In 1980, the GFOA published a revised, updated edition of *GAAFR* based on *NCGA Statement 1*. Unlike the 1968 edition of *GAAFR*, the 1980 edition is not an official pronouncement of the NCGA. It neither prescribes nor authoritatively interprets generally accepted accounting principles for governmental units. Instead, it provides detailed guidance to apply the principles in *NCGA Statement 1* to the accounting and financial reporting activities of state and local governments. Thus, NCGA Statements and Interpretations replaced *GAAFR* as the official pronouncements dealing with GAAP. With over 30,000 copies in print, *GAAFR* is widely used as a guide by state and local governmental accountants and to a lesser extent by certified public accountants.

Additional Accomplishments of the NCGA. The NCGA issued six additional statements, one of which we discuss later in the chapter. The others either deal with special topics or are beyond the scope of this and the following chapter. The NCGA also issued eleven interpretations. In addition, it started a research project to develop a conceptual framework for governmental accounting and financial reporting standards. This resulted in the 1981 issuance of *Concepts Statement 1*, which provides guidance in the future establishment of accounting and financial reporting principles for state and local governments.

FASB Involvement

Because of growing concern about the reliability and relevance of the financial reports of governmental units in the 1970s, many people urged the Financial Accounting Standards Board to become involved in the nonbusiness sector. In response to these requests, the FASB (1) sponsored a research study dealing with the conceptual issues of financial accounting in nonbusiness organizations; (2) issued a discussion memorandum in 1978 (based on the research study); (3) held public hearings on the issues set forth in the discussion memorandum; (4) decided in 1979 to develop one or more Statements of Financial Accounting Concepts on the objectives of financial reporting by nonbusiness organizations; (5) issued in 1980 *Statement of Financial Accounting Concepts No. 4*, "Objectives of Financial Reporting by Nonbusiness Organizations"; and (6) in 1983 proposed amendments to its *Statements of Financial Accounting Concepts No. 2* and *No. 3* to apply them to nonbusiness organizations as well as business enterprises. (These amendments were subsequently finalized in *Statement of Financial Accounting Concepts No. 6*).

Statement of Financial Accounting Concepts No. 4 did not establish any new accounting standards, nor did it place the FASB in a standard-setting role for state and local governmental units. The statement outlined helpful objectives for developing improved standards for financial reporting.

The Creation of the GASB

The NCGA operated under several handicaps. It never had adequate financing to build and retain a sufficient staff and to support an adequate system of due process. Furthermore, its close ties to the GFOA, which primarily constitutes preparers of financial statements, gave the appearance of a lack of independence. Because of these handicaps, it seemed logical that the NCGA should be disbanded and that the FASB should assume sole responsibility for issuing reporting standards for governmental units. This alternative was opposed by governmental accounting groups.

Much discussion and committee work led to the creation in 1984 of a new standard-setting body, the Governmental Accounting Standards Board (GASB) to succeed the NCGA, which was dissolved in June 1984. The Financial Accounting Foundation (FAF), which oversees the FASB, also oversees the GASB. Its five-member board (appointed for five-year terms) includes a full-time chairman and is located in the same Stamford, Connecticut, headquarters as the FASB.

The AICPA Recognizes the GASB

In 1986, the AICPA adopted a resolution that specified the GASB as the designated body to establish accounting principles for state and local governmental units, enforceable under Rule 203 of the AICPA's code of professional ethics. Under this rule, an auditor must communicate any departures from GAAP in his or her audit report.

The GASB's Accomplishments to Date

Since its inception in 1984, the GASB has divided its efforts between long-term projects and current problems requiring immediate attention.

Long-Term Projects. The major long-term project involves a reexamination of accounting and financial reporting for government. A discussion memorandum, "An Analysis of Issues Related to Measurement Focus and Basis of Accounting—Governmental Funds," was issued in 1985. In 1987, "Objectives of Financial Reporting," a major achievement in building a solid foundation for this financial reporting project was attained as a result of the issuance of Concepts Statement No. 1.

Current Issues Addressed. The GASB has addressed approximately ten current issues deemed to be pressing problems. As a result, one GASB interpretation and six GASB Statements of Governmental Accounting Standards have been issued. (Some issues still have exposure drafts outstanding.) Of those, five deal with specialized areas that are beyond the scope of this book. The other two are discussed:

1. *GASB Statement No. 1,* "Authoritative Status of NCGA Pronouncements and AICPA Audit Guide," states that all NCGA pronouncements issued and currently in effect are considered to be generally accepted accounting principles until their status is changed by a subsequent GASB pronouncement. The financial reporting guidance contained in the audit guide (since revised) continues in force.
2. *GASB Statement No. 6,* "Accounting and Financial Reporting for Special Assessments" (1987), eliminates one of the eight types of funds. As a result, special assessments are now accounted for in certain of the other seven fund types. (Fund types are discussed later.)

The GASB Codification of Governmental GAAP. In 1984, the GASB codified all existing governmental accounting and financial reporting standards in a joint effort with the GFOA. This book, *Codification of Governmental Accounting and Financial Reporting Standards,* is periodically updated for subsequent changes. The second (and most recent) update is as of June 15, 1987. The result is a useful and accessible reference previously not available. In referring to governmental GAAP, the AICPA's governmental audit guide cites the GASB codification rather than the various NCGA Statements, NCGA Interpretations, and GASB Statements in force at the time of the codification. This makes the most sense, and for this reason we do the same, citing the codification in the same manner as in the audit guide (for example, "GASB Cod. sec. xxx"), after first citing it in full.

AN OVERVIEW: MAJOR DIFFERENCES BETWEEN GOVERNMENTAL AND PRIVATE-SECTOR REPORTING

As this section makes clear, governmental financial reporting is different from private-sector reporting in the following major respects:

- It contains no mechanism for enforcing compliance with GAAP.

- It has no uniform requirement for audited annual financial statements.
- It has several shortcomings compared with private-sector reporting.

The Lack of a Mechanism for Enforcing Compliance with GAAP

In the private sector, publicly owned corporations must follow accounting standards as a result of legal requirements imposed by the Securities and Exchange Commission. No comparable enforcement mechanism exists for the governmental sector. Instead, the 50 states have the sovereign right to impose accounting and financial reporting requirements on governmental units within their jurisdiction. Thus, the rule-making bodies to date, being private organizations, have had no power over state and local governmental units. The states have been inconsistent in requiring their local governmental units to follow generally accepted accounting principles. Consequently, many governmental units issue financial reports that do not comply with GAAP in one or more respects. (However, governmental units that are audited by outside certified public accountants want to comply with GAAP, because the auditors must address whether GAAP has been followed.)

The major area of accounting for which governmental units do not follow generally accepted accounting principles is that of pension plans. Numerous state and local governmental units use the "pay-as-you-go" system, which is the cash basis of accounting. The dollar amount of the unfunded liabilities pertaining to pension plans that use this system is staggering. Consequently, to the extent that the financial statements of these governmental units do not reflect liabilities for these unfunded future obligations, such financial statements are grossly misleading.

No Requirement for Audited Annual Financial Statements

Many governmental units are audited annually by certified public accountants or governmental audit agencies as a result of state laws, charter provisions, or voluntary action. In addition, the Single Audit Act of 1984 requires an independent audit of all recipients of general revenue-sharing funds of $100,000 or more in any fiscal year. (Special rules apply to amounts of less than $100,000.)

However, the financial statements of many state and local governmental units do not need to be audited annually. Such units may issue securities to the public without the public's having the benefit of audited financial statements. In the private sector, a corporation that issues securities (stocks and bonds) to the public must (1) register the sale of such securities with the Securities and Exchange Commission (unless a statutory exemption is available); (2) maintain its books in accordance with generally accepted accounting principles; and (3) have its financial statements audited annually by a certified public accountant. The GFOA has issued a pronouncement, *Disclosure Guidelines for Offerings of Securities by State and Local Governments*, that it recommends be used when offering securities to investors. As with GASB Statements, however, compliance is voluntary.

Financial Reporting Shortcomings

Prior to 1979, most annual financial reports served the needs of government officials more than the needs of investors and other outsiders. Such reports contained masses of detail and were therefore quite difficult for the average citizen to understand. It was almost impossible to obtain a clear picture of either the overall financial condition or the operations of governmental units. General Motors, for example, could issue an annual report having ten pages of financial statements and notes that presented an understandable picture of its financial condition and operations, whereas the city of Detroit would issue an extensive financial report having over a hundred pages of financial statements, notes, and supporting schedules that few people could understand.

This manner of governmental reporting was criticized in the 1970s, when several major cities and counties had widely publicized, severe, and seemingly sudden financial crises. In response to this serious shortcoming, the GASB Codification calls for the presentation of specified financial statements, formally called **General Purpose Financial Statements,** in the annual financial reports of governmental units. Such statements give readers a summary overview of financial position and operations. Although the annual financial reports still contain masses of detail, the addition of the general purpose financial statements has been a giant step forward in financial reporting. The specific requirements pertaining to these financial statements are presented and discussed later in the chapter.

Despite these improvements, financial reporting by governmental units is far below the level of reporting for the private sector. In a survey in 1986 of nearly 500 governmental units (out of more than 80,000), 28% of the opinions rendered by auditors contained qualifications for departures from generally accepted accounting principles. The reasons for the qualified opinions varied; the most common ones were the improper accounting for fixed assets, revenues and expenditures, and pensions, in that order.[4]

THE NATURE OF GOVERNMENTAL OPERATIONS

Governmental operations are unique for several reasons:

1. Their absence of a profit motive
2. Their extensive legal requirements

[4]Cornelius E. Tierney and Philip T. Calder of Arthur Young & Co., *Governmental Accounting Procedures and Practices* (New York: Elsevier Science Publishing Company, Inc., 1986), pp. 239, 252.

3. Their diversity
4. Their use of fund accounting

The Absence of a Profit Motive: What to Measure?

The fundamental difference between the private sector and the governmental sector is that the former is organized and operated to make a profit for its owners, whereas the latter exists to provide services to its citizens substantially on a nonprofit basis. In the private sector, profit measurement is possible because a causal relationship exists between expenses and revenues: Costs and expenses are incurred to generate revenues. As a result, it is appropriate to compare these categories and determine profitability. The services of governmental units are not provided to generate revenues. Thus, revenues are not earned; they stand alone. This concept raises two key questions:

- Should revenues be compared with costs?
- Is some other measurement base more appropriate?

The GASB Codification states that revenues should not be compared with costs as in the private sector. Instead, it presumes that **the only appropriate measurement base is the flow of resources.** The source, or *inflow*, of resources (revenues and borrowings) is presented in a statement along with the use, or *outflow*, of resources (direct operating costs, payments for servicing debt, and payments for capital additions, all of which are referred to collectively as **expenditures**). Such a statement is, in substance, a statement of changes in financial position. In governmental accounting, however, it is called a **statement of revenues, expenditures, and changes in fund balance.** (The format of the statement is different from that used in the private sector, and it is more detailed.) The rationale for using the flow of resources as the measurement base is the presumption that the most meaningful question concerning a governmental unit's financial operations is: What resources were given to it and how were those resources used? The GASB Codification makes governmental units accountable in this respect.

Some accountants contend that in addition to measuring the flow of resources, a statement comparing revenues with costs should also be presented (including depreciation expense) even though the costs do not generate revenues as in the private sector. Such a statement would provide additional information as to **whether sufficient tax revenues were raised to cover the current costs of providing services.** (In the 1970s, many governmental units had severe financial crises from providing services far beyond the tax revenues being raised, creating substantial liabilities to be borne by future taxpayers.)

Whether an operating statement comparing revenues with the costs of providing services will be a reporting requirement in the future is conjecture; such a statement is a controversial issue. However, the improved financial reporting requirements contained in the GASB Codification (particularly the requirement to show borrowings separately from revenues in the statement of revenues, expenditures, and changes in fund balance) do provide a much better picture as to whether a governmental unit is spending beyond its means.

Extensive Legal Requirements

Governmental units are regulated by constitutions, charters, and statutes. Many legal provisions pertain to financial accounting areas. For example, certain activities or specified revenues must frequently be accounted for separately from all other operations. The uses of certain revenues may be limited. In some instances, a certain method of accounting—such as the cash basis—may be stipulated. We discuss the accounting ramifications of these requirements later in the chapter.

Diversity of Operations

Governmental operations are tremendously diverse. The GASB Codification classifies governmental operations in three broad categories:

1. **Governmental.** Operations that do not resemble commercial activities are classified in the governmental category. These operations provide primary services and are normally financed from tax revenues. Examples are education, public safety, the judicial system, social services, and administration.
2. **Proprietary.** Proprietary operations resemble commercial activities. Usually financed wholly or partially from user charges, these operations may be considered secondary services. Examples are utilities, public transportation, parking facilities, and recreational facilities. Proprietary operations usually have the objective of earning a profit or recovering a certain level of operating costs from fees charged the public for their use.
3. **Fiduciary.** Fiduciary operations pertain to accounting for assets held by a governmental unit as trustee or agent. The most common example is a pension fund for public employees.

The Use of Fund Accounting

Because of the legal requirements pertaining to financial accounting areas and the diversity of governmental operations, the use of a single set of accounts to record and summarize all the financial transactions of a governmental unit is neither legally possible nor practical. As a result, **fund accounting,** whereby certain operations are accounted for separately from other operations, is predominant in governmental accounting. The GASB Codification defines a **fund** as follows:

> A fund is . . . a fiscal and accounting entity with a self-balancing set of accounts recording cash and other financial resources, together with all

> related liabilities and residual equities or balances, and changes therein, which are segregated for the purpose of carrying on activities or attaining certain objectives in accordance with special regulations, restrictions, or limitations.[5]

Thus, from an accounting viewpoint, a governmental unit consists of all the individual funds used to account for the entity's various operations and activities.

BASIC PRINCIPLES OF THE GASB CODIFICATION

In reading the twelve basic principles of the GASB Codification (which we have grouped into seven broad categories), we must understand their relationship to the accounting principles that have been established by the FASB and its predecessor organizations. This relationship is expressed in the AICPA's governmental audit guide as follows:

> GASB pronouncements . . . constitute the primary source of GAAP for governmental units. GASB pronouncements take precedence over FASB pronouncements with regard to state and local governmental entities, but if the accounting treatment of a transaction or event is not specified in a GASB pronouncement, and the FASB has dealt with the subject, the FASB pronouncement is presumed to apply.[6]

Generally Accepted Accounting Principles, Compliance with Legal Provisions, and Conflicts between Legal Provisions and GAAP

The GASB Codification recommends the following:

> A governmental accounting sytem must make it possible both: (a) to present fairly and with full disclosure the financial position and results of financial operations of the funds and account groups of the governmental unit in conformity with generally accepted accounting principles; and (b) to determine and demonstrate compliance with finance-related legal and contractual provisions.[7]

In many cases, both objectives are satisfied through the use of a separate fund for a designated activity and the preparation of separate financial statements for the separate fund. In some cases, a legal provision may specify the use of a practice that is not in accordance with generally accepted accounting principles—for example, requiring that a certain fund maintain its books on the cash basis. In these cases, the books must

[5] *Codification of Governmental Accounting and Financial Reporting Standards* (Stamford: Governmental Accounting Standards Board, 1987), sec. 1100.102.
[6] *ASLGU* (1986 revised edition), pars. 1.7, 1.8.
[7] GASB Cod. sec. 1100.101.

be maintained according to the law. For financial reporting purposes, however, the cash basis trial balance must be adjusted (on a worksheet) to arrive at a presentation in accordance with GAAP. Financial statements would then be prepared and reported according to GAAP. The GASB Codification addresses such conflicts as follows:

> Where financial statements prepared in conformity with GAAP do not demonstrate finance-related legal and contractual compliance, the governmental unit should present such additional schedules and narrative explanations in the comprehensive annual financial report as may be necessary to report its legal compliance responsibilities and accountabilities. In extreme cases, preparation of a separate legal-basis special report may be necessary.[8]

The long-range solution to this problem is to eliminate any legal provisions that conflict with generally accepted accounting principles. Efforts are continuously made in this respect, but progress is slow.

Types of Funds

The GASB Codification, as amended by *GASB Statement No. 6*, recognizes and recommends the use of seven major types of funds, categorized into three broad areas, as follows:

Governmental Funds

1. *The General Fund*—to account for all financial resources except those required to be accounted for in another fund.
2. *Special Revenue Funds*—to account for the proceeds of specific revenue sources (other than expendable trusts or for major capital projects) that are legally restricted to expenditure for specified purposes.
3. *Capital Projects Funds*—to account for financial resources to be used for the acquisition or construction of major capital facilities (other than those financed by proprietary funds and Trust Funds).
4. *Debt Service Funds*—to account for the accumulation of resources for, and the payment of, general long-term debt principal and interest.

Proprietary Funds

5. *Enterprise Funds*—to account for operations (a) that are financed and operated in a manner similar to private business enterprises—where the intent of the governing body is that the costs (expenses including depreciation) of providing goods or services to the general public on a continuing basis be financed or recovered primarily through user charges; or (b) where the governing body has decided that periodic determination of revenues earned, expenses incurred, and/or net income is appropriate for capital maintenance, public policy, management control, accountability, or other purposes.

[8]GASB Cod. sec. 1200.113.

6. *Internal Service Funds* — to account for the financing of goods or services provided by one department or agency to other departments or agencies of the governmental unit, on a cost-reimbursement basis.

Fiduciary Funds

7. *Trust and Agency Funds* — to account for assets held by a governmental unit in a trustee capacity or as an agent for individuals, private organizations, other governmental units, and/or other funds. These include (a) Expendable Trust Funds (b) Nonexpendable Trust Funds, (c) Pension Trust Funds, and (d) Agency Funds.[9]

The number of funds used by a given governmental unit depends on legal requirements and what is practical in relation to the scope of operations. The General Fund, which usually accounts for the largest part of a governmental unit's total operations, is discussed and illustrated later in the chapter. The remaining types of funds are discussed and illustrated in Chapter 21.

Basis of Accounting

APB Statement No. 4, "Basic Concepts and Accounting Principles Underlying Financial Statements of Businesses," defines the accrual basis of accounting as follows:

> The effects of transactions and other events on the assets and liabilities of a business enterprise are recognized and reported in the time period to which they relate rather than only when cash is received or paid.[10]

Thus, the difference between the accrual basis and the cash basis is merely one of **timing.** The private sector initially developed the accrual basis concept to properly determine net income and financial position. Even though the profit motive is absent from most public-sector operations, the concept of recording items in the period to which they relate can be applied. The GASB Codification recommends using the accrual basis "to the fullest extent practicable in the government environment."[11]

Certain activities in the public sector lend themselves to the use of the accrual basis of accounting. For most activities, however, it is not practicable to use the accrual basis. Instead, a combination of the accrual basis and the cash basis is more appropriate. As a result, certain items are not recorded in the period to which they relate. Although this accounting basis might be appropriately called the "combination accrual and cash basis," the GASB Codification chose to call it the **modified accrual basis.**

[9]GASB Cod. sec. 1300.104, as amended by *Government Accounting Standards Board Statement No. 6*, "Accounting and Financial Reporting for Special Assessments" (Stamford: Governmental Accounting Standards Board, 1987).

[10]*Accounting Principles Board Statement No. 4*, "Basic Concepts and Accounting Principles of Businesses" (New York: American Institute of Certified Public Accountants, 1970), par. 35.

[11]GASB Cod. sec. 1600.103.

Accrual Basis Funds. Activities accounted for in Enterprise Funds and Internal Service Funds (proprietary funds) and Nonexpendable Trust Funds (fiduciary funds) have the objectives of profit measurement or capital maintenance. Thus, the accrual basis of accounting as conceived for private businesses is entirely suitable for these funds. Also, Pension Trust Funds (fiduciary funds) exhibit the same characteristics as pension funds established in the private sector. Thus, the accrual basis also lends itself to use with Pension Trust Funds. Accordingly, for each of these funds, revenues earned and expenses incurred may be accrued and recognized in the period to which they relate in essentially the same manner as in the private sector. For these reasons, the GASB Codification recommends the use of the accrual basis for these funds.

Modified Accrual Basis Funds. For all remaining funds (the four governmental funds and Expendable Trust Funds), the GASB Codification recommends the use of the modified accrual basis of accounting, which is described as follows:

> Revenues should be recognized in the accounting period in which they become **available and measurable** [emphasis added]. Expenditures should be recognized in the accounting period in which the fund liability is incurred, if measurable, except for unmatured interest on general long-term debt, which should be recognized when due.[12]

The reason for using the modified accrual basis of accounting for these funds may be attributed to the nature of governmental revenue sources and activities. We discuss the modified accrual basis first concerning revenues and then expenditures.

Revenues. Fund revenues are not recognized when earned (as is done under the accrual basis); the "available and measurable" criterion is used because it is more appropriate. (Most governmental operations do not "earn" revenues.) Thus, revenues are recognized when they become **"susceptible to accrual."** The term **"available"** means that a revenue source is "collectible within the current period or soon enough thereafter to be used to pay liabilities of the current period."[13]

The application of these revenue-related criteria results in (1) certain revenues being recognized entirely on the accrual basis; (2) certain revenues being recognized entirely on the cash basis; and (3) certain revenues being recognized partially on the cash basis and partially on the accrual basis. We discuss each of these revenue categories more fully below.

1. **Accrual basis revenues.** Many revenue sources may be accrued in essentially the same manner as is done in the private sector. Some of

[12] GASB Cod. sec. 1100.108 (as amended by *GASB Statement No. 6*).
[13] GASB Cod. sec. 1600.106.

the most common examples are property taxes, grants, and interfund transfers:

a. **Property taxes.** Property taxes may be precisely determined for each specific property to which a legally enforceable lien attaches. Some governmental units bill property owners in advance of the fiscal year to which the property taxes relate. For control purposes, property taxes should be recorded at the time of billing. Property tax revenues, however, should be shown as deferred revenues until the start of the fiscal year to which they pertain, because the revenues do not relate to the prior fiscal year (even though the assessment date may have been in that year).

b. **Grants and interfund transfers.** Most grants from other governmental units and interfund transfers within a governmental unit are susceptible to accrual in the period to which they relate because an irrevocable commitment exists.

2. **Cash basis revenues.** Many revenue sources may not be accrued, because governmental units cannot determine the tax receivable from individual taxpayers at each month-end. The two broad categories of such revenues are self-assessment basis revenues and such miscellaneous revenues as license and permit fees, fines, and parking meter revenues.

a. **Self-assessment basis revenues.** Self-assessment basis revenues include income taxes, sales taxes, and gross receipts taxes. The distinguishing feature of this type of revenue is that the governmental unit does not bill the taxpayer. The receivable for each revenue source at each month-end may only be estimated, because the actual amounts are unknown until taxpayer reports are received or payments are collected. It should be noted that the use of income tax withholding procedures often produces results that closely approximate the accrual basis of accounting in that tax revenues are received substantially in the period in which the income is earned by taxpayers. Even when income tax withholding procedures are used, however, the final amount to be paid to the government (or to be refunded to the taxpayer in the event of excess withholdings or estimated interim payments) is not known until several months after the year in which the taxpayer earns the income.

b. **Miscellaneous revenues.** Miscellaneous revenues include the following items:

1. **Annual business licenses.** Licenses are usually issued for new businesses at the time of payment. Because a license may not be granted, a bona fide receivable does not exist when an application is filed. Although governmental units often bill taxpayers for renewals of their annual business licenses, this billing (whether prior to or at the start of the fiscal year to which the bill pertains) is usually not relevant. The governmental unit does not know if the taxpayer will renew the license until it receives payment.

2. **Construction and home improvement permits.** Construction and home improvement permits are usually issued at the time of payment. The filing of an application does not create a bona fide receivable, because the permit may not be granted.

3. **Fines.** Most fines are collected when they are levied, which is when the amount of the fine is determined.
4. **Parking meter revenues.** The amounts of parking meter revenues are not determinable until the meters have been emptied and the receipts have been counted.

3. **Partial cash and partial accrual basis revenues.** This category merely applies the accrual concept to portions of revenues normally recognized on the cash basis. For example, sales taxes due from other governmental units or merchants that have not been received at the normal time of receipt should be accrued, providing the criteria of measurability and availability are met. Revenues received before their normal time of receipt that pertain to subsequent periods should be recorded as deferred revenues.

Expenditures. The accrual basis is used by requiring expenditures to be recognized in the period in which the liability is incurred. (This is merely a different way of saying that items should be recorded and recognized in the period to which they relate.) The strict recognition of expenditures in the period in which the liability is incurred results in the omission of prepayments and inventories from the balance sheet. Usually these items are so minor in relation to governmental operations that such omission is an insignificant departure from generally accepted accounting principles. However, if inventory is significant, the GASB Codification recommends that it be reported in the balance sheet.[14] The manner of reporting inventory in the balance sheet is discussed later in the chapter. In Chapter 21, we discuss the one specific exception to the use of the accrual basis—recognizing interest on general long-term debt when due rather than in the period in which the interest liability arises.

The AICPA Position on the Modified Accrual Basis. The AICPA governmental audit guide accepts the modified accrual basis as being appropriate and in conformity with generally accepted accounting principles.[15]

Fixed Assets and Long-Term Liabilities

Accounting for Fixed Assets. The nature of governmental operations is such that more meaningful financial reporting results if certain fixed assets are accounted for in fund accounts and all other fixed assets (referred to collectively as **general fixed assets**) are accounted for outside the funds in **account groups.** The GASB Codification recommends the following:

> Fixed assets related to specific proprietary funds or trust funds should be accounted for through those funds. All other fixed assets of a governmen-

[14] GASB Cod. sec. 1600.122.
[15] *ASLGU* (1986 revised edition), p. 59.

tal unit should be accounted for through the General Fixed Assets Account Group.[16]

Accounting for Long-Term Liabilities. As with general fixed assets, more meaningful financial reporting is possible if certain long-term liabilities are accounted for in fund accounts and all other long-term debt (referred to collectively as **general long-term debt**) is accounted for outside the funds in account groups. The GASB Codification recommends the following:

> Long-term liabilities of proprietary funds and trust funds should be accounted for through those funds. All other unmatured general long-term liabilities of the governmental unit, which includes special assessment debt for which the government is obligated in some manner, should be accounted for through the General Long-Term Debt Account Group.[17]

Certain long-term debt is excluded from governmental funds because such debt does not require the current use of financial resources of the governmental funds. Because one of the reporting objectives of the governmental funds is to reflect those liabilities to be paid from available financial resources, these liabilities must be excluded from governmental funds to accomplish this objective. Furthermore, such debt is the liability of the governmental unit as a whole and not that of any specific fund. As such, it is secured by the taxing powers of the governmental unit and not by the resources available in a specific fund.

The General Long-Term Debt Account Group is also a "self-balancing" set of accounts because the list of liabilities, maintained in account form, is balanced by accounts showing (1) amounts, if any, set aside in Debt Service Funds for repayment of the General Long-Term Debt, and (2) amounts yet to be provided for repayment of the General Long-Term Debt. The General Long-Term Debt Account Group is discussed in detail in Chapter 21.

Valuation of Fixed Assets. With respect to the valuation of fixed assets, the GASB Codification specifies the following:

> Fixed assets should be accounted for at cost or, if the cost is not practicably determinable, at estimated cost. Donated fixed assets should be recorded at their estimated fair value at the time received.[18]

Fixed assets are excluded from the governmental funds because such assets do not constitute financial resources available for spending purposes. Because one of the reporting objectives of the governmental funds is to reflect the financial resources available for spending purposes, fixed assets must be excluded from governmental funds to accomplish this objective.

[16]GASB Cod. sec. 1100.105.
[17]GASB Cod. sec. 1100.105. (as amended by *GASB Statement No. 6*).
[18]GASB Cod. sec. 1100.106.

The General Fixed Assets Account Group is not a separate fund but merely a list of a governmental unit's general fixed assets, maintained in account form. These accounts are complemented by credit accounts showing the sources by which the assets were obtained. For example, the entry to reflect the ownership of a fire truck that was purchased by the General Fund would be:

Fixed Assets — Fire Trucks	**30,000**	
Investment in General Fixed Assets (from General Fund)		**30,000**
To reflect ownership of fire truck purchased through the General Fund.		

Because of the manner of making entries, the General Fixed Asset Account Group is said to be a "self-balancing" set of accounts. The General Fixed Assets Account Group is discussed in detail in Chapter 21.

Depreciation of Fixed Assets. With respect to depreciating fixed assets, the GASB Codification recommends the following:

> Depreciation of general fixed assets should not be recorded in the accounts of governmental funds. Depreciation of general fixed assets may be recorded in cost accounting systems or calculated for cost finding analysis; and accumulated depreciation may be recorded in the General Fixed Assets Account Group [an optional treatment].
>
> Depreciation of fixed assets accounted for in a proprietary fund should be recorded in the accounts of that fund. Depreciation is also recognized in those Trust Funds where expenses, net income, and/or capital maintenance are measured.[19]

Commercial businesses record depreciation expense to match revenues with expenses, so that net income may be properly determined. Fixed assets accounted for in proprietary funds and certain trust funds also have the objectives of profitability or capital maintenance (cost recovery). Accordingly, depreciation expense is properly recorded in these funds, because income statements are prepared.

For all other funds, income statements are not presented, nor is a statement presented comparing revenues with costs (which would include depreciation expense). Instead, only a statement of revenues, expenditures, and changes in fund balance based on the "flow of resources" measurement base is presented. Accordingly, when a general fixed asset is acquired, it is reflected as an expenditure in the fund at the time of acquisition. Depreciation expense would not be recorded in this statement because it does not constitute a flow of resources.

[19]GASB Cod. sec. 1100.107.

The absence of depreciation expense in the statement of revenues, expenditures, and changes in fund balance should not be considered a departure from the accrual basis of accounting. The GASB Codification makes an important clarification regarding what is encompassed by the accrual basis of accounting:

> Unfortunately, the terms "accrual" and "accrual accounting" often are interpreted to mean "income determination accounting," and thus to connote the recognition of depreciation in the course of expense measurement. This misunderstanding likely has arisen because most literature centers on income determination and uses the terms "accrual" and "accrual accounting" in that context. It should be recognized, however, that depreciation and amortization are allocations, not accruals, and that "accrual" in a governmental fund accounting context does not mean that depreciation, amortization, and similar allocations should be recognized.[20]

This position is consistent with the AICPA's governmental audit guide, which does not state that the lack of depreciation expense in these funds is a departure from generally accepted accounting principles.

Budgets and Budgetary Accounting

Budgets. Budgets are used in the public sector for planning, controlling, and evaluating operations just as they are used in the private sector. A **budget** is merely a plan of financial operations covering a specified period of time. For all governmental, proprietary, and fiduciary funds (other than Agency Funds, which are custodial in nature), the GASB Codification recommends that "an annual budget(s) should be adopted by every governmental unit."[21]

Prepared under the direction of the governmental unit's chief executive officer, the **annual** budget is submitted to the legislative body for review, possible modification, and formal adoption. The significance of the budget for each of these funds is as follows:

Fund Type	Significance
Governmental Funds and certain Fiduciary Funds	The statutory authorization for spending an estimated amount during the subsequent fiscal year. The authorization is referred to as an **appropriation.**
Proprietary Funds and certain Fiduciary Funds	The approval of a proposed operating plan (as distinct from a statutory authorization to spend a certain amount in dollars).

[20]GASB Cod. sec. 1600.104.
[21]GASB Cod. sec. 1100.109.

A **long-term** budget covers a period of several years. Long-term budgets restricted to major capital additions and improvements are referred to as **capital** budgets.

Budgetary Accounting. Because legal limitations are imposed on certain of the funds (primarily the governmental funds) as to the amount that may be spent during a fiscal year, it is exceedingly important to monitor and control spending, so that expenditures do not exceed this limitation. The GASB Codification recommends, "The accounting system should provide the basis for appropriate budgetary control."[22]

The GASB Codification specifies the following two areas in which budgetary accounts should be used to monitor and control spending: (1) recording the annual budget in the general ledger; and (2) recording purchase order commitments in the general ledger, which is referred to as *encumbrance accounting.*

To enhance the understanding of budgetary integration in the general ledger, we use the technique, illustrated in the 1980 edition of *GAAFR*, of **printing budgetary account descriptions in all capital letters.** As a result, we can consider all budgetary accounts as a separate trial balance from the regular general ledger accounts. We also use the same account descriptions, for budgetary and actual accounts, used in the 1980 edition of *GAAFR*, because these descriptions are now used by both the AICPA (in its official solutions to the CPA examinations) and the CPA examination review courses (in their course materials).

Recording the Annual Budget. The budget for the General Fund and Special Revenue Funds is recorded in the general ledger. (The annual budget pertaining to Capital Projects Funds and Debt Service Funds is recorded in the general ledger only if it would serve a useful purpose, determined on a case-by-case basis.) Assuming a governmental unit expects its General Fund revenues to exceed its General Fund appropriations for the new fiscal year, the budget is recorded in the General Fund's general ledger as follows:

ESTIMATED REVENUES CONTROL	**1,000,000**	
APPROPRIATIONS CONTROL		**980,000**
BUDGETARY FUND BALANCE		**20,000**
To record the legally adopted annual operating budget.		

The ESTIMATED REVENUES CONTROL account is a control account. Actual revenues are recorded in individual subsidiary Revenue accounts

[22] GASB Cod. sec. 1100.109.

(and in a Revenues Control Account). The detail making up the ESTIMATED REVENUES CONTROL account is also recorded directly in the individual subsidiary Revenue accounts at the start of the year. As a result, estimated revenues may be readily compared with actual revenues throughout the year. Although revenues cannot be "controlled" in the manner that expenditures can be controlled, a governmental unit may be able to curtail spending if it appears that revenue inflows will not be reasonably close to estimated revenues.

Likewise, the APPROPRIATIONS CONTROL account is a control account. Actual expenditures are recorded in individual subsidiary Expenditures accounts, (and in an Expenditures Control account). The detail making up the APPROPRIATIONS CONTROL account is also recorded directly in the individual subsidiary Expenditures accounts at the start of the year. As a result, expenditures to date may be readily compared with the authorized spending limitation, revealing how much more may be spent.

The difference between a fund's assets and liabilities is the fund's equity. For governmental funds and fiduciary funds, this difference is recorded in a Fund Balance account. (For proprietary funds, which do not use budgetary accounts, Contributed Capital and Retained Earnings accounts are used.) A governmental unit's budget for the coming fiscal year may reflect an intention to increase (as in the above example) or decrease the fund balance amount existing at the beginning of the year. Most governmental units (with the notable exception of the federal government) try to accumulate a reasonable "surplus" in the Fund Balance account in case unforeseen adverse events occur. In recording the budget in the general ledger, the difference between the debit to ESTIMATED REVENUES CONTROL and the credit to APPROPRIATIONS CONTROL is credited (as in the above example) or debited to BUDGETARY FUND BALANCE.

Recording the budget in the general ledger does not affect the year-end balance in the Fund Balance account because the budget entry is reversed at year-end as part of the normal closing process.

Encumbrance Accounting. As stated earlier, expenditures are recognized when the fund liability is incurred, which is usually when goods are received or services are rendered. Many expenditures involve the issuance of purchase orders, whereby goods are received or services are rendered at a later date. Outstanding purchase orders are commitments for future expenditures. To monitor and control spending properly, governmental units must keep track of the amount of outstanding purchase orders. This is accomplished by recording the amount of each purchase order (including the amount of contracts entered into) in the general ledger at the time of issuance. For example, assuming a purchase order for $50,000 is issued, the following budgetary entry would be made:

ENCUMBRANCES CONTROL	50,000	
FUND BALANCE RESERVED FOR ENCUMBRANCES		50,000
To record encumbrances for purchase orders issued.		

The ENCUMBRANCES CONTROL account may be thought of as an "expenditure-to-be" account. At a later date, when the goods or services are received, the entry is reversed and the expenditure is recorded. Assume in the above example that the actual cost of the goods received under the purchase was $49,000. The following entries would be made:

FUND BALANCE RESERVED FOR ENCUMBRANCES	50,000	
ENCUMBRANCES CONTROL		50,000
To cancel encumbrances of $50,000 upon receipt of materials and rendering of services totaling $49,000.		
Expenditures	49,000	
Vouchers Payable		49,000
To record expenditures of $49,000 for goods and services which were previously encumbered for $50,000.		

Like the APPROPRIATIONS CONTROL account, the ENCUMBRANCES CONTROL account is a control account. Each encumbrance is recorded in the individual subsidiary Expenditures accounts. As a result, the remaining amount that may be legally spent at a given time is readily determined by subtracting expenditures to date and encumbrances outstanding from appropriations. (Because an Expenditures Control account is also maintained, this calculation can be done at the control level or at the detail level using the individual subsidiary accounts.)

Illustration 20-1 shows what a subsidiary ledger might look like at the departmental level. Note that the format indicates the spendable amount

Illustration 20-1
Example of a Department's Subsidiary Ledger Account

Department No. 34				
Date	Appropriation	Expenditures	Encumbrances	Remaining Spendable Amount
July 1, 19X1	$100,000			$100,000
July 19X1		$ 6,000	$7,000	(13,000)
July 31, 19X1	$100,000	$ 6,000	$7,000	$ 87,000
August 19X1		11,000	(3,000)	(8,000)
August 31, 19X1	$100,000	$17,000	$4,000	$ 79,000

remaining at the end of each month. (Only two months' activities are illustrated.) If an encumbrances column were not included, the department supervisor might erroneously conclude that $94,000 ($100,000 appropriations − $6,000 expenditures) was available for spending at July 31, 19X1. This figure is incorrect because purchase orders outstanding at July 31, 19X1, total $7,000. Thus, of the $94,000 not yet spent at July 31, 19X1, $7,000 is earmarked for the outstanding purchase orders. This leaves only $87,000 available for spending at July 31, 19X1. The objective of the procedure, of course, is to prevent spending more than has been authorized (appropriated).

From the preceding discussion and analysis, you should realize that only the debit entry recording the encumbrance is used in controlling spending. The credit to the FUND BALANCE RESERVED FOR ENCUMBRANCES account serves no control function other than to provide a credit for double-entry bookkeeping. Thus, it is merely a contra account.

Encumbrances Outstanding at Year-end. When encumbrances are outstanding at year-end, the encumbrance budgetary accounts must be closed. For example, assume a governmental unit has outstanding at year-end $5,000 of encumbrances. The following journal entry would be made:

FUND BALANCE RESERVED FOR ENCUMBRANCES....	**5,000**	
ENCUMBRANCES CONTROL..............................		**5,000**
To close out encumbrances outstanding at year-end by reversing the entry that previously recorded them.		

Governmental units generally honor purchase orders and commitments outstanding at year-end. In such cases, the GASB Codification requires that encumbrances outstanding at year-end be disclosed as a reservation of the Fund Balance account (similar to an appropriation of retained earnings for a private corporation). This requires an additional journal entry, as follows:

Unreserved Fund Balance	**5,000**	
Fund Balance Reserved for Encumbrances.........		**5,000**
To record *actual* fund balance reserve account to indicate the portion of year-end fund balance segregated for expenditure upon vendor performance.		

Thus, if a fund had a year-end total fund balance of $75,000, the fund balance would be presented in the balance sheet as follows:

FUND EQUITY	
Fund balance:	
Reserved for encumbrances	**$ 5,000**
Unreserved	**70,000**
Total Fund Balance	**$75,000**

From this presentation, financial statement readers know that $5,000 of the $75,000 total fund balance has been earmarked for encumbrances outstanding at year-end. Thus the uncommitted amount available for spending in the following year is $70,000.

At the start of the new year, the preceding two $5,000 journal entries would be reversed to reestablish budgetary control over encumbrances outstanding in the normal manner. These reversing entries are as follows:

Fund Balance Reserved for Encumbrances	**5,000**	
Unreserved Fund Balance		**5,000**
To reverse appropriation of fund balance made at the end of the prior year.		
ENCUMBRANCES CONTROL	**5,000**	
FUND BALANCE RESERVED FOR ENCUMBRANCES		**5,000**
To reestablish budgetary control over encumbrances outstanding at the end of the prior year which will be honored during the current year.		

Budgetary Comparisons — GAAP Basis. A financial reporting requirement of the GASB Codification is the preparation of "budgetary comparison statements or schedules" (as appropriate) in which budgeted data are compared with actual data for the year. Recall that under GAAP reporting, encumbrances outstanding at year-end are not reported in the statement of revenues, expenditures, and changes in fund balance. They would become expenditures in the following year and be reported as expenditures in that year. To present a meaningful comparison of actual expenditures with the budgeted expenditures, the budgeted expenditures must be prepared on a basis consistent with GAAP. To do this, amounts must be included in the following year's budget for encumbrances outstanding at the current year-end. Thus, it can be said that **encumbrances outstanding at the end of the current year "lapse," but then they are "rebudgeted" and "reappropriated" in the following year.** Without this procedure, the following year's expenditures would include amounts relating to the encumbrances outstanding at the end of the prior year, but no amount would appear in the following year's budget for these expenditures, resulting in a meaningless comparison.

To illustrate this comparison process, we assume the following data:

1. For 19X1, a governmental unit expects routine expenditures of $500,000 and also the purchase of a new fire truck for $30,000. Thus, it budgets $530,000 for 19X1 expenditures.
2. Actual spending occurs according to budget, except that the fire truck is received in early 19X2 rather than 19X1.
3. The governmental unit expects routine expenditures of $500,000 for 19X2. It also "reappropriates" or "rebudgets" an additional $30,000 to cover the fire truck for 19X2. Thus, the total budget for 19X2 expenditures is $530,000.
4. Actual spending for 19X2 occurs according to budget.

The budgetary comparison (on a GAAP basis) is as follows:

	GAAP Basis of Comparison		
			Variance
	Budget	Actual	Favorable (Unfavorable)
19X1:			
Expenditures.................	$530,000	$500,000	$30,000
19X2:			
Expenditures.................	530,000	530,000	–0–

Budgetary Comparisons — Non-GAAP "Budgetary" Basis. Most governmental units do not prepare their annual operating budgets on a basis consistent with GAAP. Thus, the following year's budget does not include amounts to honor the encumbrances outstanding at year-end. Instead, **the authorization to honor the encumbrances outstanding merely carries over to the following year.** This manner of budgeting is commonly referred to as the **non-GAAP "budgetary" basis.** To make a valid comparison to the budgeted data, the expenditures pertaining to the current-year budget must be combined with the encumbrances outstanding at year-end. Using the information in the preceding example, but assuming the non-GAAP "budgetary" basis of budgeting, the budgetary comparison would be as follows:

	Non-GAAP "Budgetary" Basis of Comparison		
			Variance
	Budget	Actual	Favorable (Unfavorable)
19X1:			
Expenditures and encumbrances ..	$530,000	$530,000	$–0–
19X2:			
Expenditures and encumbrances ..	500,000	500,000	–0–

When the annual operating budget is prepared on the non-GAAP "budgetary" basis, encumbrances and expenditures must be separated by year of appropriation. This is because current-year expenditures that resulted from encumbrances outstanding at the end of the prior year are not reported as current-year expenditures in the budgetary comparison statements. (They are reported, instead, as encumbrances in the prior year's budgetary comparison statement.) In the example dealing with the fire truck, the "Expenditures—19X1" account (or "Expenditures—Prior Year") would be charged in 19X2 when the fire truck was received.

When the budgetary comparison statement is presented on the non-GAAP "budgetary" basis, the GASB Codification still requires the presentation of a statement of revenues, expenditures, and changes in fund balance (not involving budgetary comparisons) on a GAAP basis.

Regardless of whether (a) encumbrances outstanding at year-end lapse and are reappropriated in the following year's budget, or (b) the spending authority carries over to the following year, the year-end closing entries pertaining to the encumbrances and reserving a portion of the fund balance are identical.

Financial Reporting

As discussed earlier in the chapter, the financial reporting requirements contained in the GASB Codification substantially upgraded former reporting practices. The key requirement is that financial statements be presented in the governmental unit's annual financial report (formally referred to as "The Comprehensive Annual Financial Report") using a "reporting pyramid" concept. The "pyramid" consists of four levels of financial information, each of which provide more detailed information than the previous level. Illustration 20-2 shows how this reporting pyramid might appear.

The reporting pyramid includes the following levels of financial information:

1. **Combined financial statements—Overview (General purpose financial statements).** The financial statements in the first level present the overall financial position and operating results of a governmental unit as a whole. They are referred to as the "General Purpose Financial Statements." Level 1 contains

    1. Combined Balance Sheet—All Fund Types and Account Groups.
    2. Combined Statement of Revenues, Expenditures, and Changes in Fund Balance—All Governmental Fund Types.
    3. Combined Statement of Revenues, Expenditures, and Changes in Fund Balances—Budget and Actual—General and Special Revenue Fund Types (and similar governmental fund types for which annual budgets have been legally adopted).
    4. Combined Statement of Revenues, Expenses, and Changes in Retained Earnings (or Equity)—All Proprietary Fund Types.

Illustration 20-2
The Financial Reporting Pyramid

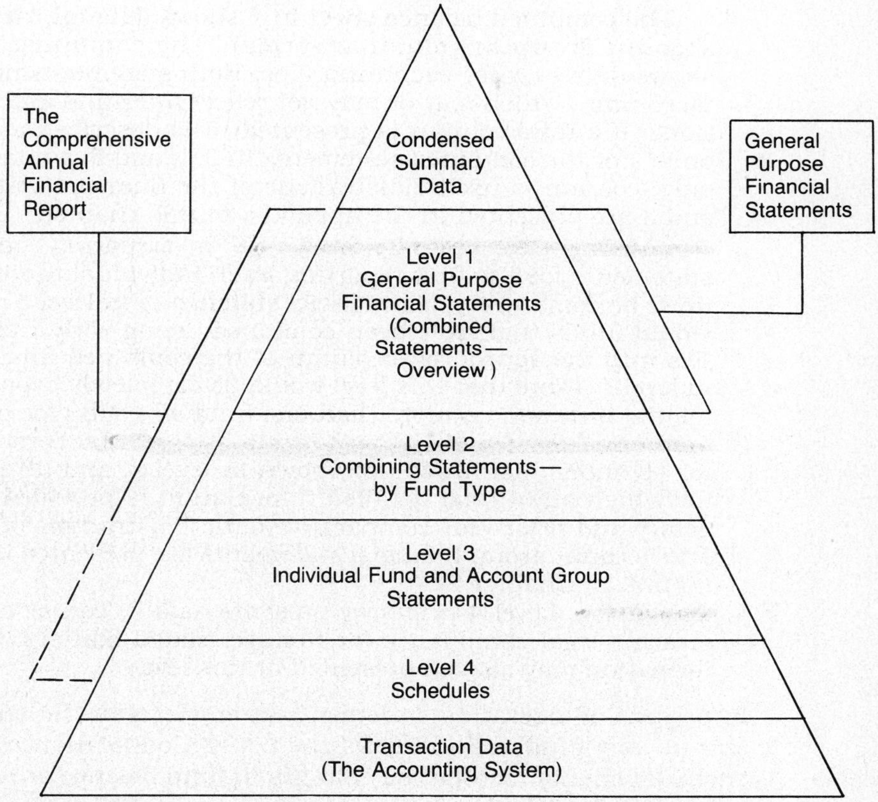

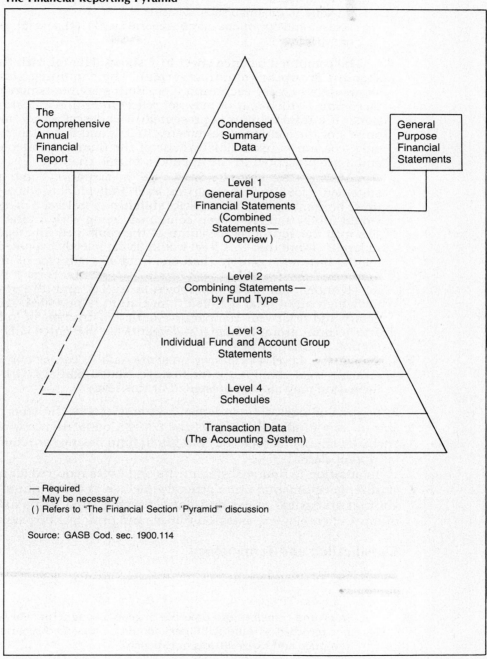

— Required
— May be necessary
( ) Refers to "The Financial Section 'Pyramid'" discussion

Source: GASB Cod. sec. 1900.114

5. Combined Statement of Changes in Financial Position—All Proprietary Fund Types.
6. Notes to the financial statements.

(Trust Fund operations may be reported in (2), (4), and (5), as appropriate, or separately.)[23]

The combined balance sheet in 1 shows data for each fund type and account group in columnar format. The combined statement in 2 shows data only for each fund type. Both statements may present a total column, which may or may not reflect interfund and similar eliminations. If a total column is presented, it is described as "memorandum only." For the combined statements in 3,4, and 5, a total "memorandum only" column is used. Illustrations of the financial statements in 1, 2, and 4 are presented in the Appendix to this chapter.

2. **Combining statements by fund type.** In preparing combined financial statements for the first reporting level, individual funds of a given type must be combined. The financial statements in level 2 present the individual funds that have been combined, along with a total column that ties into the appropriate column of the combined financial statements in level 1. (Note that this level would be completely bypassed if a governmental unit had no more than one fund for each type of fund.)
3. **Individual fund and account group statements.** Level 3 presents data for (1) individual funds not shown in level 2, and (2) individual funds for which additional detailed information is provided—such as budgetary and prior-year comparative data. Illustrations of individual fund and account group financial statements are presented later in the chapter and in Chapter 21.
4. **Schedules.** Level 4 primarily presents data in connection with demonstrating legal compliance for finance-related matters. Other useful information may also be presented at this level.

In presenting operating statements at any level in the reporting pyramid and for any fund or fund type, the GASB Codification recommends that such statements incorporate changes in fund balance or retained earnings (as appropriate).[24]

In addition to financial statements and notes required for adequate disclosure, governmental units generally include in their annual reports substantial statistical tables and data covering such items as population, number of employees, assessed values, and principal taxpayers.

Classification and Terminology

The GASB Codification recommends the following classification reporting practices:

> Interfund transfers and proceeds of general long-term debt issues [that are not recorded as fund liabilities] should be classified separately from fund revenues and expenditures or expenses.

[23]GASB Cod. sec. 1900.113.
[24]GASB Cod. sec. 2200.109.

> Governmental fund revenues should be classified by fund and source. Expenditures should be classified by fund, function (or program), organization unit, activity, character, and principal classes of objects.
>
> Proprietary fund revenues and expenses should be classified in essentially the same manner as those of similar business organizations, functions, or activities.[25]

Classifying proceeds of general long-term debt separately from fund revenues is a substantial improvement over the former practice of showing such proceeds as revenues. Such proceeds must be shown under a separate section of the operating statement of the recipient fund called Other Financing Sources. Reporting interfund transfers separately from fund revenues and expenditures or expenses is also a substantial improvement over the former practice of showing these items as revenues and expenditures or expenses.

Types of Interfund Transactions. In the GASB Codification, interfund transactions are divided into the following four types: (a) quasi-external transactions, (b) reimbursements, (c) loans or advances, and (d) transfers. Only category (c) requires no further explanation.

Quasi-External Transactions. These interfund transactions are reported as revenues, expenditures, or expenses in the particular funds, because the transactions would be treated as such if they were conducted between a fund and an organization external to the governmental unit. An example would be a city's electric utility (which would be accounted for in an Enterprise Fund) supplying electricity to the city. The city's General Fund would report expenditures, but the Enterprise Fund would report revenues in the same amount. The theory here is that the General Fund would have recorded an expenditure if it had been supplied the electricity by a private utility.

Reimbursements. Transactions in which a fund (Fund A, for example) reimburses another fund (Fund B, for example) for expenditures or expenses it (Fund B) incurs are reimbursements. The reimbursing fund (Fund A) would report expenditures or expenses, and the reimbursed fund (Fund B) would reduce its expenditures or expenses. This prevents the double reporting of expenditures or expenses and ensures that these items are reported in the correct fund.

Transfers. All interfund transactions that do not fit into one of the other three categories are called **transfers.** Transfers fit into the following two categories:

1. **Residual equity transfers.** Residual equity transfers are **nonrecurring** or **nonroutine** transfers of equity between funds made in connection

[25]GASB Cod. sec. 1800.

with the formation, expansion, contraction, or discontinuance of a fund (usually involving the General Fund and one of the Proprietary Funds). Because such transfers are of a nonoperating nature, they are reported **outside the operating statements** as direct additions to or subtractions from the fund equity accounts (Fund Balance, Contributed Capital, or Retained Earnings, as appropriate).

2. **Operating transfers.** Operating transfers are made in connection with the **normal operation** of the recipient fund. Accordingly, they are reported **within the operating statements** of the affected funds but under a separate category called Other Financing Sources (Uses).[26]

Illustration 20-3 presents how interfund transfers are presented in the operating statement of the four governmental funds. Examples of the various types of interfund transactions are given later in the chapter and in Chapter 21, where we present a detailed discussion of the individual funds and the related operating statements.

THE GENERAL FUND

Nature and Scope of Activities

The **General Fund** accounts for all revenues and expenditures of a governmental unit that are not accounted for in one of the special purpose funds. Because all other funds are special purpose funds, most activities and current operations of governmental units are financed from the General Fund. For instance, general government administration, public safety, judicial system, health, sanitation, welfare, and culture-recreation are usually accounted for in this fund.

Normally, more types of revenues flow into this fund than any other fund. For example, property taxes, sales taxes, income taxes, transfer taxes, licenses, permits, fines, penalties, and interest on delinquent taxes commonly flow into the General Fund. In addition, the General Fund may receive monies from other governmental units; such receipts are classified by the GASB Codification as follows:

> **Grant.** A contribution or gift of cash or other assets from another government to be used or expended for a specified purpose, activity, or facility.

Illustration 20-3
Summary of How Interfund Transfers Are Presented in the Operating Statement (of the Four Governmental Funds)

Type of Interfund Transaction	Section of the Operating Statement
Quasi-external transactions and reimbursements	Revenues or Expenditures
Operating transfers	Other Financing Sources and Uses
Residual equity transfers	Fund Balance

[26]GASB Cod. sec. 1800.107.

Capital grant. A contribution or gift of cash or other assets restricted by the grantor for the acquisition and/or construction of fixed (capital) assets [which would be accounted for in a Capital Projects Fund].

Operating grant. Grants that are intended to finance operations or that may be used for either operations or capital outlays at the discretion of the grantee.

Entitlement. The amount of payment to which a state or local government is entitled as determined by the federal government (e.g., the Director of the Office of Revenue Sharing) pursuant to an allocation formula contained in applicable statutes.

Shared revenue. A revenue levied by one government but shared on a predetermined basis, often in proportion to the amount collected at the local level, with another government or class of government.[27]

The General Fund often engages in a variety of transactions with other funds, as described on pages 810–811.

Comprehensive Illustration

JOURNAL ENTRIES AND FINANCIAL STATEMENTS

The June 30, 19X1, balance sheet for Funn City's General Fund is shown in Illustration 20-4.

Before proceeding with assumed transactions for the subsequent fiscal year, the following points should be understood with regard to Illustration 20-4:

Illustration 20-4

FUNN CITY
Balance Sheet — General Fund
June 30, 19X1

Assets	
Cash	$57,000
Property taxes receivable—delinquent	32,000
Less: Allowance for estimated uncollectible taxes–delinquent	(9,000)
Total Assets	$80,000
Liabilities and Fund Equity	
Vouchers payable	$26,000
Fund balance:	
Reserved for encumbrances	$20,000
Unreserved	34,000
Total Fund Balance	$54,000
Total Liabilities and Fund Equity	$80,000

[27]GASB Cod. sec. G60.501–505.

1. **Omission of prepayments and supplies inventory.** Because we assume that these items are insignificant at June 30, 19X1, they are excluded from the balance sheet.
2. **Fund Balance — Reserved for encumbrances:** The Fund Balance — Reserved for Encumbrances account signifies that a portion of the fund's assets has been earmarked for liquidation of outstanding purchase orders.
3. **Fund balance — Unreserved.** The $34,000 Unreserved Fund Balance account signifies that the fund has $34,000 of uncommitted assets available for spending purposes in the following fiscal year.

Assumed transactions and related journal entries for the fiscal year July 1, 19X1 through June 30, 19X2 are discussed in the following paragraphs.

1. Adoption of the Budget. The city council approved and adopted the budget for the year. The budget contained the following amounts:

Estimated revenues	$700,000
Authorized expenditures (including $20,000 pertaining to encumbrances existing at June 30, 19X1, which has been "reappropriated")	670,000
Estimated operating transfer in from the city-owned electric utility, which is accounted for in an Enterprise Fund	55,000
Authorized operating transfer out to the Library Debt Service Fund	75,000

As explained earlier, the adoption of the budget for the General Fund involves the use of budgetary accounts, as follows:

ESTIMATED REVENUES CONTROL	700,000	
ESTIMATED OTHER FINANCING SOURCES CONTROL	55,000	
APPROPRIATIONS CONTROL		670,000
ESTIMATED OTHER FINANCING USES CONTROL		75,000
BUDGETARY FUND BALANCE		10,000
To record the legally adopted annual operating budget.		

2. Property Taxes. Property taxes for the period July 1, 19X1 through June 30, 19X2, were levied in the amount of $500,000. Emerson estimated that $12,000 of this amount would be uncollectible. During the year, $484,000 was collected ($21,000 of which pertained to delinquent taxes of the prior fiscal year), and $8,000 of prior-year delinquent balances was written off as uncollectible. A $16,000 allowance for uncollectibles was considered necessary as of June 30, 19X2. Property taxes unpaid at the end of the fiscal year become delinquent.

As explained earlier, the accrual basis of accounting is usually appropriate for property taxes. In this case, the city's fiscal year coincides with the period to which the property taxes relate; accordingly, the property tax levy is appropriately recorded on the first day of the new fiscal year. In recording the property taxes, the estimated uncollectible amount is netted against the revenues, and the use of a Bad Debts Expense account is avoided. A Bad Debts Expense account would be inappropriate, because the General Fund has expenditures, not expenses. At the end of the fiscal year, remaining property tax receivables and the related allowance for uncollectible accounts are transferred to accounts that designate these items as relating to delinquent taxes. Thus, tax levies of the following fiscal year may be separated from the delinquent taxes.

Property Taxes Receivable—Current	**500,000**	
Allowance for Uncollectibles—Current		**12,000**
Revenues		**488,000**
To record the property tax levy.		
Cash	**484,000**	
Property Taxes Receivable—Current		**463,000**
Property Taxes Receivable—Delinquent		**21,000**
To record the collection of property taxes.		
Allowance for Uncollectibles—Delinquent	**8,000**	
Property Taxes Receivable—Delinquent		**8,000**
To write off accounts determined to be uncollectible.[a]		
Revenues	**3,000**	
Allowance for Uncollectibles—Current		**3,000**
To increase the allowance for uncollectibles—current from $12,000 to $15,000.[b]		
Property Taxes Receivable—Delinquent	**37,000**	
Allowance for Uncollectibles—Current	**15,000**	
Property Taxes Receivable—Current		**37,000**
Allowance for Uncollectibles—Delinquent		**15,000**
To transfer the fiscal year-end balances to the delinquent accounts.		

[a]The beginning of year balance in the Allowance for Uncollectibles—Delinquent account was $9,000.

[b]The Allowance accounts now total $16,000 ($1,000 remains from the beginning of the year balance.)

3. Revenues Other Than Property Taxes. The total estimated revenues for the year include an estimated **entitlement** from the federal government of $22,000. We assume these funds are used for purposes normally financed through the General Fund. The amount is assumed to be susceptible to accrual; the actual amount received midway through the year is $23,000. Revenues of $181,000 are collected from sales taxes, business licenses, permits, and miscellaneous sources. Because these revenues are not susceptible to accrual, they are accounted for on the cash basis.

Entitlement Receivable	**22,000**	
Revenues		**22,000**
To record entitlement from the federal government.		
Cash	**23,000**	
Entitlement Receivable		**22,000**
Revenues		**1,000**
To record collection of entitlement.		
Cash	**181,000**	
Revenues		**181,000**
To record revenues accounted for on the cash basis.		

4. Encumbrances Relating to the Prior Year. The goods and services relating to the purchase orders outstanding at June 30, 19X1 were received. The invoices totaled $19,000. Recall that budgetary control must be reestablished over encumbrances existing at the end of the prior fiscal year. Accordingly, the following entries are made on the first day of the new fiscal year:

Fund Balance Reserved for Encumbrances	**20,000**	
Unreserved Fund Balance		**20,000**
To reverse appropriation of fund balance made at June 30, 19X1 relating to encumbrances outstanding at June 30, 19X1, that will be honored during the current year.		
ENCUMBRANCES CONTROL	**20,000**	
FUND BALANCE RESERVED FOR ENCUMBRANCES		**20,000**
To reestablish budgetary control over encumbrances outstanding at June 30, 19X1.		

Recall that the encumbrances budgetary accounts are closed out at year-end. Thus, the preceding entry is also merely a reversing entry. The entries pertaining to the receipt of the goods or services ordered are then recorded in the normal manner, as follows:

FUND BALANCE RESERVED FOR ENCUMBRANCES	20,000	
ENCUMBRANCES CONTROL		20,000
To cancel encumbrances of $20,000 upon receipt of goods and services totaling $19,000.		
Expenditures..	19,000	
Vouchers Payable		19,000
To record expenditures of $19,000 for goods and services which were previously encumbered for $20,000		

5. Expenditures and Encumbrances Initiated During the Current Year. Purchase orders totaling $115,000 were issued during the current year. Goods and services relating to $103,000 of these purchase orders were received; invoices totaling $102,000 were received and approved. Additional expenditures of $526,000 (which did not involve the use of purchase orders) were incurred. Of the total expenditures for the year, $36,000 pertained to the purchase of supplies inventories. The city uses the "purchases" method of accounting for supplies purchases whereby expenditures are charged on acquisition.[28]

ENCUMBRANCES CONTROL	115,000	
FUND BALANCE RESERVED FOR ENCUMBRANCES		115,000
To record encumbrances on purchase orders issued.		
FUND BALANCE RESERVED FOR ENCUMBRANCES	103,000	
ENCUMBRANCES CONTROL......................		103,000
To cancel encumbrances of $103,000 upon receipt of goods and services totaling $102,000.		
Expenditures..	102,000	
Vouchers Payable......................................		102,000
To record expenditures of $102,000 for goods and services which were previously encumbered for $103,000.		
Expenditures..	526,000	
Vouchers Payable		526,000
To record expenditures for items not previously encumbered.		

[28]The GASB Codification also sanctions the use of the "consumption" method of accounting for inventories, whereby expenditures for the year are based on actual usage. Under this method, inventories on hand at year-end are reported in the balance sheet (GASB Cod. sec. 1600.122). The manner of reporting significant amounts of inventory in the balance sheet is discussed later in the chapter.

6. Disbursements (Other Than Interfund). Cash disbursements totaled $631,000.

Vouchers Payable	**631,000**	
Cash		**631,000**
To record cash disbursements other than interfund disbursements.		

7. Interfund Transactions. Each type of interfund transaction is illustrated below.

A. Quasi-External Transactions

During the year, the city's central printing department, which is operated as an Internal Service Fund, rendered billings for services to the General Fund in the amount of $11,000. Of this amount, $9,000 was paid during the fiscal year. These billings qualify for treatment as **quasi-external transactions.** Accordingly, they are treated as expenditures in the General Fund (and as revenues in the Internal Services Fund).

Expenditures	**11,000**	
Due to Central Printing Internal Service Fund		**11,000**
To record as expenditures services acquired from the Central Printing Internal Service Fund.		
Due to Central Printing Internal Service Fund	**9,000**	
Cash		**9,000**
To record payment made to Central Printing Internal Service Fund.		

B. Reimbursements

In April 19X2, the city, in anticipation of the approval of a capital project and the related sale of bonds, disbursed $7,000 to an architectural firm for preliminary work in designing a convention center. The city made the following entry in its General Fund:

Expenditures	**7,000**	
Cash		**7,000**

In June 19X2, the Convention Center Capital Projects Fund reimbursed the General Fund. The General Fund made the following entry for this **reimbursement:**

Cash	**7,000**	
Expenditures		**7,000**

C. Residual Equity Transfer

The Central Printing Internal Service Fund was terminated in May 19X2. A residual equity balance of $2,500 was transferred to the General Fund. This nonrecurring transfer may not be reflected in the operating statement of the General Fund, because it is not an operating transfer but a **residual equity transfer.** Residual equity transfers are recorded as adjustments directly to the Fund Balance account.

Cash	2,500	
Unreserved Fund Balance		2,500
To record residual equity transfer from the discontinued Central Printing Fund.		

D. Operating Transfers

The operating transfer of $55,000 to be received from the Electric Utility Enterprise Fund and the operating transfer of $75,000 to be made to the Library Debt Service Fund may be recorded on the first day of the fiscal year, because the amounts are susceptible to being accrued.

Due from Electric Utility Enterprise Fund	55,000	
Other Financing Sources		55,000
To record operating transfer to be received from the Electric Utility Enterprise Fund.		
Other Financing Uses	75,000	
Due to Library Debt Service Fund		75,000
To record operating transfer to be made to the Library Debt Service Fund.		

The following entries assume the payments were made in accordance with the authorized amounts.

Cash	55,000	
Due from Electric Utility Enterprise Fund		55,000
To record receipt of operating transfer from the Electric Utility Enterprise Fund.		
Due to Library Debt Service Fund	75,000	
Cash		75,000
To record payment of operating transfer to the Library Debt Service Fund.		

The General Fund preclosing trial balances after recording the preceding items are shown in Illustration 20-5.

Illustration 20-5

FUNN CITY
Preclosing Trial Balances—General Fund
June 30, 19X2

	Debit	Credit
Actual (nonbudgetary) accounts:		
Cash	87,500	
Property taxes receivable—delinquent	40,000	
Allowance for estimated uncollectibles—delinquent		16,000
Vouchers payable		42,000
Due to Internal Service Fund		2,000
Unreserved fund balance		56,500
Revenues		689,000
Expenditures	658,000	
Other financing sources		55,000
Other financing uses	75,000	
Totals	860,500	860,500
Budgetary accounts:		
ESTIMATED REVENUES CONTROL	700,000	
ESTIMATED OTHER FINANCING SOURCES CONTROL	55,000	
APPROPRIATIONS CONTROL		670,000
ESTIMATED OTHER FINANCING USES CONTROL		75,000
BUDGETARY FUND BALANCE		10,000
ENCUMBRANCES CONTROL	12,000	
FUND BALANCE RESERVED FOR ENCUMBRANCES		12,000
Totals	767,000	767,000

8. Closing Entries. The closing entries at June 30, 19X2 are as follows:

APPROPRIATIONS CONTROL	**670,000**	
ESTIMATED OTHER FINANCING USES CONTROL	**75,000**	
BUDGETARY FUND BALANCE	**10,000**	
ESTIMATED REVENUES CONTROL		**700,000**
ESTIMATED OTHER FINANCING SOURCES CONTROL		**55,000**
To reverse the entry previously made to record the legally adopted annual operating budget.		
Revenues	**689,000**	
Other Financing Sources	**55,000**	
Expenditures		**658,000**
Other Financing Uses		**75,000**
Unreserved Fund Balance		**11,000**
To close *actual* revenues, expenditures, and other financing sources and uses accounts into Unreserved Fund Balance.		

FUND BALANCE RESERVED FOR ENCUMBRANCES	**12,000**	
ENCUMBRANCES CONTROL		**12,000**
To close encumbrances outstanding at year-end by reversing the entry that previously recorded them.		
Unreserved Fund Balance	**12,000**	
Fund Balance Reserved for Encumbrances		**12,000**
To record *actual* fund balance reserve account to indicate the portion of the year-end fund balance segregated for expenditure upon vendor performance.		

The financial statements for the fiscal year ended June 30, 19X2, are shown in Illustrations 20-6 and 20-7.

Manner of Classifying Expenditures

The operating statement for Funn City classifies expenditures by **character** and **function.** Character refers to the fiscal period that the expenditures are presumed to benefit. Virtually all of Funn City's expenditures

Illustration 20-6

FUNN CITY
Balance Sheet—General Fund
June 30, 19X2

Assets	
Cash	$ 87,500
Property taxes receivable—delinquent	40,000[a]
Less: Allowance for estimated uncollectible taxes—delinquent	(16,000)
Total Assets	$111,500
Liabilities and Fund Equity	
Vouchers payable	$ 42,000
Due to Internal Service Fund	2,000
Total Liabilities	$ 44,000
Fund balance:	
Reserved for encumbrances	$ 12,000
Unreserved	55,500
Total Fund Balance	$ 67,500
Total Liabilities and Fund Equity	$111,500

[a]No Deferred Revenues are shown in the balance sheet. Thus, it is assumed that the $24,000 net realizable amount of the property tax receivables ($40,000 − $16,000) is expected to be collected within a relatively short time (60 days is commonly used) enabling such receipts to be "available to pay existing liabilities." If only $20,000 were expected to be collected shortly, then $4,000 of Deferred Revenues would have to be reflected.

Illustration 20-7

FUNN CITY
Statement of Revenues, Expenditures, and Changes in Fund Balance—Budget and Actual—General Fund
For the Fiscal Year Ended June 30, 19X2

	Budget[b]	Actual	Variance Favorable (Unfavorable)
Revenues:			
Property taxes	$488,000	$485,000	$ (3,000)
Intergovernmental grant	22,000	23,000	1,000
Sales taxes[a]	130,000	124,000	(6,000)
Licenses and permits[a]	45,000	38,000	(7,000)
Miscellaneous[a]	15,000	19,000	4,000
Total Revenues	$700,000	$689,000	$(11,000)
Expenditures:			
Current:			
General government[a]	$103,000	$101,000	$ 2,000
Public safety[a]	215,000	220,000	(5,000)
Sanitation[a]	50,000	49,500	500
Health[a]	40,000	41,500	(1,500)
Welfare[a]	70,000	62,700	7,300
Education[a]	185,000	176,300	8,700
Subtotal	$663,000	$651,000	$ 12,000
Capital outlay	7,000	7,000	—
Total Expenditures	$670,000	$658,000	$ 12,000
Excess of Revenues over Expenditures	$ 30,000	$ 31,000	$ 1,000
Other Financing Sources (Uses):			
Operating transfers in	$ 55,000	$ 55,000	—
Operating transfers out	(75,000)	(75,000)	—
Total Other Financing Sources (Uses)	$ (20,000)	$ (20,000)	—
Excess of Revenues and Other Sources over Expenditures and Other Uses	$ 10,000	$ 11,000	$ 1,000
Fund Balance—July 1, 19X1	54,000	54,000[c]	—
Residual equity transfer from discontinued Internal Service Fund	—	2,500	2,500
Fund Balance—June 30, 19X2	$ 64,000	$ 67,500[c]	$ 3,500

Note: Because it has been prepared in accordance with generally accepted accounting principles, the budget is presented in this statement for budgetary comparison purposes, as required under GASB Codification.

[a]These assumed amounts were not given in the transactions and journal entries.
[b]The budget includes $20,000 relating to encumbrances existing at June 30, 19X1, which amount has been "rebudgeted" during the current year. As a result, actual expenditures (including amounts relating to encumbrances existing at June 30, 19X1) may be meaningfully compared with the budget column.
[c]This is the total fund balance (reserved and unreserved portions).

were presumed to benefit the current fiscal year. Note that even the expenditures relating to encumbrances existing at June 30, 19X1 (although initially appropriated and ordered during the preceding fiscal year), benefit the year in which the goods and services are incurred. Thus, no separate categorization of these expenditures is needed. Other major categories of character classification are *Capital Outlay* (which benefits primarily future periods) and *Debt Service* (which benefits the period encompassing the useful life of the related fixed assets acquired or constructed with the proceeds of the borrowing).

Note that the operating statement shows a minor amount for the Capital Outlay category and no Debt Service category. In Chapter 21, which covers the other types of funds, the capital outlay category is also encountered in Capital Projects Funds (in which the amounts are usually not minor); the debt service category is encountered in Debt Service Funds.

When desirable, the major functions may be subdivided into **activities** and **objects.** For example, the sanitation function could be subdivided into sewage treatment and disposal, garbage collection, garbage disposal, and street cleaning. Alternatively, the sanitation function could be subdivided into employee salaries, contracted services, materials, and supplies. These other ways of classifying expenditures may be presented in the financial statements, in supporting schedules to the financial statements, or in notes to the financial statements.

Manner of Reporting Inventory

We assumed in Funn City's financial statements that the supplies inventories were insignificant at each balance sheet date. Accordingly, they were not reported in the balance sheets. When supplies inventories are significant, the GASB Codification calls for such inventory to be reported in the balance sheet. Because **supplies inventory is not an asset that is available for spending in the succeeding fiscal year,** the entry reflecting the supplies inventory must indicate clearly that the portion of the fund balance designated unreserved is not affected and is therefore available for spending in the succeeding fiscal year. The journal entries to reflect significant amounts of supplies inventories are different under the "purchases" method and the "consumption" method.

The Purchases Method. Recall that under the purchases method, all supplies acquired are immediately charged to Expenditures when received—a periodic or perpetual inventory system does not exist under the purchases method. Accordingly, the Expenditures account may not be adjusted in reporting significant amounts of supplies inventory in the balance sheet. The entry, which takes place entirely in balance sheet accounts, is as follows:

Inventory of Supplies...	**xxx**	
Fund Balance Reserved for Inventory of Supplies ..		**xxx**
To report supplies inventory in the balance sheet.		

Note that the portion of the fund balance that is designated unreserved is not affected. If the amount of supplies inventory changes from one balance sheet date to the next, the above two accounts are adjusted accordingly.

The Consumption Method. Under the consumption method, expenditures are charged based on **usage,** whether a perpetual or a periodic inventory system is used. Under a **perpetual** system, supplies inventories are automatically reported in the balance sheet because supplies are charged to an Inventory of Supplies account when acquired and then transferred to the Expenditures account as used. Under a **periodic** system, inventories are charged to the Expenditures account as they are acquired, but an entry is made at year-end to adjust the Inventory of Supplies account and the Expenditures account, so that the Expenditures account reflects usage instead of purchases. For example, assume that under a periodic system, $50,000 of supplies were acquired during the year but only $40,000 of supplies were used. The entry to adjust the Inventory of Supplies account and the Expenditures account at year-end would be as follows:

Inventory of Supplies..	**10,000**	
Expenditures..		**10,000**
To adjust the Expenditures account to reflect actual usage for the year.		

If the amount of supplies inventory changes from one balance sheet date to the next, the Unreserved Fund Balance account and the Fund Balance Reserved for Inventory of Supplies account are adjusted accordingly.[29]

SUMMARY

Accounting for state and local governmental units requires a familiarity with the pronouncements of the National Council on Governmental Accounting and the Governmental Accounting Standards Board. Because of the diverse nature of governmental operations and the extensive legal provisions of a financial nature, operations are accounted for in separate

[29]The GASB Codification sanctions an alternative practice under the consumption method, which is to establish a reserve for inventory only if "minimum amounts of inventory must be maintained and thus are not available for use (expenditure)" (GASB Cod. sec. 2200.603).

funds and account groups as opposed to a single set of books. Because of the absence of a profit motive in most governmental operations, the use of an income statement is inappropriate; accordingly, most governmental operations are presented in a statement of revenues, expenditures, and changes in fund balance, which shows in detail the sources and uses of fund resources. A modified accrual basis of accounting is used when the accrual basis is not practical. Budgetary accounts assist in controlling and monitoring spending on an interim basis.

Glossary of New Terms

Appropriation "A legal authorization granted by a legislative body to make expenditures and to incur obligations for specific purposes. An appropriation is usually limited in amount and as to the time when it may be expended."*

Budgetary Accounts "Accounts used to enter the formally adopted annual operating budget into the general ledger as part of the management control technique of formal budgetary integration."*

Encumbrances "Commitments related to unperformed (executory) contracts for goods or services."*

Expenditures "Decreases in net financial resources."*

Fund "A fiscal and accounting entity with a self-balancing set of accounts recording cash and other financial resources, together with all related liabilities and residual equities or balances, and changes therein, which are segregated for the purpose of carrying on specific activities or attaining certain objectives in accordance with special regulations, restrictions, or limitations."*

Fund Balance "The fund equity of governmental funds and Trust Funds."*

General Fixed Assets "Fixed assets used in operations accounted for in governmental funds. General fixed assets include all fixed assets not accounted for in proprietary funds or in Trust and Agency Funds."*

General Fixed Asset Account Group "A self-balancing group of accounts set up to account for the general fixed assets of a government."*

General Long-Term Debt "Long-term debt [including special assessment debt for which the governmental unit is obligated] expected to be repaid from governmental funds."*

General Long-Term Debt Account Group "A self-balancing group of accounts set up to account for the unmatured general long-term debt of a government."*

Operating Transfers "All interfund transfers other than residual equity transfers . . ."*

Quasi-External Transactions "Interfund transactions that would be treated as revenues, expenditures, or expenses if they involved organizations *external* to the governmental unit."*

Residual Equity Transfers "Nonrecurring or nonroutine transfers of equity between funds."*

**GAAFR*, 1980 edition, Appendix B.

Appendix
ILLUSTRATIONS OF SELECTED GENERAL PURPOSE FINANCIAL STATEMENTS

Illustration 20-8

NAME OF GOVERNMENT
COMBINED BALANCE SHEET—ALL FUND TYPES AND ACCOUNT GROUPS
December 31, 19X2

	Governmental Fund Types				Proprietary Fund Types		Fiduciary Fund Type	Account Groups		Totals (Memorandum Only)	
	General	Special Revenue	Debt Service	Capital Projects	Enterprise	Internal Service	Trust and Agency	General Fixed Assets	General Long-term Debt	19X2	19X1
Assets											
Cash	$255,029	$101,385	$ 31,553	$ 645,621	$ 279,296	$ 29,700	$ 216,701	$ —	$ —	$ 1,559,285	$ 1,232,930
Investments, at cost or amortized cost	65,000	37,200	—	—	—	—	$1,239,260	—	—	1,341,460	1,116,524
Receivables (net, of allowances for uncollectibles):											
Taxes, including interest, penalties, and liens	61,771	2,500	3,528	—	—	—	580,000	—	—	647,799	230,435
Accounts	8,300	3,300	—	100	24,130	—	—	—	—	35,830	43,850
Special assessments	—	—	646,035	—	—	—	—	—	—	646,035	462,035
Notes	—	—	—	—	2,350	—	—	—	—	2,350	1,250
Loans	—	—	—	—	—	—	35,000	—	—	35,000	35,000
Accrued interest	50	25	350	—	—	—	2,666	—	—	3,091	4,280
Due from other funds	12,000	—	—	—	2,000	12,000	11,189	—	—	37,189	51,220
Due from other governments	30,000	75,260	—	640,000	—	—	—	—	—	745,260	116,800
Advance to internal service fund	55,000	—	—	—	—	—	—	—	—	55,000	65,000
Inventory, at cost	7,200	5,190	—	—	23,030	40,000	—	—	—	75,420	48,670
Prepaid expenses	—	—	—	—	1,200	—	—	—	—	1,200	740
Restricted assets:											
Cash and investments, at cost or amortized cost	—	—	—	—	306,753	—	—	—	—	306,753	417,268
Fixed assets (net)	—	—	—	—	5,769,759	103,100	—	6,913,250	—	12,786,109	10,864,206
Amount available in debt service funds	—	—	—	—	—	—	—	—	12,572	12,572	5,010
Amount to be provided for retirement of:											
General long-term debt	—	—	—	—	—	—	—	—	1,687,428	1,687,428	854,990
Special assessment debt	—	—	—	—	—	—	—	—	555,000	555,000	
Total Assets	$494,350	$224,860	$681,466	$1,285,721	$6,408,518	$184,800	$2,084,816	$6,913,250	$2,255,000	$20,532,781	$15,550,208

Liabilities											
Vouchers and accounts payable	$118,261	$ 32,454	$ —	$ 49,600	$ 116,471	$ 15,000	$ 5,200	$ —	$ —	$ 336,986	$ 179,973
Contracts payable	57,600	18,300	—	119,000	26,107	—	—	—	—	221,007	503,724
Judgments payable	—	2,000	—	33,800	—	—	—	—	—	35,800	15,500
Accrued general obligation interest	—	—	—	—	14,000	—	—	—	—	14,000	14,100
Other accrued expenses	—	—	—	10,700	3,009	—	4,700	—	—	18,409	18,713
Payable from restricted assets:											
Construction contracts	—	—	—	—	—	—	—	—	—	—	145,643
Accrued interest	—	—	—	—	64,749	—	—	—	—	64,749	75,150
Revenue bonds	—	—	—	—	48,000	—	—	—	—	48,000	44,000
Deposits	—	—	—	—	64,060	—	—	—	—	64,060	55,500
Due to other taxing units	—	—	—	—	—	—	680,800	—	—	680,800	200,000
Due to other funds	24,189	2,000	—	1,000	—	10,000	—	—	—	37,189	51,220
Deferred revenues	49,500	1,396	558,045	—	—	—	—	—	—	608,941	412,951
Advance from general fund	—	—	—	—	—	55,000	—	—	—	55,000	65,000
General obligation bonds payable	—	—	—	—	700,000	—	—	—	1,700,000	2,400,000	1,610,000
Revenue bonds payable	—	—	—	—	1,798,000	—	—	—	—	1,798,000	1,846,000
Special assessment bonds payable with governmental commitment	—	—	—	—	—	—	—	—	555,000	555,000	420,000
Total Liabilities	$249,550	$ 56,150	$558,045	$ 214,100	$2,834,396	$ 80,000	$ 690,700	$ —	$2,255,000	$ 6,937,941	$ 5,657,474
Fund Equity											
Contributed capital	$ —	$ —	$ —	$ —	$1,370,666	$ 95,000	$ —	$ —	$ —	$ 1,465,666	$ 815,000
Investment in general fixed assets	—	—	—	—	—	—	—	6,913,250	—	6,913,250	5,174,250
Retained earnings:											
Reserved for revenue bond retirement	—	—	—	—	129,155	—	—	—	—	129,155	96,975
Unreserved	—	—	—	—	2,074,301	9,800	—	—	—	2,084,101	1,998,119
Fund balance:											
Reserved for encumbrances	38,000	46,500	—	1,060,521	—	—	—	—	—	1,145,021	410,050
Reserved for inventory	7,200	5,190	—	—	—	—	—	—	—	12,390	10,890
Reserved for advance to internal service fund	55,000	—	—	—	—	—	—	—	—	55,000	65,000
Reserved for loans	—	—	—	—	—	—	50,050	—	—	50,050	45,100
Reserved for endowments	—	—	—	—	—	—	160,865	—	—	160,865	119,035
Reserved for employees' retirement system	—	—	—	—	—	—	1,426,201	—	—	1,426,201	1,276,150
Reserved for debt service	—	—	123,421	—	—	—	—	—	—	12,572	(258,950)
Unreserved:											
Designated for subsequent years' expenditures	50,000	—	—	—	—	—	—	—	—	50,000	50,000
Undesignated	94,600	117,020	—	11,100	—	—	(243,000)	—	—	90,569	91,115
Total retained earnings fund balance	$244,800	$168,710	$123,421	$1,071,621	$2,203,456	$ 9,800	$1,394,116	$ —	$ —	$ 5,215,924	$ 3,903,484
Total Fund Equity	$244,800	$168,710	$123,421	$1,071,621	$3,574,122	$104,800	$1,394,116	$6,913,250	$ —	$13,594,840	$ 9,892,734
Total Liabilities and Fund Equity	$494,350	$224,860	$681,466	$1,285,721	$6,408,518	$184,800	$2,084,816	$6,913,250	$2,255,000	$20,532,781	$15,550,208

Source: Adapted from *Governmental Accounting, Auditing, and Financial Reporting* (Chicago: Municipal Finance Officers Association of the United States and Canada, 1980), pp. 126–27.

Illustration 20-9

NAME OF GOVERNMENT
COMBINED STATEMENT OF REVENUES, EXPENDITURES, AND CHANGES IN FUND BALANCES—ALL GOVERNMENTAL FUND TYPES AND EXPENDABLE TRUST FUNDS
For the Year Ended December 31, 19X2

	Governmental Fund Types				Fiduciary Fund Type	Totals (Memorandum Only)	
	General	Special Revenue	Debt Service	Capital Projects	Expendable Trust	19X2	19X1
Revenue:							
Taxes and special assessments	$ 846,800	$ 189,300	$135,362	$ —	$ —	$1,171,462	$1,117,694
Licenses and permits	103,000	—	—	—	—	103,000	96,500
Intergovernmental	186,500	831,366	41,500	1,250,000	—	2,309,366	1,256,000
Charges for services	91,000	79,100	—	—	—	170,100	160,400
Fines and forfeits	33,200	—	—	—	—	33,200	26,300
Miscellaneous	18,000	71,359	23,164	3,750	150	116,423	106,750
Total Revenues	$1,278,500	$1,171,125	$200,026	$1,253,750	$ 150	$3,903,551	$2,763,644
Expenditures:							
General government	$ 121,805	$ —	$ —	$ —	$ —	$ 121,805	$ 134,200
Public safety	258,395	480,000	—	—	—	738,395	671,300
Highways and streets	85,400	417,000	—	—	—	502,400	408,700
Sanitation	56,250	—	—	—	—	56,250	44,100
Health	44,500	—	—	—	—	44,500	36,600
Welfare	46,800	—	—	—	—	46,800	41,400
Culture and recreation	40,900	256,450	—	—	—	297,350	286,400
Education	509,150	—	—	—	2,370	511,520	512,000
Capital projects	—	—	—	1,933,765	—	1,933,765	1,075,035
Debt service:							
Principal retirement	—	—	146,000	—	—	146,000	60,000
Interest and fiscal charges	—	—	45,369	—	—	45,369	35,533
Total Expenditures	$1,163,200	$1,153,450	$191,369	$1,933,765	$ 2,370	$4,444,154	$3,305,268
Excess (Deficiency) of Revenues over Expenditures	$ 115,300	$ 17,675	$ 8,657	$ (680,015)	$ (2,220)	$ (540,603)	$ (541,624)
Other financing sources (uses):							
Proceeds of general obligation bonds	$ —	$ —	$ —	$ 902,500	$ —	$ 902,500	$ 105,000
Operating transfers in	—	—	—	74,500	2,530	77,030	89,120
Operating transfers out	(74,500)	—	—	—	—	(74,500)	(87,000)
Total Other Financing Sources (Uses)	$ (74,500)	$ —	$ —	$ 977,000	$ 2,530	$ 905,030	$ 107,120
Excess (Deficiency) of Revenues and Other Financing Sources over Expenditures and Other Uses	$ 40,800	$ 17,675	$ 8,657	$ 296,985	$ 310	$ 364,427	$ (434,504)
Fund Balance at Beginning of Year	202,500	151,035	114,764	774,636	26,555	1,269,490	1,062,994
Increase in Reserve for Inventory	1,500	—	—	—	—	1,500	—
Fund Balance at End of Year	$ 244,800	$ 168,710	$123,421	$1,071,621	$26,865	$1,635,417	$ 628,490

Source: Adapted from *Governmental Accounting, Auditing, and Financial Reporting* (Chicago: Municipal Finance Officers Association of the United States and Canada, 1980), p. 128.

Illustration 20-10

NAME OF GOVERNMENT COMBINED STATEMENT OF REVENUES, EXPENSES AND CHANGES IN RETAINED EARNINGS/FUND BALANCES—ALL PROPRIETARY FUND TYPES AND SIMILAR TRUST FUNDS
For the Year Ended December 31, 19X2

	Proprietary Fund Types		Fiduciary Fund Types		Totals (Memorandum Only)	
	Enterprise	Internal Service	Pension Trust	Nonex-pendable Trust	19X2	19X1
Operating revenues:						
Charges for services	$ 672,150	$88,000	$ —	$ —	$ 760,150	$ 686,563
Interest	—	—	28,460	2,480	30,940	26,118
Contributions	—	—	160,686	—	160,686	144,670
Gifts	—	—	—	45,000	45,000	—
Total Operating Revenues	$ 672,150	$88,000	$ 189,146	$ 47,480	$ 996,776	857,351
Operating expenses:						
Personal services	$ 247,450	$32,500	$ —	$ —	$ 279,950	$ 250,418
Contractual services	75,330	400	—	—	75,730	68,214
Supplies	20,310	1,900	—	—	22,210	17,329
Materials	50,940	44,000	—	—	94,940	87,644
Heat, light, and power	26,050	1,500	—	—	27,550	22,975
Depreciation	144,100	4,450	—	—	148,550	133,210
Benefit payments	—	—	21,000	—	21,000	12,000
Refunds	—	—	25,745	—	25,745	13,243
Total Operating Expenses	$ 564,180	$84,750	$ 46,745	$ —	$ 695,675	$ 605,033
Operating Income	$ 107,970	$ 3,250	$ 142,401	$ 47,480	$ 301,101	$ 252,318
Nonoperating revenues (expenses):						
Operating grants	$ 55,000	$ —	$ —	$ —	$ 55,000	$ 50,000
Tap fees	22,000	—	—	—	22,000	20,000
Interest	3,830	—	—	—	3,830	3,200
Rent	5,000	—	—	—	5,000	5,000
Interest and Fiscal Charges	(78,888)	—	—	—	(78,888)	(122,408)
Total Nonoperating Revenues (expenses)	$ 6,942	$ —	$ —	—	$ 6,942	$ (44,208)
Income before Operating Transfers	$ 114,912	$ 3,250	$ 142,401	$ 47,480	$ 308,043	$ 208,110
Operating transfers in (out)	—	—	—	(2,530)	(2,530)	(2,120)
Net Income	$ 114,912	$ 3,250	$ 142,401	$ 44,950	$ 305,513	$ 205,990
Retained Earnings/Fund Balances at Beginning of Year	2,088,544	6,550	1,040,800	139,100	3,274,994	3,069,004
Retained Earnings/Fund Balances at End of Year	$2,203,456	$ 9,800	$1,183,201	$184,050	$3,580,507	$3,274,994

Source: Adapted from *Governmental Accounting, Auditing, and Financial Reporting* (Chicago: Municipal Finance Officers Association of the United States and Canada, 1980), p. 131.

Review Questions

1. Distinguish between the Governmental Finance Officers Association (GFOA), the National Council on Governmental Accounting (NCGA), and the Governmental Accounting Standards Board (GASB).
2. What has been the role of the FASB and its predecessor organizations in the development of generally accepted accounting principles peculiar to state and local govenmental units?
3. For governmental units, explain the relationship between the pronouncements of GASB and FASB.
4. Must all state and local governmental units prepare their financial statements in accordance with GASB pronouncements?
5. What major steps did the NCGA take toward improving governmental financial reporting?
6. What are some unique features of the governmental sector compared with the private sector?
7. Explain the relationship between revenues and expenditures.
8. What is meant by *fund accounting*?
9. Name the seven major types of funds recommended by *NCGA Statement 1*.
10. Are general fixed assets and general long-term debt accounted for in funds? Explain.
11. When is it appropriate to depreciate fixed assets of a governmental unit?
12. Is the modified accrual basis of accounting in accordance with generally accepted accounting principles? Why or why not?
13. What is meant by *budgetary accounting*?
14. What are the two major types of interfund transfers?
15. Explain the difference between an *expenditure* and an *encumbrance*.

Discussion Cases

DC 20-1

Modified Accrual Basis of Accounting

As an accountant for the city of Tulipville, you assist the city manager in answering questions raised at city council meetings. At one meeting, a taxpayer asks why the city (which has a June 30 fiscal year-end) uses the modified accrual basis of accounting for its General Fund rather than the accrual basis, which is required for public corporations in the private sector. Furthermore, the taxpayer would like to know "the magnitude of the misstatement at the end of the recently concluded fiscal year as a result of not using the accrual basis." Assume that the city has an income tax, a sales tax, a property transfer tax, a property tax, and annual business licenses.

Required:
Respond to these questions.

DC 20-2

Comparison with Private Sector

George Jones is executive vice-president of Bottle Industries, Inc., a publicly held industrial corporation. Jones has just been elected to the city council of Old York City. Before assuming office as a member of the city council, he asks you as his CPA to explain the major differences in accounting and financial reporting for a large city compared with a large industrial corporation.

Required:

1. Describe the major differences in the purposes of accounting and financial reporting and in the types of financial reports of a large city and a large industrial corporation.
2. Why are inventories often ignored in accounting for local governmental units? Explain.
3. Under what circumstances should depreciation be recognized in accounting for local governmental units? Explain.

(AICPA adapted)

DC 20-3

Revenue Recognition

The city of Potterville, which has a calendar year-end, was awarded a $300,000 federal job development grant on December 18, 19X1. The grant is expected to be disbursed by the federal government in May 19X2.

Required:
Determine whether the grant should be accrued at December 31, 19X1.

Exercises

E 20-1

Theory and Basic Principles

Indicate whether the following statements are true or false.

1. The measurement base for governmental funds is the flow of resources.
2. For governmental funds, capital maintenance is measured rather than net income.
3. The operating statement for governmental funds is essentially a source and use of funds statement.
4. When legal provisions conflict with generally accepted accounting principles, legal provisions prevail in financial reporting.
5. When legal provisions conflict with generally accepted accounting principles, two sets of books must usually be maintained.
6. "Basis of accounting " refers to what is being measured rather than when items are recognized.

7. In revenue recognition under the modified accrual basis, "available" means collectible within the current period or soon enough thereafter to be used to pay current-period liabilities.
8. Recording depreciation in governmental funds would inappropriately mix expenditures and expenses.
9. The practice of not recording depreciation in the governmental funds is a departure from generally accepted accounting principles.
10. General long-term debt is secured by the general credit and revenue-raising powers of a governmental unit.
11. General long-term debt is a General Fund liability.
12. Operating transfers between funds affect the results of operations in both governmental and proprietary funds.
13. Quasi-external transactions are reported outside the operating statement of the affected funds.
14. Residual equity transfers are capital transfers between funds.
15. The proceeds from the sale of general fixed assets are reported as a source of financial resources.

E 20-2

Revenues

1. For the four governmental funds, revenues are recognized
   a. in the period to which they relate.
   b. when they become susceptible to accrual.
   c. when earned.
   d. when the related expenditures are recognized.
   e. none of the above
2. For the four governmental funds, revenues are
   a. matched against the cost of providing services.
   b. generated by expenditures.
   c. earned.
   d. reported in a quasi-income statement.
   e. none of the above
3. Under the modified accrual method of accounting, which of the following would be a revenue susceptible to accrual?
   a. income taxes
   b. business licenses
   c. sales taxes
   d. property taxes
   e. parking meter receipts
   f. none of the above
4. At the end of the fiscal year, a governmental unit increased its allowance for uncollectible accounts relating to property tax receivables. The entry resulted in a charge to
   a. unreserved fund balance.
   b. ENCUMBRANCES CONTROL.
   c. bad debts expense.
   d. revenues.
   e. ESTIMATED REVENUES CONTROL.
   f. APPROPRIATIONS CONTROL.

5. A city's General Fund budget for the forthcoming fiscal year shows estimated revenues in excess of appropriations. The initial effect of recording the budget results in an increase in
   a. taxes receivable.
   b. unreserved fund balance.
   c. ENCUMBRANCES CONTROL.
   d. retained earnings.
   e. BUDGETARY FUND BALANCE.
   f. none of the above

E 20-3

Expenditures and Encumbrances

1. Under the modified accrual basis, expenditures (other than the exceptions set forth in *NCGA Statement 1*) are recognized
   a. when the liability is incurred.
   b. when paid.
   c. when the related revenues are recognized.
   d. when the goods or services are ordered or contracted for.
   e. none of the above
2. Expenditures are defined as
   a. the cost of providing services.
   b. costs incurred to generate revenues.
   c. an outflow of resources.
   d. amounts arising from encumbrances.
   e. none of the above
3. When a fire truck is received by a governmental unit, it should be recorded in the general fund as a(n)
   a. appropriation.
   b. encumbrance.
   c. expenditure.
   d. expense.
   e. fixed asset.
   f. transfer to the General Fixed Assets Account Group.
4. When supplies are ordered out of the General Fund, they should be recorded as a(n)
   a. appropriation.
   b. encumbrance.
   c. expenditure.
   d. estimated expenditure.
   e. reduction of the fund balance.
5. Which of the following terms refers to an actual cost rather than an estimate in reporting for the five governmental funds?
   a. appropriation
   b. encumbrance
   c. expenditure
   d. expense
   e. none of the above
6. Wages that have been earned by the employees of a governmental unit but not paid should be recorded in the General Fund as an

a. appropriation.
b. encumbrance.
c. expenditure.
d. expense.
e. none of the above

E 20-4

Budgetary Accounting

1. Which of the following is a budgetary account in governmental accounting?
   a. fund balance reserved for encumbrances
   b. unreserved fund balance
   c. APPROPRIATIONS CONTROL
   d. estimated uncollectible property taxes
   e. expenditures
2. Authority granted by a legislative body to make expenditures and to incur obligations during a fiscal year is the definition of an
   a. appropriation.
   b. authorization.
   c. encumbrance.
   d. expenditure.
   e. none of the above
3. The actual general ledger account Fund Balance—Reserved for Encumbrances is a(n)
   a. liability in substance.
   b. budgetary account.
   c. contra account.
   d. appropriation of the fund balance.
   e. none of the above
4. An encumbrance could not be thought of as a(n)
   a. commitment.
   b. contingent liability.
   c. future expenditure.
   d. eventual reduction of the fund balance.
   e. liability of the period in which the encumbrance was created.
5. Which of the following General Fund accounts would be credited when a purchase order is issued?
   a. APPROPRIATIONS CONTROL
   b. ENCUMBRANCES CONTROL
   c. estimated expenditures
   d. vouchers payable
   e. fund balance
   f. none of the above

E 20-5

Terminology

Fill in the blanks in the following statements.

1. Under the modified accrual basis of accounting, revenues are recognized in the accounting period in which they become ____________________ and ____________________.

2. For the five governmental funds, expenditures are recognized in the period in which the fund liability is ____________.
3. Commitments related to unperformed contracts for goods and services are called ____________.
4. The use of financial resources of a fund are broadly referred to as ____________.
5. ____________ ____________ are used to establish accounting control and accountability for a governmental unit's general fixed assets and general long-term debt.
6. Accounts used to control and monitor spending on an interim basis are called ____________ ____________.
7. Items that are not accounted for in any fund are ____________ ____________ ____________ and ____________ ____________ ____________.
8. Reporting encumbrances outstanding at year-end as a reservation (or appropriation) of the fund balance indicates that a portion of the fund balance has been segregated for ____________ upon vendor performance.
9. Encumbered appropriations may or may not ____________ at year-end.
10. To honor in 19X2 encumbrances outstanding at the end of 19X1, the governmental unit may allow encumbrances to ____________, in which case it would be necessary to ____________ for these items in 19X2. Alternatively, the governmental unit could not let the encumbrances ____________, thereby allowing the spending authority to ____________ to 19X2.

E 20-6

Financial Presentation and Reporting

Fill in the blanks in the following statements.

1. The three major categories of funds are ____________, ____________, and ____________.
2. Proprietary fund revenues and expenses are recognized on the ____________ ____________ ____________.
3. For the four governmental funds, the ____________ ____________ basis of accounting is used.
4. The first level of reporting in the financial reporting pyramid presents ____________ ____________ financial statements.
5. In the operating statement, revenues are classified by ____________.
6. In the operating statement, expenditures are classified by ____________ and ____________. In addition, expenditures may be classified further by ____________ and ____________.
7. A type of interfund transfer that is classified within the operating statement is a(n) ____________ ____________.
8. A type of interfund transfer that is classified outside the operating statement (as a direct adjustment to the fund balances) is a(n) ____________ ____________.
9. A transaction in which one fund performs services for another fund and bills that fund is a ____________ ____________.
10. Budgetary comparison statements may be presented on a ____________ basis or on a ____________ basis.

E 20-7

Budgeting Practices and GAAP Reporting

Indicate whether the following statements are true or false.

1. To honor encumbrances outstanding at year-end, a governmental unit must rebudget (or reappropriate) these items in the following year.
2. Expenditures incurred in 19X2 relating to encumbrances outstanding at the end of 19X1 must be reported as expenditures in 19X2 under GAAP reporting regardless of whether the encumbrances outstanding were rebudgeted (or reappropriated) in 19X2.
3. If a governmental unit does not reappropriate or rebudget for encumbrances outstanding at year-end, the budgeting is not done on a basis consistent with GAAP reporting.
4. Encumbrances outstanding at the end of 19X1 that will be honored in 19X2 because the spending authority is carried over to 19X2 (that is, no rebudgeting or reappropriating occurred) cannot be reported as expenditures in 19X2 under GAAP reporting.
5. If encumbrances outstanding at the end of 19X1 lapse and these items are rebudgeted (or reappropriated) in 19X2, the governmental unit must cancel the unfilled purchase orders and reissue them in the following year.
6. Under GAAP reporting, encumbrances are never reported in the statement of revenues, expenditures, and changes in fund balance.
7. The manner of budgeting determines whether the budgetary comparison statement of revenues, expenditures, and changes in fund balance is prepared on a GAAP basis or a non-GAAP "budgetary" basis.
8. *NCGA Statement 1* allows expenditures related to prior-year encumbrances to be reported as adjustments to the fund balance in the manner of a prior-period adjustment.

E 20-8

Budgetary Control

The following balances are included in the subsidiary records of Tylersville's fire department at May 31, 19X2:

Appropriation—supplies	**$33,000**
Expenditures—supplies	**27,000**
Encumbrances—supply orders	**2,000**

Required:
Determine how much the fire department has available for additional purchases of supplies.

E 20-9

Revenue Recognition

Wilbur Whoops mistakenly paid his tax bill for the fiscal year ended June 30, 19X4, twice. He noticed this in June 19X4 and contacted the governmental unit. Rather than requesting a refund, he told the governmental unit to apply the overpayment of $3,000 to his taxes for the fiscal year ended June 30, 19X5. The governmental unit (which had credited Accounts Receivable $6,000) agreed to do this.

Required:
Prepare the entry or entries required by the General Fund, if any, at June 30, 19X4, relating to the overpayment.

E 20-10

Revenue Recognition

The city of Joy has the following tax assessment related accounts at its fiscal year-end, June 30, 19X7:

Property taxes receivable	$470,000
Allowance for uncollectibles	(120,000)

The net amount expected to be collected at year-end is usually collected within 60 days of the fiscal year-end. At June 30, 19X7, however, only about $200,000 is expected to be collected within 60 days, with the remaining $150,000 expected to be collected after that time over many months. The reason for the delay is a severe recession in the city's economy.

Required:
Prepare the entry or entries required for the General Fund at June 30, 19X7, if any.

Problems

P 20-1

Presentation of Financial Statements: Expenditures and Encumbrances

The city of Thrillsville has the following accounts in its preclosing trial balance at June 30, 19X5:

Account	Amount Dr.	Amount Cr.
Expenditures—Current Year	800,000	
Expenditures—Prior Year	60,000	
ENCUMBRANCES CONTROL	28,000	
APPROPRIATIONS CONTROL		902,000
FUND BALANCE RESERVED FOR ENCUMBRANCES		28,000

The city budgets on a GAAP basis. Accordingly, encumbrances outstanding at each year end ($62,000 at June 30, 19X4) are reappropriated in the following year's budget. The city council has requested that expenditures relating to such encumbrances be kept separate in the accounting records.

Required:

1. Prepare the applicable section of the budgetary comparison statement for the year ended June 30, 19X4.

2. Repeat requirement 1, but assume that the city uses the non-GAAP "budgetary" basis in budgeting.

P 20-2

General Fund: Preparing Transaction and Closing Journal Entries—Fundamentals

The city of Smileyville had the following activities pertaining to its General Fund for the fiscal year ended June 30, 19X6.

1. **Adoption of the budget.** Revenues were estimated at $1,000,000, and authorized expenditures were $950,000. (Assume no encumbrances were outstanding at June 30, 19X5.)
2. **Property taxes.** Property taxes were billed in the amount of $800,000, of which $25,000 was expected to be uncollectible. Collections were $750,000. A $22,000 allowance for uncollectibles is deemed adequate at year-end. All uncollected property taxes at year-end are delinquent.
3. **Other revenues.** Cash collections of $210,000 were received from sales taxes, licenses, fees, and fines.
4. **Purchase orders.** Purchase orders totaling $300,000 were issued to vendors and contractors during the year. For $270,000 of these purchase orders and contracts, billings totaling $268,000 were received. Cash payments totaling $245,000 were made.
5. **Payroll and other operating costs.** Expenditures for payroll and other operating costs not requiring the use of purchase orders and contracts totaled $631,000. Cash payments of $590,000 were made on these items.

Required:

1. Prepare the journal entries relating to the above items.
2. Prepare the year-end closing entries assuming that encumbrances outstanding at year-end will be honored in the following year.
3. Prepare the entry or entries that must be made on the first day of the following fiscal year.

P 20-3

Interfund Transactions

The city of Mityville had the following interfund transactions during the year ended December 31, 19X5:

1. The General Fund received a billing of $11,000 from its city-owned Water Fund, which is accounted for in an Enterprise Fund.
2. The General Fund disbursed $22,000 to its Library Debt Service Fund, so that interest could be paid to bondholders.
3. The General Fund disbursed $33,000 to start up a central purchasing fund, which is accounted for in an Internal Service Fund.
4. The General Fund received $44,000 from its Library Capital Projects Fund in repayment of money the General Fund had advanced to the architectural firm designing the library. The General Fund had charged Expenditures when the advance was made.

5. The General Fund disbursed $555,000 to its Municipal Transit Fund (accounted for in a Special Revenue Fund) as its annual subsidy.

Required:
Prepare the entries required in the General Fund.

P 20-4 General Fund: Preparing Transaction and Closing Journal Entries and a Statement of Revenues, Expenditures, and Changes in Fund Balance

Ledgerville had the following events and transactions for its fiscal year ended June 30, 19X2:

1. The budget for the year was approved. It provided for (a) $620,000 of estimated revenues; (b) $565,000 of expenditures; (c) $40,000 for servicing general long term debt (principal and interest); and (d) $30,000 to establish a central printing department that will provide services to all city departments. (The $30,000 will not be repaid to the General Fund.)
2. Items (c) and (d) above were expended in accordance with authorizations.
3. Property taxes totaling $450,000 were levied, of which $8,000 was estimated to be uncollectible. Property tax collections totaled $405,000. At year-end, the estimated allowance for uncollectibles was increased from $8,000 to $12,000. Unpaid taxes at year-end become delinquent.
4. City income taxes, sales taxes, business licenses, and fines totaled $162,000.
5. Bonds backed by the full faith and credit of the city were issued at par for $200,000 to finance an addition to city hall. (Construction is to begin in July 19X2.)
6. Some equipment accounted for in the General Fixed Assets Account Group was sold for $11,000. This transaction was not included in the budget.
7. A Capital Projects Fund was short $3,000 as a result of changes to contracts issued in connection with certain street improvements being charged to certain property owners. Authorization was given during the year to transfer funds to this fund to make up the shortage. The amount was not budgeted and will not be repaid.
8. The city received a $500,000 donation from the estate of a wealthy citizen to be used only for the acquisition of open space for parks.
9. Purchase orders and contracts totaling $280,000 were entered into. For $255,000 of this amount, invoices for goods and services totaling $254,000 were rendered. (Assume that no encumbrances were outstanding at June 30, 19X1.)
10. Payroll and other operating costs not involving the use of purchase orders and contracts totaled $282,000.
11. Cash disbursements (other than to other funds) totaled $507,000.

Required:

1. Prepare the General Fund entries for these items.
2. Prepare the closing entries at June 30, 19X2, assuming that encumbrances outstanding at year-end will be honored in the following year.

3. Prepare a statement of revenues, expenditures, and changes in fund balance for the year ended June 30, 19X2, for the General Fund that compares budgeted amounts with actual amounts. (Assume that the General Fund had a total fund balance of $100,000 at June 30, 19X1.)
4. Prepare the fund equity section of the balance sheet at June 30, 19X2.

P 20-5 COMPREHENSIVE Preparing Transaction and Closing Journal Entries and a Budgetary Comparison Statement on a GAAP Basis (Several Interfund Transactions)

The city of Postville had the following items and transactions pertaining to its General Fund for the fiscal year ended June 30, 19X3:

1. The budget for the year was as follows:

Estimated revenues	**$800,000**
Authorized expenditures (including $55,000 reappropriated for encumbrances outstanding at June 30, 19X2, which lapsed)	**725,000**
Authorized operating transfers to other funds	**50,000**

2. Property taxes were levied totaling $550,000. Of this amount, $10,000 was estimated to be uncollectible. Collections during the year were $535,000, of which $12,000 pertained to property tax levies of the prior year that had been declared delinquent at the end of the prior year. All remaining property tax receivables at the beginning of the current year totaling $4,000 were written off as uncollectible.
3. The estimated revenues for the year include an entitlement from the federal government for $34,000. During the year, $36,000 was received.
4. City income taxes, sales taxes, licenses, permits, and miscellaneous revenues totaled $222,000.
5. Purchase orders and contracts totaling $370,000 were entered into during the year. For $330,000 of this amount, invoices totaling $328,000 for goods and services were rendered. Assume that the city generally allows encumbrances outstanding at year-end to lapse but reappropriates amounts in the following year to honor the encumbrances.
6. Encumbrances outstanding at the beginning of the year totaled $55,000. The goods and services relating to these encumbrances were received along with invoices totaling $53,000.
7. Payroll and other items not involving the use of purchase orders and contracts totaled $280,000. (This amount excludes interfund billings.)
8. Cash disbursements (other than to other funds) totaled $740,000.
9. Interfund transactions consisted of the following:
   a. The Central Motor Pool Internal Service Fund was discontinued pursuant to authorization given by the legislative body at the beginning of the year. It was estimated then that the capital balance of the fund at the time of discontinuance would be $25,000. The actual amount disbursed to the General Fund during the year when the fund was discontinued was $17,000.

b. A payment of $30,000 was made to the Electric Utility Enterprise Fund to make up its operating deficit, which was initially estimated to be $35,000.
c. A payment of $15,000 was made to a Capital Projects Fund to finance a portion of certain street improvements. (This payment was equal to the amount budgeted.)
d. The Electric Utility Enterprise Fund rendered billings to the city totaling $26,000 for electricity supplied to the city by the Enterprise Fund. Cash disbursements to this fund during the year in payment of such billings totaled $22,000.

10. Assume the city uses the purchases method of accounting for acquisitions of supplies inventory, which totaled $32,000 during the year and is part of the $328,000 amount in 5, above. Assume the supplies inventory is insignificant at June 30, 19X3.

Required:

1. Prepare General Fund journal entries only for the above items.
2. Prepare the closing entries at June 30, 19X3, for the General Fund.
3. Prepare a statement of revenues, expenditures, and changes in fund balance for the year ended June 30, 19X3, that compares budgeted amounts with actual amounts. (Assume the fund balance at the beginning of the year was $100,000.)
4. Prepare the fund equity section of the balance sheet at June 30, 19X3.

P 20-6 COMPREHENSIVE Preparing Transaction and Closing Journal Entries and a Budgetary Comparison Statement on a GAAP Basis

The General Fund trial balance of the city of Solna at December 31, 19X2, was as follows:

	Dr.	Cr.
Cash	$ 62,000	
Taxes receivable—delinquent	46,000	
Allowance for uncollectible taxes—delinquent		$ 8,000
Stores inventory—program operations	18,000	
Vouchers payable		28,000
Fund balance reserved for stores inventory		18,000
Fund balance reserved for encumbrances		12,000
Unreserved fund balance		60,000
	$126,000	$126,000

Collectible delinquent taxes are expected to be collected within 60 days after the end of the year. Solna uses the "purchases" method to account for stores inventory. The following data pertain to 19X3 General Fund operations:

1. Budget adopted (including reappropriation of 19X2 items):

Revenues and Other Financing Sources:

Taxes	$220,000
Fines, forfeits, and penalties	80,000
Miscellaneous revenues	100,000
Share of bond issue proceeds	200,000
	$600,000

Expenditures and Other Financing Uses:

Program operations	$312,000
General administration	120,000
Stores—program operations	60,000
Capital outlay	80,000
Periodic transfer to Special Revenue Fund	20,000
	$592,000

2. Taxes were assessed at an amount that would result in revenues of $220,800, after deduction of 4% of the tax levy as uncollectible.
3. Orders placed but not received:

Program operations	$176,000
General administration	80,000
Capital outlay	60,000
	$316,000

4. The city council designated $20,000 of the unreserved fund balance for possible future appropriation for capital outlay.
5. Cash collections and transfer:

Delinquent taxes	$ 38,000
Current taxes	226,000
Refund of overpayment of invoice for purchase of equipment	4,000
Fines, forfeits, and penalties	88,000
Miscellaneous revenues	90,000
Share of bond issue proceeds	200,000
Transfer of remaining fund balance of a discontinued fund	18,000
	$664,000

6. Cancelled encumbrances:

	Estimated	Actual
Program operations	$156,000	$166,000
General administration	84,000	80,000
Capital outlay	62,000	62,000
	$302,000	$308,000

7. Additional vouchers:

Program operations	$188,000
General administration	38,000
Capital outlay	18,000
Transfer to Special Revenue Fund	20,000
	$264,000

8. Albert, a taxpayer, overpaid his 19X3 taxes by $2,000. He applied for a $2,000 credit against his 19X4 taxes. The city council granted his request.
9. Vouchers paid amounted to $580,000 (including $20,000 paid to the Special Revenue Fund).
10. Stores inventory on December 31, 19X3, amounted to $12,000.

Required:

1. Prepare General Fund journal entries only for the above items.
2. Prepare any required year-end adjusting entries.
3. Prepare the closing entries at December 31, 19X3.
4. Prepare a balance sheet at December 31, 19X3.
5. Prepare a statement of revenues, expenditures, and changes in fund balance for 19X3 that compares budgeted amounts with actual amounts.

(AICPA adapted)

P 20-7

General Fund: Reconstructing Transaction and Closing Journal Entries; Preparing a Budgetary Comparison Statement on a GAAP Basis

The following data were obtained from the general ledger for the General Fund of the City of Hope after the general ledger had been closed for the fiscal year ended June 30, 19X6:

	Balances June 30, 19X5	Fiscal 19X5–19X6 Charges		Balances June 30, 19X6
		Debit	Credit	
Cash	$180,000	$ 955,000	$ 880,000	$255,000
Taxes receivable	20,000	809,000	781,000	48,000
Allowance for uncollectible taxes	(4,000)	6,000	9,000	(7,000)
	$196,000			$296,000
Vouchers payable	$ 44,000	813,000	822,000	$ 53,000
Due to Internal Service Fund	2,000	7,000	10,000	5,000
Due to Debt Service Fund	10,000	60,000	100,000	50,000
Fund balance reserved for encumbrances	40,000	40,000	47,000	47,000
Unreserved fund balance	100,000	47,000	88,000	141,000
	$196,000	$2,737,000	$2,737,000	$296,000

Additional Information:

1. The budget for fiscal 19X5–19X6 provided for estimated revenues of $1,000,000, appropriations of $905,000 (including $40,000 pertaining to encumbrances outstanding at June 30, 19X5), and $100,000 to be transferred to a debt service fund.
2. Expenditures totaled $832,000, of which $37,000 pertained to encumbrances outstanding at June 30, 19X5.
3. Purchase orders issued during 19X5–19X6 totaled $170,000.
4. The city does not use delinquent accounts for delinquent taxes.

Required:

1. Using the given data, reconstruct the original detailed journal entries that were required to record all transactions for the fiscal year ended June 30, 19X6, including the recording of the current year's budget. (Hint: Use T-accounts.)
2. Prepare the year-end closing entries from the entries you have reconstructed.
3. Prepare a budgetary comparison statement of revenues, expenditures, and changes in fund balance for the current year.

(AICPA adapted)

P 20-8 General Fund: Reconstructing Transactions, Preparing Closing Entries, and Preparing a Statement of Revenues, Expenditures, and Changes in Fund Balance (Optional: Preparing a Budgetary Comparison Statement on a Non-GAAP "Budgetary" Basis)

The following summary of transactions was taken from the accounts of the Good Times School District General Fund *before* the books had been closed for the fiscal year ended June 30, 19X5:

	Postclosing Balances June 30, 19X4	Preclosing Balances June 30, 19X5
Actual accounts:		
Cash	$400,000	$ 630,000
Property taxes receivable—delinquent	150,000	180,000
Allowance for uncollectibles—delinquent	(40,000)	(80,000)
Expenditures	—	2,842,000
Expenditures—prior-year	—	58,000
	$510,000	$3,630,000
Vouchers payable	$ 80,000	$ 408,000
Due to other funds	210,000	62,000
Fund balance reserved for encumbrances	60,000	—
Unreserved fund balance	160,000	220,000
Revenues from property taxes	—	2,800,000
Miscellaneous revenues	—	140,000
	$510,000	$3,630,000

Budgetary accounts:

ESTIMATED REVENUES CONTROL	$3,000,000
ENCUMBRANCES CONTROL	91,000
	$3,091,000
APPROPRIATIONS CONTROL	$2,980,000
BUDGETARY FUND BALANCE	20,000
FUND BALANCE RESERVED FOR ENCUMBRANCES	91,000
	$3,091,000

Additional Information:

1. The property tax levy for the year ended June 30, 19X5, was $2,870,000. Taxes collected during the year totaled $2,810,000, of which $100,000 pertained to delinquent balances as of June 30, 19X4. Of the June 30, 19X4, delinquent balances, $30,000 was written off as uncollectible. Unpaid taxes become delinquent at the end of the fiscal year.
2. Encumbrances outstanding at each year-end are always honored in the following year. However, the encumbrances are not rebudgeted or reappropriated in the following year. The spending authority merely carries over to the following year. On May 2, 19X5, commitment documents were issued for the purchase of new textbooks at a cost of $91,000. Only this encumbrance is outstanding at June 30, 19X5. Other purchase orders issued during the year totaled $850,000, with invoices having been rendered for $847,000.
3. An analysis of the transactions in the Vouchers Payable account for the year ended June 30, 19X5, follows:

Balance, June 30, 19X4	$ 80,000
Expenditures pertaining to the prior year's budget	58,000
Expenditures pertaining to the current year's budget	2,700,000
Cash disbursements	(2,430,000)
Balance, June 30, 19X5	$ 408,000

4. During the year, the General Fund was billed $142,000 for services performed on its behalf by other city funds.

Required:

1. Using the data presented above, reconstruct the original detailed journal entries that were required to record all transactions for the fiscal year ended June 30, 19X5, including the recording of the current year's budget. (Hint: Use T-accounts.)
2. Prepare the closing entries at June 30, 19X5.
3. Prepare a statement of revenues, expenditures, and changes in fund balance for fiscal 19X4–19X5 (GAAP basis).
4. *Optional:* Prepare a budgetary comparison statement for fiscal 19X4–19X5 (non-GAAP "budgetary" basis).

(AICPA adapted)

P 20-9

CHALLENGER Preparing Adjusting and Closing Entries; Preparing Balance Sheet and Budgetary Comparison Statement on a GAAP Basis (Non–General Fund Transactions Improperly Recorded in General Fund)

The General Fund trial balances of the Blackboard School District at June 30, 19X7, are as follows:

BLACKBOARD SCHOOL DISTRICT
General Fund Trial Balances
June 30, 19X7

	Dr.	Cr.
Actual accounts:		
Cash	$ 60,000	
Taxes receivable—current year	31,800	
Allowance for uncollectibles—current-year taxes		$ 1,800
Inventory of supplies (June 30, 19X6)	10,000	
Buildings	1,300,000	
Bonds payable		500,000
Vouchers payable		12,000
Operating expenses:		
Administration	24,950	
Instruction	601,800	
Other	221,450	
Capital outlays (equipment)	22,000	
Debt service (interest)	30,000	
State grant revenue		300,000
Revenues from tax levy, licenses, and fines		1,008,200
Fund balance reserved for inventory		10,000
Unreserved fund balance		470,000
Totals	$2,302,000	$2,302,000
Budgetary accounts:		
ESTIMATED REVENUES CONTROL	$1,007,000	
APPROPRIATIONS CONTROL		$1,000,000
BUDGETARY FUND BALANCE		7,000
Totals	$1,007,000	$1,007,000

Additional Information:

1. The recorded allowance for uncollectible current-year taxes is considered sufficient. Unpaid taxes become delinquent at year-end.
2. During the year, the local governmental unit gave the school district 20 acres of land for a new grade school and a community playground. The unrecorded estimated value of the land donated was $50,000. In addition, a state grant of $300,000 was received, and the full amount was used in payment of contracts pertaining to the construction of the grade school. Purchases of classroom and playground equipment costing $22,000 were paid from general funds of the school district.

3. On July 1, 19X2, a 5%, 10-year serial bond issue in the amount of $1,000,000 for constructing school buildings was issued. Principal payments of $100,000 must be made each June 30, along with interest for the year. All payments required through June 30, 19X7, have been made.
4. Outstanding purchase orders for operating expenses not recorded in the accounts at year-end were as follows:

Administration	$1,000
Instruction	1,400
Other	600
Total	$3,000

The school district honors encumbrances outstanding at each year-end and reappropriates amounts in the following year's budget. No encumbrances were outstanding at June 30, 19X6.

5. Appropriations for the year consisted of the following:

Current:	
Administration	$ 25,200
Instruction	600,000
Other	222,300
Capital outlay	22,500
Debt service:	
Principal	100,000
Interest	30,000
	$1,000,000

6. The physical inventory of supplies at year-end totaled $12,500. Supplies are charged to expenditures at the time of receipt under the purchases method. The school district reports the amount of supplies inventory on hand in its balance sheet at each year-end. (The $2,500 increase in the supplies inventory was budgeted for in the current year.)

Required:

1. Prepare the appropriate adjusting entry to eliminate the activities and accounts that the school district should be accounting for in separate funds or account groups outside the General Fund. (It is not necessary to prepare the entries that would be made in these other funds or account groups to account properly for these items.) (*Note: Problem 20-9 will be used in the requirement for Problem 21-9.*)
2. Prepare any adjusting entries to accounts that are properly part of the General Fund.
3. Prepare the closing entries relating to the General Fund.
4. Prepare a balance sheet at June 30, 19X7.

5. Prepare a statement of revenues, expenditures, and changes in fund balance for the year ended June 30, 19X7, comparing budgeted amounts with actual amounts. (The beginning fund balance amount must be "forced" as though a correcting entry had been made at June 30, 19X6.)

(AICPA adapted)

P 20-10

CHALLENGER Preparing Budgetary Comparison Statements from Selected Data: GAAP Basis versus Non-GAAP "Budgetary" Basis

The following information is given for the City of Budgetville:

Fund Balance at December 31, 19X1 (GAAP basis):	
Reserved for encumbrances	$ 30,000
Unreserved	70,000
Total Fund Balance	$100,000
Budgeted items for 19X2:	
Estimated revenues	$500,000
Appropriations (including $30,000 rebudgeted for encumbrances outstanding at December 31, 19X1)	480,000
Actual amounts for 19X2:	
Revenues	503,000
Expenditures (including $29,000 relating to encumbrances outstanding at December 31, 19X1)	473,000
Encumbrances outstanding at December 31, 19X2	5,000

Required:

1. Prepare a budgetary comparison statement of revenues, expenditures, and changes in fund balance for 19X2 on a GAAP basis.
2. Prepare a budgetary comparison statement of revenues, expenditures, and changes in fund balance for 19X2 on a non-GAAP "budgetary" basis. (You now have to assume that the $30,000 relating to encumbrances outstanding at December 31, 19X1, was not rebudgeted for in 19X2.) Note: The ending fund balance in the actual column must agree with the total fund balance that would be reported in the balance sheet. However, the beginning fund balance in the actual column is the $70,000 unreserved fund balance at December 31, 19X1, (the fund balance on a non-GAAP "budgetary" basis). Accordingly, you must reconcile to the December 31, 19X2, fund balance on a GAAP basis.

21

Governmental Accounting: Special Purpose Funds and Account Groups

Special Revenue Funds
Capital Projects Funds
General Fixed Asset Account Group
Debt Service Funds
General Long-Term Debt Account Group
Special Assessments
Internal Service Funds
Enterprise Funds
Agency Funds and Trust Funds
Summary Illustration

In Chapter 20, we discussed the General Fund. In this chapter, we discuss the remaining six types of funds used for governmental accounting, the General Fixed Asset Account Group, and the General Long-Term Debt Account Group. Concerning the number of funds to be used by a governmental unit, the GASB Codification states:

> Only the minimum number of funds consistent with legal and operating requirements should be established . . . since unnecessary funds result in inflexibility, undue complexity and inefficient financial administration.[1]

Certain revenues, functions, or activities of government often must be accounted for in a designated fund separate from all others. In some situations, greater accounting control may be obtained through the use of a separate fund, even though it is not required by law. In most cases, the type of fund to be used to account for the specific revenues, functions, or activities is readily determinable. In a few instances, selecting the most appropriate type of fund requires greater scrutiny.

Certain transactions or events require entries in one or more funds or account groups. For example, the decision to build a new civic center to be financed through the issuance of general obligation bonds eventually results in entries being made in a Capital Projects Fund, a Debt Service Fund, the General Fixed Assets Account Group, the General Long-Term Debt Account Group, and in some cases the General Fund.

SPECIAL REVENUE FUNDS

Special Revenue Funds account for **"the proceeds of specific revenue sources (other than expendable trusts or for major capital projects) that are legally restricted to expenditure for specified purposes."**[2] Special Revenue Funds may be used for such small activities as the maintenance of a municipal swimming pool or such gigantic operations as a state highway system. The distinguishing feature of a Special Revenue Fund is that its revenues are obtained primarily from tax and nontax sources not directly related to services rendered or facilities provided for use. In other words, revenues are *not* obtained primarily from direct charges to the users of the services or facilities. Conceptually, therefore, Special Revenue Funds are the opposite of *most* Enterprise Funds, which recover the majority of their operating costs from charges to users.

[1] *Codification of Governmental Accounting and Financial Reporting Standards* (Stamford: Governmental Accounting Standards Board, 1987), sec. 1100.104.

[2] GASB Cod. sec. 1300.104, as amended by *Governmental Accounting Standards Board Statement No. 6*, "Accounting and Financial Reporting for Special Assessments" (Stamford: Governmental Accounting Standards Board, 1987).

The GASB Codification requires the use of Enterprise Funds when the costs of providing goods or services are recovered primarily from user charges. In addition, **under certain circumstances,** which we discuss later, Enterprise Funds may be used for activities that do not recover their costs primarily from user charges. The following activities could be accounted for in either Special Revenue Funds or Enterprise Funds, depending on the individual facts, circumstances, and operating policies: off-street parking facilities, transportation systems, turnpikes, golf courses, swimming pools, libraries, and auditoriums.

Special Revenue Funds may derive their revenues from one or several sources, commonly (1) specified property tax levies, (2) state gasoline taxes, (3) licenses, (4) grants, and (5) shared taxes from other governmental units (including federal revenue sharing).

Unless legal provisions specify to the contrary, Special Revenue Funds are accounted for using the same accounting principles, procedures, and financial statements shown for the General Fund in Chapter 20. As explained there, when a governmental unit has more than one fund of a given type, combining financial statements, showing each individual fund of that type and a total column (the second level of reporting within the "reporting pyramid" concept), are prepared for financial reporting purposes. This is also the case for the other funds discussed in this chapter.

CAPITAL PROJECTS FUNDS

Capital Projects Funds account for

> financial resources to be used for the acquisition or construction of major capital facilities (other than those financed by proprietary funds and Trust Funds).[3]

Examples of major capital facilities are administration buildings, auditoriums, civic centers, and libraries. These funds do not account for the purchase of fixed assets having comparatively limited lives, such as vehicles, machinery, and office equipment, which are normally budgeted for and acquired through the General Fund or a Special Revenue Fund and recorded as expenditures.

Capital Projects Funds **do not account for the fixed assets acquired— only for the acquisition of the fixed assets.** The fixed assets acquired are accounted for in the General Fixed Asset Account Group, which we discuss later in the chapter. Furthermore, Capital Projects Funds do not account for the repayment and servicing of any debt obligations issued to raise money to finance the acquisition of capital facilities. Such debt and related

[3]GASB Cod. sec. 1300.104 (as amended by *GASB Statement No. 6*).

servicing is accounted for in the Long-Term Debt Account Group and a Debt Service Fund, both of which we discuss later in the chapter.

Capital Projects Funds are categorized as governmental funds. Recall that the measurement basis for governmental funds is sources and uses (and balances) of financial resources. Accordingly, the same financial statements that are used for the General Fund are used for Capital Projects Funds. Likewise, the modified accrual basis of accounting is used.

Establishment and Operation

Capital Projects Funds are usually established on a project-by-project basis, because legal requirements may vary from one project to another. Most capital facilities are financed through the issuance of general obligation bonds, the liability for which is recorded in the General Long-Term Debt Account Group. In many cases, some portion is financed by the General Fund or a Special Revenue Fund. Such transfers are **operating transfers,** which we discussed in the preceding chapter. The General Fund or Special Revenue Fund debits an account called Other Financing Uses, and the Capital Project Fund credits Other Financing Sources. Federal and state grants are another major source of funds.[4]

Major capital facilities are usually constructed by contracted labor. Because encumbrance accounting procedures alone are usually deemed sufficient for control purposes, recording the budgeted amounts in the general ledger is usually considered unnecessary. Construction costs incurred are charged to expenditures. At the end of each year, expenditures are closed out to the Unreserved Fund Balance account, as are any amounts recorded in accounts pertaining to bond proceeds and operating transfers in for the year. Each Capital Project Fund is terminated upon completion of the project for which it was created. Any residual equity balance should be disposed of in accordance with legal provisions (usually as a residual equity transfer to either a Debt Service Fund or the General Fund).

At the completion of the project, the cost of the facility is recorded as a fixed asset in the General Fixed Assets Account Group. Until then, any costs incurred are shown as Construction Work in Progress in the General Fixed Assets Account Group. Generally, the year-end closing entry in the Capital Projects Fund triggers the recording of an amount in the General Fixed Assets Account Group equal to the credit to the Expenditures account. (We explain more fully later in the chapter that the GASB Codification makes optional the recording in the General Fixed Assets Account Group of certain types of improvements constructed through Capital Projects Funds.)

[4]The accounting for federal and state grants is prescribed in GASB Cod. sec. G60.

Illustration

JOURNAL ENTRIES AND FINANCIAL STATEMENTS

Assume that Funn City established a Capital Projects Fund during the fiscal year ended June 30, 19X2, for the construction of a new city hall. Assumed transactions pertaining to the establishment and operation of the fund, along with the related journal entries, are as follows:

1. **Establishment of the fund.** The new city hall is expected to cost $5,000,000. The city obtained a **capital grant** from the state government of $1,500,000, of which $600,000 was contributed at the inception of the project. The remaining $900,000 is deemed to be susceptible to accrual. The General Fund contributes $500,000, of which $200,000 was contributed at the inception of the project.

Cash	600,000	
Grant Receivable from State Government	900,000	
Revenues		1,500,000
To record amounts received and due from the state government.		

Cash	200,000	
Due from General Fund	300,000	
Other Financing Sources		500,000
To record amounts received and due from the General Fund.		

2. **Sale of bonds.** The remaining $3,000,000 was obtained from the sale of general obligation bonds at par.

Cash	3,000,000	
Other Financing Sources		3,000,000
To record the sale of general obligation bonds.		

Recall that the bond liability must also be recorded in the General Long-Term Debt Account Group. That entry would be:

Amount to be Provided for:		
Payment of Bonds	3,000,000	
Bonds Payable		3,000,000

Observe that the entry normally made in the private sector for the issuance of bonds (debiting Cash and crediting Bonds Payable) is effectively made through the combination of the two preceding entries. The debit to Cash is made in the Capital Projects Fund, and the credit to Bonds Payable is made in the General Long-Term Debt Account Group.

3. **Construction-related activity.** A construction contract for $4,600,000 is authorized and signed. During the year ended June 30, 19X2, billings of $2,700,000 were rendered, and payments totaling $2,200,000 were made.

ENCUMBRANCES CONTROL	4,600,000	
FUND BALANCE RESERVED FOR ENCUMBRANCES		4,600,000
To record encumbrance on construction contract.		
FUND BALANCE RESERVED FOR ENCUMBRANCES	2,700,000	
ENCUMBRANCES CONTROL		2,700,000
To cancel part of encumbrance for project contract with general contractor for completions to date.		
Expenditures	2,700,000	
Contracts Payable		2,700,000
To record actual expenditures to date on contract with general contractor for completions to date.		
Contracts Payable	2,200,000	
Cash		2,200,000
To record payments to contractor.		

In addition to the preceding construction contract, $390,000 was incurred for the services of architects and engineers. Of this amount, $310,000 was paid. (For simplicity, we assume that encumbrance accounting procedures were not used.)

Expenditures	390,000	
Vouchers Payable		390,000
To record fees for architects and engineers.		
Vouchers Payable	310,000	
Cash		310,000
To record payment of architect and engineering fees.		

4. **Closing entries.** The appropriate closing entries at June 30, 19X2, are as follows:

Revenues	1,500,000	
Other Financing Sources ($500,000 + $3,000,000)	3,500,000	
Expenditures ($2,700,000 + $390,000)		3,090,000
Unreserved Fund Balance		1,910,000
To close out actual revenues, other financing sources, and expenditures into unreserved fund balance.		

FUND BALANCE RESERVED FOR ENCUMBRANCES	1,900,000	
ENCUMBRANCES CONTROL		1,900,000
To close encumbrances outstanding at year-end by reversing the entry that previously recorded them.		

Unreserved Fund Balance	1,900,000	
Fund Balance Reserved for Encumbrances		1,900,000
To record *actual* fund balance reserve account to indicate the portion of year-end balance segregated for expenditure upon contractor performance.		

In addition to the preceding closing entries, the partially completed capital facility must be reflected in the General Fixed Assets Account Group at June 30, 19X2. These accounts are discussed in detail later in the chapter. For now, you should know that the following entry would be made:

Construction Work in Progress	3,090,000	
Investment in General Fixed Assets from Capital Projects—		
General Obligation Bonds (60%)		1,854,000
State Grants (30%)		927,000
General Fund Revenues (10%)		309,000
To record city hall construction in progress.		

Financial Statements. The financial statements that would be prepared for the fiscal year ended June 30, 19X2, as a result of the preceding journal entries are shown in Illustrations 21-1 and 21-2.

Completion of Project in Following Year. Assume the project is completed in the following fiscal year. A cost overrun of $5,000 was made up by an operating transfer in from the General Fund. The journal entries that would be made during the fiscal year ended June 30, 19X3, follow.

Illustration 21-1

FUNN CITY
Capital Projects Fund—City Hall
Balance Sheet
June 30, 19X2

Assets	
Cash	$1,290,000
Grant receivable	900,000
Due from general fund	300,000
Total Assets	$2,490,000
Liabilities and Fund Equity	
Vouchers payable	$ 80,000
Contracts payable	500,000
Total Liabilities	$ 580,000
Fund balance:	
Reserved for encumbrances	$1,900,000
Unreserved	10,000
Total Fund Balance	$1,910,000
Total Liabilities and Fund Equity	$2,490,000

Illustration 21-2

FUNN CITY
Capital Projects Fund—City Hall
Statement of Revenues, Expenditures,
and Changes in Fund Balance
For the Fiscal Year Ended June 30, 19X2

Revenues:	
Intergovernmental—state grant	$ 1,500,000
Expenditures:	
Capital outlay	(3,090,000)
Revenues under Expenditures	$(1,590,000)
Other Financing Sources:	
Proceeds of general obligation bonds	$ 3,000,000
Operating transfer in from general fund	500,000
Total Other Financing Sources	$ 3,500,000
Excess of Revenues and Other Sources over Expenditures.	$ 1,910,000
Fund Balance, July 1, 19X1	–0–
Fund Balance, June 30, 19X2	$ 1,910,000

1. **Reestablishment of budgetary control over outstanding encumbrances:** Budgetary control must be reestablished over outstanding encumbrances on July 1, 19X2. This is done by reversing the prior year-end closing entries related to encumbrances.

ENCUMBRANCES CONTROL	1,900,000	
FUND BALANCE RESERVED FOR ENCUMBRANCES		1,900,000
To reestablish budgetary control on remainder of construction contract.		
Fund balance Reserved for Encumbrances	1,900,000	
Unreserved Fund Balance		1,900,000
To reverse appropriation of fund balance made at June 30, 19X2, relating to encumbrances outstanding at June 30, 19X2, that will be honored during the current year.		

2. **Cash receipts:** All receivables were collected, and the $5,000 needed to pay for the cost overrun was received from the General Fund.

Cash	900,000	
Grant Receivable		900,000
To record collection of grant receivable.		
Cash	305,000	
Due from General Fund		300,000
Other Financing Sources		5,000
To record collection of amounts received from the General Fund.		

3. **Construction-related activity:** The contractor submitted bills for the remainder of the contract. Additional engineering services totaled $15,000. All liabilities were paid.

FUND BALANCE RESERVED FOR ENCUMBRANCES	1,900,000	
ENCUMBRANCES CONTROL		1,900,000
To cancel remainder of encumbrance for project contract with general contractor upon completion of contract.		
Expenditures	1,900,000	
Contracts Payable		1,900,000
To record expenditures relating to billings on remainder of contract.		
Contracts Payable	2,400,000	
Cash		2,400,000
To record payments to contractor.		
Expenditures	15,000	
Vouchers Payable		15,000
To record fees for engineering services.		

Vouchers Payable	95,000	
Cash		95,000
To record payment of engineering fees. ($15,000 + $80,000 owed at June 30, 19X2).		

4. **Closing entry:** The appropriate closing entry at June 30, 19X3, is as follows:

Other Financing Sources	5,000	
Unreserved Fund Balance	1,910,000	
Expenditures		1,915,000
To close out other financing sources and expenditures into Unreserved Fund Balance.		

In addition to the preceding closing entry, the fully completed capital facility would be reflected in the General Fixed Assets Account Group at June 30, 19X3, as a result of the following entry in these accounts:

Buildings	5,005,000	
Construction Work in progress		3,090,000
Investment in General Fixed Assets from Capital projects—		
General Obligation Bonds (60%)		1,146,000
State Grants (30%)		573,000
General Fund Revenues (10% of $1,910,000 plus $5,000)		196,000
To record completed city hall in the General Fixed Assets Account Group.		

Financial Statements for Year Ended June 30, 19X3. Because all liabilities were paid by June 30, 19X3, and no assets remained, a balance sheet at June 30, 19X3, is not necessary. The operating statement for the year ended June 30, 19X3, is shown in Illustration 21-3.

Illustration 21-3

FUNN CITY
Capital Projects Fund — City Hall
Statement of Expenditures and Changes in Fund Balance
For the Fiscal Year Ended June 30, 19X3

Expenditures:	
Capital outlay	$(1,915,000)
Other Financing Sources:	
Operating transfer in from General Fund	5,000
Excess of Expenditures over Other Sources	$(1,910,000)
Fund Balance, July 1, 19X2	1,910,000
Fund Balance, June 30, 19X3	$ –0–

Other Procedural Matters

The preceding example illustrates a project cost overrun, which was made up from the General Fund. Such situations are common. The source of additional money to pay for cost overruns is specified by legal requirements or operating policy.

All the money necessary to pay for the capital improvements is usually raised at or near the inception of the project, but contractors are paid as work progresses. Excess cash, therefore, may be temporarily invested in high-quality, interest-bearing securities. In such cases, the interest income on the investments may be either credited to revenues—to be available to the Capital Projects Fund in the event of cost overruns—or transferred to the related Debt Service Fund.

GENERAL FIXED ASSETS ACCOUNT GROUP

The General Fixed Assets Account Group is created to account for a governmental unit's fixed assets that are not accounted for in an Enterprise Fund, an Internal Service Fund, or a Trust Fund. This group of accounts is not a fund, but rather a self-balancing group of accounts. For each asset recorded in the group of accounts, there is a corresponding offsetting credit descriptive of the source of the asset. A statement of general fixed assets classified by type of asset is the basic financial statement for this group of accounts. This statement may be supplemented with: (1) a statement showing these assets broken down by function, activity, or department; and (2) a statement showing the changes in the account balances for the year. A typical statement of general fixed assets classified by type of account and source is shown in Illustration 21-4.

As mentioned previously, not all improvements constructed through Capital Projects Funds must be recorded in the General Fixed Assets Account Group. According to the GASB Codification:

> Reporting public domain or "infrastructure" fixed assets—roads, bridges, curbs and gutters, streets and sidewalks, drainage systems, lighting systems, and similar assets that are immovable and of value only to the governmental unit—is optional.[5]

In practice, only a small percentage of governmental units capitalize and report "infrastructure" fixed assets in the General Fixed Assets Account Group.

Accounting Procedures

Most high-dollar general fixed assets originate from Capital Projects Funds. Most of the equipment shown in this account group originates

[5]GASB Cod. sec. 1400.109.

Illustration 21-4

FUNN CITY
Statement of General Fixed Assets
June 30, 19X2

General Fixed Assets:	
Land	$ 1,300,000
Buildings	12,900,000
Improvements other than buildings	1,100,000
Equipment	450,000
Construction work in progress	3,600,000[a]
Total General Fixed Assets	$19,350,000
Investment in General Fixed Assets from:	
Capital Projects Funds—	
General obligation bonds	$15,300,000
Federal grants	1,000,000
State grants	800,000
County grants	600,000
General Fund Revenues	560,000
Special Revenue Fund Revenues	310,000
Gifts	180,000
Special Assessments	600,000
Total Investment in General Fixed Assets	$19,350,000

[a]This is work in progress in the Capital Projects Funds.

from expenditures made through the General Fund and Special Revenue Funds. When such assets are constructed or acquired, these three classes of funds debit Expenditures. At the same time or at the end of the fiscal year, entries are made in the General Fixed Assets Account Group debiting the appropriate asset category and crediting the appropriate source investment accounts.

Entries relating to the construction of a new city hall that would be made in the General Fixed Assets Account Group were shown earlier, in the discussion of the Capital Projects Funds. A typical entry pertaining to the acquisition of equipment by the General Fund is as follows:

Equipment	47,000	
Investment in General Fixed Assets from General Fund Revenues		47,000
To record equipment purchased through the General Fund.		

General fixed assets acquired through purchase or construction are recorded at cost. Assets arising from gifts or donations are recorded at their estimated current fair values at the time of donation. On abandonment, the entry is reversed. On sale, the entry is reversed, and the sales proceeds are recorded as revenues (usually in the fund that initially acquired the asset). As discussed in Chapter 20, accumulated depreciation may be reflected for general fixed assets in the General Fixed Assets Account Group at the option of the governmental unit. Depreciation expense, however, may not be reported in the operating statements of the governmental funds.

The GASB Codification covers accounting for lease agreements and requires that *FASB Statement No. 13*, "Accounting for Leases," be followed.

DEBT SERVICE FUNDS

For discussion purposes, long-term debt of governmental units may be categorized as follows:

1. **Revenue bonds.** Revenue bonds are issued to finance the establishment or expansion of activities accounted for in Enterprise Funds. These bonds are shown as liabilities of the Enterprise Funds, because their repayment and servicing can only come from money generated from the operations of those funds.
2. **General obligation bonds serviced from Enterprise Funds.** General obligation bonds also are issued to finance establishment or expansion of activities accounted for in Enterprise Funds. They bear the full faith and credit of the governmental unit. When such bonds are to be repaid and serviced from money generated from the operations of an Enterprise Fund, the bonds should be shown as liabilities of the Enterprise Fund and as a contingent liability of the General Long-Term Debt Account Group. (We discuss these bonds more fully later in the chapter.)
3. **All other long-term debt.** All long-term debt not fitting into one of the two preceding categories is shown as a liability of the General Long-Term Debt Account Group.

Debt Service Funds **are created for long-term debt that is shown as a liability of the General Long-Term Debt Account Group.** Remember that the General Long-Term Debt Account Group is not a fund but merely a self-balancing group of accounts that keep track of all unmatured long-term debt in category 3 above. Debt Service Funds account for the matured portion of and the payment of principal and interest on such long-term debt. Although notes payable are occasionally encountered, substantially all long-term debt of governmental units consists of one of the following two major types of bonds:

1. **Term bonds** are bonds whose principal is repaid in a lump sum at their maturity date. Such a lump-sum payment is usually made possible through the accumulation of money in the Debt Service Fund on an actuarial basis over the life of the bond issue ("sinking fund"). Term bonds are less prevalent than they used to be.

2. The principal of **serial bonds** is repaid at various predetermined dates over the life of the issue. **Regular** serial bonds are repaid in equal annual installments. **Deferred** serial bonds are also repaid in equal annual installments, but the first serial payment is delayed a specified number of years. **Irregular** serial bonds are repaid in other than equal principal repayments.

On the date that a principal payment relating to general long-term debt is to be made, a liability is established in the Debt Service Fund for the amount of the payment. Simultaneously, the amount of the debt as recorded in the General Long-Term Debt Account Group is reduced by a like amount. Thus, liabilities recorded in this group are effectively transferred at their maturity dates to a Debt Service Fund for their liquidation.

An Unusual Feature. The only unusual feature of Debt Service Funds is the method of accounting for interest on the general long-term debt. **Interest is not reflected as a liability of Debt Service Fund until the date it is due and payable.** This use of the cash basis of accounting is the major exception to the accrual of expenditures in the period to which they relate. As a result, interest for the period from the last payment date to the end of the fiscal year is not reflected as a liability at the end of the fiscal year. This is because governmental units generally budget for interest on the cash basis instead of the accrual basis.

Debt Service Funds are categorized as governmental funds. Accordingly, the modified accrual basis of accounting is used, and the financial statements used for the General Fund are also used for Debt Service Funds.

Establishment and Operation

The legal provisions of a specific debt issue may require the establishment of a separate Debt Service Fund solely for that debt issue. In other cases, several debt issues may be accounted for using a single Debt Service Fund. Concerning the appropriateness of recording budgeted amounts in the general ledger, the GASB Codification states:

> it would not be necessary [to record the budget] in controlling most Debt Service Funds, where the amounts required to be received and expended are set forth in bond indentures or sinking fund provisions and few transactions occur each year.[6]

Encumbrance accounting is not appropriate because contracts are not entered into and purchase orders are not issued.

Sources of Revenues. Debt Service Funds may obtain their revenues from one or several sources. The most common is property taxes. A sepa-

[6]GASB Cod. sec. 1700.119

rate rate is levied for each bond issue or group of bond issues. In these situations, the revenues are recognized on the accrual basis. (The accounting procedures are identical to those used by the General Fund in accounting for property taxes.) Revenues obtained from sources such as shared sales taxes are customarily recorded at the time of receipt. When money is to be transferred from the General Fund, a receivable from the General Fund may be recorded at the start of the fiscal year for the amount authorized to be transferred to the Debt Service Fund. Such transfers are **operating transfers,** and the General Fund debits the Other Financing Uses account, and the Debt Service Fund credits Other Financing Sources. Payments made for principal and interest are recorded as expenditures.

Governmental units commonly use designated fiscal agents to make the payments to the bondholders. In such cases, money is transferred from the Debt Service Funds to the fiscal agents, who submit reports and canceled coupons (if used) to the governmental unit. The fee charged for such services is recorded as an expenditure of the Debt Service Fund.

The operation of Debt Service Funds pertaining to issues of **regular** serial bonds essentially involves collecting revenues and transferring monies to the fiscal agent. Significant accumulations of money requiring investment do not occur. In these cases, the journal entries to record the revenues, the expenditures, and the closing of the books parallel those used in the General Fund. Accordingly, an illustration of journal entries and financial statements for this type of Debt Service Fund is not presented.

The operation of Debt Service Funds is more complex when **deferred** serial bonds and **term** bonds are involved. Accumulated money must be invested, and bond premiums and discounts may exist on such investments. Actuarial computations are used to determine additions and earnings. The journal entries and financial statements for a Debt Service Fund pertaining to term bonds are illustrated in the following section.

Illustration

JOURNAL ENTRIES AND FINANCIAL STATEMENTS: TERM BONDS

Assume that Funn City established a Debt Service Fund on October 1, 19X1, for an 8%, $400,000 general obligation bond issue due in 20 years (the proceeds of which will be used to construct a new civic center). Interest is to be paid semiannually on March 31 and September 30. We assume that all required additions to the fund will come from the General Fund and a specific tax levy. Assumed transactions pertaining to the operation of the fund for the fiscal year ended June 30, 19X2; along with related journal entries, are as follows:

Transaction or Event	Journal Entry		
The required fund transfer from the General Fund is recorded on October 1, 19X1.	Due from General Fund....	5,000	
	Other Financing Sources		5,000
The required fund transfer is received from the General Fund.	Cash..............................	5,000	
	Due from General Fund.		5,000
Property taxes are levied.	Property Tax Receivables..	23,000	
	Allowance for Uncollectibles...........		2,000
	Revenues.....................		21,000
Property taxes are collected.[a]	Cash..............................	20,000	
	Property Tax Receivables		20,000
An investment of $8,500 is made.	Investment......................	8,500	
	Cash...........................		8,500
Cash is transferred to the fiscal agent for the March 31, 19X2, interest payment.	Cash with Fiscal Agent.....	16,000	
	Cash...........................		16,000
Interest of $16,000 and the fiscal agent's fee of $100 is charged as an expenditure on the interest due date (March 31, 19X2).	Expenditures	16,100	
	Interest Payable...........		16,000
	Accrued Liability..........		100
Interest is paid by the fiscal agent, and the fiscal agent's fee is paid.	Interest Payable..............	16,000	
	Accrued Liability.............	100	
	Cash with Fiscal Agent..		16,000
	Cash...........................		100
Interest earned on investments is accrued at June 30, 19X2.	Interest Receivable..........	450	
	Revenues.....................		450
The fiscal year-end closing entry is made.	Other Financing Sources..	5,000	
	Revenues........................	21,450	
	Expenditures		16,100
	Fund Balance Reserved for Debt Service		10,350

[a]For simplicity, we ignore the establishment of delinquent accounts at year-end.

Financial Statements. The financial statements that would be prepared for the fiscal year ended June 30, 19X2 as a result of the preceding journal entries are shown in Illustrations 21-5 and 21-6.

The following points are important for understanding the financial statements:

1. A liability for interest for the period April 1, 19X2, through June 30, 19X2, is not reflected in the statement of financial position at June 30, 19X2, in accordance with the modified accrual basis of accounting. This interest will be shown as an expenditure in the following year when the September 30, 19X2 interest payment is due and payable.
2. If all required additions are made on time and earnings on investments earn the rate assumed in the actuarial calculations, then $400,000 will be accumulated in the Debt Service Fund by the maturity date of the bonds (19¼ years from June 30, 19X2).

Illustration 21-5

FUNN CITY
Debt Service Fund—Civic Center
Balance Sheet
June 30, 19X2

Assets	
Cash	$ 400
Property tax receivables	3,000
Less: Allowance for uncollectible taxes	(2,000)
Investments	8,500
Interest receivable	450
Total Assets	$10,350
Fund Equity	
Fund balance reserved for debt service	$10,350[a]

[a]The actuarial requirement at June 30, 19X2, is $10,200.

Illustration 21-6

FUNN CITY
Debt Service Fund—Civic Center
Statement of Revenues, Expenditures, and Changes in Fund Balance
For the Fiscal Year Ended June 30, 19X2

Revenues:	
Property taxes	$21,000
Interest on investments	450
Total Revenues	$21,450
Expenditures:	
Interest on bonds	$16,000
Fiscal agent's fees	100
Total Expenditures	$16,100
Revenues over Expenditures	$ 5,350
Other Financing Sources:	
Operating transfer in from general fund	5,000
Excess of Revenues and Other Sources over Expenditures	$10,350[a]
Fund Balance, July 1, 19X1	–0–
Fund Balance, June 30, 19X2	$10,350

[a]The actuarial requirement for the year was $9,300.

3. At the maturity date of the bonds, the entire $400,000 is recorded as a liability in the Debt Service Fund by debiting the Expenditures account and crediting Bonds Payable. Simultaneously, this debt is removed from the General Long-Term Debt Group of Accounts.
4. Making all required additions and earning interest at rates at least equal to the actuarially assumed interest rate is critical to the accumulation of the $400,000 required to redeem the bonds. If a lower interest rate is actually earned, then additional money must be contributed to the fund to make up the shortage. To the extent that earnings exceed the actuarially assumed rate, future contributions may be reduced accordingly.
5. The following essential disclosures for Debt Service Funds pertain to term bonds: (a) the actuarially computed amount that should exist in the Fund Balance account as of the statement of financial position date, and (b) the actuarially computed amount of earnings that should have been earned during the current fiscal year.

GENERAL LONG-TERM DEBT ACCOUNT GROUP

The General Long-Term Debt Account Group presents a governmental unit's debt that (1) has a maturity date of more than one year at the time of issuance and (2) is not properly shown in proprietary funds (Enterprise Funds and Internal Service Funds), or Trust Funds. Such debt is shown as a liability in this account group until its maturity date, when the liability is effectively transferred to the appropriate Debt Service Fund. For governmental purposes, "long-term debt" includes the portion of long-term debt that is due and payable in the coming fiscal year.

As previously discussed, the General Long-Term Debt Account Group does not include the following types of long-term debt:

1. **Revenue bonds of Enterprise Funds,** which are recorded as liabilities of the applicable Enterprise Funds.
2. **General Obligation Bonds to be repaid and serviced from Enterprise Fund operations,** which are recorded as liabilities of the applicable Enterprise Funds. (The contingent liability must be disclosed in a footnote.)

When general long-term debt is created, an entry is made in the General Long-Term Debt Account Group crediting a descriptive liability account—for example, Serial Bonds Payable—and debiting an offsetting account called Amount to Be Provided for Payment of Bonds (Serial or Term). As money accumulates in the Debt Service Fund, the Amount to Be Provided for Payment of Bonds account is reduced to that extent, and an account called Amount Available for Payment of Bonds is debited to signify the availability of these monies. (The proceeds are recorded in the appropriate fund authorized to use the borrowings.) For financial reporting purposes,

Illustration 21-7

FUNN CITY
Statement of General Long-Term Debt
June 30, 19X2

Amount Available and to Be Provided for the Payment of General Long-Term Debt:		
Term Bonds—		
Amount available in Debt Service Funds	$ 196,000	
Amount to be provided	204,000	
		$ 400,000
Serial Bonds—		
Amount available in Debt Service Funds	$ 14,000	
Amount to be provided	2,386,000	
		2,400,000
Total Amount Available and to Be Provided		$2,800,000
General Long-Term Debt Payable:		
Term Bonds payable		$ 400,000
Serial Bonds payable		2,400,000
Total General Long-Term Debt Payable		$2,800,000

Note: Footnote disclosure is required for the contingent liability that exists for general obligation bonds recorded in Enterprise Funds.

a statement of general long-term debt is used. A typical statement of general long-term debt is shown in Illustration 21-7.

Accounting Procedures

Typical entries that would be made in the General Long-Term Debt Account Group are as follows:

Amount to Be Provided for Payment of Bonds (serial or term)	**3,500,000**	
Bonds Payable (serial or term)		**3,500,000**
To record the issuance of bonds for the new community center.		
Amount Available in Debt Service Fund	**100,000**	
Amount to Be Provided for Repayment of Serial Bonds		**100,000**
To record increase in assets available for retirement of serial bonds.		
Serial Bonds Payable	**100,000**	
Amount Available in Debt Service Fund..		**100,000**
To transfer liability to Debt Service Fund.		

SPECIAL ASSESSMENTS No Longer GAAP

Some government activities involve constructing **public improvements that benefit a specific geographical area rather than the community as a whole.** The most common examples are residential streets, sidewalks, street lighting, and sewer lines. In these cases, governmental units usually charge all or most of the costs of the improvements directly to the owners of the properties benefited. In most cases, money is collected from the appropriate property owners in installments over a period of years. In some cases, the General Fund contributes monies for part of the improvements. Such transfers are **operating transfers.**

Although construction may be started after all the necessary money has been collected, it is more common to: (a) borrow money (usually by issuing bonds); (b) use the borrowed funds to pay for the improvements; (c) collect money in installments from property owners in succeeding years; and (d) use the collected money to make principal and interest payments on the borrowings. In these cases, the borrowings are generally serial bonds, which may be either special assessment bonds or general obligation bonds. The former may be repaid only from assessments made against the applicable properties benefited, whereas the latter bear the full faith and credit of the governmental unit. To pay for the interest on outstanding bonds, the assessment payers are charged interest in installments.

Manner of Accounting

Prior to the issuance of *GASB Statement No. 6*, "Accounting and Financial Reporting for Special Assessments" in 1987, special assessments were accounted for in Special Assessment Funds. *GASB Statement No. 6* eliminated this type of fund because a much criticized nonsensical reporting result occurred with them and it was felt that the other fund types could readily accommodate special assessments.

Construction Activity. Under *GASB Statement No. 6*, **all construction activity is to be accounted for and reported like any other capital improvement—in a Capital Projects Fund.**[7] No illustrations of entries are provided here inasmuch as they would be identical to those shown earlier for Capital Projects Funds.[8]

Financing Activity: The Critical Determinant Is the Government's Obligation to Assume the Debt. The manner of accounting for Special Assessment Receivables from the property owners and the Special Assessment Bonds depends on whether or not the governmental unit is "obligated in some manner" to make good the repayment of the special assessment

[7] *GASB Statement No. 6*, pars. 15, 19.
[8] In a probably unusual and rare instance that a fund other than a Capital Projects Fund is more appropriate, that fund may be used (*GASB Statement No. 6*, pars. 15, 19).

bonds in the event of default by the assessed property owners. According to *GASB Statement No. 6:*

> The phrase *obligated in some manner* as used in this Statement is intended to include all situations *other than* those in which (a) the government is *prohibited* (by constitution, charter, statute, ordinance, or contract) from assuming the debt in the event of default by the property owner or (b) the government is not legally liable for assuming the debt and makes no statement, or gives no indication, that it will, or may, honor the debt in the event of default.[9]

In the vast majority of cases, the governmental unit is obligated in some manner. We discuss these situations in the following paragraphs. In the section on Agency Funds, later in the chapter, we discuss the situation in which the governmental unit is not obligated in any manner (and, consequently, the financing activity must be accounted for in an Agency Fund).

When the Government Is Obligated in Some Manner. In situations in which the governmental unit is obligated in some manner, *GASB Statement No. 6* requires that a Debt Service Fund be used to account for the servicing of any Special Assessment debt and the collection of Special Assessment Receivables. The Special Assessment debt is initially recorded in the General Long-Term Debt Account Group. To the extent that such debt is to be repaid from Special Assessment Receivables, a special classification, "Special Assessment Debt with Governmental Commitment," is to be used in the General Long-Term Debt Account Group. Other than this special designation, accounting and reporting for this debt is the same as for general obligation debt recorded in the General Long-Term Debt Account Group and serviced through a Debt Service Fund.[10]

The accounting procedures for Special Assessment Receivables in a Debt Service Fund are nearly the same as for other property tax receivables accounted for in Debt Service Funds (illustrated earlier). **The one significant difference is that the deferred portion of the assessment cannot be recognized as revenues until later periods because the amounts are not "available to pay current-period liabilities"** (the revenue-recognition criteria discussed in Chapter 20). To illustrate, assume a street lighting project has an estimated cost of $500,000. On July 1, 19X1, certain property owners are assessed $500,000, which is to be collected in five equal installments of $100,000 per year beginning April 1, 19X2. Interest at 12% is to be charged on the deferred portion of the assessment ($400,000). Also on July 1, 19X1, special assessment bonds having a face value of $500,000 are issued at par, with interest at 8% to be paid annually. The entries pertaining to the assessment (but not the bonds) for the years ended June 30, 19X2, and June 30, 19X3, follow.

[9]*GASB Statement No. 6*, par. 16.
[10]*GASB Statement No. 6*, pars. 15, 17.

For the year ended June 30, 19X2:

Special Assessment Receivables—Current	100,000	
Special Assessment Receivables—Deferred	400,000	
Revenues		100,000
Deferred Revenues		400,000
To record levy of assessments on July 1, 19X1.		

Cash	100,000[a]	
Special Assessment Receivables—Current		100,000
To record collection of current assessment receivables due on April 1, 19X2.		

[a]These proceeds would be used to retire a portion of the special assessment bonds.

For the year ended June 30, 19X3:

Special Assessment Receivables—Current	100,000	
Special Assessment Receivables—Deferred		100,000
To reflect the current portion at July 1, 19X2.		

Deferred Revenues	100,000	
Revenues		100,000
To recognize revenues.		

Cash	148,000[a]	
Special Assessment Receivables—Current		100,000
Revenues		48,000
To record collection of current assessment receivables due on April 1, 19X3, along with interest of $48,000 ($400,000 × 12%).		

[a]These proceeds would be used to retire a portion of the special assessment bonds and pay related interest.

In the preceding example, the $500,000 bond issue was equal to the cost of the project. In many cases, however, the project is not begun until or near the first collection date of the special assessment levy. In such cases the bond issue need be only for the amount of the deferred portion of the special assessment levy ($400,000 in the example). Accordingly, the Debt Service Fund, in recording the special assessment levy, would not credit $100,000 to Revenues; rather, it would credit that amount to the Due to Capital Projects Fund account, inasmuch as the first annual collection from the property owners would be used to pay for part of the construction costs rather than to repay a portion of the bond issue.

Manner of Recording Interest. Recall from the discussion of Debt Service Funds that: (1) Debt Service Funds are used to service debt recorded in the General Long-Term Debt Account Group, and (2) interest is recognized when due rather than in the period to which the interest relates. Because of this manner of accounting for interest, *GASB Statement No. 6* allows interest on Special Assessment Receivables to be recognized when due, inasmuch as the amounts will usually offset each other approximately. If the amounts do not, interest is to be recognized in the period to which it relates.[11]

Service-Type Special Assessments

Governmental units provide many routine services that are financed from general revenues, such as street cleaning and snow plowing. Sometimes these services are provided at more frequent intervals or provided outside the normal service area. In these cases, the affected property owners may be assessed for the incremental services. Under *GASB Statement No. 6*, such assessment revenues and the related expenditures (expenses) for which the assessments were levied are to be accounted for and reported

> in the fund type that best reflects the nature of the transactions, usually the general fund, a special revenue fund, or an enterprise fund, giving consideration to the "number of funds" principle . . .[12]

INTERNAL SERVICE FUNDS

In this section and the next, we discuss the two proprietary types of funds—Internal Service Funds and Enterprise Funds, the accounting for which parallels that of commercial businesses. The primary distinction between an Internal Service Fund and an Enterprise Fund is that **the former provides services to departments within a governmental unit or to related governmental units, whereas the latter provides services primarily to the general public.**

Various departments of a governmental unit usually require common services. Each department may hire people to perform these services or it may contract with outside vendors. It is usually cheaper, however, for the governmental unit to establish one or more separate operations to provide these services to its various departments. Internal Service Funds account for each of these separate operations in a manner that charges the total cost of an operation to the various user departments. Internal Service Funds commonly are established for motor pool operations, central purchasing and stores, maintenance services, printing and reproduction services, and data-processing services.

The objective of an Internal Service Fund is to recover the total cost of an operation from billings to the various user departments. Generally,

[11] *GASB Statement No. 6*, par. 15.
[12] *GASB Statement No. 6*, par. 14.

billings are not set at levels intended to generate significant profits—only to recover costs or generate a slight profit. The accounting principles and procedures used in private industry also lend themselves to use with Internal Service Funds, even though billings are not made to independent parties. Accordingly, the accrual basis of accounting is used, depreciation expense is recorded, and any earnings are closed out at year-end to a Retained Earnings account. The following financial statements are used:

1. A balance sheet.
2. A statement of revenues, expenses, and changes in retained earnings (or equity).
3. A statement of changes in financial position.

Simply because all costs are recovered through billings, it does not automatically follow that the services are being provided at a lower cost than would be incurred if the Internal Service Fund were not used. This determination may only be made by comparing the total cost incurred with amounts that would have been incurred if the Internal Service Fund had not been established.

Establishment and Operation of Internal Service Funds

Internal Service Funds are normally established by contributions or advances from the General Fund. Contributions are credited to a Contributed Capital account (which is considered the equivalent of a private corporation's capital stock accounts). This type of interfund transfer is a **residual equity transfer;** accordingly, the General Fund debits its Fund Balance account. Advances are credited to an Advance from General Fund account (a liability account); the General Fund debits Advance to Internal Service Fund (a receivable account). Cash is then used to purchase materials, parts, supplies, and equipment as needed to fulfill the objectives of the fund.

A significant managerial accounting issue is that of developing a cost accounting system for charging the various user departments for the costs of the operation as reflected in the statement of revenues and expenses. When billings exceed costs, some or all of the retained earnings may need to be transferred to the General Fund. When billings are below cost, an accumulated deficit may be made up through additional charges to the user departments or a transfer from the General Fund. These interfund transfers must be substantively evaluated as to whether they are **operating transfers** or **residual equity transfers.** As discussed in the preceding chapter, **nonrecurring** or **nonroutine** transfers are considered **residual equity transfers,** and all other transfers are treated as **operating transfers.**

Illustration

JOURNAL ENTRIES AND FINANCIAL STATEMENTS

Assume Funn City established a Central Printing and Reproduction Fund during the fiscal year ended June 30, 19X2. Assumed transactions pertaining to the establishment and operation of the fund, along with related journal entries, are as follows:

1. **Establishment of the fund.** The fund was established by a contribution of $40,000 from the General Fund. The operation is conducted in a facility leased on a month-to-month basis from a privately owned company.

Cash	40,000	
Contributed Capital—General Fund		40,000
To record contribution from the General Fund.		

2. **Purchase and depreciation of equipment.** Equipment costing $30,000 was acquired on July 3, 19X1. The equipment is assigned a 10-year life and no salvage value.

Equipment	30,000	
Vouchers Payable		30,000
To record purchase of equipment.		

Operating Expenses	3,000	
Accumulated Depreciation		3,000
To record depreciation expense.		

3. **Purchase and use of supplies inventory.** Supplies costing $65,000 were acquired. A physical inventory taken on June 30, 19X2, was valued at $11,000.

Inventory of Supplies	65,000	
Vouchers Payable		65,000
To record purchase of supplies.		

Operating Expenses	54,000	
Inventory of Supplies		54,000
To record cost of supplies used.		

Note that inventories are accounted for in the same manner as in a private corporation.

4. **Incurrence of operating expenses and payment of liabilities.** Various operating expenses were incurred. Of these expenses, $7,000 represented charges from the city's electric utility (an Enterprise Fund).

Operating Expenses	67,000	
Vouchers Payable		60,000
Due to Electric Utility Fund		7,000
To record operating expenses.		

Vouchers Payable	138,000	
Due to Electric Utility Fund	5,000	
Cash		143,000
To record partial payment of liabilities.		

5. **Billings and collections.** Total billings to the city's various departments were $125,000. Of this amount, $9,000 pertained to services performed for the city's electric utility and $5,000 pertained to services performed for the city's central garage (an Internal Service Fund).

Due from General Fund	111,000	
Due from Electric Utility Fund	9,000	
Due from Central Garage Fund	5,000	
Operating Revenues		125,000
To record billing to departments for services rendered.		

Cash	110,000	
Due from General Fund		102,000
Due from Electric Utility Fund		5,000
Due from Central Garage Fund		3,000
To record partial collection of amounts due from other funds.		

Because closing entries would be identical to those made for a private enterprise, they are not shown.

Financial Statements. The balance sheet and operating statement that would be prepared for the fiscal year ended June 30, 19X2, are shown in Illustrations 21-8 and 21-9.

ENTERPRISE FUNDS

According to the GASB Codification, Enterprise Funds account for

> operations (a) that are financed and operated in a manner similar to private business enterprises—where the intent of the governing body is that

Illustration 21-8

FUNN CITY
Central Printing and Reproduction Fund
Balance Sheet
June 30, 19X2

Assets	
Cash	$ 7,000
Due from general fund	9,000
Due from electric utility fund	4,000
Due from central garage fund	2,000
Inventory of supplies	11,000
Equipment	30,000
Accumulated depreciation	(3,000)
Total Assets	$60,000
Liabilities and Fund Equity	
Vouchers payable	$17,000
Due to electric utility fund	2,000
Total Liabilities	$19,000
Contributed capital	$40,000
Retained earnings:	
Unreserved	1,000
Total Fund Equity	$41,000
Total Liabilities and Fund Equity	$60,000

Illustration 21-9

FUNN CITY
Central Printing and Reproduction Fund
Statement of Revenues, Expenses, and Changes in Retained Earnings
For the Year Ended June 30, 19X2

Operating revenues:		
Charges for services		$125,000
Operating expenses:		
Supplies	$54,000	
Salaries and wages	42,000	
Lease expense	18,000	
Utilities	7,000	
Depreciation	3,000	124,000
Net Income		$ 1,000
Retained Earnings, July 1, 19X1		–0–
Retained Earnings, June 30, 19X2		$ 1,000

Note: A statement of changes in financial position would also be prepared. Because it would be similar to that prepared for a private corporation, it is not shown here.

> the costs (expenses, including depreciation) of providing goods or services to the general public on a continuing basis be financed or recovered primarily through user charges; or (b) where the governing body has decided that periodic determination of revenues earned, expenses incurred, and/or net income is appropriate for capital maintenance, public policy, management control, accountability, or other purposes.[13]

The most common type of activity accounted for in an Enterprise Fund is the public utility providing water services, electricity, or natural gas. Other activities commonly accounted for in Enterprise Funds are off-street parking facilities, recreational facilities (principally golf courses and swimming pools), airports, hospitals, and public transit systems. The language of the GASB Codification is so broad that a governmental unit may establish an Enterprise Fund for almost any activity regardless of the extent of financing obtained from user charges. In practice, however, only a small percentage of governmental units use Enterprise Funds for activities that recover less than 50% of their costs from user charges, with public transit systems probably being the most common.

Because Enterprise Funds evaluate operations from a profit-and-loss perspective, the accounting principles and procedures used in private industry for comparable activities lend themselves to use with Enterprise Funds. Accordingly, the accrual basis of accounting is used, depreciation expense is recorded, and earnings are closed out at year-end to a Retained Earnings account. The following financial statements are prepared.

1. A balance sheet (which includes all the fund's assets and liabilities).
2. A statement of revenues, expenses, and changes in retained earnings (or equity).
3. A statement of changes in financial position (most commonly prepared using a cash flow format).

Although evaluated from a profit-and-loss perspective, the activities accounted for in Enterprise Funds are not engaged in to maximize profits, as in the private sector. Instead, the intent is to raise sufficient revenues to either (1) recover costs to break even, or (2) generate profits so that capital is effectively raised to finance expansion of operations.

Establishment and Expansion

Some of the more common ways of establishing an operation to be accounted for as an Enterprise Fund or expanding the operations of an existing Enterprise Fund are as follows:

1. **Contribution from the General Fund.** An interfund transfer from the General Fund is categorized as a **residual equity transfer.** Accordingly, the General Fund debits its Unreserved Fund Balance account, and the

[13]GASB Cod. sec. 1300.104.

Enterprise Fund credits an account called Contributed Capital. Contributed Capital accounts are similar to the capital stock accounts used by private corporations in that both reflect the value of assets contributed. Thus, Enterprise Funds do not use a Fund Balance account. Contributed Capital accounts are normally shown by the source of the contribution—for example, Contributed Capital from Municipality.

2. **Loan from the General Fund.** When the General Fund makes a loan, it debits an account called Advance to Enterprise Fund and credits Cash. The Enterprise Fund debits Cash and credits Advance from General Fund (a liability account). If interest is paid on the advance, then the Enterprise Fund has interest expense and the General Fund has interest revenue.
3. **Issuance of revenue bonds.** Revenue bonds are issued by an Enterprise Fund and are repayable, with interest, only from the earnings of the operations accounted for in the Enterprise Fund. (If the bonds also have a security interest in the fixed assets of the Enterprise Fund, then they are called mortgage revenue bonds.) Revenue bonds require accounting entries only in the Enterprise Fund. Bond indenture agreements frequently restrict the use of bond proceeds to specific capital projects; therefore, the bond proceeds are deposited in a separate checking account called, for example, Construction Cash. Using a separate account provides greater accounting control to ensure that the proceeds are spent only on authorized projects. The offsetting credit is to Revenue Bonds Payable.
4. **Issuance of general obligation bonds.** General obligation bonds are issued by a governmental unit with its full faith and backing. The proceeds are transferred to the Enterprise Fund, which uses the cash in accordance with the bond indenture agreement. General obligation bonds fall into the following two categories, based on the source of their repayment and payment of related interest:
   a. **Repayable from earnings of the enterprise.** When the governmental unit intends to repay the principal and related interest from Enterprise Fund earnings, the GASB Codification recommends that such debt be reflected as a liability in the Enterprise Fund.
   b. **Repayable from taxes and general revenues.** When the bonds and related interest are to be repaid from taxes and general revenues of the governmental unit, the bond liability is shown as a liability of the General Long-Term Debt Account Group. The Enterprise Fund treats the money received as a contribution and credits the Contributed Capital from Municipality account. Thus, a liability is not reflected in the Enterprise Fund.

Unique Features of Financial Statements

Because the financial statements of Enterprise Funds are similar to those of private enterprises engaged in comparable activities, typical transactions, related journal entries, and a complete set of illustrative financial statements are not presented. Instead, we discuss the unique features of Enterprise Fund financial statements and then illustrate the balance sheet for a water utility. (The balance sheet has certain unique classification features.)

1. **Contributed capital accounts.** As mentioned previously, Enterprise Funds use Contributed Capital accounts rather than capital stock accounts.
2. **Restricted assets.** Assets that are restricted as to use are shown separately. The most common examples are:
   a. **Construction cash.** Construction cash is not available for normal operating purposes and must be identified as usable only for its designated purpose — for example, expansion of plant.
   b. **Customer deposits.** For public utilities that require their customers to make deposits to ensure payment of final statements, the deposits constitute restricted assets that are not available for normal operations. When such deposits are invested in allowable investments, the investments should also be shown as restricted assets.
   c. **Debt-related accumulations.** Some bond indenture agreements require that certain amounts of cash provided from operations be set aside in separate accounts for retirement and servicing of bonds. In some cases, monies must be set aside to cover potential future losses.
3. **Appropriation of retained earnings.** When money relating to debt retirement and servicing of bonds has been set aside pursuant to bond indenture agreements, it may be necessary to appropriate a portion of retained earnings. The appropriation indicates that a portion of the retained earnings is not available for normal operations, internal expansion, or cash transfers to the General Fund; that is, cash that might otherwise be used for such purposes has been set aside for other purposes. This practice is at variance with customary practice in private industry, where showing the restricted assets separately is deemed sufficient disclosure.

   Technically, at any balance sheet date, the appropriation should equal only the amounts set aside to cover (a) future interest expense, (b) future principal payments (above and beyond amounts deemed to have been generated from operations to date), and (c) potential future losses.
4. **Depreciation expense.** For public utilities, depreciation expense is usually a major expense because of the large capital investment required. Depreciation expense is customarily shown on a separate line of the income statement.
5. **Income taxes.** Because governmental units do not pay income taxes, no income tax expense is shown in the statement of revenues and expenses.
6. **Payments to the General Fund.** Payments to the General Fund in lieu of taxes are **quasi-external transactions,** which we discussed in Chapter 20. Accordingly, such payments are recorded as **expenses** in the Enterprise Fund and as **revenues** in the General Fund. Payments to the General Fund not in lieu of taxes but for the purpose of financing General Fund expenditures are **operating transfers.** Accordingly, such payments are recorded as **operating transfers out** by the Enterprise Fund and as **operating transfers in** by the General Fund.
7. **Inverted balance sheet format.** Some governmental utilities use an inverted format for their balance sheets. Under this presentation, fixed

assets, long-term debt, and capital balances are shown before current items to emphasize the relative importance of the investment in fixed assets and the related financing sources. However, the conventional format, which places current items first, is still more prevalent than the inverted format. A utility fund balance sheet using the conventional format is shown in Illustration 21-10.

Illustration 21-10

FUNN CITY
Water Fund
Balance Sheet
June 30, 19X2

Assets

Current Assets:			
Cash		$ 330,000	
Customers' accounts receivable, less $185,000 allowance for uncollectible accounts		2,490,000	
Due from other funds		55,000	
Unbilled accounts receivable		670,000	
Inventories of materials and supplies		240,000	
Prepaid expenses		34,000	
Total Current Assets			$ 3,819,000
Restricted Assets:			
Customers' deposits:			
Cash	$ 23,000		
Investments	512,000	$ 535,000	
Revenue bond construction account:			
Cash		188,000	
Revenue bond current debt service account:			
Cash	$ 10,000		
Investments	1,130,000	1,140,000	
Revenue bond future debt service reserve account:			
Cash	$ 70,000		
Investments	1,200,000	1,270,000	
Total Restricted Assets			3,133,000
Property, plant, and equipment:			
Land		$ 1,511,000	
Buildings		4,477,000	
Improvements other than buildings		38,870,000	
Machinery and equipment		18,440,000	
Construction in process		2,900,000	
		$66,198,000	
Less: Accumulated depreciation		(12,450,000)	53,748,000
Total Assets			$60,700,000

Illustration 21-10 (continued)

FUNN CITY
Water Fund
Balance Sheet
June 30, 19X2

Liabilities and Fund Equity		
Current Liabilities (payable from current assets):		
Vouchers payable	$ 1,347,000	
Accrued wages and taxes	73,000	
Accrued interest payable on advance from municipality	26,000	
Advance from municipality	50,000	
Total		$ 1,496,000
Current Liabilities (payable from restricted assets):		
Customer deposits	$ 535,000	
Construction contracts payable	172,000	
Accrued revenue bond interest payable	400,000	
Revenue bonds payable	1,000,000	
Total		2,107,000
Total Current Liabilities		$ 3,603,000
Liabilities Payable after One Year:		
Revenue bonds payable	$28,000,000	
Advance from municipality	650,000	
Total		28,650,000
Total Liabilities		$32,253,000
Fund Equity:		
Contributions:		
Contributions from municipality	$ 5,000,000	
Contributions from subdividers	7,880,000	
Total Contributions		$12,880,000
Retained Earnings:		
Reserved for revenue bond future debt service reserve account	$ 1,270,000	
Unreserved	14,297,000	
Total Retained Earnings		15,567,000
Total Fund Equity		$28,447,000
Total Liabilities and Fund Equity		$60,700,000

AGENCY FUNDS AND TRUST FUNDS

Agency Funds and Trust Funds are created to account for money and property received but not owned.

Agency Funds

Agency Funds act as conduits for the transfer of money. Thus, they are purely custodial in nature. Money deposited with such a fund is generally disbursed shortly after receipt to authorized recipients, such as other governmental funds, other governmental units, and private corporations. Common examples of Agency Funds are tax collection funds and employee benefit funds.

1. **Tax collection funds:** When overlapping governmental units collect tax revenues from the same source, it is usually more practical and economical for only one of the governmental units to collect the taxes and then distribute the taxes collected to the various taxing authorities. Counties commonly collect all property taxes and then distribute amounts collected to the various cities, school districts, water districts, and any other special districts.
2. **Employee benefit funds:** When governmental employees have premiums on medical and dental insurance plans withheld from their paychecks, withholdings are deposited in such funds. Periodically, the governmental unit makes a lump-sum payment from these funds to an insurance company. (The alternative to using employee benefit funds is to set up liabilities in the appropriate funds.)

Agency Funds have no unusual operating characteristics or unique accounting issues. Usually, cash is the only asset, which is completely offset by liabilities to the authorized recipients. Thus, it has no Fund Balance account. Because cash disbursements are made frequently, on many occasions throughout the year these funds have no assets or liabilities at all.

Basis of Accounting and Financial Statements. Agency funds use the **modified accrual basis of accounting.** A balance sheet is presented. However, because Agency Funds do not have operating statements, a statement of changes in assets and liabilities is prepared to report the changes in the governmental unit's custodial responsibilities. In light of their simplicity, we do not illustrate journal entries and financial statements for Agency Funds beyond the journal entries shown in the following discussion of special assessment debt for which the governmental unit is not obligated in any manner.

Special Assessment Debt for Which the Government Is Not Obligated in Any Manner. In situations in which the governmental unit is not obligated in any manner to pay off special assessment debt in the event of a default by the property owners, *GASB Statement No. 6* requires that the collection activity pertaining to the special assessment receivables and the debt service activity pertaining to the special assessment debt be accounted for in an Agency Fund. The rationale here is that the governmental unit is acting merely as an agent for the assessed property owners and the debtholders. Accordingly, the special assessment debt is not reflected as a liability in the financial statements of the governmental unit. Nor is the special assessment levy accrued as a receivable in the governmental unit's financial statements. Only the cash collections of the levy and the disbursement of this money to the debtholders is recorded in the Agency Fund.[14]

To illustrate, the entries relating to the collection of the first annual installment of $100,000 due April 1, 19X2 from the property owners (the same information used earlier in the chapter in the discussion and illustration of special assessments) are as follows:

Cash	**100,000**	
Due to Special Assessment Bondholders		**100,000**
To record collection of first annual installment from property owners.		
Due to Special Assessment Bondholders	**100,000**	
Cash		**100,000**
To distribute money to bondholders.		

Because the bonds are not reported as a liability in the governmental unit's financial statements, *GASB Statement No. 6* requires:

> The source of funds in the capital projects fund should be identified by a description other than "bond proceeds," such as "contribution from property owners."[15]

Trust Funds

Most Trust Funds involve investing and using money in accordance with stipulated provisions of trust indenture agreements or statutes. Common examples of Trust Funds include the following:

1. **Public employee pension and retirement systems:** These Trust Funds account for employer and employee retirement contributions, the investment of such contributions, and the payments to retired employees.
2. **Nonexpendable Trust Funds:** These funds account for **endowments,** the money and property given to a governmental unit. The principal must be preserved intact; only the Trust Fund income may be expended or completely used in the course of operations.
3. **Expendable Trust Funds:** These funds also account for endowments. However, the principal does not have to be preserved intact; the trust principal and income may be expended or completely used in the course

[14]*GASB Statement No. 6*, par. 19.
[15]*GASB Statement No. 6*, par. 19.

of operations. State and federal grant programs that establish a continuing trustee relationship are to be accounted for in this type of fund under the requirements of the GASB Codification.

Classification for Accounting Measurement Purposes. The GASB Codification states:

> Each Trust Fund is classified for accounting measurement purposes as either a governmental fund or a proprietary fund. Expendable Trust Funds are accounted for in essentially the same manner as governmental funds. Nonexpendable Trust Funds and Pension Trust Funds are accounted for in essentially the same manner as proprietary funds.[16]

Nonexpendable Trust Funds and Pension Trust Funds would use the **accrual basis of accounting** and present operations using a statement of revenues, **expenses,** and changes in fund balance. On the other hand, Expendable Trust Funds would use the **modified accrual basis of accounting** and present operations using a statement of revenues, **expenditures,** and changes in fund balance.

Establishment and Operation. Public employee pension and retirement trust funds have the same operating characteristics and accounting issues as private pension and retirement plans that are funded with a trustee. Accordingly, journal entries and financial statements for these funds are not illustrated. As mentioned in the preceding chapter, a major shortcoming of many such trust funds is the lack of a sound actuarial basis in accounting for contributions to meet retirement payments.

No significant accounting issues exist for state and federal grant programs accounted for in **expendable Trust Funds.** As the creators of trusts, donors of **nonexpendable Trust Funds** have the right to specify in the trust agreement the accounting treatment to be accorded specific items. Such instructions prevail over generally accepted accounting principles. In the absence of specific accounting instructions, the governing authority is state statutes, which usually conflict with GAAP in several respects. For example, most state statutes require gains and losses on the sale of trust investments to be credited or charged, respectively, to trust principal rather than to trust income. For nonexpendable trusts, separate trust funds may be established for the principal and for the income generated by the principal. (The latter fund is essentially treated as a Special Revenue Fund.) We illustrate journal entries and financial statements for this type of fund next.

[16]GASB Cod. sec. 1300.102.

Illustration

JOURNAL ENTRIES AND FINANCIAL STATEMENTS

Assume that Funn City received $100,000 from a citizen, who specifies that the principal amount should remain intact. Earnings on the principal are to be used for park beautification projects. Assumed transactions pertaining to the establishment and operation of these funds, along with related journal entries, are as follows:

Endowment Principal Nonexpendable Trust Fund

Transaction or Event	Journal Entry		
The endowment principal fund is established.	Cash	100,000	
	Operating Revenues		100,000
Investment of cash.	Investments	96,000	
	Cash		96,000
Accrual of interest on investments.	Interest Receivable	8,000	
	Operating Revenues		8,000
Amortization of bond discount on investments.	Investments	700	
	Operating Revenues		700
Collection of interest on investments.	Cash	4,500	
	Interest Receivable		4,500
To reflect liability to Endowment Revenues Fund.	Operating Transfers Out	8,700	
	Due to Endowment Revenues Fund		8,700
To close operating revenues and operating transfer out control accounts.	Operating Revenues	108,700	
	Operating Transfers Out		8,700
	Fund Balance Reserved for Endowments		100,000
Payment of part of amount due to Endowment Revenues Fund.	Due to Endowment Revenues Fund	7,500	
	Cash		7,500

Endowment Revenues Expendable Trust Fund

Transaction or Event	Journal Entry		
To reflect revenues earned by and payable from Endowment Principal Fund.	Due from Endowment Principal Fund	8,700	
	Other Financing Sources		8,700
Receipt of part of amount due from Endowment Principal Fund.	Cash	7,500	
	Due from Endowment Principal Fund		7,500

Payment of administrative expenses.	Expenditures	300	
	Cash.........................		300
Costs incurred on park beautification projects are paid.	Expenditures	6,300	
	Cash.........................		6,300
To close other financing sources and expenditures into Fund Balance Reserved for Endowments.	Other Financing Sources	8,700	
	Expenditures		6,600
	Fund Balance Reserved for Endowments.....		2,100

Financial Statements. The balance sheets and statements of revenues, expenses, and changes in fund balance that would be prepared at June 30, 19X2, for each of these funds are shown in Illustrations 21-11, 21-12, and 21-13.

SUMMARY ILLUSTRATION

Illustration 21-14 presents a summary of the individual fund and account group statements required.

Illustration 21-11

FUNN CITY
Endowment Trust Funds
Balance Sheet
June 30, 19X2

	Principal Fund (Nonexpendable)	Revenue Fund (Expendable)
Assets:		
Cash	$ 1,000	$ 900
Due from endowment principal fund		1,200
Investments..	96,700	
Interest receivable	3,500	
Total Assets	$101,200	$2,100
Liabilities and Fund Equity:		
Due to endowment revenues fund	$ 1,200	
Fund balances:		
Reserved for endowments	$100,000	$2,100
Total Fund Balance	$100,000	$2,100
Total Liabilities and Fund Equity	$101,200	$2,100

Illustration 21-12

FUNN CITY Endowment Principal Fund (Nonexpendable) Statement of Revenues, Expenses, and Changes in Fund Balance For the Year Ended June 30, 19X2	
Operating revenues:	
Gifts	$100,000
Interest income	8,700
Total revenues	$108,700
Operating expenses	–0–
Income before Operating Transfers	$108,700
Operating transfers out	(8,700)
Net Income	$100,000
Fund Balance, July 1, 19X1	–0–
Fund Balance, June 30, 19X2	$100,000

Illustration 21-13

FUNN CITY Endowment Revenues Fund (Expendable) Statement of Revenues, Expenditures, and Changes in Fund Balance For the Year Ended June 30, 19X2	
Revenues	$ –0–
Expenditures:	
Park beautification	$ 6,300
Administrative	300
Total Expenditures	$ 6,600
Revenues under expenditures	$(6,600)
Other Financing Sources:	
Operating transfer in	8,700
Excess of Revenues and Other Financing Sources over Expenditures	$ 2,100
Fund Balance, July 1, 19X1	–0–
Fund Balance, June 30, 19X2	$ 2,100

Illustration 21-14
Summary of Required Individual Fund and Account Group Financial Statements (Level 3 of the Financial Reporting Pyramid in Illustration 20-2).

		Statement Title						
Fund Type or Account Group	Basis of Accounting	Balance Sheet	Revenues, Expenditures, and Changes in Fund Balance	Revenues, Expenses, and Changes in Retained Earnings/ Fund Balance	Changes in Financial Position	Changes in Assets and Liabilities	General Fixed Assets	General Long-Term Debt
Government Funds:								
General Fund[a]	Modified accrual	X	X					
Special Revenue Funds[a] ...	Modified accrual	X	X					
Capital Projects Funds[a]	Modified accrual	X	X					
Debt Service Funds	Modified accrual	X	X					
Fiduciary Funds:								
Trust Funds—								
Expendable	Modified accrual	X	X					
Nonexpendable	Accrual	X[b]		X	X			
Pension trusts	Accrual	X[b]		X	X			
Agency		X				X		
Proprietary Funds:								
Enterprise Funds	Accrual	X[b]		X	X			
Internal Service Funds.....	Accrual	X[b]		X	X			
Account Groups:								
General Fixed Assets	N/A						X	
General Long-Term Debt..	N/A							X

Note: Budgetary comparisons must be made for funds for which an annual budget has been adopted. For funds *that budget in accordance with GAAP*, the budgetary comparison is made in the individual fund statement of revenues, expenditures, and changes in fund balance. For funds *that do not budget in accordance with GAAP*, the individual fund operating statement may not include budgetary data. Instead, a "schedule" comparing the legally adopted budget with the actual data on the budgetary basis is required in addition to the individual fund operating statement.

[a]Encumbrance accounting is normally used.
[b]The balance sheet would include fixed assets and long-term liabilities of this fund.

Review Questions

1. When would a Special Revenue Fund be used instead of the General Fund?
2. What is the relationship between a Capital Projects Fund and the General Fixed Assets Account Group?
3. Does the General Fixed Assets Account Group include all fixed assets of a governmental unit? Why or why not?
4. What is the relationship between the Debt Service Funds and the General Long-Term Debt Account Group.
5. What is the difference in meaning of the term *long-term debt* as used in the General Long-Term Debt Account Group and as used in private industry?
6. Does the General Long-Term Debt Account Group include all long-term debt? Why or why not?
7. What determines whether Special Assessment Receivables are recorded in a Debt Service Fund or in an Agency Fund?
8. Which fund would be used to account for construction activity to be financed from a special assessment to certain property owners?
9. What is the distinction between an Agency Fund and a Trust Fund?
10. What are the two types of Trust Funds?
11. In what way are Enterprise Funds and Internal Service Funds similar to commercial operations?
12. What significance may be attributed to the fact that the billings of an Internal Service Fund exceed its costs and expenses?

Discussion Cases

DC 21-1

Expenditure Recognition on Construction Contract

On January 1, 19X1, the city council of Centersville approved the construction of a new civic center. It immediately signed a construction contract having a fixed price of $10,000,000. The terms of the contract follow:

1. A payment of $2,000,000 is to be made to the contractor at the time of the signing. (The city made the payment.)
2. Progress billings are to be made each December 20 based on the percentage of completion times $7,000,000.
3. Progress payments are to be made ten days after bills are submitted.
4. Upon completion of the project, the final payment of $1,000,000 is to be made.

On December 20, 19X1, the contractor submitted a progress billing for $2,800,000 (40% of $7,000,000). The city paid this billing on December 30, 19X1.

Required:
What amount should the city report for expenditures in its Capital Projects Fund for 19X1?

Exercises

E 21-1

Differentiation of Types of Funds: Activities

1. Recreational facilities run by a governmental unit and financed on a user-charge basis most likely would be accounted for in which fund?
   a. General Fund
   b. Trust Fund
   c. Enterprise Fund
   d. Capital Projects Fund
   e. Special Revenue Fund
2. The activities of a municipal golf course that receives most of its revenues from a special tax levy should be accounted for in which fund?
   a. Capital Projects Fund
   b. Internal Service Fund
   c. Special Revenue Fund
   d. General Fund
   e. Enterprise Fund
3. A data-processing center established by a governmental unit to service all agencies within the unit should be accounted for in which fund?
   a. Capital Projects Fund
   b. Internal Service Fund
   c. Agency Fund
   d. Trust Fund
   e. Enterprise Fund
4. The activities of a municipal employees' retirement and pension system should be recorded in which fund?
   a. General Fund
   b. Special Revenue Fund
   c. Debt Service Fund
   d. Agency Fund
   e. Trust Fund
5. Receipts from taxes levied to finance sidewalk improvements would be accounted for in which fund?
   a. Special Revenue Fund
   b. General Fund
   c. Internal Service Fund
   d. Capital Projects Fund
   e. both (c) and (d)
6. A city collects property taxes for the benefit of the local sanitary, park, and school districts and periodically remits collections to these units. This activity should be accounted for in a(n)
   a. Agency Fund.
   b. General Fund.
   c. Internal Service Fund.
   d. Special Revenue Fund.
   e. none of the above

(AICPA adapted)

E 21-2

Differentiation of Types of Funds: Activities

1. The operations of a public library receiving the majority of its support from property taxes levied for that purpose should be accounted for in a(n)
   a. General Fund.
   b. Special Revenue Fund.
   c. Enterprise Fund.
   d. Internal Service Fund.
   e. none of the above
2. The proceeds of a federal grant to help finance the future construction of an adult training center should be recorded in a(n)
   a. General Fund.
   b. Special Revenue Fund.
   c. Capital Projects Fund.
   d. Internal Service Fund.
   e. none of the above
3. The receipts from a special tax levy to retire and pay interest on general obligation bonds issued to finance the construction of a new city hall should be recorded in a
   a. Debt Service Fund.
   b. Capital Projects Fund.
   c. General Fund.
   d. Special Revenue Fund.
   e. none of the above
4. The lump-sum monthly remittance to an insurance company for hospital-surgical insurance premiums collected as payroll deductions from employees should be recorded in a(n)
   a. General Fund.
   b. Agency Fund.
   c. Special Revenue Fund.
   d. Internal Service Fund.
   e. none of the above
5. The activities of a central motor pool that supplies and services vehicles for the use of municipal employees on official business should be accounted for in a(n)
   a. Agency Fund.
   b. General Fund.
   c. Internal Service Fund.
   d. Special Revenue Fund.
   e. none of the above
6. To provide for the retirement of general obligation bonds, a city invests a portion of its general revenue receipts in marketable securities. This investment activity should be accounted for in a(n)
   a. Trust Fund.
   b. Enterprise Fund.
   c. General Long-Term Debt Account Group.
   d. Special Revenue Fund.
   e. none of the above

(AICPA adapted)

E 21-3

Understanding the Interrelationship among the Funds and Account Groups for Fixed Assets

1. A new fire truck was purchased out of a city's General Fund. An entry is also required in a(n)
   a. Internal Service Fund.
   b. Capital Projects Fund.
   c. Special Revenue Fund.
   d. General Fixed Assets Account Group.
   e. none of the above
2. A city sells an unused fire station that previously was accounted for in its General Fixed Assets Account Group. An entry is also required in a
   a. General Fund.
   b. Special Revenue Fund.
   c. Trust Fund.
   d. Debt Service Fund.
   e. none of the above
3. A city built a new city hall, the construction of which was accounted for in a Capital Projects Fund. Entries relating to the new building are also required in a(n)
   a. General Fixed Assets Account Group.
   b. Enterprise Fund.
   c. Internal Service Fund.
   d. General Fund.
   e. none of the above
4. A city made certain public improvements from a special assessment. Entries relating to the improvements are optional in a(n)
   a. General Fixed Assets Account Group.
   b. Internal Service Fund.
   c. Enterprise Fund.
   d. Capital Projects Fund.
   e. none of the above
5. A city's water utility, which is accounted for in an Enterprise Fund, acquired some new fixed assets. An entry is also required in a(n)
   a. General Fixed Assets Account Group.
   b. Internal Service Fund.
   c. General Fund.
   d. Agency Fund.
   e. none of the above
6. A city's central purchasing and stores department is properly accounted for in an Internal Service Fund. When fixed assets are acquired for this department, accounting entries are required in a(n)
   a. General Fixed Assets Account Group.
   b. Internal Service Fund.
   c. General Fixed Assets Account Group and an Internal Service Fund.
   d. General Fund and the General Fixed Assets Account Group.
   e. Enterprise Fund.
   f. Enterprise Fund and the General Fixed Assets Account Group.

E 21-4

Preparing Journal Entries: Understanding the Interrelationship among the Funds and Account Groups for Fixed Assets

Required:

For each transaction discussed in Exercise 21-3, prepare the journal entry or entries (without amounts) required in the applicable funds and account groups.

E 21-5

Understanding the Interrelationship of the Funds and Account Groups for Long-Term Debt

1. A transaction in which a municipal electric utility issues bonds (to be repaid from its own operations) requires accounting recognition in a(n)
   a. General Fund.
   b. Debt Service Fund.
   c. Enterprise and Debt Service Funds.
   d. Enterprise Fund, a Debt Service Fund, and the General Long-Term Debt Account Group.
   e. none of the above
2. The liability for general obligation bonds issued for the benefit of a municipal electric company and serviced by its earnings should be recorded in a(n)
   a. Enterprise Fund.
   b. General Fund.
   c. Enterprise Fund and the General Long-Term Debt Account Group.
   d. Enterprise Fund and disclosed in a footnote in the statement of General Long-Term Debt.
   e. none of the above
3. The liability for special assessment bonds that carry a secondary pledge of a municipality's general credit should be recorded in a(n)
   a. Debt Service Fund.
   b. General Long-Term Debt Account Group.
   c. Agency Fund.
   d. Only disclosure would be made in a footnote in the statement of General Long-Term Debt.
   e. none of the above
4. The liability for special assessment bonds where the municipality is not obligated in any manner in the event of default by the property owners should be recorded in a(n)
   a. Debt Service Fund.
   b. General Long-Term Debt Account Group.
   c. Agency Fund.
   d. Only disclosures would be made in a footnote in the statement of General Long-Term Debt.
   e. none of the above
5. A transaction in which a municipality issues general obligation serial bonds to finance the construction of a fire station requires accounting recognition in the
   a. General Fund.
   b. Capital Projects and General Funds.

c. Capital Projects Fund and the General Long-Term Debt Account Group.
d. General Fund and the General Long-Term Debt Account Group.
e. none of the above

6. Several years ago, a city established a sinking fund to retire an issue of general obligation bonds. This year, the city made a $50,000 contribution to the sinking fund from general revenues and realized $15,000 in revenue from sinking fund securities. The bonds due this year were retired. These transactions require accounting recognition in the
   a. General Fund.
   b. Debt Service Fund and the General Long-Term Debt Account Group.
   c. Debt Service Fund, the General Fund, and the General Long-Term Debt Account Group.
   d. Capital Projects Fund, a Debt Service Fund, the General Fund, and the General Long-Term Debt Account Group.
   e. none of the above

(AICPA adapted)

E 21-6 Preparing Journal Entries: Understanding the Interrelationship among the Funds and Account Groups for Long-Term Debt

Required:

For each of the transactions discussed in Exercise 21-5, prepare the journal entry or entries (without amounts) required in the applicable funds and account groups.

E 21-7 Determining Financial Statements, Basis of Accounting, and Accounts Used

1. Which financial statement is recommended for the four governmental funds?
   a. a statement of revenues, expenses, and changes in retained earnings
   b. a statement of costs of providing services
   c. a statement of cash receipts and disbursements
   d. a statement of revenues, expenditures, encumbrances, and changes in fund balance
   e. a statement of revenues, expenditures, and changes in fund balance
   f. a statement of changes in financial position
2. Which financial statement is recommended for proprietary funds?
   a. a statement of revenues, expenses, and changes in retained earnings
   b. a statement of costs of providing services
   c. a statement of cash receipts and disbursements
   d. a statement of revenues, expenditures, encumbrances, and changes in fund balance
   e. a statement of revenues, expenditures, and changes in fund balance
   f. a statement of changes in financial position
3. A statement of changes in financial position is prepared for which fund?
   a. General Fund
   b. Special Revenue Fund
   c. Capital Projects Fund

d. Debt Service Fund
e. none of the above

4. Which of the following funds or account groups uses the accrual basis of accounting?
   a. Agency Fund
   b. Special Revenue Fund
   c. General Long-Term Debt Account Group
   d. Debt Service Fund
   e. Internal Service Fund
5. Which of the following funds uses the modified accrual basis of accounting?
   a. Enterprise Fund
   b. Debt Service Fund
   c. Internal Service Fund
   d. Nonexpendable Trust Fund
   e. none of the above
6. Which of the following funds records depreciation expense?
   a. Capital Projects Fund
   b. Agency Fund
   c. Special Revenue Fund
   d. Internal Service Fund
   e. Debt Service Fund
   f. none of the above
7. Which of the following funds does not have a fund balance?
   a. Agency Fund
   b. Special Revenue Fund
   c. Internal Service Fund
   d. Capital Projects Fund
   e. none of the above
8. An Expenditures account does not appear in which fund?
   a. Capital Projects Fund
   b. Debt Service Fund
   c. Special Revenue Fund
   d. Internal Service Fund
   e. none of the above
9. Encumbrances accounts would not be used in which of the following funds?
   a. Special Revenue Fund.
   b. Capital Projects Fund.
   c. Internal Service Fund.
   d. none of the above

E 21-8

Preparing Journal Entries Relating to General Long-Term Debt

The following transactions occurred during Bondsville County's fiscal year ended June 30, 19X2:

1. On October 1, 19X1, general obligation term bonds having a face value of $1,000,000 and an interest rate of 8% were issued. Interest is payable semi-

annually on April 1 and October 1. The $980,000 proceeds were used for the construction of a new courthouse.

2. On January 1, 19X2, the county transferred $16,000 from the General Fund to a Debt Service Fund for sinking fund purposes.
3. The Debt Service Fund immediately invested this money, and by June 30, 19X2, the county's fiscal year-end, $1,000 of interest had been earned on these investments.
4. On March 27, 19X2, $40,000 was transferred from the General Fund to the Debt Service Fund to meet the first interest payment.
5. On April 1, 19X2, the Debt Service Fund made the required interest payment of $40,000. (A fiscal agent is not used.)

Required:
Prepare the journal entries that would be made in all of the appropriate funds and account groups for these transactions.

Problems

P 21-1

Capital Projects Fund

On August 1, 19X2, the city of Atlantis authorized the issuance of 6% general obligation serial bonds having a face value of $8,000,000. The proceeds will be used to construct a new convention center that is estimated to cost $8,300,000. Over the last several years, the Unreserved Fund Balance account in the city's General Fund has been approximately $300,000 greater than is prudently needed. Accordingly, this excess accumulation will be used to pay for the remainder of the construction cost. A Capital Projects Fund, designated the Convention Center Construction Fund, was established to account for this project.

The following transactions occurred during the fiscal year ended June 30, 19X3:

1. On August 4, 19X2, a payment of $180,000 was made out of the General Fund to Ace Architectural Company. This payment was for the design of the convention center. (This $180,000 for architect's fees was part of the $8,300,000 total estimated cost of the Convention Center.) The Expenditures account was charged on the books of the General Fund.
2. On September 5, 19X2, a construction contract was entered into with Nautilus Construction Company in the amount of $8,100,000.
3. On October 2, 19X2, the city deposited $120,000 ($300,000 – $180,000 paid to the architect) into the Convention Center Construction Fund.
4. On December 1, 19X1, one-half of the authorized bond issue was sold at 101. The bond premium was properly transferred to a Debt Service Fund.
5. On April 30, 19X3, Nautilus submitted a billing of $2,100,000 for work completed to date. Only $1,900,000 was paid.
6. On June 1, 19X3, the first seminannual interest payment on the bonds was made. (Principal payments are deferred until December 1, 19X4.)

7. On June 20, 19X3, the city was awarded an irrevocable federal grant totaling $1,000,000 to help finance the cost of the convention center. Payment will be received within 60 days. The city had applied for this grant in May 19X1, with slight expectation of receiving it. Accordingly, it obtained authorization for a bond issue of $8,000,000 instead of $7,000,000.

Additional Information:

8. The city intends to use a Special Revenue Fund to account for the operations of the convention center upon completion of the project.
9. The city does not record budgets for capital projects in Capital Projects Funds.

Required:

1. For the above transactions, prepare the entries that should be made in the Convention Center Construction Fund for the year ended June 30, 19X3. (Also, show the appropriate General Fund entry for items 1 and 3.)
2. Prepare the appropriate closing entries at June 30, 19X3.
3. Prepare a balance sheet at June 30, 19X3.
4. Prepare a statement of revenues, expenditures, and changes in fund balance for the year ended June 30, 19X3.

P 21-2

Debt Service Fund and General Long-Term Debt Account Group (Journal Entries Only)

The city of Promises had the following transactions during its fiscal year ended June 30, 19X4.

1. General obligation serial bonds having a face value of $100,000 matured during the year and were redeemed. (Money was transferred from the General Fund to the Debt Service Fund to redeem this debt.)
2. Total interest paid on serial bonds during the year was $80,000. (Money was transferred from the General Fund to the Debt Service Fund to pay this interest.)
3. General obligation term bonds having a face value of $500,000 were issued for $505,000. The proceeds are for construction of a new fire station, which is expected to cost $500,000. The $5,000 premium, which will not be used for construction purposes, was properly transferred to the Debt Service Fund.
4. A cash transfer of $10,000 was made from the General Fund to a Debt Service Fund in connection with a sinking fund requirement pertaining to general obligation term bonds.
5. Special assessment bonds having a face value of $400,000 were issued at par. The proceeds are for construction of residential street improvements. (The city is liable for this debt in the event of default by the assessed property owners.)
6. General obligation serial bonds having a face value of $800,000 were issued at par. The proceeds will provide working capital for the General Fund.

Required:
Prepare journal entries for each of the above transactions in all appropriate funds or account groups. Use the following headings for your workpaper:

Transaction Number	Journal Entries	Amount Dr.	Amount Cr.	Fund or Account Group

P 21-3 Debt Service Fund: Preparing a Statement of Revenues, Expenditures, and Changes in Fund Balance from Selected Information—No Journal Entries Involved

The following information relating to the city of Debtville's Debt Service Fund is provided for the year ended December 31, 19X2:

Interest:	
Interest owed at December 31, 19X1 (none past due)	$ 160,000
Interest payments made at due dates during 19X2	700,000
Interest owed at December 31, 19X2 (none past due)	130,000
Cash received from the General Fund to pay interest	700,000
Property Taxes:	
Property tax assessments made in 19X2 (to be collected by the Debt Service Fund)	566,000
Property tax collections by the Debt Service Fund	550,000
Allowance for uncollectible accounts:	
December 31, 19X1	4,000
December 31, 19X2	5,000
Accounts written off during 19X2 (from 19X1 assessments)	2,000
Property tax receivables:	
December 31, 19X1	26,000[a]
December 31, 19X2	40,000[b]
Long-Term Debt:	
Cash received from the General Fund to pay for the retirement of debt principal	400,000
General long-term debt that matured during 19X2 and was paid off	1,000,000
Miscellaneous:	
Gain on sale of investments	11,000
Interest on investments	75,000
Fund balance, December 31, 19X1 (all reserved for debt service)	621,000

[a]At December 31, 19X1, the entire net realizable amount of the property tax receivables was expected to be collected within 60 days, the time period the city uses in determining whether revenues are "available."

[b]At December 31, 19X2, $25,000 of the net realizable amount of the property tax receivables are expected to be collected after 60 days.

Required:

Prepare a statement of revenues, expenditures, and changes in fund balance for 19X2. (Hint: Use T-accounts for calculations pertaining to property tax revenues.)

P 21-4 Special Assessments

On January 2, 19X5, Pine City's council officially approved a three-year special assessment project for a street-improvement program. Approval of this project was based on the following information:

1. Issuance of $9,000,000 serial bonds at face amount, as follows:

Amount	Rate	Maturity Date
$2,000,000	7%	December 31, 19X5
3,000,000	7%	December 31, 19X6
4,000,000	7%	December 31, 19X7

2. Interest expense on the serial bonds for 19X5, 19X6, and 19X7 is estimated at $630,000, $490,000, and $280,000, respectively.
3. Assessments of $9,000,000 will be levied, payable over a three-year period by property owners benefitting from the project, with $3,000,000 due on June 30, 19X5, 19X6, and 19X7, respectively. Interest, to be charged at the simple rate of 10% on the deferred installments, from June 30, 19X5, to the due dates, is expected to be as follows:

Due Dates	Interest
January 2, 19X6	$300,000
June 30, 19X6	300,000
January 2, 19X7	150,000
June 30, 19X7	150,000

4. Signing of a construction contract for a fixed fee of $10,500,000, with progress billings based on the percentage of completion times $10,000,000 to be computed every November 30, payable on December 15. Completion estimates are 35% at November 30, 19X5, an additional 35% on November 30, 19X6, and the final 30% on November 30, 19X7. Sixty days after completion, the remaining $500,000 is to be paid.
5. Investment of temporary funds in certificates of deposit, at an estimated interest rate of 10%.
6. Interest revenue on the certificates of deposit for 19X5, 19X6, and 19X7 is estimated at $1,000,000, $850,000, and $450,000, respectively.
7. The city is legally obligated to assume all or part of the debt in the event of default by the assessed property owners.
8. For revenue recognition purposes, Pine City considers revenues as "available" when the funds are collectible within 60 days of year-end.

During 19X5, Pine City had the following transactions and adjustments relating to this street-improvement project:

1. January 2: Signing of construction contract.
2. January 2: Issuance of serial bonds and receipt of $9,000,000 proceeds.
3. January 2: Levy of special assessments.
4. January 2: Purchase of $9,000,000 certificate of deposit, due December 31, 19X5, yielding interest of $900,000.
5. June 30: Collection of $3,000,000 on current portion of special assessments.
6. July 1: Purchase of $3,000,000 certificate of deposit, due December 31, 19X5, yielding interest of $120,000.
7. November 30: Receipt of progress invoice from contractor for a payment of $4,000,000, indicating 40% completion.

8. December 20: Payment of $50,000 to contractor for removal of old street signs, erroneously omitted from contract.
9. December 31: Collection of $12,000,000 principal and $1,020,000 interest on certificates of deposit.
10. December 31: Payment of contractor's November 30 progress invoice.
11. December 31: Payment of $2,000,000 matured serial bonds, plus interest on the $2,000,000.
12. December 31: Adjusting entries for interest payable on serial bonds and interest receivable on special assessments.

Required:

1. In chronological order, prepare journal entries pertaining to the foregoing transactions and adjustments. Indicate the appropriate fund or account group in which the entry or entries would be made.
2. Prepare year-end closing entries where appropriate.

(AICPA adapted)

P 21-5

Agency Fund (Resulting from a Special Assessment)

On January 2, 19X1, the city council of Walkerville approved a six-year special assessment project for a sidewalk improvement program. Transactions during 19X1 and other information pertaining to this project follow:

1. Jan. 2, 19X1: 10% serial bonds having a face amount of $500,000 were issued at their face amount. (The city is not obligated in any manner in the event of default.)
2. Jan. 2, 19X1: A construction contract having a fixed price of $600,000 was signed.
3. Jan. 2, 19X1: Special assessments were levied totaling $660,000, of which $60,000 is expected to be uncollectible. Beginning July 1, 19X1, interest at 10% is to be charged on the deferred installments of $550,000, of which $110,000 is due annually each July 1 beginning July 1, 19X2, along with accrued interest.
5. July 1, 19X1: The current portion of the assessment ($110,000) became due and collections of $101,000 were made.
6. July 1, 19X1: A disbursement of $100,000 was made to the Capital Projects Fund.

Required:
Prepare the entries required in the Agency Fund for 19X1.

P 21-6

Internal Service Fund

The city of Paradise had the following transactions relating to its newly established Central Printing Internal Service Fund during the fiscal year ended June 30, 19X1:

1. A contribution of $100,000 was received from the General Fund to establish the Internal Service Fund.

2. Machinery and equipment costing $80,000 was purchased and paid for by the Internal Service Fund. These items were placed in service on January 4, 19X1, and have an estimated useful life of 10 years. (All machinery and equipment in the General Fixed Assets Account Group is depreciated using a 10-year life.)
3. Materials and supplies of $18,000 were ordered using purchase orders. For $14,000 of these purchase orders, the materials and supplies were received at a cost of $14,300. Payments totaling $9,500 were made on these billings.
4. Total billings for the year were $60,000. Of this amount, $7,000 was billed to the city's water utility, which is operated in an Enterprise Fund. The remaining amount was billed to various departments in the General Fund. Of these billings, $32,000 was collected from the General Fund and $5,500 was collected from the water utility.
5. Salaries and wages totaling $49,000 were paid.
6. The city's electric utility, which is operated as an Enterprise Fund, billed the Internal Service Fund $900. Of this amount, $700 was paid.
7. Materials and supplies on hand at June 30, 19X1 were counted and costed at $3,800.
8. A subsidy of $5,000 was received from the General Fund near the end of the fiscal year in recognition of the fact that the first year of operations was a start-up year at a loss. In addition, $10,000 was received from the General Fund near the end of the fiscal year as a tempory advance to be repaid (without interest) during the following fiscal year.

Required:

1. Prepare the appropriate journal entries for the above transactions in the Internal Service Fund.
2. Prepare the year-end closing entry.
3. Prepare a balance sheet at June 30, 19X1.
4. Prepare a statement of revenues, expenses, and changes in retained earnings for the year ended June 30, 19X1.

P 21-7

Enterprise Fund (Journal Entries Only)

The following activities pertain to Enterprise Funds:

1. City A contributed $1,000,000 to a newly established Enterprise Fund formed to provide off-street parking facilities.
2. City B established an Enterprise Fund to account for its municipal golf course, which would be built using the proceeds of $3,000,000 of general obligation bonds and be repaid from golf course earnings. The bonds were issued at a premium of $50,000.
3. City C established an Enterprise Fund to account for its municipal swimming pools to be built using the proceeds of $2,000,000 of general obligation serial bonds to be repaid from taxes and general revenues. The bonds were issued at a discount of $25,000.
4. City D operates a water utility in an Enterprise Fund. To expand operations, the city issued $5,000,000 of revenue bonds at a premium of $40,000.
5. City E operates an electric utility in an Enterprise Fund, which made a $500,000 payment in lieu of taxes to the city's General Fund.

6. City F operates an airport in an Enterprise Fund, which made a $600,000 payment to the city to finance General Fund expenditures.
7. City G discontinued its municipal golf course, which was accounted for in an Enterprise Fund. The land was sold to a residential home developer. All outstanding liabilities were paid, and the remaining $750,000 cash was disbursed to the General Fund. (The Enterprise Fund had $300,000 in its Capital Contribution from Municipality account and $450,000 in its Retained Earnings account just before the disbursement.)
8. City H operates a public transit system in an Enterprise Fund. The transit system usually recovers approximately 60% of its costs and expenses from user charges. During the current year, the Enterprise Fund received an $800,000 subsidy from the General Fund.
9. City I operates an electric utility in an Enterprise Fund. During the year, the city redeemed $500,000 of its electric utility's revenue bonds.
10. City J operates a gas utility in an Enterprise Fund. During the year, the city redeemed $1,000,000 of its general obligation serial bonds, which were issued many years ago to finance expansion of the gas utility. The bonds were to be repaid from taxes and general revenues.

Required:

For each transaction, prepare the necessary journal entries for all the funds and account groups involved. Use the following headings for your workpaper:

Transaction Number	Journal Entries	Amount		Fund or Account Group
		Dr.	Cr.	

P 21-8

COMPREHENSIVE (All Funds and Account Groups) Preparing Journal Entries for Typical Transactions

The village of Starville had the following transactions for the year ended December 31, 19X3.

1. Property taxes were levied in the amount of $500,000. Of this amount, $100,000 is a special levy for the servicing and retirement of serial bonds issued 15 years ago for the construction of a fire station. It was estimated that 2% of the total amount levied would be uncollectible. An Agency Fund is used.
2. The village received its share of state sales taxes on gasoline. The $33,000 share can be used only for street improvements and maintenance. During the year, the village spent $31,000 for this purpose. (The village used its own work force.)
3. On March 31, 19X3, general obligation bonds bearing interest at 6% were issued in the face amount of $500,000. The proceeds were $503,000, of which $500,000 was authorized to be spent on a new library. The remaining $3,000 was set aside for the eventual retirement of the debt. The bonds are due in 20 years, with interest to be paid on March 31 and September 30 of each year.
4. A construction contract in the amount of $490,000 was entered into with Booker Construction Company to build the new library. Billings of $240,000 were submitted, of which $216,000 was paid.

5. On September 30, 19X3, the interest due on the library bonds was paid using the money from the General Fund.
6. On November 30, 19X3, the fire station serial bonds referred to in (1) above were paid off ($60,000), along with interest due at that time ($36,000).
7. On July 31, 19X1, 8% special assessment bonds having a face value of $90,000 were issued at par; the proceeds will be used for a street lighting project. Interest is paid annually each July 31. (The village has pledged to pay off these bonds in the event the assessed property owners default.)
8. Assessments were levied totaling $100,000 for the residential street lighting project; the village contributed $7,000 out of the General Fund as its share. Of the $100,000 assessed, $10,000 was collected, with the remaining $90,000 to be collected in succeeding years.
9. A General Fund transfer of $8,000 was made to establish an Internal Service Fund to provide for a central purchasing and stores function.
10. During the year, the Internal Service Fund purchased various supplies at a cost of $6,500. Of this amount, $4,400 was billed to the city's various departments at $5,500.
11. A Capital Projects Fund having a fund balance of $2,000 was terminated. The cash was sent to the General Fund as required.
12. A local resident donated marketable securities with a market value of $80,000 (the resident's cost was $44,000) under the terms of a trust agreement. The principal is to remain intact. Earnings on the principal are to be used for college scholarships to the needy students. Revenues earned during 19X3 totaled $7,500, of which $7,000 was disbursed for scholarships.
13. The village water utility billed the General Fund $6,600.
14. A new fire truck costing $22,000 was ordered, received, and paid for. The old fire truck (which cost $8,000) was sold for $1,500.

Required:
For each transaction, prepare the necessary journal entries for all of the appropriate funds and account groups involved. Use the following headings for your workpaper:

Transaction Number	Account Titles and Explanation	Amount Dr.	Amount Cr.	Fund or Account Group

P 21-9

Additional Requirement for Problem 20-9

Required:
Prepare the entries that would be made in the other funds and account groups in Problem 20-9 to account properly for the items that should not be accounted for in the General Fund.

22

Accounting for Nonprofit Organizations

AN OVERVIEW OF ACCOUNTING FOR NONPROFIT ORGANIZATIONS

In Chapters 20 and 21 we were concerned with one type of nonprofit organization—governmental units. In this chapter we focus on the remaining types of nonprofit organizations, which increasingly represent a significant segment of the U.S. economy. Billions of dollars, representing voluntary contributions and millions of hours of donated services, flow into these organizations annually. We consider the following organizations:

1. Colleges and universities
2. Hospitals
3. Voluntary health and welfare organizations (for example, United Way and the American Heart Association)
4. Other nonprofit organizations (for example, labor unions, political parties, private foundations, professional and religious organizations)

We do not include in our discussion the types of entities that operate essentially as commercial enterprises for the direct economic benefit of members or shareholders—for example, employee benefit and pension plans, mutual insurance companies, mutual banks, credit unions, trusts, and farm cooperatives.

Many nonprofit organizations have grown in size and influence and have developed from individually operated entities to organizations of national and international scope. Along with this growth has come an increasing awareness of the nature and importance of the roles of nonprofit organizations and the need for improved accounting standards and reporting practices. Many constituencies need full knowledge of an organization's activities and how well the organization is meeting its goals. **Constituencies** include governing boards, creditors, donors and prospective donors, granting agencies, oversight committees of federal, state, and local legislative bodies, regulatory governmental agencies, national headquarters of organizations with local chapters, and accrediting agencies.

In this chapter, we introduce the generally accepted accounting principles that apply specifically to nonprofit organizations. In addition to the individual treatment of selected types of nonprofit organizations, our presentation compares the various types of nonprofit organizations, emphasizing differences in fund structure, revenue recognition, investment valuation, and the content and format of financial statements.

THE DEVELOPMENT OF GENERALLY ACCEPTED ACCOUNTING PRINCIPLES

Early Development

Statements of generally accepted accounting principles promulgated by the Financial Accounting Standards Board (FASB) and its predecessor bodies generally have applied only to business enterprises. For example, *Accounting Research Bulletin No. 43*, which is a 1953 restatement and revision of all Accounting Research Bulletins issued up to that time and which is still in force, states that

> except where there is a specific statement of a different intent by the committee, its opinions and recommendations are directed primarily to the business enterprises organized for profit.[1]

The early development of accounting principles specifically for nonprofit organizations was largely undertaken by nonprofit industry groups outside the accounting profession. Accounting manuals representing a codification of industry practices and the delineation of reporting problems were developed by colleges and universities, religious organizations, hospitals, country clubs, museums, and voluntary health and welfare organizations. The manuals provided guidance in accounting for specific types of nonprofit organizations. Not surprisingly, this piecemeal process, representing a compilation of practices, resulted in inconsistencies.[2]

Development of the Audit Guides

Increased public awareness of the nonprofit sector of our economy in the 1960s largely brought on the increased recognition by the accounting profession of the shortcomings of the industry-developed manuals. The American Institute of Certified Public Accountants (AICPA) developed and issued the following four audit guides in the early 1970s through the early 1980s: *Audit Guide for Voluntary Health and Welfare Organizations; Hospital Audit Guide; Audits of Colleges and Universities;* and *Audits of Certain Nonprofit Organizations.* These guides, and subsequent amendments in the form of Statements of Position (SOPs), provided the substantial authoritative support required for all generally accepted accounting principles for nonprofit organizations. The fifth edition of the *Hospital Audit Guide* states:

[1]*Accounting Research and Terminology Bulletins*, Final Edition (New York: American Institute of Certified Public Accountants, 1961), Intro., par. 5.

[2]Malvern J. Gross, Jr., "Nonprofit Accounting: The Continuing Revolution," *Journal of Accountancy*, June 1977, p. 67.

> This audit guide is published for the guidance of members of the Institute in examining and reporting on financial statements of hospitals. It represents the considered opinion of the Committee on Health Care Institutions and as such contains the best thought of the profession as to the best practices in this area of reporting. Members should be aware that they may be called upon to justify departures from the Committee's recommendations.[3]

GAAP for Nonprofit Organizations and the FASB

In 1979, the FASB announced plans to extract the specialized accounting principles and practices set forth in these guides and Statements of Position and issue them as FASB statements, after appropriate study. As an interim measure, in 1979 it issued *FASB Statement No. 32*, "Specialized Accounting and Reporting Principles and Practices in AICPA Statements of Position and Guides on Accounting and Auditing Matters." *FASB Statement No. 32* accorded the status of "preferable accounting principles" to the special accounting and reporting practices set forth in the guides and Statements of Position when applying *APB Opinion No. 20*, "Accounting Changes" (that is, when justifying a change in accounting principle).[4]

On the Horizon

The development of a set of uniform generally accepted accounting principles (GAAP) for nonprofit organizations based on a logical conceptual framework is apparently gaining momentum. In the late 1970s, the FASB published a research report, *Financial Accounting in Nonbusiness Organizations: An Exploratory Study of Conceptual Issues.* Under the broad scope of the study, government is considered a type of nonbusiness organization. The report's author, Robert N. Anthony, states its purpose as follows:

> This study attempts to identify the problems that would be involved in arriving at one or more statements of objectives and basic concepts of financial reporting of nonbusiness organizations. It identifies certain issues that need to be addressed in arriving at such statements and the principal arguments, pro and con, that are advanced in connection with each issue. It does not recommend how any of these issues should be resolved.[5] In 1980, the FASB issued such a statement of concepts, "Objectives of Financial Reporting by Nonbusiness Organizations."[6] Although the statement did not establish any new accounting standards, its purpose was to

[3]*Hospital Audit Guide*, Fifth Edition (New York: American Institute of Certified Public Accountants, 1985), inside cover.

[4]*Statement of Financial Accounting Standards, No. 32*, "Specialized Accounting and Reporting Principles and Practices of AICPA Statements of Position and Guides on Accounting and Auditing Matters" (Stamford: Financial Accounting Standards Board, 1979), pars. 2, 10.

[5]Robert N. Anthony, *Financial Accounting in Nonbusinesss Organizations: An Exploratory Study of Conceptual Issues* (Stamford: Financial Accounting Standards Board, 1978), p. 7.

[6]*Statement of Financial Accounting Concepts, No. 4*, "Objectives of Financial Reporting by Nonbusiness Organizations" (Stamford: Financial Accounting Standards Board, December 1980).

set forth objectives for financial reporting to help in the development of improved standards.

Looking beyond the statement of concepts stage to the future, it is likely that the FASB will impose more aggregated financial reporting on nonprofit organizations. The focus will be on meeting the needs for financial information of external providers of resources, emphasizing information for assessing financial viability and cost of service.

THE CHARACTERISTICS OF NONPROFIT ORGANIZATIONS

Nonprofit organizations vary in their size, scope, geographical influence, and objectives. Most of them, however, share certain common characteristics. We consider these characteristics now to provide an important frame of reference within which to explain their current and prospective accounting and reporting practices.

Objective

The objective of nonprofit organizations is to provide various types of services to their membership or to society as a whole. Often, the fees charged to the users of their services are less than the expenditure incurred to provide the services. For example, many hospitals and private colleges and universities cannot meet operating expenditures through patient fees and student tuition alone. The difference must be provided by such private and public funding as federal and state governments, philanthropic organizations, and individuals. These *external providers* perceive the nonprofit organization as a public-service agency accomplishing goals for the public good.

In contrast, an important objective of a business enterprise is to generate a satisfactory amount of income in relation to its resource or equity base. The emphasis is on income, and success is generally measured by the ability of the business enterprise to achieve acceptable rates of profitability, the benefits from which accrue to specific equity interests. Nonprofit organizations are not owned by an individual proprietor or investor but by the organization's membership or the general public.

The financial viability of a business organization is judged by its ability to meet its maturing obligations and to retain and attract new capital through earnings. The nonprofit organization is also judged by its ability to meet its commitments and obligations, but unlike business, the second concern is with the nature of the resource inflows and any restrictions on their use. Nonprofit organizations that generate their resources principally from services as opposed to gifts are considered more financially viable. They are less vulnerable to changes in donor attitudes and other external factors beyond their control. The greater the restrictions as to use that providers place on their donations, the more difficult it is for the organization to meet new objectives.

The traditional matching concept used to determine net income does not apply to a nonprofit organization as it does to a business enterprise. For many of the activities of nonprofit organizations, no essential causal relationship exists between the incurrence of an expense and the generation of revenue. For example, generally there is no direct relationship between contributions, grants and governmental appropriations, and the services provided by the nonprofit organization. Such resource inflows are not *earned*, in the general definition of the term. The difference, then, between revenue and expense does not have the same meaning to the nonprofit organization as it does to the business enterprise.

Reporting Emphasis

The financial statements of nonprofit organizations disclose information about the flows of funds, solvency, and liquidity, like that of business enterprises. Nonprofit organizations, however, place greater emphasis on the nature of resource inflows and the degree of resource transferability. Anthony states:

> An important distinction in some [nonprofit] organizations is between hard money (e.g., revenues from services rendered) and soft money (e.g., annual gifts); the higher the proportion of hard money, the firmer the financial foundation.[7]

Regarding the transferability of resources he states

> Resource transferability refers to the organization's freedom to use resources for various purposes; the greater the proportion of resources that is restricted to specified uses, the more difficult it is to change direction or to meet new needs.[8]

Financial statements for nonprofit organizations must also disclose compliance with a number of *spending mandates*, such as conditions of grants, gifts, and bequests. The organization must provide assurance that the resources have been used for the intended purposes. **Externally imposed spending mandates provide the rationale for fund accounting and reporting.**

FRAMEWORK OF ACCOUNTING

Organizational Objectives and User Needs

The accounting and financial reporting for nonprofit organizations must be adapted to the objectives of each organization and the needs of the

[7]*Financial Accounting in Nonbusiness Organizations*, p. 49.
[8]*Financial Accounting in Nonbusiness Organizations*, p. 49.

users of the financial information. Clearly, the organization's accounting system must ensure compliance with all external restrictions and all internal designations by the governing board (for example, funds designated for student loans, construction, and future equipment acquisitions). As mentioned earlier, the necessity to comply with spending mandates is the rationale for fund accounting. *Fund accounting* permits financial resources to be classified for accounting and reporting purposes in accordance with their intended use, as directed either by the externally imposed restrictions or by the governing board.

An essential accounting differentiation exists between externally imposed spending mandates and designations imposed internally by the governing board. External restrictions are long-term, usually irrevocable restraints on the uses of resources, but the governing board may change the designation of unrestricted funds at a later date. Knowing which funds are restricted is important to a user assessing the transferability of the organization's resources.

A Comparative Overview of the Fund Groups

The assets, liabilities, fund balances, and changes in the fund balances of a nonprofit organization may be classified into the following six basic self-balancing fund groups:

1. Current Funds (unrestricted and restricted)
2. Plant Funds
3. Endowment and Similar Funds
4. Agency Funds
5. Annuity of Life Income Funds
6. Loan Funds

Illustration 22-1 compares the types of funds used in nonprofit organizations as recommended by the audit guides. The rest of this section introduces these funds.

1. **Funds in support of current operations:**
   - **Current Unrestricted Fund** (for hospitals, **Unrestricted Fund**) accounts for all resources over which the governing board has discretionary control to use in carrying on the operations of the organization, except for unrestricted amounts for investments in plant that may be accounted for in a separate fund. For example, colleges and universities account for investment in plant in a Plant Funds Group, whereas voluntary health and welfare organizations generally account for investment in plant in a separate fund, Land, Building, and Equipment. Note that the governing board may designate portions of the Current Unrestricted Fund for specific purposes. As part of this type of action, it may set up separate accounts for such designations within this fund and thus segregate portions of it within the Fund Balance section of the Unrestricted Fund balance sheet. Because the board has the power to reverse its actions, these funds are never included in a restricted fund.

Illustration 22-1
Overview of Funds Used in Nonprofit Organizations

Purpose for Fund	Colleges and Universities	Hospitals	Voluntary Health and Welfare Organizations[a]
1. Funds in support of current operations	Current Unrestricted Fund	Unrestricted Fund (includes investment in plant and long-term debt)	Current Unrestricted Fund
	Current Restricted Fund	Specific Purpose	Current Restricted Fund
2. Funds with resources in support of fixed asset renewal, replacement, and expansion	Plant Funds Group:[b] Investment in Plant		Land, Building, and Equipment
	Plant Funds Group:[b] Unexpended; For Renewals and Replacement; For Retirement of Indebtedness	Plant Replacement and Expansion	
3. Funds providing accountability for fiduciary responsibilities	Endowment and Similar Funds	Endowment	Endowment
	Annuity and Life Income Funds	Annuity	Loan and Annuity
	Loan Funds	Loan Funds	
	Agency Funds		Custodian

[a]The audit guide for certain nonprofit organizations does not specify a fund structure. However, illustrations included in the guide's financial statements do show the use of funds similar to voluntary health and welfare organizations for complex operations.
[b]All funds in this group are considered one fund.

- **Current Restricted Fund** (for hospitals, **Specific Purpose Fund**) accounts for those resources currently available for use, but expendable only for purposes specified by a donor or grantor. Resources received by this fund are credited initially to a Fund Balance. When the funds are expended for the intended use as designated by the donor, the Fund Balance is reduced and an appropriate revenue account is credited.
- **Investment in Plant:** There is considerable diversity in accounting for plant assets. Colleges and universities account for investment in plant through a Plant Funds Group. Hospitals account for investment in plant as part of their Unrestricted Fund, and voluntary health and welfare organizations generally use a separate fund for plant assets.

2. **Funds with resources in support of renewal, replacement, and expansion of fixed assets:**
   - For colleges and universities, **Plant Funds Group** accounts for unexpended funds to be used for acquisition of fixed assets; funds set aside for renewal and replacement of those assets; funds designated for debt service charges and for the retirement of indebtedness; and funds expended for fixed assets. These funds will be addressed in more detail later in the chapter.

- For hospitals, **Plant Replacement and Expansion Fund** accounts for resources committed to future expansion and replacement of a hospital's fixed assets. Amounts received are credited directly to the Fund Balance. When appropriate expenditures are made in accordance with a donor's wishes, the amount is transferred to the Unrestricted Fund.

3. **Funds providing accountability for fiduciary responsibilities of the organization:**
   - **Endowment, Annuity, Loan, and Agency Funds** are treated similarly in all nonprofit organizations. Appropriate illustrations are provided later in Appendix D to the chapter.

ACCOUNTING FOR COLLEGES AND UNIVERSITIES

Colleges and universities provide educational services, including teaching and research. They may be public, profit-oriented, and private nonprofit institutions. Financial statements for public institutions reflect generally accepted accounting principles used for governmental units and those specified by *Audits of Colleges and Universities.* Financial statements for profit-oriented institutions reflect generally accepted accounting principles for businesses and also those specified in the audit guide. Our study focuses primarily on nonprofit institutions, and we give primary attention to these organizations.

Overview

Colleges and universities should generally include three basic types of financial statements:

- A balance sheet
- A statement of current funds revenues, expenditures, and other changes
- A statement of changes in fund balances

The balance sheet is usually presented in "pancake" form as in Illustration 22-2 in which each fund appears stacked on one another. (This illustration is discussed more fully later.) The major funds groups discussed earlier are arranged on the balance sheet in the following manner:

Current Funds:
  Current Unrestricted Fund
  Current Restricted Fund
Plant Funds:
  Unexpended Plant Funds
  Renewals and Replacement Funds
  Retirement of Indebtedness Funds
  Investment in Plant
Loan Funds
Endowment and Similar Funds:
  Endowment Funds

Illustration 22-2

PARKMOOR COLLEGE
Balance Sheet
June 30, 19X1
with Comparative Figures at June 30, 19X0

Assets	19X1	19X0
Current funds:		
Unrestricted:		
Cash	$ 210,000	110,000
Investments	450,000	360,000
Accounts receivable, less allowance of $18,000 both years	228,000	175,000
Inventories, at lower of cost (first-in, first-out basis) or market	90,000	80,000
Prepaid expenses and deferred charges	28,000	20,000
Total Unrestricted	1,006,000	745,000
Restricted:		
Cash	145,000	101,000
Investments	175,000	165,000
Accounts receivable, less allowance of $8,000 both years	68,000	160,000
Unbilled charges	72,000	—
Total Restricted	460,000	426,000
Total Current Funds	1,466,000	1,171,000
Loan funds:		
Cash	30,000	20,000
Investments	100,000	100,000
Loans to students, faculty, and staff, less allowance of $10,000 current year and $9,000 prior year	550,000	382,000
Due from unrestricted funds	3,000	—
Total Loan Funds	683,000	502,000
Endowment and similar funds:		
Cash	100,000	101,000
Investments	13,900,000	11,800,000
Total Endowment and Similar Funds	14,000,000	11,901,000
Annuity and life income funds:		
Annuity funds:		
Cash	55,000	45,000
Investments	3,260,000	3,010,000
Total Annuity Funds	3,315,000	3,055,000

Liabilities and Fund Balances	19X1	19X0
Current funds:		
Unrestricted:		
Accounts payable	$ 125,000	100,000
Accrued liabilities	20,000	15,000
Students' deposits	30,000	35,000
Due to other funds	158,000	120,000
Deferred credits	30,000	20,000
Fund balance	643,000	455,000
Total Unrestricted	1,006,000	745,000
Restricted:		
Accounts payable	14,000	5,000
Fund balances	446,000	421,000
Total Restricted	460,000	426,000
Total Current Funds	1,466,000	1,171,000
Loan funds:		
Fund balances:		
U.S. government grants refundable	50,000	33,000
University funds:		
Restricted	483,000	369,000
Unrestricted	150,000	100,000
Total Loan Funds	683,000	502,000
Endowment and similar funds:		
Fund balances:		
Endowment	7,800,000	6,740,000
Term endowment	3,840,000	3,420,000
Quasi-endowment—unrestricted	1,000,000	800,000
Quasi-endowment—restricted	1,360,000	941,000
Total Endowment and Similar Funds	14,000,000	11,901,000
Annuity and life income funds:		
Annuity funds:		
Annuities payable	2,150,000	2,300,000
Fund balances	1,165,000	755,000
Total Annuity Funds	3,315,000	3,055,000

Life income funds:			Life income funds:		
Cash	15,000	15,000	Income payable	5,000	5,000
Investments	2,045,000	1,740,000	Fund balances	2,055,000	1,750,000
Total Life Income Funds	2,060,000	1,755,000	Total Life Income Funds	2,060,000	1,755,000
Total Annuity and Life Income Funds	5,375,000	4,810,000	Total Annuity and Life Income Funds	5,375,000	4,810,000
Plant funds:			Plant funds:		
Unexpended:			Unexpended:		
Cash	$ 275,000	410,000	Accounts payable	10,000	—
Investments	1,285,000	1,590,000	Notes payable	100,000	—
Due from unrestricted current funds	150,000	120,000	Bonds payable	400,000	—
			Fund balances:		
			Restricted	1,000,000	1,860,000
			Unrestricted	200,000	260,000
Total Unexpended	1,710,000	2,120,000	Total Unexpended	1,710,000	2,120,000
Renewals and replacements:			Renewals and replacements:		
Cash	5,000	4,000	Fund balances:		
Investments	150,000	286,000	Restricted	25,000	180,000
Deposits with trustees	100,000	90,000	Unrestricted	235,000	200,000
Due from unrestricted current funds	5,000	—			
Total Renewals and Replacements	260,000	380,000	Total Renewals and Replacements	260,000	380,000
Retirement of indebtedness:			Retirement of indebtedness:		
Cash	50,000	40,000	Fund balances:		
Deposits with trustees	250,000	253,000	Restricted	185,000	125,000
			Unrestricted	115,000	168,000
Total Retirement of Indebtedness	300,000	293,000	Total Retirement of Indebtedness	300,000	293,000
Investment in plant:			Investment in plant:		
Land	500,000	500,000	Notes payable	790,000	810,000
Land improvements	1,000,000	1,110,000	Bonds payable	2,200,000	2,400,000
Buildings	25,000,000	24,060,000	Mortgages payable	400,000	200,000
Equipment	15,000,000	14,200,000	Net investment in plant	38,210,000	36,540,000
Library books	100,000	80,000			
Total Investment in Plant	41,600,000	39,950,000	Total Investment in Plant	41,600,000	39,950,000
Total Plant Funds	43,870,000	42,743,000	Total Plant Funds	43,870,000	42,743,000
Agency funds:			Agency funds:		
Cash	50,000	70,000	Deposits held in custody for others	110,000	90,000
Investments	60,000	20,000			
Total Agency Funds	110,000	90,000	Total Agency Funds	110,000	90,000

Source: Adapted from *Audits of Colleges and Universities*, 2nd ed. (New York: American Institute of Certified Public Accountants, 1975), Exh. 1, pp. 108–110.

Term Endowment Funds
Quasi-Endowment Funds
Annuity and Life Income Funds:
Annuity Funds
Life Income Funds
Agency Fund

The Current Funds Group, consisting of resources expendable for operating purposes, includes the asset, liability, and activity accounts necessary to record daily operations. For example, expenditures for instruction, research, extension programs, and auxiliary enterprise activities would be accounted for in the Current Funds Group. In many ways, this group operates in the same manner as the general fund of a city.

Within the group, unrestricted funds that have not been designated by the governing board for loan, investment, or plant purposes may be expended for operating purposes. For example, the governing board may transfer unrestricted funds to a **Quasi-Endowment Fund,** in which such funds serve as endowments until some other more suitable purpose is determined. The board may decide to transfer funds to Loan Funds for supplemental governmental appropriations, to Plant Funds for expansion or rehabilitation, or use them for debt retirement. In such cases, the receiving fund would credit the unrestricted fund's balance for these board-designated transfers. Board-designated funds should be accounted for as unrestricted, since the distinction between the balances that are externally restricted and those that are internally designated should be maintained in the accounts and disclosed in the financial statements. This disclosure is clearly important to the balance sheet user who attempts to assess transferability.

Restricted current funds are also available for operating purposes, but they are restricted by donors or other outside agencies as to the specific purpose for which they may be expended. Restricted current funds are augmented through gifts, endowment income, contracts, grants and appropriations received from private organizations or governments (for research, public service, or other restricted purposes), and income and gains from investments of restricted current funds. Earnings and contributions are not recognized as revenue until expended for the intended purpose. The amounts of earnings or contributions are credited to a Fund Balance account.

A second primary financial statement, the statement of current funds, revenues, expenditures, and other changes, shows the flow of funds only through the Current Funds Group. Illustration 22-3 shows such a statement. Two points are important for understanding this illustration:

1. Revenues for restricted current funds are recognized only to the extent that they were expended for the intended purpose. (In contrast, revenue earned by unrestricted or board-designated funds should be recognized when earned.)

Illustration 22-3

PARKMOOR COLLEGE
Statement of Current Funds Revenues, Expenditures, and Other Changes
Year Ended June 30, 19X1
with Comparative Figures for 19X0

	19X1			19X0
	Unrestricted	Restricted	Total	Year Total
Revenues:				
Educational and general:				
Student tuition and fees	$2,600,000		2,600,000	2,300,000
Governmental appropriations	1,300,000		1,300,000	1,300,000
Governmental grants and contracts	35,000	425,000	460,000	595,000
Gifts and private grants	850,000	380,000	1,230,000	1,190,000
Endowment income	325,000	209,000	534,000	500,000
Sales and services of educational departments	90,000		90,000	95,000
Organized activities related to educational departments	100,000		100,000	100,000
Other sources (if any)				
Total educational and general	5,300,000	1,014,000	6,314,000	6,080,000
Auxiliary enterprises	2,200,000		2,200,000	2,100,000
Expired term endowment	40,000		40,000	
Total Revenues	7,540,000	1,014,000	8,554,000	8,180,000
Expenditures and mandatory transfers:				
Educational and general:				
Instruction and departmental research	2,820,000	300,000	3,120,000	2,950,000
Organized activities related to educational departments	140,000	189,000	329,000	350,000
Sponsored research		400,000	400,000	500,000
Other separately budgeted research	100,000		100,000	150,000
Other sponsored programs		25,000	25,000	50,000
Extension and public service	130,000		130,000	125,000
Libraries	250,000		250,000	225,000
Student services	200,000		200,000	195,000
Operation and maintenance of plant	220,000		220,000	200,000
General administration	200,000		200,000	195,000
General institutional expense	250,000		250,000	250,000
Student aid	90,000	100,000	190,000	180,000
Educational and General Expenditures	4,400,000	1,014,000	5,414,000	5,370,000
Mandatory transfers for:				
Principal and interest	90,000		90,000	50,000
Renewals and replacements	100,000		100,000	80,000
Loan fund matching grant	2,000		2,000	
Total Education and General	4,592,000	1,014,000	5,606,000	5,500,000
Auxiliary enterprises:				
Expenditures	1,830,000		1,830,000	1,730,000
Mandatory transfers for:				
Principal and interest	250,000		250,000	250,000
Renewals and replacements	70,000		70,000	70,000
Total Auxiliary Enterprises	2,150,000		2,150,000	2,050,000
Total Expenditures and Mandatory Transfers	6,742,000	1,014,000	7,756,000	7,550,000
Other transfers and additions/(deductions):				
Excess of restricted receipts over transfers to revenues		45,000	45,000	40,000
Refunded to grantors		(20,000)	(20,000)	
Unrestricted gifts allocated to other funds	(650,000)		(650,000)	(510,000)
Portion of quasi-endowment gains appropriated	40,000		40,000	
Net Increase in Fund Balances	$ 188,000	25,000	213,000	160,000

Source: Adapted from *Audits of Colleges and Universities*, 2nd ed. (New York: American Institute of Certified Public Accountants, 1975), Exh. 3, pp. 114–15.

2. Unlike most other nonprofit organizations, colleges and universities do not depreciate exhaustible fixed assets. The audit guide states:

> The reason for this treatment is that these statements present expenditures and transfers of current funds rather than operating expenses in conformity with the reporting objectives of accounting for resources received and used rather than the determination of net income. Depreciation allowance, however, may be reported in the balance sheet and the provision for depreciation reported in the statement of changes in the balance of the investment-in-plant subsection of the plant funds group.[9]

3. Because the emphasis is on the flow of funds, the term "expenditure" is used rather than "expenses".
4. Unrestricted resources that had previously been transferred to Plant Funds or Quasi-Endowment Funds and are now being returned should be reported as transfers and not as revenues.
5. All student tuition and fees are recognized as revenues. To the extent that students are granted fee remission, generally in connection with scholarships, the waived amounts are recorded as expenditures for scholarships.

Loan Funds are usually established to provide loans to students, faculty and staff of colleges and universities. Loan Funds are generally revolving; that is, repayments of principal and interest are loaned to other individuals. Illustration 22-4 shows their sources and uses.

Notes receivable are carried at face value, less an allowance for doubtful notes. Provisions for doubtful notes are charged directly to the Loan Fund's Equity account. All other transactions that affect this fund's Equity account are also credited or charged directly to that account.

The college is simply a fiscal agent for assets that are not actually its property. An **Agency Fund** accounts for these assets. For example, a college may act as fiscal agent for the assets of student government and of faculty

Illustration 22-4
Sources and Uses of Loan Funds

Sources	Uses
Gifts, bequests, and government advances	Loans written off
Interest on loan notes	Deductions to provide appropriate allowances for uncollectible loans
Income from endowment funds	Interfund transfers
Interfund transfers	Refunds to grantors
Income, gains, and losses on investment of Loan Funds	Administrative and collection costs

[9] *Audits of Colleges and Universities*, 2nd ed. (New York: American Institute of Certified Public Accountants, 1975), pp. 9–10.

and staff organizations. The net assets of such a fund would appear as a **liability,** because the college has no equity in the fund.

For most nonprofit organizations, the **Endowment Funds Group** includes funds for endowments and for term endowments. College and university boards also designate Quasi-Endowment Funds, and therefore the title of this is funds group Endowment and Similar Funds.

Endowment Funds are established by donors that have stipulated that the principal is nonexpendable. The income generated from the endowment usually may be expended by current operating funds. Term Endowment Fund principal becomes expendable at some specified time or after a designated event. These funds are then available for operating needs. Quasi-Endowment Funds are internally designated by the board rather than externally restricted. The board may expend the principal at any time.

Legal restrictions in the endowment instrument determine the accounting for each fund's principal, income, and investments. Each endowment is accounted for as a separate fund, but the resources are generally pooled for investment purposes unless restrictive convenants limit investments to certain types of securities.

Annuity and Life Income Funds of a college consists of assets contributed to it with the stipulation that the college, in turn, promises to pay a certain sum periodically to a designated individual, usually for the remainder of his or her life. On the death of that person, the unexpended assets of the Annuity Fund are transferred to the college's Current Unrestricted Fund, Current Restricted Fund, or Endowment Fund, as specified by the donor.

At the date of the contribution, the assets are accounted for at their fair market value, an Annuities Payable account is credited for the current value of the liability (based on life expectancy tables), and the balance is credited to the annuity's Fund Balance account.

Investment income and gains or losses are credited or charged to the Liability account. Annuity payments are also charged to Liability. The liability and the fund balance are periodically adjusted to record the actuarial gain or loss due to recomputation of the liability based on revised life expectancy of the donor.

The essential difference between Annuity Funds and Life Income Funds is that for the latter the principal remains intact, and all income is distributed to the beneficiary. Annuity Fund distributions are fixed, whereas distributions of Life Income Funds reflect all fund earnings.

Colleges and universities include investment in plant within a **Plant Funds Group,** which accounts for both unexpended and expended resources. This group consists of:

> (1) funds to be used for the acquisition of physical properties for institutional purposes but unexpended at the date of reporting; (2) funds set

> aside for the renewal and replacement of institutional properties; (3) funds set aside for debt service charges and for the retirement of indebtedness on institutional properties; and (4) funds expended for and thus invested in institutional properties.[10]

Illustration 22-5 discloses in more detail the nature of the funds flows for the accounts in the Plant Funds Group.

The illustrated balance sheet in Illustration 22-2 shows how a college's Plant Funds Group is presented. The following points are important for understanding Illustration 22-2:

1. The first two funds are, in effect, unexpended plant funds. Frequently, they are summarized or combined and disclosed as Unexpended Funds for financial reporting purposes.
2. Unexpended plant funds include both externally restricted and internally designated funds.
3. The Investment in Plant Fund is in effect the Expended Plant Fund. The resources are carried at cost and, because colleges and universities do not depreciate their assets, no contra Asset account exists for accumulated depreciation. This fund's residual equity is referred to as Net Investment in Plant, not Fund Balance.

Illustrated transaction entries for the various funds are presented and explained in the appendixes to this chapter.

Pledge Disclosure and Accounting

Gifts and bequests can represent a significant source of funds to a college or university. **Pledges** of gifts may be disclosed in the notes to the financial statements or they may be reported within the financial statements. If the latter approach is used, they should be accounted for at their net realizable value and credited to Unrestricted Revenues, Deferred Income, Current Restricted Funds, or Plant Funds. The pledge receivable should be presented net of an appropriate allowance for uncollectible pledges.

Illustration

PLEDGE DISCLOSURE AND ACCOUNTING FOR A PLEDGE COLLECTED OVER SEVERAL YEARS

Pledge revenue should be recognized in the year in which the pledge or installment of the pledge is received. The donor's intention determines its future accounting. For example, beginning this year, several donors have agreed to give a total of $25,000 a year for four years for normal operating

[10]*Audits of Colleges and Universities*, p. 44.

Illustration 22-5
Plant Funds Group for Colleges and Universities: Subgroup Funds Flows

Inflows	Outflows
Unexpended Plant Funds	
Bond sales proceeds	Disbursements
Private donations	Investment losses
Restricted government appropriations	Return of unrestricted amounts to unrestricted current funds
Income and gains from the investment of unexpended funds	Transfers: Investment in plant
Transfers from other fund groups	
Renewals and Replacement Funds	
Mandatory and voluntary transfers from current funds	Investment losses
Income and gains from the investment of funds	Return of unrestricted amounts to unrestricted current funds
	Expenditures not capitalized
	Capitalized expenditures for renewals and replacements
Retirement of Indebtedness Funds	
Transfers from current funds for principal and interest payments	Payments on principal and interest
Income and gains from the investment of funds	Trustees fees and expenses
Gifts, grants and government appropriations restricted to debt retirement	Investment losses
Transfers from other fund groups as directed by donors (such as expired term endowments, annuity, and life income funds)	
Investment in Plant	
Current fund equipment replacements	Disposal
Gifts of plant assets	Abandonment
Transfers from unexpended plant and renewals and replacement funds	Sale of plant assets
Debt retirement	

expenses. Therefore, only $22,500 should be recorded as revenue in the current year, as shown in the following entry:

Pledges Receivable	100,000	
Allowance for Uncollectible Pledges		10,000
Pledge Revenue		22,500
Deferred Pledge Revenue		67,500

Illustration 22-6

PARKMOOR COLLEGE
Statement of Changes in Fund Balances
Year Ended June 30, 19X1

	Current Funds					Plant Funds			
	Unrestricted	Restricted	Loan Funds	Endowment and Similar Funds	Annuity and Life Income Funds	Unexpended	Renewal and Replacement	Retirement of Indebtedness	Investment in Plant
Revenues and other additions:									
Educational and general revenues.......	$5,300,000								
Auxiliary enterprises revenues............	2,200,000								
Expired term endowment revenues.....	40,000								
Expired term endowment—restricted.						50,000			
Gifts and bequests—restricted...........		370,000	100,000	1,500,000	800,000	115,000		65,000	15,000
Grants and contracts—restricted.......		500,000							
Governmental appropriations—restricted......................................						50,000			
Investment income—restricted..........		224,000	12,000	10,000		5,000	5,000	5,000	
Realized gains on investments—unrestricted.................................				109,000					
Realized gains on investments—restricted......................................			4,000	50,000		10,000	5,000	5,000	
Interest on loans receivable................			7,000						
U.S. government advances.................			18,000						
Expended for plant facilities (including $100,000 charged to current funds expenditures)................................									1,550,000
Retirement of indebtedness................									220,000
Accrued interest on sale of bonds.......								3,000	
Matured annuity and life income funds restricted to endowment........				10,000					
Total Revenues and Other Additions................................	7,540,000	1,094,000	141,000	1,679,000	800,000	230,000	10,000	78,000	1,785,000

Expenditures and other deductions:									
Educational and general expenditures.	4,400,000	1,014,000							
Auxiliary enterprises expenditures	1,830,000								
Indirect costs recovered		35,000							
Refunded to grantors		20,000	10,000						
Loan cancellations and write-offs			1,000						
Administrative and collection costs			1,000					1,000	
Adjustment of actuarial liability for annuities payable					75,000				
Expended for plant facilities (including noncapitalized expenditures of $50,000)						1,200,000	300,000		
Retirement of indebtedness								220,000	
Interest on indebtedness								190,000	
Disposal of plant facilities									115,000
Expired term endowments ($40,000 unrestricted, $50,000 restricted to plant)				90,000					
Matured annuity and life income funds restricted to endowment					10,000				
Total Expenditures and Other Deductions	6,230,000	1,069,000	12,000	90,000	85,000	1,200,000	300,000	411,000	115,000
Transfers among funds—additions/ (deductions):									
Mandatory:									
Principal and interest	(340,000)							340,000	
Renewals and replacements	(170,000)						170,000		
Loan fund matching grant	(2,000)		2,000						
Unrestricted gifts allocated	(650,000)		50,000	550,000		50,000			
Portion of unrestricted quasi-endowment funds investment gains appropriated	40,000			(40,000)					
Total Transfers	(1,122,000)		52,000	510,000		50,000	170,000	340,000	
Net increase/(decrease) for the year	188,000	25,000	181,000	2,099,000	715,000	(920,000)	(120,000)	7,000	1,670,000
Fund balance at beginning of year	455,000	421,000	502,000	11,901,000	2,505,000	2,120,000	380,000	293,000	36,540,000
Fund Balance at End of Year	$ 643,000	446,000	683,000	14,000,000	3,220,000	1,200,000	260,000	300,000	38,210,000

Source: Adapted from *Audits of Colleges and Universities*, 2nd ed. (New York: American Institute of Certified Public Accountants, 1975), Exh. 2, pp. 112–13.

Donated Services

Colleges and universities operated by religious groups generally account for the value of **donated services** provided by members of the religious group. The value of services performed (perhaps by comparison with lay salaries) are recorded as an expenditure with an equivalent credit to gift revenues.

Investments

Colleges and universities generally account for **investments** (exclusive of investments in physical plant) at cost or at market value if they are received as gifts; the *Audits of Colleges and Universities* provides an alternative. The investments may also be reported in the financial statements at market value, if this valuation basis is used by all funds. Unrealized gains and losses measured using this alternative basis should be reported in the same manner as realized gains and losses.

ACCOUNTING FOR HOSPITALS

As providers of health services, hospitals may be voluntary nonprofit, government owned, or owned by investors and operated on a proprietary basis. The term **hospital** extends to teaching hospitals, extended care facilities, and nursing homes.

Overview

Hospitals should generally include four types of financial statements:

- A balance sheet
- A statement of revenues and expenses
- A statement of changes in financial position.
- A statement of changes in fund balances

Like colleges and universities, the balance sheet for a hospital is generally presented in pancake form as in Illustration 22-7. Although the basic text of the *Hospital Audit Guide* addresses only unrestricted and restricted funds, the balance sheet example shows a number of restricted funds including specific purpose, plant replacement, and expansion and endowment funds. Again, the basic separation between unrestricted and restricted funds is similar to that for colleges and universities. Only resources that are restricted by external donors and grantors are accounted for in restricted funds; board-designated funds are unrestricted.

The following fund structure for hospitals is based on the *Guide's* example and includes extensions reflecting other purposes for which resources may be restricted:

Unrestricted Fund
Restricted Funds:
- Specific Purpose Fund
- Plant Replacement and Expansion Fund
- Endowment Funds
- Annuity Funds
- Loan Funds

Unlike colleges and universities, hospitals do not use a current funds group. For operating purposes, they use an Unrestricted Fund, which comprises Unrestricted Assets and Liabilities, including Property, Plant, and Equipment, Accumulated Depreciation, and related liabilities. Assets designated by the governing board are also included in this fund.

One of the essential differences between accounting for colleges and universities and accounting for hospitals is in how each accounts for fixed assets. Colleges and universities have a complex group of funds called the Plant Funds Group, which includes funds for plant-in-service, unexpended funds for plant, renewals and replacement funds, and the debt which relates to the fixed assets. Also, colleges and universities do not depreciate their fixed assets. In contrast, hospitals account for their investment in plant and related long-term debt in the Unrestricted Fund. Hospitals also depreciate their plant and equipment. Externally restricted resources for plant replacement and expansion are accounted for separately in a restricted fund titled Plant Replacement and Expansion.

Hospitals also use a **Specific Purpose Fund,** which is similar to the restricted current funds subgroup used by colleges and universities in that it accounts for resources externally restricted by donors or other outside agencies as to the specific purpose for which they may be expended. It differs from the restricted current funds subgroup in that it does not ultimately expend the resources for the specific purpose. The spending unit is the Unrestricted Fund. Like Current Restricted Funds of colleges and universities, earnings and contributions to the Specific Purpose Fund are credited to Fund Balance and not to revenue. Interfund transfers are effected from the Specific Purpose Fund to the Unrestricted Fund as the resources are expended. Also, similar treatment may be found in accounting for plant and endowment funds; the expending fund is the Unrestricted Fund.

The statement of revenues and expenses in Illustration 22-8 reports on the operations of the Unrestricted Fund. Flows of funds between the Unrestricted Fund and the other restricted funds are reported as revenue or expense on this statement. However, transfers from the Plant Expansion and Replacement Fund are recorded by the Unrestricted Fund as charges to Fixed Assets with a corresponding credit to Fund Balance.

The statement of revenues and expenses resembles a performance statement for a profit-oriented firm more than a nonprofit entity. Histori-

Illustration 22-7

BRENMARR HOSPITAL
Balance Sheet
December 31, 19X1
with Comparative Figures for 19X0

Unrestricted Funds

Assets	19X1	19X0
Current:		
Cash	$ 133,000	$ 33,000
Receivables	1,382,000	1,269,000
Less estimated uncollectibles and allowances	(160,000)	(105,000)
	1,222,000	1,164,000
Due from restricted funds	215,000	—
Inventories (if material, state basis)	176,000	183,000
Prepaid expenses	68,000	73,000
Total Current Assets	1,814,000	1,453,000
Other:		
Cash	143,000	40,000
Investments	1,427,000	1,740,000
Property, plant, and equipment	11,028,000	10,375,000
Less accumulated depreciation	(3,885,000)	(3,600,000)
Net Property, Plant, and Equipment	7,143,000	6,775,000
Total	$10,527,000	$10,008,000

Liabilities and Fund Balances	19X1	19X0
Current:		
Notes payable to banks	$ 227,000	$ 300,000
Current installments of long-term debt	90,000	90,000
Accounts payable	450,000	463,000
Accrued expenses	150,000	147,000
Advances from third-party payors	300,000	200,000
Deferred revenue	10,000	10,000
Total Current Liabilities	1,227,000	1,210,000
Deferred revenue–third-party reimbursement	200,000	90,000
Long-term debt:		
Housing bonds	500,000	520,000
Mortgage note	1,200,000	1,270,000
Total Long-Term Debt	1,700,000	1,790,000
Fund Balance	7,400,000	6,918,000
Total	$10,527,000	$10,008,000

Restricted Funds

Specific purpose funds:			Specific purpose funds:		
Cash	$ 1,260	$ 1,000	Due to unrestricted funds	$ 215,000	$ —
Investments	200,000	70,000	Fund balances:		
Grants receivable	90,000	—	Research grants	15,000	30,000
			Other	61,260	41,000
				76,260	71,000
Total Specific Purpose Funds	$ 291,260	$ 71,000	Total Specific Purpose Funds	$ 291,260	$ 71,000
Plant replacement and expansion funds:			Plant replacement and expansion funds:		
Cash	$ 10,000	$ 450,000	Fund balances:		
Investments	800,000	290,000	Restricted by third-party payors	$ 380,000	$ 150,000
Pledges receivable, net of estimated uncollectible	20,000	360,000	Other	450,000	950,000
Total Plant Replacement and Expansion Funds	$ 830,000	$ 1,100,000	Total Plant Replacement and Expansion Funds	$ 830,000	$ 1,100,000
Endowment funds:			Endowment funds:		
Cash	$ 50,000	$ 33,000	Fund balances:		
Investments	6,100,000	3,942,000	Permanent endowment	$ 4,850,000	$ 2,675,000
			Term endowment	1,300,000	1,300,000
Total Endowment Funds	$ 6,150,000	$ 3,975,000	Total Endowment Funds	$ 6,150,000	$ 3,975,000

Source: Adapted from *Hospital Audit Guide* 5th ed. (New York: American Institute of Certified Public Accountants, 1985), Exh. A, pp. 40–41.

Illustration 22-8

BRENMARR HOSPITAL
Statement of Revenues and Expenses
Year Ended December 31, 19X1
with Comparative Figures for 19X0

	19X1	19X0
Patient service revenue	$8,500,000	$8,000,000
Allowances and uncollectible accounts (after deduction of related gifts, grants, subsidies, and other income—$55,000 and $40,000) (Notes 3 and 4)	(1,777,000)	(1,700,000)
Net Patient Service Revenue	6,723,000	6,300,000
Other operating revenue (including $100,000 and $80,000 from specific purpose funds)	184,000	173,000
Total Operating Revenue	6,907,000	6,473,000
Operating expenses:		
Nursing services	2,200,000	2,000,000
Other professional services	1,900,000	1,700,000
General services	2,100,000	2,000,000
Fiscal services	375,000	360,000
Administrative services (including interest expense of $50,000 and $40,000)	400,000	375,000
Provision for depreciation	300,000	250,000
Total Operating Expenses	7,275,000	6,685,000
Loss from operations	(368,000)	(212,000)
Nonoperating revenue:		
Unrestricted gifts and bequests	228,000	205,000
Unrestricted income from endowment funds	170,000	80,000
Income and gains from board-designated funds	54,000	41,000
Total Nonoperating Revenue	452,000	326,000
Excess of revenues over expenses	$ 84,000	$ 114,000

Source: Adapted from *Hospital Audit Guide* 5th ed. (New York: American Institute of Certified Public Accountants, 1985), Exh. B, p. 42.

cally, hospitals have been viewed more as businesses than nonprofit organizations. The focus has been on their viability as going concerns and the maintenance of their capital. Thus the focus is on "expenses" and not expenditures, with the latter depicting funds flows. Also unlike colleges and universities, hospitals depreciate their plant, displaying the depreciation prominently as an operating expense.

As the statement of revenues and expenses in Illustration 22-8 shows, the primary source of funds to a hospital comes from the end users: the patients. And unlike revenues in business, the patient revenue is calculated using established standard rates. Deductions from "gross" patient revenues include adjustments for charity services, contractual adjustments from third-party payer agreements (such as Blue Cross and Medicare), bad debts, and other administrative adjustments.

Other operating revenue includes grants for research and education that are not restricted by donors, and tuition charged nursing students by nursing schools run by the hospital.

Nonoperating revenue includes gifts, grants, and bequests that are not restricted by donors. Other sources include donated services, gains on sale of hospital properties, and unrestricted income from endowments.

Hospitals are also expected to include a statement of changes in financial position, as in Illustration 22-9. Note that this statement only presents fund flows for the Unrestricted Fund, the fund under the management of the governing board of the hospital. The format is conventional and the mechanics of its construction can be reviewed in any intermediate accounting text. The fourth primary statement for hospitals is the statement of changes in fund balances, an example of which is shown in Illustration 22-10.

Donated Services, Medicine, and Supplies

Many hospitals receive the donated services of individuals. The *Hospital Audit Guide* provides that the fair value of donated services should be reflected when there is the equivalent of an employer–employee relationship and an objective basis exists for valuing such services. Hospitals operated by religious orders generally record the difference between the fair value and the amount paid for the services of members of the order as donated services. The difference is recorded as expense with the credit to Nonoperating Revenue.

Donated medicines and supplies which normally would be purchased by the hospital should be recorded at their fair market value with a credit to Operating Revenue. In contrast, donations of property and equipment are recorded at their fair market value with a credit to the Unrestricted Fund Balance.

Pledge Disclosure and Accounting

Many nonprofit hospitals are continually involved in fund-raising activities. Pledges of income should be accounted for in the financial statements and should be classified as either unrestricted or restricted. If unrestricted, the pledge revenue, net of a provision for uncollectibles, should be included in the financial statements in the period in which the pledge is made as nonoperating revenue. If parts of a pledge apply to future periods, then the credit should be to Deferred Revenue or as additions to restricted funds.

Illustration 22-9

BRENMARR HOSPITAL
Statement of Changes in Financial Position of Unrestricted Fund
with Comparative Figures for 19X0
Year Ended December 31, 19X1

	19X1	19X0
Funds provided:		
Loss from operations	$ (368,000)	$ (212,000)
Deduct (add) items included in operations not requiring (providing) funds:		
Provision for depreciation	300,000	250,000
Increase in deferred third-party reimbursement	110,000	90,000
Revenue restricted to property, plant, and equipment replacement transferred to plant replacement and expansion fund	(230,000)	(200,000)
Funds Required for Operations	(188,000)	(72,000)
Nonoperating revenue	452,000	326,000
Funds Derived from Operations and Nonoperating Revenues	264,000	254,000
Decrease in board-designated funds	210,000	—
Property, plant, and equipment expenditures financed by plant replacement and expansion funds	628,000	762,000
Decrease in working capital	—	46,000
	$1,102,000	$1,062,000
Funds applied:		
Additions to property, plant, and equipment	$ 668,000	$ 762,000
Reduction of long-term debt	90,000	90,000
Increase in board-designated funds	—	210,000
Increase in working capital	344,000	—
	$1,102,000	$1,062,000
Changes in working capital:		
Increase (decrease) in current assets:		
Cash	$ 100,000	$ (50,000)
Receivables	58,000	75,000
Due from restricted funds	215,000	(100,000)
Inventories	(7,000)	16,000
Prepaid expenses	(5,000)	1,000
	361,000	(58,000)
Increase (decrease) in current liabilities:		
Note payable to banks	(73,000)	50,000
Accounts payable	(13,000)	10,000
Accrued expenses	3,000	2,000
Advances from third-party payors	100,000	40,000
Deferred revenue	—	2,000
	17,000	104,000
Increase (Decrease) in Working Capital	$ 344,000	$ (46,000)

Source: Adapted from *Hospital Audit Guide* 5th ed. (New York: American Institute of Certified Public Accountants, 1985), Exh. E, pp. 46–47.

Illustration 22-10

BRENMARR HOSPITAL
Statement of Changes in Fund Balances
Year Ended December 31, 19X1
with Comparative Figures for 19X0

	19X1	19X0
Unrestricted Funds		
Balance at beginning of year	$6,918,000	$6,242,000
Excess of revenues over expenses	84,000	114,000
Transferred from plant replacement and expansion funds to finance property, plant, and equipment expenditures	628,000	762,000
Transferred to plant replacement and expansion funds to reflect third-party payor revenue restricted to property, plant, and equipment replacement	(230,000)	(200,000)
Balance at End of Year	$7,400,000[a]	$6,918,000
Restricted Funds		
Specific purpose funds:		
Balance at beginning of year	$ 71,000	$ 50,000
Restricted gifts and bequests	35,000	20,000
Research grants	35,000	45,000
Income from investments	35,260	39,000
Gain on sale of investments	8,000	—
Transferred to:		
Other operating revenue	(100,000)	(80,000)
Allowances and uncollectible accounts	(8,000)	(3,000)
Balance at End of Year	$ 76,260	$ 71,000
Plant replacement and expansion funds:		
Balance at beginning of year	$1,100,000	$1,494,000
Restricted gifts and bequests	113,000	150,000
Income from investments	15,000	18,000
Transferred to unrestricted funds (described above)	(628,000)	(762,000)
Transferred from unrestricted funds (described above)	230,000	200,000
Balance at End of Year	$ 830,000	$1,100,000
Endowment funds:		
Balance at beginning of year	$3,975,000	$2,875,000
Restricted gifts and bequests	2,000,000	1,000,000
Net gain on sale of investments	175,000	100,000
Balance at End of Year	$6,150,000	$3,975,000

[a]Composition of the balance may be shown here, on the balance sheet, or in a footnote.

Source: Adapted from *Hospital Audit Guide* 5th ed. (New York: American Institute of Certified Public Accountants, 1985), Exh. C, p. 43.

Investments

Prior to 1978, most hospitals carried their investments at cost with market prices noted in the financial statements. In 1978, *Statement of Position 78-1* on accounting by hospitals for certain marketable equity securities was issued by the Accounting Standards Division of the AICPA. *Statement of Position 78-1* amended the *Hospital Audit Guide* to recommend that nonprofit hospitals apply the provisions of *FASB Statement No. 12*, which states that marketable securities should be carried at the lower of aggregate cost or market.

The accounting for investment income, gains, and losses varies depending on the funds that are involved. Unrestricted (or board-designated) funds disclose unrestricted income from endowment funds and realized gains and losses in the statement of revenues and expenses. Realized gains or losses of investments held by endowment funds are credited directly to the fund's principal. For restricted funds, income and net realized gains on investments should be credited to the restricted fund balance, unless they are legally available for unrestricted purposes. If available to unrestricted funds, the income and gains should be reported as nonoperating revenue in the statement of revenues and expenses. If legal restrictions apply, losses in excess of gains should be charged to Restricted Fund Balance.

Comparison of Accounting Practices

The fourth primary statement for hospitals is the statement of changes in fund balances as shown in Illustration 22-10. This statement can be compared with similar statements for colleges and universities as follows:

1. **Funds structure:** The funds structure of both types of nonprofit organizations is similar. However, hospitals include investment in plant in the Unrestricted Fund. Colleges and universities include investment in plant in their *Plant Funds Group*.
2. **Restricted and unrestricted distinction:** For both types of nonprofit organizations, a clear distinction is made between restricted funds and unrestricted funds. Board-designated funds are accounted for as unrestricted funds.
3. **Donated services:** The difference between the fair market value of donated services and the amount actually paid may be recognized by both types of nonprofit organizations.
4. **Depreciation of fixed assets:** Hospitals depreciate fixed assets; colleges and universities do not.
5. **Restricted contributions:** Both types of nonprofit organizations recognize restricted contributions and earnings as revenues only in the period in which they are expended for their designated purpose.

VOLUNTARY HEALTH AND WELFARE ORGANIZATIONS

Voluntary health and welfare organizations provide a broad scope of public services in the areas of health, social welfare, and community services.

Such organizations include the American Red Cross, the American Heart Association, Goodwill Industries, the Cancer Society, Planned Parenthood, United Way, and many others dedicated to serving human needs and the public good.

Overview

The financial statements usually provided by voluntary health and welfare organizations include:

- A balance sheet
- A statement of support, revenues and expenses, and changes in fund balances
- A statement of functional expenses

The principal sources of revenue for voluntary health and welfare organizations are public contributions made either directly or through the United Way, and government grants. The following funds structure for these organizations is based on the example in *Audit Guide for Voluntary Health and Welfare Organizations* and includes extensions reflecting other purposes for which resources may be restricted:

Current Unrestricted Fund
Current Restricted Fund
Land, Building, and Equipment Fund
Endowment Funds
Loan and Annuity Funds
Custodian Funds

The balance sheet in Illustration 22-11 shows the content of these funds for a voluntary health and welfare organization. The first two funds, the Current Unrestricted Fund and the Current Restricted Fund, are comparable to the Current Funds Group for colleges and universities and the Unrestricted Fund/Specific Purpose Fund for hospitals.

Pledges are reported net of an allowance for uncollectibles. Pledges that relate to a future period are reported in the Contributions Designated for Future Periods account in the Current Unrestricted Fund.

Custodian Funds are equivalent to Agency Funds of colleges and universities and hospitals. They account for assets received by an organization to be held or disbursed only on instructions of the person or organization from whom they were received.

Although the statement of support, revenue, and expenses and changes in fund balances, shown in Illustration 22-12, does not include the value of donated services, many voluntary health and welfare organizations require extensive use of volunteers in providing the organization's program services. However, because of the difficulty of measuring the value of volunteer services, donated services are often not recorded as revenue and expense. The fair market value of donated materials and facilities use should be listed as support when they are received and as expenses when used.

Illustration 22-11

THE CHAMANAUDE FOUNDATION
Balance Sheets
December 31, 19X1 and 19X0

Assets	19X1	19X0	Liabilities & Fund Balance	19X1	19X0
CURRENT FUNDS					
Unrestricted					
Cash	$2,207,000	$2,530,000	Accounts payable	$ 148,000	$ 139,000
Investments			Research grants payable	596,000	616,000
For long-term purposes	2,727,000	2,245,000	Contributions designated for future periods	245,000	219,000
Other	1,075,000	950,000	Total Liabilities and Deferred Revenues	989,000	974,000
Pledges receivable less allowance for uncollectibles of $105,000 and $92,000	475,000	363,000	Fund balances:		
Inventories of educational materials, at cost	70,000	61,000	Designated by the governing board for:		
			Long-term investments	2,800,000	2,300,000
Accrued interest, other receivables and prepaid expenses	286,000	186,000	Purchases of new equipment	100,000	—
			Research purposes	1,152,000	1,748,000
			Undesignated, available for general activities	1,799,000	1,313,000
			Total Fund Balance	5,851,000	5,361,000
Total	$6,840,000	$6,335,000	Total	$6,840,000	$6,335,000
Restricted					
Cash	$ 3,000	$ 5,000	Fund balances:		
Investments	71,000	72,000	Professional education	$ 84,000	$ —
Grants receivable	58,000	46,000	Research grants	48,000	123,000
Total	$ 132,000	$ 123,000	Total	$ 132,000	$ 123,000
LAND, BUILDING, AND EQUIPMENT FUND					
Cash	$ 3,000	$ 2,000	Mortgage payable, 8% due 19XX	$ 32,000	$ 36,000
Investments	177,000	145,000	Fund balances:		
			Expended	484,000	477,000
Pledges receivable less allowance for uncollectibles of $7,500 and $5,000	32,000	25,000	Unexpended—restricted	212,000	172,000
Land, buildings, and equipment, at cost less accumulated depreciation of $296,000 and $262,000	516,000	513,000	Total Fund Balance	696,000	649,000
Total	$ 728,000	$ 685,000	Total	$ 728,000	$ 685,000
ENDOWMENT FUNDS					
Cash	$ 4,000	$ 10,000	Fund Balance	$1,948,000	$2,017,000
Investments	1,944,000	2,007,000			
Total	$1,948,000	$2,017,000	Total	$1,948,000	$2,017,000

Source: Adapted from *Audit Guide for Voluntary Health and Welfare Organizations* (New York: American Institute of Certified Public Accountants, 1974), Exh. C, pp. 46–47.

Illustration 22-12

THE CHAMANAUDE FOUNDATION
Statement of Support, Revenue and Expenses and Changes in Fund Balances Year Ended December 31, 19X1 with Comparative Total for 19X0

	19X1				Total All Funds	
	Current Funds		Land, Building, and Equipment Fund	Endowment Fund		
	Unrestricted	Restricted			19X1	19X0
Public support and revenue:						
Public support:						
Contributions (net of estimated uncollectible pledges of $195,000 in 19X1 and $150,000 in 19X0)	$3,764,000	$162,000	$ —	$ 2,000	$3,928,000	$3,976,000
Contributions to building fund	—	—	72,000	—	72,000	150,000
Special events (net of direct costs of $181,000 in 19X1 and $163,000 in 19X0)	104,000	—	—	—	104,000	92,000
Legacies and bequests	92,000	—	—	4,000	96,000	129,000
Received from federated and nonfederated campaigns (which incurred related fund-raising expenses of $38,000 in 19X1 and $29,000 in 19X0)	275,000	—	—	—	275,000	308,000
Total Public Support	4,235,000	162,000	72,000	6,000	4,475,000	4,655,000
Revenue:						
Membership dues	17,000	—	—	—	17,000	12,000
Investment income	98,000	10,000	—	—	108,000	94,000
Realized gain on investment transactions	200,000	—	—	25,000	225,000	275,000
Miscellaneous	42,000	—	—	—	42,000	47,000
Total Revenue	357,000	10,000	—	25,000	392,000	428,000
Total Support and Revenue	4,592,000	172,000	72,000	31,000	$4,867,000	$5,083,000
Expenses:						
Program services:						
Research	1,257,000	155,000	2,000	—	$1,414,000	$1,365,000
Public health education	539,000	—	5,000	—	544,000	485,000
Professional education and training	612,000	—	6,000	—	618,000	516,000
Community services	568,000	—	10,000	—	578,000	486,000
Total Program Services	2,976,000	155,000	23,000	—	3,154,000	2,852,000
Supporting services:						
Management and general	567,000	—	7,000	—	574,000	633,000
Fund raising	642,000	—	12,000	—	654,000	546,000
Total Supporting Services	1,209,000	—	19,000	—	1,228,000	1,184,000
Total Expenses	4,185,000	155,000	42,000	—	$4,382,000	$4,036,000
Excess (deficiency) of Public Support and Revenue over Expenses	407,000	17,000	30,000	31,000		
Other changes in fund balances:						
Property and equipment acquisitions from unrestricted funds	(17,000)	—	17,000	—		
Transfer of realized endowment fund appreciation	100,000	—	—	(100,000)		
Returned to donor	—	(8,000)	—	—		
Fund Balances, beginning of year	5,361,000	123,000	649,000	2,017,000		
Fund Balances, end of year	$5,851,000	$132,000	$696,000	$1,948,000		

Source: Adapted from *Audit Guide for Voluntary Health and Welfare Organizations* (New York: American Institute of Certified Public Accountants, 1974), Exh. A, pp. 42–43.

The statement of functional expenses, as in Illustration 22-13, provides further detail of the expenses included in Illustration 22-12. Another important attribute of this statement is that the expenses are identified with particular programs and supporting services.

Restricted contributions of voluntary health and welfare organizations are given recognition as revenue immediately upon receipt of the contribution. The recognition of revenue is required without regard to whether the contribution had been used or the restrictions met. This approach implies that the critical event for revenue recognition is the donation and not the expenditure.

The Land, Building, and Equipment Fund (Plant Fund) accounts for expended and unexpended funds and the Fund Balances separate the unrestricted from the restricted amounts. Land, buildings, and equipment are carried at cost and buildings and equipment are depreciated.

Investments

Investments are recorded at cost (or at market value, if donated) and reduced to market value if market is below cost. The determination of a decline in market value is computed on a portfolio basis and is generally accomplished through the use of a contra asset Allowance for Decline in Market Value account.

Investments may also be carried at market value. If they are, however, the unrealized gains or losses are included in revenues or other expenses of the appropriate fund and presented in the statement of support, revenue, and expenses and changes in fund balances.

The disposition of investment income, including realized (or unrealized, if carried at market value) gains and losses depends on the fund involved. If the investment income was earned on investments of unrestricted funds, then it should simply be reported as unrestricted revenue. If the income and net realized gains is earned on investments of restricted funds, (other than Endowment Funds), then it should be reported as revenue of the restricted funds. However, if it is available for unrestricted purposes, the income should be included in the Current Unrestricted Fund.

Realized losses on investments in restricted funds in excess of gains should be reported as a loss in the statement of support, revenue, and expenses and changes in fund balance of the restricted fund unless legal restrictions require otherwise.

Investment income from Endowment Funds, unless restricted to a specific purpose by the donor, is available for unrestricted purposes and should be included in the revenues of the Current Unrestricted Fund.

Comparison of Accounting Practices

Accounting for voluntary health and welfare organizations can be compared to accounting for colleges and universities and to hospital accounting as follows:

Illustration 22-13

THE CHAMANAUDE FOUNDATION
Statement of Functional Expenses
Year Ended December 31, 19X1
with Comparative Totals for 19X0

	19X1								Total Expenses	
	Program Services					Supporting Services				
	Research	Public Health Education	Professional Education and Training	Community Services	Total	Management and General	Fund Raising	Total	19X1	19X0
Salaries	$ 45,000	$291,000	$251,000	$269,000	$ 856,000	$331,000	$368,000	$ 699,000	$1,555,000	$1,433,000
Employee health and retirement benefits	4,000	14,000	14,000	14,000	46,000	22,000	15,000	37,000	83,000	75,000
Payroll taxes, etc.	2,000	16,000	13,000	14,000	45,000	18,000	18,000	36,000	81,000	75,000
Total Salaries and Related Expenses	51,000	321,000	278,000	297,000	947,000	371,000	401,000	772,000	1,719,000	1,583,000
Professional fees and contract service payments	1,000	10,000	3,000	8,000	22,000	26,000	8,000	34,000	56,000	53,000
Supplies	2,000	13,000	13,000	13,000	41,000	18,000	17,000	35,000	76,000	71,000
Telephone and telegraph	2,000	13,000	10,000	11,000	36,000	15,000	23,000	38,000	74,000	68,000
Postage and shipping	2,000	17,000	13,000	9,000	41,000	13,000	30,000	43,000	84,000	80,000
Occupancy	5,000	26,000	22,000	25,000	78,000	30,000	27,000	57,000	135,000	126,000
Rental of equipment	1,000	24,000	14,000	4,000	43,000	3,000	16,000	19,000	62,000	58,000
Local transportation	3,000	22,000	20,000	22,000	67,000	23,000	30,000	53,000	120,000	113,000
Conferences, conventions, meetings	8,000	19,000	71,000	20,000	118,000	38,000	13,000	51,000	169,000	156,000
Printing and publications	4,000	56,000	43,000	11,000	114,000	14,000	64,000	78,000	192,000	184,000
Awards and grants	1,332,000	14,000	119,000	144,000	1,609,000	—	—	—	1,609,000	1,448,000
Miscellaneous	1,000	4,000	6,000	4,000	15,000	16,000	21,000	37,000	52,000	64,000
Total Expenses before Depreciation	1,412,000	539,000	612,000	568,000	3,131,000	567,000	650,000	1,217,000	4,348,000	4,004,000
Depreciation of buildings and equipment	2,000	5,000	6,000	10,000	23,000	7,000	4,000	11,000	34,000	32,000
Total Expenses	$1,414,000	$544,000	$618,000	$578,000	$3,154,000	$574,000	$654,000	$1,228,000	$4,382,000	$4,036,000

Source: Adapted from *Audit Guide for Voluntary Health and Welfare Organizations* (New York: American Institute of Certified Public Accountants, 1974), Exh. B. p. 44–45.

1. **Funds structure:** The funds structure of all three types of nonprofit organizations is similar. However, voluntary health and welfare organizations account for investment in plant in a separate fund called Land, Buildings, and Equipment. These organizations also use a Custodian Fund, which is similar to the Agency Funds of the other organizations.
2. **Restricted and unrestricted distinction:** Like the other types of nonprofit organizations, a clear distinction is made between restricted funds and unrestricted funds.
3. **Donated services:** The value of donated services, materials and facilities may be recognized by all three types of nonprofit organizations.
4. **Depreciation of fixed assets:** Like hospitals, voluntary health and welfare organizations depreciate their fixed assets.
5. **Restricted contributions:** Unlike the other two types of nonprofit organizations, voluntary health and welfare organizations recognize restricted contributions as revenue immediately upon receipt.

ACCOUNTING FOR OTHER NONPROFIT ORGANIZATIONS

Other nonprofit organizations are those nonprofit units other than colleges and universities, voluntary health and welfare organizations, hospitals, and state and local governments. These organizations include:

Cemetery organizations	Political parties
Civic organizations	Private and community foundations
Fraternal organizations	Private elementary and secondary schools
Labor unions	Professional associations
Libraries	Public broadcasting stations
Museums	Religious organizations
Other cultural institutions	Research and scientific organizations
Performing arts organizations	Social and country clubs
Trade associations	Zoological and botanical societies

An authoritative guide, *Audits of Certain Nonprofit Organizations*, including *Statement of Position 78-10*, was issued by the AICPA in 1981. Like the other guides, extensive illustrations of financial statements are provided in its index.

Overview

Nonprofit organizations in this group should generally provide three basic types of financial statements:

- A balance sheet
- A statement of activity
- A statement of changes in financial position

The presentation formats vary depending on the complexity of the organization and the need to distinguish between externally restricted and unrestricted assets, liabilities, and fund balances.

As with the hospital guide, the guide for other nonprofit organizations does not specify a funds structure; but a review of its illustrative financial statements shows that a typical funds structure would include the following funds:

Current Unrestricted Fund
Current Restricted Fund
Plant Funds (Land, Building, and Equipment)
Endowment
Loan and Annuity

The extent to which the various funds are used depends on the complexity of the organization and the requirements imposed by external donors and grantors.

The financial statements of three types of other nonprofit organizations are illustrated: a country club, a performing arts organization, and a research and scientific group. The financial statements of the country club clearly resemble those of a profit-oriented organization. With some exceptions the terminology and format of the balance sheet (shown as Illustration 22-14) could be used for that of a profit-oriented entity. What distinguishes the unit as nonprofit is the terminology in the equity section, in which the phrase "Cumulative Excess of Revenue over Expenses" is used rather than "Retained Earnings." The country club's statement of revenue, expenses, and changes in cumulative excess of revenue over expenses, shown in Illustration 22-15, closely resembles that of a statement of income and retained earnings. Although not apparent, depreciation is included in the various expenses. It is also important to note that **accrual-basis accounting** is used. The statement of changes in financial position, shown in Illustration 22-16, reflects the same format as that used for profit-oriented firms.

The financial statements of the performing arts organization also reflect accrual basis accounting and depreciation is reflected in its activity statement. However, unlike the country club, the equity section of its balance sheet, in Illustration 22-17, shows how externally imposed restrictions on funds are presented for plant funds and endowment funds. The statement of activity in Illustration 22-18 closely resembles the statement of revenues and expenses of a hospital; revenues derived from sources other than operations are presented separately. The performing arts organization also includes a statement that delineates expenses by function, Illustration 22-20, which is similar to the one presented by voluntary health and welfare organizations.

The third illustrated unit is a research and scientific group. Like the performing arts organization, it uses fund accounting for its restricted funds, but it combines all the assets and liabilities and simply discloses the restrictions in the fund balance, shown in Illustration 22-22, much like an appropriations-of-fund balance. The statements also show that accrual basis accounting is used and depreciation expense is taken. And,

Illustration 22-14

DRY CREEK COUNTRY CLUB
Balance Sheet
March 1, 19X1 and 19X0

	19X1	19X0
Assets		
Current assets		
Cash	$ 44,413	$ 37,812
Investments	289,554	388,007
Accounts receivable, less allowances of $5,000 in 19X1, and $6,000 in 19X0	71,831	45,898
Inventories, at lower of cost (FIFO) or market	27,930	28,137
Prepaid expenses	19,154	13,948
Total Current Assets	452,882	513,802
Property and equipment, at cost		
Land and land improvements	1,085,319	1,098,828
Buildings	1,331,590	1,200,585
Furniture, fixtures, and equipment	274,761	254,540
	2,691,670	2,553,953
Less accumulated depreciation	864,564	824,088
	1,827,106	1,729,865
Other assets		
Deferred charges	15,077	16,524
Beverage license	10,500	10,500
	25,577	27,024
	$2,305,565	$2,270,691
Liabilities and Membership Equity		
Current liabilities		
Accounts payable and accrued expenses	$ 61,426	$ 63,600
Deferred revenues—initiation fees	15,677	7,755
Due to resigned members	16,400	12,900
Taxes	20,330	23,668
Total current liabilities	113,833	107,923
Membership equity		
Proprietary certificates, 500 at $1,500 each—no change during the years	750,000	750,000
Cumulative excess of revenue over expenses	1,441,732	1,412,768
	2,191,732	2,162,768
	$2,305,565	$2,270,691

Source: Adapted from *Audits of Certain Nonprofit Organizations* (New York: American Institute of Certified Public Accountants, 1981), Exh. 3, p. 114.

Illustration 22-15

DRY CREEK COUNTRY CLUB
Statement of Revenue, Expenses, and Changes in Cumulative Excess of Revenue over Expenses
Years Ended March 1, 19X1 and 19X0

	19X1	19X0
Revenue		
Dues	$ 590,000	$ 600,000
Restaurant and bar charges	270,412	265,042
Greens fees	171,509	163,200
Tennis and swimming fees	83,829	67,675
Initiation fees	61,475	95,220
Locker and room rentals	49,759	49,954
Interest and discounts	28,860	28,831
Golf cart rentals	26,584	24,999
Other—net	4,011	3,893
Total Revenue	1,286,439	1,298,814
Expenses		
Greens	241,867	244,823
House	212,880	210,952
Restaurant and bar	153,035	136,707
Tennis and swimming	67,402	48,726
General and administrative	533,838	690,551
Net (gains) losses on investments	98,453	(95,813)
Total Expenses	1,307,475	1,232,946
Excess (deficiency) of revenue over expenses before capital additions	(21,036)	65,868
Capital additions		
Assessments for capital improvements	50,000	—
Excess (deficiency) of Revenue over Expenses after Capital Additions	28,964	65,868
Cumulative excess of revenue over expenses—beginning of year	1,412,768	1,346,900
Cumulative Excess of Revenue over Expenses—End of Year	$1,441,732	$1,412,768

Source: Adapted from *Audits of Certain Nonprofit Organizations* (New York: American Institute of Certified Public Accountants, 1981), Exh. 3B, p. 115.

again, the statement of changes in financial position, shown in Illustration 22-24, is very much like all of the others presented earlier.

Pledge Disclosure and Accounting

Pledges which are legally enforceable represent a significant source of revenue for many other nonprofit organizations. Measurement and disclosure requirements are the same as colleges and universities.

Illustration 22-16

DRY CREEK COUNTRY CLUB
Statement of Changes in Financial Position
Years Ended March 31, 19X1 and 19X0

	19X1	19X0
Sources of funds		
Excess (deficiency) of revenue over expenses before capital additions	$ (21,036)	$ 65,868
Capital additions	50,000	—
Excess (Deficiency) of Revenue over Expenses after Capital Additions	28,964	65,868
Add-back provision for depreciation, which does not affect working capital	40,476	61,618
Total from Operations	69,440	127,486
Decrease in deferred charges—net	1,447	—
Total Sources	70,887	127,486
Applications of funds		
Purchases of property and equipment	137,717	84,377
Increase in deferred charges—net	—	8,909
Total applications	137,717	93,286
Increase (Decrease) in Working Capital	$ (66,830)	$ 34,200
Changes in the components of working capital are summarized as follows:		
Increase (decrease) in current assets		
Cash	$ 6,601	$ (70,928)
Investments	(98,453)	98,813
Accounts receivable	25,933	5,000
Inventories	(207)	8,112
Prepaid expenses	5,206	2,056
	(60,920)	43,053
(Increase) decrease in current liabilities		
Accounts payable and accrued expenses	2,174	(5,597)
Deferred revenues—initiation fees	(7,922)	(3,517)
Due to resigned members	(3,500)	(2,700)
Taxes	3,338	2,961
	(5,910)	(8,853)
Increase (Decrease) in Working Capital	$ (66,830)	$ 34,200

Source: Adapted from *Audits of Certain Nonprofit Organizations* (New York: American Institute of Certified Public Accountants, 1981), Exh. 3C, p. 116.

Donated Services

Donated services represent a significant resource that allows many nonprofit organizations to carry on their activities. However, accounting recognition is seldom given to the imputed value of these services. The principal

Illustration 22-17

GARDEN VALLEY BALLET
Balance Sheet
June 30, 19X1 and 19X0

	19X1	19X0
Assets		
Current assets		
Cash	$216,074	$169,466
Marketable securities	266,330	50,967
Accounts receivable, net of allowance for doubtful accounts	70,051	26,685
Grants receivable	—	6,100
Other	39,378	13,441
Total Current Assets	591,833	266,659
Noncurrent assets		
Investments and endowment funds cash	267,869	256,648
Property and equipment at cost, net of accumulated depreciation	55,061	40,226
Rent and other deposits	3,839	9,130
	$918,602	$572,663
Liabilities and Entity Capital		
Current liabilities		
Accounts payable and accrued expenses	$111,150	$166,351
Deferred revenues—subscriptions	297,430	193,042
Deferred revenues—grants	42,562	—
Current portion of long-term debt	50,000	50,000
Total Current Liabilities	501,142	409,393
Long-term debt	32,000	69,740
Contingencies		
Entity capital		
Plant fund	33,061	38,594
Endowment funds	267,869	256,648
Unrestricted funds	84,530	(201,712)
	$918,602	$572,663

Source: Adapted from *Audits of Certain Nonprofit Organizations* (New York: American Institute of Certified Public Accountants, 1981), Exh. 6A, p. 132.

problem is measuring their value. The *Audits of Certain Nonprofit Organizations* suggests that donated services should be reported as an expense (and of course, as revenue) when all the following circumstances exist:

1. The services performed are significant and essential to the organization and would be performed by salaried personnel if volunteers were not available. The organization would continue this program or activity if volunteers were not available.

Illustration 22-18

GARDEN VALLEY BALLET
Statement of Activity
Years Ended June 30, 19X1 and 19X0

	19X1	19X0
Revenue and support from operations		
Admissions	$1,557,567	$1,287,564
Dividends and interest	21,555	2,430
Net realized gains and losses	54,700	18,300
Tuition	242,926	130,723
Concessions and other support	103,582	68,754
	1,980,330	1,507,771
Production costs	476,982	427,754
Operating expenses	797,044	685,522
Ballet school	473,658	301,722
Neighborhood productions	378,454	81,326
General and administrative expense	390,487	469,891
	2,516,625	1,966,215
Deficiency from Operations	(536,295)	(458,444)
Donated services, materials, and facilities	—	8,000
Annual giving	150,379	78,469
Grants	702,368	678,322
Fund-raising costs	(35,743)	(50,454)
	817,004	714,337
Excess from current endeavors	280,709	255,893
Capital additions	11,221	18,250
Total Increase in Entity Capital	$ 291,930	$ 274,143

Source: Adapted from *Audits of Certain Nonprofit Organizations* (New York: American Institute of Certified Public Accountants, 1981), Exh. 6B, p. 133.

2. The organization controls the utilization and duties of the donors of the services. It can influence the activities of the volunteers (including control over the volunteers' time, location, duties, and performance) in a way comparable to the control it would exercise over paid employees with similar responsibilities.
3. The organization has a clearly measurable basis for the amount to be recorded.
4. The program services of the reporting organization are not principally intended for the benefit of the organization's members.

Essentially, an employee–employer relationship must exist between the organization and its volunteers, and objective measurement or valuation of the services must be possible. These circumstances are most often met only by organizations operated by religious groups. In such cases, the

Illustration 22-19

GARDEN VALLEY BALLET
Statement of Changes in Entity Capital
Years Ended June 30, 19X1 and 19X0

	Endowment Funds	Plant Fund	Unrestricted Funds	Total
Entity capital—June 30, 19X9	$238,398	$43,214	$(462,225)	$(180,613)
Excess from current endeavors	—	(4,620)	260,513	255,893
Capital additions	18,250	—	—	18,250
Entity capital—June 30, 19X0	256,648	38,594	(201,712)	93,530
Excess from current endeavors	—	(5,533)	286,242	280,709
Capital additions	11,221	—	—	11,221
Entity capital—June 30, 19X1	$267,869	$33,061	$ 84,530	$ 385,460

Source: Adapted from *Audits of Certain Nonprofit Organizations* (New York: American Institute of Certified Public Accountants, 1981), Exh. 6B, p. 133.

value of the services is determined by subtracting the amounts paid to or on behalf of the religious personnel from the amount of compensation that would be paid to lay persons.

Accounting for restricted contributions by other nonprofit organizations uses an approach whereby revenue is recognized upon expenditure of restricted or unrestricted funds, and unexpended amounts are credited to deferred revenue and not to a Fund Balance account. *Audits of Certain Nonprofit Organizations* states:

> If a donor restricted a contribution . . . to be used for a specific program service, and the organization subsequently . . . incurred expenses for that particular program service, the . . . obligation imposed by the restriction should be deemed to have been met even if unrestricted funds were used. Management should not avoid recognizing the restricted contribution as support in that period simply because it chose to use dollars attributed to unrestricted funds at the time the expense was incurred. . . . Current restricted gifts, grants, bequests, and other income should be accounted for as revenue and support in the statement of activity to the extent that expenses have been incurred for the purpose specified by the donor or grantor during the period. The balances should be accounted for as deferred revenue or support in the balance sheet outside the fund balance section until the restrictions are met.

Illustration 22-20

GARDEN VALLEY BALLET
Schedule of Functional Expenses—Supplementary Schedule
Year Ended June 30, 19X1
(with Comparative Totals for 19X0)

	Program Services					Support Services			
Item of Expense	Production Costs	Operating Expenses	Ballet School	Neighborhood Productions	Total Program Services	General and Administrative	Fund Raising	Total Year Ended 19X1	Total Year Ended 19X0
Salaries, payroll taxes, and employee benefits..	$219,370	$464,570	$388,113	$306,026	$1,378,079	$260,755	$15,782	$1,654,616	$1,312,504
Professional fees	7,864	—	2,785	—	10,649	15,624	—	26,273	21,722
Supplies......................	15,628	17,128	—	3,728	36,484	25,823	—	62,307	43,784
Telephone....................	—	—	—	—	—	10,725	1,211	11,936	10,783
Postage and shipping....	—	—	—	—	—	3,816	14,439	18,255	15,622
Occupancy	—	258,622	82,760	5,478	346,860	41,540	1,527	389,927	322,147
Rental and maintenance of equipment............	—	56,724	—	—	56,724	6,927	2,784	66,435	52,764
Printing and publications	—	—	—	—	—	10,381	—	10,381	10,078
Travel	—	—	—	—	—	5,824	—	5,824	4,728
Conferences, conventions, and meetings............	—	—	—	—	—	2,783	—	2,783	1,568
Membership dues	—	—	—	—	—	756	—	756	2,064
Scenery.......................	154,682	—	—	35,540	190,222	—	—	190,222	143,523
Costumes....................	79,438	—	—	27,682	107,120	—	—	107,120	70,762
Depreciation and amortization.............	—	—	—	—	—	5,533	—	5,533	4,620
Total, year ended June 30, 19X1..	$476,982	$797,044	$473,658	$378,454	$2,126,138	$390,487	$35,743	$2,552,368	
Total, year ended June 30, 19X0..	$427,754	$685,522	$301,722	$ 81,326	$1,496,324	$469,891	$50,454		$2,016,669

Source: Adapted from *Audits of Certain Nonprofit Organizations* (New York: American Institute of Certified Public Accountants, 1981), Exh. 8F, p. 137.

Illustration 22-21

GARDEN VALLEY BALLET
Statement of Changes in Financial Position
Years Ended June 30, 19X1 and 19X0

	19X1	19X0
Funds provided by		
Excess from current endeavors	$280,709	$255,893
Add expenses not requiring outlay of working capital in current period		
Depreciation	5,533	4,620
Other deferred charges	—	7,500
Funds Provided from Current Endeavors	286,242	268,013
Increase in long-term debt	12,260	—
Other	5,291	—
Capital additions	11,221	18,250
Total Funds Provided	315,014	286,263
Funds applied		
Increase in noncurrent investments and cash	11,221	—
Acquisition of property, plant, and equipment	20,368	4,362
Reduction of long-term debt	50,000	25,280
Total Funds Applied	81,589	29,642
Increase in Working Capital	$233,425	$256,621
Changes in the components of working capital		
Increase (decrease) in current assets		
Cash	$ 46,608	$220,342
Marketable securities	215,363	42,312
Accounts receivable	43,366	21,269
Grants receivable	(6,100)	—
Other	25,937	15,413
Increase in Current Assets	325,174	299,336
(Increase) decrease in current liabilities		
Accounts payable and accrued expenses	55,201	36,149
Deferred revenues—subscriptions	(104,388)	(78,864)
Deferred revenues—grants	(42,562)	—
(Increase) in Current Liabilities	(91,749)	(42,715)
Increase in Working Capital	$233,425	$256,621

Source: Adapted from *Audits of Certain Nonprofit Organizations* (New York: American Institute of Certified Public Accountants, 1981), Exh. 6D, p. 135.

Investments

Unlike colleges and universities, hospitals, and voluntary health and welfare organizations, other nonprofit organizations establish a valuation practice that depends on the nature of the security and the ability and intention to hold the securities to maturity. *Statement of Position 78-10,*

Illustration 22-22

SDI RESEARCH GROUP
Balance Sheet
June 30, 19X1 and 19X0

Assets	19X1	19X0
Current assets		
Cash	$ 125,000	$ 115,000
Certificates of deposit	200,000	210,000
Accounts receivable	372,000	346,000
Unbilled contract revenues and reimbursable grant expenses	488,000	390,000
Prepaid expenses and other current assets	40,000	38,000
Total Current Assets	1,225,000	1,099,000
Property, plant, and equipment		
Land and building	220,000	220,000
Furniture and equipment	167,000	156,000
Leased property under capital leases	479,000	479,000
	866,000	855,000
Less—accumulated depreciation and amortization	259,000	185,000
	607,000	670,000
	$1,832,000	$1,769,000

Liabilities and Fund Balance	19X1	19X0
Current liabilities		
Accounts payable and accrued expenses	$ 418,000	$ 388,000
Restricted grant advances	261,000	210,000
Obligations under capital leases	88,000	82,000
Total Current Liabilities	767,000	680,000
Noncurrent capital lease obligations	309,000	397,000
	1,076,000	1,077,000
Fund balance		
Unrestricted	458,000	419,000
Net equity in fixed assets	298,000	273,000
Total Fund Balance	756,000	692,000
	$1,832,000	$1,769,000

Source: Adapted from *Audits of Certain Nonprofit Organizations* (New York: American Institute of Certified Public Accountants, 1981), Exh. 10A, p. 153.

Illustration 22-23

SDI RESEARCH GROUP
Statement of Revenues, Expenses and Changes in Fund Balance
Years Ended June 30, 19X1 and 19X0

	19X1	19X0
Revenues		
Contract revenues—U.S. government	$ 5,958,000	$5,578,000
Restricted grants—foundations and individuals	4,752,000	4,172,000
Other, including interest	43,000	41,000
	10,753,000	9,791,000
Expenses		
Research and development		
Environmental	5,263,000	4,997,000
Health	2,992,000	2,766,000
National defense	1,166,000	938,000
Management and general	1,103,000	985,000
Contract and grant procurement	165,000	151,000
	10,689,000	9,837,000
Excess (deficiency) of Revenues over Expenses	64,000	(46,000)
Fund Balance, beginning of year	692,000	738,000
Fund Balance, end of year	$ 756,000	$ 692,000

Source: Adapted from *Audits of Certain Nonprofit Organizations* (New York: American Institute of Certified Public Accountants, 1981), Exh. 10B, p. 154.

included within the audit guide, provides that investments should be reported as follows:

- Marketable debt securities, when there is both the ability and intention to hold the securities to maturity, should be reported at amortized cost, market value, or the lower of amortized cost or market value.
- Marketable equity securities and marketable debt securities that are not expected to be held to maturity should be reported at either market value or the lower of cost or market value.
- Other types of investments, for example, real estate or oil and gas interests, should be reported at either fair value or the lower of cost or fair value.

The application of a particular valuation method should be based on each of the three groups identified above.

When the lower of cost or market valuation basis is used, and the investment is classified as noncurrent, adjustments should be charged or credited directly to Fund Balance. If the investment is classified as current,

Illustration 22-24

SDI RESEARCH GROUP
Statement of Changes in Financial Position
Years Ended June 30, 19X1 and 19X0

	19X1	19X0
Financial resources were provided by		
Excess (deficiency) of revenues over expenses	$ 64,000	$ (46,000)
Add—expenses not requiring current outlay of working capital—depreciation and amortization	74,000	26,000
Working Capital Provided by (used in) Operations	138,000	(20,000)
Financing of fixed asset additions through capital leases	—	397,000
Total Resources Provided	138,000	377,000
Financial resources were used for		
Acquisition of property, plant and equipment	11,000	481,000
Reduction of noncurrent capital lease obligations	88,000	—
Total Resources Used	99,000	481,000
Increase (Decrease) in Working Capital	$ 39,000	$(104,000)
Changes in working capital were represented by		
Increase (decrease) in current assets—		
Cash	$ 10,000	$ (14,000)
Certificates of deposit	(10,000)	(40,000)
Accounts receivable	26,000	10,000
Unbilled contract revenues and reimbursable grant expenses	98,000	42,000
Other	2,000	(1,000)
	126,000	(3,000)
(Increase) decrease in current liabilities—		
Accounts payable and accrued expenses	(30,000)	(23,000)
Restricted grant advances	(51,000)	4,000
Obligations under capital leases	(6,000)	(82,000)
	(87,000)	(101,000)
Increase (Decrease) in Working Capital	$ 39,000	$(104,000)

Source: Adapted from *Audits of Certain Nonprofit Organizations* (New York: American Institute of Certified Public Accountants, 1981), Exh. 10C, p. 155.

then adjustments should be reflected in the statement of activity in the same manner as realized gains or losses. Investments held in Current Restricted Funds should normally be considered current investments.

Accounting for investment income or loss depends on the nature of the fund. Unrestricted investment income from all funds should be reported as revenue in the statement of activity. This includes unrestricted gains and losses on investments of unrestricted and restricted funds.

Restricted income, including gains and losses, from investments of Current Restricted Funds and restricted Plant Funds should be reported as **deferred** amounts in the balance sheet. Restricted expendable income from investments of endowment funds should also be deferred on the balance sheet.

Investment income of endowment funds that must be added to the principal as stipulated by the donor should be reported as capital additions. Gains and losses should also be reported as capital additions or deductions.

Accounting for Fixed Assets

The accounting for fixed assets of other nonprofit organizations is similar to that for hospitals and voluntary health and welfare organizations. Purchased fixed assets are recorded at cost and at fair value if acquired through donation. However, inexhaustible collections owned by museums, art galleries, botanical gardens, libraries, and similar entities need not be capitalized. If historical cost is not available or if alternative valuation methods outlined in *Statement of Position 78-10* cannot be used, then the term "collections" should appear on the balance sheet, referenced to a note that describes the collections.

Although fixed assets are depreciated, only exhaustible fixed assets are depreciated. Landmarks, monuments, cathedrals, historical treasures, and structures used for worship need not be depreciated.

A COMPARATIVE SUMMARY

Funds Structure

The nature of the accounting system for nonprofit organizations depends on the complexity of each organization and its external mandates. Many of the nonprofit organizations use some form of fund accounting system in order to ensure compliance with all external restrictions and all internal designations by the governing board. In some cases, non–fund accounting is used when there are not externally imposed restrictions or when the external donor will permit a simple "appropriation" of Fund Balance disclosing the restrictions. Illustration 22-25 shows the funds structures of all nonprofit organizations.

Basis of Accounting

All nonprofit organizations must use accrual basis accounting for financial reporting purposes. However, this does not preclude organizations from using cash basis accounting throughout the period if it is cost-effective. The system need only be adjusted to accrual basis when preparing the financial statements.

Illustration 22-25
Comparative Summary of All Nonprofit Organizations

Colleges and Universities	Hospitals	Voluntary Health and Welfare Organizations	Other Nonprofit Organizations
Funds Structures			
Current Unrestricted Fund Current Restricted Fund Plant Funds Group Endowment and Similar Funds Annuity and Life Income Funds Loan Funds Agency Funds	Unrestricted Fund Specific Purpose Fund Plant Replacement and Expansion Fund Endowment Funds Annuity Funds Loan Funds	Current Unrestricted Fund Current Restricted Fund Land, Buildings, and Equipment Fund Endowment Funds Loan and Annuity Funds Custodian Funds	Depending on complexity, could be similar to voluntary health and welfare organizations, although not specified by the audit guide
Basis of Accounting			
Full accrual method for all types of nonprofit organizations			
Financial Statements			
Balance sheet Statement of changes in fund balances Statement of current funds revenues, expenditures, and other changes	Balance sheet Statement of changes in fund balances Statement of revenues and expenses Statement of changes in financial position	Balance sheet Statement of support, revenues and expenses, and changes in fund balance Statement of functional expenses	Balance sheet Statement of activity Statement of changes in financial position
Pledges			
Recorded, net of allowance for uncollectible pledges, *or* Disclosed in notes to financial statements	Recorded, net of allowance for uncollectible pledges	Recorded, net of allowance for uncollectible pledges	Recorded **if legally enforceable,** net of allowance for uncollectible pledges
Donated Services			
Generally recognized by colleges and universities operated by religious groups Generally record the difference between the fair value and the amount paid for the services of members of the order as donated services. The difference is recorded as expenditures with the credit to gift revenues.	Should be reflected only when there is an equivalent of an employer-employee relationship and an objective basis for valuation. Generally record the difference between the fair value and the amount paid for the services as donated services. The difference is recorded as expense with the credit to nonoperating revenue.	Same as hospitals The difference is recorded as expense with the credit to support	Same as hospitals but with the additional requirements that services must be essential and would be performed by salaried personnel if volunteers were not available. Same as for voluntary health and welfare organizations The difference is recorded as expense with the credit to support

Investments			
At acquisition cost (at market value at donation) or at market value	Lower of aggregate cost or market	At acquisition cost adjusted for market decline or at market value	Marketable debt securities held to maturity: • amortized cost • market value • lower of amortized cost or market value Marketable equity securities and marketable debt securities not held to maturity: • market value • lower of cost or market Other types: • fair value • lower of cost or fair value
Restricted Contributions			
Contributions are credited to an appropriate Fund Balance account. When the restrictions are met or lapse, the amount is transferred to unrestricted operating revenues for hospitals and to current restricted fund revenue for colleges and universities		Contributions are recognized as revenue immediately upon receipt. The recognition of revenue is required without regard to whether the contributions had been used or the restrictions met.	Revenue is recognized upon expenditure of restricted funds, and unexpended amounts are credited to deferred revenue and not to a Fund Balance account.
Fixed Assets			
Recorded at cost or fair value if donated	Recorded at cost or fair value if donated	Recorded at cost or fair value if donated	Recorded at cost or fair value if donated, except for inexhaustible assets, which may be simply listed in the footnotes.
Depreciation *not* taken	Depreciation taken	Depreciation taken	Depreciation taken on exhaustible fixed assets only. Excludes landmarks, monuments, cathedrals, or historical treasures.
Use a Plant Funds Group of funds including: Investment in Plant, Unexpended Plant Funds, Renewals and Replacement Funds and Retirement of Indebtedness Funds.	1. Investment in Plant, Accumulated Depreciation, and related liabilities are accounted for in the Unrestricted Fund 2. Externally restricted, unexpended resources for plant replacement and expansion are accounted for separately in a restricted fund—Plant Replacement and Expansion	Fixed assets used in operations are accounted for in a Plant Fund, unless donor restrictions require unexpended funds in a restricted fund.	Same as voluntary health and welfare organizations

Some nonprofit organizations use an encumbrance system for outstanding purchase orders and other commitments. However, the encumbrances should not be reported as expenses nor included as liabilities in the financial statements. However, like governmental units, the nonprofit organization may designate a portion of Fund Balance that is committed.

Financial Statements

All nonprofit organizations require a balance sheet, as well as a statement or statements that show revenues, expense (or expenditures), and changes in Fund Balance for the reporting period. Hospitals and other nonprofit organizations also require a statement of changes in financial position. Voluntary health and welfare organizations also require a very specialized statement which delineates functional expenses.

Pledges

Pledge receivables and related revenue, deferred income, or increases in Fund Balance are generally recorded by all nonprofit organizations. A valuation reserve — an allowance for uncollectible pledges — must also be estimated and offset against the receivable. As an exception, colleges and universities permit disclosure of the pledge receivable in the footnotes as an alternative to its recording. Other nonprofit organizations require recording the pledge receivable only if it is legally enforceable.

Donated Services

The value of donated services are generally recognized in the financial statements of nonprofit organizations but only if there is an equivalent of an employer–employee relationship and there is an objective basis for valuation. Other nonprofit organizations impose a further restriction that the services must be essential and would be performed by salaried personnel if volunteers were not available.

Investments

As Illustration 22-25 shows, the valuation practices for investments are diverse among the various types of nonprofit organizations. However, the principal methods are (1) lower of cost or market and (2) market value. If the latter method is used, unrealized gains or losses must be recognized in the financial statements.

Restricted Contributions

There are three methods for accounting for restricted contributions. One method, currently used by voluntary health and welfare organizations, recognizes the restricted contribution as revenue immediately upon receipt. The second method, used by colleges and hospitals, requires a credit to Fund Balance until the restrictions are met, at which time the Fund Balance is charged and Revenue is credited. The third method, used by all other nonprofit organizations, requires an initial credit to Deferred Revenue and subsequently to Revenue when restrictions have been met.

Fixed Assets

As Illustration 22-25 shows, fixed assets are generally recorded at cost. However, other nonprofit organizations provide an exception for inexhaustible assets. Also with the exception of colleges and universities, depreciation is recognized by all other nonprofit organizations.

Glossary of New Terms

Agency Fund "Funds received and held by an organization as fiscal agent for others."*

Annuity Fund A fund that includes gifts of money or other property given to an organization on the condition that the organization bind itself to make periodic stipulated payments that terminate at a specified time to the donor or other designated individuals.

Custodian Funds Funds received and held by an organization as fiscal agent for others.

Deferred Revenue and Support "Revenue or support received or recorded before it is earned, that is, before the conditions are met, in whole or in part, for which the revenue or support is received or is to be received."*

Designated Funds Unrestricted funds set aside for specific purposes by action of the governing board.

Endowment Funds "The fund in which a donor has stipulated in the donative instrument that the principal is to be maintained inviolate and in perpetuity and only the income from the investments of the fund may be expended."*

Expendable Funds "Funds that are available to finance an organization's program and supporting services, including both unrestricted and restricted amounts."*

Fund "An accounting entity established for the purpose of accounting for resources used for specific activities or objectives in accordance with special regulations, restrictions, or limitations."*

Fund Group "A group of funds of similar character for example, operating funds, endowment funds, annuity funds, and life income funds."*

Investment Pool "Assets of several funds pooled or consolidated for investment purposes."*

Loan Funds "Resources restricted for loans. When both principal and interest on the loan funds received by an organization are loanable, they are included in the loan fund group. If only the income from a fund is loanable, the principal is included in endowment funds, while the cumulative income constitutes the loan fund."*

**Statement of Position 78-10.*

Market Value Unit Method A method of allocating realized and unrealized gains (or losses) and income to participating funds in an investment pool.

Pledge "A promise to make a contribution to an organization in the amount and form stipulated."*

Quasi-Endowment Funds "Funds that the governing board of an organization, rather than a donor or other outside agency, has determined are to be retained and invested. The governing board has the right to decide at any time to expend the principal of such funds."* Also called designated funds.

Renewal and Replacement Funds A fund within the Plant Fund Group of colleges and universities that represents unexpended resources held for renewal and replacement of plant assets.

Resource Transferability The nonprofit organization's freedom to use resources for various purposes.

Restricted Funds "Funds for which use is restricted by outside agencies or persons as contrasted with funds over which the organization has complete control and discretion."*

Revenues "Gross increases in assets, gross decreases in liabilities, or a combination of both from delivering or producing goods, rendering services, or other earning activities of an organization during a period, for example, dues, sale of services, ticket sales, fees, interest, dividends, and rent."*

Support "The conveyance of property from one person or organization to another without consideration, for example, donations, gifts, grants, or bequests."*

Term Endowment "A fund that has all the characteristics of an endowment fund, except that at some future date or event, it will no longer be required to be maintained as an endowment fund."*

Unexpended Plant Fund A fund within the Plant Fund group of colleges and universities that represents unexpended resources for the acquisition of plant assets.

Unrestricted Funds "Funds that have no external restrictions on their use or purpose — that is, funds that can be used for any purpose designated by the governing board, distinguished from funds restricted externally for specific purposes (for example, for operations, plant, or endowment)."*

Appendix A
ILLUSTRATED CURRENT FUNDS GROUP TRANSACTIONS: COLLEGES AND UNIVERSITIES

The following sections illustrate the accounting for Current Funds Group transactions.

Illustration

UNRESTRICTED CURRENT FUNDS SUBGROUP TRANSACTIONS

The following journal entries pertain to financial events and transactions of Andover University's Unrestricted Current Funds for the year ended June 30, 19X2.

1. Student tuition and fees billed for the year were $8,000,000, which was used for educational and general purposes. Prior experience shows that $100,000 of this billing will be uncollectible. At year-end, $800,000 remains uncollected.

Cash	7,200,000	
Accounts Receivable	800,000	
Expenditures — Instruction	100,000	
Revenue — Student Tuition and Fees		8,000,000
Allowance for Bad Debts		100,000

2. Unrestricted government appropriations for the year amounted to $5,000,000, all of which have been collected.

Cash	5,000,000	
Revenue — Government Appropriations		5,000,000

3. Unrestricted gifts and private grants received during the period amounted to $50,000.

Cash	50,000	
Revenue — Gifts and Private Grants		50,000

4. Unrestricted income from endowment and similar funds amounted to $185,000.

Cash	185,000	
Revenue — Endowment Income		185,000

5. Auxiliary enterprise revenue included $175,000 from student residence halls; $200,000 from cafeterias; and $750,000 from the college store sales. All billed amounts have been collected except for $50,000 in student residence fees. Of this amount, an estimated $5,000 will be uncollectible.

Cash	1,075,000	
Accounts Receivable	50,000	
Expenditures — Auxiliary Enterprises	5,000	
Revenue — Auxiliary Enterprises		1,125,000
Allowance for Bad Debts		5,000

6. Term endowment funds that are now available for unrestricted use amount to $300,000.

Cash	300,000	
Revenue — Endowment Income		300,000

7. Purchases of materials and supplies amounted to $800,000 for the year. A perpetual inventory is used. Purchases of $150,000 remain unpaid at year-end.

Materials and Supplies Inventory	**800,000**	
Cash		**650,000**
Vouchers Payable		**150,000**

8. Operating expenditures are incurred and assigned as shown in the following journal entry. Note that $2,250,000 of these expenditures are unpaid vouchers payable at year-end.

Expenditures—Instruction	**3,500,000**	
Expenditures—Research	**1,200,000**	
Expenditures—Academic Support	**3,000,000**	
Expenditures—Student Services	**380,000**	
Expenditures—Operation and Maintenance of Plant	**1,120,000**	
Expenditures—Institutional Support	**500,000**	
Cash		**7,450,000**
Vouchers Payable		**2,250,000**

9. Use of materials and supplies is assigned as shown in the following journal entry:

Expenditures—Instruction	**300,000**	
Expenditures—Research	**150,000**	
Expenditures—Academic Support	**50,000**	
Expenditures—Student Services	**25,000**	
Expenditures—Institutional Support	**120,000**	
Materials and Supplies Inventory		**645,000**

10. The university's student aid committee granted student tuition and fee reductions of $200,000.

Expenditures—Student Aid	**200,000**	
Accounts Receivable		**200,000**

11. The trustees have specified that certain Current Fund revenues must be transferred to meet the debt service provisions relating to the university's institutional properties, including amounts set aside for debt retirement, interest, and required provisions for renewal and replacement. For this year, these mandatory transfers total $550,000.

Transfers—Plant Funds	**550,000**	
Cash		**550,000**

12. Auxiliary enterprises expenditures amount to $650,000.

Expenditures—Auxiliary Enterprises........	**650,000**	
Vouchers Payable (Cash)..................		**650,000**

13. Closing entries are not illustrated. Revenues, expenditures, and transfers are merely closed to the Fund Balance account.

Illustration

RESTRICTED CURRENT FUNDS SUBGROUP TRANSACTIONS

The following journal entries pertain to financial events and transactions of Andover University's Restricted Current Funds for the year ended June 30, 19X2.

1. Restricted gifts in the amount of $100,000 were received from the Wollaston Foundation to be used for student aid.

Cash..	**100,000**	
Fund Balance[11]		**100,000**

2. A $750,000 federal government grant was received for library acquisitions in science and engineering.

Cash..	**750,000**	
Fund Balance....................................		**750,000**

3. Federal government contracts were awarded to certain academic departments to develop training programs and instructional institutes for child care and development. These contracts amounted to $1,500,000 and included a provision for reimbursement to the university of indirect costs of $75,000. The contract payments were collected.

Cash..	**1,500,000**	
Fund Balance....................................		**1,500,000**
Fund Balance..	**75,000**	
Cash..		**75,000**

The latter entry transfers the indirect cost recovery to the Unrestricted Current Fund, which would acknowledge receipt of the payment with the following entry:

[11]Subsidiary accounts would usually show the sources, purposes, and applications of restricted resources.

Cash	75,000	
Revenue—General		75,000

4. Expenditures incurred were for: student aid, $85,000; instruction (library acquisitions), $700,000; training programs and instructional institutes, $1,425,000. At year-end, 10% of the expenditures remain unpaid.

Expenditures—Student Aid	85,000	
Expenditures—Instruction	700,000	
Expenditures—Instruction	1,425,000	
Cash		1,989,000
Vouchers Payable		221,000
Fund Balance	2,210,000	
Revenue—Student Aid		85,000
Revenue—Instruction		2,125,000

5. Closing entries are not illustrated. (Because total revenues equal total expenditures, these accounts offset each other in the closing entry.)

Appendix B
ILLUSTRATED PLANT FUNDS GROUP TRANSACTIONS: COLLEGES AND UNIVERSITIES

The following sections illustrate accounting for Plant Funds Group transactions.

Illustration

PLANT FUNDS GROUP TRANSACTIONS

The following journal entries pertain to transactions of Andover University's Plant Fund Group for the year ended June 30, 19X2. First we illustrate Unexpended Plant Fund activities.

1. A major fund-raising drive for new laboratory equipment generated $300,000 cash and $250,000 in marketable securities.

Cash	300,000	
Marketable Securities	250,000	
Fund Balance—Restricted		550,000

2. The university received a federal grant of $1,000,000 for the construc-

tion of a new classroom wing for the science department. The grant requires the university to match the government appropriation.

Cash	**1,000,000**	
Fund Balance — Restricted		**1,000,000**

3. The university's governing board directed a transfer from Unrestricted Current Funds for the construction of the new classroom wing for the science department. The $1,000,000 transfer complied with the government's building grant.

Cash	**1,000,000**	
Fund Balance — Restricted		**1,000,000**

4. The addition to the science department building was completed during the year and cost the university $2,500,000. A mortgage was signed for $500,000.

Cash	**500,000**	
Mortgage Payable		**500,000**
Construction in Progress	**2,500,000**	
Cash		**2,500,000**
Mortgage Payable[12]	**500,000**	
Fund Balance — Restricted	**2,000,000**	
Construction in Progress		**2,500,000**

5. Income from pooled investments totaled $25,000.

Cash	**25,000**	
Fund Balance — Unrestricted		**25,000**

6. A planned expansion of the university's sports stadium was abandoned because of cutbacks in available federal funds. The governing board directed the return of $400,000 to Unrestricted Current Funds.

Fund Balance — Unrestricted	**400,000**	
Cash[13]		**400,000**

7. Expenses of $20,000 were incurred in connection with fund-raising activities for the new science department classroom wing and laboratory equipment.

[12]This entry transfers the building cost and mortgage to the Investment in Plant Fund account.
[13]The Unrestricted Current Fund would credit the Transfers — Unexpended Plant Fund account.

Fund Balance—Unrestricted	20,000	
Cash		20,000

Now we cover Renewals and Replacement Fund activities.

1. Income from pooled investments totaled $15,000.

Cash	15,000	
Fund Balance—Unrestricted		15,000

2. The governing board transferred cash to the Renewals and Replacements Fund for equipment replacement in the science department, $80,000.

Cash[14]	80,000	
Fund Balance—Unrestricted		80,000

3. Replacement equipment was purchased for the science department for $78,000.

Fund Balance—Unrestricted[15]	78,000	
Cash		78,000

The Retirement of Indebtedness Fund has the following activity:

1. Income earned from pooled investments amounts to $10,000.

Cash	10,000	
Fund Balance—Unrestricted		10,000

2. The governing board transferred $250,000 to the Retirement of Indebtedness Fund for interest and principal payments on debt. The debt payments were made.

Cash	250,000	
Fund Balance—Unrestricted		250,000
Fund Balance—Unrestricted	250,000	
Cash		250,000

[14]The Unrestricted Current Fund would charge the Transfers—Plant Funds Renewals and Replacements account.
[15]This entry transfers the equipment cost to the Investment in Plant Fund account.

The Investment in Plant Fund has the following activity:

1. Completed science building is transferred from Unexpended Plant Fund (see transaction 4, Unexpended Plant Fund).

Building (science)	**2,500,000**	
Mortgage Payable		**500,000**
Net Investment in Plant		**2,000,000**

2. Replacement equipment is transferred from the Renewals and Replacement Fund (see transaction 3, Renewals and Replacement Fund).

Equipment (science)	**78,000**	
Net Investment in Plant		**78,000**

3. Mortgage payable is reduced (see transaction 2, Retirement of Indebtedness Fund).

Mortgage Payable	**250,000**	
Net Investment in Plant		**250,000**

4. The university received an art collection and several rare books for its library. The appraised values were $325,000 for the art collection and $200,000 for the rare books.

Valued Collections—Art	**325,000**	
Valued Collections—Rare Books	**200,000**	
Net Investment in Plant		**525,000**

5. The laboratory equipment that was replaced was sold for $30,000. The recorded value of the equipment was $55,000.

Net Investment in Plant[16]	**55,000**	
Equipment (science)		**55,000**

[16]The sales proceeds could be accounted for by the Unrestricted Current Fund or by the Unexpended Plant Funds, depending on the disposition of the funds.

Appendix C
ILLUSTRATED UNRESTRICTED FUND TRANSACTIONS: HOSPITALS

Illustration

UNRESTRICTED FUNDS TRANSACTIONS

The following journal entries pertain to the financial events and transactions of Charleston Memorial Hospital's Unrestricted Fund for the year ended June 30, 19X1:

1. Gross billings to patients for the year were assigned as shown in the following entry:[17]

Accounts Receivable	**4,050,000**	
Revenues — Daily Patient Services		**3,000,000**
Revenues — Other Nursing Services		**750,000**
Revenues — Other Professional Services.		**300,000**

Typically, more detailed revenue accounts are maintained by specific revenue producing segments (for example, Daily Patient Services: Cardiac Unit).

2. Adjustments to gross revenue include contractual adjustments of $500,000 with third-party payers and approved charity adjustments of $200,000.

Charity Service	**200,000**	
Contractual Adjustments	**500,000**	
Accounts Receivable		**700,000**

3. Collection of accounts receivable totaled $3,350,000.

Cash	**3,350,000**	
Accounts Receivable		**3,350,000**

4. Inventory acquisitions, including materials and supplies, amounted to $700,000. One-fourth of the approved invoices remain unpaid at year-end.

[17]Generally, hospitals bill their patients at standard rates, even though collectibility is questionable. This procedure provides management with more useful information and also facilitates as the calculation and support of reimbursement claims submitted to third-party payers (such as Medicare, Medicaid, and Blue Cross).

Materials and Supplies Inventory	**700,000**	
Cash		**525,000**
Vouchers Payable		**175,000**

5. Use of the materials and supplies inventory is assigned as shown in the following entry:

Expenses—Nursing Services[18]	**190,000**	
Expenses—Other Professional Services	**75,000**	
Expenses—General Services	**300,000**	
Expenses—Fiscal Services	**10,000**	
Expenses—Administrative Services	**5,000**	
Materials and Supplies Inventory		**580,000**

6. Salaries and wage expenses incurred for the year total $2,200,000. Of this amount, $176,000 is accrued at year-end.

Expenses—Nursing Services	**1,000,000**	
Expenses—Other Professional Services	**700,000**	
Expenses—General Services	**300,000**	
Expenses—Fiscal Services	**150,000**	
Expenses—Administrative Services	**50,000**	
Cash		**2,024,000**
Accrued Salaries and Wages		**176,000**

7. Other operating expenses processed through the voucher system are assigned as shown, including $18,000 of approved but unpaid vouchers at year-end.

Expenses—Nursing Services	**75,000**	
Expenses—Other Professional Services	**50,000**	
Expenses—General Services	**30,000**	
Expenses—Fiscal Services	**25,000**	
Expenses—Administrative Services	**20,000**	
Cash		**182,000**
Vouchers Payable		**18,000**

8. The provision for estimated uncollectible accounts is $125,000.

Provision for Uncollectible Accounts	**125,000**	
Allowance for Uncollectible Accounts		**125,000**

[18] In practice, hospitals maintain detailed expense control accounts and even more detailed subsidiary accounts for managerial control purposes.

9. Depreciation expense for the year is $350,000. This provision is based on historical cost, which conforms with generally accepted accounting principles. Hospitals may compute depreciation expense based on replacement cost for internal management purposes.

Expense—Depreciation[19]	**350,000**	
Accumulated Depreciation		**350,000**

10. Interfund transfers for the year to the Unrestricted Fund are recorded as shown.[20]

Cash	**945,000**	
Revenue[21]—Other Revenue: Transfers from Specific Purpose Fund		**320,000**
Revenue—Nonoperating Revenue: Transfers from Endowment Fund		**125,000**
Fund Balance—Unrestricted Fund: Transfers from Plant Renewal and Replacement Fund		**500,000**

11. Closing entries are not shown. Revenues, expenses, charity services, contractual adjustments, and the provision for uncollectibles are merely closed to the Fund Balance account.

[19]Generally, for reporting purposes, depreciation is not charged to the functional areas (for example, Expenses—Nursing Services). For internal management purposes, depreciation is charged to subsidiary expense accounts by cost center.

[20]Receipts of restricted resources by the Specific Purpose, Plant Renewal and Replacement, and Endowment funds are credited directly to the respective Fund Balance. All subsequent earnings from investments of these resources are also credited to Fund Balance. When the Unrestricted Fund expends resources for the designated purpose, the affected restricted fund charges Fund Balance and credits Cash or an interfund payable. The Unrestricted Fund acknowledges receipt of the transfer by a charge to Cash and a credit to Other Revenue—Transfers.

[21]The following entries would be recorded by the other funds reflecting transfers to the Unrestricted Fund:

Specific Purpose Fund:		
Fund Balance	320,000	
Cash		320,000
Plant Renewal and Replacement Fund:		
Fund Balance	500,000	
Cash		500,000
Endowment Fund:		
Fund Balance	125,000	
Cash		125,000

Appendix D
ILLUSTRATED TRANSACTIONS FOR ENDOWMENT AND SIMILAR FUNDS, AGENCY FUNDS, ANNUITY FUNDS, LIFE INCOME FUNDS, AND LOAN FUNDS

Endowment and Similar Funds

Illustration

ENDOWMENT AND SIMILAR FUNDS GROUP TRANSACTIONS

The following journal entries pertain to transactions of Andover University's Endowment and Similar Funds Group.

1. The Quincy family established an Endowment Fund, the income from which should be used to maintain the university's rare books collection. This permanent endowment does not restrict the investment of the funds.

Cash	**350,000**	
Fund Balance—Endowment		**350,000**

2. The university's board of trustees directed the accounting officer to establish a quasi-endowment fund of $200,000. The income is to be used to maintain the campus theater. No restrictions were imposed on the investment of the funds. The transfer was made from Unrestricted Current Fund.

Cash	**200,000**	
Fund Balance—Endowment[22]		**200,000**

3. The Coulomb Corporation established an Endowment Fund in the amount of $150,000, the income from which will augment a professorial chair in electrical engineering. The endowment instrument stipulates that all income and investment gains are expendable for salary augmentation for five years. At the end of the fifth year, the principal is to be used to replace equipment in the engineering laboratories.

Cash	**150,000**	
Fund Balance—Term Endowment		**150,000**

[22]Unrestricted Current Fund:

Transfers—Endowment and Similar Funds	200,000	
Cash		200,000

4. Investment earnings from pooled investments totaled $19,500, received as shown:

Cash	19,500	
Fund Balance—Endowment		6,500
Fund Balance—Term Endowment		8,000
Fund Balance—Quasi-Endowment		5,000

5. Salary augmentation payments for the professorial chair in electrical engineering amount to $6,500.

Fund Balance—Term Endowment[23]	6,500	
Cash		6,500

Agency Funds

Illustration

AGENCY FUND TRANSACTIONS

The following journal entries pertain to Andover University's Agency Fund transactions.

1. Student government fees collected during the registration process are deposited in the student government fund.

Cash	25,000	
Fund Balance—Agency (liability)		25,000

2. Income earned from student government fund investments amounted to $2,000.

Cash	2,000	
Fund Balance—Agency		2,000

3. Authorized disbursements for the period amounted to $7,500.

Fund Balance—Agency	7,500	
Cash		7,500

[23]Restricted Current Fund:

Cash	6,500	
Fund Balance—Endowment Fund		6,500
Then, as expended:		
Fund Balance—Endowment Fund	6,500	
Revenue—Instruction		6,500

4. Fund maintenance charges were $350.

Fund Balance—Agency	350	
Cash		350

Annuity Funds

Illustration

ANNUITY FUNDS GROUP TRANSACTIONS

The following journal entries show Andover University's Annuity Funds Group transactions.

1. Phyllis Sims donated $250,000 to the university with the stipulation that she receive $20,000 per year for the rest of her life. Thereafter, the principal should be used to provide student aid. The actuarial value of the annuity is $85,000.

Cash	250,000	
Annuities Payable		85,000
Fund Balance—Annuity		165,000

2. Net investment gains for the period were $24,000, and investment income was $14,000.

Cash	38,000	
Annuities Payable		38,000

3. Payments to annuitant Phyllis Sims were $20,000.

Annuities Payable	20,000	
Cash		20,000

4. There was a periodic adjustment for the actuarial gain due to recomputation of the liability based on revised life expectancies of all annuitants.

Annuities Payable	53,500	
Fund Balance—Annuity		53,500

5. Annuitant Josh Gaylord died. The annuity was transferred to the Endowment Funds Group according to the provisions of the gift instrument.

Annuities Payable	1,500	
Fund Balance—Annuity	23,000	
Cash		24,500

Life Income Funds

Illustration

LIFE INCOME FUNDS GROUP TRANSACTIONS

The following journal entries show Andover University's Life Income Fund Group transactions.

1. Gerald Baumann established a Life Income Fund, which specified that at his death the principal is to be transferred to the Unrestricted Current Fund group and used at the discretion of the board of trustees.

Cash	50,000	
Investments	150,000	
Fund Balance—Life Income		200,000

2. Income earned on investments amounted to $15,000.

Cash	15,000	
Income Payable		15,000

3. Life Income Fund distributions amounted to $15,000.

Income Payable	15,000	
Cash		15,000

4. The Erika Meagher Life Income Fund was transferred to Endowment Funds in accordance with the provisions of the gift instrument.

Fund Balance—Life Income	100,000	
Cash		100,000

Loan Funds

Illustration

LOAN FUND TRANSACTIONS

The following journal entries show Andover University's Loan Fund transactions.

1. A fund-raising drive for student loan funds generated $750,000.

Cash	750,000	
Fund Balance—Loan		750,000

2. The board of trustees directed the use of $200,000 of Unrestricted Current Funds for low interest real estate loans to the faculty.

Cash[24]	200,000	
Fund Balance—Loan		200,000

3. Loans to students and faculty totaled $500,000. An allowance for uncollectible loans was established for 1% of this amount.

Notes Receivable	500,000	
Cash		500,000
Fund Balance—Loan	5,000	
Allowance for Doubtful Loans		5,000

4. Excess cash of $400,000 was invested in marketable securities.

Investments	400,000	
Cash		400,000

5. Investment income earned amounted to $8,000.

Cash	8,000	
Fund Balance—Loan		8,000

[24]Unrestricted Current Funds:

Transfer—Endowment Fund	200,000	
Cash		200,000

6. Certain notes having a face amount of $25,000 proved to be uncollectible and were written off.

Allowance for Doubtful Loans	25,000	
Notes Receivable		25,000

7. Administrative and collection costs for the period amounted to $4,000.

Fund Balance—Loan	4,000	
Cash		4,000

Appendix E
INVESTMENT POOLS

Nonprofit organizations frequently pool the investments of their various funds. Pooling provides several advantages, including increased investment flexibility, enhanced protection of fund principal through broad diversification, and, in some cases, lower investment costs.

Nonprofit organizations commonly use both pooled and nonpooled investments. Provisions in a gift instrument may prohibit participation in pooled investment schemes. In some cases, several pools are used so that different investment objectives may be accommodated. For example, certain endowment funds may be invested in one investment pool to obtain a high rate of investment income and protection of principal. Other funds could be placed in investment pools with a goal of capital appreciation.

The use of investment pooling requires careful attention to an accounting system that ensures equitable determination of principal, allocation of realized and unrealized gains or losses, and income. The method most generally in use and one specified in the audit guides is the market value unit method.

The **market value unit method** assigns units in the investment pool to individual participating funds. The number of units assigned to a participating fund is calculated on the basis of the market value of the total assets of the pool when the specific fund enters the pool. This method is similar to the method used with open-end investment trusts or mutual funds.

Illustration

INVESTMENT POOL TRANSACTIONS

1. Four funds of Andover University form an investment pool and contribute cash as shown in the following schedule:

Quasi-Endowment Fund	$ 20,000
Endowment Fund	30,000
Unrestricted Fund	40,000
Plant Fund Group	10,000
	$100,000

An arbitrarily determined value per unit is selected. Subsequently, value per unit is determined by dividing the current market value of all net assets in the investment pool by the number of outstanding units.

Fund	Unit Value	Units	Market Value
Quasi-Endowment Fund	$10	2,000	$ 20,000
Endowment Fund	10	3,000	30,000
Unrestricted Fund	10	4,000	40,000
Plant Fund Group	10	1,000	10,000
		10,000	$100,000

2. During the first quarter, the board of trustees authorizes the withdrawal of $10,000 of the Quasi-Endowment Fund's investment in the pool. Calculation of the number of units withdrawn is as follows:

$$\text{units withdrawn} = \frac{\text{amount withdrawn}}{\text{market value per unit}} = \frac{\$10{,}000}{\$10} = 1{,}000 \text{ units}$$

Market value per unit is from the previous valuation date. After the withdrawal, the investment pool contains the following funds:

Fund	Unit Value	Units	Market Value
Quasi-Endowment Fund	$10	1,000	$10,000
Endowment Fund	10	3,000	30,000
Unrestricted Fund	10	4,000	40,000
Plant Fund Group	10	1,000	10,000
		9,000	$90,000

The following funds made additional investments to the investment pool during the second quarter:

Plant Fund Group	$15,000
Life Income Funds Group	30,000

The value per unit of funds currently in the investment pool is calculated as follows:

$$\text{market value per unit} = \frac{\text{total market value}}{\text{units outstanding}} = \frac{\$108{,}000}{9{,}000} = \$12$$

The units allocated to each additional investment are determined by dividing the amount of each additional investment by the corresponding current unit value:

Fund	Addition	Units
Plant Funds Group	$15,000	1,250
Life Income Funds Group	30,000	2,500

Immediately after this transaction, the fund includes the following:

Fund	Unit Value	Units	Market Value
Quasi-Endowment Fund	$12	1,000	$ 12,000
Endowment Fund	12	3,000	36,000
Unrestricted Fund	12	4,000	48,000
Plant Fund Group	12	2,250	27,000
Life Income Funds Group	12	2,500	30,000
		12,750	$153,000

Income distributions, including gains or losses on sales of investments, is allocated by dividing the total income available by the total units.

Review Questions

1. Compare the objectives of nonprofit organizations with those of business organizations.
2. Discuss why nonprofit organizations place greater emphasis on the nature of resource inflows and the degree of resource transferability.
3. Financial statements of nonprofit organizations distinguish between restricted and unrestricted funds. Why is this separation important?
4. Many nonprofit organizations recognize depreciation expense even though income is not a stated objective. What are some arguments in support of this practice?
5. Argue against the recognition of depreciation for nonprofit organizations.
6. How do nonprofit organizations account for pledges?
7. Compare the accounting and reporting of fixed assets by hospitals and colleges and universities.
8. Explain why contributed services are generally not given accounting recognition.
9. Describe how accounting for quasi-endowments differs among the various nonprofit organizations.
10. What common characteristics are shared by governmental units and the nonprofit organizations discussed in this chapter?
11. Outline the historical development of generally accepted accounting principles for nonprofit organizations.
12. Identify the differences in the content of current operating funds that exist among the various nonprofit organizations.

13. Describe the differences in accounting for restricted revenue among colleges, hospitals, voluntary health and welfare organizations, and other nonprofit organizations.
14. Why do voluntary health and welfare organizations use a financial statement that discloses their functional expenses?

Discussion Cases

DC 22-1

Defining User Needs and Meaningful Financial Statements

The Stecca Foundation is a nonprofit health and welfare organization concerned with public nutrition. Its program services include research, public education, and professional education and training.

The governing board has asked certain public accounting firms to submit proposals to review the foundation's accounting system—including its internal controls—and to perform an audit of its financial statements for the current year. The organization has never been audited. The governing board is acting in compliance with new state legislation that requires audits of all health and welfare organizations by public accountants.

Your accounting firm is submitting a proposal. In reviewing the foundation's most recent financial statements, you discover that they were prepared on a cash basis and that the activity statement is simply a cash receipts and disbursements statement. The balance sheet discloses only one asset—cash—and a Fund Balance. The organization owns a significant amount of fixed assets, including a large office building and other real properties.

Required:
Prepare the part of the proposal that sets forth your recommended changes in the organization's financial reporting system. Your recommendations should represent a careful delineation of user needs, internal and external, and how the statements and system should be designed to meet these particular needs.

DC 22-2

Responding to the Issue of Depreciation Expense

The board of the Stecca Foundation has reviewed your proposals concerning the organization's financial reporting system and has asked you to expand on certain proposal recommendations.

The recommendation that generated the most concern from the board members concerned the accounting for depreciation expense. Arguments centered on the belief that income is not an objective and no causal relationship exists between depreciation and revenue.

Required:
Defend your recommendation that depreciation expense be recognized in the accounts and included in the financial statements.

DC 22-3

Accounting for Donated Services

Andersson Medical Services is a voluntary medical service organization that renders limited medical assistance to the elderly residing in several cities in the western United States. The organization receives funding from United Way, other philanthropic organizations, and various government agencies. The medical and lay staff—including doctors, registered nurses, medical technicians, and lay persons who assist the medical staff—are all volunteers.

Peter Karppinen, the organization's director, wishes to consult with you concerning the possible inclusion of the value of donated services in his organization's financial statements. Apparently, his current accountant feels that "it simply cannot be done."

During the conversation, Karppinen develops several points that he believes represent sufficient support for including donated services in the financial statements. First, he argues that the fair value of the services of the doctors, nurses, and medical technicians is readily determinable. Second, the inclusion of the donated services would show more accurately the amount of services rendered to its various programs, which, in his opinion, would assist him in obtaining additional funding, especially from philanthropic organizations. He also argues that the inclusion of the value of donated services may assist him in competing more effectively for matching grants, because he can argue that the organization's matching contribution is the value of its human resources.

Required:
Respond to Karppinen in writing, outlining current accounting practices concerning accounting for donated services and carefully develop the essential rationale for the current accounting practice.

Exercises

E 22-1

Voluntary Health and Welfare Organizations: Accounting for Revenue and Expense

Delta House is a voluntary welfare organization funded by contributions from the general public. During 19X3, unrestricted pledges of $900,000 were received, half of which were payable in 19X3, with the other half payable in 19X4 for use in 19X4. It was estimated that 10% of these pledges would be uncollectible. In addition, Tom Walker, a social worker on Delta's permanent staff, earning $20,000 annually for a normal workload of 2,000 hours, contributed an additional 800 hours of his time to Delta House at no charge.

Required:
How much should Delta House report as net contribution revenue for 19X3 with respect to the pledges?

a. $0
b. $405,000
c. $810,000
d. $900,000

How much should Delta House record in 19X3 for contributed service expense?

a. $8,000
b. $4,000
c. $800
d. $0

E 22-2

Voluntary Health and Welfare Organizations: Accounting for Expenses

Revere Foundation, a voluntary health and welfare organization supported by contributions from the general public, included the following costs in its statement of functional expenses for the year ended December 31, 19X3:

Fund-raising	$500,000
Administrative (including data processing)	300,000
Research	100,000

Required:
Revere's functional expenses for 19X3 program services included:

a. $900,000
b. $500,000
c. $300,000
d. $100,000

E 22-3

Voluntary Health and Welfare Organizations: Accounting for Contributions

Helping Hand Center, a voluntary health and welfare organization, received a cash donation in 19X3 from a donor specifying that the amount donated be used in 19X5.

Required:
The cash donation should be accounted for as:

a. support in 19X3.
b. support for 19X3, 19X4, and 19X5, and as a deferred credit in the balance sheet at the end of 19X3 and 19X4.
c. support in 19X5, and no deferred credit in the balance sheet at the end of 19X3 and 19X4.
d. support in 19X5, and as a deferred credit in the balance sheet at the end of 19X3 and 19X4.

E 22-4

Universities: Accounting for Gift Revenue

During the years ended June 30, 19X0 and 19X1, Santa Cruz University conducted a cancer research project financed by a $2,000,000 gift from an alumnus. This entire amount was pledged by the donor on July 10, 19X9, although he paid only $500,000 at that date. The gift was restricted to the financing of this particular research project. During the two-year research period, the university's related gift receipts and research expenditures were as follows:

	Year ended June 30	
	19X0	19X1
Gift receipts	$1,200,000	$ 800,000
Cancer research expenditures	900,000	1,100,000

Required:
How much gift revenue should Santa Cruz University report in the Restricted column of its statement of current funds revenues, expenditures, and other changes for the year ended June 30, 19X1?

a. $0
b. $800,000
c. $1,100,000
d. $2,000,000

E 22-5

Colleges and Universities: Accounting for Tuition and Fees

For the fall semester of 19X1, Westmoor College assessed its students $2,300,000 for tuition and fees. The net amount realized was only $2,100,000 because of the following revenue reductions:

Refunds occasioned by class cancellations and student withdrawals	$ 50,000
Tuition remissions granted to faculty members' families	10,000
Scholarships and fellowships	140,000

Required:
How much should Westmoor report for the period for unrestricted current funds revenues from tuition and fees?

a. $2,100,000
b. $2,150,000
c. $2,250,000
d. $2,300,000

E 22-6

Colleges and Universities: Accounting for Revenues

During the years ended June 30, 19X4 and 19X5, Cabrillo University conducted a major scientific research project. During 19X5 the university received a corporate gift of $1,500,000, the use of which was left to the discretion of the university's governing board. The governing board restricted this gift to the major research project. During the two-year research period, expenditures for the scientific research projects were as follows:

	Year Ended June 30	
	19X4	19X5
Gift receipts	$700,000	$1,000,000

Required:
How much gift revenue should Cabrillo report in the restricted column of its statement of current funds revenues, expenditures, and other changes for the year ended June 30, 19X5?

a. $0
b. $700,000
c. $1,000,000
d. $1,700,000

E 22-7

Hospitals: Accounting for Contributions and Fund Classifications

On July 1, 19X4, Good Shepherd Hospital's governing board designated $200,000 for expansion of out-patient facilities. The $200,000 will be expended in the fiscal year ended June 30, 19X7.

Required:
In Good Shepherd's June 30, 19X5 balance sheet, this cash should be classified as a $200,000

a. Restricted current asset.
b. Restricted noncurrent asset.
c. Unrestricted current asset.
d. Unrestricted noncurrent asset.

(AICPA adapted)

E 22-8

Hospitals: Accounting for Contributions and Fund Classifications

El Camino Hospital's property, plant, and equipment (net of depreciation) consist of the following:

Land	$ 500,000
Buildings	10,000,000
Movable equipment	2,000,000

Required:
What amount should be included in the restricted fund grouping?

a. $0
b. $2,000,000
c. $10,500,000
d. $12,500,000

(AICPA adapted)

E 22-9

Hospitals: Accounting for Contributions and Donated Services

During the year ended December 31, 19X1, Middlefield Hospital received the following donations stated at their respective fair values:

Employee services from members of a religious group	$100,000
Medical supplies from an association of physicians (these supplies were restricted for indigent care and were used for such purpose in 19X1)..	30,000

Required:
How much revenue (both operating and nonoperating) from donations should Middlefield report in its 19X1 statement of revenues and expenses?

a. $0
b. $30,000
c. $100,000
d. $130,000

E 22-10

Hospitals: Accounting for Revenues

Under Homestead Hospital's established rate structure, the hospital would have earned patient service revenue of $6,000,000 for the year ended December 31, 19X3. However, Homestead did not expect to collect this amount because of charity allowances of $1,000,000 and discounts of $500,000 to third-party payors. In May, 19X3, Homestead purchased bandages from Loredo Supply Co. at a cost of $1,000. However, Loredo notified Homestead that the invoice was being cancelled and that the bandages were being donated to Homestead. At December 31, 19X3, Homestead had board-designated assets consisting of cash $40,000 and investments $700,000.

Required:
For the year ended December 31, 19X3, how much should Homestead record as patient service revenue?

a. $6,000,000
b. $6,500,000
c. $5,000,000
d. $4,500,000

For the year ended December 31, 19X3, Homestead should record the donation of bandages as

a. A $1,000 reduction in operating expenses.
b. Nonoperating revenue of $1,000.
c. Other operating revenue of $1,000.
d. A memorandum entry only.

How much of Homestead's board-designated assets should be included in the unrestricted fund grouping?

a. $0
b. $40,000
c. $700,000
d. $740,000

Problems

P 22-1

Country Clubs: Transactions and Preparation of Financial Statements

The balance sheet for Parrville Country Club for the fiscal year ended March 31, 19X1, is presented below:

PARRVILLE COUNTRY CLUB
Balance Sheet
March 31, 19X1

Assets	
Current Assets:	
Cash	$ 45,000
Investments—at market	290,000
Accounts receivable, less allowances of $25,000	70,000
Inventories	25,000
Prepaid expenses	20,000
Total Current Assets	$ 450,000
Property and Equipment—at cost:	
Land and land improvements	$1,010,000
Buildings	1,330,000
Furniture, fixtures, and equipment	275,000
	$2,615,000
Less—Accumulated depreciation	(860,000)
	$1,755,000
Other Assets:	
Deferred charges	$ 52,000
Beverage license	40,000
	$ 92,000
Total Assets	$2,297,000
Liabilities and Membership Equity	
Current Liabilities:	
Accounts payable and accrued expenses	$ 62,000
Deferred revenues—initiation fees	15,000
Due to resigned members	16,000
Taxes	20,000
Total Current Liabilities	$ 113,000
Membership Equity:	
Proprietary certificates, 500 at $1,500 each	$ 750,000
Cumulative excess of income over expenses	1,434,000
	$2,184,000
Total Liabilities and Membership Equity	$2,297,000

Transactions for the year ended March 31, 19X2, were as follows:

1. Members were billed as follows for the year.

Initiation fees	$ 83,000
Annual dues	660,000
Restaurant and bar charges	155,550
Greens fees	160,000
Tennis and swimming fees	93,250
Locker and room rentals	51,000
Golf cart rentals	21,500

2. Pro shop cash sales for the year were as follows:

Golf cart rentals to guests	$ 5,500
Miscellaneous	3,500

3. Collections on accounts receivable totaled $1,150,000 for the year. Uncollectible accounts amounted to $4,200.
4. Additions to the voucher register for the year totaled $1,165,500, charged as follows:

Greens	$245,000
House expenses	160,000
Restaurant and bar	120,500
Tennis courts and swimming pool	70,000
General and administrative expenses	560,000
Dues to resigned members	10,000

5. Vouchers paid during the year amounted to $1,150,000.
6. Capital additions funded by short-term notes:

Land improvements	$150,000
Golf carts	200,000
Office machines	50,000

   Payments on these notes for the year were $230,000, providing principal reductions of $200,000 and interest of $30,000.
7. Received from the bank the proceeds of a $350,000 short-term loan dated March 31, 19X2.

Additional Information:

1. Accrued expenses at March 31, 19X2 should be $70,000. The necessary adjustment should provide for the following charges:

House expenses	$ 3,000
Restaurant and bar expenses	3,500
General and administrative expenses	1,500

2. Deferred revenues—Initiation Fees should have a $25,000 balance at March 31, 19X2.
3. The market value of the investments at March 31, 19X2 was $315,000. No investment transactions were made during the year.
4. Depreciation for the year was assigned as follows:

Buildings	$120,000
Furniture, fixtures, and equipment	23,500

Depreciation should be allocated to program services and general and administrative expenses as follows:

Greens expenses	$ 3,500
House expenses	81,500
Restaurant and bar expenses	45,000
Tennis courts and swimming pool expenses	12,000
General and administrative expenses	1,500

5. Inventories and prepaid expenses should have the following balances at March 31, 19X2:

Inventories	$ 20,000
Prepaid expenses	18,000

These adjustments should be assigned to program services and general and administrative expenses in the following manner:

House	$ 3,000
Restaurant	2,500
General and administrative	1,500

Required:

1. Prepare journal entries for the above transactions.
2. Prepare a balance sheet and a detailed statement of revenues, expenses, and changes in cumulative excess of revenue over expenses for the year ended March 31, 19X2.

P 22-2

Sports Clubs: Transactions and Preparation of Activity Statement

In 19X0, a group of merchants in Sunnyview City organized the Committee of 100 to establish the Bay View Sports Club, a nonprofit sports organization for the city's youth. Each of the committee's 100 members contributed $1,000 toward the club's capital and in turn received a participation certificate. In addition, each participant agreed to pay dues of $200 per year for the club's operations. All dues have been collected in full for the fiscal year ended March 31. Members who have discontinued their participation have been replaced by an equal number of new members through a transfer of the participation certificates. The club's April 1, 19X4, trial balance follows:

	Debit	Credit
Cash	$ 9,000	
Investments (market value equals cost)	58,000	
Inventories	5,000	
Land	10,000	
Building	164,000	
Accumulated Depreciation—Building		$130,000
Furniture and Equipment	54,000	
Accumulated Depreciation—Furniture and Equipment		46,000
Accounts Payable		12,000
Participation Certificates (100 at $1,000 each)		100,000
Cumulative Excess of Revenue over Expenses		12,000
	$300,000	$300,000

Club transactions for the year ended March 31, 19X5 were as follows:

1. Collections of dues from participants amounted to $20,000.
2. Snack bar and soda fountain sales receipts totaled $28,000.
3. Interest and dividends received were $6,000.
4. Additions to the voucher register were as follows:

House expenses	$17,000
Snack bar and soda fountain expenses	26,000
General and administrative expenses	11,000

5. Vouchers paid totaled $55,000.
6. Assessments for capital improvements not yet incurred, $10,000 (assessed on March 20, 19X5; none collected by March 31, 19X5; deemed 100% collectible during the year ended March 31, 19X6).
7. Unrestricted bequests received amounted to $5,000.

Additional Information:

1. Investments are valued at market, which amounted to $65,000 at March 31, 19X5. No investment transactions were made during the year.
2. Depreciation for the year was as follows:

Building	$4,000
Furniture and equipment	8,000

This depreciation was allocated as follows:

House expenses	$9,000
Snack bar and soda fountain expenses	2,000
General and administrative expenses	1,000

3. A physical inventory at March 31, 19X5, revealed that $1,000 worth of supplies remained in the snack bar and soda fountain.

Required:

1. Prepare journal entries for the above transactions.
2. Prepare the appropriate activity statement for the year ended March 31, 19X5.

P 22-3

University Current Funds: Transactions Analysis and Preparation of Statement of Changes in Fund Balances

A partial balance sheet for St. Juliann University at the end of its fiscal year (July 31, 19X4) is as follows:

ST. JULIANN UNIVERSITY
Balance Sheet — Current Funds
July 31, 19X4

Assets	
Current Funds:	
Unrestricted:	
Cash	$200,000
Accounts receivable — student tuition and fees, less $15,000 allowance for doubtful accounts	360,000
Prepaid expenses	40,000
Total Unrestricted	$600,000
Restricted:	
Cash	$ 10,000
Investments	210,000
Total Restricted	$220,000
Total Current Funds	$820,000
Liabilities and Fund Balances	
Current Funds:	
Unrestricted:	
Accounts payable	$100,000
Due to other funds	40,000
Deferred revenue — tuition and fees	25,000
Fund balance	435,000
Total Unrestricted	$600,000
Restricted:	
Accounts payable	$ 5,000
Fund balance	215,000
Total Restricted	$220,000
Total Current Funds	$820,000

The following financial events and transactions occurred during the fiscal year ended July 31, 19X5:

1. Cash collected from student tuition totaled $3,000,000. Of this amount, $362,000 was outstanding at July 31, 19X4; $2,500,000 was for current-year tuition; and $138,000 was for tuition applicable to the semester beginning in August 19X5.

2. Deferred revenue at July 31, 19X4, was earned during the year ended July 31, 19X5.
3. July 31, 19X4, accounts receivable that were not collected during the year ended July 31, 19X5, were declared uncollectible and were written off against the allowance account. At July 31, 19X5, the Allowance for Doubtful Accounts was an estimated $10,000.
4. During the year, an unrestricted grant of $60,000 was awarded by the state. This state grant was payable to St. Juliann sometime in August 19X5.
5. During the year, unrestricted cash gifts of $80,000 were received from alumni. St. Juliann's board of trustees allocated $30,000 of these gifts to the student loan fund.
6. During the year, investments costing $25,000 were sold for $31,000. Restricted fund investments were purchased for $40,000. Investment income of $18,000 was earned and collected during the year.
7. Unrestricted general expenses of $2,500,000 were recorded in the voucher register. At July 31, 19X5, the unrestricted Accounts Payable balance was $75,000.
8. The restricted Accounts Payable balance at July 31, 19X4, was paid.
9. The $40,000 due to other funds at July 31, 19X4 was paid to the Plant Fund as required.
10. One-quarter of the prepaid expenses at July 31, 19X4, which pertain to general education expenses, expired during the current year. No additions to prepaid expenses were made during the year.

Required:

1. Prepare general journal entries for the foregoing transactions for the year ended July 31, 19X5. Number each entry to correspond with the indicated transaction number. Organize your answer as follows:

		Current Funds			
		Unrestricted		Restricted	
Entry No.	Account	Dr.	Cr.	Dr.	Cr.

2. Prepare a statement of changes in fund balances for the year ended July 31, 19X5.

(AICPA adapted)

P 22-4 Hospitals: Transactions Analysis and Preparation of Statement of Revenue and Expense

Children's Hospital had the following financial events and transactions pertaining to its unrestricted fund for the year ended June 30, 19X2:

1. Gross billings to the patients for the year were as follows:

Daily patient services	$2,500,000
Other nursing services	750,000
Other professional services	300,000
	$3,550,000

2. Adjustments from gross revenues were as follows:

Contractual adjustments with third-party payers	$ 500,000
Approved charity and free-care adjustments	175,000
Discounts and allowances to hospital staff	7,800

3. Collections of accounts receivable totaled $2,000,000.
4. Inventory acquisitions, including materials and supplies, amounted to $350,000. One-fifth of the approved invoices remain unpaid at year-end. The hospital uses a perpetual inventory system.
5. Use of materials and supplies from inventory was assigned as follows:

Nursing services	$ 190,000
Other professional services	75,000
General services	235,000
Fiscal services	6,000
Administrative services	2,500

6. The following salary and wage expenses were incurred for the year:

Nursing services	$ 990,000
Other professional services	550,000
General services	175,000
Fiscal services	120,000
Administrative services	25,000

7. Other operating expenses processed through the voucher system were as follows:

Nursing services	$ 65,000
Other professional services	35,000
General services	17,500
Fiscal services	6,500
Administrative services	3,500

8. The provision for estimated uncollectible accounts was $154,000.
9. Depreciation of buildings and equipment was as follows:

Buildings	$ 185,000
Equipment	120,000

The depreciation of the building is based on appraisals by qualified appraisers. Appraisals were necessary several years ago because historical records were destroyed before the hospital prepared its first set of accrual basis financial statements.

10. Interfund transfers for the year to the Unrestricted Fund were as follows:

Specific purpose fund	$ 110,000
Plant renewal and replacement fund	300,000
Endowment fund	45,000

11. Other data are as follows:

	June 30	
	19X1	19X2
Accrued general services expenses	$35,000	$23,000
Prepaid administrative services expenses	10,000	18,500

Required:
Prepare the appropriate journal entries, post to T-accounts, and draft a statement of revenues and expenses for the Unrestricted Fund.

P 22-5

Hospitals: Preparation of Statement of Revenues and Expenses and Writing Appropriate Disclosures

The following selected information was taken from the books and records of Merrcy Hospital (a voluntary hospital) as of and for the year ended June 30, 19X2:

1. Patient service revenue totaled $16,000,000, with allowances and uncollectible accounts amounting to $3,400,000. Other operating revenue aggregated $346,000, and included $160,000 from specific purpose funds. Revenue of $6,000,000 recognized under cost-reimbursement agreements is subject to audit and retroactive adjustment by third-party payors. Estimated retroactive adjustments under these agreements have been included in allowances.
2. Unrestricted gifts and bequests of $410,000 were received.
3. Unrestricted income from endowment funds totaled $160,000.
4. Income from board-designated funds aggregated $82,000.
5. Operating expenses totaled $13,370,000, and included $500,000 for depreciation computed on the straight-line basis. However, accelerated depreciation is used to determine reimbursable costs under certain third-party reimbursement agreements. Net cost reimbursement revenue amounting to $220,000, resulting from the difference in depreciation methods, was deferred to future years.
6. Also included in operating expenses are pension costs of $100,000, in connection with a noncontributory pension plan covering substantially all of Merrcy's employees. Accrued pension costs are funded currently. Prior service cost is being amortized over a period of 20 years. The actuarially computed value of vested and nonvested benefits at year-end amounted to $3,000,000 and $350,000, respectively. The assumed rate of return used in determining the actuarial present value of accumulated plan benefits was 8%. The plan's net assets available for benefits at year-end was $3,050,000.
7. Gifts and bequests are recorded at fair market values when received.
8. Patient service revenue is accounted for at established rates on the accrual basis.

Required:

1. Prepare a formal statement of revenues and expenses for Merrcy Hospital for the year ended June 30, 19X2.
2. Draft the appropriate disclosures in separate notes accompanying the statement of revenues and expenses, referencing each note to its respective item in the statement.

P 22-6

University Current Funds: Transactions Analysis and Preparation of Statement of Changes in Fund Balances

A partial balance sheet of Studyville University is shown below.

STUDYVILLE UNIVERSITY
Partial Balance Sheet
June 30, 19X0

Assets	
Current Funds:	
Unrestricted:	
Cash	$210,000
Accounts receivable—student tuition and fees, less $9,000 allowance for doubtful accounts	341,000
State appropriations receivable	75,000
Total Unrestricted	$626,000
Restricted:	
Cash	$ 7,000
Investments	60,000
Total Restricted	$ 67,000
Total Current Funds	$693,000
Liabilities and Fund Balances	
Current Funds:	
Unrestricted:	
Accounts payable	$ 45,000
Deferred revenues	66,000
Fund balance	515,000
Total Unrestricted	$626,000
Restricted:	
Fund balance	$ 67,000
Total Restricted	$ 67,000
Total Current Funds	$693,000

The following financial events and transactions occurred during the fiscal year ended June 30, 19X1:

1. On July 7, 19X0, a $100,000 gift was received from an alumnus. The alumnus requested that one-half the gift be used for the purchase of books for the university library and the remainder be used for the establishment of a scholarship fund. The alumnus further requested that the income generated by the scholarship fund be awarded annually as a scholarship to a qualified disadvantaged student. On July 20, 19X0, the board of trustees resolved that the funds of the newly established scholarship fund would be invested in savings certificates. On July 21, 19X0, the savings certificates were purchased.
2. Revenue from student tuition and fees for the year ended June 30, 19X1, amounted to $1,900,000. Of this amount, $66,000 was collected in the prior year and $1,686,000 was collected during the year ended June 30, 19X1.

In addition, at June 30, 19X1, the university had received $158,000 cash, representing fees for the session beginning July 1, 19X1.

3. During the year ended June 30, 19X1, the university collected $349,000 of the outstanding accounts receivable at the beginning of the year. The balance was determined to be uncollectible and was written off against the allowance account. At June 30, 19X1, the allowance account was increased by $3,000.
4. During the year, interest charges of $6,000 were earned and collected on late student fee payments.
5. During the year, the state appropriation was received. An additional unrestricted appropriation of $50,000 was made by the state but had not been paid to the university as of June 30, 19X1.
6. An unrestricted gift of $25,000 cash was received from alumni of the university.
7. During the year, investments of $21,000 were sold for $26,000. Investment income of $1,900 was received.
8. During the year, unrestricted operating expenses of $1,777,000 were recorded. At June 30, 19X1, $59,000 of these expenses remained unpaid.
9. Restricted current funds of $13,000 were spent for authorized purposes during the year.
10. The accounts payable at June 30, 19X0 were paid during the year.
11. During the year, $7,000 interest was earned and received on the savings certificates purchased in accordance with the board's resolution in item 1.

Required:

1. Prepare journal entries to record the above transactions for the year ended June 30, 19X1. Number each journal entry to correspond with the transaction described above.

   Organize your answer sheet as follows:

	Current Funds					
	Unrestricted		Restricted		Endowment Fund	
Accounts	Dr.	Cr.	Dr.	Cr.	Dr.	Cr.

2. Prepare a statement of changes in fund balances for the year ended June 30, 19X1.

(AICPA adapted)

P 22-7

Voluntary Health and Welfare Organizations: Preparation of a Statement of Support, Revenues, and Expenses and Changes in Fund Balances and a Balance Sheet

Following are the adjusted current funds trial balances of Westwinds Association for Handicapped Children, at June 30, 19X4:

WESTWINDS ASSOCIATION FOR HANDICAPPED CHILDREN
Adjusted Current Funds Trial Balance
June 30, 19X4

	Unrestricted Dr.	Unrestricted Cr.	Restricted Dr.	Restricted Cr.
Cash	$ 40,000		$ 9,000	
Bequest receivable			5,000	
Pledges receivable	12,000			
Accrued interest receivable	1,000			
Investments (at cost, which approximates market)	100,000			
Accounts payable and accrued expenses		50,000		1,000
Deferred revenue		2,000		
Allowance for uncollectible pledges		3,000		
Fund balances, July 1, 19X3:				
Designated		12,000		
Undesignated		26,000		
Restricted				3,000
Transfers of endowment fund income		20,000		
Contributions		300,000		15,000
Membership dues		25,000		
Program service fees		30,000		
Investment income		10,000		
Deaf children's program	120,000			
Blind children's program	150,000			
Management and general services	45,000		4,000	
Fund-raising services	8,000		1,000	
Provision for uncollectible pledges	2,000			
	$478,000	$478,000	$19,000	$19,000

Required:

1. Prepare a statement of support, revenue, and expenses and changes in fund balances, presenting each current fund separately, for the year ended June 30, 19X4.
2. Prepare a balance sheet, presenting each current fund separately as of June 30, 19X4.

P 22-8

Preparation of a Statement of Changes in Financial Position

Presented below are the June 30, 19X5 and 19X4, balance sheets of Discovery Foundation, a nonprofit research and scientific organization:

DISCOVERY FOUNDATION
Balance Sheets
June 30, 19X5 and 19X4

Assets:		
Current assets:		
Cash	$ 650,000	$ 630,000
Accounts receivable	744,000	712,000
Unbilled contract revenues and reimbursement grant expenses	976,000	780,000
Prepaid expenses	80,000	76,000
Total Current Assets	2,450,000	2,198,000
Investments and endowment fund cash	840,000	780,000
Property, plant, and equipment		
Land and building	440,000	40,000
Furniture and equipment	334,000	312,000
Leased property under capital leases	958,000	958,000
Total Property, Plant, and Equipment	1,732,000	1,710,000
Less accumulated depreciation and amortization	518,000	370,000
Net Property, Plant, and Equipment	1,214,000	1,340,000
Total Assets	$4,504,000	$4,318,000
Liabilities and Fund Balances:		
Current liabilities:		
Accounts payable	$ 836,000	$ 776,000
Restricted grant advances	522,000	420,000
Obligations under capital leases	176,000	164,000
Total Current Liabilities	1,534,000	1,360,000
Noncurrent capital lease obligations	618,000	794,000
Total Liabilities	2,152,000	2,154,000
Fund balances:		
Unrestricted	916,000	838,000
Net equity in property, plant, and equipment	596,000	546,000
Endowment	840,000	780,000
Total Fund Balances	2,352,000	2,164,000
Total Liabilities and Fund Balances	$4,504,000	$4,318,000

Excerpts from Discovery Foundation's Notes to Financial Statements:

Revenue Recognition: Substantially all of the organization's revenue is derived from restricted grants and cost-plus-fixed-fee contracts. Revenue is recognized based on the proportion of project expenses incurred to total anticipated project expenses (percentage-of-completion method). Losses on contracts are recognized when identified.

Fund Balance: Of the $188,000 increase in fund balances from 19X4 to 19X5, $128,000 represents the results of current operating activities, and $60,000 represents capital additions from interest earned in Endowment Fund investments. The Endowment Fund, in the principal amount of $700,000, was received in 19X2. The donor of this fund specified that principal and accumulated interest not be expended until 19X0, at which time the fund, including accumulated interest, will be used for environmental research projects. Net equity in property, plant, and equipment is the carrying value of all property, plant, and equipment less related noncurrent liabilities to finance their acquisition. There were no dispositions of property, plant, and equipment during the year.

Lease Commitments: The organization uses scientific equipment under capital leases expiring in 19X1 that provide for the transfer of ownership of the equipment at the end of the lease term. The related future minimum lease payments as of June 30, 19X5, for subsequent fiscal years, are as follows:

19X6	$188,000
19X7	188,000
19X8	188,000
19X9	188,000
19X0	188,000
19X1	20,000
Total	960,000
Less amount representing interest	(166,000)
Present value of minimum lease payments	$794,000

Required:

Prepare the statement of changes in financial position, including the schedule of changes in working capital, for the year ended June 30, 19X5.

V

Partnerships

23

Partnerships: Formation and Operation

AN OVERVIEW OF PARTNERSHIPS

A **partnership** is an association of two or more persons who contribute money, property, or services to carry on as co-owners of a business, the profits and losses of which are shared in an agreed-upon manner. The term **person** refers to individuals, corporations, and even other partnerships. Indeed, most partners are individuals. Partnerships that comprise one or more partnerships or corporations usually are formed to combine managerial talent and financial resources to conduct a specific undertaking—for example, the design and development of a large shopping center. Such partnerships are commonly referred to as *joint ventures.* Regardless of whether the partners are individuals, other partnerships, or corporations, the accounting and tax issues are the same.

Chapters 23 to 25 deal with **general partnerships**—that is, partnerships in which each partner is personally liable to the partnership's creditors if partnership assets are insufficient to pay such creditors. In Appendix A of this chapter we briefly discuss **limited partnerships,** in which certain partners (called *limited partners*) are not personally liable to the partnership's creditors if partnership assets are insufficient to pay such creditors.

Introduction to the Professional Corporation

Why They Were Created? Traditionally, the partnership form of organization has been used by small retail establishments and businesses that are considered the professions—for example, public accounting, law, and medicine. Such professions could not incorporate under the existing laws. In the late 1960s, more and more professionals recognized that much greater tax benefits were available with the corporate form of organization, primarily with respect to pension, profit-sharing, medical, and insurance plans. Consequently, many professional people made considerable efforts to urge legislation that would allow professional businesses to incorporate. Their efforts were so successful that each of the 50 states now has some form of legislation on the books, under the broad category of **professional corporations,** enabling professional businesses to incorporate.

Their Explosive Growth. Initially, the Internal Revenue Service (IRS) did not recognize professional corporations as corporations for federal income tax reporting purposes. In 1969, however, after a continuous series of court defeats, the IRS issued regulations recognizing the professional corporation as a corporation for federal tax purposes. As a result of this change, many existing partnerships (as well as many sole proprietorships) have incorporated. Furthermore, substantial numbers of new businesses, which would have been conducted as either partnerships or sole proprietorships, have chosen the professional corporation form of business. Even one of the "Big 8" public accounting firms had plans in 1982 to change from a partnership to a professional corporation. In 1984, tax legislation designed to achieve parity became effective, enabling partnerships and sole proprietorships to obtain almost the same tax benefits available to professional corporations. Thus, a great deal of the advantage of incorporating was eliminated. As a result, the mushrooming growth of the professional corporation form of business ended, and some shift (although not explosive) away from the professional corporation form has occurred.

Because an accountant rendering services to a professional can expect to encounter a professional corporation as often as a partnership, a limited discussion of professional corporations is included at the end of this chapter. The advantages and disadvantages of professional incorporation must be carefully weighed against the advantages and disadvantages of either the partnership or sole proprietorship form of organization. Furthermore, the accountant can expect to be a key consultant in choosing the form of organization. (According to the latest IRS publications, over 1.5 million partnerships exist, which is over a 50% increase in the last 20 years.)

Major Features of the Partnership Form of Business

Ease of Formation. Forming a partnership is a relatively simple process. The partners merely put their agreement into writing concerning who contributes assets or services, who performs which functions in the business, and how profits and losses are shared. The written document is called the **partnership agreement.**

Thus, compared with the corporate form of business, a partnership need not prepare articles of incorporation, write bylaws, print stock certificates, prepare minutes of the first meeting of the board of directors, pay state incorporation fees, or register stocks.

Potential Noncontinuity of Existence. Historically, the possibility that the operations of a partnership could not continue after the death or withdrawal of a partner (with the business subsequently liquidated) was considered a major disadvantage of the partnership form of organization. In practice, this problem occurs only for small partnerships. Even then, some steps can be taken to minimize the impact of the loss of a partner. For example, life insurance proceeds on the death of a partner can be used to settle with the deceased partner's estate, thus conserving the assets of the business so that the remaining partners can continue the operation. For larger partnerships, this feature usually is not significant. Some of the largest partnerships have more than 1,000 partners. Obviously, the loss of one or even several partners in a partnership of such size has minimal impact on the day-to-day operations of the business.

Difficulty in Disposing of Interest. An ownership interest in a partnership is a personal asset, as is the ownership of stock in a corporation. No formal established marketplace exists for the sale of a partnership interest, however, as for the sale of stock in a publicly owned corporation. Accordingly, a partner who wishes to sell or assign his or her partnership interest will have more difficulty finding a buyer than a shareholder who wishes to sell stock in a publicly owned corporation. To make this process even more difficult, the person buying a partnership interest does not have the automatic right to participate in the management of the business—the consent of the remaining partners is necessary.

Unlimited Liability. If a partnership's assets are insufficient to pay its creditors, the creditors have recourse to the personal assets of any and all general partners of the partnership. This characteristic contrasts sharply with the corporate form of organization, in which the personal assets of the shareholders are insulated from the corporation's creditors. This is undoubtedly the major disadvantage of the partnership form of organization.

Mutual Agency. The partnership is bound by each partner acting within the scope of partnership activities. Thus, each partner acts as an agent for the partnership in dealing with persons outside the partnership.

Sharing of Profits and Losses. Profits and losses are shared among the partners in any manner to which the partners agree.

Nontaxable Status. Unlike a corporation, a partnership does not pay income taxes. Instead, partnerships must file with the IRS an information return on Form 1065, which shows the partnership's taxable income and each partner's share of such income. Each partner then reports and pays taxes on his or her share of the partnership's taxable income. These procedures eliminate the undesirable "double taxation," which is a feature of corporations. That is, the earnings of the corporation are taxed and then the dividends of the corporation are also taxed—whereas partnership income is taxed only once, at the individual partner level.

Concluding Comments. For professionals, the form of organization of a partnership is simple and flexible compared with that of a professional corporation, which is generally considered complex and cumbersome. The partnership form is still common largely because it is "a more effective way to relate to each other."

Partnerships often begin with great enthusiasm and rosy expectations. Keeping the partnership going is much harder. In many cases, the partners must seek the help of a professional business therapist (often a psychologist) because they cannot work together harmoniously.

Incorporating a Partnership

Many corporations began as partnerships. Then at some point in the enterprise's existence, the advantages of incorporation outweighed the advantages of the partnership form of organization. When a partnership incorporates, its assets are transferred to the corporation, which assumes the partnership's liabilities. One technical point should be noted: The corporation's board of directors is responsible for placing a value on the assets transferred to the corporation. In theory, the assets can be revalued to their current values, and this is often done. However, if the corporation ever decides to register its common stock with the Securities and Exchange Commission, the SEC will insist that assets transferred to the corporation be carried at the partnership's historical cost, adjusted for depreciation and amortization. In other words, no upward revaluation of assets on incorporation is allowed. (Presumably, a downward revaluation would be permitted if appropriate.)

FORMATION OF A PARTNERSHIP

The Uniform Partnership Act

Before discussing the partnership agreement in detail, some understanding of the laws that govern partnerships is necessary. Although each of the 50 states has laws pertaining to partnerships, most states have adopted the Uniform Partnership Act (UPA) or a variation thereof as a means of governing partnerships. In this text, we consider the UPA the governing statute.

The UPA is reasonably comprehensive in defining the consequences of a partnership relationship. For our purposes, its more relevant sections pertain to:

1. Relations of partners to one another.
2. Relations of partners to persons dealing with the partnership.
3. Dissolution and winding up of the partnership.

Some sections of the UPA cannot be circumvented merely by contrary provisions or omissions in the partnership agreement. For example, Section 15 imposes joint liability on all general partners for partnership debts. If a partnership agreement contained a provision excusing certain general partners from joint liability, then that provision of the agreement would be inoperable, and creditors could seek recourse from any partner.

Other sections of the UPA apply only when a partnership agreement is silent. For example, suppose a partnership agreement is silent with respect to remuneration for partners who are active in the management of the business. If one of the active partners should claim subsequently to be entitled to remuneration for services, then the dispute would be settled against that partner in a court of law. Section 18 expressly provides that unless otherwise stated in the partnership agreement, "no partner is entitled to remuneration for acting in the partnership interest." A partner's remuneration for managerial services would have to be provided for in the partnership agreement.

On the other hand, the UPA is not so comprehensive that it provides for every possible provision that otherwise could be included in a partnership agreement. For example, Section 27 discusses certain consequences of the sale by a partner of his or her partnership interest. Although a partner need not give the remaining partners the first opportunity to acquire the partnership interest, neither does the UPA prevent a partnership agreement from containing a clause to the effect that if a partner desires to sell any or all of his or her interest, the remaining partners must be given the right of first refusal.

Selected sections of the Uniform Partnership Act appear in Appendix B of this chapter.

The Partnership Agreement

The partnership agreement is merely a written expression of what the partners have agreed to. Because state laws govern the consequences of partnership relationships, however, the partnership agreement should be prepared by an attorney who is experienced in partnership law. This is essential for the following reasons:

1. Mandatory provisions of the UPA may be included or referred to, so that partners are aware of and somewhat familiar with partnership law.
2. Provisions that conflict with the UPA can be avoided.
3. Optional provisions that do not conflict with the UPA can be considered for possible inclusion.

A well-written partnership agreement should be a guide to the partners' relationship and any allowable variations from the UPA to which they have agreed. It should also minimize potential disputes among the partners.

In addition to essential legal provisions, the partnership agreement should include the following:

1. The partnership's exact name and designated place of business.
2. The names and personal addresses of each partner.
3. The date on which the partnership was formed.
4. The business purpose of the partnership.
5. The duration of the partnership.
6. A list of the assets contributed by each partner and the related agreed-upon valuation of those assets to the partnership.
7. The basis of accounting to be used (for example, the accrual basis, the cash basis, or some variation of either of these methods).
8. The partnership's accounting year-end for purposes of closing the books and dividing the profits and losses.
9. The specific procedures for sharing profits and losses.

10. The amounts that partners can periodically withdraw from the business and any related conditions for such withdrawals (for example, a certain amount per month or an amount up to a percentage of current-period earnings).
11. Provisions for settling with a partner (or a partner's estate) who withdraws from the partnership through choice, retirement, or death.

An accountant can assist persons who are in the preliminary stages of forming a partnership in the following ways:

1. By explaining the cash basis and accrual basis of accounting.
2. By explaining and illustrating the numerous alternative methods available for sharing profits and losses and the appropriateness of each method. (A significant portion of this chapter is devoted to this subject.)
3. By discussing the tax ramifications compared with other methods of organizing the business. (This subject is also discussed later in the chapter.)

The Partnership as an Entity

The business of the partnership should logically be accounted for separately from the personal transactions of the partners. Although partnerships are not separate legal entities with unlimited lives, as is the case for corporations, this does not prevent partnerships from being accounted for as separate, operating, business entities.

Although partners legally must contribute additional cash or property to the partnership to satisfy the claims of creditors, this does not mean that the partnership is inseparable from the partners. It is a common banking practice for certain top officers of corporations to guarantee personally loans made to the corporation. Thus, the fact that additional collateral for creditors exists is irrelevant.

Income tax laws do not determine sound accounting theory. They do treat partnerships as separate reporting entities, although not as separate tax-paying entities. Most partnerships are considered separate business entities in that they prepare monthly financial statements for internal use. Some of the large public accounting firms even publish annual reports, complete with financial statements, for use by their partners, employees, and other interested parties.

Applicability of Generally Accepted Accounting Principles

To study partnerships, we must make an important transition from corporate accounting (in which generally accepted accounting principles are almost always followed) to partnership accounting (in which generally accepted accounting principles need not be and often are not followed). The professional pronouncements of the American Institute of Certified Public Accountants (AICPA) and the Financial Accounting Standards Board (FASB) apply to businesses that present their financial statements in accordance with generally accepted accounting principles. Such businesses include (1) publicly held corporations, which must present their financial statements in accordance with generally accepted accounting principles; (2) nonpublicly held corporations, which usually present their financial statements in accordance with generally accepted accounting principles (often pursuant to requirements of loan agreements with financial institutions); and (3) partnerships and sole proprietorships that choose to present their financial statements in accordance with generally accepted accounting principles.

When a partnership does not maintain its books in accordance with generally accepted accounting principles, such a departure usually falls into one of the following categories:

1. **Cash basis instead of accrual basis.** The cash basis of recording receipts and expenses is often more efficient and economical than the accrual basis.
2. **Prior-period adjustments.** To achieve greater equity among the partners, prior-period adjustments are often made even though the items do not qualify as such under *FASB Statement No. 16*, "Prior Period Adjustments."
3. **Current values instead of historical cost.** When the ownership of the partnership changes, it is sometimes more expedient to reflect assets at their current values than to continue to reflect them at their historical cost.
4. **Recognition of goodwill.** To accommodate a partner's wishes, goodwill may be recognized on the admission or retirement of a partner, even though a business combination has not occurred.

Categories 3 and 4 are discussed and illustrated in Chapter 24 on changes in ownership.

Partners' Accounts

Capital Accounts. Each partner has a **capital account,** which is created when the partner contributes assets to the partnership. The account is increased for subsequent capital contributions and decreased for withdrawals. In addition, the account is increased for the partner's share of earnings and decreased for the partner's share of losses.

Traditionally, accountants have not attempted to maintain a balance sheet distinction between contributed capital and earnings that have been retained in the partnership, as is customary for corporations. This is primarily because the partnership's earnings do not reflect any salary expense for the partners (they are owners, not employees), and therefore they must be evaluated carefully. If the corporate form of business were used rather than the partnership form, the corporation's earnings would be lower than those reported by the partnership, because the services performed by the partners would be performed by salaried officers and employees of the corporation. Earnings under the corporate form of business would also be lower because of income tax. To avoid the implication that the earnings retained in the partnership are comparable to the retained earnings of a corporation, a Retained Earnings account is considered inappropriate for partnerships. Accordingly, the earnings or losses of a partnership are added or subtracted, respectively, to the capital accounts of the individual partners.

Drawing Accounts. Typically, partners do not wait until the end of the year to determine how much of the profits they wish to withdraw from the partnership. To meet personal living expenses, partners customarily withdraw money on a periodic basis throughout the year. Such withdrawals could be charged directly to the capital accounts of the individual partners. However, a special account called the **drawing account** is used to charge current-year withdrawals. In substance, the drawing accounts are contra capital accounts. At year-end, each partner's drawing account is closed to that partner's capital account. The maximum amount partners may withdraw during the year is usually specified in the partnership agreement.

Loan Accounts. Partners may make loans to the partnership in excess of their required capital contributions. Section 18 of the UPA provides that unless otherwise agreed to by the partners, "a partner, who in aid of the partnership makes any payment or advance beyond the amount of capital which he agreed to contribute, shall be paid interest from the date of the payment or advance." Interest on partners' loans to the partnership is a bona fide borrowing expense of the business, is treated as interest expense in the general ledger, and enters into the determination of the profit or loss.

If a partnership loans money on an interest-bearing basis to a partner, the interest is recorded as interest income in the general ledger. It also enters into the determination of the profit or loss.

Recording the Initial Capital Contributions

The following two fundamental principles are deeply rooted in partnership accounting:

1. Noncash assets contributed to a partnership should be valued at their current values.
2. Liabilities assumed by a partnership should be valued at their current values.

These principles achieve equity among the partners, an objective that is repeatedly stressed in partnership accounting. If these principles were not followed, the subsequent operations would not reflect the true earnings of the partnerships, and certain partners would be treated inequitably.

For example, assume a partner contributed to a partnership marketable securities with a current market value of $10,000 and a cost basis to the individual partner of $7,000. If the marketable securities were later sold by the partnership for $12,000, the recorded gain on the partnership's books would be $2,000, which is the amount of appreciation that occurred during the period that the partnership held the asset. However, if the marketable securities had been valued on the partnership's books at the partner's cost basis of $7,000, the recorded gain would be $5,000. This would result in the other partner's sharing in an additional $3,000 of profit; the appreciation that occurred before the asset was contributed to the partnership. Current values must be used to prevent such inequities. The partnership agreement normally indicates the agreed-upon valuation assigned to noncash assets contributed and liabilities assumed.

The entry to record initial capital contributions for an assumed two-person partnership is shown below using the following assumed facts:

Assets Contributed and Liabilities Assumed	Adjusted Basis[a]	Current Value
By partner A:		
Cash	$23,000	$23,000
Marketable securities	7,000	10,000
	$30,000	$33,000
By partner B:		
Cash	$ 5,000	$ 5,000
Land	15,000	20,000
Building, net	25,000	35,000
Note payable, secured by land and building	(20,000)	(20,000)
	$25,000	$40,000

Entry to record initial contributions:		
Cash	28,000	
Marketable Securities	10,000	
Land	20,000	
Building	35,000	
Notes Payable		20,000
Capital, Partner A		33,000
Capital, Partner B		40,000

[a]"Adjusted basis" means each partner's historical cost, as adjusted for depreciation and amortization previously recorded for income tax reporting purposes.

The adjusted basis column is completely irrelevant for purposes of recording the initial capital contributions in the general ledger, but it is significant for income tax reporting. Income tax aspects are discussed later in the chapter.

METHODS OF SHARING PROFITS AND LOSSES

Section 18 of the UPA specifies that profits and losses are shared equally unless otherwise provided for in the partnership agreement. Because the sharing of profits and losses is such an important aspect of a partnership relationship, it would be rare to find a partnership agreement that did not spell out the divisions of profits and losses in detail. The formula that is used to divide profits and losses is arrived at through negotiations among the partners. Whether or not it is fair does not concern the accountant.

Profits and losses can be shared in many ways. Partners should select a formula that is sensible, practical, and equitable. Most profit and loss sharing formulas include one or more of the following features or techniques:

1. Sharing equally or in some other agreed-upon ratio.
2. Imputed salary allowances to acknowledge time devoted to the business.
3. Imputed interest on capital investments to recognize capital invested.
4. Expense sharing arrangements.
5. Performance criteria to recognize above- or below-average performance.

Note that the computations to determine the allocation of profit and loss among the partners are made on worksheets. The only journal entry that results from this process is to close the Profit and Loss Summary account to the capital accounts of the partners, using the amounts determined from the worksheet computations.

Ratios

Under the *ratio method*, each partner is allocated a percentage of the profits and losses. For example, partner A is to receive 60% and partner B is to receive 40% of the profits and losses. These percentages are then expressed as a ratio. Thus, profits and losses are shared between A and B in the ratio 3:2, respectively. If the partnership of A and B had profits of $100,000, the entry to record the division of the profits would be as follows:

Profit and Loss Summary	**100,000**	
Capital, Partner A		**60,000**
Capital, Partner B		**40,000**

An infrequently used variation of this method is to specify one ratio for profits and a different ratio for losses. Because profit and loss years may alternate, it is extremely important that profit or loss for each year be determined accurately in all material respects whenever this variation is used.

Salary Allowances and Ratios

Sometimes certain partners devote more time to the business than other partners. In these cases, a frequently used method for sharing profits and losses is to provide for salary allowances, with any residual profit or loss allocated in an agreed-upon ratio. For example, assume partner A devotes all of his time to the business, and partner B devotes only one-third of her time to the business. The partners could agree to provide for salary allowances in relation to the time devoted to the business—for example, $30,000 to partner A and $10,000 to partner B. All remaining profits or losses could then be divided in the agreed-upon ratio—that is, 3:2, respectively.

Using these salary allowances and a residual sharing ratio of 3:2 for partner A and partner B, respectively, the partnership would divide $100,000 in profits in the following way:

		Allocated to	
	Total	Partner A	Partner B
Total profit	$100,000		
Salary allowances	(40,000)	$30,000	$10,000
Residual profit	$ 60,000		
Allocate 3:2	(60,000)	36,000	24,000
	$ -0-	$66,000	$34,000

The general ledger entry to divide the profits would be as follows:

Profit and Loss Summary	100,000	
Capital, Partner A		66,000
Capital, Partner B		34,000

Remember that partners are owners, not employees. Accordingly, it is not appropriate to charge a Salary Expense account and credit Accrued Salary Payable. However, some partnerships do record salary allowances in this manner. Although not technically correct, it does not affect the final profit and loss allocations. In these cases, cash distributions that relate to salary allowances are charged to Accrued Salary Payable. Any remaining credit balance in a partner's Accrued Salary Payable account at year-end is then transferred to that partner's capital account.

In the above example, the total profit was greater than the total salary allowances of $40,000. What if that were not the case? Profit of only $25,000 would be shared as follows:

		Allocated to	
	Total	Partner A	Partner B
Total profit	$ 25,000		
Salary allowances	(40,000)	$30,000	$10,000
Residual loss	$(15,000)		
Allocate 3:2	15,000	(9,000)	(6,000)
	$ -0-	$21,000	$ 4,000

The general ledger entry to divide the profits would be as follows:

Profit and Loss Summary	25,000	
Capital, Partner A		21,000
Capital, Partner B		4,000

Another way of handling this situation would be if the partners agreed not to use a residual sharing ratio in the event profits were less than the total salary allowances. In this case, the first $40,000 of profit would be divided in the ratio of the salary allowances. Using the above example, a profit of $25,000 would be divided as follows:

		Allocated to	
	Total	Partner A	Partner B
Total profit	$25,000		
Salary allowances—up to $40,000 in a 3:1 ratio	(25,000)	$18,750	$6,250
	$ –0–	$18,750	$6,250

Large and moderately sized partnerships usually function with an administrative hierarchy. Partnership positions within such a hierarchy have greater responsibilities than positions outside the hierarchy. To compensate the partners who assume these greater responsibilities, salary allowances commonly are used and their amounts are correlated to the various levels of responsibility within the hierarchy.

Imputed Interest on Capital, Salary Allowances, and Ratios

When partners' capital investments are not equal, the profit sharing formula frequently includes a feature that recognizes the greater capital investment of certain partners. Accordingly, interest is imputed on each partner's capital investment. For example, a profit and loss sharing formula could specify that interest be imputed at 10% of each partner's average capital investment. To illustrate how this procedure is applied, assume the following profit sharing formula and average capital investments:

	Partner A	Partner B
Profit sharing formula:		
Salary allowances	$30,000	$10,000
Interest on average capital balance	10%	10%
Residual profit or loss (3:2)	60%	40%
Average capital investments	$10,000	$40,000

Profits of $100,000 would be divided as follows:

	Total	Allocated to Partner A	Partner B
Total profit	$100,000		
Salary allowances	(40,000)	$30,000	$10,000
Interest on average capital investments	(5,000)	1,000	4,000
Residual profit	$ 55,000		
Allocate 3:2	(55,000)	33,000	22,000
	$ –0–	$64,000	$36,000

The general ledger entry to divide the profits would be as follows:

Profit and Loss Summary	100,000	
Capital, Partner A		64,000
Capital, Partner B		36,000

Remember that the partner's capital investments are just that—they are not loans to the partnership. Accordingly, it is not appropriate to charge an Interest Expense account and an Accrued Interest Payable account. However, some partnerships do record imputed interest in this manner. This procedure is not technically correct, but it does not affect the final profit and loss allocations. In these cases, cash distributions that relate to imputed interest are charged to Accrued Interest Payable. Any remaining credit balance in a partner's Accrued Interest Payable account at year-end is then transferred to that partner's capital account.

In the above example the profit was greater than both the total of the salary allowances of $40,000 and the total of imputed interest of $5,000. A profit of only $25,000 would be divided as follows:

	Total	Allocated to Partner A	Partner B
Total profit	$ 25,000		
Salary allowances	(40,000)	$30,000	$10,000
Interest on average capital investments	(5,000)	1,000	4,000
Residual loss	$(20,000)		
Allocate 3:2	20,000	(12,000)	(8,000)
	$ –0–	$19,000	$ 6,000

The general ledger entry to divide the profits would be as follows:

Profit and Loss Summary	25,000	
Capital, Partner A		19,000
Capital, Partner B		6,000

Order of Priority Provision. Alternatively, the partners could agree not to use a residual sharing ratio in the event profits did not exceed the total of the salary allowances and the imputed interest on average capital balances. In this case, the partners must agree on **the priority of the various features.** If the partnership agreement gives salary allowances priority over imputed interest on capital balances, the first $40,000 of profit would be divided in the ratio of the salary allowances, and the next $5,000 would be divided in the ratio of the imputed interest amounts. Using the profit sharing formula and data given in the preceding example, a profit of only $42,000 would be divided as follows:

		Allocated to	
	Total	Partner A	Partner B
Total profit	$42,000		
Salary allowances	(40,000)	$30,000	$10,000
Available for interest on capital	$ 2,000		
Interest on average capital investment 1:4	(2,000)	400	1,600
	$ -0-	$30,400	$11,600

Note: If interest on capital had priority over salary allowances, the division of the $42,000 profit would result in Partner A being allocated $28,750 ($1,000 for interest and $27,750 for salary) and Partner B being allocated $13,250 ($4,000 for interest and $9,250 for salary).

In the preceding examples, interest was imputed on the average capital investments. Although this is apparently the most equitable method, using the beginning or ending capital investments are other options. Whenever this imputed interest on capital feature is used, the partnership agreement should specify whether the beginning, average, or ending capital balances should be used. Furthermore, if the partnership agreement calls for using average or ending capital investments, it should define specifically how the average or ending capital investments are determined. Only the capital account or the capital account and the drawing account of each partner may be used. For the average capital balance method, the method of computing the average must be selected—that is, using daily balances, beginning of month balances, or end of month balances.

The following assumptions and capital account activities illustrate the computation of an average capital investment.

1. The drawing account activity is considered in arriving at the average capital investment for the year.
2. An average capital investment for each month is used to arrive at the average capital investment for the year.

Capital, Partner X

	50,000	1/1/X5
	10,000	4/1/X5
	2,000	11/15/X5

Drawings, Partner X

6/30/X5	6,000	
9/15/X5	6,000	
12/31/X5	6,000	

Computation

Month	Monthly Averages
January	$ 50,000
February	50,000
March	50,000
April	60,000
May	60,000
June	60,000
July	54,000
August	54,000
September	51,000
October	48,000
November	49,000
December	50,000
	$636,000
Average capital investment for 19X5 ($636,000 ÷ 12)	$ 53,000

Capital Balances Only

Many international accounting firms allocate profits and losses *solely* on the basis of capital balances. In these cases, each partner must maintain a specified capital balance, which is correlated to the level of responsibility assumed in the partnership. This method is not only easy to apply, but it can prevent certain inequities from occurring among partners if the partnership is liquidated. These potential inequities are discussed in Chapter 25, which deals with partnership liquidations.

Expense-Sharing Arrangements

Sometimes a small partnership operates as a confederation of sole proprietorships, in that the profit-sharing formula entitles each partner to all net billings generated by that partner. Expenses are then allocated to partners on the basis of total floor space, amount of billings, or some other arbitrary method. This arrangement is common when two or more sole proprietorships form a partnership, with each partner maintaining former clients. Any net billings from clients obtained after the formation of the partnership may be assigned either to the partner responsible for obtaining the client or to a common pool to be allocated to all partners on some arbitrary basis.

Performance Methods

Many partnerships use profit- and loss-sharing formulas that give some weight to the specific performance of each partner, to provide incentives to perform well. Some examples of areas in which performance criteria may be used are listed below:

1. **Chargeable hours.** Chargeable hours are the total number of hours that a partner incurred on client-related assignments. Weight may be given to hours in excess of a norm.
2. **Total billings.** The total amount billed to clients for work performed and supervised by a partner constitutes total billings. Weight may be given to billings in excess of a norm.
3. **Write-offs.** Write-offs consist of the amount of uncollectible billings. Weight may be given to a write-off percentage below a norm.
4. **Promotional and civic activities.** Time devoted to the development of future business and to the development of the partnership name in the community is considered promotional and civic activity. Weight may be given to time spent in excess of a norm or to specific accomplishments resulting in new clients.
5. **Profits in excess of specified levels.** Designated partners commonly receive a certain percentage of profits in excess of a specified level of earnings.

An additional allocation of profits to a partner on the basis of performance is frequently referred to as a **bonus.** As with salary allowances and imputed interest, a bonus should not be charged to an expense account in the general ledger, although some partnerships improperly do this.

Subsequent Changes in Methods of Sharing Profits and Losses

If the partners subsequently agree to change the method of sharing profits and losses, equity dictates that assets be revalued to their current values at the time of the change. To illustrate, assume partners A and B shared profits and losses equally, and at a later date they agree to share profits and losses in a 3:2 ratio, respectively. Suppose also that the partnership holds a parcel of land that is carried on the books at $60,000 but now has a current value of $80,000. Partner A would receive a greater share of the profit on the land (when it is later sold) than if the land were sold before the method of sharing profits and losses was changed. This is not equitable because the land appreciated $20,000 while the profits and losses were shared equally.

An alternative to revaluing the land to its current value would be to stipulate in the new profit sharing formula that the first $20,000 of profit on the sale of that parcel of land is to be shared in the old profit and loss sharing ratio. Under this method, the partnership avoids making an entry that would be at variance with generally accepted accounting principles. However, this is not a major reason for selecting this alternative if revaluing assets is more practical.

When the profit and loss sharing formula is revised, the new formula should contain a provision specifying that the old formula applies to certain types of subsequent adjustments arising out of activities that took place before the revision date. Examples are:

1. Unrecorded liabilities existing at the revision date.
2. Settlements on lawsuits not provided for at the revision date, even though the liability may not have been probable as to payment or reasonably estimable at that time.
3. Write-offs of accounts receivable existing as of the revision date.

Regardless of the fact that some of these items would not qualify as prior-period adjustments under *FASB Statement No. 16*, "Prior Period Adjustments," greater equity usually would be achieved among the partners by using the old sharing formula. Because partnerships need not follow generally accepted accounting principles, the will of the partners may prevail.

FINANCIAL REPORTING

Because partnerships are not publicly owned, their financial statements are prepared primarily for internal use. Such statements normally include all of those that a corporation prepares, except for the statement of changes in stockholders' equity, for which a statement of changes in partners' equity is substituted.

One common reason for making partnership financial statements available to outside parties is to borrow money from financial institutions. (Under the Uniform Partnership Act, partnerships can hold debt in the partnership name rather than in the names of its individual partners.) Financial statements made available to outside parties should be converted to the accrual basis if the cash basis is used for book purposes. (Most partnerships use the cash basis as a matter of convenience.) Because partnership earnings are not comparable to what they would have been had the business been organized as a corporation, an indication to this effect should be made in the footnotes to the financial statements.

Some accountants have suggested that a partnership's income statement should reflect an imputed amount for salaries that would have been paid to the partners had the corporate form of business been used. Presumably, such an approach would state the "true earnings" of the partnership. In our opinion, this is a somewhat futile exercise involving substantial subjectivity. Furthermore, from a technical standpoint, consideration should also be given to (1) additional payroll taxes; (2) deductions for fringe benefits (primarily pension and profit sharing plans), which are not available to partners; and (3) income taxes. It would seem sufficient to state in a footnote that, because the partnership form of organization is used, the earnings must be evaluated carefully because, conceptually, earnings should provide for equivalent salary compensation, return on capital invested in the partnership, retirement, and payroll-type fringe benefits.

Virtually all partnerships maintain strict confidentiality of their financial statements. International public accounting partnerships that do issue financial statements to interested parties commonly show the following:

1. The financial statements are converted from the cash basis to the accrual basis of accounting.
2. An inputed amount for salaries is not reflected in the income statement.
3. A footnote to the financial statements indicates that the firm's earnings are not comparable to those of a corporation.
4. The financial statements are prepared in accordance with generally accepted accounting principles, and the notes to the financial statements are complete as to required disclosures—for example, disclosures of accounting policies, lease commitments, and segment information.

The income statement of small partnerships commonly shows how the profit or loss is divided. The allocation can be shown immediately below net income, as follows:

A & B PARTNERSHIP
Income Statement
For the Year Ended December 31, 19X1

Revenues	$1,000,000
Expenses	(900,000)
Net Income	$ 100,000

Allocation of net income to partners:

	Partner A	Partner B
Salary allowances	$30,000	$10,000
Imputed interest on capital	1,000	4,000
Residual (3:2)	33,000	22,000
Total	$64,000	$36,000

Furthermore, a small partnership's statement of changes in partners' equity is often shown *by partner* as follows:

A & B PARTNERSHIP
Statement of Changes in Partners' Equity
For the Year Ended December 31, 19X1

	Partner A	Partner B	Total
Beginning capital	$25,000	$ 85,000	$110,000
Contributions	5,000	—	5,000
Drawings	(10,000)	(15,000)	(25,000)
Net income	64,000	36,000	100,000
Ending capital	$84,000	$106,000	$190,000

INCOME TAX ASPECTS

Other than dividing the profits and losses among the partners in accordance with the profit sharing formula, accounting for the operations of a partnership presents no unusual problems. The income tax aspects of partnerships, however, are much more involved. An accountant providing services to a partnership must have a solid grasp of partnership tax concepts to serve his or her clients adequately. The following discussion will not make you an expert in partnership taxation; it will only provide a basic understanding of partnership taxation.

Equity versus Tax Basis

A partner's interest in a partnership is a personal, capital asset that can be sold, exchanged, assigned, or otherwise disposed of. From a financial accounting viewpoint, a partner's equity in the partnership is the balance in his or her capital account net of any balance in his or her drawing account. If a partner were to sell his or her interest in the partnership, the gain or loss from a partnership accounting viewpoint would be determined by comparing the proceeds to his or her equity at the time of sale. The gain or loss from an accounting viewpoint, however, is not important. The sale is a personal transaction; therefore, any gain or loss is not reflected in the partnership's general ledger. In this respect, it is similar to the sale of stock by a shareholder of a corporation—it does not enter into the operations of the business entity. From the selling partner's viewpoint, the relevant objective is to determine the amount of the taxable gain or loss.

Contributing Assets. The tax laws are not structured around a partner's equity as recorded in the partnership general ledger. Thus, to determine the amount of gain or loss for tax purposes on the sale of a partner's interest in a partnership, we must be familiar with the concept of tax basis. For tax purposes, a partner's interest in a partnership is referred to as that partner's **tax basis.** Tax basis is an asset-related concept; if a partner contributed $5,000 cash to a partnership, his or her tax basis in the partnership is $5,000. (Coincidentally, this would be the amount credited to his or her capital account in the general ledger, but this fact is irrelevant from a tax standpoint.) If a partner contributes equipment to a partnership, then that partner's tax basis in the partnership increases by the adjusted tax basis of the equipment immediately before the contribution or transfer. The adjusted tax basis of the equipment is the partner's historical cost less any depreciation previously deducted for income tax reporting purposes. Thus, if equipment that cost the partner $10,000 had been depreciated $2,000 in the partner's business before the contribution or transfer, the adjusted basis would be $8,000. Accordingly, the partner's tax basis in the partnership would increase by $8,000.

If the equipment was completely paid for at the time of the contribution or transfer to the partnership, the amount credited to the partner's capital account in the general ledger would depend on the current value assigned to the equipment and agreed to by the partners. This current value could be more or less than the $8,000 adjusted tax basis. Thus, it would only be a coincidence that the credit to the partner's capital account increases by the amount of the adjusted tax basis at the time of the contribution or transfer.

No Step-up or Step-down in Tax Basis. For tax purposes, any difference between the current value and the adjusted tax basis at the time of the contribution or transfer to a partnership is not recognized. In other words, no gain or loss must be reported. The adjusted tax basis of the asset (in the hands of the partner immediately before the contribution or transfer) is not stepped up or stepped down on transfer to the partnership. Accordingly, the adjusted tax basis of each asset contributed to a partnership merely carries over to the partnership for tax reporting purposes. To the extent that future depreciation and amortization expenses are different for book (general ledger) reporting purposes than for tax reporting purposes, the book income or loss must be adjusted (on a worksheet) to arrive at taxable income.

Contribution Liabilities. This concept of tax basis is slightly more involved if the contributed asset has a debt attached to it that is assumed by the partnership. Suppose the equipment had a $3,000 installment note payable attached to it, for which the partnership assumed responsibility. The contributing partner's tax basis still increases by $8,000 (the amount of the adjusted tax basis of the asset at the time of the contribution or transfer). The fact that the partnership has assumed responsibility for payment of the debt, however is significant from a tax viewpoint. The tax law says the other partners (by becoming jointly responsible for the payment of this debt), in substance, have given money to this partner. Accordingly, their tax bases should be increased and the tax basis of the partner who contributed the liability should be decreased by the amount of money deemed to have been given constructively to the partner. The profit and loss sharing ratio is used to determine this deemed amount. For example, if a three-person partnership shared profits equally, then the tax basis of the partner contributing the equipment and the related $3,000 liability would be reduced from $8,000 to $6,000 (two-thirds of $3,000) and the tax basis of each of the other partners would be increased by $1,000 (one-third of $3,000). This procedure is used even though the creditor could seek personal recourse from the partner who contributes the liability to the partnership.

Keeping Track of Each Partner's Basis. Because a partner's tax basis cannot be determined by using the amounts recorded in the general ledger capital accounts, each partner must determine his or her own individual tax basis in the partnership on a memorandum tax basis outside the general ledger. In summary, each partner's tax basis can be determined when the partnership is formed by adding the first three of the following categories and subtracting the fourth category.

- Cash contributed to the partnership by a partner.
- Add—A partner's adjusted tax basis in any noncash property contributed or transferred to the partnership.
- Add—A partner's share of any liabilities assumed by the partnership that were contributed by other partners.
- Less—The other partners' share of any liabilities assumed by the partnership that the partner contributed to the partnership.

Comprehensive Illustration. To further demonstrate the application of these procedures for determining a basis, we assume the same facts related to the formation of a partnership as in the example on page 995. In addition, we assume that partners A and B share profits and losses in a 3:2 ratio, respectively. The adjusted tax basis of each partner is shown below.

	Adjusted Basis		
	Partner A	Partner B	Total
Cash contributed	$23,000	$ 5,000	$28,000
Noncash assets contributed:			
Marketable securities	7,000		7,000
Land		15,000	15,000
Building		25,000	25,000
	$30,000	$45,000	$75,000

	Adjusted Basis		
	Partner A	Partner B	Total
Adjustment to **tax** basis for liabilities of $20,000 assumed by the partnership[a]	12,000	(12,000)	
Basis	$42,000	$33,000	$75,000

[a]The adjustment to each partner's tax basis is 60% of $20,000, because partner A assumes a 60% responsibility for the $20,000 liability contributed by partner B.

In reviewing the above illustration, one major point should be understood. Partner A's $42,000 tax basis plus partner B's $33,000 tax basis equals the partnership's tax basis in the assets of $75,000 for tax reporting purposes. This equality always exists. Note also that the sum of the tax bases of the assets immediately before the transfer ($30,000 for partner A's assets and $45,000 for partner B's assets) also equals the partnership's tax basis in the assets for tax reporting purposes.

Subsequent Adjustments to Each Partner's Tax Basis

The personal tax basis of each partner's interest in the partnership is adjusted as subsequent partnership activity takes place. Such activities can be grouped as follows:

1. **Contributions and distributions (withdrawals).** If a partner subsequently contributes additional assets to the partnership, the tax basis of that partner's interest in the partnership increases. If the partner withdraws assets from the partnership, the tax basis of that partner's interest in the partnership decreases. (It can never be less than zero.)
2. **Profits and losses.** To the extent that there are profits, each partner's tax basis of interest in the partnership increases by that partner's share of the partnership's taxable income. To the extent that there are losses, each partner's tax basis of interest in the partnership decreases by that partner's share of the partnership's loss for tax reporting purposes.
3. **Changes in partnership liabilities.** Tax laws effectively treat partnership liabilities as personal liabilities of the partners. For example, if a partnership borrowed $1,000 from a financial institution, the partnership's assets would increase by $1,000. The same result could be produced if one of the partners were personally to borrow the $1,000 from the financial institution and then make an additional capital contribution of $1,000. The form of each transaction is different, but the substance is the same.

   Thus, an increase in a partnership's liabilities is treated as an additional capital contribution by the partners. This increase is shared among the partners, and each partner's tax basis in the partnership increases. A decrease in a partnership's liabilities is treated as a distribution of partnership assets to its partners. This decrease also is shared among the partners, and each partner's tax basis in the partnership decreases.

In the example given in the preceding illustration we showed a $12,000 adjustment to the tax bases of partners A and B as a result of partner B's contributing a $20,000 liability to the partnership. In a different approach to this adjustment, we assume that (1) instead of partner B's contributing the $20,000 liability to the partnership, the partnership borrowed $20,000 from a financial institution, and (2) the partnership then distributed that $20,000 to partner B, who paid off his personal loan of $20,000. The adjustments to the tax basis of each of the partners are as follows:

	Adjustments to Basis	
	Partner A	Partner B
Borrowing of $20,000 by the partnership (60% to partner A and 40% to partner B)	$12,000	$ 8,000
Distribution of $20,000 to partner B		(20,000)
Net change to basis	$12,000	$(12,000)

Note that the net effect on each partner's tax basis is still $12,000.

The determination of a partner's tax basis in a partnership is relevant when a partner disposes of some or all of his or her partnership interest. This situation is discussed more fully in Chapter 24 on ownership changes.

Net Operating Loss Carrybacks and Carryforwards

Because partnerships are not taxable entities, they do not have net operating loss carrybacks or carryforwards. However, when a partner's share of a partnership's loss for a given year exceeds the excess of the partner's nonbusiness income over nonbusiness deductions (excluding personal exemptions as deductions), this net amount is a net operating loss that can be carried back three years and then forward seven years on the partner's individual income tax return. The excess of nonbusiness deductions (excluding personal exemptions as deductions) over nonbusiness income does not increase the net operating loss because it is not business related.

THE PROFESSIONAL CORPORATION

A complete discussion of the legal aspects and tax laws related to professional corporations is beyond the scope of this book. In general, the professional corporation form of business is available to professionals who render personal service—for example, accountants, architects, attorneys, dentists, optometrists, physicians, real estate brokers, and veterinarians. A professional corporation must act like a corporation and maintain a corporate appearance throughout its existence. For example, shareholders' and directors' meetings must be held and minutes of these meetings must be maintained. From a tax standpoint, the professional corporation is subject to tax laws that apply to corporations, including provisions related to (1) the reasonableness of compensation paid to shareholder-employees; (2) the reasonableness of accumulated earnings; and (3) the restrictions on amounts that can be deducted for pension and profit sharing plans.

Tax Advantages to Incorporation

Under the partnership form of organization, only employees of the partnership can participate in fringe benefits such as pension, profit sharing, medical, and insurance plans. Because partners are not employees, they cannot participate in these plans. The tax laws do allow professionals to provide for their retirement through the use of H.R. 10 (Keogh) plans. A self-employed professional operating as a sole proprietor or a member of a partnership may take a deduction for contributions to a qualified Keogh plan. The earnings on funds invested in a qualified Keogh plan are not taxed currently. As funds from the plan are distributed during retirement years (presumably when the recipient is in a much lower income tax bracket), the distributions are reported for income tax purposes.

By having the partnership become a professional corporation, the partners become employees of the corporation, even though they are also its shareholders. They can then participate in pension, profit sharing, medical, and insurance plans. (Pension and profit sharing plans are the major fringe benefits by far.)

Pre-1984 Tax Advantages. Prior to 1984, the contributions allowed under Keogh plans were substantially below the maximum contributions allowed to corporate employees. Thus, in a professional corporation, more pretax dollars could be set aside to earn money that is not currently taxable, enabling a professional to provide much more generously for retirement than through the partnership or sole proprietorship forms of organization. These tax advantages were the major impetus for the explosive shift to the professional corporation.

Parity Achieved in 1984. Such disparities were inequitable, and many individuals and organizations (notably the tax section of the New York State Bar Association) worked to achieve parity so that deductions for profit-sharing and pension plans would be the same for all people who work, regardless of whether they are self-employed or work for a corporation. As a result, beginning in 1984, the maximum annual Keogh plan deductions were made the same as deductions for profit-sharing and pension plans allowed for corporate employees. (For profit-sharing plans, the maximum annual deduction is $30,000; for pension plans, the maximum annual benefit is $90,000.) As a further effort to achieve parity, the new law eliminated or changed many of the special limitations affecting Keogh plans. Thus, the major reasons for using a professional corporation have been eliminated.

The Remaining Tax Advantages. The only remaining significant tax advantages associated with professional corporations are medical and insurance plan deductions. Even though the major tax advantages for using professional corporations were eliminated, only a slight shift away from the professional corporation form of business has occurred. Nontax factors favoring incorporation (discussed shortly) largely account for this.

The Double Tax Disadvantage Is Easily Avoided. Recall that one disadvantage of the corporate form of business is the double taxation of earnings—that is, the corporation's earnings are taxed and then corporate dividends are taxed. This disadvantage is usually of little significance to a professional corporation, which can enter into employment contracts with its shareholder-employees and adopt bonus plans, applying primarily to shareholder-employees, whereby salaries and bonuses can be paid to the extent necessary to eliminate any income that would be taxable at the corporate level. (Such compensation must still pass the IRS's tests of reasonableness to be allowed as a tax deduction and must not be deemed dividends rather than compensation.) In this way, the professional corporation form avoids or substantially mitigates the double tax.

Nontax Advantages to Incorporation

Unlimited versus Limited Liability. The incorporation of a partnership does not automatically insulate the former partners' personal assets from the corporation's creditors. Shareholder-employees are still responsible for liabilities that arise out of acts they perform (or acts that are performed under their supervision) while rendering professional services as employees of the professional corporation. Certain states impose joint and several liability on all shareholders for professional services rendered by the professional corporation or its employees. Other states require personal participation for a shareholder of a professional corporation to be held individually liable. Note that shareholder-employees are not individually responsible (in most states) for liabilities that arise out of acts not involving rendering professional services (such as an automobile accident incurred in delivering an audit report to a client). In summary, some limited liability protection is obtainable by incorporating.

Impracticality of Accountants Incorporating

Accounting firms that operate on a multistate basis find it impractical to incorporate because of licensing and qualification requirements. For example, many of the states' professional corporation statutes and corresponding accounting regulations require that all shareholders be licensed to practice in the state of incorporation. Primarily for this reason, virtually all of the national, multistate, and regional public accounting firms have retained the partnership form of organization.

SUMMARY

For all practical purposes, the partnership form of organization can be accounted for as a separate entity. The primary objective of partnership accounting is to achieve equity among the partners. Because the partnership form of organization is unique, the procedures that can be used to achieve such equity are quite flexible. A solid grasp of income tax concepts and rules is required before an accountant can expect to serve a partnership properly. In addition, an accountant must be familiar with the advantages and disadvantages (tax and nontax factors) associated with professional corporations.

Selected References

"Estate Planning Perils for CPA Partners and Shareholders," by Bernard Barnett. *Journal of Accountancy* (January 1986), 68–76.

"Financing with R&D Partnerships Reduces Risk," by John W. Hardy. *Management Accounting* (January 1984) 56–59.

"How to Choose the Right Form of Doing Business," by Robert E. Engle. *Management Accounting* (January 1985), 44–47.

"Mediating Partnership Disputes," by Morton J. Levy. *Journal of Accountancy* (December 1984), 136–140.

"Partnership Agreements: Realities into Formalities," from a speech by Herman J. Lowe. *Journal of Accountancy* (September 1986) 158–66.

"Profit Allocation in CPA Firm Partnership Agreements," by Akshay K. Talwar. *Journal of Accountancy* (March 1986), 91–95.

"The Unique Tax Characteristics of Partnerships," *Journal of Accountancy* (April 1984), 100–112.

Appendix A
LIMITED PARTNERSHIPS

An explosive increase in the use of limited partnerships has occured in recent years. Such partnerships are used as investment vehicles by passive investors. A **limited partnership** consists of a general partner and limited partners. Unlike the general partner, a limited partner's liability is limited to his or her cash investments. Furthermore, a limited partner plays no role in the management of the partnership, this being the complete responsibility of the general partner. Two types of limited partnerships have been extremely popular in recent years: real estate partnerships and research and development (R&D) partnerships.

SYNDICATES FOR REAL ESTATE

Real Estate Limited Partnerships

Real estate limited partnerships (RELPs) are formed by companies that package real estate investments. Such companies, which generally have real estate experience, are commonly referred to as *sponsors* or *syndicators.* These companies employ securities brokers to sell interests in the limited partnerships to individual investors. The sponsor or an affiliated company is usually the general partner. The partnership then acquires rental apartments, shopping centers, or office buildings (the most common investments). Sponsors generally receive an up-front fee, an annual management fee, and a share of the income and appreciation. The general partner controls when the property is sold. (The average life of such partnerships is seven to twelve years.) It is difficult for limited partners to get their money out of the partnership until liquidation, because they cannot readily sell their interests. They must personally find a buyer. This is a major drawback for many investors. However, such investments appear to be ideal for persons with little or no real estate experience or who do not want the headaches associated with property management.

Although real estate investment packages can take any form of ownership (such as a corporation, a general partnership, or a real estate investment trust), limited partnerships have the unique advantage of limited liability (to the limited partners) and the ability to pass through the partnership income or loss to the partners.

Investing in RELPs. There are two types of syndications: public and private. Public partnerships must be registered with the SEC, which reviews the registration statement (as opposed to approving the offering) before interests may be sold to investors. In addition, each state has investor-eligibility requirements. Generally, an investor needs either a net worth of $75,000 (excluding one's home) or a gross income of $30,000 and a net worth of $30,000 (excluding one's home). Private partnerships (which are not registered with the SEC) account for a much bigger portion of real estate partnerships and require much wealthier investors. In public partnerships, the minimum required investment is generally $5,000, but may be as low as $2,000 (to accommodate Individual Retirement Account investments). The minimum investments in private partnerships generally range from $30,000 to $150,000. As a result, small investors who otherwise are unable to invest individually in real estate are able to pool their resources and invest in shopping centers and large apartment complexes.

Unique Tax Feature. Special tax laws apply to real estate. Typically, real estate partnerships borrow from a financial institution most of the money needed to acquire the real estate. This increase in liabilities may be added to the bases of all partners (including the limited partners), even though the limited partners are not personally obligated to repay the loan if the partnership cannot repay the loan (as might happen if the project is not properly managed or the real estate declines in value). As a result, the limited partners can write off for tax purposes more than their cash investments. (However, the Tax Reform Act of 1986 did impose some limited restrictions in this respect.) Such partnerships are commonly considered the only "true" tax shelter, because the depreciation write-off is considered a paper loss, not an economic loss.

Popularity from 1981 to 1986. During the period 1981 to 1986, highly leveraged real estate limited partnerships were immensely popular because of the combination of short depreciable lives (15 to 19 years) allowable during these years under the Internal Revenue Code and the taxation of capital gains at rates 60% less than ordinary income tax rates. In fact, so much money poured into these investments that the three most important things to look for in real estate were no longer "location, location, and location." Instead, they became "tax benefit, tax benefit, and tax benefit." However, the Tax Reform Act of 1986 lengthened depreciable lives on real estate approximately 50% and eliminated the favorable tax treatment on capital gains. In addition, the right to shield other income using partnership losses is being phased out. As a result, these types of investments lost much of their appeal, and unleveraged (or "income-oriented") partnerships became more attractive. In these partnerships, sound property management and good cost control are important, inasmuch as healthy returns cannot be obtained merely by having favorable tax laws.

Potential Pitfalls. In addition to the business risks of the syndicator buying an undesirable property, paying too much for a property, having an insufficient cash flow from operations to service debt (in a highly leveraged partnership), and not properly managing the property, there are several other risks that are unique to this form of organization. In a limited partnership, controls over the general partner are quite limited in comparison to controls over management in the corporate form of business, which has a board of directors, an audit committee, and corporate officers. Many unscrupulous general partners have enriched themselves at the expense of the limited partners. Attempting to obtain information from a limited partnership in financial difficulty can be exasperating. Trying to replace a general partner for inadequate performance can sometimes be difficult.

Master Limited Partnerships. **Master limited partnerships** (MLPs) are unique in that their ownership units (commonly called *shares*) are traded on the stock exchanges, usually the New York Stock Exchange or the American Stock Exchange. Thus, the limited partners can readily dispose of their shares, and this ability gives them liquidity not available in other limited partnerships. Introduced by the oil and gas industry in the early 1980s, the concept has spread to real estate and other industries.

Many types of incorporated businesses took steps in 1986 to disincorporate into MLPs, mainly in an attempt to avoid the double taxation of corporate income taxes; MLPs are taxed only once—at the individual partner level. (See the article below for a closer look at the rise in the number of master limited partnerships.)

A burdensome problem for accountants of such partnerships is allocating the partnership's income or loss to each of the limited partners, who may have purchased their shares at different times.

PERSPECTIVE

Tax Reform's Tax Dodge
Master Limited Partnerships

With the tax bill's passage, individual tax rates will be lower than corporate rates for the first time in decades. Does that mean wealth is better held in a noncorporate form? Several shrewd minds seem to think so.

From oil companies to a motel chain, from home builders to a mortgage banker to Boone Pickens' Mesa Petroleum, firms that can get all or part of their assets out of corporate form and into something else are doing so. Reports Keith Wilson, a manager at Price Waterhouse: "The tables are crammed full of [disincorporation] deals due out before year-end that haven't been filed with the SEC."

What kinds of deals? Several large public companies are disincorporating by putting their assets into master limited partnerships. But these are MLPs with a difference. They are not intended to self-liquidate over time, like royalty trusts. Instead, the idea is for them to be active, growing businesses with units that trade on the exchanges, like corporate shares.

Unlike corporations, however, the MLPs will pass profits and losses directly through to their owners. Thus the owners will skip corporate income taxes and pay only individual taxes—at a top rate of 28%—on the assets' earnings. Single taxation at reduced rates. Attractive attraction.

Example: UDC-Universal Development, a Chicago home builder, converted to an MLP in July 1985. As a corporation it paid nearly 50% of its earnings in taxes. Now it pays nothing. As before the conversion, UDC reinvests 25% of pretax earnings in the business, yet has three times as much earnings available for distribution to investors. By 1988, when tax reform's final rates kick in, the effective top rate on the earnings UDC's shareholders receive will have fallen to 28%. In 1984, UDC's last full year as a corporation, the effective rate on distributed earnings for top-bracket taxpayers—corporate plus individual taxation—was 75%.

"There were no midnight flashes," says UDC Chief Executive Gary Rosenberg, a tax and securities lawyer. "Orthodox value analysis drove us to it. We were generating a great deal of positive cash flow that we didn't need in the business. The result is a much higher yield." Whereas UDC paid out 6% of earnings in 1984, now the company is paying out 72%. Rosenberg, not coincidentally owns 20% of the company.

Tax Reform's Tax Dodge *(continued)*

Two other home builders have gone UDC's route. McLean, Va.-based NVHomes became an MLP last April. Now the smallish (1985 sales, $114 million) builder has announced its intention to take over $566 million (sales) Ryan Homes, a corporation. Outside brains rumored to be behind the deal: Drexel Burnham Lambert. True or not, the fellows at Drexel are definitely involved in Motel 6's MLP conversion. With the backing of Drexel and Kohlberg Kravis Roberts, the buyout people, Motel 6 is expected to sell $100 million worth of partnership units in this lodging chain to the public before year's end. Drexel plans to be at the forefront of financing MLP operating companies.

Some companies are combining the incorporated and disincorporated forms. Commonwealth Financial Group, a $1.6 billion (assets) Houston mortgage banker, is putting its mortgage origination and servicing division, a cash cow, into an MLP. The firm is expected to sell 38% of the MLP, worth $230 million or so, to the public soon. Likewise, Freeport-McMoRan sold all of its sulfur, phosphate and geothermal operations, bundled into an MLP, to the public in June for $238 million.

Will the public receive these deals as eagerly as Wall Street appears set to promote them? The advantages are obvious: yields of 9% or 10%—which beat yields on most stocks and bonds—plus the ability to grow. Nor does changing the legal form of ownership, from a corporation to a limited partnership, pose a liability problem. For the limited partners, liability is no more than the amount of the investment. And in partnerships where there is substantial depreciation (as with Motel 6) or mortgage servicing rights to amortize (like Commonwealth), the tax benefits work to reduce the individual partners' tax bills.

Are there no pitfalls? Of course there are. Dangerous ones.

Because of the intricacies of partnership taxation, it may be difficult for investors who get a fat quarterly check to tell whether an MLP is really growing soundly or is actually liquidating itself slowly, and giving back to investors part of their own money. "I'd be careful," warns UDC's Rosenberg. "Very high yields often come at the expense of the future."

It's also important that general partners and their limited partners have what's called "commonality of interest." That means the general partners shouldn't get rich at the limited partners' expense. Big fees to the general partners are always a warning. Advises Price Waterhouse's Wilson: "I'd examine the relationship and the fees closely."

There's also the danger that Congress could shut down the MLP game. How? Simply by taxing large limited partnerships as if they were corporations. Congress has toyed with this idea for several years, and some Treasury officials favor the move. But absent such drastic action, disincorporation seems certain to flourish.

Source: Laura Saunders, "Tax Reform's Tax Dodge," Reprinted by permission of *Forbes* magazine, October 20, 1986, p. 103, © Forbes Inc., 1986.

Research and Development Limited Partnerships

Research and development limited partnerships are used typically by start-up companies that do not have sufficient money to conduct research and development. The start-up company is the general partner, and the investors are the limited partners. The money invested by the limited partners is used for research and development of a carefully defined product.

Advantages for Investors. Investors can write off for tax purposes their share of the money spent each year on research and development (that is, their share of the partnership's loss). Thus, they obtain immediate tax deductions. If the investors had invested directly in the start-up company, the research and development expenses would not flow through to them. Instead, such expenses would just give the start-up company a net operating loss carryforward, which might not be utilized for several years.

If the product is successfully developed, the limited partners may receive cash, common stock, or royalties from the start-up company. (Typically, the start-up company has exclusive rights to the developed product.)

Advantages for Start-up Companies. The owners of the start-up company generally retain all or a much greater ownership percentage in the start-up company.

Risks for Investors. Because there is no assurance that the product will be successfully developed, the limited partners have no guarantee that they will recover their investment.

Appendix B
THE UNIFORM PARTNERSHIP ACT

The Uniform Partnership Act has 45 sections that are separated into the following seven parts:

Part I Preliminary provisions
Part II Nature of partnership
Part III Relations of partners to persons dealing with the partnership
Part IV Relations of partners to one another
Part V Property rights of a partner
Part VI Dissolution and winding up
Part VII Miscellaneous provisions

The UPA is approximately 14 pages long and can be found in law library books that contain all of the various uniform acts. Because of its length, the UPA is not set forth here in its entirety. However, two of the sections are presented here to give you an idea of the content of the UPA.

Part III: Relations of Partners to Persons Dealing with the Partnership

Sec. 15. (Nature of Partner's Liability.)
All partners are liable:

a. Jointly and severally for everything chargeable to the partnership under sections 13 and 14.
b. Jointly for all other debts and obligations of the partnership; but any partner may enter into a separate obligation to perform a partnership contract.

Part IV: Relations of Partners to One Another

Sec. 18. (Rules Determining Rights and Duties of Partners.)
The rights and duties of the partners in relation to the partnership shall be determined by the following rules:

a. Each partner shall be repaid his contributions, whether by way of capital or advances to the partnership property and share equally in the profits and surplus remaining after all liabilities, including those to partners, are satisfied; and must contribute toward the losses, whether of capital or otherwise, sustained by the partnership according to his share in the profits.
b. The partnership must indemnify every partner in respect of payments made and personal liabilities reasonably incurred by him in the ordinary and proper conduct of its business, or for the preservation of its business or property.
c. A partner, who in aid of the partnership makes any payment or advance beyond the amount of capital which he agreed to contribute, shall be paid interest from the date of the payment or advance.
d. A partner shall receive interest on the capital contributed by him only from the date when repayment should be made.
e. All partners have equal rights in the management and conduct of the partnership business.
f. No partner is entitled to remuneration for acting in the partnership business, except that a surviving partner is entitled to reasonable compensation for his services in winding up the partnership affairs.
g. No person can become a member of a partnership without the consent of all the partners.
h. Any difference arising as to ordinary matters connected with the partnership business may be decided by a majority of the partners; but no act in contravention of any agreement between the partners may be done rightfully without the consent of all the partners.

Review Questions

1. Define *general partnership.*
2. How is a partnership defined?

3. Why is it advisable to use an attorney's services in preparing a partnership agreement?
4. What is the function of the partnership agreement?
5. What essential items should be set forth in the partnership agreement?
6. Must partnerships follow generally accepted accounting principles? Why or why not?
7. What common features may be structured into a profit and loss sharing formula?
8. Can partners be paid salaries?
9. What performance criteria may be incorporated into a profit sharing formula?
10. What is the function of the drawings account? Is it really necessary?
11. How are loans from a partner to a partnership accounted for on the partnership's books?
12. Why might it be appropriate to use the old profit and loss sharing formula in certain transactions instead of the new formula?
13. In what broad areas do partnerships commonly deviate from generally accepted accounting principles?
14. Should partnership financial statements be prepared so that partnership earnings are comparable to what they would have been if the corporate form of business had been used? Why or why not?
15. What is the purpose of keeping track of a partner's tax basis?
16. Define *adjusted tax basis.*
17. Is it possible to use a partner's capital account balance to determine that partner's tax basis? Why or why not?
18. How does the professional corporation differ from the normal corporate form of business?
19. What advantages does the professional corporation form of business have over the partnership form of business?
20. Does a shareholder of a professional corporation have limited liability?

Discussion Cases

DC 23-1

Planning for Settlement in the Event of a Partner's Death

Cross and Penn are in the process of forming a partnership. Each partner desires to obtain control of the business in the event of the death of the other partner and to make settlement with the deceased partner's estate in an orderly manner with little conflict and minimal taxation.

Required:
How might the partners accomplish these objectives?

DC 23-2

Preparing the Partnership Agreement

Nichols and Dimer have formed a partnership. They personally prepared the partnership agreement to save legal costs, but they ask you to study the agreement for completeness when you record the initial capital contributions in the general ledger.

Required:
How would you respond to this request?

DC 23-3

Dividing Profits and Losses

Barr and Courtner, both lawyers, have decided on the partnership form of organization for their new business. They have asked your advice on how the profits and losses should be divided and have provided you with the following information:

1. Initial capital contributions:	
Barr	$20,000
Courtner	80,000
2. Time devoted to the business:	
Barr	75%
Courtner	100%

3. Personal facts:
   Barr has an excellent reputation in the community. Substantially all new clients will come from her efforts.
   Courtner is strong technically and is an excellent supervisor of staff lawyers who are expected to do most of the detailed legal research and initial preparation of legal documents.

Required:
How would you advise the partners to share profits and losses?

DC 23-4

Recording the Initial Capital Contributions

High and Lowe have agreed to form a partnership in which profits are divided equally. High contributes $100,000 cash, and Lowe contributes a parcel of land, which the partnership intends to subdivide into residential lots on which to build custom homes for sale. Data regarding the parcel of land are as follows:

Cost of land to Lowe (acquired three years ago)	**$100,000**
Current market value, based on most recent county property tax assessment notice	**120,000**
Appraised value, based on recent appraisal by independent appraiser	**150,000**

Lowe feels the land should be recorded on the partnership books at $120,000. High feels the land should be recorded at $100,000 so that the tax basis to Lowe carries over to the partnership. Neither feels the current appraised value is appropriate because an objective, verifiable transaction has not occurred. They have asked your advice on how to record the land.

Required:

1. How would you respond?

2. Assuming the land is sold two years later for $140,000 (the land having been overappraised by $10,000), would this change your answer in requirement 1?

DC 23-5

Selecting the Form of Business Organization

Sam Seeker has invested $600,000 in a new business venture, in which two, possibly three, former business associates will join him. He has purchased the patent rights to a revolutionary adhesive substance known as "sticko." He is considering the various forms of business organization he might use in establishing the business. You have been engaged to study the accounting and business problems he should consider in choosing either a general partnership or a corporation. Seeker requests specific advice on the following aspects as they relate to one of these two forms of business organization.

1. Personal liability if the venture is a disaster.
2. The borrowing capacity of the entity.
3. Requirements for operating a multi-state business.
4. The recognition of the entity for income tax reporting purposes and major income tax considerations in selecting one of these forms of business organization.

Required:
Discuss the legal implications of each above-mentioned form of organization for each specific aspect on which Seeker requests advice.

(AICPA adapted)

Exercises

E 23-1

Dividing the Profit or Loss: Partnership Agreement Is Silent

The partnership of Hatter and Widden had earnings of $40,000 for the year. Hatter devotes all of her time to the business, and Widden devotes 50% of his time to the business. Hatter's average capital balance was $60,000, and Widden's average capital balance was $30,000. The partnership agreement is silent regarding the distribution of profits.

Required:

1. Prepare a schedule showing how the profit should be divided.
2. Prepare the entry to divide the profit.

E 23-2

Dividing the Profit or Loss: Performance Features and Ratio

The partnership of Maxe and Lisle has the following provisions in its partnership agreement:

1. Maxe, who is primarily responsible for obtaining new clients, is to receive a 30% bonus on revenues in excess of $200,000.

2. Lisle, who is primarily responsible for administration is to receive a 30% bonus on profits in excess of 50% of revenues, as reflected in the general ledger.
3. All remaining profits or losses are to be divided equally.

Additional Information:

Revenues for the year	$280,000
Operating expenses	120,000

Required:

1. Prepare a schedule showing how the profit or loss should be divided for the year.
2. Prepare the entry to divide the profit or loss for the year.

E 23-3

Dividing the Profit or Loss: Ratio and Salary Allowances

The partnership of Darden and Louis shares profits and losses in a ratio of 7:3, respectively, after Louis receives a $10,000 salary allowance.

Required:

1. Prepare a schedule showing how the profit or loss should be divided, assuming the profit or loss for the year is
   a. $30,000.
   b. $6,000.
   c. $(10,000).
2. Prepare the entry to divide the profit or loss in situations (a) to (c) of requirement 1.

E 23-4

Dividing the Profit or Loss: Ratio, Salary Allowances, and Imputed Interest on Capital

The partnership of Eddy and MacDonald has the following provisions in the partnership agreement:

1. Eddy and MacDonald receive salary allowances of $19,000 and $11,000, respectively.
2. Interest is imputed at 10% of the average capital investments.
3. Any remaining profit or loss is shared between Eddy and MacDonald in a 3:2 ratio, respectively.

Additional Information:

Average capital investments:	
Eddy	$ 60,000
MacDonald	100,000

Required:

1. Prepare a schedule showing how the profit would be divided, assuming the partnership profit or loss is
   a. $76,000.
   b. $42,000.
   c. $(14,000).
2. Prepare the entry to divide the profit or loss in situations (a) to (c) of requirement 1.

E 23-5

Dividing the Profit or Loss: Ratio, Salary Allowances, and Imputed Interest on Capital—Order of Priority Specified

Assume the information provided in Exercise 23-4, except that the partnership agreement stipulates the following **order of priority** in the distribution of profits:

1. Salary allowances (only to the extent available).
2. Imputed interest on average capital investments (only to the extent available).
3. Any remaining profit in a 3:2 ratio. (No mention is made regarding losses.)

Required:
The requirements are the same as for Exercise 23-4.

E 23-6

Recording Initial Capital Contributions

On May 1, 19X7, Booker and Page formed a partnership. Each contributed assets with the following agreed-upon valuations:

	Booker	Page
Cash	$80,000	$ 20,000
Machinery and equipment	50,000	60,000
Building	—	240,000

The building is subject to a mortgage loan of $100,000, which is assumed by the partnership. The partnership agreement provides that Booker and Page share profits and losses 40% and 60%, respectively.

Required:

1. Prepare the journal entry to record the capital contributions of each partner.
2. *Optional:* Assuming that no difference exists between the agreed-upon valuation of each asset contributed and its related adjusted basis, determine the tax basis of each partner on May 1, 19X7.

E 23-7

Puzzle: Determination of Partnership Net Income

Forrester, a partner in the Woods Partnership, has a 30% participation in partnership profits and losses. Forrester's capital account had a net decrease of $60,000 during calendar year 19X4. During 19X4, Forrester withdrew $130,000 (charged against her capital account) and contributed property valued at $25,000 to the partnership.

Required:
Determine the partnership's net income for 19X4.

(AICPA adapted)

E 23-8

Understanding the Impact of the Salary Allowance Feature

Partners Max and Minn share profits and losses equally after each has been credited with annual salary allowances of $15,000 and $12,000, respectively. Under this arrangement, Max benefits by $3,000 more than Minn in which of the following circumstances?

a. Only if the partnership has earnings of $27,000 or more for the year.
b. Only if the partnership does not incur a loss for the year.
c. In all profit or loss situations.
d. Only if the partnership has earnings of at least $3,000 for the year.

(AICPA adapted)

E 23-9

Determination of Tax Basis of Each Partner

Evers, Glade, and Marsh have formed a partnership by combining their respective sole proprietorships. The profit and loss sharing ratio is 4:3:3, respectively. The assets and liabilities contributed to the partnership are as follows:

	Adjusted Basis	Current Value
Evers:		
Cash	$50,000	$50,000
Accounts receivable	20,000	20,000
Glade:		
Land	30,000	40,000
Marsh:		
Equipment	20,000[a]	25,000
Equipment note payable	10,000	10,000

[a]Original cost of $27,000 minus $7,000 of depreciation taken to date.

Required:

1. Determine the tax basis of each partner's interest in the partnership.
2. What is the tax basis of each noncash asset in the hands of the partnership?
3. Prepare the general ledger entry to record these contributions.
4. Assume that Glade decided to quit the partnership one day after it was formed and received cash in full satisfaction of his capital account balance. What gain or loss, if any, should Glade report for tax purposes?

E 23-10

Subsequent Changes in Tax Basis of Each Partner

The tax basis of Reed, Storey, and Teller at the beginning of their partnership year was $50,000, $35,000, and $65,000, respectively. Profits and losses are shared equally.

Additional Information:

Additional cash capital contributions:	
Reed	$18,000
Storey	10,000
Teller	4,000
Withdrawals during the year:	
Reed	6,000
Storey	12,000
Teller	5,000
Profits for the year:	
From the general ledger	30,000
From the tax return	33,000

Required:

1. Determine the tax basis of each partner at year-end, assuming no change in partnership liabilities.
2. Determine the tax basis of each partner at year-end, assuming that the only change in liabilities during the year was a $24,000 bank loan obtained at year-end. (The $24,000 borrowed, along with $6,000 cash on hand, was used to purchase equipment costing $30,000.)

Problems

P 23-1

Dividing Profits: Interest on Capital, Bonuses, and Salary Allowances

Horn and Sax are in partnership. The activity in each partner's capital account for 19X1 is as follows:

Horn

		20,000	1/1
		8,000	2/12
5/25	4,000		
		7,000	10/19
12/10	2,000		
		1,000	12/30
		30,000	12/31

Sax

		30,000	1/1
3/23	5,000		
7/10	5,000		
9/30	5,000		
		18,000	12/5
12/30	23,000		
		10,000	12/31

A drawings account is not used. The profit for 19X1 is $200,000.

Required:

Divide the profit for the year between the partners using each of the following formulas:

a. Beginning capital balances.
b. Average capital balances. (Investments and withdrawals are assumed to have been made as of the beginning of the month if made before the middle of the month, and assumed to have been made as of the beginning of the following month if made after the middle of the month.)
c. Ending capital balances.
d. Bonus to Horn equal to 20% of profit in excess of $150,000; remaining profit divided equally.
e. Salary allowances of $45,000 and $35,000 to Horn and Sax, respectively; interest on average capital balances imputed at 10%; any residual balance divided equally. (Investments and withdrawals are treated as explained in part b.)

P 23-2 Dividing Profits: Revision of Profit-sharing Agreement—Prior Period Adjustments

The partnership of Browne, Silvers, and Tanner was formed in 19X5. The partnership agreement specified that profits and losses were determined on the accrual tax basis and were divided as follows.

	Browne	Silvers	Tanner
Salary allowances	$15,000	$15,000	$5,000
Bonuses (percentage of profits in excess of $90,000)	20%	20%	
Residual profit or loss	40%	40%	20%

On January 1, 19X9, the partnership agreement was revised to provide for the sharing of profits and losses in the following manner:

	Brown	Silvers	Tanner
Salary allowances	$20,000	$20,000	$15,000
Bonuses (percentage of profits in excess of $110,000)	20%	20%	10%
Residual profit or loss	35%	35%	30%

The partnership books show a profit of $145,000 for 19X9 before the following errors were discovered:

1. Inventory at December 31, 19X7, was overstated by $7,000.
2. Inventory at December 31, 19X8, was understated by $8,000.
3. Inventory at December 31, 19X9, was understated by $18,000.
4. Depreciation expense for 19X9 was understated by $5,000.

Required:

1. Divide the profit among the partners for 19X9, assuming the partnership agreement calls for any prior years' errors to be treated as prior-period adjustments.
2. Assuming the reported profits for 19X7 and 19X8 were $85,000 and $110,000, respectively, prepare the proper adjusting entry to correct the capital balances as of January 1, 19X9. The old profit sharing agreement is used for these items.

P 23-3 Combining Two Partnerships: Recording the Initial Capital Contributions

The partnerships of Hill & Mounds and Flatt & Level began business on July 1, 19X1; each partnership owns one retail appliance store. The two partnerships agree to combine as of July 1, 19X4, to form a new partnership known as Four Partners Discount Stores.

The following additional information is available:

1. **Profit and loss ratios.** The profit and loss sharing ratios for the former partnerships were 40% to Hill and 60% to Mounds, and 30% to Flatt and 70% to Level. The profit and loss sharing ratio for the new partnership is Hill, 20%; Mounds, 30%; Flatt, 15%; and Level, 35%.
2. **Capital investments.** The opening capital investments for the new partnership are to be in the same ratio as the profit and loss sharing ratios for the new partnership. If necessary, certain partners may have to contribute additional cash and others may have to withdraw cash to bring the capital investments into the proper ratio.
3. **Accounts receivable.** The partners agreed that the new partnership's allowance for bad debts is to be 5% of the accounts receivable contributed by Hill & Mounds, and 10% of the accounts receivable contributed by Flatt & Level.
4. **Inventory.** The opening inventory of the new partnership is to be valued by the FIFO method. Hill & Mounds used the FIFO method to value inventory (which approximates its current value), and Flatt & Level used the LIFO method. The LIFO inventory represents 85% of its FIFO value.
5. **Property and equipment.** The partners agree that the land's current value is aproximately 20% more than its historical cost, as recorded on each partnership's books.

   The depreciable assets of each partnership were acquired on July 1, 19X1. Hill & Mounds used straight-line depreciation and a 10-year life. Flatt & Level used double-declining balance depreciation and a 10-year life. The partners agree that the current value of these assets is approximately 80% of their historical cost, as recorded on each partnership's books.
6. **Unrecorded liability.** After each partnership's books were closed on June 30, 19X4, an unrecorded merchandise purchase of $4,000 by Flatt & Level was discovered. The merchandise had been sold by June 30, 19X4.
7. **Accrued vacation.** The accounts of Hill & Mounds include a vacation pay accrual. The four partners agree that Flatt & Level should make a similar accrual for their five employees, who will receive a one-week vacation at $200 per employee per week.

The June 30, 19X4, postclosing trial balances of the partnerships appear below:

	Hill & Mounds Trial Balance June 30, 19X4		Flatt and Level Trial Balance June 30, 19X4	
Cash	$ 20,000		$ 15,000	
Accounts receivable	100,000		150,000	
Allowance for doubtful accounts		$ 2,000		$ 6,000
Merchandise inventory	175,000		119,000	
Land	25,000		35,000	
Buildings and equipment	80,000		125,000	
Accumulated depreciation		24,000		61,000
Prepaid expenses	5,000		7,000	
Accounts payable		40,000		60,000
Notes payable		70,000		75,000
Accrued expenses		30,000		45,000
Hill, capital		95,000		
Mounds, capital		144,000		
Flatt, capital				65,000
Level, capital				139,000
Totals	$405,000	$405,000	$451,000	$451,000

Required:

1. Prepare the journal entries to record the initial capital contribution after considering the effect of the above information. Use separate entries for each of the combining partnerships.
2. Prepare a schedule computing the cash contributed or withdrawn by each partner to bring the initial capital account balances into the profit and loss sharing ratio.

(AICPA adapted)

P 23-4 Combining Three Sole Proprietorships: Dividing the Profit for the First Year of Operations

Arby, Bobb, and Carlos, who are attorneys, agree to consolidate their individual practices as of January 1, 19X3. The partnership agreement includes the following features:

1. Each partner's capital contribution is the net amount of the assets and liabilities assumed by the partnership, which are as follows:

	Arby	Bobb	Carlos
Cash	$ 5,000	$ 5,000	$ 5,000
Accounts receivable	14,000	6,000	16,000
Furniture and library	4,300	2,500	6,200
	$23,300	$13,500	$27,200
Allowance for depreciation	$ 2,400	$ 1,500	$ 4,700
Accounts payable	300	1,400	$ 700
	$ 2,700	$ 2,900	$ 5,400
Capital contribution	$20,600	$10,600	$21,800

Each partner guaranteed the collectibility of receivables.

2. Carlos had leased office space and was bound by the lease until June 30, 19X3. The monthly rental was $600. The partners agree to occupy Carlos's office space until the expiration of the lease and to pay the rent. The partners concur that the rent is too high for the space and that a fair rental value would be $450 per month. The excess rent is charged to Carlos at year-end. On July 1, the partners move to new quarters with a monthly rental of $500.
3. No salaries are paid to the partners. The individual partners receive 20% of the gross fees billed to their respective clients during the first year of the partnership. After deducting operating expenses (excluding the excess rent), the balance of the fees billed is credited to the partners' capital accounts in the following ratios: Arby, 40%; Bobb, 35%; and Carlos, 25%.

   On April 1, 19X3, Mack is admitted to the partnership; Mack receives 20% of the fees from new business obtained after April 1, after deducting expenses applicable to that new business. Expenses (excluding the excess rent) are apportioned to the new business in the same ratio that total expenses, other than bad debt losses, bear to total gross fees.
4. The following information pertains to the partnership's activities in 19X3;
   a. Fees are billed as follows:

Arby's clients	$ 44,000
Bobb's clients	24,000
Carlos's clients	22,000
New business:	
Prior to April 1	6,000
After April 1	24,000
Total	$120,000

   b. Total expenses, excluding depreciation and bad debt expenses, are $29,350 including the total amount paid for rent. Depreciation is computed at the rate of 10% on original cost. Depreciable assets purchased during 19X3, on which one-half year's depreciation is taken, total $5,000.
   c. Cash charges to the partners' accounts during the year are as follows:

Arby	$ 5,200
Bobb	4,400
Carlos	5,800
Mack	2,500
	$17,900

   d. Of Arby's and Bobb's receivables, $1,200 and $450, respectively, proved to be uncollectible. A new client billed in March for $1,600 went bankrupt, and a settlement of 50 cents on the dollar was made.

Required:

1. Determine the profit for 19X3.
2. Prepare a schedule showing how the profit for 19X3 is to be divided.
3. Prepare a statement of the partners' capital accounts for the year ended December 31, 19X3.

(AICPA adapted)

P 23-5

Computation of Billings and Determination of Profits

Funn and Kidd, architectural designers and interior decorators, combined May 1, 19X8, agreeing to share profits as follows: Kidd, two-thirds; Funn, one-third. Funn contributed furniture and fixtures, $3,000, and cash, $2,000; Kidd contributed cash, $500.

They plan to submit monthly bills and make the following arrangements with their clients:

1. The firm employs draftspersons who are paid on an hourly basis. Time spent on client assignments is billed to clients at their hourly rate plus 125% for overhead and profit.
2. Partners' time on jobs is billed at $10 an hour.
3. A 10% service fee is charged on purchases of furniture, drapes, and so on, installed on the jobs. (As an accommodation to their clients, Funn and Kidd pay the vendors and charge their clients for these purchases; however, they would like to have their operating statements exclude from their revenues the amounts paid to vendors.)
4. No service fee is charged on taxis, telephone, and other expenses identifiable to jobs and charged to clients.

Voucher register totals for May are given below:

Credits:	
Vouchers payable	**$3,469**
Taxes withheld—Federal income	**93**
Taxes withheld—FICA	**27**
Total	**$3,589**
Debits:	
Purchases and expenses chargeable to clients	**$1,615**
Partners' drawings (Funn, $100; Kidd, $125)	**225**
General expenses	**549**
Salaries	**1,200**
Total	**$3,589**

The first debit column is analyzed in the voucher register as follows:

Purchases subject to 10% fee:		
Client M, Job 51	**$1,210**	
Client H, Job 52	**320**	**$1,530**
Expenses chargeable to clients:		
Client M, Job 51	**$ 23**	
Client M, Job 54	**7**	
Client H, Job 52	**19**	
Client L, Job 53	**36**	**85**
		$1,615

Client M has not yet authorized Funn and Kidd to do job 54. The partners are confident, however, that the job will be authorized, and the above expenses, as well as charges for time spent by a draftsperson and Funn on preliminary designs, will be billed and collected. Assume it is proper to consider this an unbilled account receivable.

The payroll analysis is summarized below. Partners' time on jobs, charged to the jobs at $10 an hour, is summarized in the payroll analysis for convenience in posting costs to job sheets, although the partners are not paid for direct time on jobs.

Job	Secretary	Draftspersons	Funn	Kidd
51		$ 312	$240	$300
52		276	120	230
53		304	130	320
54		48	240	
		$ 940	$730	$850
Nonbillable				
General office	$160	40		
Idle time		60		
Total payroll	$160	$1,040		

Journal entries recorded $25 depreciation on furniture and fixtures and the $54 employer's share of federal and state taxes.

There were no cash receipts other than the original investment. The cash disbursements journal shows the following totals:

Debit:	
Vouchers payable	$2,373
Credit:	
Cash	$2,358
Discount on purchases	15

Required:

1. Compute the billings to clients for May.
2. Prepare a worksheet for the month, showing the opening balances, the transactions for the month, and an adjustment trial balance at month-end.
3. Divide the profit for the month.
4. Prepare a statement of changes in partners' capital for the month.

(AICPA adapted)

P 23-6*

Converting from Cash to Accrual Basis

The partnership of Green, Redd, and White engaged you to adjust its accounting records and convert them uniformly to the accrual basis in anticipation of admitting Frost as a new partner. Some accounts are on the accrual basis and others are on the cash basis. The partnership's books were closed at December 31, 19X6 by the bookkeeper, who prepared the following trial balance:

*The financial statement information presented for problems accompanied by asterisks is provided on Model 23 (filename: Model23) of the software disk that is available for use with the text, enabling the problem to be worked on the computer.

GREEN, REDD, AND WHITE
Trial Balance
December 31, 19X6

	Debit	Credit
Cash	$ 10,000	
Accounts Receivable	40,000	
Inventory	26,000	
Land	9,000	
Buildings	50,000	
Accumulated Depreciation—Buildings		$ 2,000
Equipment	56,000	
Accumulated Depreciation—Equipment		6,000
Goodwill	5,000	
Accounts Payable		55,000
Allowance for Future Inventory Losses		3,000
Green, Capital		40,000
Redd, Capital		60,000
White, Capital		30,000
Totals	$196,000	$196,000

Your inquiries disclosed the following:

1. The partnership was organized on January 1, 19X5, with no provision in the partnership agreement for the distribution of partnership profits and losses. During 19X5, profits were distributed equally among the partners. The partnership agreement was amended effective January 1, 19X6, to provide for the following profit-and-loss ratio: Green, 50%; Redd, 30%; and White, 20%. The amended partnership agreement also stated that the accounting records should be maintained on the accrual basis and that any adjustments necessary for 19X5 should be allocated according to the 19X5 distribution of profits.
2. The following amounts were not recorded as prepayments or accruals.

	December 31	
	19X6	19X5
Prepaid insurance	$700	$ 650
Advances from customers	200	1,100
Accrued interest expense		450

   The advances from customers were recorded as sales in the year the cash was received.
3. In 19X6, the partnership recorded a $3,000 provision for anticipated declines in inventory prices. You convinced the partners that the provision was unnecessary and should be removed from the books.
4. The partnership charged equipment purchased for $4,400 on January 3, 19X6 to expense. This equipment has an estimated life of 10 years. The partnership depreciates its capitalized equipment under the double-declining balance method at twice the straight-line depreciation rate.
5. The partners established an allowance for doubtful accounts at 2% of current accounts receivable and 5% of past due accounts. At December 31, 19X5, the partnership had $54,000 of accounts receivable, of which only $4,000 was past

due. At December 31, 19X6, 15% of accounts receivable were past due, of which $4,000 represented sales made in 19X5 that were generally considered collectible. The partnership had written off uncollectible accounts in the year the accounts became worthless, as follows:

	Account Written Off in	
	19X6	19X5
19X6 accounts	$ 800	
19X5 accounts	1,000	$250

6. Goodwill was recorded on the books in 19X6 and credited to the partners' capital accounts in the profit and loss ratio in recognition of an increase in the value of the business resulting from improved sales volume. The partners agreed to write off the goodwill before admitting the new partner.

Required:
Prepare a worksheet showing the adjustments and the adjusted trial balance for the partnership on the accrual basis at December 31, 19X6. All adjustments affecting income should be made directly to partners' capital accounts. Number your adjusting entries. (Prepare formal journal entries and show supporting computations.)

(AICPA adapted)

P 23-7*

Preparing Worksheets to Arrive at Current Trial Balance

The Joker & Laffer Company is a partnership that has not maintained adequate accounting records because it has been unable to employ a competent bookkeeper. The company sells hardware items to the retail trade and also sells wholesale to builders and contractors. As Joker & Laffer's CPA, you prepare the company's financial statements as of June 30, 19X2.

The company's records provide the following postclosing trial balance at December 31, 19X1:

THE JOKER & LAFFER COMPANY
Postclosing Trial Balance
December 31, 19X1

	Debit	Credit
Cash	$10,000	
Accounts Receivable	8,000	
Allowance for Bad Debts		$ 600
Merchandise Inventory	35,000	
Prepaid Insurance	150	
Automobiles	7,800	
Accumulated Depreciation—Automobiles		4,250
Furniture and Fixtures	2,200	
Accumulated Depreciation—Furniture and Fixtures		650
Accounts Payable		13,800
Bank Loan Payable (due January 2, 19X2)		8,000
Accrued Liabilities		200
Joker, Capital		17,500
Laffer, Capital		18,150
Totals	$63,150	$63,150

You collect the following information at June 30, 19X2:

1. Your analysis of cash transactions, derived from the company's bank statements and checkbook stubs, is as follows:

Deposits:	
Cash receipts from customers	**$65,000**
($40,000 of this amount represents collections on receivables including redeposited protested checks totaling $600)	
Bank loan, January 2, 19X2 (due May 1, 19X2, 5%)	**7,867**
Bank loan, May 1, 19X2 (due September 1, 19X2, 5%)	**8,850**
Sale of old automobile	**20**
Total Deposits	**$81,737**
Disbursements:	
Payments to merchandise creditors	**$45,000**
Payment to Internal Revenue Service on Laffer's 19X2 declaration of estimated income taxes	**3,000**
General expenses	**7,000**
Bank loan, January 2, 19X2	**8,000**
Bank loan, May 2, 19X2	**8,000**
Payment for new automobile	**7,400**
Protested checks	**900**
Joker, withdrawals	**5,000**
Laffer, withdrawals	**2,500**
Total Disbursements	**$86,800**

2. The protested checks include customers' checks totaling $600 that were redeposited and an employee's check for $300 that was redeposited.
3. At June 30, 19X2, accounts receivable from customers for merchandise sales amount to $18,000 and include accounts totaling $800 that have been placed with an attorney for collection. Correspondence with the client's attorney reveals that one of the accounts for $175 is uncollectible. Experience indicates that 1% of credit sales will prove uncollectible.
4. On April 1, 19X2, a new automobile was purchased. The list price of the automobile was $7,700, and $300 was allowed for the trade-in of an old automobile, even though the dealer stated that its condition was so poor that he did not want it. The client sold the old automobile, which cost $1,800 and was fully depreciated at December 31, 19X1, to an auto wrecker for $20. The old automobile was in use up to the date of its sale.
5. Depreciation is recorded by the straight-line method and is computed on acquisitions to the nearest full month. The estimated life for furniture and fixtures is 10 years and for automobiles is three years. (Salvage value is ignored in computing depreciation. No asset other than the care in item 4 was fully depreciated prior to June 30, 19X2.)
6. Other data as of June 30, 19X2 are the following:

Merchandise inventory	**$37,500**
Prepaid insurance	**80**
Accrued expenses	**166**

7. Accounts payable to merchandise vendors total $18,750. A $750 credit memorandum was received from a merchandise vendor for returned merchandise; the company will apply the credit to July merchandise purchases. Neither the credit memorandum nor the return of the merchandise had been recorded on the books.
8. Profits and losses are divided equally between the partners.

Required:

Prepare a worksheet that provides, on the accrual basis, information regarding transactions for the six months ended June 30, 19X2, the results of the partnership operations for the period, and the financial position of the partnership at June 30, 19X2. (Do not prepare formal financial statements or formal journal entries, but show supporting computations when necessary.)

(AICPA adapted)

24

Partnerships: Changes in Ownership

AN OVERVIEW OF CHANGES IN OWNERSHIP

A business conducted as a partnership usually has changes in ownership during its existence. In this chapter, we discuss changes in ownership that do not result in the termination of the partnership's business activities. Such changes in ownership may be categorized as follows:

1. **An increase in the number of partners.**
   a. **Admission of a new partner.** More partners may be needed to serve clients properly, or additional capital may be required above and beyond the personal resources of existing partners.
   b. **Business combinations.** Two partnerships may combine in such a manner that a pooling of interests occurs—that is, the partners of each individual partnership become partners in a larger, combined business.
2. **A decrease in the number of partners.**
   a. **Willful or forced withdrawal.** A partner may withdraw from a partnership in order to (a) engage in another line of work; (b) continue in the same line of work but as a sole proprietor; or (c) retire. In addition, a partner may be forced out of a partnership for economic reasons or for not having performed adequately the responsibilities entrusted to him or her.
   b. **Death or incapacity.** Aside from death, a partner may become so seriously ill that he or she cannot continue partnership duties.
3. **Purchase of an existing partnership interest.** A partner may decide to sell his or her partnership interest to someone outside the partnership.

The first two categories may generate issues of how to treat each partner equitably when (1) tangible assets have current values different from book values, and (2) intangible elements exist. For simplicity, we discuss these issues separately. The third category consists entirely of personal transactions conducted outside the partnership. Because no partnership accounting issues are associated with this category, we discuss it only briefly at this point, before discussing the first two categories.

Purchase of an Existing Partner's Interest

The purchase of an interest from one or more of a partnership's existing partners is a personal transaction between the incoming partner and the selling partners. No additional money or properties are invested in the partnership. In this respect, it is similar to the sale of a corporation's stock by individuals. The only entry that is made on the partnership's books is an entry to transfer an amount from the selling partner's Capital account to the new partner's Capital account. For example, assume the following information:

1. A and B are in partnership and share profits and losses equally.
2. A and B have Capital account balances of $30,000 each.

3. C purchases B's partnership interest for $37,500, making payment directly to B.

The entry to record the transaction on the books of the partnership is as follows:

Capital, Partner B	**30,000**	
Capital, Partner C		**30,000**

The purchase price paid by C is completely irrelevant to the entry recorded on the books, regardless of why C paid more than the book value of the partnership interest. The fact that the partnership may have undervalued tangible assets or possible superior earnings power is not relevant to the accounting issues. A personal transaction has occurred, which is independent of accounting for the business of the partnership.

Alternatively, C could purchase a portion of each existing partner's interest in the partnership. For example, assume that C purchased one-third of A's interest for $12,500 and one-third of B's interest for $12,500, making payments directly to A and B. The entry to record the transaction on the books is as follows:

Capital, Partner A	**10,000**	
Capital, Partner B	**10,000**	
Capital, Partner C		**20,000**

Again, the purchase of an existing partnership interest is a personal transaction between the old and the new partners.

An Increase or Decrease in the Number of Partners: Methods to Prevent Inequities

The number of partners in a partnership may increase or decrease without the purchase of an existing partner's interest. Recall that in Chapter 23 we stated that to prevent partners from being treated inequitably as a result of revisions to the profit and loss sharing formula, either the partnership assets should be revalued to their current values or the new profit and loss sharing formula should include a special provision whereby the old profit and loss sharing formula would be used in specified instances. Because a change in ownership of a partnership produces a new profit and loss sharing formula, the same techniques to prevent inequities may be applied to situations of changes in ownership. In addition, we introduce a new method—the **bonus method**—that also may be used to prevent inequities.

TANGIBLE ASSETS HAVING CURRENT VALUES DIFFERENT FROM BOOK VALUES

Admission of a New Partner

In most cases, a partner is admitted into a partnership by making a capital contribution to the partnership. In accounting and attorney partnerships, virtually all the partners admitted make substantial contributions after spending years in lower levels of the business obtaining the necessary training and experience. A capital contribution creates a new partner's interest. In substance, this is similar to a corporation issuing additional shares of its stock to new stockholders.

One of the three available methods of preventing an inequity must be applied when a new partner is admitted. Each method, although different procedurally, produces the same result. To illustrate how each method would be applied to a situation in which a new partner is admitted into a partnership by making a capital contribution, assume the following facts:

1. The partnership of A and B desires to admit C.
2. The Capital accounts of A and B are $25,000 each.
3. Profits and losses are shared equally between A and B. On admission of C, profits and losses are shared equally among the three partners.
4. All the partnership's assets have carrying values equal to their current values, except for a parcel of land that is worth $12,000 more than its book value of $100,000.
5. Because the current value of the existing partner's equity is $62,000 ($25,000 + $25,000 + $12,000), A and B agree to admit C into the partnership on contribution of $31,000 cash.

The credit to be made to the new partner's Capital account regarding the $31,000 capital contribution may be determined only after the partners agree on one of the following three methods.

Revaluing of Assets Method. Under the **revaluing of assets method,** the parcel of land merely is written up to its current value using the following entry:

Land	**12,000**	
Capital, Partner A		**6,000**
Capital, Partner B		**6,000**

Because the old partners shared profits and losses equally until C was admitted, each of their Capital accounts is increased by 50% of the upward revaluation. The entry to record C's contribution is as follows:

Cash	31,000	
Capital, Partner C		31,000

The revaluing of assets method is the simplest of the three methods. Although it is not in accordance with generally accepted accounting principles, this disadvantage is usually not important to the partnership form of business. If the partners agree to this method, the new partnership agreement should specify that the new partner is to receive a one-third interest in the new net assets of the partnership **after the land has been written up by $12,000,** thus receiving a full credit to his Capital account for the $31,000 capital contribution.

Not covering **Special Profit and Loss Sharing Provision Method.** Under the **special profit and loss sharing provision** approach, the land is carried at its historical cost. However, the new profit and loss sharing formula contains a provision that (a) acknowledges that the land's current value is $12,000 in excess of its book value at the time of C's admission, and (b) specifies that the old partners are entitled to share equally in the first $12,000 profit on the sale of the land. Assuming the land is sold for a $15,000 profit several years after C is admitted to the partnership, the profit on the sale would be divided as follows:

	Total	Partner A	Partner B	Partner C
First $12,000	$12,000	$6,000	$6,000	
Excess over $12,000	3,000	1,000	1,000	$1,000
	$15,000	$7,000	$7,000	$1,000

The entry to record C's contribution is the same as shown in the preceding method. If the partners agree to this method, the new partnership agreement should state that the new partner is to receive a full credit to his Capital account for the $31,000 capital contribution, **with no revaluation made to the assets of the partnership.**

The Bonus Method. Under the **bonus method,** no adjustment is made to the carrying amount of the land, nor is any special provision included in the new profit and loss sharing formula because the land is worth more than its book value. When the land subsequently is sold, C will receive one-third of the *entire* profit. From an equity viewpoint, C is not entitled to one-third of the first $12,000 profit; therefore, C's Capital account is reduced at his admission by the amount that will be credited to his Capital account in the event the land is sold for $12,000 in excess of its current book value. Thus, one-third of $12,000, or $4,000, of C's $31,000 initial capital contribution is not credited to his Capital account. Instead, the $4,000 is credited to the old partners' Capital accounts. The $4,000 is shared by partners A and B in the old profit and loss sharing ratio. The entry to record C's admission into the partnership is as follows:

Cash	**31,000**	
Capital, Partner A		**2,000**
Capital, Partner B		**2,000**
Capital, Partner C		**27,000**

Assuming the land is sold for a $15,000 profit several years after C is admitted to the partnership, the profit on the sale would be divided as follows:

	Total	Partner A	Partner B	Partner C
Total profit	**$15,000**	**$5,000**	**$5,000**	**$5,000**

In this situation, C initially gives up part of his capital contribution, only to recover at a later date the amount given up. The old partners initially receive a bonus, but on the subsequent sale of the land, they would not be allocated all of the first $12,000 profit. In this sense, "bonus" is a misnomer because it is not permanent. If the partners agree to the bonus method, the new partnership agreement should state that the new partner is to receive a one-third interest in the new net assets of the partnership of $81,000 ($50,000 + $31,000), **with no revaluation to be made to the partnership assets.**

The following points are important for understanding the three methods:

1. If the land subsequently is sold for $112,000 (which is $12,000 more than its $100,000 book value immediately before C was admitted into the partnership), the individual Capital account balances will be identical under each method. Thus, each method ensures that partners A and B share equally in the first $12,000 of profit on the sale of the land. Furthermore, each method ensures that partners A, B, and C share equally on any profit on the sale of the land in excess of $12,000.
2. The exact method chosen depends on the personal whims of the partners. Often an incoming partner desires to have the full amount of his or her capital contribution credited to his or her Capital account, if only for psychological reasons. The method agreed upon by the partners should be specified in the new partnership agreement.
3. If the new profit and loss sharing formula includes a feature providing for imputed interest on capital investments, then the second method would result in an inequity to the old partners, because their individual Capital accounts would be less than that of the new partner.
4. The key to achieving the same result with each method is the assumption that the partnership assets actually are worth the agreed-upon amounts. If they are not, then these methods do not always prevent inequities from occurring. We discuss this situation more fully below.

Because the determination of the current values of assets is so subjective, the possibility exists that the land is not really worth $12,000 more than its book value. What if shortly after C is admitted into the partnership the land is sold for only $9,000 more than its book value immediately before C was admitted? Would each method still treat each partner equitably? The answer is no. Partner C would not be treated equitably under the revaluation of assets method because he would be allocated one-third of the book loss of $3,000; he would effectively lose $1,000 of his initial $31,000 capital contribution. Partner C would not be treated equitably under the bonus method because he would not recoup all of the $4,000 bonus he initially gave to the old partners. He would recoup only $3,000 (one-third of the $9,000 book profit) and therefore lose $1,000 of his initial $31,000 capital contribution. However, under the special provision in the new profit and loss sharing method, C cannot lose any of his initial capital contribution; he is best protected under this method.

The land may actually have a current value $12,000 more than its book value immediately before C is admitted into the partnership, but then subsequently decline in value after C is admitted. The same question must be asked: Would each method treat each partner equitably? Under the special provision in the new profit and loss sharing formula, partners A and B would be treated inequitably because they would share the entire loss of value that occurred after C was admitted. From an equity viewpoint, C should share in this loss of value, and he does so only under the revaluation of assets method and the bonus method.

Obviously, each partner strives to select the method that best protects his or her personal interest. Often there is a conflict between an incoming partner and the old partners concerning which method to use. The ultimate resolution takes place through negotiation. In large partnerships—such as the national accounting firms—differences between current values and book values usually are ignored for the sake of simplicity. Of course, such partnerships usually do not have significant amounts of land and depreciable assets, which are most likely to have current values different from book values.

Business Combinations

Historically, business combinations are thought of as occurring only between corporations. However, a large number of business combinations involve partnerships, especially public accounting partnerships. Business combinations in the public accounting sector range from a two-person partnership combining with a sole proprietorship to a large international firm such as Klynveld, Main, Goerdeler, combining with another large international firm, Peat, Marwick, Mitchell & Co. (See the article on page 1043.) Although *APB Opinion No. 16*, "Accounting for Business Combinations," was intended primarily for combinations among corporations, paragraph 5 of that pronouncement states that "its provisions should be applied as a general guide" when two or more unincorporated businesses combine.[1] Accordingly, business combinations among unincorporated accounting entities may be classified as either purchases or pooling of interests. Whether the substance of a combination is one or the other depends on whether or not the owners of the combining businesses continue as owners in the new, enlarged business.

If the owners of one business do not continue as owners of the enlarged business, a **purchase** has occurred. Purchases do not increase the number of partners. Thus, no change in ownership of the acquiring partnership occurs, and such transactions do not concern us here. The acquiring firm merely applies the provisions of *APB Opinion No. 16* with respect to the assets acquired. The assets of the acquiring business are not revalued to their current values.

If the owners of both businesses continue as owners of the enlarged business, a **pooling of interests** has occurred. Pooling of interests results in an increase in the number of partners; thus, the issues associated with changes in ownership exist. If the assets of either or both of the combining firms have current values different from their book values, then one of the methods of preventing inequities from occurring must be used (revaluing the assets, using a special provision in the new profit and loss sharing formula, or the bonus method). A strict application of the pooling of interests procedures does not permit the revaluing of assets of either combining firm. If the partners revalue the assets, however, they may do so and depart from generally accepted accounting principles. These three methods are procedurally the same as when a new partner is admitted, other than through a business combination.

PERSPECTIVE

Peat Marwick Merges Its Way to the Top

A few years ago, Coopers & Lybrand was the biggest of the Big Eight accounting firms. Then Arthur Andersen & Co. muscled its way to No. 1. Now the honors go to Peat, Marwick, Mitchell & Co. But instead of doing it through internal growth, as has been the case in the past, Peat is getting there the easy way. It's combining with a firm nearly as large as itself in what will be the biggest merger in accounting history.

On Sept. 3, Peat Marwick announced that it would combine with Klynveld Main Goerdeler. The new firm will have worldwide revenues of $2.7 billion, nearly twice that of Andersen. "We will be the largest firm in virtually every country in the world," boasts Larry D. Horner, Peat's U.S. chairman.

[1] *Accounting Principles Board Opinion No. 16*, "Accounting for Business Combinations" (New York: American Institute of Certified Public Accountants, 1970), par. 5.

Peat Marwick Merges Its Way to the Top *(continued)*

Falling Behind

Like all professions, accounting has become increasingly competitive since the late 1970s, when the government forced the industry to abandon internal strictures against advertising. Many firms, unaccustomed to the rough-and-tumble marketing tactics that have since become commonplace, have been unable to keep pace. That's one reason Price Waterhouse and Deloitte Haskins & Sells proposed a merger in 1984 that would have made them No. 1. However, the deal fell through at the last minute, when Deloitte's European partners balked at what they perceived as a loss of power.

By contrast, Amsterdam-based Klynveld Main Goerdeler has been shopping for a merger partner for some time. The partners have been dissatisfied with the growth rate of the firm's U.S. affiliate, KMG Main Hurdman. When KMG surveyed potential U.S. clients, the firm was surprised to discover that many had never heard of them. "It would have been difficult for us to become No. 1, 2, or even No. 8," concedes Paul H. Boschma, the firm's international chairman. "So we decided a megamerger would be the best alternative."

For its part, Peat Marwick reinforces its international presence and picks up a nice roster of midsize U.S. clients from KMG Main Hurdman. Besides, being No. 1 never hurts.

Source: Stuart Weiss and Mark Maremont, "Peat Marwick Merges Its Way to the Top," reprinted from the September 15, 1986 issue of *Business Week*, p. 52, by special permission, © 1986 by McGraw-Hill, Inc.

Decrease in Number of Partners

If a partnership's assets have current values different from their book values when a partner withdraws from a partnership, the partners are not treated equitably unless this difference in value is considered in settling with the withdrawing partner or his estate. In these situations, each method of preventing an inequity is available. To illustrate how each method would be applied in such a situation, we assume the following facts:

1. A, B, and C are in partnership.
2. The Capital accounts of all three partners are $25,000 each.
3. Carrying values of the partnership's tangible assets equal their current values, except for a parcel of land that is worth $12,000 more than its book value.
4. Profits and losses are shared equally.
5. C decides to withdraw from the partnership.

Revaluing of Assets Method. Under the revaluing of assets method, the land is merely written up to its curent value using the following entry:

Land	12,000	
Capital, Partner A		4,000
Capital, Partner B		4,000
Capital, Partner C		4,000

Each of the partners' Capital accounts is increased by one-third of the upward revaluation, because the partners shared profits and losses equally until C decided to withdraw from the partnership. The entry to record C's withdrawal from the partnership is as follows:

Capital, Partner C	29,000	
Payable to Partner C		29,000

As indicated previously, this is the simplest of the three methods. The fact that it departs from generally accepted accounting principles may be of little concern to the partnership.

Special Profit and Loss Sharing Provision Method. Under the special profit and loss sharing provision approach, the land is carried at its historical cost. However, the new profit and loss sharing formula contains a provision that (a) acknowledges that the land's estimated current value is $12,000 in excess of its current book value and (b) specifies that the withdrawing partner is entitled to one-third of the first $12,000 profit on the sale of the land. The entry to record C's withdrawal from the partnership is as follows:

Capital, Partner C	25,000	
Payable to Partner C		25,000

Effectively, there is a contingent liability with respect to the amount that is to be paid to C upon sale of the land. This method has limited application in situations involving withdrawing partners. If different appraisals of current value of partnership assets exist, this method may be a practical alternative to the other two methods, especially if such assets are expected to be sold within a relatively short period of time. Normally, however, this method is impractical, because a withdrawing partner does not want to wait until such assets are disposed of to obtain his or her final settlement from the partnership.

The Bonus Method. Under the bonus method, no adjustment is made to the carrying amount of the land, nor is any special provision included in the new profit and loss sharing formula because the land is worth more than its book value. Consequently, when the land is later sold, A and B share all the profit. From an equity viewpoint, A and B are not entitled to one-third of the first $12,000 profit; therefore, their Capital accounts are reduced at C's withdrawal by the amount that represents C's share of the $12,000 of unrealized profit. Thus one-third of $12,000, or $4,000, is charged to the Capital accounts of the old partners in their respective profit and loss sharing ratio. A and B will recoup this bonus to C later if the land is sold for $12,000 in excess of its current book value. The entry to record the bonus and C's withdrawal from the partnership is as follows:

Capital, Partner A	**2,000**	
Capital, Partner B	**2,000**	
Capital, Partner C		**4,000**
To record the bonus to the withdrawing partner.		
Capital, Partner C	**29,000**	
Payable to Partner C		**29,000**
To record the withdrawal of partner C.		

In this situation, A and B give up part of their Capital account balances, only to recover at a later date the amounts given up. Thus, the bonus is not permanent, because it is effectively recovered later.

The following points are important for understanding these three methods:

1. If the land is later sold for $112,000 ($12,000 more than its $100,000 book value immediately before C withdrew from the partnership), the settlement to C is the same under each method. Also, the Capital account balances of A and B are identical under each method. Thus, each method ensures that the withdrawing partner receives one-third of the first $12,000 profit on the sale of the land. Furthermore, each method ensures that C does not share in any of the profit on the sale of the land in excess of $12,000.
2. The real problem is obtaining reasonable assurance of the current values of partnership assets. If the agreed-upon values are overstated, then the revaluing the asset method and the bonus method result in an excess settlement to the withdrawing partner. However, under the special profit and loss sharing provision method, no such excess payment is possible; thus, A and B are best protected under this method. If the agreed-upon values are understated, then none of the methods protects the withdrawing partner. The remaining partners share the entire increase above the agreed-upon value.
3. If the land declined in value after C withdrew, then C would not be treated equitably under the special profit and loss sharing provision method, because he would be sharing in a loss that occurred after he withdrew.

In all the preceding examples, the partnership's tangible assets were undervalued. When tangible assets have curent values less than their book values, the first method—whereby the assets are written down—makes the most sense. (This procedure would be in accordance with generally accepted accounting principles.) The second choice would be the bonus method. The use of the special profit and loss sharing provision method would usually be impractical.

INTANGIBLE ELEMENT EXISTS

We restricted our discussion in the preceding section to situations in which a partnership's tangible assets have current values different from their book values. In the next section, we discuss situations in which either the existing partnership or an incoming partner possesses an intangible element. In discussing these situations, we assume that all partnership tangible assets have current values equal to their book values. Although this assumption is not necessarily realistic, it allows us to concentrate on the issue of accounting for this intangible element.

The discussion of intangible elements usually has wider application than the earlier discussion of tangible assets, because most partnerships—other than those engaged in real estate development—do not have substantial investments in the types of assets that appreciate or depreciate, such as inventory, land, buildings, and equipment. The largest asset for such partnerships is usually accounts receivable.

Intangible elements are usually associated with an existing partnership. The most common intangible element is a partnership's superior earnings. Obviously, a partner's interest in such a partnership is worth more than its book value. Even when a partnership has only average earnings, a partner's interest may be worth more than its book value to an incoming partner merely because the organization already has clients and the potential to develop superior earnings.

An incoming partner may also possess intangible elements. For example, the incoming partner may have a successful sole proprietorship business with superior earnings power. He or she may have individual potential that the existing partners are willing to pay for. This is similar to situations in which corporations pay one-time bonuses to executives to induce them to work for them, or in professional sports in which a rookie may receive a one-time bonus just for signing with a particular team.

In these situations, whether the existing partnership or an incoming partner possesses the intangible element, the intangible element is referred to as **goodwill.** The accounting issue is how to compensate the partner or partners who have created or possess the goodwill. If there is no compensation, the other partner or partners share unfairly in a portion of the partnership's future earnings.

The general approach to compensating the appropriate partners parallels that for situations in which tangible assets have current values different from book values — that is, we may apply the same three methods that we discussed and illustrated in the preceding section of the chapter. However, the first method is called **recording the goodwill** rather than revaluing of assets. Other than this descriptive change, the three methods are procedurally the same.

In the following material on the treatment of intangibles, note that the larger the partnership, the less the partners are inclined to compute the value of goodwill. For example, in the interest of simplicity, most national public accounting firms completely ignore goodwill for all changes in ownership situations. Instead, a simpler approach is adopted whereby an incoming partner initially accepts a lower than normal profit and loss sharing percentage; that percentage is increased on a sliding scale over a period of years until the incoming partner eventually shares profits and losses equally with other partners. Such an approach has the same overall effect as the three mechanical methods of dealing with goodwill, although the exact effect on each partner would be different.

Admission of a New Partner: Existing Partnership Possesses Goodwill

Traditionally, advanced accounting textbooks have approached the issue of goodwill by presenting a set of assumed facts regarding (1) the capital contribution made by the incoming partner; (2) the percentage interest the incoming partner receives in the partnership's net assets; and (3) whether the net assets in that percentage interest include or exclude the value of the goodwill. Given all this information, we can determine (as if trying to solve a puzzle) which method the partners have used to compensate the partner or partners who have created or possess the goodwill. Under the valuing of the goodwill method, the value of the goodwill may then be determined and recorded on the books of the partnership. Under the bonus method, the amount of the bonus given to the old partners or the new partner may then be determined and recorded on the books of the partnership. This approach implies that (1) the value of the goodwill and the amount of the bonus given are derivatives of these given amounts and percentages, and (2) the partners arrive at the ownership percentages without agreeing to the value of the goodwill. This implication is completely misleading.

Although the goodwill and the amount of the bonus, or both, may be determined using this approach, the normal procedure when a partner is admitted into a partnership is obscured. The normal process, the sequence of which may vary, is as follows:

1. The value of the existing goodwill is agreed upon between the old partners and the new partner.
2. One of the available accounting methods designed to compensate the partner or partners who have created or possess the goodwill is selected.
3. The profit and loss ratio is agreed upon.
4. The capital contribution of the incoming partner is agreed upon.

Once these items are agreed upon, each partner's Capital account balance may be computed (using the appropriate accounting method selected). After determining each partner's Capital account balance, we may then express each partner's interest as a percentage of the partnership's net assets (as defined). Thus, the ownership percentage of each partner in the partnership's net assets is a *derived* amount—not the agreed-upon value of the goodwill. Accordingly, in the following illustrations, the value of the goodwill will be given.

In the first illustration, the partnership possesses the goodwill. To illustrate the application of the three methods of compensating the old partners for the goodwill they have created, we assume the following information:

1. A and B are in partnership, sharing profits equally.
2. C is to be admitted into the partnership.
3. A, B, and C agree that the partnership will generate superior earnings of $10,000 for one year after C's admission.
4. C contributes $30,000 cash to the partnership.
5. Profits and losses are to be shared among A, B, and C in a ratio of 4:4:2, respectively.
6. A and B have capital account balances of $32,500 and $27,500, respectively (for a total of $60,000), immediately before admitting C.

Recording the Goodwill Method. Under the recording the goodwill method, C's admission into the partnership results in the recording of the entire amount of the agreed-upon goodwill in the partnership's books, as follows:

Goodwill	**10,000**	
Capital, Partner A		**5,000**
Capital, Partner B		**5,000**
To record the agreed-upon value of the goodwill, shared equally between the old partners using their old profit and loss sharing ratio.		

The entry to record C's capital contribution of $30,000 is as follows:

Cash	**30,000**	
Capital, Partner C		**30,000**
To record C's capital contribution.		

The following points are important for understanding the preceding entries:

1. It can be stated that C has a 30% interest in the net assets of the partnership ($30,000 ÷ $100,000 total of the capital accounts).

2. The recording of goodwill in this manner is not in accordance with generally accepted accounting principles, because the goodwill did not result from the purchase of a business.
3. The goodwill will be amortized over a one-year period, because the partnership is expected to produce superior earnings only for one year.
4. Because of the goodwill amortization in the year after C's admission, earnings will be $10,000 lower than if goodwill had not been recorded on the books.
5. Effectively, $10,000 of future profits have been capitalized into the Capital accounts of the old partners. In this respect, the partners have guaranteed that they alone will receive the first $10,000 of future earnings (determined without regard to the goodwill amortization expense).
6. If $10,000 of superior earnings result in the following year, then such superior earnings completely absorb the goodwill amortization of $10,000.
7. If the superior earnings in the following year are less than $10,000, then C effectively loses a portion of his initial capital contribution of $30,000. This is because the normal earnings of the partnership must absorb a portion of the goodwill amortization, and C cannot share in a portion of the normal earnings.

To illustrate how this method may favor the old partners over the new partner if the entire amount of the superior earnings does not materialize, assume that during the year after C's admission, only $8,000 of superior earnings materialized. These superior earnings would absorb only $8,000 of goodwill amortization. The remaining $2,000 of goodwill amortization would be absorbed by normal earnings. Thus, C would not share in $2,000 of normal earnings. Because C's profit and loss sharing percentage is 20%, he effectively loses $400 (20% of $2,000) of his $30,000 initial capital contribution.

Special Profit and Loss Sharing Provision Method. Under the special profit and loss sharing provision method, no entry is made on the partnership's books with respect to the goodwill. As under the previous method, C's Capital account is credited with the full amount of his capital contribution of $30,000. It can be stated that C has a one-third interest in the partnership's net assets ($30,000 ÷ $90,000 total of the Capital accounts). The new profit and loss sharing formula would stipulate that the old partners are entitled to share (in accordance with their old profit and loss sharing ratio) in the first $10,000 of earnings in excess of a specified amount, the specified amount being the expected normal earnings for the year after C's admission into the partnership.

If the superior earnings of $10,000 do not materialize during this year, then the old partners will have credited to their Capital accounts only the superior earnings that do materialize. Of course, the normal earnings and any earnings above the $10,000 of superior earnings during the next year would be shared in accordance with the new profit and loss sharing ratio.

This method protects the new partner's initial capital contribution of $30,000 in the event superior earnings of $10,000 do not materialize. Obviously, the old partners would prefer the previous method, under which they are assured of the first $10,000 of earnings, regardless of whether such earnings are superior earnings.

The Bonus Method. Under the bonus method, no entry is made on the partnership's books with respect to goodwill. Unlike the previous two methods, C does not receive a full credit to his Capital account for his capital contribution of $30,000, because he must give a bonus to the old partners. The amount of the bonus given to the old partners is C's profit and loss sharing percentage of 20% times the agreed-upon value of the goodwill of $10,000. Thus, the bonus given the old partners is $2,000, which they share in their old profit and loss sharing ratio as follows:

Cash	**30,000**	
Capital, Partner A		**1,000**
Capital, Partner B		**1,000**
Capital, Partner C		**28,000**
To record C's capital contribution and to record the bonus to the old partners.		

The following points are important for understanding the above entry:

1. It can be stated that C has a 31.11% interest in the partnership's net assets ($28,000 ÷ $90,000 total of the Capital accounts).
2. Generally accepted accounting principles are followed by not recording goodwill on the books.
3. If superior earnings of $10,000 materialize in the year following C's admission, then C shares in these superior earnings. His share is $2,000 (20% of $10,000). Consequently, he recoups the bonus he initially gave to the old partners.
4. The bonus method compensates the old partners currently for the portion of the superior earnings that will later be credited to the new partner's Capital account. Thus, if all the superior earnings materialize, the bonus is temporary.
5. If the superior earnings in the year following C's admission are less than $10,000, then C effectively loses a portion of his initial capital contribution of $30,000. This is because he does not share in the amount of superior earnings that he thought would materialize, for which he was willing to give a bonus to the old partners.

If the entire amount of superior earnings does not materialize, the bonus method may favor the old partners over the new partner. Assume that during the year following C's admission, only $8,000 of superior earnings materialized. C's share of the $8,000 of superior earnings that did materialize would be $1,600 (20% of $8,000). Because he gave a bonus of

$2,000, he only recouped $1,600 of the bonus, effectively losing $400 of his initial capital contribution of $30,000.

Approach if the Value of Goodwill Is Not Given. Assume that the partners in their negotiations agree upon an amount for the goodwill, but that they do not state this amount in the new partnership agreement. Instead, knowing the amount of agreed-upon goodwill, they merely calculate the percentage that the incoming partner has in the partnership's net assets. In these situations, the accountant may determine the goodwill using the available information regarding the individual ownership percentage the new partner has in the partnership's net assets. We demonstrate the general approach using the information in our example.

If the value of the goodwill is to be recorded on the partnership's books and the new partner has a 30% interest in the net assets (tangible and intangible) of the partnership, the goodwill implicit in the transaction could be determined as follows:

1. Divide C's $30,000 capital contribution by his 30% interest in the net assets to arrive at $100,000.
2. Subtract from the amount determined in step 1 the sum of the Capital account balances of the old partners immediately before C is admitted ($60,000) plus C's capital contribution ($30,000). Thus, the goodwill would be $10,000 ($100,000 − $90,000).

Alternatively, if goodwill is not to be recorded on the partnership's books and the new partner has a 31.11% interest in the net assets (tangible assets only) of the partnership, the bonus to be given and the related goodwill implicit in the transaction could be determined as follows:

1. Determine the total tangible net assets of the partnership including C's contribution ($60,000 + $30,000).
2. Multiply the amount determined in step 1, $90,000, by C's given ownership percentage in the partnership's net assets ($90,000 × 31.11% = $28,000).
3. Subtract the $28,000 determined in step 2 from C's $30,000 capital contribution to determine the $2,000 bonus that is to be given to the old partners.
4. Divide the $2,000 bonus by C's profit and loss sharing percentage of 20% to obtain the value of the goodwill implicit in the transaction, or $10,000.

Admission of a New Partner: New Partner Possesses Goodwill

Although in most situations the existing partnership has created the goodwill, an incoming partner may possess goodwill. To illustrate the three methods of compensating an incoming partner for goodwill, assume the following information:

1. A and B are in partnership, sharing profits equally.
2. C is to be admitted into the partnership.

3. A, B, and C agree that C is expected to generate superior earnings of $10,000 for one year following his admission.
4. C contributes $30,000 cash to the partnership.
5. Profits and losses are to be shared among A, B, and C in a ratio of 4:4:2, respectively.
6. A and B have Capital account balances of $32,500 and $27,500, respectively (a total of $60,000), immediately before admitting C.

Recording the Goodwill Method. Under the recording the goodwill method, the entire amount of the agreed-upon value of the goodwill is credited to C's Capital account, along with his capital contribution of $30,000, as follows:

Goodwill	**10,000**	
Cash	**30,000**	
Capital, Partner C		**40,000**
To record the agreed upon value of the goodwill and C's capital contribution.		

Compared with the situation in which the old partners created the goodwill, the roles are now reversed. The new partner will receive the first $10,000 of future earnings (determined without regard to the goodwill amortization expense), even if superior earnings do not materialize. If the superior earnings of $10,000 do not materialize, then the old partners will lose the subsequent increases to their Capital accounts that they would have received. In this situation, it can be stated that C has a 40% interest in the partnership's net assets ($40,000 ÷ $100,000 total of the Capital accounts).

Special Profit and Loss Sharing Provision Method. Under the special profit and loss sharing provision method, no entry is made on the partnership's books with respect to the goodwill. C would receive a credit to his Capital account equal to his capital contribution of $30,000. It can be stated that C has a one-third interest in the partnership's net assets ($30,000 ÷ $90,000 total of the Capital accounts). The new profit and loss sharing formula would stipulate that the new partner is entitled to receive the first $10,000 of earnings in excess of a specified amount. That amount would be the expected normal earnings for the year after C's admission into the partnership. If superior earnings of $10,000 do not materialize during this year, then the new partner will have credited to his Capital account only the superior earnings that do materialize. In this situation, this method protects the old partners' capital balances that existed when C was admitted into the partnership.

The Bonus Method. Under the bonus method, no entry is made on the partnership's books with respect to goodwill. Because the new partner possesses the goodwill, the old partners give a bonus to him. The amount of the bonus given to the new partner is the total of the old partners' profit and loss sharing percentage of 80% times the agreed-upon value of the goodwill, which is $10,000. Thus, the bonus given the new partner is $8,000, recorded as follows:

Cash	**30,000**	
Capital, Partner A	**4,000**	
Capital, Partner B	**4,000**	
Capital, Partner C		**38,000**
To record C's capital contribution and to record the bonus given to him.		

It can be stated that C has a 42.22% interest in the partnership's net assets ($38,000 ÷ $90,000). Compared with the situation in which the old partners created the goodwill, the roles now are reversed. The old partners will recoup the bonus they gave to the new partner only if superior earnings of $10,000 materialize. To the extent that the superior earnings are less than $10,000, then the old partners will lose a portion of the balances that existed in their Capital accounts immediately before C was admitted.

Approach if the Value of Goodwill Is Not Given. If the agreed-upon value of the goodwill is not available (an unusual situation), the accountant may determine this amount so long as information is available regarding the individual ownership percentage the new partner has in the partnership's net assets. We demonstrate the general approach using the information in our example.

If the value of the goodwill is to be recorded on the partnership's books and the new partner has a 40% interest in the net assets (tangible and intangible) of the partnership, the goodwill implicit in the transaction could be determined as follows:

1. Divide the total of the old partners' Capital accounts by their total interest in the net assets ($60,000 ÷ 60%) to arrive at $100,000.
2. Subtract from the amount determined in step 1 the sum of the Capital account balances of the old partners immediately before C is admitted ($60,000) plus C's tangible capital contribution of $30,000. Thus, the goodwill would be $10,000 ($100,000 − $90,000).

Alternatively, if goodwill is not to be recorded on the partnership's books and the new partner has a 42.22% interest in the net assets (tangible assets only), the bonus to be given by the old partners and the goodwill implicit in the transaction could be determined as follows:

1. Determine the total net assets of the partnership, including C's tangible contribution ($60,000 + $30,000).

2. Multiply the amount determined in step 1, $90,000, by C's given ownership percentage in the partnership's net assets ($90,000 × 42.22% = $38,000).
3. Subtract from the $38,000 amount determined in step 2 C's tangible capital contribution of $30,000 to arrive at the $8,000 bonus that C receives from the old partners.
4. Divide the $8,000 bonus by the old partners' combined profit- and loss-sharing percentage of 80% to obtain the value of the goodwill implicit in the transaction, or $10,000.

Business Combinations

When two businesses combine in such a manner that the owners of each separate business continue as owners in the enlarged business (substantively, a pooling of interests) and when one of the businesses possesses goodwill, then we may apply the same three methods that have been illustrated in this section to compensate the partners of the business possessing the goodwill. Procedurally, these three methods are the same as in situations in which a new partner is admitted other than through a business combination. The mechanics are more involved, however, as the number of combining partners increases.

A Decrease in the Number of Partners

If a partnership possesses unrecorded goodwill when a partner withdraws from the partnership, the withdrawing partner is not treated equitably unless this difference in value is considered in settling with the withdrawing partner or his estate. In these situations, each of the methods of compensating the partner is available—the recording the goodwill method, the special profit and loss sharing provision method, and the bonus method. To illustrate how each of these methods would be applied in such a situation, assume the following facts:

1. A, B, and C are in partnership, sharing profits equally.
2. The Capital accounts of A, B, and C are $40,000, $30,000, and $20,000, respectively.
3. All the partnership's tangible assets have carrying values equal to their current values.
4. C withdraws from the partnership.
5. The partners agree that the partnership currently has unrecorded goodwill of $15,000.

Recording the Goodwill Method. Under the recording the goodwill method, goodwill is recorded on the books and shared among the partners in their profit-and-loss ratio, as follows:

Goodwill	**15,000**	
Capital, Partner A		**5,000**
Capital, Partner B		**5,000**
Capital, Partner C		**5,000**
To record the agreed-upon value of goodwill existing at the time of C's withdrawal from the partnership.		

The entry to record C's withdrawal is as follows:

Capital, Partner C	**25,000**	
Payable to Partner C		**25,000**

An alternative to recording all the goodwill is to record only C's share of the goodwill, which is $5,000. The entry is as follows:

Goodwill	**5,000**	
Capital, Partner C		**5,000**

Whether all or a portion of the goodwill is recorded is irrelevant from an equity standpoint—both methods produce the same result with respect to the withdrawing partner. As previously indicated, the goodwill method is not in accordance with generally accepted accounting principles, but the partners need not follow generally accepted accounting principles. If superior earnings of $15,000 do not materialize after C's withdrawal, the remaining partners lose a portion of their capital balances that existed at the time of C's withdrawal as a result of writing off the goodwill.

Special Profit and Loss Sharing Provision Method. Under the special profit and loss sharing provision method, goodwill is not recorded on the books. Instead, C's withdrawal is conditional on the new profit and loss sharing formula between A and B, which contains a provision that C is to share in one-third of future earnings in excess of a specified level for a certain period of time. If past superior earnings have been largely dependent on C's efforts, the partnership may not be able to generate superior earnings after C withdraws. Accordingly, this method best protects the remaining partners in the event superior earnings do not materialize during the stipulated period of time after C's withdrawal.

The Bonus Method. Under the bonus method, the old partners give a bonus to the withdrawing partner. The bonus equals C's share of the agreed-upon value of the goodwill, which is one-third of $15,000, or $5,000. The bonus is shared between the remaining partners in their respective profit and loss sharing ratio as follows:

Capital, Partner A	**2,500**	
Capital, Partner B	**2,500**	
Capital, Partner C		**5,000**
To record the bonus to C on his withdrawal from the partnership.		

This method does not deviate from generally accepted accounting principles. If $15,000 of above-normal earnings do not materialize during the stipulated period of time after C withdraws, however, then the remaining partners do not recoup all of the bonus they gave to C.

Spin-off Situations. A partner may withdraw from a partnership and then immediately commence business in the same line of work as a sole proprietor. In such a situation, the withdrawing partner often requests the partnership's clients and customers that he or she personally has been serving to give their future business to the newly formed sole proprietorship. When this happens, the method selected for equitably treating the withdrawing partner should be accompanied by provisions that protect the remaining partners from any loss of clients and customers as a result of the withdrawing partner forming a sole proprietorship. In other words, the remaining partners must guard against recording goodwill or paying a bonus and also losing clients or customers to the newly formed sole proprietorship.

LEGAL AND TAX ASPECTS OF CHANGES IN OWNERSHIP

Legal Aspects

Although a thorough discussion of the legal aspects of a change in ownership of a partnership is properly the subject of an upper-division course on business law, a brief discussion of the major legal aspects is appropriate at this point.

Section 29 of the Uniform Partnership Act (UPA) states that "the dissolution of a partnership is the change in the relation of the partners caused by any partner ceasing to be associated in the carrying on as distinguished from the winding up of the business." This definition implies that dissolution occurs only when a partner withdraws from a partnership. Section 41(1) of the UPA (which also is concerned with dissolution) refers to a partnership that admits a partner as being the "first or dissolved partnership." Accordingly, any change in ownership (whether by withdrawal of a partner, admission of a new partner, or a business combination that is in substance a pooling of interests) legally dissolves the existing partnership. Because we are dealing with changes in ownership that do not terminate the business activities of the partnership, a new partnership must be formed immediately to continue the business of the dissolved partnership.

The fact that a legal dissolution has occurred is meaningless in terms of continuity of existence; the business continues to operate just as though no change in ownership had occurred. However a legal dissolution does have personal significance to new partners, withdrawing partners, continuing partners, and creditors of the dissolved partnership.

Admission of a Partner. With respect to an incoming partner, Section 17 of the UPA provides that "a person admitted as a partner into an existing partnership is liable for all the obligations of the partnership arising before his admission as though he had been a partner when such obligations were incurred, except that his liability shall be satisfied only out of partnership property." This provision insulates the personal assets of the new partner from creditors' claims existing at the new partner's admission.

In practice, the existing partners usually insist that an incoming partner be jointly responsible for all such preexisting partnership debts. If the new partner agrees to this, Section 17 of the UPA may be circumvented by including a provision in the new partnership agreement to that effect. Because of the possibility of undisclosed liabilities (actual or contingent), the new partner in these situations should limit his or her responsibilities to the liabilities that are set forth in a scheduled exhibit to the partnership agreement.

Withdrawal of a Partner. With respect to a withdrawing partner, Section 36(1) of the UPA provides that "the dissolution of the partnership does not of itself discharge the existing liability of any partner." Section 36(2), however, provides that a withdrawing partner may be relieved of his or her responsibility for such debt if and only if the creditor expressly releases the partner from this responsibility by entering into an agreement to that effect between the withdrawing partner and the person or partnership continuing the business. Some court cases have held that a withdrawing partner may be liable for debts incurred after his or her withdrawal unless prior notice was given of that withdrawal. Notice usually must be given directly to persons who have dealt with the partnership. For persons who have not dealt with the partnership, a notice usually may be given by publication in a newspaper or some other appropriate manner.

Tax Aspects

The general ledger entries to the Capital accounts of the partners in connection with the revaluation of assets, recording the goodwill, or the bonus method are not significant from a tax viewpoint. The only tax significance of such entries is the existence of unrealized gains (when partners' Capital accounts increase) and unrealized losses (when partners' Capital accounts decrease). In general, until the partnership interest is disposed of, such gains and losses are not reportable for tax purposes.

Withdrawal of a Partner. When a withdrawing partner receives cash from either the partnership or persons to whom his or her partnership interest was sold, the determination of the withdrawing partner's gain or loss for income tax reporting purposes is made by comparing the proceeds to his or her tax basis. The *proceeds* are the sum of cash received plus the share of existing partnership liabilities for which he or she is relieved of responsibility. (The assumption of the partner's share of the liabilities by the remaining partners is treated as a distribution of money to the withdrawing partner.) To illustrate, we assume the following:

1. The withdrawing partner has a capital balance of $20,000.
2. The withdrawing partner is to receive a $5,000 bonus.
3. The partnership has liabilities of $24,000.
4. The partnership shares profits and losses equally.
5. The withdrawing partner's tax basis is $27,000.

The withdrawing partner's taxable gain is calculated as follows:

Proceeds:	
Cash distribution ($20,000 + $5,000 bonus)	**$25,000**
Relief of partnership liabilities (⅓ × $24,000)	**8,000**
Total Proceeds	**$33,000**
Withdrawing partner's tax basis	**27,000**
Taxable Gain	**$ 6,000**

When a withdrawing partner receives noncash consideration, the tax laws are complex; a discussion of these laws is beyond the scope of this chapter.

Admission of a Partner. The procedures for determining an incoming partner's tax basis are the same as those illustrated in the preceding chapter on the formation of partnerships. The incoming partner's tax basis equals the sum of (1) the amount of cash contributed, (2) the adjusted basis of any noncash assets contributed, and (3) the share of any partnership liabilities for which he or she is jointly responsible, (4) less the old partners' share of any liabilities the new partner contributes to the partnership. As when a partnership is formed, the profit and loss sharing ratios are used to adjust each partner's tax basis for any liabilities relieved of or assumed.

When a partner is admitted by directly purchasing a partner's interest, the incoming partner's tax basis is the sum of the cash paid plus the share of any partnership liabilities for which he or she is jointly responsible. The incoming partner's tax basis need not coincide with the selling partner's tax basis, because the amount paid is a negotiated amount. The partnership may elect to adjust the tax basis of the partnership assets to reflect the difference between the tax basis of the incoming partner and that of the selling partner. (No entries are made in the general ledger—the difference is kept on a memorandum.)

The amount of the increase or decrease in tax basis affects only the incoming partner. For example, assume that an incoming partner's tax basis exceeds that of the selling partner and this difference is allocable to merchandise inventory, a building, unrealized receivables, and goodwill. In future years, the incoming partner's share of earnings is adjusted by (1) treating the amount allocable to inventory as additional cost of goods sold (as the inventory is sold), (2) treating the amount allocable to the building as additional depreciation expense, and (3) treating the amount allocable to the unrealized receivables as a reduction of revenues (as the accounts receivable are collected). Although the goodwill is assigned a tax basis, the incoming partner's share of the earnings would not be adjusted for the amount allocable to goodwill, because goodwill is not deductible for income tax reporting purposes.

This election to adjust the tax basis of the assets is much more common in small partnerships than in large partnerships because the partnership—not the individual incoming partner—must do the record keeping, and most large partnerships do not bother with this record-keeping function. If the election is made to adjust the tax basis of the partnership assets, the sum of the tax bases of each partner will equal the partnership's tax basis in its assets. If the election is not made, this equality will not exist, and the difference will exist until the partner disposes of his or her interest.

SUMMARY

The determination of the journal entry to reflect a change in the ownership of a partnership is to some extent an after-the-fact mechanical process using the terms and methods selected by the partners. A far more important role for the accountant when a change in ownership is contemplated is explaining and illustrating the various methods (and their ramifications) of dealing with situations in which assets have current values different from book values and/or intangible elements exist. The accountant may even assist partners in determining the amount of any goodwill by demonstrating some of the common methods that may be used to calculate goodwill. Remember that in these situations the accountant is only an advisor. It is not his or her role to select a method for determining the amount of goodwill or to select one of the three methods available for achieving equity among the partners.

Review Questions

1. What is the primary objective of accounting for changes in the ownership of a partnership?
2. What three methods are available for achieving equity among partners when a change in ownership occurs?
3. Does each method of achieving equity always treat each partner equitably in every situation?
4. Under the bonus method, is the bonus temporary or permanent?
5. Is recognizing goodwill on the admission of a partner into a partnership considered to be in accord with generally accepted accounting principles?
6. Describe a business combination of two partnerships that would be, in substance, a pooling of interests.
7. Is a business combination that is in substance a purchase deemed a change in ownership with respect to the acquiring partnership?
8. How does an accountant know whether the bonus method, the special profit and loss sharing provision method, or the recording the goodwill method should be used to reflect a change in ownership?
9. Under the recording the goodwill method, substantively, what has occurred?
10. Under the bonus method, substantively, what has occurred?
11. What is the significance of a legal dissolution when a partner is admitted into a partnership? when a partner withdraws?
12. When a partner withdraws from a partnership after many years as a partner and such partner has a gain on the liquidation of his or her interest, is such gain treated as a capital gain for income tax reporting purposes?

Discussion Cases

DC 24-1

Admission of a Partner: Evaluation of the Bonus Method

Gentry and Royals are in partnership, and they are contemplating the admission of Squires into the partnership. Gentry and Royals have proposed that Squires give a $20,000 bonus to them as a condition of admittance. Squires feels that this bonus is ridiculous considering that (1) all tangible assets have fair market values equal to their book values; (2) all partners will be devoting 100% of their time to the partnership business; (3) future profits and losses are to be shared equally; (4) Squires' capital contribution is to be 50% of the existing partnership capital of $100,000 immediately before his admission; and (5) his tax basis would be reduced by $20,000. Squires has asked you as his accountant to counsel him on this matter.

Required:

How would you respond to this request?

DC 24-2

Admission of a Partner: Adherence to Generally Accepted Accounting Principles

Castle and Hurst are partners in the process of negotiating with Randolph regarding his admission into the partnership. Agreement has been reached regarding the value of goodwill that the existing partnership possesses. However, the partners disagree as to whether the goodwill should be recorded on the books. Castle and Hurst feel goodwill should be recognized and recorded on the books at Randolph's admission. Randolph feels it is improper to record goodwill because it was not bought and paid for. Furthermore, Randolph contends that it is senseless to record goodwill, because it is not deductible for income tax purposes. They have asked you as the partnership's accountant to settle this disagreement.

Required:
How would you respond to this request?

DC 24-3

Admission of a Partner: Role of the Accountant

Disnee and Walters are partners contemplating the admission of Duckett as a partner. They have requested that you, the partnership's accountant, determine how this should be done.

Required:
How would you respond to this request? Be specific about the advice you would give to the partners.

DC 24-4

Admission of a Partner: Role of the Accountant

Berry and Knott are partners contemplating the admission of Farmer into the partnership. Berry and Knott believe the partnership possesses goodwill of $60,000, whereas Farmer believes the partnership possesses goodwill of only $20,000. As the partnership's accountant, you have been asked to determine the amount of goodwill that the partnership possesses.

Required:
How would you respond to this request?

Exercises

E 24-1

Admission of a Partner: Calculation of Required Contribution

Partners Angel, Bird, and Crow share profits and losses 50:30:20, respectively. The April 30, 19X5, balance sheet is as follows:

Cash	$ 40,000
Other assets	360,000
	$400,000

Accounts payable	$100,000
Capital, Angel	74,000
Capital, Bird	130,000
Capital, Crow	96,000
	$400,000

The assets and liabilities are recorded and presented at their respective fair values. Dove is to be admitted as a new partner with a 20% capital interest and a 20% share of profits and losses in exchange for a cash contribution. No goodwill or bonus is to be recorded.

Required:

1. Determine how much cash Dove should contribute.
2. Prepare the entry to record Dove's admission.

(AICPA adapted)

E 24-2

Admission of a Partner: Recording the Goodwill Method

Abbey and Landly are partners with capital balances of $80,000 and $40,000, and they share profits and losses in the ratio of 2:1, respectively. Deere invests $36,000 cash for a one-fifth interest in the capital and profits of the new partnership. The partners agree that the implied partnership goodwill is to be recorded simultaneously with the admission of Deere.

Required:

1. Calculate the total implied goodwill of the firm.
2. Prepare the entry or entries to record the admission of Deere.

(AICPA adapted)

E 24-3

Admission of a Partner: The Bonus Method

Cord and Stringer are partners who share profits and losses in the ratio of 3:2, respectively. On August 31, 19X4, their Capital accounts were as follows:

Cord	$ 70,000
Stringer	60,000
	$130,000

On that date, they agreed to admit Twiner as a partner with a one-third interest in the capital and profits and losses, for an investment of $50,000. The new partnership will begin with a total capital of $180,000. ← Key to question

Required:
Prepare the entry or entries to record the admission of Twiner.

(AICPA adapted)

E 24-4

Admission of a Partner: Recording the Goodwill Method and the Bonus Method

Waters is admitted into the partnership of Dunes, Kamel, and Sanders for a total cash investment of $40,000. The capital Accounts and respective percentage interests in profits and losses immediately before Waters's admission are as follows:

	Capital Accounts	Percentage Interests in Profits and Losses
Dunes	$ 80,000	60
Kamel	40,000	30
Sanders	20,000	10
	$140,000	100

All tangible assets and liabilities are fairly valued. Waters receives a one-fifth interest in profits and losses and a 20% interest in the partnership's net assets.

Required:

1. Prepare the entry to record Waters' admission into the partnership, assuming goodwill is to be recorded.
2. Prepare the entry to record Waters' admission into the partnership, assuming no goodwill is to be recorded.

E 24-5

Admission of a Partner: Determining Bonus and Goodwill from Interest in Net Assets

Ball and Batt are partners, share profits and losses equally, and have capital balances of $30,000 and $20,000, respectively, All tangible assets have current values equal to book values. Glover is admitted into the partnership. Determine the entry to record Glover's admission in each of the following independent situations:

1. Glover contributes $10,000 cash for a 10% interest in the new net assets of the partnership of $60,000.
2. Glover contributes $10,000 cash for a 10% interest in the new net assets of the partnership, with Glover to receive a credit to his Capital account equal to his full cash contribution.
3. Glover contributes $10,000 for a one-sixth interest in the new net assets of the partnership of $60,000.
4. Glover purchases 10% of each existing partner's interest for a total cash payment of $10,000 to the existing partners.
5. Glover contributes $10,000 cash for a 20% interest in the new net assets of the partnership of $60,000.
6. Glover contributes $10,000 cash for a 20% interest in the new net assets of the partnership, with the old partners not to have any decrease made to their Capital accounts.

E 24-6

Retirement of a Partner

On June 30, 19X1, the balance sheet for the partnership of Oakley, Pine, and Woods, together with their respective profit and loss ratios, were as follows:

Assets, at cost	$180,000
Oakley, loan	$ 9,000
Oakley, Capital (20%)	42,000
Pine, Capital (20%)	39,000
Woods, Capital (60%)	90,000
	$180,000

Oakley has decided to retire from the partnership. By mutual agreement, the assets are to be adjusted to their current value of $216,000. It was agreed that the partnership would pay Oakley $61,200 for his partnership interest, including his loan, which is to be repaid in full.

Required:

1. Prepare the required entries assuming goodwill is to be recorded on the partnership's books. (Note: Two alternative amounts may be recorded for goodwill. Prepare entries under each alternative.)
2. Prepare the entries assuming that goodwill is not to be recorded on the partnership's books.

(AICPA adapted)

E 24-7

Calculation of Gain on Sale of Partnership Interests

The Capital acounts of the partnership of Fender, Hood, and Shields on May 31, 19X5, are presented below with their respective profit and loss ratios:

Fender	$200,000	1/2
Hood	150,000	1/3
Shields	100,000	1/6
	$450,000	

On May 31, 19X5, Wheeler was admitted into the partnership when she purchased for $120,000 an interest from Fender in the net assets and profits of the partnership. As a result of this transaction, Wheeler acquired a one-fifth interest in the net assets and profits of the firm. Assume that implied goodwill is not to be recorded. Fender's tax basis just prior to the sale was $180,000.

Required:

1. What is the gain realized by Fender on the sale of a portion of this interest in the partnership to Wheeler?

2. Is the gain calculated in requirement 1 a gain for book purposes, a gain for tax purposes, or both?
3. Prepare the entry required on the partnership's books.
4. What is Fender's gain or loss if he retires on December 31, 19X5? (Assume no change in Fender's Capital account or tax basis for the seven months ended December 31, 19X5; also, assume that the partnership had no liabilities at December 31, 19X5.)

Problems

P 24-1

Admission of a Partner: Tangible Assets Undervalued and Goodwill Exists

Fields and Hill are in partnership, share profits and losses in the ratio 4:1, respectively, and have capital balances of $22,500 each. Tangible assets of the partnership have a fair value of $15,000 in excess of book value. Mounds is admitted into the partnership for a cash contribution of $30,000. The new profit and loss sharing formula is Fields, 56%; Hill, 14%; and Mounds, 30%. The value of the partnership's existing goodwill is agreed to be $10,000.

Required:

1. Prepare the required entries assuming the tangible assets are to be revalued and the goodwill is to be recorded on the partnership's books.
2. Prepare the required entries assuming that the bonus method is to be used with respect to the undervalued tangible assets and the goodwill.

P 24-2

Retirement of a Partner: Tangible Assets Undervalued and Goodwill Exists

The April 30, 19X5, balance sheet of the partnership of Arbee, Karl, and MacDonald is as follows. The partners share profits and losses in the ratio 2:2:6, respectively.

Assets, at cost	$100,000
Arbee, loan	$ 9,000
Capital, Arbee	15,000
Capital, Karl	31,000
Capital, MacDonald	45,000
	$100,000

Arbee retires from the partnership. By mutual agreement, the assets are to be adjusted to their fair value of $130,000 at April 30, 19X5. Karl and MacDonald agree that the partnership will pay Arbee $37,000 cash for his partnership interest, exclusive of his loan, which is to be paid in full. No goodwill is to be recorded.

Required:

1. Prepare the entry to record the revaluation of assets to their fair value.
2. Prepare the entry to record Arbee's retirement.
3. What is the implicit goodwill?

(AICPA adapted)

P 24-3 Business Combination: Each Partnership Has Undervalued Tangible Assets and Goodwill

The partnership of A, B, C, and D has agreed to combine with the partnership of X and Y. The individual Capital accounts and profit and loss sharing percentage of each partner are shown below:

	Capital Accounts	Profit and Loss Sharing Percentages Now	Proposed
A	$ 50,000	40	28
B	35,000	30	21
C	40,000	20	14
D	25,000	10	7
	$150,000	100	70
X	$ 60,000	50	15
Y	40,000	50	15
	$100,000	100	30

The partnership of A, B, C, and D has undervalued tangible assets of $20,000, and the partnership of X and Y has undervalued tangible assets of $8,000. All the partners agree that (1) the partnership of A, B, C, and D possesses goodwill of $30,000, and (2) the partnership of X and Y possesses goodwill of $10,000. (Assume that the combined businesses will continue to use the general ledger of A, B, C, and D.)

Required:

1. Prepare the entries required to reflect the combination, assuming tangible assets are to be revalued and goodwill is to be recorded.
2. Prepare the entries required to reflect the combination, assuming the bonus method is to be used with respect to the undervalued tangible assets and the goodwill.

P 24-4 Calculation of Tax Basis of New Partner and Adjustment to Old Partners' Tax Bases: Admission by Capital Contribution into the Partnership

Bishop and Knight are in partnership; share profits and losses in the ratio 3:2, respectively; and have capital balances of $80,000 and $60,000, respectively. They admit Rook into the partnership for a cash contribution of $50,000, of which $10,000 is to be credited to the Capital accounts of the old partners as a bonus. The new profit and loss sharing percentages are Bishop, 45%; Knight, 30%; and Rook, 25%. The partnership has $60,000 of liabilities at Rook's admission. Rook became jointly responsible for these liabilities at his admission pursuant to a provision in the new partnership agreement.

Required:

1. Prepare the entry required on the partnership's books.
2. Calculate the tax basis of Rook's interest in the partnership.
3. Calculate the required adjustment to the tax basis of each of the old partners as a result of Rook's admission.
4. What is Bishop's tax basis after Rook's admission?

P 24-5 Calculation of Tax Basis of New Partner and Determination of Old Partner's Proceeds and Taxable Gain: Admission by Purchase of Existing Partner's Interest

Board and Checker are in partnership, share profits and losses equally, and have capital balances of $60,000 and $40,000, respectively. Kingmee purchases all of Checker's interest for $50,000 and agrees to be jointly responsible for all existing partnership liabilities, which total $14,000.

Required:

1. Prepare the entry required on the partnership's books.
2. Calculate the tax basis of Kingmee's interest in the partnership.
3. Calculate the adjustment, if any, to Board's tax basis as a result of Kingmee's purchase of Checker's interest.
4. Assuming Checker's tax basis was $47,000 when he sold his interest, determine the proceeds he received on the sale of his interest and his taxable gain, if any.

P 24-6 COMPREHENSIVE Admission of New Partners: Withdrawal of Old Partner and Division of Profits

You have been engaged to prepare the June 30, 19X2, financial statements for the partnership of Ash, Cherry, and Douglas. You have obtained the following information from the partnership agreement, as amended, and from the accounting records.

1. The partnership was formed originally by Ash and Burch on July 1, 19X1. At that date:
   a. Burch contributed $400,000 cash.
   b. Ash contributed land, a building, and equipment with fair market values of $110,000, $520,000, and $185,000, respectively. The land and buildings were subject to a mortgage securing an 8% per annum note (interest rate of similar notes at July 1, 19X1). The note is due in quarterly payments of $5,000 plus interest on January 1, April 1, July 1, and October 1 of each

year. Ash made the July 1, 19X1, principal and interest payment personally. The partnership then assumed the obligation for the $300,000 balance.

c. The agreement further provided that Ash had contributed a certain intangible benefit to the partnership because of her many years of business activity in the area serviced by the new partnership. The assigned value of this intangible asset plus the net tangible assets she contributed gave Ash a 60% initial capital interest in the partnership.
d. Ash was designated the only active partner, at an annual salary of $24,000 plus an annual bonus of 5% of net income after deducting her salary but before deducting interest on partners' capital investments (see below). Both the salary and the bonus are to be recorded as operating expenses of the partnership.
e. Each partner is to receive a 10% return on average capital investment; such interest is to be an expense of the partnership.
f. All remaining profits or losses are to be shared equally.

2. On October 1, 19X1, Burch sold his partnership interest and rights as of July 1, 19X1, to Cherry for $370,000. Ash agreed to accept Cherry as a partner if he would contribute sufficient cash to meet the October 1, 19X1, principal and interest payment on the mortgage note. Cherry made the payment from personal funds.
3. On January 1, 19X2, Ash and Cherry admitted a new partner, Douglas. Douglas invested $150,000 cash for a 10% capital interest based on the initial investments (tangible and intangible) at July 1, 19X1, of Ash and Burch, plus Douglas' capital contribution of $150,000. At January 1, 19X2, the book values of the partnership's assets and liabilities approximated their fair market values. Douglas contributed no intangible benefit to the partnership.

   Similar to the other partners, Douglas is to receive a 10% return on his average capital investment. His investment also entitled him to 20% of the partnership's profits or losses as defined above. For the year ended June 30, 19X2, however, Douglas would receive one-half his pro rata share of the profits or losses.
4. The accounting records show that on February 1, 19X2, the Other Miscellaneous Expenses account had been charged $3,600 for hospital expenses incurred by Ash's eight-year-old daughter, Fern.
5. All salary payments to Ash have been charged to her drawing account. On June 1, 19X2, Cherry made a $33,000 withdrawal. These are the only transactions recorded in the partners' drawing accounts.
6. Presented below is a trial balance, which summarizes the partnership's general ledger balances at June 30, 19X2. The general ledger has not been closed.

	Debit	Credit
Current Assets	$ 307,000	
Fixed Assets	1,285,000	
Current Liabilities		$ 104,100
8% Mortgage Note Payable		285,000
Ash, Capital		515,000
Cherry, Capital		400,000
Douglas, Capital		150,000
Ash, Drawing	24,000	

Cherry, Drawing	33,000	
Douglas, Drawing	–0–	
Sales		946,900
Cost of Sales	695,600	
Administrative Expenses	28,000	
Other Miscellaneous Expenses	11,000	
Interest Expense	17,400	
Totals	$2,401,000	$2,401,000

Required:

Prepare a worksheet to adjust the net income (loss) and partners' Capital accounts for the year ended June 30, 19X2, and to close the net income (loss) to the partners' Capital accounts at June 30, 19X2. Supporting schedules should be in good form. Amortization of goodwill, if any, is to be over a 10-year period. (Ignore all tax considerations.) Use the following column headings and begin with balances from the books as shown:

	Net Income (Loss)	Partners' Capital			Other Accounts	
		Ash	Cherry	Douglas	Amount	
Description	(Dr.) Cr.	(Dr.) Cr.	(Dr.) Cr.	(Dr.) Cr.	Dr. (Cr.)	Name
Book balances at June 30, 19X2	$194,900	$515,000	$400,000	$150,000		

(AICPA adapted)

25

Partnerships: Liquidations

AN OVERVIEW OF PARTNERSHIP LIQUIDATIONS

The termination of a partnership's business activities is known as **liquidation.** A partnership may be liquidated for many reasons—for example, the original agreed-upon term of existence has expired, the business is not as successful as expected, or the partnership is in serious financial difficulty. Although a partnership in serious financial difficulty may attempt rehabilitation either by filing under Chapter 11 of the Bankruptcy Reform Act of 1978 or through a troubled debt restructuring outside of bankruptcy court, such courses of action for partnerships do not entail any significant special problems not already discussed for corporations. Consequently, we restrict our discussion in this chapter to the process of liquidation.

The liquidation process for partnerships is in several respects identical to the liquidation process for corporations. Over a period of time, the noncash assets of the business are converted into cash (the realization process), creditors are paid to the extent possible, and remaining funds, if any, are distributed to the owners (partners). Partnership liquidations, however, are different from corporate liquidations in the following respects:

1. Because partners have unlimited liability, any partner may be called upon to contribute additional funds to the partnership if partnership assets are insufficient to satisfy creditors' claims.
2. To the extent that a partner does not make good a deficit balance in his or her Capital account, the remaining partners must absorb such deficit balance. Absorption of a partner's deficit balance gives the absorbing partners legal recourse against the partner.

The special problems created by these two situations are discussed throughout this chapter.

Liquidations may be categorized broadly as lump-sum liquidations and installment liquidations.

1. In *lump-sum liquidations,* no distributions are made to the partners until the realization process is completed, when the full amount of the realization gain or loss is known.
2. In *installment liquidations,* distributions are made to some or all of the partners as cash becomes available. Thus, cash distributions are made to partners before the full amount of the realization gain or loss is known.

Within each category, a variety of situations may arise concerning the ability of the partnership and the individual partners to satisfy the claims of partnership creditors. Before discussing each situation in detail, we discuss some general aspects of liquidations.

Procedures for Minimizing Inequities among Partners

Sharing of Gains and Losses. Gains and losses incurred on the realization of assets may be allocated among the partners in the manner they have agreed to in the partnership agreement. If the partnership agreement is silent with respect to the sharing of gains and losses during liquidation, then the Uniform Partnership Act (UPA) treats such gains and losses in the same way as preliquidation profits and losses—that is, gains and losses are allocated in accordance with the profit and loss sharing formula. Most partnerships follow the profit and loss sharing formula in distributing gains and losses incurred during liquidation. This is the most equitable manner for the following reasons:

1. The cumulative profit and loss of a partnership during its existence is the difference between total capital contributions and total capital withdrawals. Accordingly, the cumulative profit or loss of a partnership during its existence should include start-up periods, normal operating periods, and wind-down periods.
2. Certain gains and losses recognized during the liquidation process actually may have ocurred during normal operating periods. This would be the case when (a) land or buildings have been held for several years and appreciated in value prior to the liquidation, and (b) certain accounts receivable should have been written off as uncollectible before liquidation. The use of a method other than the profit and loss sharing formula would result in inequities among the partners.

If a partner's Capital account is not sufficient to absorb his or her share of the losses incurred in liquidation, Section 18 of the UPA provides that "each partner . . . must contribute towards the losses . . . sustained by the partnership according to his share in the profits." In other words, a partner must contribute additional funds to the partnership to eliminate any deficit balance in his or her Capital account created by losses incurred through normal operations or in the liquidation process. If such a partner does not have the personal resources to eliminate this deficit, the remaining partners must absorb the capital deficit, resulting in inequities to them. A basic procedure that may minimize such potential inequities is discussed in the next section.

Advance Planning when the Partnership is Formed. Although every partnership commences business under the "going concern" concept, it would be unrealistic if the partners did not acknowledge the possibility that the partnership may have to be liquidated at some time. It is in the interest of each partner, therefore, to take prudent steps to minimize the possibility of inequities occurring in liquidation. Inequities among partners may arise during liquidation if a deficit balance is created in a partner's Capital account (as a result of losses incurred during the conversion of noncash assets into cash), and that partner cannot contribute capital to eliminate the deficit. The partners who do not have deficit balances in their Capital accounts must absorb the deficit balance of the partner who does. In other words, they must absorb losses greater than their agreed-upon profit and loss sharing percentage.

Because a partnership has no control over its partners' personal affairs, it has no assurance that its partners will have sufficient personal funds to contribute if a deficit balance is created during liquidation. Accordingly, the partnership should be operated in a manner that minimizes the possibility of a deficit balance occurring. If the partnership agreement specifies that all partners' capital balances are to be maintained in the profit and loss sharing ratio, then a partnership may incur losses on the conversion of noncash assets into cash up to the total equity of the partnership, without creating a deficit balance in any partner's Capital account. This safeguard is so important that many partnerships (including most of the international accounting partnerships) require Capital accounts to be maintained in the profit and loss sharing ratio. Furthermore, as cash is available for distribution to the partners (a situation that occurs only if losses during liquidation are less than the total partnership equity), such cash may be distributed to the partners in the profit and loss sharing ratio with complete assurance that no inequities will result. In such situations, the liquidation process is quite simple. Unfortunately, not all partnerships use such a provision. Partners in such partnerships needlessly expose themselves to potential inequities in the event of liquidation, making the liquidation process much more complex.

Although the potential for inequities occurring during liquidation cannot be completely eliminated, a partnership that requires Capital accounts to be maintained in the profit and loss sharing ratio has taken a big step toward minimizing any potential inequities that may arise.

Rule of Setoff. When a partnership has a loan outstanding **to a partner,** the partnership receivable should be subtracted, or *set off,* from the partner's Capital account. It would not be equitable to assume that the receivable is uncollectible (even though the partner may not have sufficient personal assets to repay the loan) and thereby allocate the loss among all the partners. The partner's Capital account less the receivable represents the partner's true capital investment.

When a partner has a loan outstanding **to the partnership,** the loan does not rank on an equal level with other partnership liabilities. Section 40 of the UPA states that the *order of payment* to creditors and partners during liquidation is as follows:

(I) Those owing to creditors other than partners.
(II) Those owing to partners other than for capital and profits [loans].
(III) Those owing to partners in respect of capital.
(IV) Those owing to partners in respect of profit.

When profits and losses are closed to the partners' Capital accounts at each year-end, the last two categories may be considered one amount, which is the balance in each partner's Capital account. Although this section of the UPA implies that partners' loans are paid off before any cash distributions are made to partners in liquidation of their capital balances, a strict application of this order of payment could result in inequities among the partners. For example, a partner with a loan to a partnership could be repaid the loan, a deficit balance could be created in his or her Capital account at a later date because of losses on the realization of assets, and the partner might not be able to make a capital contribution to eliminate that deficit balance. The other partners would have to absorb such partner's deficit balance and thus incur a greater portion of the losses during liquidation than they originally agreed to. The legal doctrine of **setoff**—whereby a deficit balance in a partner's Capital account may be set off against any balance existing in his or her loan account—has been incorporated into accountants' procedures for determining which partners should receive cash as it becomes available. These procedures effectively treat the loan as an additional capital investment. The mechanical procedures, which are different in lump-sum liquidations and installment liquidations, are discussed and illustrated later in the chapter.

The Statement of Realization and Liquidation

Because normal operations do not take place during the liquidation period, traditional financial statements are not appropriate. Instead, the partners prefer to have a statement that provides information on the following:

1. Gains and losses on the realization of assets, including the impact of such gains and losses on the partners' Capital accounts.
2. Payments that have been made to creditors and partners.
3. The noncash assets still to be converted into cash.

Accordingly, accountants have devised a statement called the **statement of realization and liquidation** to provide this information. The statement is entirely historical; it reflects only the actual transactions that have occurred during the liquidation period up to the date of the statement. If the liquidation process takes place over several months, the statement is updated periodically as noncash assets are converted into cash and payments are made to creditors, partners, or both. Other than the allocation of realization gains and losses among the partners and the exercising of the right of setoff, the statement is essentially a summary of cash inflows and outflows.

Liquidation Expenses

Certain costs incurred during the liquidation process should be treated as a reduction of the proceeds from the sale of noncash assets—for example, costs to complete inventory, sales commissions and shipping costs related to the disposal of inventory, escrow and title transfer fees associated with the sale of real property, and costs of removing equipment. Other liquidation costs should be treated as expenses. It is preferable to make a reasonable estimate of these expenses at the beginning of the liquidation process and record an estimated liability in the general ledger at that time, adjusting the liability as necessary during the liquidation process. Recording the estimated liability at the inception of the liquidation process minimizes the possibility of making excess cash distributions to partners. Any cash available for distribution to partners should be set aside in an amount equal to the remaining estimated liability so that it is not distributed to partners.

LUMP-SUM LIQUIDATIONS

In a **lump-sum liquidation,** all noncash assets are converted to cash and outside creditors are paid in full before cash is distributed to the partners. Thus, the full amount of the gain or loss on realization of assets is known before the partners receive any cash distributions. Lump-sum liquidations are rare or nonexistent, because partners liquidate their loan and Capital accounts as cash becomes available for distribution. Usually, partners have personal needs for cash, and there is no sound business reason for waiting until the very last asset is converted to cash before distributing any cash to the partners. We illustrate several lump-sum liquidations for instructional purposes only.

Partnership Is Solvent and All Partners Are Personally Solvent

In the first three illustrations in this section, (1) the partnership is solvent (the fair value of partnership assets is sufficient to satisfy outside creditors' claims), and (2) all partners who must make capital contributions have either sufficient loans to the partnership (for purposes of exercising the right of setoff) or are personally solvent, so that the capital deficit from losses incurred during the realization process is eliminated by contributions.

Illustration

LOSS ON REALIZATION DOES NOT CREATE A DEFICIT BALANCE IN ANY PARTNER'S CAPITAL ACCOUNT

To illustrate how the statement of realization and liquidation is prepared in a lump-sum liquidation, assume partners A and B share profits and losses in the ratio 3:2, respectively, and the balance sheet of the partnership at the beginning of the liquidation process is as follows:

A AND B PARTNERSHIP
Balance Sheet
May 31, 19X5

Cash	$ 5,000	Liabilities	$20,000
Noncash assets	70,000	Loan, Partner B	3,000
		Capital:	
		Partner A	37,000
		Partner B	15,000
	$75,000		$75,000

Also, assume during June 19X5 that (1) the noncash assets of $70,000 are converted into $40,000 cash, resulting in a $30,000 loss, which is distributed 60% to partner A ($18,000) and 40% to partner B ($12,000); (2) outside creditors are paid in full; and (3) the remaining cash is distributed to the partners. The statement of realization and liquidation covering the entire liquidation period would be prepared as in Illustration 25-1. The following points are important for understanding Illustration 25-1.

1. The format of the statement does not combine the loan account of partner B with his Capital account. The loan is a bona fide loan and not a capital investment.
2. Cash distributions were made in accordance with the priority set forth in Section 40 of the UPA.

Illustration 25-1

A AND B PARTNERSHIP
Statement of Realization and Liquidation
June 19X5

	Assets		Outside	Loan	Partners' Capital	
	Cash	Noncash	Liabilities	B	A (60%)[a]	B (40%)[a]
Preliquidation balances	$ 5,000	$70,000	$20,000	$3,000	$37,000	$15,000
Realization of assets and allocation of loss	40,000	(70,000)			(18,000)	(12,000)
Subtotal	$45,000	$ -0-	$20,000	$3,000	$19,000	$ 3,000
Cash distributions:						
Outside creditors	(20,000)		(20,000)			
Partner's loan	(3,000)			(3,000)		
Partners' capital	(22,000)				(19,000)	(3,000)
Postliquidation balances	$ -0-		$ -0-	$ -0-	$ -0-	$ -0-

[a]Denotes profit and loss sharing percentage.

Illustration

LOSS ON REALIZATION CREATES A DEFICIT BALANCE IN ONE PARTNER'S CAPITAL ACCOUNT: RIGHT OF SETOFF EXERCISED

Assume the information in the preceding illustration, except that partner B's loan account is $10,000 instead of $3,000 and his Capital account is $8,000 instead of $15,000. The statement of realization and liquidation would be prepared as shown in Illustration 25-2. The following points are important for understanding Illustration 25-2:

1. The fact that partners' loans are assigned a higher priority for repayment than partnership Capital accounts under Section 40 of the UPA is not significant if a partner with a loan account also has a deficit balance in his or her Capital account—that is, the full amount of the loan is not paid before payments are made to partners in liquidation of their Capital accounts.
2. The $4,000 deficit in partner B's Capital account after the realization loss of $30,000 on the noncash assets means that partner B must contribute $4,000 to the partnership, so that he can fully absorb his share of the loss on realization.
3. Partner B did not contribute $4,000 to the partnership to eliminate his Capital account deficit, because he could exercise the right of setoff whereby $4,000 was transferred from his loan account to his Capital account.

Illustration 25-2

A AND B PARTNERSHIP
Statement of Realization and Liquidation
June 19X5

	Assets		Outside	Loan	Partners' Capital	
	Cash	Noncash	Liabilities	B	A (60%)[a]	B (40%)[a]
Preliquidation balances ...	$ 5,000	$70,000	$20,000	$10,000	$37,000	$ 8,000
Realization of assets and allocation of loss	40,000	(70,000)			(18,000)	(12,000)
Subtotal	$45,000	$ -0-	$20,000	$10,000	$19,000	$ (4,000)
Right of setoff exercised...				(4,000)		4,000)
Subtotal	$45,000		$20,000	$ 6,000	$19,000	$ -0-
Cash distributions:						
Outside creditors	(20,000)		(20,000)			
Partner's loan..............	(6,000)			(6,000)		
Partners' capital..........	(19,000)				(19,000)	
Postliquidation balances..	$ -0-		$ -0-	$ -0-	$ -0-	

[a]Denotes profit and loss sharing percentage.

4. Each partner received the same amount of cash in Illustration 25-1 and 25-2. For all practical purposes, partner B's loan account is the equivalent of an additional capital investment for liquidation purposes.

Illustration

LOSS ON REALIZATION CREATES A DEFICIT BALANCE IN ONE PARTNER'S CAPITAL ACCOUNT: RIGHT OF SETOFF EXERCISED AND ADDITIONAL CAPITAL CONTRIBUTION IS REQUIRED AND MADE

Assume the information in the preceding illustration, except that the loss on the realization of the noncash assets is $50,000 rather than $30,000. This additional $20,000 loss will result in partner B's having a capital deficit, which is not completely eliminated on his exercising the right of setoff. Assume that partner B is personally solvent and makes the required capital contribution to eliminate the remainder of his capital deficit. The statement of realization and liquidation would be prepared as shown in Illustration 25-3.

Partnership Is Solvent and at Least One Partner Is Personally Insolvent

In the next two illustrations, at least one partner is personally insolvent and unable to make a capital contribution to eliminate his or her capital

Illustration 25-3

A AND B PARTNERSHIP
Statement of Realization and Liquidation
June 19X5

	Assets		Outside	Loan	Partners' Capital	
	Cash	Noncash	Liabilities	B	A (60%)[a]	B (40%)[a]
Preliquidation balances ..	$ 5,000	$70,000	$20,000	$10,000	$37,000	$ 8,000
Realization of assets and allocation of loss	20,000	(70,000)			(30,000)	(20,000)
Subtotal	$25,000	$ –0–	$20,000	$10,000	$ 7,000	$(12,000)
Right of setoff exercised..				(10,000)		10,000
Subtotal	$25,000		$20,000	$ –0–	$ 7,000	$ (2,000)
Cash contribution by B ..	2,000					2,000
Subtotal	$27,000		$20,000		$ 7,000	$ –0–
Cash distributions						
Outside creditors	(20,000)		(20,000)			
Partner's capital..........	(7,000)				(7,000)	
Postliquidation balances.	$ –0–		$ –0–		$ –0–	

[a]Denotes profit and loss sharing percentage.

deficit. In such circumstances, the remaining partners must absorb the capital deficit of the insolvent partner in their respective profit and loss sharing ratio. If this, in turn, causes a capital deficit for an absorbing partner, then that partner must make a capital contribution to eliminate the deficit. If such partner also is personally insolvent, then his or her capital deficit must be absorbed by the remaining partners, using their respective profit and loss sharing ratio.

The absorption of a partner's deficit capital balance by other partners is a violation of the UPA, in that the partner who cannot eliminate his or her deficit capital balance has broken the terms of the partnership agreement. The other partners have legal recourse against the personal assets of the defaulting partner. This situation raises the question of how such claims against the personal assets of the defaulting partner are treated in relation to claims of personal creditors of the defaulting partner. In the next section of the chapter, we answer this question and discuss situations in which the **partnership is insolvent** and at least one partner is personally insolvent.

Illustration

LOSS ON REALIZATION CREATES A DEFICIT BALANCE IN ONE PARTNER'S CAPITAL ACCOUNT: RIGHT OF SETOFF EXERCISED AND ADDITIONAL CAPITAL CONTRIBUTION IS REQUIRED BUT NOT MADE

Assume partners A, B, C, and D share profits in the ratio 4:2:2:2, respectively. The partnership's balance sheet at the beginning of the liquidation process is as follows:

A, B, C and D PARTNERSHIP
Balance Sheet
June 30, 19X5

Cash	$ 10,000	Liabilities	$157,000
Noncash assets	290,000	Loan:	
		Partner B	10,000
		Partner C	5,000
		Partner D	2,000
		Capital:	
		Partner A	70,000
		Partner B	30,000
		Partner C	20,000
		Partner D	6,000
	$300,000		$300,000

Assume also that during July 19X5 the noncash assets realize $210,000 cash, resulting in a realization loss of $80,000, which is shared among the partners (using the profit and loss sharing ratio 4:2:2:2) as follows: A, $32,000; B, $16,000; C, $16,000; and D, $16,000. The realization loss creates a deficit in D's Capital account, which is not completely eliminated through his exercising the right of setoff. D must make an additional capital contribution of $8,000 but is unable to do so. As a result, his $8,000 capital deficit must be allocated to partners A, B, and C in their profit and loss sharing ratio of 4:2:2, respectively. Assuming all cash was distributed in July 19X5, the statement of realization and liquidation would be prepared as shown in Illustration 25-4. The following points are important for understanding Illustration 25-4:

1. Because partner D was unable to eliminate the deficit balance in his Capital account, the remaining partners had to bear a greater percentage of the realization loss than their individual profit and loss sharing percentages. For example, partner A suffered a total loss of $36,000 ($32,000 + $4,000). This represents 45% of the $80,000 total realization loss, which is greater than her stipulated profit and loss sharing percentage of 40%. Partners A, B, and C needlessly exposed themselves to this additional $8,000 loss by not employing the fundamental safeguard provision of maintaining Capital accounts in the profit and loss sharing ratio.
2. The illustration assumes that partner D was unable to make any of the required contribution. If a partial contribution had been made, then a smaller deficit balance would have had to be absorbed by the remaining partners.
3. A partner with a deficit balance may indicate that he is unable to eliminate completely the deficit balance when it is created but that he might be able to make a capital contribution at a later date (which may or may not be specified). If partner D had indicated this, the available $220,000 cash could have been distributed to the outside creditors and the remaining partners. The partnership books then could be kept open until partner D makes a capital contribution or it subsequently is determined that he cannot make a payment after all. This procedure could result in a lengthy delay in completing the partnership liquidation. There is no sound reason for keeping the partnership books open indefinitely, thereby delaying the completion of the liquidation process, merely because of partner D's uncertain financial situation. When partner D's Capital account deficit was created (and not completely eliminated through exercising the right of setoff), he became liable for his deficit to the other partners. Accordingly, if partner D later makes a capital contribution, he makes the payment directly to the other partners. Consequently, in situations involving lump-sum liquidations in which a partner cannot immediately eliminate his or her capital deficit, the accountant should complete the liquidation process by transferring the capital deficit to the Capital accounts of the remaining partners (using their respective profit and loss sharing ratios). The partnership books may then be closed, and the liquidation process can be completed.

Illustration 25-4

A, B, C, and D PARTNERSHIP
Statement of Realization and Liquidation
July, 19X5

	Assets		Outside	Partners' Loans			Partners' Capital			
	Cash	Noncash	Liabilities	B	C	D	A (40%)[a]	B (20%)[a]	C (20%)[a]	D (20%)[a]
Preliquidation balances..	$ 10,000	$290,000	$157,000	$10,000	$5,000	$2,000	$70,000	$30,000	$20,000	$ 6,000
Realization of assets and allocation of loss.........	210,000	(290,000)					(32,000)	(16,000)	(16,000)	(16,000)
Subtotal..................	$220,000	$ –0–	$157,000	$10,000	$5,000	$2,000	$38,000	$14,000	$ 4,000	$(10,000)
Right of setoff exercised..						(2,000)				2,000
Subtotal..................	$220,000		$157,000	$10,000	$5,000	$ –0–	$38,000	$14,000	$ 4,000	$ (8,000)
Absorption of D's capital deficit..............							(4,000)	(2,000)	(2,000)	8,000
Subtotal..................	$220,000		$157,000	$10,000	$5,000		$34,000	$12,000	$ 2,000	$ –0–
Cash distributions:										
Outside creditors........	(157,000)		(157,000)							
Partners' loans............	(15,000)			(10,000)	(5,000)					
Partners' capital..........	(48,000)						(34,000)	(12,000)	(2,000)	
Postliquidation balances..	$ –0–		$ –0–	$ –0–	$ –0–		$ –0–	$ –0–	$ –0–	

[a]Denotes profit and loss sharing percentage.

Illustration

LOSS ON REALIZATION CREATES A DEFICIT BALANCE IN ONE PARTNER'S CAPITAL ACCOUNT—ABSORPTION BY OTHER PARTNERS CREATES A DEFICIT BALANCE IN ANOTHER PARTNER'S CAPITAL ACCOUNT

Assume the information in the preceding illustration, except that the noncash assets are sold for only $170,000. This results in a realization loss of $120,000 rather than $80,000. The $120,000 realization loss is allocated among the partners (using the profit and loss sharing ratio 4:2:2:2) as follows: A, $48,000: B, $24,000; C, $24,000; and D, $24,000. In addition to the previously described consequences to partner D, the greater loss results in partner C being unable to absorb fully his share of partner D's deficit balance. Thus, partner C has a deficit balance that he cannot eliminate through setoff or contribution. His capital deficit, in turn, must be allocated to partners A and B in their respective profit and loss sharing ratio of 4:2. (Partners A and B have legal recourse against the personal assets of partners C and D—such recourse is discussed in the next section of this chapter.) Assuming all cash was distributed in July 19X5, the statement of realization and liquidation would be prepared as shown in Illustration 25-5.

Partnership Is Insolvent and at Least One Partner Is Personally Solvent

In the next two illustrations, the partnership is insolvent—that is, the loss on the realization of noncash assets is greater than the total of the partners' capital (including their loan accounts). Because unlimited liability is a feature of the partnership form of organization, creditors may seek payment from any or all of the partners as individuals.

Illustration

LOSS ON REALIZATION CREATES A DEFICIT BALANCE IN CERTAIN PARTNERS' CAPITAL ACCOUNTS—ALL PARTNERS ARE PERSONALLY SOLVENT

In this illustration, all the partners are personally solvent, and the partners with deficit capital balances contribute funds to the partnership to eliminate their capital deficits, enabling creditors to be paid in full by the partnership. Using the same preliquidation balances that are given for Illustration 25-5, assume the noncash assets of $290,000 are sold for $130,000, resulting in a realization loss of $160,000. The realization loss is shared among the partners (using the profit and loss sharing ratio 4:2:2:2) as follows: A, $64,000; B, $32,000; C, $32,000; and D, $32,000.

Illustration 25-5

A, B, C, and D PARTNERSHIP
Statement of Realization and Liquidation
July 19X5

	Assets			Partners' Loans			Partners' Capital			
	Cash	Noncash	Outside Liabilities	B	C	D	A (40%)[a]	B (20%)[a]	C (20%)[a]	D (20%)[a]
Preliquidation balances	$ 10,000	$290,000	$157,000	$10,000	$5,000	$2,000	$70,000	$30,000	$20,000	$ 6,000
Realization of assets and allocation of loss	170,000	(290,000)					(48,000)	(24,000)	(24,000)	(24,000)
Subtotal	$180,000	$ –0–	$157,000	$10,000	$5,000	$2,000	$22,000	$ 6,000	$ (4,000)	$(18,000)
Right of setoff exercised					(4,000)	(2,000)			4,000	2,000
Subtotal	$180,000		$157,000	$10,000	$1,000	$ –0–	$22,000	$ 6,000	$ –0–	$(16,000)
Absorption of D's capital deficit							(8,000)	(4,000)	$ (4,000)	16,000
Subtotal	$180,000		$157,000	$10,000	$1,000		$14,000	$ 2,000	$ (4,000)	$ –0–
Right of setoff exercised					(1,000)				1,000	
Subtotal	$180,000		$157,000	$10,000	$ –0–		$14,000	$ 2,000	$ (3,000)	
Absorption of C's capital deficit							(2,000)	(1,000)	3,000	
Subtotal	$180,000		$157,000	$10,000			$12,000	$ 1,000	$ –0–	
Cash distributions:										
Outside creditors	(157,000)		(157,000)							
Partner's loan	(10,000)			(10,000)						
Partners' capital	(13,000)						(12,000)	(1,000)		
Postliquidation balances	$ –0–		$ –0–	$ –0–			$ –0–	$ –0–		

[a]Denotes profit and loss sharing percentage.

After exercising the right of setoff, partner A has a capital balance of $6,000; partner B has a loan balance of $8,000; and partners C and D have capital deficits of $7,000 and $24,000, respectively. At this point, the available $140,000 cash may be distributed to outside creditors. Assuming partners C and D contribute funds to the partnership to eliminate their capital deficits, the $31,000 cash then may be distributed to outside creditors and partners A and B. The statement of realization and liquidation would be prepared as shown in Illustration 25-6.

In this Illustration we assume that partners C and D made additional cash contributions to the partnership, thereby eliminating their capital deficits. Thus, the partnership could make the remaining $17,000 payment to the outside creditors. Creditors occasionally take legal action against some or all of the partners as individuals when the creditors do not receive full satisfaction from the partnership. As a result, a partner personally may make payments to partnership creditors. Such payments should be reflected in the general ledger and on the statement of realization and liquidation as a reduction of partnership liabilities and an additional capital contribution by that partner. A partner's personal payments to creditors are in substance the equivalent of a cash contribution to the partnership that the partnership then distributes to the creditors.

Illustration

LOSS ON REALIZATION CREATES A DEFICIT BALANCE IN CERTAIN PARTNERS' CAPITAL ACCOUNTS—CERTAIN PARTNERS ARE PERSONALLY INSOLVENT

Before illustrating in detail a situation in which a partnership is insolvent and certain of its partners are personally insolvent, we discuss the following legal questions raised in such circumstances:

1. If partnership creditors initiate legal proceedings against a partner who is personally insolvent, what would be the legal status (priority of payment) of such claims in relation to the claims of that partner's personal creditors?
2. If a partner is personally insolvent and unable to eliminate the deficit balance in his or her Capital account, thereby causing other partners to absorb that deficit balance (which is a breach of the partnership agreement entitling the wronged partners to legal recourse against the defaulting partner), what is the legal status of such claims in relation to the claims of that partner's personal creditors?
3. If a partner is personally insolvent, to what extent may such partner's personal creditors obtain payments from the partnership?

The answers to the first two questions are found in Section 40(i) of the UPA:

Illustration 25-6

A, B, C, and D PARTNERSHIP
Statement of Realization and Liquidation
July 19X5

	Assets		Outside	Partners' Loans			Partners' Capital			
	Cash	Noncash	Liabilities	B	C	D	A (40%)[a]	B (20%)[a]	C (20%)[a]	D (20%)[a]
Preliquidation balances...	$ 10,000	$290,000	$157,000	$10,000	$5,000	$2,000	$70,000	$30,000	$20,000	$ 6,000
Realization of assets and allocation of loss..........	130,000	(290,000)					(64,000)	(32,000)	(32,000)	(32,000)
Subtotal..................	$140,000	$ –0–	$157,000	$10,000	$5,000	$2,000	$ 6,000	$ (2,000)	$(12,000)	$(26,000)
Exercise right of setoff				(2,000)	(5,000)	(2,000)		2,000	5,000	2,000
Subtotal..................	$140,000		$157,000	$ 8,000	$ –0–	$ –0–	$ 6,000	$ –0–	$ (7,000)	$(24,000)
Distribution to outside creditors..........	(140,000)		(140,000)							
Subtotal..................	$ –0–		$ 17,000	$ 8,000			$ 6,000		$ (7,000)	$(24,000)
Contributions by C and D	31,000								7,000	24,000
Subtotal..................	$ 31,000		$ 17,000	$ 8,000			$ 6,000		$ –0–	$ –0–
Cash distributions:										
Outside creditors	(17,000)		(17,000)							
Partner's loan	(8,000)			(8,000)						
Partner's capital...........	(6,000)						(6,000)			
Postliquidation balances...	$ –0–		$ –0–	$ –0–			$ –0–			

[a]Denotes profit and loss sharing percentage.

Where a partner has become bankrupt or his estate is insolvent, the claims against his separate property shall rank in the following order:
(I) Those owing to separate creditors,
(II) Those owing to partnership creditors,
(III) Those owing to partners by way of contribution.

The answer to the third question is found in Section 40(b) of the UPA, which specifies that partnership creditors have first claim on partnership assets. Consequently, these two sections of the UPA are consistent with the longstanding court procedure of **marshalling of assets,** which is summarized as follows: Partnership creditors have first priority as to partnership assets, and personal creditors of an insolvent partner have first priority as to the personal assets of such partner. However, the Bankruptcy Reform Act of 1978 modified this doctrine so that partnership creditors now share on a pro rata basis with personal creditors of an insolvent partner in the distribution of the personal assets of such partner.

Application of Marshalling of Assets. To illustrate how the marshalling of assets procedure is applied, assume the information in Illustration 25-6 with respect to partners' balances after (1) the realization loss of $160,000 is distributed; (2) the right of setoff is exercised; and (3) payment of $140,000 is made to outside creditors, leaving $17,000 owed to such creditors. At this point, the partners' accounts are as follows:

Partner	Loan Balance	Capital Balance
A		$ 6,000
B	$8,000	
C		(7,000)
D		(24,000)

Assume the personal status of each partner (exclusive of interest in or obligation to the partnership) is as follows:

Partner	Personal Assets	Personal Liabilities	Personal Net Worth (Deficit)
A	$50,000	$25,000	$25,000
B	4,000	15,000	(11,000)
C	16,000	6,000	10,000
D	20,000	33,000	(13,000)

1. Partner D has a capital deficit and is personally insolvent. Thus, none of his personal assets is available for contribution to the partnership, because his personal creditors are entitled to all his personal assets. Consequently, his $24,000 capital deficit must be absorbed by part-

ners A, B, and C in their respective profit and loss sharing ratio, 4:2:2. Partner A's share is $12,000; partner B's share is $6,000; and partner C's share is $6,000.
2. Partner C had a $7,000 capital deficit, which increased to $13,000 when he absorbed his share of partner D's capital deficit. Partner C has a personal net worth of $10,000. Thus, he can contribute $10,000 to the partnership, leaving a $3,000 deficit, which must be absorbed by partners A and B in their respective profit and loss sharing ratio of 4:2. Partner A's share is $2,000 and Partner B's share is $1,000.
3. Partner B had a loan balance of $8,000. However, his Capital account was charged with $6,000 when partner D's capital deficit was written off and $1,000 when partner C's capital deficit was written off. Thus, $7,000 must be transferred from his loan account under the right of setoff to eliminate his capital deficit. This leaves $1,000 in his loan account, which, when distributed to him, is available to his personal creditors because he is personally insolvent.
4. Because partner A has the largest personal net worth, let us assume that partnership creditors took legal action against her (as opposed to proceeding against partner C, who is the only other personally solvent partner from whom they could collect anything). The creditors collected the $17,000 owed them from partner A personally. Partner A had a capital balance of $6,000, which was reduced by $12,000 for her share of partner D's capital deficit and $2,000 for her share of partner C's capital deficit. This gives her a capital deficit of $8,000. Her $17,000 payment to the partnership creditors, however, is the equivalent of a capital contribution. Thus, her Capital account deficit is eliminated, and she now has a positive capital balance of $9,000.
5. This leaves the partnership with $10,000 cash, which is distributed to partner B ($1,000 in payment of his loan) and partner A ($9,000 in liquidation of her capital balance).

Illustration 25-7 summarizes the preceding sequence of events in a statement of realization and liquidation.

INSTALLMENT LIQUIDATIONS

In an **installment liquidation,** the conversion of noncash assets into cash takes place over a period of time. As a result, the partnership realizes greater proceeds than would be possible in a quick liquidation. Because of the lengthier conversion period, cash may become available for distribution to partners long before the last noncash asset is sold. In such situations, the partners usually want cash distributed as it becomes available.

The Two Worst-Case Assumptions

If Capital accounts are not maintained in the profit and loss sharing ratio, cash may not be distributed to the partners on some arbitrary basis such as the profit and loss sharing ratio, the capital balances ratio, or personal

Illustration 25-7

A, B, C, and D PARTNERSHIP
Statement of Realization and Liquidation
July 19X5

	Assets			Partners' Loans			Partners' Capital			
	Cash	Noncash	Outside Liabilities	B	C	D	A (40%)[a]	B (20%)[a]	C (20%)[a]	D (20%)[a]
Preliquidation balances	$ 10,000	$290,000	$157,000	$10,000	$5,000	$2,000	$70,000	$30,000	$20,000	$ 6,000
Realization of assets and allocation of loss	130,000	(290,000)					(64,000)	(32,000)	(32,000)	(32,000)
Subtotal	$140,000	$ -0-	$157,000	$10,000	$5,000	$2,000	$ 6,000	$ (2,000)	$(12,000)	$(26,000)
Exercise right of setoff				(2,000)	(5,000)	(2,000)		2,000	5,000	2,000
Subtotal	$140,000		$157,000	$ 8,000	$ -0-	$ -0-	$ 6,000	$ -0-	$ (7,000)	$(24,000)
Distribution to outside creditors	(140,000)		(140,000)							
Subtotal	$ -0-		$ 17,000	$ 8,000			$ 6,000		$ (7,000)	$(24,000)
Absorption of D's deficit							(12,000)	(6,000)	(6,000)	24,000
Subtotal	$ -0-		$ 17,000	$ 8,000			$ (6,000)	$ (6,000)	$(13,000)	$ -0-
Capital contribution by C	10,000								10,000	
Subtotal	$ 10,000		$ 17,000	$ 8,000			$ (6,000)	$ (6,000)	$ (3,000)	
Absorption of C's deficit							(2,000)	(1,000)	3,000	
Subtotal	$ 10,000		$ 17,000	$ 8,000			$ (8,000)	$ (7,000)	$ -0-	
Exercise right of setoff				(7,000)				7,000		
Subtotal	$ 10,000		$ 17,000	$ 1,000			$ (8,000)	$ -0-		
Capital contribution by A			(17,000)				17,000			
Subtotal	$ 10,000		$ -0-	$ 1,000			$ 9,000			
Cash distributions:										
Partner's loan	(1,000)			(1,000)						
Partner's capital	(9,000)						(9,000)			
Postliquidation balances	$ -0-			$ -0-			$ -0-			

[a]Denotes profit and loss sharing percentage.

needs. Such a distribution might result in later inequities to certain partners. For example, cash may be distributed to a partner who may not be able to return such cash to the partnership if a deficit balance subsequently is created in his or her Capital account as a result of future losses on the conversion of noncash assets into cash. Such partner's deficit balance would have to be allocated to partners who have credit balances, and those partners would have to bear a greater portion of the loss than their profit and loss sharing percentages. To prevent this potential inequity accountants use two worst-case assumptions to determine which partners should receive available cash at any particular time. These assumptions are as follows:

1. **First worst-case assumption:** All noncash assets are assumed to be completely worthless. Thus, a hypothetical loss equal to the carrying values of noncash assets is assumed to have occurred. On a worksheet, the hypothetical loss is allocated to the partners' Capital account balances existing at that time.
2. **Second worst-case assumption:** If, as a result of the first worst-case assumption, a partner's Capital account is in a deficit position (on the worksheet only), we assume that such partner is not able to make contributions to the partnership to eliminate the hypothetical deficit. (This assumption is made regardless of the partner's personal financial status.) Accordingly, the hypothetical deficit balance is allocated to the partners who have credit balances, using their respective profit and loss sharing ratio. If, in turn, this process creates a hypothetical deficit balance in another partner's Capital account, then such hypothetical deficit balance is allocated (on the worksheet only) to the remaining partners who still have credit balances. This process is repeated until only partners with credit balances remain on the worksheet. Cash may then be distributed to the partners who have credit balances on the worksheet.

The result of these two assumptions is that cash is distributed only to the partners who have capital balances sufficient to absorb their share of (1) the maximum potential loss on noncash assets, and (2) any capital deficiencies that may result to other partners as a result of a maximum loss on noncash assets. In other words, payments may safely be made to such partners with full assurance that the money will not have to be returned to the partnership at some later date in the event of future realization losses.

Under this method of distributing cash to the partners, the Capital accounts are brought into the profit and loss sharing ratio. This is usually accomplished only after several cash distributions have been made. Once the capital accounts have been brought into the profit and loss sharing ratio, cash distributions may be made in the profit and loss sharing ratio. The two worst-case assumptions need not be used for any future cash distributions, because their use would produce the same result as the profit and loss sharing ratio.

Applying the two worst-case assumptions shows that a partner's Capital account (on the worksheet) is reduced for any loans the partnership has outstanding to the partner. Also, a partner's Capital account (on the worksheet) is increased for any loan the partner may have outstanding to the partnership; this automatically provides for the hypothetical exercising of the right of setoff.

Illustration

LOSS ON REALIZATION CREATES A DEFICIT BALANCE IN CERTAIN PARTNERS' CAPITAL ACCOUNTS: ONE PARTNER IS PERSONALLY INSOLVENT

To illustrate how these two worst-case assumptions are applied to an installment liquidation, assume the following:

1. The partnership of A, B, C, and D has the same preliquidation balances as shown in Illustration 25-7.
2. The noncash assets of $290,000 are sold as follows:

Date	Book Value	Proceeds	Loss
July 14, 19X5	$183,000	$168,000	$(15,000)
August 12, 19X5	70,000	25,000	(45,000)
September 21, 19X5	37,000	27,000	(10,000)
	$290,000	$220,000	$(70,000)

3. Cash was distributed to outside creditors and partners as it was available.
4. Partner D could contribute only $4,000 to the partnership during the liquidation proceedings. His remaining $2,000 Capital account deficit had to be absorbed by the other partners.

The statement of realization and liquidation would be prepared as shown in Illustration 25-8. The cash distributions to partners were determined from the **schedule of safe payments** shown in Illustration 25-9, which is a supporting schedule to Illustration 25-8. The schedule of safe payments shows the cash distributions that may be made safely to individual partners in light of the objectives of minimizing potential inequities and limiting the legal exposure of the accountant. The following points are important for understanding both illustrations:

1. The statement of realization and liquidation reflects only the historical transactions as recorded in the general ledger. Although the statement covers the entire liquidation period, it was started when the liquidation process began and then periodically updated as noncash assets were sold and cash distributions were made.

Illustration 25-8

A, B, C, and D PARTNERSHIP
Statement of Realization and Liquidation
July 1, 19X5 through September 21, 19X5

	Assets		Outside	Partners' Loans			Partners' Capital			
	Cash	Noncash	Liabilities	B	C	D	A (40%)[a]	B (20%)[a]	C (20%)[a]	D (20%)[a]
Preliquidation balances	$ 10,000	$290,000	$157,000	$10,000	$5,000	$2,000	$70,000	$30,000	$20,000	$ 6,000
Realization of assets and allocation of loss	168,000	(183,000)					(6,000)	(3,000)	(3,000)	(3,000)
Subtotal	$178,000	$107,000	$157,000	$10,000	$5,000	$2,000	$64,000	$27,000	$17,000	$ 3,000
July cash distribution:										
Outside creditors	(157,000)		(157,000)							
Partner's loan	(10,000)[b]			(10,000)[b]						
Partners' capital	(11,000)[b]						(10,667)[b]	(333)[b]		
Subtotal	$ –0–	$107,000	$ –0–	$ –0–	$5,000	$2,000	$53,333	$26,667	$17,000	$ 3,000
Realization of assets and allocation of loss	25,000	(70,000)					(18,000)	(9,000)	(9,000)	(9,000)
Subtotal	$ 25,000	$ 37,000			$5,000	$2,000	$35,333	$17,667	$ 8,000	$(6,000)
Exercise right of setoff						(2,000)				2,000
Subtotal	$ 25,000	$ 37,000			$5,000	$ –0–	$35,333	$17,667	$ 8,000	$(4,000)
Cash contribution by D	4,000									4,000
Subtotal	$ 29,000				$5,000		$35,333	$17,667	$ 8,000	$ –0–
August cash distribution:										
Partner's loan	(3,750)[b]				(3,750)[b]					
Partners' capital	(25,250)[b]						(16,833)[b]	(8,417)[b]		
Subtotal	$ –0–				$1,250		$18,500	$ 9,250	$ 8,000	
Realization of assets and allocation of loss	27,000	(37,000)					(4,000)	(2,000)	(2,000)	(2,000)
Subtotal	$ 27,000	$ –0–			$1,250		$14,500	$ 7,250	$ 6,000	$(2,000)
Write-off of D's deficit							(1,000)	(500)	(500)	2,000
Subtotal	$ 27,000				$1,250		$13,500	$ 6,750	$ 5,500	$ –0–
Final cash distribution:										
Partner's loan	(1,250)				(1,250)					
Partner's capital	(25,750)						(13,500)	(6,750)	(5,500)	
Postliquidation balances	$ –0–				$ –0–		$ –0–	$ –0–	$ –0–	

[a]Denotes profit and loss sharing percentage.
[b]See Illustration 25-9.

Illustration 25-9
Supporting Schedule to Illustration 25-8

A, B, C, AND D PARTNERSHIP
Schedule of Safe Payments to Partners

	Partner			
	A (40%)[a]	B (20%)[a]	C (20%)[a]	D (20%)[a]
Computation to determine how available cash on July 14, 19X5 should be distributed:				
Capital and loan balances at cash distribution (from Illustration 25-8)—				
Capital	$64,000	$27,000	$17,000	$ 3,000
Loan		10,000	5,000	2,000
Total	$64,000	$37,000	$22,000	$ 5,000
First worst-case assumption—Assume full loss on noncash assets of $107,000	(42,800)	(21,400)	(21,400)	(21,400)
Subtotal	$21,200	$15,600	$ 600	$(16,400)
Second worst-case assumption—Assume D's deficit must be absorbed by A, B, and C	(8,200)	(4,100)	(4,100)	16,400
Subtotal	$13,000	$11,500	$ (3,500)	$ –0–
Repeat second worst-case assumption—Assume C's deficit must be absorbed by A and B	(2,333)	(1,167)	3,500	
Cash to be distributed to each partner	$10,667	$10,333[b]	$ –0–	
Computation to determine how available cash on August 12, 19X5 should be distributed:				
Capital and loan balances at cash distribution (from Illustration 25-8)—				
Capital	$35,333	$17,667	$ 8,000	
Loan			5,000	
Total	$35,333	$17,667	$13,000	$ –0–
First worst-case assumption—Assume full loss on noncash assets of $37,000	(14,800)	(7,400)	(7,400)	(7,400)
Subtotal	$20,533	$10,267	$ 5,600	$ (7,400)
Second worst-case assumption—Assume D's deficit must be absorbed by A, B, and C	(3,700)	(1,850)	(1,850)	7,400
Cash to be distributed to each partner	$16,833	$ 8,417	$ 3,750[c]	$ –0–

[a]Denotes profit and loss sharing percentage.
[b]Of this amount, $10,000 is deemed a repayment of the loan.
[c]All of this amount is deemed a repayment of the loan.

2. The schedule of safe payments to partners reflects the assumptions that were made at those dates when cash was available for distribution to partners. The purpose of the schedule is to determine which partners should receive the cash that is available at those dates.
3. The payments that may be made to partners, as shown on the schedule of safe payments, are first applied as a reduction of a partner's loan and

then as a reduction of his or her capital in the statement of realization and liquidation.

4. After the first cash distribution to partners on July 14, 19X5, the Capital accounts of partners A and B are in their respective profit and loss sharing ratio of 4:2. All future cash distributions to these two partners are in this 2:1 ratio.
5. After the second cash distribution to partners on August 12, 19X5, the Capital accounts of partners A, B, and C (which includes partner C's loan account balance) are in their respective profit and loss sharing ratio of 4:2:2. All future cash distributions to these three partners are in this 4:2:2 ratio.
6. Obviously, the schedule of safe payments is prepared only after cash is available for distribution to partners. Thus, it may be used only when the partnership is solvent.

Cash Distribution Plan

When cash is available for distribution to partners, a schedule of safe payments to partners must be prepared using the two worst-case assumptions (except for the final payment, of course). The result of distributing cash to partners in the sequence resulting from the use of the two worst-case assumptions is to bring the Capital accounts into the profit and loss sharing ratio. (As demonstrated earlier in the chapter, a partner's loan to the partnership is, in substance, part of that partner's capital investment.) Once the Capital accounts are in this ratio, all future cash distributions to partners are made in the profit and loss sharing ratio.

By understanding the result of this process, we may analyze the relationship of the Capital accounts at the beginning of liquidation to determine which partners receive cash as it becomes available. The analysis results in a **cash distribution plan.** A cash distribution plan has the advantage of informing partners at **the beginning of the liquidation process** when they will receive cash **in relation to the other partners.**

Understanding the methodology underlying the preparation of a cash distribution plan requires an intuitive understanding of the fact that when the capital accounts are not in the profit and loss sharing ratio, one or more partners have capital balances sufficient to absorb his, her, or their share of losses that exceed the partnership's net worth, whereas one or more other partners have capital balances sufficient to absorb only his, her, or their share of losses that are less than the partnership's net worth. To illustrate this fact, we present the following comparative analysis:

		Partner			
	Total	W (40%)	X (30%)	Y (20%)	Z (10%)
Actual preliquidation capital and loan balances	$100,000	$48,000	$33,000	$11,000	$ 8,000

	Total	Partner W (40%)	X (30%)	Y (20%)	Z (10%)
Hypothetical capital and loan balances in the profit and loss sharing ratio of 4:3:2:1..	$100,000	$40,000	$30,000	$20,000	$10,000
Percentage relationship of actual balances to hypothetical balances		120%	110%	55%	80%

Only partners W and X (because their actual balances exceed the balances that would exist if balances were kept in the profit and loss sharing ratio) could absorb their share of losses greater than the partnership capital of $100,000. On the other hand, partners Y and Z (because their actual balances are less than the balances that would exist if balances were kept in the profit and loss sharing ratio) could absorb only their share of losses that are less than the partnership capital of $100,000.

Ranking the Partners. The percentage line of the analysis above ranks the partners in terms of which partner could absorb the largest loss to which partner could absorb the smallest loss. The ranking in this example is W, X, Z, and Y—that is, partner W (who has the highest percentage) can absorb the largest loss, and partner Y (who has the lowest percentage) can absorb the smallest loss. This ranking can be readily proved by calculating the exact loss needed to eliminate each partner's capital and loan balance. We divide each partners' capital and loan balance by his or her profit and loss sharing percentage. Continuing with our example, this calculation is as follows:

	Partner W	X	Y	Z
Actual preliquidation capital balances	$ 48,000	$ 33,000	$11,000	$ 8,000
Profit and loss sharing percentage	40%	30%	20%	10%
Loss absorption potential.	$120,000	$110,000	$55,000	$80,000
Ranking..........................	1	2	4	3

Note that a loss of $120,000 would eliminate the capital and loan balance of partner W (the highest ranking partner), whereas for partner Y (the lowest ranking partner) a loss of only $55,000 would eliminate his capital and loan balance.

Ranking the partners in this manner reveals the order in which cash should be distributed to the partners as it becomes available. Distributing cash in this order brings the capital balances into the profit and loss sharing ratio on a step-by-step basis, as follows:

1. **Distribution to highest ranking partner:** Distribute sufficient cash to partner W so that his capital balance is brought into the profit and loss sharing ratio with the next highest ranking partner (partner X).
2. **Distribution to two highest ranking partners:** Distribute sufficient cash to partners W and X in their respective profit and loss sharing ratio of 4:3 so that their capital balances are brought into the profit and loss sharing ratio with the next highest ranking partner (partner Z).
3. **Distribution to three highest ranking partners:** Distribute sufficient cash to partners W, X, and Z in their respective profit and loss sharing ratio of 4:3:1 so that their capital balances are brought into the profit and loss sharing ratio with the next highest ranking partner (partner Y).

Only the exact amount of cash distributed at each stage in this sequence needs to be determined. The calculations are shown in Illustration 25-10. The following points are important for understanding this illustration:

1. The cash distribution plan is operable only after outside creditors have been paid in full.
2. The schedule reflects only the order in which cash distributions to partners will be made *if* cash is available for distribution to the partners.
3. The sequence of distributing cash in the cash distribution plan coincides with the sequence that would result if cash were distributed using the schedule of safe payments.

SUMMARY

Liquidating a partnership consists of converting the partnership's noncash assets into cash, paying cash to creditors to the extent possible, and distributing any remaining cash to the partners. In lump-sum liquidations, no distributions are made to the partners until the realization process is completed, when the full amount of the gain or loss on realization of the partnership assets is known. In these cases, cash is distributed to the partners who have credit balances in their capital and loan accounts.

In installment liquidations, distributions are made to some or all of the partners as cash becomes available; thus, cash is distributed to partners before the full amount of the gain or loss on realization of the partnership assets is known. In these cases, cash distributions are made to partners in such a manner that the capital and loan balances of the individual partners are brought into line with the profit and loss sharing ratio.

To the extent that a partner must absorb some or all of another partner's capital account deficit, the absorbing partner has legal recourse against the personal assets of the partner who could not make good the

Illustration 25-10

W, X, Y, AND Z PARTNERSHIP
Schedule of Cash Distribution to Partners

	Partner			
	W	X	Y	Z
Preliquidation capital and loan balances	$48,000	$33,000	$11,000	$8,000
Ranking	1	2	4	3
Step 1: Cash to be distributed to W:				
Balances, per above	$48,000	$33,000		
Balances in profit and loss ratio of 4:3 using X's actual balance as the base	44,000[a]	$33,000		
	$ 4,000			
Step 2: Cash to be distributed to W and X:				
Balances, per above	$44,000	$33,000		$8,000
Balances in profit and loss ratio of 4:3:1 using Z's actual balance as the base	32,000[b]	24,000[c]		$8,000
	$12,000	$ 9,000		
Step 3: Cash to be distributed to W, X, and Z:				
Balances, per above	$32,000	$24,000	$11,000	$8,000
Balances in profit and loss ratio of 4:3:2:1 using Y's actual balance as the base	22,000	16,500	$11,000	5,500
	$10,000	$ 7,500		$2,500

After this distribution, all Capital accounts would be in the profit and loss sharing ratio of 4:3:2:1. Accordingly, all future cash distributions would be made in this ratio.

Summary of cash distribution plan:

	W	X	Y	Z
First $4,000	$ 4,000			
Next $21,000 (4:3)	12,000	$ 9,000		
Next $20,000 (4:3:1)	10,000	7,500		$2,500
Any additional amounts (4:3:2:1)	40%	30%	20%	10%

[a] $33,000 × 4/3.
[b] $8,000 × 4/1.
[c] $8,000 × 3/1.

deficit balance through setoff or contribution. The settlement of claims pursuant to legal recourse is governed by the marshalling of assets principle. Partners may greatly minimize the possibility of having to absorb another partner's deficit balance by specifying in the partnership agreement that capital balances are to be maintained in the profit and loss sharing ratio.

Glossary of New Terms

Rule of Setoff The subtraction of a partner's deficit balance in his or her Capital account from the balance of any loan outstanding to the partnership. Also, the subtraction of a partnership's loan to a partner from the partner's capital account.

Marshalling of Assets A legal doctrine whereby a partnership's creditors are given first claim on partnership assets, and personal creditors of an insolvent partner are given first claim on such partner's personal assets.

Review Questions

1. How are partnership liquidations different from corporate liquidations?
2. What is the significance of maintaining partners' Capital accounts in the profit and loss sharing ratio?
3. How is a deficit balance in a partner's Capital account disposed of if that partner is unable to eliminate the deficit through setoff or contribution?
4. In what ratio should realization gains and losses during liquidation be shared among the partners? Why?
5. Explain how the rule of setoff is applied.
6. What is the function of the statement of realization and liquidation?
7. In what order does the UPA specify that cash distributions are to be made to creditors and partners during liquidation?
8. Is the order in question 7 strictly followed in all situations? Why or why not?
9. Explain the marshalling of assets doctrine.
10. Under what conditions may cash be distributed to partners on the installment basis rather than in a lump sum?
11. When a partnership is insolvent and some partners have positive Capital account balances, whereas other partners have deficit balances, against which partners may creditors proceed personally to obtain full payment of their claims?
12. How is a partner's personal payment to partnership creditors treated on the partnership's books?

Discussion Cases

DC 25-1

Manner of Sharing Realization Losses During Liquidation

Jennings and Nelson recently formed a partnership under the following terms:

	Jennings	Nelson
Capital contributions	$80,000	$20,000
Time devoted to the business	100%	100%
Profit and loss sharing formula—		
Interest rate on capital over $20,000	10%	10%
Residual profit and loss	50%	50%

You have been hired as the partnership's accountant. While closing the partnership books for the first month of operations, Jennings casually mentions to you that he feels a "good and equitable" partnership agreement was negotiated between himself and Nelson.

Required:
How would you respond to this comment?

DC 25-2

Manner of Sharing Realization Losses During Liquidation

Harper, McCord, and Stringer are attempting to form a partnership in which profits and losses are shared in the ratio 4:4:2, respectively. They cannot agree on terms of the partnership agreement relating to potential liquidation. Harper feels it is a waste of time to have any provisions relating to liquidation, because the prospective partners firmly believe that the business will be successful. McCord feels that in the event of liquidation, any realization losses should be shared in the ratio of the capital balances, because this method allows each partner to absorb losses in relation to his or her capacity to absorb such losses. Stringer feels any liquidation losses should be shared equally, because if the business is not successful it will most likely be the fault of each partner. As the accountant who will be keeping the partnership's books, you have been asked to settle this dispute.

Required:
How would you respond to this request?

DC 25-3

Procedures for Distributing Available Cash to Partners

The partnership of Dials and Winder is in the process of liquidation, which is expected to take several months. Dials, who is in need of cash, wants cash distributed to the partners as it is available. Winder feels that no cash should be distributed to either partner until all the assets are sold and the total realization gain or loss is known. Thus, the partnership would not distribute cash to a partner and later request a capital contribution to absorb any capital deficits created by realization losses.

Required:
Evaluate the positions of each partner.

DC 25-4

Procedures for Distributing Available Cash to Partners

The partnership of Jurnell, Ledgley, and Post is in the process of being liquidated. The trial balance immediately after the sale of a portion of the noncash assets and full payment to outside creditors is as follows:

Cash	$20,000	
Note Receivable from Ledgley	14,000	
Other Assets	36,000	
Loan, Jurnell		$ 5,000
Capital:		
Jurnell		11,000
Ledgley		20,000
Post		34,000
	$70,000	$70,000

Jurnell wants the available cash distributed to her to pay off her loan—she cites Section 40(b) of the UPA, which states that partners' loans have priority over partners' capital. Ledgley wants the cash distributed to him, because he has the largest capital investment. Post feels it should be distributed equally, which is how profits and losses are shared.

Required:

1. Evaluate the positions of each partner.
2. Who should receive the $20,000 available cash?

Exercises

E 25-1

Lump-sum Liquidation: Solvent Partnership Having Partners' Loans—All Partners Personally Solvent

Partners Hall, Lane, and Tower share profits and losses in the ratio 3:2:1, respectively. The partners voted to liquidate the partnership when its assets, liabilities, and capital were as follows:

Cash	$ 2,000	Liabilities	$20,000
Noncash assets	78,000	Loans:	
		Hall	5,000
		Tower	10,000
		Capital:	
		Hall	20,000
		Lane	15,000
		Tower	10,000
	$80,000		$80,000

Assume that all the noncash assets were sold for $36,000, and all cash was distributed to outside creditors and partners.

Required:
Prepare a statement of liquidation and realization.

E 25-2

Lump-sum Liquidation: Insolvent Partnership Having Loans to and from Partners—All Partners Personally Solvent

Partners Bass, Singer, and Tennor share profits and losses equally. The partners voted to liquidate the partnership when its assets, liabilities, and capital were as follows:

Cash	$ 14,000	Liabilities	$ 80,000
Note receivable from		Loans:	
Tennor	11,000	Bass	4,000
Other noncash assets	120,000	Singer	16,000
		Capital:	
		Bass	15,000
		Singer	15,000
		Tennor	15,000
	$145,000		$145,000

Assume the following:

1. All the noncash assets of $120,000 were sold for $54,000.
2. Tennor instructed the partnership to write off the $11,000 he borrowed from the partnership.
3. All partners could eliminate any deficits in their Capital accounts through set-off or contribution, or both.
4. All cash was distributed to outside creditors and partners.

Required:
Prepare a statement of realization and liquidation.

E 25-3

Lump-sum Liquidation: Solvent Partnership Having Loans to and from Partners—Certain Partners Personally Insolvent

Partners Criss, Kross, and Zigge share profits and losses in the ratio 3:3:2, respectively. The partners voted to liquidate the partnership when its assets, liabilities, and capital were as follows:

Cash	$ 1,000	Liabilities	$34,000
Note receivable from Zigge	9,000	Loan:	
Other noncash assets	75,000	Kross	15,000
		Capital:	
		Criss	11,000
		Kross	10,000
		Zigge	15,000
	$85,000		$85,000

Assume the following:

1. All the noncash assets of $75,000 were sold for $43,000.

2. Zigge was personally insolvent and unable to contribute any cash to the partnership.
3. Criss and Kross were both personally solvent and able to eliminate any deficits in their Capital accounts through setoff or contribution.
4. All cash was distributed to outside creditors and partners.

Required:
Prepare a statement of realization and liquidation.

E 25-4

Lump-sum Liquidation: Insolvent Partnership Having Loans from Partners—Certain Partners Personally Insolvent

Partners Cattie, Deere, Fox, and O'Hare share profits and losses in the ratio 5:2:2:1, respectively. The partners voted to liquidate the partnership when its assets and liabilities were as follows:

Cash	$ 15,000	Liabilities	$165,000
Noncash assets	235,000	Loans:	
		Deere	7,000
		Fox	5,000
		O'Hare	3,000
		Capital:	
		Cattie	40,000
		Deere	16,000
		Fox	10,000
		O'Hare	4,000
	$250,000		$250,000

Assume the following:

1. All the noncash assets were sold for $135,000.
2. Cattie contributed $5,000 to the partnership after the noncash assets were sold. He has no additional funds above and beyond what is needed to satisfy personal creditors.
3. All other partners were personally solvent and made capital contributions as necessary to eliminate deficits in their Capital accounts.
4. All cash was distributed to outside creditors and partners.

Required:
Prepare a statement of realization and liquidation.

E 25-5

Insolvent Partnership and Insolvent Partners—Theory

Q, R, S, and T are partners sharing profits and losses equally. The partnership is insolvent and is therefore being liquidated; the status of the partnership and each partner is as follows:

Partner	Partnership Capital Balance	Personal Assets (Exclusive of Partnership Interest)	Personal Liabilities (Exclusive of Partnership Interest)
Q	$15,000	$100,000	$40,000
R	10,000	30,000	60,000
S	(20,000)	80,000	5,000
T	(30,000)	1,000	28,000
	$(25,000)		

Required:
Select the correct response to the question below.
Assuming the Uniform Partnership Act applies, the partnership creditors:

a. must first seek recovery against S because she is personally solvent and has a negative capital balance.
b. will not be paid in full regardless of how they proceed legally because the partnership assets are less than the partnership liabilities.
c. must share R's interest in the partnership on a pro rata basis with R's personal creditors.
d. have first claim to the partnership assets before any partner's personal creditors have rights to the partnership assets.

(AICPA adapted)

E 25-6 Installment Liquidation: Solvent Partnership Having Partner's Loan—First Cash Distribution to Partners

Partners Deeds, Grant, and Trusty share profits and losses in the ratio 6:3:1, respectively. The partners voted to liquidate the partnership when its assets, liabilities, and capital were as follows:

Cash	$ 1,000	Liabilities	$35,000
Noncash assets	94,000	Loan:	
		Trusty	10,000
		Capital:	
		Deeds	30,000
		Grant	15,000
		Trusty	5,000
	$95,000		$95,000

Assume that noncash assets with a book value of $74,000 were sold for $54,000.

Required:
Determine how the cash available after this sale should be distributed.

E
25-7

Installment Liquidation: Solvent Partnership—First Cash Distribution to Partners

Partners Springer, Sumner, and Winters share profits and losses in the ratio 5:3:2, respectively. The partners voted to liquidate the partnership when its assets, liabilities, and capital were as follows:

Cash	$ 40,000	
Other assets	210,000	
Liabilities		$ 60,000
Capital:		
Springer		48,000
Sumner		72,000
Winters		70,000
	$250,000	$250,000

The partnership will be liquidated over a long period of time. Cash is to be distributed to the partners as it becomes available. The first sale of noncash assets having a book value of $120,000 realized $90,000.

Required:
Determine how the available cash should be distributed to the partners after this sale.

(AICPA adapted)

E
25-8

Installment Liquidation: Solvent Partnership with Partnership's and Partner's Loans—First Cash Distribution to Partners

Partners Castle, King, and Queen share profits and losses in the ratio 4:4:2, respectively. The partners voted to liquidate the partnership when its assets, liabilities, and capital were as follows:

Cash	$ 20,000	
Note Receivable from Castle	10,000	
Other Assets	170,000	
Liabilities		$ 50,000
Loan from King		30,000
Capital:		
Castle		37,000
King		15,000
Queen		68,000
	$200,000	$200,000

The partnership will be liquidated over a long period of time. Cash will be distributed to the partners as it becomes available. The first sale of noncash assets having a book value of $90,000 realized $50,000.

Required:
Determine how the available cash should be distributed to the partners after this first sale.

(AICPA adapted)

Problems

P 25-1*

Lump-sum Liquidation: Solvent Partnership Having Partner's Loan — All Partners Personally Solvent

Partners Rockne and Stone share profits in the ratio 3:2, respectively. The partners agreed to liquidate the partnership when the assets, liabilities, and capital were as follows:

Cash	$ 6,000	Liabilities	$27,000
Noncash assets	44,000	Loan:	
		Stone	6,000
		Capital:	
		Rockne	14,000
		Stone	3,000
	$50,000		$50,000

Assume the following:

1. Rockne agreed personally to take certain equipment having a book value of $5,000. (The partners estimated the current value of this equipment at $6,500.)
2. Stone agreed personally to take certain office furniture having a book value of $3,000. (The partners estimated the current value of this at $2,000.)
3. All other noncash assets were sold for $25,000.
4. Liquidation expenses of $1,000 were incurred.
5. Cash was distributed to outside creditors and partners.

Required:
Prepare a statement of realization and liquidation.

P 25-2*

Lump-sum Liquidation: Solvent Partnership Having Partners' Loans — Certain Partners Personally Insolvent

Partners Duke, Lord, Noble, and Prince share profits and losses in the ratio 4:3:2:1, respectively. The partners agreed to liquidate the partnership when it had assets, liabilities, and capital as follows:

Cash	$ 10,000	Liabilities	$ 78,000
Noncash assets	140,000	Loans:	
		Duke	4,000
		Lord	3,000
		Capital:	
		Duke	10,000
		Lord	10,000
		Noble	30,000
		Prince	15,000
	$150,000		$150,000

*The financial statement information presented for problems accompanied by asterisks is also provided on Model 25 (filename: Model25) of the software disk that is available for use with the text, enabling the problem to be worked on the computer.

Assume the following:

1. The noncash assets were sold for $90,000.
2. Duke is personally insolvent.
3. Lord contributed $2,000 cash to the partnership; he had no other available funds in excess of amounts needed to satisfy personal creditors.
4. All cash was distributed to outside creditors and partners.

Required:
Prepare a statement of realization and liquidation.

P 25-3*

Lump-sum Liquidation: Insolvent Partnership Having Partners' Loans—Certain Partners Personally Insolvent

Partners Oates, Ryley, and Wheatman share profits and losses in the ratio 3:3:2, respectively. The partners agreed to liquidate the partnership when assets, liabilities, and capital were as follows:

Cash	$ 5,000	Liabilities	$48,000
Noncash assets	85,000	Loans:	
		Oates	10,000
		Ryley	3,000
		Capital:	
		Oates	11,000
		Ryley	10,000
		Wheatman	8,000
	$90,000		$90,000

Assume the following:

1. The noncash assets were sold for $29,000.
2. Outside creditors of the partnership proceeded against Wheatman and collected from her $14,000 that the partnership was unable to pay.
3. The partnership incurred liquidation expenses of $4,000, which were paid personally by Ryley.
4. Oates is personally insolvent.
5. Ryley and Wheatman (who are both personally solvent) make a personal settlement between themselves.

Required:
Prepare a statement of realization and liquidation.

P 25-4

Installment Liquidation: Schedule of Safe Payments—First Cash Distribution to Partners

On January 1, 19X2, the partners of Allen, Brown, and Cox, who share profits and losses in the ratio of 5:3:2, respectively, decide to liquidate their partnership. The partnership trial balance at this date is as follows:

	Debit	Credit
Cash	$ 18,000	
Accounts Receivable	66,000	
Inventory	52,000	
Machinery and Equipment	249,000	
Accumulated Depreciation		$ 60,000
Allen, Loan	30,000	
Accounts Payable		53,000
Brown, Loan		20,000
Allen, Capital		118,000
Brown, Capital		90,000
Cox, Capital		74,000
	$415,000	$415,000

The partners plan a program of piecemeal conversion of assets in order to minimize liquidation losses. All available cash, less an amount retained to provide for future expenses, is to be distributed to the partners at the end of each month. The liquidation transactions for January 19X2 follow:

1. $51,000 was collected on accounts receivable; the balance is uncollectible.
2. $38,000 was received for the entire inventory.
3. $2,000 of liquidation expenses were paid.
4. $50,000 was paid to outside creditors, after offset of a $3,000 credit memorandum received on January 11, 19X2.
5. $10,000 cash was retained in the business at the end of the month for potential unrecorded liabilities and anticipated expenses.

Required:
Prepare a schedule of safe payments showing how cash was distributed to the partners as of January 31, 19X2.

(AICPA adapted)

P 25-5*

Installment Liquidation: Schedule of Safe Payments and Statement of Realization and Liquidation

Partners Barley, Flax, and Rice share profits and losses in the ratio 6:3:1, respectively. The partners decided to liquidate the partnership on June 30, 19X5, when its assets, liabilities, and capital were as follows:

Cash	$ 10,000	Liabilities	$ 42,000
Noncash assets	130,000	Loans:	
		Barley	4,000
		Flax	1,000
		Capital:	
		Barley	84,000
		Flax	5,000
		Rice	4,000
	$140,000		$140,000

Assume the following:

1. On July 1, 19X5, liquidation expenses were estimated at approximately $3,000. Actual liquidation expenses totaled only $2,500 and were paid as follows:

July 31, 19X5	$1,000
August 31, 19X5	1,000
September 30, 19X5	500
	$2,500

2. Noncash assets were sold as follows:

Date	Book Value	Proceeds
July 11, 19X5	$ 30,000	$ 36,000
August 14, 19X5	40,000	28,000
September 27, 19X5	60,000	44,000
	$130,000	$108,000

3. Partners were able to eliminate any deficits in their Capital accounts through setoff or contribution as deficit balances occurred.
4. Cash was distributed to outside creditors and partners as it was available.

Required:
Prepare a statement of realization and liquidation, including supporting schedules showing how cash was distributed to creditors and partners as it was available.

P 25-6

Installment Liquidation: Schedule of Cash Distribution

Partners Brickley, Glass, Steele, and Woods decide to dissolve their partnership. They plan to sell the assets gradually to minimize losses. They share profits and losses as follows: Brickley, 40%; Glass, 35%; Steele, 15%; and Woods, 10%. The partnership's trial balance as of October 1, 19X0, the date on which liquidation begins, is shown below.

	Debit	Credit
Cash	$ 200	
Receivables	25,900	
Inventory, October 1, 19X0	42,600	
Equipment (net)	19,800	
Accounts payable		$ 3,000
Brickley, Loan		6,000
Glass, Loan		10,000
Brickley, Capital		20,000
Glass, Capital		21,500
Steele, Capital		18,000
Woods, Capital		10,000
	$88,500	$88,500

Required:

1. Prepare a statement as of October 1, 19X0, showing how cash will be distributed among partners by installments as it becomes available.
2. On October 31, 19X0, $12,700 cash was available to partners. How should it be distributed?

(AICPA adapted)

P 25-7

Installment Liquidation: Schedule of Cash Distribution

Partners Arbuckle, Beltmore, and Tanner want you to assist them in winding up the affairs of their partnership. You gather the following information:

1. The June 30, 19X2, trial balance of the partnership is as follows:

	Debit	Credit
Cash	$ 6,000	
Accounts Receivable	22,000	
Inventory	14,000	
Plant and Equipment (net)	99,000	
Note Receivable—Arbuckle	12,000	
Note Receivable—Tanner	7,500	
Accounts Payable		$ 17,000
Arbuckle, Capital		67,000
Beltmore, Capital		45,000
Tanner, Capital		31,500
	$160,500	$160,500

2. The partners share profits and losses as follows: Arbuckle, 50%; Beltmore, 30%; and Tanner, 20%.

The partners are considering an offer of $100,000 for the accounts receivable inventory and for plant and equipment as of June 30. The $100,000 would be paid to the partners in installments, the number and amounts of which are to be negotiated.

Required:
Prepare a cash distribution schedule as of June 30, 19X2, showing how the $100,000 would be distributed as it is available.

P 25-8*

Installment Liquidation: Schedule of Cash Distribution and Statement of Realization and Liquidation

Assume the facts in Problem 25-7, except that the partners decide to liquidate their partnership instead of accepting the offer of $100,000. Cash is distributed to the partners at the end of each month.

A summary of the liquidation transactions follows:

July

1. Collected $16,500 on accounts receivable; the balance is uncollectible.
2. Received $10,000 for the entire inventory.
3. Paid $1,000 liquidation expenses.
4. Retained $8,000 cash in the business at month-end.

August

1. Paid $1,500 liquidation expenses. As part payment of his capital, Tanner accepted a piece of special equipment that he developed that had a book value of $4,000. The partners agreed that a value of $10,000 should be placed on the machine for liquidation purposes.
2. Retained $2,500 cash in the business at month-end.

September

1. Received $75,000 on sale of remaining plant and equipment.
2. Paid $1,000 liquidation expenses.
3. No cash retained in the business.

Required:

Prepare a statement of realization and liquidation.

(AICPA adapted)

26

Estates and Trusts

AN OVERVIEW OF ESTATES AND TRUSTS

In this chapter, we consider the role accountants play in the administration of estates and trusts. Before proceeding into this subject, however, we discuss briefly the role accountants may play in estate planning, which takes place before an individual dies.

Estate Planning

People commonly make plans for the orderly transfer of their property upon death to relatives, other persons, organizations, or trusts to be set up for the benefit of relatives. Such forethought is known as **estate planning** and is done under the guidance of attorneys, often working closely with accountants. The attorney's role centers around preparing wills and, in many cases, trust agreements (discussed in detail later in the chapter). The accountant's role consists of suggesting planning techniques consistent with the objective of minimizing *transfer costs* (federal estate taxes, state inheritance taxes, and fees and expenses). In this capacity, an accountant often determines expected transfer costs under various options. An accountant may also play an important role in advising his or her client on accounting matters pertaining to trusts that are to be established.

Participation by accountants in estate planning is usually limited to cases in which individuals are wealthy or moderately wealthy. The Tax Reform Act of 1976 substantially overhauled the federal estate and gift tax laws, and an estimated 98% of all estates became exempt from estate and gift tax laws. However, inflation was lowering this percentage. Furthermore, certain inequities were perceived to exist still. To address these two areas, further changes were enacted in the Economic Recovery Tax Act of 1981, and an estimated 99.5% of all estates are now exempt from estate and gift tax laws. An accountant participating in estate planning must have substantial expertise in estate and gift taxes—a complex area of the tax laws. A detailed discussion of these laws and the use of planning techniques to minimize transfer costs is properly the subject matter of a tax course. However, a brief discussion of the estate and gift tax laws is included later in the chapter.

The Trust Feature of Estate Planning

Frequently a will contains a provision for the establishment of a trust, whereby certain designated property of the decedent's estate is to be transferred to a **trustee** when the person dies. The trustee holds legal title to the property and administers it for the benefit of one or more other persons, who are called **beneficiaries.** Thus, the trustee serves in a position of trust with respect to the beneficiaries. This is a fiduciary relationship, and the trustee is commonly referred to as a **fiduciary.** (Recall another type of fiduciary relationship discussed in Chapter 19 in connection with companies in bankruptcy proceedings.) The person creating the trust is referred to as the **trustor** (also known as the **grantor, donor, creator,** and **settlor**). The legal document creating the trust is the **trust agreement.** Trust beneficiaries are of the following two classes:

1. **Income beneficiary.** An income beneficiary is entitled to the income earned by the trust's assets, which are referred to as the trust **principal,** or **corpus.**
2. **Principal beneficiary.** A principal beneficiary is entitled to the principal, or *corpus*, of the trust, which is distributed according to the terms of the trust agreement (usually at the specified termination date of the trust). A principal beneficiary is also known as a **residuary beneficiary** or **remainderman.**

The income and principal beneficiaries may or may not be the same person. A common arrangement is to name one's spouse as the income beneficiary for his or her remaining life and name one's children as the principal beneficiaries. Another common arrangement is to name one's minor children as both income and principal beneficiaries, with some or all of the income to be used for their support and the principal to be distributed to them when they reach a specified age.

The Basic Accounting Problem

Regardless of whether the income and principal beneficiaries of a trust are the same person or persons, **it is necessary to account for the separate interests of each class.** The manner of accomplishing this task is the subject of this chapter. The requirement of correct separate accounting for the interests of each class is the reason for the special theories and techniques for accounting for the administration of estates and trusts by fiduciaries. Otherwise, quite simple record-keeping procedures would be adequate.

Accounting for the separate interests of each class of beneficiaries is even more difficult because there is a built-in clash of interests between the two classes. When the principal and income beneficiaries are not the same person or persons, the clash revolves around who gets what. When the principal and income beneficiaries are the same person or persons, the clash concerns the timing of distributions. Frequently, disputes between these interests lead to litigation.

Although a trust may be established by a transfer of property to the trustee during the transferor's lifetime (known as an **inter vivos** trust), we deal solely with trusts that are created by a gift made in the will of a decedent (known as a **testamentary trust**). Thus, we must consider the administration of a decedent's estate in connection with the establishment of a trust.

Relationship between an Estate and a Testamentary Trust

All the states have enacted some form of legislation concerning the administration of trusts. State statutes pertaining to trusts are operative, in most cases, only to the extent that they do not conflict with the terms of a trust agreement. Twenty states have adopted the Revised Uniform Principal and Income Act (of 1962) either in its entirety or with modifications; accordingly, we base our discussion on this act. Under this act, testamentary trusts are deemed to be created at the time of a person's death, even though the property to be placed in trust usually is not actually distributed to the trustee until some time after the person dies.[1] Property to be placed in trust becomes subject to the trust at the time of death; the rights of the income beneficiary are also established at the time of death. Therefore, the interests of the income beneficiary of the trust must be accounted for separately from the interests of the principal beneficiary of the trust **during the period of the estate administration,** as well as after the property is actually transferred to the trustee. (Some trust agreements simplify matters by specifying that the rights of the income beneficiary do not begin until the assets are actually transferred to the trustee.)

For accounting purposes, we treat the estate and the trust as separate accounting entities. (Conceptually we view each of these entities as comprising two accounting entities—a "principal entity" and an "income entity.") For tax-reporting purposes, estates and trusts both are treated as taxable entities. However, they are not legal entities in the sense that corporations are legal entities.

PRINCIPAL VERSUS INCOME

When a testamentary trust is established, every transaction must be analyzed to determine if it relates to principal or income. An incorrect determination has important legal consequences to a fiduciary. If it is later determined that income has been overstated and the fiduciary cannot recover the amount of an overpayment from the income beneficiary, then the fiduciary must make up the deficiency. In turn, if the error was made by the accountant or was based on the bad advice of the fiduciary's legal counsel, then these persons may be professionally responsible to the fiduciary.

Manner of Analyzing Transactions

Reference to the Trust Agreement. In determining whether a transaction pertains to principal or income, **generally accepted accounting prin-**

[1]Revised Uniform Principal and Income Act, U.L.A. Volume 7A, Section 4 (St. Paul: West Publishing Co.).

ciples are not the point of reference. The trustor may create his or her own definition of income. In other words, the trustor may specify the receipts that are to be income and the receipts that are to be principal. Likewise, the trustor may specify disbursements that are to be treated as charges against income and disbursements that are to be treated as reductions of the principal. Accordingly, all transactions must be analyzed as to the decedent's intent.

Because the decedent is not available, the first step is to determine if the decedent's intent is expressed in the trust agreement. Unfortunately, a common shortcoming of estate planning is that trust agreements usually do not explain in detail the treatment to be accorded specific types of receipts and disbursements. Many potential problems can be avoided if the decedent's personal accountant, who should have a knowledge of his or her client's properties, participates in the preparation of the trust agreement sections that pertain to accounting matters.

Reference to State Law. If the treatment of an item cannot be resolved by referring to the trust agreement, the second step is to find out what the state law is on the subject. Again, generally accepted accounting principles are not the point of reference. The Revised Uniform Principal and Income Act specifically addresses the principal versus income treatment of several items. Much of the impetus for revising the original Uniform Principal and Income Act (of 1931) resulted from the development of new forms of investment property, the treatment of which was not specified in state statutes. The treatment accorded many items specifically dealt with in the act produces income results that would be obtained if generally accepted accounting principles were applied. For numerous other items, however, the treatment produces results that are quite contrary to generally accepted accounting principles. For example, the act provides that the following items be treated as increases and decreases, respectively, to the trust principal instead of to income:

1. Gains and losses on the sale of corporate securities.
2. Gains and losses on the sale of rental property.
3. Bond discounts (with certain exceptions) and bond premiums.

We present the general thrust of the act's accounting requirements later in the chapter. Section 5 of the act calls for income during the administration of an estate to be determined in the same manner that income is to be determined by a trustee in administering a trust. Thus, the act applies to estates as well as trusts.

Reference to Case Law. If the treatment of an item is not covered in state law, the third step is to determine if the courts have encountered and ruled on the same problem. If so, the answer is found in case law. If the answer cannot be found there, then the fiduciary may petition the court for a determination.

The Accountant's Role in Analyzing Transactions. When the treatment to be accorded an item is not clearly set forth in the trust agreement or state statutes, the accountant does not determine whether an item pertains to principal or income. This is the function of the fiduciary, the fiduciary's legal counsel, or the courts. The accountant's role would be expanded, of course, when the trust agreement specifies that income is to be determined in accordance with generally accepted accounting principles. Such cases are the exception and not the rule.

Manner of Record Keeping

Because the interests of the principal beneficiary and the income beneficiary must be accounted for separately, it is necessary to identify the assets and transactions pertaining to principal and those pertaining to income. Conceptually, we may view the assets and transactions pertaining to principal as belonging to a separate accounting entity and do likewise for the assets and transactions pertaining to income. Thus, a trust may be viewed as comprising two entities, each with a self-balancing set of books.

One method of record keeping is physically to maintain separate journals and general ledgers for each conceptual entity. An alternate method is to use one set of books for both entities but to use separately identified columns in the journals and separately identified accounts in the general ledger for principal and income. This technique allows separate trial balances to be prepared for each conceptual entity, just as though two general ledgers were used. In practice, this technique is quite simple to work with, largely because cash is usually the only type of asset common to both principal and income. Regardless of which method is used, it is not necessary to use one bank account for cash pertaining to principal and another bank account for cash pertaining to income, unless the trust agreement requires it. When only one set of books is used, the separation of the total cash balance is reflected in the general ledger through a Principal Cash ledger account and an Income Cash ledger account. One set of books is generally used in practice. We illustrate this manner of record keeping later in the chapter.

Cash Basis Versus Accrual Basis

At the Beginning and the End of the Income Beneficiary's Rights. In most respects, the Revised Uniform Principal and Income Act provides for the use of the accrual basis in determining at the time of the person's death the assets that are to be treated as part of the trust principal. The purpose, of course, is to establish a reasonably fair and practical starting point to determine income for the income beneficiary. Specifically, the following items are to be included as part of the trust principal at the time of death:

1. Amounts due but not paid at the time of death (Section 4[a]).
2. Prorations of amounts not due at the time of death that pertain to periodic payments, including rents, interest, and annuities (Section 4[b]).
3. Corporate distributions declared for which the date of record precedes the person's death (Section 4[e]).

The cash basis is specified for all other items (Section 4[c]). In a somewhat parallel manner, the act provides in most respects for the use of the accrual basis on termination of an income interest, to effect a reasonably fair and practical cutoff of the income beneficiary's interest (Sections 4[d] and [e]).

Accounting Periods between the Beginning and the End of the Income Beneficiary's Rights. For accounting periods between the beginning and the end of the income beneficiary's rights, the accrual basis in most respects does not fit in with the underlying objective of the fiduciary, which is to account for the **flow of assets in and out of his or her control.** Accordingly, with one major exception, the cash basis is considered more appropriate for such accounting periods. However, the accrual basis offers much better measuring results when determining the income of a business in which principal is invested.

At the End of the Estate Administration. When the income rights of the income beneficiary are established at the time of the person's death, the end of the estate administration is not relevant to the income and principal beneficiaries. Using the accrual basis is therefore unnecessary at the end of probate administration. Of course, if the trust agreement provides that income rights do not start until the end of the estate administration, then accrual techniques would be appropriate.

ACCOUNTING FOR ESTATES

Probate Administration

When a person dies, his or her property and liabilities (collectively referred to as the **estate**) must be administered, regardless of whether the person died with a will (referred to as having died **testate**) or without a will (referred to as having died **intestate**). Each state has laws concerning the affairs of decedents, commonly known as **probate law** or the **law of decedent estates.** A Uniform Probate Code exists, but only two states have adopted it. Accordingly, uniformity among the states in this area is negligible. The objectives of probate laws are to (1) discover and make effective the decedent's intent in the distribution of his or her property, (2) gather and preserve the decedent's property, and (3) provide for an efficient and orderly system of making payments of estate debts and distributions in the course of liquidating estates. If the decedent does not have a will, property is distributed according to state inheritance tax laws.

Under the probate laws, the affairs of decedents must be administered by fiduciaries who are subject to the control of the state **probate courts** (referred to in a few of the states as **surrogate courts** or **orphans' courts**). The following two terms are used for estate fiduciaries:

1. An **executor** is named in the decedent's will to serve as the decedent's personal representative in administering his or her estate and is appointed by the court to serve in that capacity.
2. An **administrator** is appointed by the court when (a) a person dies intestate, (b) a person does not name anyone in his or her will, (c) the person named in the decedent's will refuses to serve as executor, or (d) the court refuses to appoint the person named in the will.

The title to a decedent's property is subject to the possession of the fiduciary and the control of the court, even though title passes at the time of death to the person or persons to whom the property is to be distributed. In short, the probate court serves as guardian of the estate. If a person dies testate, his or her will has no legal effect until it has been "probated." **Probate** is the act by which the court determines if the will submitted to it meets the statutory requirements concerning wills. If the court so determines, then it issues a certificate or decree that enables the terms of the will to be carried out. The will is said to have been "admitted to probate."

Basically, an estate fiduciary must (1) take an inventory of the decedent's assets; (2) settle the claims of the decedent's creditors; (3) prepare and file the applicable income, estate, and inheritance tax returns; (4) distribute the remaining assets as gifts as provided for in the will; and (5) make the appropriate accountings to the court.

Gift Terminology

A gift of personal property by means of a will is called a **legacy.** The recipient of a legacy is called a **legatee.** Legacies are classified as follows:

1. A **specific legacy** is a gift of specified noncash items. For example, "my automobile to my son, Harvey."
2. A **demonstrative legacy** is a gift of cash for which a particular fund or source is designated from which payment is to be made. For example, "$1,000 to my sister, Christine, out of my savings account."
3. A **general legacy** is a gift of cash for which no particular fund or source is designated from which payment is to be made. For example, "$2,000 to my brother Chad."
4. A **residual legacy** is a gift of all personal property remaining after distribution of specific, demonstrative, and general legacies. For example, "the balance of my personal property to my wife, Ann Marie."

If the balance of the estate assets after payment of estate liabilities, taxes, and administrative expenses is insufficient to make good all of various types of legacies, then the legacies are deemed to be null and inoperative in the reverse of the above order (referred to as the process of **abatement**).

A gift of real property by means of a will is called a **devise.** The recipient of a devise is called a **devisee.** Devises are classified as specific, general, or residual devises. Estate assets to be transferred to a trustee pursuant to the establishment of a testamentary trust may be any type of legacy or devise. The most common type of legacy given to a trustee is a residual legacy, which we illustrate later in the chapter.

Inventory of Decedent's Property

The estate fiduciary's first major task in administering the estate is to take an inventory of the decedent's property. Each item must then be valued at its current market value for federal estate and state inheritance tax purposes (using state inheritance tax or private appraisers, as required), and the appropriate tax forms must be filed. (We discuss these in more detail in the following section.) In addition, the estate fiduciary must submit to the probate court an inventory of the decedent's property that is subject to probate administration. Not all items included for estate tax and state inheritance tax purposes are subject to probate administration. Many states allow real property to pass directly to the beneficiaries (or to the trustee, in the case of real property placed in trust), bypassing probate administration. Likewise, many states allow certain types of personal property—such as personal effects, clothing, household items, and a limited amount of cash—to pass directly to beneficiaries outside of probate. State probate law must be consulted to determine which items are subject to probate administration; an attorney's services are usually used for this. Although required only by some states, a separate schedule should list the items not subject to probate administration, if only for the record.

In general, the following items are subject to probate administration:

1. Cash in checking and savings accounts, cash in a safety deposit box, and cash on hand.
2. Investments in stocks and bonds.
3. Interest accrued on bonds through the date of the person's death.
4. Dividends declared on stocks prior to the person's death.
5. Investments in businesses and partnerships.
6. Life insurance proceeds that name the estate as the beneficiary.
7. Notes and accounts receivable, including interest accrued through the date of the person's death.
8. Accrued rents and royalties receivable.
9. Advances to those named in the will as beneficiaries, including interest accrued through the date of death.
10. Unpaid wages, salaries, and commissions.
11. Valuables such as jewelry and coin collections.

12. Real estate not specifically exempted (the most common exemption is property held in joint tenancy, because all rights in such property immediately pass to the surviving tenant at the time of death).

Even though other items may be includible for federal estate tax and state inheritance tax purposes, the fiduciary's accountability to the probate court includes only the items subject to probate administration. The fiduciary must take control of these items for estate preservation purposes.

Payment of Estate Liabilities

The liabilities of the estate must be paid before any distributions are made to beneficiaries. Probate laws usually require the estate fiduciary to publish promptly notices in newspapers for a certain period of time calling for persons having claims against the decedent to file them within a specified period of time or be barred forever. The estate fiduciary is responsible for determining the validity of claims filed. If the estate assets are insufficient to pay all liabilities, payment must be made in accordance with the priority provided for in state law. This general order of priority is as follows:

1. Funeral expenses.
2. Estate administration expenses.
3. Allowances for support of the decedent's spouse and dependent children for a specified period of time.
4. Expenses of the deceased's last illness.
5. Wages owed to employees of the decedent.
6. Debts owed to the federal, state, or local government that have priority under federal or state law.
7. Lien claims.
8. All other debts.

Tax Matters

The estate fiduciary is responsible for preparing and filing tax returns for the decedent and the decedent's estate.

Decedent's Final Income Tax Return. A final income tax return must be filed for the decedent, covering the period from the date of the decedent's last income tax return to the date of death. Any taxes owed are paid from estate assets.

Taxation of Estate Income. An estate is a taxable entity, which comes into being at the time of the person's death. Estate income taxes must be filed annually on federal Form 1041 (U.S. Fiduciary Income Tax Return) until the estate is terminated upon discharge of the fiduciary by the probate court. The gross income of an estate is computed in the same manner as that of an individual. In addition to deductions for expenses relating to the generation of income, a deduction is allowed for net income currently distributable to beneficiaries. As a result, the estate is taxed only on the remaining net income not currently distributable. The beneficiaries, in turn, are taxed on the currently distributable net income. The tax rates that apply to estates are those that apply to trusts:

Taxable Income	Tax Rate
First $5,000	15%
Over $5,000	28%

The concept of estate income for tax reporting purposes differs in many respects from the concept of estate income for fiduciary reporting purposes. Accordingly, working paper adjustments to fiduciary book income amounts are usually necessary to arrive at gross income and deductions for income tax reporting purposes.

State Inheritance Taxes. Most states impose an inheritance tax on the value of property to be distributed to each individual heir. This tax is based on the **right to receive or inherit** property; thus, the burden of taxation falls on the recipient of the property. Although the taxes are paid to the state out of the estate assets, the estate fiduciary either seeks reimbursement from the individual heirs (when noncash assets are distributed) or reduces proportionately the amount to be distributed to each individual heir (when cash is distributed). The tax rates and allowable exemptions are based on the relationship of the heir to the decedent, with tax rates increasing and exemptions decreasing as the relationship becomes more distant. It is quite common, however, for wills to provide specifically that state inheritance taxes be paid out of the residue of the estate, so that the entire burden of taxation falls on the heirs who receive the residue.

Federal Estate Taxes. Unlike state inheritance taxes, the federal estate tax is based on the **right to give** property. The burden of taxation, therefore, falls entirely on the estate and not on each individual heir. Of course, this merely reduces the amount of the residue of the estate that otherwise would be distributed to heirs. (Some state probate codes require the federal estate tax to be borne by each heir, as with the state inheritance taxes.) Assuming a decedent has made no gifts during his or her lifetime, estate taxes are calculated in the following manner:

1. The total value, or **gross estate,** of the decedent's property is determined at the time of death or, if the estate fiduciary elects, at a date six months after death. Property sold within six months of the person's death is valued at its selling price. (Recall that the gross estate for federal estate tax purposes is usually greater than the probate estate.)
2. The taxable estate is determined by making the following deductions from the gross estate determined in step 1:

  a. Liabilities of the estate.
  b. Administrative expenses, including funeral expenses, court costs, and attorney fees.
  c. Casualty and theft losses during the administration of the estate.
  d. A **marital deduction** (a term used to describe **a transfer between spouses** that is exempt from transfer taxes). The marital deduction is unlimited; thus, any amount may be used.
  e. Charitable contributions.
3. The estate tax rates are then applied to the taxable estate to arrive at the **gross estate tax.** The estate tax rates are graduated from 18% on taxable estates of $10,000 to a maximum of 50% on taxable estates in excess of $2,500,000.
4. Certain specified tax credits—such as state death taxes (with limitations) and the unified transfer tax credit—are subtracted from the gross estate tax to arrive at the **net estate tax.**

The *unified transfer tax credit* is the equivalent of an exemption. The following table shows the amount of the unified transfer tax credit and the related exemption equivalent:

Unified Transfer Tax Credit	Exemption Equivalent
$192,800	$600,000

Accordingly, a single individual may transfer a taxable estate of $600,000 and incur no federal estate tax.

Because a surviving spouse may take a marital deduction for any amount, all federal estate taxes otherwise payable can be deferred until the death of that surviving spouse. Thus, the tax law treats a married couple as a single economic unit.

To use the unified credit fully, the marital deduction amount chosen generally is small enough to leave a taxable estate equal to the $600,000 exemption equivalent of the unified transfer tax credit. (The taxable estate of $600,000 is then placed in a trust for the decedent's children.) For example, assume that (1) Henry Steele passed away, (2) his gross estate is $3,700,000, and (3) all deductions other than the marital deduction are $100,000. With a marital deduction amount of $3,000,000, the taxable estate is $600,000, resulting in a gross estate tax of $192,800. However, because of the unified transfer tax credit of $192,800, no net estate tax is payable. The unified transfer tax credit can also be used on the death of Steele's surviving spouse (who was transferred $3,000,000). Thus, the exemption equivalent of $600,000 is really $1,200,000 for a married couple.

The calculation of estate taxes is substantially more complicated when the decedent has made gifts during his or her lifetime. One of the major changes in the Tax Reform Act of 1976 was to unify the previously separate estate and gift tax rate schedules into a combined transfer tax system, so that lifetime transfers and transfers at death are no longer taxed at different rates. The unified transfer tax credit is labeled as such because it also may be applied against gift taxes due on lifetime gifts. The amount of any unused credit is then applied against the gross estate tax.

The Opening Entry

Once an inventory of the decedent's property that is subject to probate administration has been compiled, the opening entry for the "principal entity" of the estate is made. The entry consists of debits to the various assets and a credit to an Estate Principal account. This account is merely a balancing account that facilitates the double-entry bookkeeping system. It does not reflect the "net worth" of the estate, inasmuch as the decedent's liabilities are not recorded as part of the opening entry. Liabilities are recorded in the books when they are paid, and such payments are eventually reflected as reductions to the Estate Principal account. This manner of accounting reflects the fiduciary's role, which is to **administer the decedent's assets,** rather than attempting to establish and account for the net worth of the estate. As expected, no opening entry pertains to the "income entity."

Transactions Pertaining to Principal

Transactions pertaining to principal are recorded by debiting or crediting the appropriate asset account and crediting or debiting, respectively, an account that is descriptive of the transaction. Transactions pertaining to principal may be grouped as follows:

1. **Transactions that increase principal:**
   a. Assets subsequently discovered
   b. Gains on disposition of principal assets
2. **Transactions that decrease principal:**
   a. Losses on disposition of principal assets
   b. Payments of debts and certain taxes
   c. Payment of funeral expenses
   d. Payment of administrative expenses
   e. Distributions of gifts
3. **Transactions that do not affect principal:**
   a. Disposition of principal assets at their carrying values
   b. Receipts of amounts to be given to legatees (which are reflected as liabilities until paid)
   c. Disbursements of amounts held by legatees, as described in category (3)b
   d. Payments of amounts chargeable to a beneficiary (which are reflected as receivables until collected)

The nonasset accounts that are debited or credited in categories 1 and 2 are nominal or temporary accounts that are eventually closed to the Estate

Principal account. (Some finer points concerning principal transactions are discussed later in the chapter.)

Transactions Pertaining to Income

The accounting techniques used for the principal entity are also used for the income entity. An income asset account is debited or credited, and the other half of the entry is to an account that substantively explains the transaction. Initially, the income entity has no assets. Revenues, expenses, and distributions to income beneficiaries are closed periodically to an Estate Income account, which accumulates undistributed earnings.

A detailed discussion of the various types of income transactions and charges made against income is delayed until after the illustration of estate accounting. For simplicity, the illustration limits income transactions to interest on savings and bond investments, cash dividends on corporate stock investments, and interest on a partnership investment.

Illustration

THE OPENING ENTRY AND SUBSEQUENT TRANSACTIONS

David Diamond died testate on March 27, 19X1, with the following provisions in his will:

1. The decedent's residence and household items are left to his wife, Krystal Diamond, who assumes the mortgage on the residence.
2. Cash of $150,000 is to be given to Krystal Diamond.
3. All the corporate stocks are to be given to the decedent's alma mater, Krebitsville University, to be used for scholarships in accounting.
4. The decedent's automobile is to be given to Ruby Diamond, the decedent's sister.
5. The residual balance of the estate is to be placed in trust with the following terms:
   a. *Trustee:* Coral Point Bank
   b. *Income beneficiary:* Krystal Diamond, wife of the decedent, for the remainder of her natural life.
   c. *Principal beneficiaries:* Jade and Opal Diamond, the only two children of the decedent. The principal is to be distributed at the later of: (a) the date of death of Krystal Diamond, or (b) when both Jade and Opal Diamond reach the age of 25. (If Krystal Diamond dies before both children reach the age of 25, then the children succeed her as income beneficiaries until they both reach the age of 25.)
   d. The accrual basis is to be used in determining principal at the time of death.
6. State inheritance taxes are to be paid out of the residue of the estate and not by the individual heirs, except for the case of the automobile given to Ruby Diamond.

7. The decedent's personal financial advisor, Jack Cass, is named executor of the estate.

The estate of David Diamond consists of the following items, each listed at its current value:

Assets Subject to Probate Administration:		
Cash (including checking and savings accounts)		$ 70,000
U.S. government and corporate bonds—face value, $350,000; cost, $341,000		337,000
Corporate stocks—cost, $38,000		63,000
Life insurance (payable to the estate)		100,000
Investment in partnership of Diamond, Ring, and Stone:		
Capital account balance at date of death, net of drawings	$84,000	
Share of profits from close of preceding partnership accounting period to date of death	14,000	
Share of partnership goodwill deemed to exist at date of death (calculated according to the terms of the partnership agreement)	22,000	120,000
Accrued interest receivable on bonds		10,000
Accrued interest receivable on savings accounts		2,000
Dividends declared on corporate stocks		1,000
Automobile		7,000
Total		$ 710,000
Assets Not Subject to Probate Administration:		
Residence and household items		240,000
Duplex rental unit (cost, $75,000) subject to secured loan of $55,000		110,000
Total Estate Assets		$1,060,000
Liabilities to Be Paid out of Probate Estate:		
Outstanding balance on credit cards		$ 1,100
Medical expenses pertaining to illness		3,700
State and federal income taxes for the period January 1, 19X1 to March 27, 19X1		5,500
Total		$ 10,300
Liabilities Not to Be Paid out of Probate Estate:		
Mortgage on residence		30,000
Mortgage on duplex rental unit		55,000
Total Estate Liabilities		$ 95,300

In reviewing the items making up the estate, note that we have assumed that the decedent's residence, household items, and the duplex rental unit are not subject to probate administration of the state probate law.

Consequently, the residence and household items pass immediately to the decedent's surviving spouse outside probate, and the duplex rental unit passes immediately to the trustee outside of probate. None of these items is accounted for in the administration of the estate. Accounting for the depreciable assets of a trust (such as the duplex rental unit used in this illustration) is discussed and illustrated later in the chapter.

The opening entry in the estate books follows.

Principal Cash	70,000	
Investment in Bonds	337,000	
Investment in Stocks	63,000	
Life Insurance Receivable	100,000	
Investment in Partnership of Diamond, Ring, and Stone	120,000	
Accrued Interest Receivable on Bonds	10,000	
Accrued Interest Receivable on Savings Accounts	2,000	
Dividends Declared on Corporate Stocks	1,000	
Automobile	7,000	
Estate Principal		710,000

No liabilities are recorded, because the accounting concerns the administration of estate assets.

Assumed transactions and related journal entries pertaining to activities completed by the executor during the administration of the estate from March 27, 19X1, to June 30, 19X2, are as follows:

Transaction	Entry		
1. Subsequent discovery of a checking account.	Principal Cash	700	
	Asset Subsequently Discovered		700
2. Receipt of life insurance proceeds.	Principal Cash	100,000	
	Life Insurance Receivable		100,000
3. Receipt of proceeds from liquidation of investment in partnership, along with interest to date of receipt.	Principal Cash	120,000	
	Income Cash	4,000	
	Investment in Partnership		120,000
	Interest Income		4,000
4. Receipt of interest on bonds.	Principal Cash	10,000	
	Income Cash	18,000	
	Accrued Bond Interest Receivable		10,000
	Interest Income		18,000
5. Receipt of interest on savings accounts.	Principal Cash	2,000	
	Income Cash	6,000	
	Accrued Interest Receivable on Savings Accounts		2,000
	Interest Income		6,000

Transaction	Entry		
6. Receipt of cash dividends on corporate stocks. (Receipts pertaining to dividends declared during the estate administration accrue to the legatee.)	Principal Cash	4,000	
	Accrued Dividends Receivable		1,000
	Liability to Krebitsville University		3,000
7. Payment of credit card, medical, and income tax liabilities.	Debts of Decedent	10,300	
	Principal Cash		10,300
8. Payment of funeral and administrative expenses.	Funeral and Administrative Expenses	11,000	
	Principal Cash		11,000
9. Payment of $49,300 inheritance taxes, $300 of which is to be borne by Ruby Diamond, who received the decedent's automobile.	Inheritance Taxes	49,000	
	Receivable from Legatee, Ruby Diamond	300	
	Principal Cash		49,300
10. Distribution of automobile as gift (a specific legacy) and collection of related inheritance taxes from legatee.	Principal Cash	300	
	Legacies Distributed	7,000	
	Receivable from Legatee, Ruby Diamond		300
	Automobile		7,000
11. Distribution of corporate stocks as gift (specific legacy) to Krebitsville University, along with dividend receipts pertaining to dividends declared and received during the estate administration.	Legacies Distributed	63,000	
	Liability to Krebitsville University	3,000	
	Investment in Stocks		63,000
	Principal Cash		3,000
12. Sale of a portion of the bonds to raise cash. (Current value at Diamond's death was $9,600.)	Principal Cash	9,800	
	Investment in Bonds		9,600
	Gain on Sale of Principal Asset		200
13. Distribution of cash (general legacy) to Krystal Diamond.	Legacies Distributed	150,000	
	Principal Cash		150,000
14. Payment of income taxes relating to estate income.	Estate Income Tax Expense	4,600	
	Income Cash		4,600
15. Payment of administration expenses pertaining to income.	Administration Expenses	300	
	Income Cash		300
16. Distributions to income beneficiary of trust.	Distributions to Income Beneficiary	18,000	
	Income Cash		18,000

We assume that no estate taxes are owed because of the use of the unlimited marital deduction. If estate taxes had been paid, the entry would appear as follows:

Estate Taxes	xxx	
Principal Cash		xxx

Illustration

CHARGE AND DISCHARGE STATEMENTS

Continuing with our illustration, the only remaining task for the estate fiduciary is to submit an accounting to the probate court with a request to distribute the residual balance of the estate to the trustee, Coral Point Bank. Trial balances for the principal entity and the income entity as of June 30, 19X2, are presented in Illustration 26-1. Charge and discharge

Illustration 26-1

ESTATE OF DAVID DIAMOND
Trial Balance — Principal
June 30, 19X2

	Debit	Credit
Cash	$ 93,200	
Investments in bonds	327,400	
Estate principal		$710,000
Asset subsequently discovered		700
Gain on sale of principal asset		200
Debts of decedent	10,300	
Funeral and administrative expenses	11,000	
Inheritance taxes	49,000	
Legacies distributed	220,000	
Totals	$710,900	$710,900

ESTATE OF DAVID DIAMOND
Trial Balance — Income
June 30, 19X2

	Debit	Credit
Cash	$ 5,100	
Interest income		$ 28,000
Estate income tax expense	4,600	
Administrative expenses	300	
Distributions to income beneficiary	18,000	
Totals	$ 28,000	$ 28,000

statements, which portray the activity of these entities through June 30, 19X2, are shown in Illustration 26-2. The charge and discharge statements are usually accompanied by supporting schedules—such as the detail of the decedent's debts paid and the detail of legacies distributed. Because they are quite simple, such schedules are not presented.

Illustration

CLOSING ENTRIES FOR THE ESTATE

Assuming the probate court authorizes the distribution of the residual Diamond estate assets to the trustee, the entries to record the distributions and close the estate books are as follows:

Illustration 26-2

ESTATE OF DAVID DIAMOND
Jack Cass, Executor of the Estate
Charge and Discharge Statements
March 27, 19X1–June 30, 19X2

First, as to Principal:		
I charge myself as follows:		
Assets per inventory	$710,000	
Assets discovered	700	
Gain on asset realization	200	$710,900
I credit myself as follows:		
Debts of decedent paid	$ 10,300	
Funeral and administrative expenses paid	11,000	
Inheritance taxes paid	49,000	
Legacies distributed	220,000	(290,300)
Balance of the estate:		
Principal cash	$ 93,200	
Investment in bonds	327,400	$420,600
Second, as to Income:		
I charge myself as follows:		
Interest received on bonds	$ 18,000	
Interest received on savings accounts	6,000	
Interest received on partnership investment	4,000	$ 28,000
I credit myself as follows:		
Estate income taxes paid	$ 4,600	
Administrative expenses paid	300	
Distributions made to income beneficiary	18,000	(22,900)
Balance of the estate:		
Income cash		$ 5,100

Transaction	Entry		
17. Distribution of residual estate assets of principal entity to Coral Point Bank, trustee.	Legacies Distributed............	420,600	
	Principal Cash..................		93,200
	Investment in Bonds..........		327,400
18. Distribution of residual estate assets of income entity to Coral Point Bank, trustee.	Distribution to Trustee for Income Beneficiary...........	5,100	
	Income Cash		5,100
19. Closing of nominal accounts of principal entity into estate principal.	Asset Subsequently Discovered	700	
	Gain on Sale of Principal Asset	200	
	Estate Principal....................	710,000	
	Debts of Decedent		10,300
	Funeral and Administrative Expenses.......................		11,000
	Inheritance Taxes		49,000
	Legacies Distributed..........		640,600
20. Closing of nominal accounts of income entity.	Interest Income	28,000	
	Estate Income Tax Expense		4,600
	Administrative Expenses....		300
	Distributions to Income Beneficiary....................		18,000
	Distribution to Trustee for Income Beneficiary.........		5,100

ACCOUNTING FOR TRUSTS

Accounting for trusts is identical to accounting for estates, except that a Trust Principal account is used rather than Estate Principal for the principal entity, and a Trust Income account is used rather than Estate Income for the income entity to accumulate undistributed earnings. The nature of the transactions is also different. An estate fiduciary is concerned primarily with cleaning up the affairs of a decedent and making proper distributions of estate property. A trustee, on the other hand, is concerned primarily with prudently managing a pool of assets in accordance with the powers granted to him or her by the trust agreement. This task usually involves buying and selling trust assets. Trustees must make periodic accountings to the principal and income beneficiaries and the probate court. A charge and discharge statement similar to the one illustrated for estates is used. Upon termination of the life of the trust, the trustee distributes the assets of the trust principal to the remainderman, makes a final accounting to the court, and requests to be discharged.

Using the illustration from the preceding section, the entries to record the receipt of the gifts from the estate of David Diamond are as follows. This is the principal entity:

Principle Cash..	93,200	
Investment in Bonds	327,400	
Trust Principal......................................		420,600

This is the income entity:

Income Cash	5,100	
Trust Income		5,100

Transactions Pertaining to Principal

Early in the chapter we summarized the general thrust of the accounting requirements of the Revised Uniform Principal and Income Act regarding principal transactions. Some finer points of principal transactions are as follows:

1. The costs of investing and reinvesting principal assets are charged against principal.
2. The costs of preparing property for rental or sale are charged against principal.
3. Taxes levied on gains or profits allocated to principal are charged against principal.
4. The costs incurred in maintaining or defending any action to protect the trust or trust property or ensure title to any trust property are charged against principal.
5. Extraordinary repairs or costs incurred in making capital improvements paid for out of principal may be recouped from income through depreciation charges.
6. Trustee's fees and costs relating to the periodic accounting to the court of jurisdiction (court costs, attorney fees, and accounting fees, for example) are shared equally between principal and income.
7. Liquidating dividends are considered to be principal.
8. Stock dividends go to principal, not income.

Transactions Pertaining to Income

As mentioned earlier, under the Revised Uniform Principal and Income Act, interest and cash dividends are considered income transactions. The act also includes the following as income: rents, loan prepayment penalties, lease cancellation charges, lease renewal fees, and the net profits of any business in which principal is invested. Losses of any business in which principal is invested are charged to principal, because no provision exists for loss carryforward or carryback into any other calendar or fiscal year for purposes of calculating net income. Profits and losses of such businesses are to be determined using generally accepted accounting principles.

Among other things, the act includes as charges against income the interest expense on trust liabilities (such as a mortgage on a trust rental property), property taxes, insurance premiums, ordinary repairs, depreciation expenses (including depreciation charges pertaining to extraordinary repairs), income taxes attributable to trust income, a share of trustee fees and costs relating to periodic accounting to the court, and any other ordinary expense incurred in connection with the administration, management, or preservation of trust property. (Depreciation and unusual charges are discussed in detail in the following paragraphs because of the unique manner in which journal entries are recorded.)

Depreciation. Under the act, depreciation is mandatory and results in preserving the estate principal for the principal beneficiaries. However, under many state statutes, depreciation is provided at the discretion of the trustee. When depreciation is to be provided, a portion of the income entity's revenue flow must go to the principal entity. Because we view the trust as comprising two entities, the accounting entries to record depreciation produce results as if the principal entity had sent a bill to the income entity for the use or consumption of the depreciable asset. The entries are as follows:

1. To record depreciation:

	Income Entity		Principal Entity	
Depreciation Expense.................	1,000			
Due to Principal................		1,000		
Due from Income........................			1,000	
Accumulated Depreciation.				1,000

2. To record payment:

Due to Principal.........................	1,000			
Income Cash.....................		1,000		
Principal Cash...........................			1,000	
Due from Income..............				1,000

Whether or not to provide depreciation should be thoroughly explored in estate planning. Depreciation charges may deprive an income beneficiary of income necessary to maintain the standard of living intended by the decedent. Depreciation makes no sense if the properties are appreciating in value, as is the case with many rental properties. If depreciation is to be provided, it should be computed based on the current value of the property when it becomes subject to the trust.

Unusual Charges against Income. The Revised Uniform Principal and Income Act states:

> If charges against income are of unusual amount, the trustee may by means of reserves or other reasonable means charge them over a reasonable period of time and withhold from distribution sufficient sums to regularize distributions [Section 13(b)].

The provision is somewhat ambiguous and open-ended. Under the "by means of reserves" approach, the trustee must anticipate and estimate expected unusual charges before they are incurred. Charges are then made against income over a reasonable period of time prior to their incurrence, resulting in the buildup of a "reserve," or estimated liability. The cash distributable to the income beneficiary during these periods is limited; thus, funds accumulate from which to make the expenditure when it actually arises. Under the "by other reasonable means" option, the trustee can possibly have the principal entity make the expenditure when it arises but record the expenditure as a deferred charge, which is subsequently amortized against income.

The entries under each approach for an unusually large expenditure, such as the painting of an apartment building exterior, are as follows:

1. **Accumulation Method:**
   a. Periodic charge.

	Income Entity		Principal Entity	
Estimated Painting Expense	1,000		(no entry)	
Estimated Future Liability.		1,000		

   b. Actual payment.

	Income Entity		Principal Entity	
Estimated Future Liability	5,000		(no entry)	
Income Cash		5,000		

2. **Amortization Method:**
   a. Actual payment.

	Income Entity		Principal Entity	
Painting of Building	(no entry)		5,000	
Principal Cash				5,000

   b. Periodic amortization.

	Income Entity		Principal Entity	
Painting Expense	1,000			
Due to Principal		1,000		
Due from Income	(no entry)		1,000	
Painting of Building				1,000

SUMMARY

The fundamental function of estate and trust fiduciaries is to administer assets under their control rather than attempting to determine the net worth of an estate or trust. Accordingly, accounting for estates and trusts involves accounting for assets rather than accounting for net worth. As a result, special bookkeeping practices and accountability statements are used for estates and trusts that are quite unlike those found in commercial enterprises. Furthermore, the cash basis of accounting suffices in most instances.

Generally accepted accounting principles have virtually no application to estates and trusts. Trust income (including trust income during the administration of an estate) is determined according to the terms and provisions of the trust agreement. If the trust agreement is silent on the treatment to be accorded an item, then state statutes control. An accountant rendering services to a trust must recognize that his or her role is a passive one when it comes to determining the treatment to be accorded items that are not clearly set forth in the trust agreement or state statutes. Decisions on such matters should be referred to legal counsel or the courts. In most cases, an accountant rendering services to an estate or trust must also have expertise in estate, inheritance, and trust taxation.

Glossary of New Terms

Administrator A person appointed by the court to administer the affairs of a decedent when an executor is not appointed.

Demonstrative Legacy A gift of cash for which a particular fund or source is designated from which payment is to be made.

Devise A gift of real property.

Devisee The recipient of a devise.

Estate The property of a decedent.

Estate Planning The making of plans for the orderly transfer of one's property on death as desired, with a view toward minimizing transfer costs.

Executor A person who is named in a will to serve as the decedent's personal representative in administering the estate and who is appointed by the court to serve in that capacity.

General Legacy Gifts of cash for which no particular fund or source is designated.

Income Beneficiary The party to a trust who is entitled to the income earned on trust assets.

***Inter Vivos* Trust** A trust created during a person's life.

Intestate A term used to refer to having died without a will.

Legacy A gift of personal property.

Legatee The recipient of a legacy.

Principal Beneficiary The party to a trust who is entitled to the trust principal.

Probate The act by which a probate court determines if a decedent's will meets the statutory requirements concerning wills.

Probate Court Courts in the state court system that have jurisdiction over the affairs of decedents.

Remainderman The party to a trust who is entitled to the trust principal.

Residual Legacy A gift of all personal property remaining after distribution of specific, demonstrative, and general legacies.

Testamentary Trust A trust that comes into being on a person's death, pursuant to provisions in the decedent's will.

Testate A term used to refer to having died with a will.

Trust An arrangement in which property is transferred to a person, called a trustee, who holds title to the property but administers the property for the benefit of other parties, who are called the beneficiaries.

Trustee That party to a trust who takes title to trust property and administers the property for the benefit of others.

Trustor The party to a trust agreement who created the trust. (Also referred to as a settlor, grantor, donor, or creator.)

Specific Legacy A gift of specified noncash items.

Selected Reference

"Estate Planning Perils for CPA Partners and Shareholders," by Bernard Barnett. *Journal of Accountancy* (January 1986), 68–76.

Review Questions

1. What role do generally accepted accounting principles play in determining trust income? Explain.
2. How do we determine whether a transaction pertains to principal or income?
3. What is the nature of the relationship between a trust income beneficiary and a trust principal beneficiary?
4. What are legacies and devises?
5. Are estate liabilities recorded in the opening entry for an estate? Why or why not?
6. An estate fiduciary may have to deal with what four types of taxes?
7. Under the Revised Uniform Principal and Income Act, when do the rights of income beneficiaries begin?
8. When is the accrual method used in accounting for estates and trusts?
9. What is the function of probate administration?
10. State the major tasks of an estate fiduciary.
11. Describe the accountant's role with respect to distinguishing between principal and income transactions.
12. Must assets and transactions pertaining to income be accounted for in separate general ledgers? Explain.

Discussion Cases

DC 26-1

Estate Planning

Your client, Jan Landers, has asked your advice on accounting matters with respect to her attorney's preparation of a testamentary trust agreement. Jan wants all her residential rental property holdings placed in trust for the benefit of her husband (as income beneficiary) and her children (as principal beneficiaries).

Required:
On what points should you advise your client? (Assume you are located in a state that has adopted the Revised Uniform Principal and Income Act without modification.)

DC 26-2

Role of the Accountant

An attorney who is an acquaintance of yours has suggested that you attend a meeting that may lead to some work for you. At the meeting, you are informed that: (1) Ken Dall died approximately one year ago; (2) the attorney is serving as the executor of the estate; (3) the residual balance of the estate is to be placed in trust; and (4) the trustee is Barbara Dall, Ken's widow. Mrs. Dall describes the nature of the trust assets as bonds, residential rental properties, and the stock of a wholly owned corporation, which continues to operate. She requests that you become the accountant for the trust and, in that capacity, do the following:

1. Maintain the books and records.
2. Make all accounting decisions.
3. Prepare the fiduciary income tax returns.
4. Prepare the annual financial statements.

Required:
How would you respond to this request? Elaborate on the points you should discuss with Mrs. Dall.

Exercises

E 26-1

Estates: True or False

Indicate whether the following statements are true or false. Explain any false answers.

1. An estate is a taxable entity.
2. An estate is a legal entity.
3. The probate estate is usually smaller than the estate for federal estate tax purposes.
4. One function of an estate fiduciary is to account for the estate in a manner that continually reflects the estate's net worth.
5. Federal estate taxes are effectively borne by the residual beneficiaries of the estate.

6. State inheritance taxes are based on the right to give away one's property.
7. The Estate Principal account reflects the net worth of the estate at a given point in time.
8. Accounting for estates revolves around the administration of the decedent's assets.
9. The probate court essentially serves as the guardian of the estate.
10. A legacy is a gift of real property.

E 26-2

Estates: Fill-in Statements

Fill in the missing words for the following items.

1. An estate fiduciary who is named in a decedent's will is called a(n) __________ .
2. An estate fiduciary who is appointed by the probate court when no person is named in a decedent's will is called a(n) __________ .
3. A gift of personal property is called a __________ .
4. A gift of real property is called a __________ .
5. The four types of legacies are __________ , __________ , __________ , and __________ .
6. A person who dies without a will is said to have died __________ .
7. A person who dies with a will is said to have died __________ .
8. State laws dealing with the affairs of decedents are commonly known as __________ __________ .
9. Federal estate taxes are based on the right to __________ property.
10. State inheritance taxes are based on the right to __________ property.

E 26-3

Trusts: True or False

Indicate whether the following statements are true or false. Explain any false answers.

1. When the income beneficiary and the principal beneficiary are the same person, no built-in clash of interests exists as in trusts in which these beneficiaries are not the same person.
2. The rights of an income beneficiary begin when assets are actually transferred to the trustee.
3. In trust accounting matters, the terms of the trust agreement prevail over generally accepted accounting principles.
4. When the accounting treatment of an item is not clearly specified in the trust agreement, reference is made to generally accepted accounting principles.
5. The Revised Uniform Principal and Income Act of 1962 is somewhat outdated because it is based on generally accepted accounting principles in effect at that time.
6. When reference must be made to state laws to distinguish trust principal from trust income, it is the accountant's role to interpret those laws concerning accounting matters.
7. The Revised Uniform Principal and Income Act specifies the use of the accrual basis for many items at the commencement of a trust.

8. Accounts and transactions pertaining to trust income must be accounted for in a separate ledger to prevent commingling of accounts and transactions with that of trust principal.
9. If the answer to an accounting question cannot be found by referring to the trust agreement, state law, or case law, then reference is made to generally accepted accounting principles.
10. Trustors may specify their own definition of net income, even if this definition is contrary to state laws pertaining to trust principal and income.

E 26-4

Trusts: Fill-in Statements

Fill in the missing words for the following items.

1. The person creating a trust is commonly called the ____________ .
2. Trusts established pursuant to the provisions of a will are called ____________ trusts.
3. Trusts established during a person's life are called ____________ trusts.
4. The party taking title to trust assets is called the ____________ .
5. The two classes of trust beneficiaries are the ____________ beneficiaries and the ____________ beneficiaries.
6. Another term for trust principal is trust ____________ .
7. The basis of accounting that is used in most respects when an income beneficiary's rights are established is the ____________ basis.
8. Depreciation is ____________ under the Revised Uniform Principal and Income Act.
9. When the accounting treatment of an item is in doubt, the first place to look is the ____________ ____________ .
10. The ____________ basis of accounting is used during the administration of a trust but not at the beginning and end of an income beneficiary's rights.

E 26-5

Estates: Preparing Journal Entries

Emory Feldspar died on May 12, 19X1, with a provision in his will for the establishment of a testamentary trust. His estate had the following assets subject to probate administration:

	Current Value
Cash in checking and savings accounts	$ 42,000
Investment in U.S. government bonds	387,000
Coin collection	11,000
Bond interest receivable	6,500
Total	$446,500

The estate fiduciary had the following receipts and disbursements from May 12, 19X1, to January 20, 19X2:

1. Personal liabilities totaling $2,200 were paid.
2. Funeral expenses of $1,800 were paid.

3. Federal estate taxes of $37,000 were paid.
4. State inheritance taxes of $14,000 were paid. Of this amount, $400 is to be borne by the legatee receiving the coin collection, and $1,100 is to be borne by the legatee (Children's Hospital) that is to receive $25,000 cash.
5. Administrative expenses of $3,000 were paid.
6. A note receivable of $2,000 was discovered in September 19X1.
7. The note receivable in item 6 was collected in December 19X1, along with $150 interest.
8. Interest on bonds was received totaling $22,000.
9. Bonds having a current value of $60,500 at Feldspar's death were sold for $58,800.
10. The coin collection was distributed to the specified legatee, and the legatee reimbursed the estate for the inheritance taxes at that time.
11. Cash of $23,900 was distributed to Children's Hospital ($25,000 specified in the will – $1,100 state inheritance taxes).
12. Estate income taxes for the period May 12, 19X1, to December 31, 19X1, totaling $3,800 were paid.
13. Cash of $10,000 was distributed to the income beneficiary of the trust, Pearl Feldspar.

Required:

1. Prepare the opening and subsequent transaction journal entries for the estate.
2. Prepare closing journal entries as of January 20, 19X2.

E 26-6

Trusts: Preparing Journal Entries

Following are the 19X3 transactions of a trust that has investments in corporate bonds and an apartment house:

1. Rental receipts totaled $38,500.
2. Property taxes of $1,400 were paid.
3. Mortgage payments of $15,500 were made. Of this amount, $14,900 pertained to interest and $600 pertained to principal. (Assume that the mortgage liability is reflected as a liability in the trust general ledger only on a memorandum basis.)
4. Normal operating costs of the apartment totaling $7,300 were paid.
5. The exterior of the apartment building was painted in January 19X3 for $2,100, and payment was made at that time. The apartment exterior is painted approximately every seven years. (Assume that this qualifies as an "unusual amount," as that term is used in Section 13[b] of the Revised Uniform Principal and Income Act.)
6. The annual depreciation charge on the apartment is $4,500.
7. Bond investments having a face value of $50,000 matured during the year and were redeemed. (These bonds had a current value of $48,800 when they became subject to the trust.)
8. Federal trust income taxes pertaining to the prior year were paid totaling $450.
9. Estimated federal trust income tax payments for the current year were paid totaling $1,850.

10. The $2,200 trustee's fee for the year was paid.
11. Interest receipts on bond investments totaled $14,400.
12. Cash distributions totaling $9,000 were made to the income beneficiary.

Required:

1. Prepared the trust transaction journal entries for the year.
2. Prepare the year-end closing entries.

Problems

P 26-1

Estates: Preparing Charge and Discharge Statements

The will of Tom Ford, deceased, directed that his executor, Wayne Pilgrim, liquidate the entire estate within two years of the date of Ford's death and pay the net proceeds and income, if any, to the Children's Town Orphanage. Ford, who never married, died February 1, 19X4, after a brief illness.

An inventory of the decedent's property subject to probate administration was prepared, and the fair market value of each item was determined. The preliminary inventory, before the computation of any appropriate income accruals on inventory items, follows:

	Fair Market Value
Monument Valley Bank checking account	$ 6,000
$60,000 of 8% Bootville City school bonds, payable January 1 and July 1, maturity date of July 1, 19X8	59,000
2,000 shares of Rider Corporation capital stock	220,000
Term life insurance, beneficiary—estate of Tom Ford	20,000
Personal residence ($75,000) and furnishings ($15,000)	90,000

The following transactions occurred during 19X4:

1. The interest on the Bootville City bonds was collected. The bonds were sold on July 1 for $59,000, and the proceeds and interest were paid to the orphanage.
2. The Rider Corporation paid cash dividends of $1 per share on March 1 and December 1, as well as a 10% stock dividend on July 1. All dividends were declared 45 days before each payment date and were payable to stockholders of record as of 40 days before each payment date. On September 2, Pilgrim sold 1,000 shares at $105 per share, and paid the proceeds to the orphanage.
3. Because of a depressed real estate market, the personal residence was rented furnished at $300 per month commencing April 1. The rent is paid monthly, in advance. Real estate taxes of $900 for calendar year 19X4 were paid. The house and furnishings have estimated lives of 45 and 10 years, respectively. The part-time caretaker was paid four months' wages totaling $500 on April 30 for services performed, and he was released.
4. The Monument Valley Bank checking account was closed; the $6,000 balance was transferred to an estate bank account.

5. The term life insurance was paid on March 1 and deposited in the estate bank account.
6. The following disbursements were made:
   a. Funeral expenses, $2,000.
   b. Final illness expenses, $1,500.
   c. April 15 income tax remittance, $700.
   d. Attorney's and accountant's fees, $12,000.
7. On December 31, the balance of the undistributed income, except for $1,000, was paid to the orphanage. The balance of the cash on hand derived from the estate principal was also paid to the orphanage on December 31.

Required:
Prepare Charge and Discharge Statements, separating principal and income, together with supporting schedules, on behalf of the executor for the period February 1, 19X4, through December 31, 19X4. The following supporting schedules should be included:

1. Original Principal of Estate
2. Gain or Loss on Disposal of Estate Assets
3. Funeral, Administration, and Other Expenses
4. Debts of Decedent Paid
5. Legacies Paid or Delivered
6. Assets (Corpus) on Hand, December 31, 19X4
7. Income Collected
8. Expenses Chargeable to Income
9. Distributions of Income

(AICPA adapted)

P 26-2

Estates: Preparing Charge and Discharge Statements

Ron Ho died in an accident on May 31, 19X1. His will, dated February 28, 19X0, provided that all just debts and expenses be paid and that his property be disposed of as follows:

1. Personal residence is devised to Donna Ho, widow. (Real property is not subject to probate administration in the state in which the deceased resided.)
2. U.S. Treasury bonds and Bubb Company stock is to be placed in trust. All income to go to Donna Ho during her lifetime, with right of appointment on her death.
3. Happe Company mortgage notes are bequeathed to Lulu Ho Waters, daughter.
4. A bequest of $10,000 cash goes to Dave Ho, son.
5. Remainder of estate is to be divided equally between the two children.

The will further provided that during the administration period, Donna Ho was to be paid $800 a month out of estate income. Estate and inheritance taxes are to be borne by the residue. Dave Ho was named executor and trustee.

An inventory of the decedent's property was prepared. The fair market value of all items as of Ho's death was determined. The preliminary inventory, before the computation of any appropriate income accruals on inventory items, is as follows:

Personal residence property	$145,000
Jewelry—diamond ring	9,600
Oahu Life Insurance Company—term life insurance policy on life of Ron Ho; beneficiary, Donna Ho, widow	120,000
Marble Trust Company—8% savings account, Ron Ho, in trust for Lelani Waters (grandchild), interest credited January 1 and July 1; balance May 31, 19X1	400
Hilo National Bank—checking account; balance May 31, 19X1	141,750
$200,000 U.S. Treasury bonds, 10%; interest payable March 1 and September 1	200,000
$10,000 Happe Company first mortgage notes, 12%, 19X5; interest payable June 30 and December 31	9,900
800 shares Bubb Company common stock	64,000
700 shares Maui Manufacturing Company common stock	70,000

The executor opened an estate bank account, to which he transferred the decedent's checking account balance. Other deposits, through July 1, 19X2, were as follows:

Interest collected on bonds:	
$200,000 U.S. Treasury—	
September 1, 19X1	$10,000
March 1, 19X2	10,000
Dividends received on stock:	
800 shares Bubb Company—	
June 15, 19X1, declared May 7, 19X1, payable to holders of record May 27, 19X1	800
September 15, 19X1	800
December 15, 19X1	1,200
March 15, 19X2	800
June 15, 19X2	800
Net proceeds of June 19, 19X1, sale of 700 shares of Maui Manufacturing Company	68,810
Interest collected on Happe Company first mortgage notes—June 30, 19X1	600

Payments were made from the estate's checking account through July 1, 19X2, for the following items:

Funeral expenses	$ 2,000
Assessments for additional 19X0 federal and state income tax ($1,700) plus interests ($110) to May 31, 19X1	1,810
19X1 income taxes of Ron Ho for the period January 1, 19X1, through May 31, 19X1, in excess of estimated taxes paid by the decedent	9,100
Federal and state fiduciary income taxes, fiscal year ended June 30, 19X1 ($75), and June 30, 19X2 ($1,400)	1,475
State inheritance taxes	28,000
Monthly payments to Donna Ho: 13 payments of $800	10,400
Attorney's and accountant's fees	25,000
Payment of interest collected on Happe Company mortgage notes that accrues to legatee	600

The executor waived his commission. However, he wanted his father's diamond ring in lieu of the $10,000 specific legacy. All parties agreed to this in writing, and the court's approval was secured. All other specific legacies were delivered by July 15, 19X1.

Required:
Prepare Charge and Discharge Statements for principal and income, and supporting schedules, to accompany the attorney's formal court accounting on behalf of the executor of the Estate of Ron Ho for the period May 31, 19X1, through July 1, 19X2. The following supporting schedules should be included:

1. Original Capital of Estate
2. Gain on Disposal of Estate Assets
3. Loss on Disposal of Estate Assets
4. Funeral, Administration, and Other Expenses
5. Debts of Decedent Paid
6. Legacies Paid or Delivered
7. Assets (Corpus) on Hand, July 1, 19X2
8. Proposed Plan of Distribution of Estate Assets
9. Income Collected
10. Distribution of Income

(AICPA adapted)

P 26-3

Trusts: Treatment of Disputed Items

You have been assigned by a CPA firm to work with the trustees of a large trust in the preparation of the first annual accounting to the court. The income beneficiaries and the remaindermen cannot agree on the proper allocation of the following items on which the trust agreement is silent:

1. Costs incurred in expanding the garage facilities of an apartment house owned by the trust and held for rental income.
2. Real estate taxes on the apartment house.
3. Cost of casualty insurance premiums on the apartment house.
4. A 2-for-1 stock split of common stock held by the trust for investment.
5. Insurance proceeds received as the result of a partial destruction of an office building that the trust owned and held for rental income.
6. Costs incurred by the trust in the sale of a tract of land.
7. Costs incurred to defend title to real property held by the trust.

Required:
Locate a copy of the Revised Uniform Principal and Income Act in your library. Indicate the allocations between principal and income to be made for each item, using the act as the point of reference. Be sure to quote the applicable section of the act. (The purpose of this problem is to force you to search out items in the act, a task that is necessary in actual practice.)

P 26-4

Trusts: Preparing Journal Entries and Charge and Discharge Statements

The postclosing combined trial balance for the principal entity and the income entity of a trust as of December 31, 19X3, is as follows:

	Debit	Credit
Principal Cash	$ 3,500	
Income Cash	800	
Investments in Bonds	123,400	
Investment in E & T Corporation Common Stock	86,200	
Duplex Rental Unit	95,000	
Accumulated Depreciation on Duplex Rental Unit		$ 12,000
Trust Principal		296,100
Trust Income		800
Totals	$308,900	$308,900

Following are the 19X4 trust transactions:

1. Rental receipts were $11,500.
2. Property taxes of $1,000 were paid.
3. Mortgage payments of $6,500 were made. Of this amount, $5,800 pertained to interest and $700 pertained to principal. (The mortgage liability of $57,500 on the duplex at December 31, 19X3, is recorded in the trust general ledger on a memorandum basis.)
4. Normal operating costs of the duplex rental unit totaling $600 were paid.
5. New carpeting was installed in both units of the duplex in January 19X4 at a cost of $1,800, with payment being made at that time. (New carpeting is installed approximately every ten years.)
6. The annual depreciation charge on the duplex is $2,000. (Of the $95,000 value assigned to the duplex when it became subject to the trust, $15,000 was assigned to land, and $80,000 was assigned to the building, carpets, and drapes. The $80,000 is depreciated over 40 years.)
7. Bonds investments having a face value of $25,000 matured during the year and were redeemed. (These bonds had a $25,500 current value when they became subject to the trust.)
8. Bonds having a face value of $20,000 were purchased in the open market for $19,000 on July 1, 19X4. The maturity date of the bonds is June 30, 19X9.
9. Interest receipts on bond investments totaled $9,800.
10. E & T Corporation declared a 10% stock dividend on April 1, 19X4. The trust held 200 shares of E & T's common stock prior to this declaration. (The market price of E & T's common stock increased $30 per share during 19X4.)
11. Cash dividends of $3,300 on E & T Corporation's common stock were received.
12. The $1,500 trustee's fee for the year was paid.
13. Attorney's and accountant's fees for periodic judicial accounting totaling $1,200 were paid.
14. Cash distributions totaling $8,000 were made to the income beneficiary.
15. "Due to" and "due from" accounts are settled at year-end.

Required:

1. Prepare the trust transaction journal entries for the year.
2. Prepare the year-end closing entries.
3. Prepare Charge and Discharge Statements for the year for trust principal and trust income.

27

Installment Sales, Franchises, and Consignments

Accounting for Installment Sales

Accounting for the Business Franchise

Accounting for Consignments

Summary

Certain businesses conduct operations in a manner that demands special or delayed revenue recognition practices. In this chapter, we discuss accounting for installment sales, business franchises, and consignments.

ACCOUNTING FOR INSTALLMENT SALES

In some sales transactions in which credit is granted, the terms provide for the collection of the sales price in installments over an extended period of time. Such sales are commonly referred to as **installment sales.** The terms and conditions of installment sales may vary widely, as follows:

1. **Collection period:** A collection period of from one to three years is common for installment sales in the retail furniture and appliance businesses. For the retail land sales business, the collection period may be as long as 10 or 15 years.
2. **Cash down payment:** Some installment sales require a fairly high cash down payment (ranging from 20% to 40% of the sales price), forcing the buyer immediately to have a material equity in the purchased item. On the other hand, some installment sales require only a nominal cash down payment, such as 5% of the sales price.
3. **Seller's recourse in the event of default:** If the buyer defaults on payment of the receivable, the seller's only recourse may be to repossess the item. In other cases, the seller may have recourse against other assets of the purchaser.

Accordingly, installment sales usually produce more uncertainty than noninstallment sales regarding the ability and willingness of the buyer to make full payment. Furthermore, the ability and willingness of the buyer to make full payment may change over the extended period of collection. For some installment sales, this uncertainty is so great that no reasonable basis exists for estimating the degree of collectibility of the receivable. In such cases, prudence dictates that a more conservative approach be used to report such transactions than that used for credit sales in which collection of the sales price is reasonably assured. Two methods may be used to effect a more conservative treatment—the installment method and the cost recovery method.

The Installment Method

Under the **installment method,** a sale is recorded, but the gross profit on the sale is recognized in the income statement only in proportion to the payments received on the purchase price. In this way, recognition of the gross profit is delayed (through the use of deferral accounts), and the receivable is carried at a conservative value over the credit period. (The unrecognized deferred gross profit at any point in time is shown in the balance sheet as an offset to the receivable.)

Theoretically, the gross profit should be reduced by direct selling expenses (such as commissions) when determining the amount of profit to be deferred. Practice varies in this respect. (In *FASB Statement No. 66*, "Accounting for Sales of Real Estate," the illustrations dealing with the recognition of profit on retail land sales under the installment method treat selling expenses as a reduction of gross profit.[1]) The matching concept may also be used as an argument in favor of subtracting a pro rata portion of general and administrative expenses from the gross profit. The conventional installment method, however, treats these expenses as period costs for reasons of conservatism and simplicity, thereby avoiding the need to make complex and arbitrary allocations.

Whether or not an individual installment sale should be accounted for under the installment method is a decision based on the terms and conditions of the sales contract. *APB Opinion No. 10—1966*, "Omnibus Opinion," states that the installment method of accounting is inappropriate "unless the circumstances are such that the collection of the sales price is not reasonably assured."[2]

Thus, the selection of the installment method cannot be an arbitrary decision; the use of the method must be justified to be in accordance with generally accepted accounting principles. The installment method is not widely used for installment sales for financial reporting purposes. For income tax reporting purposes, however, use of the installment method for installment sales is quite widespread. Income tax aspects are discussed more fully later in the chapter.

In addition to sales of manufactured products, the installment method (or the cost recovery method, which is discussed later), may have to be used in the following two special areas:

1. **Sales of real estate.** This topic is dealt with in *FASB Statement No. 66*. Briefly, if certain specified criteria are not met (some of which set forth minimum amounts or down payment levels), the installment method is mandatory. (In certain situations the cost recovery method may be used instead of the installment method.)[3]
2. **Franchise fee revenues.** This topic is dealt with in *FASB Statement No. 45*. Briefly, the installment method or the cost recovery method is mandatory when the franchise fee revenue is to be paid over an extended period and there is no reasonable basis for estimating the collectibility of the receivable.[4] (The wording in *FASB Statement No. 45* is slightly different from that in *APB Opinion No. 10*, but it is substantively the same criterion.)

[1] *Statement of Financial Accounting Standards, No. 66*, "Accounting for Sales of Real Estate" (Stamford: Financial Accounting Standards Board, 1982), p. 62.
[2] *Opinions of the Accounting Principles Board, No. 10*, "Omnibus Opinion" (New York: American Institute of Certified Public Accountants, 1966), par. 12.
[3] *FASB Statement No. 66*, pars. 22, 47.
[4] *Statement of Financial Accounting Standards, No. 45*, "Accounting for Franchise Fee Revenue" (Stamford: Financial Accounting Standards Board, 1981), par. 6.

Illustration

THE INSTALLMENT METHOD

To illustrate the application of the installment method of accounting and the related financial statement presentation, we assume the following facts for a sale that may be properly accounted for under the installment method:

1. Sales price	$100,000
2. Cost of goods sold	$ 60,000
3. Gross profit	$ 40,000
4. Gross profit percentage ($40,000 ÷ $100,000)	40%
5. Sales date	January 1, 19X1
6. Payment terms:	

Cash down payment at date of sale	**$10,000**
Installment payments of $2,500 per month over 36 months, beginning January 31, 19X1 and ending December 31, 19X3	**$90,000**
Annual interest rate to be charged on outstanding balance...	**10%**

7. All monthly payments, along with interest on the unpaid balance, are made on time. Accordingly, cash collections are as follows:

	19X1	19X2	19X3	Total
Down payment	$10,000			$ 10,000
Installment payments	30,000	$30,000	$30,000	90,000
Total	$40,000	$30,000	$30,000	$100,000
Interest on average unpaid balance:				
10% of $75,000	$ 7,500			$ 7,500
10% of $45,000		$ 4,500		4,500
10% of $15,000			$ 1,500	1,500
				$ 13,500

The journal entries that would be recorded for this transaction for 19X1, 19X2, and 19X3 are as follows:

19X1:		
Cash	10,000	
Installment Receivables — 19X1	90,000	
Installment Sales		100,000
To record installment sale.		

Cost of Installment Sales	60,000	
Inventory		60,000
To relieve inventory for goods sold on the installment basis.		
Deferral of Gross Profit (an income statement account)	36,000	
Deferred Gross Profit—19X1 (a contra asset account)		36,000
To defer the recognition of gross profit on installment sale (40% of $90,000). (The Deferral of Gross Profit account is closed to retained earnings at year-end along with the other income statement accounts.)		
Cash	37,500	
Installment Receivables—19X1		30,000
Interest Income		7,500
To record collections on installment receivable, along with related interest on average outstanding balance.		
Deferred Gross Profit—19X1	12,000	
Recognition of Deferred Gross Profit (an income statement account)		12,000
To recognize gross profit based on cash collected on sales price (40% of $30,000).		
19X2:		
Cash	34,500	
Installment Receivables—19X1		30,000
Interest Income		4,500
To record collections on installment receivable, along with related interest on average outstanding balance.		
Deferred Gross Profit—19X1	12,000	
Recognition of Deferred Gross Profit		12,000
To recognize gross profit based on cash collected on sales price (40% of $30,000).		
19X3:		
Cash	31,500	
Installment Receivables—19X1		30,000
Interest Income		1,500
To record collections on installment receivable, along with related interest on average outstanding balance.		
Deferred Gross Profit—19X1	12,000	
Recognition of Deferred Profit		12,000
To recognize gross profit based on cash collected on sales price (40% of $30,000).		

The financial statements for 19X1, 19X2, and 19X3 would reflect the following accounts and amounts as a result of these journal entries:

Income Statement

	19X1	19X2	19X3
Installment sale	$100,000		
Cost of installment sale	(60,000)		
Gross profit	$ 40,000		
Less—Deferral of gross profit	(36,000)		
Add—Recognition of deferred gross profit	12,000	$12,000	$12,000
Gross profit recognizable	$ 16,000	$12,000	$12,000
Interest income	7,500	4,500	1,500

Balance Sheet

	December 31,		
	19X1	19X2	19X3
Installment receivable	$ 60,000	$30,000	
Less—Deferred gross profit	(24,000)	(12,000)	
Installment receivable, net of deferred gross profit	$ 36,000	$18,000	

Presentation of Financial Statements

In presenting accounts relating to installment sales accounted for under the installment method in the financial statements, the following finer points require discussion.

Installment Sales and Regular Sales. If a company has sales that are not accounted for under the installment method, then these sales and their related cost of goods sold and gross profit should be shown in the income statement separately from the accounts relating to the installment sales accounted for under the installment method. This presentation may be made (a) vertically, by showing the regular sales, cost of sales, and gross profit either above or below the accounts relating to the sales accounted for under the installment method; or (b) horizontally, by showing one column for regular sales, another column for installment sales accounted for under the installment method, and a total column. The vertical presentation is generally used in comparative-year financial statements. Likewise, in the balance sheet, normal trade receivables would be shown separately from installment sale receivables.

Classification of Deferred Gross Profit. We showed The Deferred Gross Profit account in the preceding illustration as a deduction from installment receivables in the balance sheet. The Deferred Gross Profit account is substantively an asset valuation allowance. Under the provisions of *APB Opinion No. 12—1967*, "Omnibus Opinion," asset valuation allowances must be shown as deductions from the assets to which they relate.[5] *FASB Statement No. 66*, "Accounting for Sales of Real Estate," also requires this presentation for real estate sales accounted for under the installment method.[6] (These pronouncements disallow the previously accepted alternative presentation of showing the deferred gross profit as a deferred credit immediately above the stockholders' equity section.)

Classification of Installment Receivables as Current Assets. A company that uses an operating cycle of more than one year as the basis for classifying current assets and current liabilities on its balance sheet classifies installment receivables as current assets under the provisions of *ARB No. 43* (dealing with the definition of working capital), provided the installment sales "conform generally to normal trade practices and terms within the business.[7] In such cases a company will often show: (a) parenthetically in the balance sheet, the amount of installment receivables maturing within one year, or (b) in the notes to the financial statements, the maturity of the installment receivables by year. A company that uses a one-year time period as the basis for classifying current assets and current liabilities on its balance sheet must separate the installment receivables into current and noncurrent portions. Likewise, the related deferred gross profit must be separated into current and noncurrent portions.

Defaults and Repossessions

A seller customarily retains a security interest in items sold on the installment basis to be able to repossess them if and when purchasers default on their payments. Repossessed items become part of the used goods inventory. In many cases, reconditioning costs are incurred to increase the salability of the repossessed item. When repossession occurs, the seller must (1) write off the balance of the unpaid installment receivable; (2) eliminate the balance in the Deferred Gross Profit account; and (3) assign a value to the repossessed item. At first we might conclude that the carrying value of the receivable (the installment receivable net of the related deferred gross profit) should be the amount to be assigned to the repossessed item. Under this approach, no gain or loss is reported at the time of the repossession. If accounting is to be a mirror of economic events, however, such an approach cannot be justified. The amount to be assigned to the repossessed item must be related to its current value, which may be quite different from the carrying value of the receivable. When the current value of the repossessed

[5]*Opinions of the Accounting Principles Board, No. 12*, "Omnibus Opinion" (New York: American Institute of Certified Public Accountants, 1967), par. 3.
[6]*FASB Statement No. 66*, par. 60.
[7]*Accounting Research Bulletin No. 43*, "Restatement and Revision of Accounting Research Bulletins" (New York: American Institute of Certified Public Accountants, 1953), ch. 3, par. 4.

item is above or below the carrying value of the receivable, a gain or loss, respectively, should be reported at the time of repossession.

To illustrate the entry required when the current value of a repossessed item is below the carrying value of the receivable, assume the following facts at the time of repossession:

Installment receivable	$30,000
Deferred gross profit	(12,000)
Carrying value	$18,000
Current value of the repossessed item	$16,000

The journal entry to reflect the repossession is as follows:

Inventory—Repossessed Items	16,000	
Deferred Gross Profit	12,000	
Loss on Repossession	2,000	
Installment Receivable		30,000
To record repossession of inventory sold on the installment basis.		

Note that if the current value of the repossessed item had been $20,000 (instead of $16,000), a gain of $2,000 on repossession would have been reported rather than a loss of $2,000.

The key element in determining whether a gain or loss has resulted is the *current value* of the repossessed item. There are two generally accepted approaches to determining the current value of repossessed items. The first approach is to estimate the selling price of the repossessed item and subtract from the estimated selling price (a) a normal gross profit margin on used items of this type, and (b) anticipated reconditioning costs, if any. The merit of this approach is that it results in a valuation that should theoretically equal the amount the seller would have been willing to pay in the open market for the item in the condition found.

Under the second approach, which is a variation of the first approach, estimated selling costs and anticipated reconditioning costs, if any, are subtracted from the estimated selling price to determine the current value. Thus, estimated selling costs are substituted for a normal gross profit margin in the subtraction process. The second approach produces the **net realizable value** of the repossessed item. This valuation is slightly higher than under the first method. We prefer the first method primarily because financial statement users normally expect inventory reported in the balance sheet to generate a contribution margin—not simply recover the carrying value and the estimated selling costs. The first method also gives a more conservative valuation. Under both approaches, reconditioning costs incurred are charged to the assigned current value.

Other Installment Sales Considerations

Detailed Record Keeping. Considering that the gross profit rate varies from year to year, the accounting system must segregate the installment receivables and deferred gross profit by years. We assumed a perpetual inventory system in our illustration of the installment method. A company that uses a periodic inventory system must maintain sufficient inventory records that the cost of installment sales may be determined apart from the cost of regular sales.

Imputation of Interest. If the terms of the installment sale provide for no interest to be paid on the outstanding installment receivable or for an unreasonably low interest rate, then a reasonable interest rate must be imputed using the provisions of *APB Opinion No. 21*, "Interest on Receivables and Payables." For example, if we changed the assumed facts in the preceding illustration so that no separate interest payments were required, then it would be necessary to determine how much of the $100,000 sales price actually represents interest. The remainder would then be reported as the sales price. The amount determined to be interest would then be amortized to income over the credit period. Assuming no separate interest payments are required and that $11,000 is determined to be the amount of the imputed interest, the installment sale would be recorded as follows:

Cash	**10,000**	
Installment Receivable	**90,000**	
Deferred Interest Income (a contra asset account)		**11,000**
Installment Sales		**89,000**
To record installment sale.		

Because a portion of the purchase price is allocated to interest, the gross profit is reduced from $40,000 to $29,000.

Trade-ins. When a trade-in is accepted as part payment, the item traded in should be valued in inventory at its current value. As with repossessions, the current value is the estimated selling price of the item, less: (a) estimated reconditioning costs, and (b) a normal gross profit margin on used items of this type (which normally is more than sufficient to cover estimated reselling costs). This value should be used regardless of the actual amount allowed to the customer on the trade-in. If the amount allowed to the customer exceeds the current value of the trade-in, the excess should be treated as a reduction of the sales price. (Some companies keep track of overallowances on trade-ins by using a contra sales account called Overallowances on Installment Sales.) In determining the gross profit to be recognized, the current value of the trade-in is treated as equivalent to a cash down payment. To illustrate, assume the following facts:

Sales price of item sold	$10,500
Cost of installment sale	6,300
Gross profit	$ 4,200
Trade-in allowance granted	$ 1,100
Cash down payment	1,000
Installment payments to be made	8,400
	$10,500
Estimated reconditioning costs of item traded in	$ 120
Estimated selling price of item traded in after reconditioning	$ 900
Normal gross profit margin on used items of this type	20%

The current value assigned to the trade-in and the amount of the overallowance are calculated as follows:

Trade-in allowance granted			$1,100
Less—Current value of item traded in:			
Estimated selling price of item traded in		$900	
Less—Estimated reconditioning costs	$120		
Gross profit to be realized on resale (20% of $900)	180	(300)	(600)
Overallowance given on item traded in			$ 500

The entries to record the sale and the related cost of goods sold (assuming a perpetual inventory system) are as follows:

Cash	1,000	
Inventory—Trade-ins	600	
Installment Receivables	8,400	
Installment Sales ($10,500 − $500 overallowance)		10,000
Cost of Installment Sales	6,300	
Inventory—New		6,300

Because a $500 overallowance was given on the trade-in, the gross profit on the sale is reduced from $4,200 to $3,700. The amount of gross profit that is immediately recognizable is 16% of $3,700, or $592. The 16% was derived by dividing the sum of the $1,000 cash down payment and the $600 value assigned to the item traded in by the $10,000 recorded sales price.

Income Tax Aspects

Sections 453, 453A, and 453B of the Internal Revenue Code deal with the use of the installment method. For sales of personal property regularly sold or otherwise disposed of on the installment plan (that is, by dealers in personal property), dealers **may elect to use** the installment method of reporting for all such sales. For casual sales of personal property by nondealers and sales of real estate, the installment method is the normal method of reporting such sales; however, the taxpayer **may elect not to use** the installment method and thereby report the entire gross profit in the year of sale.[8] The installment method is not applicable to sales at a loss.

As stated earlier, many companies having installment sales use the installment method only for income tax reporting purposes. In such cases, a company has deferred income tax credits reported in its balance sheet. Companies that present classified balance sheets (showing current assets and current liabilities) must follow the provisions of *APB Opinion No. 11*, "Accounting for Income Taxes," which requires that deferred income tax credits be classified in the same way as the related installment receivables.[9]

Accordingly, if a company (1) uses an operating cycle longer than one year as the basis for classifying current assets and current liabilities on its balance sheet, and (2) classifies all its installment receivables as current assets, then all related deferred income tax credits are to be classified among current liabilities. If a company uses a one-year period as the basis for classifying current assets and current liabilities on its balance sheet, then that portion of the deferred income tax credits relating to the installment receivables due within one year should be classified among current liabilities. For example, if 23% of the total installment receivables were classified as current, then 23% of the deferred income tax credits related to the installment receivables would be classified as current.

The Cost Recovery Method

APB Opinion No. 10 also sanctions the use of the cost recovery method for installment sales.[10] Far more conservative than the installment method, the cost recovery method allows no recognition of gross profit until cash collections on the sales price equal the cost of the goods sold. All collections in excess of the seller's cost of the goods sold then cause the recogni-

[8] The Tax Reform Act of 1986 curtailed the tax deferral benefits previously available for installment sales (the "proportionate-disallowance rule"). As a result, that portion of the installment sale (with some exceptions allowed) that is deemed to have been constructively received through borrowings related to the installment obligations is not allowed installment treatment.

[9] *Opinions of the Accounting Principles Board, No. 11*, "Accounting for Income Taxes" (New York: American Institute of Certified Public Accountants, 1967), par. 57. (In 1980 the FASB issued *Statement of Financial Accounting Standards, No. 37*, "Balance Sheet Classification of Deferred Income Taxes," which amends par. 57 of *APB Opinion No. 11*. This amendment is a clarification, and it does not change the requirements of par. 57 as it pertains to classifying deferred income tax credits relating to installment receivables.)

[10] *APB Opinion No. 10*, fn. 8 to par. 12.

tion of profit equal to the amount of cash collected. Because most practicing accountants and academicians consider the cost recovery method too conservative, it is rarely encountered in practice.

The accounts used under the cost recovery method are the same as those previously illustrated for the installment method. The amounts are different from those previously shown only because the gross profit is recognized at a much later date under the cost recovery method. Accordingly, we do not illustrate the detailed journal entries. Using the assumed information given in the illustration of the installment method, the income statement under the cost recovery method would be as follows:

Income Statement

	19X1	19X2	19X3
Installment sale	$100,000		
Cost of installment sale	(60,000)		
Gross profit	$ 40,000		
Less—Deferral of gross profit	(40,000)		
Add—Recognition of deferred gross profit		$10,000	$30,000
Gross profit recognizable	$ –0–	$10,000	$30,000
Interest income	7,500	4,500	1,500

ACCOUNTING FOR THE BUSINESS FRANCHISE

The business franchise industry now generates in excess of $300 billion in sales, accounting for approximately one-third of all U.S. retail trade. It is a dynamic industry that began with gas stations, continued with hotels, motels, hamburgers, real estate, and brake repair, and most recently evolving into home computer stores, business brokerages, dental centers, vision centers, and photo finishing stores.

Although the business franchise does not generate new generally accepted accounting principles, it does present certain unique conditions that require the careful application of current principles. Furthermore, the accounting and reporting problems presented by these conditions relate to the franchisor, not the franchisee.

Distinguishing Features of a Franchise

Business franchises are distinguished from other business arrangements in the following ways:

a. The relation between the franchisor and franchisee is contractual, and an agreement, confirming the rights and responsibilities of each party, is in force for a specified period.

b. The continuing relation has as its purpose the distribution of a product or service, or an entire business concept, within a particular market area.
c. Both the franchisor and franchisee contribute resources for establishing and maintaining the franchise. The franchisor's contribution may be a trademark, a company reputation, products, procedures, manpower, equipment, or a process. The franchisee usually contributes operating capital as well as the managerial and operational resources required for opening and continuing the franchised outlet.
d. The franchise agreement outlines and describes the specific marketing practices to be followed, the contribution of each party to the operation of the business, and sets forth certain operating procedures that both parties agree to comply with.
e. The establishment of the franchised outlet creates a business entity that will, in most cases, require and support the full-time business activity of the franchisee. (There are numerous other contractual distribution arrangements in which a local business person becomes the "authorized distributor" or "representative" for the sale of a particular good or service, along with many others, but such sale usually represents only a portion of the person's total business.)
f. Both the franchisee and franchisor participate in a common public identity. This identity is achieved most often through the use of common trade names or trademarks and is frequently reinforced through advertising programs designed to promote the recognition and acceptance of the common identity within the franchisee's market area.[11]

In addition to these distinctions, we must also understand the legal and operational relationships between the franchisor and franchisee. The following provisions are commonly found in **franchise agreements:**

1. Rights to use trademark, trade name, processes, and so on transferred to the franchisee.
2. The amount and terms of payment of the initial franchise fee.
3. The amount and terms of the continuing franchise fee. The amount of this fee is usually based on a percentage of the franchisee's gross revenues.
4. Services to be provided by the franchisor initially and on a continuing basis. The services may include personnel training, operating manuals, bookkeeping and financial services, and quality control programs.
5. Provisions for acquisition of inventory, supplies, and equipment from franchisor or a designated supplier.
6. Provisions for cancellation, reacquisition, or acquisition of the franchise.

The **franchise** is thus a contractual agreement between two parties, the *franchisor* and the *franchisee*, the ultimate purpose of which is to expand the distribution channels of the franchisor's products, services, or both. Clearly, franchising is a marketing strategy that provides the franchisor with the necessary capital for expansion and a shift in investment risk.

[11]*FASB Statement No. 45*, pp. 11–12.

Specific provisions of the agreement establish certain rights; the amount and terms of payment of an initial franchise fee; the amount and terms of payment of continuing franchise fees, the nature of the franchisor's commitment; provisions for the acquisition of inventory, supplies, and equipment from the franchisor; and cancellation, reacquisition, and acquisition of the franchise.

The franchisor's accounting and reporting problems arise from the unique and frequently complex provisions of the franchise agreement. These provisions must be carefully analyzed to ensure appropriate applications of generally accepted accounting principles.

The franchisor's accounting and reporting problems focus on such matters as (1) when to recognize revenue (a timing problem), (2) separating the various kinds of revenue (a classification problem), (3) the collectibility of the receivable representing the franchisee's unpaid portion of the initial franchise fee (a valuation problem), (4) accounting for costs, and (5) disclosing to financial statement users information that is unique or significant to franchisors (a disclosure problem).

Revenue Recognition

The franchisor generates revenue from (1) the sale of the initial franchise in the form of the **initial franchise fee,** (2) the sale of fixtures, equipment, inventory and supplies to the franchisee, and (3) **continuing franchise fees** charged the franchisee based on the operation of the franchise. Essentially, the initial franchise fee represents consideration for establishing the franchise relationship and for such services as site selection, architectural and design assistance, shop or store layout, training, and staff assistance when the franchise business is opened.

The revenue-recognition problem concerns this initial fee, which is payment for certain intangible rights and services. No discrete time occurs at which "title passes" and revenue is recognized, as occurs with the sale of inventory, equipment, and so on. The franchise agreement may specify that the initial fee is to be paid completely or partially in cash; it may be paid completely or partially on the date the agreement is signed, on the date the franchisee commences business, or periodically thereafter. The fee may or may not be refundable under the terms of the agreement. In the 1960s, franchisors commonly recognized the initial fee revenue at the date the agreement was signed, even though significant costs had yet to be incurred by the franchisor.

Because questionable accounting practices were employed during the 1960s, the American Institute of Certified Public Accountants issued an accounting industry guide, *Accounting for Franchise Fee Revenue.* This guide promulgated a concept of revenue recognition for franchisors called **substantial performance.** Because authoritative guidance is now provided by *FASB Statement No. 45,* the guide was withdrawn by the AICPA. (The provisions of *FASB Statement No. 45* are not significantly different from the guide.) In accordance with *FASB Statement No. 45*, substantial performance by the franchisor represents the consummation of the transaction and is evidenced when

> (a) the franchisor has no remaining obligation or intent—by agreement, trade practice, or law—to refund any cash received or forgive any unpaid notes or receivables; (b) substantially all of the *initial services* of the franchisor required by the franchise agreement have been performed; and (c) no other material conditions or obligations related to the determination of substantial performance exist.[12]

Substantial performance has been interpreted by the profession as the point at which the franchisee begins operations. Most franchisors have rendered the required services by that time. Of course, recognizing substantial performance at this time also results in a more conservative determination of income than would occur at the date the franchise agreement is signed.

Recognition of revenue at any other time—earlier or later—carries with it the burden of demonstrating that the alternative time best reflects income for the franchisor. Some franchise arrangements clearly support a time other than when the franchisee begins operations.

It is important to observe that although in most cases the conditions for substantial performance are met when the franchisee commences operations, certain conditions may require careful judgment. This could be the case, for example, if the franchisor has little business experience, particularly in franchise operations. Little or no relevent experience or, for that matter, a poor record of franchise operations may require a more conservative interpretation of substantial performance. Similar concerns would be appropriate if an experienced franchisor develops a new and different franchise venture or expands an existing franchise operation into a new geographic area.

Other revenue-recognition methods may be used in certain franchise accounting situations, including (1) recognition of revenue over the life of the contract, (2) percentage of completion, and (3) installment and cost recovery. If the first method is appropriate, revenue would be recognized evenly over the life of the contract. For example, if the initial fee amounted to $150,000 and the franchise life were 15 years, the franchisor would recognize $10,000 of the initial fee as revenue each year for 15 years. In this instance, the initial fee would be viewed as a prepayment for use of the franchise over the franchise period. However, most franchise agreements show little or no indication that the initial franchise fee includes compensation for any intangible benefits associated with membership in the franchise system. This method would be particularly difficult to defend if the

[12]*FASB Statement No. 45*, par. 5.

franchisor incurred significant costs for initial services and if adequate continuous fees were charged over the life of the contract. However, if the evidence shows that the initial fee includes significant compensation for intangible rights conveyed to a franchisor—and this would be more clearly evidenced when large fees are charged for franchise renewals—this method may be preferable to substantial performance.

Although percentage of completion is generally associated with construction accounting, the method may be applied to other situations. A particular strength of the method is that it recognizes effort spent and, hence, revenue earned between the date of the franchise agreement and the date the franchisee begins business. Of course, judgment must be used in estimating the cost of services performed over the total expected cost of services. When the initial fee is for initial services only, this method generally provides results similar to those of the substantial performance method.

Installment sales and cost recovery methods may be used only under exceptional circumstances. In essence, no reasonable basis exists for estimating the degree of collectibility of the receivable. (For a complete discussion of this subject, see the first section of this chapter, "Accounting for Installment Sales."

The initial franchise fee frequently includes charges to the franchisee for fixtures, equipment, and inventory. In these cases, the relevant portion of the fee pertaining to these items should be separated, and the revenue and related costs should be matched when title passes, even if it occurs before the opening date of the franchise.

Collectibility of the Receivable

After it has been concluded that substantial performance has occurred and the initial franchise fee has been separated into charges for fixtures, equipment, and inventory, the next important accounting question concerns the collectibility of the receivable. The following circumstances make this process especially difficult:

1. Unpaid franchise notes may be significant to the individual franchisee and payment may depend upon the franchisee's future operations, or current or prospective capitalization, or a combination thereof.
2. The franchisee may be inexperienced in business with a consequent effect on his credit standing.
3. The franchise agreement, which is important as a basis for making collection estimates, may require interpretation by legal counsel as to uncertainties.
4. The credit standing of guarantors or other indirect sources of credit to the franchisee may require investigation.[13]

[13]Committee on Franchise Accounting and Auditing of the American Institute of Certified Public Accountants, *Accounting for Franchise Fee Revenue*, an AICPA Industry Accounting Guide (New York: American Institute of Certified Public Accountants, 1973), pp. 9–10.

The first two circumstances raise basic concerns in estimating the collectibility of the receivable. In the first case, if little or no cash has been paid by the franchisee and reliance is based solely on the success of future operations, the uncertainty of collection may indeed be quite high because the franchisee has nothing at risk. In the second case, the probability of failure may be quite high because inexperience is a major contributor to business failure. The likelihood that the franchisor will repurchase the franchise should also be carefully assessed. This requires study of the franchise agreement and recent behavior of the franchisor. Obviously, if the probability of repurchase is high, it is less likely that the receivable will be collected.

Accounting for Franchise Costs

The *matching concept* requires that costs directly related to revenues be reported in the accounting period in which the revenue transaction occurred. The concept presumes a cause-and-effect relationship between revenue and expense. Other costs that are not directly associated with the revenue transaction are generally expensed when incurred.

Franchisors are likely to encounter different circumstances when trying to match costs and revenues. Costs and revenues may show irregular and nonrecurring patterns, and because we are dealing with services and intangibles, the sources of revenues may not be as readily identifiable. This is especially true for transactions involving initial franchise fees. Some costs may be incurred before or after the revenue is recognized.

Generally, franchisors should defer direct costs and relate them to specific franchise sales for which revenue has not yet been recognized. Indirect costs that are regular and recurring, and that are incurred regardless of the level of sales, should be expensed as incurred. Costs that exceed anticipated revenues less estimated additional costs should not be deferred.

Illustration

ACCOUNTING FOR THE FRANCHISE

Frank Riggs enters the four-wheel-drive vehicle parts sales business at the retail level by signing a franchise agreement with Specialty 4-Wheel Drive Parts, Inc. The franchisor provides Riggs with assistance in site selection, shop layout, equipment and building fixtures, inventory, operating manuals, personnel training, and advertising.

The franchise agreement includes provisions for an initial franchise fee as payment for site selection assistance, shop layout, shop equipment and building fixtures, initial inventory, use of operating manuals, and training of personnel. The initial fee is $150,000, of which $20,000 is payable when the agreement is signed, and $130,000 is payable in five non-interest-bearing notes of $26,000 each, one note to be paid on each anniversary date of the opening. The agreement also includes a provision for a continuing franchise fee of $10,000 per year in return for Riggs's use of Specialty's accounting system and advertising and the right to purchase parts.

Assumed transactions and related journal entries pertaining to activities completed by Specialty in the first year of the franchise agreement are shown in Illustration 27-1.

Disclosure

In addition to customary disclosure requirements, franchisors must disclose relevant information pertaining to franchising. In this regard, *FASB Statement No. 45* states:

> *Significant commitments and obligations:* The nature of all significant commitments and obligations resulting from franchise agreements, including a

Illustration 27-1
Accounting for the Franchise

Transactions	Entry		
1. Franchisor incurred direct costs related to the franchise prior to the store opening.	Deferred Franchise Expenses...	12,000	
	Accounts Payable................		12,000
2. The franchise agreement was signed. The credit ratings of all franchisees entitle them to borrow at the current interest rate of 15%. The present value of an ordinary annuity of five annual receipts of $26,000 each, discounted at 15%, is $87,156.	Cash....................................	20,000	
	Notes Receivable....................	130,000	
	Discount on Notes Receivable ($130,000 − $87,156).......		42,844
	Equipment Sales................		65,000
	Sales (inventory).................		15,000
	Unearned Franchise Fee Revenue..........................		27,156
The following additional information pertains to equipment and inventory sold to the franchisee:	Cost of Equipment Sold..........	35,000	
	Cost of Goods Sold	8,000	
	Inventory		43,000
Sales Price / **Cost**			
Equipment and fixtures........ $65,000 $35,000			
Inventory......... 15,000 8,000			
3. The store was opened.	Unearned Franchise Fee Revenue............................	27,156	
	Franchise Fee Revenue......		27,156
	Franchise Expenses...............	12,000	
	Deferred Franchise Expenses		12,000
4. The continuing franchise fee was received.	Cash....................................	10,000	
	Continuing Franchise Fee Revenue..........................		10,000

description of the services that the franchisor has agreed to provide . . . that have not yet been substantially performed, shall be disclosed.

Use of installment or cost recovery method: If no basis for estimating the collectibility of specific franchise fees exists, the notes to the financial statements shall disclose whether the installment or cost recovery method is being used to account for the related franchise fee revenue. Furthermore, the sales price of such franchises, the revenue and related costs deferred (both currently and on a cumulative basis), and the periods in which such fees become payable by the franchisee shall be disclosed. Any amounts originally deferred but later recognized because uncertainties regarding the collectibility of franchise fees are resolved also shall be disclosed.

Segregation of franchise revenues: Initial franchise fees shall be segregated from other franchise fee revenue if they are significant. If it is probable that initial franchise fee revenue will decline in the future because sales predictably reach a saturation point, disclosure of that fact is desirable. Disclosure of the relative contribution to net income of initial franchise fees is desirable if not apparent from the relative amounts of revenue.

Franchisor-owned outlets: Revenue and costs related to franchisor-owned outlets shall be distinguished from revenue and costs related to franchised outlets when practicable. That may be done by segregating revenue and costs related to franchised outlets. If there are significant changes in franchisor-owned outlets or franchised outlets during the period, the number of (a) franchises sold, (b) franchises purchased during the period, (c) franchised outlets in operation shall be disclosed.[14]

ACCOUNTING FOR CONSIGNMENTS

Manufacturers and distributors who market their products through dealers cannot always enter into agreements that require the dealers to purchase their products outright when the items are shipped. Instead, an owner may enter into a **consignment agreement,** whereby the owner ships inventory to a dealer but retains title until the dealer sells it. Inventory of an owner in the possession of another is called **consigned inventory.** The owner may not report any profit on the transaction because a sale has not yet occurred.

In legal terms, the owner is called the **consignor,** and the dealer is called the **consignee.** The rights and duties of each party are usually set forth in the consignment agreement. For example, the consignee typically must give the consignor's property reasonable care and make periodic accountings (or notifications of sales) to the consignor. (You may want to refer to a law textbook covering consignments for a more detailed discussion of the relationship between a consignor and a consignee and the corresponding rights and duties of these parties.)

[14]*FASB Statement No. 45*, pars. 20–23.

In Perspective

Consignments are infrequently used in marketing products largely because of the now common use of **flooring plan** lines of credit offered to dealers by financial institutions (including finance subsidiaries of manufacturers). Briefly, the usual features of these flooring plans include the following:

1. Dealers borrow money from financial institutions to purchase certain individual inventory items from manufacturers or distributors.
2. The borrowings are secured by the individual items purchased.
3. Borrowings to purchase an individual inventory item must be repaid when the dealer sells the item or within a specified period of time, whichever occurs first.
4. The manufacturer or distributor agrees to pay a portion of the dealer's financing costs under the flooring plan.

Automobiles, recreational vehicles, farm machinery, major home appliances, and television sets are almost always carried by dealers under flooring plans rather than under consignment agreements. In the publishing and record industries, it is common practice to sell inventory to retail outlets under terms that allow the retail outlets to return the inventory if they do not sell it—a practice that, in substance, is the equivalent of a consignment. For these industries, allowances for sales returns are established when sales to the retail outlets are recorded.

Responses to our inquiries have led us to conclude that consignments are limited to cases in which (1) a dealer is not financially strong enough to enter into flooring arrangements with financial institutions; (2) the salability of a new product is in doubt, and dealers are reluctant to devote floor space to it (this was the case with microwave ovens several years ago); and (3) a manufacturer is attempting to rekindle interest in a product that had a poor image when originally introduced.

Accounting Procedures

The procedures used to account for consignments should reflect the substance of the consignment agreement. Not only has the use of consignments declined considerably over the years, but the terms and substance of consignment agreements have changed. We first discuss the traditional arrangements between a consignor and a consignee and then a new arrangement, which we call the modern arrangement.

The Traditional Arrangement. Traditionally, the substance of consignment agreements has been that the consignee merely acts as the consignor's agent, for which the consignee earns a commission on sale of the consigned inventory. When the consignee made credit sales, the resultant receivable was the property of the consignor, with the consignor bearing any collection loss. (Sometimes the consignee guaranteed the collectibility of the receivable, in which case the consignee was referred to as a *del credere* agent.) As called for in the consignment agreement, the consignee periodically rendered an accounting to the consignor. Such a report—known as an **account sale**—showed the sales made for the consignor's account less the commission on the sales earned by the consignee and any other charges incurred by the consignee to be borne by the consignor. Typically, the consignee remitted a check to the consignor for the net amount on this report when it was submitted. Under this traditional arrangement, the accounting procedures resulted in the consignor reporting in the income statement (1) sales at the amount for which the consignee sold the consigned inventory to the ultimate customer; (2) the consignor's cost of the inventory sold; (3) the commission expense (paid to the consignee); and (4) any freight or other incidental costs incurred. The consignee's income statement reflected only commission revenues and selling expenses not reimbursable by the consignor. Responses to our inquiries have led us to believe that this type of arrangement is no longer widely used, if at all. Accordingly, we do not illustrate the related accounting procedures.

The Modern Arrangement. The substance of most consignment arrangements currently consists of a purchase of the consigned inventory by the consignee from the consignor—when the consignee sells the consigned inventory to the ultimate customer. At that time, the consignee pays the consignor an agreed-upon amount. (Often the consignor bills the consignee at the time of shipment so that the consignee can make ready payment; the consignor does not record the billing as a sale, however, until the consignee notifies the consignor that the consigned inventory has been sold.) On receipt of consigned inventory, the consignee makes only a memorandum entry—the purchase is recorded when the consignee sells the consigned inventory. Furthermore, when the consignee sells on credit, the resultant receivable is the property of the consignee; there is no continuing involvement by the consignor. Under this arrangement, the accounting procedures result in both the consignor and the consignee reporting sales and cost of goods sold.

Illustration

THE MODERN CONSIGNMENT ARRANGEMENT

Assume that a manufacturer ships inventory with a manufacturing cost of $1,000 to a dealer at an agreed upon billing price of $1,500. The manufacturer pays $30 for shipping charges. The dealer later sells the inventory for $1,800 and notifies the consignor of the sale and makes payment. Illustra-

Illustration 27-2
Journal Entries for a Modern Consignment Arrangement

Consignor's Books (the manufacturer)			Consignee's Books (the dealer)		
Shipment of inventory to dealer on consignment:					
Finished Goods on Consignment	1,000		Memorandum entry only		
Inventory—Finished Goods		1,000			
Payment of freight costs on shipment to consignee:					
Finished Goods on Consignment	30		No entry		
Cash		30			
Sale of inventory by consignee:					
No entry			Cash	1,800	
			Sales		1,800
			Purchases	1,500	
			Accounts Payable (to consignor)		1,500
Notification of sale to consignor and payment of billing price:					
Cash	1,500		Accounts Payable	1,500	
Sales		1,500	Cash		1,500
Cost of Consignment Goods Sold	1,030				
Finished Goods on Consignment		1,030			

tion 27-2 shows the journal entries that would be recorded on the books of the consignor and the consignee. The following points are important for understanding this illustration:

1. The consigned inventory remains on the consignor's books until the consignee notifies the consignor that the consigned inventory has been sold, which causes the consignee to purchase the consigned inventory from the consignor.
2. The consignee made payment to the consignor at the time of notification, although sometimes, payment is made shortly after notification.

SUMMARY

Installment Sales

Under the installment method, gross profit is recognized to the degree that collections on the sales price relate to the total selling price. The installment method may be used only when collection of the sales price is not reasonably assured. Deferred gross profit is reported as a deduction from the installment receivable. In the event of a default and repossession, a gain or loss is reported, determined by comparing the carrying value of the receivable with the current value of the repossessed item. The current value of the repossessed item is its estimated selling price less a normal gross profit margin for used goods of that type and any anticipated reconditioning costs. An allowable alternative approach to determining current value is to use the item's net realizable value. The value assigned to an item received on a trade-in is its current value, which is determined in the same manner as in cases of repossession. An overallowance on a trade-in is subtracted from the selling price.

Franchises

Franchising, which is an important part of our economy, presents certain inherent accounting and reporting problems. Because of its unique nature, current generally accepted accounting principles must be carefully applied.

The accounting and reporting problems confronted by the franchisor are (1) determining when to recognize revenue (a timing problem), (2) properly separating the various kinds of revenue (a classification problem), (3) estimating the collectibility of the receivable representing the franchisee's unpaid portion of the initial franchise fee (a valuation problem), (4) accounting for costs, and (5) disclosing important financial information unique to the franchise.

The initial fee revenue is recognized when conditions of substantial performance are met. Generally, such conditions are satisfied when the franchisee commences operations. When the initial franchise fee includes charges for equipment, inventory, and so on, these amounts must be segregated from the initial franchise fee and separately stated.

The receivables must be carefully valued. When little or no cash has been paid by the franchisee, the risk of noncollection is quite high because the franchisee has risked nothing. The franchisee's lack of business experience must also be considered in the estimation process.

Direct costs should be deferred and related to the specific franchise sale, and indirect costs should be expensed as incurred. Costs should not be deferred when they exceed anticipated revenues, less estimated additional costs.

Consignments

A consignment is a transfer of possession of inventory from its owner (called the consignor) to another party (called the consignee). Because the transfer is not an outright sale, no profit is recorded by the owner at the time of the transfer. Instead, profit is recorded by the consignor when the consignee sells the inventory to the ultimate customer. Under the modern arrangement, a sale is recorded between the consignor and the consignee (at a billing price agreed upon in advance) when the consignee sells the inventory.

Glossary of New Terms

Consignee The party holding possession of inventory—but not ownership—in a consignment arrangement.

Consignment A transfer of possession of inventory from an owner (the consignor) to another party (the consignee) to facilitate the sale of the inventory.

Consignor The owner of inventory in a consignment arrangement.

Continuing Franchise Fee "Consideration for the continuing rights granted by the franchise and for general or specific services during its life."*

Franchise Agreement A contract between a franchisor and a franchisee that specifies the legal and operational relationship between them. Some common provisions found in franchise agreements are (a) rights transferred by the franchisor; (b) the amount and terms of payment of initial franchise fees; (c) amount or rate and terms of payment of continuing franchise fee or royalty; (d) services to be rendered by the franchisor initially and on a continuing basis, (e) acquisition of inventory, supplies, or equipment, and terms of payment; and (f) cancellation, reacquisition, or acquisition of franchise.

Initial Franchise Fee "Consideration for establishing a franchise relationship and providing some initial services. Occasionally, the fee includes consideration for initially required equipment and inventory, but those items usually are the subject of separate consideration."*

Substantial Performance "Substantial performance for the franchisor means that (a) the franchisor has no remaining obligation or intent—by agreement, trade practice, or law—to refund any cash received or forgive any unpaid notes or receivables; (b) substantially all of the *initial services* of the franchisor required by the franchise agreement have been performed; and (c) no other material condition or obligation related to the determination of substantial performance exists."*

Review Questions

1. What basic condition must exist for the installment method to be used for financial reporting purposes?
2. How are selling expenses for an installment sale treated when the sale is recorded under the installment method for financial reporting purposes?

**FASB Statement No. 45*, app. A.

3. How is deferred gross profit relating to installment sales reported in the balance sheet?
4. Define *current value* as it is used in connection with defaults and repossessions occurring on installment sales.
5. How are overallowances on trade-ins reported when reporting installment sales?
6. Summarize the major features distinguishing a business franchise from other business arrangements.
7. Accounting practice specifies the nature of the disclosures required in the financial reports of franchisors. Identify the required disclosures.
8. List some common provisions specified in franchise agreements.
9. Conceivably, continuing franchise fees could be less than the incremental costs associated with these fees. How would this condition affect the recognition of the initial franchise fee?
10. Describe the four principal accounting problems associated with franchises.
11. Describe the concept of substantial performance as used in franchise accounting.
12. Identify the approaches for revenue recognition, other than substantial performance, and discuss the conditions under which they could be used.
13. In what principal ways does a franchisor generate revenue?
14. What factors should be considered in valuing receivables?
15. Describe the accounting for costs associated with franchises.
16. Explain why a consignment may not be recorded as a sale.
17. How has the use of consignments changed over the years?
18. Explain the differences in the consignor's income statement under the traditional arrangement and under the modern arrangement.
19. How do we determine whether to account for consignments under the traditional arrangement or under the modern arrangement?

Discussion Case

DC 27-1

Installment Sales: Theory—Classification of Deferred Gross Profit

DGP Company has recently allowed customers to purchase items on the installment basis. In preparing the year-end financial statements, the company is considering separating the Deferred Gross Profit account into the following categories: (1) an allowance for uncollectibles, shown as an offset to the installment receivables; (2) a Deferred Income Taxes account, shown immediately below its long-term debt; (3) an Unrealized Profit account, shown immediately above Stockholders' Equity.

Required:
Evaluate the theoretical soundness of this approach. (Ignore the presentational requirements of the professional pronouncements.)

Exercises

E 27-1

Installment Sales: Determining the Year-end Balance of Deferred Gross Profit Account

Sellit Corporation, which began business on January 1, 19X1, appropriately uses the installment method for financial reporting purposes. The following data were obtained for 19X1 and 19X2:

	19X1	19X2
Installment sales	$350,000	$420,000
Cost of installment sales	280,000	315,000
General and administrative expenses	35,000	42,000
Cash collections on installment sales in:		
19X1	150,000	125,000
19X2		200,000

Required:
Determine the balance in the Deferred Gross Profit control account at December 31, 19X2.

(AICPA adapted)

E 27-2

Installment Sales: Determining Gain or Loss on Repossession

Gann Company appropriately uses the installment method for financial reporting purposes. In 19X4, a customer who purchased merchandise in 19X2 defaulted. At the date of the default, the balance of the installment receivable was $12,000, and the repossessed merchandise had a fair value of $8,200. Data for 19X2 are as follows:

Installment sales	$700,000
Cost of installment sales	560,000
General and administrative expenses	70,000

Required:
Assuming that the repossessed merchandise is recorded at its current value, determine the gain or loss on repossession.

(AICPA adapted)

E 27-3

Installment Sales: Determining Gain or Loss on Repossession

Valuex Company repossessed equipment in 19X3 that it had sold for $60,000 on the installment basis in 19X1. The company appropriately used the installment method for financial reporting purposes. At the time of the repossession, the installment receivable was $40,000, and the deferred gross profit was $12,000.

The company expects to resell the repossessed item for $30,000 (after it incurs reconditioning costs of $400). The company's normal gross profit margin on sales of used equipment of this type is 10%. The company also expects to incur a 3% sales commission on the resale. The customer was granted a trade-in allowance of $1,500 when the equipment was initially sold; of this amount, $600 was determined to be an overallowance.

Required:

1. Determine the gain or loss at the time of repossession.
2. Prepare the journal entry to be made at the time of repossession.

E 27-4

Installment Sales: Trade-in and Over-Allowance

Marginex Company sold equipment to a customer on the following terms:

a. Sales price	$75,000
b. Cash down payment	2,000
c. Allowance granted on item traded in	3,000
d. Installment payments over 30 months	70,000

The manufacturing cost of the equipment sold is $54,500. Assume that the use of the installment method is appropriate. The estimated selling price of the item traded in (after expected reconditioning costs of $300) is $3,500. The company's normal profit margin on the sale of used items of this type is 20%.

Required:
Prepare the journal entries to be made at the time of the sale. (Assume that a perpetual inventory system is used.)

E 27-5

Installment Sales: Determining Installment Receivables and the Current Portion of the Installment Receivables from the Amount of Deferred Income Taxes

The Fernwood Company sells household furniture. Customers who purchase furniture on the installment basis make payments in equal monthly installments over a two-year period, with no down payment required. Fernwood's gross profit on installment sales equals 60% of the selling price of the furniture.

For financial accounting purposes, sales revenue is recognized when the sale is made. For income tax purposes, however, the installment method is used. There are no other book and income tax accounting differences, and Fernwood's income tax rate is 50%.

Fernwood's December 31, 19X1, balance sheet includes a deferred tax credit of $30,000 arising from the difference between book and tax treatment of the installment sales, of which $14,000 is classified as a current liability.

Required:

1. Determine the total amount of installment accounts receivable at December 31, 19X1.

2. Determine the amount of installment receivables that should be classified as current assets.

(AICPA adapted)

E 27-6

Franchises: Revenue Recognition

On January 1, 19X3, William Fong signed an agreement to operate a franchise of Herbie's Hot Dogs, Inc., for an initial franchise fee of $40,000. Of this amount, $15,000 was paid when the agreement was signed, and the balance is payable in five annual payments of $5,000 each beginning January 1, 19X4. The agreement provides that the down payment is not refundable and no future services are required of the franchisor. Fong's credit rating indicates that he can borrow money at 15% for a loan of this type.

Required:
Prepare the appropriate journal entry for the franchisee to record the acquisition of the franchise on January 1, 19X3.

(AICPA adapted)

E 27-7

Franchises: Revenue Recognition

On December 31, 19X2, Piper Pizza, Inc., signed an agreement authorizing Bill Banks to operate as a franchise for an initial franchise fee of $50,000. Of this amount, $20,000 was received when the agreement was signed, and the balance is due in three annual payments of $10,000 each beginning December 31, 19X3. The agreement provides that the down payment (representing a fair measure of the services already performed by Piper) is not refundable and substantial future services are required of Piper Pizza. Bank's credit rating is such that collection of the note is reasonably certain. At December 31, 19X2, the present value of the three annual payments discounted at 14% (the implicit rate for a loan of this type) is $23,220.

Required:
Prepare the appropriate journal entry for Piper Pizza, Inc., on December 31, 19X2, the date the agreement was signed.

(AICPA adapted)

E 27-8

Consignments: Determining Proper Year-end Inventory Amounts

Norr Company is a manufacturer that markets its products through dealers, sometimes using consignment arrangements. At December 31, 19X1, Norr and one of its dealers, Nee Company, took a physical count of inventory in their possession. The amounts were $1,000,000 for Norr and $50,000 for Nee. The following additional information is available:

1. Of the $50,000 of inventory counted by Nee, $8,000 of this amount represents the billing price of inventory on consignment from Norr. (Norr's manufacturing cost is $6,000.)

2. On December 30, 19X1, Nee sold inventory that it had obtained from Norr on consignment at a billing price of $2,500. Norr's manufacturing cost was $2,000. Nee notified Norr of this sale on January 6, 19X2.
3. At December 31, 19X1, inventory in transit between Norr and Nee that is being shipped on consignment at a billing price of $1,400 has a manufacturing cost of $1,000.

Required:
Determine the correct amount of inventory to be reflected in each company's balance sheet at December 31, 19X1.

Problems

P 27-1

Installment Sales: Basic Journal Entries

The Pay-Later Company, which reports on a calendar year-end, sold equipment on October 1, 19X1, to a customer on the following terms:

a. Sales price	$80,000
b. Cash down payment	$ 8,000
c. Installment payments over 24 months, beginning October 31, 19X1	$72,000
d. Annual interest rate charged on outstanding balance (to be paid each month)	10%

The manufacturing cost of the equipment is $50,000. Assume the use of the installment method is appropriate and that all payments are made on time.

Required:

1. Prepare the appropriate journal entries for 19X1, 19X2, and 19X3. (Assume a perpetual inventory system is used.)
2. Prepare an income statement for 19X1, 19X2, and 19X3 using the amounts from the journal entries in requirement 1.

P 27-2

Installment Sales: Default and Repossession

The Easy-Credit Company sold equipment on July 1, 19X1, to a customer on the following terms:

a. Sales price	$50,000
b. Cash down payment	$ 2,000
c. Installment payments over 48 months, beginning July 31, 19X1	$48,000
d. Annual interest rate charged on outstanding balance (to be paid each month)	10%

The manufacturing cost of the equipment is $30,000. The company appropriately used the installment method to report the transaction. The purchaser defaulted on its November 30, 19X2, payment, and the company repossessed the equipment on December 20, 19X2. The estimated selling price of the repossessed equipment (after expected reconditioning costs of $300) is $23,000. The company's normal profit margin on the sale of used items of this type is 20%.

Required:

1. Prepare the journal entries made at the time of the sale. (Assume a perpetual inventory system is used.)
2. Prepare the journal entry made at the time of the repossession.

P 27-3

Installment Sales: Determining Realizable Gross Profit and Interest Income (Equal Installment Payments Include Interest)

On July 1, 19X1, Leader Computers, Inc., sold computer equipment with a book value of $15,000 to Modem, Inc., for $20,000. Because the collection of the sales price was questionable, Leader retained title to the equipment until Modem made the last payment. Modem made a down payment of $2,000 and signed an 8% note due in eight equal quarterly payments of $2,457 each, including interest, beginning September 30, 19X1. During July 19X1, Leader incurred $750 selling expenses in the sale of this equipment. Assume that (1) the 8% interest rate is reasonable, (2) all payments are made in accordance with the agreement, and (3) the installment method is appropriate for financial reporting purposes.

Required:
Prepare a schedule of all income and expenses for the above transaction for the year ended June 30, 19X2. (Ignore income taxes.)

(AICPA adapted)

P 27-4

Installment Sales: Determining Year-end Balance in Gross Profit Account and Dealing with a Repossession

Conservo Company uses the installment method for financial reporting purposes. Selected data follow:

	December 31, 19X4	December 31, 19X5
Installment receivables — 19X3	$100,000	$ 70,000
Installment receivables — 19X4	280,000	230,000
Installment receivables — 19X5		420,000
Deferred gross profit — 19X3	37,000	
Deferred gross profit — 19X4	112,000	
Installment sales — 19X5		600,000
Cost of installment sales — 19X5		390,000
Initial down payments made on 19X5 installment sales		110,000

On October 1, 19X5, the company repossessed equipment that it had sold in 19X4 for $15,000, of which $6,000 had been collected. The company credited Installment Receivables — 19X4 and debited Inventory — Repossessed Equipment for the unpaid balance. The current value of the equipment at the repossession date was $4,500.

Required:

1. Calculate the year-end balances in the Deferred Profit accounts. (Do each year separately.)
2. Make the appropriate adjustment needed for the repossession.
3. Prepare a partial income statement for 19X5.

P 27-5

Franchises: Revenue Recognition

Julius, Inc., sells fast-food franchises to independent operators throughout the United States. The contract with the franchisee generally includes the following provisions:

a. The franchisee is charged an initial fee of $100,000. Of this amount, $50,000 is payable when the agreement is signed, and a $10,000 non-interest-bearing note is payable at the end of each of the five subsequent years.
b. The initial franchise fee collected by Julius is refunded and the remaining obligation canceled if, for any reason, the franchisee fails to open the franchise.
c. In return for the initial franchise fee, Julius agrees to (1) assist the franchisee in selecting the location for the business, (2) negotiate the lease for the land, (3) obtain financing and assist with building design, (4) supervise construction, (5) establish accounting and tax records, and (6) provide expert advice, over a five-year period, on such matters as employee and management training, quality control, and promotion.
d. In addition to the initial franchise fee, the franchisee must pay to Julius a monthly fee of 2% of sales. This fee is a payment for menu planning, recipe innovations, and the privilege of purchasing ingredients from the franchisor at or below prevailing market prices.

The management of Julius estimates that the value of the services rendered to the franchisee when the contract is signed amounts to at least $20,000. All franchisees to date have opened their locations at the scheduled time, and none has defaulted on any of the notes receivable.

The credit ratings of all franchisees would entitle them to borrow at the current interest rate of 16%. The present value of an ordinary annuity of five annual receipts of $10,000 each, discounted at 16%, is $32,743.

Required:

1. Discuss the alternatives that Julius might use to account for the initial franchise fee. Evaluate each by applying generally accepted accounting principles to this situation, and give illustrative entries for each alternative.
2. Given the nature of Julius's agreement with its franchisees, when should revenues be recognized? Discuss the question of revenue recognition for both the initial franchise fee and the additional monthly fee of 2% of sales, and give illustrative entries for both types of revenue.

P 27-6

Franchises: Revenue Recognition and Disclosure

Glazer's Inc., has established franchised outlets that bake and sell various types of donuts. Holly Doe entered into an agreement for a Glazer's franchise on March 10, 19X1, for a term of 10 years. The agreement included the following provisions:

a. An initial franchise fee of $100,000 is to be paid as follows: $20,000 cash at the opening of the store; the balance in eight non-interest-bearing notes of $10,000 each, one note to be paid on each anniversary date of the opening.
b. The initial franchise fee includes charges for store equipment, fixtures, and inventory. The cost of the equipment and fixtures to Glazer's is $15,000; the estimated salable value is $20,000. The cost of the inventory and supplies to Glazer's is $5,500, and the estimated wholesale price to the franchisee is $7,000.
c. Continuing fees are ½% of gross revenue. These fees are for the right to use the Glazer's trademark for the duration of the franchise, the privilege of buying inventory and supplies at or below recognized market prices, advertising, quality control visitations, use of the Glazer's accounting and reporting system for franchisees, and management assistance.
d. Incremental costs associated with the initial franchise fee are $32,000, which does not include the costs of equipment, fixtures, and inventory. Minor costs associated with the franchise are not accrued. The estimated annual continuing costs are $275.

Additional Information:
The store opened for business on June 30, 19X2. Store revenues for the six months ended December 31, 19X2 amounted to $500,000. The credit rating of the franchisee would entitle him to borrow at the current interest rate of 15%.

Required:

1. Prepare a schedule that shows the income recognized by Glazer's Inc., in regard to the franchise, through December 31, 19X2. The schedule should disclose fully the nature of the revenue and expense items.
2. Prepare a disclosure statement included in Glazer's annual report. Assume that Glazer's has only one franchise agreement.

P 27-7

Consignments: Preparing Journal Entries

Ace Company is an appliance distributor. In December 19X1, the following events occurred between the company and one of its dealers, Selmore Company:

1. Inventory costing $100,000 was shipped to Selmore at a total billing price of $150,000. Of these amounts, inventory costing $7,000 was shipped on consignment at a billing price of $10,000.
2. Ace incurred shipping costs of $1,100 on inventory shipped to Selmore. Of this amount, $100 pertained to goods shipped on consignment.
3. Ace received remittances of $135,000 from Selmore. Of this amount, $8,000 pertained to the sale of consigned inventory by Selmore. The manufacturing

cost for all inventory totaled $90,000, of which $6,000 pertained to the consigned inventory sold.

4. Ace received notification from Selmore that inventory on consignment at a billing price of $3,300 was sold by Selmore, but the remittance was not made to Ace until January 19X2. (Ace's manufacturing cost was $2,200.)

Required:
Prepare the journal entries recorded on each company's books for these transactions.

APPENDIX

Student Manual for Using Electronic Spreadsheet Templates

GENERAL MATTERS

Introduction

Almost all companies with subsidiaries (and the outside independent auditors of these companies) now use software programs to perform both consolidation of financial statements and translation of foreign currency financial statements. Although some companies and some auditors use an internally developed software program, the common practice is to use one of the more popular, commercially developed electronic spreadsheet software packages. Accordingly, accounting majors need to obtain some hands-on experience in performing consolidations and translations using an electronic spreadsheet software package to be prepared for their future work environment.

What Is an Electronic Spreadsheet?

An **electronic spreadsheet** is merely an accountant's working paper on a video screen (called a **monitor**). Amounts and account descriptions are entered on the screen through a keyboard (very similar to a typewriter keyboard), just as a pencil is used to enter these items onto a working paper. To have ready control over entering data on the screen, it is necessary to divide the screen into columns and rows. Thus, the screen can be thought of as a matrix or grid system. Each column and row is labeled alphabetically or numerically. The intersection of a given column and a given row is referred to as a **cell**. For example, Cell A7 refers to the intersection (or the coordinate) of Column A and Row 7. For most accounting applications, column widths are designed so that nine to twelve characters can be entered into a cell.

The Cursor. The location of the **cursor** (also called a pointer or a highlighter) on the screen determines which cell is the **active cell.** Data can be entered into (or erased from) only the active cell. The cursor is moved around on the video screen using the four arrow keys (up, down, left, or right) located in the lower right corner of the keyboard.

The Template Approach

Companies using a spreadsheet package usually design spreadsheets to be used for specific applications (such as budgeting and consolidating financial statements). A spreadsheet configured for a specific application is called a **template**. Typically, the template is stored on a diskette and loaded into the computer's memory when the application is to be performed. The user then merely enters data into the computer and completes the applicable task. Thus the templates are used over and over again, making it unnecessary for the user to set up the design and configuration of the spreadsheet each time the task is to be performed. Since designing and programming a template is an involved and time-consuming task, the software industry now offers templates to be used with spreadsheet packages. With templates available, users need only a minimal understanding of an electronic spreadsheet software package. Although a thorough understanding of spreadsheet software is desirable, that is beyond the scope of this appendix.

Using Templates but with Some Programming Required

The *Electronic Spreadsheet Templates* diskette available for use with this text was designed to be used with any version of LOTUS 1-2-3 spreadsheet software on an IBM PC (or IBM XT or IBM AT) computer. (See page 1202 for system requirements.) The diskette contains templates for these chapters:

Chapter	File Name	Description
1	MODEL1	Combining statement worksheet
3	MODEL3	Consolidating statement worksheet
4	MODEL4	Consolidating statement worksheet
5	MODEL5	Consolidating statement worksheet
6	MODEL6	Consolidating statement worksheet
7–10	MODEL7	Consolidating statement worksheet
15	MODEL15T	Foreign currency translation worksheet
15	MODEL15R	Foreign currency remeasurement worksheet
16	MODEL15T	Foreign currency translation worksheet
19	MODEL19	Statement of affairs
23	MODEL23	Partnership trial balance worksheet
25	MODEL25	Partnership statement of realization and liquidation

Templates for all the chapters are purposely not 100% complete. Accordingly, the student must do a limited amount of "programming." For the consolidation templates, for example, for any additional asset or liability accounts that you add, you must insert formulas at certain locations in order that these accounts cross-total on the spreadsheet. (These templates contain space for these additional accounts.) Depending on the problem selected, you will need to add from one to six additional asset or liability accounts. By designing the templates in this manner, you gain some spreadsheet "programming" experience. (Instructions for writing formulas and entering data appear on page 1191.)

Purchasing a Personal Diskette

A master templates diskette is available to students from the instructor. However, you will have to purchase your own diskette on which to copy this master and save your work. First, it is more convenient to have your own copy of the master templates diskette than to share the master with classmates. Second, when working a problem on the computer you may have to stop the session before you have completed the problem, and unless you wish to begin the problem all over again from scratch, you must save your work from that session to your personal diskette. Do not save your work to the master templates diskette obtained from your instructor; it would not have nearly enough space to accommodate the files for all students, and you risk erasing a model from the master.

Before making your copy of the master or saving your recent work to this personal diskette, first make sure that the diskette is formatted for the IBM PC (or IBM AT or IBM XT) computer. If it is, no formatting is necessary. If it is not, read and perform the steps that follow. Remember that formatting a diskette erases all previous files on that diskette, if there were any, so be sure to copy files you wish to save to another diskette first. For this reason, do **not** attempt to format the master diskette from the instructor. The master will take up about 230KB of disk space on a $5\frac{1}{4}$-inch, double-sided, double-density 360KB diskette.

Formatting. To format a disk, perform the following steps:

1. Put the Lotus 1-2-3 and operating system diskette in Drive A (they should both be on the 1-2-3 diskette) and close the flap.
2. Turn on the computer (the unit that has the disk drives).
3. Time and date prompts will appear. To bypass them, press ⟨**ENTER**⟩ twice. (⟨**ENTER**⟩ is discussed more fully on page 1184.)

   Note: Your system disk may have been configured to automatically bypass these prompts and take you to 1-2-3 directly. If so, once in 1-2-3 press /**QY** to get to the system prompt (A⟩). (The slash (/) key is discussed on page 1185.)

4. When the A⟩ prompt appears, put the diskette you wish to format in Drive B and close the flap.
5. Type the following:

FORMAT B: ⟨ENTER⟩

Caution: Be sure to insert a space after **FORMAT**.

6. After formatting, the computer will ask you whether you want to format another disk. If yes, follow the instructions on the screen. If no, press **N**.

Copying the Master Templates Diskette. The following steps are necessary for copying the master templates diskette to your personal diskette.

1. Put the LOTUS 1-2-3 and operating system diskette in Drive A and close the flap.
2. Turn on the computer.
3. Press ⟨**ENTER**⟩ twice to bypass the time and date prompts, if they appear.

Caution: Do not load LOTUS 1-2-3 at this point. (Loading 1-2-3 is discussed in a later section.) If your system disk has been configured to load 1-2-3 automatically, press **/QY** to get to the system prompt (A⟩).

4. When the A⟩ prompt appears, remove the system diskette from Drive A.
5. Put the master templates diskette in Drive A and close the flap.
6. Put your personal diskette, the one that will hold your copy of the master, in Drive B.
7. Type the following:

COPY A:*.* B: ⟨ENTER⟩

Caution: Remember to add a space after **COPY** and one before **B:**.

Using Macros

A **macro** is a stored instruction. By invoking (using) a macro, you can execute a complex and involved instruction by typing only a few keys. The templates for Chapters 1 through 15 contain several macros. By using them you can perform several operations quickly, and easily:

1. Upload problem data from the lower portion of the template into the worksheet portion of the template (thus not having to enter this data manually).

Caution: Amounts for retained earnings and dividends must be entered **manually**.

2. Automatically post the primary elimination entry to the worksheet. (For models 3 through 7, space is provided in the middle section of the worksheet for preparing this elimination entry.)
3. Simplify the entering of data in columns.

4. "Freeze" or lock in column titles or row descriptions along the top or left edge of the screen.

   Caution: Use this macro only after you no longer need access to the frozen area. Otherwise, you must undo the macro (using the command / **Worksheet Title Clear**, or **/WTC**) to gain access.

Each template's macros are stored (along with instructions for using the macros and a description of each macro) at the bottom of the template. Macros are easy to use. Each macro is assigned a letter of the alphabet. To invoke the macro stored in letter E, for example, merely press and hold down the ALT key (located below the left shift key). While holding this key down, press the letter E. (Some of the more involved macros take about ten seconds to be executed.)

As you proceed to use one template and then the next, it is recommended that you make a hard-copy printout of each template before using it on the computer. This will enable you to review the template in its entirety and readily see which macros are available to you on a particular template.

Accounting Instructions

Before working your first problem on the computer, do the following:

1. Work the problem manually. This should be unnecessary for subsequent problems. If your first problem is a consolidations problem, you most likely will perform the following steps:
   a. Make any necessary adjustments to the parent's and subsidiary's financial statements.
   b. Prepare any required analyses for purposes of developing elimination entries.
   c. Prepare all elimination entries.
2. Make sure the elimination entries you prepare balance as to debit and credit totals.

By working the first problem manually before working the problem on the computer, you will be able to concentrate solely on how to use the computer once you start using it. This will make your initial learning process go much more smoothly.

Computer-Related Aspects of the Assignments

For most problems, working a problem using the computer consists of the following steps:

1. Loading the operating system and the LOTUS 1-2-3 electronic spreadsheet software program into the computer's memory.

   Note: If your computer has a hard disk (such as on the IBM AT), in most cases the LOTUS 1-2-3 program (and possibly the operating system program) is stored on the hard disk. Accordingly, it is not necessary for you to insert a disk containing LOTUS 1-2-3 (or possibly a disk containing the operating system program) for loading purposes. **Be sure to inquire about this.**

2. Loading the desired template into the computer's memory.
3. Entering your name on the spreadsheet in the space provided.
4. Entering the problem number on the spreadsheet in the space provided.
5. Entering the appropriate company name or names and year-end date in the heading section of the worksheet (spaces are provided).
6. Entering the appropriate company name or names in certain columns (spaces are provided).
7. Determining whether additional asset and liability accounts need to be added to the worksheet section of the templates.
8. Adding the appropriate additional asset and liability accounts.
9. Entering formulas in certain columns of the worksheet of any accounts in step 8 that you added, so that amounts will cross-total.

Caution: You do not have to enter or modify any formulas for vertical totals as a result of adding one or more accounts. (Ignore all accounts that you do not need for your particular problem.)

10. Entering financial statement amounts in certain columns of the worksheet (either manually or using macros).
11. Entering elimination entries in the appropriate elimination columns (either manually or using a macro) for consolidation problems.
12. Making a hard-copy printout of the completed problem.

The following sections explain how to do each of the preceding tasks in a step-by-step manner. However, you will be much more comfortable and efficient in using the computer if you first read this material once or twice thoroughly *before* proceeding to work on the computer.

USING LOTUS 1-2-3

Getting Started

Entering Data and Commands. Using an electronic spreadsheet requires the entering of data and commands into the computer's memory. The keyboard key that performs this function is labeled ←┘ and is called the ⟨**RETURN**⟩ key in some manuals and the ⟨**ENTER**⟩ key in others. Because the latter term describes the exact function of the key, this key is called the ⟨**ENTER**⟩ key in this appendix. To enter data and commands, follow these steps in sequence:

1. Obtain the LOTUS 1-2-3 spreadsheet software program and the operating system diskette for the IBM PC (or IBM AT or IBM XT) computer. It would also be a good idea to have the 1-2-3 manual available as a reference.
2. Insert the LOTUS 1-2-3 and operating system diskette into Drive A and close the flap.
3. Insert your personal diskette, containing your copy of the templates diskette, into Drive B and close the flap.

Caution: When the computer is accessing either disk drive, the appropriate red light comes on. Never attempt to remove or replace a diskette when either of these lights is on.

4. Turn on the computer. (It may take up to 75 seconds while the computer checks its circuits before Drive A begins to operate.)
5. **Load the operating system and 1-2-3.** After checking its circuits, the computer will automatically search Drive A and load the computer's operating system. (This step takes about 20–30 seconds.) Time and date prompts will appear. To bypass them, press ⟨**ENTER**⟩ twice. (The operating system may have been configured to load 1-2-3 directly, eliminating this option.) Next, the computer will call up the 1-2-3 menu, and you will see "1-2-3" as the highlighted option on the screen. Press the ⟨**ENTER**⟩ key to load the 1-2-3 program. (Loading 1-2-3 can take from 10 to 40 seconds.) After 1-2-3 has been loaded, the LOTUS copyright information will appear. Then press any key, and within five seconds column titles (labeled alphabetically) and row titles (labeled numerically) will appear on the screen. During this step, 1-2-3 also reads Drive B to see what 1-2-3 files are there.
6. **Load a template.** This step involves using the keyboard to build a 1-2-3 command.

Building Commands. You build a command by stringing together subcommands in the proper order. Each subcommand has a name, consisting of one or more command keywords, such as **Copy**, **Erase**, **File**, and **Print**. These command keywords (approximately 200 of them) are organized into a logical multilevel hierarchy called a **menu system.** Generally, each level of the menu system has several command keywords from which a choice is to be made. To indicate to the computer that you wish to build a command, press the / (slash) key. At this point, the top-level menu would be displayed in the upper left corner of the monitor (called the control panel). You would then make a choice from this top-level menu, after which the second-level menu would appear. You would then proceed through this level and lower levels as necessary to complete your command. For example, the command

/ **Worksheet** (1st level) **Global** (2nd level)

Format (3rd level) **Currency** (4th level)

would be used to specify the use of dollar signs and commas when amounts are entered into the spreadsheet.

Making Command Keyword Choices. There are two ways to select a command keyword from any level of the command menu:

a. **"Point and pick" method.** To minimize errors and to make building commands as "user-friendly" as possible, 1-2-3 uses a cursor (or highlighter) within the control panel. For simplicity, we refer to this cursor as the **menu pointer.** (It should not be confused with the cell cursor, which is used later in entering labels, values [amounts], and formulas.) Using the arrow keys (on the numeric keypad to the right of the alphabetic keyboard), move the menu pointer to the command keyword of your choice. You have *pointed to* a command keyword when you see that command keyword highlighted on the monitor. To *pick* that option, press the ⟨**ENTER**⟩ key.
b. **"First-letter-only" method.** At each level of the command menu, press the first letter of the command keyword of your choice. (The chosen command keyword does not have to be highlighted in the menu line—but you must be able to see that command keyword in the menu line.)

Comparative Note: The "first-letter-only" method of selecting command keywords is much quicker than the "point and pick" method because it is not necessary to either move the menu pointer or use the ⟨**ENTER**⟩ key. However, it *is* easier to make a typing mistake.

We shall present both "point and pick" and "first-letter-only" explanations for a few critical 1-2-3 commands.

Caution: When using the keyboard, press and release the keys quickly. Pressing a key slowly or holding it down produces multiple entries for the key.

If you make a mistake using the keyboard, go to step 7 (page 1188), which explains how to correct such mistakes. Then return to step 6.

Load the consolidation template into the computer's memory by pressing the following keys:

Keys to be Pressed	Explanation and Guidance
/	By pressing the / (slash) key, you are telling 1-2-3 that you want to build up a command, using command keywords. After pressing /, see on the screen the top-level menu of command keywords: **Worksheet Range Copy Move File Print Graph Data Quit**

Use the four arrow keys on the numeric keypad to point to your next menu choice, which is to be the command keyword File. (Use the right and left arrows for moving across a single line of menu choices to highlight an option; use the up and down arrows on a multi-line menu.) Or press the single letter F.

F

By pressing the F key or by pressing ⟨**ENTER**⟩ after pointing to File on the menu, you are telling 1-2-3 to access the File command. You want to load the consolidation template that is stored on the diskette in Drive B. After selecting File, the following menu choices appear on the prompt line of the monitor:

Retrieve Save Combine Xtract Erase List Import Directory

The Retrieve command should appear highlighted on the screen. If it is not, you can point to it by pressing the left and right arrow keys to move the menu pointer. Or you can just press the single letter R.

R

By selecting the Retrieve command, you are telling 1-2-3 to load a 1-2-3 file from a diskette into the computer's memory. Next, you will see the prompt:

Enter name of file to retrieve:

Notice that the file name **MODEL1** is highlighted under the prompt. Assume, however, that you want to load Model 4 (the file name is MODEL4).

MODEL4
and/or
⟨**ENTER**⟩

Typing MODEL4 (the file name under which the template for Chapter 4 is stored on the data diskette) and then pressing ⟨**ENTER**⟩ loads that file into the computer's memory. If instead you use the arrow keys so that MODEL4 becomes highlighted under the file name prompt, you only need to press ⟨**ENTER**⟩ (Loading a template takes 10–20 seconds.)

After 1-2-3 has retrieved the desired template from the diskette, it will appear on the screen. Note that the cell cursor is positioned in cell A1 and that the contents of that cell (TEMPLATE:) is displayed on the cursor coordinate line (the top line in the upper left corner of the screen). Note also that the contents is preceded by ', an apostrophe. The apostrophe signifies that a **label** (text string) is stored in this cell.

Summary: In step 6, you loaded one of the templates by building and entering a command. If you used the "point and pick" method, which requires the use of the arrow keys and the ⟨**ENTER**⟩ key for each step in building the complete command, your process was as follows:

/ File ⟨ENTER⟩ Retrieve ⟨ENTER⟩ MODEL4 ⟨ENTER⟩

If you used the "first-letter-only" method, which requires typing only the first letter of each command keyword, your process was as follows:

/FR MODEL4 ⟨ENTER⟩

7. **Correct any keyboard mistakes.** The manner of making corrections depends on whether you: (a) are building commands; (b) typing labels, values, or formulas **to be entered** into a cell, or (c) **have entered** an incorrect label, value, or formula into a cell.

a. Making corrections when building commands:

Keys to be Used	Location on Alphabetic Keyboard	How They Work
⟨**ESCAPE**⟩	Labeled **Esc** in upper left corner.	Cancels the last command keyword choice that you selected. Repeated pressing takes you backward through the main command menus, **one subcommand at a time.**
⟨**CONTROL**⟩ and ⟨**BREAK**⟩	Labeled **Ctrl** above left shift key. Labeled **Break** (on front) and **Scroll Lock** (on top) in upper right corner.	Cancels with one stroke the **entire command sequence constructed to this point.** To execute, first hold down the ⟨**CONTROL**⟩ key and *then* press the ⟨**BREAK**⟩ key.

b. Making corrections when typing labels, values, or formulas that have not yet been entered into a cell:

Keys to be Used	Location on Alphabetic Keyboard	How They Work
⟨**BACKSPACE**⟩	Labeled ← in upper right corner (a very large key) to left of the ⟨**NUM LOCK**⟩ key.	Erases the last character typed. Repeated pressing erases other characters in the line, one character at a time, in right-to-left (LIFO) order.
⟨**ESCAPE**⟩	Labeled **Esc** in upper left corner.	Cancels the entire text line that you have typed, allowing you to begin that line again.

c. Erasing labels, values, or formulas that have been entered into a cell:

Command	Explanation and Guidance
/ Range ⟨ENTER⟩ Erase ⟨ENTER⟩ or **/RE**	Erases the contents of a cell. (Cell cursor must first be moved to that cell.) Note: LOTUS 1-2-3 assumes here that the range (the extent of data to be erased) is just the cell to which you have moved the cell cursor. A range is expanded using the arrow keys, enabling multiple cells to be erased simultaneously.

8. **Print a hard copy of the template.** At this point, it will be useful to instruct the computer to print out a hard copy of a template in model form. This takes about five minutes. You can then study the entire template before entering any data relating to the assigned problem. If the cell cursor is not already in cell A1, use the arrow keys to move it there now. Jump ahead to page 1195, which gives instructions for printing a hard copy of solutions. Then come back to this section and proceed from here.

   In reviewing the hard copy of the template, note the following items:

   a. **General instructions and cautions** are located in the upper left corner of each template. Read them carefully.
   b. The order of the items comprising the templates is as follows:
      i. The worksheet.
      ii. Analysis and journal entry section (included only for templates for Chapters 3–10).
      iii. Problem data section (included only for templates for Chapters 1–16).
      iv. Macros: instructions, explanations, and the stored instructions.
   c. In the worksheet section of the template, whenever a zero (**0**) shows, there is a formula stored in the cell at that location. **Formulas** are used to arrive at subtotals, totals, and cross-totals. (How to write formulas is explained later.)
   d. Everything printed except the zeros are called **labels**. At this point, there are no **values** (amounts) in the worksheet section of the template. If there were, the worksheet would not be a model but a finished document.

Moving the Cell Cursor

Note that LOTUS 1-2-3 displays only a small portion of the template at one time on the monitor, even though the entire template is stored in the computer's memory. Any section of the template can be displayed merely by moving the cell cursor to the desired section. Familiarize yourself with cursor movement by doing the following:

1. If the cell cursor is not at cell A1, then use the directional arrow keys (in the numeric keypad) to move it there.
2. Press the down arrow key and hold it down until you reach cell A45. Note that the contents of cell A45 are displayed on the cursor coordinate line (the top line in the upper left corner of the screen).
3. Using the right arrow key, move the cell cursor to cell B45. Note that this cell is blank and that the cursor coordinate line is blank except for the coordinate of the cell cursor (B45). Later in this assignment, you will have to enter a value in this and many other cells. (Instructions are provided on p. 1193.)
4. Using the right arrow key, move the cell cursor to cell F45. Note that the contents of this cell is a zero, but that the cell cursor coordinate line displays the following:

   F45: (**B45+C45+D45−E45**)

   This means that the above formula (which produces a value) is stored in this cell. Thus as values (amounts) are entered in cells B45, C45, D45 and E45, the cross-total of these four cells will appear in cell F45. Cross-totaling and totaling are done automatically by the computer wherever formulas are stored.

The GOTO Key. When you need to pass over a great number of rows or columns to get to a particular cell, it is more efficient to use the **GOTO** key. Here is how to operate the GOTO feature:

The GOTO key is labeled **F5**, one of the keys located to the left of the alphabetic keyboard. After pressing the GOTO key, the prompt line (the second line from the top in the upper left corner) displays the following:

ENTER address to go to: (your current position)

This means that 1-2-3 is prompting us to enter the coordinate to which we want to move the cell cursor. Assume that you want to position the cell cursor at coordinate A57. Press the following:

A57 ⟨ENTER⟩

The cell cursor is now positioned at cell A57.

Other Cell Cursor Movement Keys. The following keys (all of which are located on the numeric keypad) are other convenient and time-saving ways to move the cell cursor:

Key	What It Does
PgUp	Moves the cell cursor up one screen (20 rows).
PgDn	Moves the cell cursor down one screen (20 rows).
HOME	Moves the cell cursor to cell A1.

END Moves the cell cursor to the boundary of the active (or used) portion of the spreadsheet—this key **must** be used in conjunction with one of the arrow keys **or** the HOME key, **with the END key typed first** and held down while the other key is typed. For example:

END HOME	Moves cell cursor to the bottom right section of spreadsheet.
END →	Moves cell cursor to right boundary of the row that the cell cursor is on.

Cell Protection

To prevent the accidental altering or erasing of labels and formulas, each of the models has been **cell protected.** When a cell is protected, the user is prevented from: (a) altering or erasing the contents of a cell, and (b) entering a label, formula, or value into an empty cell. Trying to do so causes the computer to beep. Of course, those cells that you need to use in preparing your solution have been **unprotected**. You can readily determine if a cell is unprotected as follows:

1. **Cells having labels, values, or formulas.** For unprotected cells, the labels, values, and formulas are shown in the template in a much brighter display than that used for the protected cells. (They stand out nicely.)
2. **Unused cells.** For these cells, the cell cursor coordinate line has the letter U (for "unprotected") displayed whenever the cell cursor is located in an unprotected cell.

Cell Protection Using the Range Command. Once the cell protection option has been activated for an entire model (or template), as has been done for each of the models on templates diskette and your copy of it, individual cells may have their protection removed or added using the Range command as follows:

Command	Explanation
/RU	To unprotect a cell.
/RP	To protect a cell.

For either command, the cell cursor must be in the cell you wish to unprotect or protect.

Entering Labels, Formulas, and Values

The templates for Chapters 1–10 have been designed so that columns B through F are each 11 characters wide. Each cell can be programmed to contain: (1) a label (such as a column heading, an account description, an instruction, your name, or a problem number); (2) a value (such as 500);

or (3) a formula (such as a listing of cells whose values are to be totaled or cross-totaled). Note that the number of characters needed for a formula in a cell is not restricted by the width of that cell.

Entering Labels. For these templates you must enter several labels—your name, the problem number, the name of the company or companies, and in most cases several account descriptions. To perform these tasks, it is first necessary to understand (1) how to enter labels into a cell, and (2) when to use the ' (apostrophe) symbol so that 1-2-3 knows you are entering a label. Without the apostrophe, 1-2-3 might interpret your string of characters as a value (an amount).

1. Move the cell cursor to cell A52. This is a blank line to be used for entering an additional asset account to the balance sheet. Assume that we want to add the account Installment Receivables on this row. The caption "Installment Receivables" contains 23 characters and is to be indented one space from the left boundary of cell A52. Because column A has been designed to hold only 17 characters, the caption must be abbreviated: for example, "Installment Rec." With one space for indenting and one period at the end, there are 17 characters. (Use the **space bar** for indenting.)

   As you press the letter keys (remember to indent one space), the letters appear on the third line from the top in the upper left corner of the screen. This line is called the **edit line,** and its purpose is to allow you to see what you have typed. (If you make any typing mistakes, use the ⟨**BACKSPACE**⟩ or ⟨**ESCAPE**⟩ keys.)
2. Press the ⟨**ENTER**⟩ key and "Installment Rec." appears in two places: the cursor coordinate line and cell A52.
3. If you made a mistake, try it again. (It is not necessary to erase your mistake from the cell to try again; but if you desire to do so, press **/RE** ⟨**ENTER**⟩ which you should recall is the erase command.)
4. After you have entered the label correctly, erase the contents of cell A52.
5. Move the cell cursor to cell E16, where the year-end of the company is to be inserted.

   Whenever you write a label whose first character in the cell is not a letter of the alphabet or a blank space as a result of using the space bar, you must begin that string of characters with an apostrophe ('). In this way, 1-2-3 knows you are entering a label rather than a value. So to enter 12/31/X1 in cell E16, type:

   '12/31/X1 ⟨ENTER⟩

6. **Specific labels.** The following labels would have to be entered for MODEL4:
   a. Your name (cells E2 and F2).
   b. The problem assignment number (cell E4).

   Caution: Assume you are working Problem 4-2 in Chapter 4. If you try to enter 4-2, LOTUS 1-2-3 will think you are trying to enter a value and will not accept this (it beeps). It is necessary to alert 1-2-3 that you intend to enter a label instead of a value. Accordingly, you must begin with ' (an apostrophe); then type 4-2.

c. The parent company's name (cells C14 and D14).
d. The parent company's year-end (cell E16).
e. The parent company's name and the subsidiary company's name (cells B19 and C19).
f. Account descriptions for assets (rows 52 through 55).
g. Account descriptions for liabilities (row 60).

The labels to be entered vary depending on the particular template.

Note: When working a problem on the computer and you cannot complete the problem at one sitting, you can store the partially completed solution (at any stage of completion) on your personal diskette and then return to the computer at a later time to complete the assignment. Refer to page 1200 for instructions on saving a partially completed solution on a diskette.

Entering Formulas. For any asset or liability account that you add to the balance sheet, you must enter a formula in column F, so that amounts on these rows will cross-total. You do not need to write any formulas for subtotals and totals. Before entering any formulas, move the cell cursor to cell F45, the intersection of the column labeled "Consolidated" and the row labeled "Cash." The formula for this cell is displayed in the upper left corner of the screen. For accounts that you add, you must write formulas such as these. Assume that you have added the account Goodwill to row 53. You would write the formulas for cell F53 as follows:

Position Cell Cursor At	Press These Keys
F53	**(B53+C53+D53−E53) ⟨ENTER⟩**

At this point, you would enter formulas for any balance sheet accounts that you had to add to the template.

Caution: When writing formulas, be sure to (1) enclose the formulas within parentheses and (2) use no space characters within the formulas.

Note: You may use either upper- or lowercase letters when you enter formulas. But if you enter lowercase letters, 1-2-3 will automatically convert them and store them as upper-case.

Entering Values. Continuing with Model 4 as an example, you would enter values only in columns B through E. No values would be entered into column F, since the appropriate cells in this column contain formulas to make the amounts cross-total automatically. Also, no values need be entered at any total or subtotal, since these cells already contain formulas so that amounts will automatically total. **You can readily see on the screen where formulas have been placed, since a zero (0) is displayed there. (Entering values at these locations would destroy the formulas.)**

With column widths of 11 characters in columns B through F in Model 4, LOTUS 1-2-3 will accept up to eight numeric characters for a value. (Two positions are required for commas, automatically inserted by 1-2-3, and one space must be left blank for spacing between columns.) Because negative amounts are shown in parentheses and space must be provided for the left parenthesis, only seven numeric characters can be accepted when entering negative amounts. Enter values by pressing the numeric keys and then the ⟨ENTER⟩ key. For example, move the cell cursor to cell B23 and enter the value **500** using the numeric keyboard, and then press ⟨**ENTER**⟩.

> **Caution:** Because the numeric keyboard is used both for moving the cell cursor and entering values, it is necessary to press the **NUM LOCK** key (located directly above the numeric keyboard) when you want to enter values.
>
> The disadvantage of this arrangement is that when you want to move the cell cursor to another cell (after having entered a value in your present cell), it is necessary to: (a) press the **NUM LOCK** key again (to go back to the "moving the cell cursor" mode); (b) press the appropriate arrow keys to move the cell cursor to your desired cell; and (c) press the **NUM LOCK** key to go to the "entering values" mode. **For most of the templates, a special purpose macro (/N) is available to circumvent this disadvantage.**

Using the arrow keys, note how this value is totaled and cross-totaled in the income statement and also carried forward to the analysis of retained earnings and then to the retained earnings account in the balance sheet. Now move the cursor to cell B23 and press **/RE** ⟨**ENTER**⟩**,** which erases the 500 value. While entering values, remember the following points:

1. **Enter values as you would on a calculator.** Thus, enter **8700**, not $8,700. LOTUS 1-2-3 will automatically insert commas when it displays your values, and display the values right-justified (as would a calculator).

   Summary caution for entering values:

   a. **Never** enter commas.
   b. **Never** enter dollar signs.
   c. **Never** enter spaces (via the space bar).

2. **Entering negative values.** Use a minus sign when entering a negative value (as you would on a calculator). A negative amount of $3,200 would be entered as **−3200** (the minus sign must be entered first); LOTUS 1-2-3 will automatically display the negative value as (3,200). Thus you *never* need to enter parentheses.

Caution: For Models 1 through 7, only certain accounts in columns B and C (the parent and subsidiary company columns) require the use of negative values:

Income Statement and Statement of Retained Earnings:	All debit balances.
Balance Sheet—Assets:	All credit balances (such as Accumulated Depreciation).
Balance Sheet—Liabilities and Equity:	All debit balances (such as Bond Discount).

Accordingly, you would *not* use a minus sign in any column other than columns B and C.

3. For values containing the number 1 (6100, for example), be sure to use the 1 in the numeric keyboard—not the lowercase letter *l* next to the letter *k*.
4. **Entering elimination entries.** Enter only the values; do *not* try to code the values. Thus, enter **300000**—not 300,000(1). LOTUS 1-2-3 has no facility to allow the coding of entries in a worksheet. After you have obtained a hard copy printout of a completed problem, you can *manually* code elimination entries.

In working a problem using Model 4, values in columns B through E would be entered manually. This is best done by entering all required values in column B and then proceeding to the next column (making sure the balance sheet balances in column B before proceeding to the next column). As each value is entered, the computer automatically subtotals, totals, and cross-totals the values. If you have entered labels, formulas, and values properly, the balance sheet should balance in column F. Also, the debit and credit postings in the two elimination columns (at the bottom of worksheet section of the spreadsheet) should agree. You would then make a printout of the appropriate sections of the spreadsheet, as explained in the following section.

Reminder: You can save substantial time by using macros to enter data in columns B and C (and for templates for Chapters 3–10, columns D and E, as well).

Reminder: Be sure to use only those income statement and balance sheet accounts that you need for working your particular problem. Ignore all other accounts.

Printing a Hard Copy of the Solution

Overview. You can print (or file on a diskette) all or any portion of the electronic spreadsheet. To obtain a general familiarity with a particular template, first print the entire template. In printing the solution to a specific problem, however, it usually would *not* be necessary to print the **problem data** and **macro information,** both of which are contained in the **lower** sections of the templates. Accordingly, print only the worksheet portion of the template and any supporting information or conceptual analysis, both of which are contained in the **upper** sections of the templates. Below are the widths of the various sections of each of the templates in characters per line:

	Section of Template			
Model	**Worksheet**	**Conceptual Analysis**	**Problem Data**	**Macros**
1	72	n/a	105	72
3	72	72	105	72
4	72	105	105	72
5	72	105	105	72
6	72	94	105	72
7	105	105	127	72
15T	71	n/a	71	60
15R	71	n/a	71	60
19	124	n/a	n/a	60
23	88	n/a	n/a	66
25	120	n/a	n/a	60

The area to be printed must be designated as a rectangle. The rectangle is defined by indicating: (a) the cell in the upper left corner of the rectangle, and (b) the cell in the lower right corner of the rectangle. How to enter the coordinates that define this rectangular area is explained on page 1197.

Printer Capabilities. Some printers output 128 characters per line (which for convenience we refer to as **wide** printers). Other printers output only 80 characters per line (which we refer to as the **standard** printers). Wide printers can print all or any portion of the spreadsheets in one step. In contrast, standard printers require two steps if the section to be printed is more than 80 characters per row. These two steps might be to print out, for example, columns A through F and then print out columns G through I. However, the use of the **compressed printing option,** which uses a smaller type size, enables 132 characters to be printed on a standard printer. This option is explained on page 1199. We suggest you use it but only after you have mastered the basics of printing a hard copy.

Connecting the Printer to the Computer. There are various ways to connect the printer to the computer. Determine which arrangement is true for the computer you are using.

1. **Manual hookup.** This involves taking the cord attached to the printer and plugging the other end of it in the back of the monitor.

Caution: In doing this, be sure that you do not disconnect any plugs in the back of the monitor, as you may disconnect the monitor from the computer's memory and destroy what is on the screen.

Caution: It may be necessary to obtain assistance to connect the printer to the monitor. The connecting plug must be positioned properly.

2. **Designated computer for printing.** In this arrangement, the computer closest to the printer is designated to be used only for printing purposes. To print, you must store the material to be printed on your personal diskette (assuming you are already using a different computer) and then load it into the designated computer for printing. (No movement of cords and plugs is necessary.)
3. **Electronic hookup.** In this arrangement, one or more rows of computers are assigned to a specific printer. Only one of the computers can be connected to the printer at a time.

Printing Instructions. Follow these steps in proper sequence:

1. Connect the printer to the computer.
2. Position the paper properly in the printer.
3. Turn on the printer. If the "ready" or "on-line" indicator on the printer is not on, then press the printer button that will turn it on.
4. Press the following keys in the sequence indicated:

Keys to be Pressed	Explanation and Guidance
/	Tells 1-2-3 to display the top-level menu.
P	To select the "Print" command. After the letter *P* is pressed, the prompt line displays the following menu choices: **Printer File** 1-2-3 is prompting you to select one of the above subcommands. Pressing the F key selects the File subcommand; pressing the P key selects the Printer subcommand.
P	Since you want to print, press the P key. The prompt line then displays the following menu choices: **Range Line Page Options Clear Align Go Quit** Each of these menu choices stands for a possible printing suboption.
R	To specify the Print Range, the upper left and lower right coordinates of the print area. The first coordinate of the Print Range then appears:

Enter Print range: A1

A1 identifies the current location of the cell cursor. For our purposes, ignore this cell location and type over it.

Select one of the printer methods below:

A. Using a wide (128 characters) printer: If you use a wide printer and, for example, desire to print the entire template for Model 4 (which has 105 characters per row in its widest section), proceed as follows:

A1..I325 ⟨ENTER⟩ Cell A1 is the upper left corner of the template. Cell I325 is the lower right corner of the template. (Cell I325 need not be visible on the screen when we specify the cell.) Specifying I325 tells 1-2-3 to print the entire template at one time.

B. Using a standard (80 characters) printer: If you use a standard printer and, for example, desire to print the entire template for Model 4 (which has 105 characters per row in its widest section), you will need to print one portion of the spreadsheet within the 80-character limitation and then repeat the procedure for the remainder of the spreadsheet. To define the first print area, in the last part of step 4 define the Print Range as follows:

A1..F325 ⟨ENTER⟩ Cell A1 is the upper left corner of the spreadsheet. Cell F325 is a convenient place to set the lower right corner of the rectangular print area. (This Print Range will allow you to print the first six columns, or 72 characters per line.) Then proceed to step 5; when you are finished with step 5, return to this place in step 4.

While the computer is printing the first portion of the spreadsheet, as soon as the flashing WAIT message in the upper right corner of the screen stops, you can prepare the commands for printing the remainder of the spreadsheet. The menu will list a series of options (beginning with Range). Press R for Range and specify the Print Range as follows:

G1..I325 ⟨ENTER⟩ Cell G1 is the upper left corner of the unprinted portion of the spreadsheet. Cell I325 is the lower right corner of that portion. Proceed to step 5.

5. Once you have entered the print range, the previous higher level menu choices (beginning with Range) reappear. (The range you entered has been remembered, however.) You could now select Go, and the spreadsheet would be sent to the printer. However, to print a spreadsheet that is longer than one page in a continuous format, it is first necessary to

override one of the built-in printing instructions. To do so, press the following keys:

Keys to be Pressed	Explanation and Guidance
O	Press the letter O to request one of the special printing Options.
O	Press the letter O to request one of the special print options grouped under the command keyword Other.
U	Pressing U specifies that the format should be Unformatted (ignoring the page breaks throughout the templates). Then the previous higher level menu containing the command keyword Other reappears to allow you to select additional print options.
Q	Because no additional print options are needed, tell the computer that you are finished selecting print options by pressing Q for Quit. Then the previous higher level menu (beginning with the option Range) reappears. You are now ready to select Go.
G	This command sends the spreadsheet to the printer.

Naturally, you can always use the "point and pick" method of building the command: moving the menu cursor to each option **and pressing ⟨ENTER⟩ for each selection:**

/ Print Printer Range A1..I325 Option Other Unformatted Quit Go

Using the Compressed Printing Option

A standard 80-characters-per-row printer uses a normal type size of 10 pitch. Most of these printers also have the capability to use a smaller type size of 16.5 pitch, which allows 132 characters per row to be printed. There are two manners by which to use this compressed printing option, both of which require you to obtain certain information:

A. **Using LOTUS 1-2-3:** Look up in the printer's manual the nine-digit code applicable to the printer used in your computer lab. (For example, one of the Okidata printers is assigned the code \015\027\071.) The command for selecting this option follows:

   / Printer Print Options Setup \000\000\000 (or **/PPOS**\000\000\000)

   (Be sure to type in the three backslashes.)

   The above command changes the **default** setting in the printer's memory—not the computer's memory. Note that you must be connected to the printer to execute this command. The printer will stay in this new setting until someone changes it back to its original default setting (10-pitch type, 80 characters per row). This is usually done for most printers by turning the printer off and then back on again.

B. **Using the operating system:** Some utility programs, when used with the operating system, allow you to obtain compressed printing. Approximately five steps must be executed; check with the utility program's manual. Choose this route only if the LOTUS 1-2-3 route cannot be executed.

Saving a Completed or Partially Completed Solution

If you wish to save a completed or partially completed problem on your personal diskette, then you must assign a specific file name to that problem, such as PROB42 if you are working Problem 4-2 in Chapter 4.

> **Caution: Never** save your solution under a file name beginning with MODEL—this would destroy this or other models on the diskette and prevent you from using that template for working a different problem. To prevent accidental destruction of any of your templates, follow carefully the following instructions for assigning file names and for filing solutions.

File Names. File names in LOTUS 1-2-3 can be up to eight characters long. However, the characters can consist only of letters of the alphabet (A through Z) and numbers (0 through 9). Accordingly, you **cannot use dashes, periods, other forms of punctuation, or blank spaces;** the computer will reject these as improper file names by beeping. Note that above we suggest using PROB42 as an example—not an improper file name such as PROBLEM 4-2 or PROB. 4-2 (both of which have three rule infractions—see whether you can identify them). If you type in lowercase letters in assigning a file name, LOTUS 1-2-3 will automatically convert them to upper case.

Instructions for Saving Your Work. To save a completed or partially completed solution on your personal diskette, do the following:

Keys to be Pressed	Explanation and Guidance
/	To display the top-level menu.
F	To select the File command.
S	To select the subcommand Save within the File command.
	At this point, 1-2-3 tries to be helpful by displaying on the monitor the names of any of the files already on your personal diskette, which contains a copy of the master templates. The display should be:
	MODEL1 MODEL3 MODEL4 MODEL5 MODEL6

and so forth, with MODEL1 highlighted. You must assign a file name that is different from any of the file names you may have on your personal diskette, so as to avoid destroying one of your saved files.

Caution: Be sure you do not press the ⟨ENTER⟩ key at this point—this would destroy one of your saved files.

Assuming you select PROB42 as your file name; proceed as follows:

PROB42	To indicate the file name you wish to assign to your solution.
⟨ENTER⟩	To begin the filing process (takes about 10–20 seconds). Watch for the blinking WAIT in the upper right corner of the screen to return to READY.

Using the "point and pick" method of building the command, the sequence is as follows: **/ File ⟨ENTER⟩ Save ⟨ENTER⟩ PROB42 ⟨ENTER⟩.**

To terminate your session with 1-2-3, call for the main menu by pressing /. Then select Quit (or press **Q**). When 1-2-3 asks for a confirmation, select Yes (or type **Y**). **Be sure to save your work from your current session before quitting.**

Starting Again Where You Previously Stopped. Assume you later return to the computer to finish Problem 4-2, which you filed in its partially completed stage as previously instructed. Load the PROB42 file from your personal diskette (rather than the original MODEL4 file from the templates diskette), thereby enabling you to begin where you left off earlier. The command would be: **/FS PROB42 ⟨ENTER⟩.**

Filing a Solution a Second (or Third) Time. Suppose you are either unable to complete Problem 4-2 at the end of the second session or you have completed it and want to file your completed solution. Again, it will be necessary to file the solution on your personal diskette. This time, however, you will be **replacing** the existing PROB42 file with the file from your latest session, rather than creating it. In replacing an existing file, an additional step is added to the previously shown filing instructions. The complete process is as follows:

Keys to be Pressed	Explanation and Guidance
/FS PROB42 ⟨ENTER⟩	Same explanation as previously shown. After pressing these keys, the prompt line shows: **Cancel Replace**

1-2-3 is merely checking to see if you want to update (replace) the PROB42 file. If you really do not want to replace PROB42, abort (Cancel) this command.

R By pressing R, you are confirming that you want the file replaced. The old PROB42 file is destroyed and is replaced by the new PROB42 file.

Other Technical Points Concerning Files. Some other technical points that may be of interest are as follows:

Commands	Explanation and Guidance
/ **Worksheet** ⟨**ENTER**⟩ **Erase** ⟨**ENTER**⟩ **Yes** (or /**WEY**)	This command erases only the screen — it does not erase any files on the diskette.
/**File** ⟨**ENTER**⟩ **Erase** ⟨**ENTER**⟩ **Worksheet** (file name) ⟨**ENTER**⟩ **Yes** (or /**FEW** file name **Y**)	This command erases a file on the diskette. After Worksheet (or W) is selected, it is necessary to "point" to the file name to be erased — all file names on the diskette are displayed (or can be displayed) to allow a choice to be made. By using the right arrow key to move the menu pointer all the way to the right, file names not initially displayed become displayed.

SYSTEM REQUIREMENTS

- IBM PC (or IBM XT or IBM AT with 360 KB drive)
- Two double-sided, double-density disk drives for IBM PC; one floppy disk drive for IBM XT or IBM AT
- 256 K RAM of memory
- LOTUS 1-2-3 System disk, version 1A or 2
- 80-column, parallel printer (if worksheets are to be printed)

INDEX

A 7
B 8
C 9
D 0
E 1
F 2
G 3
H 4
I 5
J 6

(continued from front endpapers)

P10-5 1. Carrying value of investment at Dec. 31, 19X7, $292,667; Gain on disposal, $26,500
P10-6 1. Parent's dilution, $225,000
P10-7 1. Parent's accretion, $40,000
P10-8 1. Dec. 31, 19X5 investment balance, $855,000
4. Gain on extinguishment of debt, $2,400; Minority interest, income statement, $70,050; Consolidated net income, $864,050; Consolidated assets, $4,742,100; Consolidated retained earnings, $2,764,450; Minority interest, balance sheet, $284,650
P10-9 1. Dec. 31, 19X5 investment balance, $853,950
4. (Same check figures as for P10-8)
P10-10 2. Minority interest at Dec. 31, 19X2, $17,000
P10-11 2. Minority interest at Dec. 31, 19X2, $227,800
P10-12 2. Minority interest at Dec. 31, 19X1, $13,600
P10-13 2. Minority interest at Dec. 31, 19X1, $95,200
P10-14 2. Minority interest at Dec. 31, 19X1, $3,600
5. Consolidated net income, $278,000; Consolidated assets, $1,029,000
P10-15 Cash flow from: Operations, $108,000; Investing, $(77,000); Financing, $(16,000)

E11-1 2. $38,000
E11-2 2. $207,000
E11-3 2. $31,000
E11-4 1. $9,977,480; 2. $1,132,520
E11-5 1. $580,000 and $20,000
2. $567,391 and $32,609
P11-1 1. $584,000; 2. $30,000
P11-2 1. $1,080,700; 2. $21,800
P11-3 1. $687,600; 2. $21,400
P11-4 1. $878,000 and $10,000
2. $868,352 and $19,648
P11-5 1. $450,000 and $40,000
3. $430,851 and $59,149
4. Controlling interest balance at Dec. 31, 19X1, $1,157,533; Minority interest balance at Dec. 31, 19X1, $205,447
P11-6 2. $223,000

E12-1 1. Goodwill, $55,000
E12-2 Income tax expense, $12,000
E12-3 Income tax expense, $–0–
E12-4 Income tax expense, $–0–
E12-5 b. $25,000
E12-6 1a. $2.80; 1b. $2.82
E12-7 1a. $13.75; 1b. $14.25
E12-8 1a. $2.24; 1b. $2.42
P12-1 1. Goodwill, $82,000
P12-2 Income tax expense, $20,000
P12-3 1. Income tax expense, $20,000 plus $30,000
P12-4 1. Income tax expense, $90,000 plus $30,000
P12-5 1. Parent's income tax expense, $202,400; Subsidiary's income tax expense, $60,000
3. Consolidated net income, $497,600
P12-6 1. Parent's income tax expense, $698,000; Subsidiary's income tax expense, $100,000
3. Consolidated net income, $797,000
P12-7 1a. $1.62; 1b. $1.65
P12-8 1a. $0.81; 1b. $0.83
P12-9 1a. $1.62 and $1.40; 1b. $1.67 and $1.43

E13-4 Operating profit, $320,000
E13-5 1. Segments A, B, D, and G
2. 75% test is not satisfied
E13-6 S. America, Australia, Middle East
E13-7 19X6 loss from discontinued operations, $150,000; 19X7 gain on disposal of discontinued operations, $78,000
P13-1 1. Segments B, C, D, E, and G
P13-2 Consolidated operating profit, $99,200
P13-3 Segment A's operating profit, $290,000; Consolidated operating profit, $350,000
P13-4 1. Consolidated operating profit, $444,000; Segment A's operating profit, $196,000
2. Segment A's operating profit, $206,000; Consolidated operating profit, $455,600
P13-5 U.S. operating profit, $587,600; Consolidated operating profit, $717,600
P13-6 Segment G, $200, $200, and $500
Segment H, $200, $100, and $200
P13-7 Loss from discontinued operations, $(810,000); Net income, $270,000

E14-1 1. Direct rate at Dec. 31, 19X1, 1 peso equals $0.005
E14-2 Credit retained earnings $160,000
E14-3 a. $10,000—Adverse
b. $25,000—Favorable
E14-4 Brazil, Net monetary liability position; Mexico, Net monetary asset position; Belgium, Net liability position; Ireland, Net asset position

E15-3 2a. $30,000; 2b. $63,000
E15-4 a. $180,000; b. $217,000
E15-5 a. $8,000; b. $(40,000)
P15-1 1a. $42,000; 1b. $13,000—Favorable
2a. $70,000; 2b. $10,000 gain
P15-2 1. Net income, $72,000; Translation adjustment $(157,000)
P15-3 1. Net income, $203,000; Gain from remeasurement, $219,000
P15-4 1. Net income, $420,000; Translation adjustment, $155,000
P15-5 1. Net income, $454,000; Loss from remeasurement, $(161,000)

E16-3 1. Parent records $9,000 loss
2. Subsidiary records $100,000 loss in widgettas
E16-4 1. Dividend receivable, $1,500,000
2. F.C. transaction gain, $78,930

(continued on back endpapers)

(continued from p. 1210)

P16-1 Vendor A: $200 transaction gain at July 31, 19X1
Customer A: $125 transaction loss at July 30, 19X1
P16-2 Vendor A: $1,000 transaction gain at June 30, 19X1
Customer A: $300 transaction loss at June 30, 19X1
P16-3 Dec. 31, 19X1: Offsetting $2,400 gain and loss; Jan. 15, 19X2; Offsetting $800 gain and loss
P16-4 June 30, 19X3, two $1,500 adjustments; July 30, 19X3, two $500 adjustments
P16-5 Capitalized cost of equipment $481,000
P16-6 June 30, 19X1 transaction gain, $24,000; Dec. 31, 19X1 transaction gain, $36,000
P16-7 Sit. A: Two $50,000 amounts that offset in St. Eq.
Sit. B: Net $40,000 charge to St. Eq.
Sit. C: Net $40,000 credit to income
Sit. D & E: Net of $–0– in income
P16-8 1. F.C. transaction gain of $50,000
P16-9 1. Current year translation adjustment, $(79,000)
2. Defer $62,000 of intercompany profit
3. Dec. 31, 19X5 investment balance, $600,000
4. Parent has $21,000 F.C. transaction loss
5. Consolidated net income, $1,437,000; Consolidated assets, $5,008,000

E17-3 $60,000 each quarter
E17-4 $1,100,000
E17-5 Expense in second quarter
P17-1 First-quarter income tax expense, $200,000; Second-quarter income tax expense, $220,000
P17-2 First-quarter bonus expense, $14,000 or $8,000; Second-quarter bonus expense, $5,000 or $4,000
P17-3 3. Revised estimated annual tax rate, 42.36%; Second-quarter income tax expense, $170,160

There are no key figures for Chapter 18

E19-4 1. No gain on restructuring
E19-5 1. Gain on restructuring, $80,000
3. No gain on restructuring
E19-6 1. No gain on restructuring
2. $60,000; 3. 3%
E19-7 1. Gain on restructuring, $40,000
E19-8 1. Gain on restructuring, $75,000
E19-9 Gain on restructuring, $7,000,000
E19-10 Gain on restructuring, $2,500,000
E19-11 $156,000 available to unsecured creditors
P19-1 1. Gain on restructuring, $176,000
P19-2 1. Gain on restructuring, $300,000
P19-3 1. Gain on restructuring, $440,000
P19-4 2a. Future interest expense, $–0–
2b. Future interest expense, $9,000,000
P19-5 3. Future interest expense, $323,000
4. Approx. effective interest rate, 5%
5. 19X1 interest expense, $163,850
P19-6 2. Gain on restructuring, $375,000
3. Future interest expense, $150,000
P19-7 2. No entry required
3. 5% of the face amount
P19-8 1. Discount, $19,773,720
Gain on restructuring, $254,773,720
2. First-year interest expense, $42,033,942
P19-9 1. Deficiency to unsecured creditors, $18,200
P19-10 1. Deficiency to unsecured creditors, $41,000

E20-8 $4,000
E20-9 Defer $3,000 of revenues
E20-10 Defer $150,000 of revenues
P20-1 1. $42,000 favorable variance
2. $12,000 favorable variance
P20-2 2. Total expenditures, $899,000; Total revenues, $988,000
P20-4 2. Credit unreserved fund balance, $32,000
3. June 30, 19X2 fund balance, $102,000
P20-5 2. Credit unreserved fund balance $66,000
3. June 30, 19X3 fund balance, $183,000
P20-6 3. Credit unreserved fund balance, $34,000
4. Total assets, $158,000; Total fund balance, $136,000
P20-7 3. Total expenditures, $832,000; June 30, 19X6 fund balance, $188,000
P20-8 3. Excess of revenues over expenditures, $40,000; June 30, 19X5 fund balance, $260,000
4. Fund balance available for appropriation at June 30, 19X5 (non-GAAP "budgetary basis"), $169,000
P20-9 5. July 1, 19X6 fund balance (corrected retroactively), $80,000
June 30, 19X7 fund balance (corrected), $90,500
P20-10 1. Excess of revenues over expenditures, $30,000
2. Excess of revenues over expenditures, $54,000; Dec. 31, 19X2 fund balance (non-GAAP "budgetary basis"), $125,000

P21-1 3. June 30, 19X3 fund balance, $3,020,000
P21-3 Revenues (under) expenditures, $(1,076,000)
P21-4 2. Credit unreserved fund balance, $5,650,000 (in Capital Projects Fund); Credit fund balance reserved for debt service, $790,000 (in Debt Service Fund)
P21-5 Only 5 and 6 requires entries
P21-6 June 30, 19X1 retained earnings, $600

E22-1 b. $405,000; a. $8,000
E22-2 d. $100,000
E22-3 d.
E22-4 c. $1,100,000
E22-5 c. $2,250,000
E22-7 d.
E22-8 a. $–0–
E22-9 d. $130,000
E22-10 a. $6,000,000
c. Other operating revenue of $1,000
d. $740,000